DRAMA
CRITICISM

Guide to Gale Literary Criticism Series

For criticism on	Consult these Gale series
Authors now living or who died after December 31, 1959	*CONTEMPORARY LITERARY CRITICISM (CLC)*
Authors who died between 1900 and 1959	*TWENTIETH-CENTURY LITERARY CRITICISM (TCLC)*
Authors who died between 1800 and 1899	*NINETEENTH-CENTURY LITERATURE CRITICISM (NCLC)*
Authors who died between 1400 and 1799	*LITERATURE CRITICISM FROM 1400 TO 1800 (LC)* *SHAKESPEAREAN CRITICISM (SC)*
Authors who died before 1400	*CLASSICAL AND MEDIEVAL LITERATURE CRITICISM (CMLC)*
Black writers of the past two hundred years	*BLACK LITERATURE CRITICISM (BLC)*
Authors of books for children and young adults	*CHILDREN'S LITERATURE REVIEW (CLR)*
Dramatists	*DRAMA CRITICISM (DC)*
Hispanic writers of the late nineteenth and twentieth centuries	*HISPANIC LITERATURE CRITICISM (HLC)*
Native North American writers and orators of the eighteenth, nineteenth, and twentieth centuries	*NATIVE NORTH AMERICAN LITERATURE (NNAL)*
Poets	*POETRY CRITICISM (PC)*
Short story writers	*SHORT STORY CRITICISM (SSC)*
Major authors from the Renaissance to the present	*WORLD LITERATURE CRITICISM, 1500 TO THE PRESENT (WLC)*

ISSN 1056-4349

DRAMA
CRITICISM

Criticism of the Most Significant and Widely Studied
Dramatic Works from All the World's Literatures

VOLUME 6

Lawrence J. Trudeau, Editor

Margaret Anne Haerens, Christine Slovey
Associate Editors

GALE

DETROIT • NEW YORK • TORONTO • LONDON

STAFF

Lawrence J. Trudeau, *Editor*

argaret Haerens, Christine Slovey, *Associate Editors*

Debra A. Wells, *Assistant Editor*

Marlene S. Hurst, *Permissions Manager*
Margaret A. Chamberlain, Maria Franklin, *Permissions Specialists*

Susan Brohman, Diane Cooper, Michele Lonoconus, Maureen Puhl,
Shalice Shah, Kimberly F. Smilay, Barbara A. Wallace,
Permissions Associates

Sarah Chesney, Edna Hedblad, Margaret McAvoy-Amato,
Tyra Y. Phillips, Lori Schoenenberger, Rita Valazquez,
Permissions Assistants

Victoria B. Cariappa, *Research Manager*

Julie C. Daniel, Tamara C. Nott, Michele P. Pica,
Norma Sawaya, Cheryl L. Warnock, *Research Associates*

Mary Beth Trimper, *Production Director*
Deborah Milliken, *Production Assistant*

Sherrell Hobbs, *Macintosh Artist*
Randy Bassett, *Image Database Supervisor*
Robert Duncan, *Scanner Operator*
Pamela Hayes, *Photography Coordinator*

Library of Congress Catalog Card Number 92-648805
ISBN 0-8103-9288-7
ISSN 1056-4349

Printed in the United States of America
Published simultaneously in the United Kingdom
by Gale Research International Limited
(An affiliated company of Gale Research Inc.)
10 9 8 7 6 5 4 3 2 1

Contents

Preface

*D*rama Criticism (*DC*) is principally intended for beginning students of literature and theater as well as the average playgoer. The series is therefore designed to introduce readers to the most frequently studied playwrights of all time periods and nationalities and to present discerning commentary on dramatic works of enduring interest. Furthermore, *DC* seeks to acquaint the reader with the uses and functions of criticism itself. Selected from a diverse body of commentary, the essays in *DC* offer insights into the authors and their works but do not require that the reader possess a wide background in literary studies. Where appropriate, reviews of important productions of the plays discussed are also included to give students a heightened awareness of drama as a dynamic art form, one that many claim is fully realized only in performance.

DC was created in response to suggestions by the staffs of high school, college, and public libraries. These librarians observed a need for a series that assembles critical commentary on the world's most renowned dramatists in the same manner as Gale's *Short Story Criticism* (*SSC*) and *Poetry Criticism* (*PC*), which present material on writers of short fiction and poetry. Although playwrights are covered in such Gale literary criticism series as *Contemporary Literary Criticism* (*CLC*), *Twentieth-Century Literary Criticism* (*TCLC*), *Nineteenth-Century Literature Criticism* (*NCLC*), *Literature Criticism from 1400 to 1800* (*LC*), and *Classical and Medieval Literature Criticism* (*CMLC*), *Drama Criticism* directs more concentrated attention on individual dramatists than is possible in the broader, survey-oriented entries in these Gale series. Commentary on the works of William Shakespeare may be found in *Shakespearean Criticism* (*SC*).

Scope of the Series

By collecting and organizing commentary on dramatists, *DC* assists students in their efforts to gain insight into literature, achieve better understanding of the texts, and formulate ideas for papers and assignments. A variety of interpretations and assessments is offered, allowing students to pursue their own interests and promoting awareness that literature is dynamic and responsive to many different opinions.

Each volume of *DC* presents:

- 8-10 entries

- authors and works representing a wide range of nationalities and time periods

- a diversity of viewpoints and critical opinions.

Organization of an Author Entry

Each author entry consists of some or all of the following elements, depending on the scope and complexity of the criticism:

- The **author heading** consists of the playwright's most commonly used name, followed by birth and death dates. If an author consistently wrote under a pseudonym, the pseudonym is listed in the author heading and the real name given in parentheses on the first line of the introduction. Also located at the beginning of the introduction are any name variations under which the dramatist wrote, including transliterated forms of the names of authors whose languages use nonroman alphabets.

- A **portrait** of the author is included when available. Most entries also feature illustrations of people, places, and events pertinent to a study of the playwright and his or her works. When appropriate, photographs of the plays in performance are also presented.

- The **biographical and critical introduction** contains background information that familiarizes the reader with the author and the critical debates surrounding his or her works.

- The list of **principal works** is divided into two sections, each of which is organized chronologically by date of first performance. If this has not been conclusively determined, the composition or publication date is used. The first section of the principal works list contains the author's dramatic pieces. The second section provides information on the author's major works in other genres.

- Whenever available, **author commentary** is provided. This section consists of essays or interviews in which the dramatist discusses his or her own work or the art of playwriting in general.

- Essays offering **overviews and general studies of the dramatist's entire literary career** give the student broad perspectives on the writer's artistic development, themes and concerns that recur in several of his or her works, the author's place in literary history, and other wide-ranging topics.

- **Criticism of individual plays** offers the reader in-depth discussions of a select number of the author's most important works. In some cases, the criticism is divided into two sections, each arranged chronologically. When a significant performance of a play can be identified (typically, the premier of a twentieth-century work), the first section of criticism will feature **production reviews** of this staging. Most entries include sections devoted to **critical commentary** that assesses the literary merit of the selected plays. When necessary, essays are carefully excerpted to focus on the work under consideration; often, however, essays and reviews are reprinted in their entirety.

- As an additional aid to students, the critical essays and excerpts are often prefaced by **explanatory annotations**. These notes provide several types of useful information, including the critic's reputation and approach to literary studies as well as the scope and significance of the criticism that follows.

- A complete **bibliographic citation**, designed to help the interested reader locate the original essay or book, precedes each piece of criticism.

- The **further reading list** at the end of each entry comprises additional studies of the dramatist. It is divided into sections that help students quickly locate the specific information they need.

Other Features

- A **cumulative author index** lists all the authors who have appeared in *DC* and Gale's other Literature Criticism Series, as well as cross-references to related titles published by Gale, including *Contemporary Authors* and *Dictionary of Literary Biography*. A complete listing of the series included appears at the beginning of the index.

- A **cumulative nationality index** lists each author featured in *DC* by nationality, followed by the number of the *DC* volume in which the author appears.

■ A **cumulative title index** lists in alphabetical order the individual plays discussed in the criticism contained in *DC*. Each title is followed by the author's name and the corresponding volume and page number(s) where commentary on the work may be located. Translations and variant titles are cross-referenced to the title of the play in its original language so that all references to the work are combined in one listing.

A Note to the Reader

When writing papers, students who quote directly from any volume in *Drama Criticism* may use the following general formats to footnote reprinted criticism. The first example pertains to material drawn from periodicals, the second to materials reprinted from books.

[1]Susan Sontag, "Going to the Theater, Etc.," *Partisan Review* XXXI, No. 3 (Summer 1964), 389-94; excerpted and reprinted in *Drama Criticism*, Vol. 1, ed. Lawrence J. Trudeau (Detroit: Gale Research, 1991), pp. 17-20.

[2]Eugene M. Waith, *The Herculean Hero in Marlowe, Chapman, Shakespeare and Dryden* (Chatto & Windus, 1962); excerpted and reprinted in *Drama Criticism*, Vol. 1, ed. Lawrence J. Trudeau (Detroit: Gale Research, 1991), pp. 237-47.

Suggestions are Welcome

Readers who wish to suggest authors to appear in future volumes of *DC*, or who have other suggestions, are cordially invited to contact the editor.

Acknowledgments

The editor wishes to thank the copyright holders of the excerpted criticism included in this volume and the permissions managers of many book and magazine publishing companies for assisting us in securing reprint rights. We are also grateful to the staffs of the Detroit Public Library, the Library of Congress, the University of Detroit Mercy Library, Wayne State University Purdy/Kresge Library Complex, and the University of Michigan Libraries for making their resources available to us. Following is a list of the copyright holders who have granted us permission to reprint material in this volume of *DC*. Every effort has been made to trace copyright, but if omissions have been made, please let us know.

COPYRIGHTED EXCERPTS IN *DC*, VOLUME 6, WERE REPRINTED FROM THE FOLLOWING PERIODICALS:

America, v. 150, April 14, 1984. © 1984. All rights reserved. Reprinted with permission of America Press, Inc., 106 West 56th Street, New York, NY, 10019. —*Black American Literature Forum,* v. 21, Winter, 1987, for an interview with Amiri Baraka by Sandra G. Shannon. Copyright © 1987, by the author. Reprinted by permission of the author. —*Black Creation,* v. 4, Winter, 1973, for an interview with Ed Bullins by Richard Wesley. Copyright 1973, by the Institute of Afro-American Affairs. Reprinted by permission of the authors. —*CLA Journal,* v. XVI, September, 1972. Copyright 1972, by The College Language Association. Used by permission of The College Language Association. —*The Classical Journal,* v. 73, February-March, 1978. Reprinted by permission of the publisher. —*Comparative Drama,* v. 15, Winter, 1981-82. Copyright © 1982, by the Editors of Comparative Drama. Reprinted by permission of the publisher. —*Critical Quarterly,* Autumn, 1978; Spring, 1985. Copyright © 1978, 1985, by Manchester University Press. Reprinted by permission of Basil Blackwell Limited. —*Cross Currents,* Dobbs Ferry, v. 42, Summer, 1990. Copyright 1990, by Association for Religion and Intellectual Life, Inc. Reprinted by permission of the publisher. —*The Drama Review,* v. 14, No. 2, Winter, 1970, for "LeRoi Jones' Slave Ship" by Stefan Brecht. Copyright © 1970, *The Drama Review*. Reprinted by permission of *The Drama Review,* the author, and The MIT PressJournals. —*ELR,* v. 8, Autumn, 1978. Copyright © 1978, by *English Literary Renaissance*. Reprinted by permission of the publisher. —*Financial Times,* March 30, 1995. © Financial Times Limited 1995. Reprinted by permission of the publisher. —*The Guardian,* March 30, 1995. © The Guardian. Reprinted by permission of the publisher. —*Harper's,* v. 233, September, 1966. Copyright © 1966, by *Harper's Magazine*. All rights reserved. Reprinted by special permission. —*The Hudson Review,* v. XVII, Autumn, 1964. Copyright © 1964, renewed 1992, by The Hudson Review, Inc. Reprinted by permission of the publisher. —*The Independent,* March 31, 1995. Reprinted by permission of the publisher. —*Kansas Quarterly,* v. 12, Fall, 1980, for "The Art of History in Tom Stoppard's *Travesties,*" by Carol Billman. Copyright © 1980, by *Kansas Quarterly*. Reprinted by permission of the publisher and the author. —*The Kenyon Review,* n.s., v. XV, Spring, 1993 for "Václav Havel: The Once and Future Playwright" by Robert Skloot. Copyright 1993, by Kenyon College. All rights reserved. Reprinted by permission of the author. —*Modern Drama,* v. XVII, June, 1974; v. 20, March, 1977; v. XVI, December, 1977; v. XXV, December, 1982. Copyright 1974, 1977, 1982, by Modern Drama, University of Toronto. Reprinted by permission of the publisher. —*Modern Philology,* v. 69, August, 1971. © 1971, by The University of Chicago. Reprinted by permission of the University of Chicago Press. —*The Nation,* New York, v. 145, November 13, 1937; v. 210, February 2, 1970. Copyright 1937, renewed 1965; 1970, by *The Nation Magazine*/The Nation Company, Inc. Reprinted by permission of the publisher. —*National Review,* New York, v. XVII, March 23, 1965. © 1965, by National Review, Inc., 150 East 35th Street, New York, NY, 10016. Reprinted with permission of the publisher. —*The New Leader,* v. LXVI, December 26, 1983. © 1983, by The American Labor Conference on International Affairs, Inc. Reprinted by permission of the publisher. —*The New Republic,* v. LXXXII, March 13, 1935; v. 185, December 23, 1981; v. 190, March 12, 1984. © 1935, renewed 1963; 1981; 1984, by The New Republic, Inc. Reprinted by permission of *The New Republic*. —*New York Magazine,* v. 14, January 12, 1981; v. 14, November, 1981; v. 16, December 5, 1993. Copyright © 1996 K-III Magazine Corporation. All rights reserved. Reprinted with the permission of *New York* Magazine. —*The New York Times,* v. LXXXV, December 15, 1935; November 21,

COPYRIGHTED EXCERPTS IN *DC,* VOLUME 6, WERE REPRINTED FROM THE FOLLOWING BOOKS:

Amiri Baraka
1934-

(Born Everett LeRoy Jones; has also written as LeRoi Jones and Imamu Amiri Baraka.) American poet, dramatist, short story writer, novelist, essayist, critic, and editor.

INTRODUCTION

A seminal figure in the development of contemporary black literature, Baraka is a controversial writer. According to some scholars, he succeeds both W. E. B. Du Bois and Richard Wright as one of the most prolific and persistent critics of twentieth-century America. His works, which cover a wide variety of literary genres, often concern such political issues as the oppression of blacks in white society and the oppression of the poor in a capitalist society. He received worldwide acclaim for his first professional production, "Dutchman," in 1964, and his subsequent work for the theater has provoked both praise and controversy. Various movements and philosophies have shaped Baraka throughout his life, from the Beat movement of the late 1950s to Marxist-Leninist thought which he has embraced most recently. The only constant in his life is change, making a study of his writing both a complex and challenging endeavor.

BIOGRAPHICAL INFORMATION

Born Everett LeRoy Jones in New Jersey in 1934, Baraka excelled in his studies, graduating from high school at the age of fifteen. He enrolled in Howard University in 1952 and just before beginning his first year, started spelling his name LeRoi. At Howard, Baraka studied with such famous black scholars as E. Franklin Frazier, Nathan A. Scott, Jr., and Sterling A. Brown who is regarded as the patriarch of African-American literary critics. Despite these exceptional teachers, Baraka found Howard University stifling and flunked out in 1954. He then joined the United States Air Force. In 1957, after being dishonorably discharged, he moved to New York's Greenwich Village and became part of the Beat movement. That same year he married Hettie Roberta Cohen and together they founded *Yūgen*, a magazine forum for Beat poetry. During the next few years, he also established himself as a music critic, writing about jazz for *downbeat*, *Metronome*, and the *Jazz Review*. Baraka first received critical acclaim as a poet, for his collection *Preface to a Twenty Volume Suicide Note. . .* , which was published in 1961.

In 1960, he was invited to Cuba by the New York chapter of the Fair Play for Cuba Committee and the visit changed the young writer's life. Baraka came to understand that politics had a place in art and he made it his life's work to incorporate his political, social, and spiritual beliefs

into his writing. He would no longer be content with art for art's sake, but would use poetry and drama to teach the people, opening their eyes to reality as Baraka saw it. Following the murder of Black Muslim leader Malcolm X in 1965, Baraka divorced his white wife and move to Harlem. He dissociated from the white race and dedicated himself to creating works that were inspired by and spoke to the African-American community. This same year, he founded the Black Arts Repertory Theatre/School in Harlem. He married Sylvia Robinson, a black woman, in 1966. Around this time, Baraka's hatred of whites peaked. When a white woman asked him what whites could do to help blacks, he retorted, "You can help by dying. You are a cancer." In 1968, he converted to Islam and changed his name to Imamu Amiri Baraka, meaning "blessed spiritual leader."

In 1974, in another radical shift, Baraka dropped the spiritual title of Imamu and declared himself an adherent of Marxist-Leninist thought. Rejecting Black Nationalism as racist in its implications, he now advocated socialism as a viable solution to the problems in America. He also repudiated his past anti-Semitic and anti-white statements. He concluded: "Nationalism, so-called, when it says 'all non-blacks are our enemies,' is sickness or criminality, in fact a form of fascism." In the fall of 1979, he joined the Africana Studies Department at State University of New York at Stony Brook as a teacher of creative writing. His autobiography was published in 1984 and *Money: A Jazz Opera* (1982) was one his latest dramas produced.

MAJOR WORKS

"Dutchman" is widely considered Baraka's masterpiece in the drama genre. The play received an Obie Award for best Off-Broadway play and propelled the playwright into the public eye. "Dutchman" centers around an interracial encounter between Lula, an attractive, flirtatious white woman, and Clay, a young, quiet, well-dressed black intellectual. The seemingly random meeting on a New York subway ends with Lula murdering Clay. "Dutchman" is considered by many critics to be Baraka's first successful integration of the themes and motifs of earlier, less-successful works, merging mythical allusions, surrealistic techniques, and social statement. Another of Baraka's well-known plays, "The Toilet," is set in the bathroom of an urban high school and concerns a white homosexual boy who gets beaten up by a gang of black boys for sending a love letter to the leader of the black gang. The play is exemplary of several recurring themes in Baraka's work: the drama of the sensitive, isolated individual pitted against the social code of his community; marginalized individuals' self-hatred as perpetuated by society; and the failure of love, or of the ability to love in our society. During Baraka's period of Black Nationalism, he produced a series of works with increasingly violent overtones which called for blacks to unite and establish their own nation. Experimenting with ritual forms in his dramas, he wrote *Slave Ship: A Historical Pageant*, a vivid recreation of the passage of slaves to America that relies heavily on powerful images and music to help convey its meaning. His drama since 1974 reflects Baraka's latest political commitments to Marxist-Leninist-Maoist thought and Communism. *S-1* and *The Motion of History* are reminiscent of the agit-prop dramas of the 1930s, particularly in their appeals to working-class solidarity and in their suggestion that working class revolution is society's only hope.

CRITICAL RECEPTION

Critics have praised "Dutchman" for its "power," "freshness," and "deadly wit." Others were outraged by its vulgar language, its perpetuation of interracial hostility, and its portrayal of whites. "The Toilet" also met with mixed reviews, described by one critic as an "obscene, scatological, bloody confrontation of the races." Many scholars, including William J. Harris, have observed that critical assessment of Baraka's work has fallen into two general camps. Harris remarked: "The white response. . . has been either silence or anger—and, in a few cases, sadness. . . . One general complaint is that Baraka has forsaken art for politics. . . . The reaction to Baraka in most of the black world has been very different from that in the white. In the black world Baraka is a famous artist. . . ." Whatever the reaction to Baraka, no one is left unaffected by his works. People bristle at his depictions of "white America," critics assert, because he mirrors the ugly facets of American society.

---

*PRINCIPAL WORKS

PLAYS

A Good Girl Is Hard to Find 1958
"Dante" 1961; also produced as "The Eighth Ditch" 1964
"The Baptism" 1964
"Dutchman" 1964
"The Slave" 1964
"The Toilet" 1964
"Experimental Death Unit #1" 1965
"J-E-L-L-O" 1965
A Black Mass 1966
"The Death of Malcolm X" 1966
"Arm Yourself or Harm Yourself: A One-Act Play: A
    Message of Self-Defense to Black Men" 1967
"Great Goodness of Life (A Coon Show)" 1967
"Madheart: A Morality Play" 1967
"Slave Ship: A Historical Pageant" 1967
"Home on the Range" 1968
Police 1968
*Four Black Revolutionary Plays: All Praises to the Black
    Man* 1969
"Resurrection in Life" 1969
Bloodrites 1970
Junkies Are Full of Shhh. . . 1970
Columbia The Gem of The Ocean 1973
A Recent Killing 1973
The New Ark's A-Moverin 1974
*The Sidnee Poet Heroical or If in Danger of Suit, The Kid
    Poet Heroical* 1975
S-1 1976
The Motion of History 1977
The Motion of History and Other Plays 1978
Selected Plays and Prose of Amiri Baraka/LeRoi Jones
    (dramas and prose) 1979
"The Sidnee Poet Heroical: In 29 Scenes" 1979
"What Was The Relationship of the Lone Ranger to the
    Means of Production: A Play in One Act" 1979
Dim'Crackr Party Convention 1980
Boy & Tarzan Appear In A Clearing! 1981
Money: A Jazz Opera 1982
"Song: a One Act Play about the Relationship of Art to
    Real Life" 1983

OTHER MAJOR WORKS

Preface to a Twenty Volume Suicide Note. . . . (poetry)
    1961
Cuba Libre (essay) 1961
Blues People: Negro Music in White America (essay)
    1963
The Dead Lecturer: Poems (poetry) 1964
"The Revolutionary Theatre" (essay) 1965; published in
    periodical *Liberator*

The System of Dante's Hell (novel) 1965
Home: Social Essays (essays) 1966
Black Art (poetry) 1967
Black Music (essay) 1967
Tales (short stories) 1967
*Black Magic: Sabotage, Target Study, Black Art; Collect-
    ed Poetry, 1961-1967* (poetry) 1969
Black Spring (screenplay) 1968
*In Our Terribleness (Some Elements and Meaning in Black
    Style)* (poetry) 1970
It's Nation Time (poetry) 1970
A Fable (screenplay) 1971
Raise, Race, Rays, Raze: Essays since 1965 (essays) 1971
Strategy and Tactics of a Pan-African Nationalist Party
    (essay) 1971
Supercoon (screenplay) 1971
Kawaida Studies: The New Nationalism (essay) 1972
Spirit Reach (poetry) 1972
Afrikan Revolution (poetry) 1973
Crisis in Boston! (essay) 1974
Hard Facts: Excerpts (poetry) 1975
*Three Books by Imamu Amiri Baraka (LeRoi Jones): The
    System of Dante's Hell, Tales, The Dead Lecturer*
    (novel, short stories, and poetry) 1975
AM/TRAK (poetry) 1979
Selected Poetry of Amiri Baraka/LeRoi Jones (poetry)
    1979
"Afro-American Literature and Class Struggle" (essay)
    1980; published in periodical *Black American Litera-
    ture Forum*
"Confessions of a Former Anti-Semite" (essay) 1980;
    published in periodical *Village Voice*
In the Tradition: For Black Arthur Blythe (poetry) 1980
Reggae or Not! (poetry) 1981
In the Tradition (poetry) 1982
"Sounding" (poetry) 1982; published in journal *Black
    American Literature Forum*
*The Descent of Charlie Fuller into Pulitzerland and the
    Need for Afro-American Institutions* (essay) 1983
The Autobiography of LeRoi Jones (autobiography)
    1984
Daggers and Javelins: Essays, 1974-1979 (essays)
    1984
"Wailers" (poetry) 1985; published in periodical *Calla-
    loo*
"Why;s/Wise" (poetry) 1985; published in periodical
    Southern Review
The Music: Reflections on Jazz and Blues (essay) 1987
"Reflections" (poetry) 1988; published in periodical *Black
    Scholar*

*Works before 1967 were published under the name LeRoi Jones.

AUTHOR COMMENTARY

The Revolutionary Theatre (1965)

SOURCE: "The Revolutionary Theatre," in *Home: Social
Essays*, William Morrow & Co., Inc., 1966, pp. 210-15.

[*In the following essay, a reprint of the original which
appeared in* Liberator *in 1965, Baraka outlines the goals
and responsibilities of Black Revolutionary Theatre.*]

The Revolutionary Theatre should force change; it should
be change. (All their faces turned into the lights and you
work on them black nigger magic, and cleanse them at
having seen the ugliness. And if the beautiful see themselves, they will love themselves.) We are preaching virtue again, but by that to mean NOW, toward what seems the
most constructive use of the world.

The Revolutionary Theatre must EXPOSE! Show up the
insides of these humans, look into black skulls. White
men will cower before this theatre because it hates them.
Because they themselves have been trained to hate. The
Revolutionary Theatre must hate them for hating. For
presuming with their technology to deny the supremacy of
the Spirit. They will all die because of this.

The Revolutionary Theatre must teach them their deaths.
It must crack their faces open to the mad cries of the poor.
It must teach them about silence and the truths lodged
there. It must kill any God anyone names except Common
Sense. The Revolutionary Theatre should flush the fags
and murders out of Lincoln's face.

It should stagger through our universe correcting, insulting, preaching, spitting craziness—but a craziness taught
to us in our most rational moments. People must be taught
to trust true scientists (knowers, diggers, oddballs) and
that the holiness of life is the constant possibility of wid-
ening the consciousness. And they must be incited to strike
back against *any* agency that attempts to prevent this wid-
ening.

The Revolutionary Theatre must Accuse and Attack anything that can be accused and attacked. It must Accuse
and Attack because it is a theatre of Victims. It looks at
the sky with the victims' eyes, and moves the victims to
look at the strength in their minds and their bodies.

Clay, in **"Dutchman,"** Ray in **"The Toilet,"** Walker in
"The Slave," are all victims. In the Western sense they
could be heroes. But the Revolutionary Theatre, even if it
is Western, must be anti-Western. It must show horrible
coming attractions of *The Crumbling of the West*. Even as
Artaud designed *The Conquest of Mexico,* so we must
design *The Conquest of White Eye,* and show the mission-
aries and wiggly Liberals dying under blasts of concrete.
For sound effects, wild screams of joy, from all the peoples of the world.

The Revolutionary Theatre must take dreams and give them
a reality. It must isolate the ritual and historical cycles of
reality. But it must be food for all those who need food, and
daring propaganda for the beauty of the Human Mind. It is
a political theatre, a weapon to help in the slaughter of these
dim-witted fatbellied white guys who somehow believe that
the rest of the world is here for them to slobber on.

This should be a theatre of World Spirit. Where the spirit

can be shown to be the most competent force in the world. Force. Spirit. Feeling. The language will be anybody's, but tightened by the poet's backbone. And even the language must show what the facts are in this consciousness epic, what's happening. We will talk about the world, and the preciseness with which we are able to summon the world will be our art. Art is method. And art, "like any ashtray or senator," remains in the world. Wittgenstein said ethics and aesthetics are one. I believe this. So the Broadway theatre is a theatre of reaction whose ethics, like its aesthetics, reflect the spiritual values of this unholy society, which sends young crackers all over the world blowing off colored people's heads. (In some of these flippy Southern towns they even shoot up the immigrants' Favorite Son, be it Michael Schwerner or JFKennedy.)

The Revolutionary Theatre is shaped by the world, and moves to reshape the world, using as its force the natural force and perpetual vibrations of the mind in the world. We are history and desire, what we are, and what any experience can make us.

It is a social theatre, but all theatre is social theatre. But we will change the drawing rooms into places where real things can be said about a real world, or into smoky rooms where the destruction of Washington can be plotted. The Revolutionary Theatre must function like an incendiary pencil planted in Curtis Lemay's cap. So that when the final curtain goes down brains are splattered over the seats and the floor, and bleeding nuns must wire SOS's to Belgians with gold teeth.

Our theatre will show victims so that their brothers in the audience will be better able to understand that they are the brothers of victims, and that they themselves are victims if they are blood brothers. And what we show must cause the blood to rush, so that pre-revolutionary temperaments will be bathed in this blood, and it will cause their deepest souls to move, and they will find themselves tensed and clenched, even ready to die, at what the soul has been taught. We will scream and cry, murder, run through the streets in agony, if it means some soul will be moved, moved to actual life understanding of what the world is, and what it ought to be. We are preaching virtue and feeling, and a natural sense of the self in the world. All men live in the world, and the world ought to be a place for them to live.

What is called the imagination (from image, magi, magic, magician, etc.) is a practical vector from the soul. It stores all data, and can be called on to solve all our "problems." The imagination is the projection of ourselves past our sense of ourselves as "things." Imagination (Image) is all possibility, because from the image, the initial circumscribed energy, any use (idea) is possible. And so begins that image's use in the world. Possibility is what moves us.

The popular white man's theatre like the popular white man's novel shows tired white lives, and the problems of eating white sugar, or else it herds bigcaboosed blondes onto huge stages in rhinestones and makes believe they are dancing or singing. WHITE BUSINESSMEN OF THE WORLD, DO YOU WANT TO SEE PEOPLE REALLY DANCING AND SINGING??? ALL OF YOU GO UP TO HARLEM AND GET YOURSELF KILLED. THERE WILL BE DANCING AND SINGING, THEN, FOR REAL!! (In **"The Slave"**, Walker Vessels, the black revolutionary, wears an armband, which is the insignia of the attacking army—a big red-lipped minstrel, grinning like crazy.)

The liberal white man's objection to the theatre of the revolution (if he is "hip" enough) will be on aesthetic grounds. Most white Western artists do not need to be "political," since usually, whether they know it or not, they are in complete sympathy with the most repressive social forces in the world today. There are more junior birdmen fascists running around the West today disguised as Artists than there are disguised as fascists. (But then, that word, *Fascist,* and with it, *Fascism,* has been made obsolete by the words *America,* and *Americanism.*) The American Artist usually turns out to be just a super-Bourgeois, because, finally, all he has to show for his sojourn through the world is "better taste" than the Bourgeois—many times not even that.

Americans will hate the Revolutionary Theatre because it will be out to destroy them and whatever they believe is real. American cops will try to close the theatres where such nakedness of the human spirit is paraded. American producers will say the revolutionary plays are filth, usually because they will treat human life as if it were actually happening. American directors will say that the white guys in the plays are too abstract and cowardly ("don't get me wrong . . . I mean aesthetically . . .") and they will be right.

The force we want is of twenty million spooks storming America with furious cries and unstoppable weapons. We want actual explosions and actual brutality: AN EPIC IS CRUMBLING and we must give it the space and hugeness of its actual demise. The Revolutionary Theatre, which is now peopled with victims, will soon begin to be peopled with new kinds of heroes—not the weak Hamlets debating whether or not they are ready to die for what's on their minds, but men and women (and minds) digging out from under a thousand years of "high art" and weak-faced dalliance. We must make an art that will function so as to call down the actual wrath of world spirit. We are witch doctors and assassins, but we will open a place for the true scientists to expand our consciousness. This is a theatre of assault. The play that will split the heavens for us will be called THE DESTRUCTION OF AMERICA. The heroes will be Crazy Horse, Denmark Vesey, Patrice Lumumba, and not history, not memory, not sad sentimental groping for a warmth in our despair; these will be new men, new heroes, and their enemies most of you who are reading this.

On Black Theater (1978)

SOURCE: "On Black Theater," in *Theater,* Vol. 9, No. 2, Spring, 1978, pp. 59-61.

[*In the essay, below Baraka discusses the commercializa-tion of American theatre and the role of the Black theatre as an alternative to traditional American theatre.*]

At the end of 1975, beginning of 1976, I wrote two plays. The shorter one is called **S-1,** and the other which is called **The Motion of History** is about four hours long. I'm not writing plays regularly—perhaps that's why they come out so long. I'm now writing a play called *The Factory* that I hope to have produced soon. We have a workshop called "The Yenan Theater Workshop" that meets in New York. We're getting ready to do a poetry reading of revolution-ary poetry from around the world, and then we're going to orchestrate it with music. We're going to put it together so we can do it in Soho, in a little theater that seats about eighty people.

I talked to Woody King [a theater producer] last night about directing Langston Hughes' *Scottsboro Limited,* which is a play that's sort of been covered-over. Very few people know about it. It was printed in 1932 in a pamphlet called *Scottsboro Limited.* Langston during the thirties was very strong, an incredibly strong, incredibly beautiful writer. I'm interested in bringing that thirties work into people's minds. It's much closer to what I want to do— being a Marxist—than the stuff that he did before and after. In the thirties he was very strong, very clear, fear-less, and that's what I want to raise up.

Reading that verse play of Langston's (*Scottsboro Limit-ed*) makes me realize how effective poetic drama can be. I used to write drama consciously as poetry—when I start-ed writing drama, I tried to write poetry. And then later on I just tried to write dialogue. Hughes used a rhyme scheme, but the context of it makes it move. It's the kind of rhyme heard on the street—it's like playing the dozen, it's a very close kind of rhyme scheme. This is the time to bring that back. The Depression that's here is not going to let up, it's going to get worse. Beyond that real deep Depression there's a war, another war.

Everything in this country is in the main controlled by a very few people, mostly millionaires and the bourgeois capitalists. And as you become less and less clearly use-able in their terms—theater as a commodity—you have less and less use for them, and they make less and less *of* you. That's something that I had to understand; I knew it theoretically, but having to understand it in a real life practical way is another thing. The only way you can deal with it is the way I tried to deal with it when I was very young, which is to do it yourself. Get it on, get it up, publish it, whatever. If you're interested in making a statement, you have to make it independent of any kind of . . . angel. You have to do it *outside* of the commer-cial things . . .

There's a whole tradition of American writing that's gen-erally obscured by the academics, and by those people who come into urban centers thinking they're writers, because a lot of them have been shaped by the academic conception of what constitutes art and writing. For the most part that's a right-wing conception. When we go to school we learn from anthologies that are tilted to the right. We learn about Ezra Pound, who was a Fascist. We learn about T.S. Eliot, who was a Royalist. But in terms of the whole other stream of writing—they always hold up Henry James over Melville, for instance. They say that Mark Twain, who was a democrat, is "awkward" and "cynical," see that Jack London is obscure. But to actually see that stream as a progressive stream of American writ-ing, and then to align yourself consciously with it, gives you more strength.

I don't think there was any such thing as American drama until the early twentieth century. People like O'Neill and Howard and Rice initiated American drama. The time they initiated it is the same time they began to talk about Blacks realistically. I mean more realistically than say, minstrel caricature. American drama doesn't exist in any human dimension at all before that. It's not until they can begin to talk about Black people in any kind of way approximat-ing humanity or reality that American theater exists. It doesn't exist just because of that—it's the fact that they've managed to disconnect themselves from European models sufficiently to create an American drama. An American drama has to deal with America, and you cannot deal with America without the question of the Afro-American, you cannot deal with America without the question of slavery, because the country's built on it.

Now if the slave master's culture does not develop a the-ater until 1918 or 1920, then Black theater will have to develop a little later. The Black theater movement of the sixties paralleled the Black liberation movement, as the arts generally parallel the development of society. The Black theater movement actually developed out of, and took its shape from, the development of the Black liber-ation movement. The people who were talking about Black art were essentially people effected by Malcolm X, people who wanted to make a distinction in art that Malcolm made in the whole question of political struggle—let's say the distinction between Malcolm X and Martin Luther King and Roy Wilkins.

So the people who were talking about Black art were try-ing to make the same kind of distinction about what their art should be—a weapon of change, let's say, as opposed to the Civil Rights art of Ellison, Baldwin, Hansberry. And the problem was and is that there is no really revo-lutionary political organization in this country—I mean there is no political party in this country to guide or direct the struggle. In order for the people to win their struggle, they cannot just rise up spontaneously, because this coun-try is not spontaneously governed. And ditto for the Black arts movement, because it was not characterized by any kind of scientific development either. It was mostly spon-taneous, eclectic—a little Mao and a little Elijah Moham-med and a little Che Guevara, a little of this, mix them all up and you don't have anything, you've just got some phrase-mongering. So what happens? The movement rises and falls; with spontaneity it's always going to rise and fall, until we get a revolutionary party, a Marxist-Leninist political party that can be the focal point of the struggle for the people, to lay out the things we should be doing, where our emphasis should be put, to actually guide the people themselves in the struggle against this system.

Some Black theaters went the route of the antipoverty thing, accepting grants so they can exist as long as that exists. Others went the foundation route, you know, the Ford-Rockefeller thing: the New Lafayette, the Negro Ensemble Company. NEC is sort of the flagship of the grants. NEC was actually the Black folks that were left in the Village once the Black arts movement had cried out that we were all leaving the Village, once all the people who were the best known writers left downtown, saying: "We're going to Harlem, we're going to start a theater in Harlem." Then all the people who argued that there was no such thing as Black theater, that there was no such thing as Black art were put in charge of it by Rockefeller. Rockefeller determined that since these niggers were making all this noise about Black theater, then "We need us a Black theater." But Black skin is the only prerequisite for this Black theater. Those people never believed in theater of change, theater of revolution, but they do meet the minimum requirement, which is that they be Black.

You can have a theater that has Black people in it, you can have Black directors, Black actors, Black everything, but suppose the theater is just the same kind of bourgeois decadent theater that you see on Broadway or Off-Broadway. Ultimately, it depends on the content. Skin color doesn't determine political content.

What revolutionaries would do is teach a revolutionary message through Black theater. They would actually make the theater a weapon for the liberation of Black people. That would be the purpose of Black theater. But if you're going to have a Black theater that only shows Black people aspiring to be in this system and do the same thing as the middle-class white majority, then the Blackness of their theater is finally irrelevant.

The popular theater of our time is television, and it's absolutely controlled. The major theme on television, if we analyzed it, would be, I guess, "Police are your friends," on the evening programs; I don't know about the daytime TV. Those images control a lot of people's consciousness. Now they don't ultimately control consciousness because they're unreal, and the people have to come away from those television sets and deal with reality. So you've got the reality versus the illusion the bourgeois can create. But at the same time, the people who are talking about change and transforming society have at least got to raise up some images that criticize the images that the rulers put out, and also put out alternative images. Theater can put out an alternative image, and I think in the sixties that's what the whole Black theater thing was doing.

Now they've transformed the whole Black theater thing into what it would be in commercial, bourgeois theater, which is namely skin. They take *The Wizard of Oz* and make *The Wiz*. They take *Guys and Dolls* and they make a Black musical. They bring back *Porgy and Bess, Bubbling Brown Sugar*, music, song, and dance. The bourgeoisie have the theater now, and the people who want to do it—Black or White—have to create an alternative to that.

Interview with Baraka (1987)

SOURCE: An interview in *Black American Literature Forum*, Vol. 21, No. 4, Winter, 1987, pp. 425-33.

[*In the following interview with Sandra G. Shannon, Baraka explores his own vision as director of his dramas.*]

[Shannon]: *The questions that I'd like to ask you today are specifically oriented toward directing. My first question is this: I see that you have directed several of your own sixties' plays. What motivated you to want to direct your own works?*

[Baraka]: Well, because directing was something that I hadn't done, but I always had a great appreciation for directing. Also, I thought that I could give the work an added kind of accuracy in terms of the interpretation. I like to direct actually. Directing is more work that people might think.

Does directing, for you, involve everything—such as teaching the actors how to convey a particular point in your works, incorporating music . . . ?

Well, I think that first it has to do with helping the actors understand the play and to understand the characters because I think that if they don't understand what the play is about and what all of the characters are about . . . in particular, they've got to have some insight into their own characters. But they've got to know the whole play. They've got to know all the relationships, the history of the characters. Like a life situation, they have to know it like that and be in tune with it.

How is the fact that they know the play portrayed in the way they act? How can you tell they know the play?

Well, because their motivations ring true. What they do seems real or justifiable or legitimized in some kind of way. They have to understand the play, and I think too often you see people just sort of sleepwalking through a play or going through these kinds of formal blocking moves stage left and downstage right, and you don't see any acting going on. You see mostly people being placed on different parts of the stage.

So you're saying that a certain amount of what they portray comes from within?

Yeah. There has to be an understanding. To me, it's like a piece of music. You can't play it if you don't understand it. Or if you can't read the notes and it's a written piece of music, you're in trouble. I think you have to know the composer's intentions, what feelings the composer was trying to transmit. The same thing with the play—you have to know what the playwright was trying to say.

What directors have you worked with?

Well, I've liked quite a few people's directing, but the director that I've liked best has been Gil Moses, who did **"Slave Ship."** To me, he's one of the most intelligent and innovative directors that I've known. But I've had some other good directors. At the Black Arts, we had a guy named Jim Campbell—very good director. He's now a principal of an elementary school.

What do you think makes a good director?

Understanding the play and being able to put that in dramatic terms—to transpose it from literary terms to dramatic terms, which sometimes calls for things that the playwright has not seen that are obvious from the interpretation.

Do directors consult you? Do you feel it necessary that they consult you, or do you just leave them alone?

I usually leave them alone, but I think good directors always want to know what the playwright thinks, even if they don't agree with him. There are a lot of good directors around now, for example, the guy who's directing this play of mine at NYU named George Ferrinks. He's a white director. He's a good director. He's Hungarian. He understands texts, and he can improvise. Glenda Dickerson, a black woman who is out here with us at Stony Brook, is an excellent director.

What makes your job as a director easier?

Well, what makes it easier is if you have all of the resources to translate a play from literature into drama and into theater without a hassle. And the principal of those resources is actors—people who are intelligent. You've got some who are intelligent; you've got some who are sort of mediocre; and you've got some whom you shouldn't get stuck with under any circumstances.

To what extent do you get involved in the music which becomes part of the play?

See, music has ideas in it. People think that it's only if they hear lyrics that ideas are being communicated. That's not true. There are ideas in the music—what the composer wants to say, what he feels, what kind of emotional parallel music conjures up. There are all kinds of ideas and thoughts and feelings, of course, in music. And so the music, to me, is an added dramatic dimension—as narrator, as actor. Music, to me, is as much alive as the actors. It has as much importance.

So the concept, then, that you tried to get from the use of Sun Ra or, say, Albert Ayler was a certain disorderliness, unpredictability, anti-establishment feeling?

With Sun Ra, I wanted the feeling of some kind of otherwordly wisdom or dimension, which changes sometimes

to fear, terror, contemplation of the laboratory, contemplation of what wisdom and knowledge really are [refering to his play **Black Mass**.] With Ayler, it was the kind of power and force that he has which is so striking when you hear him live. I've used him when I've wanted improvisation added to the text; in other words, let the musician look at the play and improvise. I've done that a few times. But I think that's interesting because the play is as much a generator of emotions as any other kind of thing. And if you have a musician improvising off the emotions he gets from the play, then it creates a kind of improvised life of the play at the same time that you have a kind of stated life of the play.

How do you deal with such production limitations as space and budget?

Well, you just have to do other things. You have to do things that don't require space, and you have to do things that are cheap. That's been my story all of my life—all of my theatrical life. There were a couple of times I thought I was going to have some money. We were supposed to do a jazz opera in the Paris opera and the Berlin opera, and the Americans got to the French to cancel it. They were going to spend a million and a half francs on it.

Oh really! What did the Americans say?

They said it was an anti-American play.

*Your 1960s' plays leave much room for the creative director—for example, **Black Mass**. I listened to the album. I read the play. But I cannot understand how the beast is portrayed on stage. Do you settle for a facsimile of the hideous creature, or do you expect some other rigid interpretation?*

How is it interpreted on the stage? I guess you could say that it is up to the imagination of the director. But what we did was take grease paint and paint all over the guy, and we had a red mask, which was turned into a tail like a dinosaur's tail. That was Ben Caldwell's design. I thought that it was something with room for improvisation.

In "The Slave" what stage props did you suggest to depict the surrounding race wars and the ultimate bombing of Easley's home?

The sound was going on throughout the play.

Was that an album or a sound track?

It was taped. Largely war sounds—shots, bombs—and, near the end of the play, it gets closer and closer and closer, and then there is the very final scene where they're up close with near hits, near misses, and direct hits. Then we actually had to use the kind of explosion techniques that you use in theater: smudge pots, a soft ceiling with plaster up in it that you could release, a blackout, turning chairs and stuff over, pulling down false walls—simple stage techniques. It was gradually a kind of closing in of war sounds.

Did you ever use colors to capture a particular effect? To what extent were colors involved? For example, if you would like to portray fire, did you just splatter orange and red?

You mean real fire and burning?

Yes.

Well, again, we used different kinds of pots and things for fire—things that can actually burn. And sometimes to get a fire effect, we used lights. But we usually used pots that were turned on, usually electrically. The stage manager or the lighting person would handle that. It was a simple process, although those kinds of things can be dangerous.

In "Experimental Death Unit #1," your stage notes call for "a white man's head still dripping blood." Can you explain how this was translated to the stage?

There was a friend of mine, a white painter, who made an exact facsimile of the actor's head out of papier-mâché, and it was so life-like that it actually created a kind of sensation. A guy named Dominique Capobianco molded papier-mâché face masks. He's an artist at Rutgers. He made papier-mâché heads that were exactly like the actors'. We had a special kind of dramatic effect that we used wherein the actors who were supposed to be beheaded would twist their heads down in their chests and pull up some kind of jackets we had. And they would fall so they were upstage and you couldn't see their heads, and then the guy who was cutting them off would look like he'd cut one off and he had the head already inside his coat. When he'd cut like that, you couldn't see the head struck and then he'd go down and his body would cover the dead man's body and he'd take the head out from under his coat and then come up with the head.

Ingenious!

Well, theater people think of these things. When you get theater people and you've got a project, you discuss it. That's why set designers, prop people, lighting people—these people are key to directors. No theater production is a one-person operation. That's absurd. Some of the technical aspects of these things I wouldn't begin to be able to put together. I could just say, "I think it should be like this," and that would be the way it was done. You've got people who know the theater. That's why, in really doing heavyweight theater, you've got to have some skilled people with you to really bring it off.

I can imagine "Slave Ship" called for a lot of ingenuity.

Yeah. That's why I say Gil Moses, to me, . . . I directed **"Slave Ship"** first in Newark at the Spirit House, and that was like . . . I mean we had on-and-off lights: "Click, click." It was nothing but the first floor of a house that I had torn the walls of down. We had almost nothing at all to work with. But when Gil took it on and when he used his imagination and the kind of the technical resources that were available to us at the Brooklyn Acade-

my, which were quite a bit, we were really able to do something good.

*In 1967 you directed **"Great Goodness of Life: A Coon Show"** at the Spirit House in Newark. Can you recall how you portrayed Attorney Breck? "A bald-headed smiling house slave in a wrinkled dirty tuxedo crawls across the stage; he has a wire attached to his back leading off-stage. A huge key in the side of his head. We hear the motors 'animating,' his body groaning like tremendous weights. He grins, and slobbers, turning his head slowly from side to side. He grins. He makes little quivering noises."*

Well, we were pretty faithful to that. Actually, we had . . . who played that? L. Earl Jay played that, I think, when we did it in New York. Are you talking about the wires and the big key in his head and stuff like that? Well, we made a hat like a hairpiece or something like that. Anyway, it sat up on his head and had a big key in it that whirled around—the key actually whirled around. It sort of fit over his head like a strap on top of his head. In other words, the key was the cap, and he put the cap on and then the key was attached to it on one side. It was like a rod coming down, off the cap and then the key stuck out of the rod. In the rod was the kind of mechanism that turned the key. And it was a key that you actually did wind up, and it was spring-loaded so that when you wound it up—when the attorney pushed the starter that he had on—it actually would turn: "Ch-ch-ch." It would look like the little toy soldiers or little robots that you see for kids.

*Returning to your means of adapting to various limitations, at any time did your street plays, **"Arm Yourself, Or Harm Yourself"** and **Police** encounter obstacles because of uncertain conditions due to temporary settings?*

Yeah. Real police came into this loft where we were rehearsing. They had told us something about we weren't supposed to read poetry down in the cellar in Newark. There was some controversy around that, but, in those days, the Newark police were the worst on the planet. That was one of the reasons that we were so quick to get a black mayor. That was the only kind of respite that we got from the Negroes that had been running the city. They did cool out the police, and they couldn't have stayed in there if they hadn't because the people had demonstrated in 1967 what they would do. Police ran up in my rehearsal and actually took a script out of my hand. We were rehearsing and police came in there. That's the kind of harrasment outside in the street. We had to do plays, and we were never quite sure how we would be greeted by the powers that be—the police, etc. One time we did **Junkies Are Full of Shhh** . . . and a woman started beating the junky—started beating the dope pusher like she thought it was really happening. She started whipping Yusef Iman's butt. We had to pull her off him. She was going to beat him up. I guess her child had gotten involved in drugs. It's always uncertain outside.

Several prominent actors showed up in your early plays. Can you talk about the contributions of, say, Barbara Teer or Al Freeman?

Well, Barbara did **"Experimental Death Unit #1,"** and as it turned out, the guy who was directing it first was a nut. I mean, he was absolutely a maniac and he and Barbara got to talking and he slapped her.

You're talking about Tom Hackensack?

Right. He slapped her face, and then I had to take over the direction. I thought she did a very very good job myself. That was one of the plays that I directed both downtown and up at the Black Arts. I think it came off all right. We did it at this benefit down at the Saint Mark's Theater, and we had the resources and stuff. I thought it was a good experience. There were a lot of things I learned directing then. Now, interestingly enough, Barbara—when we first started working—said there was no such thing as Black Theater. She said theater was theater. We used to stand out there and argue—she and this guy named McBeth, who later got to be head of the Lafayette. They were both opposed to the concept of Black Theater. They said it didn't exist. They said it was just theater. Later on, it is interesting that they came to understand the fact that there is such a thing as Black Theater and that they have gotten a great deal of success in Black Theater. Barbara is a good actress and a very capable director.

I don't know what she is doing now with the National Black Theater. But that was something that we called for in the 1968 Black Power Conference—a National Black Theater. The Negro Ensemble is the Negro Ensemble. But we need a theater that can encompass, coast to coast, the best actors, the best directors, the best playwrights, the best set designers, the best musicians who would tour the country and play to our people all over the country. That's what we need definitely.

I noticed that your wife was a member of the cast of **Black Mass.** *To what extent has she helped in shaping and developing your 1960's plays?*

Well, my wife certainly has a great deal of influence on me—I guess just like everybody else's wife or husband has on them. We had just met some months before that. I was making a movie which never got seen by anybody except the FBI. They have records of this movie that we made and the images in it, and nobody has ever seen it. It's fantastic.

Did they confiscate it?

No. They were just watching when we made it. We didn't know it, but when I got the Freedom of Information Act papers, they had listed it in there. They saw us shooting out in the yard, and I had nooses hanging off the trees and people in KKK costumes marching. We had met not long before the time of **Black Mass,** and I think that it was subsequent to **Black Mass** that we began to see each other. But she has been a very strong influence upon me in terms of . . . you know, a lot of times you bounce concepts off people whether you know it or not. People do shape your concepts. In a lot of my earlier plays, the black woman is not dealt with well at all. And I think that she has been

very very forceful in terms of trying to make me understand that, which I hope I have understood, and just generally in terms of helping me to give some weighty attention to black people's real problems rather than the problems of one sector of the black middle class, which, I think, is another one of my tendencies—to make my problems everybody's problems or my own kinds of concepts sort of automatically all black people's. So, I think she's helped clarify—to the extent that it can be called clarified—that thing. It's a continuing influence obviously. We work together. She was in the Spirit House Movers when it first began. Then the organization that we put together got in the way of that, and she wasn't in the Movers later on. Now we are working together with this group called Blue Ark that we have. We do poetry and we work usually with three musicians, and she's a part of that and hopefully we are going to do some more dramatic work together.

How were the changes in your ideology—that is, from nationalist to Marxist—reflected on stage?

I had a big falling out with the woman who played Lula when I directed **"Dutchman"** in Newark when I first came back to Newark in 1966. This white woman—I can't think of her name—she said something that I didn't like, and I said, "Well, you know. I don't even like white people. I don't even know why I'm standing here arguing with you." That kind of stupid stuff. Certainly, during my post-nationalist phase, I would not be involved in some kind of crazy stuff like that. I mean, when you just crack people over the head because you get angry with them, and then you take them out the worst way you can. I don't think I would do that. It was the nationalism certainly that fueled that kind of approach. I guess people can tell you stories about that. I used to do a lot of that.

I think the most important change has been in terms of the content of the plays—the line, the political line, the ideological line that comes out of the plays. I think that is the real critical change—from plays that pretty much focus on kicking white folks' asses and getting them off ours to trying to find a way to bring in the more complex reality that we live, which obviously is full of white supremacy, racism, and exploitation, with black people being on the bottom of the heap. But I think that what that is really is what I try to talk about: how it got to be the way that it is, and, I guess, what we can do about it—and that we can survive it.

OVERVIEWS AND GENERAL STUDIES

Lloyd W. Brown (essay date 1980)

SOURCE: "Drama," in *Amiri Baraka,* Twayne Publishers, 1980, pp. 135-65.

[In the following excerpt, Brown demonstrates Baraka's poignant use of dramatic form and his careful integration of plot, character, and setting. Brown also comments on

Baraka's manipulation of such traditional forms as the morality play to criticize conventional social structures, values, and beliefs.]

The Early Plays

"The Baptism," first produced in 1964, is a useful introduction to Baraka's drama because it includes features that dominate the earlier plays and others that foreshadow subsequent developments in Baraka's dramatic art. Set in a church, the play is actually a modern morality drama about a young boy who is accused by an old woman of masturbating while pretending to pray. As the action unfolds it centers on a growing contest for the soul—and body—of the boy. The contest pits the old woman and the minister of the church against a homosexual who is contemptuous of his opponents' hypocrisy toward sex and who expresses a frank need for love and for an honest sexuality. The minister and the old woman are revolting not simply because they are puritanical but because their puritanism is a thin disguise for sexual desires (for the boy in this case) that they are unable to express frankly. As the contest becomes violent they strike the homosexual to the ground and in turn they are cut down by the boy who now claims to be the Son of God. At this point the play ends abruptly: the boy is carried off by a motorcyclist who is supposed to be a "messenger" of the boy's father.

As a morality play centered on a moral struggle between love and puritanism **"The Baptism"** exploits an old dramatic tradition with special ironic effects. The usual conflict between good and evil in the morality play tradition of Christian culture appears here with significant modifications. The forces of evil are now associated with the Christian Church itself; love and charity are embodied by the homosexual, a conventional figure of moral and sexual "perversion." And given the ambiguous figure of the boy himself (child figure and Christ archetype) then the moral struggle takes on an ironically twofold meaning: it is traditional insofar as it involves a contest for the soul of the human individual; and it is antitraditional in that Christianity is no longer an unquestioned symbol of goodness but is actually associated with evil. Indeed the most crucial outcome of the play's moral conflict is the degree to which Christianity emerges as an inherently corrupting tradition which makes it impossible for the individual to experience love and sexuality to the fullest, except on nonconformist or rebellious terms. Social traditions in the play are inherently destructive because they sanction a pervasive lovelessness and a neurotic fear of sex and feeling. The church is the main target in this regard because it is the institution which embodies these traditions.

The morality design of the play is, therefore, basically ironic in conception. Baraka recalls the old morality traditions of early Christian drama in order to attack those traditions and the Christian ethic that they espoused. And insofar as **"The Baptism"** subverts Christian morality and art, it anticipates the use of the morality play format in Baraka's black nationalist, anti-Western drama. For in those later plays, as we shall see, political conflicts take on the

form of moral contests in which a Western dramatic tradition (the morality play) becomes a device for rejecting the West itself. Moreover, this subversive, antitraditionalist use of tradition is reflected in the play's title. The ritual of baptism is no longer an initiation into the established conventions of religious belief and social morality. It has now become a ritual of exposure and subversion, one directed against the conventions themselves.

Similarly the ritual of religious sacrifice acquires a new significance in the play. The minister and the old woman insist that the boy must be "sacrificed" in order to atone for his sexual "sin." But their demand is really a hypocritical evasion. The choice of the boy as sacrificial victim allows them to evade the consequences of their destructive attitudes towards sexuality. It enables them to divert attention from the repressed sexual longings that are so manifest in their "moral" rhetoric—especially in the old woman's suggestively detailed account of the boy's sin: "You spilled your seed while pretending to talk to God. I saw you. That quick short stroke. And it was so soft before, and you made it grow in your hand. I watched it stiffen, and your lips move and those short hard moves with it straining in your fingers for flesh. . . . Your wet stickly hand. I watched you smell it."

In effect the planned sacrifice allows them to avoid the sinfulness of their own hypocrisy and the emotional destructiveness of their puritanism by treating "sinfulness" as a problem that can be solved through the ritual sacrifice—of another. Indeed the very idea of ritual, whether of baptism or sacrifice, is associated in the play with elaborate systems of hypocrisy and self-evasion. Hence Baraka's adaptation of such rituals for the form of his play amounts to the ironic use of ritual as a form of protest and rebellion—against established rituals (systems) and their associated social values. And here too **"The Baptism"** anticipates Baraka's black nationalist drama where the idea of ritual and the forms of established ritual are associated with the culture that is being rejected by the play.

Both as morality play and as ritual drama **"The Baptism"** is distinguished by a marked emphasis on the idea of role playing. The characters have no names as such. They are presented as types (old woman, minister, homosexual, boy and messenger); and as such they are social roles reflecting the cultural values that are central to the play's themes. In this instance each character's personality reflects a theatrical self-consciousness about her or his role: the minister is the sanctimonious voice of Christianity; the old woman energetically acts out her identity as the symbol of female chastity; the homosexual deliberately exaggerates his role as a "queen" in order to emphasize his calculated contempt for social convention; and the boy moves self-consciously from being the familiar symbol of childhood innocence to being a Christ-child.

On the whole this pointed presentation of characters as roles has the effect of emphasizing the degree to which the conventions and values attacked in the play have encouraged individuals to assume roles that reflect social norms instead of giving free play to honest feeling. In this sense the stereotypical nature of such roles is a form of social realism, for it underscores the limiting and deforming effects of established traditions on the human personality. This, too, explains the significance of self-conscious role playing in the other plays. In each instance the issue of roles reflects the dramatist's careful integration of his theme with his sense of dramatic art: the role playing of dramatic theater is also a symptom of social reality.

Altogether, then, **"The Baptism"** is an impressive example of Baraka's early ability to synthesize dramatic form and theme. And this synthesis is linked with the play's major theme—the failure of love in contemporary society. The very issue of forms, roles, and rituals is crucial in the play because they have become empty shells in the absence of any real feeling. Consequently moral statements and declarations of love are invariably hypocritical, particularly when they are made by self-consciously traditional figures. The role of the homosexual is therefore particularly ironic in this regard: the alleged pervert emerges as the healthiest of the lot because he frankly expresses his commitment to love and because he refuses to accept the puritan antithesis between flesh and spirit. He is the subversive outsider, pitted against the minister who is the loveless, and unlovable, apostle of Christian "love" and "charity." The homosexual's candor about love and sex (he does not disguise his erotic interest in the boy) amounts to a virtue. On the other hand the minister and the old woman attempt to disguise their love for the boy with the rhetoric of puritan morality. In so doing they corrupt their sexual response to the boy. Their puritanism has transformed it into mere prurience. As in *Preface to a Twenty Volume Suicide Note* puritan hypocrisy has turned love into an evil thing. This kind of transformation is also the burden of the later, black nationalist plays where white racism and black self-hatred are linked to the general fear of love in society. It also dominates the theme of an early work like **"The Toilet,"** where, as in **"The Baptism,"** the general failure of love is thrown into sharp relief by the role of the homosexual as subversive outsider.

Originally produced in 1964, **"The Toilet"** is set in an urban high school toilet. The plot is rudimentary. Ray Foots leads a group of boys in crude horseplay which rapidly culminates in violence. The victim of the violence is Karolis, a sensitive boy who is accused of having written a love letter to Foots. Karolis surprises Foots by refusing to deny the accusation and by insisting on fighting him. Discomfited by Karolis's honesty and belligerence Foots tries to avoid the fight on the ground that Karolis has already been badly beaten by members of the gang. But Karolis persists, beats Foots, who has to be rescued by the other boys, and is battered into unconsciousness by the gang. Karolis is left lying on the toilet floor, but after a brief interval Foots sneaks back in tears to cradle Karolis's head in his arms.

The toilet setting remains throughout the play as its dominant symbol. Its appearance and smells suggest the ugliness and fifth that Baraka attributes to his characters' social and moral milieu. In turn this vision of America as toilet defines the personalities of the characters themselves. The choice of toilet as setting shrewdly duplicates the usual adolescent preference for the toilet as the stage for a certain kind of brutish bravado or for covert rebelliousness. In individual terms the filth and stench represent the unsavory personalities of Foots and his gang. Finally the privacy of the toilet lends itself to the theme of repression—the repression of love—which runs throughout the play.

The moral corruption that is suggested by the toilet setting is associated here with a kind of perverted masculinity. Foots and his gang represent a cult of manhood which takes the form of mere brutishness. This brutishness is reflected in the inane but violent dialogue and by an intense, neurotic need to dominate others in verbal jousting or in improvised forms of boxing and basketball. In turn this corrupted maleness is attributed to the failure of love in Foots's world. As in **"The Baptism"** the theme of moral and emotional corruption is heightened by a sense of irony. In this instance the irony is centered on the name "Love" borne by a member of Foots's gang. And as in **"The Baptism"** this irony is intensified by the fact that it is the alleged pervert, the homosexual, who emerges as the most humane of these young males going through the traditional rites of passage into manhood.

Karolis's humanism and heroism consist of the fact that he has the kind of courage which enables him to express his love in the incriminating letter and to affirm that love in the face of hostility. Ironically, the sleazy privacy of the toilet has become the setting for a certain kind of public declaration or self-revelation, one that strikes at the guilty secrecy with which society perceives love and with which Foots eventually responds to love. By a similar token the conventionally "masculine" hero, Foots, emerges as an antihero: he is contemptible in his fearful need to deny and punish Karolis's love, and is pathetic, at best, in that final moment of his belated, and secret, demonstration of love.

Finally, that secrecy ends the play on a note of unequivocal realism. It confirms the continuation of these prevailing social codes which encourage a guilty secrecy about sex and emotional experience. The toilet setting therefore remains crucially significant to the very end. It defines the filthiness that results from the denial of feeling in Foots and his kind. Foots's declaration of love at the end is actually corrupted by the social values which dictate secrecy; and the toilet symbolizes the persistent corruptions which result from those values. The play's setting is therefore a dynamic force in the action of the play and in the experience of the characters. And on this basis it reflects a rather impressive grasp of theater as the total integration of setting, action and character.

"Dutchman," first produced and published in 1964, also reflects a rather self-conscious use of setting. Here the setting is a subway, "heaped," according to the playwright, "in modern myth." The subway is less intimately involved in the personalities and action of the play than is the toilet in **"The Toilet."** In **"Dutchman"** the setting owes its significance to the manner in which it evokes mythic materials that are, in turn, interwoven with the play's themes and action. The winner of the Obie award for the best off-Broadway production of 1964, **"Dutchman"** has perhaps been the most widely discussed of Baraka's plays; and this popularity is attributable, in part, to the interest of critics in the role of myth in the play.

In examining **"Dutchman"** as mythic drama it is important to take seriously Baraka's description of the setting as one that is "heaped" in myths. Any approach that singles out one mythic theme will miss the degree to which the play's structure depends in part on the interweaving of several myths. The underground setting recalls the holds of the slave ships, and this image is reinforced by the title itself: the first African slaves were reportedly brought to the New World by Dutch slave traders. The image of slavery is further reinforced by the possibility that the underground setting refers to the famous "underground railway" which assisted runaway slaves on their way from the South to the North. The Dutch reference may also be linked with the legend of the Flying Dutchman—the story of a ship doomed to sail the seas forever without hope of gaining land. This ship is also supposed to be a slave-trading vessel. In turn the theme of retribution in the legend of the Flying Dutchman links the idea of a curse with the history of slavery. Slavery insured the loss of American innocence quite early in American history. That is, it undermined the American's claim to some special kind of functional idealism. And here the complex formation of images and myths include biblical myth, for like the descendants of Adam and Eve after the biblical fall, contemporary Americans must cope with the consequences of a prior curse—in this instance the curse of slavery.

Finally, Adam and Eve have their counterparts in the play. The black Clay (Adam) and the white Lula (Eve) are both linked by America's fearful fascination with the sexual juxtaposition of the black man and the white woman. Clay is the black American Adam, tempted by the forbidden fruit of Lula's white sexuality. On her side, Lula's sexual fascination with his blackness is interwoven with her racial condescension toward him. The play's plot revolves around the ethnosexual implications of Baraka's handling of myths. As a white American Lula is both the forbidden sexual fruit and the Flying Dutchman, compelled by the curse of racism and historical slavery, to engage in a series of repetitive actions that reflect the recurrent guilt, fascination, and hatred with which whites view blacks in the society. Hence she boards the subway train, engages Clay in conversation (on race and sex), then stabs him to death when his initial attraction changes to scornful resentment at her racial condescension. And after Clay's body has been removed she prepares to engage another young black man who has just boarded the train.

The total effect of the play's mythic structure is twofold. It creates the impression of continuity in the issues with which the myths are associated—racial oppression, destructive sexual attitudes, and an emotionally paralyzing puritanism. But the structure also heightens our awareness of the characters as social types. Notwithstanding Baraka's well-known disclaimer [in *Home: Social Essays*, 1966] Lula and Clay are not simply unique individuals. They are clearly archetypal figures representing social traditions (racial and sexual) and exemplifying the behavior that results from those traditions. Lula, for example, is at pains to emphasize that she is a type; and she feels old because as a type she represents generations of attitudes. She also perceives Clay as a type whose personality seems quite open to her because he belongs to a well-known pattern.

Lula and Clay are both types in this sense. And at the beginning of the play they are clearly presented, on the basis of their interaction, as racial and sexual stereotypes—Lula the white goddess and white liberal, and Clay the naively middle-class black stud. This stereotypical dimension is a calculated aspect rather than mere defect of the play. It arises from the perception and behavior of the characters who have chosen to limit their humanity within the confines of racial and sexual stereotypes that have been molded by social conventions. They are deliberately acting out predetermined roles instead of attempting to comprehend and communicate with each other's humanity. The built-in element of theater operates at a conscious level in the play. Hence Lula elaborates upon her self-description as a type by remarking that she is an actress, and Clay suggests that their encounter has proceeded as if it had been written as a script. As in **"The Baptism"** role playing is not simply a theatrical device; it is also deliberately chosen pattern of social behavior. The protagonists' choice of stereotypical roles is a symptom of their limitations; and in turn, the roles which they choose are intrinsic to the dramatic structure of the play itself.

Moreover they are presented and judged on their acceptance of these roles, and on their ability to look beyond the pretence in their own roles and in the roles of the other. Lula is very conscious of her role as the white goddess of America's racial mythology and chooses to revel in the destructiveness of that role. By a similar token she is incapable of dealing with Clay when he ceases to be an Uncle Tom and a black stud. Her white indifference to the humanity of blacks and to the essence of their culture is epitomized by her shallow interpretation of the blues as mere "belly-rub" music. On his side Clay fails initially, insofar as he accepts Lula's stereotypical attitudes and insofar as he caters to those attitudes by being the black stud and Uncle Tom. This failure proves fatal in the long run because it allows Lula to establish the kind of interaction that leads to his death: having subordinated himself to her sexual fantasies and her liberal condescension, he inevitably drives her to destructive anger by asserting his humanity.

However, Clay's failure is not complete. He gains a limited triumph in that very assertion of humanity which makes his death inevitable. At first he shifts from the bland, self-effacing acquiescence of the Uncle Tom to the covert hostility which allows him to agree, sarcastically, when Lula assumes that black history and black music evolved out of big happy plantations in the slave-holding South. This covert hostility is soon replaced by open resentment. He castigates Lula's one-dimensional image of blacks and mocks her inability to realize that in many instances the blacks who seem to conform with this image are really rejecting her by subversively acting out her fantasies. They are playing roles based on "lies."

Clay's own interpretation of the blues reflects his own growth from mere role playing to a complex rebel: the blues are not mere "belly-rub" music but the expression of complex experiences ranging from joy and sorrow to despair and rage. As Clay interprets the blues he himself grows into a complex humanity and away from the racial and sexual perspectives of Lula and her "type." In the process we discover in his character the same kind of rebelliousness that he attributes to the blues tradition. Lula destroys Clay the rebel because his rebellion threatens her by destroying the stereotypes and myths that are essential to her own sexual and racial roles.

Yet Clay also fails in the end because, although his rebellious perspectives are substantial enough, his identity as a rebel is incomplete. Even as he expounds on the power and integrity of black music, Clay unfavorably compares himself with the musician as ethnic artist. Clay himself is a poet whose art lacks, in his opinion, the ethnic integrity of black, grass-roots forms like the blues: as a derivative of Western literature his own writings are a "kind of bastard literature," and his poetry is an escape from direct rebellious action. His words as poet have become a contemptible substitute for the act: "Safe with my words, and no deaths, and clean, hard thoughts, urging me to new conquests."

Clay's bitter self-analysis is based on two familiar and recurrent themes in Baraka's work. As a black writer and intellectual Clay is caught up in a cultural conflict which paralyzes him, limiting his capacity for rebellious action, despite his intellectual awareness of the need for rebellion. On the one hand he is drawn to Lula's ethnocentric white culture, but on the other hand he responds to the black ethnicity represented by the blues. His death, therefore, represents the self-destructive consequences of this kind of moral and intellectual paralysis. Second, Clay's ineffectuality as rebel stems in part from the fact that his poetic art is self-contained rather than actively committed to social action. His is literary art for art's sake. He suffers from a fascination with words for their own sake. As Clay himself admits, blacks "don't need all those words." On this basis it is easy to see the close connections between the theme of rebellion in **"Dutchman"** and the advocacy of change in the more explicitly revolutionary plays of a later period. Given Clay's limitations, the issues of rebellion and change are curtailed in this play. Here the question is not one of advocating change as such. This is to come in the later plays. In **"Dutchman"** we are offered an analysis of those things which make rebellion and change little more than imagined possibilities in the lives of Clay and his "type," but which will become urgent options when the idea of rebellion combines word and act.

Despite its setting—a revolutionary race war—**"The Slave"** is closer to **"Dutchman"** than to the later revolutionary plays in that here, too, we have a work that analyzes the potential rebel. The subject of analysis in this case is

Walker Vessels, the leader of the blacks in the race war. The action centers on his encounter with his former wife, Grace Easley, and her present husband, Bradford (both white), when he returns to Grace's home at the height of the fighting. It is a violent encounter that is marked by racial recriminations on both sides, and the sounds of the race war outside provide the background for this personal conflict. The confrontation ends with the house collapsing under shell fire. Grace dies just after realizing that her two children by Walker are dead, either as the result of Walker's war or directly by his hands.

It is easy enough to see the play, on its literal level, simply as another black militant fantasy of racial revenge. But such an approach does not really do justice to the more complex and interesting features of the work. Here, as in **"Dutchman,"** the play's conflicts center on the tensions within the black protagonist. Although the play's action emphasizes the desirability of radical change, it is actually more significant as an extended analysis of those attitudes which stimulate or retard the capacity for radical ethnic change within the black psyche. In this regard we should view Grace and Bradford not simply as representatives of the white world around Walker but also as embodiments of his white, Western perspectives, those perspectives which inhibit his racial pride by encouraging self-hatred. As a poet, for example, Walker feels that his art has been compromised by a certain dependency on the Western tradition. Hence the white Easley is expected to recognize Walker's poetry and literary tastes because they both share the same intellectuality. Walker hates Easley as the white enemy outside, but he loathes and fears him as the symbol of the "whiteness" within himself.

Grace is comparable with Bradford Easley in this respect. She is the image of that white femininity that has historically attracted a certain kind of self-hating black male. Thus Walker's previous marriage to her represents a self-destructive obsession. It is an obsession that has formed the racial triangle of black man, white woman, and white man—even in Shakespeare. As Walker muses aloud to his two antagonists, "Remember when I used to play a second-rate Othello? . . . You remember that, don't you, Professor No-Dick? You remember when I used to walk around wondering what that fair sister was thinking? . . . I was Othello . . . Grace there was Desdemona . . . and you were Iago."

In short, the black imitation of whites is represented by the Iago-Easley figure of treachery—treachery to one's racial identity. And the self-destruction that is inherent in that treachery is embodied by the half-man (Professor No-Dick) whose alleged impotence represents Walker's crippled humanity as a black. In reviling Grace and man-handling Easley during their confrontation Walker tries to exorcise his crippling white self-perception. The contrast in the play between the strong, masterful black Walker and the weak white Easley has little to do with Baraka's alleged "endorsement of the stereotype of Negro sexuality" [*Black Music,* 1968]. It represents, instead, an internal conflict—within Walker—between an assertive racial integrity and the stunted awareness that results from the denial of one's black identity.

Easley, then, personifies the cultural values and racial attitudes that compromise Walker's role as revolutionary. This point is implicit in the title. Having progressed from the status of a slave in the prologue (where he addresses the audience in the guise of a field slave), Walker is going through a transitional stage in which he now recognizes his continuing intellectual serfdom as it is incarnated in Easley, his cultural alter ego. The "race war" of the plot is, therefore, less important as a literal happening than it is significant as an allegorical background for the conflicts within Walker. Indeed the manner in which Baraka presents Walker at the beginning and conclusion of the play emphasizes the allegorical nature of the race war. The physical violence and the emotional confrontations in the play are actually a projection of Walker's subjective experience as a split personality. And in keeping with that subjective context, these events assume a dreamlike form if they are viewed in relation to the words of Walker Vessels when he appears in the prologue as an old field slave: "We know, even before these shapes are realized, that these worlds, these depths or heights we fly to smoothly, as in a dream, or slighter, when we stare dumbly into space, leaning our eyes just behind a last quick moving bird, then sometimes the place and twist of what we are will push and sting, and what the crust of our stance has become will ring in our ears and shatter that piece of our eyes that is never closed."

Walker is actually preparing his audience for a "dream," a self-revealing vision that will disturb and awaken. And since this is to be a form of self-revelation then it will shatter that apathy ("stupid longing not to know") which characterizes the slave mentality. The shattering of this apathy can create "killers" (real revolutionaries) or "foot-dragging celebrities," who exploit their "militant" image for personal gain. Applied to the events that follow the prologue Walker's remarks imply that the race war incidents and the confrontation with Grace and Bradford Easley are the elements of a vision that reveals Walker's divided ethnic consciousness to himself and to the audience. That consciousness includes a capacity for revolution, for the radical reshaping of his ethnic perception.

In this connection, Walker's physical relationship with the main action of the play strongly suggests that the latter is a kind of dream sequence: he is an old man in the prologue, and at the end of the introductory speech he "assumes the position he will have when the play starts." If this physical transformation (from old field slave to Walker Vessels) suggests that there is a "fading in" to the main-action dream sequence, then the physical change at the end of the play is equally suggestive: as Walker the rebel leader stumbles out, he becomes "the old man at the beginning of the play"—signifying the "fading out" of the dream.

All of this brings up the question of Walker's actual identity. He himself points to his ambiguity in the prologue: "I am much older than I look . . . or maybe much younger. Whatever I am or seem . . . to you, then let that rest. But figure, still, that you might not be right." He is warning against a literal approach to his character, for he is really an archetype of the black experience. He is therefore both older and younger than he looks because he incorporates the past and the present; and his dream opens up future possibilities. The "old" field-slave personality is the key to this archetypal role. That role is ambiguous. In one sense his servile status symbolizes the subjection to white images and cultural values. But in another sense his identity as a *field* slave points up rebellious potential. In this latter regard he recalls Malcolm X's interpretation of the field slave's image in black history. Unlike the "house Negro" who loved the white slave-master, the "field Negroes" hated the master and were always eager to rebel or run away from slavery.

Malcolm X's field Negro and Baraka's field slave are the same archetype. He is characterized by a predisposition toward rebellion. And as such an archetype Walker represents both past and present ("older" and "younger") militancy. To return to the words of the prologue Walker's ideas involve the rediscovery of a long history of black militancy and resistance: "Old, old blues people moaning in their sleep, singing, man, oh, nigger, nigger, you still here, as hard as nails, and takin' no shit from nobody." Walker's consciousness of black dreams of rebellion and his interest in the blues as a tradition of resistance confirm his own rebellious predisposition. And in turn that predisposition lends itself to dreams of revolution—the kind of dream that constitutes the main action of the play.

Walker's capacity to dream of revolution in specific terms and his growing sense of commitment take him beyond Clay's rather muddled impulses in **"Dutchman."** But in general Walker is comparable with Clay in that he too suffers from a destructive split-consciousness. As in Clay's case this division stems from the unresolved tensions between his identity as a militant black and his continuing involvement with (white) cultural norms that inhibit his militant potential. And like Clay, Walker is hamstrung by a frustrating dichotomy between word and action. Hence his failure as a poet is not only caused by a self-hating imitation of white models. His poetry has also failed because it exists apart from his dreams of revolutionary change. The (literary) word and (revolutionary) action remain separate in his character. Hence whether it is considered as a literal event or, more interestingly as Walker's fantasy, the race war remains an inchoate happening rather than a concrete action informed by a shaping revolutionary imagination.

Black Revolutionary Drama

Baraka's involvement in the black nationalist movement stimulates a significant shift in his drama. In his black revolutionary plays theater is no longer a process of reenacting or analyzing tensions, or conflicts, between the revolutionary idea or word and the political act. It attempts, instead, to be an example of the dramatic art as political action. That is, theater itself is a political activity by virtue of the fact that the play has become a form of political advocacy. But although the theater of political advocacy would seem to fulfill Baraka's ideological ideals—as black aesthetician and later as scientific socialist—the plays of this period seldom meet the criteria which he himself admires in Maoist aesthetics. Many of the plays are ideologically "correct," from Baraka's black nationalist viewpoint, but they seldom approximate that "highest possible perfection of artistic form" which Baraka is later to demand of political art.

A basic problem, one that is seldom resolved in this period, is that Baraka finds it difficult to use drama for sociopolitical purposes while maintaining convincing dramatic forms. Consequently, too, many of the plays are little more than the kind of bombast that appears in the preface to his *Four Black Revolutionary Plays*: "We are building publishing houses, and newspapers, and armies, and factories / we will change the world before your eyes."

A. *Short Pieces*

Many of the plays of this period are little more than agit prop. As we have already noted, several of these remain unpublished; and on the basis of these shorter pieces it appears that Baraka is not often interested in the play's dramatic design. At other times potentially interesting dramatic forms (street theater and ritual drama, for example) lack thematic substance. Some works are mainly polemics against white racism. **"Home on the Range"** (1968), for example, depicts members of a white suburban family through the eyes of a black burglar. They appear as a collection of dim-wits who talk gibberish. **"The Death of Malcolm X"** (1969) dramatizes the events leading up to Malcolm X's assassination as a white conspiracy involving brainwashed blacks. But the more interesting plays are less concerned with white society as such and are more involved with examining the black experience itself from a black nationalist point of view.

"Experimental Death Unit #1" (1965) belongs to this latter group. It depicts a street scene during an apparent black revolt. A patrol of black soldiers encounters a black prostitute and her two white customers and kills all three. The symbolism is obvious enough. Prostitution represents the broader historical experience in which blacks barter their humanity in order to be accepted or merely tolerated by white society (*Four Black Revolutionary Plays*).

The title of **"Arm Yourself or Harm Yourself"** (1967) sums up the simple message: blacks who hesitate to arm themselves against violent whites (particularly the police) are choosing suicide. The suicidal nature of nonviolence is, therefore, emphasized by the death of three brothers at the hands of the police—as they stand on the street debating the merits of armed militancy versus nonviolence.

Police (1968) is partly based on pantomime. It centers on the dilemma of a black police officer whose job places him in the role of killing blacks on behalf of whites. He is hated by those whites, and he is despised by the blacks who eventually drive him to suicide during a riot. The police officer's life symbolizes the split loyalties which afflict many blacks. His death becomes the black community's symbolic ritual of expunging self-hatred and racial treachery. Significantly, the self-hatred that destroys the

police officer is associated with older blacks. The young blacks are the revolutionaries. They drive the police officer to suicide, and at the end of the play they promise to return in order to take care of "some heavy business." The events of the play spark the promise of fundamental changes that are associated with a new (young) consciousness.

Black youth also spearhead the revolution in *Junkies Are Full of SHHH . . .* (1971). Here Damu and Chuma set out to rid the community (Newark) of drug pushers. In the process they kill the whites who control the drug traffic, and Bigtime, the principal black drug pusher. The play concludes with Bigtime's body being pulled out to be displayed on the street as a message to the community.

These plays are all linked by the fact that they are street theater. Their setting is primarily or exclusively the streets of black neighborhoods. Their themes are rooted in the "street" experience (prostitution, police actions, rioting, and drug traffic). And they are obviously aimed at those people whose lives are influenced by these street experiences. Moreover, as the rather grisly ending of *Junkies* demonstrates, street theater of this kind treats the street as a kind of medium, a communications device that may be used destructively (by junkies) or constructively (by young revolutionaries spreading their message). Consequently, the very idea of street theater exploits the familiar image of the street itself as a living dramatic environment, an environment that offers its audience a variety of messages. The play's setting defines its scope and action.

In addition to the theater of the street, Baraka also produced a number of other short pieces which are really based on ritualistic pantomime, dance, and chant. These are the plays of the later black nationalist period in which the emphasis is on the celebration of blackness rather than on exorcising white racism or black self-hatred. In this vein *Bloodrites* (1971) is a ritual dance. It features groups of blacks dancing around (white) devil figures and chanting black power slogans in Swahili. The devils wither away in exhaustion while the blacks gain increasing strength from their dance and chants. *Black Power Chant* (1972) is precisely what its title signifies: a group of dancers chant black power slogans as they move about on the stage. *Ba-Ra-Ka*, too, is based on song, dance, and political slogans.

On the basis of theme these plays are undistinguished. They never move beyond the obvious. The really interesting feature of such plays lies in their design and impact as spectacle. Dance (act) and chant (word) are integrated within highly stylized forms of ritual. And despite the intellectual thinness of these works they represent Baraka's continuing interest in ritual as drama, an interest that has obviously grown from the satiric subversiveness of **"The Baptism"** to the use of ritual as a legitimate medium in its own right. Here it is the medium of celebration, drawing upon the rhetoric of black power slogans, as well as the rhythms of black dance and music. In the process this kind of theater is intrinsically bound up with the experience that it celebrates: it is a an expression of black power—a symptom of the movement rather than simply an enactment of it.

B. *The Longer Plays*

Despite their obvious flaws Baraka's short plays are generally more interesting than most of his black nationalist dramas. These shorter works provide some direct clues to Baraka's dramatic imagination in terms of street theater, ritual drama, and theater as a committed art form. And as such they offer the audience a relatively more stimulating experience of theater than much of what Baraka has produced since the first major plays. The longer black nationalist pieces, however, reflect no significant innovations in Baraka's dramatic writing, although their themes are more ambitious than those of the shorter works.

Black Mass (1966), a science fantasy in the Frankenstein tradition, is typical of the limited achievement of the longer plays. As the title indicates, this is another example of Baraka's ritual drama. In this case the ritual is based on the religious myth, "Yacub's History," in the Nation of Islam (previously known as the Black Muslims). Here the idea and function of ritual are closer to the satiric themes of **"The Baptism"** than they are to the themes of celebration in the short black nationalist plays. The title is therefore ironic: it confirms the evil connotations of black mass (black magic) and black identity in white, Christian culture; but at the same time it defines evil on an antiChristian, antiwhite basis. Hence the evil in the play is really caused by a black scientist, Jacoub, who creates the first white being, a creature that quickly turns out to be a monster. The beast corrupts and destroys blacks—including Jacoub himself—by tainting them with its whiteness.

The beast represents Jacoub's moral bankruptcy and his racial self-betrayal. In creating the beast Jacoub panders to what the black nationalist perceives as a sterile need to create for the sake of creation. Jacoub does not envisage his creation in any functional sense. And on this basis his scientific talent belongs to that tradition of a narrow, self-serving rationalism which Baraka repeatedly attacks in his writings. But Jacoub's scientific narrowness is not only suspect on this moral basis. It is also reprehensible because it reflects his racial self-hatred. Creating for the sake of creating, whether in art or in science, is a "white" Western value system, and in catering to such a value system Jacoub betrays his racial and cultural tradition—a functional tradition, as defined in black nationalist terms. Thus the cries of the white beast ("White! . . . White! . . . Me . . . Me . . .") reflect Jacoub's self-destructiveness. Although the cries express the racist's megalomania in one sense, they also express that racial self-deprecation which has historically eroded black pride and cultural values. As Jacoub's fellow scientists warn him, his undertaking negates human feeling and decency and represents "the emptiness of godlessness," because it involves the betrayal of his ethnic and moral integrity.

The moral and ethnic implications of Jacoub's personality are also linked with Baraka's perception of time and history. Jacoub's invention involves the "discovery" of time; but, as his colleagues protest, time is merely a demon that turns human beings into "running animals." Jacoub's obsession with time is therefore suspect because it implies the subordination of the human personality to the rigid categories (exemplified here by time) of a narrow, rationalistic view of experience. And in ethnic terms this obsession is another symptom of Jacoub's racial self-hatred: his rationalism is clearly identical to that scientifically defined concept of time and history which Baraka repeatedly attributes to white, Western culture, and which associates "progress" and the very idea of human "development" with clock time.

Finally, the play contrasts Jacoub's rationalism with a more integrated and complex perception of science—science as complete knowledge encompassing reason, spirit and feeling, rather than as a narrow technology dedicated to the creation of systems for their own sake. The "compassionless abstractions" that Jacoub's colleagues deplore in him are therefore "anti-life" because they represent the "substitution of thought" for feeling. At this point Baraka's familiar redefinition of magic, especially black magic ("black mass"), is crucial. The "true" scientists (Jacoub's colleagues) are magicians in that here, as in the *Black Magic* poems, magic represents knowledge as an integrated and creative process. On the other hand, Jacoub's fragmented approach to science as an enclosed system is destructive. His is a limited kind of knowledge in that it is divorced from humanistic concerns and moral values. This kind of science is a perverted and destructive kind of "magic," and Baraka ironically invests it with all the negative connotations with which white, technological cultures have responded to nonwhite traditions of "science." That is, he is now treating Jacoub's "white" science as evil magic, as a form of "witchcraft" or "superstition." The very idea of black magic therefore emerges from the play as an ironically ambiguous concept. It connotes (a) the black nationalist ideal of a creatively integrated approach to knowledge and experience, and (b) the evil magic which Western culture and blacks like Jacoub develop from a limited approach to science—at the same time that they reject the nonwhite ideal of knowledge as mere "superstition" and "black magic."

On the whole the themes of *Black Mass* are full of complex possibilities. But the play is badly flawed. Quite apart from the theatrically unconvincing plot and the self-defeating shrillness, Baraka fails to exploit fully the idea of ritual that his title so deliberately invokes. The play's ambitious complex of themes therefore remain unlinked with the kind of formal, ritualistic design that is promised by the work's title and religious background.

"Great Goodness of Life," subtitled "A Coon Show," is one of Baraka's better black nationalist plays. While *Black Mass* harks back, unsuccessfully, to the satiric use of ritual form in **"The Baptism," "Great Goodness of Life"** continues Baraka's earlier interest in the theater's role playing as a symptom of social roles. The idea of the "coon show" is therefore bound up with the play's presentation of racial types. Blacks and whites are satirically presented as stereotypes which they have imposed upon themselves as well as upon others. The racial role playing of society is actually an extended coon show in which white racism fosters a sense of superiority by attributing the subhuman coon role to blacks. And in their turn blacks reinforce their inferior status by playing this attributed role. The coon in this show is Court Royal; and the setting, a courtroom, heightens the impression of a "show" or piece of theater by virtue of the dramatic nature of judicial proceedings.

Court Royal has been accused by the white court of having harbored a murderer. He knows nothing about the crime with which he is charged, but as a racially timid and conservative black he is easily intimidated into accepting the court's final edict: he must expiate his "crime" by shooting the murderer, and as a result his soul will be "washed white as snow." Court Royal complies with the edict, then celebrates his freedom and "white" soul without once reacting to the fact that the young "murderer" claims him as father in the moment of death. As the play ends Court Royal suddenly assumes a lively pose and announces to Louise (off-stage) that he is going to the bowling alley for a while.

That closing vignette contrasts with the opening scene which is set outside an old log cabin, presumably in a rural setting that is far removed from the urban environment of a bowling alley. The shifts in time and place are comparable with similar changes in **"The Slave."** The juxtaposition of past and present, black rural roots and black urban present, dramatizes the continuity and the pervasiveness of the destructive attitudes represented by the coon show. And as in **"Dutchman"** these continuities are reflected in the play's deliberate emphasis on social types and role playing: by their very nature the stereotypes of the coon show underscore the enduring nature of the racial attitudes that they embody.

In his other major black nationalist play Baraka returns once again to a dramatic form that he first utilizes in his early drama. **"Madheart"** (1966) is subtitled "A Morality Play," and it therefore recalls the morality play tradition upon which **"The Baptism"** draws. In **"Madheart"** the "moral" conflicts of the morality drama are defined in terms of black nationalism. They center on an ethnosexual battle for the black male's soul, or more precisely, for his sexual allegiance. At the same time these conflicts involve a struggle for the racial integrity of the black everywoman who is torn between the old desire to imitate white models of femininity and the new black insistence on racial pride and black beauty.

The ethical and ethnic struggles of the play's themes are developed within an unconvincingly melodramatic plot. Black Man and Black Woman vanquish the seductive arrogance of the (white) Devil Lady. Then they undertake, in the spirit of black unity, to "take care" of the sick ones—Mother and Sister—who are still fascinated with white standards of sexual beauty. On the whole the moral tensions of the play are linked with the black male's consciousness and personality. He feels compelled to destroy the "whiteness" of Sister's self-hating images of white femininity, not only for her own sake, but for his own: he needs to eradicate from within himself his destructive obsession with the white woman as a supposedly superior

being. He is both repelled by and fascinated with the white woman (Devil Lady) for these reasons. And this fascination-abhorrence is emphasized by the scene in which he destroys Devil Lady. The manner of the execution is both a form of revenge and a kind of self-betrayal: he thrusts arrows, a spear and a stake into her genitals, thereby tainting the act of execution with the suggestive connotations of rape.

In this connection it is significant that Devil Lady is presented as a masked figure. The white mask suggests not only a white presence as such but a white image imposed upon and accepted as a sexual norm by black men and women. And in this latter sense the "execution" of Devil Lady is really an act of self-cleansing by the black man and his ally, Black Woman. In turn this cleansing has implications that go beyond the immediate sexual issue. The Devil Lady image represents white culture at large as it is interpreted from a black nationalist viewpoint—a culture in which moral and social values, as well as goods, are marketed through the media by the exploitation of the (white) woman's sexual image. In the inelegant language of Baraka's Devil Lady, "My pussy rules the world through newspapers. My pussy radiates the great heat."

The sexual issues that Baraka explores here are not essentially innovative insofar as they are related to the black experience. But in linking these issues with the broader social context as well as with the racial theme, he offers a potentially complex and interesting view-point of his subject. Despite that potential, however, **"Madheart"** is unconvincing at best and more often than not is offensive and bombastic. The main problem stems from the dramatist's sexual perceptions, especially his perception of female sexuality and female roles in society. On one level, for example, it is possible to justify the manner in which Black Man executes Devil Lady by indicating that this reflects his lingering fascination with the white woman's sexuality even in the very moment at which he attempts to expunge the myth of white (sexual) superiority from his consciousness. But on another level, it is difficult to escape the conclusion that this kind of crude genital violence reflects a deeper, disturbing response to female sexuality as such, irrespective of race. It is the kind of response in which the ideal woman is the subjugated woman and in which the most attractive form of female sexuality is one that is accessible, for whatever reason, to a neurotically masculine need to engage in repetitive rites of phallic domination.

In effect the rather shrill themes of ethnic regeneration amount to little more than a thinly disguised rehashing of certain male preconceptions that Baraka, black nationalism notwithstanding, shares with nonblack men. Black Man's disposal of Devil Lady bears all the hallmarks of old, universal traditions of masculine dominance. So does Black Man's relationship with Black Woman. From a certain point of view that relationship is no more satisfactory than the ethnosexual order of things that it is supposed to replace. Both the "new" black man and the "new" black woman have disposed of their sexual and racial self-loathing in order to reaffirm all the traditional values of masculine superiority and feminine submissiveness. He therefore demonstrates his need for her by slapping her, and his new sense of "manhood" depends upon her submission to him and to her defined role as mother: "'I want you, woman, as a woman. Go down' (*He slaps her again.*) 'Go down, submit, . . . to love . . . and to man, now, forever.'" She assures him of this newly found "strength" by submitting to his strength—and his sperm: "I am your woman, and you are the strongest of God. Fill me with your seed."

The sexual ideal that Baraka espouses here is also advocated in his political essays. Indeed *Kawaida Studies* reflects his personal confusion and distress at the possibility that the conventions of female subordination may be replaced by new sexual roles based on equality. The black woman, he insists, is the black man's "divine complement." As for sexual equality, "We do not believe in 'equality' of men and women. We cannot understand what devils and the devilishly influenced mean when they say equality for women. We could never be equals . . . nature has not provided thus." And according to this natural scheme of things the black woman must inspire her man and teach the children. Curiously enough it does not strike Baraka the black nationalist that a political ideology which demands equality for blacks while denying equality to women is self-contradictory. And this contradiction severely limits the scope and depth of **"Madheart."**

On the whole **Black Mass, "Great Goodness of Life,"** and **"Madheart"** are centered primarily on attacks upon white society and white attitudes among blacks. And Baraka develops these attacks in a generally less interesting way than the manner in which he handles themes of ethnic growth and celebration in the other major plays of his black nationalist period—**"Jello"** and **"Slave Ship."** "Jello" was written in the middle 1960s and was originally scheduled to be published with the other works that eventually appeared in **Four Black Revolutionary Plays** in 1969. But the publisher balked and the play finally appeared separately in 1970. It is a satiric parody of "The Jack Benny Show," featuring all the main characters of the original television show—Jack Benny, his black valet Rochester, Dennis, Mary, and the announcer Don Wilson.

In **"Jello"** Rochester is no longer the surly but basically compliant servant. He is now a black militant who stages his own rebellion by refusing to work for Benny. He quits his job after robbing Benny and the others. The effectiveness of the play depends in part on its close parody of the original show. Baraka captures the style and personalities of the Jack Benny program. Indeed the play self-consciously underscores this similarity: hence Rochester is able to "rebel" with relative ease because for much of the proceedings his antagonists assume that his actions are all part of "The Jack Benny Show" itself, that the entire incident is just a joke.

In turn this leads to another aspect of the play's effectiveness. The well-developed scenes in which Rochester's victims believe that this is all in fun have a twofold effect. They dramatize the degree to which "reality" and "fanta-

sy" are blurred in Rochester's world. White fantasies about blacks are part of a social reality in which the "good" black is the docile Uncle Tom (the old Rochester) and in which the idea of black militancy is something of a joke. And, ironically, such fantasies make it difficult for whites to recognize the validity of militant claims when blacks do break away from the docile stereotype. Moreover, the banal fantasies of television, including programs like "The Jack Benny Show," are mirrors of that general insipidity which Baraka consistently attributes to American culture at large. In this regard **"Jello"** is comparable with **"Home on the Range,"** where the gibberish of the white suburban family is presented as an echo of television. Finally, the realism of the play allows the audience to perceive convincing links between Rochester, the new militant, and Rochester, the old Uncle Tom. Despite his compliance the original Rochester is sufficiently saucy in his relationship with Jack Benny to suggest a certain predisposition toward rebelliousness. And Baraka's militant really brings out into the open the rebelliousness that seems to lurk under the surface of the Uncle Tom image.

As in **"The Slave"** the militant's violence implies a previous, long-standing potential for revolt. Unlike **"The Slave,"** however, **"Jello"** is a literal statement in the sense that Rochester is no mere dreamer of revolutions, as Walker Vessel's is. Rochester's actions are not invested with those ambiguities which confirm the suspicion, in **"The Slave,"** that the race war is an imaginary event taking place in Walker's fantasies. Indeed in **"Jello"** there is a sustained emphasis on the contrast between (white) fantasies and (black) action. Consequently Rochester is an unreal or imaginary rebel only when he is perceived through eyes that can see him only as Benny's lackey, as the comically irreverent but fundamentally docile Uncle Tom. Thus while the play gradually strips away Benny's white liberalism to expose the racism with which he views Rochester, it simultaneously forces whites to awaken slowly from their racial fantasies and to see Rochester's personality and actions as they really are. In effect the play seeks to confront whites with what is really happening, notwithstanding deeply rooted needs to ignore or distort the realities behind black militancy.

Despite Rochester's personal success in forcing the recognition of his actions and new attitudes, **"Jello"** as a whole avoids that facile wish-fulfillment which too often mars Baraka's black nationalist writings. Thus although Rochester escapes with the stolen money and compels his victims to recognize him as he is, his triumph is counterbalanced by the continuity of the social order against which he is rebelling. Thus before he is knocked out and robbed by Rochester, Jack Benny's announcer (Don Wilson) assures the television audience that "The Jack Benny Show" will return as usual the following week. The announcement amounts to an assurance of continuity—the persistence of white fantasies even after the revelation of black attitudes. Indeed the play as a whole is a wry tribute to the power of the media, especially television, in reinforcing and perpetuating entrenched viewpoints in white America: Rochester's individual rebellion, like the actual revolts of the 1960s, has become a television "event," recognizable

as an actual experience with disturbing implications for
the white audience but easily transformed into an entertaining spectacle that leaves old fantasies untouched after
the initial moment of disturbance. Hence the play as a
whole balances the celebration of a black revolutionary
idealism against the persistence of certain social attitudes
in white America. But, paradoxically, the intransigence of
white attitudes actually heightens the importance of Rochester's rebellion by underscoring the need for black modes
of perception that arise from a new black awareness instead of depending upon the old, and continuing, white
indifference. This blend of revolutionary idealism and
social realism is rare in Baraka's black nationalist writings, and it is largely responsible for the success of **"Jello"** as a complex drama and entertaining theater.

"Slave Ship," (1967), "a historical pageant," is one of
Baraka's more successful experiments in ritual drama. The
plot is minimal. It consists of images, dances, and pantomime together with sporadic dialogue; all is designed to
dramatize the physical and psychic experiences of slavery
from the holds of the slave ships to contemporary American society. The play's real strength lies in the audiovisual impact of its materials. Much of the action takes place
in darkness or half-light. This suggests the hold of a slave
ship, and the relative lack of lighting accentuates the variety of sounds upon which Baraka builds his themes and
his dramatic effect—African drums, humming of the slaves,
cries of children and their mothers, shouts of slave drivers, and cracking sounds of the slaver master's whip.

The succession of audiovisual forms is integral to the
pattern of ritual upon which Baraka bases his historical
pageant. The sights and sounds of the slave ship remain
throughout, but they alternate from time to time with other
forms which depict successive stages of black American
history—the plantation of the slaveholder, the nonviolent
civil rights movement, and the black nationalist movement. History itself becomes a succession of rituals, particularly the ritual of suffering which gives way after repeated cycles to the new rituals of racial assertion and
cultural awakening. The music which dominates the play
is integral to the ritualistic pageantry of history. At first
the main sounds are those of the African drum, accentu-
ating the fresh African memories of the new slaves. Then
as the plot moves toward the contemporary period the
sounds of the African drum are gradually integrated with
the musical forms that evolved in black American history
since slavery. And this musical progression culminates in
the blues and jazz idioms both as forms of protest and as
the celebration of black nationalism. By a similar token
the humming of the slaves in the holds of the slave ships
gradually gives way to the sounds of protest and eventual
triumph.

But throughout all of this the audience is always in touch
with the persistent sounds and sights of the slave ship
itself, for this is the setting that remains for the duration
of the play, and the subsequent historical epochs are actually superimposed upon it in sequence. The historical
pageant is, therefore, both progressive in direction (moving from slavery to the black nationalism of the 1970s)

and circular (reinforcing a sense of the moral and social
continuities of the society: the slavery of the past exerts a
powerful influence on the circumstances of the present).
Moreover, the persistence of the slave ship images has the
effect of defining history itself as movements (progressive
and cyclical) through time. Similarly the ritualistic forms
of the play (dance, chant, and pantomime) are each a
microcosm of the historical process: each synthesizes the
materials inherited from a previous generation with the
experiences of the contemporary period. And by extension this kind of synthesis characterizes the play as a whole.
As a pageant that combines past and present experiences,
traditional forms and new materials, it reenacts the historical process as Baraka defines it.

Socialist Drama

"Slave Ship" predates Baraka's major socialist dramas by
several years. But the play's historical themes, and historically defined structure, make it a direct forerunner of *The
Motion of History* and *S-1*. And this remains true despite
the fact that **"Slave Ship"** is not committed to socialist
ideology. The perception of history in all three plays is
intrinsic to Baraka's emphasis on the theater as a teaching
device. In black nationalist drama like **"Slave Ship"** the
reenactment of history fulfills a major assumption of black
nationalism: the full understanding of black history is crucial to a vital sense of black identity because the crippling
of black pride in the past has been partly the result of
white distortions of black history. Moreover, the very
process of reenactment becomes a form of celebration, the
celebration of that black ethnicity which emerges from the
exploration of the past.

On the whole this approach to the play as teaching device
and as celebration is similar to the fundamental premise of
Baraka's socialist drama, although in the latter there is a
far more explicit self-consciousness about the teaching role.
The norms of "scientific socialism" reflect a certain commitment to education: the inevitability of the socialist revolution is partly the consequence of politically enlighten-
ing the masses. Art, especially dramatic art, facilitates the
revolutionizing process by depicting the past and its impact on the present. While the black nationalist's historical sense enhances the discovery and celebration of a
distinctive black culture, the historical perspectives of
scientific socialism encourage the social awareness that
will hasten revolution across racial lines. As Baraka himself describes *The Motion of History* and *S-1*, "both plays
are vehicles for a simple message, viz., the only solution
to our problems . . . is revolution! And that revolution is
inevitable. *The Motion of History* brings it back through
the years, focusing principally on the conscious separation
created between black and white workers who are both
exploited by the same enemy."

Both plays also reflect a continuing weakness in Baraka's
committed art. In this socialist phase, as in the black nationalist period, he suffers from a tendency to indulge in
ideological wish-fulfillment at the expense of social realities. Hence the earlier habit of exaggerating the depth
and breadth of black nationalism in America has been

replaced by unconvincing images of one great socialist rebellion in all the countries of the world (*The Motion of History*) and by the highly unlikely spectacle of the American labor union movement as an anticapitalist, prorevolutionary force. Of course these "weaknesses" are less troublesome if we are inclined to accept the underlying purpose of such plays: they are concerned less with strict social realism as such, and more with the advocacy of social change.

The realities that invite "scientific" analysis in these plays are the facts of history, the kind of historical data that forms the plot of *The Motion of History*. The play is actually a series of historical vignettes. The first act depicts scenes from the early civil rights movement of the 1950s and 1960s in order to attack the futility and self-destructiveness of nonviolent protest. Thereafter the play interweaves the ethnic and labor union movements of the twentieth century with past rebellions. The earliest slave uprisings, the abolitionist movement, and the political conflicts of the Reconstruction period are all dramatized as responses to a repressive caste system that is based on class and economics rather than race. Racial conflicts that do occur are portrayed as the outcome of a deliberate policy, by the ruling elite, of stimulating racial divisiveness in order to prevent solidarity among the working classes.

Like **"Slave Ship,"** *The Motion of History* dramatizes the "motion" of history on two levels. The multiple historical episodes which form most of the play emphasize the cyclical nature of American history by presenting exploitation and rebellion as continuing features of the society. But the play's conclusion emphasizes a progressive movement toward the kind of radical change that will dispense with the traditional cycles of continuing repression and abortive rebellion. And by emphasizing history as a progressive force, the play's theme and structure dramatize the "inevitability" of socialist revolution as the culminating result of that progression.

S-1 is less heavily dependent on historical data than is *The Motion of History*. There are a limited number of scenes that depict examples of judicial and political repression in America's past. But on the whole the plot centers on a mythical incident that is historically significant because it is an extension of the old repressiveness and because it hastens the historical inevitability of revolutionary reaction among the masses. The thin plot centers on the passage of a law (*S-1*) that severely limits political activities and freedom of expression. Revolutionary groups organize resistance to the passage of the law, and after it comes into effect they plan widespread defiance of it. The play concludes on an optimistic note: the revolutionaries celebrate their unity and purpose. The play's real strength, and one of its few merits as theater, lies in Baraka's ability to integrate his dramatic form with the conflicts that constitute his political scenes.

In this regard *S-1* achieves a limited success of the kind that *The Motion of History* never approaches. Thus Baraka is able to eke out some sense of the dramatic from the series of confrontations on which the play's plot is based.

The judicial debates on the merits of the new law, in the Supreme Court, are enhanced by the inherently dramatic setting of the courtroom; and this setting is again exploited to effect in the trial of Red (one of the revolutionary leaders) on charges of treason. In a similar vein Congress provides the setting for another series of confrontations—the debates between "liberals" and "conservatives" about the law and the current social unrest. The dramatic experience centers here on the interaction of ideas. This is the theater of ideological positions rather than one of character and situation, and in this respect *S-1* is the culmination of a trend that has been developing in Baraka's dramatic writings since his earlier black nationalist plays.

This kind of drama does have its built-in limitations, of course. The characters are rudimentary types conceived in very broad terms, so broad indeed that the revolutionary figures of *S-1* are indistinguishable not only from each other but from their counterparts in *The Motion of History*. Scenes in which ideological conflicts are presented are severely underdeveloped, largely because the extreme sketchiness of the characterization limits the possibilities of the very confrontations that are supposed to dramatize the clash of ideas. And as a result of all this the audience is left with a theater of rhetoric in which potentially interesting situations and personalities are inundated with a flood of repetitive statements from all sides of the political landscape. Ironically enough Baraka's lack of emotional control in his ideological statements and his increasing indifference to characterization have resulted in a thin, one-dimensional drama that contravenes his own ideal of dramatic art as one that fuses word, act, and idea. Instead what he has produced is largely a loosely connected series of scenes filled with the shopworn clichés of reactionaries and revolutionaries alike. At its worst this method exemplifies the predominance of ideological word over dramatic art, the very kind of imbalance that Baraka himself abhors in theory. Curiously enough, at this stage of his career as dramatist his theory of effective drama is less compatible with the kind of plays that he prefers to write, and it is more appropriate to the early plays which he does not choose to mention in his introduction to *The Motion of History and Other Plays*.

"DUTCHMAN"

PRODUCTION REVIEWS

Edith Oliver (review date 4 April 1964)

SOURCE: "Over the Edge," in *The New Yorker*, Vol. XL, No. 7, April 4, 1964, pp. 78-9.

[*In the following excerpt, Oliver praises the "deadly wit and passionate wild comedy" of "Dutchman," but felt that the anger expressed by the black character, while justifiable, was ineffective.*]

LeRoi Jones whose **"Dutchman"** is the final one-acter of

*Robert Hooks and Jennifer West as Clay and Lula in the 1964
Cherry Lane Theatre production of "Dutchman."*

"Three at the Cherry Lane," is an original and talented young dramatist. For about three-quarters of the way, his play has a kind of deadly wit and passionate wild comedy that are his alone, and then, sad to say, he almost literally sends it all up in smoke, under what I feel is the mistaken impression that in order to have point and impact a good story must be given general and even symbolic implications. Himself a Negro, Mr. Jones presents a young Negro who is accosted in the subway and subjected to a sort of mocking seduction by a crazy, though fascinating, blonde in a tight-fitting jersey dress. At first, the girl seems just a nutty bohemian type and scarcely dangerous—which, indeed, she turns out to be. She begins by needling him and trying to provoke him in every way, and ends up by goading him with such trigger words as "Uncle Tom" and "nigger." Finally, he can stand it no longer and tells her off in an outburst of fury that goes on for quite a while and encompasses all the anger of the Negro against white people. There is no doubt that this anger is justified, but there is also no doubt, I think, that in this case it is inartistic, weakening the character and the play. Up to the time of the outburst, the boy has been winning every round anyway, and it just won't do to suddenly cast him as the representative of the exploited telling off his exploiters. Much of what he says, however deeply felt it may be, has been said before. There are echoes of James Baldwin's essays, and even of Adrienne Kennedy's "Funnyhouse of a Negro." At any rate, somewhere in the middle of the

harangue the rage sounded hollow to me—cooked up rather than real—and I stopped trusting the playwright. It is too bad to see a writer as gifted and as one-of-a-kind as Mr. Jones forcing himself into any sort of familiar mold. Still, the pre-outburst dialogue could scarcely be funnier or more painful or fuller of surprises, and even much of the monologue is forceful and satisfying to an invective fan like me. The language and some of the business are as rough as any I've ever been exposed to in the theatre, and both seemed to me entirely appropriate to the characters and the situation.

Mr. Jones has written two wonderful parts, and Jennifer West and Robert Hooks do them justice. Miss West is remarkably vivid and willful and funny and strange, and Mr. Hooks is good, too, recording any number of changes in emotional temperature and not letting one word of his scathing lines go to waste. The actors who play the silent, onlooking passengers display an indifference to the lethal vendetta taking place before their eyes that surely marks them as marrow-deep New Yorkers enjoying public transportation.

John Simon   (review date Autumn 1964)

SOURCE: A review of "Dutchman," in *The Hudson Review,* Vol. XVII, No. 3, Autumn, 1964, p. 424.

[*In the following unfavorable review, Simon condemns what he considers to be an overtly allegorical plot, simplistic symbols, and pretentious language in "Dutchman."*]

In LeRoi Jones's **"Dutchman"** an intellectual, artistic young Negro is picked up on the subway by a weird, taunting white temptress. He is to take her along to a party he is going to, in exchange for which she'll later take him home and to her bed. The girl provokes him with jeers at his attempts to become assimilated into white society and culture; hers in a vicious combination of inviting nymphomania and castrating rejections. He finally explodes in a philippic hurled as much at some other white passengers as at the girl herself; when she further provokes him into swinging at her, it is she who pulls out a switchblade knife, kills him, and, with the help of the other passengers, dumps the body onto an empty platform. As the play ends, she has spotted another well-dressed, bookish young Negro who has just boarded the subway car, and she prepares to repeat the entire bloody ritual.

That the play is preposterous on the literal level is obvious enough. Yet allegory or symbolism, to be effective, must first function properly on the literal level. But does **"Dutchman"** work even figuratively? Does the white society woo the Negro with a mixture of promises and rebuffs only to destroy him utterly when he shows his just resentment? Perhaps. But it looks to me as if resentment were finally beginning to pay off. Whites, moreover, have been treating Negroes with a simpler, though no less damnable, cruelty. They have been neither so Machiavellian, nor so psychotic, as **"Dutchman"** implies. Add to this

Jones's often consciously arty language and the vacuity of his symbols: the girl plies her victims with apples, an assembly-line Eve; the title presumably refers to the Flying Dutchman, but whether this describes the girl, fatally traveling up and down the subway line, or the boy, needing to be redeemed by the true love of a white girl, is unclear and, in either case, unhelpful. **"Dutchman"** [is] merely propaganda, which can add some fuel to a sometimes necessary fire; [it is] not truth, which alone can free us from our eternal enemy, ignorance.

CRITICAL COMMENTARY

Tom S. Reck (essay date 1970)

SOURCE: "Archetypes in LeRoi Jones' 'Dutchman,'" in *Studies in Black Literature,* Vol. 1, No. 1, Spring, 1970, pp. 66-8.

[*In the following article, Reck examines archetypal symbolism in "Dutchman," and argues that Baraka's play pities the white world, leaving Lula stuck in it and setting Clay free through death.*]

Most viewers and readers of LeRoi Jones' play **"Dutchman"** acknowledge its power and recognize the timeliness of the theme. No one has really shown, however, how the elements of myth which it contains make it, at least in a literary way, considerably more than a topical drama of American Racial strife. *Newsweek* magazine in its review gave token recognition to the quality of myth which raises **"Dutchman"** "above sociology" to something that is "perennial among men: the exploitation of one another for satisfaction of dreams and hungers"; but it did not analyze Jones' use of myth very specifically.

The stage action of **"Dutchman"** is simply this: a white girl encounters a black man on a New York subway. When he refuses to fit her erotic dream of the primitive black, she proceeds to taunt him with her sharp mind and her beautiful body until he drops his white disguise to become a Negro and deliver a tirade against the claim that whites can ever understand what being a Negro means. His attack ends in his own ruin, however, when she suddenly murders him.

Jones' early stage directions point toward his purpose to build his message on legend and mythology. He describes the setting as "the flying underbelly of the city" and notes that the subway is "heaped in modern myth." **"Dutchman"** is, in fact, worked around the most archetypal of all myths: the seduction of the male by the beautiful but deadly female, with particular inference to the myth of Adam and Eve in the Garden of Eden. The name of the Negro male, Clay, seems to suggest an Adam and an Everyman; and the white temptress, Lula, is not only a direct descendent of Lilith, Circe, and Delilah, but particularly of Eve. When she enters the subway car, Jones has her eating an apple, which she soon will offer to Clay ("You want this?"). Clay later muses that "eating apples is always the first step" and will even ask: "Hey, what was in those apples?"

As the fall of Adam may be sexual allegory, Clay's destruction is also sex-oriented. Lula's opening remark is ". . . . I'd turned around and saw you staring through the window in the vicinity of my ass and legs." She obscenely provokes his frenzy with: "Let's rub bellies on the train. The nasty. The nasty. Do the gritty grind, like your ol' raghead mammy. Grind till you lose your mind."

Yet the girl versus boy is only surface; it is only symbolic of white versus black. She refuses to let him be white by damaging his self-image with "God you're dull" and by accusing him of crawling "through the wire" and making tracks "to my side." When he is finally black, however, ("Kiss my black ass"), she kills him. The black man is first condemned when he emulates the white (he is destined to be only a poor imitation anyway). And if he is willing to be totally black, he gets death rather than ridicule. A form of survival if he submits to imitation; death when true to his own nature. With Lula as an Eve and with Clay as a kind of Everyman, Jones seems to be saying that the Negro is man in a natural and primitive and virtuous state: Adam, as it were, before the fall. He is tempted to corruption by white socialization, represented by Eve/Lula and the apples.

Yet it is the white world which Jones seems to finally pity. So the play's title implies, although no one has apparently recognized it. The title is obvious reference to the myth of the Flying Dutchman, condemned to sail the seven seas through eternity, denied the peace of a death. After Clay's murder, Lula moves to apparently repeat the pattern against another Negro male, a device that a number of critics have objected to as theatrical and contrived. Yet, the repetition is essential, since like the ancient Dutchman, she has been condemned by her own bigotry and frustration to act out this ritual through eternity, accompanied now by the hideous screaming of the twentieth-century subway.

Robert L. Tener (essay date 1972)

SOURCE: "Role Playing as a Dutchman," in *Studies in Black Literature,* Vol. 3, No. 3, Autumn, 1972, pp. 17-21.

[*Tener refutes the widely-held belief that the title of Baraka's play "Dutchman," refers to the legend of the Flying Dutchman.*]

Although the critical material on LeRoi Jones' dramatic works has been steadily accumulating, one of his best plays has not received the varied attention it deserves. **"Dutchman"** has intrigued a few critics like Harold Clurman, Hugh Nelson, Susan Sontag, Sister Mary John Carol Blitgen, and John Ferguson. Each has sought to interpret the complex events leading to Clay's murder. For Blitgen, Nelson, and Ferguson the title refers to the legend of the Flying Dutchman. The most comprehensive treatment of this point of view is provided by Professor Nelson [in "LeRoi Jones' **'Dutchman'**: A Brief Ride on a Doomed Ship," *Education Theatre Journal,* March, 1968]. His thesis is that Jones had converted the legend to a modern myth in order to reveal the "symbolic relationship of Clay and Lula."

Professor Nelson draws parallels equating the subway car of the play with the legendary sailing ship and its doomed crew. The most important, yet awkward, parallel equates Lula with the cursed Captain. The problem in this parallel is caused by the necessity to explain the reversal of sexual roles. According to the Wagnerian version of the legend, the curse on the Captain can be removed only if he is released by the love of a pure woman. Lula, in her surrogate role, therefore, has to find the love of a pure man. As Nelson points out, Lula cannot be released by Clay's love. She can only use him. Professor Nelson concludes, then, that the legend is "an indication of the doomed fatality of the situation and of the characters who live through it." For Nelson the mythical pattern of the play involves the heroine's quest for redemption (Lula needs to be taken as a human being not as a sex machine), the discovery of the proper object of her quest (Clay), her apparent failure through betrayal (Clay cannot respond properly to her), the violent denouement (the quarrel), and the last minute union of the lovers in death.

A closer analysis of the play suggests that other views are possible without the necessity of the subsitute sex scheme to make the old legend apply. Indeed the play needs to be examined as part of that body of literature that treats the duel of the sexes. Its immediate dramatic ancestors are Strindberg's *Miss Julie,* Ionesco's *The Lesson,* and Albee's *Who's Afraid of Virginia Woolf*? Against this background the legend of the Flying Dutchman appears too barren a myth to explain the ambiguities in the play.

The title of the play suggests a possible interpretation that has heretofore been ignored. No definite article precedes the title. The play is called **"Dutchman,"** not "The Dutchman." The implication of this omission is that Jones had no specific individual or legend at hand. Instead, it is more likely that what he intended is the theatrical term meaning a strip of cloth used to hid the crack between the seams of flats, or, in a more general sense, a contrivance used to hide a defect of some kind.

From this perspective the play acquires a meaning different from what Professor Nelson has suggested. The theme of the play is anchored to the defects in character and in personality of a black man and a white woman and to the devices which they use to hide those defects. Both Lula and Clay have lost their identities as human beings and use role playing to hide their loss and subsequent alienation from meaningful relationships between man and woman. Inasmuch as Clay is black, the play also reflects the historical relationships between blacks and whites on an abstract, highly generalized level. In this sense the subway (on which the action develops) is similar to the underground railroad of slave days that carried slaves north to their freedom and to their new identities. The subway

is obviously a train and it is underground. It takes Clay and Lula somewhere, perhaps to freedom. But that freedom is defined differently for them. The train takes Clay to his death; it frees him from his self-imposed dependence on the devices of clothing and white middle class values. It takes Lula to other victims. She can find herself only in the repetitive killing of others. As Harold Clurman pointed out in his review of **"The Toilet"** and **"The Slave,"** Lula is the "concise and piercing dramatic image for the killer our society generates through its metallic emptiness" [*The Naked Image,* 1966].

Lula has as her heritage both the Lilith and the Eve patterns. She is female and equal to man; she is the temptress and needs to determine man's reactions to her. Her first role or device to hide her emptiness is to be the aggressive seductress searching for a man. Once she has discovered him, she defines the situation between them in sexual and political terms. She maniupultes Clay's reactions by telling him lies and deducing part of his life style from the stereotyped pattern his clothing suggests he has become accommodated to. Her second strategy is to pretend to be the white liberal intellectual who sees the world in terms of labels. Not being able to accept meaningful relationships, she tells lies to create illusions and to give meaning to the situations which she helps develop. She turns relationships into games, especially the sexual feelings between men and women. With her hand on Clay's knee she says that he is going to a party and that she is a poetess.

But she is also a creative puppet master. Conceiving a dramatic event, she develops the dialogue, creates the situations, and then, because she has substituted knowledge of the stereotype for knowledge of the real Clay, wants him to act and even become the character she has created falsely. She is an author in search of a character who is necessary to her creative abilities. As a consequence of this quality in her role playing, her relationship to Clay tends to be ritualistic and depends on sexual and political attitudes, on the game of a false white liberality, and on her desire to substitute her illusions of life for what she senses is already dead.

Although she plays other roles to hide what she is, the early incidents in the play have presented her defect. She is one of the living dead. Like Clay, she is the product of her racial past. Embedded in her are the desires of the white master who wants to exploit the sexual resources of the black slave, who wants to shape the image of the black man according to his white vision. By that act of manipulation, the master loses his identity. The relationship between a master and his slave is frequently characterized by the tendency of the master to lose his human identity in treating his slave and to exploit the slave through habit. In the end he cannot relate to the slave like one human being to another. He responds to what he senses is a thing, a piece of property. In this sense Lula cannot love.

Having lost her identity, literally having no valid historical roots which enable her to relate to Clay, she becomes bored. In the next instant she turns sharply on Clay, rejects him, then shifts to him the burden of their incipient sexual involvement. She accuses him of trying to get fresh with her. In the historical context of racial America, her actions are equivalent to jamming the black into a dangerous, ambiguous position which many whites would interpret as damaging the honor of a white woman. In the past some whites would have lynched a black man caught in such an act. Clay's response to her actions cannot be divorced from the historical consequences. He has become a type which she knows well.

She pretends also to be the new white liberal who appeared on the American scene in the 1960's. She knows how blacks should act and what it means to be black. In this mask she attacks his stereotyped clothing and reveals her digust with him because he has not resisted the pressures of white society. Believing that she knows what his identity should be and how he should find himself, she tells him what he is not while ignoring what he might wish to be. Hers is here again the role of the racist killer. She sneers at his lack of tradition; she ridicules his acceptance of white middle class values. But like Clay, she too has lost her historical antecedents which gave her life meaning. As an actress of dead roles, she symbolizes the white attitudes which Jones has come to attack so often in his plays.

Helene Keyssar (essay date 1981)

SOURCE: "Lost Illusions, New Visions: Imamu Amiri Baraka's 'Dutchman,'" in *The Curtain and the Veil: Strategies in Black Drama,* Burt Franklin & Co., 1981, pp. 147-76.

[*In the following excerpt, Keyssar argues that Baraka has portrayed the main characters of "Dutchman" realistically, not just symbolically, thereby intensifying their effect on the audience.*]

There is, as in most drama, an attempt in **"Dutchman"** to change the spectator's way of looking at the world. **"Dutchman,"** however, works in such a way that for spectators as well as stage characters, changes in perspective vary according to whether one is black or white. **"Dutchman"** makes manifest the ambivalent intentions that have been disguised or latent in earlier black dramas. While **"Great Goodness of Life"** and other black revolutionary dramas urge the need for separate dramatic strategies for black and white audiences by aiming their intentions only at black spectators, **"Dutchman"** acknowledges the encounter of two worlds and two modes of seeing within the one world it constructs onstage and within the space of the audience for which it is played. The play presumes our differences and confronts them; some elements of its strategy will work similarly on black and white spectators, but its essential strategic devices affect not what black and white spectators share as human beings, but what separates us as black and white Americans.

In **"Dutchman,"** the imprisoning paradoxes that black dramas had been revealing for forty-five years are boldly and baldly thrust at the audience; in the world of twentieth-century urban America that Baraka synthesizes and mythologizes, it becomes an insult to call a black man middle class. It is also possible in this world at once to perceive a black man as middle-class, a bastard, and the son of a "social-working mother." This is a play in which not to be a nigger is to be a "dirty white man," and in which, as **"Dutchman"** goes on to expose, not to dance with Lula, the drama's emissary from the white middle class, is to choose death as your partner.

For the many spectators who have witnessed productions of **"Dutchman"** since its first performance in 1964, it has remained singular, baffling, and troubling. For forty-five minutes we listen to a white woman, Lula, delineate what it means to have "made it" in modern America, to be middle-class. But Lula not only catalogs middle-class attributes—having an education, being able to make appropriate small-talk, wearing a three-button suit—she presents the other main character, the black man, Clay, to himself and to us as a model of these characteristics. While some, particularly those who are black among the audience, may be suspicious and angered from the beginning of the play by Lula's easy assumptions, it is not until Clay's long and explosive speech near the end of **"Dutchman"** that white spectators are fully forced to acknowledge their disorientation and black spectators are led to unmuted fear. At the end of Clay's speech, he warns Lula and the audience that the day may come when black Americans are indeed accepted into the fold of white middle-class society, and that will be a day when "all of those ex-coons will be stand-up Western men, with eyes for clean hard useful lives, sober, pious and sane, and they'll murder you." This is not simply a threat that the rage of black people against racism will eventually and inevitably explode, it is a warning that the very central image of the good American life, the open door to the middle class, is not only a deceptive fantasy but a death wish if realized.

The inclusion of blacks and whites in the world of **"Dutchman"** is not, then, the "integrated" world of Lorraine Hansberry's *A Raisin in the Sun*. It is a world in which a black man and a white woman meet in the rushing anonymity of the subway, engage in conversation at once intimate and estranged, and come to a mutual recognition through violent action. Clay, the black man, and Lula, the white woman, are in the same physical place, but neither they nor we ever see them as alike. Lula attempts to seduce, taunt, bewilder Clay; Clay tries to ignore, rebuff, enjoy, and humor Lula. Finally, only rejection is possible. Clay's refusal is violently verbal; Lula's literally murderous: She kills him. In the end, we learn from this play that black people cannot rest peacefully in the same world with white people like Lula.

Although there may be a moral to **"Dutchman,"** the play is not a fable. Baraka has urged that we regard his **"Dutchman"** characters as human beings, not primarily as symbolic figures: Lula, Baraka has said, "does not represent anything—she is one" [Doris Abramson, *Negro Playwrights in the American Theatre, 1925-1959,* 1969]. Lula is not a fantasy or an emblem; she is not a character created by a synthesis of Baraka's understanding of important elements in the white American character (or even just the white American female character). Nor is she a figure like Edward Albee's young man in *The American Dream*—a creature who could never exist in the real world but who functions as a kind of flag to illustrate what that world is elementally like. Lula and Clay are real people, or, in theatrical terms, realistic characters, who can and do exist. We could not encounter Albee's young man on a subway train; we can and do, find people like Clay and Lula on a subway every day, even if we do not recognize them.

Creating the understanding that Lula is one of the people who ride the subway and is not *only* a representative of them, is central to Baraka's strategy. The playwright wishes to prohibit the audience from maintaining an intellectual distance from Lula and Clay. We are not to be allowed to say, "Well, yes, she does represent elements of American society, but there is no one around really like her." Literary symbols can trouble an audience, but they do not frighten us as would "real" people, because they cannot act like a real people.

Yet Baraka's intention is not limited to our recognition of Lula and Clay as a real white woman and a real black man. The subway on which we discover Lula and Clay is, according to Baraka's stage directions, "heaped in modern myth." From its title, **"Dutchman,"** through its use of apples and its allusions to places like "Juliet's tomb," Baraka's play is "heaped in myth." We are to perceive Lula and Clay, then, as real *and* mythical figures. This is not a contradiction. As anthropologists have shown us, myth is not a false or fictitious description of events in the world; rather, it is an expression of the particular, common, basic, and necessary ways in which men and women relate to each other and the world around them. The power and magic of myth are that it isolates and enables us to acknowledge those structures of human relationship that define who and how we are in the world. This power and magic are at the core of Baraka's strategy in **"Dutchman."**

"THE TOILET"

PRODUCTION REVIEWS

Howard Taubman (review date 17 December 1964)

SOURCE: "'Slave' and 'Toilet' by LeRoi Jones Open," in *The New York Times,* December 17, 1964, p.51.

[*In the following excerpt, Taubman calls Jones an angry and gifted playwright.*]

LeRoi Jones is one of the angriest writers to storm the theater—and one of the most gifted. On the evidence of his new one-acters, **"The Slave"** and **"The Toilet,"** one wonders whether his rage is not at war with his instincts as an artist.

In both halves of the double bill, which opened last night at the St. Marks Playhouse, Mr. Jones has exciting and moving things to say. Once again, as in **"Dutchman,"** he discloses a sure grasp of the theatrical image.

But he cannot resist the urge to shock by invoking violence and all the obscenities he can think of. There are times when these shock tactics perform no useful dramatic function, when they clarify no meaning, when they merely set up needless resistance to what the play is saying.

When Mr. Jones sets out to be literal, he is about as unsubtle as the law will allow.

"The Toilet" occurs in a toilet of a boys high school. Larry Rivers has obliged the author by designing a retreat with all the equipment you would find in a men's room. Leo Garen has staged the opening moments of the play to indicate realistic use of the equipment. Mr. Jones and his colleagues apparently assume that nothing can be left to an audience's imagination.

The students, nearly all of them Negro, drift into the toilet. Again Mr. Jones, his director and his actors are nothing if not realistic. The talk is latrine language. The boys are ugly, mindless, full of bravado and violence. They are waiting for a fight to be fought between two boys. Meanwhile, the Negroes assail each other and are particularly vicious to a white boy who has drifted into the room.

Karolis, apparently a Puerto Rican, is finally hauled in, already bloodied from a beating he has received en route to the arena. Foots, a bright boy, whom a teacher has called "a credit to his race," is waiting to take on Karolis. Foots is angry because Karolis has sent him a love letter. Though badly hurt, Karolis rises to fight, and as he is getting the better of Foots, the other Negroes savage him.

For all its violence and "ritual filth," to use Mr. Jones's phrase, **"The Toilet"** ends on a note of tenderness. The denouement of the play is moving as only a natural dramatist can make it, and underneath its coarseness there runs a strong sense of the needless debasement of human beings. One is sure, however, that Mr. Jones could have made his points without the shock tactics.

Henry Hewes (review date 9 January 1965)

SOURCE: "Crossing Lines," in *The Saturday Review,* New York, Vol. XLVIII, No. 2, January 9, 1965, p. 46.

[*In this review of "The Toilet," Hewes finds that while the gratuitous violence and obscenities may scare off many viewers, the play is nonetheless "a vivid and indelible work of art."*]

LeRoi Jones's two new plays confirm the impression this thirty-year-old playwright made last season with his **"Dutchman"** and **"The Baptism."** Mr. Jones is less an astute dramatic craftsman than he is a Negro creatively expressing his portion of a total anger that his race has had to suppress in the centuries since the first slave-owner committed an injustice on the grounds that the Negro was subhuman. His plays are poetic and prophetic views of the total situation by one individual human being in search of a vital identity.

"The Toilet," written in 1961 (before **"Dutchman"**), is deliberately as unrelievedly obscene a play as Mr. Jones can make it. Against the smelly and profane background of urinals and scrawled-upon lavatory walls we watch a bunch of Negro high school students as they demonstrate the insensitivity, the foul language, and the exercise of gratuitous violence one finds among groups of boys attempting to maintain tough-guy status and a supermasculine virility. Amid all this, the necessity has arisen for a washroom fight between a white boy and a Negro honor student to whom he has written a homosexual love letter. The action is brutal, an example of how society can force people to behave at their worst. But if Mr. Jones deplores this, he also recognizes its essential reality as he seems to present the white boy's extreme pain and humiliation as being somehow inherent in his attempt to reach across the battle lines of moral and racial taboo. Furthermore, his tender ending tells us that only as two non-group-associated individuals can their genuine feelings be shared.

Director Leo Garen has staged the play beautifully and unevasively. Larry Rivers has constructed a realistic men's room, complete with urinals, on the small St. Marks Playhouse stage. And the performances are most convincing. Where the play has difficulty is in its violence, which goes on much longer than necessary to make its dramatic point (although not as long as did the Living Theater's *The Brig*) and its deliberately redundant use of the sort of unimaginative obscene vocabulary adolescent boys use to show that they are one of the gang. Because of this unpleasantness many will walk out. Those who stay are not likely to feel sufficiently rewarded with esthetic or intellectual gratifications. Yet they will have experienced a vivid and indelible work of art.

Myrna Bain (review date 23 March 1965)

SOURCE: "Everybody's Protest Play," in *National Review*, New York, Vol. XVII, March 23, 1965, pp. 249-50.

[*In the following excerpt, Bain calls "The Toilet" "straight bathroom drama, with little if any plot and absolutely no uplift."*]

Did you know the exclamation point was dead? Or that the Western white man had failed to realize "the idealization of rational Liberalism"? Or even that these questions could possibly be serious points for stage adaptation? Probably not. But for playwrights Lorraine Hansberry and Le-Roi Jones, the theater is a perfect place to act out these serio-comic problems.

Mr. Jones, the latest bombshell among the hip writers, is

currently enjoying a successful run at the St. Mark's Playhouse with his two one-act plays, **"The Slave"** and **"The Toilet."** Anarchic and prurient in tone, language and style, these two plays present a nightmare of twisted logic that will probably, by next season, descend in waves on Shubert Alley.

Played in the hermetic atmosphere of a small theater-in-the-round, **"The Toilet,"** first up, locks the audience in with the oddest collection of subway marauders, basketball junkies and cool boppers to be seen anywhere outside of the hallways of Boys High. And these eleven boys, all of them mentally and linguistically retarded, leave the viewer with the decided impression that if Jones is not trying to prove that Negroes are "inherently inferior" to whites, he certainly is not making any effort to clear up any misconceptions. For this play is straight bathroom drama, with little if any plot and absolutely no uplift.

The curtain rises on five urinals and a rusty sink. And the first character to enter, Ora (described in the script as "short, ugly, crude, loud"), ought to set the mood sufficiently; but just in case you don't get the message, Ora next engages in a bit of highly graphic mime action ("He enters, looks around, then with one hand on his hip, takes out his penis and urinates . . ."). As I said, this is done in mime action, but it was the only concession made to sensibility for the rest of the play.

Gradually the other characters "bop" on stage. And it becomes apparent that a murder or near-murder is going to be the central act of the play. LeRoi Jones has always been fascinated with murder; there was a killing in his previous production, **"Dutchman."** In **"The Toilet,"** Jones portrays the stylistic obscenities of the boys as the "natural" flowering of their primitive natures, but there is one added touch in this and the other play, **"The Slave"**—the white characters (there are two in each play) are characterized in such a devitalized fashion that all the brutalities appear almost "necessary." The two in **"The Toilet"** function as alternate and unsightly copies of the nine Negro boys. And their lines are so written that, when the first one is "sounded" out of the room and the other dragged in, bleeding and battered, his possible death horrifies but does not necessarily repel you.

CRITICAL COMMENTARY

Robert L. Tener (essay date 1974)

SOURCE: "The Corrupted Warrior Heroes: Amiri Baraka's 'The Toilet,'" in *Modern Drama,* Vol. XVII, No. 2, June, 1974, pp. 207-15.

[*Below, Tener claims that "The Toilet" explores the negative affects of white society on the maturing process of black boys.*]

At the time that Baraka was composing **"The Toilet,"** most blacks did not have black heroes to emulate in shap-

A scene from "The Toilet."

ing their psyches. They had primarily white mythic or historical or athletic or artistic models. But the feeling was abroad that the white culture was dying and that the dependency on white models could only destroy the black identity. James Baldwin had pointed out in *The Fire Next Time* that "white people cannot, in the generality, be taken as models of how to live. Rather, the white man is himself in sore need of new standards, which will release him from his confusion and place him once again in fruitful communion with the depths of his own being." Much later Eldridge Cleaver emphasized in *Soul on Ice* that the white race had lost its heroes. Its youth had come to see that its historical white heroes such as George Washington and Thomas Jefferson were really arch-villains. Young whites began to "recoil in shame from the spectacle of cowboys and pioneers . . . galloping across a movie screen shooting down Indians like Coke bottles."

As Amiri Baraka himself suggested in "The Myth of a 'Negro Literature,'" most negro literature is mediocre because it imitates white literature and models, its creators not being able to maintain "their essential identities as Negroes." What was of most importance apparently to Baraka at the time of that essay (first given as an address in 1962) was to maintain a black identity among blacks without its being weakened through the imitation of white

models and to make certain that black art reflects "the experiences of the human being, the emotional predicament of the man, as he exists, in the defined world of his being."

Does **"The Toilet"** offer the viewer the new black identity or does it reveal the black psyche dehumanized by its imitation of white models? It would seem in **"The Toilet"** that Baraka is trying to show how the black youths, except for Foots, act according to their inner vision of what is a man, an image affected by the white mythic heroes, and have, consequently, lost some of their dignity and worth as black boys. They have been corrupted by the white society. In addition it also seems possible that Baraka is intending to reflect the black experience under the eroding influence of the white middle class society which not only debases the black identity but also destroys the vitality of the white group. The only two positive characters in the play are Ray (the name Karolis uses for Foots, the gang leader) and Karolis. Both have some dignity as human beings and are involved emotionally with each other. Ray resists fighting Karolis; he returns after the gang members have left to share himself with Karolis. On the other hand Karolis is willing to fight Foots but loves Ray, as though he senses the split identity of the young gang leader. Of importance also is Baraka's strategic conception of Karolis, the only white in the play, as a homosexual. The characterization suggests perhaps the demoralization and confusion of standards for behavior within the white system.

The operating world of the gang is the urine stinking toilet in a high school with white and black students. It is a male world. Here, the image of a man, derived partly from heroes in the outer world, stigmatized by the stench of man's excremental functions and his sexual confusions, is incompletely expressed by the boys. That image is an epic one minus its heroism. It captures the heroic warrior from a classic past with its emphasis on physicality, but it is transmuted by the alchemy of the white dream into the picture of a fighter or athlete. It is reflected in the gang's emphasis on physical contact, in their tough talk, their games, their actions, their assumptions, and especially in their limitations.

The male relationships in their world are given in terms of physical contact. It is boy strength versus boy strength as muscle tests muscle. Love holds the door against Ora who thumps the door but does not get angry; Holmes and Love spar a few minutes with each other, then Hines joins in the action. In another instance Holmes and Ora square off, after Ora has already punched Holmes, *"both laughing and faking professional demeanor."* Love and Hines play an imaginary game of basketball. In all of these examples the physical involvement shifts its emotional strength, always threatening to move from fun to violence. Ora nudges Karolis with his foot or he pushes Karolis into Foots. In turn Foots pushes Karolis away. Except in the relationship with Karolis, the rules of the physical contact game do not allow the contact to turn into serious fighting. Their function apparently is to allow the gang members to express in an acceptable but restricted manner their contradictory impulses to be both dominant and dominated, to be both independent as well as bound by some cohesive force. Ora clearly threatens the group physically, but he cannot subdue George and he accepts Foots as the leader.

The emphasis on physical contact, like that expressed in the training of some warrior or athlete, is reinforced in their male world by their excessively tough language. But it is a young male world activated by the image of man as a fighter-hero who battles the forces of evil mechanically (not all know why Karolis must be forced to fight) and who ignores the effects of his sexual changes. But such a warrior-athlete, if he is successful, is rewarded with sexual adulation, his female counterpart being reduced to serving him. The inhabitants of this male arena talk about the two characteristics of a man related to that image: fighting (what all their physical contact is directed towards as though they were going through a training process) and sex (what their changing glandular systems are preparing them for).

Their talk about fighting is always done in the context of their still being boys. The proposed fights are imagined, not real. Those in between are affairs of honor, involving an imagined or felt ideal, and following a definite ritual, borrowed possibly from white western movies or Batman

comics. When Foots asks Knowles to stop drumming on the walls, Knowles threatens to drum on Foots' head. Ora threatens to "stomp mudholes" in Farrell's head if he doesn't shut up.

The central incident, however, is a matter of honor. The gang has dragged Karolis to the toilet room where he is supposed to fight their leader Foots. According to Hines the gang does not intend to beat him up. But by the time that they get him to his destiny, he has been considerably mauled. Foots pays homage to Ora who has hit Karolis by saying "You a rough ass cat, Shot. He sure don't look like he's in any way to fight anybody." But Foots is supposed to fight Karolis because the white boy had written him a letter calling him beautiful and saying "that he wanted to blow him." The talk among them is of killing as though the fighting were to be for real on some battlefield. But it is not. When Karolis pulls himself up unsteadily and says that he wants to fight Foots, Knowles exclaims "You mean that sonofabitch wasn' dead?" Or when Foots comes in and first sees Karolis on the floor, he asks "Damn! What'd you guys do, kill the cat?" Even Karolis says "I want to kill you" to Foots. All such comments refer not to the actual destruction of a human being but more than likely to an emphasis on fighting, hitting, or beating up, to some process not likely to end in death but which releases their internal tensions. Their language thus continually suggests that they are in a probationary period when all their actions are training sessions for the real thing. In the world of the play, however, they can never have the real thing.

But it is their language about sex and their sexual terms that most readily reveals their participation in a male world where their concept of maleness is affected by the masculine images provided by a white society. In the first place the emphasis is on their talking about sex; nowhere in the play do they actually engage in sexual activities. While they are not necessarily virgins or neophytes, they are certainly in that transition period where they lose their sexual innocence. But their uncertain sense of masculinity and of heroism has not taught them how to cope with their ambivalent sexual feelings and responses or how to express them. Under their internal pressures they play the game of the dozens in which they insult each others mothers. As Ora says, he would "rub up against" Love's mother, and Love replies "Ora, you mad cause you don't have a momma of your own to rub up against." But it is a game. They do not rub up against real women, not yet. They are not free enough of their maternal-female image to develop a separate sexual-female concept. In their rhetorical playing, the force is on talk and male dominance, as in the love of tall talk on the American frontier. Their language does not reflect the subtleties of the sexual feelings between men and women and the ways in which those feelings permeate all other relationships. Their vocabulary reveals their almost new yet crude concern for their penises, a self-interest which bothers them somewhat, perhaps even embarrasses them. They relish the names for their sexual masculinity which has suddenly become important to them. Perhaps that is why they want Foots to fight a duel with Karolis. As Perry says, Karolis wanted to "blow him" and Ora calls the white boy a "dick licker."

Their sexual reactions have yet to be directly transferred to women. They do not discuss going with girls, or bedding with them, or marrying them. They are still boys and apparently embarrassed or confused by their bodies and sexual stirrings. They conceive of sex in the terms of comic books, of sexual relationships in the metaphors of the white mythic heroes. They relate sex to their male egos and their need to dominate. Almost in retaliation for their changing selves, they stress their obvious maleness to each other in ritualized language which is often euphemized. They refer to a penis as a "joint." In the toilet or commode, like little boys they want to play with their urine. Even Ora, the most obviously physical boy, tends to giggle and grin as he pees over the seat of a commode; he flushes all the urinals in a row when he leaves. Hines tells Holmes that Love is in the toilet "pulling his whatchamacallit". And when Holmes asks him why he doesn't get Gloria to do that, Love says "She-et. [*Grinning.*] Huh. I sure don't need your ol' lady to be pullin' on my joint. [*Laughs. . . .*]". They even call each other "cocksucker," a term which when it applies to them is less pejorative, perhaps even complimentary, than the term "dick licker" which they apply to Karolis.

When Love says that Karolis never bothered him, Ora turns his reply into the dozens by saying that Karolis always tells everybody that "he bangs the hell out of Caroline, every chance he gets." Holmes answers by asking if that's the name of Love's mother. Even Ora calls his own penis a "nice fat sausage" for Karolis. Such excessive use of euphemisms suggests their sense of embarrassed delight and highly limited response to their sexual organs. For them it is insulting to be compared with a girl. Knowles says to Ora, after Karolis had struggled to his feet, "Shit, Big Shot, you must hit like a girl."

Their range of emotional responses to each other is apparently limited by their inner sense of manhood. They tend to eschew girls; they emphasize physical touch; they pretend to play basketball. In general they tend to transfer their sexual impulses into such games as the dozens, bluff, or the affair of honor. Their reaction to their emotions and to the problems of personal involvement with each other suggests the same mechanical quality that strikes one in the behavior of the Lone Ranger, Superman, or any of the other mythical heroes of white society.

The actions of the gang members, furthermore, strengthen their unconscious imitation of such models. The boys stress agility, strength, a super-masculinity. They feel insulted by the thought of a white boy calling one of them beautiful and wanting the pleasure of intimacy. Perhaps their unconscious image of a super, but false, masculinity can best be seen in their relationship with their leader Foots.

It is Foots whom Karolis says that he wants to kill, not Ray. The implication is that Karolis sees Foots as two different persons: Ray, a human being, beautiful, whom he wishes to be involved with; and Foots, a stereotyped leader of a gang of corrupt heroes. Like Foots, Karolis has some dimension to his development in the play. But the other persons are nearly caricatures in Baraka's strategy.

They are hardly the models for black dignity. Their stereotyping is most obvious. Foots, the leader, is short and intelligent. On the other hand Ora is short and ugly. Most of the others are tall, like Hines who is "big" and "husky." Foots does not rule the gang through physical strength. He cannot even break Karolis' choke hold. Instead he rules by cleverness, by wit, or by some charisma he holds for the other boys. The authorities in the high school, whom he mocks, find him smart, a credit to his race. In explaining why he is late for the duel, Foots says that he was detained by Van Ness, symbol of the high school authorities, who wanted him to help keep all the unsavory boys in line. Foots directly implies in his statement that his gang are some of the "unsavory . . . elements." Neither the gang members nor the high school authorities, apparently, accept Foots as a person. Rather both groups see him as an agent whom they can exploit for some particular quality he has, perhaps his cleverness or sure intelligence. Whatever it is, their relationship with him is mechanical and stereotyped.

What does Foots receive from them? From the high school authorities, he probably gets a good laugh; what he receives from his gang cannot be so easily answered. In terms of his reaction to Karolis, what Foots desires is some acceptance of himself as a young man, a recognition of his feelings. Karolis has appealed to him in a way that his gang friends cannot. The white boy sees beauty and love in him. Instead of trying to use Ray, Karolis is willing to risk his person for the black boy's love. As a human being needing and responding to love, Foots has to return, therefore, to the beaten boy. In the solitude of the room, the loneliness and stench intensifying his compassion, as Ray he holds Karolis' head in his arms. At that moment with another human being, Ray expresses a mature tenderness and love which his mythic destiny had denied him with his gang. The relationship between the two has to be private to be meaningful, to take place in a toilet in order for it to rise above the stereotyped and artificial responses of the other boys.

In its dramatic strategies **"The Toilet"** implies Amiri Baraka's awareness of how a white society has affected the lives of black boys. At a critical time in their passage from boyhood to manhood, their conceptions of manly behavior, conditioned as they are by the mythic heroes of a white culture, have made them incapable of responding fully as complete human beings. They have no expression for beauty, for compassion, for selfless love. No black music penetrates their world; no blues affects their body rhythms. To all appearances the gang members are alienated from the world at large. Their center of operations is a crude and foully smelling toilet room where they stand revealed as rough caricatures of mythical heroes, like puppets created in some lesser image of an imperfect dream.

They leave the room carrying their wounded, Foots, after what has been a mock battle of honor. The stage is left for those who have some acceptance of their new sexual feelings; the future belongs to Foots. He leaves the gang for love and tenderness. He is needed for himself, not for his leadership qualities or his ability to be a credit to his race. He has become a man, or at least he alone has the possibility of becoming a man. In his past are the unhuman mythical heroes of his gang. Perhaps his future is to be a human being, black, a different kind of model for his gang.

Werner Sollors (essay date 1978)

SOURCE: "Amiri Baraka (LeRoi Jones)," in *Essays on Contemporary American Drama,* edited by Hedwig Bock and Albert Wertheim, Max Hueber Verlag, 1981, pp. 105-22.

[*In this excerpt, which appeared originally in Sollers' book* Amiri Baraka/LeRoi Jones: The Quest for a "Populist Modernism," *the critic calls "The Toilet" a play about race and acceptance for blacks in a white world.*]

"The Toilet," first performed in 1962, is set in an urban high school and deals . . . with loving self-expression in terms of homosexuality. The one-act play contrasts the homosexual relationship of two protagonists with the hostile and threatening, all-male outside world. . . . Homosexuality is viewed positively by Baraka both as an outsider-situation analogous to, though now also in conflict with, that of Blackness, and as a possibility for the realization of "love" and "beauty" against the racial gang code of a hostile society. But there is [another] element of race consciousness in the play.

In the course of the one-act play, Black student Ray Foots has to deny and denounce his love for white student James Karolis. Although Ray had written him a love note, he feels compelled in the presence of other students to deny his own feelings, to act tough, and to let the other students rough up his beloved. Only after the others leave the latrine can Foots express his feelings by cradling the beaten Karolis. In **"The Toilet,"** the Black protagonist has to choose between his generic identity as "Foots" and his individual peculiarity as "Ray." While Foots denotes a "lower" kind of "plebeian" existence, that is closer to the ethnic roots and the soil, "Ray" suggests a more spiritual personality with a cosmic genealogy.

On one level, **"The Toilet"** is the affirmation of Ray's individual self-expression—of a person different from that majority which defines his reality negatively. **"The Toilet"** contrasts the possibility of the free expression of homosexual love, as admission of "any man's beauty," not only with the repression of this freedom of the protagonists through a "social order," but, more than that, with a total inversion of the positive metaphor of homosexuality into the perversion of sadism.

"The Toilet" is undoubtedly an indictment of a brutal social order, depicted fittingly against the background of a filthy latrine. This time, however, in Baraka's familiar confrontation of outsiders with the group, the representatives of the "social order" are young Black males; they are the kind of group Baraka increasingly attempted to speak

for, and with whom he tried to identify, in opposition to "Liberals."

The approach to the play as a perverted "love story" is thus challenged by an interpretation of the majority-minority relations that inform **"The Toilet."** With this focus, the function of homosexuality and the roles of Ray Foots and James Karolis appear in a different light. Instead of representing love and the situation of the outsider, homosexuality now becomes a metaphor for acceptance in the white world. In other words, homosexuality becomes the gesture of individual assimilation, of trying to rise above the peer group, of "liberal" betrayal. As a consequence, the identity of a down-to-earth "Foots" would now seem somewhat more desirable than that of the lofty "Ray," who has removed himself from his ethnic reality. For, if the "love story" is a sentimentalization of "Ray," the "black-and-white story" is a bitter acceptance of Foots. And this acceptance, which implies a painful exorcism of interracial and homosexual love, was increasingly felt to be necessary by Baraka.

Henry C. Lacey (essay date 1981)

SOURCE: "Die Schwartze Bohemien: '*The Terrible Disorder of a Young Man,*'" in *To Raise, Destroy, and Create: The Poetry, Drama, and Fiction of Imamu Amiri Baraka (Le Roi Jones),* The Whitston Publishing Company, 1981, pp. 27-39.

[*In the following chapter excerpt, Lacey states that race is not a central theme of "The Toilet" and Baraka's involvement with the Beat movement is evident.*]

[**"The Toilet"**] derives much of its power from Baraka's faithful presentation of the experiences of the adolescent boy. The writer's ability in this area is seen again, and perhaps to best advantage, in the stories of *Tales.* Everything *belongs* in this extremely naturalistic play. The earthy language, rivaling even that heard in **"The Baptism,"** is a real and necessary part of this world of young, primarily black, urban school boys. The language of **"The Toilet"** emphasizes the intense but misguided efforts of these adolescents to assert their manhood. Likewise, the setting, a "large bare toilet of gray rough cement . . ." and resembling "the impersonal ugliness of a school toilet or a latrine of some institution," is right for this work. The setting is symbol of our bleak and viciously regulated world. In retrospect, even the strong introductory stage directions do not seem excessive. The play opens with these instructions: *"The actors should give the impression frequently that the place smells."* After seeing one of the actors urinate into one of the commodes, *"spraying urine over the seat,"* we are ready for the first lines of **"The Toilet."**

As pointed out by Paul Witherington in "Exorcism and Baptism in LeRoi Jones's 'The Toilet'" [*Modern Drama,* Sept. 1972], the boys wish to show their masculinity by discarding all maternal or "soft" values. At the same time, however, they are driven to find means of expressing love within the group. Consequently, the boys have a real need for affection as well as a fear of the demands of love. Their thwarted libidinal urge is expressed in the form of violence. The dialogue, often funny and firmly rooted in the black idiom, not only focuses on universally identifiable character types (the bully, the coward, the "signifier"). It simultaneously probes the various ways by which the boys enforce the taboo against tenderness.

Driven to deny impulses which they consider "unmanly," the boys exhibit hostility in varying forms throughout the play. These actions culminate in the desperate actuality of physical violence against Karolis. However, the violence takes a more subtle appearance in the early stages of the drama. The boys engage in name-calling and the well known ghetto game, "the dozens," at the start of the action. Both activities serve to shield the participants from the greatly feared overt expression of love, an expression that is ironically manifested in the very need for the gang. Yet, the boys feel that as long as they can call one another "bastid" or "cocksucka," they remain safely within the boundaries of masculine behavior. The same motivating factor is in evidence in the playing of "the dozens," a game in which the participants exchange slurs about one another's parents. The slurs are usually of a sexual nature and directed against the mother. Witherington is perhaps correct in seeing this game as additional evidence that the boys are attempting to exorcise maternal values. It is no less indicative of their desire to show their hardness, their ability to give and take the most crushing blows short of actual violence. The winner of "the dozens" competition is invariably the "man" who through his sheer poetic skill and bawdy imagination can force his opponent to actual violence, or worse, tears. . . .

Although repressed behavior is seen in all the boys, with the exceptions of Karolis and Farrell, it is most glaringly present in the brutal Ora. Ora evinces an absolute horror of compassion, and justly so. If we consider the controlling metaphor for love in the drama, i.e., homosexuality, Ora shows himself most vulnerable to its expression. We see it, first, in his frequently invoked appellations ("cocksucka," "dick licker"). He, furthermore, attempts to engage in oral sex with Karolis and is only interrupted by Ray's entrance. Ora is a latent homosexual. In terms of the metaphorical implications of the play, however, he has a tremendous desire to express love. Because his world does not allow this expression, he inverts his desire. While the callous Oras can live with this necessary inversion, the sensitive Rays cannot.

Foots/Ray is Baraka's earliest presentation of the skinny, intelligent, bug-eyed, middle-class black boy who figures so prominently in the author's writings. We see him as a young child in "Uncle tom's Cabin: Alternate Ending" (*Tales*). In some of the stories, even the name Ray is used. Much of the writer's own life went into these various portraits.

Ray is the middle-class black boy who is torn between two cultures. The dramatist's description of him as "manic" is not extreme. His psychic trauma stems from the schizoid nature of his existence. His problem will be articulated later by Clay in **"Dutchman."** We get our first glimpse of Ray's problem and the boys' understanding of it in Hines's statement concerning Ray's whereabouts. Hines says:

> I think he's still in Miss Powell's class. You know if he missed her class she'd beat his head, and then get his ol' lady to beat his head again.

The white teachers take a special interest in Ray because he is "one" worth saving. The other boys are lost causes. The knowledge of his special treatment causes Ray intense feelings of guilt. Hence, his tremendous desire to belong to his black peers. His feeble attempts to laugh at this situation only serve to intensify our appreciation of his pain:

> That goddamn Van Ness had me in his office. He said I'm a credit to my race. (*Laughs and all follow.*) He said I'm smart-as-a-whip (*imitating Van Ness*) and should help him to keep all you unsavory (*again imitating*) elements in line. (*All laugh again*).

This halting laughter reveals the insecurity of all concerned. Ray is whiter. His homelife most assuredly is closer to that of the teachers than to the black peers. His good grades are sure to lead him to college and a comfortable niche in mainstream society. His upwardly mobile mother, the stereotypical Yiddish mother in blackface, will be there to counter every backsliding move on his part. In spite of these things, he manages to hold onto his role as leader. He does it through sheer intellectual prowess and the actor's ability to project a consummate "macho" image, which is all the more important to Ray because of his fragile physique.

Whereas the gang will tolerate a bourgeois intellectual as a leader, it will never accept a leader whose masculinity is in doubt. Consequently, Ray must deny his relationship with Karolis in order to belong. He must be Foots, not Ray. At the height of the fury, Karolis tells the gang members as much:

> [. . .] his name is Ray, not Foots. You stupid bastards. I love somebody you don't even know.

Karolis understands that his lover is "Foots" only when he surrenders to the gang's debased concept of manhood. The nickname itself implies a plodding, lock-stepped entanglement. "Ray," on the other hand, implies freedom and the light of the spirit, able to shine only when free of the restraining pressures of the group.

"The Toilet," despite its violence and ugliness, does conclude on an optimistic note. After the climactic confrontation, the boys leave Karolis bleeding on the urine-soaked toilet floor. Ray manages to sneak back to his side undetected. The play ends in silence, but with the following stage directions:

> *. . . the door is pushed open slightly, then it opens completely and FOOTS comes in. He stares at Karolis'*

body for a second, looks quickly over his shoulder then runs and kneels before the body, weeping and cradling the head in his arms.

In this markedly maternal gesture, Ray rejects the "macho" role demanded by the gang and asserts another understanding of "manhood." The real man is again the individual with the strength to divorce himself from the inhibiting influence of the majority. In these early works that individual is the homosexual. In the ensuing works the black American takes over this role, as Baraka becomes increasingly convinced that "any black American, simply by virtue of his blackness is weird, a nonconformist in this society."

Though this play has little explicit to say concerning the issue of race, the final scene causes some critics to see the whole work as a statement on race relations. Even Baraka himself seems to have forgotten the real issue of the play. Speaking of the conclusion, he says:

> When I first wrote the play, it ended with everybody leaving. I tacked the other ending on; the kind of social milieu that I was in dictated the kind of rapproachment. It actually did not evolve from the pure spirit of the play. I've never changed it of course, because I feel that now that would only be cute. I think you should admit where you were even if it's painful, but you should also understand your development and growth. . . . But that was ground that I walked on and covered, I can't deny it now.

Baraka is, of course, right in saying that the Beat milieu dictated the concluding scene, but he is wrong in implying that "that kind of rapprochment" should be read "racial rapprochment." Were Karolis black or Ray white, the play would carry the same thematic weight. Basically, **"The Toilet"** is no more concerned with race than is **"The Baptism."** A measure of the writer's total involvement in his milieu is seen in his ability to populate his works with blacks and whites, even in conflict, and yet not be obsessed with race as central theme.

Although **"The Baptism"** and **"The Toilet"** are obviously products of the same period in the writer's development, their dissimilarity in style is worthy of comment. **"The Baptism"** is in no way an attempt at "representational" drama. Markedly expressionistic in technique, the work is evidence of the writer's awareness of the absurdists, who gained prominence in the '50's and '60's. Like the works of the absurdists, **"The Baptism"** is a conscious rejection of realistic theatre. This anti-realism is effected in a number of ways. First, the existence of the characters as "believable" examples of everyday humanity is purposely undercut by their lack of personal names. Minister, boy, old woman, etc. bear testimony to the depersonalizing consequences of modern society. The fragmented, often nonsensical, speech of the characters, strikingly similar to some of the more private lyrics of Baraka, is exemplary of the conscious cacophony of the absurdists. The general effect of distortion and unreality is enhanced also by the abundance of raw sounds, especially "moaning" and "screaming." Because of these and other

effects, **"The Baptism"** frequently approaches the realm of cartoon. The humor is, however, balanced by the viewer's unsettling knowledge that the play images the chaos of his own life. Finally, **"The Baptism"**, like the best works of the absurdists, is impervious to any definitive analysis. The play, like the world of which it is a part, refuses to yield an absolutely logical meaning. This is not the case with **"The Toilet."**

"The Toilet" is a drama of extreme realism, or naturalism. Everything about the play is intended to enhance the viewer's belief in the actuality of the situation. The setting is of extreme importance in that it grounds the viewers in the tactile. Indeed it is no accident that Baraka emphasizes the solidity of the scene (*"The scene is a large bare toilet built of gray rough cement."*). Like the setting, the other aspects of the drama, characterization, diction, and action, express the same concreteness. The boys are all flesh and blood "types" with particular names. They also speak an understandable, earthy idiom. Furthermore, their actions, urinating intermittently, and giving the "impression frequently that the place smells," add to the viewer's illusion that he is secretly observing life in a public school "john" in all its squalor. **"The Toilet,"** unlike **"The Baptism,"** offers a meaning as explicit as its technique.

"SLAVE SHIP:
A HISTORICAL PAGEANT"

PRODUCTION REVIEWS

Clive Barnes (review date 22 November 1969)

SOURCE: A review of "Slave Ship," in *The New York Times,* November 22, 1969, p. 22.

[*In the review below, Barnes outlines the political message of "Slave Ship," and praises Baraka's provocative delivery of his black militant outlook.*]

LeRoi Jones's new play, **"Slave Ship,"** . . . raises for a white critic somber and awful problems. It is a strong, strange play that once seen will never be forgotten. But to regard it simply as a work of art and to sidestep nimbly its implications would be nothing but dishonest.

This is a propaganda play. It is a black militant play. It is a racist play. It purports to counsel black revolution. It is a "get whitey" play. Its attitudes are ugly and prejudiced, and its airily total condemnation of the white American is as sick as a Ku Klux Klanner at a rally.

To an extent it is a celebration of the death of white liberalism. Some people might see in it a hymn to the assassination of Martin Luther King's moderation, for it is also a sad celebration of the death of black liberalism. The play says to hell with moderation—an eye for an eye, a tooth for a tooth—away with the idea of a black man being a white man who has had an unfortunate accident in the color of his skin, and burn, baby, burn.

Were I black I would, I think, be militant. But I am not black, and my concerns are for justice, not revenge. Every white man, every black man, seeing this play is forced to look at himself very carefully in the mirror of his heart.

Is black racism less reprehensible than white racism? You cannot possibly see **"Slave Ship"** without confronting this question, for it is a play that is as much a political statement as a work of art. What are you going to choose?

If you are like me you will perhaps decide that black racism is less reprehensible because it is more understandable. To be brought to a country as a fettered slave is very different from arriving as even the poorest immigrant.

Also, black racism is perhaps a taken affair. It may be part of the business of establishing racial pride. The shooting that this play clearly advocates has luckily not yet started. If it ever does then we will all have decisions to make far more important than the consideration of a play.

Mr. Jones is a clumsy, fantastically gifted playwright. I understand his political concerns, but, as a drama critic rather than a man, I cannot but observe wryly that if he could spare the time and energy to the business he could be a most unusual playwright.

"Slave Ship" is riveting. But it is riveting on two accounts for its deliberately segregated audience. The whites feel shame, compassion and that kind of pointless guilt that can have no absolution because it has no cause. The blacks—and here I am guessing—feel shame, compassion and a certain self-righteous satisfaction in the discomfiture of whitey. It is—ritually turning the other cheek—their all too civil right.

The play is set in the hold of a ship and the conscience of a nation. We see the slaves, chained, humiliated, treated like animals, behaving like animals, being brought in long and tortuous pain to America. We witness—painfully and, yes exhaustingly witness—their degradation.

Mr. Jones, helped by the emphatically realistic staging of Gilbert Moses and the violently brilliant acting of the cast, has already made his point. And what follows is almost a predictable extension of his basic theme of slavery.

Using a very free-styled theatrical form, he shows African tribal vignettes, a coon-like Uncle Tom, a black uprising and a very telling scene suggesting the rejection of Christianity. The play ends with the symbolic destruction of white America. Whitey is got—black panther banners are unfurled. This scared and horrified me. I am whitey.

The play looks as if it has been thrown together like a casual omelette. Yet Mr. Jones's command of the medium and control of his craft is sufficient to insure that although the play is artistically as ragged as burlap, it remains re-

markably effective. But I wonder whether he worries about its artistic effectiveness.

Mr. Jones is a poet of politics. I would like to call him brother, but I am too smart to be that presumptuous. Are we all, including Mr. Jones, going to be too smart? Peace **"Slave Ship"**—do your thing.

Harold Clurman   (review date 2 February 1970)

SOURCE: A review of "Slave Ship," in *The Nation,* New York, Vol. 210, No. 4, February 2, 1970, p. 125.

[*Clurman finds "Slave Ship" a masterpiece of living theater.*]

From what I had read about [**"Slave Ship"**] after its first performance at the Brooklyn Academy of Music I expected it "to scare me to death." Nothing of the sort happened. I was fascinated by the play—full of raucous sound but very few words—as a theatrical phenomenon.

It begins with a picture of the sufferings inflicted on Africans being shipped in the filthy holds of boats to be sold as slaves in America. It proceeds to equally horrendous scenes in the slave markets of the South. It then turns to the consequences of Nat Turner's rebellion. Following this we witness the false place of religious prayer meetings among the blacks and their later determination to rise against oppression.

None of this is "new" except for the excellence of Gilbert Moses' direction, guided by the arrangement of Eugene Lee's construction of the playing areas. These are on several levels: the ship's deck and hold (later used for the auction of slaves) and various other platforms placed all about us and from which players speak, music is played, semi-choral movement and song are projected. The audience is caught in the overall ferment, made aware of an enormous ground swell which is at once obscure and throbbing with gigantic energy. One realizes the possibility of a frenzied and overpowering outbreak.

This does not signify "kill all whites!"; it implies a situation from which great devastation may ensue. What affected me most, however, was not any ideological pronouncement or triumph of stagecraft; the outstanding factor was the quality of the cast. Some of the players have enough stage experience to do justice to individual roles in other than mass dramas, but here all the actors move together, adjust to one another with a seemingly spontaneous coordination and unity which can be achieved only when a common inspiration of blood and brain, heart and flesh inform the whole. This therefore, apart from any other consideration, is *theatre.*

Such groups as the Living Theatre aim at similar attainments, but the results for the most part are forced, unsightly and sympathetic only by an extra stretch of will. The very sophisticated and artful Grotowski ensemble arrives at something like this coherence in "wildness." The **"Slave Ship"** company is in the purest sense of the term *tribal*, hence unassumingly impressive.

CRITICAL COMMENTARY

Stefan Brecht   (essay date 1970)

SOURCE: "LeRoi Jones' 'Slave Ship,'" in *The Drama Review,* Vol. 14, No. 2, Winter, 1970, pp. 212-19.

[In the following excerpt, Brecht explores the images in Baraka's play, "Slave Ship."]

The production [of **"Slave Ship"**] is spectacle, the play being imagist & exhortatory. It does not develop: it shows. Its style is somewhat epic—what little interaction exists is either demonstrative (commiseration, rape) or semi-ritualistic, having the form of recall (Christians vs. Africans: the child-ignoring preacher vs. the member of the tribe pressing the child on his attention)—& the rhythm is the uneven, leisurely one of telling, not the drive of process. The music underscores this epic rhythm, but also builds up the emotional intensities. (The play does not afford much scope for Archie Shepp's marvelous lyricism.) These intensities attach to the affects to whose representation the acting is devoted: suffering & affection, degradation & dignity. The acting style is idealizing naturalism—more or less the same as "socialist realism" or Broadway (minus Jewish irony). Its sentimentality & bathos strike me as the most "European" thing about the production's form. But I think they naturally result from the effort required by Jones' Africanism: an effort to recover & express a *basic* humanity (male & female), which is conceived of as by nature *simple*. This old-fashioned European notion of savages ironically & even tragically engenders artificial culture-products of a complex sort: stereotypes of sincere insincerity. Reductionism can never furnish the basic, & in any event the basic is never simple, if for no other reason than that human existence is inappropriate to human essence.

Though historical in content, the play is not historical drama. It evokes history metaphorically: as information about the essence of a present state. It exposes the audience to the action of successive images of a human condition. Each image identifies a dimension of this condi-

Cover for the mimeographed script of "Slave Ship."

tion, present but subsidiary in the other images. Image no. 1 (about twenty minutes) identifies its genesis, no. 2 its nature, no. 3—the last—its immanent overcoming. The condition is that of the audience: slavery. Being, like all human conditions, one of alienation, its dramatic form is a dialectic of identity: deprivation of identity, alienation, retrieval of identity—a struggle in mind. It resolves into a feast with the audience over which the theatre officiates, revealing itself as active participant in the life imaged. The theatrical evocation of a still actual history turns out to be an act of (political-artistic) participation in a communal life comprising the theatre & the audience.

The play conceives of identity as communal natural identity, which it in turn defines as cultural identity animated by sexual identity through the generation of pride by love.

Slavery is identified by the first image as forcible removal from *home;* by the second, as destruction of *family,* pride, & culture; by the third, as un-Christian *revolt.*

In the first image, the slaves are brought aboard one by one. In the hold (which is under the stage, we have to bend to see), they are segregated by sex. The white man rapes a black woman: the blacks restrain sex among themselves. Wives manage to join husbands, chastely. There is love, suffering, song. The agitated suffering provides the keynote while the guard on deck listens, rapes, laughs, sleeps: a powerfully nervous rhythm, orchestrated by Shepp. I do not think Gil Moses has directed this well. Yet its valuable aspect, in the context of contemporary European theatre (e.g., the Living Theatre), is that it's not abstract. Just as Jones reminds us of concrete love, so he reminds us of real suffering, tangible unfreedom, physical attempts at liberation—instead of obliterating natural life with psychological reflections or metaphysical analyses.

The second image theatrically, though not analytically, correlates the destruction of the family (a mock marriage, selling man & wife apart, etc.) with cultural alienation, which is portrayed by the two classic species (cf. Frazier, Keil) of the cultural house-nigger, the self-abasing clown who has turned his existence into its own denial (the tolerable bad nigger) & the gibbering preacher (the good nigger) who in a foreign tongue (scat) preaches the message which denies his essence. The plantation Tom (Garret Morris: a virtuoso performance, but perhaps less profound than Tim Pelt's portrayal of the preacher) betrays a conspiracy for a pork chop; the Reverend (could Jones have King in mind?) obstinately disregards a wounded baby pressed on his attention, stepping over it as he preaches. Both are shown as maniacs; they have lost their minds. Nostalgic racial memories of the homeland evoke the destroyed identity: male & female pride in their respective chores of home- & war-making, expressed in integral culture: dance, song, prayer.

The third image is of revolt, but the play shows the Afro-American in revolt from the first crossing of the gangplank. From the beginning until now, not acceptance or inertia, but superior brute force abetted by treason have kept him down. This is a historically incorrect idealization

(cf. Du Bois & Genovese vs. Aptheker) which is valid, within the framework of Jones' conception of identity, as revelation of the repressive power that generated inertia & acceptance, & also valid insofar as Jones is using history as symbol for present condition. They resist being loaded into the hold; in the hold they work at ridding themselves of their shackles; in America they sullenly plan assassinations. The point is not merely to give heart, but that no new cultural identity emerged from the alienation into slavery.

Identity is tied to communality. The community is shown as integral, especially in the hold: many spontaneous gestures of concern for & succor of others; a perennial unreasoned orientation toward collective suffering & collective revolt, & by nature religion—itself a collective self-awareness relative to revered familial forces (and implicitly contrasted to the Christian alienation of man from nature).

The family is shown as the living cell of community, its love the community's energy. Acting & directing stress male supremacy. The woman stands silently behind her man. (But finally all take arms.) Seeing the destruction of the family as major evil & as root-danger to identity is a personal thing with Jones (cf. his beautiful account of his youth) & part of a trend (cf. the Black Muslim). This male suprematism seems to fit better into the revolt against decadent European civilization than does the idolization of the small family. But for Jones it's a matter of what's natural & therefore good & black. The play upholds the "petty-bourgeois" values of heterosexual love, monogamy, male leadership, parental child-rearing, as sources of *communal* strength—& as nourishing place of that pride, which for Jones is the core of personal identity & the source of cultural being.

The final revolt is a genocidal call to arms to the young Afro-American audience—a call for the killing of the white man. But the only enemy killed is a black man. This may be significant. Not only because of the alleged killings of Malcolm X by Black Muslims & of Black Panthers by Karenga's men, but because it suggests that Jones' stress on cultural community identity may ultimately override his advocacy of social revolt. There is a symbolic overthrow of Uncle Sam. The play joins the present with clenched fists, hymns, new flags. It not only joins the present, it joins actuality—unlike *Paradise Now,* & in the opposite sense from that recently fashionable "audience participation" which invites the audience to join the play. This audience, having enjoyed the play, joins in, walks out dancing.

Kimberly W. Benston (essay date 1976)

SOURCE: "'Slave Ship': Vision Meets Form," in *Baraka: The Renegade and the Mask,* Yale University Press, 1976, pp. 243-54.

[*In the excerpt below, Benston explores Baraka's use of music throughout his work, especially in "Slave Ship."*]

In his drama Baraka has constantly used music. In **"Jello,"** Rochester dances soul-steps while robbing Bennie. In *A Recent Killing*, dances and songs help fill empty dramatic spaces and serve as entertainment. In **"Home on the Range,"** music becomes a metaphor for judgment and apocalypse in the wild "nigger" party. The most interesting use of music before **"Slave Ship"** is in **"Dutchman,"** where Lula's dance, Clay's discussion of the blues and Charlie Parker, and the Negro conductor's final soft-shoe are crucial theatrical and thematic elements of the play.

It is with **"Slave Ship,"** however, that Baraka elevates music to the dual position of central metaphor and primary theatrical vehicle. . . . The drama of **"Slave Ship"** is fundamentally the same as that of *Blues People:* African Spirit endures Western (specifically, American) oppression and rises to perfection in musical form. The genius of Baraka's play lies in the manner in which the complex black music aesthetic is given precise theatrical embodiment.

These, then, are the primary forces that inform the nature and use of music in **"Slave Ship."** As one might expect from this diverse background, music operates on many levels and in many ways to give form to Baraka's thought in the play. Every effect of feeling and every physical condition is portrayed through sound. The props call for ship "noises," ship "bells," sea "splashing," whip and chain "sounds." The slave-characters evoke the state of misery with constant moans, cries, curses—all bare intonations which, rather than describing a condition, become its essence. Baraka's observation in the poem "Ka'Ba," that "our world is full of sound," is concretized in **"Slave Ship"**: here, sound fully becomes the world.

The experience of the play, then, is less one of watching than of listening. If sound is the world's substance, then the particular organization of sound into music is the world in process. Music in **"Slave Ship"** is the form of idealized historicity as projected by the successive "pageant" images. Thus religious, civilized Africa is the music and dance-oriented rite of the opening image. Africa survives on the slave ship and in America in the incessant drumbeats, ritual chants, and tribal dances that remain a basic means of expression among the slaves. On the slave ship, the life of the black people is assured almost thoroughly through the rising "chant-moan of the women [. . .] like mad old nigger ladies humming forever in deathly patience," and in the percussional beating upon planks and walls. The white man's being *is* his hideous laughter; the entire Middle Passage is composed by Baraka as a sound-war between this laughter and the music of the black collective will (which is also internally threatened by "the long stream of different wills, articulated as screams, grunts, cries, songs, etc."). At times, the "laughter is drowned in the drums," but these moments are always followed by silence (a stand-off) or the rise of white laughter (repression). The tribal humming endures; the African civilization is brought to America with the slaves.

The musical expression of the Afro-American does not simply parallel history; again, it is the complexity of the slaves' alienated existence. The gospels, presaged by the patient moans of women in the hold, take over as the constant undertone of black resistance. The traitorous Tom's shuffling, jeffing "dance" represents the degradation of the masked dancer of the opening fertility rite. Yet subversively, in darkness, the pure and ancient culture remains, juxtaposed to the Tom image:

> *(Lights off . . . drums of ancient African warriors come up . . . hero-warriors. Lights blink back on, show shuffling black man, hat in his hand, scratching his head. Lights off. Drums again. Black dancing in the dark, . . . scratching his head. Lights off. Drums again. Black dancing in the dark, with bells, as if free, dancing wild old dances. Bam Boom Bam Booma Bimbam Boomama boom beem bam. Dancing in the darkness . . . Yoruba Dance/lights flash on briefly, spot on, off the dance. Then off.)*

With the suppression of the plantation revolt, African war drums subside into "the sound of a spiritual," a song of American experience and African spirituality: "Oh, Lord Deliver Me . . . oh Lord." White laughter howls in triumph; for a moment, it drowns out what has now become the complex African/American musical fusion.

Now, modern rhythms: the gibberish of the preacher-Tom takes up the gospel's "Jesus, Jesus, Jesus . . ."; against him, the African/American voices sing new notes—jazz and blues scatting—and "new-sound" horns scream the old war chants. The drums persist as the unvarying keeper of the old rhythms. As the community coalesces once again, the original humming gathers and reaches toward climax. White laughter rises sporadically above the swelling sounds of chant, scream, hum, scat, horns, drums; all is "mixed with sounds of [the] slave ship." History gathers all its imagined moments in an anarchy of sonority and becomes imminently apocalyptic. The chant of "when we gonna rise/up" grows with the music; "the white man's laughter is heard trying to drown out the music, but the music is rising."

Eventually, the chant becomes song; African drums, slave-ship noises, and contemporary visionary jazz (Sun Ra, Archie Shepp) become one poem of black experience, one tangible weapon of black revolt. The preacher's voice "breaks" before he dies; the white man gasps on his laughter as the horde descends. Finally, the triumph—spiritual and physical—is expressed as dance. Again, this is an African/American synthesis, "Miracles'/Temptations' dancing line" merging with African movement in a "new-old dance": what Baraka amusingly but pointedly calls "Bogalooyoruba." The improvisational essence of this Afro-American musical sensibility becomes the ultimate statement of transcendence, and this is the audience's achievement. The quickly created "party" is an ecstasy of "fingerpop, skate, monkey, dog" in which each participant's thing is everyone's thing and individual improvisation becomes communal form: in the words of the street-wise saying, 'everything is everything.'

Music is thus strength, memory, power, triumph, affirmation—the entire historical and mythical process of Afro-

American being. The mythical curve of return to primordial power is enacted in the dance, for the final dance of the audience in the womblike hold returns us to the site of the whirling fertility goddess. By integrating the spectator with the opening dance, Baraka has moved **"Slave Ship"** out of drama and into ritual; that is, he has reversed the process by which the Western (particularly Greek) theatre evolved from rite to drama. In Greek theatre, the spectators became a new and different element added to original ritual. The dance was not only danced but also watched from a distance; it became a "spectacle." Whereas in ritual nearly all were worshippers acting, the spectators added the elements of watching, thinking, feeling, not-doing. The *dromenon* or rite, something actually done by oneself, became *drama,* a thing also done but abstracted from one's doing. The members of Baraka's audience, on the contrary, are transformed from spectators of drama as "a thing done" but apart from themselves, to partakers of ritual, "a thing done" with no division between actor and spectator. Just as the opening African ritual is refashioned at the end into a higher act, one of communal triumph as well as celebration, so the audience is brought to a higher role. No longer merely observers of an oft-forgotten tradition, they themselves now perform a ritual, affirming by their deed the complete communality of the theatrical event. The collectivity of ritual has supplanted the individuation of drama.

The final rite, with its mimed cannibalistic aspect, is apocalyptic in both a mythical and a religious sense. In its mythical dimension, the ending completes the absorption of the natural, historical cycle into mythology. Its mythical movement is one of comic resurrection and integration, completed by the marriage of the spectator into community and the birth of the "old-new" black nation. This fertility ritual clearly has a religious dimension that has been prepared for by the continuous prayers to Obatala and Jesus, curses of the "Godless, white devil," and litanies such as "Rise, Rise, Rise, etc." Indeed, by creating basic images of resurrection with accompanying sensations of magic, charm, and incantation, Baraka returns the black audience to the most fundamental religious ground of tribal ceremony from which sprung the two greatest epochs of Western theatre (Greek and Christian), and which gave life to the archetypical African spirit. The spectators are as integral a part of the work as the congregation of a black Baptist church is of its service, and they function in much the same way. The nationalist myth of African-inspired renewal and Afro-American triumph is taken up by the audience because Baraka has called upon the community's shared aesthetic—the genius for musical improvisation.

This re-creation of the mythical and religious through music points Baraka's art toward the Nietzschean Dionysian state. Here the end of individuation becomes possible, for the Dionysian essence for Nietzsche was a musical one: "In song and dance man expresses himself as a member of a higher community; he has forgotten how to walk and speak and is on the way toward flying into the air, dancing" [*The Birth of Tragedy,* trans. Walter Kaufman, 1967]. By claiming African roots in their totality, the black community controls its destiny as Clay, the middle-class greyboy, could not. Now, Baraka's black heroes, not the witch-devil Lula,

dance in triumph. The tragedy-burdened slave ship of **"Dutchman"** has become the dance-filled celebration of **"Slave Ship";** musical transcendence has risen from the spirit of tragedy.

FURTHER READING

AUTHOR COMMENTARY

Reilly, Charlie. *Conversations with Amiri Baraka.* Jackson: University Press of Mississippi, 1994, 271 p.
    Collection of twenty-five interviews covering Baraka's life and career.

OVERVIEWS AND GENERAL STUDIES

Andrews, W. D. E. "The Marxist Theater of Amiri Baraka." *Comparative Drama* 18, No. 2 (Summer 1984): 137-61.
    Concludes that Baraka's Marxist plays are his least effective dramas.

Benston, Kimberly W., ed. *Imamu Amiri Baraka (LeRoi Jones): A Collection of Critical Essays.* Englewood Cliffs, N.J.: Prentice-Hall, Inc., 1978, 195 p.
    A collection of essays by noted critics, including overviews of Baraka's career, a biographical essay, music criticism, and articles focusing on Baraka's prose, his poetry, and his drama.

Bigsby, C. W. E. "LeRoi Jones." In *Confrontation and Commitment, A Study of Contemporary American Drama: 1959-66,* pp.138-55. Kansas City: University of Missouri Press, 1967.
    Covers Baraka's early career up to 1967 and calls him talented though lacking in discipline.

Brown, Lloyd W. *Amiri Baraka.* Boston: Twayne Publishers, 1980, 180 p.
    Study of Baraka's poetry, prose, and drama.

Hudson, Theodore R. *From LeRoi Jones to Amiri Baraka: The Literary Works.* Durham: Duke University Press, 1973, 222 p.
    Biographical and critical study of Baraka and his work.

Islam, Syed Manzoorul. "The Ritual Plays of Amiri Baraka (LeRoi Jones)." *Indian Journal of American Studies* 14, No. 1 (January 1984): 43-55.
    Describes ritualistic use of cruelty "with a graphic exactness that borders on repulsion," especially in the plays "Slave Ship," "The Slave," and "Dutchman."

Marranca, Bonnie. "Leroi Jones (Amiri Baraka)." In *American Playwrights: A Critical Survey,* edited by Bonnie Marranca and Gautam Dasgupta, pp. 121-33. New York: Drama Book Specialists, 1981.
    Outlines the prevailing themes of Baraka's plays.

Sarma, M. Nagabhushana. "Revolt and Ritual in the Plays of LeRoi Jones." *Osmania Journal of English Studies* XI, No. 1 (1974-75): 1-9.

> Discusses "Revolutionary Theatre" and Baraka's place in it.

Sollors, Werner. *Amiri Baraka/LeRoi Jones: The Quest for a "Populist Modernism."* New York: Columbia University Press, 1978, 299 p.

> Sollors traces the development of Baraka's work through the four major political and aesthetic phases of his life.

Werner, Craig. "Brer Rabbit Meets the Underground Man: Simplification of the Consciousness in Baraka's "Dutchman" and "Slave Ship." *Obsidian: Black Literature in Review* 5, No. 1 & 2 (1979): 35-40.

> Werner identifies a continuum in Baraka's drama in which "Dutchman" represents the failure of "obsessive comtemplations of contradictions and consciousness" as

a reaction to stereotyping and white oppression. This failure necessitates a simplified reaction—"a clearly defined vision of the threat to black survival posed by a genocidal white world"—which is presented in "Slave Ship."

"DUTCHMAN"

Levesque, George A. "LeRoi Jones' 'Dutchman': Myth and Allegory." *Obsidian: Black Literature in Review* V, No. 3 (1979): 33-40.

> The criticism of "Dutchman" is analyzed, supporting some of it and disagreeing with other conclusions.

Weisgram, Dianne H. "LeRoi Jones' 'Dutchman': Inter-racial Ritual of Sexual Violence." *American Imago* 29, No. 3 (Fall 1972): 215-32.

> Explores, in-depth, the sexual roles of the lead characters in Baraka's famous play.

Additional coverage of Author's life and career is contained in the following sources published by Gale Research: *Black Literature Criticism*; *Contemporary Authors*, Vols. 21-24 (rev. ed.); *Contemporary Authors Bibliographic Series*, Vol. 3; *Contemporary Authors New Revision Series*, Vols. 27, 38; *Contemporary Literary Criticism*, Vols. 1, 2, 3, 5, 10, 14, 33; *Concise Dictionary of American Literary Biography 1941-1968*; *Dictionary of Literary Biography*, Vols. 5, 7, 16, 38; *Dictionary of Literary Biography Documentary Series*, Vol. 8; *Discovering Authors, Major 20th Century Writers*; *Poetry Criticism*, Vol. 4.

Francis Beaumont
1584-1616

John Fletcher
1579-1625

INTRODUCTION

During the brief period of their collaboration, Beaumont and Fletcher were among the most successful playwrights of the Jacobean stage. Together they helped establish and define the dramatic genre of tragicomedy, which became the most popular form of the period. Their partnership began around 1606-1607 with the comedy *The Woman Hater* and ended when Beaumont retired from the theater around 1613 or 1614. During that time they produced some dozen plays together, including *Philaster, or Love Lies a-Bleeding, The Maid's Tragedy,* and *A King and No King.* In addition, they individually composed such plays as Beaumont's *The Knight of the Burning Pestle* and Fletcher's *The Faithful Shepherdess.* After Beaumont's retirement, Fletcher went on to produce dozens of plays both singly and jointly with several other writers, most notably Philip Massinger and William Shakespeare. He later succeeded Shakespeare as the principal playwright for the King's Men, the leading acting troupe in London.

BIOGRAPHICAL INFORMATION

Beaumont and Fletcher both had distinguished backgrounds. Fletcher was born in 1579 at Rye in Sussex, the son of Anne Holland Fletcher and Dr. Richard Fletcher, an Anglican minister. In the course of his career Dr. Fletcher became Chaplain to the Queen, Dean of Peterborough, Bishop of Bristol, Bishop of Worcester, and eventually Bishop of London. Fletcher's uncle Giles Fletcher was a diplomat and the author of a book on Russia (which the dramatist later drew upon for his play *The Loyal Subject*); his cousins Giles, Jr., and Phineas Fletcher were poets. Fletcher attended Cambridge University and earned a bachelor's degree in 1595 and a master's three years later. Beaumont was born in 1584 at Grace-Dieu in Leicester to Francis and Anne Pierrepoint Beaumont. The Beaumonts were connected to some of the most prominent families in England, including the royal Plantagenet family. They had strong Catholic loyalties, however (in 1605 Beaumont's cousin Anne Vaux was implicated in the Gunpowder Plot, a Catholic attempt to assassinate King James), and they suffered greatly from the penalties laid against members of that faith. Beaumont's father, a lawyer, judge, and member of Parliament, died when his son was fourteen. Beaumont attended Oxford University and subsequently studied law at the Inner Temple in London. During his student years he

Francis Beaumont

composed a burlesque for the Inner Temple's Christmas revels and published the narrative poem *Salmacis and Hermaphroditus* in 1608.

By 1606 Beaumont and Fletcher were actively writing for the stage, and by 1609-1610, with the production of *Philaster,* they were working for the King's Men—a remarkably rapid ascent to the top of their profession. In 1611 *A King and No King* was staged at Court before royalty. Despite such success, Beaumont left the theater sometime during 1613 or 1614 when he married the heiress Ursula Isley. Since Beaumont and Fletcher collaborations continued to be produced as late as 1616, he may have continued to write at his country estate. (Or, these late works may simply have been composed but not staged before his retirement.) He died in 1616 and was buried in the Poet's Corner of Westminster Abbey. Fletcher continued to write for the stage for another nine years, remaining highly productive right up until his death of the plague in 1625.

John Fletcher

MAJOR WORKS

Beaumont and Fletcher are acknowledged innovators of the dramatic form of tragicomedy, in which a potentially tragic plot results in a happy ending. Of their three finest collaborations, *Philaster, A King and No King,* and *The Maid's Tragedy,* the first two are examples of this new genre. Although not published until 1620, *Philaster* was almost certainly performed at least a decade earlier. (It was mentioned by John Davies of Hereford in his 1610 work *Scourge of Folly.*) The play concerns the actions of Philaster, a prince whose kingdom has been usurped, and his love for Arathusa, the daughter of the tyrant who displaced him. Philaster is attended by Bellario, a young girl who is in love with him and disguises herself as a male page in order to be near him. Hearing rumors that Arathusa and Bellario are having an affair, Philaster attacks the supposed lovers in a jealous rage and wounds them both. At the end of the play, Bellario reveals that she is a woman, Philaster and Arathusa are united, and Philaster regains his kingdom. *A King and No King* centers on King Arbaces, an unstable and excessively proud ruler who, after an absence of many years, falls in love with his sister Panthea, whom he had last seen as a child. Much of the action revolves around his wild vacillations between abhorrence of his incestuous desires and his urge to fulfill them. In the end it is revealed that Arbaces and Panthea are not related after all: he is the son of Gobrias, the Lord Protector, while she is in actuality the queen. Thus, al-

though he is not king, Arbaces is free to consummate his love. *The Maid's Tragedy,* like *A King and No King,* was written around 1611; unlike the other play, however, *The Maid's Tragedy,* as its title indicates, does not resolve happily. In this work, Amintor, despite his betrothal to Aspatia, is commanded by the King to marry another woman, Evadne. On their wedding night Evadne reveals that she is the King's mistress—a liaison she intends to continue—and the marriage is merely a device to protect her reputation. The play explores the various effects of this state of affairs: Amintor's humiliation, Aspatia's grief, and the rage of Evadne's brother Melantius, who convinces his sister of her degradation. At Melantius' instigation, she murders the King in his bed and then commits suicide. Aspatia, in her desolation, disguises herself as a man and provokes a fight with Amintor, during which she is killed. When he discovers the identity of the person he has slain, Amintor takes his own life.

CRITICAL RECEPTION

Although they were greatly admired throughout the seventeenth century, the plays of Beaumont and Fletcher have since fallen in critical estimation. Commentators have often viewed them as evidence of a decline in dramatic art, judging them degraded versions of the great tragedies and comedies of the Elizabethan period. They have been characterized as skillful but highly artificial constructions designed to satisfy the increasingly decadent tastes of Jacobean and Caroline audiences. Today, they are of interest to scholars as transitional plays spanning the gap between the works of Shakespeare and Ben Jonson and the dramas of such Restoration playwrights as John Dryden. Numerous critics have argued that Beaumont and Fletcher exerted a significant influence on Shakespeare, noting that, in his late romances, the elder dramatist was following the lead of his younger contemporaries. Shakespeare and Fletcher are known to have collaborated on the romance *The Two Noble Kinsmen,* and, although there is much debate on the subject, many hold that Shakepeare's *Cymbeline* was patterned after *Philaster.* During the Restoration period, the plays of Beaumont and Fletcher were among the first works staged, and some commentators have contended that Dryden's form of "heroic tragedy" is indebted to the "extravagant passion" (as Robert Turner phrased it) depicted in Beaumont and Fletcher's tragicomedies. Modern critics have also scrutinized the plays of Beaumont and Fletcher for what they tell of Jacobean social conditions and concerns. John Danby, for example, has analyzed them as productions designed for an aristocratic audience and therefore reflective of the views of that class. Mary Grace Muse Adkins, on the other hand, has detected in the sympathetic depiction of common people in *Philaster* a change in the political atmosphere of the period. Ronald Broude has explored the seventeenth-century conceptions of providence and the divine right of kings expressed in *The Maid's Tragedy.* And William C. Woodson has read *A King and No King* as a critique of Protestant beliefs in that time of great religious contention. Other topics addressed by critics include the presentation of ethics and morality in the plays and the influence of the

highly popular masque form on the tragicomedies of Beaumont and Fletcher.

PRINCIPAL WORKS

PLAYS BY BEAUMONT AND FLETCHER

The Woman Hater c. 1606
Love's Cure, or The Martial Maid c. 1607
Philaster, or Love Lies a-Bleeding c. 1609
The Coxcomb c. 1609
Cupid's Revenge c. 1611
The Maid's Tragedy c. 1611
A King and No King c. 1611
The Captain c. 1611
The Scornful Lady c. 1615
Thierry and Theodoret (with Philip Massinger) c. 1615
Beggars' Bush (with Massinger) c. 1615
Love's Pilgrimage c. 1616

PLAYS BY BEAUMONT

The Knight of the Burning Pestle c. 1607
The Noble Gentleman (later revised by Fletcher) c. 1607
The Masque of the Inner Temple and Gray's Inn 1613

PLAYS BY FLETCHER

The Faithful Shepherdess c. 1608
The Woman's Prize, or The Tamer Tamed c. 1611
The Night Walker, or The Little Thief c. 1611
Bonduca c. 1611
Valentinian c. 1612
Monsieur Thomas, or Father's Own Son c. 1612
Four Plays, or Moral Representations in One (with Nathan Field) c. 1612
Cardenio (with William Shakespeare) 1612-1613
The Two Noble Kinsmen (with William Shakespeare) 1612-1613
Henry VIII (with Shakespeare) 1613
The Honest Man's Fortune (with Massinger and Field) c. 1613
Wit without Money c. 1614
The Mad Lover c. 1616
The Queen of Corinth (with Massinger and Field) c. 1617
The Jeweller of Amsterdam (with Massinger and Field) c. 1617
The Knight of Malta (with Massinger and Field) c. 1618
The Loyal Subject 1618
The Humorous Lieutenant, or Demetrius and Enanthe c. 1619
The Bloody Brother, or Rollo Duke of Normandy (with Massinger and others) c. 1619
Sir John van Olden Barnavelt (with Massinger) 1619
The Custom of the Country (with Massinger) c. 1619
The False One (with Massinger) c. 1620
Women Pleased c. 1620
The Island Princess c. 1621

The Double Marriage (with Massinger) c. 1621
The Pilgrim c. 1621
The Wild Goose Chase c. 1621
The Prophetess (with Massinger) 1622
The Sea Voyage (with Massinger) 1622
The Spanish Curate (with Massinger) 1622
The Little French Lawyer (with Massinger) c. 1623
The Maid in the Mill (with William Rowley) 1623
The Devil of Dowgate, or Usury Put to Use 1623
The Lovers' Progress 1623
A Wife for a Month 1624
Rule a Wife and Have a Wife 1624
The Elder Brother (with Massinger) c. 1625
The Fair Maid of the Inn (with Massinger and others) 1626

OVERVIEWS AND GENERAL STUDIES

Suzanne Gossett (essay date 1971)

SOURCE: "Masque Influence on the Dramaturgy of Beaumont and Fletcher," in *Modern Philology,* Vol. 69, No. 1, August, 1971, pp. 199-208.

[*In the essay below, Gossett examines how the tradition of court masques influenced the tragicomedies of Beaumont and Fletcher.*]

The masque has recently received new critical attention. Books on the subject have appeared, important masques have been reprinted, and the 1968 volume of *Renaissance Drama* dealt exclusively with this form. The relation of the masque to the Jacobean drama still needs reexamination, however, with emphasis not merely on mechanical connections—who borrowed an antimasque from whom—but on the stylistic influence of the masque on the new tone of drama in the Jacobean period. From this viewpoint the contribution of Beaumont and Fletcher is central, particularly since they developed and popularized the other characteristic Jacobean form, tragicomedy.

Both masque and tragicomedy existed in England before the reign of James I, but they changed noticeably around 1605-8. For the sixth of January 1604/5 Ben Jonson produced *The Masque of Blackness,* the first of his series of great Jacobean masques. Shakespeare's *Cymbeline* and Beaumont and Fletcher's ***Philaster*** soon followed.

The simultaneous emergence of these two extravagant forms was not accidental. Both are romantic, even antirealistic. Laurels go to the poet who manipulates the situation most spectacularly, not, as in realistic drama, to the one who best conceals his controlling hand. Furthermore, the leading authors of Jacobean masques and tragicomedies knew each other's work. Beaumont and Fletcher were "sons of Ben," and in 1608 the King's Men may have hired both Jonson and the collaborators to write for the Blackfriars theater.

Under these conditions the Jacobean masque did not remain isolated at court, performed once or twice and forgotten. Increasingly it penetrated the plays of the time. But as the masque grew from a single entry of disguised visitors to a spectacular dramatic performance, the process of adaptation became more complex. The masque in *The Tempest* sufficiently indicates that a dramatist introducing Juno and Ceres, Nymphs and Sicklemen, faces a different problem from one introducing Romeo and some friends to dance. In one case the entry is an episode in a continuing drama; in the other, it is a complete shift of style and genre within the framework of a play.

Beaumont and Fletcher are usually thought to have worked masques into their plays in order to please their audience, and certainly, from their earliest works to **The Fair Maid of the Inn,** Fletcher's last play, specific connections to current court productions can be traced. The select audience in the private theater thus basked in reflected glory, feeling that they were in touch with spectacular, aristocratic entertainment. But—and this was long ignored or denied— there was also aesthetic logic to the collaborators' use of masques. Beaumont and Fletcher's chief contribution to Jacobean drama was their continued experimentation with the tragicomic form. As early as the preface "To the Reader" of **The Faithful Shepherdess,** Fletcher attempted to define tragicomedy, and, no matter what the inadequacies of his definition, it demonstrated a self-conscious awareness of innovation. As Beaumont and Fletcher slowly explored the possibilities of tragicomedy, they must have been struck by its similarities to the much-discussed masque.

In the typical Jacobean masque a set of masquers suffers harm, imprisonment, or enchantment by an evil force. When some higher power, usually a god or the King, overcomes this force, the masquers make their appearance. This pattern is already found in *The Masque of Blackness* (1604/5) and *The Masque of Beauty* (1607/8). In the first the masquers, to lose their black color, must find the right country, whose name ends in "Tania," where there is a "greater Light"; in the second the masquers cannot be seen until, with the aid of the moon, "*Nights* black charmes are flowne" and "*the* Scene *discouer'd*" (*Jonson,* 7:186). Late masques follow the same pattern. In *Love Freed from Ignorance and Folly* (1611) the Sphinx imprisons the masquers; in *Pleasure Reconciled to Virtue* (1619) Hercules vanquishes Comus and the pigmies before the masquers can appear. The masquers are always romanticized figures like gods, goddesses, or knights.

This pattern is to some extent the pattern of comedy, for the audience at once understand that the virtuous force, the King or his substitute, will prove stronger than the evil. Northrop Frye [in *The Anatomy of Criticism,* 1957] describes masque as a subdivision of comedy:

> The total *mythos* of comedy, only a small part of which is ordinarily presented, has regularly what in music is called a ternary form . . . the hero's society is a Saturnalia, a reversal of social standards which recalls a golden age in the past before the main action of the play begins. . . . Thus we have a stable and harmonious

order disrupted by folly, obsession, forgetfulness, "pride and prejudice," or events not understood by the characters themselves, and then restored. . . . The Jacobean masque, with the antimasque in the middle, gives a highly conventionalized or "abstract" version of it.

In certain of the more solemn masques, however, the genre, insofar as masque has a genre explicable in dramatic terms, seems to be tragicomedy. The actors are always of high rank, as they must be in tragicomedy. In both forms the main characters usually come from a romantic, distant place. The danger, which may seem slight to us, is serious by implication, since only the intervention of a god or king can overcome it. A central problem of all tragicomedy is raising this danger to a level sufficient to distinguish the play from comedy; in masques this is often done by treating the danger as moral or psychological. In both masque and Fletcherian tragicomedy a disproportion exists between the difficulty and the effort required to overcome it. In masques the King appears and a great enchantress vanishes, or the mere mention of Nature and her true creations banishes alchemy and its imperfect creations; in tragicomedy someone repents and a seemingly insoluble dilemma collapses. The laws of necessity are no longer the laws of cause and effect.

Frye does not anatomize tragicomedy as a separate *mythos,* but he does comment that in some masques, as "we move further away from comedy, the conflict becomes increasingly serious, and the antimasque figures less ridiculous and more sinister." While the masque was a subtype of romantic tragicomedy before the antimasque became prominent, the growing use of antimasque figures at Whitehall provided further opportunities for the dramatists at Blackfriars. Since writers of tragicomedy sought to create what Miss Doran calls "the mixture . . . of tragic and comic episodes, and of feelings appropriate to these," those feelings which did not ultimately figure in the tragicomic synthesis could usefully be attached to antimasque figures [Madelaine Doran, *Endeavors of Art: A Study of Form in Elizabethan Drama,* 1964]. Dangerous human propensities—disruptive social, moral, or psychological forces— were embodied, given force, and then transcended. The effect, escape from potential danger or tragedy, recalls modern psychological methods for dealing with such forces in the individual. Furthermore, the antimasque figures were inherently ambiguous. They represented dangerous forces, beastliness or false nature, but did so in a reassuringly comic manner. Yet the pattern of danger and escape was already basic to the masque before the antimasque became prominent, so that even when antimasque figures began to resemble types from city comedy, the general implications of masque for tragicomedy remained.

The masques in Beaumont and Fletcher's plays helped overcome another difficulty of tragicomedy: destroying conventional comic and tragic expectations. The concealed denouement is often considered the central and distinguishing characteristic of Beaumont and Fletcher's tragicomedy. The audience should have no idea how or whether the dilemma will be solved. Normally a play creates a set of tragic or comic expectations, but in tragicomedy both must be kept in uneasy balance. Beaumont and Fletcher abjured any helpful reference to the way things really happen, while their technique of surprise inhibited them from furnishing the audience decisive information unknown to the characters (as in *Measure for Measure*). They found another way to destroy comic or tragic expectations by shifting the entire play into a mode formal enough to be free of conventional logic. Their dramas are organized formally, as Mizener has illustrated, and within this formal organization constant shifts from the familiar to the fantastic disorient the audience [Arthur Mizener, "The High Design of *A King and No King*," *Modern Philology* 38, 1940].

Masques throughout the Beaumont and Fletcher canon create these shifts from real to unreal, remind us of the factitious nature of the performance, and destroy conventional comic or tragic expectations. A full masque was not essential for achieving these results, and in practice masques introduced into plays had to be abbreviated. A masque in a drama could not lead to one or two hours of reveling with the ladies, and its author could not hope for elaborate scenery or complex machinery. What remained, then, was a short, spectacular entertainment, normally including some music, dancing, and the entry of fabulous or exotic characters.

The abbreviation of the masque impelled by theatrical circumstances might suggest that isolated masque elements could occasionally be as effective as "full" masques. Thorndike, who did not differentiate masques from masque elements, counted "distinct masque elements occurring in eighteen of their plays" [A. H. Thorndike, *The Influence of Beaumont and Fletcher on Shakspere*, 1901]. These masque elements, isolated bits of the masque requiring less preparation than a full masque, help fashion the abrupt changes of mood and meaning in a Beaumont and Fletcher tragicomedy. They may appear alone or together with a full masque; in either case, such elements permit a particularly continuous and flexible penetration of the masque into the drama. Repeated shifts to the more formal style serve as reminders of the artifice of the play, constantly pulling the audience back from the brink of serious involvement. In this way masques and masque elements can resolve a critical difficulty of tragicomedy, and Beaumont and Fletcher exploit them with increasing frequency throughout their careers.

Three of Beaumont and Fletcher's best plays illustrate the uses of the masque just described. The masque in *The Maid's Tragedy* recalls specific productions of Ben Jonson; it also complicates the issue of whether the play is a tragedy. In *Philaster* suggestions of a masque act as a pivot in what becomes a standard method, turning the play toward a tragicomic conclusion. *The Mad Lover* contains an antimasque and masque elements; various parts of a conventional masque, distributed throughout the play, establish its tone. All three plays indicate that the masque was not intended merely to flatter an audience.

The Maid's Tragedy begins with a wedding masque, a "detailed reproduction of court entertainments" [David Laird, "The Inserted Masque in Elizabethan and Jacobean Drama," 1955]. Beaumont and Fletcher borrow much of the material for this sea masque with its presiding moon goddess, hostile, personified Night, and final compliment to the greater sun, from Jonson's celebrated masques of *Beauty* and *Blackness*. But the masque in *The Maid's Tragedy* has a specific dramatic function, and details from Jonson are subordinated to the needs of the whole. Though the resemblances adequately indicate an awareness of masque successes of the time, the aesthetic implications of the masque for the drama remain the primary concern of the authors. The affinity between masque and tragicomedy is peculiarly apparent in this tragedy.

Many critics have noted how little difference there is between this tragedy and Beaumont and Fletcher's tragicomedies. For example, Miss Ellis-Fermor writes: "The plays which conform to Fletcher's definition of tragicomedy . . . are not essentially different in respect of mood, characterization or style from those, like *The Maid's Tragedy* . . . which, by reason they do not 'want deaths,' are classed as tragedies" [Una Ellis-Fermor, *The Jacobean Drama*, 4th ed., 1964]. Ashley Thorndike created a list of archetypal Beaumont and Fletcher characters, and *The Maid's Tragedy* contains the faithful friend, the poltroon, the self-sacrificing maiden, the lily-livered hero, and the evil woman, all typical of their tragicomedy. The play, then, is a tragedy leaning toward the tragicomic not in its conclusion but in its conduct.

The relation of the masque to the rest of *The Maid's Tragedy* has been repeatedly noted. Reyher, who praised the masque as "une des chefs-d'oeuvre du genre," thought nevertheless that "il ne se rattache que de très loin à l'action" [Paul Reyher, *Les masques anglais*, 1909]. Opinion has gradually changed. Miss Bradbrook remarks that the "'sudden storm' rising on the marriage night, is not entirely irrelevant" and finds a "felt fusion" between the masque and the play [M. C. Bradbrook, *Themes and Conventions of Elizabethan Tragedy*, 1960]. Clifford Leech takes the escape of Boreas as a bad omen for the marriage being celebrated [*The John Fletcher Plays*, 1962]. Most recently Inga-Stina Ewbank has commented that the masque has "a peculiar, strongly ironical, bearing on the action of the play." She concentrates on the sharp contrast between the masque and the wedding night manqué which immediately follows. "In *The Maid's Tragedy*, then, the authors have seized on the assumptions of the traditional marriage masque—prenuptial chastity, bridal bliss and royal integrity—and contrasted them with a corrupt reality ["'These Pretty Devices': A Study of Masques in Plays," in *A Book of Masques in Honour of Allardyce Nicoll*, 1967]. This sort of analysis can be taken further; themes and figures of the opening masque reverberate throughout *The Maid's Tragedy*.

The masque opens as Night rises in mists, saying:

> Our raign is come; for in the raging Sea
> The Sun is drown'd, and with him fell the day.

The crucial actions of the play take place in Night's reign; all the movement of the plot is summarized in the change from Amintor's wedding night with Evadne to the night when Evadne murders the King her lover in his bed. Night defies and hates the sun and closes the masque by wishing to see "another wild-fire in his Axletree" (I, i). Cynthia then points out "a greater light, a greater Majestie" (I, i). This, like much of the commentary the masque provides, is ironic; the King-sun is full of the wild fire of lust.

The masque is curiously inappropriate to a wedding. The titular goddess is Cynthia, cold and moonlike. She too reminds us of what the night brings and will bring to the characters:

> Gaz'd on unto my setting from my rise
> Almost of none, but of unquiet eyes.
>
> [I, i]

Lovers, though expected to remain awake, are not usually called unquiet, and Evadne the next morning says ambiguously that she has had ill rest.

Neptune looses the winds, but unfortunately Boreas escapes and is not yet recaptured as the masque ends. Neptune is not afraid:

> Let him alone, I'le take him up at sea;
> He will not long be thence.
>
> [I, i]

Yet Eolus soon comes to tell him that Boreas has

> rais'd a storm; go and applie
> Thy trident, else I prophesie, ere day
> Many a tall ship will be cast away.
>
> [I, i]

This angry and unleashed force may prove more dangerous than its would-be controllers assume. Should we not see the application, it is stated for us in act IV as Melantius accosts his sister Evadne and describes the danger to anyone who would encourage her daring while he is alive:

> by my just Sword, h'ad safer
> Bestride a Billow when the angry North
> Plows up the Sea.
>
> [IV, i]

Melantius is the force unreckoned by the King, the cold north wind blowing on this wedding arrangement.

The three songs in the masque are ostensibly in accord with the marriage celebration, yet each represents an ironic comment on a major character. The first song tells the day not to steal night away:

> Till the rites of love are ended,
> And the lusty Bridegroom say,
> Welcome light of all befriended.
>
> [I, i]

Amintor's rites of love are nonexistent. The second song celebrates the blushes and coy denials of the bride in

Spenserian terms. The irony is patent. Finally, the third song urges:

> Bring in the Virgins every one
> That grieve to lie alone:
> That they may kiss while they may say, a maid.
>
> [I, i]

This anticipates the scene immediately following, in which Aspatia and Dula, the two virgins, express their reactions to the marriage. Dula, openly grieving to lie alone, is rebuked by the "maid," Evadne, and Aspatia expresses her grief by kissing not Evadne but Amintor, who consequently feels "her grief shoot suddenly through all my veins" (II, i).

The songs are ironic, while most of the masque action is anticipatory. The tone is decidedly threatening: in addition to the storm there is Night's curse, a "wild-fire in his Axletree; / And all false drencht" (I, i), only slightly alleviated by Cynthia's final compliment to the King. This compliment has been evaluated for us in the first dialogue, where Strato the poet says the masque will be "as well as Mask can be. . . . Yes, they must commend their King, and speak in praise of the Assembly, bless the Bride and Bridegroom, in person of some God; th'are tyed to rules of flattery" (I, i). Strato's comment makes us dubious, even cynical, before the masque begins.

The entire play is introduced against a ritual setting. The court wedding, patronized by the monarch, celebrated with a masque, was standard at the courts of Elizabeth and James. As the play continues, actions become less and less ritualistic, and presupposed normal conditions disappear. The King is the first to forego a ritual action:

> We will not see you laid, good night Amintor,
> We'l ease you of that tedious ceremony.
>
> [I, i]

Aspatia's willow song is a ritual of the abandoned lover, but when she promises to search for "some yet unpractis'd way to grieve and die" (II, i), she suggests a real passion. Most important, the central ritual, Amintor's wedding night, is destroyed. Even before he knows why, or quite believes that Evadne denies him, he says:

> Hymen keep
> This story (that will make succeeding youth
> Neglect thy Ceremonies) from all ears.
>
> [II, i]

The destruction of this ritual, he fears, will destroy all future order in the world. Thus, in addition to commenting specifically on the action, the masque by its very formality establishes a background contrast to the increasingly frenzied play.

By 1611, then, Beaumont and Fletcher's methods of working with a masque encompassed complex commentary on the play and continual reverberation. Partly because *The Maid's Tragedy* starts with a masque we are unable to tell from the tone whether it will prove a tragedy or a tragi-comedy. The gods seem to have things in control, just as Neptune, the king figure, expects to capture Boreas. All is formal and ritual; the press of evil need not lead the action to an inevitably tragic conclusion. We are deceived in terms of death and destruction, but not radically wrong in terms of mood. Moreover, the play opens at one remove, with the stage audience standing between us and the masque. Thus in content and in form the masque inhibits tragic involvement and is largely responsible for the classification of this play with *Philaster* and other tragicomedies. Whether Beaumont and Fletcher originally intended this effect, they understood how to use it profitably thereafter.

In *The Maid's Tragedy* a formal masque, more appropriate to the tone of tragicomedy, obscures ultimate tragedy. In *Philaster* the tragicomic outcome is enhanced by an enormously suggestive masquelike moment, suggestive because it shows the young dramatists' awareness of their own technique and implies that the Jacobean audience were expected to catch brief hints of masque out of their usual context.

The crucial point of the play occurs at the beginning of the fifth act. Though Arethusa the princess, Bellario the page, and Philaster the dispossessed heir are reconciled, the latter two are prisoners and can expect nothing but death. Arethusa has convinced the King to assign the captives to her, and there is some expectation of a turn in events, much obscured by a pathetic prison scene. Finally the King bids the prisoners brought forth:

> *Enter* Phil. Are. *and* Bell. *in a Robe and Garland.*
> *King.* How now, what Mask is this?
> *Bell.* Right Royal Sir, I should
> Sing you an Epithalamium of these lovers,
> But having lost my best ayres with my fortunes,
> And wanting a celestial Harp to strike
> This blessed union on; thus in glad story
> I give you all. These two fair Cedar-branches,
> The noblest of the Mountain, where they grew
> Straightest and tallest, under whose still shades
> The worthier beasts have made their layers, and slept
>
> . . . . .
>
> Till never pleas'd fortune shot up shrubs,
> Base under brambles to divorce these branches;
> And for a while they did so, and did raign
> Over the Mountain, and choakt up his beauty
> With Brakes, rude Thornes and Thistles, till thy Sun
> Scorcht them even to the roots, and dried them there:
> And now a gentle gale hath blown again
> That made these branches meet, and twine together,
> Never to be divided: The god that sings
> His holy numbers over marriage beds,
> Hath knit their noble hearts, and here they stand
> Your Children mighty King, and I have done.
> *King.* How, how?
> *Are.* Sir, if you love it in plain truth,

> For there is no Masking in't; This Gentleman
> The prisoner that you gave me is become
> My keeper, and through all the bitter throws
> Your jealousies and his ill fate have wrought him,
> Thus nobly hath he strangled [*sic*], and at length
> Arriv'd here my dear Husband.
> *King.* Your dear Husband! call in
> The Captain of the Cittadel; There you shall keep
> Your wedding. I'le provide a Mask shall make
> Your Hymen turn his Saffron into a sullen Coat,
> And sing sad Requiems to your departing souls:
> Bloud shall put out your Torches, and instead
> Of gaudy flowers about your wanton necks,
> An Ax shall hang like a prodigious Meteor
> Ready to crop your loves sweets.
>
> [V, i]

This little scene provides one of the most interesting examples of the technique of using aspects of a masque to shift a play from tragedy to tragicomedy. It is based on the assumption that the audience would be fully aware of masques, aware of their basic ingredients and of their appropriateness to weddings. Only with such a background can the counterpoint irony of the passage be appreciated. As soon as he sees the three young people, the King's question alerts us to these implications. Bellario may have been dressed as Hymen, as the passage suggests, but the evidence is insufficient. The first quarto does not mention the robe at all, merely the "Boy, with a garland of flowers on's head." However, his speech is the "presenter's" speech with which most brief masques begin, and the allegorical nature of it, abstracting the general situation from Arethusa's and Philaster's predicaments, emphasizes the division between this section and the straightforward dramatic action of the rest of the play. Though the two protagonists are not treated as gods, they become allegorical figures, representatives of their positions in life and society, as members of the English royal family became symbols of themselves when they took part in masques (e.g., Prince Henry's role in Jonson's *Masque of Oberon*). Of course the comparison of the King to the sun was a standard masque formula.

Though Arethusa, afraid of further irritating her father by this extensive make-believe, reasserts the reality with "there is no Masking in't," it is the King who concludes the scene with the reelaboration of each masque element. He attempts to deny the presence of a masque and, by implication, the possibility of a tragicomic conclusion to the lovers' trials. He enumerates each element: the conventional nuptial occasion for the masque, with Hymen as chief actor, the epithalamium which he desires to transform into a requiem, the ever-present torches, the flowers. The last lines, "An Ax shall hang like a prodigious Meteor / Ready to crop your loves sweets," replace the references in wedding masques to the love rites to follow. *Hymenaei* (1606), which contains all of these elements, ends with an epithalamium which contains references to the "fayre and gentle strife / Which *louers* call their *life*." The entire scene is viewed in perspective, with a backdrop of the conventional giving poignant irony to the situation of the royal lovers.

In this early experimental play Beaumont and Fletcher establish the procedures which govern their exploitation of the masque in conjunction with tragicomedy. Masque elements occur at the play's moment of greatest tension. The three young people assert that they are indeed presenting a wedding masque; the King tries to deny it and to reimpose the tragic sequence of events. He is not successful. As he orders the masquers removed, messengers announce that Prince Pharamond has been captured by the citizens. The city mutinies, the court rallies to Philaster, and the King must first beg Philaster to quiet the rebels and then accept him as son and heir. The intervening scene of the citizens with Pharamond is comic, anticipating Fletcher's later use of comic characters as a contrast to solemn masquers. The masque thus becomes a watershed in the play; the action stops and turns upon itself. Style and tempo shift, and the audience lose the deep involvement of the pathetic fourth act. This shift ensures the triumph of tragicomedy.

The two early plays adumbrate most of the significant effects of masques on Beaumont and Fletcher's dramaturgy. Only the antimasque was not yet fully operative. In *The Mad Lover,* one of Fletcher's most successful later tragicomedies, masque and antimasque both enter completely into the play, until it is difficult to separate play and masque. The masque resembles Jonson's *Lovers Made Men,* which appeared a month later. This reversal of normal indebtedness suggests that Fletcher had become so adept at creating masque material for his plays that Jonson was not above borrowing from him.

The play concerns the warrior Memmon, who falls so in love with the princess Calis on first sight that he agrees to her teasing suggestion that he send her his heart as a proof of love. At once he begins to contemplate the other world, instructing his lieutenant Chilax to die and meet him in Elysium two days later. As he tries to convince himself that the joys of love are as great or greater after death, Memmon attacks the flesh and yearns for

> Pure Love,
> That, that the soul affects, and cannot purchase
> While she is loaden with our flesh.
>
> [II, i]

He is, however, increasingly mad and beastlike, resembling "a Dog / Run mad o'th' tooth-ache" (II, i). Stremon, one of his soldiers, arranges a show in the hope of curing Memmon. The idea is taken from his mad ravings:

> h'as divers times
> Been calling upon *Orpheus* to appear
> And shew the joyes: now I will be that *Orpheus,*
> And as I play and sing, like beasts and trees
> I wou'd have you shap't and enter.
>
> [III, i]

Act IV opens as Memmon begins to face the possibility that Calis may not love him in the other world either. Orpheus enters announcing that he has come not the joys but *"the plagues of love to show."* As Eumenes says,

"This Song / Was rarely form'd to fit him" (IV, i). Memmon is threatened with plagues in Hell if he dies with his love unreturned. When he doubts that his passage to Elysium could be denied after his sacrifice, Charon arrives to corroborate Orpheus, singing that *"'tis too foul a sin. He must not come aboard"* (IV, i). Orpheus then presents a "masque" of beasts, and explains that each one died of a foolish love: "This Ape with daily hugging of a glove, / Forgot to eat and died" (IV, i).

The beasts are basic antimasque figures. Here they represent Memmon's beastlike inner state. In fact, they represent the beast-like state of most of the lovers in the play. Syphax, who also falls in love with the princess, is scorned by his sister: "Fye beast" (II, i). Chilax's wanton love for Venus's priestess leads him into a scrape in which he finally appears disguised as a woman in the oracle's box. These transformations are epitomized in the antimasque.

The presentation by Stremon ends simply enough with the adjuration "O love no more, O love no more" (IV, i). In the fifth act a spectacle of true love occurs which is, effectively, the masque or formal show corresponding to the antimasque. The princess Calis, who has fallen in love with Memmon's brother, goes to the temple and sings a prayer to Venus. Meanwhile Chilax and the priestess, caught unprepared, decide to send Chilax to impersonate the oracle. After their hurried conversation Calis speaks, or perhaps even sings, her second supplication, *"O Divine Star of Heaven,"* which is in the same rhythm as her first. As Chilax begins "I have heard thy prayers," there is thunder and music, "the temple shakes and totters," and Venus descends (V, i). The unforeseen appearance of a real goddess had occurred previously in plays as well as in masques. But the presence of a masque earlier in the play, and the balance created between the disorder of beasts and the order of goddesses, makes the provenance more likely to be the masque. We find ourselves in an almost indefinable position vis-à-vis the reality of the play. Orpheus was Stremon, but this appears to be Venus; the unreal is as real as the real. This effect prepares us to see all difficulties removed, to have the tragicomic experience forced upon us. Laws of expectation are no longer operative. We rest in a state of pleasurable, formal anticipation, waiting to see how Calis, as Venus promised, will be pleased with the dead.

Like *Philaster, The Mad Lover* pivots on the masque moments, though now there are several of them. There is no dance or transformation scene in the literal masque sense, yet all the characters are transformed after Venus's appearance. The dead Polybius lives; the mad Memmon is once again the glorious warrior; the "princess" Chilax married is retransformed into Chloe his whore. The movement of the play thus approximates the movement of a masque with its transformation scene after the intervention of a god.

Act V, which substitutes for the masque, depends noticeably upon song and rhymed, clearly metered poetry. After Calis's song and prayer Venus speaks in the same tetrameter. Memmon meets Chilax disguised in the priestess's robes, takes him for a slain warrior, and demands a song of his death. Memmon's friends reply with a battle song intended to show him what he must once again become, in a retransformation.

The masque and masquelike elements of *The Mad Lover* repeat the action of the play and elaborate it. They are not necessary to the plot. Even Venus merely prophesies, does not act. Nevertheless, the masque does more than please the audience. The play moves between formal episodes which qualify its tone, clarify its themes, and point out its contrasts. The movement and structure are perfectly controlled, so that those who did not just enjoy watching the ape wave his tail could see in the beasts and in Venus simple but visually effective symbols of the main theme.

Thus, in all three of these plays by Beaumont and Fletcher, artistic logic united masque with tragicomedy. Eventually Fletcher's plays began to follow a formula, but he deserves credit for its creation. The influence of the court masque on Beaumont and Fletcher was deep. By its inherently tragicomic nature and its abrupt romanticizing of a situation threatening to become simply tragic or comic, the masque proved a major asset in the search for the difficult balance which creates tragicomedy. This tragicomedy, in turn, became more and more masquelike. Once the relationship is seen as aesthetically sound and not merely fortuitous, we can better understand why Beaumont and Fletcher, now often slighted, were so highly esteemed in their own time.

Arthur Kirsch (essay date 1972)

SOURCE: "Beaumont and Fletcher," in *Jacobean Dramatic Perspectives,* The University Press of Virginia, 1972, pp. 38-51.

[*In the essay that follows, Kirsch examines the artificiality of the characters and situations in Beaumont and Fletcher's work.*]

Indebted to both [Giovanni Battista] Guarini and [Ben] Jonson, the theatrical style which Beaumont and Fletcher and their collaborators created at once encompasses and dilutes the polarities of romance and satire. Fletcher's actual definition of tragicomedy reads very much like Guarini's, from which it was clearly borrowed. "A tragie-comedie," he wrote in the preface to *The Faithful Shepherdess* (1608), "is not so called in respect of mirth and killing, but in respect it wants deaths, which is inough to make it no tragedie, yet brings some neere it, which is inough to make it no comedie: which must be a representation of familiar people, with such kinde of trouble as no life be questioned; so that a God is as lawful in this as in a tragedie, and meane people as in a comedy." As in the case of Guarini, among the natural consequences of such a conception of a play is a self-conscious emphasis upon plot and style, and like Guarini, Beaumont and Fletcher have an exceptional interest in declamatory rhetoric—in their case directly derived from Senecan declamations—and in copious and intricate plots organized less on causal

than on spatial principles. Where their practice diverges significantly from Guarini's is in their lack of interest in an overall providential pattern. [Guarini's] *The Pastor Fido* . . . is designed to culminate in a recognition scene which verifies the comic dispensation of the art both of the Creator and the dramatist; *The Faithful Shepherdess,* as all of Beaumont and Fletcher's subsequent plays, though nominally devoted to providential precepts, in fact makes little use of them to organize the action.

Beaumont and Fletcher's debt to satirical comedy leads in a similar direction. As Eugene Waith has shown [in *The Pattern of Tragicomedy in Beaumont and Fletcher,* 1952], many of the most notable characteristics of Fletcherian tragicomedy have roots in Jonson's and [John] Marston's practice: the atmosphere of evil, Protean characterizations, extreme and schematic oppositions of emotions as well as characters, moral dilemmas that are acute but disengaging, and kaleidoscopic plots. In Jonson and Marston, however, these features are at least intended to serve the purposes of satire. In Beaumont and Fletcher, though a detritus of satire remains, there is no comparable sense of purpose, and the same characteristics receive an abstracted and more formal emphasis. As with the debt to Guarini, the net result is frequently less meaning and more art, plays with effects of unusual virtuosity but also unusual self-consciousness.

This stress upon artifice for its own sake is confirmed by the testimony of Beaumont and Fletcher's contemporaries. James Shirley, who was perhaps their best critic as well as a devoted disciple, wrote in the preface to the 1647 collection of their works [*Comedies and Tragedies Written by Francis Beaumont and John Fletcher Gentlemen*]:

> You may here find passions raised to that excellent pitch and by such insinuating degrees that you shall not chuse but consent, & go along with them, finding your self at last grown insensibly the very same person you read, and then stand admiring the subtile Trackes of your engagement. Fall on a Scene of love and you will never believe the writers could have the least roome left in their soules for another passion, peruse a Scene of manly Rage, and you would sweare they cannot be exprest by the same hands, but both are so excellently wrought, you must confesse none, but the same hands, could worke them.

> Would thy Melancholy have a cure? thou shalt laugh at *Democritus* himselfe, and but reading one piece of this *Comick* variety, finde thy exalted fancie in Elizium; And when thou art sick of this cure, (for excesse of delight may too much dilate thy *soule*) thou shalt meete almost in every leafe a soft purling passion or *spring* of sorrow so powerfully wrought high by the teares of innocence, and *wronged Lovers,* it shall perswade thy eyes to weepe into the streame, and yet smile when they contribute to their owne ruines.

Here is theatrical plenty, and Shirley's description reveals not only the variety of passions which Beaumont and Fletcher were able to exploit, but also the unusual sophistication of their effects. The insistence in this description upon the recognition of artifice goes beyond the traditional capacity of Elizabethan drama to be simultaneously realistic and symbolic, to make us aware of the analogies between the stage and the world, and to involve us in the action and at the same time to keep us detached enough to make judgments about it. Shirley places decisive stress upon detachment, upon the constant recognition of the play as a play, as the work of an artist. It is a matter of emphasis, but a crucial one. To Shirley, as to virtually all of their contemporaries, the excellence of Beaumont and Fletcher rested not simply in their ability to capture an audience, but in their capacity to do so with an elegance that was self-revealing.

Perhaps the most transparent example of this artfulness occurs in *Philaster,* in the scene which gave the play its subtitle, "Love lies a Bleeding." Philaster has come upon Arathusa in the woods. She is attended by Bellario, his own page. Unaware that Bellario is Euphrasia in disguise (and in love with him), Philaster misinterprets the meeting and launches a passionate diatribe against faithlessness:

> Let me love lightning, let me be embrac't
> And kist by Scorpions, or adore the eyes
> Of Basalisks, rather then trust the tongues
> Of hell-bred women. Some good god looke downe
> And shrinke these veines up; sticke me here a stone
> Lasting to ages, in the memory
> Of this damned act.
>
> (IV.v.27-33)

At a word from Arathusa, however, he quickly reverses his mood:

> I have done;
> Forgive my passion: Not the calmed sea,
> When *Eolus* locks up his windy brood,
> Is lesse disturb'd then I; I'le make you know't.
>
> (IV.v.41-44)

In a replay of a scene in *The Faithful Shepherdess,* he then offers his sword to Arathusa and Bellario to kill him. Both of course refuse and Philaster, in a counterturn, prepares to use the sword to "performe a peece of Justice" upon Arathusa. At that moment, however, a "countrey fellow" enters and the situation becomes quite remarkable:

Countrey Fellow. There's a Courtier with his sword drawne, by this hand upon a woman, I thinke.

Philaster. Are you at peace?

Arathusa. With heaven and earth.

Philaster. May they divide thy soule and body.
[Philaster *wounds her.*]

Countrey Fellow. Hold dastard, strike a woman! th'art a craven: I warrant thee, thou wouldst be loth to play halfe a dozen venies at wasters with a good fellow for a broken head.

Philaster. Leave us good friend.

Arathusa. What ill-bred man art thou, to intrude thy selfe

Upon our private sports, our recreations.

Countrey Fellow. God uds me, I understand you not; but I know the rogue has hurt you.

Philaster. Persue thy owne affaires; it will be ill To multiply blood upon my head, which thou Wilt force me to.

Countrey Fellow. I know not your rethoricke, but I can lay it on if you touch the woman.

[*They fight.*]

Philaster is wounded and, hearing the court party approaching, runs off. The country fellow demands a kiss from Arathusa, and only after he learns that she is a princess does he lose his fine uncouth country poise. His last words are: "If I get cleare of this, I'le goe to see no more gay sights" (IV.v.80-97, 142-43).

The scene was evidently very popular—it is not only referred to in the subtitle of the play but pictured in a woodcut on the title page of the first edition (1620)—and it constitutes a paradigm of Fletcherian dramaturgy. It is entirely contrived to allow for striking if not sensational contrasts of emotion. The whole situation is false and improbable, and since we know it is, we consciously follow the ebb and flow of Philaster's passion, responding to his diatribes and laments as declamatory exercises. The intervention of the country fellow italicizes the wholly self-regarding theatricality of the scene even further. In the peculiar dialectic of Fletcherian dramaturgy the country fellow would seem to represent a popular ideal of honor which Philaster at that point lacks, but at the same time his emphatic outlandishness serves to qualify any serious apprehensions we might develop about Philaster and Arathusa and thus to preserve the mood of tragicomedy. His honorable uncouthness is finally an urbane joke, a conceit which paradoxically insulates the boundaries of Beaumont and Fletcher's world of gay sights and protects its private sports and recreations. His appearance not only assures us that any wound Arathusa receives has been made with a pasteboard sword, but absolutely compels us to become conscious of the preciousness of the entire scene.

The scene is an extreme instance, but it is nonetheless typical of the play as well as of much of Beaumont and Fletcher's subsequent work. Their later tragicomedies and tragedies are more carefully modulated, more versatile, more elegant, but not fundamentally different in kind. They rarely employ so stark a device to define and emphasize their theatrical conceits: the juxtapositions of characters and scenes, or of contrasting emotions within a character, are more integrated with one another and more graceful; but their essential purposes and effects remain the same as *Philaster*'s. *The Maid's Tragedy,* the play which is usually acknowledged as their masterpiece and which certainly exhibits their resources to great effect, is a case in point, and an especially important one, I think, both because a few critics have been inclined to see a different kind of accomplishment in it and because an understanding of the effect of Beaumont and Fletcher's characteristic tragicomic patterning upon an ostensive tragedy is very suggestive in interpreting plays of other seventeenth-century dramatists.

Three scenes in *The Maid's Tragedy* were especially celebrated by contemporary audiences and may stand as typical examples of its dramaturgy: Amintor's and Evadne's wedding night (II.i), Aspatia mourning with her maids (II.ii), and the quarrel between Amintor and Melantius (III.ii). The first scene, the wedding night, is a typical Fletcherian dramatic conceit—an outrageous and multiple inversion of conventional expectations. The scene is set in bed-chamber and begins, traditionally enough, with a maid making bawdy comments which apparently embarrass Evad-ne. A pathetic melody is counterpointed to the bawdy by the presence of Aspatia, the maid whom Amintor was supposed to marry until the King ordered him to marry Evadne. Amintor meets Aspatia outside the chamber and asks Evadne to come to bed: "Come, come, my love, / And let us loose our selves to one another" (II.i.149-50). But she protests, and after a protracted discussion Amintor assures her that she could preserve her maidenhead one more night by other means if she wished. She answers, "A maidenhead *Amintor* at my yeares" (ll. 198-99). The scene continues with a number of similarly sensational turns. Evadne swears that she will never sleep with him, not because she is coy but because she does already "enjoy the best" of men, with whom she has "sworne to stand or die" (ll. 301-02). Amintor furiously demands to know who the man is so that he may "cut his body into motes" (l. 304). Evadne obligingly informs him that "'tis the King" (l. 309), and that the King had ordered their marriage to mask his own affair with her. Amintor responds to his cuckoldom by turning royalist:

> Oh thou has nam'd a word that wipes away
> All thoughts revengefull, in that sacred word,
> The King, there lies a terror, what fraile man
> Dares lift his hand against it, let the Gods
> Speake to him when they please: till when let us
> Suffer, and waite.

>   (ll. 313-18)

In a final turn, Amintor begs Evadne that for the benefit of his honor they may pretend before the court to have fulfilled the rites of a wedding night. She agrees and he coaches her on how she should behave in front of morning visitors:

> And prethee smile upon me when they come,
> And seeme to toy as if thou hadst been pleas'd
> With what I did. . . .
> Come let us practise, and as wantonly
> As ever longing bride and bridegroome met,
> Lets laugh and enter here.

>   (ll. 360-62, 63-65)

The scene, as John F. Danby has shown [in *Poets on Fortune's Hill,* 1952] is like a dramatized metaphysical conceit, a rich exploration of progressively inverted Petrarchan images culminating in a demand that the lover either literally kill himself for his mistress or serve her as

a pandar and a cuckold (which he does). In dramatizing this conceit, however, the scene exhibits many of the usual trademarks of Fletcherian tragicomedy: the constant peripeties, the discontinuous characterization (Evadne appears alternately as virgin and whore), the systematic betrayal of conventional expectations; and despite the apparent burden of "metaphysical meaning," the emphasis is still upon display and expertise. The scene's outrageousness, like that of the country fellow's in *Philaster,* points finally to itself, at once insulating the action from belief as well as ridicule and italicizing its artifice. It is entirely appropriate that the final turn should show us two actors preparing themselves to "act" the "scene" which we had expected them to act in the first place.

Immediately following this episode, and in counterpoint to it, is the scene showing Aspatia in mourning with her maids. It has no witty turns and its pace is deliberately measured, designed to depict a static tableau of Aspatia's grief. Typically, we are conscious of the scene as a tableau since one of Aspatia's maids is embroidering a picture of the wronged Ariadne on the island of Naxos, and Aspatia, applying the scene to herself, tells the maid how a grief-stricken woman should really appear:

> Fie, you have mist it there *Antiphila,*
> You are much mistaken wench:
> These colours are not dull and pale enough,
> To show a soule so full of miserie
> As this poore Ladies was, doe it by me,
> Doe it againe, by me the lost *Aspatia,*
> And you will find all true but the wilde Iland,
> Suppose I stand upon the Sea breach now
> Mine armes thus, and mine haire blowne with the wind,
> Wilde as the place she was in, let all about me
> Be teares of my story, doe my face
> If thou hadst ever feeling of a sorrow,
> Thus, thus, *Antiphila* make me looke good girle
> Like sorrowes mount, and the trees about me,
> Let them be dry and leaveless, let the rocks
> Groane with continuall surges, and behind me,
> Make all a desolation, see, see wenches,
> A miserable life of this poore picture.

>   (II.ii.61-78)

Charles Lamb remarked in *Specimens of English Dramatic Poets* [1808] that, in contrast to Shakespeare, the finest scenes in Fletcher are "slow and languid. [Their] motion is circular, not progressive. Each line resolves on itself in a sort of separate orbit. They do not join into one another like a running hand. Every step that we go we are stopped to admire some single object, like walking in beautiful scenery with a guide." This description captures perfectly the statuesque and self-regarding quality of the scene with Aspatia. The setting of that scene is the island of grief which Aspatia at once describes and represents. She is the guide to the scenery as well as its emblem, and because she is both, the pathos she elicits calls for a sophisticated response: we are meant to feel her grief, but even more to admire it as a virtuoso example of passionate theater portraiture. There are comparable portraits everywhere in Fletcher's plays, though those which occur in scenes marked by witty turns of speech and action are more changeable and less sustained. The distinction of Aspatia's scene is its static emphasis, an emphasis that became increasingly important in the plays of [John] Webster and [John] Ford.

The third of the scenes in *The Maid's Tragedy* that were especially admired in the seventeenth century is the one dealing with the quarrel between Amintor and Melantius (III.ii). The scene is particularly important because it reveals so transparently the dynamics of the Fletcherian patterning of action. It is composed entirely of the kinds of turns and counterturns of love, honor, friendship, &c. which were to become the staples of Caroline and Restoration drama. The scene begins with Melantius questioning Amintor about the strangeness of his behavior. Amintor refuses to explain until Melantius threatens to dissolve their friendship, at which point Amintor confesses that Evadne, who is Melantius' sister,

> Is much to blame,
> And to the King has given her honour up,
> And lives in whoredome with him.
>
>   (III.ii.128-30)

Melantius responds by drawing his sword:

>   shall the name of friend
> Blot all our family, and stick the brand
> Of whore upon my sister unreveng'd.
>
>   (ll. 139-41)

Amintor, however, welcomes death as a relief from his sorrows and in any case refuses to draw upon his friend, but after Melantius calls him a coward, he does draw his sword. Melantius immediately reflects that "The name of friend, is more then familie, / Or all the world besides" (ll. 172-73), and sheaths his sword. When Amintor does likewise, they are reconciled; but Melantius threatens to kill the King, and Amintor then draws his sword, both because he is opposed to regicide and because he does not wish his cuckoldom to become known. Melantius draws his sword, and after further discussion, they both sheath their weapons and their dance finally ends.

[Thomas] Rymer's comment upon this scene in *The Tragedies of the Last Age* was that "When a Sword is once drawn in Tragedy, the Scabbard may be thrown away." The remark is myopic but revealing, for Beaumont and Fletcher are clearly not interested in tragic decorum. In the quarrel between Brutus and Cassius [in Shakespeare's *Julius Caesar*] which was probably the model for their scene the turns of action and sentiment grow out of the characters of the two men, their evolving relationship with one another, and their particular situation. Amintor and Melantius are not comparably defined, nor is their quarrel. What characters they have are largely postulates for the turns and counterturns in which they are engaged, for theirs is a choreographic abstraction of the Shakespearian scene, a *pas de deux* in which movements of swords and declamations upon friendship have equal meaning. The substance of their quarrel *is* its design.

John F. Danby has been in such designs and in the kind of scenes that elicit them "not only literary entertainment, but literature aware of itself as a symptom rather than a reflection of the dangerous reality surrounding it—aware of a world that cannot be trusted, and in which the mind is forced back upon itself to make a world of its own, by belief, or resolve, or art." Danby argues that for Beaumont and Fletcher this reality is composed of absolutes—among them, Honor, Kingship and Petrarchan Love—"which have to be chosen among and which it is nonsence to choose among." He contends further that Beaumont and Fletcher are interested not in assessing any of these absolutes separately but in opposing them, for their "best work" and "main interest" lie "in the conflict of the absolutes and the contortions it imposes upon human nature." On the basis of these assumptions he concludes that *The Maid's Tragedy,* in particular, is a searching expression of the disorientation of values in Jacobean society, conveyed through exceptionally subtle characterizations. Evadne, for example, "a study in radical perversity . . . is more compelling than Lady Macbeth, and more subtle"; Melantius, though the soul of honour, is essentially a representative of "the simplifying madness of war"; and Aspatia "represents that large and immovable continent of the traditional morality from which the 'wild island' of Beaumont's dramatic world detaches itself."

There is a great deal in these arguments which deserves attention. Danby's consideration of the relationship of Beaumont and Fletcher to their social milieu certainly helps explain their extraordinary popularity and his particular analyses of Fletcherian wit are often acute. For a number of reasons, however, it is difficult to accept his general assessment of Beaumont and Fletcher's intrinsic achievement. In the first place, it is a fallacy common in criticism of the plays which he discusses to see a theatrical style which is self-conscious and which can be entirely self-regarding as necessarily a reflection of Jacobean *angst*. Danby may well be correct in his assumptions about the sociological sources of Fletcherian drama, but the critical issue is whether these sources are meaningful parts of the plays themselves. James's court and the general decay of Elizabethan standards may have encouraged the enshrinement of absolutes "which have to be chosen among and which it is nonsense to choose among," but in the actual scenes in *The Maid's Tragedy* and *Philaster* in which protagonists make such choices, the real emphasis is upon the contrivance with which the choices are posed and disposed rather than upon what they represent. It is difficult, and we are not intended, to take either the absolutes or the protagonists very seriously. The choices are indeed empty of meaning, and not because they are the expression of an empty or disoriented society, but because the alternatives they pose are essentially rhetorical counters in a theatrical display. The quarrel scene between Amintor and Melantius asserts absolutely nothing about Kingship or Honor, either negatively or positively. Inherited ideas of kingship or honor are adverted to solely to provide opportunities for debate and turns of action. In this respect the old judgment, held by both Coleridge and Eliot, that Beaumont and Fletcher's plays are parasitic and without inner meaning, seems just.

Nor do Beaumont and Fletcher, either in *The Maid's Tragedy* or *Philaster,* really explore the stress which the conflicts they contrive place upon human nature, as Danby also claims, for psychologically considered, the characters in these plays simply do not have sufficient substance to explore. They are all primarily elements in a spatial design and they follow completely from the design, not the design from them. They are accordingly portrayed with radical discontinuities, capable of Protean change, like Evadne, or with consistent but stereotyped humours, like Melantius (honor) or Aspatia (grief), which are equally in the service of a peripetetic action. The true contortions of Beaumont and Fletcher's situations in these plays are thus rhetorical and theatrical, and their ultimate stress is less upon the nature of the participants than upon the artifice which employs them.

A case can and should be made for the possibilities of such artifice, but on different ground and with different plays, for it is in their comedies, it seems to me, rather than in works like *The Maid's Tragedy,* that Beaumont and Fletcher's real achievement lies. Plays like *The Scornful Lady, The Humourous Lieutenant,* and *The Wild Goose Chase,* apparently more trivial than the tragicomedies and tragedies, are at the same time less guilty of trifling with ideas and need neither excuses nor footnotes about baroque mentality to explain them. They explain and justify themselves, and the reason is that as with the Restoration comedies of manners of which they are precursors, as indeed with all good plays, their artifice and their subjects give substance to each other.

The Scornful Lady was written by Beaumont and Fletcher in collaboration and shows Beaumont's influence in its satiric emphasis and in its strong humours characterizations. *The Humourous Lieutenant,* written by Fletcher alone, mixes comedy with threats of tragedy, while *The Wild Goose Chase,* also an unaided Fletcherian work, is more strictly a comedy of intrigue. At the heart of all three plays, however, is a sexual combat in which one lover wittily and persistently foils the attempts of another to make him or her submit to love and marriage. In *The Scornful Lady* the Lady of the title resists Elder Loveless's efforts to make her acknowledge her love, and the bulk of the play consists of their intrigues against one another. In *The Humourous Lieutenant* Celia toys contrarily with the true passion of her lover and frustrates the villainous passion of his father. In *The Wild Goose Chase* three witty couples spawn intrigues and counter-intrigues: in two of them it is the women who have the "brave spirit" of contention, in the third it is Mirabel, the man. The theme of wit combat is not in itself new—Shakespeare, among others, had represented it with obvious mastery in *Much Ado About Nothing*—but Beaumont and Fletcher make it peculiarly their own because the peripeties of action and feeling, the declamations, the intricate intrigues, the discontinuous, Protean characterizations, in short, the characteristics which are bred by their tragicomic style, are also and precisely the characteristics which express the comic manners of a witty couple. .

The Scornful Lady depicts these manners with perhaps the greatest insight. The Lady—she has no other name—is represented as a woman whose humour does not permit her to submit to a man, even one she loves. In a series of encounters she alternately spurns and appears to favor her lovers while they correspondingly praise or vilify her. The most remarkable of these scenes is the one which eventually leads her to relent. Elder Loveless, who has already been duped and rejected by her, comes to her house to mock her and boast of his escape from bondage:

> Neither doe I thinke there can bee such a fellow found i' th' world, to be in love with such a froward woman: if there bee such, th'are madde, *Jove* comfort um. Now you have all, and I as new a man, as light, & spirited, that I feel my selfe clean through another creature. O 'tis brave to be ones owne man. I can see you now as I would see a Picture, sit all day by you, and never kiss your hand, heare you sing, and never fall backward; but with as set a temper as I would heare a Fidler, rise and thanke you.

> (IV.i.224-34)

At first unmoved by such diatribes, the Lady after a while appears to be deeply affected. She asks to speak "a little private" with him and accuses him of perjuring himself; he laughs at her "set speech," her "fine *Exordium*"; she kisses his hand and swoons into the arms of her sister, who has just entered the room. Predictably, Elder Loveless then reverses course completely, railing upon himself as passionately as he had upon her and vowing that it was only a trick, that he always has loved her:

> for sooner shall you know a generall ruine, then my faith broken. Doe not doubt this Mistres: for by my life I cannot live without you. Come, come, you shall not greeve, rather be angry, and heape infliction on me: I wil suffer.

> (ll. 275-79)

Suffer indeed he does as the Lady, her sister, and her maid proceed to break into laughter and the Lady tells him he has been finely fooled. He then rails upon her in earnest:

> I know you will recant and sue to me, but save that labour: I'le rather love a Fever and continual thirst, rather contract my youthe to drinke, and safe dote upon quarrells, or take a drawne whore from an Hospital, that time, diseases, and *Mercury* had eaten, then to be drawne to love you.

> (ll. 366-73)

He flees and at precisely that moment, the Lady asks her servant Abigail to recall him: "I would be loth to anger him too much: what fine foolery is this in a woman, to use men most frowardly they love most?" Abigail agrees, remarking, "this is still your way, to love being absent, and when hee's with you, laugh at him and abuse him. There is another way if you could hit on't" (ll. 383-85, 392-94).

The scene is a perfect counterpart of the debate between Amintor and Melantius or the wedding night of Amintor

Fletcher's definition of tragicomedy:

TO THE READER

If you be not reasonably assured of your knowledge in this kind of poem, lay down the book, or read this, which I would wish had been the prologue. It is a pastoral tragicomedy, which the people seeing when it was played, having ever had a singular gift in defining, concluded to be a play of country hired shepherds in gray cloaks, with curtailed dogs in strings, sometimes laughing together, and sometimes killing one another; and, missing Whitsun-ales, cream, wassail, and morris-dances, began to be angry. In their error I would not have you fall, lest you incur their censure. Understand, therefore, a pastoral to be a representation of shepherds and shepherdesses with their actions and passions, which must be such as may agree with their natures, at least not exceeding former fictions and vulgar traditions; they are not to be adorned with any art, but such improper ones as nature is said to bestow, as singing and poetry; or such as experience may teach them, as the virtues of herbs and fountains, the ordinary course of the sun, moon, and stars, and such like. But you are ever to remember shepherds to be such as all the ancient poets, and modern, of understanding, have received them; that is, the owners of flocks, and not hirelings. A tragi-comedy is not so called in respect of mirth and killing, but in respect it wants deaths, which is enough to make it no tragedy, yet brings some near it, which is enough to make it no comedy, which must be a representation of familiar people, with such kind of trouble as no life be questioned; so that a god is as lawful in this as in a tragedy, and mean people as in a comedy. Thus much I hope will serve to justify my poem, and make you understand it; to teach you more for nothing, I do not know that I am in conscience bound.

JOHN FLETCHER.

John Fletcher, an address to the reader prefacing
The Faithful Shepherdess, *c. 1609.*

tication of our response to them enables us to appreciate both the artifice (theirs and the dramatists') of the ballet which they dance and the meaning behind it.

The Humourous Lieutenant, a full-blown tragicomedy, is less consistent and less penetrating than *The Scornful Lady,* but the portrait of its heroine Celia has some of the same virtues. Unlike the Lady, Celia is in part a romantic figure, very much in love with Demetrius and usually very willing to say so. But she also, like the Lady and indeed like most of Fletcher's women, has a brave streak in her, and it is this part of her character that is most prominent in the play. When Demetrius's father, King Antigonus, pursues her with lecherous designs while Demetrius is away fighting, alternately tempting and threatening her, she resists with a high spirit, declaiming satirically and at length on the corruption of courtiers and kings. Persuaded as much by her energy as her chastity, Antigonus eventually becomes her convert, praising the virtue which he had before suspected. At this point Demetrius comes home, and unaware of the full situation, suspects her himself. She then turns upon him: "he's jealous; / I must now play the knave with him, [though I] dye for't, / 'Tis in me nature" (IV.viii.54-56). A quarrel ensues in which she castigates him for his lack of faith and he contritely asks her forgiveness. Antigonus himself is obliged to command that she forgive him.

Celia swings between extremes of romance and satire which appear incompatible, but her character, if not profound, is nevertheless of a piece. Her diatribes are the other side of the coin of her love, for she is motivated by love as much in the satiric condemnations of Antigonus's lust as in the criticism of Demetrius's faithlessness. The extremes through which she travels are thus plausible and though they are also exaggerated they still denote a coherence of feeling. She is indeed still capricious, but the caprice is clearly hers, not simply the dramatist's.

The Wild Goose Chase is less concerned with the psychology of its characters than either *The Scornful Lady* or *The Humourous Lieutenant*. Its emphasis is upon the spirit which they display and the contrasts they create rather than upon their motivations. Oriana pursues the witty and reluctant Mirabel, Pinac and Belleur chase the equally witty and reluctant sisters, Lillia-Bianca and Rosalura. Each group is in counterpoint to the others and within each the lovers continuously adopt opposing postures, some conscious, some not. Their *pas de deux* are symmetrically balanced and end only after the exhaustion of every contrast of every movement. Once again, however, stylization has a relation to content. Mirabel, Lillia-Bianca, and Rosalura (as well as Celia and the scornful Lady) look forward to the heroes and heroines of Restoration comedy. Like their descendants, they habitually don masks which reflect not only their pleasure in acting roles, but their need to do so in order to respond to the requirements of their personal relationships. Their wit, thus, expresses their sexual identity as well as their social grace, and the consciously elegant patterns which their courtships form at least begin to represent the nature of their society as well as the art of the dramatist.

and Evadne. Like them it consists of extreme turns and counterturns, of characters whose emotions oscillate violently, of declamations which are at once passionate and contrived. Like them also, it calls repeated attention to the artifice of its own construction. The difference is that whereas in *The Maid's Tragedy* the extreme discontinuities of character and the turns of passionate debate which are their consequence can be accepted only as theatrical conventions, in *The Scornful Lady* they represent credible human behavior. Elder Loveless's contortions are the reflection of a young man in love, while the artifices of the Lady are the expression of a woman who finds herself incapable of accepting not only the love of a man but the reality of her own feelings. Interacting with one another, the two form a pattern representing the dynamics of a recognizable human relationship. Their perversities, their posturings, conscious and otherwise, spring from something resembling psychological integrity. Thus the sophis-

It is no doubt curious that the pattern of tragicomedy which Beaumont and Fletcher crystallized should have produced less merit in the tragedies and tragicomedies themselves than in the comedies, but it is nonetheless true. Without either the vision of fortunate suffering which informs Shakespeare's dispassion or the moral clarity which informs [Thomas] Middleton's, the detachment and self-consciousness which Beaumont and Fletcher's style breeds turn in upon themselves when applied to a serious subject; and this was to be a most damaging legacy in seventeenth-century drama, affecting playwrights like Webster, Ford, and [John] Dryden, as well as comparative hacks like [Philip] Massinger and Shirley. In their tragicomedies and tragedies Beaumont and Fletcher's men in action are essentially formal devices, theatrical fragments, and no amount of special pleading can mend them or give them human dimension. It is only in some of their comic writing that Beaumont and Fletcher can truly be said to have held a mirror up to nature, and it is no accident that it was in this genre that they left their most enduring legacy to the repertory of the English stage. [William] Congreve was born of many parents, but not least among them were Beaumont and Fletcher, who were the first, as Dryden saw, to represent "the conversation of gentlemen."

Robert Y. Turner   (essay date 1984)

SOURCE: "Heroic Passion in the Early Tragicomedies of Beaumont and Fletcher," in *Medieval & Renaissance Drama in England,* Vol. I, 1984, pp. 109-30.

[*In the following essay, Turner examines* The Faithful Shepherdess, Philaster, *and* A King and No King *in light of tragicomic depictions of heroism and "extravagant passion."*]

In *The Faithful Shepherdess* (*ca*. 1608), *Philaster* (*ca*. 1609), and *A King and No King* (*ca*. 1611), Beaumont and Fletcher create their distinctive tragicomic effects by holding up for admiration characters who act with passionate disregard for the dictates of reason. Their intense passions impart an outsized—one could say heroic—dimension to them, but a heroism that lies more in desires than in deeds. This is not to say that these characters are unwilling to act; they are all too willing to lay their lives on the line for what they believe to be matters of life or death. So frequently do they proclaim their willingness that twentieth-century readers have been inclined to discount their heroic intensity and overlook a feature central to Beaumont and Fletcher's notion of tragicomedy. As a result, critics concentrate upon "high design," "pattern," surprising endings, and liken the plays to "roller-coaster rides." For most of us, extreme perturbations, such as the wrath of Achilles or the jealousy of Othello, fit the dimensions of epic or tragedy but appear less worthy of serious consideration when they dissipate in the tides of good fortune characteristic of tragicomedy. Even so, a willingness to die for love or honor meets the requirements of

tragicomedy, which, as Fletcher wrote [in his preface to *The Faithful Shepherdess,* 1608], "wants deaths, which is inough to make it no tragedie, yet brings some neere it, which is inough to make it no comedie." Beaumont and Fletcher were not unaware of the slight ridiculousness of a character's gesture at tragic grandeur during the course of events moving inexorably toward happiness. Indeed, the serio-comic is the very chord to be sounded in tragicomedy. Yet the playwrights' interest, as I see it, lay more in the exploration and judgment of ethical conduct than in an adjustment of tones for the sake of some imposed design. Before Fletcherian tragicomedy hardened into formula, the plays raised questions about assumed values and showed difficulties in assessing behavior by even the most accepted standards.

Beaumont and Fletcher's most provocative case for extravagant passion is *A King and No King*. If Arbaces's reason and will were strong enough to temper his desire for Panthea, his putative sister, then he would either remain the illegitimate king or be replaced. If his passion were to challenge all moral, legal, and religious prohibitions against incest, then he would discover his real father and become a real king through marriage to the princess and true heir to the throne. This bizarre testing of kingship reverses traditional wisdom about a ruler's exercise of self-control. From Erasmus's *The Education of a Christian Prince* to James I's *Basilicon Doron* in the sixteenth century, one finds the dictum that a king must rule himself before he can rule others properly. At the end of Lyly's *Campaspe,* Alexander masters his desire for Campaspe and gives her to Apelles: "It were a shame *Alexander* should desire to commaund the world, if he could not commaund himselfe" (V.iv.150-51). Implicit in Prince Hal's rejection of Falstaff is the exercise of self-control necessary to a successful ruler. Throughout most of *A King and No King* this standard seems to be appropriate, for Beaumont and Fletcher withhold the facts of Gobrius's plan and Arbaces's parentage. Not only Mardonius, the trustworthy captain and adviser, but Arbaces himself and his sister recoil from the prospects of incest. Until the final disclosures, the paradox of the title seems to refer to Arbaces's failure as a real king, since he cannot control his passions, as the temperate Tigranes manages to do. Arbaces, in his penultimate speech of the play, praises Tigranes for being temperate, no doubt a speech to reassure the audience that the drama hardly champions irresponsible submission to one's feelings. And by affirming the customary rule of temperance, the play strengthens its case for Arbaces's conduct as exceptional. The very strangeness of his circumstances, the odd way in which he becomes heir, then to be superseded by Panthea, insists upon its characteristic as being exceptional. Primarily, however, the dramatists arrange events to show that even the most unquestioned standards need not apply absolutely. In view of the details, the play resists the charge that it encourages the audience to take Arbaces's behavior as a license for indulgence. Instead, it cautions against the assumption that human beings behave in similar ways in similar circumstances or can be readily judged by the same standards.

I

Arbaces, in effect, proves himself worthy to be a real king by feeling a love so strong that he challenges all prohibitions, even to the extent of risking eternal damnation. Entangled as Arbaces's love is with the topic of incest, his love has not been seen as clearly as it might within the respectable tradition of heroic love, embodied in epical romance and tragicomedy. If we understand this connection, the charge of sensationalism against the play loses some of its force. Sidney's *Arcadia* makes a suitable starting place because it exerted the most direct impact of any work upon the young playwrights, providing as it did the story for *Cupid's Revenge* (ca. 1607), in all probability their earliest collaboration. Even though *Cupid's Revenge* is a tragedy, resemblances with the first tragicomedy they wrote together, *Philaster,* indicate that the same story served as model for that play too. Fletcher probably wrote *The Faithful Shepherdess* by himself between these two collaborations; it is a pastoral tragicomedy that takes many of its events from the third book of Spenser's *The Faerie Queene,* although Fletcher certainly knew [Giovanni Battista] Guarini's *Il Pastor Fido,* which directed his interest toward the fashionable new genre. All three sources feature at least one character who feels a love so intense that he cannot resist it and is driven to extraordinary actions, which to sober eyes would be intemperate and impractical. Guarini's tragicomedy resembles the two English epics in its concern to show how apparently dangerous passions, deviating as they do from the approved rules of conduct, eventually solve problems of state and coordinate with some divine plan, revealed by an oracle or other supernatural means. In *A King and No King* Beaumont and Fletcher remove the heroic character from his customary romantic or pastoral setting, excise all intimations of divine approval, and populate Arbaces's environment with sober commentators like Mardonius and Ligones or temperate characters like Tigranes, thereby intensifying the problematic aspect of Arbaces's outsized passion and extravagant behavior.

From the beginning of the young playwrights' collaboration, they showed a fascination with the operations of passion, especially romantic passion. For *Cupid's Revenge* they selected from Book Two of *The Arcadia* some stories of entangled lives made turbulent by passion and linked them together by the figure of Cupid, who asserts his intention to get revenge against the whole family of Hidaspes when she orders destruction of all his statues. The theme linking five central characters concerns the irresistible and ruthless power of Cupid and is in itself simple: Cupid rules all. He signifies love, of course, but the ways the characters behave under his control suggest that he signifies passions in general: greed, ambition, vindictiveness, selfless devotion, as well as love. The play derives its interest less from the theme than from the complicated ways by which the characters move relentlessly toward destruction under the control of passion. It is in the dramatists' later plays that they explore the implications of passion's control: its effect upon identify and its potentiality for beneficial, as well as for destructive, consequences.

One problem involved in the control by passion can be seen from the ways in which Elizabethans and Jacobeans, as well as ourselves, use the term "passion." The second and third meanings listed in the *Oxford English Dictionary* signify on the one hand any vehement, commanding, or overpowering emotion, such as love, hatred, joy, grief, or anger, and on the other hand a state of being passive, of being acted upon. To speak of someone as passionate, we mean that he is driven or possessed, as if the passion were somehow separate from the person, who should try to reinstate control. At the same time the joy or love or grief or hatred is "inside" and intimately a part of the person. We talk as if one is not entirely himself when he is in the throes of passion, and yet those passions are identifiably his very own. Implied in this seemingly contradictory usage is a question of identity and a question of judgment. Is the character "himself" when he controls his passions, or are his passions attributes of "himself"? The question can be rephrased as a matter of judgment: should he not control his passions if he wishes to become fully "himself"? Such questions lie at the heart of *A King and No King*. Arbaces believes that his passionate desire for Panthea should be controlled, and he tries but cannot master this intense feeling, which is the very attribute that confirms his identity as king.

To pose the issue of control in that way, the playwrights needed to draw upon their reading of *The Arcadia,* as well as *Il Pastor Fido* and *The Faerie Queene.* Although *Cupid's Revenge* does little more than testify to their interest in the possibilities in romantic passion for exciting dramatic episodes, their work with their source indicates a careful and sensitive reading. The stories for the play run intermittently through Book Two of *The Arcadia.* Sidney narrated the events by a variety of means: King Basilius learns part of the story from Plangus and writes what he learns on paper which is later read by Pyrocles; Philoclea tells part of the story to Pyrocles; Pyrocles (disguised as Zelmane), who has been involved in another part of the story, tells it to Philoclea. This fragmented narrative, which the characters must piece together, suggests a relationship between the inner story and those who are telling and hearing it. When Beaumont and Fletcher chose to substitute stage names for the central characters, the fact that they selected the names from minor but morally appropriate characters from other sections of Book Two reveals their acute understanding of the text. It appears unlikely that they failed to notice how the problem of love experienced by the tragic characters of the inner story was related to the main characters of the outer story. Like Hidaspes of the inner, Musidorus of the outer feels contempt for love and chastises his devoted friend and cousin Pyrocles, who has fallen in love with Philoclea and, to be near her, has taken the degrading disguise of an Amazon: "forsooth love, love, a passion and the basest and fruitlessest of all passions . . . is engendered betwixt lust and idleness." Pyrocles responds that men have claimed love to be the "highest power of the mind"; any faults associated with love "be not the faults of love but of him that loves, as an unable vessel to bear such a liquor." Musidorus, of course, comes to realize that he can no more resist love than can Pyrocles. Since both princes are rare vessels, marked from birth by divine prophecy for extraordinary deeds, they fall in love with princesses of appropriate beauty and virtue, who feel love with appropriate intensity.

Yet Sidney complicates their story to embody our traditional ambivalence toward passion. The heroic princes, driven by their love, perform heroic deeds in defense of Philoclea and Pamela, but they also engage in devious shifts to avoid King Basilius and Queen Gynecia, who have retreated from their proper roles as rulers of Arcadia out of fear of an ominous prophecy. The princes' intrigues almost cost them their honor and lives, but at the same time their love and consequent actions help fulfill the prophecy, so that at the end of *The Arcadia* the reader sees how their heroic passions, dangerous in themselves, coordinate with their heroic deeds, peace in Arcadia, marriage, and divine plan. The distinction between heroic love and sheer lust is a thin one, unclear until the ultimate outcome in marriage and political harmony. Whether or not the end justifies the means, Sidney's narrative, as it slowly unwinds, cautions against hasty judgment. What appears devious or imprudent at one point fits into an overall beneficent pattern at another point. Beaumont and Fletcher exploit a similar evolving narrative that requires shifting judgments when they compose their major tragicomedies.

This pattern of destiny, working through the young lovers to solve problems of state, underlies Guarini's *Il Pastor Fido,* Britomart's quest for Artegall in Books Three, Four, and Five of *The Faerie Queene,* and Beaumont and Fletcher's *Philaster*. Part of the outline can be discerned in *A King and No King,* although the playwrights remove the dimension of divine prophecy and locate the controls solely in Gobrius's planned gamble on the quality of Arbaces's passion. In all probability, the strong resemblance between the main story of *The Arcadia* and Guarini's *Il Pastor Fido* helped encourage Fletcher's close attention to the tragicomedy. At the outset of Guarini's play, a divine oracle predicts that the burden of yearly sacrifice of a nymph to Diana will be lifted only when two lovers of divine ancestry are married. Difficulty arises because the only two such descendants, Silvio and Amarillis, feel little love for one another, but Mirtillo, a shepherd of foreign origin, loves Amarillis enough to offer his life to save her from execution. He feels such intense passion that he persists in his devotion despite the religious sanction of her betrothal to Silvio, despite the legal prohibitions of Arcadia, and despite the fact that Amarillis refuses to give him any sign of her love. With no assurance beyond his own feelings, he persists and without hesitation offers his life to save her from death, an offer that sets in motion the disclosures to bring about a happy ending. This extreme passion, at odds with any practical calculations of normal conduct, then turns out to be in harmony with the social and religious forces of Arcadia, in both Sidney's and Guarini's work.

Likewise, in *Philaster* the love of Arethusa and Philaster, not the arranged marriage of Arethusa to Pharamond, solves the political difficulties of Sicily and Calabria and thus appears to have the endorsement of the gods. In *A King and No King* the planned marriage of Panthea to Tigranes is stopped by Arbaces's unnatural love for his sister, but this love eventually solves the difficulties of rulership in Iberia and ends in marriage. Such resemblances would be less striking if there were other English comedies written before 1608-09 which dramatize solutions to political difficulties by private loves. Robert Greene's *James IV* (*ca.* 1592) is the only early extant comedy that approximates the scope of this pattern. In tragedies, such as Marston's *Sophonisba* (*ca.* 1605) or Shakespeare's *Antony and Cleopatra* (*ca.* 1607), private love does affect matters of state, but the comedies tend to conform to the humanists' definition of the genre that limits issues to domestic problems of ordinary families.

Fletcher's *The Faithful Shepherdess,* written about the same time as *Cupid's Revenge,* does not embody the full scope of Guarini's tragicomic design that gives sanction to Mirtillo's extreme passion. Without problems of state and without a divine oracle to burden them, the shepherds and shepherdesses concern themselves with controlling their passions. In effect, Fletcher narrows the focus to explore the problem raised by Cupid's irresistible power. His pastoral characters align themselves on a spectrum from the utterly controlled—or chaste—Clorin and Amoret to the utterly lustful Cloe and the Sullen Shepherd. Most of the characters lose themselves temporarily to passion and then undergo purgations and cures. The very movement of the play from dusk to dark to dawn, from the public work area into the dark woods surrounding the magical grounds of a holy well and back to Clorin's cabin, follows the psychological pattern of release, confusion, and reassertion of order. Thus described, the play would appear to endorse the customary thinking about passions as dangerous energies to be controlled, thereby the contrary of *A King and No King,* where Gobrius's plan rests on the hope that Arbaces's passion will be too intense to be controlled.

In this regard Thomas Wright's *The Passions of the Mind in General,* first printed in 1601, and again in 1604, 1620, 1621, and 1630, can serve as a popular contemporaneous account of traditional thinking about control over passions to gloss Fletcher's tragicomedy. Wright, a Jesuit, followed Aquinas's division of the soul into its various faculties, the appetites into the concupiscible and irascible, and saw man's central problem to be one of governing them as the king governs his state. Reason, he writes, in its proper role

> like an Empresse was to gouern the body, direct the senses, guide the passions as subjects and vassals, by the square of prudence, and the rule of reason, the inferior parts were bound to yeeld homage, and obey.

Many of Fletcher's shepherds talk about self-control in the same way. Clorin, dedicated to the memory of her beloved shepherd, excludes the "lustful" turpentine from her medicinal herbs because it would "intice the vaines, and stirre the heat / To civill muteny, scaling the seate / Our reason moves in, and deluding it / With dreames and wanton fancies" (II.ii.36-40). Like Thomas Wright, she uses the metaphor of governing the lower faculties by the higher reason. Daphnis behaves as a textbook example when he prepares to meet Cloe in the dark woods. Fletcher gives him a soliloquy that depicts his use of the square of prudence and the rule of reason:

> I charge you all my vaines
> Through which the blood and spirit take their way,
> Locke up your disobedient heats, and stay
> Those mutinous desires, that else would growe
> To strong rebellion.
>
> (II.iv.16-20)

His straightforward talk to his "vaines" prefigures Tigranes's soliloquy in *A King and No King,* which dramatizes the mastering of his passion for Panthea and earns him the right to be praised as temperate. Other shepherds in *The Faithful Shepherdess,* however, experience more trouble in governing their mutinous desires. Angered by Amoret's apparently wanton behavior, Perigot stabs her in a moment of abandonment to his irascible passions. Cloe and Alexis give free reign to their concupiscible passions and suffer appropriate misfortune. Alexis, at the very moment of their rendezvous, is wounded "in the thigh" by the Sullen Shepherd and must undergo a cure by Clorin, the chaste shepherdess, who administers herbs and advice about self-control.

Thomas Wright divides the passions into the ordinate, which are moderated according to reason in harmony with the virtuous motions of the will, and the inordinate or perturbations, which blind the reason by distorting the imagination and causing "all those vices which are opposite to prudence," such as the rashness exhibited by Perigot. This distinction, Wright is cautious to explain, does not counsel mortification of the passions, as the Stoics would. Wright recalls the Scriptures' exhortation to be angry and sin not (Ps. 4:4) or "With fear and trembling work your salvation" (Phil. 2:12). Christ's zeal in chasing the money-lenders from the Temple shows how passions can be enlisted in the service of goodness. The shepherd Thenot, who remains content to worship Clorin for her devotion to the memory of her dead lover, is a negative example of this point because he mortifies his passions for a life of idolatry. To cure him, Clorin pretends to cast off her chaste life, dedicated to curing wounded shepherds, and disillusions Thenot by her wanton advances.

Thus Thomas Wright's commentary on the control of passion applies to most of the episodes in Fletcher's pastoral tragicomedy, but it bears little revelance for Amoret, who like Clorin belongs to an order different from those of her fellow shepherds. More than Clorin, Amoret has claim to the faithful shepherdess of the title and center of Fletcher's interest, although Clorin too is admirable for her chastity and virtuous deeds. One would be hard put to find the square of prudence or the rule of reason guiding Amoret's devotion to Perigot after he has stabbed her twice, and yet the play holds up her unswerving love for our wondrous approval. Her difficulties arise from Amarillis's exercise of magic and thus do not lend themselves to measurement by the square of prudence, which is ill-equipped to take account of events that fail to meet nor-

mal expectations. Amarillis desires Perigot, who loves only Amoret. To possess him, Amarillis transforms herself by magic to look exactly like Amoret. As the false Amoret, she exhibits wanton behavior that surprises and angers Perigot to the point of abandoning her. Subsequently, when the true Amoret comes upon him in the dark woods, he gives way to an "irascible perturbation" and stabs her. With appropriate miraculousness, the River God suddenly appears to save the wounded Amoret and cure her. Despite Perigot's ill-treatment, she remains faithful to him and rejects the River God's offer of love. Again she meets Perigot in the dark woods, and again he stabs her, and again she remains unwavering with a devotion that rises above any normal response and certainly beyond any calculations by the square of prudence, if not the rule of reason.

Tasso in the *Discourses on the Heroic Poem* (1594) discusses the exceptional feelings of the heroic character and defines love itself, with a nod to Aquinas, as appropriate to heroes: "If love is not merely a passion and a movement of the sensitive appetite but also a noble habit of the will, as Saint Thomas thought, love will be praiseworthy in heroes and consequently in the heroic poem." Tasso removes love, at least in part, from the realm of passion and places it in the will and the realm of action. In this light, Amoret's constancy—she remains "true" to Perigot, as this faithfulness is sometimes expressed—can be interpreted as an heroic act of will that arises from choice, and not simply a given passion. Fletcher could have inserted a speech to explicate Amoret's faithfulness as an exertion of will, for other shepherds interpret their actions by mental faculties. Or he could have postulated a princess in disguise as a shepherdess to diminish the mysteriousness in the source of her constancy. One would accept without question a princess who feels heroically, as Pyrocles's defense of love indicates when he says to Musidorus that the vessel into which the liquor of love is poured determines its quality. This connection, cast in the form of a test, governs Beaumont and Fletcher's later play about Arbaces's identity. Or one could see Amoret, as well as the chaste Clorin, in the tradition of the long-suffering wives like Dekker's Grissil or his Bellamont in *The Honest Whore.* Bellamont and Grissil remain chaste and constant despite extreme provocations, but Dekker's plays raise few questions about the psychological determinations of their conduct. In *The Faithful Shepherdess,* Amoret and Clorin behave in a context of psychological commentary, from the Priest of Pan's first blessing as he sprinkles holy water on his flock to help them tame their wanton fires until his final summary on events of the play. This context leads us to make a distinction between ordinary passions, which appear wanton and need control, and rare or heroic love, so elevated and powerful that by its very nature it is exempt from the dangers of wantonness. Fletcher intimates a divine dimension in this distinction in the Priest of Pan's final speech:

> All your strength,
> Cannot keepe your foot from falling,
> To lewd lust, that still is calling,
> At your cottage, till his power,
> Bring againe that golden howre,

Of peace and rest, to every soule.
May his care of you controle,
All diseases, sores or payne . . .
Give yee all affections new,
New desires and tempers new,
That yee may be ever true.

(V.v.201ff.)

The play does not insist upon a divine causation that divides the shepherds into saints and sinners, somewhat like Calvin's division of the elect and the reprobate. Almost as an afterthought, the Priest of Pan's speech touches on a note that Guarini sounds loudly in making his faithful shepherd a descendant of divine ancestors, who fulfills the oracle by his heroic devotion to Amarillis. Fletcher leaves open the possibility that Amoret's heroic love, either an exercise of will or a noble passion, may be, like grace, a divine gift.

The major source for his pastoral tragicomedy was Book Three of Spenser's *The Faerie Queene* on the virtue of chastity, not Guarini's *Il Pastor Fido,* as the title suggests. W. W. Greg proposed [in *Pastoral Poetry and Pastoral Drama,* 1906] that the young Fletcher intended his play to rival Guarini's, not to imitate it; so he deliberately looked elsewhere for inspiration. He no doubt took the episodes concerning the true and false Amoret from Spenser's true and false Florimel. Amoret's very name, of course, derives from the twin of Belphoebe. Their mother, Chrysogonee, made fertile by sunbeams, gives birth to her twin daughters in the Garden of Adonis. Belphoebe joins Diana for her education; Amoret joins Venus. Belphoebe becomes a chaste huntress, who helps cure the squire Timias, wounded in the thigh as he fights three "foule fosters" (probably representing lust of the eye, ear, and flesh). Her counterpart in Fletcher's play is Clorin, destined to remain unmarried and loyal to the memory of her dead lover; she cures Alexis, wounded in the thigh when he lusts for Cloe. Thenot, who worships Clorin without hope of response, embodies another aspect of Timias, who loves Belphoebe. And Amoret, like her namesake, embodies chastity in love and marriage, her future with Perigot, as the end of the play indicates.

But it is to Spenser's arrangement of his characters in relation to chastity and especially to Britomart, that we must look to understand the influence upon Fletcher's thinking about heroic passion. Belphoebe and Amoret, as Thomas Roche has explained [in *The Kindly Flame: A Study of the Third and Fourth Books of Spenser's "Faerie Queene,"* 1964], must be differentiated from Britomart, who exhibits psychological experiences of a well-rounded character; the twins are archetypes or universals, whose emblematic natures are disclosed in their adventures. Britomart, whose quest for her loved one, Artegall, constitutes the central adventure of Book Three, reveals a remarkable power to realize the potentialities of the virtue of chastity, as she confronts a variety of characters either controlled by their wanton passions or struggling to control them. Spenser's narrator, in commenting on the many versions of love, sounds much like Pyrocles talking to Musidorus:

Wonder it is to see, in diuerse minds,
How diuersely loue doth his pageants play,
And shewes his powre in variable kinds:
The baser wit, whose idle thoughts alway
Are wont to cleaue vnto the lowly clay,
It stirreth vp to sensuall desire,
And in lewd slouth to wast his carelesse day:
But in braue sprite it kindles goodly fire,
That to all high desert and honour doth aspire.

(III.v.i)

This commentary avoids discussing the way passions should be controlled by the rule of reason and the square of prudence and attributes instead the quality of passion to the quality of the "vessel" into which it is poured. Like Fletcher's shepherds, such characters are identified by the quality of their love more than by strength of will.

Britomart, like Sidney's two heroes, is marked from the outset for greatness. When she first views Artegall in Merlin's magic mirror, she falls instantly in love, and Merlin interprets her glance into the charmed glass as "the streight course of hevenly destiny" (III.iii.xxiv.3). For all that, Spenser insists upon the physically passionate aspect of her love:

Sithens it hath infixed faster hold
Within my bleeding bowels, and so sore
Now ranckleth in this same fraile fleshly mould,
That all mine entrailes flow with poysnous gore,
And th'vlcer groweth daily more and more.

(III.ii.xxxix.1-5)

Beaumont and Fletcher stress this feature of passion more with Arbaces than Fletcher does with Amoret. Unlike Arbaces's amorous passion, Britomart's inspires her to a series of virtuous exploits, so that her deeds and the supernatural sanction help establish her identity as heroic; Arbaces's valorous exploits on the battlefield occur before he experiences the test of passion that determines his regal identity. Britomart begins her adventures with the stamp of nobility; Arbaces's passion warrants this stamp. Fletcher must have felt the challenge of basing identity upon feelings when he confined all the varieties of passion to shepherds without regard to external endorsement by a social hierarchy. According to his preface to the quarto of *The Faithful Shepherdess,* the differentiations caused problems for his audience who expected to see "a play of country hired shepheards, in gray cloakes, with curtail'd dogs in strings." Instead, they should "remember Shepherds to be such, as all the ancient Poets and moderne of understanding have received them: that is, the owners of flockes and not hyerlings." In other words, the audience should not conceive them as base rustics for whom the passions of love would be inappropriate. Theater-goers were accustomed to seeing a princess feel heroic passion, but not to seeing extraordinary passion itself as a fundamental differentiating characteristic.

It is hardly surprising that Beaumont and Fletcher, given the poor reception of *The Faithful Shepherdess* and *The Knight of the Burning Pestle,* plays written individually, would in their collaborations be attracted to stories about misunderstandings and failures of judgment. Both *Philaster* and *A King and No King,* although they continue Fletcher's interest in the value of intense passion, concern themselves as much with characters who fail to understand and judge those passions adequately. These plays hold up characters like Amoret for the audience's admiration but also dramatize in detail obtuse characters who fail to admire them. Many episodes turn upon the difference between those who take a mundane outlook and those who acknowledge the exceptional. Mundane characters expect the usual to occur and guide their lives by the square of prudence; characters of heroic dimensions, driven by their extreme passions, attempt and achieve what would otherwise seem impossible.

The initiating predicament in *Philaster* moves the play toward Guarini's model and away from the schematized variations derived from Spenser. In both *Il Pastor Fido* and *Philaster,* the rulers arrange an obviously wrongheaded marriage for interests of state. Unlike Guarini, Beaumont and Fletcher reveal almost immediately to the audience that Princess Arethusa's true love could solve the difficulties between Sicily and Calabria. She loves not Pharamond, the vain prince of Spain selected by her father, but Philaster, the true heir to the throne of Sicily, displaced by her father. When Arethusa first discloses her true feelings to Philaster, Beaumont and Fletcher pitch their dialogue at a high degree of intensity: love for Arethusa and Philaster is a matter of life or death. Arethusa says that she must either have her "wishes" "or I dye, by heaven I die" (I.ii.55). Philaster matches her vehemence with his response: "Love you, / By all my hopes I doe, above my life" (I.ii.92-93). To underline the exceptional quality of Arethusa's passion, Beaumont and Fletcher give her several references to the hand of the gods:

> You Gods that would not have your doomes
>   withstood,
> Whose wholy wisedomes at this time it is,
> To make the passions of a feeble maide,
> The way unto your Justice; I obay.
>
>   (I.ii.31-34)

Elsewhere she says, "'Tis the gods, / The gods, that make me so" in explaining to Philaster the intensity of her love for him. By showing in the second scene of the play how the intense passion of the hero and heroine could solve political difficulties and by intimating the approval of the gods, the playwrights move swiftly to provide external endorsements and win the audience's acknowledgement of the value of their feelings. Convinced of this evaluation, the audience then watches the wrongheaded characters fumble toward a similar outlook by the end of the play. The happy conclusion thus becomes as much an agreement in judgment as it is a joining of the lovers in marriage.

Once the solution to the initial difficulties is suggested by Arethusa's possible marriage to Philaster, the playwrights introduce a series of intervening events that nicely exploit the implications of the opening scenes. As one might expect, the hero and heroine, who declare so readily their

willingness to die for their love, are put to the test. The action moves into a forest not unlike the dark and magical woods of *The Faithful Shepherdess,* where restraints fall away and confusion reigns. They are pushed to the test by misunderstandings and mistrust that fail to take account of exceptional behavior and extraordinary love. The complication is triggered by Megra's slander of Arethusa. At the moment when Megra's lust is being exposed, she deflects attention to Arethusa by exploiting what from Megra's viewpoint is a probability: Arethusa's lust for her attractive young page, Bellario. Megra's slander unintentionally enlists Dion in her cause. He is the sensible, plain speaker who serves throughout the first section of the play the role of the reliable commentator, the role that Mardonius takes in *A King and No King* and Ismenus takes in *Cupid's Revenge.* When Dion hears Megra's accusation, he is willing to believe the worst since he knows the ways of the world and takes the opportunity to turn Philaster against Arethusa for the practical purpose of regaining his throne. Dion miscalculates, for he fails to take account of Philaster's extraordinary love that has become a defining part of himself. Far from agreeing to wrest the throne from Arethusa's father, Philaster sees himself to be a rejected lover, not a displaced ruler, and envisions a life apart from society in the forest. There he comes upon Arethusa in the arms of her page Bellario. He gives what he sees the worst interpretation, as Perigot does to the "facts" about the false Amoret.

Just as Perigot stabs the true Amoret in his anger, so Philaster stabs Arethusa in his despair, but unlike the shepherd, both Arethusa and Philaster, true to their earlier statements about the value of their love, request death from one another in their dismay over their situation. Philaster takes up his sword and asks Arethusa to help guide it to execute "justice," when suddenly the Country Fellow enters, speaking prose, eager to catch a glimpse of the King and his courtiers hunting in the forest. Like Philaster who earlier comes upon Bellario comforting the faint Arethusa, the Country Fellow misinterprets what he sees and rushes to rescue a helpless woman from a dastardly attacker. His prosaic outlook throws into relief the operatic behavior of the hero and heroine, whose intense passions allow for no thoughts of moderation or practicality. The intrusion of the Country Fellow dislocates the audience's attitude by introducing everyday standards that move events from the edge of tragedy toward comedy. They are thus shaken from a frame of mind which has adjusted to the scope of Philaster's outlook—that his love for Arethusa is indeed a matter of his identity and thus a matter of life or death. The title page of the quarto, which exhibits a woodblock of the episode, confirms the centrality of this moment in the play, a moment that dramatizes "the danger, not the death." Our involvement in the heroic passion of Philaster and Arethusa suddenly has been qualified; the upshot of this qualification does not become clear until the final moments of the play when we discover the true identity of Bellario and the effects of her passion.

The extent to which the audience shares Philaster and Arethusa's outlook can be measured by our judgment of

Philaster as he flees for his life, having been wounded by the Country Fellow. He wounds in turn Bellario to create a decoy for the King's party of searchers. Certainly Philaster's action is practical, but we judge him as small when he instinctively tries to preserve his life. The play has had its way with us, so that we take the heroic gestures of self-sacrifice by Arethusa and Bellario to be the standard of conduct. When Philaster comes to a full recognition of their willingness to die for their love, their integrity needs no "facts" to reverse his judgment. He assumes his earlier heroic stance, purified of practical calculations, when he offers his life to the King: "By the Gods it is a joy to die, / I find a recreation in't" (V.iii.103-04). The comic aspect of this extravagance fades somewhat if Philaster is compared with Pharamond, who trembles for his life when taken captive by the threatening but jolly citizens. The retreat into the forest, then, provides the occasion for Arethusa and Bellario to affirm their integrity as they lay their lives on the line, and for Philaster to regain his when he regains his judgment of their true worth. It would not be farfetched to describe the play as the education of Philaster, who awakens to the actuality of total devotion, the consequence of heroic passion.

Yet the play ends not with Philaster's enlightenment and subsequent marriage, but with the disclosure of Bellario's identity. This disclosure can be described as the playwrights' "trick" by those who find the facts about Euphrasia essential to the happy ending, but it is the King, not Philaster, who needs such facts and pushes to the ultimate revelation. Philaster has been convinced of Arethusa's trustworthiness. The King, throughout the play, has failed to take account of the exceptional. It is he who proposes the "practical" marriage of Arethusa to Pharamond, and it is he who believes Megra's accusation, thereby refusing to give the benefit of the doubt to his own daughter. Like him, Dion is practical; he seizes the opportunity of slander to lie in order to motivate Philaster; and he too never suspects the extraordinary passion and equally extraordinary conduct of his own daughter. The final disclosures enlighten those who fail to trust and interpret conduct by standards based upon ordinary behavior. In cases of slander like Megra's, there can usually be no facts to decide the issue of chastity for convincing doubters. The very nature of the trick, the improbability of a situation where the page turns out to be a woman, makes the very point that a "trick" is necessary where trust should prevail. Judgment should take into account behavior that can transcend the average, the probable, and even the practical. What Philaster relearns in the forest both the King and Dion learn with the final disclosure about Bellario.

By ending the play not with marriage but with disclosure, the playwrights address the problem of judging heroic passion in the perspective of tragicomedy, admirable from the tragic or heroic, grandiose from the comic or practical viewpoint. Although the emphasis comes down on the heroic and exceptional, the play can hardly be accused of rejecting Thomas Wright's square of prudence and rule of reason. Bellario's very career points to the bi-fold judgment provoked by the play. She could have prevented all

the difficulties consequent upon Megra's slander by revealing her own identity as Euphrasia. But the absoluteness which governs her dedication to her vow governs her love for Philaster and leads to her willingness to sacrifice her life to save his, a willingness that opens his eyes to her loyalty and reverses the tragic chain of events. Guarini adapts Aristotle's dictum about the best plot for tragedy so that, in the best plot for tragicomedy, the cause of tragic danger becomes the cause of the comic resolution. Bellario's intense devotion works both ways; so does Philaster's love for Arethusa. The complexity of the tragicomic design thus evokes a complexity of judgment. Neither unqualified approval nor unqualified disregard of heroic behavior or practical behavior will do. As we have seen, Bellario, Arethusa, and Philaster, through their willingness to sacrifice themselves, push events to the brink, but so do Dion and the King's practical calculations. The heroic characters' willingness to sacrifice themselves leads to the happy ending, but so do the actions by the Country Fellow, Dion, and the citizens. *Philaster* dramatizes a picture of human conduct that neither fully endorses Thomas Wright's standards for controlling passions, nor rejects them; it is a picture that urges the audience to take account of the exceptional.

II

A King and No King, placed in the context of Beaumont and Fletcher's earlier plays and their sources, can be seen as a provocative reworking of their interest in extraordinary passion as a basis of heroic identity rather than as a dangerous force to be mastered, extraordinary insofar as it drives a character beyond all calculations of prudence and the accepted laws of reason to ultimately beneficial results. By casting this passion in the form of incest, the playwrights present their case at its most challenging because incest is probably as horrifying a consequence as one could imagine in arguing the case against uncontrolled passion. Unlike Arethusa's love for Philaster, seen from the outset with political and divine endorsements, Arbaces's love for his sister runs counter to all sanctions. Only the love of Guarini's faithful shepherd compares with Arbaces's in the number of prohibitions apparently against his love, but Mirtillo feels an inner conviction about his passion that Arbaces lacks. Stripped of all supports, Arbaces's passion is the thing itself, irresistible before the ultimate taboo. Dramatized in these all-or-nothing terms, it is the stuff of tragedy, unlike Arethusa's love for Philaster, which is typical of romance. In this later play, Beaumont and Fletcher reduce the trappings of romance for the sake of verisimilitude characteristic of tragedy: no retreats into the forest, no oracles, no priests, no magic wells. Arbaces's situation fits literally the requirements implied by the name of the genre, *tragi-*comedy, more evocative of Seneca than of Sidney. The features of comedy and romance—the slapstick evoked by Bessus's ridiculous pursuit of honor and the strong-willed maiden in disguise—separate themselves for the most part into subplots to serve as contrasts with the episodes concerning incestuous passion. The only way to resolve Arbaces's problem happily is for the playwrights to shift the terms of the opposition: things are not what they seem. It is this shift which has annoyed critics and made the play more provoking than provocative. The case against incest, so fiercely presented through the first four acts, turns out not to be the case at all.

Moreover, the disclosures alter the mode from the verisimilitude of tragedy to the implausibilities characteristic of romantic comedy, involving secret parents and a babe exchanged at birth. Yet this mixture, so strange to a palate accustomed to tragedy or comedy, may be part of the playwrights' generic arrangement. The cause of the reversal, Arbaces's extraordinary passion, is the very same cause of the initial difficulty, a fact that indicates some care about genre in the planning. And, too, the dramatic irony works upon the audience to strengthen the provocative impact, not as it works in *Philaster* with the audience against the misjudgments of wrongheaded characters. This provocation, as I see it, leads the audience to reconsider their understanding about passion: not to abandon their principles about the need for restraints, but to apply their principles with flexibility by acknowledging the possibility of exceptions. Both *Philaster* and *A King and No King* resemble one another in their focus upon judgment, but the later tragicomedy uses devices more directly disturbing to the audience, cast in a role comparable to Dion's in *Philaster*.

Four acts of the play make the case for Thomas Wright's moderation of the passions. The very source of the names of Tigranes, Panthea, and Gobrius, taken from Xenophon's *Cyropaedia,* gives external support for this plan. At least one of the playwrights had studied this epical narrative about a practical and temperate soldier and king, who never suffered defeat. Scattered through the eight books are passages of advice like this one:

> And by making his [Cyrus's] own self-control as an example, he disposed all to practise that virtue more diligently. For when the weaker members of society see that one who is in a position where he may indulge himself to excess is still under self-control, they naturally strive all the more not to be found guilty of any excessive indulgence.

> (III.i.30)

This passage could have appeared in Erasmus's *The Education of a Christian Prince* or King James's *Basilicon Doron*. Certainly, the character of Cyrus, as it emerges from his prudent management of his troops, his exercise of temperance, his piety and his loyalty, could be taken by sixteenth-century rulers as an ideal. Arbaces, who conquers the Armenian forces not by a cautious deployment of his troops but by a challenge of Tigranes to single combat, strikes us as a rash contrast. Beaumont and Fletcher, as if to enforce this impression, never disclose why Arbaces's Iberian army was fighting the Armenians, aside from the glory of the enterprise. Cyrus, on the other hand, fights for payment of tribute money, for loyal supporters, for self-defence, but not for mere personal honor. Thomas Wright could have explained Cyrus's actions by the square of prudence and the rule of moderation, but not Arbaces's.

Panthea in the *Cyropaedia,* the beautiful wife of Abradates of Susa, no doubt attracted Beaumont and Fletcher by her resemblance to the faithful shepherdess Amoret. Xenophon's Panthea remains true to her noble husband even to the point of killing herself at his funeral after he dies an honorable death in battle, fighting for Cyrus. Earlier her husband fights on the side against Cyrus, and she is taken prisoner by Araspas, one of Cyrus's captains. Araspas becomes enraptured of her beauty and urges Cyrus to view his rare captive. Cyrus, characteristically prudent, refuses to be tempted because he knows the danger in beauty. Araspas disagrees, arguing that beauty need not cause love since love is a matter of free will:

> But of beautiful things we love some and some we do not; and one loves one, another another; for it is a matter of free will, and each one loves what he pleases. For example, a brother does not fall in love with his sister, but someone else falls in love with her; neither does a father fall in love with his daughter, but somebody else does; for fear of God and the law of the land are sufficient to prevent such love.

> (V.i.10)

This discussion about the control of passions happens to be the very topic which occupied Beaumont and Fletcher from their collaboration upon *Cupid's Revenge*. Araspas's mistaken argument, which cites incest to clinch his belief in man's ability to control his passions, could well have been the seed for *A King and No King*. As events turn out, Araspas finds that he loses control, falls in love with Panthea, and brings shame upon himself by threatening her in order to win her submission.

Tigranes, the primary example of self-control in *A King and No King,* takes his name from one of Cyrus's captains, who joins Cyrus after Cyrus has outmaneuvered and conquered Tigranes's father, the King of Armenia. In the play it is Arbaces who conquers Tigranes, the King of Armenia. Xenophon's Tigranes pleads with Cyrus for his father's release from imprisonment, saying that the King has been punished by fear and has learned discretion (III.i.16-18). By implication, the son too has learned a lesson from his father's mistake in refusing to pay tribute to Cyrus. Cyrus accepts Tigranes's argument, releases the King, and gains Tigranes's loyalty, for Tigranes follows Cyrus throughout the *Cyropaedia* as a stalwart supporter. The point to be stressed in the similarity between Xenophon's character and the dramatic Tigranes is his secondary role. The dramatic character masters his passion for Panthea and thereby serves as the embodiment of temperance to contrast with Arbaces. As admirable as Tigranes is, he never escapes the fact that he remains Arbaces's prisoner throughout the play, already defeated in single combat when the play begins, released at the conclusion to return to rule Armenia with Spaconia as his queen. This secondary position casts a shadow over his self-control: does he control his passions not so much because his will is stronger but because his passions are weaker? If Tigranes were meant to serve as our standard of judgment, then Gobrius's plot to bring about the happy ending must be viewed as wrongheaded. Yet, had Arbaces followed Tigranes's example and behaved temperately, the true ruler would have been deprived of the Iberian throne, and Arbaces would have lacked the final sanction as king.

Gobrius, the third name to be derived from the *Cyropaedia*, belongs to aggrieved fathers in both the drama and the epic. Xenophon's Gobrius gets revenge upon his Assyrian king, who killed Gobrius's son in anger for besting him in a hunt. In short, Gobrius suffers from a ruler who could not control his temper. Beaumont and Fletcher's Gobrius protects his son from Queen Arane's attempt to kill him by fostering an uncontrollable passion in his son for Queen Arane's daughter. Like Panthea and Tigranes, the dramatic counterpart serves a thematic purpose the very opposite to that of his namesake.

From the outset of the play, Beaumont and Fletcher give indications that the problem of judging Arbaces lies at the center of the dramatic action. Before he sees his sister and falls in love with her, he behaves in ways that defy a simple favorable or unfavorable judgment. Like Araspas, he thinks he can control love, confident that when Tigranes sees Panthea, he will want to marry her. To help guide our attitude toward Arbaces, the playwrights use the trustworthy old captain, Mardonius, whose prudent outlook resembles Cyrus's, so that he could very well have stepped from the *Cyropaedia,* although he has no namesake there. When Arbaces boasts about his victory in a style reminiscent of Tamburlaine, Mardonius undercuts his vainglory and at the same time shows the justness of tempered praise: "Would you but leave these hasty tempers, which I doe not say take from you all your worth, but darken um, then you would shine indeede" (I.i.360-62). He speaks with a voice of moderation, neither endorsing Arbaces's extreme behavior nor overlooking his heroism. From among his balanced comments one can be chosen for its portentous, although unintended, irony: "Yet I would have you keepe some passions, least men should take you for a god, your vertues are such" (I.i.364-65). In some ways Mardonius sounds like a moderating interlocutor from a Senecan tragedy, but in all probability he was modeled after Shakespeare's Enobarbus [in *Antony and Cleopatra*], whose prudence and scepticism help the audience adjust to Antony's extravagant passions and behavior. Enobarbus's practical soldiership cannot finally take the full measure of Antony's stature, as Enobarbus comes to realize after he defects and thus dies of a broken heart from his misjudgment. *A King and No King,* as a tragicomedy, does not push matters that far. Mardonius is put to the test when Arbaces discloses his incestuous desires in Act Three. As we would expect, Mardonius recoils in horror but does not abandon his leader in total disgust. It is Gobrius, not Mardonius, who possesses the fullest grasp of events, and as Gobrius's viewpoint comes to dominate events in the last section of the play, Mardonius as spokesman for received values fades in importance.

Bessus, the low comic figure, for all his apparent irrelevance to the audience's problem of gauging their attitude toward the protagonist, does affect it. An utter coward, Bessus runs by mistake toward the enemy in battle and shares inadvertently in Arbaces's victory. With impudent boasts, he exploits his good fortune—boasts which bear an uncomfortable resemblance to Arbaces's speeches about his triumph over Tigranes. Whereas the contrast between the low comic coward and the valorous king remains the dominant impression, the similarity is strong enough to affirm the critical reservations expressed by Mardonius of Arbaces. Later in the play, a parallel works in the opposite way to enforce a contrast. Bessus, in his effort to thrive, shows himself to be the amoral courtier, ever eager to please his king. He listens to Arbaces's tortured confession of incestuous feelings without so much as the blink of an eye and promptly agrees to serve as go-between with Panthea. As an afterthought, to impress Arbaces with his efficiency, Bessus volunteers to solicit the King's own mother. Now it is Arbaces's turn to recoil in horror at the moral insensitivity of another character.

Yet it is Bessus's pursuit of honor that dominates the dramatic life of this character and creates, although obliquely, the strongest impact upon the audience's responses to the question of Arbaces's identity as king. Bessus's boasts about his soldiership make him the victim of slapstick for those who cannot abide his obvious hypocrisy. Despite the humiliations, he persists in his pursuit of "honor" with a comic resilience that helps win the audience's good-natured indulgence of his shortcomings. His efforts to buy the testimonies of authorities about his honor and his transparent evasions of challenges to prove his valor give comfort to the audience that things are what they seem. No one mistakes Bessus's character; he cannot gain a reputation for qualities he does not have. Just as the audience takes comfort in Mardonius's voice of moderation, so they feel reassured by the ease of judging Bessus. He appears to live in a world where deceptions never work, where reputations coordinate with inner qualities, where identities are unmistakable. Bessus could hardly be described as "a coward and no coward."

Even in the first four acts when Mardonius and Bessus exert their influence, the audience should resist being seduced by their simplified version of the world because it has overheard Gobrius talking to Arane about secret past events. Why does Arane want to kill her own son? This question hangs over subsequent events and should caution against hasty estimates about the way things are. Beaumont and Fletcher introduce Ligones in Act Five to renew this caution. From the viewpoint of the main story, Ligones would appear to be a totally extraneous character; the presence of Spaconia's father makes no difference to the outcome of the play. Ligones suddenly arrives from Armenia, expecting to confirm his worst speculations about his daughter, whose love for Tigranes has led her to risk her reputation, if not her life, by following him into captivity. The father discovers Spaconia living in prison with Tigranes and places the worst interpretation upon the situation, calling his daughter a whore on the assumption that she and Tigranes are behaving as ordinary mortals would behave. But the audience knows Spaconia to be far from ordinary in the intensity of her love and character. Appropriately Tigranes has proposed that she become his queen. The reversal of Ligones's judgment when he learns that his daughter is hardly a whore but a queen occurs just before Arbaces learns that his would-be incest is in fact love for a princess and that he is no king. Ligones's enlightenment thus prefigures the reversal in Arbaces's outlook and, of course, the audience's. Both Ligones and the audience must come to terms with the fact that extreme passion leads to royalty. Neither Spaconia nor Arbaces was born of royal blood, but their intense love leads them to royal marriages.

Shortly after Ligones's misjudgment, Arbaces makes a similar misinterpretation. When Gobrius says that he is Arbaces's father, Arbaces places the worst interpretation upon the Queen's conduct, only to learn like Ligones that others need not confirm one's usual expectations. The two cases of mistaken judgment, occurring so near one another in the final act of the play, show how the playwrights are preparing the audience for the final disclosures, all of which caution against absolute judgments. Events thus encourage a flexibility of outlook that allows for the unpredictable in human affairs, not only the odd happening, such as Arbaces's exchange at birth, but the exceptional passion, such as Arbaces's love for Panthea.

If the final act of **A King and No King** were lost, we would no doubt read the remaining four acts to be endorsing temperance as an ideal for human conduct. The unsuspected facts of Arbaces's birth and Gobrius's plot, introduced in Act Five, throw us off balance and remove our confidence in judging all cases by one standard: temperate conduct need not be best for all in all circumstances. This outlook in some ways recalls Fletcher's viewpoint in **The Faithful Shepherdess,** where Amoret and Clorin remain exempt from the problems of the other characters who struggle to control their passions. In both plays some characters show themselves to be outstanding exceptions to general rules of conduct, although Amoret calls into question prudence, not restraint, as Arbaces does. But the sudden readjustment of attitude evoked by the disclosures of Gobrius's plot has no counterpart in **The Faithful Shepherdess**; instead, it recalls the sudden interruption of the deadly serious moment between Philaster and Arethusa by the Country Fellow. There the dislocation of tone throws us off balance to make us realize that our outlook has been too narrowly focused; we must readjust to include, in the earlier play, the everyday viewpoint of the Country Fellow, in the later, the bizarre facts of Arbaces's birth and reassessment of his irresistible passion. Granting the comparison, we still feel that Gobrius's narrative disturbs us far more than the intrusion of the Country Fellow, for we suddenly become aware of the hands of the playwrights manipulating us. We become conscious of the play as an arrangement of events, a consciousness that imparts a hypothetical, even playful, dimension to a drama that for four acts maintains typical dramatic illusion.

To be sure, in all drama we remain somewhat aware that we are attending to a fiction, but style can intensify the verisimilitude; Beaumont and Fletcher, with the improbable facts that solve Arbaces's problem, suddenly call attention to the contrived story, as if to catch us off guard. By breaking through the alternatives for development that Arbaces's story seems to require, the play risks the charge

of triviality, and its playwrights the charge of being cynical entertainers. The logic of Arbaces's situation dictates either that he succumb to his passion, an act that would lead to his death, or that he master his passion either by renunciation or by suicide. Tigranes has removed himself, in effect, as a partial solution, husband to Panthea, by managing to redirect his love to Spaconia. The playwrights' actual solution coordinates the esthetic response, to use rough terminology, with the moral response: the sudden shift of tone catches us unprepared, as if to warn us to be on the *qui vivre,* to be alert to the exceptional.

Coleridge, using Beaumont and Fletcher's tragedies to compare unfavorably with Shakespeare's, complained that they are founded "on some out-of-the-way accident or exceptional to the general experience of mankind." As usual, he placed his finger on an important critical issue. If Beaumont and Fletcher's tragedies exhibit their fascination with the unusual or exceptional, how much moreso do their tragicomedies, for the genre itself encourages this attention. Tragicomedy, as Guarini embodied it in *Il Pastor Fido,* not only takes account of the unusual, but holds it up for praise. "Wonder" is a characteristic response to his form. The heroic, as it appears in the tragicomedies of Beaumont and Fletcher, must be differentiated from the heroic as Sidney describes it in *An Apology for Poetry:* not as an example to admire and imitate, but an exception to be wondered at. Giason Denores protested Guarini's new amalgam because in his view there were only two dramatic genres, tragedy and comedy, sanctioned by nature and the ancients. Guarini countered by urging a flexibility toward changing circumstances: since Christians experience an outlook on life different from that of Greek and Roman audiences, it is only natural that their dramas should take new forms to render their new experiences. It is hardly surprising that Beaumont and Fletcher also see in the tragicomic genre the potentiality for encouraging a flexibility of response toward the surprising and outstanding, a readiness for the wondrous exception.

PHILASTER

Mary Grace Muse Adkins (essay date 1946)

SOURCE: "The Citizens in *Philaster*: Their Function and Significance," in *Studies in Philology,* Vol. XLIII, No. 1, January, 1946, pp. 203-12.

[*In the following essay Adkins regards Beaumont and Fletcher's treatment of the commons in* Philaster *as indicative of the "shifting political current" in the Jacobean period.*]

The aristocratic sympathies of Francis Beaumont and John Fletcher are a commonplace of criticism—sympathies de-

Title page of the 1620 edition of Philaster.

rived naturally from their gentle birth and fostered by the demands of a drama which under royal patronage was becoming increasingly restricted in subject-matter and audience. The purpose of this paper is not to dispute the dictum but to analyze *Philaster* as an exception which apparently has gone unnoticed, and to demonstrate that, even as an exception, the play is significant in showing the direction of the political winds in early seventeenth-century England.

In what may be called the political aspect of the plot of *Philaster,* the citizens are the dominant force. They are the means by which the usurping king of Sicily is deposed, the interloper Pharamond shipped back to Spain, and Philaster restored to his rightful inheritance. The result is not achieved by a *tour de force* at the end. Their importance is announced in the first scene and referred to at occasional intervals; the audience is not only not allowed to forget them, but is compelled to think of them as being an integral part of a well planned play.

In the opening conversation between two courtiers, Dion and Cleremont, the potency of the people's will is suggested. The Spanish prince Pharamond, says Dion, will find it difficult, even through marriage with Princess Arethusa, to keep the crown of Sicily, "the right Heir . . . living, and living so vertuously, especially the people admiring the bravery of his mind, and lamenting his injuries."

The reigning king is, in intention, a king by divine right. Though not unaware that the hydra-headed public must be appeased (as witness the rumor, reported by Dion, that "the King labours to bring in the power of a Foreign Nation to aw his own with"), he does not willingly concede their importance. In publicly proclaiming Pharamond his heir, his major purpose, he tells Pharamond, is

>   to confirm
> The Nobles, and the Gentry of these Kingdoms,
> By oath to your succession.

Indeed, his lofty conception of a king's estate, which brooks no demur even from noble or gentry, would do credit to James himself. In substance, his grandiose speeches claim for him the same illimitable, if vague, authority which James claimed in theory. To him apparently, as to James, "royal authority was . . . a mystery, not to be explained or argued about, but to be piously accepted with a 'mystical reverence.'" In the hunting scene in Act IV, when his demand that the lost Arethusa be found and brought to him proves futile, he exclaims in anger:

>   what am I not your King?
> If I, then am I not to be obeyed?

And he swells to rhetoric when he has to repeat his demand:

>   'tis the King
> Will have it so, whose breath can still the winds,
> Uncloud the Sun, charm down the swelling Sea,
> And stop the Flouds of Heaven.

Stripped of its bombast, it is a claim to absolute power, not different in essence from that claimed by James. One who exercises authority by divine right is only a step from godhood, as James himself avowed [in "A Speach to the Lords and Commons of the Parliament at White-Hallon Wednesday the XXI of March. Anno 1609"]:

> For Kings are not onely GODS Lieutenants vpon earth, and sit vpon GODS throne, but euen by GOD himselfe they are called Gods. . . . In the Scriptures Kings are called Gods, and so their power after a certaine relation compared to the Diuine power. . . . Kings are iustly called Gods, for that they exercise a manner or resemblance of Diuine power vpon earth: For if you wil consider the Attributes to God, you shall see how they agree in the person of a King.

It is usual enough, of course, that a usurping monarch should have to yield, finally, to the rightful heir. What is surprising about this play is that the citizens are made the agents of justice. In Shakespeare's *Richard II,* for example, though frequent lip service is paid to "the people," they do not enter as characters; the destiny of Richard, and of England, is clearly in the hands of the masterful Bolingbroke and the supporting barons. It is true that in *Philaster* the real instigators of the revolt are Dion and Cleremont, but the courtiers' part is unobtrusive; it is mentioned in only two places, and there not prominently. The citizens are given the dominant role. In fact, to interpret for the audience the mood and temper of the people seems to be Dion's main function in the political plot. Upon the king's threat to imprison Philaster, Dion murmurs, ". . . you dare not for the people." He promises Philaster that he will

> conjure up
> The rods of vengeance, the abused people,

who shall restore the kingdom to its rightful owner.

In Act III, when Megra's slander against Arethusa has received general acceptance in the court, Dion and Cleremont, no longer bound by loyalty to Arethusa or desirous of her union with Philaster, sigh impatiently for Philaster to rise and claim his own, saying that "the Gentry do await it, and the people." Philaster entering at this juncture, they urge revolt upon him in the name of "the Nobles, and the people." The importance of the people as a political force is further shown when Philaster is carried off to prison for his attack upon Arethusa in anger at her supposed misconduct: Cleremont is worried lest "this action lose . . . *Philaster* the hearts of the people."

It does not. In Act V the instigation to rebellion bears fruit. The citizens take Pharamond prisoner and rise in a mutiny which threatens the king as well. That mighty sovereign, who a moment before was angrily denouncing the newly reunited Philaster and Arethusa, now pleads with Philaster in a frenzy of fear:

> Calm the people,
> And be what you were born to: take your love,
> And with her my repentance, and my wishes,
> And all my prayers, by the gods my heart speaks this:
> And if the least fall from me not perform'd,
> May I be struck with Thunder.

In plot alone the part of the citizens is given equal importance with the conventional devices by which the romantic story is developed to its happy ending. But from an analysis of the citizens themselves and their relation to other characters, emerge some interesting facts—not to say discrepancies—which make the indisputable importance of "the people" all the more surprising. The courtiers who are quietly responsible for the rebellion seem to have the usual aristocratic contempt for the character and the intelligence of the common people. In the opening scene of the play Dion speaks of the "multitude . . . that seldom know any thing but their own opinions," a line which the context suggests is intended to characterize them as ignorant, uninformed, emotionally unstable. It is true that in Act V Dion apostrophizes them as "brave followers," as "fine dear Country-men," but the terms are an expression of his delight at their revolt. His real opinion is voiced in a comment to Cleremont:

> Well my dear Country-men, what ye lack, if you continue and fall not back upon the first broken shin, I'le have you chronicled, . . . prais'd, and sung in Sonnets, and bath'd in new brave Ballads, that all tongues shall troule you in *Saecula Saeculorum* my kind Can-carriers.

Another Lord also fears their cowardice and instability of purpose:

> What if a toy take 'em i'th' heels now, and they run
> all away, and cry the Devil take the hindmost?

The citizens, in fact, except for the serious business of securing the kingdom, are made objects of more or less kindly ridicule. They display the rough bawdy humor found in many plays of the middle class. And their Captain, who is their chief spokesman, comports himself with a bluff heartiness reminiscent of Simon Eyre in [Thomas Dekker's] *The Shoemaker's Holiday*. A seventeenth-century aristocratic audience would no doubt have found in him a target for pleasantly condescending mirth.

An important contrast in attitude, however, is afforded by Philaster, who treats the citizens with grave respect. His manner towards them is restrained, moderate, sincere. It has none of the contemptuous implications of the courtiers'; none of the bombast of the king's; nothing suggesting the weakness of character that distinguishes him in the purely romantic plot. When he has rescued Pharamond and calmed the popular frenzy, he dismisses the citizens with quiet courtesy and firmness:

> Good my friends go to your houses and by me have
>   your pardons, and my love,
> And know there shall be nothing in my power
> You may deserve, but you shall have your wishes.
> To give you more thanks were to flatter you,
> Continue still your love, and for an earnest
> Drink this.

So, one might conclude, the relations between sovereign and subject should be. One can almost imagine Queen Elizabeth, in diplomatic mood, tactfully and shrewdly ensuring the loyalty of the middle class, which contributed so largely to Tudor strength. And the citizens go as requested, praising Philaster and rejoicing in their good fortune. The political action ends here. The remainder of the play disposes of various unfinished business in the romantic plot. It is an impressive ending for the citizens, demonstrating their power and, as well, the desirable relationship between a ruler and his people.

Such, it seems to me, must be the impression left by the citizens if the play is read carefully. One can grant that *Philaster* is primarily romantic in interest, its major appeal directed to the fashionable audiences in the Jacobean theatres; can recognize that the outspoken criticism of the king is, after all, criticism of a usurper (and, as such, to be welcomed by a lawfully reigning king); must admit that the courtiers are really, albeit unobtrusively, responsible for the rebellion and that they are contemptuous of the human agents they use to consummate it—yet the fact remains that in the political action of the play the citizens are the decisive force. Their importance is not only admitted; it is made emphatic. And that fact has at least the significance of a straw in the wind. The play ends with pious moralizing of the king:

Let Princes learn
By this to rule the passions of their blood,
For what Heaven wills, can never be withstood.

He finds it expedient to attribute certain events to Heaven, but even a seventeenth-century audience must have seen that Heaven had appointed the citizens as its agents. In the first of the play no king could have been more plainly an absolute monarch in intention; in the last none could be more clearly amenable to the popular will. It was the seventeenth-century Puritans that about forty years after the first performance of *Philaster* were to make a practical demonstration of popular sovereignty.

This recognition of the power of the people and the fallibility of the sovereign appears to be Beaumont's rather than Fletcher's. In the passages quoted the significant speeches are commonly attributed to Beaumont. Seven other plays in which the relation of ruler and subject is mentioned seem to offer confirmation that Fletcher's views were uncompromisingly royalist. Of one, *A King and No King,* Beaumont and Fletcher are joint authors. In this play there is little of political implication, since the personal rather than the kingly qualities of Arbaces are stressed, and since, after some talk of conquest at the beginning, it is largely a story of romantic love. But in Act II, as the king returns triumphantly to his own country, the citizens (London citizens, need it be said?) turn out to greet him. Everything he says to them, though egotistical, is conciliatory in tone. His first speech is particularly significant:

I thank you all, now are my joyes at full, when I behold you safe, my loving Subjects; by you I grow, 'tis your united love that lifts me to this height: all the account that I can render you for all the love you have bestowed on me, all your expences to maintain my war, is but a little word, you will imagine 'tis slender paiment, yet 'tis such a word, as is not to be bought but with your bloods, 'tis Peace.

The citizens, though obviously intended to offer comic entertainment, are shown as at least aware that their money has paid for the war; they are perhaps even a little complacent over their value in the kingdom.

Of *Valentinian, The Loyal Subject,* and *The Island Princess* Fletcher is sole author. Valentinian talks grandiosely of himself as absolute in power, above the reproaches of men and even of gods, who "as they make me most, they mean me happiest." This exalted conception is also held by his loyal follower Aecius, who declares that

Majesty is made to be obeyed,
And not to be inquired into.

In *The Island Princess* there is the same conception of royalty, stated by the Princess herself:

though I be
A Princess, and by that Prerogative stand free
From the poor malice of opinion,
And no ways bound to render up my actions,
Because no power above me can examine me.

In *The Loyal Subject,* in spite of the criticism of the Duke made by Theodore and the soldiers, the royalist view is maintained by the uncritical loyalty of Archas throughout and by Theodore's retraction at the end. There is no doubt as to Fletcher's intention to uphold royalty at any cost; he wants us to think of the Duke as a noble, generous ruler, temporarily misled by false counsel.

In three plays of divided authorship the passages which deal with the power of the citizens or the obligations of the sovereign are not from Fletcher's hand. Field is considered responsible for the scene in *The Bloody Brother* in which Rollo, Duke of Normandy, has to ingratiate himself with the citizens, lest they learn that he murdered his brother wantonly and not in self-defense, as he claims. To Jonson is attributed the nobleman's comment that a prince may send troublesome nobles to the block, but that when they (kings) "once grow formidable to their Clowns, and Coblers, ware then, guard themselves." In *Thierry and Theodoret* two passages which suggest that kings have an obligation to their subjects and are under some necessity of restraint, are attributed to Massinger. Believed to be also by Massinger is a passage in *The False One* which, though it clearly shows a subject's loyalty, is characterized by a blunt independence, an insistence on the right of free opinion.

That Fletcher's attitude is thoroughly royalist seems clear from the evidence of these six plays, as well as of the two in which he had a slight share with Beaumont. *Valentinian,* the play in which blind loyalty is most stressed, is by Fletcher alone. And no passage which lays strong emphasis upon a king's obligation to his subjects can certainly be attributed to Fletcher.

And what of Beaumont? Are we to conclude that he had love and admiration for the common people, the London citizens? The evidence of his plays seems to warrant no such inference. The good-natured tolerance of the middle class shown in *The Knight of the Burning Pestle* is far removed from positive expression of approval, and is doubtless to be explained on the basis of temperament rather than of social conviction. My belief is that Beaumont, consciously, was a royalist, though, unlike historical dramatists, he did not have to face the issue squarely even in his plays, since they are romantic in scene and story, far removed from the conflicts between James and his subjects. As Wilhelm Creizenach points out [in *The English Drama in the Age of Shakespeare,* 1916], the attitude of submissive loyalty is particularly noticeable in plays based on English history. But to further statements— ". . . not one among the dramatists appears to doubt that the duty of the subjects lies in submission, and that kings are responsible to God alone for the manner in which they rule"; "it goes without saying that the downtrodden multitude is never allowed the right to revolt against bad government"—I must at least raise the question of exception. I believe that Beaumont, whether knowing or caring about the implications in his plays, is giving evidence of the changing temper of the English people. He must have been aware of Elizabeth's fear of the Puritans as a political force, young though he was when she died. And he could hardly have failed to be aware, when *Philaster* (1608/ 1610) and *A King and No King* (1611) were acted, of the frequent clashes between James and the Puritans, James and Parliament. It is possible, if we accept 1609 or 1610 as the date of its composition, that *Philaster* had its inception at a time when James himself temporarily relaxed his extreme claims. Though James angrily dissolved his first Parliament in February, 1611, "determined henceforth to carry on affairs free from the vexatious cavilling of a Parliament [G. M. Trevelyan, *England under the Stuarts,* 1914], the dissolution itself was the unhappy outcome of earlier, and unsuccessful, attempts at compromise. In both 1609 and 1610 he had adopted a conciliatory attitude. One reason was his desperate need of money. Another was the resentment in the House of Commons over James Cowell's *The Interpreter,* which asserted that the King of England was an absolute king, and therefore had plenary legislative power. Since no book could be printed without a license, every book treating of politics seemed to have the sanction of the state, and the Commons was determined to defeat this apparent attack upon its prerogative. *The Interpreter* was denounced by the House in 1610, and shortly thereafter James suppressed it by royal proclamation. The year before, however, he had disclaimed it publicly. Early in 1609 he sent a message to Parliament by the Earl of Salisbury, then lord treasurer, acknowledging that "he had noe power to make laws of himselfe, or to exact any subsidies without the consent of his 3 estates," and even that the crown had been set on his head by the common law. His own later speech, in March, struck the same conciliatory note, mainly in his emphasis upon the important distinction between the powers possessed by the king in theory and those he found it judicious to exercise in practice. The Parliamentary victory was far in the future—so far, in fact, that many Royalists failed to see the storm gathering upon the distant horizon—but even then to acute observers the winds of change were blowing. It seems not implausible to number Francis Beaumont among those observers, and to see in *Philaster* a recognition, however slight, of the shifting political current.

Harold S. Wilson   (essay date 1951)

SOURCE: *"Philaster* and *Cymbeline,"* in *English Institute Essays, 1951,* edited by Alan S. Downer, Columbia University Press, 1952, pp. 146-67.

[*In the essay below, Wilson counters assertions by previous critics that Shakespeare's* Cymbeline *was modeled after* Philaster. *He accounts for similarities between the plays by stressing that the "situations of the romantic plays of Shakespeare and Beaumont and Fletcher are the materials of romance which they and every other playwright of their time used in common."*]

At the beginning of the present century Professor A. H. Thorndike advanced two notable contentions in his book *The Influence of Beaumont and Fletcher on Shakespeare*

[1901]. The first was that Beaumont and Fletcher had introduced a new dramatic genre to the Jacobean stage during the first decade of the seventeenth century, the genre of the heroic romance, with such plays as *Philaster, The Maid's Tragedy,* and *A King and No King*. This contention has scarcely been challenged since he so ably presented it, and certainly not successfully challenged. His second contention, however—that Shakespeare followed the fashion set by Beaumont and Fletcher in writing *Cymbeline, The Winter's Tale,* and *The Tempest*—has proved more controversial, though this contention still carries enough weight to have gained the notice of Granville-Barker [in his *Prefaces to Shakespeare, Second Series,* 1935] and to have been recently endorsed, with some qualifications, by critics of the distinction of Una Ellis-Fermor [in her *Jacobean Drama,* 1936] and E. M. W. Tillyard [in his *Shakespeare's Last Plays,* 1938]. I should like to re-examine Professor Thorndike's second contention in this paper, with particular reference to the analogy he draws between *Philaster* and *Cymbeline*.

First, however, we should notice, for the sake of dismissing them, certain gratuitous assumptions which color Professor Thorndike's argument and which have also commended themselves to various later writers. There is the assumption that Shakespeare's latest plays represent a diminution of Shakespeare's dramatic powers, an assumption based upon the feeling that *Cymbeline* and the plays which followed it are somehow inferior to *Antony and Cleopatra* and the other tragedies, an assumption common to Professor Thorndike and Lytton Strachey [in his *Books and Characters,* 1922], but incapable of real demonstration, since the last plays are very different in form and purpose from the great tragedies. Then there is the view (to quote Professor Thorndike) "that Shakspere almost never invented dramatic types. In his earliest plays he was a versatile imitator of current forms, and in his later work he was constantly adapting dramatic types used by other men." Shakespeare, it would seem, lacked the ability, so conspicuous in Beaumont and Fletcher, to mold his own dramatic form. Fortunately, he was clever at imitation and quick to follow the changing fashions set by others. If the Jacobean audiences demanded romances of the Beaumont and Fletcher cut, Shakespeare was their humble servant.

This part of Professor Thorndike's hypothesis is, of course, designed to bolster his main argument that *Cymbeline* is imitated from *Philaster* and Shakespeare's last group of plays from the Beaumont and Fletcher type of romance. These assumptions are unsupported by any real examination of the development of Shakespeare's dramatic form. It is simply asserted that Shakespeare was an "adapter and transformer" of other men's work, and we are expected to take this extraordinary assertion as self-evident.

Finally, there is the circumstance, fortunate for Professor Thorndike's argument, that it has not proved possible to establish by external evidence whether *Philaster* preceded *Cymbeline* or *Cymbeline* preceded *Philaster*. Both plays belong to the period 1608-1610; that is all we may safely assert about their dating. Professor Thorndike, of course, thinks it extremely likely that *Philaster* came first; but if

John Dryden on Beaumont and Fletcher:

Beaumont and Fletcher, . . . had, with the advantage of Shakespeare's wit, which was their precedent, great natural gifts, improved by study: Beaumont especially being so accurate a judge of plays, that Ben Johnson, while he lived, submitted all his writings to his censure, and, 'tis thought, used his judgment in correcting, if not contriving, all his plots. What value he had for him, appears by the verses he writ to him; and therefore I need speak no farther of it. The first play that brought Fletcher and him in esteem was their *Philaster*: for before that, they had written two or three very unsuccessfully, as the like is reported of Ben Johnson, before he writ *Every Man in his Humour*. Their plots were generally more regular than Shakespeare's, especially those which were made before Beaumont's death; and they understood and imitated the conversation of gentlemen much better; whose wild debaucheries, and quickness of wit in repartees, no poet can ever paint as they have done. Humour, which Ben Johnson derived from particular persons, they made it not their business to describe: they represented all the passions very lively, but above all, love. I am apt to believe the English language in them arrived to its highest perfection; what words have since been taken in, are rather superfluous than ornamental. Their plays are now the most pleasant and frequent entertainments of the stage; two of theirs being acted through the year for one of Shakespeare's or Johnson's: the reason is, because there is a certain gaiety in their comedies, and pathos in their more serious plays, which suits generally with all men's humours. Shakespeare's language is likewise a little obsolete, and Ben Johnson's wit comes short of theirs.

John Dryden, in his An Essay of Dramatic Poesy, *1668.*

some unlooked-for evidence should one day turn up to show that *Cymbeline* preceded *Philaster,* his hypothesis would be in a sad plight.

Yet although Professor Thorndike's case depends in some measure upon the question of dating and the apparatus of critical assumption that we are agreed, I hope, to dismiss as irrelevant or worse, his argument does not rest simply upon these insubstantial grounds. He bases his contention chiefly upon his demonstration that Beaumont and Fletcher did introduce a new type of dramatic romance to the Jacobean stage during the first decade of the seventeenth century, a type of play different from anything Shakespeare had written before *Cymbeline,* and upon a detailed analysis of the plot, characterization, style, and stage effects of *Philaster* and *Cymbeline* designed to show that the resemblances between these two plays cannot be accidental. To quote his summing up,

there are enough specific similarities to make it very probable that one play was directly suggested by the other. When we remember that both plays were written at nearly the same time, for the same company, and by dramatists who must have been acquainted, the probability approaches certainty. . . . It is not only prac-

tically certain that *Philaster* was written for the King's Men while Shakespere was still writing for that company; it is also probable that it was written before *Cymbeline*. In that case we could not escape the conclusion that Shakespere was indebted to *Philaster.*

Professor Thorndike assumes, with little further argument, that *The Winter's Tale* and *The Tempest* belong to the same type as *Cymbeline* and must therefore reflect a less specific, but still definite, influence of Beaumont and Fletcher. With the latter suggestion we need not much concern ourselves, for the weight of Professor Thorndike's argument rests upon the analogy he traces between *Philaster* and *Cymbeline*. We shall accordingly treat that analogy as providing the only substantial ground of his conclusions.

Though it is a great commonplace, it may be remarked by way of preliminary that analogies are often misleading. In literary criticism, especially, they are dangerous tools. With something less than metaphysical ingenuity, one may draw analogies, more or less striking, between Sophocles' Queen Jocasta and the Wife of Bath or between *Paradise Lost* and *Tom Jones;* and what has actually been done with Shakespeare's *Tempest* in this line almost passes belief. By a tactful selection of criteria, it would not be too difficult to argue that both *Cymbeline* and *Philaster* are imitated from Robert Greene's *James IV* or from *King Lear*. The analogy with *Lear,* to take but one example from those here suggested, might go like this: Cymbeline is Lear, with one ungrateful daughter instead of three. He is also the father of Arethusa. Iachimo is Edmund, turning his attentions upon Cordelia and Edgar, who are at once Imogen and Posthumus, Arethusa and Philaster. And surely Belarius is an unmistakable Kent, a little damaged by his long exile, whose *alter ego* is Bellario's father, the Lord Dion. So we might go on; but we have all played this game and need not further remind ourselves that analogy hunting comes easy to an irresponsible fancy.

Part of the trouble with Professor Thorndike's analogy between *Philaster* and *Cymbeline* is the highly selective nature of his criteria for comparison and a certain ambiguity about the criteria themselves. This is how Professor Thorndike compares the plots of the two plays:

The historical narrative and the Italian expedition of Posthumus have no parallels in *Philaster,* and most of the Megra affair and the rising of the mob in *Philaster* have no parallels in *Cymbeline*. In the main, however, the plots are strikingly similar.

Imogen, heiress to the throne, is destined by her royal father to marry his boorish step-son, Cloten; but she is wedded to a noble youth, Leonatus Posthumus. Arethusa, only daughter of the King of Calabria, is likewise destined by her father to marry the boorish Spanish prince, Pharamond, but she is in love with Philaster the rightful heir. Leonatus is favorably contrasted by the courtiers with Cloten, and so Philaster is contrasted with Pharamond. Both Leonatus and Philaster are driven from court by the royal fathers. As he is leaving Arethusa's apartments, Philaster has an encounter with Pharamond, and as Leonatus is leaving Imogen, he has an encounter with Cloten. In the absence of Leonatus,

Iachimo tries to seduce Imogen, and Pharamond makes similar proposals to Arethusa. Both are repulsed. Iachimo slanders Imogen to Leonatus, and Arethusa is falsely accused to Philaster by Dion. Imogen is brought to despair by Leonatus' letter charging her with unfaithfulness, and Arethusa is likewise in anguish when similarly upbraided to the face by Philaster. Each lover has a passionate soliloquy in which he denounces his mistress and all womankind. Imogen leaves the court in disguise to seek Leonatus and, after dismissing Pisanio, loses her way; and Arethusa parts from the hunting party to wander "O'er mountains, through brambles, pits, and floods." Both, because falsely slandered, wish to die. Each king is very much disturbed at his daughter's absence. Cymbeline accuses Pisanio of knowing where she is, and so Calabria accuses Dion. Arethusa is wounded by Philaster, and Imogen is struck down by Leonatus. Finally the disentanglements of the two plots are made in similar ways. In *Philaster,* Bellario explains that in spite of her page's clothes she is a woman, and Megra confesses that she has falsely slandered Arethusa. In *Cymbeline,* Imogen explains and Iachimo confesses. In *Philaster,* all are forgiven, even Megra and Pharamond; so in *Cymbeline* Iachimo is pardoned; and in each play the lovers are happily united under the king's favor.

These parallels indicate a close similarity between the two plots, yet after all the similarity does not lie so much in the stories as in the situations. The basis of the Imogen story is probably the ninth novel of the second day in the Decamerone. This story, the story of Iachimo's trick, forms no part of *Philaster.* To this Iachimo-Imogen story, however, Shakspere added a dozen or so situations which are almost exact counterparts of situations in *Philaster.*

But a group of dramatic "situations" do not constitute a dramatic action. The situation of Philaster in the opening of his play roughly corresponds to the situation of Hamlet; the situation of Bellario approximates that of Shakespeare's Julia and Viola; and we might easily multiply similar parallels from *Much Ado* and other of the earlier Shakespearean comedies. But this does not mean that the plot of *Philaster* derives in any part from Shakespeare. The situations of the romantic plays of Shakespeare and of Beaumont and Fletcher are the materials of romance which they and every other playwright of their time used in common. To select certain stock romance situations from two plays like *Philaster* and *Cymbeline* and to conclude from this that one play must be imitated from the other is like comparing, let us say, the David of Verocchio and the Statue of Liberty and concluding that because they contain similar materials the one must be imitated from the other.

By means of this innocent confusion between "plot" and "situation," Professor Thorndike has, in fact, largely avoided comparing the conduct of the action in the two plays. Had he done so with any care, he must surely have concluded that they were very different.

Let us notice some of these differences. The plot of *Cymbeline* is a double plot in this sense: it is the story of what happened to Imogen and of what happened to her brothers. The two stories are not parallel and do not grow out of each other; each story has a separate exposition, a sep-

arate climax, and a distinct culmination. After we have followed Imogen's story for two whole acts, she wanders into her brothers' story by accident, and from then on the two stories are cleverly sandwiched together to produce a finely complicated climax.

The plot of *Philaster* is nothing like this. From beginning to end it is one story, the story of what happened to Philaster, and the fates of Arethusa and Bellario-Euphrasia are parallel and contrasted plot elements that depend upon Philaster's fate and support his story. The controlling idea of *Philaster,* again, has nothing to do with Shakespeare's *Cymbeline,* but rather finds its proper parallel in Fletcher's own *Faithful Shepherdess*. There we find disinterested love represented in Clorin; normal love in the pairs of Amoret and Perigot, Alexis and the reformed Chloe, Daphnis and the reformed Amarillis; lust in the Sullen Shepherd and the unregenerate Amarillis and Chloe. So in *Philaster,* Bellario-Euphrasia stands for disinterested love, Philaster and Arethusa for normal love, Megra and Pharamond for lust.

The main sources of *Cymbeline* are clear enough. Shakespeare retells, whether at first or second hand, the story of the ninth novel of the second day in Boccaccio's *Decameron* and adds certain materials from [Raphael Holinshed's *Chronicles of England, Scotland and Ireland*] for his framework and second plot. The sources of *Philaster* are by no means so clear (though no scholar likes to admit that the authors may have made up the story themselves); but it is at least clear that *Philaster* is not derived from Boccaccio or Holinshed. Shakespeare must have had a fine time with his sources if he had to watch the plot of *Philaster* constantly while he was juggling with Boccaccio and Holinshed. According to Professor Thorndike, Shakespeare would have had to turn from Boccaccio's story to elaborate traits and situations for Imogen suggested by the two characters of Arethusa and Bellario; and in modeling his Posthumus upon Philaster he must surely have felt embarrassed to recognize in Philaster traits of his own Hamlet.

But the really essential and decisive difference between the two plots lies in Shakespeare's technique of preparation as distinguished from the Beaumont and Fletcher technique of surprise. [Samuel Taylor Coleridge in his "Characteristics of Shakespeare"] long ago pointed it out: "Expectation in preference to surprize. . . . As the feeling with which we startle at a shooting star, compared with that of watching the sunrise at the pre-established moment, such and so low is surprize compared with expectation."

In *Cymbeline* we are prepared to grasp the implications of each situation as it arises, as the actors themselves are not. The effect of such preparation is cumulative. We first see Posthumus's protestation of fidelity to Imogen:

> I will remain
> The loyal'st husband that did e'er plight troth.

We then learn of the Queen's poison plot, but neither the Queen, who gives the poison to Pisanio, Pisanio, who gives it to Imogen, nor Imogen, who ultimately takes it, knows what we learn from Cornelius, that it is actually but a sleeping potion. We witness the wager scene, learn all the circumstances of Iachimo's attempt, and see his successful ruse of concealment in Imogen's chamber whereby he betrays both Imogen and Posthumus. From then on (II, iii) we are prepared to observe the mounting irony of the succeeding action. Cloten comes in the morning with his musicians to serenade Imogen, and we have the comic moment of his emphatic rejection. But the comedy is sharply interrupted by Imogen's discovery of the loss of her bracelet; and her premonitory

> I hope it be not gone to tell my lord
> That I kiss ought but he

reminds us poignantly that the consequences are likely to be far worse than even she knows. With all her high courage, she has no chance of avoiding the snare laid for her; we have seen it, but she has not.

The ensuing scenes gradually increase the sense of horror impending and closing in on its victim. We see Pisanio receive his instructions from Posthumus to kill Imogen on the way to Milford Haven; and though we are slightly reassured by Pisanio's

> I am ignorant in what I am commanded,

Imogen's rapturous outburst,

> O, for a horse with wings! Hear'st thou, Pisanio?
> He is at Milford Haven!

marks for us the beginning of her deepest pathos. The moment of her realization that she has been betrayed is supported for us by her impassioned denial and appeal to Pisanio, whose device of disguising her as a page brings about the reunion with her brothers at the cave of Belarius. Here, for a moment the idyllic setting and the gentleness of her welcome bring a lull in Imogen's misfortunes; but the other shadow of the plot against her, set in motion by Pisanio's parting gift of the Queen's poison, soon closes in again. The sleeping Imogen is placed beside the headless body of Cloten, and she wakens, but dimly realizing her surroundings at first, as she finds the corpse half-concealed with flowers, and the flowers soaked in blood; then the dawning realization that there is no head, that the clothes, the very limbs seem to be her husband's, that Pisanio, as she thinks, has murdered him.

We know better; but it is not this knowledge that matters at the moment, it is Imogen's suffering. And all that separates it from the pathos of Lear's attempts to revive the dead Cordelia is that we are spared the recognition of the inevitability of it all. It comes close to tragedy, so close that in the reunion of Imogen and Posthumus at the end there can be no rejoicing, but only tenderness and tears. It is tragedy subdued to a gentler, a sentimental key, with a consequent loss of intensity. But it is by no means the Beaumont and Fletcher vein of sentimentality.

The opening situation of *Philaster* shows the hero in love with the Princess Arethusa, whose father intends to marry her to the cowardly Pharamond. Philaster presents his devoted page Bellario to Arethusa as a liaison in forwarding their love. Here is the first major difference in method. Bellario is represented to us as Bellario, a page. We do not learn her proper sex or identity or why she is devoted to Philaster until the very end; so complete is her disguise that her own father, Dion, does not recognize her; indeed, he never gives his daughter a thought, beyond casually mentioning near the beginning of the play (I, i, 333-35) that she has gone on a pilgrimage. We witness Imogen's disguise as a page and fully understand the circumstances of it. All the time she is disguised, our awareness of her identity allows us to understand not merely her actions but also her feelings, and this deepens the pathos of her predicament, especially in the denouement. There is no surprise and no trick about Imogen's disguise; the intention is to let us see all the springs of her actions and to feel the full significance for her of each following situation as it arises.

Bellario's situation actually offers considerable psychological possibilities, but they are deliberately ignored. Bellario loves Philaster and must act as his representative with the woman he loves, who (unlike Viola with the Duke and Olivia [in Shakespeare's *Twelfth Night*]) also loves him. Furthermore, Bellario is falsely accused of illicit relations with Arethusa, and the man Bellario loves believes the calumny. Philaster unhesitatingly takes the word of Megra and the nobles against Arethusa, whom he loves, and the page, whose single-hearted devotion to himself he has already remarked. When he passionately accuses Bellario face to face, she sadly protests her innocence and her devotion to Philaster; but neither of them seeks an explanation of the misunderstanding, and Philaster's suspicions are but lulled, to rouse with new welcome when he finds Bellario bending over the fainting Arethusa in the hunting scene. He dismisses Bellario (though one might expect a man of such strong feelings to direct his first violence against her; as usual, she seeks no explanation or vindication, but sadly departs), and Philaster exhorts Arethusa to kill him. Since she declines, he wounds her. Philaster, himself wounded by the countryman who intervenes to protect Arethusa, then comes upon Bellario sleeping from exhaustion and wounds her as she lies asleep with this remarkable explanation:

> Hark! I am pursued. You gods,
> I'll take this offer'd means of my escape:
> They have no mark to know me but my blood,
> If she [i.e., Arethusa] be true; if false, let mischief light
> On all the world at once! Sword, print my wounds
> Upon this sleeping boy! I ha' none, I think,
> Are mortal, nor would I lay greater on thee.

The next instant Philaster repents what is surely the most astonishing lapse in any hero of Jacobean romance (though no comment is made upon it anywhere in the play) and urges Bellario to lay the blame for wounding Arethusa upon him, which she, of course, fails to do, taking it upon herself to protect him; then he crawls out of the bushes, where he has impulsively hidden, and assumes it himself, and both of them are arrested.

All of this is, of course, the most evident artifice, and we are not to pause and ask why Bellario and Arethusa and Philaster act at any particular moment as they do. The action is full of excitement, swift turns, and surprises; logical motivation and consistency of character are neglected, that each turn of the plot may be more unexpected than the last.

When the denouement comes, we see the King reconciled to the marriage of Arethusa and Philaster. There has perforce been some preparation for this through Philaster's quelling the popular uprising in his favor and the final discrediting of Pharamond. But the authors have one surprise left. The discredited Megra spitefully renews her accusation of Bellario. The king at once credits Megra and is bent only upon getting a confession from Bellario. He orders the page to be stripped and tortured. Philaster, who must be prevented from spoiling things, is tricked into an oath not to interfere. He offers to kill himself, but no one pays much attention to him. As Bellario is about to be stripped, she is obliged to break her oath (of which we hear now for the first time) and reveal herself as Euphrasia, the Lord Dion's daughter, dedicated to a hopeless love. She assures them that her love is selfless.

> Never, sir, will I
> Marry; it is a thing within my vow;
> But, if I may have leave to serve the princess,
> I shall have hope to live.

She, at least, has been consistent, and her role is the only element in the play which might tempt one to take it seriously. The beautiful lines she earlier speaks to Philaster:

> Alas, my lord, my life is not a thing
> Worthy your noble thoughts! 'tis not a life,
> 'Tis but a piece of childhood thrown away

are of a piece with her modest renunciation at the end; but the picture of a tranquil *ménage-à-trois* with which the play closes is again too much for solemnity. "I, Philaster," says Arethusa majestically,

> Cannot be jealous, though you had a lady
> Drest like a page to serve you; nor will I
> Suspect her living here.—Come, live with me;
> Live free as I do. She that loves my lord,
> Cursed be the wife that hates her!

We might similarly consider the treatment of Arethusa. Her good name is traduced to her lover, as Imogen's is to Posthumus. But even to suggest the comparison is to see at once its absurdity. Arethusa makes a few rhetorical protestations when she is required to act:

> And I (the woful'st maid that ever lived,
> Forced with my hands to bring my lord to death)
> Do by the honour of a virgin swear
> To tell no hours beyond it!

But woeful she is not, unless in the figure she cuts beside the more attractive Bellario, who is obviously the feminine lead. For the most part, Arethusa preserves an inconspicuous calm throughout the tempestuous action to which she is submitted that at least saves her from being altogether ridiculous. Philaster is charming in his way, but he is closer to *opéra bouffe* or even musical comedy than to tragedy. Posthumus is not one of Shakespeare's strong characters. He is necessarily absent from the action during the middle part of the play, and he is built up for the climax by rather artificial means. But he has dignity and force in the difficult wager scene, and in the end he seems a fitting husband for Imogen, which is all that need be required of him. He lacks the volatility of Philaster, and certainly he is not half so much in love with easeful death. But he belongs in a serious play, and the other does not.

The other characters of *Philaster* are little more than conveniences of the plot. The King is a good cardboard tyrant, refreshing in his imperiousness because he always seems to know his own mind—which can hardly be said of Shakespeare's Cymbeline—even when he changes it abruptly as the plot requires. Since neither monarch has any clearly marked character, neither needs to reform in order to accept the culmination of events and preside benevolently at the end. Megra is a stock villainess, "a lascivious lady," like Chloe in *The Faithful Shepherdess,* except that she does not reform; and Pharamond is a stock villain, the cowardly lecher. Beaumont and Fletcher do not run the risk of puzzling their audience—to say nothing of later readers—with the subtler characterization of a Cloten, a bully too dull to know fear. Pharamond is lecherous, boastful, cowardly, and nothing more. The Calabrian lords are a faint and ineffectual chorus, with the prize for fatuity going to Dion, who leads the attempt to turn Philaster from his allegiance to the King by swearing that he has seen Arethusa's misbehavior with the page Bellario.

Thus, to belittle *Philaster* is not, of course, to do it justice. It is not meant to be a study of human pathos or human character, for all the high-pitched emotional tone of the piece, even to the relatively slight extent that *Cymbeline* is. *Philaster* is a lively series of incidents contrived with great ingenuity to provide constant excitement and surprise and to issue agreeably with the recognition and reward of virtue, the dismissal of the wicked in disgrace. And it is nothing more. *Cymbeline* is, by comparison, more old-fashioned in method, more complicated, and altogether more ambitious. At least as ingeniously plotted, it employs an utterly different method in the conduct of the action: preparation of the audience to perceive the dramatic ironies of situation, the pathos of character, the joys and sorrows of reunion; it aims at effecting the gratification of expectancy rather than the shock of surprise. *Cymbeline* admits all kinds of ancient romance conventions and stage devices in which Beaumont and Fletcher were little interested—stately pageants, riddles, masques, the god from the machine. The younger dramatists seem to have regarded such effects as unnecessary. Their new technique in the dramatic romance was actually a remarkable simplification of existing stage conventions. In *Philaster,* apart from the ingenious plotting there is scarcely any conspicuous stage device used save that of disguise—and that in the single example of Bellario. But they carried their economy much further, virtually eliminating character study and stripping the play down to the bare essentials of swift emotional dialogue and clever plot. One might say, if the figure would hold, that *Cymbeline* is a stately and somewhat overloaded Elizabethan matron, bejeweled and brocaded, with filmy laces, ruff, farthingale, and pelisse, old-fashioned and stiff in fashionable Jacobean society, but still imposing; *Philaster* is a court shepherdess under the Stuarts, sophisticated to extreme simplicity and as shallow as her simplicity would make her seem.

Cymbeline has fully as much artifice as *Philaster,* or more, as the foregoing figure would suggest, but it is directed to a more serious end. *Philaster* is written in the middling mood of pure recreation. Its stormy passions, its perils and reverses, are never meant to be taken seriously. It is like a ride on a roller coaster. It is breathless and exciting, and the whole technique is directed to keeping the roller coaster going through its dizzy swerves and plunges and recoveries, until the ride comes to a delicious end with everybody safe and sound and pleased with the fun—and it may be very good fun, if you happen to like it. Some people do not, and denounce it as a fraud or a menace; but this is not fair to the operators of the entertainment. They had no nefarious design upon the art of the drama, but only strove to amuse people and to make some money in the process.

We have now considered the plots and the characters of the two plays and found them to be in important ways unlike. I am enough of an Aristotelian to think that the action of a play is its essence, that the characters tend to take their natures from the nature of the action—if the playwrights know their business, that is, as Shakespeare and Beaumont and Fletcher undoubtedly do. The characters of a play like *Cymbeline* are not extracted from suggestions in someone else's play and "stuck on" to the action as one mounts postage stamps in an album. Rather, the impression of character, however impressive or unimpressive it may be, emerges from the developing action, emerges as we watch the characters act. This impression of individual and recognizable characters is very much stronger and subtler in *Cymbeline* than in *Philaster*; and so it is not likely that any of the characters of *Cymbeline* is "imitated," in any meaningful sense, from the characters of *Philaster*.

It remains to speak of Professor Thorndike's two other criteria, the "style" (or, more precisely, the verse) of the two plays, and the "stage effects"; and this we may do rather briefly. If anyone believes that the verse of one play may be at all successfully imitated from the verse of another play which has an essentially different theme and structure, he does not, to my mind, have a very clear conception of what poetry is like. And as for the stage effects, if Shakespeare, who had been writing successful plays for at least fifteen years before Beaumont and Fletcher started, had to be prompted by these juniors in order to avail himself of the pageantry of the court masques in his

last plays, then he must surely have suffered something like that mental crisis and indeed collapse, before or during his famous "last period," of which some critics would fain persuade us. Nothing short of a mental breakdown could explain this extraordinary loss of initiative and command over one of the familiar elements of stage technique that Shakespeare had made skillful use of in plays like *A Midsummer Night's Dream* and indeed most of the earlier comedies. The hypothesis of a mental collapse during Shakespeare's later years might attract us, were it not for the fact of the plays that he wrote during that time. Of course, there are those who say that the Earl of Oxford wrote them for him.

"The question of Beaumont and Fletcher's influence on Shakespeare," writes Dr. Tillyard, "has, in fact, been warehoused rather than disposed of for good." This paper has attempted to take it out of the warehouse and air it a little. But it has also, I hope, a relevance to the more general issue . . . of sources and analogues and what use we should make of them in literary criticism. The principle which this paper tends to support, it seems to me, is that the first and best analogue in considering any author's work is that author's other work. Our first critical obligation is to try to understand the author's whole work in all its interrelations. There are, to be sure, many aids to doing this outside the *corpus* of the author, and the study of his work in relation to its indubitable sources is one of the most important. But we must not confuse sources with partial analogues, nor should we venture to introduce the vague and dubious conception of "literary influence" to explain such partial analogues. For a great author like Shakespeare, we must never lose sight of the aim to comprehend his work as an organic and interrelated whole, growing as a tree grows from a young sapling until it towers above the forest. When we treat some casual or conjectural circumstance—that Beaumont and Fletcher may have written *Philaster* for Shakespeare's company; that this play or others like it enjoyed such popular success that Shakespeare was bound to imitate them—as of decisive critical importance, we not only imply a decided disparagement of Shakespeare's ability; we disregard the vital principle that Shakespeare's dramatic art was a continuous growth. If we would understand *Cymbeline,* or any other play of Shakespeare's, we must consider it primarily in relation to the whole body of his work, in relation to this only indubitable evidence of his artistic growth. And the same holds for Beaumont and Fletcher. The best clue to *Philaster* is not in *Cymbeline* or any other play of Shakespeare, but in the other plays with which Beaumont and Fletcher, those enterprising and estimable collaborators, graced the Jacobean stage.

John F. Danby (essay date 1952)

SOURCE: "Beaumont and Fletcher: Jacobean Absolutists," in *Poets on Fortune's Hill: Studies in Sidney, Shakespeare, Beaumont & Fletcher,* Kennikat Press, 1952, pp. 152-83.

[*In the following essay, Danby explores the ways in which* Philaster *reflects the concerns and tastes of an aristocratic audience.*]

> After all, Beaumont and Fletcher were but an inferior sort of Shakespeares and Sidneys.
>
> C. LAMB, *Specimens of an English Dramatic Poetry*. Note on *Maid's Tragedy*

Charles Lamb's judgment is not likely to be reversed however much the plays of Beaumont and Fletcher are re-read or re-assessed. But something less than justice is done them if the Shakespeare comparison is made prematurely or in the wrong way. In any such comparison they will naturally come out on the wrong side; and they have rarely been read without the motive of comparison in mind. Coleridge, for example, wrote [in his *Lectures on Shakespeare*]:

> The plays of Beaumont and Fletcher are mere agregations without unity; in the Shakespearian drama there is a vitality which grows and evolves itself from within— a key-note which guides and controls the harmonies throughout.

And Lamb [in his note on **The Two Noble Kinsmen**]:

> Fletcher's ideas moved slow; his versification, though sweet, is tedious; it stops every moment; he lays line upon line, making up one after the other, adding image to image so deliberately that we see where they join: Shakespeare mingles everything, he runs line into line, embarrasses sentences and metaphors; before one idea has burst its shell another is hatched and clamours for inclusion.

The more recent reports on their work are in much the same vein. On the question of dramatic workmanship generally Miss Ellis-Fermor [in her *Jacobean Drama,* 1936] repeats Coleridge's charge: Beaumont and Fletcher sacrifice everything to situation and immediate effect. Lamb's criticism of their verse has been made again, in other words, by Mr. T. S. Eliot [in his *Selected Essays*]: imagery in the Beaumont and Fletcher verse amounts merely to dead flowers of speech planted in sand. Neither as dramatists nor as poets do they seem to have the roots that clutch. Yet at the beginning of this century Shakespeare's last plays were commonly regarded as having been strongly influenced by Beaumont and Fletcher. And at any time after the death of James I (Fletcher too died in 1625) something like the following comparisons would be made by the polite and instructed reader:

> When Jonson, Shakespeare, and thyself did sit,
> And sway'd in the triumvirate of Wit,
> Yet what from Jonson's oil and sweat did flow,
> Or what more easy Nature did bestow
> On Shakespeare's gentler muse, in thee full grown
> Their graces both appear; yet so, that none
> Can say, here Nature ends and Art begins;
> But mixt, like th'elements, and born like twins.
> [John Denham, "On Mr. Fletcher's Works"]

Denham need carry no authority, but he is a reminder of the Caroline rating which, as a phenomenon of taste and choice, calls for understanding. There was a time when Beaumont and Fletcher seemed the universal geniuses, combining qualities which avoided on the one hand Jonson's laboured calculation of effect and on the other Shakespeare's merely random happiness:

> Manners and scenes may alter, but not you;
> For yours are not mere humours, gilded strains;
> The fashion lost, your massy sense remains.
> [J. Berkenhead, "On the Happy Collection of Master Fletcher's Works"]

The judgment is no doubt a mental aberration. But it was broadspread in the seventeenth century, typical of a class and a time.

I propose now to look at the position Beaumont and Fletcher occupied in their contemporary world; then, to examine what they actually did in one of their serious plays; finally, bearing in mind their present-day neglect, when practically all the other Jacobeans have had their vogue, to hazard a fresh placing of their work from the point of view of a modern observer.

I

The social positioning of Beaumont and Fletcher has often been noticed. So has the timing of their appearance. The provenance of what they put into their plays has also been commented on. What is most lacking, in their case, would seem to be that which is most needed—the linking of these things significantly, so as to make possible the right groupings and the appropriate comparisons.

Professor A. Harbage [in his *Cavalier Drama*] has pointed to their special position among dramatists of their time:

> In the reign of James a greater number of the writers seem to have been gentlemen by birth, but there is no change in the status of their occupation. Typical of this group was John Fletcher, well-born, and well-nurtured but *déclassé*; he lacked patrimony, his father had died in debt and in royal disfavour. Most dedicatory epistles . . . were suggestive of mendicancy, and could scarcely be written by the gentle according to the strictures of the day. The one true exception to our rule is Francis Beaumont, his father a judge in a family still prospering. But Francis was a younger son. . . .

The best sketch of Bishop Fletcher and son (Harrington only portrays the father) is given by Bishop Goodman, that anxious whitener of sepulchres wherever possible:

> Doctor Fletcher, dean of Peterborough, he was made almoner and Bishop of Bristol . . . he was afterwards preferred to London; and there he married my Lady Baker, a very handsome, beautiful woman. . . . Here many libels were made against him: I remember part of one of them: "We will divide the name of Fletcher; / He, my Lord F.; and she, my Lady Letcher." I think

he had a check from the Queen, and died for sorrow.
His son was a poet to a playhouse.

> [*The Court of King James*]

Bishop Goodman's professional charity was apt to fail when confronted with failure. He obviously regarded the son's career as a fitting appendage to the father's disgrace. Harrington is kinder to the man by including in his contempt most of the courtier-Bishop's contemporaries:

> What shall I say for him? *Non erat hoc hominis vitium sed temporis?*
>
> [*Nugae Antiquae*]

The original judgment of Lamb at the head of this chapter may be more fully understood in a social than in a literary sense (though it has the literary implication too). It is important either way that Beaumont and Fletcher had a Bishop and a Judge for their fathers and not a bricklayer or a small country-tradesman. The Great House, however, was not around them, as it was around Sidney: they were, after all, an inferior sort of Sidneys. The Great House was some distance away behind them, or, as an ambition, some distance in front of them: Beaumont actually did marry well and retire from the stage; Fletcher had to be content with the playhouse and the Mermaid. These he maybe succeeded in converting into something agreeable to the court *élite*—an urban substitute for Wilton and Penshurst.

The precise social placing of Beaumont and Fletcher carried with it specific differences of endowment and interest and intention as compared with those with which the popular dramatist worked. Something more, however, must be added. Beaumont and Fletcher were inferior Sidneys of the second generation. The work done within the Great House itself is different from that work which is based on it (as 'literature') but which is actually done outside its walls by persons whose right of admittance might be a matter for conjecture, for a public that would certainly, in most cases, be excluded. The distinctions are not merely snobbish. The declension is real. In Sidney's day the Great House had been a centre of culture in its own right, independent of the Court. Sidney draws a picture of it in the opening pages of the *Arcadia*—itself a typical achievement of the Great House in literature. There Lord Kalander can comment critically and with sharp detachment on the sillinesses of King Basilius, who, in leaving his palace and shirking his responsibilities, has fallen away from the standards the Great House expected the Palace to uphold. The Great House and its literature (the *Arcadia, The Faerie Queene,* the Pastorals, and the petrarchan sonnet-sequences) belonged to the polite Renaissance and to something consciously European. Its works were to stand comparison with those of Greece and Rome, France and Italy: epics in prose or verse compendiously analysing love and the ideal man. Beaumont and Fletcher take over from this tradition the matter of the Arcadian and pastoral and petrarchan, together with the conscious intention of the Great House to achieve literature—the intention, as it becomes with them in fact, to make the popular drama literary. In their case,

however, the declension has to be reckoned in: a twofold degeneration, what Harrington would see as *vitium hominis et temporis.*

The Jacobean phase can best be seen, as the Victorians saw it, in a sinister light. In both politics and letters the Court asserted itself disastrously, to upset a precarious balance. James's claim to the kingly prerogative was not the attempt to retain something which had been granted Elizabeth. It was a bid for something Elizabeth herself had never pretended to, and which (on the terms maintained by James) had never existed. The structure behind Elizabeth's rule had been a confederation of Great Houses. Her power was merely the exertion in a single person of the reason, the competence, the influence, and the desert upon which this confederation (ideally) based itself. In the person of James the Court usurped the place the Great House had occupied. Thereby what Greville called 'the strong middle wall' was broken. Looking at the disgusting shambles of James's dramatic entertainment for the King of Denmark, Harrington remarked that it was different 'in our Queen's days'. Commenting more widely, a Lord Kalander could have noted almost item by item how James was behaving like Basilius in his dotage. This political depression of the Great House and the values it represented is paralleled in the literary field by James's taking over the Chamberlain's men and making them King's Players, and by his attaching other of the actors' companies to the Queen and the Prince. The influence of the Court seems to have vulgarized both the politics and the literature of the Great House. It coarsened the technique of government and perverted taste.

It is this that makes the timing of Beaumont and Fletcher as important as the placing. The *déclassé* son of the Bishop and the younger son of the Judge are James's unconscious agents. They are capturing the Great House literature for the courtier, writing for adherents of a Stuart king rather than for Tudor aristocrats. Their work, from one point of view, represents a snobbish vulgarization and a sectional narrowing of the great tradition.

In this Beaumont and Fletcher are not alone, nor are they unrespectable. They occupy very much the same social and literary position as Donne. Donne himself was a marginal beneficiary of the Great House tradition, who survived, depressed and now utterly dependent, to write subserviently under the conditions inaugurated by James.

Donne in his *Satyres* can claim rightly:

> With God and with the Muses I conferre.

Or again:

>   On a huge hill,
> Cragged, and steep, Truth stands . . .
> Keep the truth which thou hast found; men do not stand
> In so ill case here, that God with his hand
> Sign'd Kings blanck-charters to kill whom they hate,
> Nor are they Vicars but hangmen to Fate.

This has the tone and independence of Kalander and the Great House. In *The Sunne Rising* (still in the pre-Jacobean period) Donne can also write:

> If her eyes have not blinded thine,
>   Looke, and tomorrow late, tell me,
>   Whether bot th'India's of spice and Myne
>   Be where thou left'st them, or lie here with mee.
> Aske for those Kings whom thou saws'st yesterday,
> And thou shall heare, All here in one bed lay.
>   She is all States, and all Princes, I,
>   Nothing else is.
>   Princes doe but play us; compar'd to this,
>   All honor's mimique; All wealth alchimie.

It is the same Donne that writes the *Satyres* and *Songs and Sonets*. In the *Satyres* he takes his stand on truth and his own independent experience, on a kind of dignity which he feels due both to God and the Muse. In *Songs and Sonets,* in spite of the different content, there is a similar tone. *The Sunne Rising* gets an immediate sanction. It has tenderness, playfulness, impatience, and pride, vigorous courage and tough reasonableness. Its components, matched with hyperbole and conceit, lie well together with each other and with the form in which they are expressed. One feels confident that the poet would put things in right order of priority. Even the final hyperbole is not a lie, or a merely poetic truth. Hyperbole will eventually become one of the main Jacobean vehicles of self-persuasion: here it is the witty stretching of plain sense in order to take in more truth:

> She is all States, and all Princes, I,
>   Nothing else is.

—'She is all the States I care about and am a loyal member of; and I am sole ruler as well as subject in this State, complete servant and complete King. Nothing else is—is important, is as much, is so completely known.'—The 'over'-statement that is presented to a first glance as an extravagance resolves itself, on a second glance, into an interesting exploration of what is generally accepted and acceptable. The effect is carried by the rich ambiguities of 'is', itself capable of meaning everything or nothing: everything if we regard it as saying 'has real Being', nothing if we see it as needing always an extension before it can mean anything; everything and nothing as it means 'is' or 'seems'.

'Is' and 'seems' and the ambiguities playing through them set up a frame that contains what immediately follows—with its almost unnoticeable inversion of what Dr. Richards has called *vehicle* and *tenour*:

> Princes doe but play us; compar'd to this,
>   All honor's mimique; All wealth alchimie.

—Love is both an assertion and a surrender of the will, a resolved belief and a rapture. Rule, honours, and token currency are secondary phenomena, social shadows or derivatives or a language for or an expression of the primary society which two lovers form. None of them can stand in their own right, or can be so immediately known,

as love can, to be more than provisionally true. They are means not ends. Their usurpation of the central position in the world would be a perverse tyranny. They command not belief, but, at the most acquiescence; their claim over us is felt not as a rapture but as coercion. Again the hyperbole is on the surface only: the direction in which it works is towards an interesting exploration of sense.

In all this Donne is in the great tradition of Sidney. He writes as the poet above the need or the desire to sing at doors for meat, as the poet exploring truth and investigating the metaphysic of love: love not as a petrarchan convention but as the key to what conventions are about. Within ten years the tone and truth of Donne's verse change. The 'truth' he was dedicated to in the *Satyres* becomes the fabrication of the compliments he there despised. The mistresses of the *Songs and Sonets* become the patronesses of the *Verse Letters*. There the riches of 'mine' and 'India', 'America' and 'coins', become suddenly concretized to the moneys he desperately needed:

> She that was best and first originall
> Of all fair copies, and the generall
> Steward to Fate; she whose rich eyes, and breast,
> Guilt the West Indies, and perfum'd the East;
> Whose having breath'd in this world, did bestow
> Spice on those Isles, and bade them still smell so,
> And that rich Indie which doth gold interre,
> Is but as single money, coyn'd from her:
> She to whom this world must itself refer,
> As Suburbs, or the Microcosme of her,
> Shee, shee is dead; shee's dead: when thou knowst
>   this,
> Thou knowst how lame a cripple this world is.

Donne here is adding image to image rather than writing poetry; and the imagery is repetitious, commercial, mercenary. What he says, furthermore, is now felt as only poetically true. The hyperboles do not extend sense: they balance permissively on a convention or a fashion of compliment.

Beaumont and Fletcher provoke comparison with the later Donne. *Non erat hoc hominis vitium sed temporis.* They are involved in the same degeneration of a tradition, impelled by similar bread-and-butter needs. It was economic pressure that deflected Donne from the metaphor of *Songs and Sonets* to the conceits of the *Anniversaries*. It was the urge of the younger son to exploit the India of the stage, the desire of the *déclassé* to rehabilitate himself in court circles (the memory and the ambition of the Great House still working in each of them) which drove Beaumont and Fletcher to descend on the popular theatre and wrest it from its popular way to something they could approve of and make their social equals applaud. This of course makes their descent on the playhouse much more consciously a social strategy than in all likelihood it was. There is, however, the fact that two of the earliest plays they wrote were, first, a burlesque of what the popular audience approved, **The Knight of the Burning Pestle** which was not well received, and second, **The Faithful Shepherdess,** a literary pastoral of which Fletcher wrote to one of James's new baronets:

This play was never liked, unless by few
That brought their judgments with 'em.
['To that Noble and true Lover of
Learning, Sir Walter Aston Knight']

Compared with the tradition digested naturally into the drama of Shakespeare the Sidneian world is itself a narrow thing. It is conscious and classical and avoids contacts with what in the *Arcadia* would be called the Helots. The world of Beaumont and Fletcher is still narrower. The difference is that between Penshurst and Wilton and the Court or Blackfriars. The former were European and national at the same time. The latter became something local and sectional.

Beaumont and Fletcher's social affiliations, then, are the same as Donne's; their literary tradition goes back on one side, but on the new Jacobean terms, to the Elizabethan Great House. They operate at a time when the tradition is already degenerating; they are themselves, in fact, prime agents in the degeneration—in the adaptation of platonism and petrarchanism to an inferior end and audience. Their ambition and their strategy can be represented as being a twofold invasion. On the one hand they will capture the popular playhouse, on the other they will gate-crash court society. The Sidneian matter supplied protective colouring for the latter; their dramatic facility ensured success in the former. Their work is brilliantly opportunistic. They are quick to catch and reflect back the lights of their social and literary environment. But they are not to be regarded solely as followers of fashions and tastes. Their social significance in the early Jacobean period goes deeper. They had the power to be formers of attitudes, initiators rather than mimics. They supplied the basis of what will later develop into the Cavalier mentality. In this respect their work can be compared with that of Byron. Later people—not in literature but in actual life—play out Beaumont-and-Fletcherism in their own biographies. Kenelm Digby is one of their heroes in the flesh. The early part of Herbert of Cherbury's autobiography reads like one of their plays.

It is evasive, therefore, to regard their art as merely the creation of a 'fairy world'. Their plays strike roots deep into a real world—the world of their time and of the embryonic Cavalier. Their 'unreality' for us amounts to a criticism of much more than the two dramatists concerned. It is a judgment too of the habits of mind of an actual section of a historical society—a world, in spite of its heritage of charity from the Middle Ages and of instructed reason from the Great House, soon to be confronted with the situation of dictated choice in the midst of civil conflict, a world of radical self-division and clashing absolutes: the world ready to split in every way which Beaumont and Fletcher's serious plays symbolize.

We might turn now to one of these serious plays. Our purpose will be to look for signs of consistency and method. Our leading idea will be, they are not organized, as Shakespeare's plays are, by metaphor—'a key-note which guides and controls the harmonies throughout'—but rather by that which organizes Donne's *Anniversaries,* the hy-

perbole and the conceit. And it is the experience organized by hyperbole and conceit which strikes the roots that clutch Beaumont and Fletcher's time. What these roots were we shall also attempt to say.

II

The central situation in **Philaster** involves three people. Arethusa, the princess, is the only child of the King. Philaster, legitimate heir to part of the Kingdom, is in love with her. Bellario is Philaster's 'page', sent by him to Arethusa to serve as their means of communication. The events of the play are set in motion by the arrival, at the Court, of Pharamond, the Spanish prince, who comes seeking the hand of Arethusa. This touches off, first, the rebellion story: the group of courtiers led by Dion are unwilling for Philaster's legitimate claims to be put on one side, as Philaster himself is too. Secondly, Pharamond's incontinence while at the Court (the reverse side, as in *Songs and Sonets,* of the idealistic petrarchan woman-worship) leads to the calumny which will start rotating the relations between the three in the central triangle. Pharamond is discovered early in his stay with a loose waiting-woman who avoids publicity by accusing Arethusa of similar looseness with Bellario, and thus blackmails the King into silence. This lie is repeated to Philaster by Dion. Dion is intent on Philaster's leading the popular revolt and breaking with Arethusa.

A larger frame is sketchily suggested for the central happenings in the play: the King, like Henry IV, is aware of the guilty means whereby he has come to the throne and is depriving Philaster of his just inheritance. He sees his misfortunes as part of a providential punishment for his sins. Arethusa too feels that providence is at work—in her case, a providence working through romantic love for the restoration of justice.

The retention of this traditional providence supervising the working out of the plot might be significant. It is not what we think of as the typically Beaumont-and-Fletcherian. It seems rather to be a gesture in the direction of something Shakespearian. (Philaster is moved by the spirit of his 'father' as Hamlet was, and the King's guilty conscience is reminiscent of Claudius as well as Henry IV.) Though the King, Arethusa, and the courtiers more than once underline it in their speeches, it might be intended merely as a familiar colouring for the story, the better to insinuate what was essentially new. The references to providence, in any case, belong to the outer shell of the play. The inner core, wherein the novelty consists, and in which the main seriousness of the dramatists is displayed, is the platonic or petrarchan triangle of the lovers. It is the happenings here that I propose to concentrate attention on. These provide almost all the 'situations' and 'dramatic effects' to which Beaumont and Fletcher are said to sacrifice everything: coherence of character, moral integrity, artistic unity.

The basis of the emotional attitudes throughout is a prevailing disposition to wilful belief, belief as an all-or-nothing reaction, consciously directed, an absolute self-commitment. The typical Beaumont and Fletcher situations turn on the divisions that such rival absolutes bring about when the central characters find themselves between two or more of them.

In *Philaster* (as in the plays generally) one of these absolutes is the King. At one point in the play the King's absoluteness is given a satiric or comic turn. The princess Arethusa is lost in the forest and her father is commanding that she shall be found:

> KING. I do command you all, as you are subjects,
>   To show her me! What! am I not your King?
>   If ay, then am I not to be obeyed?
> DION. Yes, if you command things possible and
>   honest.
> KING. Things possible and honest! Hear me, thou,
>   Thou traitor, that do'st confine thy King to
>   things
>   Possible and honest! show her me,
>   Or let me perish if I cover not
>   All Sicily with blood.
> DION. Indeed I cannot,
>   Unless you tell me where she is.
>
>   (IV. ii.)

But brute facts call the King's bluff and he is forced at length to realize his limitations:

>   Alas! What are we Kings!
> Why do ye gods place us above the rest,
> To be served, flattered, and adored, till we
> Believe we hold within our hands your
>   thunder,
> And when we come to try the power we have
> There's not a leaf shakes at our threatenings?
> I have sinned, 'tis true, and here stand to be
>   punished
> Yet would not thus be punished: let me
>   choose
> My way, and lay it on!
> DION. He articles with the gods. Would somebody
>   would draw bonds for the performance of
>   covenants betwixt them.
>
>   (IV. ii.)

We have said that this passage is comic or satiric. To be so definitive is maybe over-precipitate. There seems, rather, to be a mixture, or a confusion, or a wavering between intentions in its treatment. Clearly, however, the scene cannot be claimed for full seriousness. The King is not Lear, and Dion is neither Kent nor the Fool. The significant thing is the way the characters fling themselves into disparate roles, adopting one extreme stance after another with all-or-nothing wilfulness. The roles have nothing in common except the wilfulness behind them. The King will be absolute King, the King will be patient sinner suffering the strokes of the gods. Dion (who could have been made a Lord Kalander or a Kent) remains the debunking commentator on both, not disinterested but uninterested in what he says. Neither Dion

nor the King seem to have anything in common, not even common humanity, nor the common relationship of King and subject. Instead, they both seem to be embodiments, as it were, of the attitudes they voice—attitudes, again, that the romantics would accuse of having no organic interconnection, and between which transition can only be made by violent self-galvanizations of the will.

If the scene itself is not to be taken seriously, the frequent occurrence of such scenes in the plays must be. It is profoundly symptomatic of Beaumont. Though he is not being clearly satirical or comic, and while the total effect is too confused for full artistic seriousness, there is no doubt that seriousness is intended. The point is that Beaumont's mind works like the minds of his characters, and he is involved in quandaries similar to theirs. He lacks the supporting strength of an independent position from which to see with detachment what he is writing about. Sidney had this strength and support through membership of the Great House: his portrait of Basilius, therefore, is steady and unequivocal. Jonson and Shakespeare had the strength and independence of yet another tradition which enabled them to comment on Kingship, in plays like *Sejanus* or *King Lear,* with equal unmistakability. Beaumont has no steady ground to stand on. His attitude to the King, therefore (to take the single example of this scene), inevitably wavers. Beaumont himself is surrounded by the clamorous absolutes which have to be chosen among and which it is nonsense to choose among. But choice is dictated for him. He is himself deeply engaged in the attitudes he is writing about, and in the attitude of mind which makes 'attitudes' important. He is responding deeply to something in his environment. He is a part of his contemporary situation in a pejorative sense.

There is also the fact of Beaumont's adolescence which is relevant here. His concern with attitudes and choice is adolescent—the adolescent as the parvenu to the adult world who brings with him all the virgin will to be convinced, but who has not yet had the time to acquire the wisdom that would illuminate what he is choosing and bring relevant order to his convictions. Beaumont and Fletcher's work indicates the collapse of a culture, an adult scheme is being broken up and replaced by adolescent intensities. It is this which makes the Caroline rating of their work, as compared with that of Jonson and Shakespeare, such a bad augury.

The scene with Dion and the King is about as bad as Beaumont and Fletcher can be. It does, however, reveal the kind of forces among which even their good scenes are set, and the kind of 'situation' we have to deal with in reading them. These 'situations' have much to do with 'psychology', but little to do with the naturalism of consistent character-portrayal. The psychology is that of a blind compulsion to be certain and to be convinced. It is the psychology, too, of a time when action was demanded on the basis of the conviction entertained; and when loyalties were being solicited by widely different authorities.

Kingship is only one of the absolutes in the general Beaumont and Fletcher environment. They are not interested in assessment of any of the absolutes separately, and are weakest when they pretend to be. Their best work is done where their main interest lies—in the conflict of the absolutes and the contortions it imposes on human nature.

In Act I, Scene i, this typical inner setting is swiftly arranged. Philaster comes into the Presence to challenge Pharamond's right to replace him as heir to the throne. He begins by making his obeisances to the King:

> Right noble sir, as low as my obedience,
> And with a heart as loyal as my knee
> I beg your favour.

The King gives him permission, within the bounds proper to a subject, to say what he will. Philaster then immediately turns on Pharamond, and threatens him with hyperbolical rebellion if ever he should take the throne. The King intervenes to check him; Philaster's defiance collapses:

> I am dead, sir; you're my fate. It was not I
> Said I was wronged.

The King thinks Philaster must be possessed. Philaster rejoins that he is possessed—and with his father's spirit:

> It's here, O King,
> A dangerous spirit! now he tells me, King,
> I was a King's heir, bids me be a King,
> And whispers to me, these are all my
>   subjects . . .
> But I'll suppress him; he's a factious spirit,
> And will undo me. Noble sir, your hand;
> I am your servant.
> KING. Away! I do not like this:
> I'll make you tamer, or I'll dispossess you
> Both of your life and spirit. For this time
> I pardon your wild speech, without so much
> As your imprisonment.

There is no suggestion of satire here. The King is one of the absolutes Philaster recognizes. The demands of justice (the 'spirit' of his father) are another. But there is no moral conflict in Philaster. He can live absolutely in either the one loyalty or the other. It is a law of the Beaumont world that absolute committal removes the need for moral deliberation, and supervenes on conflict by suppression of one of the warring terms. The courtiers, Philaster's friends, for example, are bent on revolt:

> shrink not, worthy sir,
> But add your father to you; in whose name
> We'll waken all the gods, and conjure up
> The rods of vengeance, the abused people,
> Who, like raging torrents . . .

But Philaster does not so much as feel the pressure of their rhetoric:

> Friends, no more;
> Our ears may be corrupted; 'tis an age
> We dare not trust our wills to.

The audience is left, at the end of this first scene, with an exciting sense of an either-or world, and of a hero who will be all-or-nothing whichever way he is thrown: for it is obvious he won't (in the normal sense of the word) decide. There is this, and a further sense besides—something that comes through in Philaster's words last quoted: the sense that this is not only literary entertainment, but literature aware of itself as a symptom rather than a reflection of the dangerous reality surrounding it—aware of a world that cannot be trusted, and in which the mind is forced back upon itself to make a world of its own, by belief, or resolve, or art:

> 'tis an age
> We dare not give our wills to.

The other sphere in which the absolutes manifest themselves for the Beaumont hero we are introduced to in the scene immediately following. Arethusa sends for Philaster. Up to now neither he nor the audience have had any inkling of what is to take place. But Arethusa is in love with Philaster. The scene is a minor example of the stunts with situation which characterize all the Beaumont and Fletcher plays: the subject cannot woo the princess, so the princess will declare her love to the subject. More than this, it is an interesting example of Beaumont's technique exerting itself on a more serious level. Its congruency with what has gone before it and with what will follow after helps to credibilize the incredibles later to be handled.

Arethusa's inversion of propriety is justified by invoking the overruling power of the gods. She is driven by forces larger than human:

> 'tis the gods,
> The gods that make me so; and, sure, our love
> Will be the nobler and the better blest,
> In that the secret justice of the gods
> Is mingled with it.
>
>   (I. ii.)

But this divine sanction is in fact supererogatory: love itself is an absolute for the Beaumont and Fletcher lovers.

Secondly, there is the teasing way in which the proposal is made. Philaster assumes (the audience is already aware of what is in Arethusa's mind) that a declaration of love is the last thing that will be made in the interview. And Arethusa's first words seem to bear out his fears. Why, she asks, has he laid scandal on her in a public place, and called the great part of her dowry in question? Philaster's reply is similar to his original reaction to the King:

> Madam, this truth which I shall speak will be
> Foolish; but for your fair and virtuous self,
> I could afford myself to have no right
> To anything you wished.

Notwithstanding, Philaster confesses he is loath to give

> His right unto a sceptre and a crown
> To save a lady's longing.

He is still unaware that Arethusa is in love with him. Arethusa then says she must have both kingdoms, and even more. Philaster must turn away his face while she tells him the full length of her demands. At this Philaster flies into heroics:

> I can endure it. Turn away my face!
> I never yet saw enemy that looked
> So dreadfully but that I thought myself
> So great a basilisk as he; or spake
> So horribly but that I thought my tongue
> Bore thunder underneath, as much as his;
> Nor beast that I could turn from: shall I then
> Begin to fear sweet sounds? a lady's voice
> Whom I do love? Say, you would have my life;
> Why, I will give it you; for 'tis to me
> A thing so loathed, and unto you that ask
> Of so poor use, that I will make no price:
> If you entreat I will unmovedly hear.

This is wit according to Dr. Johnson's formula: contrary ideas yoked together by violence. It is witty in that what the audience knows is love on Arethusa's part, Philaster takes to be hate; what he thinks is a demand about to be made on him the audience knows is an offer about to be made to him. Philaster's misapprehension has been successfully raised at this point to hyperbolical proportions. And in one and the same speech we see his heroism and his helplessness, his worth and his sense of worthlessness asserted.

But a measure of depth and seriousness can be recognized in the admittedly adolescent mood in which the hero and the scene are conceived. The part somehow seems to become greater than the whole, the contortions of the hero more important than the forces that produce them. The fact that Philaster is labouring under a misapprehension does not make for complacency in the spectator; and the heroics—on a fair reading—are not received as ridiculous. From this point of view the scene works like a joke that has been pushed too far: except that it never has been a joke. Arethusa's apparently teasing lack of straightforwardness is in keeping with her situation. She must be assured that Philaster would in any case give himself utterly before she can offer herself utterly to him. The point is in that 'utterly'—the adolescent all-or-nothing terms in which the commitments are conceived.

The scene in any case works two ways. There is the joke that it will all have a happy ending. There is also the sense, fatal to our taking the joke at its face value, that happiness as a conclusion to what the scene reveals is an irrelevance. Philaster's heroic and pathetic self-contortion, his insistent readiness to give himself utterly (misapprehension or no) to love or death, are part of a tragi-comedy that cannot really be happy.

There is a final aspect of the Beaumont and Fletcher manner which this scene illustrates, a factor which still further assists belief in Philaster's reactions later. This is the monadic self-enclosure of the characters—part of the petrarchan convention of love, or a part of the native adolescence of Beaumont's mind. The lover can be completely insulated within his love, regardless of the beloved. Love is not necessarily a mutual contract, it can be a private direction of the will, like prayer; or a service, like virtue, that justifies itself by being its own reward. This quality comes out in the scene when Arethusa has finally confessed her love to Philaster, and he replies:

> Madam, you are too full of noble thoughts
> To lay a train for this contemned life,
> Which you may have for asking: to suspect
> Were base, where I deserve no ill. Love you!
> By all my hopes, I do, above my life!
> But how this passion should proceed from you
> So violently, would amaze a man
> That would be jealous.

The world of Beaumont is a violent, extreme, arbitrary, sudden, and wilful thing, ready at any moment to be inverted, or to swing from one contrary to another. We have seen how the external plot is arranged so that opposite pulls can be exerted at any minute on the main characters, and how—with Philaster in the first scene—the loyalty of the subject is absolute but never complete, since it can only be maintained by an actively willed suppression of the disloyalty he also shares in. Here, the opposites are introjected into the heart of what might seem the only single certainty and purity the Beaumont lovers can find. Love itself, in the moment of its most open and utter declaration, is recognized to be an incalculable force, ambivalently sinister in its possibilities: binding and yet disruptive:

> how this passion should proceed from you
> So violently, would amaze a man
> That would be jealous.

Philaster sees the chaste and hitherto inaccessible model of womanhood suddenly proposing to him. He is overwhelmed, but of course ready to accept. In the midst of his confusion he is able to note the possible ambiguity of Arethusa's behaviour for an interpreter that 'would be jealous'. His 'amazement' is another stroke of wit, and an oddly serious one. He loved Arethusa apart from any hope of reciprocation: in spite of her impossibility and almost because of it. (The 'psychology' is the same here as in Marvell's poem.) Now that the Impossible She is so possible, the possibility might itself argue an imperfection. Philaster will love her, of course, on the new terms still. But these will require suppression of the interpretation just glimpsed. A fresh tension is thereby introduced. And when Arethusa is calumniated, as she is soon to be, the scales will tilt again, the disruption will begin, and inverted petrarchanism show itself in near-obscenity and disgust of life. The conception in this scene prepares us to accept Philaster's subsequent misbelief of Arethusa.

It is a scene well contrived within the limits of the initial sonneteerish postulates. It might even be claimed to carry more conviction then Leontes' jealousy, or the somersault of Posthumus; though, it must be added, Shakespeare was not really interested in the postulates Beaumont adopted,

and does not seem to have bothered overmuch with the
mechanics appropriate to them.

Act II springs the trap which has been prepared for Philaster's love. Arethusa is accused of intimacy with Bellario,
the Viola-like page Philaster sent her. (In justice to Beaumont's workmanship it might be pointed out that again we
have been prepared for the sort of thing the calumniators
report: In Act II, Scene iv, misconduct with pages is represented as almost habitual in court circles.) Act III is
devoted to Philaster's reception of the report, his interview with Bellario (who is in love with him) and his encounter with Arethusa herself.

Close analysis of this act (a most effective one) would not
carry insight into Beaumont's technique much further.
There is no increment of growing wisdom in the situation
as it develops. Beaumont's plays, in fact, have no developing revelations, crowded as they are with surprises
and fresh turns. For all the increasing violence and cleverness of their movement they seem to get nowhere. The
return is always to the original starting-point: the petrarchan
nexus, the adolescent all-or-nothingness, the willed and
rigid stance on one set of assumptions maintained by the
resolved suppression of another, the sense of an arbitrary
outer world and a dissociated inner one, of rifts that cannot be bridged but must be desperately overleapt, the mêlée
of absolute claims and exaggerated postures—an agony of
self-scision based on misapprehension and brought back
(by the external contrivances of the plot) to a 'happy'
conclusion: a curious sense, typical of decadence, of something at once more primitive and more sophisticated than
the normal.

But while it does not further insight into the essential
Beaumont situation Act III is a good example of what we
have called the 'extended conceit'. This is particularly
true of the scene between Philaster and Bellario.

Philaster has just received his friend Dion's account of
Arethusa's scandalous behaviour. He is soliloquising on
the theme 'What the eye doesn't see'; how, for animals,
nothing is but what is seen; but for man, nothing is (at
times) but what is not:

> O that like beasts we could not grieve ourselves
> With what we see not! Bulls and rams will fight
> To keep their females, standing in their sight:
> But take 'em from them and you take at once
> Their spleens away; and they will fall again
> Unto their pastures; growing fresh and fat;
> And taste the waters of the springs as sweet
> As 'twas before, finding no start in sleep;
> But miserable man—
>
> (III. i.)

—and at this point Bellario enters. The rest of the speech
(it can be imagined well enough) will be demonstrated in
action on the stage rather than compressed into metaphor.
Philaster is amazed that Bellario, the monster of lust and
ingratitude, should still look outwardly the same as he has
always done:

> See, see, you gods,
> He walks still; and the face you let him wear
> When he was innocent is still the same,
> Not blasted! Is this justice? do you mean
> To intrap mortality, that you allow
> Treason so smooth a brow? I cannot now
> Think he is guilty.

The speech carries on the ruminations of the soliloquy. It
works too a kind of trick with intellectual mirrors, animating all the confusions between 'is' and 'seems' in which
mortality can so easily entrap itself, precipitating Philaster
into the midst of these confusions, where he finds himself
choosing again—hurling himself on the desperate other
side of the gulf he has opened out before himself: he
cannot now think Bellario is guilty. The volte-face is well
executed, and restores both sides of Philaster's self-division to equal status; the prerequisite for Beaumont's strongest occasions.

The remainder of the scene is constructed wittily along
similar lines. Beaumont exploits fully the device of dou-
ble-consciousness (or even double-talk) which is expressive of something central in his conception. The divided
man confronts the integral, and mistakes it. Bellario is
really innocent. Philaster thinks instead he is the consummate actor of innocence. Philaster will therefore act the
part to compete with this, and hoist the engineer with his
own petard. The mirror effects begin to multiply.

Philaster inquires how Bellario has been treated while with
Arethusa:

> Tell me, my boy, how doth the princess use thee?
> For I shall guess her love to me by that.

Bellario gives his innocent account of all Arethusa's fav-
ours. Philaster is caught by the reviving shock of his love
and disgust. He recovers and presses Bellario harder. We
are shown the familiar reverse side of petrarchan idealism.
The catastrophic overthrow of his love (only possible by
reason of his 'noble' mind and the 'virtue' it would es-
pouse) releases an unmanageable and compulsive evil
within him. Philaster is as much bound now to the most
squalid prurience as he was formerly to the chastest adoration. And the agent of his overthrow, whom he would
make the pander to his itch for obscenities, is the innocent
'page' he regards as his greatest friend, and who (beneath
it all) is really a girl faithfully in love with him—and thus
doubly incapable of disloyalty. It is easy to see what the
generation which produced the metaphysicals saw in such
scenes as this. It is the 'conceit' perfectly stage-managed,
without the overt imagery of conceit:

> PHIL. She kisses thee?
> BEL. Not so, my lord.
> PHIL. Come, come, I know she does.
> BEL. No, by my life.
> PHIL. Why then she does not love me. Come, she
>   does:
>   I bade her do it; I charged her by all charms
>   Of love between us, by the hope of peace

We should enjoy, to yield thee all delights
Naked as to her bed; I took her oath
Thou should'st enjoy her. Tell me, gentle boy,
Is she not parallelless? is not her breath
Sweet as Arabian winds when fruits are ripe?
Are not her breasts two liquid ivory balls?
Is she not all a lasting mine of joy?

BEL. Ay, now I see why my disturbed thoughts
Were so perplexed: when first I went to her
My heart held augury. You are abused;
Some villain hath abused you: I do see
Whereto you tend. Fall rocks upon his head
That put this to you! 'tis some subtle train
To bring that noble frame of yours to nought.

PHIL. Thou think'st I will be angry with thee. Come,
Thou shalt know all my drift; I hate her more
Than I love happiness, and placed thee there
To pry with narrow eyes into her deeds.
Hast thou discovered? is she fallen to lust,
As I would wish her? Speak some comfort to
me.

BEL. My lord, you did mistake the boy you sent:
Had she the lust of sparrows or of goats,
Had she a sin that way, hid from the world,
Beyond the name of lust, I would not aid
Her base desires: but what I came to know
As servant to her, I would not reveal,
To make my life last ages.

The code of Honour sets a final and inescapable trap for its observers. Absolute loyalty forbids any telling of tales, even when a friend or a lover commands. Honour itself can thus ally with deception. Philaster has to proceed to threats:

oh, my heart!
This is a salve worse than the main disease.
Tell me thy thoughts; for I will know the least
                    (*Draws his sword*)
That dwells within thee, or rip thy heart
To know it: I will see thy thoughts as plain
As I do now thy face.

At the climax of his rage he returns to the thought with which he began on first seeing Bellario.

The rest of the scene solves the problem of Philaster's transition from threatening Bellario's life to sending him away still loved but still thought to be the deceiver. The moves are worked with the same skill, but still continuing within the narrow and violent compass of the petrarchan and adolescent postulates. The note on which Philaster ends is the second return to the dilemma of what things are and what they seem. This time the resolution seems magnanimous:

Rise, Bellario:
Thy protestations are so deep, and thou
Dost look so truly when thou utter'st them,
That, though I know them false as were my hopes,
I cannot urge thee further. But thou wert
To blame to injure me, for I must love
Thy honest looks, and take no revenge upon

Thy tender youth: a love from me to thee
Is firm, whate'er thou dost . . .
            . . . But, good boy,
Let me not see thee more: something is done
That will distract me, that will make me mad
If I behold thee.

The mood, however, is not one of firm resolve. It is rather the passing stability of exhaustion in the midst of fever. All the items of Philaster's self-division are still present. Only the informing energies that usually stir them to conflict are absent. The verse moves to the rhythm of a relaxed exhaustion. In the lull of the violent fit Philaster is at length able to hold together all the opposites. He can call up again the absolute of his affection for the page, and recognizes too that it will be overthrown at any moment by 'distraction'. Occasions like this show how firmly Beaumont has hold on what he is doing, and how consistent is his conception.

What is it that Beaumont is doing? To analyse the serious scenes that ensue would tell us little more than is already apparent from those examined so far. Philaster sees Arethusa, in a subdued mood he confesses himself her slave, her

creature, made again from what it was
And newly-spirited.
                                        (III. ii.)

Then, stirred again, he reviles both himself and her. He echoes Donne's *A Lecture upon a Shadow*:

all the good you have is but a shadow,
I' the morning with you, and at night behind you.

He goes off into the forest which provides a fitting backdrop for the Beaumont and Fletcher worlds, both inner and outer. Here the court hunts, and court ladies disappear into convenient brakes. Here the normal countryman can comment on his betters in much the same vein as Harrington commented on the hunting parties of James and the King of Denmark. Here a brute creation seems to pursue the rational. Lovers wound themselves and wound each other, and seek death in the pastoral environment they otherwise long for as the asylum from their conflicts and confusions. At times the Beaumont vision strikes through the verse. There is resonance, for example, in Arethusa's cry at the end of Act III, Scene ii, when Philaster has left her and she is called to join her father's hunting:

I am in tune to hunt!
Diana, if thou canst rage with a maid
As with a man, let me discover thee
Bathing, and turn me to a fearful hind,
That I may die pursued by cruel hounds,
And have my story written in my wounds.

The forest, above all, is where the heroes and heroines get lost, with the lostness that is recurrent in Beaumont:

Where am I now? Feet, find me out a way,
Without the counsel of my troubled head:

I'll follow you boldly about these woods,
O'er mountains, through brambles, pits, and floods,
Heaven, I hope, will ease me: I am sick.

(IV. iii.)

And in the same forest where all seems confused, the feet
of the plot somehow find a way, and bring everything to
a happy ending. The fourth act is as clever in its transitions from the climaxes of the third as it is in its preparation for the surprises and dénouement of the fifth.

III

We have concentrated our commentary on the petrarchan
part of the play, and on only a part of that. There is much
else in Beaumont and Fletcher that has received more
attention. It is, however, the treatment of the love-triangle
which, it seems to me, belongs particularly to their seriousness both as conscious analysts and unconscious symptoms of a particular human plight. The dramatists (or
Beaumont alone, if he was solely responsible) attain in
their handling of the petrarchan a personal inflection which
is both distinctive and distinguished. The main roots that
clutch in their work strike down through this into the heart
of their time.

The petrarchan matter indicates their derivation. They are
in the tradition which began with the Great House, the
source of the Arcadian, Heroic, and Pastoral, as well as of
the sonnet sequences, the literature of the Elizabethan *élite*.
Their derivation is important from the social as well as
from the literary point of view. Or rather, the literary
importance does not exist apart from the social. That both
Shakespeare and Beaumont and Fletcher went to the same
Arcadian and Romance sources at about the same time
means two things, not one. Different interests were involved, and different intentions, and these were in part the
result of differences in their respective social placings. On
a superficial glance alone, it is obvious that Beaumont and
Fletcher, as 'inferior Sidneys', the shabby genteel of the
Great House, cannot usefully be compared with Shakespeare until the important prior distinctions between the
two have first been made. Their prime affiliations are not
with the tradition in which Shakespeare wrote but with the
tradition—however degenerate—of the Sidneians and the
metaphysicals.

A close examination of ***Philaster*** only brings out more
clearly the difference in content and conception between
their romances and those of Shakespeare's last period. On
their own ground Shakespeare could not compete with
them. Nor would he, one can suppose, have been minded
to. The intensely narrowed world in which they are at
home is one which Shakespeare's maturity cannot be conceived as entering. At the same time it is evident that
Beaumont and Fletcher could have learnt nothing to their
essential purposes from Shakespeare's last plays. Their
own romances are a genre peculiar to themselves, in spite
of the surface lights from *Antony, Lear, Othello, Hamlet,*
and possibly *Troilus,* which they reflect. If it is a case of
influence one on another it would seem likely that the

Victorians were right, and that Shakespeare was the debt-
or. Paradoxically, in a case like this it is easier to imagine
the greater taking a cue from the lesser—and then going
off on its own. *The Winter's Tale* and *Cymbeline* do resemble the Beaumont romances. Structural resemblance
we should not expect, but resemblance in the incidentals
and externals there certainly is. However, Shakespeare's
last plays, internally, belong to the body of his own writing, and through that to the tradition in which they were
produced. Their framework is the large metaphor his work
had established for him before Beaumont and Fletcher
began to write.

Beaumont and Fletcher are dramatic opportunists. ***Philaster,*** besides its petrarchan core, has quick and successful
utilizations of the large themes of the maturer drama; the
theme of rebellion, of the guilty King on the throne, the
theme of the King John who turns to a Falconbridge, in
time of trouble. (Philaster gathers up the roles of Falconbridge, Hal, and Hamlet as ancillary to his main role of
lover-hero.) But it is the petrarchan core which is important for the final assessment of the two dramatists.

We have said that it is by reason of the petrarchan matter, as they treat it, that their work strikes roots into their
time. Petrarchanism is an important aspect of the Renaissance. It held out the opportunity to concentrate on a
territory sealed off from the other realities, social, ethical, or religious. It hinted seductively that a social code,
the basis of morality, the effects of religious discipline,
could all be found in the ceremonial cult of Stella or
Astrea. Ideal love would be in itself a liberal education.
It would be open, also, only to such as had the leisure
and the facilities of the Great House around them. Petrarchanism was both insulated and aristocratic. In the
case of Beaumont the insulation works to make the large
traditional themes marginal, reducing them to convenient
plot-ingredients.

The roots of petrarchanism, however, strike deeper than
this, particularly in the Beaumont and Fletcherian drama.
Its real importance there is that the central love-triangle,
conflict and self-contortion in the setting of the absolutes,
presented a small-scale model and a disguise for the larger situations of real life: situations of dictated choice, of
self-commitment, of wilful belief that looks like headstrong
denial—situations suited to the extremities of the emotional partisan. (The reign of James brought the question
of partisanship to the forefront in almost every sphere.) In
the person of Philaster the embryonic Cavalier could live
through in pantomime what he would later have to live
through in fact except that the terms would be changed.
The Beaumont hero feels himself already 'fated'. He is
cut off from the social past and the neighbourly present
and his future includes only death. He is absolved from
the need to exert rational control, and incapable of compromise. He is self-enclosed in the splintering world of
the contending absolutes, and all the violence of activity
these call out can only end in self-destruction. The fated
lover-hero of the Beaumont drama is one of the great
premonitory symbols of the seventeenth century.

Thus plays like *Philaster* are not merely passively addressed to the tastes of their audience. They play an active role. They catch at the half-felt or the unconscious and give it expression. Beaumont and Fletcher do not cater superficially, they shape for their audience the attitudes and postures the audience is not wholly aware yet that they will need. On a most cursory view, of course, as we have tried to show, Beaumont and Fletcher clearly aimed at a two-level appeal. Their plays could easily compete with the popular theatre in dramatic stir and skill; they had something to offer, too, to the aristocrat whose poetic reading was Donne, whose private pastime was the Sonnet, and whose connoisseurship was reserved for 'wit'.

The main poetic feature of Beaumont and Fletcher is their adaptation to the stage of the sonneteer's material and the sonneteer's 'conceit'. The primary affiliation of their drama is with the Sidneians and the metaphysicals. That this should have been overlooked may be a result of the recent concentration, in criticism, on the *imagery* of poetry: the fashion for what Dr. I. A. Richards has called 'metaphor-hunting'. Clearly, poetry is not to be limited to the devising of *imagery* narrowly conceived. Our indifference to the poetry of Sidney, Spenser, and Jonson, with its accompanying exaltation of Donne, Herbert, and Marvell, may eventually be recognized as a by-product of Mr. T. S. Eliot's personal pamphleteering for what—even in him—was to be merely a chapter in his own poetic development. In any case, the absence of 'verbal texture' in Beaumont and Fletcher's verse is not decisive. Their words are stretched in the frame of their situations, and it is the frame which gives them the manifoldness of 'wit'. Their achievement was to make dramatic situation perform the work of metaphysical conceit.

A play like *Philaster,* we have said, further, leaves one with a sense of something at once more sophisticated and more primitive than the normal, of something we associate with decadence. Each of the operative words here can bear fuller expansion.

The world they construct is a product of sophistication. Sophistication implies immediate viability within a restricted circle; a degree of knowledgeability in the extreme, which yet never reaches as far as wisdom; a specialness of insight and an extreme localization of field; an intensity that fails to bring breadth of view, and which breadth of view would render impossible. Beaumont's work has this sophistication. It comes, I have argued, from his concentration on the petrarchan matter, with interests even more circumscribed than those of Sidney. And even Sidney's tradition was narrower, less mixed, and less ancient than that of Shakespeare. It would be wrong, however, to think of Beaumont and Fletcher as deliberately constructing a 'fairy world'. Their artefact is more sinister and more serious than that. It is more like the *Anniversaries* than Hans Andersen.

The world into which Beaumont and Fletcher fit, as the Victorians used to insist, however clumsily and vaguely, is the world of James I and fermenting civil war. They can be regarded from one point of view as unconsciously fight-

ing a rearguard action on behalf of the Court, compensating with advances in Blackfriars for the retreats in Westminster. The importance of Philaster is that he foreshadows figures in real life: figures of the same class and temper as Kenelm Digby, who married, *ad maiorem gloriam amoris,* an alleged courtesan.

In history as in the Beaumont drama the setting for the main actors was one in which all-or-nothing, and either-or, were continually presented as the alternatives for choice. The absolutes of Justice for the subject, Loyalty to the King, Faith in God, Obedience to Church Discipline—a medley of incompatible demands surrounded the individual. Behaviour could no longer be regulated by agreed social habits, or by decent mutualizations of differences as between souls naturally Christian. The outer world and the inner world were beginning to exhibit the phenomena of fissure. In such a situation belief does tend to become wilful and hyperbolical, resting on suppressions and assertions combined. The Philaster hero focusses all this, and becomes the kind of Byron-model for his generation. In him the conflicts, self-divisions and desperate stands, the distraction and the longing for certainty, the bewildered lostness and the violence which will destroy what it loves and finally turn on itself—pathetically and comically jumbled, all the agonies and irresponsibilities meet.

And yet Lord Falkland can be seen as part of Beaumont's world, as well as Kenelm Digby. He too was one who did not want civil war, and yet was confronted with it. He did not wish to take sides, yet when all were fighting he must fight too, and only one side could be taken. And the story goes that on the eve of Newbury he prepared himself as if for his own burial, went out to battle in clean linen, was lost at the head of his cavalry among the opposing ranks, and was discovered next day dead on the field—the kind of suicide without self-slaughter a Philaster would have willed for himself, or Arethusa wished:

> I am in tune to hunt!
> Diana . . . let me discover thee
> Bathing, and turn me to a fearful hind,
> That I may die pursued by cruel hounds,
> And have my story written in my wounds.

The primitive quality in the play is what we should expect from a decaying or collapsing culture. It is congruent, too, with what we have called the adolescent in Beaumont's conception. Both the primitive and the adolescent indicate a reversion to the premature imposed on a civilization by the new and unmanageable developments taking place inside it. Beaumont was only twenty-four when *Philaster* was written. It is not likely that he should have become maturer as he got older. His adolescence lent itself to the requirements of the time more than Jonson's detached satire could do, or Shakespeare's socially unuseable inclusiveness of comprehension. What we call the modern world was about to launch on a phase when the adolescent and the wilful had special survival value. Since Beaumont's day our society has become increasingly partisan, increasingly juvenile in its wilfulness and its unwisdom. Beaumont and Fletcher are, in an unfortunate sense, the first of the moderns. Their counterpart in the nineteenth century, we suggested, was Byron. A contemporary parallel to their work might be that of Graham Greene. The decadence they reflect has been a condition permanent since their time, and, if anything, apt to be aggravated.

THE MAID'S TRAGEDY

Michael Neill   (essay date 1970)

SOURCE: "'The Simetry, which Gives a Poem Grace': Masque, Imagery, and the Fancy of *The Maid's Tragedy*," in *Renaissance Drama,* Vol. 3, 1970, pp. 111-35.

[*In this essay, Neill contends that the wedding masque functions as a structural element in* The Maid's Tragedy, *involving the "ironic manipulation of running imagery, which links the masque not only to the wedding night, but to the action of the play as a whole."*]

Masques are a commonplace feature of the drama written for the private playhouses of the Jacobean and Caroline periods. Their spectacular appeal to an audience, which (whatever the statistical details of its composition) was nearly dominated in matters of taste by a genteel coterie, is obvious. Thanks to the work of Enid Welsford and M. C. Bradbrook, it is now generally recognized that in the hands of the more intelligent dramatists "these pretty devices" may also have important structural functions. Miss Welsford [in *The Court Masque,* 1927] has shown that the ritualistic qualities of masque, as well as helping to universalize the significance of the action, may provide an essential method of controlling the audience's response to apparently melodramatic episodes. Professor Bradbrook [in *Themes and Conventions of Elizabethan Tragedy,* 1960] has discussed the use of masques as a variety of the play-within-the-play device, designed to create "ironic interplay" of various kinds.

Oddly enough, however, very little attempt has been made until recently to examine the structural purpose of one of the most elaborate masques-within-the-play, the wedding masque in *The Maid's Tragedy*. Professor Bradbrook remarks that "the masque . . . with its description of the sudden storm rising on the wedding night, is not entirely irrelevant"; and W. W. Appleton [in *Beaumont and Fletcher: A Critical Study,* 1956] finds a "prophetic irony" in Cynthia's promise to provide such entertainment for the company

> As may for ever after force them hate
> Our brother's glorious beams, and wish the night.
> (I.ii.153-154)

Otherwise the critical silence would suggest that Beaumont and Fletcher's masque has been regarded as a spectacular irrelevance. In an essay ["'These pretty devices':

Title page of the 1619 edition of The Maid's Tragedy.

A Study of Masques in Plays"] printed in *A Book of Masques* [1967] Inga-Stina Ewbank attacks this generally implicit view: she notes the way in which the highly conventional themes and imagery of this masque are echoed in the following scene, so that the idealized masque ritual becomes a foil for the corrupt action of the wedding night. And she detects further heavy irony in the conventional tribute to the sovereign with which the masque concludes. In general she claims for it "a . . . strongly ironical bearing on the action of the play," though the scope of her paper does not allow her to argue the case in detail.

The failure of other critics to give sympathetic attention to the function of the masque is particularly surprising since constructive skill is perhaps the only talent that Beaumont and Fletcher are widely granted today: and yet here, in a play that is usually cited as their most successful tragedy, we are faced with a structural excrescence of unique proportions—and in the exposition, where dramatic economy is most important. Far from attempting to minimize the weight given the masque by its elaborate proportions, the dramatists actually go out of their way to emphasize it in the action and dialogue of Act I. Indeed, with the excep

---

Samuel Taylor Coleridge on Beaumont and Fletcher:

In the romantic drama, Beaumont and Fletcher are almost supreme. Their plays are in general most truly delightful. I could read the **Beggar's Bush** from morning to night. How sylvan and sunshiny it is! **The Little French Lawyer** is excellent. Lawrit is conceived and executed from first to last in genuine comic humor. **Monsieur Thomas** is also capital. I have no doubt whatever that the first act and the first scene of the second act of the **Two Noble Kinsmen** are Shakspeare's. Beaumont and Fletcher's plots are, to be sure, wholly inartificial; they only care to pitch a character into a position to make him or her talk; you must swallow all their gross improbabilities, and, taking it all for granted, attend only to the dialogue. How lamentable it is that no gentleman and scholar can be found to edit these beautiful plays!

Samuel Taylor Coleridge, an extract dated 17 February 1833, from his Table Talk, *in* Coleridge on the Seventeenth Century, *edited by Roberta Florence Brinkley, Greenwood Press, 1968.*

---

tion of some brief narrative which reveals Amintor's desertion of Aspatia and sketches in his friendship with Melantius, it would be fair to say that the masque is the real dramatic subject of the first act. In view of the care taken to focus the audience's attention upon the masque, it is at least reasonable to assume that its physical prominence is deliberate, that it corresponds to an intended structural significance.

The purpose of this essay is to show that the "felt fusion" between masque and play action in *The Maid's Tragedy,* of which Professor Bradbrook speaks, is a real thing; that the masque is part of a carefully worked out dramatic scheme; and that this scheme involves (among other things) the ironic manipulation of running imagery, which links the masque not only to the wedding night but to the action of the play as a whole. Elsewhere in her *Themes and Conventions,* Professor Bradbrook remarks that the final test of the decadence of the Beaumont and Fletcher plays is their lack of any kind of "verbal framework." I shall argue that a complete reading of *The Maid's Tragedy* does involve the recognition of significant "linguistic patterns," though they are not perhaps of quite the kind that Professor Bradbrook meant.

I

In the first set of encomiastic verses which he contributed to the 1647 folio, William Cartwright singled out Fletcher's constructional skill for particular praise:

None can prevent the Fancy, and see through
At the first opening; all stand wondring how
The thing will be until it is; which thence
With fresh delight still cheats, still takes the sence;
The whole designe, the shadowes, the lights such
That none can say he shewes or hides too much.

By "Fancy" Cartwright apparently means something like "design" or "plot," though of a rather specialized kind. The context suggests that the senses of "witty conceit" and "something delusive" are also relevant. Fletcher's "Fancy" is not only a "designe," but a thing which "with *fresh delight* still *cheats* . . . the sence." The term thus neatly embraces three of the most distinctive features of Fletcher's plots: the paradoxical perversions of familiar social situations from which the plays begin; the working out of these paradoxes in a logically articulated sequence of further structural conceits; and the elaborate tissues of deception, dissimulation, and error, rising naturally out of the situational paradoxes, which serve to keep up the audience's interest in the unfolding design.

The social conceits, on which the fancies of plays like *A King and No King* or *A Wife for a Month* are built, are immediately and more or less adequately suggested by their titles. The fancy of *The Maid's Tragedy* is rather more complicated and could be covered only partially by the subtitles which suggest themselves: "A Wife and No Wife," "A Maid and No Maid," or "A Marriage and No Marriage." But it is, I believe, only in terms of the conceited kind of design which Cartwright calls a "fancy" that we can properly discuss the dramatic method and meaning of the play, and so avoid making critical demands that are inappropriate to the dramatists' artistic intention. More specifically, I believe that it is only in its relation to such a controlling fancy that we can fully realize the function of the obtrusive wedding masque.

Of course the masque does have simple, literal functions: it is designed to set the play in a certain milieu and to establish the appropriate social tone. As part of a sequence of wedding festivities, ending with the banquet in Act IV, scene ii, it provides an ironic foil to the revenge action. But these are limited and static uses; more important is what we might call its kinetic function, as part of a dynamic pattern of verbal and dramatic ironies. It embodies, in striking visual terms, a group of images, whose equivocal significance the play exploits through a series of paradoxes and reversals, both structural and rhetorical. The ironic nature of this development compels repeated recollection and re-examination of the masque: it becomes the central and dominating image of the whole work, an epitome of its structural fancy.

The reason for the general critical neglect of the ironic patterns of action and imagery in *The Maid's Tragedy* seems to me to be fairly indicated by Eliot's complaint that "the blossoms of Beaumont and Fletcher's imagination draw no sustenance from the soil, but are cut and slightly withered flowers stuck into the sand [T. S. Eliot, *Selected Essays,* 1953] The language of the Fletcher plays obviously lacks the poetic intensity of the best Elizabethan and Jacobean work, and it does not appear to be organized in patterns which can be called (except in the broadest sense) morally significant. But this is not to say that the plays lack any organizational principle except that of melodramatic opportunism. The marriage masque in *The Maid's Tragedy* is as conventional as the imagery which links it to the play as a whole: but this conventionality is appropriate to the fanciful design of the play, which consists in the juggling of equally conventional social situations. The familiarity of the rhetoric vouches for the fundamental ordinariness of the basic situations. But what the play does, of course, is to turn these situations inside out, and the language of the play is made to go through a corresponding series of inversions and perversions. The patterns are patterns of wit.

By the very nature of its conventional ritual, a wedding masque ought to define the images it presents. In its sophisticated way it remains a kind of magical rite, performed to ensure the success and fertility of the union it celebrates. The unconventional thing about this most conventional of masques is that it fails to establish the proper definitions. This means, as far as the language of the play is concerned, that it initiates a pattern of equivocation and semantic inversion which is the rhetorical analogue of the repeated peripeties of the plot structure. At the same time it ironically predicates the disasters and confusions of the subsequent action. Implicitly its action is related to the fate of the play action: it is not magic which has failed, but magic which has gone astray. I must emphasize that this connection is only implicit: if we stopped to consider it, it would seem absurd. But the implication is necessary if the ironical symmetry is to be effective. The sleight of hand is possible only because the dramatists are juggling with two levels of illusion: in life mundane reality conventionally transcends stage reality at the conclusion of a masque (the presence of the king visibly affects the actions of the masquers), but when the mundane reality is itself a play there is no felt reason why the relationship should not be reversed and the masque "determine" the fate of its audience. Queen Night, and Cynthia, after all, who control the revels and see the stage audience as their "servants" (I.ii.151), are as "real" to the theater audience as Amintor and Evadne themselves.

II

A stock theme of revels, both in England and on the Continent, as Miss Welsford points out, is the arrival of night and the gradual approach of dawn. Allusion to the presence of night, whether simply in the setting (like the "obscure and cloudy nightpiece" of *Blacknesse*) or through the presence of a goddess (Queen Night herself or one of the Moon deities), is an obvious device for the blurring of artifice and reality which is essential to the effectiveness of masque. The particular appropriateness of such allusions in wedding entertainments is equally obvious. In choosing Queen Night as the presenter of their wedding masque, Beaumont and Fletcher may perhaps have been influenced by the published accounts of the entertainments at two Italian weddings in 1608. One of these, the Florentine *Notte D'Amore* was to be extensively adapted by Jonson for his *Vision of Delight* (1617) and again by Davenant in *Luminalia* (1638). But the idea might just as well have been borrowed from the conventions of the epithalamium, of which this masque is in effect a dramatized version. A regular feature of epithalamia is the poet's entreaty that the departure of day be hastened and the

reign of night begin; and the appeal is normally followed by the announcement that the wished-for night has in fact arrived. Queen Night's "Our reign is come . . . I am the Night" (I.ii.122-124) at once signalizes the beginning of the masque and anticipates the end of the revels in the entry to the nuptial night itself. The visual context of the announcement and the terms in which it is made suggest an ambiguity which is also native to the epithalamium tradition—an ambiguity which the dramatists go on to exploit.

The eighteenth stanza of Spenser's "Epithalamion," for instance, while welcoming Night as the friend and protectress of lovers, implies that night conceals not only love but evil: it may stand not only for the joys of marriage but for death. And stanza 19 consists of a series of charms invoked against the sinister possibilities of the dark. So, when Beaumont and Fletcher's Night "rises in *mists*," we may take them as standing for Spenser's "deluding dreames" and phantasms (as in the Mantuan *intermezzo* of 1608) or, more generally, for "misconceived dout" and "hidden feares." In fact the imagery of Night's opening lines tends to support her identification with evil and confusion:

> Our reign is come; for in the *quenching* sea
> The sun is *drown'd,* and with him *fell* the Day.
> (I.ii.122-123; italics added)

There is a quite deliberate irony in the juxtaposition of this ominous visual and verbal imagery with Evadne's greeting to Melantius ("Your presence is more joyful than this *day*" l. 120; italics added), an irony which is complicated by the fact that her apparent hyperbole turns out to be a heavily sarcastic litotes.

The doubts thus created are deepened rather than dispelled when Queen Night is joined by her co-presenter, the Moon Goddess, Cynthia. As the patron of virginal chastity, Cynthia/Diana may seem to preside somewhat incongruously over a ritual of consummation. In fact, of course, she has a second aspect as the patron of generation and childbirth and is so invoked in Spenser's poem and in the Epithalamium from *Hymenaei*. But in both of these her connection with fertility is given considerable emphasis, whereas here it is not so much as alluded to. Indeed, Cynthia's rather tart rebuke to Night's insinuations about her relationship with Endymion (ll. 168-170) can only tend to identify her with the virgin Diana. If we make this identification, Neptune's offering of the revels as "a solemn honour to the moon" (l. 211) becomes heavily ironical; and the irony is perfectly, if perversely, fulfilled in a wedding night which remains completely chaste, though the chastity results from the vows of whoredom, not virginity. As an ironic celebration of chastity, the masque is relevant to both Amintor's love relationships: each is a match but no match which this wedding-and-no-wedding ensures will never be consummated, except in death.

The initial uncertainties concerning the nature of Queen Night herself are partially resolved by the conversation between the two goddesses, in which Night is presented as the friend, and Day as the enemy of lovers. Night's proposal that they should "hold their places and outshine the day" (l. 145) even promises to fulfil the conventional lovers' wish (expressed here in the masque songs) that the night may never end. Cynthia has to remind her that the gods' decrees may not be broken in this way but suggests instead that they "stretch their power" over fleeting time by means of an entertainment, designed

> To give our servants one contented hour,
> With such unwonted solemn grace and state,
> As may for ever after force them hate
> Our brother's glorious beams, and wish the night.
>
> (ll. 151-154)

In effect the masque is to be, like Spenser's "Epithalamion," "for short time an endlesse moniment" which will raise to time a nobler memory / Of what these lovers are" (ll. 173-174). If we read the masque with the irony that its ambiguities invite, it can be seen to do exactly this.

Pre-eminent among the servants for whose delight the revels are offered are the lovers themselves, Evadne and Amintor; and conventionally of course it is the bride and groom who will most hate the advent of dawn and "wish the night." This defining association of Night with happiness, love, and sexual consummation is continued in the nuptial songs which separate the three dances of the revels. The masquers make repeated appeals for the extension of Night's reign:

> Joy to this great company!
>   And no day
> Come to steal this night away,
>   Till the rites of love are ended.
>
> (ll. 219-222)

> Hold back thy hours, dark Night, till we have done;
>   The Day will come too soon:
> Young maids will curse thee, if thou steal's away,
> And leav'st their losses open to the day:
>   Stay, stay, and hide
>   The blushes of the bride.
>
> (ll. 233-238)

> Hesperus, be long a-shining,
> Whilst these lovers are a-twining.
>
> (ll. 257-258)

By contrast with "gentle Night," Day is rude, abrupt, and inquisitive: the reward which Cynthia offers the sea-gods for their performance is flood tides which will hide their dwellings from the hateful eye of Day (ll. 265-269).

The process of definition, then, is one which inverts, according to the familiar conceit of epithalamia and love poetry in general, the conventional symbolism of night and day, light and dark. But the definition remains incomplete and equivocal. The masquers who are conjured up by Cynthia represent the winds and the sea-gods. Both wind and sea supply conventional metaphors for the passions; so that the dances in which the masquers are led by Neptune may be seen as analogous to the ordered

dance in which Reason sets the rebellious humours and affections of *Hymenaei*. But this symbolism of marital harmony is upset by the escape of Boreas, who proves unamenable to the power of Neptune's "music to lay a Storm." His raising of a tempest which threatens the destruction of "many a tall ship" *before day* implicitly calls in question the real nature of Night (ll. 259-262). The storm stands for an outbreak of unbridled passion which is realized in the discord of the wedding night which follows, and even more disastrously in the slaughter of the second "wedding night" in Act V. Further, the presence among the dancers of Proteus, the shape changer, may also have ironic implications, in views of the web of dissimulation and deception which complicates the subsequent action.

The conventionally circular structure of the masque allows the dramatists to wind up its action with a recapitulation of its opening sequence, which concentrates in a single dramatic emblem the ambiguity of the whole piece. Night, now appropriately called "dead Night" (l. 273) announces her departure with a second and even more malevolent reference to her murderous quarrel with Day, and then vanishes once more "into mists" (l. 287):

> Oh, I could frown
> To see the Day, the Day that flings his light
> Upon my kingdom and condemns old Night!
> Let him go on and flame! I hope to see
> Another wildfire in his axletree,
> And all fall drench'd.
>
> (ll. 275-280)

The immediate effect of the various uncertainties about the significance of the masque action is to give substance to the visual and verbal ambiguities surrounding the figure of Queen Night on her first appearance. Night is described by Cynthia as "queen of shadows" and in the context of a dramatic performance "shadows" may refer not only to the literal shadows of darkness but to the shadows of theatrical illusion: as the presenter of a masque, Night is queen of its actor / shadows and acted illusions. In a wider sense the "shadows" may stand (like the symbolic mists out of which she rises) for delusive appearance and concealed evil. The unfolding ironies of the plot are to reveal Night as the presiding deity of the Rhodian court, Queen of its shadows in both these senses. The whole of the ensuing play action can be seen as the process by which the ambiguities of the masque are ironically elaborated and finally resolved.

The process begins in Act II, scene i: in its opening sequence Dula's bawdy identification of night with love and consummation is contrasted with Aspatia's melancholy association of night with death (ll. 104-105). The juxtaposition extends the ambiguity of the masque-artifice to the play-reality and gives a somewhat sinister ambivalence to the removal of the wedding torches (l. 114). The ambivalence is supported by a subdued play with the two senses of "death" which, though it becomes explicit only occasionally, underlies a great deal of the action of *The Maid's Tragedy* and is an essential feature of its witty fancy. Just as the rhetoric of love poetry can convert Night, the symbol of death, so it can convert death itself to its own metaphorical ends. On her wedding night a maid "dies" in two senses: there is the "death" of sexual climax and the consequent "death" of her virgin self: in the morning she is reborn as a wife. These are the deaths which the bride songs of the masque lead us to expect for the supposed maid, Evadne:

> Stay, and confound her tears and her shrill cryings,
> Her weak denials, vows, and often-dyings.
>
> (I.ii.241-242)

> they may kiss while they may say a maid:
> To-morrow twill be other kissed and said.
>
> (I.ii.255-256)

Thus, the full pathos of Aspatia's rebukes to Evadne and Amintor depends on an implicit comparison between the literal death which she foresees for herself and the nuptial death of which she has been cheated (II.i.94-105, 116-118)—the allusion being clinched by the association of the funeral hearse, around which the maids will watch one night, with the marriage bed, around which maids gather to prepare the bride, and of the mourning garlands of yew, ivy, and willow (ll. 77-78, 108, 124) with the bride's floral coronet.

The ironic hints in the first 130 lines of the scene are partially substantiated by the ominous recurrence of tears on the wedding day, so lightly dismissed in Act I, scene i. And the omen is amply fulfilled in the wedding night, in terms which constantly send us back to the masque. Amintor's ineffectual deprecation of "the vapours of the night" (l. 146) immediately recalls the mists surrounding Queen Night, with their symbolism of doubt, confusion, evil, and possibly also of death. In one way, of course, the scene is to dispel the mists of deception and error by revealing the true nature of Amintor's "maid and wife"; but against this is set his decision that they must both dissemble (ll. 355 ff.). Again, Amintor's jocose "I mean no sleeping" (l. 154) may remind us of Cynthia's claim to be "gazed on . . . Almost of none but of *unquiet* eyes" (I.ii.159; italics added); but this night is to be unquiet for its lovers in quite another sense from the one intended. Even more important are the ways in which the scene produces a perverted realization of two of the masque's most conventional epithalamic tropes. Evadne's declaration that her refusal of conjugal rights is "not for a night / Or two . . . but ever" (ll. 210-211) amounts to an ironic fulfilment of the conventional wish for the indefinite extension of the night of bliss: these "joys of marriage," such as they are, are granted for ever. At the same time Cynthia's prediction that her servants will come to "wish the night" is morbidly realized in Amintor's desire for death at Evadne's hands (ll. 327-333). The substitution of literal for sexual death suggests an ironic equation of Amintor's situation with that of the woman he has betrayed.

If night proves as hateful as its symbolic connection with death threatens, day, nevertheless, remains as unwelcome as the masque songs predict. The two morning scenes (II.ii and III.i) contrast Aspatia's lamentation with the inner misery of Amintor. The imagery of her laments makes of the sun, Cynthia's brother and Night's antagonist, a further agent of destruction and death. Rather than credit the faith of a man, she says, one should believe the impossible, that

> the sun
> Comes but to kiss the fruit in wealthy autumn,
> When all falls blasted.
>
> (II.ii.20-22)

The image reflects, with ironic aptness, firstly on the King, whom the mandatory flattery of the masque has styled a greater sun (I.ii.283), and whose kiss has in fact blasted the fruitfulness of Evadne's marriage, and next on Evadne herself, whom Amintor has previously hailed as bringing a kind of day at midnight (II.i.142-144). In the second of these scenes, the hostility attributed to the searching eye of day is painfully embodied in the blundering curiosity of the courtiers and the jealous enquiries of the King. Their jokes about the troublesomeness of the night (III.i.2-4) and Diphilus' cheerful shout to his sister that "the night will come again" (ll. 16-17) are heavy with unconscious irony, an irony which is heightened by the fact that it is actually Amintor whom Diphilus has heard approaching.

In this scene (as throughout the play) the night/day antithesis is given considerable rhetorical emphasis. But the ironies are not always as clear-cut as in the cases we have been considering, and it would be pointless to labor them all. In general, we can say that they function chiefly as insistent reminders of the central paradoxes of the play's fancy. The final resolution of these paradoxes begins with the perverted second "wedding-night." The preparation for this begins in Act IV, scene i, Evadne's conversion scene. Here the play with the literal and metaphorical senses of death becomes brutally explicit. Evadne, who has been introduced in the hackneyed trope of love poetry as "a lady . . . that . . . strikes dead with flashes of her eye" (I.i.74-76), and for whom the bridal dyings have been promised, now quite literally "has death about her." Her relationship with the King has "poisoned" her virtue and "murdered" the honor of her family; and, according to Melantius, she can redeem herself only by resolving to kill the King in fact. When she hesitates, her brother responds with a sarcasm that demands death for her "dyings":

> An 'twere to kiss him dead, thou'dst smother him:
> Be wise and kill him.
>
> (IV.i.159-160)

The conceit is elaborately worked out in Act V, where Evadne fulfils her vow.

In Act IV, scene ii, the King presents Amintor and Evadne with a second marriage entertainment, in the shape of a banquet, which is the structural equivalent of Act II's masque. The feast ends with his urging the couple once more to the bridal chamber: "It grows somewhat late.—/ Amintor, thou wouldst be a-bed again" (ll. 221-222). But the conversation which follows, between Melantius and his brother, sharply points up the difference in the two situations:

This were a night indeed
To do it in: the King hath sent for her.

(IV.ii.276-277)

And as though Diphilus' exclamation were not sufficient to establish the night/death conceit on which their revenge is to be built, Melantius is made to echo it a few lines later (ll. 288-290).

With Act V the night, in fulfilment of Diphilus' promise to his sister in Act III, scene i, "is come again." Its opening scene is evidently designed as an ironical inversion of the wedding night. The gentleman's obscene banter as he ushers the King's whore to the royal bed corresponds to the bawdy nudging of Dula during the preparation of the bride; just as the dialogue between the two gentlemen at the end of the scene, with its boasting and speculation on the King's sexual prowess, recalls the horse-play outside the bridal chamber in Act III, scene i. The "good-nights" of the gentleman and Evadne ominously echo the repeated "good-nights" of Act I, scene ii and Act II, scene i; and the gentleman's farewell picks up the conventional wish for the perpetuation of the marriage night ("A good night be it, then, and a long one" V.i.2)—a wish which is about to be fulfilled for the lovers of the play with an exactitude that he scarcely anticipates. The King's insistent "to beds" (V.ii.33, 38, 43) ironically repeat the groom's invitations to his bride in II.i.152, 155-156, 194, 277; while his mounting horror as he becomes aware of Evadne's real purpose, his protestations that she is "too sweet and gentle for such an act" and his despairing plea for "pity" all parallel Amintor's response to Evadne's unmasking. The allusions to the earlier action show the scene as a grotesque travesty of a wedding night and thus give its *doubles entendres* on love and death an intensified ironic force. As she trusses up the sleeping King, Evadne actually seems to recall Melantius' sarcastic quibble:

I dare not trust your strength; your grace and I
Must grapple upon even terms no more.

(V.ii.25-26)

And she recklessly pursues the conceit by referring to her knife blows as "love-tricks" (l. 91). The whole perverted love act reaches its climax in the King's expiring "Oh! I die" (l. 99). In ironic fulfillment of the second masque song, Night stays to cover the kisses ("love-tricks") of the lover, to "hide all" and make the cries of the murdered King as ineffectual as those of the dying bride. In this scene the symbolism of night becomes for the first time completely unequivocal (though the context provides ironic reminders of its original association with amorous fulfilment):

The night grows horrible; and all about me
Like my black purpose.

(V.ii.1-2)

The abortive night of love is succeeded by the consummatory night of death.

In the final scene Evadne appears, "her hands bloody, with a knife," to announce to her husband

joys,
That in a moment can call back thy wrongs . . .

(V.iv.109-110)

The joys she envisages are in fact nothing less than the "marriage-joys" so insistently referred to in the first three acts. The blood and the knife she offers as tokens, not of death but of "rites" which have "washed her stains away" and, she implies (ll. 112-113, 117-123), restored her maidenhood, so that their marriage may be rejoined. Thus, she announces her revenge in words which echo the hymeneal shout in the first masque song:

Joy to this great company!

(I.ii.219)

Joy to Amintor! for the King is dead.

(V.iv.128)

And she goes on to make the last of the play's formal invitations to the marriage bed (ll. 152-157). When, however, Amintor rejects the symbolism of her love tokens ("Black is thy colour now"), Evadne bids her husband farewell with a speech that finally accepts death as the only consummation possible for her:

Amintor, thou shalt love me now again:
Go, I am calm. Farewell and peace forever!
Evadne, whom thou hatest, will die for thee.

(V.iv.169-171)

The death of Evadne, bride and no maid, is carefully contrived to parallel that of Aspatia, maid and no bride. Aspatia's equation of sexual and actual death, at II.ii.22-26, is realized through her absurd duel with Amintor in Act V, scene iv, which can be seen as an ironic literalization of the metaphorical battle of bride and groom. Quite properly, as the conventions of the trope require, Aspatia offers only a token resistance (V.iv.101 ff.). And her line as she falls recognizes a pathetic irony in her death in the house of the man who was to have become her husband:

There is no place so fit
For me to die as here.

(ll. 106-107)

In its final act *The Maid's Tragedy* is revealed as at once dramatized epitaph and epithalamium; the disturbing ambiguities of the masque have been elaborated into a structure of verbal and dramatic ironies which, whatever the difference of scale, is fundamentally of the same order, in its witty conjunction of opposites, as Herrick's "Upon a maid that dyed the day she was married":

That Morne which saw me made a Bride,
The Ev'ning witnest that I dy'd.
The holy lights, wherewith they guide
Unto the bed the bashful Bride;
Served, but as Tapers, for to burne,

And light my Reliques to their Urne.
This *Epitaph,* which here you see,
Supply'd the *Epithalamie.*

Evadne's intention is that the night of death should blot out the dishonor of the actual wedding night: the blackness of the deed, by a final paradoxical twist, is to make her fair again.

> Am I not *fair?*
> Looks not Evadne beauteous in these rites now?
> Were those hours half so lovely in thine eyes
> When our hands met before the holy man:
> I was too *foul* within to look *fair* then.
>   (V.iv.117-122; italics added)

The italicized words belong to a strain of light/dark imagery so closely related to the basic Night/Day opposition that it may be appropriate to deal with it now. The symbolic hostility of Night and Day in the masque was clearly meant to be paralleled in the staging by spectacular use of chiaroscuro. The presence of the "fair Queen," "Bright Cynthia" in the company of dull, black Night, the "Queen of Shadows," calls for visual realization of the paradox which the moon goddess promises to achieve in her revels ("our music may . . . make the east break day / At midnight" I.ii.214-216). In the play action this visual opposition is continued in the alternation of nocturnal and daytime scenes; and it is a consistent theme of the poetry. The masque's paradox of brightness in blackness, fairness in foulness, is typically embodied in Evadne and in that false sun, the King. The Night Goddesses salute the assembled court beauties (among whom the bride is pre-eminent) as "a troop brighter than we," whose "eyes know how / To shoot far more and quicker rays" than Cynthia herself (ll. 136-143); and Night's figure recalls the first description of Evadne as a lady "that bears the light above her and strikes dead / With flashes of her eye" (I.i.75-76), while her comparison of their beams of beauty with the dawn (ll. 134-135) looks forward to Amintor's conventional greeting of his bride as Aurora (II.i.142-144).

The first scene, with its references to the "fair Aspatia" (l. 60) and "the fair Evadne" (l. 76) establishes the two as rivals in fairness. Evadne's triumph in this contest, signalized by Amintor's tribute to the "lustre" of her eye, proves however to be a matter of appearance only. When Amintor asks "what lady was there, that men call *fair* and virtuous . . . that would have shunned my love?" (II.i.263-265; italics added), he is in fact stumbling towards his later characterization of her as "that *foul* woman" (IV.i.206; italics added). And by Act III it is Aspatia whom he recognizes as genuinely "fair" (III.i.235). There is an irony beyond that which the King intends in his reference to Evadne's "black eye" (III.i.147) as a token of her quickness in the sports of love. For hitherto it has been the brightness, the fieriness of her eyes which has been insisted on as an epitome of her fairness. But the blackness on which the King fixes, we know by now, corresponds to an inner blackness—the foulness of illicit lust. If there is any

true whiteness about Evadne it is the proverbial whiteness of leprosy (III.ii.183; IV.i.201). And once Melantius has penetrated Amintor's mask of dissimulation, her blackness becomes a persistent rhetorical theme; in Melantius' castigations:

> that desperate fool that drew thee
> From thy fair life.
>   (IV.i.51-52)

> The burnt air, when the Dog reigns, is not fouler
> Than thy contagious name.
>   (IV.i.60-61)

> Thy black shame . . .
>   (IV.i.113)

and then in her own bitter self-denunciation:

> Would I could say so to my black disgrace!
>   . . . . .
> There is not in the compass of the light
> A more unhappy creature.
>   (IV.i.181-186)

> A soul as white as Heaven . . .
>   . . . . .
> I do present myself the foulest creature . . .
>   (IV.i.222-232)

> I am hell,
> Till you, my dear lord, shoot your light into me,
> The beams of your forgiveness.
>   (IV.i.234-236)

> All the dear joys here, and above hereafter,
> Crown thy fair soul! Thus I take leave, my lord;
> And never shall you see the foul Evadne,
> Till she have tried all honour'd means, that may
> Set her in rest and wash her stains away.
>   (IV.i.281-285)

There is of course a special irony in the fact that the King continues to see her (IV.ii.64) as "fair Evadne" (by which he means fair to himself and foul to her husband), since her conversion has effectively restored the word from the perverted sense he gives it.

The imagery of the regicide scene carries on the fair / foul, light / dark oppositions (V.ii. 45, 50, 59, 62-65, 74-80, 87, 90), now chiefly in reference to the King whose foulness has corrupted Evadne's fairness, and whose death alone may restore it: "Am I not fair? / Looks not Evadne beauteous in these rites now?" Amintor's reply to this question is crucial: he coldly denies that one evil can cancel out another; for him Evadne remains foul beneath her fairness: "Black is thy colour now" (V.iv.135). The effect of the last scene is in fact to define beyond argument (as the masque failed to do) the key terms of the play's fancy. And in that damning "Black" (in which is concentrated the traditional symbolism of both sin and death) is implied the ultimate resolution of the central ambiguity of Night—

a resolution achieved in Amintor's judgment of Evadne's murder:

> And to augment my woe,
> You now are present, stain'd with a king's blood
> Violently shed. *This keeps night here,*
> And throws an unknown wilderness about me.
>
> (V.iv.147-150; italics added)

The lines point to the scene as the final ironic realization of the conventional epithalamic appeal which has haunted the action of the play, "Hold back thy hour, dark night . . . Stay, and hide all"; the appeal is granted as the four lovers of the play slip into the illimitable night of death.

Two further linguistic patterns, associated with the masque and important for the working out of Beaumont and Fletcher's fancy, deserve some comment. One involves images of blushing, and the other, images of storm. The second masque song, in the fashion of an epithalamium, appeals to Night to "stay, and hide / *The blushes of the bride*" (I.ii.237-238; italics added). These conventional tokens of maidenly modesty acquire an increasingly ironic significance as the play develops. In Act II, scene i, Amintor attributes Evadne's obstinacy to "the coyness of a bride" (l. 163); but Evadne shortly disabuses him (ll. 213-217) and cruelly spells out the real meaning of the color on her face:

> Alas, Amintor, think'st thou I forbear
> To sleep with thee, because I have put on
> A maiden's strictness? Look upon these cheeks,
> And thou shalt find the hot and rising blood
> Unapt for such a vow.
>
> (II.i.290-294)

The revelation gives a bitterly ironic twist to Aspatia's complaint at the beginning of the scene which follows:

> Good gods, how well you look! Such a full colour
> Young bashful brides put on.
>
> (II.ii.2-3)

But the greatest ironies are reserved for Act III with Strato's unwittingly tactless banter: "O call the bride, my lord, Amintor, / That we may see her blush" (III.i.76-77) and the King's vicious probing

> I should think, by her black eye,
> And her red cheek, she would be quick and
> stirring . . .
>
> (III.i.147-148)

As he perfectly well knows, her blushing is a token not of chastity but guilt: it is the result not of maiden bashfulness but excess of blood, in the sense of lust. Despite this, Evadne's blushes, like the fire in her eye, continue to be used for purposes of dissimulation—Amintor endeavors to fob off the curious Melantius with a complimentary reference to the "inevitable colour" of her cheeks (III.ii.76-77); while Evadne herself responds to his attacks with the tokens of bashful innocence (IV.i.3, 5). The foolish old

Calianax imagines the restoration of Aspatia's happiness in terms of the same image: "I shall revenge my girl, / And make her red again" (III.ii.333-334). Blushing is seen, then, as a sign of health, as well as of fairness and innocence—the health which the "leprous" Evadne, for all her superficial color, conspicuously lacks. For this reason there is an ironic appropriateness in the fact that the meaning ascribed to blushes is precisely inverted in Act IV. Melantius' reply to Evadne's "You would make me blush" (IV.i.3) implies that blushing reveals guilt rather than bashful innocence. And this cynical interpretation is maintained through Act IV, scene ii (ironically the scene of the second wedding entertainment, where the coy blushes of the bride would be appropriate):

CALIANAX   If he deny it,
          I'll make him blush.
                                   (IV.ii.7-8)

AMINTOR   Here, my love,
          This wine will do thee wrong, for it will set
          Blushes upon thy cheeks; and, till thou dost
          A fault, 'twere pity.
                                   (IV.ii.68-71)

KING   . . . Calianax,
          I cannot trust this: I have thrown out words,
          That would have fetch'd warm blood upon
               the cheeks
          Of guilty men, and he is never moved.
                                   (IV.ii.95-98)

The King's is the last overt reference in the play to blushing, but I think it is clear that the red of the blood upon Evadne's hands as she enters in Act V, scene iv is meant to recall the earlier insistence upon the redness of her cheeks. The King has connected that redness with lustful excess of blood (III.i.148), and Evadne ironically describes his murder as a medicinal bleeding to purge his surfeit of passionate blood (V.ii.41-46). At the same time the bleeding is intended to "wash her stains away" (IV.ii.285), to "make her red again" in Calianax' phrase. In Act V, scene iv she offers the red upon her hands as an emblem of restored fairness and maiden innocence. The ambivalence of redness cannot, however, any more than that of blackness, survive the assassination of the King: in Amintor's eyes it stands only for lust and sanguinary corruption. Evadne has simply committed the one sin that may "outname thy other faults" and the stain of lust is deepened by the stain of "a king's blood / Violently shed" (ll. 148-149).

In my discussion of the masque, I pointed out that its dance of wind and sea gods could be seen as symbolizing the reasonable ordering of the passions necessary to nuptial harmony, and that this symbolism was compromised by the escape of Boreas. Like the other evil auguries of the masque, his storm is realized in the play action and its realization marked by a series of images. Sea and storm imagery runs through Aspatia's extended laments in Act II, scene ii. Its first appearance, seemingly incidental, is as part of the elaborate comparative figure at Act II, scene ii, lines 17 ff. But her "ruined merchant" (merchant vessel) must recall Aeolus' prophecy of the wreck of "many a tall ship," and the recollection becomes even more apparent in the elaborate tableau of Dido and Aeneas which she sets up a few lines later (ll. 31 ff.). Aspatia identifies herself with the deserted Dido and pictures herself standing, helpless before the elements

> upon the sea-beach now,
> Mine arms thus, and mine hair blown with the
>   wind,
> Wild as that desert . . .
>   let the rocks
> Groan with continual surges; and behind me,
> Make all a desolation.
>
> (ll. 68-77)

Amintor she casts as the faithless Aeneas, on whose departing ship she calls down a storm:

> Could the gods know of this,
> And not, of all their number, raise a storm?
>
> (ll. 49-50)

The irony is, of course, that the wind god Boreas has raised just such a tempest as she despairs of and that it has already struck Amintor in the preceding scene. The wedding night has been stormily "troublesome" in a sense that Diphilus at III.i.3 does not guess.

In Act II, scene i, Amintor feels his inner storm of passion mocked by the peacefulness of the elements. His complaint reflects ironically on Aeolus' advice to Neptune "to strike a calm" for the bridal night (I.ii.264):

> Why is this night so calm?
> Why does not Heaven speak in thunder to us,
> And drown her voice?
>
> (II.i.253-254)

Appropriately, the height of Amintor's passion is expressed in his threat to cut the body of Evadne's lover "into motes, / And scatter it before the northern wind" (II.i.304-305)— where the reference to Boreas is felt less as a literal threat than as an ironic metaphor for his ungoverned rage. And in Act IV, scene i, when Melantius plots the revenge which Amintor's royalism has prevented, the motif occurs again as a metaphor for the revenger's unbridled fury against Evadne's seducer:

> By my just sword, h'ad safer
> Bestrid a billow when the angry North
> Ploughs up the sea . . .
>
> (ll. 76-78)

The storm so ominously raised by Boreas is not in fact to be allayed until the last scene of the play, after the destruction of "many a tall ship." For Amintor, Evadne's murder of the King has

> touch'd a life
> The very name of which had power to chain

> Up all my rage, and calm my wildest wrongs.
>
> (V.iv.136-138)

The image explicitly identifies his storm of rage on the wedding night with Boreas' breaking of his chain in the masque, and it signals the destruction of his last restraints. He finds himself in the "unknown wilderness" of Aspatia's tableau in Act II, scene ii, the psychological desert left by the violent winds of passion (V.iv.150). True calm of mind is possible now only when all passion is finally spent in death—as Evadne, at the last, comes to realize:

> Go; I am calm. Farewell, and peace for ever.
>
> (V.iv.170)

III

In the second of the encomiums which he contributed to the 1647 Folio, William Cartwright returned to the praise of Fletcher's constructive genius:

> Parts are so fitted unto parts, as doe
> Shew thou hadst wit, and Mathematicks too.

Fletcher, in Cartwright's admiring view, excelled all his contemporaries in mastery of "the simetry, which gives a Poem grace." In this essay I have been concerned to reveal something of the formal symmetry of *The Maid's Tragedy*. I have tried to show how it extends as Cartwright claims, to all the parts—to the rhetoric as much as to the characters and the plotting. The symmetry of the whole is primarily a symmetry of inversions and oppositions—love and death, marriage and adultery, appearance and reality—produced by the dramatists' juggling of familiar social situations. The rhetorical symmetry is designed to elaborate these structural conceits in terms of patterns of imagery whose effectiveness is paradoxically dependent on their very conventionality. Certainly, these patterns are of a different order from those we find in, say, Webster; and there is a good deal of force in Eliot's criticism that the language lacks a "network of tentacular roots reaching down to the deepest terrors and desires." But the criticism is only a half-truth. The imagery of *The Maid's Tragedy* is conventional rather than imaginative, but the conventionality is the consequence of a particular constructive function: it corresponds to the social familiarity of the situations out of which the plot, with its fanciful twists and witty counterturns, grows. There is a network of roots, but not of the kind that Eliot or Professor Bradbrook were looking for—its spread is wider and shallower.

The wedding masque justifies its formal prominence by the way in which its fundamental oppositions and ambiguities prefigure the development of the whole elaborate edifice of structural and rhetorical conceits. It provides, in effect, the necessary exposition of the play's "fancy," an exposition which predicates the "fate" of the play. In this it combines an oracular ambivalence, ensuring that "none can prevent the fancy," with a mathematic precision that justifies Cartwright's enthusiastic puff:

The whole designe, the shadowes, the lights such
That none can say he shewes or hides too much.

Beaumont and Fletcher have suffered more than most from neglect of the principle that criticism should move towards, rather than from, evaluative comparisons. An attempt to set that right need not, of course, involve any radical change in our assessment of their worth as dramatic poets, but it ought to enhance our respect for their virtues as theatrical craftsmen.

Ronald Broude (essay date 1989)

SOURCE: "Divine Right and Divine Retribution in Beaumont and Fletcher's *The Maid's Tragedy*," in *Shakespeare and Dramatic Tradition: Essays in Honor of S. F. Johnson,* edited by W. R. Elton and William B. Long, University of Delaware Press, 1989, pp. 246-63.

[*In the essay below, Broude examines Jacobean views on providence, justice, and the divine right of kings as depicted in* The Maid's Tragedy.]

We are accustomed to regarding **The Maid's Tragedy** (ca. 1608-11) as a play about the divine right of kings. The immunities conferred by kingship have a prominent part in the play, and the dilemma faced by the play's central character, Amintor, depends upon a conflict between the code of personal honor and a concept of monarchy that holds the person of the king to be inviolable.

Surprisingly, in view of the importance that the theme of kingship—or, more specifically, regicide—is thought to have in *The Maid's Tragedy,* there has been little agreement about what—if anything—the play says about kings, their responsibilities, and their privileges. During the reign of Charles II, influential members of the court seem to have felt that *The Maid's Tragedy,* with its portrayal of a lustful king slain by the woman he has seduced, was a play inimical to the interests of the Crown, and, accordingly, Edmund Waller undertook to rewrite Beaumont and Fletcher's most successful tragedy, providing two alternative endings in both of which the King's life is spared. On the other hand, Samuel Taylor Coleridge, at least partially on the basis of his reading of *The Maid's Tragedy,* characterized Beaumont and Fletcher as "the most servile *jure divino* royalists." J. St. Loe Strachey, however, vigorously contested this view, observing [in the introduction to the Mermaid edition of Beaumont and Fletcher's plays, 1887] that the portrayals of kings in the plays of Beaumont and Fletcher demonstrate attitudes quite different from the blind respect for royalty that Coleridge seems to have seen in works such as *The Maid's Tragedy*. More recently, John Danby [in *Poets on Fortune's Hill,* 1954] has sought to show that the royalist views enunciated by characters in the Beaumont and Fletcher plays were not necessarily the views of the playwrights themselves but were, rather, one of the several absolutes, conflicts between which furnished these proto-cavalier dramatists with dramatically effective situations.

What Beaumont and Fletcher's original audience may have thought of the regicide in *The Maid's Tragedy* we cannot say with certainty, for we have no contemporary comment on this aspect of the play. This lack of comment, however, may in itself be significant, for it suggests that the killing of the King in *The Maid's Tragedy* was not viewed by Jacobean playgoers with undue alarm. Indeed, had *The Maid's Tragedy* contained any matter which could have been regarded as politically objectionable, it is highly unlikely that the Master of the Revels would have allowed it to reach the stage: James I was, after all, a sovereign particularly sensitive to the privileges of royalty, and, as the author *The Trew Law of Free Monarchies,* he had propounded one of the most extreme statements of the theory of divine right to have been published during the Renaissance.

Plays in which wicked kings are killed are not uncommon in the drama of the English Renaissance—witness Saturninus, slain in *Titus Andronicus*; Piero, in *Antonio*'s *Revenge*; and Claudius, in *Hamlet.* What is unusual in *The Maid's Tragedy*'s treatment of regicide is the stress placed upon the view that the royal person is sacred. Other plays in which regicide occurs adroitly avoid reminding their audiences of the idea—sanctioned by approved doctrine under James—that a subject raising his hand against his lawful sovereign is guilty not only of treason but also of impiety. Regicide—even tyrannicide—was simply too sensitive a subject to deal with directly on the Stuart stage.

Perhaps, however, it was just this "forbidden" element in the regicide theme that made it attractive to Beaumont and Fletcher—and that helped to make *The Maid's Tragedy* popular with their audiences. For the courtier playgoers for whom Beaumont and Fletcher wrote, *The Maid's Tragedy* may well have provided much needed relief from the pressures—both intellectual and psychological—imposed by an unnecessarily rigid and unrealistically restrictive theory of royal privilege, a theory that, given the circumstances obtaining in the English court, could be questioned by the king's adherents neither openly nor directly.

But to prove successful, a play dealing with regicide was obliged to maintain a delicate balance between the dramatically effective and the politically objectionable. In *The Maid's Tragedy,* such a balance is carefully maintained by diverting attention from the political implications of the killing of the King. In so far as possible, the King's death is "depoliticized": the conflict in which the King plays so important a part is treated as a private rather than a public matter, and his transgressions are represented as injuries to his victim's personal honor and sexual vanity instead of crimes that affect the welfare of the commonwealth. Character and motivation are also artfully manipulated, so that the question of regicide, having been exploited for maximum dramatic effect in the second, third, and fourth acts, is tactfully forgotten when the King is actually killed in the fifth. Finally, the central issue of the play—the entrapment of Amintor into a tragic marriage intended to conceal the liaison of the King and Evadne—is portrayed as part of a larger complex of events over which the heavens preside and that they direct towards the punishment of the adulterous king. Here again, however, political questions are eschewed, for the heavens seem to be punishing not a king who is an adulterer but an adulterer who happens to be a king. As the heavens' program works itself out, Amintor is spared the cruel necessity of choosing between the dishonor of wittoldom and the guilt of regicide, and the King's death, when it does come, assumes a significance altogether different from that it would have had, had Amintor, after mature deliberation, elected to kill the King himself.

But if Beaumont and Fletcher were successful in their own day in making of *The Maid's Tragedy* a play that both is and is not about the rights of kings, their success has not been altogether able to withstand the passage of time. The strategies that they employed to render their treatment of regicide acceptable to their Jacobean audiences depended in large part upon the conventions of action and character that were peculiar to the Renaissance English stage and that did not survive the closing of the theaters in 1642. It is, therefore, not surprising that these strategies should have failed to have their intended effect when the theaters reopened after the Restoration. For audiences of the Restoration and succeeding generations, Amintor's forcefully expressed views on the inviolability of the royal person naturally suggested that *The Maid's Tragedy* was a play about the divine right of kings. Moreover, like much literature that seeks to exploit the sensational aspect of forbidden questions while avoiding the potentially embarrassing implications of their answers, *The Maid's Tragedy* has suffered from the weakening of the taboos that had made its carefully wrought equivocations so during to the courtier playgoers for whom it was written; to modern audiences, the play may well seem wanting in the integrity of vision that is expected of great tragedy. To recover some measure of the meaning that *The Maid's Tragedy* may have had for its original audience, it is necessary to read the play within the context of both the Jacobean political theory upon which it draws and the Jacobean dramatic conventions within which it was conceived. The insight to be gained is well worth the effort.

The limits of royal power and the immunities and privileges attaching to kingship—the theme with which *The Maid's Tragedy* seems to promise that it will deal—were issues much in men's minds circa 1610, the approximate date of *The Maid's Tragedy's* composition. The accession of James I had brought to the English throne a rigid theoretician who claimed for the Crown broader rights and greater privileges than had been either asserted in Tudor theory or implied by Tudor practice. Changes in the social structure of England, however, had given new standing to a middle class that ascribed to Parliament and the Law powers at least as great as those of the Crown. Social differences, economic pressures, and political confrontations served to aggravate the conflict between the Crown and the institutions in which were seen to lie alternative sources of power. Eventually, this conflict—and the antagonisms that it reflected—was to prove a cause of civil war; during James's reign, however, rival claims were still in the process of being staked and basic issues were still only tentatively defined.

Sixteenth-century English political thought had consisted of disparate (and sometimes mutually inconsistent) elements drawn from a broad range of traditions—from theology, from law, from speculative politics, and from custom. The views that had received official sanction—and that had been disseminated in forms ranging from learned treatises to simple sermons and homilies—had been those which supported the Tudors in their effort to establish a strong central government which would secure the Tudor dynasty from feudal upheavals of the sort that had toppled in turn their Lancastrian and Yorkist predecessors. Notwithstanding the sixteenth century's interest in—and astute application of—the principles of *Realpolitik,* approved Tudor theory had grounded its concept of kingship upon a medieval cosmology that represented the structure of the commonwealth as the political manifestation of the divine order that permeated and informed the universe. To each member of the commonwealth (as to each being in the universe) God was supposed to have assigned a place and a function. The place of the king in the commonwealth had been understood to be analogous to that of God in the universe: the king's function was to serve as God's deputy on earth, to maintain order in the body politic, and to punish those who transgressed the law. Theories that sought the mandate for kingship in the assent of those governed or in a system of mutual obligations between sovereign and subject had not been unknown in sixteenth-century England—indeed, they had been reflected in some of England's most venerable institutions—but Tudor theorists had preferred to regard royal power as flowing directly from God: the king and the magistrates, it was asserted, held offices ordained by God, and the power that they exercised was therefore His.

Failure on the part of the king to seek out and prosecute all malefactors had been considered an extremely serious matter, for unpunished crime had been understood to lay upon the entire commonwealth a burden of collective guilt. Especially grave was the situation created when the king himself violated the laws that it was his duty to uphold. Nevertheless, Tudor theory, consistent with its emphasis on the importance of civil order and its fear of riot and insurrection, had assumed the position that no royal malfeasance—neither negligence in the pursuit of malefactors nor misconduct by the sovereign himself—could justify the use of force against the legitimate king. The wicked king, it had been argued, was a punishment visited by the heavens upon an unworthy people; to resist such a king was therefore to resist the will of the heavens. The subject of such an evil sovereign was advised to accept God's will and to obey his lawful ruler. Only if his king commanded a course of action manifestly contrary to the word of God could the subject refuse to obey; such refusal, however, rendered him liable to whatever punishment the sovereign thus thwarted might choose to inflict. Called by modern scholars the "doctrine of non-resistance," this insistence upon the immunity of the king from reprisals by his subjects and the obligation of subjects to obey even tyrannical kings had been a prominent feature of "official" Tudor theory; it had been especially valuable in helping to maintain political stability during the uncertain early years of the English Reformation.

With the accession of Mary Tudor in 1553, English Protestants, who for the most part had been staunch in their support of the doctrine of non-resistance under Henry and Edward, had begun to reconsider their position. The sources of royal power were reexamined, and the view that the king derives his authority from "the people," who, if he abuses the trust placed in him, may remove him from office, had been revived and elaborated. The duty of a good Christian living under an impious king had been studied, and it had been suggested, tentatively at first but later more forcefully, that passive resistance might not in all cases be a sufficient response to the ungodly exercise of royal power: tyrannicide had been openly discussed. With the death of Mary in 1558, English Protestants' interest in tyrannicide had understandably waned, but on the continent Reformers and Counter-Reformers alike had become intensely concerned with defining the circumstances that might justify active opposition to a legitimate but despotic ruler; some of the Catholic documents in this bitter exchange of pamphlets and treatises had been unmistakably addressed to the Catholic subjects of England's Protestant queen. Concern with tyrannicide had not, however, been purely speculative; events such as the deposition of Mary Stuart in Scotland and the assassination of William of Orange in the Netherlands had served to keep tyrannicide a topic of current if not continuously immediate interest for Englishmen.

The broad range of ideas on kingship to which Englishmen had been exposed during the sixteenth century all but precluded the possibility of a favorable reception for views on royal authority as militant as those professed by James I when he ascended the English throne in 1603. As James VI of Scotland, the new English king had waged a long and bitter struggle to impose upon the unruly Scots nobility the same sort of strong monarchy that the Tudors had created in England a century earlier, and, accordingly, his conception of the divine right of kings had become too firmly fixed to permit comfortable adjustment to the very different political conditions obtaining in his new kingdom. James's views, which his subjects could read in his published speeches and in *The Trew Law of Free Monarchies,* went well beyond the familiar model presented by "official" Tudor theory. For James, the king derived his authority directly from God and was therefore responsible to no earthly power. The king, James argued, stood above the law, for laws were established in the king's name, and might be altered, suspended or revoked at his pleasure. The king might obey his own laws if he chose, but he was under no obligation to do so, and he might without reproach ignore them when it suited him. To all intents and purposes, then, royal power was absolute, untrammeled by institutions of any sort: this, indeed, is what James meant by a "free" monarchy.

To be sure, the king would be called to account before God both for his own conduct and for the welfare of his subjects, and severe punishment would certainly be visited upon the ruler found to have failed in his duty. Sometimes, James admitted, invoking a commonplace of Tudor doctrine, this punishment would take the form of an insurrection raised by God among the subjects of the wicked

sovereign; all good Christians, however, were urged not to participate themselves in such mutinies, for, they were warned, subjects who overthrow their king are instruments of God which, having served His purpose, will be delivered up to the punishments prescribed for rebels.

Although *The Maid's Tragedy* draws upon political theories that would have been familiar to Englishmen during the first decade of James's reign, it does so in ways that effectively remove the play from the context of contemporary political controversy. *The Maid's Tragedy* presupposes no more than superficial acquaintance with either James's views or the premises of sixteenth- or early seventeenth-century political thought; it avoids serious discussion of both abstruse and controversial aspects of political theory; and it alludes to royal privileges and immunities only in the simplest and most general terms. No attempt is made to examine the issues most likely to be of current interest—the limits of the king's powers and the relationship of royal authority to the laws of the realm. Nor is there any balanced presentation of conflicting views: the broad yet vague claims made on behalf of royal privilege by Amintor, the King, and Evadne are nowhere countered—not even in 3.2, the crucial scene in which Amintor reveals his predicament to Melantius—by reference to the obligations inherent in the office of kingship or to possible (if not universally acceptable) courses of action open to subjects whose king fails in his duty.

The concepts of kingship upon which *The Maid's Tragedy* draws are applied to a situation so apolitical and so unusual that they seem to have little if any relevance to the real world of politics. In *The Maid's Tragedy,* a king and his mistress propose to make use of the privileges and immunities of the royal office in a cynical attempt to keep their illicit relationship secret: they depend upon the position of the King both to compel a loyal subject's participation in their scheme and to shield them from the subject's wrath when he discovers how he has been deceived. But Tudor-Stuart political theory does not contemplate the flagrant and premeditated abuse of royal authority in an essentially private matter such as this. Traditional theory assumes that, unlike the King in *The Maid's Tragedy,* most sovereigns whose subjects complain of them will have some measure—or at least some pretext—of justice on their side. Moreover, the wrongs to which English political thought addresses itself are political wrongs—abuses on a large scale involving the consciences, lives, or property of substantial numbers of subjects. Aside from the scandal of his personal life, however, the King in *The Maid's Tragedy* remains a cipher: we do not know, in political terms, whether he has been been a good king or a bad one, whether his policies have been wise or foolish, his kingdom prosperous or impoverished. He seems, in fact, to exist in a political vacuum; the sins for which he dies are private sins, and his death, in so far as a king's death can be, is without political significance. The situation presented in *The Maid's Tragedy* is, then, an artificial one sufficiently removed from the realities of English politics to make the application of political theory to it a harmless academic exercise, an exercise in the tradition of the *controversiae,* which, as Eugene Waith has shown [in

The Patterns of Tragicomedy in Beaumont and Fletcher,
1952], play so interesting a part in the drama of Beaumont
and Fletcher.

Although *The Maid's Tragedy* assiduously avoids discussion of specific topics that might have been construed to
have relevance to Jacobean politics, the importance accorded the question of royal immunity in the second, third,
and fourth acts requires that, if the play is not to appear
a *pièce à thèse* on the limits of royal privilege, the killing
of the King must not seem the considered act of a morally
responsible character who has carefully reviewed the arguments both for and against regicide. The King has committed serious crimes, and he must certainly be made to
pay for them, but Amintor, who has suffered most from
the King's malfeasance and has had to decide whether or
not to revenge himself upon his sovereign, cannot be made
the immediate instrument of the King's punishment: having affirmed his belief in the inviolability of the royal
person, Amintor cannot reverse himself without calling
into question the adequacy of the doctrine of royal immunity. The punishment of the King is accordingly accomplished through the joint efforts of three characters among
whom the functions of exposing the King and putting him
to death are carefully distributed: Amintor reveals the
King's crimes to Melantius; Melantius plans and sets in
motion the machinery of retribution, and Evadne executes
Melantius's instructions. Great care is exercised in managing the details of circumstance and character that would
have shaped an audience's perception of the significance
of the characters' actions, so that the likelihood of any
incident's assuming embarrassing political implications is
effectively minimized.

The character of Amintor and the circumstances in which
he is placed are manipulated in such a way as to make his
reluctance to proceed against the King both credible and
acceptable to a Jacobean audience. The particulars that
define the injury that Amintor has suffered are carefully
selected and arranged so that he cannot take action against
the King without changing from an innocent victim to a
villain revenger. The conventions of the Renaissance English stage recognized only one sort of crime for which
revenge might be sanctioned—a felony (usually but not
always murder) secretly committed against an immediate
blood relative. Judged in accordance with these conventions, the injuries that the King has done Amintor—commanding him to break his vows to Aspatia and marrying
him to the dishonored Evadne—although grave, would not
have been regarded by a Jacobean audience as serious
enough to warrant revenge. Thus the question of justifiable regicide does not really arise in *The Maid's Tragedy,* for regardless of whether Evadne's lover be a king or
a commoner, Amintor lacks sufficient cause to take action
against him.

Nor does Amintor's character—a skillful blend of engag-
ing virtues and serious flaws—suggest that he will be likely to repair the damage that the King and Evadne have
done his honor. Amintor can be generous, brave, and stead-
fast in his loyalty to principles in which he believes, but
he can also be petty, weak, and strangely indifferent to the

demands of the honor he professes to value so highly. In
2.1, we see him—under great stress, it is true—disgrace-
fully agreeing to act the role of satisfied husband for which
the King and Evadne have cast him; he defends his decision with the thoroughly unacceptable argument that hon-
or is merely a matter of appearances:

> Me thinkes I am not wrong'd,
> Nor is it ought, if from the censuring world
> I can but hide it—reputation
> Thou art a word, no more. . . .
>
> (2.1.331-34)

These sentiments are in perfect harmony with those which
underlie Amintor's plea in 3.1 that Melantius not revenge
himself upon the King lest it

> shame me to posterity. . . .
> It will be cald
> Honor in thee to spill thy sisters blood
> If she her birth abuse, and on the King
> A brave revenge, but on me that have walkt
> With patience in it, it will fix the name
> Of fearefull cuckold.
>
> (3.2.216, 223-28)

We are reminded by these speeches that Amintor has already compromised his honor by acceding to the King's
command and abandoning Aspatia, already his troth-plight
wife. As we have observed, Renaissance Englishmen were
unlikely to have regarded royal authority as having power
sufficient to compel a subject to disobey the dictates of
his own conscience, nor were they likely to have regarded
the plea of obedience to a royal command as absolving a
subject from responsibility for his own actions. Amintor
himself shares these views: as he acknowledges,

> It was the King first mov'd me to't, but he
> Has not my will in keeping.
>
> (2.1.130-31)

Nevertheless, Amintor has allowed his honor to be stained
because of his undiscriminating allegiance to the Crown
and because of an ignoble preference for present comfort—the King's favor, alliance with his friend Melantius,
and marriage to a much admired woman—to the disad-
vantages of incurring royal displeasure while keeping his
word to Aspatia. For an audience sensitive to such failings, Amintor's inability to redeem his honor by taking
action against the King would seem neither surprising nor
out of character.

The passive role that Amintor must play if *The Maid's
Tragedy* is safely to avoid politically compromising issues
determines the course that his career follows. Amintor's
tragedy conforms to the pattern associated with such similar tragic figures as Richard II and Lear, and audiences
acquainted with the persecutions that these noble but flawed
characters impotently endure must have found the shape
of Amintor's tragedy familiar. Like Richard and Lear,
Amintor can see the immediate cause of his misery in an
ill-considered choice—in Amintor's case, the decision to

obey the royal command and marry Evadne instead of Aspatia. This decision—like those of Richard and Lear, superficially tenable but tainted by elements of self-indulgence and moral irresponsibility—opens Amintor to persecution by powerful and implacable enemies; it seems also to deprive him of the ability effectively to take the initiative in determining his own fate. Reduced to theatrical displays of self-pity and futile rage, Amintor must look to others to right the wrongs he has suffered. Only when he has been rescued from the consequences of his fatal choice is Amintor able to regain the moral composure with which bravely to confront his tragedy.

Melantius, who provides the impetus for action against the King, is presented as a veteran warrior, less naive and more adept at intrigue than he would like others to believe, but nevertheless decidedly more comfortable with simple deeds than with complex ideas. Forced to choose between the rival claims of friendship and family solidarity, Melantius quickly decides upon the priority of his loyalties and acts in accordance with the decision he has made. His preference for action allows him little opportunity for the sort of prolonged meditation that might be construed as an embarrassing discussion of regicide, and this quality permits the playwrights to accomplish almost without our noticing it the dangerous transition from deliberation on Amintor's plight to action against the King.

Particular attention has been given to the details that show Melantius to be not only a gentleman concerned with the honor of his family but also a just and pious man who accepts the part he must play in the King's punishment fully aware of what will be required of him. In depicting the revenge that Melantius effects, the playwrights are careful "to touch all the bases." Although quick to act, Melantius is not over hasty: having heard—and believed—Amintor's accusations, he nevertheless seeks confirmation of what his friend has told him: having bullied a confession from Evadne, he patiently allows her to corroborate Amintor's charges by herself identifying the King as her lover. Assured of the King's guilt, Melantius rightly perceives that the King's crimes are offenses against the heavens and that the revengers are the agents of the gods' vengeance: "All the gods require it [i.e., the killing of the King]," Melantius tells his sister: "They are dishonored in him" (4.1.144-45). Finally, having successfully contrived the King's death and secured the safety of himself and his followers, Melantius casts aside the dissimulation that he has so skillfully employed, accepting responsibility for all that he has done and submitting his cause for judgment. Melantius has sought no material benefit for himself from the King's death; he is prepared to serve the new king as a loyal subject. That his actions have been scrupulous and his cause just is suggested by the choric observations of Strato ("He looks as if he had the better cause, . . . I do beleeve him noble . . ." [5.2.14, 19]) and by the promptness of Lysippus in pardoning him.

Evadne, to whom falls the actual killing of the King, is a character so filled with contradictions and so lacking in moral substance that it is difficult to attach moral significance to the regicide she commits. When we first see her,

she is proud of her position as the King's mistress, but she is not altogether comfortable with the burdens that the necessity of concealing her liaison have placed upon her. She pities Amintor, yet she is able cold-bloodedly to make him accept the cruel realities of the shameful position into which she has helped to maneuver him. Her confession to Melantius is extracted by brute force instead of being freely given, and her "reformation" seems dictated as much by fear of her irate brother as by sincere repentance. Although Evadne accepts the killing of the King as a form of penance, she sees it also as a way of winning Amintor. Unlike Melantius, Evadne is quite unaware that the King has offended the gods and that in punishing him she is acting as the heavens' agent; instead, she sees herself as avenging her much-injured husband, her dishonored brother, and her own lost purity. Her suicide, which she regards as proof of her love for Amintor, is merely another indication of her emotional instability and inability to recognize the moral principles that should be guiding her actions; having substituted love for ambition as her *summum bonum,* she dies, like another "reformed" criminal who seeks belatedly to avenge his own victim, in a mist. She is, to use the familiar image that James employs in *The Trew Law,* an instrument that the heavens have employed to scourge a wicked king and that, having served its purpose, will be cast into the fire.

Perhaps the most effective means by which *The Maid's Tragedy* contrives not to be a play about divine right is by being a play about divine retribution. The chain of incidents by which the adultery of the King and Evadne is revealed and the adulterers are punished is conceived and presented in accordance with the formulaic sequence of events that on the Renaissance English stage was reserved for portrayals of the ways in which the heavens bring secret crimes to light and mete out justice to secret criminals. There is the secret crime exposed by the miscarriage of the very scheme intended to conceal it; there is the twist of plot by which the criminals are made the instruments of their own undoing; and there is the liberal use of dramatic irony to underline the limitations of the cunning in which the criminals have trusted to help them escape retribution. For a Jacobean audience, the presence of these conventions of action and dramaturgy would have indicated unequivocally that *The Maid's Tragedy* belongs to the tradition of plays concerned with the implementation of God's Justice and the operation of Divine Providence.

All of the events that constitute the action of *The Maid's Tragedy* have their origin in the adultery of the King and Evadne. To provide against exposure should Evadne conceive, the lovers devise the ingenious stratagem of marrying Evadne to Amintor, a highly regarded young man whose respect for the Crown will, they cynically assume, protect them from his wrath when he learns how he is being used. This cruel ploy backfires, however, when Amintor, having discovered the truth about his bride, proves too transparent to hide it from his friend Melantius. Having satisfied himself of the King's guilt and his sister's dishonor, Melantius does not hesitate in deciding between his allegiance to the King who has betrayed him and his duty to the gods and his own honor; he binds Evadne by oath to kill the

King, and sets about himself to secure support for his enterprise. When the King next commands Evadne to his bed, all the circumstances of their illicit relationship combine to aid her in fulfilling her vow. The courtiers who guide Evadne to the royal chamber are told that it is the King's pleasure that "none be neere," and, obeying what they take to be their sovereign's command, they are too far away to hear him when he calls for help. Tied to the bed lest his strength prove too great for Evadne, the King at first thinks his bonds part of a new amorous game; when he has at last been convinced of Evadne's fatal intent, it is too late for him to offer effective resistance. But the ultimate irony of the King's death lies in the fact that in summoning Evadne to his bed on this occasion, the King has been the instrument of his own punishment.

Evadne, too, finds that irony attends her end. Having sought to redeem herself before Amintor, whose merits she has belatedly recognized, Evadne finds him appalled by the regicide that she proudly confesses to him: the same uncritical respect for the royal person upon which she and the King had earlier relied now condemns her in Amintor's eyes. Disappointed by Amintor's unexpected yet predictable response, Evadne kills herself.

As is often the case in Renaissance English plays dealing with divine retribution, the plot of *The Maid's Tragedy* consists of a chain of incidents in which each link is a logical but not inevitable consequence of the preceding one. Events grow out of one another in obedience to rigorously applied principles of cause and effect, but at crucial junctures a higher power determines which course among several equally plausible ones events will follow. That the direction that events take at these crucial junctures is not only consistent but also yields a conclusion that affirms the very justice that the adulterers have sought to circumvent suggests that the higher power is not chance but Divine Providence.

The elaborate machinery of crime and retribution that the liaison of the King and Evadne sets in motion not only brings about the punishment of the two adulterers but also claims the lives of Aspatia, Amintor, and Melantius, the three characters who have suffered most from the adulterers' ill-conceived attempt at concealment. The tragedies of these "victims," who, with best meaning incur the worst, are shaped by the same principles of cause and effect and the same fatal combinations of character and circumstance that determine the careers of the King and Evadne.

Aspatia, who has never recovered from the severe depression induced by Amintor's betrayal, remains ignorant of the failure of Amintor's marriage. Resolving to seek her death at Amintor's hands, she disguises herself as her soldier brother and delivers a challenge to the unhappy young man to whom she had thought she would be married. Aspatia's motives are difficult to identify: on the one hand, she seems prompted by a sincere desire to end her suffering, but, on the other, she seems attracted by the idea of a perverse vengeance, which will fix upon Amintor the responsibility for terminating literally the life that his broken promise has already figuratively destroyed. De-

clining to defend herself, Aspatia receives the fatal wound she has sought; before expiring, however, she reveals herself to Amintor, and the two exchange expressions of love. Amintor, whose intense suffering has already suggested thoughts of suicide, proves unable to withstand this latest blow; taking up the sword by which Aspatia has died, he slays himself. Melantius, seeing the corpse of the youth whose friendship he had valued more than his own family's honor, prepares to take his own life; restrained, he vows that

> I will never eate
> Or drinke, or sleepe, or have to doe with that
> That may presrve life, this I sweare to keepe.
>   (5.3.288-90)

There is no reason to suppose that Melantius will not honor this oath.

It is the untimeliness of Aspatia's response to her painful situation that puts the seal of tragedy upon events that to all appearances might otherwise have yielded a happy conclusion. When Aspatia confronts Amintor with her challenge, the King has already met his death, and Melantius has already received his pardon; in another instant, Evadne, having been rejected by Amintor, will kill herself. The sense of tragedy is heightened by the feeling that a matter of moments has made the difference between the happy outcome that for a brief minute had seemed possible and the catastrophe we witness. Lysippus, who, intuiting the justice of his brother's death, had expressed the hope that "heaven forgive all" (5.2.22), now, surveying the bloody scene, realizes that his hope had been vain; soberly, he draws the moral implicit in the events we have watched unfold:

> May this a faire example be to me,
> To rule with temper, for on lustfull Kings
> Unlookt for suddaine deaths from God are sent,
> But curst is he that is their instrument.
>   (5.3.292-95)

For a Jacobean audience, conditioned by religious training, by political propaganda, and by repeated exposure to plays embodying orthodox views on divine retribution and kingship, Lysippus's comments would have constituted an appropriate—indeed, a self-evident—interpretation of the tragedies of the King, Evadne, Aspatia, Amintor, and Melantius. The adultery of the King and Evadne has offended the heavens, and the adulterers must certainly be punished. The punishment of the King by means of human agents, however, necessarily entails a new offense. The deaths of Aspatia, Amintor, and Melantius make up the price required by the heavens in order to wipe out both the transgression of which the adulterers have been guilty and the transgression that must be committed in punishing them.

For a modern audience, skeptical about the operation of Divine Providence and reluctant to regard kingship as sacrosanct, the temptation is strong to dismiss Lysippus's curtain speech as post facto moralizing that has no organic relationship to the events of the play. To discount Lysippus's comments, however, is to run the danger of reading the play not as tragedy but as a study of neurotic characters who suffer the inevitable consequences of their own self-indulgence, weakness, and perversity. It is, however, the validity within the world of *The Maid's Tragedy* of the principles that Lysippus invokes—the sanctity of kingship and the concern of divine Providence to affirm this sanctity even while punishing a wicked king—that creates the tragic predicament in which Aspatia, Amintor, and Melantius find themselves.

To acknowledge the operation of Divine Providence in *The Maid's Tragedy,* however, is not necessarily to acquiesce in the justice that Divine Providence is represented as upholding. Christian acceptance of the heavens' will is not the only possible response to the glimpse we are granted of an inscrutable power that insists that even criminal rulers may not be deposed without penalty and that exacts a terrible price in suffering and death in return for maintaining order in the universe. Horror and outrage are responses equally appropriate to the spectacle of stern laws being implemented pitilessly, and such responses are not necessarily incompatible with the pious awe and enlightened resignation that such "demonstrations" of God's justice were traditionally supposed to induce. In *The Maid's Tragedy*—as in similar Elizabethan and Jacobean plays—important elements of our response depend upon the discrepancy between what, on the one hand, we, as mortals with limited vision, perceive as "just" with respect to particular characters and situations, and what on the other hand, we are asked to accept as the manifest will of the omniscient and omnipotent powers whose Purpose is by definition identical with Justice. The more rigid, repressive, and arbitrary seem the principles we are required to acknowledge as established by these powers for the common good or the glory of God, the greater is the potential for tragedy. In Jacobean England, the tension between the extreme and uncompromising views on royal authority that James espoused and the broad range of alternative positions readily accessible to well-informed Englishmen provided favorable conditions for the creation of tragedy, which, by portraying a universe which functions in strict obedience to royalist principles, could generate situations in which intense and seemingly unmerited suffering might be seen to confirm the criticism of these principles implicit in the existence of rival political theories. *The Maid's Tragedy* adroitly exploited this tension, simultaneously affirming and questioning the religious and political doctrines upon which the events it portrays depend for their meaning.

A KING AND NO KING

Arthur Mizener (essay date 1940)

SOURCE: "The High Design of *A King and No King*," in *Modern Philology,* Vol. XXXVIII, No. 2, November, 1940, pp. 133-54.

[*In this essay Mizener argues that rather than seeking to imbue* A King and No King *with moral significance, Beaumont and Fletcher simply aimed to "generate in the audience a patterned sequence of responses, a complex series of feelings and attitudes so stimulated and related as to give each its maximum effectiveness."*]

It is *A King and No King* which [John] Dryden [in "The Grounds of Criticism in Tragedy"] described as "the best of [Beaumont and Fletcher's] designs, the most approaching to antiquity, and the most conducing to move pity." Apparently it was the play's power to move him which determined this opinion, for he added: " 'Tis true, the faults of the plot are so evidently proved, that they can no longer be denied. The beauties of it must therefore lie. . . . in the lively touches of the passion." These remarks come very close to implying that a play can be formally ordered, given design, in terms of "the lively touches of the passion" rather than assuming, as most neoclassic theory does, that these "lively touches" are minor elements which have by their nature to be subordinated to a design largely determined by the plot. And Dryden goes on to do some very queer things to the seventeenth-century concept of Nature in order to defend Beaumont and Fletcher on something like these grounds. ["The beauties of [*A King and No King*] must therefore lie either in the lively touches of the passion; or we must conclude, as I think we may, that even in imperfect plots there are less degrees of Nature, by which some faint emotions of pity and terror are raised in us: . . . for nothing can move our nature, but by some natural reason, which works upon passions. And, since we acknowledge the effect, there must be something in the cause."] The reason for this stretching of the neoclassic theory is that Dryden feels *A King and No King* to be a better play than it can be shown to be by any analysis based on the strict interpretation of neoclassic theory which [Thomas] Rymer adopted [in The *Tragedies of the Last Age Considered,* 1692]. This is in effect to argue that the play is not a bad example of the best kind of tragedy but a good example of an "inferior sort of tragedies."

Throughout the nineteenth century, however, the possibility of explaining the success of the Beaumont and Fletcher plays (for they are all alike in this respect) in this way was lost sight of. The nineteenth-century critics were intent on showing that all successful plays were functional in terms of character as they conceived it and presented the human situation in terms of their moral predilections. They therefore undertook to show, and nothing is easier, that *A King and No King* was defective in plot, that is, that it was not formally ordered in terms of the narrative, and that, where it was not defective in plot, it was painfully lacking in regard for nineteenth-century decorum. This conclusion ought to have proved, as Rymer's conclusion ought to have, that Beaumont and Fletcher's play was a failure. Yet the best of the nineteenth-century critics continued to admit that the play in some sense succeeds. [William] Hazlitt is a good example; he found, on the one hand, that "what may be called the love-scenes. . . . have all the indecency and familiarity of a brothel," and, on the other, that the play was "superior in power and effect" ["Lectures on the Dramatic Literature of the Age of Elizabeth"].

The more or less explicit contradiction in these nine-teenth-century judgments between the theoretical conclusion and the actual response to the play is the result of the assumption that narrative form is the only kind of form a play can have, that the narrative form must therefore of necessity be the bearer of the play's meaning and value, and that "the lively touches of the passion" must be subordinated to it. With the very greatest kind of plays this assumption is probably justified, for in the final analysis we are not satisfied to be moved by what we find on consideration not to be natural or morally true in the deepest sense. But there are not very many plays of this kind, and Beaumont and Fletcher's are not among them. Their plays are of a different kind, and critics who analyze them on an assumption not relevant to this kind are bound, if they are at all sensitive, to land in a contradiction between what they prove by analysis and what they feel about the plays.

It is the object of this essay to try to define the kind of play Beaumont and Fletcher wrote and to try to show how successfully they did so. The primary concern of their kind of play is to order its material, not in terms of narrative form, but in terms of what might be called emotional or psychological form. Beaumont and Fletcher's aim was to generate in the audience a patterned sequence of responses, a complex series of feelings and attitudes so stimulated and related as to give to each its maximum effectiveness and yet to keep all in harmonious balance. The ultimate ordering form in their plays is this emotional form, and the narrative, though necessarily the ostensible object, is actually with them only a means to the end of establishing this rich and careful arrangement of responses.

There is nothing particularly novel about the idea that a complex of emotions generated by a loosely bound set of scenes—loosely bound, that is, as narrative—was the primary object of a Jacobean play. The consequences of approaching Beaumont and Fletcher this way have not, however, been very much considered. Yet Beaumont and Fletcher, perhaps more skilfully than most of their contemporaries, directed all the resources of their plays to the induction of such complexes of emotions; they learned, as so many Jacobean dramatists did not, how to manage character and event so that they became useful to this kind of play rather than irrelevant or at best intolerably confused. This is not to say that Webster, for example, constructed a less valuable pattern of responses. I mean only that Beaumont and Fletcher showed more skill in using narrative elements such as character and event to this end. While Webster, Ford, and Tourneur frequently sacrificed the narrative to the demands of emotional form, Beaumont and Fletcher not only showed less willingness to lose the advantage of the representational illusion of an ordered narrative but succeeded in finding out how to use it to further the effect of the emotional form.

It is probably at least in part because Beaumont and Fletcher constructed the narrative so carefully as a means of supporting and enriching the emotional form that critics have been able to suppose it was the end, the ultimate ordering form, and not merely a means, in their plays. There is not

Title page of the 1619 edition of A King and No King.

much chance that a critic will focus his attention exclusively on the narrative in Webster, for example. But the skill with which Beaumont and Fletcher construct the narrative of their plays invites just this kind of misunderstanding.

There is plainly another reason, however, why critics have been unwilling to approach Beaumont and Fletcher as they approach Webster. Webster, though his range of feelings is narrow, appears sincere; it is felt that the mood his plays explore is serious. Critics are willing, therefore, not only to pass over the defective narrative in his plays but even to forgive him what are at least for us faults of the emotional form. But, though the range of feelings presented in a Beaumont and Fletcher play is by no means narrow, the lightness of the mood which seems to lie behind their emotional effects offends many critics.

I do not intend in this paper to argue with this judgment of the moral shortcomings which are supposed to inhere in the mood which Beaumont and Fletcher project with such skill in their plays. It has already been discussed too much at the expense of ignoring the skill itself. Beaumont and Fletcher succeeded in writing plays embodying a mood into which their audience could enter wholeheartedly, and so found "(that which is the only grace and setting forth of a Tragedy) a full and understanding Auditory." And the dramatic presentation of that mood was accomplished through the use of a set of moral and dramatic conventions which were understood and accepted in Beaumont and Fletcher's day. Many of the charges, for example, which are made against their plays are the result of a failure to remember that "it was the letter and not the spirit of action that counted with Elizabethan [and to an even greater extent Jacobean] audiences" [M. C. Bradbrook, *Themes and Conventions in Elizabethan Tragedy*]. The substitution of one woman for another, the repentance of villains, such tricks of plot as those by which an Arbaces or an Angelo is freed from the guilt of his evil impulses apparently had for these audiences no "moral valency" at all. It is perfectly understandable that such a baroque art as Beaumont and Fletcher's should offend critics of a serious cast of mind. But if there is to be any understanding of the exact nature of the mood embodied in their best plays, we shall simply have to grant them their right to the moral and dramatic conventions of their day by means of which that mood is given body and life. It will be time enough to condemn the mood of their plays, if we wish to, after they are understood.

A reader normally notices the narrative of a play first, and as you examine the narrative of *A King and No King* you are surprised—if you have read the textbooks—not only to discover how carefully planned the plot is, but to realize that there is a moral plainly implicit in that plot. To be sure, Beaumont and Fletcher are not particularly in earnest about it; they apparently care for it not so much because it is moral as because it can be used to arouse certain feelings in the audience. Nonetheless it is there, as it were, to justify the play at this level of interest. Arbaces, for all his good qualities, is so domineering and proud that Gobrias feels he cannot reveal the truth until Arbaces' pride has been broken. He chooses as his means for breaking that pride, Panthea. If Arbaces comes to love Panthea enough, Gobrias is to be thought of as reasoning, his sense of omnipotence will be destroyed, and he will gladly give up his claim to royal birth. This scheme is a particularly clever one for Gobrias to have devised because it will also serve his desire to retain a high place for his son by making him Panthea's husband. The psychology of character in this plot is simplified, as it so often is in Elizabethan plays, and one may question the probability of many of the incidents which the dramatists force to play into Gobrias' hands, as Shakespeare forces chance to favor Iago and not to favor Romeo and Juliet. But these are the conventional short cuts of all drama of the period; grant them, and this central plot is tightly knit.

Parallel to this main plot runs the minor story of Tigranes, Spaconia, and Lygones. It is attached to the main plot not only by the careful interrelation of the characters but by the balancing of the emotional relations between the four characters. In general, this subplot is used as a contrast to the main plot. It is the Everlasting's canon against incest which hinders Arbaces and Panthea, and the helplessness of Arbaces' earthly power to destroy that canon is emphasized; what hinders Tigranes and Spaconia is mainly a lack of earthly power, the Everlasting being, presumably, a sup-

porter of romantic love. Finally, there is the comic subplot built around Bessus. Bessus' plight is the comic version of Arbaces'. Like Arbaces, Bessus is boastful, and his troubles, like Arbaces', are the consequences of his boastfulness.

It is impossible not to admire the ingenuity of this construction; yet most readers will probably feel that it is more ingenious than satisfying. The difficulty is most apparent in the case of Bessus; for all their skilful management of it, Beaumont and Fletcher do not seem really to care about the parallel between Bessus and Arbaces. The complex comparison of the attitudes of different kinds of people in the same basic dilemma in the typical Shakespeare play gives the reader a sense not only that the possible implications of the comparison are almost as multitudinous as those of life itself but that Shakespeare is serious about those implications. The form of the narrative, once one has granted the conventions of the Elizabethan theater, is a correlative of Shakespeare's own sense of the world; it is both verisimilar and meaningful. The reader feels none of this fundamental seriousness in Beaumont and Fletcher's parallel, and he does not because their narrative is not the correlative of a serious sense of the world, but only of a convenient and conventional one. Most of the Jacobean dramatists gave up trying to make their plays accord with both "reality and justice," with the moving and significant worlds of their imagination and the always more or less—but in their apprehensions unconquerably—discordant facts of the actual world. Most of them set about organizing the worlds of their plays in accord with their ideas of justice; but they succeeded only at the expense of keeping the narrative in accord with their sense of reality. Beaumont and Fletcher so organized the world of their plays, too, if one can describe the underlying mood which determined the pattern of the emotional form of their plays as a sense of justice. But they did not, in the process, allow the narrative form to lose all formal order. They gave the narrative of their plays a pattern; but it is not a morally significant pattern, and its great complexity is not determined by any complexity of meaning but exists because a complex narrative is itself exciting, as well as the means of providing the maximum number of exciting moments.

It is for this reason that the reader feels none of the seriousness, finds none of the moral significance, in the parallel between Arbaces and Bessus which he does in the structurally similar parallels in Shakespeare's plays. And this same lack of significance can be traced through the rest of the play's structure. There is no serious meaning to be found in the elaborate interrelation of the main plot and the subplot. And in the main plot the light of our attention is, if the narrative were actually the means for giving the play form and significance, in the wrong place: Gobrias' scheming, which provides the trial of Arbaces and Panthea, is so in the shadow that we are scarcely able to detect it, and the tragic moral implications of that trial are not only never fully developed, but sometimes scandalously neglected; Beaumont and Fletcher's only contingent interest in them is most apparent when the characters are moralizing most violently. We are forced into the realization that, despite the care and skill with which Beaumont and Fletcher have constructed the narrative of this play, they are interested not so much in having it carry a serious meaning as in using it to support and enrich an emotional form; this is the significant form of the play. In spite of their great care for the narrative, the focus of attention in *A King and No King,* as in all their plays, is the emotional form, just as it is in the plays of any typical Jacobean dramatist. No more than in the case of Webster or Tourneur or Ford, therefore, is it a really relevant objection to Beaumont and Fletcher that the feelings displayed by a character or generated in the audience by a scene are found, on close examination, to be out of proportion to the narrative situation which ostensibly justifies their existence.

The successful creation of a formal structure of this kind depends, in the first place, on an ability to display with elegance, with a kind of detached eloquence, the attitudes presented. It depends, in the second place, on an ability to vary and repeat these attitudes in such a way as to give the pattern which they form richness and interest. The coolness, the artificiality, the "insincerity" of the emotional displays in Beaumont and Fletcher's plays is the deliberately calculated means by which they give the necessary weight to the particular attitude presented. Consider, for example, Arbaces' great speech in the first scene of Act III of *A King and No King*:

My sister!—Is she dead? If it be so,
Speak boldly to me, for I am a man,
And dare not quarrel with divinity;
And do not think to cozen me with this.
I see you all are mute, and stand amazed,
Fearful to answer me: it is too true,
A decreed instant cuts off every life,
For which to mourn is to repine: she died
A virgin though, more innocent than sleep,
As clear as her own eyes; and blessedness
Eternal waits upon her where she is:
I know she could not make a wish to change
Her state for new; and you shall see me bear
My crosses like a man. We all must die;
And she hath taught us how.

This speech would verge on the extravagant in almost any play. It is in a manner the simplicity and grandeur of which is reserved by the greatest dramatists for the moment when the hero becomes morally certain of the tragic fact of the play, in this case the death of Arbaces' sister. "Detached from its context," to quote [T. S. Eliot, in his *Selected Essays, 1917-1932*] . . . , "this looks like the verse of the greater poets." But if you turn to the context of the speech, you find that it is not, as it would be in "the greater poets," any such climactic speech; it is not, that is to say, the poetic exploitation of a situation carefully built up in terms of plot and character; it has not, in this sense, any roots in the soil of the narrative form. And when you look at the speech more closely, you detect in it a kind of elegant and controlled exaggeration which is almost never found in Shakespeare's verse, as if the dramatists and their audience wished to make the most they could of a partic-

ular feeling short of allowing it to become patently absurd in its exaggeration, because their interest was in that feeling and not in the character and situation of which it is supposedly the result.

What this speech shows, in other words, is that Beaumont and Fletcher had a highly developed sense of just how far they could push a given feeling without pitching the whole speech over the edge into the abyss of absurdity. Their insistence on retaining for the speech its appearance of being justified by situation and character is largely owing to their realization that by giving the speech an appearance of justification they could push the feeling a good deal further without producing this disaster. Thus, though neither the kind nor degree of response demanded by this speech is actually justified in terms of Arbaces' character and the situation, Beaumont and Fletcher show an immense and deceptive ingenuity in making it appear that it is. And they elaborate this deception with such ingenuity because by doing so they can lull themselves and the audience into accepting and enjoying a kind and degree of emotion which would otherwise seem merely absurd. Consider this ingenuity for a moment. Arbaces knows that his sister is not dead but kneeling before him, and he knows too that he is in love with her. Looked at from the point of view of the narrative, therefore, these are the words of a proud man driven to playing for time in a desperate situation, and there is much in the speech which, for an audience with its attention not fixed directly on the moral significance of character, will encourage this view of its purpose. It is clever dramatic irony on the authors' part, for example, to have the man who has just discovered himself desperately in love with his sister say that for him she is dead. It may seem to the audience simply further evidence of the authors' concern for the moral implications of character that Arbaces, who has always thought of himself as a godlike hero, should, in this moment of discovering his own sinfulness, realize that "I am a man / And dare not quarrel with divinity." And Arbaces' tender concern for his sister's virginity may easily be thought to have no other function than to reveal his revulsion from his incestuous impulse. Even his closing words may appear to be a necessarily concealed prayer for strength to bear his own crosses.

All this is calculated to encourage an audience to believe that this stimulating speech is no more than a legitimate exploitation of character and situation, that the excitement really has been justified by them. Yet on careful examination it is quite clear that character and situation are not the center of Beaumont and Fletcher's interest here, that everything in the speech is primarily directed to arousing in the audience a feeling which is both in degree and in kind not so justified. The speech lacks the tone of irony and bitterness which it must have if it is to be taken as the words of a man in the midst of self-discovery. Its tone is one of elegiac simplicity and dignity, of graceful pathos. It was plainly written with a view to extracting all the pity possible from the thought of a sister dead, in spite of the narrative irrelevance of that pity at this point. All the details of the speech, including those discussed in the previous paragraph, are so presented as to demand of the audience, not such a response as the situation and character might be justified in demanding, but a response which could be justified only if Panthea were really dead, and only then if this were the culminating disaster of the play for Arbaces.

This is the characteristic relationship in Beaumont and Fletcher between the narrative and "the lively touches of the passion." A dramatic situation is created which, usually with some ingenuity, is made to appear to justify the speech; that speech is then written, not so much for the purpose of exploiting the feelings which grow out of character and situation, the feelings which in terms of the narrative justify the speech—though that purpose is never wholly neglected. It is written primarily to exploit a feeling which contrasts with, parallels, or resolves the patterned sequences of emotions which have, in precisely the same way, been exploited in the speeches which form its context.

Arbaces' speech is climactic, then, not in the sense that it forms a climax in the narrative development; any reader looking at it in its context will see that its appearance of climaxing a tragic narrative is a skilfully devised trick. It is climactic in the sense that it resolves a complex sequence of emotional tones, the tension of which has become almost intolerable. The sequence is worth looking at closely, since it is, in little, a Beaumont and Fletcher play: the method of its construction is the method they use in dealing with the larger units of the play as a whole.

This sequence begins with an introductory passage in which Arbaces' supposed mother, Arane, kneeling before him, is graciously forgiven for having plotted his death. Panthea then kneels before Arbaces and speaks as if the whole purpose of her life had been fulfilled by the mere privilege of looking at him; the attitude is adoration, an emotion ostensibly justified by the fact that Arbaces is supposedly Panthea's kingly brother; but it is plainly out of all proportion to this narrative justification. Arbaces' response to this speech is in startling contrast, not only with Panthea's words, but with his treatment of Arane a moment before, though Arane would have murdered him and Panthea is all adoration.

> *Gobrias.* Why does not your majesty speak?
> *Arbaces.* To whom?
> *Gobrias.* To the princess.

Panthea then strikes another note, trembling fear that Arbaces looks upon her as "some loathed thing." Once more Gobrias intervenes.

> *Gobrias.* Sir, you should speak to her.
> *Arbaces.* Ha!

And once more Panthea strikes in, now with the attitude of one conscious of her unworthiness, who pleads for a word of kindness for simple mercy's sake.

This time it is Tigranes who is shocked by Arbaces' apparent brutality and who urges him to speak. Tigranes, Arbaces' prisoner and the man he has chosen for his sister's husband, is secretly pledged to Spaconia. Through-

out this scene the theme of his growing love for Panthea gradually emerges until, for a moment near the end, it dominates the scene. This speech is its first appearance; Arbaces answers it with a long aside which makes it clear to the audience that he has been confounded by the discovery that he is passionately in love with his own sister. This aside is followed by an aside from Tigranes in which he indicates *his* growing love for Panthea.

Once more Panthea speaks; this time with half-jesting pathos she begs Arbaces to speak, if only to save her modesty. Now it is Mardonius, the bluff soldier, who urges Arbaces to speak; and, with another startling shift in emotional tone, Arbaces turns to Panthea with grave courtesy.

> You mean this lady: lift her from the earth;
> Why do you kneel so long?—Alas,
> Madam, your beauty uses to command,
> And not to beg! What is your suit to me?
> It shall be granted; yet the time is short,
> And my affairs are great.—But where's my sister?
> I bade she should be brought.

The tension of this moment is then held through a series of short speeches, each of which seems inevitably to be the last which can be spoken before Arbaces must publicly recognize Panthea:

> *Mardonius (aside).* What, is he mad?
> *Arbaces.* Gobrias, where is she?
> *Gobrias.* Sir?
> *Arbaces.* Where is she, man?
> *Gobrias.* Who, sir?
> *Arbaces.* Who! hast thou forgot? my sister.
> *Gobrias.* Your sister, sir!
> *Arbaces.* Your sister, sir! Some one that hath a wit,
>   Answer where is she.
> *Gobrias.* Do you not see her there?
> *Arbaces.* Where?
> *Gobrias.* There?
> *Arbaces.* There! Where?
> *Mardonius.* 'Slight, there: are you blind?
> *Arbaces.* Which do you mean? that little one?
> *Gobrias.* No, sir.
> *Arbaces.* No, sir! Why, do you mock me? I can see
>   No other here but that petitioning lady.
> *Gobrias.* That's she.
> *Arbaces.* Away!
> *Gobrias.* Sir, it is she.
> *Arbaces.* 'Tis false.
> *Gobrias.* Is it?
> *Arbaces.* As hell! by Heaven, as false as hell!

And then, after the anger and fear and bewilderment of this sequence, after the intolerable pitch of tension that has been reached and then held through this virtuoso passage, the sequence is resolved by Arbaces' astonishing elegy for his dead sister.

Throughout this passage Beaumont and Fletcher are concerned primarily neither to develop the characters nor to bring out the moral implications of the action. Their primary concern is to arouse in the audience, at each step, the feeling which is a psychologically dramatic successor to the feeling aroused by the previous speech. And this purpose requires the introduction of a series of attitudes on the part of the characters which makes it appear, from the point of view of the narrative, that these characters are not only strained to the breaking point for a mere momentary effect which comes to nothing but made to speak at great length while only apparently advancing the plot.

The scene-by-scene and act-by-act construction of the play has the same purpose in view and the same consequences. The remainder of the first scene of Act III, for example, is made up of a series of passages of exactly the same kind as the one analyzed above; and each of these passages is adjusted to the preceding and succeeding passages with the same care for the emotional pattern in the audience's mind as is shown in the arrangement of the individual speeches within these passages. As soon as the elegiac mood of Arbaces' speech which closes the first passage has been exhausted, Gobrias once more reminds the king that Panthea is his sister. At this Arbaces takes another line:

> Here I pronounce him traitor,
> The direct plotter of my death, that names
> Or thinks her for my sister. . . .

In terms of the narrative, Arbaces is here displaying the passionate side of his nature, established in Act I. In terms of the emotional form, this speech is a skilful modulation of the pathos of his previous elegiac speech; for, though this is the impassioned anger of a man unaccustomed to denial, it is asserted on a hopeless case, against nature itself; the more angry Arbaces becomes, the more pathetic he appears, "a sight most pitiful in the meanest wretch, / Past speaking of in a king."

After a speech from Panthea, Arbaces is given a third modulation of pathos:

> I will hear no more.
> Why should there be such music in a voice,
> And sin for me to hear it. . . . ?

a speech which ends with his sinking exhausted on the throne.

At this pause Tigranes steps forward to address Panthea. The passage which follows is beautifully balanced against the preceding passage. Panthea, distracted by grief and uncertainty, is yet gentle and gracious; the simple pathos which has been hers from the start shows in this passage with a new and touching dignity. Tigranes is eager to show his devotion to her but is restrained by the presence of Spaconia, whose asides are at once a choral commentary on the dialogue and, as the expression of another much-wronged woman's sorrows, a kind of complementary grief to Panthea's. The passage, so far as the feelings presented are concerned, is a variation on the previous one, with Tigranes replacing Arbaces. Gradually Arbaces recovers,

and the audience's attention is brought back to his feeling—now jealous suspicion of Tigranes—by the series of ominously cryptic questions which he asks. Tigranes becomes more and more angry under this questioning, and Arbaces more and more certain that his jealousy is justified, until, in helpless rage, he orders Tigranes imprisoned.

As the clashing anger of this passage dies away, Gobrias once more reminds Arbaces of the presence of his sister, and, in immediate and striking contrast to his anger of the moment before, Arbaces turns to Panthea, kneels, and begs her forgiveness. Panthea kneels with him, and there follows a passage of suspiciously extravagant affection, tense with the audience's knowledge that certainly Arbaces and perhaps Panthea are playing with fire in this attempt to pretend that their mutual feelings are only natural. Arbaces kisses Panthea "to make this knot the stronger" and then, with a brief aside—"I wade in sin, / And foolishly entice myself along"—turns abruptly away and orders Panthea imprisoned. Thus the scene shifts back to anger and violence, though to a kind subtly different from that of the exchange between Arbaces and Tigranes a moment before. As Panthea is carried off to prison, Arbaces returns to the despairing rage at his own powerlessness which appeared in his second speech in the scene, though now that feeling is more despair than rage:

> Why should you, that have made me stand in war
> Like Fate itself, cutting what threads I pleased,
> Decree such an unworthy end of me
> And all my glories?

At the end of this speech, once more faint with exhaustion, he is led off by Mardonius, and the emotional pattern of the scene is completed with a Hamlet-inspired dying fall:

> Wilt thou hereafter, when they talk of me,
> As thou shalt hear, nothing but infamy,
> Remember some of these things? . . . .
> I prithee, do;
> For thou shalt never see me so again.

From the narrative point of view this scene is full of wild starts and changes on the part of the characters and of bewildering and apparently profitless backing and filling on the part of the story. But in terms of the audience's psychology the form of the scene is firm and clear, for all its richness and variety.

The form of the act can also be defined only in these terms. Miss Bradbrook has remarked that the coarsening of the poetic fiber can be clearly seen in Beaumont and Fletcher's blurring of the tragic and comic. In the sense that the contrasting of the tragic and comic, like the contrasting of other moods in the audience, has no serious functional purpose in terms of the narrative, this comment is true. But in terms of the emotional form, Beaumont and Fletcher's comic contrasts are clear cut and carefully calculated. The first scene of Act III, for example, is followed by a comic scene in which Bessus faces the ridiculous consequences of his newly acquired and embarrassing reputation for courage, as Arbaces has just faced the tragic fact of his sudden and passionate love for Panthea. This contrast, as Miss Bradbrook suggests, proves nothing morally, and there appears to be little justification for the considerable space which is devoted to the rather pointless business of Bessus' cowardice; in terms of the narrative, in other words, the variation from tragic to comic here and throughout the play seems to be purposeless and random. The scene can, in fact, be justified only in terms of the psychology of the audience; its relationship to the previous scene is of the same kind as the relationship which exists between speech and speech within the scene. In terms of the narrative, such justification as it has is tricky but meaningless, but psychologically it shifts the audience's attention to a set of feelings, parallel but of a different kind, and it also prevents the law of diminishing returns from asserting itself, as it would if the dramatists attempted to follow scene i immediately with scene iii.

After this comic scene, however, it is possible to return to the tragic theme of Panthea and Arbaces. The basic form of scene iii is simpler than that of scene i; the audience watches Arbaces slowly working himself up to the point where he can request Mardonius' aid in fulfilling his shameful desire, and presumably it thrills to Mardonius' manful refusal and pities Arbaces as he wilts before Mardonius' righteousness. Scarcely has Arbaces repented his request when Bessus enters and Arbaces is once more tempted. Bessus accepts the commission eagerly, so eagerly that Arbaces is horrified and once more repents. The scene is Beaumont and Fletcher's version of the familiar good-angel, bad-angel scene and, in the way it plays down the larger implications of such a scene, it is an instructive example of the skill with which Beaumont and Fletcher collected the cash while only pretending not to let the credit go.

Probably Beaumont and Fletcher's very real talent for narrative construction shows most clearly in the act-by-act organization of the play. The complicated story which is necessary for their kind of play, if the emotional climaxes it requires are not to be obviously arbitrary and therefore difficult to accept, is handled with such ease and with so very little direct exposition, and the narrative interest is so carefully carried over when new material is introduced, that only detailed analysis is likely to reveal how elaborate the plot really is. Yet, for all this display of narrative skill, Beaumont and Fletcher build their play around emotional, rather than narrative, climaxes. The climax of Act I, for example, is clearly Arbaces' display of passionate anger; true, this passionate quality is the "tragic flaw" in Arbaces' character, but it is not the cause of his tragic dilemma; it exists not so much for the sake of the action as a whole as because, in conjunction with the plot, it provides some sort of narrative justification for Arbaces' extravagant and varied emotions, which are so important a part of the emotional form. The climax of Act II is perhaps Spaconia's display of pathos; in any event, there is no narrative climax in this act, no obligatory scene. The last three acts have similar climaxes, each a little tenser

than its predecessor. In so far as they depend on suspense—on whether Arbaces will yield to desire—they depend on the narrative for their effect. But in the sense that the narrative is the local habitation of an important meaning, as in *Doctor Faustus,* which has some superficially comparable scenes, and the climaxes moments when the choice between good and evil must be made, they are not narrative climaxes at all. Once more Beaumont and Fletcher are in these scenes using the narrative effect of suspense to support and enrich an emotional climax, rather than using emotional effects to support and enrich a narrative climax.

The climax of the third act is the first meeting between Panthea and Arbaces, with its elaborate emotional composition, its use of events as one more way of inducing a patterned sequence of psychologically effective attitudes in the audience. The climax of the fourth act is the second meeting between the two lovers, a meeting perceptibly tenser for the audience than that of the third act because Arbaces' confession to Panthea and Panthea's "For I could wish as heartily as you, / I were no sister to you" bring the two so much closer to disaster. This sequence reaches its logical culmination in the fifth act, when Arbaces finally surrenders to his desire. The expectation of action aroused by Arbaces'

> It is resolved: I bore it whilst I could;
> I can no more. Hell, open all thy gates,
> And I will through them: . . . .

is held suspended through a passage between him and Mardonius in which he displays the tortured cynicism of his determination to do what he knows to be sin, and through a passage in which he accuses Gobrias of having fostered his love for Panthea. The audience's attention is then partly deflected from the expectation that Arbaces will act on his sinful desire by the first part of Gobrias' revelation and Arbaces' anger at Arane as he understands Gobrias to be telling him he is a bastard. Each of these notes is held as long as possible, both for its own sake and for the sake of maintaining the suspense. Finally, however, Gobrias is permitted to tell Arbaces enough to make him listen to the rest, and Arbaces shifts abruptly from anger and despair to what G. C. Macaulay well called "a sudden violent patience":

> I'll lie, and listen here as reverently (*Lies down*)
> As to an angel: if I breath too loud,
> Tell me; for I would be as still as night.

Gobrias' story is quickly told, Arbaces rises almost mad with joy, and on this note the play is quickly brought to an end.

The ordering form of *A King and No King*—and it is the form of all the tragedies and tragicomedies that Beaumont and Fletcher wrote together—is a pattern of responses in the mind of the audience, a subtle and artful arrangement of "the lively touches of the passion." Like *A King and No King,* the typical Beaumont and Fletcher play is an excitingly elaborate affair of lath and plaster whose imposing pretense that it is a massive narrative structure is in part a device for making the audience accept the elaboration and in part a means of adding to the excitement by the charm of its own ingenuity. Its characters and narrative are given the maximum of decorative elaboration, and, though Beaumont and Fletcher are careful that the decoration shall always appear to be a part of some functional detail in the narrative, actually the significant and ordering form of the structure is not the narrative pattern, clever as that always is, but the pattern of decoration. Just as in another kind of play the meaning implicit in character and situation is intensified by a subordinate pattern of more narrowly poetic effects, so in Beaumont and Fletcher these carefully ordered poetic effects are made richer and more complex by the narrative pattern. If the ideal play of the critical imagination of the nineteenth century may be said to have been functional in terms of character and narrative, then Beaumont and Fletcher's plays are strictly baroque.

Most critics would, I believe, agree that plays which are functional in terms of Nature, in the widest sense of the word, constitute a superior kind; if they do, then Beaumont and Fletcher's baroque plays represent an inferior kind. But that kind is certainly superior to the kind represented by the ideal play of the nineteenth-century critics' imagination, which is functional in terms of character only in a very mundane and individualist sense, and in terms of a nature whose vitality has been dissipated by a scientific and utilitarian conception of it. There is something to be said for Rymer's attitude toward Beaumont and Fletcher; he knew what they were up to and damned them by comparison with a kind of play whose superiority is at least arguable. But the nineteenth century, misunderstanding them, damned their plays as bad examples of a kind which they do not represent and which is inferior to the kind they do.

There is not much to be gained from a discussion of Beaumont and Fletcher's plays which assumes that they represent a kind they do not, nor is the situation visibly improved if the critic goes on to offer a simple moralistic explanation of their failure to be something their authors never sought to make them. It seems to me obvious that there is something radically wrong with the usual approach to Beaumont and Fletcher when it can lead so acute a critic as Miss Bradbrook into the assumption of a simple relationship between the historical, the strictly literary, and the moral kinds of decadence.

We would be nearer to understanding Beaumont and Fletcher and thus to being able to judge them justly if we had never strayed from the conception of their purpose, which lies behind Herrick's lines for the First Folio:

Here's words with lines, and lines with Scenes
　consent,
To raise an Act to full astonishment;. . . .
Love lyes a bleeding here, *Evadne* there
Swells with brave rage, yet comely every where,
Here's a *mad lover,* there that high designe
Of *King and no King.* . . . .

Robert K. Turner, Jr.　(essay date 1958-1960)

SOURCE: "The Morality of *A King and No King,*" in *Renaissance Papers 1958, 1959, 1960,* edited by Peter G. Phialas and George Walton Williams, The Southeastern Renaissance Conference, 1961, pp. 93-103.

[*In the essay below, Turner asserts that* A King and No King *presents an immoral value system in which "indulgence becomes not only respectable but very nearly sanctified."*]

Many of our greatest critics of Renaissance literature have commented upon the sense of defeat, spiritual emptiness, and decadence which sets the tone of Jacobean drama. The relationship of Beaumont and Fletcher's tragicomedies to the spirit of their age is variously expressed, perhaps most typically by Miss Ellis-Fermor who sees them as romantic escape literature from a reality of despondency and anxiety [Una Ellis-Fermor, *The Jacobean Drama,* 1953]. Miss Bradbrook feels that the slackening of the moral fibre which these plays reflect had a deleterious effect upon their literary quality. "The final test of these plays," she says, "is their language and here they are strikingly apart from the earlier drama. There is no verbal framework of any kind; the collapse of the poetic is to be directly related to the collapse of the moral structure, for they were interdependent" [M. C. Bradbrook, *Themes and Conventions of Elizabethan Tragedy,* 1935]. Professor Arthur Mizener, however, defends the playwrights against a specific charge of immorality by pointing out that they were no more immoral than anybody else: ". . . I cannot believe," he writes,

> that the attitude toward life implied by Beaumont and Fletcher's plays is not a reflection of the attitude which dominated the society for which they wrote and of which they were a part, rather than the result of any special immorality in them. Unlike Webster and Jonson, they were not seriously in revolt against the values of a large part of their world. Their plays are complex and delicate projections of one of the attitudes widespread in their day, just as Dekker's plays are a confused and crude projection of another. The moral quality implicit in both is not primarily a personal, but a group attitude . . . [*Modern Philology* XXXVIII, 1940].

It is generally agreed that the dramatists had an unusually well developed sense of theater; the tragicomedies are held to be very skillfully constructed to the end of exploiting all of the emotional possibilities of their rather gaudy themes. Yet the consensus remains that these plays, lacking any high seriousness of intention, are morally shabby.

Some light can be cast not only on this judgment but also on the reasons for the contemporary popularity of the tragicomedies by examining one of them, *A King and No King,* from the intellectual point of view of the Jacobean audience. During the preceding age tragedy had shared little of its popularity with tragicomedy, although the "mongrel" form, to use Sidney's epithet, was being acted at least as early as the mid-sixteenth century. One aspect of Elizabethan tragedy was its general lack of sentimentality; it was founded on a tough code in which sin was invariably paid

---

Ashley H. Thorndike on the uniqueness of Beaumont and Fletcher's romances:

Beaumont and Fletcher, like Shakspere and all other Elizabethan dramatists, took their material where they could find it, and availed themselves of whatever had found favor on the stage. There can be no doubt, however, that their plays seemed very different to the spectators of their day from any which preceded. This is true of their comedies, with which as a class we shall have little to do, and it is still more true of their tragi-comedies and tragedies which I shall include by the term romances. In the period 1600-1615 there are certainly few plays by other authors that resemble these romances. They are nothing like the revenge plays which were prevalent at the beginning of the period, nor the "tragedies of blood" of Webster and Tourneur, nor Chapman's Bussy d' Ambois and Byron, nor the classical tragedies of Jonson and Shakspere. Neither are they like Macbeth, Othello, or Lear, tragedies which deal with one main emotion and center about one character. If they differ from the plays which immediately preceded or were contemporary with them, they differ still more from the earlier chronicle-histories or tragedies. Beaumont and Fletcher, in fact, created a new dramatic form, the heroic romance. . . . [Their] romances were distinguished by much that was new in situations, plots, characters, and poetic style.

Ashley H. Thorndike, in his The Influence of Beaumont and Fletcher on Shakspere, *1901.*

---

for with death. As we all know, human evil was explained in terms of a Christianized version of Peripatetic doctrine: sin resulted from a victory of Will over Reason, the conflict of these two psychological factors being one of the most disastrous legacies of Adam's fall from grace. The nature of sin was in part determined by the degree of stimulation received by the Will from the passions: if the stimulation was great enough to cause Will to override a reluctant Reason, venial sin resulted, but if the stimulation was so great that Reason itself became perverted and enslaved by Will, mortal sin resulted. Thus, as Professor Lily Campbell has explained [in *Shakespeare's Tragic Heroes,* 1959], tragic heroes were distinguished from villains by the extent to which reason played a part in the commission of their sins. But the point to be emphasized here is that in Elizabethan tragedy, although salvation was open to the protagonist who was not tainted with mortal sin, there was no human happiness for him; the tragic view saw in the universe a system of unalterable justice which demanded the life of the protagonist as payment for his evil deeds.

In the tragic system of values, the unspeakable crime of incest led straight to mortal sin, yet it is just this crime which provides the focal point of *A King and No King.* Arbaces, brilliant young king of Iberia and Beaumont and Fletcher's protagonist, has not seen his sister Panthea since her childhood, having been many years away at the wars. When he returns home victorious, her beauty strikes him such a blow that he falls hopelessly and irretrievably in love with her. Turning on this central situation, the play develops a conventional conflict between Arbaces' pas-

sion-stimulated Will and his reluctant Reason, and Beaumont and Fletcher enhance the dramatic value of this conflict by making Arbaces a man of high psychological complexity. He is "vain-glorious and humble, and angry and patient, and merry and dull, and joyful and sorrowful, in extremities, in an hour" (I, i, 88-90). To emphasize his internal conflict further, they construct the play, as Professor Mizener has shown, in the manner of the old moralities, with Mardonius, a loyal follower, as the good and Bessus, a foolish coward, as the evil angel. Mardonius is all that is reasonable and humane in Arbaces' personality; Bessus, who also has the comic characteristics of the Vice, is all that is unreasonable and bestial. Thus, Arbaces stands between Mardonius and Bessus very much as Prince Hal stands between the Lord Chief Justice and Falstaff [in Shakespeare's *1* and *2 Henry IV*].

These relationships are made quite clear in the play. Mardonius, the bluff and outspoken old soldier, is cast in the role of Arbaces' mentor; it is he who can discern and preserve the virtue that is intermixed with Arbaces' folly. Therefore, he is necessary to Arbaces, and both he and the king know it:

> *Arb.* How darest thou so often forfeit thy life?
>   Thou knowest it is in my power to take it.
> *Mar.* Yes, and I know you wo'not; or if you do,
>   You'll miss it quickly.
> *Arb.*   Why?
> *Mar.* Who shall then tell you of these childish
>   follies,
>   When I am dead? who shall put-to his power
>   To draw those virtues out of a flood of
>   humours,
>   Where they are drown'd, and make 'em shine
>   again?
>   (IV, ii, 166-173)

Being an honorable man, Mardonius is completely honest. Although he loves the king, his attitude toward him is ambivalent—"thy valour and thy passions sever'd, would have made two excellent fellows in their kinds" (I, i, 177-179)—and he will not demean himself by flattering. He is never in doubt, as Gobrias and Bacurius temporarily are, about Bessus' true nature. Thus, Mardonius serves symbolically as a projection of Arbaces' Reason, a quality which, according to Arbaces, binds man's actions with curious rules, restricting and confining the Will. It is just this function that Mardonius performs with respect to Arbaces on the narrative level of the play.

Bessus, the airy, thin, unbodied coward, operates on two levels, and his dual roles reinforce and inform one another. He is, of course, the comic relief, and as such his buffoonery stands in contrast to the high emotionalism of the Arbaces theme. Furthermore, on a much debased level, he exhibits, and at the same time parodies, Arbaces' boastfulness. But in his direct relationship to Arbaces himself, he becomes much more sinister. Unlike Mardonius, he does not seek literally to control the king, but he does suggest foolishly (and amusingly) that at least from his own point of view he can be set on the same level with him. "By my troth, I wished myself wi' you," he says to Arbaces with regard to the combat in which Tigranes was vanquished (I, i, 227), and, in replying to Panthea's question about the king's health, he states that Arbaces is as well "as the rest of us that fought are" (II, i, 81). Nobody takes this very seriously, of course, but apparently the dramatists want us to see Bessus as something more than just a humorous poltroon. His bestiality is several times hinted at: to Bacurius he is "Captain Stockfish" (specifically because he is the object of much cudgelling), and when the king rages he slinks away like an animal (I, i, 298). But his sub-human qualities are revealed most clearly in the excellent scene in which Arbaces seeks a bawd to approach Panthea, first in Mardonius and then in him (III, iii). The passionate and heavy mood of the king's conversation with Mardonius is broken when Bessus enters making a ridiculous jest. "Away you fool! the King is serious, and cannot now admit your vanities," cries Mardonius. But Arbaces is quite ready to reject Reason and to surrender to Will. He interjects, "No; let him stay, Mardonius, let him stay; I have occasions with him very weighty, and I can spare you now." Mardonius once gone, the king can speak without the hedging that characterized his earlier approach to the question. Previously Arbaces had stated that "he that undertakes my cure must first o'erthrow divinity, all moral laws . . ." (III, i, 188-189), and Bessus is not only willing but eager to serve him. Bessus' bland equanimity in the face of the terrible proposition so horrifies Arbaces that he recoils:

> But thou appear'st to me, after thy grant,
> The ugliest, loathed, detestable thing,
> That I have ever met with. . . .
> Hung round with curses, take thy fearful flight
> Into the deserts; where, 'mongst all the monsters,
> If thou find'st one so beastly as thyself,
> Thou shalt be held as innocent.
>
> (III, iii, 163-165, 184-187)

Arbaces, driving Bessus out, resolves to control his passions, but Bessus takes no fearful flight. The king has only temporarily renounced the domination of his Will, and Bessus remains on the scene just as Arbaces' unlawful lust continues to burn.

Tigranes, a captured prince intended at first by Arbaces to be Panthea's husband, is also used symbolically to comment on Arbaces' plight. The parallel between the two is strongly enforced. Like Arbaces, Tigranes is a young and powerful king. He too falls in love with Panthea at first sight, and his passion is also illicit, only it is so in terms of a breach of faith with Spaconia, a lady of his own land, rather than a breach of fundamental moral law. He is acutely aware of his own humanity—"I know I have the passions of a man" (V, ii, 90-91)—and he conceives of his desertion of Spaconia as something "unmanly, beastly" (IV, ii, 28), in other words, as a lapse from human status. Nevertheless, through Reason he masters his desire for Panthea and returns honorably to Spaconia. He appears as about what we would expect Arbaces to be were he not so much ruled by his passions; however, Tigranes has been overcome by Arbaces, and as a prisoner he must endure the indignities

and insults that Arbaces, often unwittingly, subjects him to. Mardonius recognizes Arbaces' victory over his noble enemy as the cause of the king's downfall (IV, ii, 117); in a sense, by defeating Tigranes the king has subjugated the better half of himself and has on the symbolic level enslaved himself just as on the narrative level he has enslaved Tigranes. Tigranes' remark that Arbaces' treatment of him violates "the law of nature, and of nations" (III, i, 238) thus acquires special meaning.

The symbolic relationship of Mardonius, Bessus, and Tigranes to Arbaces helps to emphasize the alteration which his character undergoes during the course of the action. As Professor Mizener has pointed out, Arbaces is a man who is being purged of pride, and the imagery of the play suggests that the authors conceived of this purgation in terms of a descent of the chain of being. At the outset, Arbaces thinks of himself as a hero-king who is especially favored of the gods; in fact, as a king he stands in a relationship to his enemies and his subjects roughly equivalent to that in which a god stands with respect to mankind in general. His victorious arm is "propt by divinity" (I, i, 133); his mission has been to "teach the neighbour-world humility" (I, i, 138), and his conquest of Tigranes has been "an act fit for a God to do upon his foe" (I, i, 144-145). Simply because she is his sister, Panthea "deserves the empire of the world" (I, i, 168). In his orgy of self-glorification, he sets himself on a level with the gods by degrading his followers to the level of animals: when Mardonius reproaches him for boasting, he retorts:

> Will you confine my words? By Heaven and earth,
> I were much better be a king of beasts
> Than such a people! If I had not patience
> Above a god, I should be call'd a tyrant
> Throughout the world. . . .
>
> (I, i, 239-243)

Those who cross him lose claim to humanity. Once again to the censuring Mardonius he says,

> O, that thy name
> Were great as mine! would I had paid my wealth
> It were as great, as I might combat thee!
> I would through all the regions habitable
> Search thee, and, having found thee, with my sword
> Drive thee about the world, till I had met
> Some place that yet man's curiosity
> Had miss'd of; there, there would I strike thee dead:
> Forgotten of mankind, such funeral rites
> As beasts would give thee, thou shouldst have.
>
> (I, i, 288-296)

And Mardonius, who always speaks honestly, must admit that there is some truth in Arbaces' exaggerated opinion of himself:

> Sir, that I have ever loved you
> My sword hath spoken for me; that I do,
> If I be doubted, I dare call an oath,
> A great one, to my witness; and were

You not my King, from amongst men I should
Have chose you out, to love above the rest:
Nor can this challenge thanks; for my own sake
I should have done it, because I would have loved
The most deserving man, for so you are.

(I, i, 323-331)

In fact, it is only Arbaces' passions that keep men from taking him to be a god (I, i, 370-372).

But such language as we have just heard Arbaces use is a characteristic of him only when he is in the grip of his passions; a shift in his mood results in a change in his concept of himself. He then becomes a man among men, concerned about the world's opinion (I, i, 489-490). His sudden love for Panthea makes him especially aware of his manhood. He sees himself no longer as semi-divine but as palpably human ("for I am a man, and dare not quarrel with divinity" [III, i, 122-123]). In fact, the initial shock of his meeting with Panthea pushes him far down the chain of being. "Am I what I was?" he asks himself, and, as he stares at his kneeling sister through an extraordinary silence, Mardonius asks,

Have you no life at all? for manhood sake,
Let her not kneel, and talk neglected thus:
A tree would find a tongue to answer her,
Did she but give it such a loved respect.

(III, i, 99-102)

As Arbaces tries to regain his former dominant status, once again his language becomes that of the hero-king:

She is no kin to me, nor shall she be,
If she were ever, I create her none:
And which of you can question this? My power
Is like the sea, that is to be obey'd,
And not disputed with. . . .

(III, i, 157-161)

To this absurdity the sycophantic Bessus answers for Arbaces' own Will, "No, marry, she is not, an't please your majesty; I never thought she was; she's nothing like you" (III, i, 166-167). For the last time the king thinks of himself as super-human: "I stood stubborn and regardless by and, like a god incensed, gave no ear to all your prayers" (III, i, 273-275). However, as he later recognizes, sin has robbed him of his god-like power (III, iii, 90-94).

Mardonius knows that Arbaces' lust is a scourge justly laid upon him by Heaven (III, iii, 2-4). Indeed, the scourge is applied so heavily that Arbaces fears that he has slipped through the level of humanity to the level of the beasts. Figuratively he becomes a bull, an animal whose destructive power and overt sexuality are especially appropriate to Arbaces' state. That part of himself which he has given over to lust he acknowledges as bestial; his resistance to lust, which deteriorates with increasing rapidity, is "all that's man" about him (IV, iv, 21). Having lost his Reason through his rejection of Mardonius, he has lost "the only difference between man and beast" (IV, iv, 65). Why, then, he asks himself, should he not enjoy the freedom of the beast, since

"who ever saw the bull fearfully leave the heifer that he liked, because they had one dam?" (IV, iv, 136-138).

Throughout the play the corrupting power of the Will, manifesting itself primarily as lust, is imaginatively equated with poison, infection, and disease. Thus, Panthea begs the overwrought Arbaces to speak to her, even though the speech be "poison'd with anger, that may strike me dead" (III, i, 98). To Arbaces Panthea is a witch, a poisoner, "for she has given me poison in a kiss" (III, i, 312); yet he recognizes that she is a perfect woman and is evil only because he makes her so. To her pathetic question, "Alas, sir, am I venom?", he replies,

Yes, to me;
Though, of myself, I think thee to be in
As equal a degree of heat or cold
As nature can make; yet, as unsound men
Convert the sweetest and the nourishing'st meats
Into diseases, so shall I, distemper'd,
Do thee. . . .

(IV, iv, 27-32)

An earlier occurrence of this idea brings the disease imagery into conjunction with the beast imagery:

You are fair and wise,
And virtuous, I think; and he is blest
That is so near you as your brother is;
But you are nought to me but a disease,
Continual torment without hope of ease.
Such an ungodly sickness I have got,
That he that undertakes my cure must first
O'erthrow divinity, all moral laws,
And leave mankind as unconfined as beasts
Allowing them to do all actions
As freely as they drink, when they desire.

(III, i, 182-192)

Arbaces' lust not only infects Panthea in stimulating a responding passion in her, but, like the plague, it permeates the atmosphere in which all of his followers move. Mardonius comments,

This love, or what a devil it is, I know not, begets
more mischief than a wake. I had rather be well beaten,
starved, or lousy, than live within the air on't.

(IV, ii, 217-220)

Under the circumstances, it is not surprising to find Bessus associated with the idea of disease. To him Arbaces says,

Thou hast eyes
Like flames of sulphur, which, methinks, do dart
Infection on me. . . .

(III, iii, 165-167)

This imagery, which is linked to the narrative level of the play through the attempt of Arane, the queen mother, to poison Arbaces, is especially apparent in the discovery scene. There Arbaces, whose passion will not let him hear Arane and Gobrias out, rails at her:

Adulterous witch,
I know now why thou wouldst have poison'd me;
I was thy lust, which thou wouldst have forgot:
Thou wicked mother of my sins and me,
Show me the way to the inheritance
I have by thee, which is a spacious world
Of impious acts, that I may soon possess it!
Plagues rot thee as thou liv'st, and such diseases
As use to pay lust recompense thy deed!

(V, iv, 160-168)

To the discovery scene the theme being developed and the imagery, which is organic to it, convey tragic implications. The imagery is drawn from the same subject matter, if not presented with the same poetic skill, as that which dominates, for instance, *Hamlet, King Lear, The Duchess of Malfi,* and *The White Devil*; it is used with great skill to link the narrative and the symbolic levels of the drama, to create and sustain the atmosphere in which the action takes place, and to lend a unity to the whole composition, increasing its emotional impact. On the level of theme, Beaumont and Fletcher show Arbaces' Reason so crumbling before his Will that at the beginning of the discovery scene he stands on the lip of mortal sin. He announces:

It is resolved: I bore it whilst I could;
I can no more. Hell, open all thy gates,
And I Will thorough them: if they be shut,
I'll batter 'em, but I will find the place
Where the most damn'd have dwelling. Ere I end,
Amongst them all they shall not have a sin,
But I may call it mine: I must begin
With murder of my friend, and so go on
To an incestuous ravishing, and end
My life and sins with a forbidden blow
Upon myself!

(V, iv, 1-11)

Later in the scene, however, the tragic mood is completely dispelled; Arbaces learns that he is not Panthea's brother, and thus his illicit lust is transformed into legitimate love. Not only that, even though the revelation of his true parentage makes him no king, his marriage to Panthea will restore him to the throne. With the incest problem sidestepped, it turns out that Will, not Reason, had been right all along, a point driven home by Bessus' fatuous, yet significant, remark—"Why, if you remember, fellow-subject Arbaces, I told you once she was not your sister; ay, and she look'd nothing like you" (V, iv, 293-295).

Thematically the play turns out to be a kind of philosophical pipedream in which Will has its way while Reason stands by and nods approvingly. Punishment for surrender to the passions vanishes, a complete subversion of the moral and intellectual code which had formed the basis for tragedy. It is for this reason, I believe, that *A King and No King* and the other tragicomedies, in which much the same thing happens, seem immoral—indulgence becomes not only respectable but very nearly sanctified. And it is no wonder that these plays gained a quick popularity. What member of a society which was characterized by a "falling off in the general discipline" would not like to see his own licentious fantasies symbolically projected with such dramatic effectiveness? Not only was it titillating, but it must have been rather a relief to learn that there was a world where the ideals and standards of Christian humanism did not hold—where technicalities existed which permitted one to sleep with one's sister or perhaps to gorge on such other exotic emotional confections as suited one's palate without having to pay with a fatal moral bellyache that might last an eternity.

William C. Woodson (essay date 1978)

SOURCE: "The Casuistry of Innocence in *A King and No King* and Its Implications for Tragicomedy," in *English Literary Renaissance,* Vol. 8, No. 3, Autumn, 1978, pp. 312-28.

[*In the following essay, Woodson counters previous critical estimations of* A King and No King, *arguing that the play presents a "morally coherent dramatic sequence." Beaumont and Fletcher's drama, he maintains, presents an ironic critique of Protestant beliefs regarding the "paradox of innocent sinners."*]

While Beaumont and Fletcher's *A King and No King* (1611) is generally recognized as a landmark in the development of Jacobean tragicomedy, it is also true that the play has perplexed virtually all its commentators beginning with Thomas Rymer [in *The Tragedies of the Last Age Considered,* 1692]. Written only a short time after the authors' *Philaster* (c. 1609), *A King and No King* clearly abandons the meandering romance structure of the earlier tragicomedy. Yet while the presence of a new dramatic logic is widely acknowledged, it has not been convincingly identified: the consensus is with Mizener, that the play has no "morally significant pattern," and with Ristine, that rational dramatic meaning has been sacrificed "for theatrical effects" [Arthur Mizener, in *Modern Philosophy* XXXVIII, No. 2, 1940]. Thus the play languishes in the suburbs of disapproval, a supposed piece of episodic theatricalism, intended primarily for a coterie audience which presumably took prurient delight in the dramatization of threatened incest.

Against this critical orthodoxy, however, it may be submitted that Fletcher's tragicomedies, including *A King and No King,* gained considerable popularity at the public Globe theater, where it is far less likely that a naughty topic could undo the traditional need for meaningful dramatic coherence in the action. Nor could Fletcher, as principal dramatist for the King's Men, afford to cater exclusively to a decadent coterie. What criticism has not offered, in short, is an estimate of the play's appeal to its historical middle-class audience at the Globe, whose applause is actually remarked on the title page of the first quarto (1619). This general audience, I assume, expected, and certainly in this play was given, a morally coherent dramatic sequence.

I

The significant innovation Beaumont and Fletcher brought to the conventional tragicomic formula of the triumph of the innocents was to borrow from the Puritans their casuistry regarding the immutability of election. What is more surprising, in view of the authors' disrepute, is that they framed the jeopardizing action in a context of a providential concern for the elect. Thus they may be regarded as the first British dramatists to make explicit structural use of the theological assumptions of "poetic justice," which in turn is among their major legacies to the Restoration stage. Curiously, however, because the excessive sentimentality of the recovery of innocence is burlesqued throughout the subplot, Beaumont and Fletcher probably did not endorse the moral laxness with which they imbued the main action, and I will explore this discrepancy also as a secondary but decisive feature of the play.

Unlike the riddling moral dilemmas which critics find in Shakespeare's "problem plays," the main action of *A King and No King* presents a casuistical situation that is rather simple to solve once the key is established. The play threatens again and again the consummation of an incestuous courtship between the young king Arbaces and Panthea; only in the last scene of the fifth act is it revealed that the supposed brother and sister are not related. Rymer, whose critical displeasure with the play has had lasting influence, considered the happy ending a violation of tragic expectations and argued that the protagonists deserve tragic suffering for their intended sin, not the prospect of marriage. His attack on the play as an inadequate *tragedia di lieto fin* assumes that the play in fact establishes unambiguously evil intentions for the courtship. But the sympathetic presentation of Arbaces and Panthea systematically frustrates a rigorous interpretation like Rymer's and compels instead a sentimentally lax interpretation of the wrongdoing, for the play follows a casuistical pattern in which the young innocents are merely jeopardized by an alien and unwanted desire. Thus, as Rymer complained, there is no indication that they are tragically purged of pride by their ordeal. On the contrary, in order to share in the joyful conclusion the audience is required to forgive them at once, on the charitable assumption that they have preserved their wonderful innocence intact. A strong indication that the audience accepted the conclusion with joy and relief is found on the title page of the first quarto, where an emblem depicts the benevolent hand of God emerging from the clouds to settle the crown on Arbaces' head. The emblem suggests the sentimental theme of the play, the transcendent power of the hero's innocence to find divine favor in the midst of jeopardy, and thus it displays the theological basis for the hope of rescue which unifies the action.

It would appear obvious, then, that a rhetorical interpretation of the play indicates the choice of benevolent and lax moral principles. The choice is made difficult, however, because Elizabethan scholarship conventionally recognizes only a rigorous set of moral principles which derive from an ecumenical conflation of Roman Catholic and Aristotelean moral thinking. It is necessary to note, therefore, that the Reformers consistently rejected the established Catholic casuistry so as to develop a new moral system more in keeping with their special attitude towards justification and forgiveness of the sinner. When the Council of Trent affirmed the legalistic basis of rigorous casuistry, the distinction between mortal and venial sin, it did so largely because the Reformers denied the doctrine that some sins were in their nature minor, while others were by definition major. All sins, the Reformers insisted, were equally mortal and so equally jeopardized one's salvation.

If with this change the Reformers made their casuistry more rigorous, as was their hope, they also made it more lax, as their critics said, for now the external and legal fact of sin was potentially secondary to the psychological feeling of the individual—and a subjective belief in one's own rectitude could understandably lead to a lax accounting for sin. This casuistical topic of assurance and justification is admittedly complex, but Calvin's reluctance to discuss it was not shown in England by William Perkins and his followers, who "made it into a commonplace of the religious life" and thereby established a wide knowledge of the principles of the new casuistry in Jacobean London [see Basil Hall, "Calvin against the Calvinists," in *John Calvin,* Courtenay Studies in Reformation Theology I, ed. G. E. Duffield, 1966].

The decidedly lax dramatic pattern of temptation and rescue in the new tragicomedy follows the paradigmatic case in Puritan casuistry of the justified man who nevertheless sins because of the imperfect nature of all mankind. For a justified individual, however, these occasional lapses would pose a mild danger, because at the moment of ceasing from sin, he would be assured of his original justification. In fact, the possibility of instant rescue from sin is implicit in this system, for when the inward assurance of justification has not been seriously damaged or discarded, it provides ready pardon for trespasses against the moral law. While repentance is still important, a pragmatic measure of the original justification would be the duress of the penitential experience. Moreover, as Richard Field and his fellow Puritans admit, satisfaction "is so imputed unto us, as that it freeth us from all punishment whatsoever" [Richard Field, *Of the Church,* 1606]. This view of divine justice, as Field states later, significantly differs from the Tridentine position regarding mortal sin, which entails a required period of expiation, precisely what Rymer considered the necessary tragic suffering in Panthea and Arbaces.

Tragic suffering, however, is not required for what Perkins calls "sins of infirmity." By this term Perkins means exclusively the sins of the regenerate. Perkins in effect distinguishes between the existential and essential selves, and he finds in the case of regenerate that outward sinful acts or passing desires do not necessarily damage the inward essence: "A sinne of infirmitie is, when there is a purpose in the heart not to sinne: and yet for all this, the sinne is committed, by reason the will is overcarried by temptation, or by violence of affection, as by feare, anger, lust" [*A Commentarie . . . on Galatians*]. In discussing such cases, the primary question was the extent to which sin has harmed faith and grace: "the man that is regenerate, sinneth neither when he would, because hee is restrained by the grace of God that is in him: nor in what manner he would, partly because he sinneth not with al his hart, the strength of his flesh beeing abated by the Spirit; and partly for that beeing fallen, he lies not still, but recovers himselfe by speedie repentance" [*The Whole Treatise of the Cases of Conscience*]. The popular audience would be generally familiar not only with the laxity implied by this casuistry, but also with its related assumption of a providential concern for the "children of God": "If he cast them into the fire, it is not to consume them, but to purge and refine them. . . . He presseth us, that we might cry: we crie, that we may be heard: we are heard, that we might be delivered. So that here is no hurt done: we are worse scared, then hurt" [Arthur Dent, *The Plain Man's Path-Way to Heaven,* 1607]. This passage by Arthur Dent, the great popularizer of Puritanism, aptly summarizes the moral sequence of the action in *A King and No King* and relates it to immediate concerns of the vast majority of Londoners. Thus in structuring the tragicomedy Beaumont and Fletcher were not appealing simply to a decadent coterie audience, as is commonly alleged, but rather they were directing their play to the widest possible interests.

Because of its new moral assumptions Beaumont and Fletcher's tragicomedy, of course, lacks the pattern of penitential remorse which is common in earlier prototypes of the genre. Chapman's *The Gentleman Usher* (pub. 1606), for example, is directly allied with the morality play tradition, since it enacts the mortification of the errant characters before they are extended literary sympathy. Thus the erring Duke Alphonso is granted dramatic reinstatement only after his explicitly painful conversion from sin; the religious emphasis of the moment is reinforced by the wicked character Medice, an unchristened former gypsy king, who flees from the scene of forgiveness to "hide . . . from the sight of heaven" because he has a soul which he regards as being "too foul to expiate" (V.iv.280, 273). Dramatic sympathy for Leontes in *The Winter's Tale* similarly follows sixteen years of expiation, while in *The Tempest* Prospero intentionally arouses guilt and remorse in his enemies so as to share with them the lesson of forgiveness. Unlike these characters who must be purged of pride, however, Arbaces and Panthea are established at the outset as wonderfully innocent characters who are rescued from the jeopardy of sin before their sentimental innocence is irrecoverably lost. Many critics, not seeing how *A King and No King* breaks with tradition, have felt that the sudden recovery of the protagonists is a cheap contrivance that illogically abandons the tragic burden of the play. But that is to judge character and action apart from the new casuistry, which integrally relates the fortunate discovery, the theme and the narrative meaning of the play to the dominant fact of the enduring and triumphant innocence of the characters.

The decisive moral innocence of Arbaces and Panthea is dramatically suggested by making them childlike. As may be seen in Dent's reference, the association of childhood with moral innocence was familiar in contemporary theology. "At the board," wrote Hooker, "it very well becometh children's innocency to pray, and their elders to say Amen"

[*The Works of Richard Hooker*]. "Children in maliciousnesse," according to [Thomas Wilson's] *The Christian Dictionary* (1612), indicated the low degree of sin said to obtain in the regenerate: "Such as be like little children, voyde of malice, and unharmefull. 1 Cor. 14, 20. *But as concerning maliciousnesse be ye children.*" Children's moral transgressions, because they lacked malice, thus were defined in the *Dictionary* as "foolishnes or folly," precisely the terms used in the play to describe the actions of Arbaces and Panthea. Bishop John Earle's character "A Child" [in his *Microcosmography*, 1633] reveals a remarkably prelapsarian belief in a child's innocence: "His soul is yet a white paper unscribbled with observations of the world, wherewith, at length, it becomes a blurred notebook. He is purely happy, because he knows no evil, nor hath made means by sin to be acquainted with misery." These morally sentimental attitudes towards childhood are carefully invoked by *A King and No King,* which seeks directly to be "a proof / Whether the gods have care of innocents" (IV.iv.62-63).

The childlike innocence of Arbaces accordingly is asserted throughout the play. His prayer for "tears / Enough to wash me white, that I may feel / A childlike innocence within my breast" (I.i.456-58) comes early in the play so as to clearly establish the moral status that the audience hopes he will recover. Thus when he kneels "with the obedience of a child" (V.iv.183) to hear the revelation of his true identity, the dramatic expectation that he will recover his innocence is fulfilled. Panthea, six years younger than Arbaces, is scarcely nubile. She also is introduced as being "arm'd" with "innocence" (II.i.75), but later confesses during the temptation that "Children and fools are ever credulous, / And I am both" (IV.iv.42-43). Mardonius, the blunt captain who is Arbaces' closest friend, knowns of his desires but regards them primarily as "childish follics" (IV.ii.172).

Yet because they are marriageable, Arbaces and Panthea are not, from a chronological standpoint, children, despite continual assertions in the play to that effect. Danby properly calls attention to their adolescence, which he finds revealed especially in their desire to regain the "petrarchan nexus" of their self-idealizing personalities [John Danby, *Poets on Fortune's Hill*, 1952]. But while Danby thus corroborates the pattern of perfect recovery in the play, his secular analysis does not account for the psychological fear of sin that prevents Arbaces from enacting his desires. For although Arbaces resists as best he can, he and the audience know from the first that he is being tempted into damnation. Consequently the sudden claim to recovered innocence that he and Panthea share at the conclusion cannot be based on petrarchan assumptions, nor on the prelapsarian beliefs of Bishop Earle; rather, their claim to innocence rests squarely on the Puritan casuistry of forgiveness for sins of infirmity.

The supposedly incestuous courtship which begins in Act III now may be seen to follow a remarkably clear pattern of infirm temptation and full recovery. When Arbaces returns to court from years of war, he and Panthea are the melodramatic victims of love at first sight. Arbaces complains that Cupid has given him an "ungodly sickness" which can be cured only by deeds that will "O'er throw divinity, all moral laws, / And leave mankind as unconfin'd as beasts" (III.i.197-98). He fights temptation, but he cannot expel it, and soon he kisses Panthea. He then rejects his foolishness and, to protect them both temporarily, he orders her under house arrest. As the scene ends he prays to the inscrutable power above for mercy and assistance.

His precarious situation worsens at his next appearance, for he tries to enlist his friend Mardonius as his pander, even though the idea is morally repugnant, "To do a sin that needs must damn us both / And thee too" (III.iii.79-80). Mardonius refuses the role, warns him against sin, and leaves him alone on stage. The scene develops as an obvious tableau of morality, for when the comic Bessus enters, he offers to "do anything without exception, be it a good, bad, or indifferent thing" (ll. 140-41). Still unconfirmed in sin, Arbaces cautions that what he intends "Thy conscience will not suffer thee to do" (l. 145). Consequently he is taken by surprise when Bessus offers gleefully to arrange "a bout," and the resulting shock revives moral strength in Arbaces. He rightly accuses Bessus of being a demonic tempter, an accusation which Bessus counters with the offer to help Arbaces to his mother, too. The calculated contrast between the turpitude of Bessus and the naiveté of Arbaces has major significance now and in the conclusion of the play. At present it relieves Arbaces' moral jeopardy:

My mother!—Heaven forgive me to hear this;
I am inspir'd with horror.—I hate thee
Worse than my sin, which, if I could come by,
Should suffer death eternal. . . .

(III.iii.172-75)

Thus recovered from temptation, Arbaces beats the demonic Bessus from the stage with an equivocal curse that ironically will return to haunt him: "If thou find'st one so beastly as thyself, / Thou shalt be held as innocent" (ll. 183-84). "I will not do this sin," he resolves, "I'll press it here till it do break my breast" (ll. 192-93).

In spite of this encouraging resolution Arbaces almost succumbs to sin twice more in the play. When he meets Panthea alone late in the fourth act, he finally confesses the full scope of his feelings to her. She, however, would rather be "in a grave sleep with my innocence / Than welcome such a sin" (IV.iv.89-90). True to the casuistical pattern of the temptation, Arbaces recovers, asks her prayers, and bids farewell. Then quite unexpectedly she confesses that she loves him in return. They hold hands, and as the tension grows, they kiss. She is startled to feel "a sin growing upon my blood," an image Arbaces repeats: "Sin grows upon us" (ll. 159, 164). The image of sin as an alien presence opposed to their essential selves is determinative for the casuistical meaning of the play. The scene ends with the lovers fleeing from each other, and so momentarily from temptation.

As the play gathers momentum towards its apparent resolution, sin is seriously jeopardizing these young charac-

ters. Indeed, it might seem that Arbaces finally repudiates his remaining innocence. So impious is his tragic declaration that the bracketed part of the speech was omitted from the seven quartos following the first and from the folio of 1679:

Enter Arbaces *with his sword drawn.*
It is resolv'd. I bore it whilst I could;
I can no more. [Hell, open all thy gates,
And I will through them; if they be shut,
I'll batter 'em, but I will find the place
Where the most damn'd have dwelling. Ere I end,
Amongst them all they shall not have a sin
But I may call it mine.] I must begin
With murder of my friend, and so go on
To an incestuous ravishing, and end
My life and sins with a forbidden blow
Upon myself.

(V.iv.1-11)

The spark of remaining innocence reveals itself to a sympathetic audience in his moral repulsion at the "forbidden" deeds he feels compelled to do. More importantly, even at this late stage, his proclaimed resolution to enter remorselessly into sin is not irrevocable. To help establish the tentative quality of his commitment to sin, the pace of the action slows immediately. Mardonius pleads with him to put up his sword, and the extended conversation that follows (ll. 11-61) not only lowers the dramatic tension, but it also puts Arbaces in an altogether different frame of mind: "Why should the hasty errors of my youth / Be so unpardonable, to draw a sin / Helpless upon me?" (ll. 62-64). The authors skillfully manage the transition from Arbaces as the seemingly resolved sinner to Arbaces as the infirm victim of sin, and so prepare the audience for the happy conclusion.

The remainder of the play serves to complete the dramatic reinstatement of Arbaces as an innocent childlike character. Gobrius now steps forward to announce that he is Arbaces' father, who gave Arbaces at birth to the Queen to raise. The pathetic reconciliation of the child to his father is both a dramatic and a moral representation for the sympathetic audience: "Bring it out, good father; / I'll lie and listen here as reverently / As to an angel" (ll. 198-200). Thus by special intervention the extreme jeopardy of an infirm sinner is happily redeemed, and at the end of the long explanation Arbaces halloes the court to enter and be "Partakers of my joy!" (l. 262).

The sympathetic response of the audience at the conclusion has been carefully guided by the moral characterization of Arbaces. Sin does not have for him a significant or painful duration because he never abandons his belief in his innocence. His redemption from improper behavior relieves the anxious audience and creates a dramatic situation in which it is possible to forgive the wrongdoing. Easy forgiveness already has been extended to other characters, precisely on grounds of their supposed infirmity. Arbaces forgave the Queen her wicked plots in exactly these casuistical terms: "As far be all your faults from your own soul / As from my memory; then you shall be / As white as innocence herself" (III.i. 51-53). Another lover was forgiven his infidelity with similar unquestioning generosity:

> Good sir, be pleas'd
> To think it was a fault of love, not malice,
> And do as I will do—forgive it, prince;
> I do, and can, forgive the greatest sins
> To me you can repent of.
>
>   (IV.ii.76-80)

Indeed the magnanimous mode of lax contemplation encouraged by the resolution of the jeopardy is best explained by William Perkins [in his *A Treatise of Christian Equity and Moderation*]:

> Our nature is given to take men at the worst, to deprave mens deeds and words, and to pervert them to the worst sense that may be: and this is commonly the cause of debate and dissention in the world.

> But the dutie of Christian Equitie is contrarie hereunto; namely, to thinke the best they can of all men, to construe all doubtfull actions in the better part, and to make the best sense of all doubtfull speeches, if we have any probable reason to induce us to it.

Although many critics rigorously take the play in "the worst sense that may be," the moral presentation of Arbaces and Panthea unquestionably induced the popular audience to forgive them quickly, on the casuistical assumption that they were probably innocent even in the seeming act of sin. The narrative pattern of the play thus concludes intelligibly for the audience at the Globe.

II

The sentimental satisfaction that *A King and No King* offered the Globe audience was theological in confirming the providential bias of the new casuistry and in suggesting the doctrine of the immutability of election. The peculiar pattern of jeopardy and total rescue became a leading characteristic of later Jacobean tragicomedy and probably influenced the practice of grafting poetic justice to Shakespearean tragedy during the Restoration. But if the new casuistry was thus made popular in London, it also was vigorously attacked by Catholics on the Continent, where it was sporadically insisted that Protestants were ridiculously lax in assuming easy forgiveness for sins of infirmity. Beaumont and Fletcher surely recognized this objection, for the play eschews smugness, both through the ironic presentation of Arbaces in the main plot and through the sustained parody of his innocence in the subplot, which has not been explained since Dryden wished it were "thrown away" [John Dryden, "Preface to *Troilus and Cressida*, 1679]. When this satire is considered together with the authors' previous dislike for the audience, there is good reason to believe that Beaumont and Fletcher meant all along to ridicule the sentimental taste of the London audience.

Only George Pierce Baker [in *Select Plays of Francis Beaumont and John Fletcher*] has postulated that throughout their career "Beaumont and Fletcher wrote in half-amused contempt of their public." Yet it is clear that Beaumont satirized the court and the current anti-Catholic mania in *The Woman Hater* (1606) and the vapid love of chivalric romance in *The Knight of the Burning Pestle* (1608). Some critics suspect that Fletcher was ironic in his early venture, *The Faithful Shepherdess* (c. 1608), a pastoral love play in which few characters are properly chaste. Both plays of 1608 were failures in performance. Ben Jonson blamed the audience of "fools" for the ill reception of Fletcher's play; Beaumont's commendatory verses similarly attacked the audience for its hostility to art and wit, while Chapman consoled Fletcher for cruel treatment by "the multitude, / With no one limb of any art endued . . ." [see *The Works of Beaumont and Fletcher*, ed. A. H. Bullen, 1908]. Thus if Fletcher felt martyred by the audience, and was not simply the unsuccessful ironist, then the reason for his later estrangement from the public is understandable. In either event he soon went partners with an established satirical dramatist.

Beaumont's disdain for the public was unmistakable after *The Knight of the Burning Pestle*. In verses written for the publication of *Volpone* a year earlier, he had attacked the pretentious gallants in the audience and threatened to ridicule them on the stage and have them "like it." Making good this threat, in *The Knight* Beaumont interrupts the action of a prodigal play so that Rafe, a gallant apprentice with outspoken preferences for Spanish romances, may come on stage to enact his chivalric fantasies in absurdly contrapuntal fashion to the ongoing play. Rafe's master and mistress meanwhile speak occasionally throughout the performance, revealing themselves to be "artistically and morally stupid." This was heavy-handed stuff, and in the first quarto Walter Burre took opportunity in his publisher's preface to acknowledge the play's poor reception, and to call for a second play, to "revenge his quarrel, and challenge the world either of fond and merely literal interpretation or illiterate misprision." Since Burre had published many of Jonson's plays and presumably knew the dramatists' current dislike for their audience, his preface is a valuable secondary indication of the satirical technique used in *A King and No King*—for here, the open burlesque of the audience changes to a sophisticated comment on their "merely literal" responses to the new Puritan casuistry.

Beaumont and Fletcher were by their upbringing in a position to be more than usually knowledgeable about counter-Reformation polemics. Fletcher's high-living father had been Bishop of Bristol, Worcester, and London, from which post he was removed. What is more interesting, Beaumont's grandmother received the last rites from Henry Garnet, Superior of the Jesuits in England, who also referred to Beaumont's mother as a devout Catholic. Her influence on at least one of her sons is apparent.

Beaumont's brother John, with whom he lived for a time in London, married Elizabeth Fortesque, whose entire family was imprisoned for recusancy before the marriage.

John himself is cited for recusancy in 1607, and his own son later became a Jesuit. It might be added that the dramatists' friend Ben Jonson was haled into consistory court in 1606 on charges of recusancy and of proselytizing youths to the Catholic faith.

A further piece of circumstantial evidence regarding the dramatists' anti-Puritanism is worth notice despite its uncertain provenance: the verse letter from Beaumont to Jonson (c. 1609). In the letter Beaumont familiarly alludes to and invites contempt for Matthew Sutcliffe, who was informally recognized as King James's minister of Protestant propaganda. The letter begins with banter about high times at the Mermaid Tavern and, after mockery of the Puritans' drinking wine so weak it is almost water, there comes the slap at Sutcliffe: "'Tis licquor that will finde out Sutcliffs witt, / Lye where it will, and make him write worse yet." Sutcliffe was the leading Puritan controversialist in England, and one of his major opponents at this time was Matthew Kellison, who served on the faculty at Douay [a Catholic Seminary in France]. In three book-length critiques of Reformation theology Kellison had singled out for special ridicule the casuistical paradox of innocent sinners. Sutcliffe in 1606 responded to each of Kellison's arguments and attempted to refute them all. This was a significant exchange over fundamental issues in the counter-Reformation, and while we cannot know if they read it, Beaumont and Fletcher apparently knew the tenor of Kellison's objections to sins of infirmity.

Kellison argued [in *A Survey of the New Religion,* 1603] what the play satirically demonstrates, that the doctrine of sins of infirmity leads to sentimentalism and finally to moral anarchy, since this doctrine makes the legal fact of sin only a passing jeopardy to the elect:

> . . . . soe when I am moved to sinne by the devil or my owne concupiscence, yea even then when I ame in the acte of sinne, I may apprehend that thoughe there is noe goodnesse in me of myne owne, yet Christes justice is myne, of which, if even in the acte of sinne, I assure my selfe, I maye assure my selfe also, that noe sinne can hurte mee. . . . And so the way is open to all vice and wickednes, because if a man will beleeve that he is juste, and hold faste by this faith, noe sinne can hurte him, bicause that assuraunce of justice dothe justifie him.

As we have seen, the calculated sentimental response of the audience to Arbaces is based entirely on the alluring faith in a sudden recovery of innocence. Kellison scorns the lax attitude towards sins of infirmity with a directness that is not found in the play; what makes the dramatic satire unmistakable, however, is the ironic disparagement of Arbaces' imperturbable assurance in both plots.

III

In the main action Arbaces' vacuous self-esteem is ridiculed occasionally: when the citizens mock him for bringing "peas" to their land (II.ii), and especially in the final scene of the play, when he conveys his good fortune to the court. Here his sense of moral relief transcends all bounds of common sense. The extravagant imagery of his speeches reveals an unconnected view of reality. He orders Mardonius, preposterously enough, to conduct Tigranes home "as never man went." "Shall go on's head?" Mardonius quips, but the barb goes unnoticed:

> He shall have chariots easier than air
> That I will have invented, and ne'er think
> He shall pay any ransom; and thyself,
> That art the messenger, shall ride before him
> On a horse cut out of an entire diamond
> That shall be made to go with golden wheels
> I know not how yet.
>
>   (V.iv.314-20)

This sort of fairy tale language at one level makes the happy ending an escapist's fantasy, but at an ironic level, the vain imprecision of the imagery and thought is the poetic measure of Arbaces' detachment from experience. In this light his promise to Spaconia reveals a silliness that is also morally insincere:

> She shall have some strange thing; we'll have the
>   kingdom
> Sold utterly and put into a toy
> Which she shall wear about her carelessly
> Somewhere or other.
>
>   (V.iv.323-26)

Arbaces' superficial but self-assured toying with reality is inescapably associated with the happy laxity of the play and thus with a complacently cheerful audience that accepts such laxity.

It may not be very damaging for the main plot to suggest that Arbaces' self-satisfaction has its markedly foolish side: the subplot, however, develops the comic presentation of Bessus into a witty parody of Arbaces' self-assurance. As the play ends with Arbaces' miraculous recovery from theological sin, so it begins with "Bessus' Desperate Redemption" from secular cowardice (I.i.52). Bessus, retreating in the wrong direction, fell upon the enemy and in the confusion won the day. Before this known everywhere as a coward, he now boasts he is famed for valor by "The Christian World" (I.i.42). His "conversion from a coward" (III.ii.113-14) is challenged repeatedly. Bacurius especially denies his new assurance of valor, beats him into admitting he is still a coward, and takes away the outward sign of his honor, his sword, leaving Bessus only his "impudence" to maintain his reputation (III.ii.102-60). He seeks out two casuistical "bilbo-men" (that is, two master swordsmen, with a likely pun on "Bible-men") to analyze the case of his honor. The bilbo-men decide in a definitive statement of ethical theory that his sword was "forc'd but not lost" (IV.ii.61) and therefore that he is still "a very valiant man" (l. 147). But when all three confront Bacurius with their findings, he beats and kicks the swordsmen and takes away their swords too. After he is gone they nonetheless shake hands all around "to our honors"

(V.iii.99). "We are valiant / To ourselves, and there's an end" concludes Bessus (ll. 101-02).

The weakness of Arbaces' pretension to recovered innocence is ironically exposed by his distorted reflection in Bessus, for in a reductive sense both are "valiant" to themselves. The subplot pointedly burlesques the recovered reputation that Arbaces lays claim to, on the presumption that his innocence, like Bessus' sword, was "forced but not lost" during the long temptation. In the world of the play, society forgives the sinner at his behest while it tests the bravura of a coward. Yet from a psychological standpoint there is no easy public method to detect unwarranted moral self-assurance, which is of course precisely the casuistical dilemma which Kellison had predicted for the Protestants. The potent sin of incest loses its significance in the play, therefore, because it has no importance to the conscienceless Bessus and is of no lasting consequences to the reassured Arbaces. They are both characters whom no sin can hurt, and in this ironic sense they are equals.

The interaction between Bessus and Arbaces further exposes the tendency towards anarchy in Puritan casuistry. Arbaces, it may be recalled, drove Bessus from the stage in the third act because he properly recognized him as a demonic tempter. Yet at their next meeting, during the joyful final scene, Arbaces blithely forgets the painful moral lesson he has learned and greets him cheerfully as "good Captain Bessus" (V.iv.296). With this reunion the psychology of infirmity is neatly demonstrated to be based, in its extreme laxist form, on self-willed intellectual oblivion. Arbaces has regained his innocence only at the price of dissociation from his past behavior and especially from any moral knowledge he has gained; apparently he is doomed to an unending pretence of innocence. He reveals then a necessary myopia when he greets the recognized devil of the play as his "fellow subject" and invites him to the marriage of the "innocents." But the riddling curse with which Arbaces had banished Bessus now brilliantly returns to define the paradox of their new-found equality: "If thou find'st one so *innocent* as thyself, / Thou shalt be held as *beastly*" (III.iii.183-84). Like the situation, the crucial terms (in italics) have been reversed.

The conventional scene of forgiveness in tragicomedy thus leads to an outrageous conclusion that I think intentionally undercuts the cozy moral formula of the play. By incorporating a twofold treatment of lax casuistry, *A King and No King* was at once a successful exploitation of and a fey triumph over an alien sentimental audience. Still it is disturbing to think that this play and *Macbeth* were both acted at the Globe in 1611 to the applause of the same audience, for the plays present diametrically opposed views of moral retribution. Surely the sentimental possibilities for drama permitted by the new casuistry were not missed by the authors of either play; they of all people were aware of the onset of a new epoch in English drama. Beaumont and Fletcher's irresponsibility, if it may be called such, was to understand and accept the change, rather than fight against it. Yet remarkably enough *A King and No King* demonstrates a serious recognition of the danger of laxity, and thus indicates that Beaumont and Fletcher were them-selves disturbed by the sentimental tragicomedy which their audience seemed to demand. The clear implication is that although Beaumont and Fletcher structured a casuistical action to which lax and even decadent responses are possible, the authors are not in consequence "morally hollow," as alleged by Coleridge and Eliot. If anything, the play leads to quite the opposite conclusion—that the authors disparage the sentimental myopia which their casuistical drama craftily invites.

FURTHER READING

OVERVIEWS AND GENERAL STUDIES

Andrews, Michael Cameron. "Beaumont and Fletcher." In his *This Action of Our Death: The Performance of Death in English Renaissance Drama,* pp. 72-90. Newark: University of Delaware Press, 1989.
> Investigates the emphasis on the notion of the "exemplary death" depicted in Beaumont and Fletcher's plays.

Appleton, William W. *Beaumont and Fletcher: A Critical Study.* London: George Allen & Unwin, 1956, 131 p.
> Broad survey of Beaumont and Fletcher's joint efforts, Fletcher's works alone and with other collaborators, and the history of their reception since the Restoration.

Cunningham, John E. "Beaumont and Fletcher." In his *Elizabethan and Early Stuart Drama,* pp. 73-88. London: Evans Brothers, 1965.
> Examines Beaumont and Fletcher's plays in the context of Elizabethan social, cultural, literary, and theatrical conventions.

Ellis-Fermor, Una. "Beaumont and Fletcher." In her *The Jacobean Drama: An Interpretation,* pp. 201-26. London: Methuen & Co., 1936.
> Comments that the tragicomedies of Beaumont and Fletcher differ from other Jacobean dramas by offering a "sanctuary from the agonies of spiritual tragedy and the cynicism of observant comedy."

Finkelpearl, Philip J. "Beaumont, Fletcher, and 'Beaumont & Fletcher': Some Distinctions." *English Literary Renaissance* 1, No. 2 (Spring 1971): 144-64.
> Contends that the inflated rhetoric of Beaumont and Fletcher's plays intentionally "dramatize a moral vacuum and hollow center," and are not demonstrations of the decadence of the Jacobean theater.

——. *Court and Country Politics in the Plays of Beaumont and Fletcher.* Princeton, N. J.: Princeton University Press, 1990, 263 p.
> Locates both the initial success and subsequent decline in critical estimation of Beaumont and Fletcher's plays in their political content.

Herndl, George C. "The New Meaning of Tragedy: Tourneur, Beaumont & Fletcher, Ford." In his *The High Design: English Renaissance Tragedy and the Natural Law,* pp. 218-80. Lexington: The University Press of Kentucky, 1970.

Traces the "distinctive characteristics" of Beaumont and Fletcher's drama, finding the "realism of its language [gives] substance to its fairyland characters."

Hoy, Cyrus. "The Shares of Fletcher and His Collaborators in the Beaumont and Fletcher Canon." *Studies in Bibliography* 8-15 (1956-1962).

Seven-part examination of the respective shares of Beaumont and Fletcher in their joint works and of the possibility that other writers contributed to the dramas.

Masefield, John. "Beaumont and Fletcher." *The Atlantic Monthly* 199, No. 6 (June 1957): 71-4.

Offers compact biographical information.

Mincoff, Marco. "The Social Background of Beaumont and Fletcher." *English Miscellany* I (1950): 1-30.

Places Beaumont and Fletcher within the atmosphere of change, social crisis, and revolt in the Jacobean period.

Ornstein, Robert. "John Marston. Beaumont and Fletcher." In his *The Moral Vision of Jacobean Tragedy,* pp. 151-69. Madison: University of Wisconsin Press, 1960.

Focuses particularly on Fletcher's plays, which, Ornstein claims, "indicate all too clearly the decline of the Jacobean stage after its first golden decade."

Thorndike, Ashley H. *The Influence of Beaumont and Fletcher on Shakspere.* 1901. Reprint. New York: Russell & Russell, 1965, 176 p.

Compares the characteristics, dates of composition, and stage histories of the plays of Shakespeare and of Beaumont and Fletcher. Thorndike concludes that Shakespeare was likely influenced by the younger dramatists.

Waith, Eugene. *The Pattern of Tragicomedy in Beaumont and Fletcher.* New Haven, Conn.: Yale University Press, 1952, 214 p.

Interprets the "distinctive features" of Beaumont and Fletcher's tragicomedies "in the light of certain contemporary literary forms and, ultimately, of the rhetorical tradition."

Wallis, Lawrence B. *Fletcher, Beaumont & Company: Entertainers to the Jacobean Gentry.* Morningside Heights, N.Y.: King's Crown Press, 1947, 315 p.

Presents a survey of Beaumont and Fletcher criticism from their own time to the twentieth century.

Wilson, John Harold. *The Influence of Beaumont and Fletcher on Restoration Drama.* 1928. Reprint. New York: Benjamin Blom, 1968, 156 p.

Assesses the degree to which the plots, characters, settings, and tone of Beaumont and Fletcher's plays affected those of their successors.

THE MAID'S TRAGEDY

Danby, John F. "*The Maid's Tragedy*." In his *Poets on Fortune's Hill,* pp. 184-206. Port Washington, N.Y.: Kennikat Press, 1952.

Analyzes the play as a composition aimed at an aristocratic audience.

A KING AND NO KING

Neill, Michael. "The Defence of Contraries: Skeptical Paradox in *A King and No King*." *Studies in English Literature 1500-1900* XXI, No. 2 (Spring 1981): 319-32.

Examines the play as a kind of "discordia concors" which reconciles the "contrary demands of tragedy and comedy."

Additional coverage of Beaumont's and Additional coverage of Beaumont's and Fletcher's lives and careers is contained in the following source published by Gale Research: *Dictionary of Literary Biography,* Vol. 58.

Ed Bullins
1935-

(Also wrote under pseudonym Kingsley B. Bass, Jr.)

INTRODUCTION

As the author of more than thirty plays, Bullins is regarded as one of the most significant playwrights to emerge from the Black Power Movement. His works are acclaimed for their realistic, sometimes controversial depiction of African American ghetto life. From 1967 to 1973 Bullins was the Playwright-in-Residence at Harlem's New Lafayette Theater, and it was during this period that Bullins produced some of his most popular plays, including *Goin' a Buffalo, In the Wine Time, The Duplex, Clara's Ole Man,* and *In New England Winter.*

BIOGRAPHICAL INFORMATION

Bullins was born in 1935 in Philadelphia, Pennsylvania, and he grew up on the rough streets of North Philadelphia. In 1952 he dropped out of school and joined the Navy. After three years of world travel, Bullins returned to Philadelphia. He moved to Los Angeles in 1958 and enrolled in Los Angeles City College. He continued his education at San Francisco State University, and after attending a production of *The Dutchman* and *The Slave* by the black radical Imamu Amiri Baraka (LeRoi Jones), Bullins realized that he would pursue a career in the theater. Influenced by Baraka's works and his call for black identity, he joined The Black Panthers and served as cultural director of a African American artists consortium called Black House. He eventually broke with the Black Panthers and when the director of the New Lafayette Theatre, Robert Macbeth, invited Bullins to stage *In the Wine Time* there, Bullins accepted. He moved to New York in 1967 and began his long association with the artists at the New Lafayette.

The Taking of Miss Janie, Bullins introduces and reintroduces characters such as Len, a Black Nationalist, and Sharon, his white friend whom he eventually marries. With the recurrence of characters comes the recurrence of themes; miscegenation, white/black relations and their viability, and the schism within the Black Power Movement in general. This technique also allows Bullins the opportunity to make his characters current with the changing times.

MAJOR WORKS

Bullins's work is concerned with the candid depiction of the African American experience. To this end, Bullins has created a body of work which falls into two categories: those of the "Twentieth-Century Cycle," or cycle plays, and non-cycle plays. Among the latter are *Goin' a Buffalo, Clara's Ole Man, The Pig Pen,* and *The Taking of Miss Janie.* In order to create his theater of black experience, Bullins has striven to attain a recognizable thematic and character progression throughout these plays. In this way, the audience feels an even greater affinity and connection with Bullins's people. In *The Pig Pen* and its sequel

CRITICAL RECEPTION

Although initial critical reaction to Bullins's work was generally favorable, some viewers complained that his early plays were too violent and offered an unflattering picture of African American life. Several black critics rallied to defend Bullins and attacked white critics for using "white" notions of good drama to evaluate black art. Today, Bullins is recognized as one of the leading African American playwrights in America. Commentators agree that his plays, devoid of political or revolutionary rhetoric, force viewers to examine themselves and the conditions surrounding them.

PRINCIPAL WORKS

PLAYS

Clara's Ole Man 1965
Dialect Determinism (or The Rally) 1965
How Do You Do? 1965
The Game of Adam and Eve [with Shirley Tarbell] 1966
It Has No Choice 1966
A Minor Scene 1966
The Theme is Blackness 1966
The Corner 1968
The Electronic Nigger and Others [includes *Clara's Ole Man* and *A Son, Come Home*] 1968
Goin' a Buffalo: A Tragifantasy 1968
In the Wine Time 1968
The Gentleman Caller 1969
The Man Who Dug Fish 1969
*We Righteous Bombers [as Kingsley Bass, Jr.] 1969
The Devil Catchers 1970
The Duplex: A Black Love Fable in Four Movements 1970
The Fabulous Miss Marie 1970
Four Dynamite Plays: It Bees Dat Way, Death List, The Pig Pen, Night of the Beast 1970
The Helper 1970
A Ritual to Raise the Dead and Foretell the Future 1970
Street Sounds 1970
In New England Winter 1971
Next Time 1972
The Psychic Pretenders (A Black Magic Show) 1972
You Gonna Let Me Take You Out Tonight, Baby? 1972
House Party, A Soul Happening [music by Pat Patrick] 1973
The Taking of Miss Janie 1975
Home Boy [music by Aaron Bell] 1976
I Am Lucy Terry 1976
Jo Anne!!! 1976
The Mystery of Phillis Wheatley 1976
DADDY! 1977
Sepia Star, or Chocolate Comes to the Cotton Club [music and lyrics by Mildred Kayden] 1977
Storyville [music and lyrics by Mildred Kayden] 1977
C'mon Back to Heavenly House 1978
Michael 1978
Leavings 1980
Steve and Velma 1980
Bullins Does Bullins 1988
American Griot 1990
I Think It's Gonna Work Out Fine [with Idris Ackamoor and Rhodessa Jones] 1990
Salaam, Huey Newton, Salaam 1991
Raining Down Stars: Sepia Stories of the Dark Diaspora [with Idris Ackamoor and Rhodessa Jones] 1992

OTHER MAJOR WORKS

Drama Review [editor] (anthology) 1968
New Plays from the Black Theatre [editor and contributor] (anthology) 1969
The Hungered One: Early Writings (short stories) 1971

To Raise the Dead and Foretell the Future (poetry) 1971
The Ritual Masters (screenplay) 1972
The Reluctant Rapist (novel) 1973
The New Lafayette Theatre Presents: Plays with Aesthetic Comments by Six Black Playwrights [editor] (anthology) 1974

*This work is attributed to Bullins, although he publicly denies having written it.

AUTHOR COMMENTARY

Ed Bullins with Richard Wesley (1973)

SOURCE: An Interview in *Black Creation,* Vol. 4, No. 2, Winter, 1973, pp. 8-10.

[*In the following interview with dramatist and editor Richard Wesley, Bullins examines the responsibilities of the black artist to the black community.*]

[Richard Wesley]: *What points can be made for the role of the critic in the arts?*

[Ed Bullins]: Many points can be made, though I question whether Black critics in this period are making points worthy of consideration. The critics almost without exception do not understand their role, are confused by its possibilities or, more often, are critics in name only.

How do you feel critics have failed thus far?

A critic should be some sort of intellectual/aesthetic guide to the audience, the reader, the appreciator. But in the Black Arts today you find a group of so-called critics almost devoid of original ideas and without an artistic or intellectual guiding ethos. They do shoddy newspaper journalism and call it criticism. They do not have the range of vision to exploit the demands of their craft. If Black Arts has a history, some philosophical principles, a cadre of evolving practitioners, then these things should be put in some sort of perspective by the critic. Critics do not do their study/work. They believe themselves knowledgeable but don't have a foggiest notion as to where the Black Artist is coming from and what resources that he or she is using. They have failed the Black people miserably. They are frauds, except for a small handful who don't even choose to write much criticism any longer or live and work outside the mainstream where the major Black Arts work is being done. Darwin Turner, Stephen Henderson, James Murray, Kushauri Kupa are several critics who do and attempt ably to do their jobs when their work appears. Larry Neal can be considered a strong head but he has abandoned the craft for the most part. There are numerous others working in the field with differing degrees of committment but falling short of the ideal.

Do you feel movies are stealing talent and audiences from Black Theater?

No. I feel that movies are developing talent and audiences for Black Theater. One art form complements another. It has been said by Clayton Riley that films are not an art form. This is ignorance at a very low level. And people listen to this type of misconception and believe it because they have few other choices.

How has Black Theater adapted itself to current Black thought?

Current Black thought has been reflected in some forms of Black theater. Black thought has even been anticipated by some Black theater: **We Righteous Bombers, Arm Yourself or Harm Yourself,** the Black Ritual forms developed by Robert Macbeth of the New Lafayette Theater, etc.

Some of the best minds in the Black nation are in the Black theater. And these minds affect Black thought in general.

What future do you see for Black Theater, particularly The New Lafayette?

The future of Black theater seems assured. Black theaters are mushrooming across the country. Where there were a handful of Black theater companies in the New York area alone several years ago, today there are more than twenty functioning groups.

At this point, The New Lafayette Theater continues to work. The group is engaged in stage productions, films and video tape.

Why did the New Lafayette become involved in film making?

Because there were enough members of the company interested in making quality films that the inevitable evolutionary nature of progress could not be denied.

It has been said that you (Ed Bullins) often use the New York Times to fight your battles with other blacks while still claiming to be the blackest of the black, how do you respond to that charge?

Many people read the *New York Times*. More Black people than one may suspect. Attacks are leveled from that media. Replying in kind and with authority only seems sensible. Being infrequently published by *The Amsterdam News* and Black publications like *Black World* that have leveled attacks but refused space to answer is very limiting. When I make my voice heard I choose to have it magnified to the best degree that I can.

What are some of the ways that community-based theater groups such as the New Lafayette can build up an audience capable of supporting the group? Or is it possible?

I don't know if it is possible. It will take lots of work and effort. We, at the New Lafayette, have been working at it for a half dozen years or more. When someone finds out please let us know. We'll probably be at our theater location on 137th and Seventh Ave. in Harlem, working as usual.

What is the definition of Black Theater?

I don't generally deal in definitions. Definitions seldom answer very much. Do not educate yourself in terms of definitions. Start with the thing. Look into its process. How does it work? What makes it work and be? Begin at a thing's reality, the bit of reality that one can perceive, and then work toward whatever is called definition. A label is little more than a label if the inner mystery of what a thing is is not solved. The working generalization that can be used: Black Theater is that theater, sometimes found in the Black community, that is done by Black people. (Of course there are various exceptions.) But how one discovers what Black Theater is is by going to *any* and *all* Black theaters in one's community or area; failing to discover Black Theater in your locale (Montana maybe?), then one should be prepared to travel. If travel is restricted by circumstances (again reality), then one should read *everything* that can be found concerning Black Theater. Now everything seen or read in Black Theater will not be appreciated or liked by those who see or read it; but if enough seeing and reading is done over a period of *experience formulation* then that person will *know* what he believes to be Black Theater, for that person will have experienced the *fact,* plus incorporated his preconceived notions and biases as to what Black Theater should be or is into some valid model. And with all of the above said it is left to the one who attempts to create Black Theater who might gain the actual inner insight into this revolutionary art form.

What is the role of the Black playwright?

To write plays.

Who should criticise Black Theater—Black critics or white critics?

Critics of Black Theater, for the most part, shouldn't be taken seriously, and then only with reservations, if they are not *practicing* Black Theater workers. Since whites cannot fit this condition—for how can whites *practice* Black Theater art?—then there is only need to regard them if they can aid in keeping a Black production alive. For Black critics not practicing Black Theater, Black literature and Black Art on the level of *mastership,* their sensibilities are almost exclusively rooted within the consciousness of the Black bourgeoisie—a class whose values are those of the market place and whose cultural ideals dwell in Europe—and their minds are usually filled with the garbage that that class misunderstands as intelligence. Forget about critics; the Black audience is the supreme critic of Black Theater.

Do you think there is any value in presenting "negative images" in works of Black Theater?

The cry for "positive images" as against "negative images" in Black Art during these early days of the seventies is part of the rhetorical fallout of the sixties. *Do not mistake rhetoric for inspired oratory.* If an image is grounded in truth then it is a depiction of a true phenomenon in the world. In fact, it is a real phenomenon, itself. And that is how education occurs—by confrontation of real phenomena with the learner's consciousness which creates realistic models within the mind. Nothing can really substitute for what really exists; and existence can be evaluated as positive or negative but actually the single real characteristic of existence is existence itself. But Black Theater criticism is at a very low level today, with even the supposedly knowledgeable demonstrating that they have regressed to the sloganeering of the 1930's in appealing for positive images for Black people. This invoking of the unreal was initially a 19th century Russian aesthetic philosophy imported during the 1930's depression era to aid the mythical American class struggle of blacks by showing the Black proletariat and "lumpen" struggling upwards to the glorious socialist, nonracist future. For Black people, we know that this is all a lot of old timey European jive in still-racist America. And Black people do not need so-called Black intellectuals still perpetuating that type of harmful propaganda. Little did everyone realize then that the future had been bought up piecemeal by IBM and Associates (Con Ed, General Motors, the American war machine, etc.); in fact, the ripoff of the people's future is reminiscent of how Manhattan was supposedly bought for Indian wampum. Our Black fathers and mothers paid for the future, an *in* to the American dream, with their bodies in the almost endless wars which have been waged by America against the world. And with their souls by ending up with practically nothing in the way of progress to show for these forty years except half-remembered slogans. The pseudo-political rhetoric of the Black bourgeoisie should not be mistaken for literary or dramatic criticism. This class has traditionally never studied their artistic and intellectual history, let alone the history of other non-European cultures. They'd rather exist on newspaper slogans and appear as Cultural Commissars who ride their weary mules backward at full gallop into the nineteenth century. They be afraid of truth which might expose them; such as, niggers surviving in those wilds of north America. They have always been afraid of truth, especially the truth of Black folk/niggers who are the audience of Black Theater.

What is the project you're engaged in known as the 20th Century Cycle?

The *Twentieth Century Cycle* is a series of plays about Blacks living throughout Black America. The plays are *In the Wine Time, In New England Winter, The Duplex, The Fabulous Miss Marie* and *Homeboy*. They have all been produced by now except for *Homeboy*. I have hopes of The New Lafayette Theatre doing it some time soon. The plays deal with Black lifestyles and peopleways. It explores and examines some family groups and follow them throughout their lives, in the present day and throughout history. Black literature is a survival record of Black people surviving America and this cycle of plays hopes to set the record down about some groups of people coming

through some dreadful times. These people should not be forgotten. And I hope to make some artistic statements as well. As well as do some thinking and analysing along the way. I am trying to aim straight at truth and honesty in the work, if that is possible. So I hope to invest the best of my talents into the grand design. And I hope to see that they are presented as they should be.

The artist must thrust his way outward if his expression is to penetrate the wall of oblivion. I wish to show Black people themselves and the universe and the possibility of the awesome unlimitness. And I wish to contribute at least to the future of creativity and truth.

—*Ed Bullins*

What new directions do you think your art will chart in the future?

I am going ahead of myself, if I can. I don't think I should stay still or go backward, if I can. So I am trying to stretch out into video and film. More so video. Video that can be controlled by you; video tape and self-made films as well as movies and TV. Maybe the movement is horizontal and not vertical. But it will all have depth if it can hang together in its unique components. The artist must thrust his way outward if his expression is to penetrate the wall of oblivion. I wish to show Black people themselves and the universe and the possibility of the awesome unlimitness. And I wish to contribute at least to the future of creativity and truth.

Do you have any new productions planned for the 1972-73 season?

Yes. Woodie King and I are working on a production of *The Fabulous Miss Marie* for Off-Broadway. We will produce it. It should open in March. Then, Roscoe Orman and I are working on a production at the American Place called *House Party*. A Soulful Happening, which might jump off in the spring if the pieces fall together. And it is so early in the season I can not say what may happen. It might all get out there.

What advice would you give to young writers coming up behind you?

I would tell them to write a lot, more than they dream they could ever do, and to read a lot, to almost impossible for them to imagine, and for them to live and experience and travel and try to use their minds in coordination with their bodies and reality and then they might be able some day to write a sentence. If that kind of energy can be decoded. We should listen and look at our teachers. We should go on and work out the story. We should write. Young writers should write. Not talk about it. Or think about it. Or dream about writing. But do it. And you should do it with passion, with love, and with grace. And you must do it like only you can do it. Because nobody can do what you do but you. It is never too late to tell the truth. It is never too late to show the truth. If you miss a day of writing that is one more day that you won't get it done, for your death has gained a day on you. And you have so much work to do that ten lives would only be a beginning. Write everything that you have seen, smelled and touched, if you have the heart to do so. Hearts are big and small and a man's should beat as long as it can. For work is divine. And creation is holy. And being a Black artist is the metaphor of being a soldier of the present and future in the African Nation of the West.

Ed Bullins with Charles M. Young (1975)

SOURCE: An interview in *The New York Times*, Section 2, May 18, 1975, p. 5.

[*In the interview with Charles M. Young below, Bullins reflects on his goals, the growth of African American theater, and the role of the theater as an instrument of change.*]

[Charles M. Young]: *Are you trying to reach a black or white audience?*

[Ed Bullins]: The blacks like it when the whites get put down and the whites like it when the blacks get put down. I don't write to please the audience and reassure everyone that we agree. I don't care how they feel or what they think—whether they agree or disagree—just so it makes them examine themselves. In a work like [*The Taking of Miss Janie*], the truth is open-ended. Like Hemingway said, "If I wanted to send a message, I'd go to Western Union."

Clive Barnes said you were a moral writer without moralizing. Is that true?

If a writer moralized in an amoral world, he would be a contradiction of the times. Morality changes. To say what morality is, is letting yourself in for lies. Martin Luther King was a moral man and you saw what happened to him.

You don't want to save the world with your writing?

I have no Messianic urge. Every other street corner has somebody telling you Christ or Mao is the answer. You can take any *ism* you want and be saved by it. If you're part of some movement and it fulfills you, that's cool, but I like to look at it all.

You don't define yourself as capitalist or socialist then?

Oh no. Render unto Caesar that which is Caesar's. I don't think the day will ever come when people will share equably in the fruits of production. It goes against reality. Perhaps the best we could get would be a benevolent dictatorship that would give us clean subway cars.

*What has been the reaction of other black militants to [*The Taking of Miss Janie?*]*

Are there any black militants left?

What would you do if Norman Lear offered you a million dollars to do a TV situation comedy?

They could offer me far less and I'd do it. It's not a matter of selling out. My work is just incompatible with that sort of thing. I've had offers from Hollywood and I've submitted scripts but nothing ever came of it. *Miss Janie* was originally done for a West Coast theater group and they refused it. Several theaters rejected it in New York. They gave me no constructive criticism, just statements like, "This is dreadful. I don't even want to talk about it." I'm very appreciative of Woody King and Joe Papp for producing it.

A few years ago you were harshly critical of Charles Gordone, Lonne Elder III and some of the other less radical black playwrights. Have your views moderated?

They should write more plays.

In 1972, you wrote that Gordone was "separated from reality" and Elder could "perhaps quietly disappear with grace."

Well, he did disappear with grace in Hollywood. I enjoyed *Ceremonies in Dark Old Men.* I think it was a mistake for talented playwrights to go off to Hollywood.

In that same 1972 essay, you said that black theater had profoundly influenced black culture. How has black theater changed things?

Back in the sixties, there were Imamu Amiri Baraka, myself and a few others in it. There were only three or four black theaters in the whole country. Now there are over a hundred functioning all across the country. The growth of black theater in the past ten years has had more of an impact on the artists themselves than on any vast audience. The audiences are still small, like congregations in churches, but black theater is beginning to arrive commercially.

Again in that 1972 essay, you said the black theater was a powerful instrument for changing slave mentality in black Americans. It hasn't yet reached the mass audience to do that?

Not really. The black movies which rose out of the theater have just repeated the macho stud stereotype with a lot of action and sex. It was a stupid and incestuous development, but it's dying out now. The theater writers are going on, exploring different themes, and this will be reflected more in the media as time passes.

What are the themes of these new black writers coming up?

They're writing all kinds of things about the black family and the black man's existence in the world. Some are doing ideological tracts. Marvin X is not a young play-wright, but he has just finished a play about Patty Hearst and the Symbionese Liberation Army.

Only about a third of New York City school children are reading at or above grade level. Will future audiences have the intellectual tools to understand your plays?

My plays are understandable to anyone who can look and listen. The kids are very sophisticated. They've looked at more TV and movies than the whole rest of the world has seen. Of course, you can't do Shakespeare in the ghetto. You must put on something that concerns them. We're putting on experimental, third-world plays in Harlem every day and the kids understand.

You said in an interview in 1969 that you didn't feel like an American. Is that still true?

I don't feel like an American American. I'm a black man who lives in America.

What's the distinction?

What's the difference between black music and Rodgers and Hammerstein? A scholar could tell you about notation and rhythm but we feel it as an intuition.

In a final sense, what do you hope to accomplish?

I'm creating a universe for future centuries, if there are any future centuries. When people then see my work, they will become part of what it was like in our time. I like to capture an audience. I like to spellbind them. If I lived in China, I'd like to write some of Mao's speeches, though he does pretty well for himself. I'm a pretty good propagandist when that's what I'm writing.

So it isn't what you say, it's how you say it?

Everything's been said. If you say it well, you can say anything. See, when I was young, I was stabbed in a fight. I died. My heart stopped. But I was brought back for a reason. I was gifted with these abilities and I was sent into the world to do what I do because that is the only thing I can do. I write.

OVERVIEWS AND GENERAL STUDIES

Lance Jeffers (essay date 1972)

SOURCE: "Bullins, Baraka, and Elder: The Dawn of Grandeur in Black Drama," in *CLA Journal,* Vol. XVI, No. 1, September, 1972, pp. 32-48.

[*Jeffers is an American poet, short story writer, and critic. In the following essay, he analyzes Bullins's honest*

and unsentimental depiction of the black working class in Clara's Ole Man *and* In the Wine Time.]

There are hellish depths and godly heights in the black experience that await the black artist as he charts our voyage into the future. Coltrane and Bird and Gene Ammons and Sidney Bechet and Johnny Hodges confidently exploit these heights, these depths. In black music there is a heavenly rage and an ecstatic prophecy and a danger and bottomless depth and the presence of juice and viscera that are the nerve and the sinew of experienced oppression, the bowel of the future of black life. The black musician, from the time of the spirituals, has not hesitated to touch this nerve, to feel this sinew, to dip his hand into the viscera of black life. What a tradition there is for Nina Simone to follow, a tradition centuries old and planets deep. But the black writer too often has stood timid, awed, whitened, fearful, educated, before the torrential currents of the black experience. Although our literature is massive, although our literary tradition is distinguished, although no other American writer has equalled Richard Wright's depiction of the moral horror of America—and the effectiveness of the depiction of the moral horror of the human condition is one of the primary criteria by which literature must be judged—despite the towering achievements of our literature, the black writer does not have the tradition of the black musician, for the black writer's tradition has been burdened by the defensive posture, that terror that the scorn of whites for blacks might be intensified if the black writer wrote with utter fearlessness and total recognition of the hell he sees before him: not only the hell of brutal mistreatment by whites but the hell the black man has sometimes created for himself through the *nature* of his *response* to the white man's oppression.

The black writer has hesitated, for example, to write fearlessly of our color caste; until Wright, the black writer hesitated to write fearlessly of a Bigger; until Ellison the black writer hesitated to write fearlessly of a Trueblood. The defensive posture is to react, rather than to act; the defensive posture is to be psychologically dependent on the white man, not psychologically independent. It is the black defensive posture that permits us to view with aplomb and appreciation O'Casey's *Juno and the Paycock* and Gorky's *Lower Depths* and "Twenty-six Men and a Girl" and Nexo's *Ditte*—and yet turn with horror and aversion from our own Joxers and Jack Boyles and Dittes, our own so-called lower depths. Yet it is the responsibility of the black writer to depict and analyze every aspect of black life—the lives of pimps and prostitutes, of black saints like Malcolm and Tubman and Carver, the lives of the upper reaches of the black bourgeoisie. The writer can turn his eyes from nothing human; nothing human is alien to the writer; in every human being is to be found the breadth of the human condition; in every human heart is to be found, to some degree, the angelic, the satanic, the godly, the depraved. The writer must examine everything human. The writer examines and analyzes, in depth, human motives and human behavior and human potentialities in order that he may help to direct humanity to its destiny of grandeur. This is the writer's holy charge. Only by depicting honestly every aspect of black life will the black writer help us reach our destined grandeur—and the thoughtful and resolute black writer cannot pause to consider the opinions of those who view with aversion the disorganized black life which they may see depicted on a stage.

The defensive posture, although it is diminishing, still lurks in black writers' hearts. But Bullins, instead of fearing how the white man might appraise us in the sight of the ugly and confused aspect of black life, Bullins like Elder and Baraka simply sets the white man aside and writes honestly of black reality. And this is good: for there is no need for the writer to stand fearful before the richness of his humanity. In the courage and in the cowardice of our response to oppression, in our immortal and godly endurance and in our lightless despair, in the rage of our retaliation and in the impotence of our confusion—in all of these there is the richness of our humanity, for our humanity is a mosaic, and the stones that constitute the mosaic are both dreadful and magnificent, and the writer's unashamed recognition of that which is beautiful and ugly in one's people: this is the ladder to grandeur.

In the best of Bullins' work, he is creating a tradition for black drama to follow, helping to create a fearlessness, a self-acceptance. There is no sensational spooning up of filth nor is there sentimentality; instead there is the searing eye of unsentimental analysis. And subtlety, so that when one reads *Clara's Ole Man,* one is reminded of the principle that in the presence of artistic greatness, the surface of a play does not necessarily reveal its depths; the depths are suggested rather than stated. And there is implicit direction; though Bullins' working class in his best work does not have conscious direction, one senses a kind of godly principle, a kind of holiness, and enormous energy and power, and one perceives that all that is needed is a harnessing force, a wise and compelling leadership, and sweeping changes will be made. There is another artistic principle: that a great work of art must suggest the awesome potentialities of man for growth: this principle too is a spine of Bullins' best work.

There is thus great strength and great confusion in Bullins' working class, of whom one could say: in great chaos, great strength; in great lostness, the potentiality of decisive direction; in compulsive suicide, powerful life.

In *Clara's Ole Man* we have homosexuality, dependence upon wine as an escape, hoodlums balancing themselves on the frontier of sudden death, and the imperception of the middle class, represented by a young former marine (and the armed forces to Bullins are the blunting force of human sensibility) who comes courting Clara in the absence of her "old man," but the marine does not realize that Clara's old man is Big Girl the lesbian. The marine finally clumsily unlocks the door to this truth or falls through the door upon this truth, and for his awkward blindness he is taken out to be thrashed by the hoodlums. It is as if in the developed narrative—novel, play, short story—there is often to be found the symbol of imperception, the symbol of moral blindness, for without blindness there can be no failure in human life, no death to stalk human life: thus the bourgeois aspirant's lack of percep-

tion is really the expression of a death-sleep from which he is brutally awakened through his beating by the black working class.

Awakening flutters beneath the surface of this play like a live vigorous bird loosely buried in sand. Clara is a prisoner of Big Girl and of her own weakness, but she is ashamed of her homosexual liaison, ashamed of Big Girl's coarseness, and her departure will probably follow Big Girl's ordering that her would-be suitor be taken out and beaten by the hoodlums: Clara's very presence there is a reproach to the disorder and chaos and brutality and the mis-sexuality: she is the black woman who stands on the threshhold of health: she is Man on the threshhold of harmony; she is potential order in the midst of disorder, and one is reminded of Mann's *Disorder and Early Sorrow,* the big children and the little child growing up in the moral chaos of Germany of the twenties, with never a principle of order in their lives, only sentimentality: but this is the black working-class world, harsher and potentially more orderly than Mann's middle-class world in *Disorder and Early Sorrow* and *Death in Venice,* where the middle class has lost its life principle, and in Bullins' working-class world there is the principle of potential order, and it is in Clara, in her embryonic strength soon to be born.

> In the best of Bullins' work, he is creating a tradition for black drama to follow, helping to create a fearlessness, a self-acceptance. There is no sensational spooning up of filth nor is there sentimentality; instead there is the searing eye of unsentimental analysis.
>
> —*Lance Jeffers*

It is a contradictory truth that in the midst of this world of winos and hoodlumism and irrational sexuality, Big Girl herself is a symbol of order: Big Girl the butch and the brute and the sustainer of alcoholics and hoodlums is in a sense the male leader of the household, its intellectual leader; her contorted sexuality springs not only from her encounters with black women whose weak and inadequate femininity or brutality she scorns: her distorted sexuality springs also from her compulsion to bring order out of chaos, her compulsion to be the steadying and dominating force in a world without a rudder, and to her mind, only a male can play such a role. Thus she sees herself as Clara's refuge, the refuge of the drunken aunt whose alcoholism she must support, and thus she is the place of sanctuary of the hoods; she is their cathedral to whom they escape when the white world threatens them with its law: and she is intellectual leader too: she teaches Baby Girl foul language so that Baby Girl's retarded mind can maintain a semblance of balance: she analyzes the failure of white psychiatry in the mental hospital where she works, the insane asylum which is the symbol of the insanity of the white world: and she rejects the fabricated falseness of the bourgeois aspirationist Jack: Big Girl is the powerful mother-father figure in this world: the powerful order-bringer, and she is the figure of realistic perception who deals perceptively with the world as she finds it, and when she protects the hoods, she is protecting and cultivating the seeds of a new world, for they, her sons, the anti-bourgeois, the robbers, the homeless, the carriers of an important form of black culture, it is they who are the future Soledad Brothers, these desperate and manly iconoclasts, those Attica-Soledad suckings of the future. And withal I sense in Big Girl a femininity unnourished, a femininity as seedwise as the masculinity of the hoods whose sanctuary she becomes.

In the Wine Time is a play about black manhood, and it is as if almost every black work of art is based, to a degree or almost wholly, upon the artistic principle of the consideration of the black man's manhood in America: the artistic principle of the consideration of the manhood of oppressed man. The manhood of the oppressed man is crucial: whether here or in Northern Ireland or in Bangladesh or in Toussaint's Haiti, for the oppressed man's response to oppression determines the nature of oppression or the very existence of oppression: whether the oppressed man is essentially subservient or defiant of oppression, and subservience does not necessarily imply overt Uncle Tomming, but may express itself in, let us say, an empty idleness. An artist acquaintance once told me, "If you don't work, Charley has won over you." A man may be externally proud, but internally he may actually have surrendered his manhood to the oppressor. A related kind of surrender is the thesis of Sean O'Casey's *Juno and the Paycock,* and this is instructive because the position of the Irish under the British is somewhat similar to the position of the blacks in this country, and Boyle is the man who has surrendered to the oppressor, surrendered his manhood, allowed himself to be castrated, and though his son violently resisted the castrative enemy, the British, he too ultimately patterned his manhood after his father's and thus betrayed his comrades to the authorities. There is much in this play and O'Casey's *The Plough and the Stars* to remind me of Baraka and Elder and Bullins, though Bullins' working class is a stouter working class than O'Casey's, and Bullins' view of his people and the human race is a stronger and warmer view, and Bullins in consequence a stronger playwright than O'Casey, *in the plays we now consider.* Bullins' working class is more vigorous than O'Casey's, and this black working-class vigor is an expression of immortality.

Let us add that in Bullins' working-class perspective we find the key to grandeur: for all literature, to achieve greatness, to achieve grandeur, must enter life through the most profound and realistic perspective, the perspective that is most respectful of Man and his potentialities: This is a *most* important key to understanding the grandeur of Bullins and Sholokhov and Nexo and Achebe and Silone and O'Casey.

Thus we have Cliff in *In the Wine Time,* the man who has surrendered his manhood to the oppressor: he has simply given up. He gives himself the excuse that he does not want to be a Derby Street donkey, that is, a factory worker. But he has really surrendered his manhood to his oppressor. While his wife works in a menial position, Cliff chases women, carouses, sits on the stoop and quarrels with his wife we see here Bullins' fine subtlety, for Cliff's quarreling is an expression of his profound anxiety, his profound dissatisfaction with himself, his essential suicide. Cliff is the oppressed man who has succumbed almost totally to the oppressor. And this concept of the activity or the passiveness or the mixture of activity and passiveness that exists in the oppressed man is most important in black literature or the literature of any oppressed people, for it is a key really to an understanding of the oppressed people and to the nature and the complexity of their life. Langston Hughes mastered this principle beautifully—the fusion of suicide and manhood—in his characterization of Bert in "Father and Son." We see the importance of this principle in Wright's "Big Boy Leaves Home"—or in Wright's "Down by the Riverside." And we see it masterfully handled in *In the Wine Time,* this ultimate artistic principle: the question of the black man's manhood, the question of the complex nature of his response to oppression.

And often there is another ultimate artistic principle: the earthcore strength and endurance of the Afro-American woman. Big Girl and Lou thus are sisters; each is a black woman who is a spine for life. Big Girl dominates *Clara's Ole Man,* dominates all around her, sets the tone around her, and though it seems a certainty that Clara will leave her, Big Girl's strength will continue to dominate, whether in her slum or in prison. Lou is another kind of black female strength: genuinely feminine, she has more of the pliancy which we stereotypically see as feminine: but her toughness and vision are a part of her femininity. She tells Cliff:

> You ain't no man. My daddy he worked twenty years with his hands . . . his poor hands are hard and rough with corns and calluses. He was a man . . . he worked and brought us up to take pride in ourselves and to fear God. What did I marry? I thought you was a man, Cliff. I thought because you was loud and was always fightin' and drinkin' and was so big and strong that you was a man . . . but you ain't nothin' but a lowdown and less than nothin'!

Cliff replies: "In the navy Ray can travel and see things and learn and meet lots of different—." Lou interrupts: "No!" Cliff continues: ". . . girls and make somethin' . . ." And Lou replies: "Is that what it did for you?" Cliff says: "Yeah, that's what it did for me!" And Lou replies: "Well, I don't want him to be like you." And Cliff responds: "How would you want him to be like . . . one of the Derby Street donkeys? Or one of the ditty boppers or an avenue hype . . . or . . . a drug addict . . . or what?" And Lou replies, to end the discussion: "He ain't turned out so bad so far. He's not going, Cliff." And to Ray she says: "Ray, just get it out of your mind. I'm not signin' no navy papers . . . You're too young." She senses that the armed forces are an instrument to turn potential black men into alcoholics, proud of their directionless lechery, that the armed forces are an instrument of whiteness to help black men choose nothingness and empty idleness over manhood, to choose surrender over initiative, that the armed forces are a castrative parent that will leave black men helpless, paralyzed, impotently dreaming at 30: "To be on watch," Cliff says, "on a summer night in the South Atlantic or the Mediterranean when the moon is full is enough to give a year of your life for, Ray. The moon comes from away off and is all silvery, slidin' across the rollin' ocean like a path of cold, wet white fire, straight into your eye. Nothin' like it to be at sea . . . unless it's to be in port with a good broad and some mellow booze." Bullins, we see, indirectly, subtly damns war and its instruments through Cliff and Lou, and never through a word of overt propaganda.

Cliff has one final gesture of defiance: he accepts the responsibility for the killing of Red, and thus he liberates Ray, his wife's nephew but it is also a gesture of death, the killing of Red, a suicidal gesture, an abdication of his life, an abdication of his manhood. Now he need never try to implement his dreams of conquering the world, and he releases to Ray, his, Cliff's, fragment of manhood, saying: "It's your world, Ray . . . Go on out there and claim it."

The new black playwright speaks a language of the dawn, he mirrors the vision of the young: "This is *our* world," they say: "We will take it and mold it as we will: we fear no man."

The killing of Red, like the beating of Jack in *Clara's Ole Man,* has special significance. The beating of the bourgeois aspirant Jack is the rejection of what Bullins considers the class enemy, the black man who in Bullins' view disappears into the middle class and returns to the working class only to mindlessly exploit it—as he returns to Big Girl's house to exploit Clara. The gulf of class is there, and once the gulf has been opened, there is, in Bullins' view, no bridge to cross the gulf. Red, too, although he is a son of the working class, represents to Bullins, like the pretty boy Art in *Goin' a Buffalo,* the enemy within the ranks who in a moment of crisis betrays the working class, as Art does; Red's arrogance, like his suicidal drive, is towering, for it is his suicidal need to express his insolent contempt for black people that leads to his death: his urinating in a bottle and giving the bottle to Ray to drink.

Bullins completely rejects the middle-class ethos, as his work rejects completely the white world. His rejection of the white world has in it no implicit element of a wish to belong, a rejection of the white world based on the white world's rejection of him; Bullins' rejection of whites, in his best work, is almost an afterthought, as if he were saying, this working-class black world is my world, it has never occurred to me to want another. In Bullins' rejection of the white world, the term rejection is even inexact, for he is like a man living in his own home with his own family and who does not wish to live in another man's home and with another man's family. I have my own family, my own people—why should I identify elsewhere? And the two go together in Bullins: the

rejection of the middle-class ethos and turning one's eyes completely on one's own people. In such a deep-rooted racial philosophy there is no worship of whiteness nor any strained exclusion of whiteness: whites sometimes occur in Bullins' work, and, in his best work, they are simply a natural part of the work—in Bullins' natural and unselfconscious oneness with his own class and with his own people. One must note that in certain other black plays there seems a straining to produce a genuine working-class, a straining to produce a correct racial philosophy. The dawn of grandeur is the total and natural and uncondescending acceptance of oneself. Nor does this mean that Bullins accepts Big Girl's values in his acceptance of Big Girl: it is simply that Big Girl is one of his class: or even better, Big Girl is of his humanity: but let us add that in Bullins we see an artist-as-working-class-writer, as in Sean O'Casey we see artist-as-working-class-writer though Bullins' working class is an intestine more working class, and more implicitly victorious than O'Casey's. Bullins sees the working class through working-class eyes and it is rare that we sense a false note in the dialogue and in the behavior. The complexity and implicit direction of people of the ghetto through the eyes of the black working-class artist—and this fused with the artist's conviction that man is a potential giant. What emerges is magnificence.

Nicholas Canaday (essay date 1986)

SOURCE: "Toward Creation of a Collective Form: The Plays of Ed Bullins," in *Studies in American Drama, 1945-Present,* Vol. 1, 1986, pp. 33-47.

[*In the following excerpt, Canaday traces Bullins's artistic development, asserting that his early works focus on feelings of alienation, while his later works concentrate on those of collectivity and community.*]

When Ed Bullins wrote the introduction to *The Theme Is Blackness,* a collection of his plays published in 1973, he made an important, frequently quoted statement about what he called the New Black Theatre as well as about contemporary black playwrights, many of them friends and colleagues associated with him in the New Lafayette Theatre in Harlem. The goal of that Black Theatre, encompassing all who write plays for it, is a continuity that "is achieved through *creative struggle*: ruthless dedication in creation of collective forms that will survive any single individual's life. . . . *to inspire the creation of the nation.*" Bullins then supplies considerable detail about the "collective" form of the new drama and its content, which will breathe life into the "creation of the nation." In this new Black Aesthetic the emphasis is on community.

The emphasis had been different in Bullins's earlier plays, and his introduction to *The Theme Is Blackness* also provides a comment on these earlier plays as well as a useful critical framework from which to view the evolution toward the idea of community that becomes the keystone in the Black Theatre. In the early Sixties there appeared what Bullins labels generally as "black revolutionaries"—whether in political or social relationships or the arts:

> A handful of these "revolutionaries" evolved into what can best be described as *Black artists,* using the tired and wasted Western theater form as a medium to effect the most profound changes in Black people here in America, that process termed "altering consciousness". . . .

It is not my purpose here to describe how that consciousness in black people was altered; and certainly all of us are familiar with the rhetoric concerning the death of Western Civilization in such writers as Amiri Baraka, Larry Neal, or James T. Stewart—or, frequently, as in the work of George Kent, for example, of the need for the extirpation and replacement of certain dominant motifs in Western Culture. Rather, we here first use details from several of the early plays of Ed Bullins to see him as "Black artist" within the "tired and wasted Western theater form." This means the naturalistic theatre as form, alienation as theme. But within that framework Bullins saw himself as a "misfit," and in the second part of this study we examine the "collective form" toward which he has been moving. . . .

Bullins was Playwright in Residence and the Associate Director of the New Lafayette Theatre in Harlem, between 1967 and 1973. Four of his plays, produced in 1968 and published in *Five Plays by Ed Bullins,* had young, alienated male protagonists in varying degrees of conflict with what might be thought of as the black "community." Taken in order of their production, the resolution of the conflict in each play becomes part of a significant sequence of options and possibilities.

A young man named Jack, who has just returned from three years of service with the Marine Corps (Bullins himself served in the Navy, 1952-55), is the protagonist of *Clara's Ole Man*. It is the mid-1950's, and Jack's attitude toward the black community in South Philadelphia—a place reflecting Bullins's own youthful experience—is superficial and condescending. Jack's central failure of perception has a humorous aspect: the young woman Clara who has invited him to stop by lives in the house of her "old man," a stocky domineering woman of indeterminate age named Big Girl. Jack is clearly unable to cope with that relationship or with the others who appear: the retarded sister Baby Girl, a drunken woman neighbor, a local streetfighter and two members of his gang, and a young wino drifting through.

Jack's alienation is painful. Dressed in a corduroy Ivy League suit with vest, he uses a kind of pretentious speech that has been carefully learned. When Clara, for example, is embarrassed because Baby Girl has acquired a string of nasty words from Big Girl, Jack responds: "Yes, it does seem a problem. But with proper guidance she'll more than likely be conditioned out of it when she gets into a learning situation among her peer group." The ludicrous language matches the fatuous conception of Baby Girl's future. As Jack drinks wine with the others, however, he tries without success to imitate their street talk. That effort merely brings upon him the mockery of the other young men, which he fails to comprehend. Later Jack naively reveals Clara's invitation, which brings violent abuse from the gang and jealous fury from Big Girl. When Jack realizes who in fact "Clara's ole man" is, he staggers into the yard to throw up; and the three youths, encouraged by Big Girl, follow him and brutally beat him as the play ends.

Yet despite the character of the protagonist—"proper," insensitive to these people, striving to be middle class—the play is not about the need to "come home" or reestablish roots, at least not in the community depicted. Bullins's picture is realistic: life in this neighborhood is explosive, verbally and physically abusive, punctuated by a series of jiving, superficial relationships, and covered with a patina of alcohol and violence. It is a play about alienation that shows Bullins's satiric attitude and a balancing of sympathies.

Another study of alienation, called *A Son, Come Home,* is somewhat shorter and the least naturalistic of the four plays produced in 1968, but it uses the familiar naturalistic device of the return home of the protagonist after a long absence. Michael, who had lived on Derby Street in South Philadelphia in a section called "The Bottom," comes to visit his mother in the East after having been away nine years, some of the time spent in college in California. (Bullins himself attended Los Angeles City College and San Francisco State College.) Mother is living in some kind of religious home; but, more important, she is living in a different world, recognizing her son only intermittently, never really communicating with him. The alienation of the young man Michael is even more painfully intimate than that of Jack in *Clara's Ole Man* because the understanding and support in a family relationship, to the extent that it ever existed, has disappeared. Michael says in the beginning, "Home . . . is an anachronism," but it is Michael himself, of course, who is misplaced, a misfit.

In the dialogue Michael and Mother drift by each other on topics like his present life and aspirations, his poetry, his relationship with his Aunt Sophia in California, the length of his hair, her religion, his absent father, and her lover who was with them when Michael was a teenager. In this son's return home there is no communication to be the basis for a relationship—in fact, the details suggest there was never a mutual support between son and mother—and "home" is simply an empty concept. Nor is there any resolution to the play; at the end son and mother simply say goodbye and part. Michael, unlike Jack of *Clara's Ole Man,* is self-sufficient and sophisticated, but no less sad for all that.

The resolution of the third play seems to have been conceived in anger. *Goin' a Buffalo* takes place in the early 1960's in the West Adams District of Los Angeles and involves a group of hustlers of both sexes trying to score some "grand theft dough" so they can take off for Buffalo, reportedly a high rolling, easy living, "boss" town. These characters include Curt and Rich, partners in the narcotics life, Curt's wife Pandora, a dancer at the Strip Club, and a white junkie prostitute named Mamma Too Tight, formerly Queenie Bell Mack from Mississippi. Pandora has a box in which she keeps her dope, and there is a recurrent ironic motif in the

Helen Ellis, George Miles, and Crystal Field in the first production of Goin' a Buffalo.

play about good things rather than bad coming from Pandora's box—together with certain obscene variations.

The one alienated from this community, which is again realistically presented, is a stranger named Art, a man younger than the others who has just got out of the county jail. The gullible Curt wants to bring Art into the group and makes the effort to do so during the course of the play despite Art's tough aloofness. Tough, wise, cool—Art has served in the Merchant Marine and he is the very opposite of the naive Jack in *Clara's Ole Man*; nor does he have the intellectual pretentions of Jack or of Michael in *A Son, Come Home,* although Curt tells the others (he is rather impressed) that Art reads too much, and Rich calls Art a "book-readin' faggot." Pandora's comment, in character, speaks for the whole group: "Ain't heard of nobody gettin' no money readin'." Meanwhile, Art ingratiates himself with the women by stopping Curt from beating Pandora and by telling Mamma Too Tight that most of all she needs "understanding." Yet what he is doing turns out to be playing his own game. Pandora asks him what he is waiting for, and he replies:

Me? I'm just waitin' so I won't jump into somethin' too fast . . . just sit back and look around and wait a while. You don't have to do anything . . . baby, the whole world will come to you if you just sit back and be ready for it.

Curt is impressed with his new friend, and in light of the outcome of the play his speech to Art is heavily ironic:

You're like me in a lot of ways. Man, we're a new breed, ya know. Renegades. Rebels. There's no rules for us . . . we make them as we break them.

Curt fails to understand at this point, of course, that he is describing Art but not himself.

Art betrays Curt and Rich to the police as the two make their big deal in heroin. He has now also taken over Mamma Too Tight, giving no sign that "understanding" her is of any importance to him. The last act presents Art as an entirely different person who slaps Pandora viciously when she wants to do something to help the jailed Curt. Art is in charge: he orders Pandora to get packed and be ready to go to Buffalo with him and Mamma Too Tight. A brutal takeover is the resolution to Art's alienation, a playing of the game without rules to his own advantage: deception, betrayal, violence, whatever cruelty is necessary.

In the fourth play, *In the Wine Time,* there is not one alienated male protagonist but two, the boy Ray and the older Cliff Dawson, married to Ray's Aunt Lou. The place is described as a large, northern city, but Derby Street identifies it again as Philadelphia. (Ray, the youngest protagonist in this series, would be in the early 1960's about the age of Bullins himself, born in 1935.) Ray speaks a symbolic prologue, in which he is seen on many an evening waiting on a street corner to see his ideal woman pass, who favors him with a smile. She represents his future, and it is not on Derby Street:

"Can I go with you?"

She let go of my hand and smiled for the last time.

"No, not now, but you can come find me when you are ready."

"But where?" I asked.

"Out in the world, little boy, out in the world. Remember, when you are ready, all you have to do is leave this place and come to me, I'll be waiting. All you'll need to do is search!"

But Ray's Aunt Lou fears for his innocence and vulnerability and will not permit him to join the Navy as Cliff had done at his age.

Cliff also wants to get away from this place, and the "Derby Street Donkeys," as he calls those individuals who live there place and people depicted in a panorama of drifting relationships, crime, alcohol, and violence. Some, like Lou, who works long hours in a laundry for a dollar an hour, show—and here Bullins very typically balances the possibilities—either courage and determination or donkey-like stubbornness. But Cliff wants the "big rich world out there," and he is going to school on the GI Bill to try to reach it. Yet in other moments he tells Ray not to be trapped as he is, not to fail as he has:

> Nawh . . . nawh . . . I had my crack at the world . . .
> and I made it worse, if anything . . . you youngbloods
> own the future . . . remember that . . . I had my chance.
> All I can do now is sit back and raise fat babies. It's
> your world now, boy.

The tension is resolved at the end of the play by an act of random violence. Ray's girl friend appears and announces she is now the girl friend of one of the members of a street gang. As she says of August evenings carelessly drinking and waiting for the sun to rise, "Honey, these wine times is somethin' else." In the fight that ensues Ray kills his rival in an alley, but Cliff is able to take the blame for the murder, and does, as the police arrive. For this sacrifice he makes it clear that he expects Lou to let Ray leave Derby Street. As Cliff is led away handcuffed, his words to the young man express his hope for Ray in an ironic echo of the prologue: "It's your world, Ray . . . It's yours, boy . . . Go out there and claim it."

Thus the last of these four plays of alienation seems to start again at the beginning, with the protagonist battered by the harsh realities of ghetto life. Still, Ray has learned much already, and so the full circle has spiraled to a higher beginning for him than for the other young representative male characters. Ray is far too street-wise to be humiliated like Jack in *Clara's Ole Man,* and having spoken his determined prologue he will never have the purposelessness of Michael in *A Son, Come Home*. Finally, because he has the example of Cliff's sacrifice, an act of love that frees Ray from Derby Street, he is unlikely to develop the ruthless self-centerdness of Art in *Goin' a Buffalo*. It may be that Ray will leave and then return to be a participating member of that black community that Bullins discovers and reveals in the next phase of his art and thought.

. . . . .

Even as early as 1969 Bullins saw in himself and in his career as a playwright a development that was both personal and aesthetic:

> Moving my whole art back into my original reference
> which is my people, my community fulfills me. . . . It
> makes me a peaceful, creative brother who wants to
> build, to create for the Black people and nation, where

before I was like a very disturbed cat—I was a misfit, a Western Negro-artist misfit.

> *(New Plays)*

In fact, the evolution of the Black Theatre, "playwrights consciously migrating to non-Western references" (*The Theme Is Blackness*), has a beginning virtually coterminous with black playwrights using the traditional forms and themes. Bullins's revolutionary plays, performed beginning in the 1960's, are published in *The Theme Is Blackness* (1973). The seven plays published in this volume are non-representational in form and deal with a wide variety of themes both traditional in black literature and specifically relevant to contemporary black experience. Two of the plays seem to be influenced by earlier works of Amiri Baraka, and the final one brings back Cliff Dawson in a reprise which places him in a different relationship with the community from that of *In the Wine Time*.

The title play, *The Theme Is Blackness,* is what was called in the late sixties a "happening." The directions for its performances are very brief: a speaker introduces blackness as the theme for the play, and the lights go out for twenty minutes. There may be incidental sound effects or music in the interim. The key is the speaker's introduction: "One may discover all the self-illuminating universes in creation." Thus in a paradoxical reversal of traditional imagery there is illumination in blackness. And since the play is without a traditional structure it does not articulate a theme in the traditional way.

The earliest play in the group, first performed in 1965, is called *Dialect Determinism,* and it has the black community, represented symbolically in a broad spectrum of Brothers and Sisters, assembled at a meeting. An alternate title for the play, as a matter of fact, is given by Bullins as *The Rally*. The play is essentially the entire community listening to and responding to a speech by Boss Brother. It soon becomes apparent that this putative leader will play any role in order to maintain his sway over the people. He begins by announcing that they are assembled for a great purpose, but his mumbling delivery and hesitant speech immediately undercut that assertion. And his rapidly changing guises—black nationalist, Hitler, Lenin, the Wandering Jew—reveal him to be a con man without substance or purpose. With lights rapidly changing colors, he concludes:

> Don't yawhl knows I's Martin Luther, Butterbeans
> without Susie. That I's Uncle Tom, Fred Schwarz,
> Emperor Goldwater, Lumumba, Castro, all the LBJ's,
> Lincoln Rockwell, the Birds' Turds resurrected. . . .

When the people cry for him to teach them more, he responds: "Very well, I'll give you more, everything and whatever you wish to hear." In an ironic ending, Boss Brother calls for a martyr to bind the community together; the Brothers and the Sisters surge upon the stage, stomp him to the floor, tear at him and finally strangle him with a rope that has been instantly produced.

The play is an enactment of a remark Bullins makes in the introduction to the published plays when he says that the awakening black nationalism of the sixties was pervaded with "confused tenets of dated negro radical activism." Thus the community is swayed, even buffeted, by a series of contradictory political passions, and the leaders of whatever stripe (or one leader cast in the light of whatever moment) are far more interested in their own power than in power to the people.

Two plays first performed in 1966 seem directly influenced by Amiri Baraka's 1964 plays *Dutchman* and *The Slave*. Bullins himself acknowledges a general debt in a 1969 interview with Marvin X [published as the introduction to *New Plays from the Black Theatre*]:

> I guess LeRoi Jones influenced me most directly as a playwright. . . . I had heard about LeRoi's plays and read them before I actually saw them. . . . I read the Absurd people, and I read some of the contemporary plays which aren't really contemporary.

In technique, characters, even setting in one case, the Bullins plays *A Minor Scene* and *It Has No Choice* are very similar to the Baraka plays. The action of each Bullins play, however, represents a reversal; in theme, a triumph of blackness.

Bullins's *A Minor Scene* presents two characters, Peter Black and Miss Ann instead of Clay and Lula of *Dutchman,* who have a brief encounter at a bus stop. The place is obviously similar to the subway setting of the Baraka play, and in both plays the characters are types, each name characterizing. In Bullins's play the black Peter sexually humiliates the white Miss Ann, which reverses the roles of *Dutchman,* in which Lula dominates and molds Clay at will, until he rebels at the end of the play. Bullins's play begins with the same absurd dialogue as in *Dutchman,* showing language as mere gesture, its content violating our conventional expectations. It is Peter Black who strolls up to Miss Ann in *A Minor Scene,* in contrast to Baraka's aggressive Lula. His opening speech: "Hey, you white scummy-lookin' bourgeois bitch, take me to dinner?" The anonymous encounter, though each in a deeper sense know each other well, in the urban setting is unlikely enough, his humiliation of her in this public context even more so. She keeps apologizing to him—Bullins's version of white liberal guilt is a bit different from Baraka's—despite his crude verbal abuse, and by the end of the play pleads with him to come away with her, offering to hail a taxi. Standing there fondling her, he agrees. It is a brief play, a minor scene perhaps compared to the longer *Dutchman,* but a significantly different vision.

It Has No Choice is another play that goes directly to the fundamental issue of black-white sexual tension. Its action is not an initial encounter between strangers, but like Baraka's *The Slave* it deals with the end of a relationship between a black man and a white woman. The title refers to a statement by Kafka that Steve, the strong black intellectual quotes in the play:

> You do not need to leave your room. Remain sitting at your table, simply wait. . . . The world will offer itself freely to you to be unmasked, it has no choice, it will roll in ecstasy at your feet.

Grace, in this Bullins play, has no choice, rather unlike Grace, a woman with the same name, in Baraka's *The Slave*. Here the time is truncated: the Grace of *It Has No Choice* has had a relationship with Steve for only two weeks. Grace in Baraka's play repudiates Steve's counterpart, there named Walker, and takes their two daughters when she is subsequently married to a white man. That Grace leaves her black husband Walker for the same reason that Bullins's Grace says she wants to end her relationship with Steve. But Bullins's black protagonist has a much less divided personality than Walker, with much greater emotional strength. The action of *It Has No Choice* takes place in a Southern California apartment on a Sunday morning. The lovers Grace and Steve are in bed, but the sensual tranquillity is ended by Grace's declaration that she wants to end the affair. She says she is a "silly little secretary" who has enjoyed their physical intimacy but is uncomfortable with Steve's constant reading and study, his "white and black philosophy," and his view of himself as an Afro-American. There is, in short, a large part of Steve's life from which Grace is excluded. Such was exactly the Grace-Walker relationship in the earlier Baraka play: blackness has come to be perceived as an insurmountable barrier by the white female. But the significant difference between the two plays is in the resolutions. In *It Has No Choice* Steve will not let his Grace go, but instead reminds her she freely entered into the relationship and cannot reverse her decision:

> You want to go back like nothin's happened? You want to go back like it was before . . . so you can look through me and around me and never see me . . . I love *myself* too much for that. You're mine and if you go back, you'll go back mine.

The play ends in physical violence, with the stronger Steve dominating Grace, standing over her as she sprawls on the floor. She nods weakly, acceding to his order to return the next day: "I think I'll enjoy making love to you tomorrow, darling." Grace has, it is clear, no choice.

In both of these Bullins plays derived from those of Baraka, the basic sexual tensions, the first in encounter and the second in parting, are the same as the source. The stereotypical roles are similar, as are the basic reasons for the conflict and the way each character fights. What is different is the outcome, because in the Bullins plays the strength of the black male, not only physical but also due to a fully integrated personality evincing determination and a sense of purpose, dominates the white woman. Thus the traditional racist assumptions—backed up by the power of the white society—about the black male as menial are overturned. The white world yields to blackness because it has no choice.

In the next play, *The Helper,* a major motif of the black literary tradition is used. The Helper, an invisible man watching a decadent white world, is hired to help a white couple move furniture out of an apartment they are vacating. The four members of the family involved for the most part simply ignore The Helper, talking as if he were not there. Sister, the wife, is so named because she is really still a child of her parents. She would prefer not talking to The Helper at all, and she becomes hysterical when he accidentally walks in a room while she is changing her faded jeans. Sister's one enthusiasm seems to be a campaign poster being moved off the wall, saying "In Your Soul You're Sold on Him," an obvious parody of Barry Goldwater's 1964 campaign slogan. Her husband, the sullen Buddy, is trying to get finished with the move so as to get away from Mother and Daddy. Her father is rude and crude, and he will not acknowledge The Helper's presence by the slightest sign. At the end of the play when the young people say The Helper was helpful, Daddy simply spits on the floor. Mother is a talkative, silly, domineering woman. Characteristically, she comments about The Helper: "Your sweating brings out the most gorgeous tones in you skin. I had this houseboy in Kingston . . . he was simply darling." Saying very little through all this, The Helper takes his money at the end and leaves—silent, strong, sure of himself, and yet invisible in a white world.

In an extended metaphor of contemporary black experience in America, *The Man Who Dug Fish* is essentially a clever and witty tale squarely in the "puttin' on ole massa" tradition. Three quick changes of scene in this short, impressionistic one-act play present a well-dressed black man with a fake British accent confronting a Fish Store Clerk, a Hardware Clerk, and the Assistant to the Assistant Manager of the Bank—all of them white and played by the same actor. The Man is a kind of confidence man, but instead of perpetrating a swindle for gain he makes a symbolic statement about a hidden black agenda. The title is the key to the joke: the Man buys a fish of the size that will fit into his attache case and then a shovel; at the bank he rents a safety deposit box for ten years, slips in the fish and the shovel when the Assistant is not looking, says in a cheery fashion "See you in ten years," and leaves whistling "Columbia, the Gem of the Ocean."

No matter how absurd the dialogue, each person is playing his role, but only the Man knows it. Since the Man is "impeccably dressed in the clothes of a financier," the whites serving him are properly deferential. Although this modern black man is on the inside of the establishment, the role playing is just like the slave and "ole massa," except that sly deceit has been replaced by bold effrontery. This tradition is best illustrated when the Assistant finds the supposedly empty safety deposit box heavier than he expects. The Man convinces him that it seems difficult to lift because he is sick and needs to go home. In self-pity the Assistant says that he will get attention from his wife "if she's home from the bridge club, or the country club, or the beautician's, or ladies aid society, or women's club"; they will "call the doctor if that's included in the budget this month." The Assistant suggests his illness must be due to his head or liver or kidneys, and the Man responds pointedly: "Or your heart . . . or your soul . . . my good man." That comment, of course, makes no impression on the Assistant.

The bank in this tale represents impregnable institutional America. Everyone should have a safety deposit box, says the Assistant, because they are "moth proof, radar proof,

fireproof, earthquake proof, drop proof, heist proof, dirt proof, atomic-blast and dust proof, water free, airless, and they cannot be touched by another human hand." All this confidence about the contents of the Man's box, a "still wet . . . very dead fish," together with a shovel is ironic. Of course the present functioning of impervious institutional America is the butt of this joke, but so is its future, even in the short term of ten years. "Three cheers for the red, white, and blue" are the familiar words to the melody the Man whistles as he leaves institutional America to its destiny.

The final play in this group, called *The Corner,* presents Cliff Dawson in the early 1950's before the time of the action of *In the Wine Time* but after he has returned from the Navy. The play is in four scenes that show the characteristic lifestyles of the people in the urban ghetto: violent, exploitive, with highly ritualized verbal and physical clashes. The relationships are shifting and superficial, and in the course of the play Cliff makes his decision to leave that life to Bummie, Slick, Blue, and Silly Willy. He also repudiates Stella, his street girl-friend, and leaves her to the others in an ironic legacy: "All of you deserve each other." Stella, who is drunk and whining most of the play, resents Cliff because he refuses to put his regular friend Lou on the street with her, nor will he take Stella to a motel for their sexual encounters instead of the back seat of Silly Willy's junked car or the couch in Slick's front room. Yet Stella insists that Cliff "spends money" on her even as the gang is mocking her viciously with that phrase. Her attitude brings out the worst in Cliff; he treats her with casual brutality and leaves her passed out in Silly Willy's car for the others to have.

The statement repeatedly made by Cliff, "I'm through with you niggers," is the key to the resolution of the play. Bummie thinks that he means that he will be leaving town again, but Cliff says no, that Lou is pregnant and that he intends to be in the community for a long time to come as a family man. He agrees, however, with Bummie's perception that he is changing. Although Cliff later becomes disillusioned and despairing, as made apparent in *In the Wine Time,* the decision in this play is for community and against a street life in which style has completely replaced substance. The slight difference in the retelling of Cliff's life in *The Corner* is significant. The impulse of the alienated protagonist of *In the Wine Time,* which belongs to the earlier group, had been to leave Derby Street in order to grab a piece of "the big rich world out there." Although the despair of a later part of Cliff's life is known, his motivation in *The Corner* is to be a part of a community, and thus it is appropriately one of the plays published in *The Theme Is Blackness.* Unfortunately, Cliff Dawson seems to be one so damaged by life in the ghetto that he achieves when we last see him only a kind of stoical resignation. He had been alienated, a misfit like the playwright describes himself; he had had once at least a glimpse of the possibility of community; but he was not to be a part of Bullins's new world.

Thus the "collective" form of the new drama represented in *The Theme Is Blackness* departs from the received form and theme of earlier works by black artists, including Bullins's own. "Collective" implies a reliance on motifs traditional in Afro-American literature and suggests that there is a black agenda now and into the future, still incompletely articulated and formed but compellingly real. The necessary condition for evolution, furthermore, is a community with its members sharing a common identity, healed of alienation caused by caste, class, or self-interest. In Ed Bullins's own terms, the creation of a nation.

Leslie Sanders (essay date 1986)

SOURCE: "'Dialect Determinism': Ed Bullins' Critique of the Rhetoric of the Black Power Movement," in *Studies in Black American Literature, Volume 2: Belief vs. Theory in Black American Literary Criticism,* edited by Joe Weixlmann and Chester J. Fontenot, Penkevill Publishing Co., 1986, pp. 161-75.

[*Sanders is an American-born Canadian critic. Below, she analyzes the use of rhetoric in several of Bullins's works.*]

It was Black Power rhetoric that signaled the end of the Civil Rights Movement. In the earlier movement, the language of the Black Church predominated, notably the exceptional oratory of the Reverend Martin Luther King, Jr., in which the language of the Church and that of American social ideals were brilliantly combined. In King's rhetoric, the injustice American blacks suffered and the justice they sought were made vivid; made vivid also was the mode through which their fight was conducted: confrontation through non-violence combined with the discipline of Christian charity.

The Black Power Movement explicitly rejected the non-violence of which King spoke, and its rhetoric differed accordingly. Whereas King spoke of the ballot, Malcolm X included bullets as the alternative; whereas King prayed for brotherly love from behind the bars of a Birmingham jail, Malcolm X asked what kind of men stood by while other men murdered their children. Whereas King spoke of Christianity, Malcolm X and others offered the alternative mythology of Islam, particularly its Black Muslim variant; whereas King spoke of the failure of the American Dream, Black Power advocates, influenced by analyses of colonialism, and particularly by the work of the Martinique philosopher/psychiatrist/revolutionary Franz Fanon, spoke of the dialectical relationship of oppressor and oppressed and sought to understand the Afro-American predicament as analogous to that of subject colonial peoples.

Not only the images, logic, and sources of authority of the two rhetorics differed, but also their accents: whereas the rhetoric of the Civil Rights Movement was Southern and familiar to the rural as well as to an urban audience, that of the Black Power Movement was decidedly Northern, strictly urban and often derived its logic and authority from the ethics of the streets where many of its early adherents struggled for survival.

Certainly earlier Afro-American leaders had urged defensive and even offensive violence. Nat Turner explicitly saw himself as an avenging angel; David Walker called for violence in his *Appeal* of 1829; many slaves realized that in identifying themselves with the Chosen People they were also praying for the Divine vengeance of which the Old Testament speaks. During the Red Summer of 1919, Claude McKay wrote:

> If we must die, let it not be like hogs
> Hunted and penned in an inglorious spot,
> While round us bark the mad and hungry dogs,
> Making their mock at our accursed lot.
> If we must die, O let us nobly die,
> So that our precious blood may not be shed
> In vain; then even the monsters we defy
> Shall be constrained to honour us though dead!
> O kinsmen! we must meet the common foe!
> Though far outnumbered let us show us brave.
> And for their thousand blows deal one deathblow!
> What though before us lies the open grave?
> Like men we'll face the murderous, cowardly pack,
> Pressed to the wall, dying, but fighting back!

—a poem whites found so alarming that it was read into the Congressional Record as a sign of imminent black insurrection. More than race loyalty motivated the passion with which black America followed the careers of such boxers as Jack Johnson, Joe Louis, and Muhammad Ali. What was new about the Black Power Movement's explicit advocacy of violence was its public quality. Neither was the language veiled nor were the discussions confined to the black community.

> **Most of Bullins' plays lovingly but unsparingly examine the lives of ordinary ghetto dwellers, their dreams and illusions, and particularly the way they themselves are authors of their own suffering.**
>
> —*Leslie Sanders*

While violence was central to the Movement's rhetoric, violence was far from its entirety. In the main, the Black Power Movement sought to redefine black Americans' perceptions of themselves and their relation to the larger American society. While certain advocates were completely literal about the violence they urged, more often than not, those who engaged in the rhetoric of violence proposed an imaginative testing, indulgence, and validating of fantasies that had long lain buried in the collective imagination of American blacks. As Clay says, in Amiri Baraka's landmark play *Dutchman* (1964), If Bessie Smith had killed some white people she wouldn't have needed that music. She could have talked very straight and plain about the world. No metaphors. . . . Crazy niggers turning their backs on sanity. When all it needs is that simple act. Murder. Just murder! Would make us all sane!"

Although Baraka was among the most disconcertingly literal of the advocates of violence, his work continually explores the relation of word and act, of imagination and reality. He believed then, and does now, but for different reasons, in violent revolution, but the violence he sought to exorcise in much of his poetry, prose, and drama is the internalized violence which deforms and prohibits both self-knowledge and clear judgment of the world.

. . . . .

> I went to see *The Toilet* and *Dutchman,* and when I saw *The Toilet* the whole world opened up to me because I never knew that I was right by writing *Clara's Ole Man.* . . . I didn't really find myself until I saw *Dutchman.* That was the great influence on my life. LeRoi has greatly influenced many young black artists. . . . He essentially created me as a playwright. . . .

By 1969, when Ed Bullins made these remarks to interviewer Marvin X, Bullins was at least as influential as Baraka, at least in the theatre. Playwright-in-residence at the most important black theatre of the period, the New Lafayette Theatre in Harlem, he had also edited the Black Theater issue of *The Drama Review* (Summer, 1968), a volume which immediately became the new Black Theater's manifesto, and in fact the manifesto of the Black Arts Movement. Also in 1968, he won the Vernon Rice Drama Desk Award for an evening of three plays (*Clara's Ole Man, The Electronic Nigger,* and *A Son, Come Home*) produced and directed by Robert Macbeth of the New Lafayette (but staged downtown at the American Place Theater because the New Lafayette had just burned down). In 1969 he edited for Bantam the similarly influential anthology *New Plays from the Black Theater.* More awards and grants followed, including three Obies for Distinguished Playwrighting—in 1971 for *In New England Winter* and *The Fabulous Miss Marie* and in 1975 for *The Taking of Miss Janie.* By 1972 there had been at least fifteen productions of Bullins' plays at an impressive array of New York theatres, and he is now the author of over fifty plays, at least twenty of which have been produced and over forty published.

Bullins' major work of the period in question, however, was written and developed at the New Lafayette Theatre, and almost all of his work has its Harlem audience in mind. Most of Bullins' plays lovingly but unsparingly examine the lives of ordinary ghetto dwellers, their dreams and illusions, and particularly the way they themselves are authors of their own suffering. These plays of the black experience (the term is Bullins') embody the intent of the Black Theater of the period, but they are not typical of it, except in their choice of the ghetto as setting and subject. The plays normally identified as "black theater" were what Bullins called "black revolutionary theater": plays directly about conflict, either with whites or with internalized white culture and its deforming effects on black society.

Bullins wrote in both modes, but his plays differed markedly from those of most of his contemporaries in their attitude toward the rhetoric and mythology of the Black Arts/Black Power Movement of which they were a part. In various ways, and even while using it, Bullins suggested that *rhetoric* was a substitute for action rather than a prelude to it and that it constituted an evasion rather than a revelation of the transformations upon which a healthier society could be predicated. Most of Bullins' "black revolutionary plays" depict the revolutionary scenario in order to test it. He challenges his audience to engage in the fantasies proposed, but then disturbs their fantasies by a voice within the play which comments on the vision in which the play engages.

For example, his early play *Dialect Determinism (or The Rally)* depicts a rally/church service through the eyes of a visitor who, the play suggests, remains unengaged only because it is his "first time." During the rally, Boss Brother harangues his increasingly excited audience with militant but illogical propositions ranging from "I call you Brothers for we have a common experience . . ." to "In brotherhood there is power, and all we want is power . . ." to "So as de most honest people on de face of the earth, we don't have to fool ourselves by sayin' it's some kind of holy crusade . . . if we get our chance finally to kick the hell out of somebody else for a change. . . ." He claims to be a series of messiahs ranging from Hitler to Marx to Martin Luther King, Jr., Lumumba, Castro, and even L. B. J.; he has the ghost of Malcolm X evicted when it appears to challenge him; and he finally urges the crowd to produce a martyr. Not the fools they seem, the members of the crowd turn on him in a frenzy while the visitor and a girl he picks up slip away. "Never seen my people in such high spirits. Well, good night, brother. Good night, sister. Peace be with you," says the doorman as they leave.

Dialect Determinism is characteristic Bullins: he wrote it in 1965 while at the same time closely involved with the formation of the Black Panther Party in San Francisco and in the developing of Black House, a cultural center which the Panthers used as a base. While it may be read as an attack on the Panthers (Black House dissolved in 1967 over a quarrel between the political activists and the artists who espoused cultural nationalism), there is no trace of the play's being seen as political treachery, then or later. *Dialect Determinism* is a satire about rhetoric without substance, about the dangers of a mob, about politics as emotional catharsis rather than as a reasoned guide for action. It foreshadows what Bullins was to do even more dramatically in later plays which ask the questions no one else within the Movement was asking, at least in a public forum. And he usually got away with it.

It Bees Dat Way (1970) admits a mixed audience (no more than twenty-five people and most must be white) to a room which is set as a Harlem street corner. The play consists of their being molested by pimps, prostitutes, and pickpockets. Tension erupts among the black characters, and one of them, Corny, advises the whites to leave the room before there is real danger, saying to the others,

"Dese here people ain't the ones to get . . . they ain't got nothin' . . . just like you and me . . . they just work for them that made dis mess. . . . The ones to shoot is who what made this mess." As the whites leave the room in twos and threes, Corny preaches to them: "SHOOT THE PRESIDENT . . . HE'S CUTTIN' OFF WELFARE . . . AND SENDIN' YOUR BOY TO VIETNAM . . . SHOOT YOUR GOVERNMENT . . . THEY'S THE ONES MAKIN' WAR ON YOU! . . .". As the last of the whites leave, sounds of sirens, crowds, gunfire, and riot erupt.

The impact of the play for a white audience is primarily discomforting. As the black actors are extremely aggressive, it is not likely that the average white audience member would readily make the connection between the revolution he is urged to join and the unsavory behavior of the characters he has just encountered. For black members of the audience, however, the experience the play provides is more complex. If they enjoy the discomfort of the whites in the audience, the violence that builds quickly in the confined space, they are then robbed of completing their fantasies and reminded that what they have just enjoyed is too easy: such victims have little to do with what real revolution is about.

In *Death List* (also 1970), Bullins proposed an image even more terrifying: the play consists simply of a black man cleaning and loading a rifle while calmly reading a list of sixty-eight names of black American leaders who signed an advertisement in The *New York Times* in support of the State of Israel. He punctuates his reading with comments and the refrain: "Enemy of Black People." A black woman joins him, entreating him not to fulfill the mission given him by the "Central Revolutionary Committee." Her arguments are various, but essentially she asks whether the black world of the future for which the revolution is being fought can be predicated on the ruthless violence for which the man is preparing himself. Her final accusation is that he has become the "white-created demon" of which they were warned. Her appeals are to no avail.

Notably, white reviews of the play attended only to its vicious attack on black leaders; little regard was taken of the woman's voice. Certainly the play is brutal: almost anyone, black or white, no matter how militant, would resist the inclusion of at least some of the names on the list. The play in its entirety, however, is far more than a political statement about the racial implications of U. S. support of Israel against the Palestinians.

Projected into a not-distant future in which a well-organized black revolutionary guerrilla army is conducting a consistent and presumably effective war against the United States, the play tests the revolutionary scenario at its most explicit and criticizes it in two ways. The first is a continual concern of Bullins: the fact that so much of Black Power politics was internecine rather than clearly directed at the roots of oppression. The second involves a variant of the question posed by the doctrine of non-violence, the question of whether, even when one acknowledges the necessity of violence in the name of change, violence does not simply beget itself. Bullins' abiding

question, then, is whether and in what ways the rhetoric of Black Power is an advance over the ethics of the street, where people turn against each other and where violence is the tenor of human relations.

Bullins had proposed these questions in a more extended fashion in 1969 when, under the pseudonym Kingsley B. Bass, Jr., "a twenty-four-year-old Blackman killed by Detroit police during the uprising of 1967," he wrote *We Righteous Bombers,* a reworking of *Les Justes,* Camus' meditation on terrorism and the terrorist. To Camus' plot and dialogue Bullins adds a further twist. His terrorists do not know—although in prison Jackson, the man who threw the bomb, discovers—that the Chief of Police is the Grand Duke and the man he has killed was an actor. Moreover, at the end it is suggested that while in prison Jackson chose to take the place of the prisoner who had bargained years off his sentence by becoming the executioner. Not only have the terrorists accomplished nothing, they do not even know if Jackson has remained true to them. In Bullins' play there is a question prior to the philosophical issue raised in *Les Justes* about whether violence can advance the cause of goodness and whether a man can murder with integrity. That prior question is posed as a problem of illusion: Bullins' terrorists do not even know if their target is real. *We Righteous Bombers* did not go unremarked: it was the subject of a heated symposium at the New Lafayette Theatre in which, unexpectedly, Baraka was one of Bullins' strongest defenders. Characteristically, Bullins did not attend and, at least publicly, to this day denies that he wrote the play.

The philosophical issues raised in *Bombers* are not, however, Bullins' main concern. Other issues, apparently of less significance, are actually prior, in Bullins' eyes, to the moral issue of whether a new society can be born of violence. These issues may be characterized by the question: what exactly is the reality that needs be transformed? *Street Sounds: Dialogues with Black Existence* (also 1970) exemplifies his method of inquiry. This play is a series of forty monologues by such characters as "Harlem politician," "lover man," "seduced and abandoned," "black revolutionary artist," "non-ideological nigger," "black student," "wild child," and "Harlem mother." The delineations are brief, witty, and often moving; each exposes in the character not only what he or she thinks, but what he or she conceals from him/herself. The only unremitting portrait is a self-indulgence: the black critic attacks the kinds of plays Bullins writes, accusing him of creating a negative image of the race and of bad art.

In *Street Sounds,* the voices of Black Power, whether concerned with art or with politics, are only several among a multitude, and what emerges from the play is the sense that they describe the black experience no more or less accurately than any of the others. In fact, if anything they evade what must, for Bullins, be confronted first: the tangible, day-to-day experience of pain, failure, aimlessness, being trapped. For example, the "workin' man" says:

> Yeah . . . I've been workin' on this job for years. My
> whole family does, almost, at least my mother and

sisters with me. I'm a foreman now. Make pretty good bread . . . Since we got a union now . . . tryin' to buy me a house . . . if my F.H.A. loan ever comes through. If you had'a seen me fifteen years ago . . . I was a bad nigger . . . I was out of work, bummin' around, no prospects . . . My crime partner, Tootsie, and me were trapped . . . trapped inside of ourselves, inside our surroundings, inside our experience. Yeah, those sound like some good words, you understand? I can rap them some . . . although I can't write them so good . . . Mom got me a job where she worked. And that's where I've been since. Didn't know I could or would work that hard and steady. I still drank and ran around and did other things but I worked. Tootsie didn't work steady but we still ran together. Even pulled an occasional job . . . And I grew fat. Tootsie got hisself killed last year by some broad's husband . . . and now I'm scared to death to stay out late at night because my old lady's threatened to lock me out and not let me in . . . Damn . . . I wonder what the next twenty years is going to be like.

His speech is infinitely more eloquent than that of "the rapper," who intones:

Brothers, we are slaves. Slaves in this moment of history. Nothing short of that, however we wish to disguise this fact . . . And what I am calling for is a slave revolt . . . An honest-to-god revolution. The time has come for us to throw off the shackles of the slave-masters. The time has come for us to rise up as men and rulers of our own destiny. The time has come for us to assume our roles on the world stage of revolution. . . .

The "workin' man's" eloquence, like that of many of the other characters, lies in its simplicity and concreteness: the facts of the character's daily life make his simple generalizations almost superfluous. The "rapper's" rhetoric concerns ideas so remote from the details of existence that they obfuscate the realities that must be confronted and transformed if any revolution is to succeed. Bullins insists in almost all his work that what is can only be changed by being confronted. The "rapper's" rhetoric obscures this necessity because it invites its audience to evade rather than to transcend those realities.

In several full-length plays, all of which deal with race relations, at least in part, Bullins introduces a black nationalist figure and through these figures continues his critique of the Black Power Movement's rhetoric. The three principal figures are Ernie in *The Pig Pen* (1970), Gafney in *The Fabulous Miss Marie* (1970), and Rick in *The Taking of Miss Janie* (1974). These three characters have in common their rhetoric (their insistence on defining absolutely everything in terms of the black man's struggle for liberation). They all also display arrogance and superiority towards anyone who fails to define the world as they do, and displeasure (in Gafney, amounting to prudishness) over other characters' carryings on. Ernie judges Len for his white wife while lusting after her; Gafney is disgusted by everything that occurs at Marie Horton's Christmas party; Rick attacks Peggy for being a lesbian. Yet, Bullins insists in *The Fabulous Miss Marie,* unless the militant can ally himself with the street nigger, specifically, and more generally can come to a compassionate

understanding of all aspects of the black community, his rhetoric will amount to nothing.

In *The Fabulous Miss Marie,* Gafney encounters Art, a character from another Bullins play, *Goin' a Buffalo*. Art is a ruthless con-artist and Gafney is horrified by him. At the end of the play, Art has overstepped his boundaries with Marie, who was using him as shamelessly as he was her, and she throws him out. The following interchange completes Art's dialogue with Gafney:

Gafney: Art, there you are. . . . I see you're still standing around. What are you going to be doing when the revolution comes?

Art: (*Softly*) Gafney . . . without me you won't have a revolution.

Gafney: Oh, man . . . (Gafney looks at Art, Art feints, then jabs him sharply in the nose).

Bill [the host]: Art . . . damn . . . what's going on here?

Gafney: Oww . . . you shouldn't have done that . . . Don't you know I'm non-violent . . . you stupid, ignorant nigger!

Periodically throughout the play, which takes place at Bill and Marie Horton's Christmas party, the tv shows scenes of Civil Rights marchers being beaten on the streets of some Southern town. Wanda, Marie's niece, is their only defender. The older characters, all middle-class, either fear or feign ignorance of or reject what the young people are doing, principally because they see it as threatening the world they have struggled to create for themselves. Art, of course, rejects both the non-violence and the altruism in their behavior. At first Gafney backs Wanda: "Teach sister! . . . Tell 'em where it's at!" As the play progresses, however, Gafney becomes a less and less sympathetic figure as we see that he is critical not only of Art but also of Wanda, whose life is painful and complicated, or Marie and her friends, whose illusions he does not understand. As complex as her struggles have been, Marie Horton is admirable, as tough as Art, as loving as she can be given the sorrows in her life. Wanda's plight is the most desperate, but Gafney does not take her up on her offer of herself, so concerned is he with winning his argument with Art. Thus he leaves Wanda to be exploited by both Bill and her boyfriend Marco. Love between men and women is the principal barometer of social health in Bullins' plays, and in none of them does the cultural nationalist measure well.

The Taking of Miss Janie is Bullins' retrospective on the period of the Black Power Movement and its counterpart in white society. Peggy sums up his analysis succinctly:

Peggy: We all failed. Failed ourselves in that serious time known as the sixties. And by failing ourselves we failed in the test of the times. We had so much going for us . . . so much potential . . . Do you realize it, man? We were the youth of our times . . . And we blew it. Blew it completely. Look where it all ended. Look what happened?

(They all look out at the audience)

We just turned out lookin' like a bunch of punks and freaks and fuck-offs.

Rick: It has been said: "That if one doesn't deal with reality, then reality will certainly deal with them."

Peggy: Amen.

Rick: But I am not allowing myself to be held to blame. I am not allowing myself to be other than glorious. History will vindicate me.

Peggy: Hey, man . . . you know, you never left yesterday. You're confused like all of us.

The structure of *The Taking of Miss Janie* is the story of Monty's rape of Miss Janie; the play opens just after the rape and closes with its prelude. In the interim is the story of the Sixties told episodically with breaks for monologues from each of the significant characters, some of whom appear in Bullins' earlier works. Monty, the black poet, meets white Janie in his creative-writing class and means to have her. She insists the relationship remain platonic, and for thirteen years he complies: they are close, helpful to each other, even real friends. In the meantime, Monty marries and leaves Peggy, who later marries a white man, leaves him, and becomes a lesbian. Monty also has an ongoing affair with Peggy's best friend Flossie, a good-time woman with little morality but a great deal of honesty. He drifts aimlessly, in and our of school, in and out of writing, but constant in his life is Janie. Janie, meanwhile, sleeps with many men, both black and white, has an abortion with Monty's assistance, and breaks with Lonnie, her long-time white boyfriend, a third-rate jazz player.

The one marriage that endures the Sixties is that of Len and Sharon, characters who first appear in *The Pig Pen,* Black Len is a student of black culture and history and the man responsible for the awakening of many others. Sharon is Jewish, as a young woman had been very spoiled and naive, but, as she appears in *Miss Janie,* is mature, realistic, and tolerant. Len has turned capitalist, still sees himself as the great teacher, and justifies all he does by saying he is an intellectual. Their relationship, though far from shallow, is full of compromise, which Sharon confronts more readily than does Len.

Janie, the symbol and object of Monty's obsessions, is a complex mixture of the calculated and the naive: "I'll be true to Monty. To keep our friendship alive. And perhaps our relationship will mature into the purest of loves one day. An ideal black/white love. Like sweet grapes change with age and care into a distinctive bouquet upon choice, rare wines." But she also admits to Flossie that she knows Monty's abiding interest in her is because "he's got what he wants from you . . . and he wants what he thinks he can get from me." According to Peggy, Monty is selfish and cruel. Certainly his relationship with Janie, although not without feeling, has little to do with love. Finally, Bullins concludes, behind all the talk, the romance with Mao,

Fanon, and Voodoo (as Monty hurls at Mort Silberstein in their epic battle at the end of the play), are fantasies of domination. When all was said and done, what Monty really wanted was Miss Janie—and he got her, at a high price to both of them. Self-gratification triumphed over the creativity with which the decade began. Bullins' analysis of the failure of the Sixties summarizes his attitude toward Black Power rhetoric as well.

. . . . .

Bullins does not mean to say, in all this, that what was said was of no value. In the real sense he was then and remains now a black cultural nationalist. Yet he shuns public engagement in politics and, considering his centrality to the Black Arts/Black Power Movement, made remarkably few statements which relied on the Movement's rhetoric. He sees his task as an artist as, simply, to extend people's vision of what is. Rick's cliché about reality dealing with those who fail to deal with it is also Bullins speaking. He believes people must confront first the realms in which they are the authors of their own unfreedom: their difficulty with love, with manhood, with the panaceas of drugs, crime, sex and violence, and romantic notions of machismo. Unless and until these abiding problems are confronted, political rhetoric, for Bullins, is meaningless, the violence Black Power proposed no more than the violence on any street corner in Harlem—and equally misdirected.

> **Like Malcolm X, Bullins' vision is urban, secular, and of the streets. It is there he finds home truths, and these are the abiding ones. Anything that deflects from dealing with them must be examined with care.**
>
> **—*Leslie Sanders***

His work implies not only a comment on the rhetoric of Black Power but also on the rhetoric of the Civil Rights Movement. The non-violence King proposed is equally distant from the basic experiences of the people of whom Bullins speaks. Getting beaten up makes as little sense to him as does self-indulgent aggression. He understands fully the complexity of racial oppression, and in other plays deals with it acutely. However, that oppression is only a given in the lives of his characters, never a focus. In his major work, his eye never swerves from the self, from the black community as he sees its actual existence. The black political leader who is emblem of his beliefs is Malcolm X, but in *The Pig Pen,* in which the death of Malcolm figures, only the poet Ray and a white man, Mackman, truly mourn his passing.

Like Malcolm, Bullins' vision is urban, secular, and of the streets. It is there he finds home truths, and these are the abiding ones. Anything that deflects from dealing with

Dust jacket for the Bullins plays produced in New York by the New Lafayette Theater Company in 1968.

them must be examined with care. Finally, Bullins queries the connection between the generalized analysis Black Power rhetoric proposed and the daily personal pain and complexity of individual existence. In suggesting that the former provided an evasion rather than a helpful understanding of the latter, he does not mean to negate the former's validity, only to test it and show where it is wanting. Bullins' mode of establishing the vision Black Power rhetoric proposed is contained rather in the phrase with which he prefaces most of his lists of characters: "The characters in this play are Black." He then proceeds to explore their world.

Arlene A. Elder (essay date 1988)

SOURCE: "Ed Bullins: Black Theatre as Ritual," in *Connections: Essays on Black Literatures,* Aboriginal Studies Press, 1988, pp. 101-09.

[*In the following essay, Elder explores the ritualistic elements in three of Bullins's works:* The Corner, In the Wine Time, *and* In New England Winter.]

In 1971, the African-American playwright, Ed Bullins said of himself, 'To make an open secret more public: in the area of playwrighting, Ed Bullins, at this moment in time, is almost without peer in America—black, white, or imported'. Fortunately, time has supported this boast. In a recent assessment, critic Genevieve Fabre concludes, 'Next to LeRoi Jones, Ed Bullins is probably the most important black dramatist of the last twenty years' [*Drumbeats, Masks, and Metaphor,* 1983].

Bullins's continuing success rests for some in his political stance, expressive, largely but not entirely, of the Black Power interpretation of a racist American society. For many others, it rests with his sensitivity to the artistic imperatives of Black Aesthetic theory, that is, to the return to traditional, African oral performance and African-American folk roots. These two impulses are not, of course, mutually exclusive; they are, however, difficult to reconcile successfully in a single artistic work. Such reconciliation requires not only talent but, also, a clear understanding of the purposes of one's art and of the playwright's role *vis a vis* his audience.

This dilemma of the contemporary black artist is one not lost on literary critics. Peter Bruck, for example, in an article entitled, 'Ed Bullins: The Quest and Failure of an Ethnic Community Theatre' [in *Black American Literature Forum,* 1979], quotes the following paradoxical statements by Bullins:

> I hope that all of us will . . . produce create, that is, for we are creators, revolution. And that, I think, is the true role of the revolutionary artist. Black Art is to express what is best in us and for us Black People. Black Theater is . . . a people's theater, dedicated to the continuing survival of Black people.

'How does one', Bruck asks, 'aesthetically speaking, reconcile the hope for revolution with the wish for survival? In other words, how are the two aspirations to be combined in theater politics?'

Bruck resolves the paradox satisfactorily for himself by placing Bullins's work within the historical context of Alain Locke's distinction during the 1920s between 'the drama of discussion and social analysis and the drama of expression of folk life' and seeing Bullins combining these two dichotomies. Expressing both a Marxist and a Black Aesthetic perspective, Bruck says Bullins represents:

> a new stage in the evolution of black drama. As his plays are beset with urban *lumpen* blacks and their sub-cultural lifestyle of hustling, he transcends both the realm of mere social analysis and of a mere portrayal of folk life by seeking to fuse these realms in the minute depiction of various facets of black existence.

Although the Marxist analysis is obviously useful (and, indeed a feminist perspective is called for as well), this fusion in Bullins's plays can best be understood, by examining the work through the Black Aesthetic as examples of contemporary rituals and by recognising the playwright's conscious desire to reawaken the power of this ancient form in his audience. Bullins, himself, has suggested this approach to his work. 'Perhaps', he says, 'the black artist should think in the ancient tribal patterns, in the terms of his people as tribal units, and he being the shaman, sorcerer, medicine man or witch doctor.' Acutely aware of the possible polarities of contemporary black theatre, Bullins explains, 'I was a conscious artist before I was a conscious artist revolutionary, which has been my salvation and disguise'.

Plays such as *The Corner, In the Wine Time,* and *In New England Winter,* are three works intended as part of his ongoing Twentieth Century Cycle and concern the fortunes and relationships of Cliff Dawson and his half-brother, Steve Benson. In these plays, Bullins clearly demonstrates this conscious return to the elements of traditional African oral performance and African-American folk roots. These plays, among others, reveal his ability to couch revolutionary interpretations of the black American experience in ritual form, drawing on the traditions of black oratory, narrative, street talk, mythology, and, especially, music.

. . . . .

When one reads Black Aesthetic theory, it soon becomes clear that there is no consensus of opinion as to what contemporary black rituals are, precisely, and how the literate playwright should utilise this oral and aural form. The loosest definition is that of critic Shelby Steele who views 'the ritualistic aspect' of the New Black Theatre as one of its 'most salient characteristics' separating it 'from mainstream American drama' [in *The Theater of Black Americans,* 1980]. By 'ritualistic', Steele means:

> the strong presence of *symbols, characterizations, themes* and *language styles* which are frequently repeated from play to play and over a period of time with the result that easily recognized patterns are established which have the function of reaffirming the values and particular commitment of the audience for whom the plays are written. The term *ritual* is used here in the modern sense which is looser than the traditional religious view of ritual as a rigidly prescribed unvarying pattern of spiritual observance.

It is, however, toward 'spiritual observance' that the director, Robert Macbeth, with whom Bullins had a very close association during their years together at The New Lafayette Theatre, wishes to move. Macbeth, whom Bullins credits along with Imamu Baraka as having had a profound influence upon him, has spoken very persuasively about the function of ritual in contemporary black theatre. His goal for performances at The New Lafayette suggests drama that is much more religiously oriented than what Steele has in mind. He explains:

> we would like to return to . . . those rituals that our people did in ancient times, rituals that taught the young men the essence of courage and manhood. Rituals that showed the young women their place in the history of

their people. These are plain, old, ordinary, educational ones. Then there are the more mystic ones, the more spiritual ones, and those are the ones that call upon the ancient Black gods, and call upon the spirits of the fathers, and the spirit of the ancestors to be of importance in the present as we continue. . . . I think we're preparing our people, The New Lafayette audience, for that time into parti-cipating in a ritual in which the spells are cast, in which new vibrations are created that never existed before.

The traditional African concept of art's functional significance is also important to Macbeth:

> Our people's rituals are never just for show, they're always for purpose, they're always for something . . . something for the purpose of entertainment is not part of our people's reality in that sense. When they get together, it's not for entertainment, it's for unity, for being together, for having a time together [*Black Theatre,* 1972].

Unlike Steele, Macbeth is clearly not using the term, 'ritual', in a modern sense, but in ancient terms that he is confident will have spiritual and, consequently, political consequences for the future. Macbeth's 1968 *A Black Ritual* is the type of performance he hoped would soon characterise much of black theatre. Clearly, a conventional playwright would have to revolutionise his artistic choices, even his understanding of himself as an artist and transform even the performance oriented techniques of conventional black drama to create such a theatrical experience as Macbeth's *A Black Ritual.*

Ed Bullins's plays reveal a movement toward such development, and statements by him and Macbeth place his understanding of ritual somewhere between the previous loose version by Steele and the more rigorous one of Macbeth.

Bullins's list of the 'obvious elements' that should constitute black plays shows his appreciation of the spiritual or mystical dimension of traditional performance. He calls for:

> dance, as in Black life style and patterns; Black religion in its numerous forms . . . gospel, negro spiritualism to African spirit, sun, moon, stars and ancestor worship; Black astrology, numerology and symbolism; Black mysticism, magic and mythscience; also history, fable and legend, vodun ritual ceremony, Afro-American nigger street styles, and, of course, Black music.

However, Bullins still writes plays, recognisable as such by audiences formally trained in Aristotelian dramatic principles as well as those schooled in African orature and black street styles of performance. His works, then, provide the largest number of examples of that middle ground in black drama that Robert Macbeth designates 'play form rituals' [*Black Theatre,* 1970]. The spiritual effect of these plays depends as much upon the way they are staged as upon the texts, hence upon the director almost as much as the playwright. Director Macbeth judges his production of *In the Wine Time* and other plays at The New Lafayette Theatre as revealing the company's 'ritual point of view':

> We always try to approach (the play) from the point of view of a service, a ritual of some kind, and for that reason, because we approach them that way, our plays are a little bit different in a lot of things, the timing, the way the thing gets done, the way it's staged, how it's staged, why it's staged that way.

Speaking specifically of *In the Wine Time,* he is pleased with his staging, because it:

> includes the people in there so they understand this thing is between us, among us all. . . . the thing that we begin to do immediately includes all the people who come. So all of these things are orientated around, 'Welcome, sit down, Brother, we're gonna hold hands and sing. . . .'

This statement was made in 1970. A year later, however, Macbeth [in *Black Theatre,* 1971] admits to the possibly insurmountable difficulties in the Western dramatic form, which he calls, 'really ragged' and 'very hard'; 'it doesn't serve our purposes', he realises. Of special concern is the audience's separation from the action, not just physically but, also in terms of roles and responsibilities, hence, spiritual fulfilment. 'I did want you to talk back during the play', he explains to an audience member of *In the Wine Time*. 'You were supposed to get into it. But the form is limited. It doesn't really work. The Western white form is a drawing room form. They sit around and they jive. They sit there and talk to each other. Nothing really happens.' Therefore, he desires the movement to a more traditional ritual form mentioned earlier, where audience members can participate, in playwright and theorist, Paul Carter Harrison's term, as 'spectator performers'.

. . . . .

Whatever the limitations of the 'play form ritual', Ed Bullins views theatre in the black community as 'a sanctuary for recreation of the Black spirit and African identity'. Bullins has been at work for some time on a series of twenty plays he envisions as the Twentieth Century Cycle, focusing primarily on the lives of one family and different acquaintances. The following is a commentary on three of these plays, *The Corner, In the Wine Time,* and *In New England Winter,* all of which present stages in the life of Cliff Dawson and his half-brother, Steve, and, specifically, examines them as 'play-form rituals'.

Briefly, the narrative of the three interlocking plays is as follows: *The Corner,* the shortest of the three, presents the conflicts over wine, women, and self-image of four, young, urban blacks, one of whom is Cliff Dawson, who by the end of the play has stunned his friends by deciding to quit wasting his money, his time, and life, drinking every night under the street lamp on the corner or on the back seat of a broken-down car with Stella. The reason

for this change is, most immediately, his acceptance of responsibility as the father of his other girlfriend Lou's unborn child and, of more long-range significance, his desire for a more meaningful future than that promised by hanging out on the corner.

In the Wine Time, picks up a little later in Cliff's life with Lou, when she is about three months pregnant. We learn that Cliff had, at one time, been in the Navy and is now going to night school. Bullins is still interested in evoking the atmosphere of his characters' poor, urban neighbourhood, but the most important action in the play consists of conflicts between Lou and Cliff about how to raise her nephew, Ray. The climax occurs when Ray stabs another youth, and to save him, Cliff takes the blame.

In New England Winter is set several years later, after Cliff has gotten out of prison and has lost Lou, and centres on Cliff's half-brother, Steve, mentioned in *The Corner* as having an unspecified disagreement with one of the other wine drinkers, Bummie. Here, the conflict takes the form not only of sibling rivalry between Cliff and Steve, but of two opposed lifestyles, that can be characterised simply as Western and non-Western. In the course of the play, it is revealed that Cliff has known for a long time that Lou's second child was by Steve. Nevertheless, when Steve kills Bummie, a cohort now in a robbery they have planned, Cliff once again devises a scheme to help save the younger brother.

As this synopsis indicates, these plays follow the traditional Western form of presenting a developing story. Moreover, they create individual characters who speak and interact in theatrically expected ways, and they are played out in a recognisable historical setting and time period—the late 1950s. When we analyse them as orature, however, not as literature, that is, when we examine their performance features, not just their lines of dialogue on a printed page, Bullins's ritualistic intent becomes clear.

First, despite my chronological presentation of their action, neither the plot of *In the Wine Time* nor of *In New England Winter* is actually linear. The first play opens with a dream-like reverie of Ray's about a Girl symbolic of all youth, innocence, and promise of love that cannot exist in his depressing, limiting street environment. She is the mother/lover who calls him her 'little boy' and invites him 'out in the world'. Her departure from the neighbourhood signals the end of his youth. In Act Two, the Girl, who is the romantic opposite of all the real girls he knows, reappears in a tableau as Ray talks to Cliff about her. Her reappearance signals a symbolic dance by the other characters, interrupting the realistic, chronological sequence of action and suggesting that symbolic action, psychological movement, is of the greatest importance in what, at first, appears to be a naturalistic play. 'I do not write realistic plays, no matter the style I choose' Bullins, has said [in *Black American Literature Forum,* 1979].

In New England Winter bears him out. This 'play-form ritual' consists of seven titled sequences that are not at all sequential. Like *In the Wine Time,* it, too, opens with a reverie, both of which have been published separately as pieces of fiction. Again, as in the other play, the content of this prologue is a love relationship, this time the aborted relationship between Steve and the mad Liz, during a winter in New England. It also presents, however, the carrying out of the robbery that is still being rehearsed and prepared for in the subsequent scenes of the play.

Section One pulls us into the present to the rehearsing of the robbery and to hear about what happened between Cliff and Lou while he was in prison. Sections Two and Three return us to Steve in New England with Liz. Section Four jumps to the present to further develop the conflict between the two brothers. Sections Five and Six detail Steve's break up with Liz in the past, and Section Seven gives us Steve's murder of Bummie in the present. Bullins's juxtaposition of non-sequential time periods, then, definitely distinguishes his works from those of the traditional Western 'well-made play' with its linear time requirements and demonstrates his allegiance to a symbolic, mythic, or psychological reality rather than to social realism or naturalism.

It is Bullins's allegiance to the African concept of the unity of the arts, however, and his development of representative black characters that convincingly demonstrates his commitment to revolutionary drama based on ancient forms. 'I believe my characters sometimes have multiple identities, as parts of a whole, as ever-changing, interchangeable universe (sic), as the points in a vision which expands—dreamlike', he says [in *Black American Literature Forum*, 1979].

There is a dream-like quality to the three plays under discussion, much of it contributed to, of course, by the non-linear narrative technique, but also by the reappearance, as if recalled from some dream or previous life, of characters repeated from play to play. Cliff Dawson, for example, develops from the dissatisfied, aimless street kid of *The Corner* to a father-figure for Ray in *In the Wine Time*, to one, in Bullins's terms, 'more resigned to the reality of his identity' in *In New England Winter*. Cliff's metamorphosis as an individual is hopeful, because Bullins characterises it as a rejection of the dehumanising Western values still espoused by his younger brother, Steve.

Steve, whose relationship with Cliff's wife, Lou, has been forgiven, is the plotter of the robbery being planned in the play. He is associated throughout the work with cold, snow, winter, even winter's 'Silen(ce) like death must be.' As Cliff realises, Steve resents him for being the elder and believes he had a closer relationship with their mother than he had. Steve continually compares himself favourably with Cliff, criticising his treatment of Lou and of women in general and, especially, what he perceives as his lack of seriousness.

While the spectator would expect the brothers to clash over Lou, then, their actual conflict is about their mother, a jealousy that remains unresolved, and, even more significantly, about lifestyles. Steve is anxious, methodical, future oriented; Cliff lives for the day, if not the moment,

and expresses his feelings, his love for Steve, for instance, without fear. Steve seems machine-like to Cliff:

> I'm not just talkin' about how you plan jobs, Steve. It's how you live . . . that's the part you can keep. Your bein' on time or you'll have a heart attack. Your keepin' to the schedules you make . . . whether it's takin' some bull-shit night course, gettin' your hair cut a certain time ah month . . . or waitin' for years to go see the woman you love.

When he rejects Cliff's expression of love for him, Steve explains:

> No, I can't feel . . . don't want to if I could. That's for you, big boss. Me . . . I don't have feelings, emotions, sympathy, tenderness, compassion . . . none of it . . . I don't need it . . . it slows you up. I wouldn't have any of that sickness in me if I didn't have to deal with people like you.

Yet if Steve cannot act out of love, he can out of hate. He kills Bummie in a fit of passion, and it is Cliff, ironically, who must assume leadership and plan how to save him.

Bullins's characterisation seems intended to offer his audience two opposing lifestyles and to show his preference for love and involvement in life over detached self-interest. Criticised frequently for the depressing, criminal lifestyles of his characters, their 'offensive' language, and the violence in his plays, Bullins's first reply is one establishing the authenticity of his portrayal: 'I learned how to survive. I'm a street nigger.' A later response [in *Black World*, 1974], however, indicates the cathartic, spiritual intent of his work. He explains that he wishes to make 'the members of (the) community see themselves in all their terrible ugliness in hope that from this profound glimpse they will be cleansed.'

As Paul Carter Harrison has pointed out [in *The Drama of Nommo*, 1972], this catharsis requires the natural, active involvement of the audience, a dynamic best achieved through the arts of music and dance. 'Music is one of the most effective modes of unifying the black community', Harrison observes, 'it unveils an emotional potency and spiritual force that is collectively shared. Black music articulates the cross-fertilization of African sensibility and the American experience. . . .' Critics have noted not only the actual presence of music in most of Bullins's plays but, also, the essentially musical quality of their structure. Speaking of the 1968 *Goin' a Buffalo*, Fabre [in *Drumbeats, Masks, and Metaphor*, 1973] cautions, for instance:

> One must listen to Bullins' plays as one listens to music and be drawn into the movement of broken rhythms, dramatic breaks, repeats, and lyrical crescendos. The play unfolds like a musical score; each sequence has its own key and modality, each character a voice and register.

From within Cliff and Lou's house in *In the Wine Time*, black music of the period—called rhythm 'n blues by disc jockeys at that time—is heard not too loudly, and continues throughout the play, interrupted only seldom by amusing, jive-talking commercials. Some of the recording stars of this season are King Pleasure Johnnie Otis, Fats Domino, Little Esther, Ray Charles and 'the Queen' Miss Dinah Washington. 'When MISS MINNY GARRISON raises her window, gospel music can be heard.' The mood of the later play, *In New England Winter,* is maintained by 'Modern jazz of the late fifties and early sixties, maybe Miles Davis or Cannonball or Nate Adderly.' At Liz's place, 'Joe Williams sings "Goin to Chicago" over the drug store radio and Count Basie plays throughout the remainder of the scene.' This music is not incidental but both reflective of the concerns and feelings of the characters and strategic in drawing the audience into the action, hence, in fulfilling the ritualistic intent of the plays.

As Askia Muhammed Toure comments in *Black Theatre,* 'the Black musician became and remains the major philosopher, priest, mythmaker and cultural hero of the Black nation. . . . Black music is the core of our National Culture.' Bullins's reliance upon this mode clearly indicates his understanding of the dramatic, political, and spiritual function of African orature. While LeRoi Jones's *Slave Ship* is often pointed to as the best example of black ritual drama, Ed Bullins's 'play-form rituals' constitute the largest body of works combining aspects of the Western tradition with the revitalising features of the Black Aesthetic.

THE TAKING OF MISS JANIE

PRODUCTION REVIEWS

Edith Oliver (review date 24 March 1975)

SOURCE: "Fugue for Three Roommates," in *The New Yorker,* Vol. LI, No. 5, March 24, 1975, pp. 61-3.

[*Below, Oliver offers a positive assessment of* The Taking of Miss Janie, *maintaining that "Mr. Bullins has rarely been wittier or, for that matter, more understanding and vigorous."*]

The Taking of Miss Janie, a good new play by Ed Bullins, at the Henry Street Settlement's New Federal Theatre (on Grand Street), can be most briefly described as a fugue, whose themes are the feelings and experiences of a number of young people during the nineteen-sixties. The action, which takes place in California, starts out at, and keeps returning to, a party that three black roommates, all of them college students, give for a number of their white and black friends. The principal story concerns black Monty, one of the roommates, who has met white Janie in a "creative-writing class" and invites her to the party, thereby beginning a sexless friendship that continues for

thirteen sterile years and then abruptly changes in the bed that is the setting for the prologue and the epilogue of the play. As was true of Mr. Bullins' *The Fabulous Miss Marie,* each of the leading characters, with a spotlight on him, talks at one time or another directly to the audience about what is on his mind and in his heart and, occasionally, what lies in store for him. There is Monty's roommate Rick, a militant black nationalist to whom whites are devils and "paper tigers." There is Peggy, who briefly marries Monty, quits college to support him while he writes, is abandoned by him, even more briefly marries a white "boy," and ends up a lesbian. There is Lonnie, a Jewish guitarist and Janie's lover, who leaves her after three abortions (during the time she has been refusing to sleep with Monty so that their friendship can grow into "the purest love") and ends up a religious nut and a sideman in a number of bands with "the spades." There is Sharon, another Jew and a hippie, who ends up married to Len, the third roommate, and stays married to him. There is Mort Silberstein, self-described as a leftover beat poet from the fifties and now a pusher, who is eventually beaten up and thrown out of the party. Finally, there is Flossie, a merry sexy black girl. By the time the party and play are over, we know not only what has taken place but much of what will become of all of them. At one funny moment, Peggy reminds Rick of some shootout at U.C.L.A., and he tells her angrily that that "ain't even happened yet." There are, by the way, a lot of funny moments. Mr. Bullins has rarely been wittier or, for that matter, more understanding and vigorous. *The Taking of Miss Janie* is, according to a program note, a sequel to *The Pig Pen,* his most puzzling play. This one may be his most complex, but it is clear.

The highly stylized production, under Gilbert Moses' able direction, composed as it is of dialogue, monologues, choral speech, music (the recorded music is very important), and choral movements, is completely satisfying, and so is the acting of everyone concerned.

Clive Barnes (review date 5 May 1975)

SOURCE: "Miss Janie," in *The New York Times,* May 5, 1975, p. 243.

[*Barnes is an English-born American critic. In the mixed review below, he praises the intellectual and emotional appeal of* The Taking of Miss Janie, *but concludes that the play requires a sharper focus.*]

Just about five years ago Ed Bullins wrote a play called *The Pig Pen,* which was all about a mixed party in 1965, that took place the night Malcolm X was assassinated the night of the big divide between black and white. Now Mr. Bullins has produced *The Taking of Miss Janie,* which arrived last night at the Mitzi E. Newhouse Theater of the New York Shakespeare Festival. It is described by the author as "a sequel," and once again it is about the nineteen-sixties, pot and wine parties, blacks and whites not so much together, and the face of America's violence. But there is a difference of tone.

The Taking of Miss Janie has come to Lincoln Center from Henry Street Settlement's New Federal Theater, where it was produced by Woodie King Jr. This presentation by the Shakespeare Festival represents the beginning of a new collaboration between the Festival and the New Federal Theater, which is to be offered a showcase for its more successful offerings.

It was sensible to commence the arrangement with this new Ed Bullins play, which deserves to reach a larger audience. It is a sensitive work, with vivid dialogue, a sensibility toward time and place, and possesses both an intellectual and emotional density. Its construction is unusual, yet also highly effective. This is a much more mature play than *The Pig Pen,* but the changes are not the result of growing artistic maturity.

Although Mr. Bullins is clearly a moral writer, he never moralizes. His point of view is not so much argued out on stage, but presented as a documentary, and documented truth. In *The Pig Pen,* he pinpointed the killing of Malcolm X as a kind of watershed in American black history—namely the point at which, in the view of many reasonable blacks, black nationalism became a better bet for survival than integration. In *The Taking of Miss Janie* he is concerned with a black overview of the sixties, the decade that saw the death of both Kennedys and the Rev. Dr. Martin Luther King Jr., as well as Malcolm X. The decade that opened with Camelot and, in effect, ended with Watergate.

Right at the beginning, Mr. Bullins informs us that he is telling us "a tale about the spirit of the sixties." It is the story of a rape—a friendly rape, but a rape. Janie is a white student at City College who meets Monty, a black, at a creative writing course. Monty determines to have Janie, even if he has to wait. He does. He waits 10 years and then rapes her in the aftermath of a sick and sad party.

Mr. Bullins is covering a lot of ground, and echoing out many reverberations. His suggestion that white liberalism may have a great deal to do with sexuality is possibly relevant, as is his rather cynical picture of black men obsessed with white women, and his dismal view of miscegnation. Perhaps his attitude is summed up by the black poet Monty when, quite early in the play, he asks: "How is a white broad going to dig 'Down with Whitey' poems?" Mr. Bullins has a point.

The play could do with a sharper focus, and this is not, I feel, the fault of the director, Gilbert Moses, who, helped by the building-block set by Kert Lundell, organizes the kaleidoscopic pattern of scenes with neat skill. Rather it is a failure of total clarification on the part of the playwright but the man can write like an angel. Each of the characters has a soliloquy—chiefly satirical in tenor, particularly when it comes to whites, who are depicted as even more stupid and venal than the blacks—and these, and the quick dissolving scenes, do offer the image of a period seen through the distorting glass of a special mind.

The acting was good without being especially remarkable. The most assured performances came from Adeyemi Lyth-

cott as Monty and Robbie McCauley as the black woman who marries him. But the play is adequately done and well worth bringing to Lincoln Center.

CRITICAL COMMENTARY

Samuel J. Bernstein   (essay date 1980)

SOURCE: "The Taking of Miss Janie," in *The Strands Entwined: A New Direction in American Drama,* Northeastern University, 1980, pp. 61-80.

[*In the excerpt below, Bernstein offers a thematic and structural analysis of* The Taking of Miss Janie, *focusing on the intra-racial and inter-racial relationships depicted in the play.*]

The Taking of Miss Janie, which is a long one-act play, is concerned with black/white relations in America. As its title suggests, the play focuses upon the rape of a white woman by a black man. Actually, it is a second sexual assault that is imminent when the play begins; Janie (or "Miss Janie," to use Monty's disparaging nickname, a throwback to slave/owner relationships) has already been raped by Monty once. In the prologue, which is angry and bitter in tone, Monty stalks Janie. As we move into the body of the play, a flashback, we wonder whether this second sexual attack will actually take place. When we return to the rape sequence in the epilogue, the tone is of sadness and resignation in Janie and of increasing anger in Monty. Ironically, instead of showing us the completion of the second assault, the epilogue takes us to a time that is immediately prior to the first encounter. Moreover, the epilogue seems to happen both in the present (like the prologue) and in the past. This purposeful ambiguity of both time and process reflects the tone of the entire play.

Neither the extremely theatrical and sensational rape, nor even the sexual relationship of Janie and Monty per se, is of deepest concern to Bullins. Rather, Bullins uses the relationship of the couple and their relationships with the other seven characters essentially as a means for exploring black/white relations in America. It is the vividness, the power, the violence, and the social and psychological insight that makes Bullins' exploration compelling; all of these elements are then meshed with theatrical experimentalism, making the play new and excitingly different.

Structurally, the work is divided into twelve sections; each section is then further subdivided.

Although the entire work is exposition, the *first section,* beginning with Janie's monologue, introduces us to the present situation of the two principal characters, Monty and Janie. Janie, who has just been raped by Monty, sits tearfully at the end of his bed, trying to communicate with him. She is trying to understand why Monty, who has been a close friend, would wish to mistreat her and destroy their friendship. Monty simply stalks her, calls her "bitch," and says that she knew from the start that their relationship would come to this. Janie denies this, and the point is left moot in the play itself; she claims that all she ever wanted was their friendship. Apparently, Monty is unimpressed by her denial and her entreaty to him to desist.

Section two, introduced by a slide of Monty and Janie dressed in the styles of the late fifties, is a flashback. We watch as they meet, fellow students in a creative writing class. After class, Janie expresses admiration for Monty's writing; although its bitterness repels her, she recognizes Monty's talent and sensitivity. When she asks him, "Do you call that Black Poetry?", she exhibits a naiveté that will continue to characterize her, in some measure, throughout the play. But Janie is not simply "naive"; she is a symbolically complex character; paradoxically, her portrayal, like that of the other characters, is flawed and only partially realized in the play. Along with the naiveté that enables her to enter the black world and form a friendship with Monty, there is also a shallowness and selfishness in Janie that makes it impossible for her, at least at the outset, to draw really close to Monty. Reacting against the conventional controls of her parents, she dabbles—and essentially trifles—with the lives of people she cannot possibly understand at her stage of development. Wishing to be arty and chic—and longing to partake of the more dynamic, more directed lives of the blacks—she tries desperately to interact and to belong. But her commitment is incomplete, and she protects herself with a degree of aloofness. She is a symbol of the American ethos that uses blacks but never totally accepts them; unable to fuse herself to and identify with Monty, she also represents white liberals who interact socially with blacks but essentially fail to understand or respond to them. Although Bullins' conscious intention may not have been realized in the play, he has summarized Janie's position in his interview with Charles Young [*The New York Times*, 18 May 1975],

> Janie was very dishonest. She knew what Monty wanted; he never disguised his intentions. But she still was trying to keep him as her own little slave or eunuch.

The play gives us insufficient opportunity to enter Janie's mind and to observe her maturation, which does occur; she assents, albeit sadly, to the rape. Because we do not witness her development, we find it difficult to accept her as a real human being, and her symbolic dimension is sometimes obscure. For example, her language is often trite and poetically false. She continually utters lines that are hardly believable from a fairly intelligent college student. While such triteness might indicate her shallowness, and such poetic falseness might indicate her desperate attempt to be provocative and deep like Monty and the other black characters, the lines often are simply too awkward for a realistic character. In essence, the transition back and forth from realistic character to symbol is rich and intriguing, but not always clear and smooth.

During this initial scene in the flashback, Monty coins the "Miss Janie" nickname. She objects, but he persists, saying that this name will be a secret between them. His tone is mocking rather than bitter or angry. He invites Janie to a party at his apartment. She finds the prospect of his

poetry reading an enticement to come, but she hopes that his tone will not be as despairing as it was in class.

The party is the *third* major *section* of the work. Before the guests arrive, Monty's roommates, Rick and Len, casually argue, exposing us to their divergent black politics. Rick is essentially a Black Nationalist who detests whites and attacks Len for interacting with them. His rhetoric prepares us for his mistreatment of Janie upon her arrival as the first guest. Rick first slams the door in her face, then tells her her sin was being born, and finally calls her a "devil lady." Both Monty and Len, who are more hospitable to whites, try to soften the effect of Rick's attack.

After Janie, a series of other people arrive at the party. First to arrive is Peggy, a sensitive and intelligent black woman; she also mistreats Janie, and seems to interact best with Rick. Next is Sharon, a young, middle-class white Jewish woman, who is Len's friend. She arrives at the same time as Lonnie, Janie's jazz-playing boyfriend, who is the epitome of the shallow person who feels compelled to be "hip." In Monty's very first monologue, he indicates his displeasure at Janie's inviting this white boyfriend to a party to which he invited her alone.

Flossie arrives next. She is a hard, sensual black woman of the streets, who is involved in a casual sexual relationship with Monty. She has little to say during the party, other than expressing hunger and thirst. Shortly after Flossie, Mort Silberstein arrives, a mythic figure of the 1950s beat generation, now out of date but trying to hold on to a feeling of significance. He has a bad drug habit and no available funds. He tries to manipulate a loan from Monty, telling him that the price of drugs has risen. We meet these characters singly as they arrive and meet each other; this is an extremely smooth technique for introducing characters.

While much of this party section is a matter of introductions, the black/white strain is a continual undercurrent. It appears in discussion (e.g., Lonnie's having learned black music in school) and in certain symbolic gestures (e.g., Mort Silberstein arrives singing and dancing a rock hora, and as the individuals watch, they divide into separate racial camps). The racial issue is kept at the fore, primarily by Rick's acidic commentaries on the fall of Western civilization, his jibes at the white guests (he states that he would like to pour gasoline on Janie), his Black Moslem rhetoric about pork, his repeated slurs on Jews, and his expressed dissatisfaction with his roommates over their friendliness to the alleged "devil" whites.

This section also repeats the monologue technique and the surrealism of the first section. During the party, both Monty and Janie present monologues. These monologues are clearly distinguishable from the somewhat briefer, more aggressive speeches of Rick. Monty uses his monologue to express anger at Janie for inviting Lonnie, to assert his own superiority to white males, to argue that Janie is teasing and stringing him along, and to foreshadow that he will physically dominate her in the end, no matter how long it takes. By contrast, Janie uses her monologue to tell us that she is attracted only platonically to Monty. He is sensitive, serious, and talented, and she hopes that they will form a lasting friendship. As for Lonnie, he is not talented and really means nothing to her. Therefore, she will resist Monty's sexual entreaties not because of Lonnie or because of Monty's blackness—she has "made it with black guys before"—but because she does not want to intensify, complicate, and thus spoil their potential friendship. Idealizing their "black/white love," Janie hopes that their friendship will mature "like sweet grapes change with age and care into a distinctive bouquet upon choice, rare wines." This is bad, trite poetry, surrealistically imposed here and occasionally elsewhere upon Janie's naturalistic dialogue. While Janie's desire for friendship is sincere, her banal language suggests a shallow understanding of what such a friendship would entail.

The Taking of Miss Janie **is a flawed masterpiece. Nevertheless—in its breadth; its vivid dynamic action; its structural complexity; its unique use of time; and its effective marriage of diverse styles, rhythms, and moods—it deserves respect as one of the outstanding recent contributions to the American theatre**.

—*Samuel J. Bernstein*

Examples of other significant surrealistic elements involve the use of light and motion. For example, Mort enters from the shadows, suggesting his ghostlike qualities; he is the spirit of the fifties, when activism was simpler, and his kind of beat liberalism was acceptable to blacks. Now he is only an outdated cliché. The monologues are presented in an isolated lighted spot to emphasize separate states of consciousness. Also, the dancelike motions of the characters and the changes in light take us beyond the atmosphere of this party to a consideration of the larger outside situation—American racial strife in general.

These imaginative elements complement the overall surrealistic rendering of Monty's apartment, which in Bullins' words, is "an abstract depiction of a decade of cheap living spaces." Indeed, it is only a subtle change of lighting that takes us from this party to a meeting, years later, between Janie and Monty.

Section four is concerned with this subsequent meeting between Janie and Monty. Janie does not wish to give birth to Lonnie's baby and asks Monty to help her get an abortion. By now Monty is her special friend, and she comes to him when there is no one else to turn to. He readily agrees to help her so that she will not have to tell her parents, who would be horrified. Monty offers her money and his apartment for recuperation. However, when he offers her love, she withdraws, not wishing to involve them in a way that will harm their friendship. When Monty calls her "Miss Janie," she says they are so close that she no longer even resents that old epithet.

The *fifth section* begins a steady series of monologues that punctuate the play until, in its final section, the play cyclically returns to a conversation between Monty and Janie that, paradoxically, preceded the prologue itself. Each monologue is followed by a dialogue between the monologist and a second character; often, additional related interactions, involving more characters, occur as well. In many of the monologues, time jumps forward to the future. Peggy, whose monologue begins this fifth section, concentrates on her relationship with Monty, whom she married, with whom she had a child, and from whom she is now separated. Peggy speaks in decidedly racist terms about black love, black men, and black women. She tells us that Monty is selfish and cruel and loves only himself. However, she reveals that she still wants Monty, despite the pain she has suffered, particularly in having to give up her child for adoption. She likens Monty to a con man; he married her, fathered her child, sent her to work so that he could go to school, and then left her.

Peggy's story continues in a dialogue with Flossie. She tells Flossie how she married a white boy after Monty left her, almost causing Monty to become a Black Nationalist out of jealousy and rage. She also reveals that she knows of Flossie's sex with Monty behind her back, to which Flossie answers only, "Well, you know that my thing is making it with my friend-girl's ole men, honey."

With the major focus still on Peggy, the scene permits a subdivided flashback illustration of the period of her marriage to Monty. A light comes up on another part of the stage, and a minor episode unfolds. Janie has arrived in San Francisco to visit Monty. Her arrival is interrupted by Flossie's appearance; it is obvious that Monty and Flossie are very deeply involved sexually. Here, Janie again speaks an awkward poetic line that reflects her character, yet weakens the scene:

> I didn't know you had someone besides me . . . somebody real . . . somebody black and sensual as the night who would blot out my pale image like a cloud covering a dim, far constellation.

In the execution of this flashback scene, Flossie has moved over to join Monty and Janie. Returning to Peggy, Flossie recounts Monty's sex with her and poetry reading with Janie. When Flossie calls black men evil, Peggy declares she's a Lesbian, and she and Flossie passionately embrace.

Section six is Lonnie's monologue. He, too, speaks of his past, particularly of his past with Janie. After blaming his contemporaries and himself for feeding parasitically on each other, he speaks of his long and intense relationship with Janie. He speaks of the influence Janie's parents exercise upon her (her never-ending student life is a result) and of Janie's need for independence, which drew them apart. When Janie had three abortions, he began to feel guilty; then she began to feel stifled by him, and they broke up. Although Lonnie now declares he is a member of the Baha'i World Faith, a believer in a world family of all mankind, he reiterates his anti-black prejudices that he spouted earlier at the party, including his characteristic use of the pejorative *spade*.

After his monologue, Lonnie argues with Rick. Rick calls Lonnie a devil and a Jew. Lonnie tells Rick that he has renounced his Judaism and wishes to be characterized as a human being, not a devil. But when Rick persists, Lonnie loses his temper and exits. Rick feels triumphant. With this section as with the last, it is hard to specify the time sequence. Bullins' blurring of time relationships, his detailing of the lives of minor characters (in the initial list of characters, he refers to both major and minor characters as "people"), his use of direct address to the audience, his discussion of large social themes, and the cyclical structure of the play all serve to expand the play's horizons, to reflect powerfully on the American ethos, not simply to depict the particular relationship between Monty, a black man, and Janie, a white woman.

Len, whose monologue begins *section seven,* speaks not so much of past events in his life as of the influence he has had upon others. He speaks of himself as a teacher and explains that he got Monty interested in drama and introduced Rick to Black Nationalism. Like a seer, he foretells the rise and fall of Rick as a Black Nationalist leader, and foresees the assassinations of the Kennedys, Martin Luther King, and Malcolm X. Len says to the audience: "Tonight you are looking into some of the makings of the sixties . . . which, of course, went to make the seventies." Characterizing the play as an "integrated social epic," he explains that Bullins only hinted at matters because he did not know the impacts of the "accidental associations" he depicted. Thus, surrealistically, a character looks at his author as a limited being, limited at least in comparison with himself. Len regards himself as a kind of progenerative seed upon which Bullins had only a limited perspective. "He did not know," Len says, "that through me he would discover the kernel of political truth of the era, the seminal social vision of the sweep of so much history."

From this monologue, Len proceeds to converse with Sharon. This is presumably a conversation in the distant past when Len and Sharon hardly knew each other. He describes himself as a rational intellectual, and she tells him that she does not like his revolutionary friends. She wonders if he considers her a devil, and he assures her he does not. Sharon tells him of her sexual rebellion—that she has slept with over seventy men—and he simply replies that she is a child of the times. He is deeply attracted to her.

Len moves out of the light, and *section eight* begins with Sharon's monologue. Time has passed since Len and Sharon first became involved with each other; she speaks of their marriage and the birth of their son. Essentially, she says that although times were occasionally very rough, she and Len finally worked things out. He continues to think of himself as an intellectual, but has become a middle-class businessman. Sharon is proud that they have stayed together; unlike most black/white couples, they have managed to live harmoniously. Surely, despite Len's loss of radical commitment, their lasting relationship is an optimistic note in the play.

Mort Silberstein is not, however, as enthusiastic about Sharon's marriage as she is, as he expresses in the subse-

quent dialogue with her. Mort accuses her of adding "racial suicide to cultural injury" by marrying Len. This attitude shows him to be a narrow racist, and Sharon proves him to be a hypocrite; she reveals that he is having an affair with a German girl even though superficially he is a confirmed Jewish zealot. Actually, we find he is filled with self-hatred, declaring he could never marry a Jewish girl and expressing deep resentment toward his mother who allegedly drowned him in chicken soup and tried to bury him in bagels and lox. (Bullins is less acute in treating the Jewish ethos than he is in projecting the overall relationship of blacks and whites.) Finally, Mort becomes utterly ridiculous when he explains his attachment to Nina, the German girl, by pointing to the internationalist orientation of her Marxism. He can praise Nina's internationalism but cannot accept Sharon's interracial marriage. Sharon caps the conversation by saying that the only reality for her is her black baby (i.e., in white America) and by declaring that she does not care who killed Jesus (i.e., these narrow, silly religious arguments and prejudices have no place in her mind or in her life).

Section nine emerges with a monologue by Flossie. The setting is a party at Monty's apartment. Once again, the exact time frame is difficult to establish. We do know that we are at a rather early party thrown by Monty. Instead of speaking of herself, Flossie speaks mostly of Monty, with whom she has had sex intermittently, and who treats her like a lady and enjoys her sensuality. She contends that, unlike other male friends, Monty is gaining a clear vision of himself; he is achieving emotional health. His only flaw is chasing after white girls; if he would only let himself, he and Peggy might get together. Flossie sees herself as too unsteady a companion for Monty.

Flossie's monologue shifts to dialogue with Janie. She first expresses hostility toward Janie because Janie is white and because Monty seems so allured by her. Janie, showing aloofness but a sudden hint of new maturity, counters: "Maybe he's got what he wants from you . . . and he wants what he thinks he can get from me." While such a sentiment might suggest that Janie is stringing Monty along, it is simply objective observation by an uninvolved Janie. Flossie seems impressed with Janie's hipness and pulls her aside to teach her to play The Game (i.e., the sex game). Flossie enjoys helping a girl with sexual potential, thus psychologically eliminating Janie, a white woman, as a competitor; but Janie is merely bewildered by Flossie's advice and exhortations.

Section ten begins with a monologue by Rick, presumably at the same party. He reports an old motif: his dissatisfaction with integrated social events. He particularly scorns Len for planning to marry Sharon and Monty for waiting so long for sex from Janie. To Rick, this chasing of white women epitomizes the confusion of the blacks in the sixties; stepping (as Len did earlier) outside time, Rick contends that the confusion will last into the seventies as well. He feels that the black women are also doing strange things, that "This is Babylon" and, as he said earlier, "the beginning of the end." Peggy offers to give him a ride downtown in her new sports car. Rick pompously addresses Peggy, calling her life unnatural and assessing her troubles partly as the result of Monty's sexual exploitation, association with white devils, and other psychosocial factors. Peggy accuses him of distorting the truth; they did not have parties to impress white girls. Instead, they were part of the sixties generation that believed in integration. Rick continues to deride her broken life and to blame Western culture for making her a freak. Angered now, she counters by mentioning Rick's future drug problems, his torturing of young black women, and his political problems as a powerful Cultural Nationalist. To make these points, Peggy must transcend the present and speak as a seer of the future. Rick disputes her forecast:

> . . . why don't you keep quiet about all that? It ain't even happened yet. So be cool.

Rick claims he already knows his future and that it will be "glorious." Peggy poignantly argues that "we all failed." By "we" she means the youth of the sixties, a youth with great potential; "We just turned out lookin' like a bunch of punks and freaks and fuck-offs." She goes on to tell Rick that he is living in the past. When Rick no longer wants her ride, she declares that she is going to stay at the party and have sex with Monty in memory of the relationship she had with him. She adds: "I can't just let the Miss

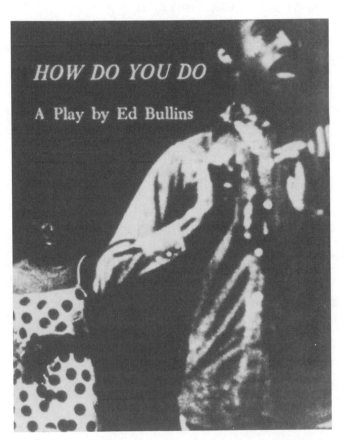

Front cover for Bullins's first play, written while he was studying creative writing at San Francisco State College.

Janie's dance off with the world, can I?" Rick encourages her and concludes with the existential line: "Ya know, it be about what you make it anyway."

The *eleventh section* begins with the last of the monologues, that by Mort Silberstein. Mort, in his hip language, a language captured as well as the black street idiom by Bullins, claims the world is confused and ugly, a bad party, "the worst party of the decade. . . . Probably the worse goddamn party in memory." Despite his social awareness, Mort is unable to direct or save himself. He is still a beat poet, after his time, and a confirmed drug addict. At the end of his monologue, he begs the audience for money to buy a fix.

As Monty enters, Mort says: "Hey, Monty. Tell these folks [the audience] how bad I need ten bucks." Monty rejects Mort's request and, in fact, rejects Mort entirely. An exchange of charges and a violent argument ensues. Monty withdraws from Mort's drugs and ultra Jewishness, and Mort refers to black people as "spades." When Mort persists in reviling black politics, Monty hits him and shouts:

> I don't want to be a whiteman, do you hear me, Mort Silberstein? I don't want to be a token Jew even. I'm me. You understand? It's taken a long time but I know that now.

In essence, Monty is saying that his self-concept is one of a black man, distinct and separate. Mort angrily tells Monty that nineteenth-century white domination and slavery suffuses Monty's consciousness. This frightens Monty. When Mort says that Monty loves Marx, Freud, and Einstein, all of whom are Jews, Monty replies that Mao, Fanon, and Voodoo are his new idols. With Mort's final insult, "You're freaky for JESUS," Monty beats him unconscious.

The other characters stir, as if from a marijuana-induced dream. Time seems to have changed once again; Monty indicates that it is now the early sixties. Everyone decides to leave the party, either to go to bed or to go home. Rick is going to the ghetto. Only Janie remains, supposedly to learn about Monty's life. Monty asks Rick to throw out Mort, which he and Flossie proceed to do. Thus ends the penultimate section.

At the beginning of *section twelve*, everyone has left the party and the scene takes on conditions reminiscent of the prologue. The only difference is that Janie's hair is combed out and she is wearing her glasses, making her all the more seductive to Monty. Contrary to what he said earlier in the play, Monty says: "I never knew it would come to this." Janie agrees that Monty's raping her after thirteen years of friendship is a shock. She expresses regret for the loss of friendship his behavior has brought. When she asks if he wants her to bathe, he simply begins to remove her clothes. She speaks of a friend of theirs who hanged herself, who resignedly gave in to death. Janie will not fight Monty because she knows him so well. She, like their friend, will give in to this inevitable ending, this symbolic death of their long friendship. Monty begins undressing her and declares his lust. Symbolically speaking of herself, she again mentions their friend: "She just put the noose over her head and felt her spirit dance away." Janie accepts the inevitable, but she is sad in her realization that this is the death of her only link with meaningful life, her platonic relationship with Monty. Monty now pushes her back and proceeds to tear off the rest of her clothes. The lights go down as the play ends.

The play's surface action defies simple analysis. A black man has raped a white woman. He has waited a long time to do so and, presumably, the intervening period in their lives and the intervening occurrences in the play help us to understand this action. However, Bullins only leads; he does not explain or define. What seems likely is that Janie wanted only a platonic friendship; however, Monty, who continuously called her "Miss Janie," an insulting name, has had a need to dominate and humilate her. Perhaps Janie represents the American ethos, to which the suppressed black has strongly ambivalent feelings. Perhaps she also represents American liberalism, with its abstract support of, yet ultimate aloofness from, the black. Since Monty, as a black American, feels that he has always been an excluded being, a second-class citizen, he has come to define his worth in terms of his ability to "make it" within, and even despite, the predominantly white cultural ethos. Although that ethos may be shallow or hollow, it must be dominated or manipulated before the black can feel triumphant.

Such attitudes, Bullins suggests, have deleterious effects on individuals and on relationships. Blacks cannot accept other blacks as desirable life partners, and true friendship between a black and a white is made difficult, if not impossible. This leads to a certain isolation for the white person who is caught in the midst of the American ethos, and a certain anger in the black who resents being riveted to the golden chains of the American dream.

It is appropriate that Bullins expresses this black/white conflict in sexual terms; miscegenation is the great fear of the racist black or white, and a false eugenics—one based on color—is the primary means by which distinction, separation, and hierarchy are maintained. Moreover, the stereotype of the vulnerable white female goddess and the supersensual black male is characteristic of American racism.

Of course, this explanation is highly speculative; the play is not a racial statement, but a vivid and truthful, if often superficially contradictory, series of impressions. Although the subject of the play is surely black/white relations in America, its intention is to present the entire racial panorama of the sixties, not to digest, differentiate, collate, or finally explain it.

At one point in the play, Rick states that this is a play about Monty's desire to rape the blonde Miss Janie. This is superficially correct; but, just as Rick's narrow racist views are based on oversimplification, so, too, is his artistic judgment inaccurate. Closer to the truth is Mort's statement:

> This is a crazy scene, ain't it? An honest-to-God creepy insane looney bin. A picture of the times, I say. And

you can't forgive the creator of this mess [God? America? Bullins?] for the confusion. That's what happens when you mix things up like this. It throws everything out of kilter. Jews, niggers, politics, Germans, time, philosophy, memory, theme, sociology, past, drugs, history, sex, present, women, faggots, men, dikes, phoneys, assholes . . . everything bunched up together.

However limited he is, and however absurd his rationalizations become, Mort is right in this monologue. Presumably, the confusion of which he speaks is the situation of America in the late sixties; and Bullins has mirrored this confusion, this craziness, in the cornucopia of this play.

Another clue to the play's aesthetic is furnished by Len in his monologue. Speaking of himself as a teacher, he praises himself for having elevated Monty's tastes, especially for stimulating his interest in drama. But this is the only time we hear mention of drama in the play. When Janie first meets Monty in creative writing class, it is his *poetry*, not his dramatic writing, that attracts her. This overlapping of the two arts is a key to Bullins' method. Poetry works largely through association, through connotation; it does not usually charge forth in clear confrontation as drama does. Similarly, the conflict of Monty and Janie is only a framework through which Bullins can express the phantasmagoria, the truly poetic complexity and subtlety of black/white relations in America. The play, then, is actually a poem in dramatic form.

In this light, the time shifts; the contradictory statements; and the intermixture of naturalism/surrealism, prose/poetry, and monologue/dialogue are assets. They enable Bullins to maintain a believable surface, to penetrate the psychology and sociology of his characters and their milieu, to leap historically as he finds it appropriate to do so, and to project the inconsistencies and confusions that exist in and around our American racial struggle.

Compounding the confusion of the play is an ambivalence in Bullins himself. Although he seems to believe in the possibility of black/white harmony (the marriage of Sharon and Len and the friendship of Monty and Janie), there is no question that strains of anti-white and anti-Jewish feeling inform the play. The anti-white feeling is clear and almost constant; the anti-Jewish orientation, more subtle, is shown in the rejection of Judaism by Sharon, Lonnie, and Mort; in the shallowness of Lonnie and Sharon; in the formulized rhetoric of pathetic Mort; and in the flippant lines concerning chicken soup and bagels and lox. Despite ambivalences, it is clearly Bullins' rage at social inequity that is the seed of his artistic vision and of his play's dynamism.

The Taking of Miss Janie is a flawed masterpiece. Nevertheless—in its breadth; its vivid dynamic action; its structural complexity; its unique use of time; and its effective marriage of diverse styles, rhythms, and moods—it deserves respect as one of the outstanding recent contributions to the American theatre.

FURTHER READING

AUTHOR COMMENTARY

Bullins, Ed. "Playwright's Journal 1975." *Confrontation,* Nos. 33-34 (Fall-Winter 1986-1987): 269-73.

> Discusses the critical reception of *The Taking of Miss Janie,* and his impressions upon winning the New York Drama Critics Circle Award for that play.

Gussow, Mel. "Bullins, the Artist and the Activist, Speaks." *The New York Times* (22 September 1971): 54.

> Offers the playwright's views on critics, the importance of theater to the black community, and playwriting as an "exact craft."

Jackmon, Marvin X. "An Interview with Ed Bullins: Black Theater." *The Negro Digest* XVIII, No. 6 (April 1969): 9-16.

> Marvin X (also known as El Muhajir) and Bullins discuss "black theater and some of the forces and personalities important to it."

BIBLIOGRAPHIES

King, Kimball. "Ed Bullins." In *Ten Modern American Playwrights: An Annotated Bibliography,* pp. 137-54. New York: Garland Publishing, 1982.

> Annotated bibliographic essay which includes primary stage sources up to *You Gonna Let Me Take You Out Tonight, Baby?,* film adaptations, and secondary sources.

Sanders, Leslie. "Ed Bullins." In *American Playwrights since 1945: A Guide to Scholarship, Criticism, and Performance,* edited by Philip C. Kolin, pp. 66-79. New York: Greenwood Press, 1988.

> Bibliographic and critical resource covering primary stage performances, fiction, anthologies, interviews, and secondary sources.

OVERVIEWS AND GENERAL STUDIES

Anderson, Jervis. "Profiles-Dramatist." *New Yorker* XLIX, No. 17 (16 June 1973): 40-4, 46, 48, 51-2, 54, 59, 61-2, 66, 68, 70, 72-9.

> Provides an overview of Bullins's life and career, especially his role in the black theater movement.

Andrews, W. D. E. "Theatre of Black Reality: The Blues Drama of Ed Bullins." *Southwest Review* 65, No. 2 (Spring 1980): 178-90.

> Compares Bullins to other influential black playwrights, especially Imamu Amiri Baraka (LeRoi Jones) and asserts that his "way of viewing life, the way of feeling the vision that informs his plays is the vision of that unique form of black music, the blues."

Giles, James. "Tenderness in Brutality: The Plays of Ed Bullins." *Players* 48, No. 1 (October-November 1972): 32-3.

> Considers loyalty and brutality as themes in several of Bullins's plays, including *Goin' a Buffalo, In the Wine Time,* and *In New England Winter.*

Herman, William. "'The People in this Play are Black': Ed Bullins." In *Understanding Contemporary American Drama,* pp. 161-95. Columbia: University of South Carolina Press, 1987.

> Offers a thematic analysis of several Bullins plays.

Lahr, John. "Black Theatre: The American Tragic Voice." *Evergreen Review* 13, No. 69 (August 1969): 55-63.

> Investigates Bullins's work as a treatise on black theater, observing that with his plays, "black theatre holds an awesome possibility for America, that of re-discovering a lost and noble form of tragedy."

Smitherman, Geneva. "Everybody Wants to Know Why I Sing the Blues." *Black World* XXIII, No. 6 (April 1974): 4-13.

> Explores Bullins's use of the blues motif as the "central mechanism for conveying his message."

THE DUPLEX

Hay, Samuel A. "'What Shape Shapes Shapelessness?': Structural Elements in Ed Bullins's Plays." *Black World* XXIII, No. 6 (April 1974): 20-6.

> Examines the dramatic structure of *The Duplex.*

Kerr, Walter. "Mr. Bullins is Himself at Fault." *The New York Times* (19 March 1972): 1, 7.

> Offers a negative review, asserting that the play does not provide adequate structure, and therefore, resolution.

Václav Havel
1936-

INTRODUCTION

Playwright, essayist, and poet Václav Havel is a major figure in Czech culture, and he is considered his country's foremost dramatist. His plays are powerful condemnations of the bureaucratization and mechanization of modern society and their effects on the individual. His keen satires depict the prevalence of cliché and official doublespeak in a totalitarian society and the chaos brought about by the disintegration of meaning. Many of Havel's works are considered absurdist black comedies because they employ grotesque and ludicrous elements that give expression to humanity's fundamental uneasiness in an inane universe. This focus on the absurd nature of existence in the modern world gives his works a universality that goes beyond his exploration of the uniquely Czech experience.

BIOGRAPHICAL INFORMATION

Havel was born into a wealthy family in Prague. Once his primary education was completed, he was denied access to higher education because of the Communist government's policy of discrimination against the bourgeoisie. Havel worked in a chemical factory and attended night classes in order to finish secondary school. Havel credits this period of his life with giving him the opportunity to "see the world 'from below,' that is, as it really is." It is from this vantage point, Havel believes, that one clearly views the absurd and comic dimensions of the world. In 1959 Havel accepted his first theater job, becoming a stagehand at Prague's Divadlo ABC (ABC Theater); the following year he moved to the highly respected avant-garde Divadlo na zábradlí (Theater of the Balustrade), eventually becoming its literary adviser. Having begun writing articles and essays in the mid-1950s, Havel wrote his first play, *Zahradní slavnost* (*The Garden Party*) in 1963, and it was produced by the Balustrade. *Vyrozumění* (*The Memorandum*) premiered in 1965, and *Ztížená možnost soustředení* (*The Increased Difficulty of Concentration*) debuted in 1968. These plays were highly acclaimed internationally. *The Memorandum* premiered in America in 1968, and Havel won the prestigious Obie Award. The same year he was honored with the Austrian State Prize for European Literature. Throughout the early 1960s Czechoslovakia had been experiencing a gradual relaxation of government controls on culture, but this abruptly ended in 1968 when troops from the Soviet Union invaded the country in order to enforce closer compliance with Soviet policies. Although Havel's works were subsequently banned and Havel himself prohibited from working in the theater, he refused to abandon his country, and he continued to write plays and political works. His resistance to the Communist regime—which included co-founding the

human rights organization Charter 77—resulted in his arrest several times in the 1970s. His plays written during this period circulated privately and premiered abroad. In 1979 Havel was sentenced to four and a half years in prison for his involvement in an organization that sought to defend individuals unjustly prosecuted by the state. In 1982 the 36th International Theatre Festival at Avignon, France, included a six-hour "Night for Václav Havel," and featured Samuel Beckett's "Catastrophe" and Arthur Miller's "I think about you a great deal," plays dedicated to Havel and written in protest of his imprisonment. Havel continued to write and to have his plays produced outside of Czechoslovakia, and he was awarded the Erasmus Prize in 1986. With the collapse of the Communist state in 1989, Havel was elected president of Czechoslovakia. When that country divided into the Czech and Slovak republics in 1993, Havel was elected president of the Czech Republic, a position he still holds.

MAJOR WORKS

The main theme in Havel's work is the relationship between the individual and the government. Associated with the absurdist playwrights Eugene Ionesco, Jean Genet, and Samuel Beckett, Havel explores the power of language and its ability to alienate and overwhelm the individual. These are the central issues in *The Garden Party, The Memorandum,* and *The Increased Difficulty of Concentration.* Three one-act plays, written after the Soviet invasion of Czechoslovakia in 1968, are semi-autobiographical. Known as the "Vaněk Plays," they all feature a dissident playwright named Ferdinand Vaněk. In "Audience," Vaněk, unable to work as a playwright, is forced to take a job at a brewery. His supervisor there offers him an easier job in exchange for composing the weekly reports to the authorities that the supervisor must file on Vaněk himself. In "Vernisáž" ("Private View") Vaněk visits former friends, an affluent couple who flaunt the material possessions they have gained by renouncing their previous opposition to the government. They attempt to convince Vaněk to recant his dissent as well. "Protest" features Staněk, a successful scriptwriter whose daughter's boyfriend has been arrested. Staněk encourages Vaněk to write a petition to protest the arrest, but he himself refuses to sign it. Throughout these three plays Vaněk is a nearly silent figure who functions as an external conscience for his interlocutors, prodding them to inadvertently admit their cowardice and hypocrisy. Havel's 1984 work, *Largo Desolato,* is a semi-autobiographical play about a philosopher driven to abuse alcohol and pills by the pressure both from officials who want him to recant his writings and from friends who themselves are unable to support his efforts but still urge him to continue. *Pokoušení (Temptation),* a 1985 variation on the Faust legend about a scientist who sells his soul to the devil for knowledge and power, is an allegory in which the state is depicted as the true devil because it corrupts science in the service of political ends. Both *Largo Desolato* and *Temptation* develop the theme of humanity's tendency toward totalitarianism, the central issue as well in "Omyl" ("Mistake"), a play written in 1983 in response to Beckett's "Catastrophe."

CRITICAL RECEPTION

Many of Havel's works have met with acclaim both at home and abroad. Michael Billington, writing of a recent production of *The Memorandum* in London, admired the play's "brutally logical satire on the use of language to enforce conformity" and observed: "The play may have grown out of experience of Czech communism: its application is universal." Similarly, Sarah Hemming, noting that *The Memorandum* was thirty years old at the time of its London performance, remarked: "As a political parable, the play seems almost prophetic: everything changes, and yet things remain the same." When the three Vaněk plays were staged together in New York under the title *A Private View,* critics praised the manner in which they effectively convey the ills of society and challenge the audience to reflect on existence in an absurd world. Overall, Havel is recognized as a powerful playwright who, as Marketa Goetz-Stankiewicz has written, not only "gives shape to some of the most important issues of our time but also a thinker who from his small place in a small country in the heart of Europe sends forth an eloquent artistic diagnosis of men living in social groups East or West."

PRINCIPAL WORKS

PLAYS

Zahradní slavnost [*The Garden Party*] 1963
Vyrozumění [*The Memorandum*] 1965
Ztížená možnost soustředení [*The Increased Difficulty of Concentration*] 1968
Spiklenci [The Conspirators] 1971
Žebrácká opera [adaptor; from the drama *The Beggar's Opera* by John Gay] 1972
*"Audience" [also known as "Interview"] 1975
*"Vernisáž" ["Private View"; also known as "Unveiling"] 1975
Horský hotel [*Mountain Hotel*; also known as *The Mountain Resort*] 1976
†*Hry 1970-1976* (play collection) 1977
*"Protest" 1978
"Omyl" ["The Mistake"] 1983
Largo desolato [*Largo Desolato*] 1984
Pokoušení [*Temptation*] 1985
Slum Clearance 1987

OTHER MAJOR WORKS

Protokoly [*Protocols*] (essays, drama, and poetry) 1966
Dopisy Olze [*Letters to Olga: June 1979 to September 1982*] (correspondence) 1983
O lidskou identitu [*In Search of Human Identity*] (essays) 1984
Dálkový výslech [*Disturbing the Peace: A Conversation with Karel Hvížďala*] (interview) 1986
Open Letters: Selected Writings (essays, speeches, correspondence) 1991

*These three plays were produced together in New York in 1983 under the title *A Private View*; they are also known by the collective title "The Vaněk Plays."

†This volume contains *Spiklenci, Žebrácká opera, Horský hotel,* "Audience," and "Vernisáž."

AUTHOR COMMENTARY

Light on a Landscape (1985)

SOURCE: "Light on a Landscape," translated by Milan Pomichalek and Anna Mozga, in *The Vaněk Plays: Four Authors, One Character,* edited by Marketa Goetz-Stankiewicz, Vancouver: UBC Press, 1987, pp. 237-39.

[*In the following essay, which was written in 1985, Havel discusses the experience of having other authors utilize his character Vaněk and coins the term "Vaněk principle" to describe the phenomenon.*]

In the 1970's it was customary (and a good custom it was) for several of my writer-friends to spend one summer weekend with me in my country cottage every year. After 1969 they all had found themselves in a situation similar to mine; that is to say, they were banned in their native country and publicly disgraced for their beliefs concerning society. At these gatherings we used to, among other things, read our new works to each other. In the course of about two days before our meeting in 1975, and mainly to have something to read on that occasion, I wrote the one-act play **"Audience."** The inspiration came from personal experience—my employment in a brewery the year before—and the play was intended, as may be evident, primarily for the entertainment of my friends. Indeed, it is little more than a dialogue between the so-called "dissident" writer Vaněk (who works in a brewery) and his superior, the brewmaster. Though the latter is invented, obviously many of my own experiences—and not only those from the brewery—went into his making.

It never occurred to me that the play might be saying something (more or less significant) to other people, people who do not know me or my situation and who are ignorant of my having worked in a brewery. As it turned out, I was—as I had, after all, been a number of times before in regard to my literary work—mistaken: the play was successful not only with my friends but, also, having by various ways soon penetrated the relatively broad consciousness of the Czech public, also won its esteem. At times, it has even happened that total strangers, people in restaurants or casual hitchhikers I picked up, not only knew it but also had extracted from it pieces of dialogue, which they then used—in addition to short quotations or paraphrases—in various situations (in some cases as a sort of password among people spiritually akin). This wide domestic acclaim naturally pleased me, the more so as it occurred under conditions which made it impossible for the play to be published or performed publicly in my country. But what pleased me most is that something apparently happened which, I think, does or should occur with all art, namely that the work of art somehow exceeds its author, or is, so to speak, "cleverer than he is," and that through the mediation of the writer—no matter what purpose he was consciously pursuing—some deeper truth about his time reveals itself and works its way to the surface.

Stimulated by this experience, I later wrote two more Vaněk plays, **"Unveiling"** and **"Protest."** All three have since been staged by many theatres in divers countries, and, in spite of the rather special and unusual circumstances from which they originated, they have turned out to be generally intelligible. The third one, **"Protest,"** however, was actually written after a discussion with my friend Pavel Kohout as a counterpoint to his "Permit" (likewise a Vaněk play). These two were originally written with the intention of having them staged together, something that eventually did happen. Later, when I was already in prison, Kohout wrote another Vaněk piece, "Morass," and at approximately the same time my friend Pavel Landovský composed "Arrest." Later still, after his release from the prison in which we had served time together, Jiří Dienstbier, another of my friends, wrote a Vaněk play as well.

If I am to make some marginal comments on the whole Vaněk series, it might, above all, be appropriate to emphasize that Vaněk is not Havel. Of course, I have transferred into this character certain of my own experiences, and I have done so more distinctly than is usual among writers. Undoubtedly, I have also implanted in him a number of my personal traits or, more precisely, presented a number of perspectives from which I see myself in various situations. But all of this does not mean that Vaněk is intended as a self-portrait. A real person and a dramatic character are entirely different things. The dramatic character is more or less always a fiction, an invention, a trick, an abbreviation consisting only of a limited number of utterances, and subordinated to the concrete "world of the play" and its meaning. In comparison with any living person, even the most enigmatic and psychologically most rounded character is hopelessly inadequate and simplistic. On the other hand, however, he should also exude something a real person cannot possibly possess: the ability always to say something perspicuous and essential about "the world as it is"—all within the context of the few lines of dialogue and the few situations that make up his entire being.

This holds true for Vaněk as well, perhaps more so than for many another dramatic character. Vaněk is really not so much a concrete person as something of a "dramatic principle": he does not usually do or say much, but his mere existence, his presence on stage, and his being what he is make his environment expose itself one way or another. He does not admonish anyone in particular; indeed, he demands hardly anything of anyone. And in spite of this, his environment perceives him as an invocation somehow to declare and justify itself. He is, then, a kind of "key," opening certain—always different—vistas onto the world in which he lives; a kind of catalyst, a gleam, if you will, in whose light we view a landscape. And although without it we should scarcely be able to see anything at all, it is not the gleam that matters but the landscape. The Vaněk plays, therefore, are essentially not plays about Vaněk, but plays about the world as it reveals itself when confronted with Vaněk. (This, I must add, is an *ex post facto* explanation. While writing **"Audience,"** I was not aware of this, and I did not plan things that way beforehand. It is only now that, removed in time and faced with Vaněk's literary and theatrical existence of several years, I have come to realize it.)

From what I have just said about Vaněk, it of course follows that the Vaněk of different plays and, even more so, the Vaněk of different authors is not always quite the same character. While it is true that as a "principle" or "dramatic trick" he moves from play to play, the principle is used differently every time, and as a character he is therefore always someone slightly different. The writers impress on him their own varied experiences, they perceive him in the framework of their individual poetics, perhaps they even project into him their varying interpretations of the man who was the original model. In short, every writer is different and writes differently; consequently, he has his own Vaněk, different from the Vaněks of the others.

For me, personally, all that remains is to be pleased that, having discovered—more unconsciously than on purpose—the "Vaněk principle," I have inspired other Czech writers who, as it happens, are also my friends, and have provided something of a key for them to use in their own way and at their own responsibility. And if the present collection of Vaněk-plays [*The Vaněk Plays: Four Authors, One Character,* 1987] says—as a whole—something about the world in which it was given us to live our lives, then the credit should be given collectively and in equal measure, to all the authors involved.

Writing for the Stage (1986)

SOURCE: "Writing for the Stage," in *Disturbing the Peace: A Conversation with Karel Hvížďala,* translated by Paul Wilson, Alfred A. Knopf, 1990, pp. 35-72.

[*The following interview was first published in 1986. Havel surveys his career and discusses the origins of several of his plays.*]

How many plays have you written by now? Could you give us a bibliographical overview?

. . . [My] first play, still juvenilia really, was a one-acter called **"An Evening with the Family"** from 1959. After I went over to the Theatre on the Balustrade, I worked with Ivan Vyskočil on a play called *Hitchhiking,* which was performed in 1961. With Miloš Macourek, I wrote a cabaret play called *Mrs. Hermannova's Best Years,* which was performed, if I'm not mistaken, in 1962. I wrote several scenes for a poetic revue called *The Deranged Turtledove,* which was also performed sometime around that period.

My first independent full-length play was *The Garden Party,* which was given its premiere in the Theatre on the Balustrade in 1963. *The Memorandum* was mounted in 1965, but I had started writing it in 1960, and then rewritten it several times. In 1968 the Balustrade performed another play of mine, *The Increased Difficulty of Concentration.* I also wrote a short radio play called *Guardian Angel* in the sixties, and in 1968 the Czechoslovak Radio broadcast it, with Josef Kemr and Rudolf Hrušínský (I never actually heard it). Also I wrote a television play called *A Butterfly on the Antennae,* for which Czechoslovak Television gave me a kind of prize. They even prepared to tape it, but, thanks to the Soviet invasion, this never happened. Later it was done by West German Television. *The Garden Party* and *The Memorandum* were published sometime in the 1960s by Mladá Fronta, along with two of my essays and a collection of typographical poetry, all under the title *Protocols.* A separate edition of *The Garden Party* had already been published by Orbis, which also later brought out *The Increased Difficulty of Concentration.* All three plays came out as well as a supplement to *Divadlo* magazine, and recently they were published together in book form under the title *The Increased Difficulty,* by the Rozmluva press in London. To make this survey complete, I should also mention a film

version of *The Garden Party,* which fortunately was never realized (I say "fortunately" because Barrandov Studios had hired a director whose poetics were not very close to mine); another unrealized film scenario, *Heart Beat* (with Jan Němec); a sound collage called *Bohemia the Beautiful, Bohemia Mine* created in Czechoslovak Radio but never broadcast (fortunately for the producers who had commissioned it), and *A Door to the Attic,* a revue based on texts by Ivan Sviták, and apparently performed later (I'm not sure about this) in Viola. In the 1970s—that is, when I was already banned—the first play I wrote was *The Conspirators* (1971), but I don't think it was very successful. Next came *The Beggar's Opera* (1972), and in 1975 two one-act plays, **"Audience"** and **"Private View,"** to which I added a third, **"Protest,"** in 1978. All three feature the same character, Vaněk. In 1976 I wrote another full-length play, called *Mountain Hotel.* Except for **"Protest,"** all these plays from my "banned" period were published by 68 Publishers in Toronto under the title *Plays.* (Unfortunately, a working version of *The Conspirators* was published by mistake; it was even worse than the final version.) After my release from prison, I wrote a miniplay in 1983 called **"The Mistake"** (it was printed by *Svědectví*); then, in 1984, came a full-length play, *Largo Desolato,* and, in 1985, *Temptation.* Both were published in Munich by *Poezie Mimo Domov. Largo Desolato* was also published earlier in *Svědectví.* Considering that I've been writing plays now for twenty-six years, I haven't written a great deal. I should perhaps add that all my plays were and still are performed by various theatres in various countries of the world, and they've also been published in foreign languages.

Do you remember how you got the idea for **The Memorandum** *and where the word "ptydepe" come from?*

I don't really like to admit this, but the idea for an artificial language called "ptydepe" was not mine: it came from my brother Ivan, who is a mathematician. Of course the play was my own idea, and I wrote it in my own way; I merely consulted with my brother in the passages on redundancy.

And how did you come up with the subject for **The Garden Party***?*

In this case, the original impulse came from Ivan Vyskočil, for a change. After the shows, we'd always sit around in some wine bar, and he would talk about all the different themes, subjects, and ideas he had for plays. The fact is that he never, at least not in those days, turned any of his ideas into plays, but he did have a bottomless supply of them, and they'd always be different, because he'd be making them up as he was talking. Once he was talking about some connections or bribery or something, I don't really remember what it was, but I do know that he challenged me to tackle the subject. I did tackle it, but I don't suppose the play that eventually came out of it has anything in common with the original impulse.

Ten years ago, when you were approaching forty, you said, in a conversation with Jiří Lederer, that sooner or later there comes a time in a writer's life when he exhausts the initial experience of the world that compelled him to write in the first place, and that that moment is a vitally important crossroads: he has to decide whether he will simply go on repeating himself, or try to find his second wind. You said that you yourself had been standing on this crossroads for some time, looking for this second wind. Now that you're almost fifty, how do you feel about this?

I still think that a writer will find himself at a crossroads, probably around the age of thirty-five. At least that's how I felt it. Your first burst of writing necessarily draws on the things you've observed and felt and understood in your youth. One day, however, this initial burst drops off, runs out of steam, and you're faced with the question: What now? How should I go on? And if you don't want simply to reproduce mechanically the things you've already accomplished, you have to take a basic step. But this is very hard to do, because you feel bound by what you've already managed to understand so far, and what you've done. You are bound, in a sense, by your own literary history, and you can't simply slip out of that history and start again from the ground up. Moreover, you've become a little more modest, you've learned a few things, you've lost your literary virginity, as it were, with the wonderful arrogance, self-confidence, the still-sharp ability to see that goes with it.

I still think that this is true. But does it apply to me? Frankly, I'm not sure I have found anything like my second wind. After those first plays, which belong to that happy period of my first outburst of creativity, and which reflect my initial experience of the world, I've written quite a few other plays, some of which I'm rather fond of. But I'm still not entirely certain that I've really rediscovered myself. I can't write the way I used to write when I was young: I'm different, the times are different, and I'm interested in different things. But I don't think I would go so far as to say that aesthetically, for instance, I'm now walking on a new path. I'm still searching, in fact—searching for that second wind. Who knows whether I'll ever find it, or whether it can even be found. I mean, I don't know whether all the other things I will eventually write will not remain anchored forever in a feeling of merely searching for the lost certainty of youth—

In an incredibly short time after you finished **Largo Desolato,** *you finished your next play,* **Temptation.** *Doesn't this indicate that you've found some new approach after all? How do you feel about your two most recent plays?*

I've always taken a long time to write plays; I write slowly and with great difficulty. Usually two or three years go by between plays, and each play goes through several drafts. I would rewrite them, restructure them, worry a lot over them, and once in a while I would give in to despair. I am definitely not a spontaneous type of author. And suddenly a very strange thing happened: in July 1984 I wrote *Largo Desolato* in four days, and in October 1985 I wrote *Temptation* in ten days. Obviously something had really changed; something had happened to me. But I'm

not reading too much into this, and I certainly don't intend to draw any long-range conclusions from a mere change in my working rhythm or method. It doesn't necessarily mean anything in itself, let alone promise anything for the future.

For now, I tend to think there were external factors at work. For instance, when I came back from prison, I had a bad case of nerves. I was constantly depressed and out of sorts; nothing gave me any pleasure. Everything became a duty. At the same time, I carried out these duties, both the real and the apparent ones, with a kind of surly stubborness. An Austrian critic wrote of one of my plays that it seemed to have been written out of the very depths of despair, and that it was my attempt to save myself. I laughed at his notion of how plays got written, but now I feel as though I should apologize to him: perhaps my writing these plays so soon after coming home from prison really was an act of self-preservation, an escape from despair, or a safety valve through which I sought relief from myself.

Another thing, more external but perhaps more important because of that. Among the various manifestations of obsessive neurosis that marked my condition after my return from prison (and perhaps still marks it), there is one that probably every dissident knows: fear for his manuscript. As long as the text into which you've put your best effort, or which you consider very important, is not safely hidden away somewhere, or reproduced and distributed in a sufficient number of copies, you live in constant suspense and uncertainty. And this does not improve with time: you never get used to the notion that your manuscript is constantly in danger. On the contrary, your fear becomes a genuinely pathological obsession. And if the original fear was merely of a house search, or a body search, to be allayed by giving the manuscript to the neighbors in the early-morning hours, before house searches traditionally begin, then over time your fear becomes broader and more general: you begin to fear that they will lock you up tomorrow, that you will die or become ill, simply that something undefined will happen to you (the more uncertain the fear, the more advanced the disease) that will make it impossible for the work to see the light of day. And as the work draws to completion, the suspense grows: you begin to fear that someone will trip you just before the finish line. You begin to look forward to the time when you will have nothing incomplete lying around. Prison merely makes fears of this kind more profound.

I think this played an important role in my case. I wrote both those plays with increasing impatience, in feverish haste, in a bit of a trance. This doesn't mean they're not finished: I would never allow something to leave my hands that I didn't think was finished. It merely means that an imp has taken up residence in me who forces me to finish in a hurry. When the play is done and safely tucked away somewhere, I don't care what anyone does to me. I'm happy; I feel I've triumphed over the world once more. As long as it's lying out there on my table as a practically illegible manuscript, I tremble, not just for the play but for myself—which is to say, for that part of my identity that would be irrevocably torn away from me if the manuscript were confiscated. That's really all I can say in general terms about my last two plays.

Now, about *Largo Desolato*: More than once I've used, and abused, a theme or an idea that comes from the world immediately around me, and so I've earned the silent or vocal rebuke of those who, justifiably or unjustifiably, felt hurt. I always regretted this, but I would never think of dropping such a theme, or of not doing it again. The thing is, I know I have no right to do so. When the drama demands something, I must respect its will and not censor it. If I did, I would be sinning against the very essence of my profession. The role of the writer is not merely to arrange Being according to his own lights; he must also serve as a medium to Being and remain open to its often unfathomable dictates. This is the only way the work can transcend its creator and radiate its meaning further than the author himself can see or perceive. And so—without wanting to—I have sometimes wounded or hurt someone.

In *Largo Desolato,* all those I may once have hurt can see an instrument of divine justice taking revenge on me for them. The damage I inflict in this play is on myself, for

a change. Everyone, including foreign drama critics, tries to see myself in its main character, the deranged Doctor Kopřiva, and many have felt sorry that I'm in such terrible shape. But the injunction not to censor the themes and the motifs that haunt me and inspire me is not something I can respect only when it concerns others, and then reject when I'm the one involved! I knew what I was letting myself in for, but I had no right not to let myself in for it. This play was inspired by my own experiences, certainly more directly than any other play I've written, and this is true not only of the individual motifs, but also about its most basic theme. I really did put a bit of my own instability into Kopřiva's instability, and in a certain sense it is a real caricature, containing elements of me and of my postprison despair. At the same time, it is not an autobiographical play; it is not about me, or only about me as such. The play has ambitions to be a human parable, and in that sense it's about man in general. The extent to which the play was inspired by my own experiences is not important. The only important thing is whether it tells people something about their own human possibilities. And anyway, if I was as badly off as Kopřiva, I couldn't have written a thing, certainly not with any ironic distance, so in fact the very existence of this play argues against its being autobiographical.

A 1976 Viennese production of "Private View."

Regarding *Temptation*: As far as I know, I don't think anyone saw me in that play. And yet it is every bit as much inspired by my personal experience, which was even more profound and painful than the experience that lay behind *Largo Desolato* (Ivan Jirous put his finger on this in his essays on those two plays). But let me approach it somewhat systematically. The plays I wrote in the 1960s tried to grasp the social mechanisms and the situation of man crushed by these mechanisms; that is, they were—as we say today—about the "structures" and the people in them. The theme of man expelled from the structures and at the same time confronting them—in other words, the theme of dissenting opposition or resistance—did not appear. This is understandable: whether we like it or not, we always take off—regardless of how far we wish to fly—from the ground we know. I was "within the structures" then (that my "view from outside" particularized the structures in one way or another is another matter). At the time I had no dissident experience—at least not in the form it took in the 1970s. Later, when I was expelled from the structures and found myself a dissident, I naturally began to explore that situation and examine it in different ways (including the very same "view from outside")! In other words, the ground from which I took off had changed. From this arose the series of Vaněk plays, three one-act plays that finally led to *Largo Desolato,* which examines what happens when the personification of resistance finds himself at the end of his tether.

After *Largo Desolato,* I didn't think I could go any further in that direction. I suddenly felt the need to begin in a completely different way, to draw from another barrel, to abandon the terrain of dissident experience (which in any case was suspected, somewhat unjustifiably, of being too exclusive). In short, I didn't want to depend so transparently on my own experience; I was tired of hearing yet again that dissidents could only write about themselves. Therefore, I decided to try writing about the structures again, as though I were inside them. I intentionally tried to re-create, to some extent, the atmosphere of my old plays. I was curious to see what would come out of it now, face to face with the present, after everything that had happened in the meantime. That was how I found the territory. What was to fill it up, however, has its own, deeper roots.

Ever since 1977, when I was first imprisoned, I'd been haunted by the Faust theme; it was in the air around me. I wasn't in jail for long that time, but even so, for various reasons, it was a difficult time for me. I didn't know what was going on outside; I could only follow the hysterical campaign against Charter 77 in the newspapers. I was deceived by my interrogators and even by my own defense lawyer. I was buffeted by strange and somewhat pyschotic states and feelings. I had the feeling that, as one of the initiators of the Charter, I had hurt many people and brought terrible misfortune upon them. I took upon myself an inordinant share of the responsibility, as though the other Chartists hadn't known what they were doing, as though I alone were to blame.

In this miserable state of mind, I began to understand, toward the end of my stay in prison, that a trap was being laid for me: a relatively innocent turn of phrase—or so I thought at the time—in one of my requests for release was to be published in a falsified version in order to discredit me. I had no idea how to stop this from happening, or how to defend myself against it. It was a very dark time for me, but then odd things began to happen. If I remember correctly, instead of the usual books, like *Far from Moscow,* I suddenly had delivered to my cell Goethe's *Faust,* and then, right after that, *Doctor Faustus* by Thomas Mann. I had strange dreams and was haunted by strange ideas. I felt as though I were being, in a very physical way, tempted by the devil. I felt that I was in his clutches. I understood that I had somehow become involved with him. The experience of having something misappropriated in this way—something I had actually thought and written, something that was true—clarified for me with fresh urgency that the truth is not simply what you think it is; it is also the circumstances in which it is said, and to whom, why, and how it is said. This is one of the themes of *Temptation*. (I've analyzed this experience at some length in my letters from prison, in letters 138 and 139.)

That was when the idea to work this Faustian material up in my own way first came to me. I returned to it several times, but I always threw out what I'd written. In fact, right up to the last minute, I simply did not know how to approach that multifaceted and essentially archetypal theme. Then, last October, I got an idea and began to play with it, to sketch it in my usual fashion, first with graphs of the entrances and exits, the scenes and the acts; then I wrote it. I actually did write the whole play in ten days. So that was how *Temptation* was written. Perhaps I have found, through this play, a new starting point; perhaps I've rediscovered myself; perhaps it is really the beginning of a new stage in my writing. A number of people have told me it's my best play, but I truly can't be the judge of that. Or perhaps, on the contrary, it's just a recapitulation of something I've already dealt with, a kind of personal revival, a résumé of what has already been. I don't know. All I can do is stand behind what I've already told you about this eternal search for a "second breath."

You say that the Faust theme had been haunting you for a long time and that you didn't dare tackle it, or didn't quite know how to deal with it. Are there any other themes that haunt you and that you haven't yet dared to tackle? After this Faust, I find no difficulty in imagining that you might give us a reworked or boiled-down Don Quixote—

Nothing since has impinged upon me quite as strongly. Occasionally I've played with the idea of using other characters, like Don Juan, Oblomov, and their like, and I've even considered throwing a number of characters like that into a single play and having them confront each other. But I've given up such ideas for the time being. . . .

You are in the situation of someone who has been persecuted for some time, a situation that not infrequently leads to a kind of self-worship. How do you fight against this danger? Doesn't it present a threat to your creative work as well?

I don't feel threatened by that particular danger. It has to do with my nature, my disposition, my general type, both as an author and as a man. I'm the kind of person who is always doubting himself. I'm far more sensitive to critical voices than I am to voices that praise me. I hear many different expressions of sympathy, solidarity, respect, and admiration; some have even invested their hope in me. People I don't know call me up and thank me for everything I'm doing. I'm delighted by such voices, of course, because they confirm that our efforts have some resonance, that we are not just crying out in the wilderness. At the same time, however, I always find them somewhat embarrassing, and I continually ask myself whether I really deserve such attention, whether I'll manage not to disappoint all those expectations and live up to all those demands. After all, what have I really accomplished? I've written a few plays, a few articles, I've done some time in prison. I ask myself these questions, and I harbor these feelings, so perhaps the danger of self-worship you raise is not my problem. But I could be wrong; something like that is probably best judged by the people around me.

OVERVIEWS AND GENERAL STUDIES

Phyllis Carey (essay date 1990)

SOURCE: "Living in Lies: Václav Havel's Drama," in *Cross Currents,* Vol. 42, No. 2, Summer 1990, pp. 200-11.

[*Carey places Havel's drama in three major phases: "the early absurdist comedies; the Vaněk morality plays; and the psychological-prison plays."*]

Americans were captivated by the 1989 election of Vaclav Havel, a human rights activist who spent almost four years in prison, as the first president of post-communist Czechoslovakia. Many who had heard that his ideas had played a vital role in the country's "Velvet Revolution" were introduced to his thinking through interviews, particularly the extended dialogue in *Disturbing the Peace,* as well as occasional pieces in the *New York Review of Books.* They learned even more from the philosophical-political essays of *Living in Truth,* and from *Letters to Olga,* the collection of fascinating, philosophical letters Havel wrote to his wife while he was in prison. Havel's political writings emphasize, among a great many other things, the "power of the powerless," the ability of seemingly impotent individuals to transform their societies through assuming responsibility for their humanity and living in truth.

Fewer Americans have been introduced to Havel's dramatic oeuvre, which provides a fascinating counterpoint to his philosophical and political thought. His plays, which have earned an international reputation and have won several awards in the U.S., were banned in Czechoslovakia between 1969 and 1989. In contrast to the moral clarity of the political essays, the plays explore the ethical ambiguity that plagues modern life regardless of its political context.

Havel, who served for a number of years as literary manager of the Balustrade Theater in Prague, has defined his dramatic goal as forcing the viewer/reader "to stick his nose into his own misery, into my misery, into our common misery, by way of reminding him that the time has come to do something about it. . . . Face to face with a distillation of evil, man might well recognize what is good" (*Disturbing the Peace*). Three major phases characterize Havel's drama: the early absurdist comedies; the Vaněk morality plays; and the psychological-prison plays.

Absurdist Plays of the 1960s

Havel's first full-length play, *The Garden Party* (1963), demonstrates his enduring interest in the many roles language plays in modern society. As Havel himself notes, the action of *The Garden Party* is controlled by cliché, which not only inundates the dialogue but becomes the objective correlative of the humans who have surrendered themselves to the bureaucratic system.

The play derives its name from a garden party at an anonymous Liquidation Office. Hugo Pludek, the would-be protagonist, seeks a career in the system, but because each bureaucrat has become merely an interchangeable functionary, Hugo ends up compromising himself out of existence, unaware that the "Hugo Pludek" he is waiting to see at the end of the play is himself. As in the game of chess that forms a recurring motif in the play, the characters move in grid-like fashion within the rigid confines of prescribed, lifeless systems—social, political and linguistic—only to checkmate their own meaningless existences. Like a political address that avoids offending any group or individual, Hugo's final speech, echoing both *Hamlet* and Beckett's *Watt,* reduces the question of being to verbal gymnastics:

> . . . we are all a little bit all the time and all the time we are not a little bit; some of us are more and some of us are more not; some only are, some are only, and some only are not; so that none of us entirely is and at the same time each one of us is not entirely; . . . I don't know whether you want more to be or not to be, and when you want to be or not to be; but I know I want to be all the time and that's why all the time I must a little bit not-be. . . .

If the language games of *The Garden Party* relativize the human out of the equation, the use of a synthetic language —*Ptydepe*—enables Havel in *The Memorandum* (1965), winner of the Obie Award (1967-68) for best foreign play, to focus on the process by which humans abdicate their humanity to linguistic and/or political systems.

Josef Gross, the Managing Director of an anonymous bureaucracy, receives a memorandum in *Ptydepe,* an artificial language designed to make human communication scientifically precise by making words as dissimilar as possible. In his attempts to get the memo translated, Gross experiences the paradoxes of bureaucracy: he can obtain the documents he needs to authorize the translation only by having the memorandum already translated. While he struggles with the irrationality of the system, he falls victim to a subordinate's power play, is demoted, but eventually convinces Maria, a secretary, to translate his memo; the message, ironically, confirms in *Ptydepe* the inadequacy of the new language, urging its liquidation. The play ends with Gross back in charge and with the prospect of a new synthetic language—*Chorukor*—which will operate on linguistic principles of similarity.

In *The Memorandum* Havel explores the scientific effort to transform language into a technological tool. Here, the drive for scientific precision contends with the apparently human need for unpredictability. The language instructor's lesson on saying "boo" in *Ptydepe* illustrates how analysis increasingly deadens spontaneity: The decision as to which *Ptydepe* expression to use for "boo" depends on the rank of the person speaking and whether the "boo" is anticipated, a surprise, a joke, or a test, as in "Yxap tseror najx." Another hilarious example of a simple expression made as complex as possible is the word "Hurrah!," which in *Ptydepe* becomes "frnygko jefr dabux altep dy savarub goz texeres."

The precision exercised on analyzing the trivial contrasts with the imprecision in expressing what may be humanly significant. The ambiguous term "whatever," deemed the most used human expression, is rendered by the shortest *Ptydepe* word, "gh." Ironically, beneath all of the scientific pretensions, body language communicates and carries much of the action.

The preoccupation with using an artificial language in *The Memorandum* draws attention to the technological propensity to focus on means instead of ends. Enormous efforts to communicate precisely are undercut by the banality of what is expressed. Knowing the system, however, enables one to participate in the illusion of power and control. Like the specialized jargon of most professionals, *Ptydepe* represents an elitist code that paradoxically limits human communication both to a small group of *cognoscenti* and to those issues that can be analyzed and labeled.

Gross is caught between the need to fit into the system and his own humanistic platitudes. When Maria, fired because she translated the message without authorization, asks for his help, Gross excuses himself on the grounds that he cannot compromise his position as the "last remains of Man's humanity" within the system. He moves Hamlet's dilemma into Camus' theory of the absurd, and as so often in a scientific age, the descriptive becomes the normative:

> Like Sisyphus, we roll the boulder of our life up the hill of its illusory meaning, only for it to roll down again into the valley of its own absurdity. . . . Manipulated, absurdity . . . automatized, made into a fetish, Man loses the experience of his own totality; horrified, he stares as a stranger at himself, unable not to be what he is not, nor to be what he is.

Gross, the would-be existentialist who is always wishing he could start his life over, cannot translate his own language into responsible action. If Pudnik is entangled in language games devoid of human integrity, Gross demonstrates that when language becomes an end in itself, even the most accurate or the most eloquent expressions become impotent.

In the tradition of Kafka, Camus, and Beckett, probably his most significant mentors, Havel explores in *The Garden Party* and *The Memorandum* the paradox of human rationality pushed to its absurd logical extreme. As in Kafka, anonymous authority figures loom behind the absurd context; as in Beckett, the habits and rituals of daily existence frequently deaden people from the horror of their predicament; as in Camus, there is occasional recognition of the absurdity. But Havel's characters, unlike those of Camus, do not rebel; rather they adapt and use the absurdity as an excuse for their own inhumanity.

The Vanek Plays

Havel wrote three one-act plays in the mid-to-late 1970s that are based on one character, a Czech writer named Ferdinand Vanek: **"Audience"** (1975); **"Private View"** (1975); and **"Protest"** (1978). (In a fascinating twist to dramatic history, three other playwrights adopted Vanek for their own plays—Jiři Dienstbier, Pavel Kohout, and Pavel Landovský.) Havel's Vanek plays focus on the role of the writer in a society whose corruption extends from the workplace to the privacy of home, and even to the professional life of writers.

"Audience" (also published with **"Private View"** under the title **"Sorry . . ."**) is probably Havel's best known work in the United States: it is often paired with *Catastrophe,* a one-act play Samuel Beckett wrote and dedicated to Havel while the latter was in prison in 1982. Although superficially simple, **"Audience"** raises complex ethical questions. Essentially a dialogue between Vanek and the increasingly drunken head-malster of the brewery where Vanek works, **"Audience"** focuses on the brewmaster's attempts to persuade Vanek to compose the brewmaster's weekly reports in exchange for an easier job. To do so, however, Vanek would, ironically, be supporting the system he is against by informing on himself.

Vanek's reluctance to accept the offer precipitates the brewmaster's assault on intellectuals, which some critics see as the heart of the play:

> It's all right if I get filthy—so long as the gentleman stays clean! The gentleman cares about a principle! But what about the rest of us, eh? He couldn't care less! . . . Principles! Principles! Sure you hang on to your flipping principles! Why not? You know damned well how to cash in on them, you know there's always a market for them, you know bloody well how to sell them at a profit! Thing is, you live on your flipping principles! But what about me? . . . Nobody's ever going to look after me, nobody's afraid of me, nobody's going to write about me, nobody's going to help me, nobody takes an interest in me! I'm only good enough to be the manure on which your flaming principles can grow!

The play ends with Vanek making a mock exit and re-entrance, starting the dialogue anew with the malster, this time readily accepting the proffered beer and joining immediately in camaraderie. The "underlying message" of the play, as Damien Jaques (drama critic of *The Milwaukee Journal*) notes, would seem to be that "artists can have principles that they refuse to violate [but] the common man doesn't have that luxury" ["Chamber's 'By Havel, for Havel' Works," *Milwaukee Journal,* 2 June 1991].

But truth, as Havel dramatizes it, is almost never so obvious. Among the inescapable ironies of **"Audience"** is that the brewmaster—rather than not having principles of his own—has merely exchanged them for the mechanics of the bureaucracy and, as a result, has become a slave to the system. Although ostensibly the one in power—he is in charge of Vanek and several other workers—he confesses himself powerless because he is a mere dispensable cog. Vanek, on the other hand, is a threat by virtue of being an authentic human being. The drunken brewmaster, a blustery administrator of the powers-that-be, ends up begging the timid Vanek to bring an actress to see him so that he can believe "I didn't live for nothing—." To "live for nothing," however, as Vanek's reticence implies, is as much a choice as to live on principle, to live for something. The ending of the play, suggesting an alternative scenario, leaves the larger "audience" with the question of which alternative is preferable.

"Living for nothing" comes in many different packages, however, as **"Private View"**—perhaps the most accessible and humorous of Havel's Vanek plays—amply illustrates. Michael and Vera are Westernized Yuppies who have invited Vanek for a "private view" of their newly redecorated apartment. That their lifestyle has become their only absolute is clear early on as Michael proudly shows Ferdinand the Madonna he has long sought in order to fit his "niche." Rather than adjusting the niche, he has traveled widely to find a Madonna the right size. Correspondingly, he and Vera fit all of life's experiences into the niches of their consumer clichés, which they try to convince Vanek are the "solution" to all of his presumed problems: he should redecorate; he should have a child; his wife should take cooking lessons, etc.

As the play progresses, Michael and Vera increasingly sound like commercials. When they reach the topic of their sex lives, they are quite willing to perform a demonstration for Vanek. As Michael notes,

> "Vera has remained as smashing as ever.... The body she's got now! It's a knockout! So fresh and young! Well, you can judge for yourself. Darling, do you mind just opening your dress a little bit? ... After we've finished our little chat, we're going to show you some more, so you'd see what sophisticated things we do to one another."

When Vanek demurs and starts to leave amidst a barrage of advice, Michael and Vera suddenly fall apart. Their facade is their existence, and with no one to impress, they lose their only reason for being. They browbeat Vanek into staying, and the play ends where it began.

"Private View" provides a glimpse of private life withdrawn and alienated from public and political concerns. Michael and Vera accuse Vanek of being a coward and a romantic because he will not compromise enough to get a socially respectable job. They, on the other hand, in substituting consumer comforts and "self-fulfillment" for social responsibility, have become dehumanized, merely part of the decoration in their apartment. The satisfaction Michael finds in the almond peeler he has brought back from the States suggests the way in which their being and purpose have been trivialized, their identity subsumed in the objects that they serve.

Havel, describing elsewhere the interdependence of the social and the private, the historical and the personal, alludes to the problem at the core of **"Private View"**:

> . . . even the most private life is oddly distorted, sometimes to the point where it becomes implausibly bizarre, the paradoxical outcome of a paralyzing desire for verisimilitude. It is obvious what has made this desire so intense: the subconscious need to compensate for the absence of the opposite pole—truth. It is as though life in this case were stripped of its inner tension, its true tragedy and greatness, its questions. (**"Stories and Totalitarianism,"** *Open Letters*)

If the "crisis of human identity" that Havel sees as the central question of all of his plays (*Living in Truth*) afflicts the bureaucrat, the blue-collar worker, and even the purely private relationships of spouses, it also afflicts writers themselves as the Vanek play **"Protest"** illustrates. Like all of his plays, **"Protest"** contains vague allusions to actual events or experiences in Havel's life.

As in the other two Vanek plays—and most of Havel's *oeuvre*—the action takes place in the language, in this case the dialogue between Vanek and Stanek, a fellow writer whose daughter is pregnant by a pop star who has just been arrested on a pretext. Stanek, who enjoys political immunity presumably because he can straddle issues, asks Vanek about protesting the pop star's arrest. When Vanek, who has already written a protest, presents Stanek with the document for his signature, Stanek's inner conflicts come to the fore. In a lengthy monologue Stanek analyzes the "subjective" and "objective" arguments for signing the protest, demonstrating through convoluted logic both how "they"—the authorities—think and how he excuses himself from taking responsibility. His speech embodies "double think," becoming a brilliant exercise in reducing morality to rationality. Stanek does not sign the document and the play ends when Stanek learns that the pop star has been released, making the protest superfluous.

Part of Stanek's rationalizing anticipates what Havel explores in greater detail in *Largo Desolato*: the widespread abdication of personal responsibility to the professionals in morality. Stanek points out that "the rest of us—when we want to do something for the sake of ordinary human decency—automatically turn to you [Vanek], as though you were a sort of service establishment in moral matters." The question of Stanek's signature, therefore, involves his claiming identity as a responsible human being, a claim he is unable to make.

Havel's Vanek, however, around whom moral issues arise, does not play the role of a moral authority; rather, he comes off as a self-ironic, timid soul whose occasional embarrassment becomes the only comment on the "bad faith" of the brewmaster, Michael and Vera, and Stanek. In all three plays Vanek, who speaks very little, becomes a sounding board for the characters' reflections on their own identities and concerns. His simplicity contrasts with their sophistication and sophistry. He occasionally questions, often offers understanding, never condemns. Rather, he allows his own integrity and motives to be questioned and attacked as the other characters attempt to implicate or discredit him. If he is an alter-ego of Havel, he is also an anti-hero, his humility and self-effacement pointing beyond the human to a standard of truth that enables the other characters to glimpse their own duplicity and that gives his own character both its quiet dignity and its self-parody.

Psychological-Prison Plays

When Havel returned from his stay in prison as a result of dissident activities, he wrote a short play (1983) in response to Beckett's *Catastrophe*. The play, entitled **"Mistake,"** foregrounds the human tendency—regardless of political system—toward totalitarianism, not only politically but privately as well. The plot is simple: four inmates in a prison—who have formed their own subsystem with their own kingpin—indoctrinate a new prisoner, who has inadvertently smoked a cigarette before breakfast, on his rights and responsibilities within the system. The new inmate, XIBOY, says nothing throughout the play, merely shrugging and looking embarrassed, to the increasing anger and frustration of the "King" and his cohorts, who finally realize that XIBOY is a "bloody foreigner." The play ends with King's "death sentence" for XIBOY.

The prison setting as a totalitarian system—although no doubt inspired by Havel's own recent experiences—underscores the human propensity not only to adapt to repressive systems but to duplicate them in subsystems, and to subjugate others, attempting to force them into uniformity. The seemingly trivial offense against "non-smokers' rights" becomes a major crime in the context of the repressive systems operating without and within and suggests a subtle challenge to the West's preoccupation with minor "rights" when larger questions of human survival and identity are at stake. The foreigner's death sentence comes about because, speaking another language literally and perhaps metaphysically, he cannot be indoctrinated and subsumed into the system. His silence and lack of complicity become a threat to the status quo.

Havel's two full-length post-imprisonment plays, *Largo Desolato* (1984) and *Temptation* (1985), further explore the themes of **"Mistake."** Unlike the relatively flat characters of Pudnik and Gross in the earlier plays, the post-imprisonment drama excavates much deeper psychological terrain. In addition, the archetype of Faust joins Ham-

let as the subtle distortions of truth become both increasingly ambiguous and perverse.

Largo Desolato, which won a Best Play Off Broadway award for 1985-86, probes the relationship between human identity and the roles one plays. Professor Leopold Nettles, an existentialist philosopher who has been under police surveillance and harassment for writing a paragraph "disturbing the intellectual peace," can escape from his dilemma by declaring that he is "not the same person who is the author of that thing." Nettles is so tortured by the expectations of his friends and by his own self-doubts, however, that he has virtually imprisoned himself within his own apartment and his own mind.

Like Vanek in **"Protest,"** Nettles has been the vicarious moral voice upon whom all his friends, who have surrendered their own voices, depend. He is their excuse not to be. Their vague expectations and dependence contribute to his identity crisis: is there a split between who he is and the roles others expect him to play? The dichotomy between Nettles's current internal torment and the image he has projected in the past is revealed through the other characters. His friend Bertram notes, "I can't escape the awful feeling that lately something inside you has begun to collapse . . . that you are tending more and more to act the part of yourself instead of being yourself."

In fact, Nettles in his desperation increasingly acts the roles that others project on him, using the same phrases they have addressed to him. Urged to put his philosophical ideas to some practical use, he ironically does just that: he uses his reputation and writings to seduce Marguerite, a young student whom he sees as "in mid-crisis about the meaning of life." Before the seduction is complete, however, the agents of the authorities appear. Nettles takes a stand, swearing that he will not disclaim his paragraphs, that he will not give up his "own human identity." The agents inform him that his protest comes too late: he has already given up his identity, and his signature, therefore, "would be superfluous." Like Stanek, Nettles has spent so much time analyzing and worrying about his image that he has lost his own identity in the process. The play ends where it began, but with Nettles taking a bow as the actor playing a role in a play about playing roles.

Largo Desolato anticipates *Temptation* in its depiction of the external and internal demons that make Nettles's existence a living hell. The prospect of going to prison seems trivial in comparison with the torment and restrictions that Nettles experiences as a result of trying to serve all of his self-imposed masters, of playing all of the roles others expect of him. As in a dysfunctional family, most of the other characters have already abdicated their identities, becoming mere stage props or interchangeable characters, as evidenced by their very names—"First Sidney" and "Second Sidney," "First Chap" and "Second Chap," "First Man" and "Second Man." *Largo Desolato* depicts the loss of human identity both by those who depend on others to save them and by those who would save others from their own burden of humanity. For Havel, there are no specialists in being human; every human is challenged to be—or not to be.

Havel's long-term interest in writing a play based on the *Faust* legend found its fruition in *Temptation,* his latest full-length play. *Temptation* is by far Havel's wordiest play as he explores in depth the question of truth and the ways truth can be perverted. Havel's Faust, Dr. Foustka, who is a scientist, has been secretly studying black magic. Fistula, who plays the Mephistopheles role, becomes his mentor and points out that "the truth isn't merely what we believe, after all, but also why and to whom and under what circumstances we say it!" Here, ironically the Devil is paraphrasing Havel, who expressed this definition of truth in a 1982 letter to his wife (*Letters to Olga* [No. 138, 347]). Later, the Deputy of the Institute in the play convolutes the definition:

> The truth must prevail, come what may. But for that very reason we must remind ourselves that looking for the truth means looking for the whole, unadulterated truth. That is to say that the truth isn't only something that can be demonstrated in one way or another, it is also the purpose for which the demonstrated thing is used or for which it may be misused, and who boasts about it and why, and in what context it finds itself.

Foustka begins his struggle with truth where Nettles left off in *Largo Desolato*; Foustka's philosophic description of modern humanity leads Marketa, a secretary at the Institute, to fall in love with him. When, his ego inflated by the "conquest," Foustka is confronted by the Director and accused of pursuing unscientific knowledge, Foustka appeals to scientific truth and morality to exonerate him. He claims that he has studied the occult in order to expose its unscientific basis. Marketa, who has believed Foustka's appeal to a higher authority as a basis for truth, ends up as Foustka's Ophelia, dismissed from the Institute and singing in madness. Foustka later learns that Fistula is a secret agent of the Institute, sent to test his fidelity to scientific truth. Foustka is finally entrapped by the complex web of lies he has woven; like Nettles, he has created his own hellish prison.

Finally aware that his attempts to manipulate the system have failed, Foustka acknowledges the devil—"here among us"—not Fistula, but "the pride of that intolerant, all-powerful, and self-serving power that uses sciences merely as a handy weapon for shooting down anything that threatens it, that is, anything that doesn't derive its authority from this power or that is related to an authority deriving its powers elsewhere." The play ends with a witches' sabbath, chaos, Foustka being set afire, and a fireman coming to put out the flames.

Temptation constantly challenges common definitions of truth while affirming its fundamental significance. Havel masterfully demonstrates how the most "truthful" expressions can be demonic when truth is instrumentalized, made a tool for some human purpose. At the same time, he creates seemingly demonic characters who see clearly the logical inconsistencies of selective duplicity. Ironically, it is a devil figure quoting Scripture who points out that living in lies carries its own rules: "You cannot serve two masters at once and deceive them both at the same time! . . . You simply must take a side!" The play suggests, moreover, that to reduce truth to the limits of rationality in turn distorts the "truths" of that rationality. *Temptation* becomes a comic-bitter indictment of the postmodern mind.

The setting of Havel's plays alternates from modern apartment interiors to anonymous bureaucracies. Although the characters all seem to be aware of "higher authorities," those in charge might as easily be representatives of free-market countries as of communist or socialist regimes. As in Beckett, Havel's perennial setting is metaphysical: the contemporary human mind, imprisoned in its rationality, substituting scientific, political, and consumer systems to fill the need for an absolute.

The question of human identity that Havel explores in all of his works is not the issue of individual self-fulfillment that seems to preoccupy Americans. Rather, it is the universal question of the human on the brink of the twenty-first century, in which technical specialization has, paradoxically, produced greater standardization, and more and more people are living in an artificial environment, seduced by the comforts of effortless existence. The question for Havel from Pudnik to Foustka is whether humans choose to be or not to be human beings, to live in truth rather than to support the lies that make them mere adjuncts of one or another system: "Human identity, simply put, is not a 'place of existence' where one sits things out, but a constant encounter with the question of how to be, and how to exist in the world" (*Letters to Olga* [No. 139, 355]).

And what is truth? Havel never tells us directly in his plays. He assumes that we will recognize the many forms of its opposite—the excuses, subterfuges, rationalizations, illusions, pretexts, sophistries—even if many of his characters do not. Truth for Havel seems inextricably linked with assuming responsibility for one's humanity. To the extent we fail, his drama implies, we live in misery; hope lies in recognizing and taking responsibility for "our common misery."

Marketa Goetz-Stankiewicz (essay date 1991)

SOURCE: "Shall We Dance?: Reflections on Václav Havel's Plays," in *Cross Currents: A Yearbook of Central European Culture,* Vol. 10, 1991, pp. 213-22.

[*In the essay below, Goetz-Stankiewicz traces the dance metaphor through Havel's plays.*]

At fifty-three the Czech playwright Václav Havel has arrived at a crossroad in his life that he hardly could have foreseen. He has been catapulted by the political events in Central Eastern Europe from his writer's desk in a quiet country house in Northern Bohemia to the president's office in Prague's Hradčany Castle, and his life has undergone a change that could hardly have been more drastic. Today his dramatic oeuvre, written over a period of about twenty-five years, comprises nine full-length and four one-act plays (in addition to some early short pieces for stage, television, and radio). When audiences will be able to see a new play by Havel is an open question.

Now, when his name as an important political figure is appearing almost daily in the international press, seems the right time to take stock of his stature as playwright and determine what he has to tell the waning twentieth century, which has seen the splitting of the atom, the rise of the computer, the mechanization of war, the development of artificial insemination, and the realization of the visions of Orwell and Kafka, on the one hand, and of Bosch and Goya, on the other.

In the postscript to a Czech edition of his plays, Havel provides us, in a typically unpretentious way, with an insight into the first stirrings of playwriting in his life. Equally typically, his statements—never couched in merely informative literal prose—also contain a miniature sample of his artistic vision: "In 1956 I was twenty. It was the moment when, for the first time in our part of the world . . . there began that strange dialectic dance of truth and lie, of truth alienated by lie and deceptive manipulation of hopes." ["Dovětek autora," *Hry 1970-1976,* 1977]. Havel feels that this historical moment was felicitous for him as a playwright. Yet despite his claim that he could not have written what he did "without this concrete inspirational background," he was aware that from the moment he started writing, his plays reached beyond the local situation. As he says in a comment for future directors of *Largo Desolato,* written almost a decade later: "Any attempts to localize the play more obviously into the environment where it was conceived . . . would harm it greatly. *Whatever would make it easier for members of the audience to hope that this play did not concern them, is directly opposed to its meaning* [Havel's italics]," ["Z poznámek Václava Havla, psaných pro inscenátory hry *Largo desolato,*" 1984]. Considering the political situation in Czechoslovakia, it is not surprising that Western theater directors and drama critics have tended not to heed the playwright's plea. With interesting and often impressive results Havel's plays have been searched for "clashes between the individual and society," for the deadening influence of "political artificial language" that no longer reflects reality, for rigid power structures and their victims, and for false values and manipulated attitudes, all giving eloquent testimony to an imaginative critic of a totalitarian political regime who was willing to go to prison for his moral convictions. The changed situation today has an odd air of déjà vu about it. In the past there was the "dissident" and "prisoner" obscuring the stature of the writer; now we have the president appearing center stage, and the playwright is literally disappearing in the wings.

When the writer Marie Winn, who translated Havel's latest plays, *Temptation* (1985) and *Slum Clearance* (1987), for the Public Theater in New York, visited Havel in Prague in the spring of 1987, he repeated to her what he had frequently said before in interviews as well as in print, namely that Czech writers "don't really like the word 'dissident.' It makes it seem like a special profession. I'm simply a playwright and it's irrelevant whether I'm a dissident or not" [*New York Times Magazine,* 25 October 1987]. Today one might ironically paraphrase Havel's words: I'm simply a playwright and it's irrelevant whether I'm a *president* or not.

In order briefly to stake out the area of Havel's writings, I would like to bring some other twentieth-century voices into the argument. They are disparate voices from various intellectual disciplines, but they have certain things in common: they reflect postmodern perceptions of the world, and they provide guideposts for orienting ourselves in Havel's dramatic universe—enjoyable and entertaining, yet on a deeper level surprisingly appropriate to contemporary ideas on humanity and its changing views of itself. The voices are drawn from literary theory, sociology, and physics. In his *Physics and Philosophy* [1958] the renowned physicist Werner Heisenberg, author of the principle of indeterminacy, raises two points that relate surprisingly to Havel's work. First, there is his discovery that every act of observing alters the object being observed; second, he notes the difficulty of rendering certain phenomena with ordinary words because "the distinction between 'real' and 'apparent' contradiction . . . has simply disappeared." Physics like philosophy, is faced with a world of potentialities or possibilities rather than one of things or facts."

When Eduard Huml, the sociologist in Havel's *The Increased Difficulty of Concentration* (written in 1968 and, compared with earlier plays, showing a refined perception of the nature of language) dictates to his secretary a treatise about human nature, his statements, though not incorrect, are altered by our observing them in the context in which they are spoken: "Various people have, at various times and in various circumstances, various needs." After pacing about thoughtfully, Huml continues the dictation: "—and thus attach to various things various values—full stop." The fact that these statements, hilariously banal tautologies, are undeniably true does not prevent them from ringing false. Havel has made language transparent and explored its double nature, though in this play the experiment is still somewhat rudimentary, and his language has not yet achieved the opaque yet mirrorlike quality of his later plays—a quality he referred to in his acceptance speech for the Peace Prize of the German Booksellers in October 1989: "Words are a mysterious, ambiguous, ambivalent, and perfidious phenomenon." They can be "rays of light in the realm of darkness" or "lethal arrows. Worst of all, at times they can be the one and the other. And even both at once!" ["Words on Words," trans. A. G. Brain, *The New York Review of Books,* 18 January 1990.]

A cluster of voices pointing in the same direction are concerned with issues of freedom and constraint, of roles and changed identities, of constellations and interdependencies. They belong to the Russian literary theorist Mikhail Bakhtin and the American-Spanish philosopher George Santayana. Both have written about the phenomenon of the carnival. Bakhtin [in *Rabelais and His World*] sees in it "liberating energy of a world opposed to all that was ready made and completed," whose humor "revives and renews because it is also directed at those who laugh." But carnival can also unleash a sense of terror because it reveals something frightening in that which seemed "habitual and secure." The notion of carnival also implies a dance of sorts, a rhythmic swaying controlled by something other than reason. Santayana's lighter but essentially similar vision of the carnival stresses its salutary aspects, its moment of freedom when the exchange of the fig leaf for the mask brings release from habitual restraint, from "custom [that] assimilates expectations" ["Carnival," in *Soliloquies in England*]. It is here that we touch upon a key metaphor in Havel's writings—the dance.

Approaching his plays with the theme of the dance in mind, we discover that another pattern or rhythm, partly a light skipping, partly a dark throbbing beat, emerges beneath the tightly structured, sober surface of his texts. Occasionally the playwright lets this mysteriously threatening rhythm burst forth in the final moments of a play (*The Mountain Resort* [1976] and *Temptation* are cases in point) and calls into question the obviously cerebral control of the rest of the play. A quick scan of the metaphor of the dance in Havel's plays is revealing. In his first play, *The Garden Party* (1963), the dance in its literal meaning is present by implication only: a party surely includes some dancing. Yet the play is permeated by another kind of dance. The protagonist, Hugo Pludek, spends most of the play learning the forms of new behavior with regard to language. He observes the strictly prescribed steps of the "official language" minuet with precisely measured steps forward and backward, carefully placed silences, and clocked pauses, according to a choreography Hugo learns to master during the course of the play. Whoever joins this dance becomes an integral part of its modulations and precisely measured movements. The whole would not be the same without him. This dance of linguistic patterns, unrelated to reality (although seemingly adhering to logic), causes the incessant merriment of the audience, who come to recognize something vaguely familiar. It is here that we have the beginnings of what Havel later called the "adventure" of theater.

In his next two plays Havel perfects his choreography of patterns and movements (or dance steps and figures). In *The Memorandum* (1965) the characters' professional rise and fall turns on their ability to learn the artificial language Ptydepe. This results in a linguistic dance of power performed by the characters, punctuated by a pattern of familiar daily movements—the common exit to the cafeteria, the icons of cutlery held high and ready for use during the ritual of consumption. These two types of prescribed movements, one new but learnable (Ptydepe), the other reassuringly familiar (the ritual lunch breaks), performed with mind and body respectively, are choreographed by Havel into one interdependent cluster of motions, a perfect artifact that recharges its own mechanism and creates its own momentum.

Havel's next play, *The Increased Difficulty of Concentration,* takes this double dance of mind and body one step further. Its mechanistic nature is brought home to the audience by a dramatic trick: the author jumbles the time sequence. Apologies for attempted seductions precede the attempt at seduction itself; characters who in scene 2 seemed well acquainted with the protagonist introduce

themselves to him in scene 5. The comings and goings of a research team collecting "scientific" data to establish a "sample" of human life (Huml's name was chosen at random) alternate with the increasing number of women who, lovingly, are trying to run his life. All this provides a dance of pseudoscientifically and pseudoerotically patterned language that the audience begins to recognize because the patterns reappear at predictable moments. Gradually the audience also realizes that the words remain, but the characters who speak them can be exchanged. In other words, the dance as such remains, but its components, the dancers, change partners and places in the configurations. A kiss on the neck becomes an icon of special devotion; lunch brought in on a tray by wife or woman friend becomes a welcome rest for the hero from the familiar patterns of tearfully extracted declarations of love, linguistic strategies of self-defense, and push-button recall of happy memories.

Before moving on to the most challenging of Havel's plays, his Faust play *Temptation,* I will call on the social scientist among my aiding voices. Since his first major work, the German sociologist Norbert Elias has not only drawn attention to dynamic "figurations" and interdependencies but has also stressed the pervasive tendency to reduce processes conceptually to states. Using the metaphor of the dance, Elias argues against statuary concepts like, say, "the individual" and "society": "One can speak about a dance in general, but no one will imagine a dance as a form outside individuals. . . . Without the plurality of individuals who are . . . dependent on each other, there is no dance" [*Über den Prozess der Zivilisation,* Vol. 1, 1976]. In his well-known essay **"The Power of the Powerless"** (1978) Havel writes about the greengrocer who puts a political slogan into his shop window not because he wants to express his political opinion but because "everyone does it" and "because these things must be done if one is to get along in life." It is not necessary, Havel argues later in the essay, to believe in these things, but if one behaves as though one did, one has accepted the situation. And "by this very fact, individuals confirm the system, fulfill the system, *are* the system." There are numerous other instances where Havel has made a similar point—explicitly in his prose, implicitly and metaphorically in his plays. The dancers *are* the dance.

In *Temptation* the Tempter and the Tempted (although it is not as clear who is who as my naming them implies) hold three razor-sharp dialogues. The former, a smudgy, non metaphysical but obviously astute fellow, makes a puzzling statement. Revealing his own familiarity with the mechanisms of Foustka's reasoning process, his "intellectual rotation," he comments on how Foustka manages to turn his pet ideas "into a sort of little dance floor on which to perform the ritual celebration of his principles." Principles on a dance floor? An intellectual ritual? Is the tight repartee of the two partners to be understood as a pas de deux of ambiguous ethics? But in a pas de deux each partner repeats in variations the steps of the other. Precisely! They dance with their feet, their bodies, their words, following fixed patterns of entrances and exits, appearing and speaking on cue. *Temptation* teems with variations on dance patterns presented as essential ingredients of human relationships. There are two key "dance" scenes: scene 3, the seduction scene, where Foustka, using his freshly discovered powers of linguistic persuasion, explains to Maggie what life is all about, whereupon she swears eternal love to him. The stage instructions for this scene (Havel's carefully planned, metronomically timed patterns of entrances and exits are, as always, of extreme importance) call for a dance at the back of the stage while the seduction dialogue takes place at the front. Partners are changed, and dancers float in and out, interrupting the wooing process. Repeatedly Maggie is being swept off to the dance floor by other partners, and Foustka's own choreographed linguistic mating dance, his "ritual celebration" (Fistula's perceptive words) of what he knows will appeal and achieve his purpose, suffers lamentable interruptions. While waiting for Maggie to return, however, Foustka is approached by another would-be partner, the Director, who, like a strutting peacock, performs another ritual of seduction, though more banal and obvious than Foustka's own, a stock package of I'd-like-to cliches complete with "home-made cherry brandy," a "collection of miniatures," "a good chat," and the possibility to "stay the night."

In the last scene of the play another dance takes place at the institute's office party, a masked ball with a "magical theme" to the evening, including not only pendants and amulets but also "a profuson of devil's tails, hoofs and chains." During the final minutes "a piece of hard rock, wild and throbbing," gets progressively louder while all figures (Foustka excepted) "succumb to the music"; "an orgiastic carnival" ensues, and the stage goes up in flames and smoke. An atavistic, primitive rhythm is unleashed, obliterating the strategic dance steps by which the rest of the play was controlled on every level. The dark and threatening side of the carnival spills onto the stage. There is, however, another variation on the dance in *Temptation*. A character called only the Dancer (literal and iconic meaning in one) appears intermittently at the flat of Foustka's woman friend and brings her flowers, leaving fits of jealousy and possible (but never proven) lies in his wake. At the end of the play he and Vilma execute some complicated tango steps at the moment when Foustka realizes that his own strategic steps of several levels of deceit had been vain and useless.

Thus Havel works with flexible figurations. His characters are parts or particles of certain groups or systems, yet they make up these systems. In the case of *The Memorandum,* Office Director Josef Gross comes full circle in the system to which he belongs. He loses his leading position, is demoted, and ultimately rises again, having learned to live within the constellation of which he is a part. If he watches his step—the English idiom fits the situation perfectly—in the dance of official dos and don'ts, if he says the right words to the right person at the right moment, if he choreographs his language suitably, he might well be able to remain on top of the bureaucratic pyramid he has climbed again at the end of the play.

Havel has remarked repeatedly that he is interested in the composition of "movements of meanings, motivations, . . .

arguments, concepts, theses and words" rather than "the actions of the characters or the progression of the plot" [*Disturbing the Peace: A Conversation with Karel Hvížďala*]. This makes him indeed a "political" playwright in the oldest sense of the adjective. At a performance of *The Memorandum* in 1965, when the protagonist at the end defended the ethical collapse of the world in the jargon of "at that time newly discovered Existentialists," a perturbed member of his audience asked Havel whether he was serious about his defense of this collapse or whether he was trying to criticize this new "Western" philosophy that represented the very opposite of what grimly cheerful official Marxism was teaching. The playwright was delighted because "that particular man was disturbed, and I could not have wished for anything better." The juggling of phrases masquerading as true statements had had the desired effect: it had unsettled a set mind. The playwright had illuminated the mechanism of phrases and revealed their rotating dance within a seemingly closed system.

In one of his letters to his wife from prison, which have now appeared as *Letters to Olga,* Havel writes of "the electrifying atmosphere that attracts me to the theatre," that makes the audience share in "an unexpected and surprising 'probe' beneath the surface of phenomena which, at the same time as it gives them new insight into their situation, does it in a way that is comprehensible, credible and convincing on its own terms." These probes "bear witness, in a 'model' way, to man's general situation in the world. . . . Such theatre inspires us to participate in an adventurous journey toward a new deeper questioning, of ourselves and the world."

What is significant about this passage is that Havel makes it quite clear that as playwright he does not seek answers but rather asks questions; he does not set out to tell us things but invites us to an "adventure." In other words, he puts himself in the same boat with the audience. But what are these adventurous quests that he proposes to us?

Another contemporary playwright might help us out here. The connections between Tom Stoppard and Václav Havel have received some (but not enough) critical attention. Stoppard's recent play *Hapgood* (1988) reveals the artistic kinship of these two playwrights in a new way. Harkening back to Heisenberg, Stoppard's espionage thriller is built around a problem that physics and human beings have in common—their dual natures. As Kerner, the physicist, explains to Blair, the spy catcher: "Every time we look to see how we get a wave pattern, we get a particle pattern. The act of observing determines reality." And later: "Somehow light is particle and wave. The experimenter makes the choice. . . . A double agent is more like a trick of light. . . . You get what you interrogate for." Apply these words to Havel's plays and you have an inkling of what they are about. As his dramatic genius has been refining itself—from the vantage point of today, *The Beggar's Opera, Largo Desolato, Temptation,* and *Slum Clearance* represent his mature period—it has become increasingly difficult to pin down what one might call the meaning of the plays. No wonder, for that is what the playwright is aiming at: "I find it a lot of fun to write various rhetorically adorned speeches in which nonsense is being defended with crystal clear logic; I find it fun to write monologues in which, believably and suggestively, truths are spoken and which are full of lies from beginning to end." Stoppard's Hapgood is perhaps a double agent, perhaps a triple agent; her identity not only remains an open question but also becomes oddly unimportant when we take up the playwright's challenge and realize that she is "like a trick of light," that her nature changes with our question. When Macheath of Havel's *The Beggar's Opera* (1972) claims to join the general whirl of petty crookedness just because he refuses to pose as a lofty hero, this attitude could well be interpreted as being either good or bad (as wave or particle), depending on the interpretation of the director or—if the latter is particularly astute about Havel's work and keeps its mystery intact—on the frame of mind of the audience. Similarly, Foustka's and architect Bergmann's voluble justifications at the end of *Temptation* and *Slum Clearance* shimmer with ambiguities. We cannot but agree to the single statements, yet we feel that the whole thing comes, uncomfortably, to more than the sum of its parts and that it is somehow false or at least suspect.

If we put the ideas gleaned from other thinkers into formulas, we get something like the following: language and reality, order and chaos, individuals as parts and initiators of systems, movement and change as constants, questions determining answers. These are obviously vast and complex issues that touch—or mold? determine?—the lives of all of us. I do not think I am stretching a point if I propose that this is the stuff that Václav Havel's plays are made of, though at first encounter they may seem to be primarily a good show, exciting theater. But now, under Havel's guidance, we shelve the abstractions that represent precisely those static intellectual clichés that he has been trying to undermine all along, and we follow him, with open eyes and open minds, into what he calls the adventure of theater.

Robert Skloot (essay date 1993)

SOURCE: "Václav Havel: The Once and Future Playwright," in *The Kenyon Review,* n.s. Vol. XV, No. 2, Spring 1993, pp. 223-31.

[*In this essay, which was written in the interim between Havel's terms as President of Czechoslovakia and of the Czech Republic, Skloot explores the political nature of Havel's plays.*]

In the short space of a few years, we have been witness to a Havel industry. Images of the Czech playwright-politician appear frequently in the West, and his words are quoted often whenever democrats of all kinds convene. His life is held up as an example of resistance to the tyrant's authority and the terrors of the state, and he is celebrated by those who have suffered brutal indignities as well as by those who have suffered not at all.

In 1992, with the fragmentation of his bipartite nation and the loss of his presidency, the simple fact of his unwavering commitment to human rights and to policies of tolerance and trust has introduced into the politics of the 1990s new spirit of both personal courage and political resolve. The mention of Havel's name is, for most observers, an occasion to chart the possibilities of changing old, repressive, tribal ways for new, humane ones, an exercise all the more needed as neighboring countries hemorrhage in an agony of self-destruction. In this essay, I want to explore the nature of political Havelism by temporarily disengaging it from the newspaper headlines and looking at a number of his plays. In doing so, I want to point out their distinctiveness as well as their problematic aspects and to ask whether, were it not for Havel's political importance, we should attend to (or attend at all) the theater of this astonishingly undramatic actor on the stage of modern history.

One result of Václav Havel's recent celebrity has been references throughout the media to his plays which, it is quite likely, have never been seen or read by most American commentators or journalists. Since 1963, when *The Garden Party* was first produced, Havel has written four short and five full-length plays which are available in English translation, the language in which I have come to know them, and several others. The remainder of Havel's artistic energy has been expended in political essays and correspondence, the latter including *Letters to Olga,* (published in English in 1988), *Disturbing the Peace* (in English, 1990) and *Summer Meditations* (in English, 1992). Havel's plays have been generally neglected by most American theaters. Because the predominant concern of most American theater has been, and continues to be, to provide entertainment for the dwindling numbers of middle-class audiences, Havel is not good "box office." For a while, smaller and "engaged" theaters and a few in universities, will produce Havel's plays as a statement of political solidarity with the momentous changes in European politics. At the same time, they will confirm the feebleness of America's theatrical art to rouse anyone to thought or action.

Aside from its political context, what is the artistic relationship between Havel's plays and those of his contemporaries? Discerning the thread that binds the plays of Czechoslovakia's ex-president to other modern playwrights is important in understanding his theater. One dramatist who comes to mind is Harold Pinter who, not surprisingly, acted in two of Havel's short plays ("**Audience**" and "**Private View**") in 1977 on the British Broadcasting Company. Pinter shares with Havel an interest in how people respond to the space in which they live, particularly the enclosed kind of space which makes Havel's "**Audience**" and *Largo Desolato* reminiscent of Pinter's *The Dumbwaiter* and, especially, *The Birthday Party*. In the latter, first produced in 1958, Pinter creates the figure of Stanley, the inarticulate recluse who is, depending on the interpretation of the text in production, destroyed by a thuggish, malevolent society or "birthed" into a culture which may not be as corrupt as it is pragmatically brutal. In fact, such opportunities for interpretation separate Pinter's plays from Havel's. Pinter's plays suffer markedly when they are "located"; Havel's, on the other hand, are conceived within a specific political context which is very difficult to separate out from the texts and their implications. Pinter, who writes in a democracy, is interested in existential freedom and is nonideological in his plays; confinement is a condition of life, not of politics. Trying to make his plays overtly political (as in the presentation of McCann's Irishness in *The Birthday Party*) restricts and diminishes them.

Havel, who wrote his plays under tyranny, is deeply ideological in both attitude and experience. His plays embody a knowledge of history and are always attached to a context; Pinter's float free and are open to multiple inferences. For Pinter, the threatening "Other" is whoever happens to be the annihilating force of the moment; for Havel, the Other is always the state which may be, depending on the depth of our compromise with its invidious demands, surprisingly benign. Pinter's people talk elliptically, trying to conceal motive and expressing a wide range of psychological subtexts; Havel's people talk ambiguously, seeking to avoid blame or shame, but expressing a very narrow choice of psychological motive. Both writers do create a very powerful sense of the sinister, and Havel's plays may be called, as Pinter's have been, "comedies of menace." Pinter frequently creates a feeling of threat through the use of an enclosed space; Havel often achieves the same effect by including in his plays a character or two, perhaps silent, who represent the omnipresent repressive state, for example Pillar in *The Memorandum,* the Two Chaps in *Largo Desolato,* and the Secret Messenger in *Temptation*.

An even closer theatrical affinity exists between Havel and the English playwright Tom Stoppard, who was born a few months after Havel, also in Czechoslovakia. Kenneth Tynan has written a splendid comparison of the lives, plays and temperaments of the two writers [in *Show People: Profiles in Entertainment,* 1979]. Suffice to say that the two playwrights share a deep mistrust of all orthodoxy and authority, and an identical delight in the liberating power of satirical language. The beginning of Stoppard's *Travesties* with its multilingual, arch use of language made both artistic and incomprehensible (to the audience) in the hands (or at the scissors) of Tristan Tzara, James Joyce and Vladimir Lenin reminds us of Havel's invention of Ptydepe, the unlearnable bureaucratic babble of *The Memorandum,* written in 1965. And, equally important, the "time slips" in *Travesties* have been an identifying feature of Havel's plays since *The Garden Party,* a theatrical device where one scene or piece of dialogue is repeatedly replayed, perhaps modified by changing who says a certain speech or who performs the repeated action.

In Stoppard's play, the "slips" are "under the erratic control" of Henry Carr, his irascible curmudgeon of a protagonist, and Carr's frequent narrative recapitulations in the performance of *Travesties* are intended by Stoppard to be metatheatrical intrusions. Havel uses the technique more

as a metaphorical device, apart from character, in order to signal either a world careening out of control (when the words and actions are accelerated), or one denuded of objective meaning, leaving its inhabitants to their meaningless lives. Stoppard has adapted Havel's *Largo Desolato,* written the introduction to *The Memorandum* in its English translation, and has dedicated his own brilliant political comedy about life under tyranny in Czechoslovakia, *Professional Foul,* to Havel. Geographically speaking, Stoppard is the cultural and national bridge between Havel and Pinter since he was born in Czechoslovakia but relocated to England at an early age. Artistically, he has been more prolific and inventive.

The third and even greater influence on Havel, of an entirely continental source, is Eugene Ionesco. With *The Bald Soprano,* first produced in 1950 and called an "anti-play" by its Romanian-born author, Ionesco began a series of theater pieces extraordinary for their antic humor and complete disregard of what can be called the logical necessities of stage realism. Well into the 1960s, his work endured as one of the dominant influences on European playwriting, and his shadow looms large as a presence in Havel's work. In a brief tribute to Havel ["Candide Had to Be Destroyed," in *Václav Havel; or, Living in Truth,* ed. Jan Vladislav, 1987], Milan Kundera asserts that

> . . . no foreign writer had for us at that time [the 1960s] such a liberating sense as Ionesco. We were suffocating under art conceived as educational, moral or political . . .

> One cannot conceive of Havel without the example of Ionesco yet he is not an epigone. His plays are an original and irreplaceable development within what is called 'The Theatre of the Absurd'. Moreover, they were understood as such by everyone at the time . . .

Looking at *The Garden Party* with its loopy dialogue, nonsensical action and its fragmentation of character (by the end of the play, the protagonist Hugo Pludek has assumed a second identity of the same name), or noting the pretentious social chatter and bourgeois accumulations in **"Private View"**, it is impossible not to perceive the Ionesco of *The Bald Soprano, The Lesson* or *Jack, or the Submission,* the first two of which were produced by Havel's Theatre of the Balustrade in the early 1960s. And Havel's use of doors in *The Increased Difficulty of Concentration* and *Largo Desolato,* in particular as an expression of the intrusions of an erratic, malignant external universe, has Ionesco's type of comic paranoia as its model. Havel, however, adds the political context missing in Ionesco, and Kundera is but one of many observers who see this Absurdism with a political face as a true moment of cultural liberation in the dark history of postwar Czechoslovakian politics.

One additional name must be mentioned in relation to Havel, though not for his structural, scenographic or linguistic similarities. It is a thematic thread that ties Pinter, Stoppard, Ionesco and Havel together with Samuel Beckett who wrote his small *Catastrophe* in 1983 to commemorate and excoriate (though subtly, minimally) Havel's lengthy and near-fatal imprisonment. This thematic line can be expressed as the well-worn theme of "respect for individual worth and the individual's need for dignity," though it is the unique genius of each of these five artists that keeps this concern meaningful and frequently moving. The painful and occasionally fanciful existence of Pinter's Stanley, of Stoppard's Henry Carr, of Ionesco's Berenger and of Beckett's Gogo and Didi are all images of their creators' devotion to the irreducible minimum of human freedom, and it is no coincidence that all of them in their personal lives (though some more than others and Beckett least of all) have committed themselves to fighting on several fronts for a humane existence for all the world's abused inhabitants.

With his election to the presidency, Havel's career in the theater was suspended, and his political commitments needed to be worked out in the "real world." In this connection, I think of the Chilean poet and politician Pablo Neruda (who took his name from a lesser-known Czech writer of the nineteenth century), for just as Neruda's Nobel Prize was earned for literature, Havel may receive his for peace.

Currently, the great attraction to Havel's writing in the West is extra-theatrical, based on its antitotalitarian ideology of tolerance and responsibility, as well as by Havel's personal drama of exemplary courage in the face of oppression. One curious result of recent events in Czechoslovakia is that Havel's political failure now aligns him better with the failure of his plays' protagonists (who share occasional details of a common biography with their author). But if we examine Havel's artistic endeavor apart from his political life, how can we measure his achievement?

Looking at Havel's plays leads even a sympathetic reader to conclude that the stylistic and structural repetitions, for example, the time warps, the repeated gestures and bits of business, the identical dreary "journeys" of the protagonists (Gross in *The Memorandum,* Huml in *The Increased Difficulty of Concentration,* Nettles in *Largo Desolato* and Foustka in *Temptation*) show Havel repeating himself too much. Thus, *Largo Desolato* and *Temptation,* Havel's last two plays, reveal a continuing preoccupation with outdated theater forms and an inability to drive his thinking or technique into a more moving creative expression than it possessed before the time of his imprisonment in 1979. In his brief tribute to Havel ["Prague—A Poem, Not Disappearing," in *Living in Truth*], Timothy Garton Ash assesses the situation thus:

> . . . I still cannot avoid a deeper disappointment. The play [*Temptation,* produced in 1986 in Vienna], even as Havel has written it, is weak. And it is weak, it seems to me, for reasons directly related to his situation. For a start, the dramaturgy and stage effects envisioned in his very detailed stage directions are stilted, and if not stilted, then dated—all stroboscopes and smoke, *circa* 1966. Not surprising if you consider that he has been unable to work in the theatre for eighteen years.

In 1986, in a culinary metaphor Brecht would have loved and perhaps agreed with, Ash concludes about *Temptation*: "The thing is overcooked."

The comparison to Ionesco now becomes useful, for it has long been noted that the best efforts of Ionesco are the early, short plays like those mentioned above. Absurdist drama, already a historical detail in the postmodern theater and unknown firsthand to anyone under thirty, was most successful when it remained playfully brief. When lengthy, as is Ionesco's work since *Exit the King* (1962), Absurdism turned turgid and not a little pompous because the fun (often touched with horror) and the spirit of invention was unsustainable. Consider the conclusions of *The Garden Party* and *Temptation,* two Havel plays separated by almost a quarter of a century. The former ends with a character hidden inside a large cupboard (eavesdroppers appear in several Havel plays), making a surprising entrance, walking down to the footlights and directly addressing the audience: "And now, without sort of much ado—go home!" For this play, essentially a cartoon, the ending is abrupt, silly and appropriate. But the ending of *Temptation,* a play that attempts to deal with some of the same themes as *The Garden Party* (the language of bureaucracy, the description of life without commitment), seems to result from an exhausted imagination that has reached a point of no return, and no advance. The concluding dance which Havel describes as "a crazy, orgiastic masked ball or witches' sabbath" is accompanied by excruciatingly loud music and an auditorium full of smoke. The stage direction reads:

> The music suddenly stops, the house lights go on, the smoke fades and it becomes evident that at some point during all this the curtain has fallen. After a very brief silence, music comes on again, now at a bearable level of loudness—the most banal commercial music possible. If the smoke—or the play itself—hasn't caused the audience to flee, and if there are still a few left in the audience who might even want to applaud, let the first to take a bow and thank the audience be a fireman in full uniform with a helmet on his head and a fire extinguisher [a major prop in *The Memorandum*] in his hand.

Temptation explores in greater measure Havel's major theme of betrayal (by society, of self), but its satirical attack on a world destined to disappear in flames is too discursive and distended, lacking precision or sting. *Temptation* features the usual Havel touches: repetitive and replayed dialogue or action, long speeches of apology for or exculpation from corruption (Havel's protagonists are frequently compromised intellectuals and/or academics), an environment of bureaucratic timeserving and political cowardice, and ample though insufficient flashes of antic wit. But, unlike Beckett whose work traced an endangered and dying universe with ever greater austerity and concision (including *Catastrophe*), Havel's proliferating scenic and linguistic excesses provide a smaller payoff.

In Tynan's essay referred to earlier, he discusses Stoppard's difficulty in expressing genuine emotion and in creating convincing female characters. These are Havel's problems too, although in his defense it could be argued that in the kind of comic universe he creates, having either would be unusual. Nonetheless Havel's comic plays, essentially cerebral and objective, exclude the opportunity for the expression of deep, genuine feeling. His world is usually one of evasion and avoidance, like the world of classical farce which it frequently resembles in its dependence on rapid entrances and exits through a multiple number of doors. At his weakest, Havel replaces feeling with activity, providing gestures instead of activated concern. When this occurs, as in the recurrent business with PUZUK the computer in *The Increased Difficulty of Concentration,* the face washing/door slamming of *Largo Desolato* or second dance sequence of *Temptation,* the plays lack, in Tynan's phrase, "the magic ingredient of pressure toward desperation."

The most common Havel story (and clearly a political one) involves the increasing pressure of a (male) protagonist to decide whether or not to betray himself or his friends. Mostly, Havel's characters fail the test miserably. But on the way to failure, the plays suggest a way to a true if limited salvation: the involvement in a genuine experience of love with a woman. Thus, in *The Memorandum,* Gross is attracted to the pure adoration of the office clerk, Maria, but he abandons her at the moment of her greatest need and marches off to lunch with his office staff. That Maria remains "happy" because "nobody ever talked to me so nicely before" does not excuse Gross's avoidance of moral action nor his failure to reciprocate Maria's genuine expression of love toward him. Similarly, at the conclusion of *The Increased Difficulty of Concentration,* Huml almost reaches an expressive emotional reciprocity with Miss Balcar who, at one moment in the final scene, is reduced to tears by her need for Huml despite the gassy academic discourse he puts between them. Though he embraces her and kisses her "gently on her tearful eyes," and she exits "smiling happily," it is clear that Miss Balcar will be the fourth of Huml's failures with women in this play and additional proof of his intellectual and political cowardice.

At the end of *Largo Desolato,* Marguerite arrives to give Leopold Nettles one final chance for rejuvenation through love. "You have given me back the meaning to my life," she tells him, "which is to give you the meaning back to yours." But their intense embrace is interrupted by the doorbell, and a terrorized Nettles leaves her immediately to chase after and to be humiliated by the two sinister chaps who inform him his gesture of "heroism" will no longer be required. Lastly, in *Temptation,* it is Marketa who serves as the abused image of innocence when her moment of courage in defending Foustka in front of their hostile bosses ends only in her summary dismissal after Foustka's betrayal of her. She returns later in the play dressed and behaving like a lunatic Ophelia, the one serious moment in the "witches' sabbath," but one deprived of tragic resonance because Havel has her return under peculiar circumstances for a last appearance as one of Foustka's tormentors.

In all of these scenes, I sense that Havel is flirting with a way to express a potentially liberating emotional occasion, liberating to his protagonists and to himself as a playwright of satirical political comedies. But in all of them, he deflects the serious tendencies of the characters and himself, preferring to avoid the entanglements of emotion with a disengaged, objective posture. It would be possible to argue that this lack of emotional commitment is the *result* of the political environment of his country, but I do not believe this is the case. Instead, I see this pattern as a refusal to extend these wonderful comedies into a more profound and troubling territory which would have serious and I think very positive results on Havel's playwriting. Havel turns back to his satire of bureaucratic and academic language in the arias of his cowardly protagonists, preferring the Ionesco "anti-play" to, say, Beckett's "tragicomedy." In this critical context, I would choose the two short pieces **"Audience"** and **"Protest"** as Havel's most successful plays, although I have a great liking for the stylish, sustained confidence of the comic ironies of *The Memorandum.* These plays are relatively brief, with all male characters, and emphasize the anguish of moral action and the fallibility of the human character, and are very funny.

In the third of his **"Six asides about culture"** (1984) [in *Living in Truth*], Havel compares the Czechs with their northeastern neighbors: "We live in a land of notorious realism, far removed from, say, the Polish courage for sacrifice." I understand Havel to refer to the Polish inclination toward the deathly side of human existence rather than his own Czech appreciation of the dark side of human organizations, and to the Polish strain of fatalism which is outside of and resistant to Havel's satirical assault on the notorious political realism of Czechoslovakia. Havel has yet to write a play as powerful as, say, Mrozek's *Tango,* that terrifying exposure of malignant brutality which, it should be mentioned, was adapted for the English stage by Tom Stoppard.

In John Webster's early seventeenth-century tragedy, *The Duchess of Malfi,* the title character confronts her state supported executioners and replies to their murderous threats with an ingenious and unlikely metaphor:

> I know that death hath ten thousand several doors
> For men to take their exits, and 'tis found
> They go on such strange geometrical hinges,
> You may open them both ways.

Havel's stage would until now has had the doors but not the death. His new, resumed life as an ex-president may include an appointment with the theater where, contemplating the murderous world around him, he will be hard pressed to avoid writing pointedly about how countries and peoples die. In his part of Europe the dire situation isn't, or isn't only, a joke.

". . . if you must have a revolution," wrote Timothy Garton Ash [in "The Revolution of the Magic Lantern," in *The New York Review of Books,* 18 January 1990], "it would be difficult to imagine a better revolution than the one Czechoslovakia had: swift, nonviolent, joyful, and funny. A laughing revolution." This revolution culminated in Havel on the balcony overlooking a huge public square, in Prague's open air, unconfined, and recorded by accredited journalists rather than hidden informers. As president, Havel's voice was aspiring and consoling, simple and moral, a deliberate rejection of the anxious volubility and fussy cowardice of his absurd protagonists. Now it appears that he has been given a new, unwanted freedom so that he may, in the words of the Israeli novelist David Grossman, "hallucinate another kind of future," or perhaps, another kind of play. For a brief political moment, Havel's was the triumph of life over art, though the future may demand otherwise.

THE MEMORANDUM

PRODUCTION REVIEWS

Jeremy Kingston (review date 29 March 1995)

SOURCE: A Review of *The Memorandum,* in *The Times,* London, 29 March 1995, p. 28.

[*In the following evaluation of a recent British production of* The Memorandum, *Kingston praises the play but finds its absurdist elements dated.*]

Written and produced in 1965 when its author, Vaclav Havel, was a relatively free man; first staged in this country 12 years later, when he had been placed under house arrest, this famous play [*The Memorandum*] is being revived at a time when he appears to have become incarcerated again, although now as his country's President.

The Velvet Revolution gives a special significance to the words spoken by the typist Maria, the only decent character in the play, trying to embolden her pusillanimous boss: "I believe that if one doesn't give way, truth must always come out in the end."

It has not done so when the play ends, and, perhaps, within the multiple ironies of the closing scene Maria herself has given way. Her boss's fatuous blatherings make her curiously happy. But on the other hand, this may be because she is leaving him to join her brother's theatre group—just such a group as the Theatre on the Balustrade, for whom *The Memorandum* was written.

Her boss is Josef Gross, who could well be known as Josef G, recalling Josef K, Kafka's hero [in *The Trial*], who woke up one morning to find himself arrested. Josef G arrives at his office to find himself being supplanted by his scheming deputy. The weapon used is a synthetic language called Ptydepe, pronounced in four syllables: P-tie-dip-py. This is supposed to increase the efficiency of inter-departmental memos and instead leads to impotence and chaos.

Havel writes amusing scenes in which this ghastly tongue is being taught, culminating in one where the instructor (John Baddeley) has suavely replaced it with another, based on directly opposite principles. But the play's real meat is the endless circling by Gross around the building, becoming ever deeper entangled in the deceit and betrayal. David Allister, in physique like a harassed Clement Attlee although twice the height, gives his voice the wobble of panic and his shoulders the hunched look of a beast of burden.

Shortly before the half-way mark the play is becalmed in repetition, and some of the Absurdist baggage has not worn well. But Sam Walters's production recovers in the second half, and the scenes between Allister and Victoria Hamilton, excellently conveying Maria's plucky goodness, are tense and eloquent.

Among the play's happier inventions is the character of Mr Pillar, played here by Ian Angus Wilkie in silence for almost the entire play, but communicating volumes by his nods, insouciant shakes of the head and ominous shrugs. In an office, or a nation, where human speech is condemned, silence may seem wise. But it fails to save Pillar. The only true course, even if it is foolhardy, is not to give way.

Michael Billington (review date 30 March 1995)

SOURCE: A review of *The Memorandum,* in *The Guardian,* 30 March 1995.

[*In this review, Billington admires the irony in* The Memorandum *as well as the play's "brutally logical satire on the use of language to enforce conformity."*]

Vaclav Havel's most durable play, ***The Memorandum,*** from 1965, gets a welcome revival at the Orange Tree Theatre, Richmond, which for two decades has treated him almost as a house author. And even if the work now seems a trifle over-extended, it reminds one, in its brutally logical satire on the use of language to enforce conformity, of what Havel once called his "spiritual kinship" with Kafka.

Havel shows Josef Gross, the managing director of a large firm, suddenly discovering a surreptitious plan to replace the native vernacular with Ptydepe: a synthetic language designed to iron out all ambiguities and evasions. But although office business is meant to be conducted in this new nonsense speak and the language is assiduously taught, almost no one can understand it. Unable to translate a memo written in Ptydepe or get the authorisation to decode it, Gross realises that "the only way to learn what is in one's memo is to know it already".

In this world of insane Catch-22 bureaucracy, Gross is demoted, then sacked but, with the discrediting of Ptydepe, finally restored to office, only to discover that an even more absurd artificial language has taken its place.

What is impressive is how many targets Havel manages to hit in the course of the play. On the one hand he attacks the linguistic perversion, conformism, surveillance and recantation that are part of any oppressive ideology: on the right, one might add, as well as the left.

But he also exposes the shallow humanism of Gross who, while prating of moral values, is the archetypal organisation man who does everything possible to save his own skin. The play may have grown out of experience of Czech communism: its application, however, is universal.

Havel's concern with symmetry makes it hard for him to end the work when he should. But his writing also has a blithe playfulness seen at its best in the very funny Ptydepe tuition scenes here conducted by John Baddeley with a donnish absorption in linguistic minutiae that suggests Alan Bennett as Shakespeare's Holofernes. In Sam Walters's astute, intelligent production David Allister's palpitating Gross confirms that the victim of conformity is also its ultimate apologist and there is an outstanding debut by Victoria Hamilton as a shy secretary punished for her misplaced sympathy.

It is, among many other things, a sharp-toothed attack on office politics written by a man who himself now seems trapped in the deadening politics of presidential office.

Sarah Hemming (review date 30 March 1995)

SOURCE: A review of *The Memorandum,* in *Financial Times,* 30 March 1995, p. 17.

[*Hemmings argues that the subject matter of* The Memorandum *is still current: "the use of language or jargon to obscure meaning has by no means vanished," she maintains.*]

One problem facing any writer in a totalitarian regime is that many words and phrases are hopelessly devalued by their official use. In *The Memorandum,* the Czech dissident playwright-turned-president Vaclav Havel tackles this dilemma head on, by making language itself the subject of the play. His 30-year-old comedy deals with a monolithic office of uncertain function, where a new language is introduced to make communications more precise and to galvanise the chronically inefficient staff. Naturally, the project is doomed. The language proves too difficult for most employees, those who do master it begin to introduce unwelcome spontaneity, and the labyrinthine rules attached to its use are utterly self-defeating.

It is a funny and very clever play, and its revival at the Orange Tree in Richmond reveals it to be just as pointed as at its premiere. The portrayal of an unwieldy bureaucracy, whose only purpose seems to be self-perpetuation, will strike many people as familiar; the use of language or jargon to obscure meaning has by no means vanished. And while the play is about language, it also uses it as a metaphor: it takes little effort to see the imposed language as communism—or any political system. As a political

parable, the play seems almost prophetic: everything changes, and yet things remain the same.

Havel focuses on Josef Gross, a mild-mannered and ineffectual managing director (a pleasing performance by David Allister), who one day receives a memo so opaque it beats even the legendary Birt-speak communications. The memo is written in Ptydepe, the new language that Gross discovers has been introduced under his feet by his grasping deputy (John Hudson) and his sinister silent sidekick (Ian Angus Wilkie). A whole new industry has grown up behind his back of translators, teachers and experts, and Gross finds himself frogmarched into the new system, struggling to keep his authority and trying, in vain, to get his memo translated.

The play's comic portrayal of a bewildering, intransigent bureaucracy and nightmarish love of control is reminiscent of Kafka, while some of its bully-boy characters and its circular progress remind of you of *Animal Farm.* In the space of 24 hours, Gross is demoted and returned to power, the useless language is introduced, discredited and another introduced to take its place, while those involved in its implementation invent rules so complex they never need to do anything.

If the play has faults they are, as you might expect, that it can be verbose and over-intellectual. But it is very droll and beautifully acted in Sam Walters's meticulous, funny production. A strong cast revels in the play's absurd humour: John Baddeley is enjoyable as a blustering teacher, Roger Llewellyn as a florid translator and Stephanie Putson as a bimbo secretary. Victoria Hamilton, meanwhile, is sweetly serious as the Havel figure, the junior secretary who bucks the system by speaking the truth—and loses her job. The programme offers a primer of essential Ptydepe words, so I can tell you that the play runs at the Zup Zot until April 29.

Paul Taylor (review date 31 March 1995)

SOURCE: A review of *The Memorandum,* in *The Independent,* 31 March 1995.

[*In the following, Taylor offers a favorable assessment of* The Memorandum.]

At the start of Vaclav Havel's *The Memorandum,* the managing director of a company is seen desultorily sorting through his in-tray, when all of a sudden he's arrested by the contents of a particular document. I use the verb advisedly, for from that moment the MD's life is turned upside-down with the abrupt arbitrariness and illogic that characterise Josef K's arrest at the beginning of *The Trial.* The memo that launches the absurdist lunacy in this 1965 play (now spiritedly revived by Sam Walters at the Orange Tree) is written in "Ptydepe". Sounding like gobbledegook, it is a synthetic language that's been designed to eradicate all ambiguity and imprecision from office discourse by making words as different as possible from each other in spelling. On lesser-used nouns, this procedure takes its toll: the word for "wombat" is 319 letters long. Vulnerable to blackmail because he innocently took the company's endorsement stamp home for the weekend, David Allister's splendidly rattled, mystified MD allows himself to be hustled into giving verbal authorisation for the Ptydepe classes that have already been functioning without his knowledge.

By so doing, he plunges his career into a dippily downward spiral and the office into situations that allowed the young Havel to theorise on the tortuous entanglements of totalitarian bureaucracy. To get a translation from Ptydepe, for example, you need an authorisation from someone who needs an authorisation from someone who, by definition, can't give it. The only way to learn what is in a memorandum, therefore, is to know it already.

Though the production can't disguise the protracted nature of the play, Walters' cast brings a biting exuberance to its bureaucratic shenanigans. Particularly enjoyable are the Ptydepe classes presided over by John Baddely's hilarious bow-tied enthusiast of a tutor. He demonstrates, say, the many intention-differentiating Ptydepe equivalents for the word "boo!" with the serene pedantry of the blinkered expert—a fact underlined when, after a power shift in the office, he's seen teaching another synthetic language (based on opposite principles) with just the same dispassionate eagerness.

The desirable goal of reverting to the country's mother tongue can't be achieved because, even when reinstated, the MD is still in hock to his enemies. They, after all, manoeuvred him into the position of authorising the now-despised Ptydepe. The saddest aspect of the whole affair is that it corrupts his human instincts, tempting him to pass off as high-minded necessity his refusal to defend Maria, the young secretary (movingly played by Victoria Hamilton) who had risked her job by translating the original memorandum for him.

This document, though couched in Ptydepe, had, it turns out, pledged full support from on high for the MD's negative stance towards the language—head office, like God, moves in mysterious ways. Curiously undated and with spot-on comic acting, *The Memorandum* gets this reviewer's endorsement stamp.

Lucy Hughes-Hallett (review date April 1995)

SOURCE: A review of *The Memorandum,* in *Plays & Players,* Vol. 24, No. 8, April 1995, pp. 32-3.

[*Below, Hughes-Hallett characterizes the mood of* The Memorandum *as one of "weary, witty disenchantment."*] Vaclav Havel's *The Memorandum* is set in the kind of office in which not only the people but even the notebooks are in danger of having their official existence denied if they lack the proper documents. The office routine is time-wasting and somewhat ludicrous but functions fairly smoothly until the deputy managing director, possibly, or possibly not, prompted by some unknown superior, introduces Ptydepe, a synthetic language designed to ensure the absolute precision of official memoranda by eliminating all the unnecessary and confusing emotional overtones of natural language. It's first rule is 'If similarity between any two words is to be minimised the words must be formed by the least probable combination of letters'. A Ptydepe department is set up to translate memos for staff who have not yet learnt the new language and evening classes instituted to make sure that they do learn it fast. Confusion follows.

The plot is circular, or rather caucus race-shaped, in that everyone ends up exactly where they started in the hierarchy of the firm, but the Ptydepe affair shakes things up enough to reveal both the funny and the sinister side of excessive bureaucracy. In Sam Walters' production the former is sensibly given prominence. The play takes the form of a Kafkaesque political allegory. One of the firm's regular employees is the staff-watcher, whose wretched job is to stand in an airless cupboard all day listening to conversations in adjoining offices; there are references to authorities 'higher up' who never appear and whose opinions, which can only be guessed at, are all-important. The two senior members of the Ptydepe department are given to behaviour strongly reminiscent of some of Pinter's thugs, putting their unshod feet up on the managing director's desk and talking across him, ignoring his nervous questions. But in this production the play's strength lies in its wit and the blend of realism and absurdity in its observation of office life: the pert secretary, Hana, played by Cindy O'Callaghan, who spends all day back-combing her hair, the rituals of coffee-making and lunch in the canteen, the frisson of embarrassment when the wrong person uses a Christian name and, most revealing of all, the tidy emptiness of the executives' desks. (When the managing director and his deputy change jobs for a spell all they have to move are their fire extinguishers.)

Our hero is Mr Gross, managing director, played with pleasant bafflement by Roger Swaine. When he objects to Ptydepe his deputy, using the kind of Alice in Wonderland logic that sounds unanswerable if you say it fast enough, persuades him to step down. Later he is as easily reinstated but the real action is taking place off-stage. The apparently bewildering shifts in the bosses' balance of power seem to reflect quite accurately the mood of the staff, as reported by Hana after her regular trips to the dairy-shop. The ambitious deputy is played fast and smoothly by John Challis but he's eclipsed by his wordless henchman Peregrine Pillar, who says nothing until the final scene but gets most of the laughs. Paddy Ward, who plays him, shrugs, grimaces and twitches with devastating precision.

John Baddely as a Ptydepe teacher is deliciously unctuous and Tony Aitken as the goody-goody of the class gives a marvellous performance, hinting in his few short scenes at a whole story of the unpopular man who tries too hard and whose world melts round him when even the teacher turns on him. But for me the real delight of the evening was Liz Crowther's performance in the tiny part of a sweet downtrodden secretary, the only character in this whole play about work who is ever actually seen to do any (and even her job consists mainly of doing her superiors' shopping). I have seldom seen anyone who looked so obviously, wholesomely good, and her reaction to Gross's cowardly refusal to help save her job—'No one ever talked to me so *nicely* before' is a moment radiant with selfless innocence in an evening whose predominant mood is one of weary, witty, disenchantment.

A PRIVATE VIEW

("THE VANĚK PLAYS")

PRODUCTION REVIEWS

John Simon (review date 5 December 1983)

SOURCE: "Farcical Worlds," in *New York* Magazine, Vol. 16, No. 48, 5 December 1983, pp. 149-50.

[*When the three Vaněk plays were staged off-Broadway in 1983, they were given the collective title* A Private View. *In the following review of that presentation, Simon declares "Protest" the best of the pieces.*]

Vaclav Havel, the Czech playwright and fighter for human rights, is utterly heroic and admirable in the latter capacity. Twice jailed (once for four and a half years) and reduced to such menial labor as working in a brewery for championing freedom in general and the unjustly prosecuted in particular, he has also proved a decent and interesting writer, even if not in a league with such fictionists as Milan Kundera, Bohumil Hrabal, and the brilliant but politically unsavory Vladimír Páral. Though, right now, he is out of jail, Havel's works cannot be openly performed or published in Czechoslovakia, which makes the Public Theater's mounting of *A Private View,* a triple bill of his one-acters, an act of justice as well as satisfaction.

In all three plays—separately conceived but forming a cohesive triptych—Vanek, the manifestly autobiographical hero, confronts representative members of his repressive society, all of whom variously pretend not to be part of the official tyranny, though all of them variously contribute to it. The names of the onstage characters have been changed (although most Czechs would recognize them); many of those mentioned in the dialogue bear their real names. In the first play ["**Interview**"], Vanek is summoned by the Head Maltster of the brewery where he funlessly rolls out the barrels. The H. M., while plying Vanek with the local brew, which the poor fellow detests but must partake of, tries to get him to inform against himself in writing, which the H. M. will pass on to the watchful and suspicious powers that be; in exchange, Vanek

will be moved to a soft office job. "Who but yourself would know the kind of things They want to know?" the H. M. argues with inexorable logic; moreover, as a writer, Vanek is just the person to put those reports in good writing. A somewhat less Kafkaesque subplot has the H. M. urging Vanek to bring a famous actress he knows to the brewery, so he, the H. M., can spend a night of love with her to console him for his dreary life. Vanek handles his boss with consummate tact, but still gets into trouble for refusing to become a self-stoolie (or is it autopigeon?), and the play ends on a grimly funny note.

In the second work ["**Private View**"], a prosperous *aparatchik* and his wife, who claim to be Vanek's best friends, invite the dramatist to dinner with the double purpose of impressing him with all their material goods, many of them brought back from the West, and of hectoring him into making his life as nice as theirs, which he, being in the political and economic doghouse, manifestly couldn't do even if he wanted to. Yet these rich and crass "friends" desperately need validation by an honest man—as the H. M. did, too—and feel likewise indignant when, for all his courtesy, he cannot quite oblige. Here again there are some wonderful ironies, but the best play is the third ["**Protest**"]: Vanek tries to get Stanek, a prosperous sellout of a fellow writer, to sign a protest petition in behalf of a young non-conformist in serious trouble. As it happens, the young man is the boyfriend of Stanek's daughter, and Stanek intended to get Vanek and his group to draft just such a protest; when, however, he is asked by Vanek to add his signature, he comes up with the most hilariously horrifying doublethink to justify his refusal.

There are three difficulties with these highly deserving plays. First, they are all a bit overlong for what they have to say, and, despite a small final twist, telegraph their endings. Second, there is, understandably but disturbingly, something self-serving here that leaves me feeling queasy: This Vanek-Havel is so patient, brave, and incorruptible, yet so tolerant of the weaknesses of others! While they are champions at what Havel, in a feuilleton entitled "The Trial," calls "the puny attempts to skate painlessly over the real dilemmas of life," you can tell by a glance at Vanek's cheap, well-worn, honest boots, the only footgear he has, that no skates have ever been clamped to them. *A Private View* contains noble and harrowing truths that needed saying, but either somebody else should have said them or the hero, even if he is, shouldn't emerge as such a saint.

Lastly, this well-designed and generally well-acted production—Stephen Keep and Richard Jordan are particularly good—is marred to a degree by Lee Grant's overdirecting. Miss Grant, an expert at Neil Simon farce, has goosed all three plays (but especially the second) into such hyperactivity that some of the real humor and horror gets lost in the nonstop shuffle.

Incidentally, for what is redundantly referred to as "a Turkish yataghan," we are given an ordinary curved saber. Vera Blackwell's translation sometimes sounds awkward but not cripplingly so.

A private performance of "Audience" in the 1970s, with Havel playing Vaněk and Pavel Landovsky as the Brewmaster.

Edith Oliver (review date 5 December 1983)

SOURCE: "Voice from Abroad," in *The New Yorker,* Vol. LIX, No. 42, 5 December 1983, p. 183.

[*The following is a highly favorable assessment of the off-Broadway production of* A Private View. *Oliver asserts: "The performance of these plays, in the impeccable translation of Vera Blackwell, is itself impeccable."*]

A Private View, at the Public, is a program of three brief one-act satires by the brave dissident Czech dramatist Vaclav Havel. Each of them is an encounter centering on a character called Vanek, who is plainly based upon the author himself. The first two plays are set in 1975, shortly before Havel was sent to prison for protesting to the government on behalf of human rights; the third was written in 1978, shortly after his release, when he was employed in a brewery, pushing empty barrels around.

"Interview," which opens the evening, takes place in the office of the Head Maltster, who is seated at his desk when Vanek enters after being summoned from his work. The maltster, pouring himself beer after beer, and getting drunker and drunker, first warns Vanek about the people around him and then, after circling the point of the interview for quite a while, offers him a promotion to an office job on a couple of conditions: first, that he bring a famous actress to the factory to meet the maltster, and this Vanek agrees to do; and, second, that Vanek prepare his own

secret report on his activities for the maltster to present to the authorities, and this Vanek refuses to do. The maltster, bursting into sobs, delivers a tirade on the intellectual's contempt for the poor working-man and then passes out, his head on his desk. As Vanek is about to go, the maltster wakes up; having forgotten all that has gone before, he greets Vanek and begins the interview over again.

In the second play, **"Private View,"** Vanek, all but down and out, visits a prosperous couple—his former best friends—in their new flat, which is furnished to the brim with artistic atrocities. The couple offer him bourbon from America, offer to play him new rock records, and offer him boundless advice on how to be as rich and happy as they are. (One way, of course, is to get rid of the "failures and has-beens," the dissident troublemakers who are Vanek's colleagues.) Angrily, he starts to leave; there are sobs and hurt feelings, and he returns. All ends with hugs and kisses and recorded music.

In **"Protest,"** Vanek has been sent for by a successful writer of television scripts who is worried to death about being overheard or spied upon or stepping out of line. He begins by saying how much he admires Vanek's courage and envies his conscience. He then tells Vanek that a young songwriter, who is his daughter's lover, has been arrested for outspokenness, and that the scriptwriter needs Vanek's help. Vanek takes a protest, already prepared, out of his briefcase, and the rest of the play is given over to Vanek's attempts to persuade the writer to sign it, and the verbal and intellectual squirming of the writer, who, of course, refuses to do so.

The performance of these plays, in the impeccable translation of Vera Blackwell, is itself impeccable, under Lee Grant's direction. Miss Grant is able to maintain the correct tone and the European Absurdist style from beginning to end, with an able American company. As Vanek, the one sane figure in a world gone mad, Stephen Keep (who looks like a young Joseph Papp) spends much of his time listening, and he does so with dramatic intensity. The other actors are Barton Heyman, Concetta Tomei, Nicholas Hormann, and Richard Jordan, and all of them are good. The scenery is by Marjorie Bradley Kellogg, the lighting is by Arden Fingerhut, and the costumes are by Carol Oditz.

Leo Sauvage (review date 26 December 1983)

SOURCE: "Dramas in Two Worlds," in *The New Leader*, Vol. LXVI, No. 24, 26 December 1983, pp. 16-17.

[*In this review of* A Private View, *Sauvage praises "Interview" and "Protest" but severely censures "Private View," stating: "The play is bad, and made worse by [director Lee] Grant's misdirection and [actress Concetta] Tomei's physical miscasting" as Vera.*]

Three one-acters written between 1975-78 by the dissident Czech playwright Vaclav Havel have had their initial New York production at Joseph Papp's Public Theater under the title of *A Private View*. The plays, which seem to be excellently translated by Vera Blackwell, premiered separately in London. Naturally, they cannot be seen in the author's own "socialist" country.

The first and last of the trio, **"Interview"** and **"Protest,"** are short tales of extraordinary dramatic power, exemplary in the sense Cervantes gave to the word. Rather unexpectedly, Havel concentrates—with bitter, yet only slightly sarcastic understanding—not on people like himself but on those who have more or less reluctantly adapted to the totalitarian system. What the conformists are still able to feel, and how they cope with it, is revealed when they are faced with a dissident playwright named Ferdinand Vanek, who is obviously Vaclav Havel himself.

Admirably acted by Stephen Keep, Vanek is a quiet, steady, sturdy symbol of human resistance. Havel, a permanent victim of the Prague regime even if he is out of jail for the moment, intends to demonstrate that the authorities have not entirely succeeded in extinguishing the emotional and moral life of their servants. Deep, or not so deep, inside, some of the submissive majority cannot help admiring, indeed envying, the dissident, however they try to wriggle out of the discomposure this causes them.

Unfortunately, there is also the second play, the title piece. Placed between the two small masterpieces, **"Private View"** comes close to spoiling the whole evening. Certainly, it upsets Havel's demonstration.

One of the jobs Vanek/Havel had to take in order to survive through the 1970s was that of a laborer handling barrels in a brewery. **"Interview"** begins when the "head maltster"—as the program identifies him—summons Vanek to his office. Looking like a George Grosz drawing of a fat bureaucrat, the chief is a former blue-collar worker who has managed to climb to a position that allows him to drink beer, fall asleep at his desk, snore, and dream of spending a night in the arms of a beautiful actress whom, he learns with rapture, Vanek knows. Though vulgar and well aware that he has to be very careful to retain his cushy spot, he is neither brainwashed nor mean. Vanek's political status doesn't seem to disturb him, except for one problem: *They* want him to write a weekly report on his worker, and he doesn't know what to say.

Eventually, he thinks of a solution. After long, embarrassed, circuitous small talk punctuated by the opening of beer bottles and interrupted by frequent trips to the toilet, he suggests that perhaps Vanek would be willing to concoct the entries to his own dossier. After all, he is a writer by profession. An easy desk job, it seems, could be arranged in exchange for these innocent flights of imagination.

"Interview" is a farce—thick, coarse, uninhibited, enthusiastically staged by Lee Grant in her directorial debut, and pushed to the limit by Barton Heyman's lavishly unrefined head maltster. But it is not devoid of meaning. When Vanek tries to slip out of the office without having relieved his superior's headache, the "interviewer" arouses himself from a moment of drunken stupor and, forgetting the previous conversation entirely, invites the disgraced intellectual in to start all over again. And Vanek, who has until now carefully kept his distance, is ready to join the man in his revels. In the eyes of Vanek/Havel, then, the dull-witted bureaucrat is not an enemy, only a sad example of Czechoslovakia's "new society."

In **"Protest,"** Vanek's presence unravels a quite different member of the unhappy group who once thought they could reap the benefits of satisfying the regime without becoming dissatisfied with themselves. Stanek, a novelist and television scenarist, and a former good friend of Vanek, has given up all independent writing in favor of his well-rewarded hack work. He has suddenly called Vanek, whom official intellectuals of course prefer to avoid, because a young songwriter lately placed under arrest happens to be the boyfriend of Stanek's daughter. Maybe, Stanek tells Vanek, a protest signed by well-known dissidents would help the young man. Vanek, although previously ignorant of his ex-friend's personal connection to the case, has come to Stanek's comfortable villa with a briefcase containing precisely such a petition. By asking Stanek whether he wants to sign it himself, he launches an exquisitely peculiar dialogue wherein the accommodationist, pen in hand, details all his good reasons for refusing. It's a great scene, superbly played by Richard Jordan as Stanek and flawlessly directed by Grant.

Like the head maltster who represents the industrial bureaucracy, the opportunist from the intellectual bureaucracy is not hopelessly corrupt—for he is as little at ease with himself as with Vanek. In **"Private View,"** by contrast, Michael and Vera, the husband and wife whose apartment Vanek is visiting for the evening, have no conscience. They are soulless, perhaps brainless, certainly tasteless profiteers. Thanks to Michael's position in the upper-class bureaucracy, they have recently traveled to the U.S., bringing back every American gadget, record and piece of furniture they could lay their hands on.

Although Michael would have access to luxuries unknown to his ordinary comrades, it is difficult to believe a high-ranking Communist would openly lead such an "Americanized" life. Surely Michael would understand that he was putting an end to his career.

More important, because it lacks the leitmotif of guilt and embarrassment that carries the other plays, **"Private View"** introduces an element of incoherence into what is supposed to be an interrelated trilogy. Michael and Vera conspire to seduce Vanek into relinquishing his principles out of friendship—or, as becomes increasingly evident, out of desires that reach beyond the bounds of normal friendship. There is an incredibly ludicrous scene where Concetta Tomei, as Vera, exhibits her breasts to Vanek while Michael, portrayed by Nicholas Hormann, vaunts their beauty. No less grotesque is the concluding sequence. When Vanek is told that breaking with fellow dissident playwright Pavel Kohout (throughout, Havel refers to the various offstage characters by their real names) would make life easier for him, he takes his coat and prepares to leave. With Vera crying hysterically on the sofa, however, and Michael swearing at his guest for turning his back on their longstanding bond of affection, Vanek comes back, not to drink beer with a head maltster this time, but to join in what is obviously going to be a triangular sex party.

The play is bad, and made worse by Grant's misdirection and Tomei's physical miscasting. I recommend, therefore, walking out after **"Interview,"** without going too far away to be back in time for **"Protest."**

Robert Brustein (review date 12 March 1984)

SOURCE: "Private Views, Public Vistas," in *The New Republic,* Vol. 190, No. 10, 12 March 1984, pp. 27-9.

[*In the evaluation below of* A Private View, *Brustein argues that Havel has made Vaněk the spokesman for his own views, and in so doing has "created for himself an insoluble problem: how to dramatize the cowardice of others and contrast it with your own heroism, without appearing impossibly self-righteous."*]

I am late in reviewing Vaclav Havel's *A Private View* at the Public Theater for reasons that suggest how political considerations can inhibit one's critical judgments. I have not greatly admired Havel's dramatic writings in the past (I found *The Memorandum,* for example, a post-Absurd-

ist contrivance hamstrung by crude linear plotting), but in view of the courageous public actions of this Czechoslovakian dissident, it somehow seemed insensitive to be making aesthetic judgments on his techniques. How does one criticize the art of a man exemplary enough to draw tributes from Samuel Beckett and Tom Stoppard without seeming to mitigate one's admiration for his personal heroism? Still, Havel is not just a symbol of political persecution, he is also a serious writer who both seeks and deserves an honest assessment. The problem is that Havel's new play is compromised by the very virtues that make him a hero to the West.

A Private View consists of three short playlets unified by its central figure, Ferdinand Vanek. When we first see Vanek [in **"Interview"**], he has arrived, cap in hand, for an interview with his bibulous boss, the head malter in a brewery. An intellectual and a playwright, Vanek has taken this job for reasons partly economic (he needs money), partly political (a troublemaker banned from editorial jobs, he needs to identify himself with working people). But his beer-soaked interrogator, alternately menacing and friendly in the manner of a Kafka bureaucrat, views him as a condescending creature from another class whose friendship with such dissidents as Pavel Kohout is [compromising] his credibility with the authorities. Guzzling bottles of brew and interrupting their conversation for frequent piss calls, the boss holds out promise of a better-paying job if Vanek will fix him up with an actress and admit his dissident sympathies. Always humble and agreeable, Vanek will arrange the assignation, but stoutly refuses to inform on himself. The boss grows more sloshed; Vanek makes another entrance to start the interview again, this time assuming the coarse macho manners appropriate to his environment.

"I am a swine and the swine go home," says Brecht's Kragler of *Drums In The Night,* another character who learns that the best defense against authority is pliancy. The second playlet [**"Private View"**], however, suggests that Vanek's self-denigration is more a modest authorial pose than a strategy for political adaptation. Here Vanek visits two friends from his past, a swinging middle-class couple in a trendy apartment festooned with vulgar objects purchased abroad. "We're having our own little private view here this evening," they tell him. And as he drinks their whiskey from the "States," munches their gourmet "grundles," and tries to admire their conversation-piece confessional and Biedermeier clock, Vanek is unwillingly drawn into the experimental lives of this advanced couple. The wife puts her hand on Vanek's crotch and exposes her breasts, while extolling the sexual prowess of her husband; before long, the couple is making love in front of him—forcing the uneasy Vanek to avert his eyes ("Won't my being around make you nervous?")

Soon they get down to the real subject of the visit, which is to rebuke him for his unorthodox politics and his dissident associates (Kohout is again mentioned as a dangerous influence), meanwhile suggesting that if Vanek would only conform he could be enjoying similar luxuries and privileges. Throughout this colloquy, Vanek remains silent, unprotesting, a figure whose very impassivity seems to make his critics furious. Finally, Vanek confesses he is sorry to have caused his friends so much trouble and anguish, and just as he adapted earlier to the proletarian camaraderie demanded by the head malter, he now sits contentedly listening to his bourgeois friends' rock records and drinking their bourbon.

The plays are apparently based on real incidents (and, according to the translator, Vera Blackwell, "real people"). But although Vanek is undoubtedly an autobiographical figure, there are significant differences between the dissident Havel and his unprotesting hero. These are even more evident in the third and final playlet of the evening, **"Protest,"** which takes place four years later, in 1979. Here Vanek—just released from a year in prison for his political activities—visits a successful writer, Stanek. In the security of his studio, Stanek is able to profess deep contempt for the authorities—"this nation is governed by scum"—but publicly he has been enriching himself by writing for TV and film. Like any other media artist, he displays both guilt and defiance regarding the moral compromises necessary to prosper in such a job. But Stanek greatly admires Vanek's integrity in regard to art and human rights, even though, having read his play about the brewery, he disapproves of the "unrealistic" ending. Now a young friend of his daughter (she is pregnant by him) has been arrested for political reasons, and Stanek wants Vanek to submit a petition for his release.

Vanek has already written such a petition and collected some signatures, including that of Pavel Kohout. It never occurs to Stanek to sign it himself. Instead he makes suggestions about how to make the document milder, less provocative, and then offers Vanek some money for his persecuted comrades (naturally he doesn't want this known). Still preternaturally mild-mannered, Vanek finally asks Stanek to become a signatory to his own petition. The panicked Stanek responds with an outpouring of shame and remorse. He had always assumed that only dissidents made protests, that when you wanted something dangerous done you turned to agents—"Can everybody become a fighter for human rights?" Filled with self-loathing, he determines to regain his lost honor and self-respect, and sign, then rehearses all the reasons why he shouldn't: he will lose his job, his son will be unable to continue with his studies, he will no longer be able to do any "backstage maneuvering." Inevitably, Stanek decides to withhold his name, and when he asks Vanek, "Are you angry?" receives the reply, "I respect your reasoning."

This Christ-like response enrages Stanek. He accuses Vanek of "benevolent hypocrisy," of "moral superiority," of hiding his contempt behind a mask of reasonableness. Still impassive, Vanek refuses to defend himself against these charges, but the issue resolves itself at the end of the play when news comes that the young man has already been released and the petition is unnecessary. Vanek assures the relieved Stanek it was his "backstage maneuvering" that produced the happy results, and, considering for a moment whether to return Stanek's donation, decides to keep the money and leave.

Clearly, Havel has created for himself an insoluble problem: how to dramatize the cowardice of others and contrast it with your own heroism, without appearing impossibly self-righteous. The playwright's strategy is to make Vanek at times a "swine who goes home," scraping before authority and conforming to whatever is demanded, at other times a model of compliant sweetness. Still, the savagery of Havel's satire on the moral dilemmas of those who lack his courage raises doubts about whether he shares his hero's charitable nature, and the difficult sacrifices he has made on behalf of human rights suggest that whatever his faults, conformity is not among them. Vanek, the character, is exonerated from Stanek's accusation of "moral superiority" by the uncritical way he behaves toward others; but the man who invented him cannot entirely escape the same charges.

It is a problem compounded by a conflict between the public and private aspects of Havel's character, between the hero who acts and the playwright who creates. I can't begin to suggest how it could be avoided, except to avoid writing about yourself altogether. But since political protest is at the very center of Havel's obsessions, this alternative would rob him of his subject. Brecht escaped the problem because he had a much less exalted view of human character ("Unhappy is the land that needs a hero"), including his own (he was willing to adopt any stratagem for survival). But without personal heroism, a once proud, progressive nation would be doomed eternally to slavish servility.

Lee Grant's production at the Public Theater strives bravely, though not always successfully, to disguise the contradictions in Havel's style and tone. Marjorie Bradley Kellogg's set is a garish false proscenium decorated with Communist worker symbols, tanks and hammers, providing an ominous reminder of the totalitarian context of the plays. Stephen Keep, looking like a latter-day Leslie Howard, manages to keep the character of Vanek modest and charming in the face of the most irritating provocations. But it is these provocations, and Vanek's gentle response to them, that ultimately undermine one's faith in the veracity of the proceedings, and leave one wishing Havel had found a more direct way to express his outrage and contrast his own behavior with that of his craven friends.

Catharine Hughes (review date 14 April 1984)

SOURCE: "Where Theater Matters," in *America,* Vol. 150, No. 14, 14 April 1984, pp. 281-82.

[*In this review of* A Private View, *Hughes offers a moderately favorable assessment of the play.*]

The first portion of the Czech dissident's three-play evening [*A Private View*] is entitled **"Interview."** Like the remaining two, both of which stand on their own but are interrelated, it features the obviously autobiographical Vanek (Stephen Keep). Initially, he is called into the office of the head maltster of the brewery to which he has been sent to perform menial labor as punishment for his nonconformist behavior. There, amid phony bonhomie, he is asked in effect to inform upon himself in writing. In exchange, he will receive a far softer office job where he will, in theory, be able to pursue his writing. Although observing "I couldn't very well inform on myself," he handles his interrogator with consummate politeness and skill as the brief play moves to its somberly funny conclusion.

In the second segment, **"A Private View,"** Vanek goes to visit his supposedly "best friend," a prosperous aparatchik, and his wife, who seek to impress him with their material possessions, their records from the West, their art and interior decoration. And not coincidentally, to convince him of the error of his dissident ways. He, too, could enjoy such things if only he would confine himself to the political straight and narrow. He cannot agree. Nor can he provide them with the salve to their conscience that such agreement would offer. A combination of bemusement and sardonic observation, he must remain true to what he believes, his worn-out shoes and clothes and his jailing notwithstanding.

"Protest," the best and concluding segment, finds Vanek at the country home of another supposed friend, this one a successful television writer Stanek (Richard Jordan). Stanek's heart, of course, is in the right place; his convenience is not. Vanek has brought with him a protest on behalf of a youthful nonconformist that he wishes Stanek to sign. As it evolves, the boy is the other writer's daughter's lover. Although his daughter is soon to bear the young man's child, a curious and at times very funny form of doublethink enables him to justify his refusal, at least to himself. For, in the end, "It doesn't seem possible that really everyone should be a fighter for human rights."

Havel has twice been jailed for his views, most recently for four and one-half years, so perhaps he can be forgiven for making his alter ego into a little too much of a paragon, a little too pure, a little too perfect. And, frankly, one does not think overly much about this when viewing *A Private View,* which has been somewhat busily directed by the actress Lee Grant. What comes through in the end is a sense of the statement Havel made to *Le Monde* in April of last year: "I am not on the side of any establishment, nor am I a professional fighter against any other. I am simply on the side of truth against lies, of good sense against nonsense, and of justice against injustice."

FURTHER READING

BIOGRAPHY

Kriseová, Eda. *Václav Havel: The Authorized Biography,* translated by Caleb Crain. New York: St. Martin's Press, 1993.
  Written by a friend and colleague of Havel, this book details the author's private and public life, touching briefly on his literary career.

AUTHOR COMMENTARY

Blair, Erica. "Doing without Utopias: An Interview with Václav Havel," translated by A. G. Brain. *Times Literary Supplement,* No. 4373 (23 January 1987): 81-3.
  Critiques both totalitarian and capitalist societies and discusses the role of art in Czechoslovakia.

Havel, Václav. "Second Wind." In *Good-bye Samizdat: Twenty Years of Czechoslovak Underground Writing,* edited by Marketa Goetz-Stankiewicz, pp. 205-10. Evanston, Ill.: Northwestern University Press, 1992.
  Discusses the writing process and the shaping of the writer.

Mestrovic, Marta. "From Prison, a Playwright Yearns for a Stage." *The New York Times* (9 April 1989): II, 5-6.
  Interview in which Havel recounts the effects of his imprisonment on his writing and assesses the state of theater in Czechoslovakia.

OVERVIEWS AND GENERAL STUDIES

Baranczak, Stanislaw. "All the President's Plays." *The New Republic* 203, No. 4 (23 July 1990): 27-32.
  Explores the relationship between Havel's "realistic plays," including the Vaněk series and *Largo Desolato,* and his "parabolic plays," most notably *The Memorandum* and *Temptation.*

Bradbrook, M. C. "Václav Havel's Second Wind." *Modern Drama* XXVII, No. 1 (March 1984): 124-32.
  Surveys Havel's post-1960s plays, which Bradbrook unifies through the theme of conscience and "the power to say NO."

Goetz-Stankiewicz, Marketa. "Václav Havel." In her *The Silenced Theatre: Czech Playwrights without a Stage,* pp. 43-88. Toronto: University of Toronto Press, 1979.
  Broad overview of Havel's dramatic output.

———. "Václav Havel: A Writer for Today's Season." *World Literature Today* 55, No. 3 (Summer 1981): 389-93.
  Traces in Havel's plays the theme of language as a tool used to annihilate the individual.

Grossman, Jan. "A Preface to Havel." *Tulane Drama Review* 11, No. 3 (Spring 1967): 117-20.
  Consideration of *The Garden Party* and *The Memorandum* by the artistic director of Prague's Balustrade Theatre, where they were first staged.

Schamschula, Walter. "Václav Havel: Between the Theater of the Absurd and Engaged Theater." In *Fiction and Drama in Eastern and Southeastern Europe,* edited by Henrik Birnbaum and Thomas Eekman, pp. 337-48. Columbus, Ohio: Slavica Publishers, 1980.
  Surveys Havel's work written prior to 1978 in order to assess the playwright's place within the theater of the absurd.

Stern, J. P. "Havel's Castle." *London Review of Books* 12, No. 4 (22 February 1990): 5-8.

> Relates events in Havel's life to aspects of his plays.

Trensky, Paul I. "Václav Havel and the Language of the Absurd." *The Slavic and East European Journal* XIII, No. 1 (Spring 1969): 42-65.

> Focuses on the use of language in *The Garden Party* and *The Memorandum*, noting Havel's association with the theater of the absurd, particularly Eugene Ionesco's work.

Vladislav, Jan, ed. *Václav Havel; or, Living in Truth.* London: Faber and Faber, 1985, 315 p.

> Important collection of essays about Havel's life and works.

THE GARDEN PARTY

Ambros, Veronika. "Fictional World and Dramatic Text: Václav Havel's Descent and Ascent." *Style* 25, No. 2 (Summer 1991): 310-19.

> Examines *The Garden Party* as the interaction of written text and theatrical performance.

Trensky, Paul I. "Havel's *The Garden Party* Revisted." In *Czech Literature Since 1956: A Symposium,* edited by William E. Harkins and Paul I. Trensky, pp. 103-118. New York: Bohemica, 1980.

> Investigates Havel's use of language in *The Garden Party.*

THE MEMORANDUM

Clardy, J. V. "Václav Havel's *The Memorandum*: A Study in the Terror of the Czechoslovak Bureaucratic World." *Cimarron Review* 6 (December 1968): 52-7.

> Reads *The Memorandum* in the context of the 1968 Soviet invasion of Czechoslovakia, characterizing it as "a terrifying account of the dehumanizing effects of Stalinistic bureaucracy."

Flannery, James W. "Taking Theatre to the Bureaucrats: An Experimental Production of *The Memorandum* by Václav Havel." *Educational Theatre Journal* 29, No. 4 (December 1977): 526-34.

> Explores the challenges and impact of staging *The Memorandum* in a non-theatrical setting.

A PRIVATE VIEW ("THE VANĚK PLAYS")

Blackwell, Vera. "Havel's *Private View*." *Cross-Currents: A Yearbook of Central European Culture* 3 (1984): 107-19.

> Analyzes the function of Vaněk in "Audience," "Private View," and "Protest," recounting the enthusiastic response the plays received at their American premiere.

Quinn, Michael L. "Ferdinand Van k, or Compliant Protest." In *Text and Presentation: The University of Florida Department of Classics Comparative Drama Conference Papers,* Vol. X, edited by Karelisa Hartigan, pp. 73-81. Lanham, Md.: University Press of America, 1990.

> Surveys the Vaněk plays and discusses the appropriation of the Vaněk character by other writers.

TEMPTATION

Goetz-Stankiewicz, Marketa. "Variations of Temptation— Václav Havel's Politics of Language." *Modern Drama* XXXIII, No. 1 (March 1990): 93-105.

> Contends that *Temptation* is the "most challenging" of Havel's critiques of language.

Beth Henley
1952-

(Full name Elizabeth Becker Henley.)

INTRODUCTION

Henley is noted for her comic yet sympathetic depictions of small-town life in the southern United States. Her best-known work is the black comedy *Crimes of the Heart,* for which she received the Pulitzer Prize for drama in 1981. In this and her other plays, Henley combines improbable plots and grotesque situations with sensitive, complex character portraits. For her depictions of Southern life, she has often been compared to such acclaimed writers as Tennessee Williams and Flannery O'Connor.

BIOGRAPHICAL INFORMATION

Henley was born in Jackson, Mississippi, to Charles Boyle Henley, an attorney, and Elizabeth Josephine Becker Henley, an actress. Her mother regularly performed at the New Stage Theatre in Jackson, and as a senior in high school, Henley participated in an acting workshop there. Initially intending to become an actress herself, Henley studied drama at Southern Methodist University in Dallas, Texas. During this time, she wrote the one-act play "Am I Blue?" which was staged in 1973. After receiving a Bachelor of Fine Arts degree in 1974, Henley studied and taught for a year as a graduate student at the University of Illinois at Champaign and acted in summer stock productions. In 1976 Henley moved to Los Angeles with her friend, director-actor Stephen Tobolowsky. Shortly thereafter Henley began her career as a playwright. Her first full-length play was *Crimes of the Heart,* completed in 1978, which won the Great American Play Contest at the Actors Theatre of Louisville, a New York Drama Critics Circle Award, a Guggenheim Award, and a Tony nomination, as well as the Pulitzer Prize.

MAJOR WORKS

Crimes of the Heart is set in a small town in Mississippi and centers on three eccentric sisters who come together in the home of the youngest, Babe, after she has shot her husband because, as Babe puts it, "I didn't like his looks." The other sisters include Meg, a would-be singer who has failed in Hollywood, and Lenny, single and desperately lonely at age thirty. Through their conversations and conflicts, the nature of the sisters' relationships and past lives are revealed. Although none have achieved the popular or critical success of *Crimes of the Heart,* Henley has written several other plays, including *The Miss Firecracker Contest* and *Abundance.* The former work concerns Carnelle Scott, a woman who views entering a local beauty pageant

as a opportunity to overcome her dubious reputation. *Abundance* centers on two mail-order brides and the clash between their dreams and the reality of their lives in the Wyoming Territory of the 1860s.

CRITICAL RECEPTION

Henley's reputation was established with *Crimes of the Heart* and *The Miss Firecracker Contest.* Many reviewers have admired the witty dialogue in Henley's plays and the smooth nonchalance of the characters' colloquial speech. In a review of *Crimes of the Heart,* John Simon praised the dialogue, noting that it is "always in character . . . , always furthering our understanding while sharpening our curiosity, always doing something to make us laugh, get lumps in the throat, care." Other critics, such as Nancy Hargrove, have investigated Henley's treatment of serious themes beneath the surface humor of her plays, noting a concern with death, strange accidents, and disasters. William W. Demastes has seen Henley's fusion of the comic and the serious as a distinctly absurdist perspective on the world, while Billy J. Harbin has interpreted the world of Henley's plays as one of "estrangement, spiritual longing and grostequerie, made all the more remarkable by the calm acceptance of the bizarre as perfectly ordinary."

PRINCIPAL WORKS

PLAYS

"Am I Blue?" 1973
Crimes of the Heart 1979
The Miss Firecracker Contest 1980
The Wake of Jamey Foster 1982
The Debutante Ball 1985
The Lucky Spot 1987
Abundance 1989
Control Freaks 1992

SCREENPLAYS

The Moon Watcher 1983
True Stories [with David Byrne and Stephen Tobolowsky] 1986
Crimes of the Heart 1987
Nobody's Fool 1987
Miss Firecracker 1990

AUTHOR COMMENTARY

Beth Henley with John Griffin Jones (interview date 1981)

SOURCE: Interview with Beth Henley, in *Mississippi Writers Talking,* by John Griffin Jones, University Press of Mississippi, 1982, pp. 169-90.

[*In the following conversation, Henley discusses her development as a playwright and her views of her craft.*]

This interview was conducted about a month before Beth won the Pulitzer Prize for her play, ***Crimes of the Heart***. At the time of our meeting, the play had been accepted for the 1981 Broadway season, having just completed a successful five-week run off-Broadway in December 1980 and January 1981. Our mothers are friends of long standing, and it was through their combined efforts that I secured the scripts of ***Crimes of the Heart*** and ***The Miss Firecracker Contest,*** and then was able to interview Beth during one of her brief visits to her childhood home in Jackson. At twenty-eight, she was not inured to the interview process. She sat in a high-backed chair with one leg under her and spoke in an open and unself-conscious way. On the Monday night in April when we got the news that

Beth had been awarded the Pulitzer Prize there was great excitement and rejoicing in our home.

[Jones]: *This is John Jones with the Mississippi Department of Archives and History, and I'm about to interview Beth Henley. We are at Beth's mother's house. This is where you grew up?*

[Henley]: Well, after the fourth grade I moved here.

Right. It's a house on Avondale in Jackson, Mississippi. Today is Tuesday, March 10, 1981. As I told you before we cut the tape recorder on, Beth, I just wanted to get some basic biographical data first, if you could tell me something about your early life, when and where you were born, your schooling and things like that.

I was born in Jackson on May 8, 1952. I went to St. Andrew's Day School for the first through the third grade, and then I went to Duling Elementary School, and then I went to Bailey Junior High School.

Did you?

Yes, did you go there?

Yes.

I went to Murrah. That's all in Mississippi. Then I went to S.M.U. in Dallas for four years. Then I did one year of graduate work at the University of Illinois.

In what?

In acting.

Theatre arts, yes. Did you act all through high school? Were you in the Murrah players, or whatever?

No. I wasn't even in the Thespians. I'm surprised. When I look back now, most of my friends were in the Thespians, but I never was.

When did you get interested in it?

Well, I did some plays at New Stage. I went to a class that they had there. I can't remember if I was actually in a play there. Yes, I was. Oh, gosh. What's that one I did with John Maxwell?

[Geno]: I can't remember.

[Henley]: *Stop The World.*

Let me mention this: With Beth and me are Chrissy Wilson from the Department, and C. C. Geno, Beth's sister. You did this play when you were in college?

[Henley]: In high school.

[Geno]: And you were in *Summer and Smoke* when you were little.

[Henley]: Right. I did *Summer and Smoke* when I was in the fifth grade.

We'll talk more about that. Are your family roots in Hazlehurst and Brookhaven, the settings of **Crimes of the Heart** *and* **Miss Firecracker**?

Right. My mother's family is from Brookhaven and my father's family is from Hazlehurst.

I see. You still have family there now?

Yes, in both places. My grandmother still lives in Hazlehurst, and some of my cousins and an uncle, my father's brother and his wife. And then in Brookhaven, my mother's mother and some great-uncles and aunts and cousins, and an uncle lives there.

That's interesting. And you would visit there a lot when you were growing up, spend summers there and things?

We'd go down there a lot on the weekends, go down for the holidays.

So you went to S.M.U. for four years?

Right.

I have some newspaper clippings written about you, and in those articles I read that that was where you took your first playwriting course.

Yes.

Your last year?

No, it was my second year.

I'm interested to get you to describe by what process you finally decided to sit down and write. Had you been thinking about it your whole life?

No. I wanted to write, I think, when I was in junior high school, but then I started reading books and I said, "No way. I could never write." It was just too hard. I wasn't even that hot in English, in grammar and spelling and stuff. Then I took a playwriting course just like you take theatre history or lighting design. It was something I thought would be fun. You had to write a play to pass, so I wrote that play.

What play?

"**Am I Blue**" is the name of it. It's a one-act.

And that was your first try?

Well, in the sixth grade I wrote a play that we tried to produce. Other than that, I was in a creative writing course in junior high school, and I remember having to read my story in front of the class. I said, "But I'm not finished," and they said, "Ah, go on and read it anyway, 'cause nobody's written anything anyway." So I got up to read and I was about half-way finished and it wasn't sounding like I wanted it to sound like. I smashed it up and threw it in the trash and ran out of the class crying. Like I thought I was really going to get in trouble, but the teacher felt so sorry for me she didn't say anything.

So that was your first production.

Yes, in that creative writing class.

Was "**Am I Blue**" *ever staged?*

Yes. My senior year—I'd written it my sophomore year—my senior year they were doing Rick Bailey's play called *Badlands* at the time, I think he's changed it to *The Bridgehead,* and they needed a companion piece to go on the bill with it. Jill Peters was a director there, and she was looking through all the old one-acts that had been written and she found mine. She said, "This is the most together play I've come across, so why don't we do it?" So I did a few rewrites on it and they did it to fill out the evening.

Hm. Have you ever or have you yet tried prose or poetry? Is playwriting your only creative concern?

No, I haven't tried them yet. I don't know if I could do them. I used to write some poetry when I was a freshman. We'd all sit down and see who could write the grossest poetry, weird poems. But that's all I did. I did that when I was a freshman. I still don't have good grammar for putting like a whole novel or whole story together. I can just write dialogue.

Do you think that's something you'd like to try? Certainly you have the ear and the eye.

To write like a novel or something?

To write prose.

I might try that. It would be a relief because once you finished it and somebody published it you wouldn't have to worry about it anymore. With a play that's where your problems just begin.

Yes. Tell me, after "**Am I Blue**" *came,* **Crimes of the Heart** *was your next one?*

Well, I wrote the book for a musical my first year after I was out of S.M.U. A friend of mine who's a really talented musician wanted to write a musical, and said, "I really like that play you wrote, so why don't you write the book for this?" So I said okay. I was working at horrible jobs all the next year after I graduated. So I wrote the book for the musical at that time, and the students did it right before I left for Illinois. It was fun because I had never been around musicians that much. It was a 1940s musical called *Parade*. It was a real exciting thing to do.

What is the book?

The book. That's just the dialogue. There's a composer and a lyricist. Somebody writes the music, somebody writes the lyrics to the music, and I wrote the lines the people actually say in between the songs.

Oh, yes. Tell me something about the genesis of **Crimes of the Heart**.

Okay. I was out in Los Angeles, I was trying to act. It was so hard trying to get a job out there. I had an acting agent, but she'd never call you up and I'd sit at home all day long. She was reduced to working at the Broadway Department Store and making calls on her lunch hour. I was working with a group of actors out there, among them Rick Bailey the playwright, and I thought I'd just write a play with parts for people around our age and we can do it as a showcase out there. I thought I may as well do something while I was sitting out there. I'd written a screenplay when I first got out there, so I was kind of in the habit of writing.

What happened to the screenplay?

The screenplay is called ***The Moonwatcher***. It takes place in Illinois, which is from when I worked there, and it's about a girl who's kind of at a crisis in her life. She's been jilted by the boy that she's in love with. She's going to have his baby but he marries somebody else and she has to give up her baby. Now she's all confused. Now, just before I left Los Angeles to go to Dallas, there was a lady who'd read the screenplay and she really liked it and is interested in it, so I'm glad it didn't just die. I thought it was kind of dead. I don't know if anything will happen to it.

What's the difference in writing a screenplay and writing a play?

I don't know. That screenplay was really just one of those gifts, you know, just came to me image after image. It seems it was a lot easier to write than any play I ever wrote because you can just say something very quickly and very vividly and move on to something else. I really enjoyed writing it, but it's just so impossible. For two years after I wrote that I couldn't get anybody to read it, much less consider producing it—you know, millions of dollars. With a play you can feasibly do it on your own. At the time that was a consideration. I wanted something that could be done.

What years are we talking about when you were in L.A. and looking for work?

Okay. I left Illinois the fall of 1976 and moved to Los Angeles. Let's see. My play, *Crimes of the Heart,* wasn't done in Louisville until 1979, so that's that many years of destitution.

Goodness. What were you doing out there during this time, besides writing?

Working at temporary jobs that I hated, trying to avoid work.

Did you ever get any work as an actress?

No, I didn't, come to think of it. I worked in a workshop, but I never got any work.

Out there with some people that you knew from S.M.U. or from Illinois?

Yes, some people from Texas, some people who were at S.M.U. ahead of me were out there.

When did you—I'm asking too many chronological questions. It's like a history test. We'll talk about the other in a minute. When did you decide to sit down and write **Crimes of the Heart**?

Let's see. I wrote that in seventy . . . Daddy died in 1978. That was right before I finished it. I wrote it in 1978.

How long did it take you?

It only took me three months to write the first draft. I had to do a lot of rewrites on it, a rewrite every production. I had to do one rewrite before it went to Louisville, and then one during rehearsals at Louisville, and then for all the other productions I've worked on it.

Were these full-fledged rewrites or just cutting?

Henley: Just mainly cutting. Like the major cut I've done is cut Uncle Watson out. I don't know if you have a script with Uncle Watson in it. I had to cut him out for the New York production. That's just like a page and a half really. But, no, the characters have remained the same. The end is what I've had to work on. It's really pretty much intact. I've added some and subtracted some.

Did it hurt your feelings when they asked you to cut your play?

No. I was overly eager at first, because I was so happy to be having it done. I was just a slave to trying to please them. I was just the opposite. Now I'm not so much.

Now you have your own opinions about it.

Right.

Will you tell me why you sat down and wrote it, what inspired you?

You mean the idea?

Well, yes.

[Henley]: I kind of had two different ideas. One was based on my grandfather, my father's father, had gotten lost in the woods in Hazlehurst. They called up. I didn't go home. I was in Dallas at the time. For three days he was lost in the woods. They had picnic tables out there, and helicopters. In the Copiah County paper they had like, "Thirty foot snake found in the search for W. S. Henley!" And they had paratroopers . . .

[Geno]: The National Guard.

[Henley]: The National Guard. The governor came down. It was just a huge deal. People were out on horseback, people were out on foot.

[Geno]: The Coca-Cola people came in their trucks and advertised free cokes.

[Henley]: Did you go down there?

[Geno]: Yes.

[Henley]: Anyway, my grandfather was just walking through the woods, and according to him was never lost. He knew where he was: Copiah County. He found this little shack. He got to this little shack, and these people brought him into town and they got to a gas station where some people were saying. "They're gonna find that old man, but he'll be dead." And he said, "No they are not! Here I am alive!" So he returned alive after three days. So I thought that would be a good idea for a play: a family crisis bringing everybody back home. It was too close or something, anyway I couldn't get a lead on writing a play about my grandfather getting lost in the woods. I had that idea: a family and everybody gets back home. Also I heard this story about Walter Cronkite was sitting up on the front porch of these rich people's house in the South, and this little black kid came up and said he wanted ice cream, and the man came down and socked him in the face and said, "Don't you ever come around to this front door again." That made such an impression on him. I thought, "God, I'd like to kill somebody for just being cruel like that to some innocent person." So that kind of gave me the idea of Zackery beating up on Willie Jay. I thought it would be interesting to write about a character who tries to kill somebody, but you'd be in their corner rather than in against them. So I kind of combined those two ideas. I guess that's what started it.

You said you were hesitant to write about your grandfather being lost in the woods in Copiah County because it is too close to you. My question is how much of your writing is bits and pieces of what you have heard, your memory, and how much is imagination?

I don't know if I could say a percentage.

No.

But some of the things I might not have heard from my family but have heard from other people in Texas or even in New York that I transposed down to the South, to Mississippi; or even in Los Angeles because that's where I live now. But a lot of them are from stories I've really heard, more in *Miss Firecracker* than *Crimes of the Heart*. I totally made that up about being hung with the cat. I never knew anyone who would shoot their husband because they didn't like their looks, and then go fix lemonade. I made all that up. I don't really.

I know that's kind of a nebulous question. Chrissy and I were talking about that on the way over here. Are there things as a writer that you won't touch, that are too close? Do you feel that as a writer you are able to deal with any emotion of anybody, you can use any family history, that everything is open to you because you're an artist? Or are you shy about talking about certain things?

I think I would prefer to disguise certain things, you know, instead of . . . I've put some things in my plays and I wondered how people would react. Usually they don't even remember saying them or doing them or something like that. For some reason I don't like to get too factual, because it's too confining. It's easier for me to deal with that area of fiction where you're not stifled by having to adhere to "I'm going to write this story to really show how my father was, or my grandmother was."

Right.

I don't think I really answered your question. I guess if it's something really good I don't feel that bad about putting it in, you know. I'll just stick it in there. I don't think I've hurt anybody's feelings so far. People always like to read themselves into your work. When it was about three sisters my sisters assumed it was going to be about them and our lives and everything. They were kind of surprised when they saw it: "That's nothing like me!"

Right. How has your family treated your success as a playwright? Do they like your work?

Oh, they love it. My mother has come up for practically all my productions. C. C. came up to New York with her husband. My mother and her new husband came up to New York. My father was the only one who didn't like it. He died before I ever made any money. I hadn't done anything and he was like, "What are you doing? You should go back to secretarial school and learn to type faster."

Yes. Your father was a Mississippi state senator, Charles Henley.

Right. Charles Henley.

And he died in 1978?

Right.

Before **Crimes of the Heart**.

Right.

I want to ask you something just to get your reaction to it. We don't necessarily have to include this in the transcript. My mother was talking with your mom about your success, and they were kidding like they do, and your mom was saying that your new play **The Wake** *was based on the death of your father and the fact that his family took a long time to bury him, which was a matter of great pain for her. They were joking, you know. Was—did you write it based on your experiences at that time?*

It's not based on any actual experience that I had at that time, except for the experience. It was definitely based on that. We were thinking then, "Gosh, this would make a great play." It was so interminable! All the family was together, and there was all this tension and all these raw emotions. That makes for a good play, I think. You know, people have an excuse to drink and an excuse to scream and an excuse to act their fullest. I thought that would be a real good idea for a play. There's not tons of similarities—I would say there are no similarities between the actual thing here. It was much grimmer than my play. My play's a real comedy. Here it was just really a drag. Maybe if you were in the play you'd look at it as a drag. I don't know.

And the guy in the play actually dies from getting kicked in the head by a mule.

A cow.

Right. Well, when you finished **Crimes of the Heart,** *did you know you had something there? Had you read extensively in the plays that have come out over the last ten years and knew that yours was something new in the art?*

I remember I was at T.R.W. in the parts department, back there after I'd written it. I had taken off from work to try to finish it; you know, temporary work. I thought, "Oh, God, I'll probably be doing this till I'm eighty." I didn't know. I mainly read old things. I missed a lot of reading when I was young, so I like to read more classical stuff. I don't read tons of contemporary plays. I didn't really know what the score was. I didn't even know they weren't doing three-act plays anymore. They told me, "They're not doing three-act plays anymore," and I went "They're not? Wow! Back when I was reading plays they were doing them." So I was real surprised that people liked it as much as they did.

You showed it to friends first. I know the story of your friend sending it to Louisville to the 1979 competition. So what happened then? Did you immediately get an agent? What happened to it after it was recognized?

Well, we had a reading at my house. It was real fun and went well. Then a friend of mine who was at the reading, her agent was trying to start a literary department out in Los Angeles. My agent, Gilbert Parker, was coming in to visit. He didn't have any scripts to read, so my friend told her agent, "Well, give him this of my friend's. It's really good." So she gave it to her agent who gave it to Gilbert. This was before it was done in Louisville. I got in that night and there was a message on my phone machine to call him. I didn't even know who he was. I didn't know who his clients were. "Mark Medoff, now I know he's written something. Paul Zindel?" He thought I was brainless beyond belief. It was so embarrassing. He got off the phone and said, "How can she write such good plays and be so . . ." I don't know if he said, "ignorant." So then he was my agent. He's real nice. He's a good agent. He just liked it from reading it.

I've also read where you said you wrote the play with the intention of playing the part of Babe in a production of it. Any truth in that?

That was in the production we were going to do. They had that publicity that I was going to give myself a part. I was kind of embarrassed by that statement. But I did have in mind with the cast we were going to have that I would play Babe. Now I'm so old I probably couldn't play Lenny. That is true.

Let me ask you this: people that I've talked to have said that acting and writing is really much the same insofar as you're under the spotlight and if it's good it sticks, is remembered. Being an actress, do you think it was any easier for you to write?

Being an actress really helped me writing plays particularly. It is the same for me in a sense. You just get into a character, and what that character wants, what are their greatest dreams, their greatest fears, what would they feel at this moment or in this scene, you can both determine. As a writer I can play a fifty-three-year-old man, or I can play a tall brunette woman, you know, as many characters as you want. The pleasure of writing is when you write, and the hell of it is to go into rehearsals. With acting your creative work is in rehearsals. It's more immediate.

Yes. In the reviews I read some critic likened Babe to a character out of Flannery O'Connor, Meg to a, I believe he says, a benign Tennessee Williams, and then Lenny from Chekhov. Are those people you've read, and did you do that consciously?

I hadn't read Flannery O'Connor. Like, in my first review in Louisville they compared me to her. I hadn't read her. Now I love her. I think she's great. I had read Tennessee Williams and Chekhov, and I think they're great. Now, what did you ask me?

If you drew that parallel consciously, or if that tradition meant anything to you when you sat down to write?

Chekhov and Shakespeare, of course, are my favorite playwrights. Chekhov, I feel he influenced me more than anyone else, just with getting lots of people on stage. I don't do anything close to what he does with orchestration. That fascinates me. I also like how he doesn't judge people as much as just shows them in the comic and tragic parts of people. Everything's done with such ease, but it hits so deep. So I guess I've got to say he influenced me more than I guess anybody.

What about the literary tradition of Mississippi, certainly with fiction. A lot of the humor you use in the two plays I've read is taking that Gothic Southern heritage and turning it upside down, you know, with the mother who hangs her cat and then herself. Do you take that old Southern eccentricity as something you are trying to satirize? Are you really conscious of that?

Well, I didn't consciously like say that I was going to be like Southern Gothic or grotesque. I just write things that are interesting to me. I guess maybe that's just inbred in the South. You hear people tell stories, and somehow they are always more vivid and violent than the stories people tell out in Los Angeles. It's always so mellow.

Right. Do you think you would have been a playwright had you grown up—there's really no way to answer that—say in California? Is your real inspiration here in Mississippi?

I don't think I'd be writing the same type of plays, but I'm not saying California is devoid of inspiration. The poet Charles Bukowski writes very well about Los Angeles. The South just suits me better.

Can you write when you're here in Mississippi?

No. I can't even breathe. I get hay fever every time I come here.

You really can't write?

I can take a few notes or something like that, but there is no way I could sit down and write in my parents' house. It's so in-and-out, you know, and there's too much going on to sit down and write.

When you come to Mississippi do you go to Brookhaven and Hazlehurst and visit the people?

I go to Hazlehurst all the time. I was there Sunday. But I don't go to Brookhaven as often.

I wanted to get you to describe what inspires your characters, your characterizations. Is it the small Southern town that interests you so? Is it something else?

I don't know, because Jackson's not really that small a Southern town. It's the one I grew up in. It's not a large metropolis. I think it's that in a small Southern town there's not that much to detract from looking at characters. If you live in Los Angeles there's just so much going on that you can't write about it. But here things are small and Southern and insular, and you get a bird's-eye view of peoples' emotions. I don't know if that's a good answer.

It is. Will you always return to Mississippi in your writing?

I'm really not sure. My next play takes place in the South, in Jackson, if I ever get to writing on it. But I'm not sure if I'll ever be able to write about Los Angeles, or if that will interest me. I just don't know. I like to write about the South because you can get away with making things more poetic. The style can just be stronger. If I could figure it out I'm sure I could do it with any place, but I haven't.

You've been in New York for a while. Does the cultural world still think things Southern are neat?

I haven't really spent a lot of time in New York because my play only ran five weeks. I was there for the rehearsals and for a few days. There were no lines of people dying to find out about me by any means. I'm not really sure about New York because I was there for only a short time.

Your play is going to run on Broadway next season?

Right. In the fall.

Let me get you to talk to this too: John Simon said that the only fear he had was that your play **Crimes of the Heart** *came from a stockpile of youthful memories, and that there was a chance—I know you remember his saying that—and that there was a chance that you would not be able to come up to what that play is ever again* [New York *Magazine,* 12 January 1981]. *What do you think about that?*

Well, I was just glad I'd finished those two other plays by that time so I didn't panic and be in total distress. I don't think *Crimes of the Heart* was as autobiographical as he was implying. It's true I'm from Mississippi, and I have two sisters, but my mother isn't dead with suicide, my sister hasn't shot her husband, you know, my sister doesn't have a missing ovary. All the characters were imaginary. I guess it is biographical in the sense that they were sisters and they are from Mississippi.

He also said, or others have said, that it is a play about adversity being triumphed over by unity and a family coming together. I've read where you said that, and then said, "I guess that's the theme of the play, that's what they tell me." Was the play defined for you by the critics?

A lot of it really was. It's much easier for me to talk about it after reading my reviews. It was like, "Oh, I see, that's what it's about," because I don't think very thematically. I think more in terms of character and story. I don't necessarily know whether I'm writing it to any end, you know, to any theme. Like, I just found out vaguely what the theme to *The Wake* might be after we had the reading. I said, "I think I may know what this play's about." See, I didn't know when I was writing it, and watching it made it much more simple.

Yes. That's one of the reasons I was anxious to talk with you, especially after reading your quote about the theme of **Crimes of the Heart.** *Many of the artists today are so concerned with art for art's sake, you know, having the right lingo when talking about "their art," that it's really great to be able to talk with someone young like you who has maybe not learned all the ropes, and maybe whose art is more spontaneous and real than the rest. You know what I mean? Is that helpful to what you are trying to do? I don't know how to make a question out of it.*

Well, I think it's helpful not to be confined by anything at the start, you know, "This is what my play's going to be about." Well, maybe that's not what your play's going to be about, maybe you don't have the vaguest idea, maybe your characters want it to be about something else. Also, I don't like the idea of a playwright sitting there saying, "This is what my play's about," because then everybody says, "Well, if the playwright says this is what it's about then this is what it's got to be about." People can have different viewpoints about it. It can mean different things to different people. If you have it in black and white that that's what you're thinking about, you might not think that's what it's about if you read it ten years from now. So I really wouldn't like to write down what I think about the theme of my play.

What about **The Miss Firecracker Contest,** *did that come quickly?*

No, that was hard to write. I was doing a lot of traveling then. Before, I didn't have anything to distract me at all. When I was writing **Crimes** there was no pressure, you know. This was harder to write because I was having to go here and there. And **The Wake** was even harder. That's too bad.

You were writing **Miss Firecracker** *during the Louisville time, or was it before that?*

No, right when I got back from Louisville I started working on it. I worked for television that summer, so I had to do that for three months. Then in the meantime there had been a production in California of **Crimes,** and then there was a production in the fall of **Crimes** that I had to go to. That was in St. Louis. Gosh. Then I got to work on **Miss Firecracker**. Then I finished it, I think.

Was the Jackson New Stage production of it the first?

The second. It was done in Los Angeles at a ninety-seat showcase theatre, the Victory Theatre.

And where is it now?

It's in Dallas.

Right. So it came harder than **Crimes,** *and* **The Wake** *was harder still?*

Right. The next one will be impossible. Actually it's not as hard, it's just getting the time and getting your mind in the place of the play. When I get to work on another play my mind goes to work on that play. Then I have to get back and read over all my notes, and that's real boring but I have to do it so my mind will be on the play.

[Jones]: *Did you have something, Chrissy?*

[Wilson]: *Yes. I just wanted to ask if you think New Yorkers can appreciate your plays as well as Southerners.*

Oh, gosh. I think Southerners would have the edge generally speaking, but I think New Yorkers can enjoy the play. They have, but I do think maybe Southerners have an edge.

[Wilson]: *You said earlier that your characters are not based on your family but maybe a caricature or exaggeration of many Southern families. When New Yorkers go to your play, do you think they think all Southern families*

are like that, or do you think a lot of Southern families are really like that?

I think a lot of Southern families are really like that. I heard people in the audience of **Crimes** say, "You know, my sister's just like that. That reminds me just of my sisters." They can relate to it like that. But I don't know.

[Wilson]: *Better than New Yorkers can.*

No, that is people from New York.

[Wilson]: They all think that.

Yes.

[Jones]: *I've read where you said your next play will be about two old friends that meet in the restroom of the Stardust Ballroom during an Iggy Pop concert. That's your California play.*

Yes. I've been trying to work that out in my brain.

Don't have anything down about it yet?

I have a few notes on it. I think that would be fun to write about. I could write about that, if I could just find the right tone to do it so it wouldn't be commenting on it or taking it lightly. You know, I'd like to make it real.

You would take it seriously?

Yes. You know, I've got to get to where I can understand the people enough to take them seriously and not make fun of them, figure out why they are doing that.

Why they are at an Iggy Pop concert with green hair.

Yes, why people become punkers.

I'd like to read that.

Yes.

Is that pretty much sweeping California? I know Steve, your boyfriend, is involved with a punk rock band.

Right. I don't know if he calls it punk rock, but I do. It's really a rock-and-roll band, the L.A. Slugs.

A good punk name.

Yes. They're real good.

Is he out there now?

No, he's here.

Yes, I've been seeing somebody wandering around. I thought that might be him.

Yes.

What about your success? I know it's changing your life, but is it changing the things you want to do? Will playwriting replace acting as your ambition?

Well, I would like to be able to do both. Like, I'm going to work in a play when I get back out to L.A. Writing is probably—it just gives you so much more freedom, because you can sit down there and you can create all this stuff and you don't have to worry about somebody writing a part that's right for you, casting other people that are good in it. You need so much to really make things work artistically as an actor. I mean, just getting cast at all is a miracle, much less in a part that you give a damn about. So I would like to write and just act in situations that I know would have some importance to me, rather than just beating my brains out to get a commercial.

[Wilson]: *Beth, could you compare your satisfaction with the production here of* **Miss Firecracker** *and the Broadway production?*

Well, they're two different plays.

[Wilson]: *Yes, but I meant just as far as the quality of the production.*

Well, I'll tell you, I was more satisfied with my production here with *Miss Firecracker* than I was with the one in New York. It's surprising. I really think it has a lot to do with having Southern actors in a play. It's such an edge they have to get in understanding these people that I just didn't see in the New York production—it was very Yankee stoic in many ways, instead of just bursting with the passion of these people. I didn't like that at all. I worked to change it, and it did improve. I just think on the whole that down here was much more fun. The show was more my vision than it actually ended up being in New York. The structure was all fine in New York. It just lacked some of the blood.

[Jones]: *Is it hard as a playwright working with directors to get your vision across?*

It's real hard. It really is.

You being young and female I was wondering if you'd gotten any condescension.

Oh, yes! I think anyone would get condescension from directors. So many of them are so insecure. I never realized it, but their jobs are really in jeopardy all the time. The producers can fire them. It's harder to get a job as a director than as an actor. They've got all sorts of responsibilities. I've had generally good relations with the directors. But if you get on their bad side then you better forget it. They won't listen to anything you say, because they don't have to. I never have had power enough to get a director fired, because usually the director is more of a name than me, or is the producer. I try to get along with them, and hopefully be with the director long enough so that we'll have a similar vision of the play.

[Wilson]: *Do you have a say in the casting?*

In New York I did. I did here as a matter of fact.

[Jones]: *What are you going to have to do about the Broadway production, are you cutting it again?*

I'm making just a few changes. Probably people who saw it wouldn't even notice them.

Are you going up there for the casting? Or have they done that?

They haven't cast it. They are trying to get the same three women who did it at the Manhattan Theatre, which would be good because they really are a good ensemble. I mean, regardless of what I said before, they worked well together. And they got good reviews, and nobody wants to tamper with success, especially if the producer really wants to go for the bucks. But they may have other engagements, and you can't book an actor this far in advance according to the rules of Equity. So, we'll have to wait and see if they will accept it again.

So, is L.A. your permanent home now?

Gosh, I still can't relate to it. I have a Mississippi driver's license, Texas license plates and Illinois car insurance. I refuse to say L.A.'s my home. I can't believe it! But now I think I'd rather live in Los Angeles than New York, just because I have a house with a garden and a car you can drive. I don't know. I guess it is, for a while.

What about someone like Miss Welty who writes very movingly about us and lives down the road? Do you think you'll ever be able to do that?

I don't know. I may. Right now there's just too much I want to do besides just come back and live here. It would just be too quiet for me.

It's not too interesting right now to you.

No, that's not true. It is. I've just got friends in Los Angeles, and it would just be hard to leave. Steve works out there.

Well, You have anything else, Chrissy? C. C., you have anything else?

[Geno]: No.

This has been nice. I appreciate your having us over and talking with us. It's been really interesting.

God. How did it compare with all those other guys? They're probably really eloquent.

No, it's perfect. That's why I wanted to talk to you. You are the authentic thing, a real creative talent. Thanks again.

OVERVIEWS AND GENERAL STUDIES

Billy J. Harbin   (essay date 1987)

SOURCE: "Familial Bonds in the Plays of Beth Henley,"
in *The Southern Quarterly,* Vol. XXV, No. 3, Spring,
1987, pp. 81-94.

[*In the following essay, Harbin examines five of Henley's plays, focusing on the "themes related to the disintegration of traditional ideals, such as the breakup of families, the quest for emotional and spiritual fulfillment, and the repressive social forces within a small southern community."*]

There emerged out of the cultural and political upheavals of the 1960s a new feminine consciousness with such fervent intellectual leaders as Betty Friedan, Pam Allen, Shulamith Firestone and Vivian Gornick. In the following decade, the "blunt" feminist rage of the movement gradually gave way to what Jan Stuart calls "a second, rounder-edged phase of feminism . . . characterized by a pragmatic . . . retrenchment which eschews yesterday's rhetoric of sexual politics" in favor of a calmer perception of the female experience "as a metaphor for the human condition" [*Essays in Feminism,* edited by Vivian Gornick, 1978]. The work of contemporary American playwrights has tended to parallel the developments of the feminist movement. Rochelle Owens, Adrienne Kennedy, Alice Childress and Megan Terry—all of whom made significant contributions to the aesthetic revolution of the 1960s—represent the first wave of the new feminine consciousness in the theatre. With ferocious energy their plays spurned traditional forms and styles and zealously dismantled taboos, but the startling originality of their work limited their productions primarily to experimental stages on the fringe of the commercial theatre and university studios. The women playwrights of the 1970s and 1980s—namely, Beth Henley, Marsha Norman, Tina Howe, Lavonne Mueller, Kathleen Tolan, Emily Mann and others—tended to turn from the radical experimentation of their predecessors and sought ways to make use of traditional structures and modes without sacrificing the integrity of what they had to say. Women playwrights wanted to get out of the small spaces to which they had largely been relegated and into the main houses. They sought to make their plays more accessible and "successful." "The answer was obvious: regroup," Tina Howe has said of her own shift from the radicalism of her early plays [in her "Antic Vision," *American Theater,* September 1985]; "Though I couldn't curb my antic vision, at least I could move it into more palatable settings."

Ironically, of the new wave of writers a young southern woman with her first full-length play made the most notable breakthrough into the commercial theatre. In 1981 Beth Henley's *Crimes of the Heart* became the first drama to receive the Pulitzer Prize prior to its Broadway opening, and she, the first woman playwright to receive the award in twenty-three years. The play's enthusiastic reception on Broadway late in the year of the drama's prestigious award brought Henley quickly into the theatrical mainstream; it also opened theatre doors across the nation to the production of her plays, particularly *Crimes of the Heart,* and thrust the dramatist into a commercial prominence long denied more experienced women writers.

Henley's achievement was viewed as a boon for all new writers because of the national attention given to the Pulitzer awards. Marsha Norman's winning of the award two years later with *'night, Mother* helped consolidate the phenomenon of a women writers movement and the emergence of a southern writers contingent. The famed success of both Henley and Norman encouraged surveyors of the arts to examine in a profusion of studies a number of new and not so new women artists as a fresh and unique force in the American theatre. However, while feminists applauded the breakthrough that the Pulitzer awards represented, they also noted that both plays were in a conventional realistic mode, and that neither challenged custom, either aesthetically or politically. They pointed out that the innovative work of earlier risk-taking dramatists, such as Megan Terry, Rochelle Owens and Maria Irene Fornés, had been ignored as influences in favor of the "safer" tradition of male realists.

Beth Henley's *Crimes of the Heart,* after its Broadway opening, was taken on a national tour and subsequently produced in regional and community theatres throughout the states; its success seemed to underscore the notion that the marketable play cannot stray far off convention's beaten path. Tina Howe says, however, that "the serious writer [must] cover her scent." Beth Henley's grave vision in *Crimes of the Heart* is both masked by and realized through a depiction of the ludicrous. Indeed, her antic imagination covers her serious tracks so successfully that the play has been acclaimed as a "constantly hilarious" piece of "homespun" humor [Clive Barnes, quoted in *New York Critics' Review* 42, 1981], or rejected as a trivial "Southern fried Gothic" farce [John Beaufort, in the *Christian Science Monitor,* 9 November 1981]. Henley's southern roots (she was born in Jackson, Mississippi), regional settings and comic emphasis upon the peculiar in ordinary situations led many critics to admire her whimsical imagination and to underestimate the significant implications of her humor. Furthermore, in productions of the play, the comic clues in the script, of which there are many, have not only been seized but enlarged upon, especially the regional dialect and eccentric character behavior, all but engulfing the serious terrain that lies beneath the ludicrous gesture. At the heart of the play, however, there is a disenchanted view of contemporary manners and morals that comic distortions of speech and character cannot blink away.

Crimes of the Heart is about lost American ideals in the larger tradition of native dramatists from Eugene O'Neill to Sam Shepard, who have explored America's shift from a stable, rural tradition of self-reliance and moral certitude to transient instability, materialistic prosperity and spiritual bankruptcy; from family and community solidarity, trust and resourcefulness to fragmentation, incommunicativeness and sterility.

Set in the present in Hazlehurst, Mississippi, the play opens in the spacious kitchen of Old Granddaddy's two-story home with Lenny, in solitary ceremony, celebrating her thirtieth birthday by sticking a candle in a crumbling cookie. The scene evokes Lenny's own image of herself as an isolated and forgotten martyr, long trapped by her own inability to evade the dominance of her grandparents, while her two sisters, Meg and Babe, fled elsewhere to do what they pleased. That there is some self-conscious pleasure in her own birthday tribute to herself, in choosing, in fact, to suffer alone, seems evident from the care she has taken to stage the ceremony; it is not spontaneous. She stopped to purchase the candles on her way home from retrieving Babe's saxophone, and her first action upon entering the kitchen (which marks the beginning of the play) becomes a deliberate ritual of fashioning with rather grim satisfaction her birthday "cake" out of the cookie and candle. Interrupted by the appearance of her neighbor and first cousin, Chick, and then Doc, she hides the birthday evidence. When they leave, she resumes her solemn, solitary party, singing "Happy Birthday" to herself twice.

The scene not only tells us something about Lenny and her circumstance, but marks the boundaries of the play's journey. The isolated Lenny of the first scene reaches by the end of the play a communion with others; she and her sisters, from their various solitary confinements, have come to discover something of value in belonging to each other. The final image of the play depicts a festive and joyful celebration of Lenny's birthday, with the three sisters reunited—tenuously, for this one moment—physically and spiritually as family.

Since birth the pathway of the three sisters has been through a bleak and sometimes dangerous terrain, with experience bringing psychological wounds more than understanding or resourcefulness. Henley captures the now traditional sense of place in southern fiction and drama: the sisters, born in Vicksburg, were torn from their home, moving with their mother to Hazlehurst "to live with Old Grandmama and Old Granddaddy." This disturbing relocation was apparently in consequence of their father's desertion, forcing the mother to seek shelter with the grandparents. Although the script does not divulge precisely when the father left, we know that the move to Hazlehurst was at least twenty years ago, when Lenny was 10, Meg, 7 and Babe, 4.

In Hazlehurst, the parental roles were soon assumed by the grandparents, for after her husband's desertion the mother withdrew into herself, "spending whole days just sitting . . . and smoking on the back porch steps." Of the father's relationship with the children, little is revealed. "Daddy was such a bastard," says Meg. "Was he?" replies Babe, "I don't remember." Lenny says that if he had not left, their mother would still be alive. But Meg tends to disagree, which indicates that even when present he was spiritually absent and that their mother had always been on a self-destructive course. An album photograph of the father smiling at the beach evokes the only other mention of him by his daughters: "Jesus . . . turn the page," exclaims Meg, "we can't do any worse than this!"

The mother's emotionless ties with her children seem to have been more primal and instinctual than loving and motherly in any ideal sense. She found shelter for them, and that done, she psychologically abandoned them, just as the father had done physically, retreating into a solitary meditation with herself, the old yellow cat her only companion. Later, she deserted them completely by committing suicide. The sisters' memories of their mother are detached and without affection, reflecting her own cold indifference to them. Says Babe, "I thought if she felt something for anyone it woulda been that old cat." The telling image Meg presents of Mama in the first act lingers throughout the play: sitting with the cat on the back porch, an anguished prisoner of herself, drawing her only wisp of comfort from endless cigarettes and the flicking of ashes "onto the . . . bugs and ants . . . passing by." This desolate portrait of the mother, the only one her daughters offer, suggests the sterility of their family ties.

The parental guidance of the grandparents was in many ways as barren as that of the natural parents. Old Granddaddy provided a roof over their heads and food for their bellies, but, like them, was not equipped to provide a stabilizing moral environment. Self-indulgence and the pursuit of material success were his primary means of combating aches of the heart and soul; he offered them to the sisters as substitutes for the familial nurturing. It was in Old Granddaddy's home, some four years after the Ma-Graths moved in, that Mama, having "a real bad day," hanged herself and her old yellow cat. On the day of her funeral, Old Granddaddy's remedy for the suffering of the three children was to stuff them with banana splits: "Why, Lenny was fourteen years old and he thought that would make it all better," Meg recalls. "Oh, I remember he said for us to eat all we wanted," responds Babe, "I think I ate about five! He kept on shoving them down us." "The thing about Old Granddaddy," continues Meg in a moment of rare insight, "is he keeps trying to make us happy and we end up getting stomach aches and turning green and throwing up in the flower arrangements."

In Henley's play, as in works of Marsha Norman, Sam Shepard and other contemporary dramatists, characters consume food to numb the pain of loneliness, familial disintegration and spiritual emptiness. Old Granddaddy's well-stocked kitchen, which serves as the single setting for *Crimes of the Heart,* emphasizes the dominance of food as opiate in the sisters' lives. Indeed, Henley's metaphoric use of food and drink as narcotics pervades the play. Food is devoured not for sustenance, but as compensation for grievances of the heart; it has no relationship to the ideal tradition of family gatherings, a sharing with others or meal-time communion. While food permeates the play, no family meal is ever served. Rather, each of the sisters forages for herself, as she has come habitually to do in life since childhood, trying to relieve her emotional losses through bodily indulgences: cokes, candy, nuts, cookies, lemonade, bourbon, vodka and cake litter the sisters' traumatic landscape. Meg pillages Lenny's chocolates, taking a bite out of each one, vainly searching for those with nuts in a box filled only with cremes. After Babe shot her husband Zackery, she gorged herself with lemonade to anesthetize the painful reality of her act: "I put the gun down on the piano and then I went out into the kitchen and made up a pitcher of lemonade . . . with lots of sugar . . . then I drank three glasses, one right after the other. They were large glasses . . . then suddenly, my stomach kind of swoll all up." Numbed into a kind of stupor by this gluttonous act, dreamily detached from the actuality of the event, she reverted to the role of the southern hostess. "Zackery," she called out as he lay in his own blood, "I've made some lemonade. Can you use a glass?" Her gracious courtesy, grotesquely inappropriate for the circumstance, suggests the behavior of a woman whose marital anguish has driven her into an act of violence.

Uprooted from their home, abandoned by their parents and cast as aliens into a strange and sometimes hostile community, the sisters throughout their lives suffer the distress of separation. Ultimately, they come to discover the regenerative power of their sisterly bonds and a place for themselves with each other, however temporary. Old Granddaddy's equating "belonging" with money or fame first led them into false values and pursuits. It was he who plotted for Babe to marry Zackery, "the richest and most powerful man in all of Hazlehurst." The day of the marriage "was his finest hour," knowing that "Babe was gonna skyrocket right to the heights of . . . society." "I was just eighteen," says Babe. "Were you happy then?" asks Meg. Babe is evasive: "Well, I was drunk on champagne punch. I remember that!" But Zackery's riches gave her no more contentment than had Old Granddaddy's banana splits on the day of her mother's funeral. With the money came Zackery, who physically abused her. She suffered in silence and alone, until she discovered a means of retaliation against Zackery and an indulgent compensation for herself: she seduced her black housemaid's fifteen-year-old son. Her seduction of Willy Jay had devastating consequences for the boy, but not, as it turns out, for Babe. Willy Jay suffers a brutal beating from Zackery, who also threatens to have him killed on sight if he should reappear. Babe's lawyer, Barnette, neatly solves the problem of any future embarrassment to Babe by shipping the terrified Willy Jay out of town "on a midnight bus—heading North."

A further complication of the plot, plucked from the well-made play tradition, has the wounded Zackery revealing that he possesses photographs of Babe's sexual encounter with Willy Jay; his intention to expose them to public view threatens the outcome of Babe's impending trial for attempted homicide. Barnette tidily resolves this problem, however, by countering Zackery's threat with one of his own: unless Zackery agrees "to settle this affair on our own terms," he will reveal Zackery's past acts of "graft, fraud [and] forgery." Thus, the consequences of Babe's acts are resolved expediently, and Meg convinces her that "we've just got to learn how to get through these real bad days here." With Meg's help, Babe starts learning.

Meg was also encouraged by her grandfather to seek her fortune, not through marriage, as in her sister's case, but Hollywood stardom. That she not only survived but eventually brings herself and her sisters to some new level of

self-awareness is a testament to her powers of endurance. It was Meg, then eleven, who discovered her mother's body, a traumatic experience that deepened the fears of an already insecure child. She responded by forcing herself to confront morbidity wherever she could find it, testing her strength to endure the confrontation and even rise above it. Babe says that Meg deliberately pored over photographs of disease-ridden victims, or stared at posters of crippled children, finishing her bizarre ritual by gorging herself with ice cream. "See," Meg would say, "I can stand it." By the time she was fourteen, her solace was no longer ice cream, but bourbon and sexual relationships, in a compulsive search to find acceptance. But she found herself incapable of feeling anything for anybody, even for Doc, who "loved her." She made use of Doc's affections by promising to marry him if he would stay with her through a vodka drinking party in the midst of hurricane Camille. When he was injured by a collapsing roof, she coldly abandoned him, fleeing to Los Angeles to pursue a singing career. Instead of stardom and the imprint of her feet "in one of those blocks of cement they've got out there" (which Old Granddaddy "thinks [is] real important"), she ended up clerking for a dog food company. Engulfed with loneliness, she became, like her mother, a helpless prisoner of herself, destined for self-destruction: "All I could do was sit around in chairs, chewing on my fingers. Then one afternoon I ran screaming out of the apartment with all my money . . . and valuables and tried to stuff it all into one of those March of Dimes collection boxes." Finally, "I went nuts. I went insane." Babe's crisis, however, saved her. Indeed, Meg begins to retrieve her life, Henley seems to say, through the admission of an inner grace that she never knew she possessed: a capacity for responding to the needs of others. Her arrival in Hazlehurst at the beginning of the play sets in motion the ultimate bonding together of the sisters. For it is Meg, despite her overt selfishness and continuing dependency upon narcotics, who brings home an awakened sense of the restorative powers of familial trust and communion: "to talk to someone . . . about our lives" she says to Babe, "[is] an important human need." Babe's positive response to open communication and nurturing indicates Henley's optimism about human relationships, especially among families.

For Lenny, the oldest of the sisters, Old Granddaddy also had plans. Her happiness, he believed, lay in the devotion of her life to his own physical comfort and well being. He had trained her well for the acceptance of her role, showing favoritism to Babe (who was the prettiest) and to Meg (the most talented) throughout their lives. Lenny had no attributes with which to make her way to success; because of her "shrunken ovary," she was not even fit for marriage. Her only appropriate function was that of nurse and housemaid to her grandparents in their old age. After the grandmother's death, and after her one prospect of marriage is rejected "because of Old Granddaddy," she seems to have become resigned to the suffocating burden of nursing her ailing grandfather. The burden doubtless became more bearable once she began to view herself as a martyr, whose sacrifice could be admired as a positive expression of some remarkable inner strength. Meg refuses, however, to indulge Lenny's claim to martyrdom. "All this responsibility keeps falling on my shoulders," Lenny says. "Well, boo hoo, hoo, hoo," Meg replies with impatience. With Babe's support, she nurtures in Lenny a sense of self-worth and resourcefulness. Lenny gathers the strength to become her "own woman." She rejects the intimidations of her cousin Chick and asserts her mastery of Old Granddaddy's domain by claiming his house as "my home!" Exhilarated by these aggressive victories, she is ready to reestablish her relationship with Charlie, indeed, to redirect her life from its narcissistic course: "My courage is up; my heart's in it; the time is right!" she rejoices, as she rushes to dial Charlie's telephone number.

Throughout the action of *Crimes of the Heart,* always apparent is the stultifying, inhibitive atmosphere of Hazlehurst, a small southern community represented by characters both seen and unseen. Chick Boyle, the MaGraths' cousin and next-door neighbor, reflects the mean-spirited mentality of the Ladies' Social League, of which she is a member and "committee head." The ideal tradition of the charitable "good neighbor," or of the social organization devoted to the cultural enlightenment and well being of the village, finds no expression in the character of Chick. Her petty bitchery, ugly manners and gossip-laden harrassment of the MaGrath sisters personify the spiritual bleakness of the community. Other Hazlehurst citizens referred to include Mrs. Porter, whose moral self-righteousness serves as the yardstick for the admission of the League's members; Lucille Botrelle, who shares her brother Zackery's proclivity for underhanded craftiness; and Doc Porter, whose relationship with Meg has not only crippled his ambitions to practice medicine (he becomes a house painter instead) but lamed him physically. It is a grotesque gallery of community portraits. Nevertheless, Henley, unlike Edward Albee, for example, does not offer an utterly "dark vision of provincial America" as "a wasteland of moral . . . despair, emptiness, and sterility" [Ima Honaker Herron, *The Small Town in American Drama,* 1969]. *Crimes of the Heart* is not without faith in the human spirit, which can be glimpsed through the sisters' remarkable endurance of suffering and their eventual move toward familial trust and unity. In the play's last scene, the sisters gather to commemorate Lenny's birthday. More importantly, they join physically and spiritually as sisters to celebrate a newly discovered fund of strength and nourishment: themselves together, not forever, but "for just this one moment," laughing and smiling.

Since *Crimes of the Heart,* Beth Henley has written four plays rooted in her southern heritage: *The Miss Firecracker Contest* (1979), *The Wake of Jamey Foster* (1983), *The Debutante Ball* (1985) and *The Lucky Spot* (1986). Henley's works also include a one-act piece, **"Am I Blue"** (1972), initially produced at Southern Methodist University. Set in New Orleans in 1968, the play examines the lives of two lonely teenagers who are deprived of both parental and peer group acceptance. Ashbe, left behind by her mother, lives with her sometimes absent alcoholic father. Like the sisters in *Crimes of the Heart,* she forages for affection and attention wherever she can find it, prowling the streets of the French Quarter, indulging in petty thievery and striking up acquaintances with other

lonely souls, such as John Polk, whom she invites back to her home for drinks. Unnurtured by family or friends, both have the fears and insecurities of those ill-prepared to take control of their own lives. They feel rejected and alone; they do not seem to belong anywhere. Ashbe cries, ". . . what's wrong with this world? I just wasn't made for it . . . everyone . . . views me as an undesirable lump." John Polk's life has been manipulated by his father, who, like the grandfather in *Crimes of the Heart,* equates success with making "good money." Nevertheless, John Polk "wanted to be a minister, or something good." He longs "to do something that's—fulfilling." By the end of the play, the two are able to establish tentative bonds of affection and understanding that have been denied them by others. In the last scene, they join together to dance *"as the lights black out and the music soars and continues to play."*

In *The Miss Firecracker Contest,* the setting (a small Mississippi town), the given circumstances (a child abandoned by her parents is reared in an alien environment) and the plot (the struggle to transcend the past) have similarities to *Crimes of the Heart* and to **"Am I Blue."** Again, the action and sense of place are highly specific: a roomy old house in which the present occupant feels estranged, surrounded by the "dreary . . . suffocating and frightening" relics of a family to which she does not belong. In the living room of her deceased aunt's home, Carnelle Scott, now twenty-four, practices her tap dancing, marching and baton twirling routines in preparation for the community's Miss Firecracker contest on the Fourth of July. Although she has lived here for fifteen years, the house remains a temporary shelter, not a home.

Like the MaGrath sisters, Carnelle had been thrust at a youthful age into a new family of strangers. Her mother had died before Carnelle was one, and "then my daddy kinda drug me around with him till I was about nine and he couldn't stand me any longer; so he dropped me off to live with my Aunt Ronelle and Uncle George and their own two children: Elain and Delmount." Like Meg, Carnelle spent her adolescent years seeking affection and acceptance in sexual relationships. She only succeeded in further alienating herself from others and in deepening her own anguish; the community contemptuously dubbed her "Miss Hot Tamale," and she contracted a venereal disease. Longing for some means of redeeming herself, she feverishly sets out to capture the Miss Firecracker crown so that she can "leave this town in a blaze of glory!"

The arrival of Elain and Delmount brings further evidence of the blighting effects of their parents' tutelage. Elain was ignored by Aunt Ronelle until she started winning beauty pageants (she gained the Miss Firecracker title at the age of seventeen), whereupon her mother told her, as Old Granddaddy told Babe, "go out and get a rich husband." But the money brought no mental peace, and Elain has now deserted her husband and children to try something else. Elain's dialogue frequently echoes that of the lyrical Blanche DuBois—"The abundance of treasures merely serves to underline the desperate futility of life"— and her rejection of wealth is merely a pose; after a sexual fling with the disease-ridden Mac Sam (a character so repugnant that Elain's action can only be attributed to lunacy or the author's antic whim), she flees back to the husband and children she detests so that she can live again "just like a queen in a castle."

Elain's brother Delmount has recently been released from a "lunatic asylum" and after a job of "scraping up dead dogs from the road" has now returned to sell the house left to him by his mother. Carnelle, now deprived of shelter, must move on; the winning of the contest offers the last desperate chance to prove to herself and the community that she is worth something.

Henley surrounds Carnelle with an assortment of peculiar people, the maimed and estranged of society, who follow her through the traumas of the contest: Carnelle's costume seamstress Popeye, who "makes little outfits" for bullfrogs and can hear voices through her eyes; Tessy, one of the "ugly" Mahoney sisters, whose virginity was plundered by Delmount in the middle of a box full of deformed cats; Mac Sam, who suffers from a venereal disease (given him by Carnelle or vice versa), alcoholism and a hacking cough that ejects "a lot of blood." Hovering over the unhappy lives of Carnelle, Elain and Delmount is the vivid image of the cancer-ridden Aunt Ronelle, who died looking like an ape, "the dreadful side effects" of a transplanted monkey's gland.

Although Carnelle does not win the contest (she places fifth out of five finalists), she perceives that "it doesn't matter" but cannot articulate why. "I just don't know," she says, "what you can . . . reasonably hope for in life." Almost as an afterthought, Henley has Mac Sam respond, "There's always eternal grace," to which Carnelle replies without much hope, "It'd be nice." Perhaps for Carnelle, as for so many of Henley's characters, the redemptive grace that comes through self-knowledge, spiritual enlightenment or nourishing bonds with others can be but dimly glimpsed and only partially realized.

The Wake of Jamey Foster presents a family of adult siblings (and their partners) who gather at the home of their newly-widowed sister Marshael Darnell Foster to attend the wake and funeral of her unfaithful, alcoholic husband. They do not gather in grief or consolation, but out of a typically southern sense of family duty. Marshael's brother Leon says that their sister Collard "always comes home when anybody dies." Around the corpse of Jamey Foster, prominently displayed in an open-lidded coffin in the living room, the family members devour, throw and trample upon food, and talk about their individual neuroses. Their familial animosities, jealousies and resentments rob them of any peace. As they juggle their plates of food and glasses of gin around the coffin, the air rife with petulant bickering, the prevailing image is that of a grotesque celebration. "Oh, hell," says Collard, as she leans over the casket eating her ham sandwich, "I may as well have one last look at the son of a bitch." A piece of ham drops on the corpse. "Ah, hell," shrugs another character, as he retrieves and eats it. Jamey Foster's wake is amply fortified with food and drink. Gin and whiskey are consumed in great quantities, along with jelly beans, choco-

late rabbits, peas, Rice Krispie bars and blueberry pie. When Marshael throws the pie *"from the upstairs landing down to the floor below,"* her rage comes from pain, and her grim suffering remains unrelieved throughout the play. She and her funeral guests end the play as they began it, floundering in isolation and low self-esteem, no more able to establish bonds with others than their parents before them. Unlike the sisters in *Crimes of the Heart* and the teenagers in *"Am I Blue,"* whose anguish is relieved through a progressive communion with each other, the Darnells remain bereft and unenlightened prisoners of their own anxieties.

Henley's recent play, *The Debutante Ball,* which has not been published, is set, like all of her full-length pieces, in her home state of Mississippi. It presents yet another variation on themes familiar from the author's earlier works. The debutante of the title, for example, is the tormented product of a family with a traumatic past, and through her mother's remarriage becomes an alien member of a new family circle.

In all of her plays, Henley takes up themes related to the disintegration of traditional ideals, such as the breakup of families, the quest for emotional and spiritual fulfillment, and the repressive social forces within a small southern community. The author's success in finding fresh explorations of these ideas in the works following *Crimes of the Heart* has been limited by the narrow range of her material. Since Henley's special concern is with the world of the "walking wounded," her later characters, intellectually and emotionally impoverished, possess little potential for change, for retrieving themselves from hopeless resignation. Unnurtured by family or peers, they reach adulthood hungering for bonds of affection, longing to connect with family, home and siblings. Trapped within their own limitations and eccentricities, they have few resources for positive action and remain essentially passive victims. Henley's modern South is a world of estrangement, spiritual longing and grotesquerie, made all the more remarkable by the calm acceptance of the bizarre as perfectly ordinary.

CRIMES OF THE HEART

PRODUCTION REVIEWS

John Simon (review date 12 January 1981)

SOURCE: "Sisterhood is Beautiful," in *New York* Magazine, Vol. 14, No. 2, 12 January 1981, pp. 42, 44-6.

[*Crimes of the Heart was first produced in 1979 at the Actors Theater of Louisville. It was then presented at several regional theaters before being staged off-Broad-*

way at the Manhattan Theater Club in late 1980 and on Broadway a year later at the John Golden Theater. Simon's enthusiastic review of the off-Broadway production, reprinted below, was an influential early assessment of the play.]

From time to time a play comes along that restores one's faith in our theater, that justifies endless evenings spent, like some unfortunate Beckett character, chin-deep in trash. This time it is the Manhattan Theatre Club's *Crimes of the Heart,* by Beth Henley, a new playwright of charm, warmth, style, unpretentiousness, and authentically individual vision.

We are dealing here with the reunion in Hazlehurst, Mississippi, of the three MaGrath sisters (note that even in her names Miss Henley always hits the right ludicrous note). Lenny, the eldest, is a patient Christian sufferer: monstrously accident-prone, shuttling between gentle hopefulness and slightly comic hysteria, a martyr to her sexual insecurity and a grandfather who takes most of her energies and an unconscionable time dying. Babe Botrelle, the youngest and zaniest sister, has just shot her husband in the stomach because, as she puts it, she didn't like the way he looked. Babe (who would like to be a saxophonist) is in serious trouble: She needs the best lawyer in town, but that happens to be the husband she shot. Meg, the middle sister, has had a modest singing career that culminated in Biloxi. In Los Angeles, where she now lives, she has been reduced to a menial job. She is moody and promiscuous, and has ruined, before leaving home, the chances of "Doc" Porter to go to medical school. She made him spend a night with her in a house that lay in the path of Hurricane Camille; the roof collapsed, leaving Doc with a bad leg and, soon thereafter, no Meg.

The time of the play is "Five years after Hurricane Camille," but in Hazlehurst there are always disasters, be they ever so humble. Today, for instance, it is Lenny's thirtieth birthday, and everyone has forgotten it, except pushy and obnoxious Cousin Chick, who has brought a crummy present. God certainly forgot, because he has allowed Lenny's beloved old horse to be struck dead by lightning the night before, even though there was hardly a storm. Crazy things happen in Hazlehurst: Pa MaGrath ran out on his family; Ma McGrath hanged her cat and then hanged herself next to it, thus earning nationwide publicity. Babe rates only local headlines. She will be defended by an eager recent graduate of Ole Miss Law School whose name is Barnette Lloyd. (Names have a way of being transsexual in Hazlehurst.) Barnette harbors an epic grudge against the crooked and beastly Botrelle as well as a nascent love for Babe. But enough of this plot-recounting—though, God knows, there is so much plot here that I can't begin to give it away. And all of it is demented, funny, and, unbelievable as this may sound, totally believable.

The three sisters are wonderful creations: Lenny out of Chekhov, Babe out of Flannery O'Connor, and Meg out of Tennessee Williams in one of his more benign moods.

But "out of" must not be taken to mean imitation; it is just a legitimate literary genealogy. Ultimately, the sisters belong only to Miss Henley and to themselves. Their lives are lavish with incident, their idiosyncrasies insidiously compelling, their mutual loyalty and help (though often frazzled) able to nudge heart-break toward heart-lift. And the subsidiary characters are just as good—even those whom we only hear about or from (on the phone), such as the shot husband, his shocked sister, and a sexually active fifteen-year-old black.

Miss Henley is marvelous at exposition, cogently interspersing it with action, and making it just as lively and suspenseful as the actual happenings. Her dialogue is equally fine: always in character (though Babe may once or twice become too benighted), always furthering our understanding while sharpening our curiosity, always doing something to make us laugh, get lumps in the throat, care. The jokes are juicy but never gratuitous, seeming to stem from the characters rather than from the author, and seldom lacking implications of a wider sort. Thus when Meg finds Babe outlandishly trying to commit suicide because, among other things, she thinks she will be committed, Meg shouts: "You're just as perfectly sane as anyone walking the streets of Hazlehurst, Mississippi." On one level, this is an absurd lie; on another, higher level, an absurd truth. It is also a touching expression of sisterly solidarity, while deriving its true funniness from the context. Miss Henley plays, juggles, conjures with context—Hazlehurst, the South, the world.

The play is in three fully packed, old-fashioned acts, each able to top its predecessor, none repetitious, dragging, predictable. But the author's most precious gift is the ability to balance characters between heady poetry and stalwart prose, between grotesque heightening and compelling recognizability—between absurdism and naturalism. If she errs in any way, it is in slightly artificial resolutions, whether happy or sad.

Melvin Bernhardt has staged it all with the same affectionate, incisive attention to detail with which John Lee Beatty designed the kitchen set, Patricia McGourty the mundane costumes, and Dennis Parichy the lighting. As for the cast, it is a dream ensemble, with only Peter MacNicol a trifle overstated as Barnette (but very good all the same). Perfection is the word for Mia Dillon's Babe, Mary Beth Hurt's Meg, Stephen Burleigh's Doc, and Julie Nesbitt's Chick; as for Lizbeth MacKay's Lenny, she goes beyond that, into the miraculous.

I have only one fear—that this clearly autobiographical play may be stocked with the riches of youthful memories that many playwrights cannot duplicate in subsequent works. I hope this is not the case with Beth Henley; be that as it may, *Crimes of the Heart* bursts with energy, merriment, sagacity, and, best of all, a generosity toward people and life that many good writers achieve only in their most mature offerings, if at all.

Scot Haller (review date November 1981)

SOURCE: "Her First Play, Her First Pulitzer Prize," in *Saturday Review,* Vol. 8, No. 11, November, 1981, pp. 40, 42, 44.

[*The following article includes a favorable assessment of* Crimes of the Heart, *as well as comments on the play by Henley and others.*]

Beth Henley can go home again, but it isn't easy. "I'm allergic to Mississippi," she drawls. "Even when I was growing up there, I'd always have these allergies to certain things. Sometimes, when I go back, my eyes swell up, and I look *horrible*. I have to leave because I just keep sneezing and sneezing."

The Mississippi countryside seems to provoke dramatic reactions from Beth Henley: It serves as the setting for her three-act play, *Crimes of the Heart,* which opens on Broadway this month. Following its much-praised off-Broadway premiere last winter, critic John Simon announced that Henley's work "restores one's faith in the theater" [*New York* Magazine, 12 January 1981]. The New York Drama Critics named *Crimes of the Heart* the best American play of the season. The Pulitzer Prize committee agreed. It gave Henley the 1980-81 award for drama, making her the first woman so honored in 23 years. Hollywood added its approval, too, buying the screen rights for $1 million. Not bad for a 29-year-old who had never before written a full-length play.

Henley's comedy has elicited comparisons with the works of such distinguished Southern writers as Eudora Welty and Flannery O'Connor, in part because she writes with wit and compassion about good country people gone wrong or whacko. *Crimes of the Heart* is set in the small town of Hazelhurst, Mississippi, five years after Hurricane Camille, and it chronicles two dizzying days in the down-home, upended lives of the MaGrath sisters. The eldest, Lenny, is a homebody celebrating her 30th birthday when she learns her horse has been killed by a lightning bolt. Middle-sister Megis visiting from Los Angeles, where she has abandoned her singing career for a job in a dog-food factory. The youngest sister, Babe, has just shot her husband "because I didn't like his stinking looks." Of course, the family wants Babe to have the best lawyer in town. Unfortunately, Babe's husband *is* the best lawyer in town. "I thought I'd like to write about somebody who shoots somebody else just for being mean," says Henley. "Then I got intrigued with the idea of the audience's not finding fault with that character, finding sympathy for her."

Although *Crimes of the Heart* is structured as a six-character, three-act, one-set comedy, Henley's accomplishment is not the resurrection of the traditional well-made play but rather the ransacking of it. She has chosen the family drama as her framework—the play takes place entirely in the MaGrath kitchen—but she has populated the household with bizarre characters. In effect, she has mated the conventions of the naturalistic play with the unconventional protagonists of absurdist comedy. It is this unlikely dramatic alliance, plus her vivid Southern vernacular, that supplies Henley's idiosyncratic voice.

In fact, the physical modesty of her play belies the bounty of plot, peculiarity, and comedy within it. Like Flannery O'Connor, Henley creates ridiculous characters but doesn't ridicule them. Like Lanford Wilson, she examines ordinary people with extraordinary compassion. Treating the eccentricities of her characters with empathy, she manages to render strange turns of events not only believable but affecting. "Most American playwrights want to expose human beings," says Jon Jory, who staged the first production of *Crimes of the Heart* in Louisville two years ago. "Beth Henley embraces them."

Henley may be the only Pulitzer Prize winner with a ponytail. Wearing a purple paisley skirt and gray blazer, she is sitting cross-legged in a corner of an office in Manhattan's theater district. Although *Crimes of the Heart* is boisterous and bawdy, its author is shy and self-effacing. Cupping a mug of coffee or twirling a wisp of brown hair, she looks like a schoolgirl in a student lounge. But her conversation displays an aptitude for tale-telling, an affection for the spoken word, and a touch of the good-old-girl as well as the poet.

"One day," she recalls, "the phone rang, and a voice said, 'This is the Associated Press. Do you know you've won the Pulitzer Prize?' My sweetie was sitting there, and he said my face went through about five different emotions, from surprise to terror to disbelief to joy. We went to this French restaurant, and I called up everybody I knew to come over, and we got drunk. Then we went back to our house and got drunk some more. The people with TV cameras were coming over to interview me. So a friend of mine put me in this nice-looking outfit and put my pearls on me. And told me not to have anything else to drink. By the time the television people came, I don't know if they thought it was liquor or just ecstasy. But my sister said she could tell I was drunk."

Born and raised in Jackson, Mississippi (Eudora Welty's hometown), Henley now lives in West Hollywood with Stephen Tobolowsky, her boyfriend since college. The daughter of a lawyer, she is the second oldest child in a family of four girls. Henley was introduced to theater by her mother, who appeared in local productions. At Southern Methodist University, she majored in theater, hoping to be an actress. She wrote one-act plays only as class assignments, and when one of those dramas, **"Am I Blue?,"** was staged at the university, the bashful playwright insisted that a pseudonym appear on the program. Following graduation in 1974, she spent a year studying for her master's at the University of Illinois and then headed to Los Angeles in search of acting jobs. "I said when I got out there, if I ever grow to like this place, I'll need psychiatric care. So now I'm afraid I need psychiatric care."

Frustrated by the lack of opportunities for an actress, Henley began work on *Crimes of the Heart*. The plot was inspired by a specific Mississippi memory: "When I was in college, my grandfather got lost in the woods on his tree farm for two nights. He fell off his horse, and it came back without him. So the whole family came together to search through the woods. Helicopters were sent out. People were coming back with 30-foot snakes found in the hunt for Henley." Her grandfather was finally recovered, unharmed, she says, "but that event, the family getting back together in the face of tragedy, started me thinking."

She showed the completed manuscript to a friend, playwright Frederick Bailey, who first met Henley while directing a summer-stock production of *A Midsummer Night's Dream* in which she played a fairy. Without her knowledge, Bailey entered *Crimes of the Heart* in the annual playwriting contest sponsored by Louisville's Actors Theater. "I had so much confidence in the play, I didn't even include a self-addressed stamped envelope," recalls Bailey. His enthusiasm was matched by artistic director Jon Jory, who selected *Crimes of the Heart* as co-winner of the 1977-78 competition. "What impressed me was this immensely sensitive and complex view of relationships," notes Jory. "And the comedy didn't come from one character but from between the characters. That's very unusual for a young writer.

"I called Beth to tell her she'd won," he remembers. "And I told her we were very interested in producing this play, but I had some suggestions to make. I asked her if that would be OK. And there was a long pause. In fact, there had been a lot of long pauses. I realized she didn't have any idea who I was."

In early 1979, Actors Theater of Louisville mounted the first production of *Crimes of the Heart* as part of its festival of new American plays. "The first preview, it was snowing," recalls Henley. "I was waiting out in the parking lot before the show. And all these people showed up, dressed up. They were paying money to see my show without having any idea what it was like. I just started crying in the parking lot." The comedy was an immediate hit, and it was produced at three other regional theaters before the Manhattan Theater Club staged it in New York last December. That production is now transferring to Broadway.

Still moonlighting as an actress on occasion, Henley represents a current trend in contemporary theater: the author/actor, a group that includes Sam Shepard, Christopher Durang, and Bill C. Davis. Henley's second career has made her particularly sensitive to the collusions and collisions that occur between performer and playwright as a show is staged. "Beth approaches a play from the point of view of theater, not literature," says Bailey. "She hears the fun in what people say," observes Melvin Bernhardt, who is directing the Broadway production. "And as an actress, she then knows how to make it stageworthy."

"I think of things I'd like to do on stage," explains Henley. "*I'd* like to come downstairs screaming or with a rope around my neck. To me, somebody sticking her head in the oven on stage, the way Babe does, is interesting."

Playwright James McClure, who has known Henley since student days at Southern Methodist, says, "Beth's is not a theoretical mind. She doesn't have a lot of pronounced opinions on art and writing. She's very matter-of-fact about the whole thing." "This is something I should be ashamed to admit," she says, "but I hadn't read Flannery O'Connor when I saw in a review that I was like her."

Though Henley strives to make her work eminently theatrical, she also makes it eminently practical to perform. "I wrote *Crimes* with the idea that I could do this as a showcase in Los Angeles. I wanted it producible. One set, small cast. In fact, in the first version, I didn't put in a birthday cake because I thought we couldn't afford to get a new cake every night. That's how cheap I was thinking."

Will Beth Henley grow into a major dramatist or will she turn out to be a one-play playwright, as critic John Simon worried in his rave review [in *New York* Magazine, 12 January 1981]? It has happened before: Where are the startling subsequent works of Robert Marasco (*Child's Play*), Jason Miller (*That Championship Season*), or D. L. Coburn (*The Gin Game*)? Henley's associates predict a long life in the theater for her: "When a writer portrays relationships as accurately as Beth does, you've got to assume she's a long-distance runner," says Jon Jory. Henley has already completed two more plays. *The Miss Firecracker Contest,* a comedy about a small-town Mississippi beauty pageant, premiered last month at the University of Illinois. Henley's third play, *The Wake of Jamey Foster,* has been optioned by director Ulu Grosbard, who will stage its first production at Connecticut's Hartford Stage Co. in January. As usual, it's a comedy about a sad state of affairs: The Southern heroine is a 33-year-old widow. "Her husband has been kicked in the head by a cow, and he's died," says Henley.

Accordingly to friends, winning the Pulitzer Prize hasn't altered her common sense or unusual sensibility. "She's never had any false pretensions," says James McClure. "Beth used to work in a dog-food factory. And when someone asked a while ago what winning the Pulitzer meant to her, she said, 'Winning the Pulitzer Prize means I'll never have to work in a dog-food factory again.'"

Ever loyal to her Southern heritage, Beth Henley is certain that Mississippi will continue to supply her with dramatic material. "I get off the plane, and the stories are just incredible," she says. "All sorts of bizarre things are going on. It's in the air. Oh, Lord, the stories I hear about just who has died in town. There are dope fiends living next door. Hermits live over here. The police are out after people breaking in windows. Somebody's drowned, and somebody's shot themselves." She pauses. "And that's just the houses on my block."

Walter Kerr (review date 15 November 1981)

SOURCE: "Offbeat—But a Beat Too Far," in *The New York Times,* 15 November 1981, Section D, pp. 3, 31.

[*Kerr notes that disbelief was his prevailing response to* Crimes of the Heart, *maintaining that Henley pushes the play's improbabilities into the realm of jokes.*]

Beth Henley's *Crimes of the Heart,* now at the "Golden after winning virtually every prize going during its run at the Manhattan Theater Club, is loaded and perhaps overloaded with quirky, casually outrageous, Mississippi-Gothic misbehavior. As I watched the three MaGrath sisters reassemble for the 30th birthday of one and for the impending death of the grandfather who'd long cared for them, I found myself often grinning at what might have been gruesome, sometimes cocking my head sharply to catch a rueful inflection before it turned into a comic one, and always, always admiring the actresses involved. I also found myself, rather too often and in spite of everything, disbelieving—simply and flatly disbelieving. Since this is scarcely the prevailing opinion, I'd best be specific.

Take a case in point. Mia Dillon plays the only one of the three who's married, and at the moment she's most decidedly stealing the limelight from the aging birthday girl, Lizbeth Mackay, and from Mary Beth Hurt, the pop singer who didn't make it and wound up in a mental institution over Christmas. Miss Dillon not only has a husband, she's shot him.

Pressed for details, she will at first only say that she's nerved herself to the deed because she never really liked his looks, though we're permitted to suspect from the outset that behind Miss Dillon's very bland countenance other motives may lurk. For the time being, however, Miss Dillon is not so much concerned with justifying her conduct as she is with checking on her newspaper coverage. After all, when the girls' mother hanged herself—and hanged the family cat alongside her, for good measure—the double death picked up national coverage whereas Miss Dillon's, thus far, is only local. The fact is not terribly upsetting; it merely seems to occupy her mind.

And, thus far, I think we're all right. We do understand the ground-rules of matter-of-fact Southern grotesquerie, and we know that they're by no means altogether artificial. People do such things and, having done them, react in surprising ways. When Miss Dillon, finally confiding some of the homelier details of the shooting to her siblings, reveals that immediately after pumping a bullet into husband Zachary's stomach she went to the kitchen and made herself a pitcher of lemonade, we're still all right. As Miss Dillon says, she had a simply terrible thirst. Shock and a terrible thirst go very nicely together. It could have— no doubt *has*—happened. And the actress is personally persuasive.

Where my doubting psyche draws the line is a few seconds further along in Miss Dillon's narrative. Having refreshed herself with lemonade, she bethought herself of her husband, lying conscious on the floor in the blood flowing from his open wound. "Zach," she called out, "I've made lemonade, do you want a glass?" I submit that we've now pressed the offbeat a beat too far, that we've chased a notion past Carson McCullers country straight through Flannery O'Connor country and on into Joke country.

How else are we to take the stretch, the literal extension of an improbable idea? The young woman has begun to

recover herself, sufficiently to think of her husband. Thinking of him, she offers him nothing but a glass of lemonade, instantly conjuring up in our own dizzy heads a vision of mixed lemonade and blood pouring out of that hole in the man. But the young woman is not totally unfeeling, she isn't meant as a monster, we are certainly not supposed to dislike her. She may be impulsive but she is naïve, ingenuous, nice. In which case her remark can only be taken as a gag.

Miss Henley, whose first play this is and whose real promise is very much in evidence, does have a beginner's habit of never letting well enough alone, of taking a perfectly genuine bit of observation and doubling and tripling it until it's compounded itself into parody. She's willing to take *advantage* of something funny, and that's got to be watched because it tends to thin out her people. Peter MacNicol is quite choice in the part of an ardent young lawyer eager to take on Miss Dillon's defense (his most powerful motive is that he detests her husband, his next most powerful that he rather likes *her*). Questioning his client, he loses track of his logic and asks, "Now where were we?," apparently so that Miss Dillon can pop back with "I just shot Zachary." That is a laugh, but I think it is a damaging one. Her untoward deed has already been mined for its full comic worth; the replay here, especially in a two-a-day rhythm, simply reduces it to the level of a vaudeville snapper.

And the person saying it inevitably becomes, on the instant, a little less real. Which is a pity, because the author has such unexpectedly true things to tell us, and show us, about this tattered family comparing notes as they munch on apples and sip cokes in a sorely scuffed green kitchen. There is, for instance, a long and perfectly played moment of hysteria that erupts from some secret source of feeling at a time when the girls don't mean to be sentimental at all. Miss Hurt has lied about herself and her lack of success to their dying grandfather. Feeling guilty, she decides she'll tell him the truth before he lapses into a coma. And that reminds Miss Mackay she's just received word he *has* lapsed into a coma. The crisscross of information strikes all three as suddenly funny and they are quite unable to contain the uprush of giddy hilarity that overtakes them. Midway in the spasm they sober up as swiftly as they've lost control, long enough for one of them to remark "It's not funny, it's really sad," a statement solemn enough to send them all off into outer space again. Director Melvin Bernhardt has orchestrated the two-way emotional collapse perfectly, and the performers stomp their way through it with alternating fits of grief and manic glee.

Miss Hurt, itchy extrovert of the trio, makes use of a variety of small but striking gestures to tell us what she's *really* like beneath her brisk and bristling airiness. Offered a piece of evidence that will seriously implicate the quick-on-the-trigger Miss Dillon, her hand instinctively recoils as though the envelope handed her might bite: we know immediately that, tough-minded as she is, she wishes no harm to her sister. She obviously *would* like to do something horrid to the wife her onetime suitor, Raymond Baker, has acquired. We watch her, fascinated, as she puts her fingernail against a jar Mr. Baker's wife has sent over, inching it toward table-edge, eyes popping in exaltation as she anticipates its lovely crash. Later, she and Mr. Baker will make exceptionally vivid the memory of a hurricane they rode out together.

Miss Mackay, the left-behind spinster who's abandoned a possible lover because she's not sure her ovaries are up to it, whips about with her hands jammed in her sweater pockets promising to make pecan pies, answering telephones and—on one satisfying occasion—taking a broom to a first cousin who's an imperious pest. (We're delighted when she so shoos the creature from the premises; when she later informs us that she's left her "up a tree, screaming," I'm afraid we've slipped from plausible cantankerousness into cartooning again.) The actress is particularly fine in her flustered exhilaration after she's forced herself to phone the man she wanted to marry and has—much to her astonishment—found him as willing as ever. It may be a shade surprising to find this particular play doling out such a readymade happy ending, but, as Miss Mackay revels in it, it's touching.

And I haven't meant to suggest that Miss Dillon is anywhere at fault as an actress in doing her playwright's bidding and plunging into caricature. She manages to be wistful, and even winning, as she looks forward to the delights of spending her days and nights in jail, with her ancient saxophone and without Zachary. And you can literally see her mind turning over—what there is of it, I mean—as she thinks back on one of her stranger mishaps and muses, "Funny I did that." She is exemplary. It's just that she's been drawn as the least literate of the three ("I'm not a liberal, I'm a Democratic") and, most of the time, has been given the broadest stage business: yawning into the telephone the moment she realizes it's her wounded husband calling from the hospital; creeping upstairs to hang herself with an obviously inadequate length of woolly twine.

Crimes of the Heart is clearly the work of a gifted writer. And, unstable as I feel it to be, it does mean to arrive at an original blend of folkways, secret despairs, sudden fun. Given the giggling and the wailing that overtake the girls regularly, it's a bit as though William Faulkner had tried his hand at writing *Little Women*. But a new mix that works is always welcome. It Miss Henley's play falls short for me, it's because its interesting characters tend to lose weight and substance as they reach farther and farther for one more brass ring. So that they can say, one after another, "Funny I did that."

John Simon   (review date 16 November 1981)

SOURCE: "Living Beings, Cardboard Symbols," in *New York* Magazine, Vol. 14, No. 45, 16 November 1981, pp. 125-26.

[*Below, Simon evaluates the Broadway production of* Crimes of the Heart, *declaring that "this is one of those rare plays about a family love that you can believe and participate in."*]

Readers can find my initial reaction to Beth Henley's *Crimes of the Heart* in the January 12 *New York* Magazine. One more Manhattan Theatre Club and now one Broadway viewing later, my fondness and admiration for the play remain undimmed, although the focus of my perception has shifted slightly. You may recall that the play concerns the three MaGrath [*sic*] sisters of Hazlehurst, Mississippi: earnest Lenny, whose forgotten thirtieth birthday this is—a timid, faintly hysterical, semivirginal young woman, dedicated to keeping hospitalized Granddaddy alive; promiscuous Meg, who started out as a singer, damaged loving "Doc" Porter's leg and ruined his chances at medical school, watched her career hit the skids in L.A., and is now visiting home after a brief nervous breakdown; and naïve Babe, who, lovelessly married to the town's most prominent and crooked lawyer, has had an awkward involvement with someone else, and has just shot her husband in the stomach, allegedly because of not liking the way he looks.

Crimes of the Heart (which also brings on amiable, uncomplicated Doc, now a house painter and married to a Yankee; Cousin Chick, a self-righteous busy-body; and Barnette Lloyd, the inexperienced but enthusiastic young lawyer who is to defend Babe, falls in love with her, and will have to give up a personal vendetta for her sake) could have been written as drama, farce, absurdist comedy, or that particularly southern genre, the winsome horror story. It does indeed partake a little of each, but is chiefly a piece of heightened realism—heightened not into symbolism or expressionism or whatever realism usually gets heightened into, but into a concentrate.

The play is an essence, *the* essence of provincial living, with everything from a father who ran off and a mother who hanged herself and her cat to an invalid grandfather and a shrunken ovary that combine to cause emotional blockage, from guilt feelings based on too much popularity to defiance caused by not enough brains, visited on one or another or all three of these young women. This is a loving and teasing look back at deep-southern, small-town life, at the effect of constricted living and confined thinking on three different yet not wholly unalike sisters amid Chekhovian boredom in honeysuckle country, and, above all, at the sorely tried but resilient affection and loyalty of these sisters for one another. However far misunderstandings, quarrels, exasperation may stretch their bond, they bounce back into embraces, Indian dances, leaps of joy, or, more simply, love.

For this is one of those rare plays about a family love that you can believe and participate in, because that love is never sappy or piously cloying, but, rather, irreverently prankish and often even acerb. Warmhearted Lenny is also an irritating fussbudget and martyr; Meg is selfish and irresponsible as well as sensible and ultimately generous; Babe, though blessed with the queer wisdom of the unreconstructed child, is also obtuse and infuriating. It is the ties of sympathy—or, if you will, the bloodline—among these three that form the play's crazy, convoluted, but finally exhilarating tracery: sisterly trajectories that diverge, waver, and explosively reunite. Laughter is squeezed from anguish as the logical consequence of looking absurd reality in the eye and just plain outstaring it. Babe's explanation of her mother's real and her own attempted suicide is the same: "a bad day"—nothing Freudian, only what happens when you do not gaze back at life unblinkingly enough.

The wonderful thing about the young author is that she understands a great deal about people and living. Thus Meg used to stare at posters of polio victims and then spend her eleemosynary dime on a bigger ice cream; during her breakdown, she was caught trying to stuff all her scant money and jewelry into a March of Dimes collection box (note the irony as well as the psychology). Thus modesty and pride wrestle to a near-standstill in Barnette's not-quite-yet-manly bosom; and thus Babe gets her satisfaction from blowing into a saxophone she may never learn to play. Miss Henley knows too how life-changing revelations arrive in grotesque little packages, as when Lenny admits over the phone her traumatizing inability to have babies and forthwith counters her swain's answer with a slight shock and vast elation: "They're not *all* little snot-nosed pigs!"

The acting of Lizbeth Mackay, Mary Beth Hurt, and Mia Dillon continues to be enchanting individually and nothing short of uplifting as an ensemble; Peter MacNicol is again effortlessly hilarious, although Melvin Bernhardt, the good director, may have unduly slowed down his scenes with Babe. John Lee Beatty's set, Patricia McGourty's clothes, and Dennis Parichy's lighting are overwhelmingly right, and the two new cast members, Sharon Ullrick and Raymond Baker, though perhaps a bit overexplicit, make their points. The play may have been ever so slightly pushed for Broadway—it did seem more at ease in the intimacy and immediacy of a smaller space—but it still makes us laugh, cry, think, and enjoy ourselves as hardly anything else around does.

Robert Brustein (review date 23 December 1981)

SOURCE: "Broadway Inches Forward," in *The New Republic*, Vol. 185, No. 3493, 23 December 1981, pp. 25-7.

[*Brustein offers a lukewarm evaluation of* Crimes of the Heart, *maintaining that while the play is whimsical and likable, it is "unlikely to survive as anything more than a stock company favorite."*]

After years of being out of service, serious American dramas are running again on commercial highways normally restricted to musicals, light comedies, and British imports. Few of these are original Broadway manufactures; almost all are products of the resident theaters. If the customary route for such plays in the past was via the Public Theater or the Mark Taper Forum, however, now their pit stop is more likely to be the Manhattan Theater Club or the Circle Rep, occasionally after early tune-ups

at the Actors Theater in Louisville. Still, it is cheering to see some native models tooling around our popular stages again. In closing itself off from the images, idioms, themes, and characters of American life, Broadway got itself in the embarrassing position of being eclipsed by its despised rival, Hollywood. What was the commercial theater offering to match the intensity of *The Godfather* or *Prince of the City,* in investigating contemporary social issues? Which industry could now be accused of being the dream factory?

Broadway has been making a little more effort in the last two years, so I wish I could be more positive about the results; but I sense defective models. A decade ago, the influential Broadway playwrights were Miller, Williams, and Albee; today the reigning figure is Lanford Wilson. Wilson, admittedly, is canny and talented. He has an eye for local color and colorful locals; he has the capacity to please a large variety of tastes. But whereas off Broadway he apprenticed himself to Tennessee Williams, Wilson made his mark on the Great White Way as a disciple of William Inge, from whom he borrowed both his mid-American types and his pastel romantic-realism. Whatever their failings, the members of the older theatrical generation usually had a surgical purpose—to cut to the center of the American malaise; Wilson and his school seem less interested in carving out the patient's tumor than in applying cosmetics to the corpse.

I speak of a school because Wilson has recently made a few disciples himself, following his demonstrated success in breaking Broadway barriers. The most recent of these is Beth Henley, whose *Crimes of the Heart* (John Golden Theater) won the Pulitzer Prize and is now a major commercial hit after two pre-Broadway productions. Only 29 years old, Miss Henley already displays enough winning theatrical manners to melt the stoniest heart (John Simon's, for example). One doesn't know whether to feel more awed by her precocity or alarmed over her early loss of innocence.

Despite the promise of the title, *Crimes of the Heart* has more to do with sentiment than with felony, though one of its three plots does involve an attempted homicide. Set in rural Mississippi "five years after Hurricane Camille," the action moves within one of those semi-transparent shabby-genteel settings that John Lee Beatty usually designs for Lanford Wilson: a kitchen with flowered scrim walls and a misty view of mimosa trees. It is the home of three sisters, all oppressed by small-town life, and too far away to go to Moscow. One is Lenny, a 30-year-old spinster who (like Wilson's spinster Sally Talley in *Talley's Folly*) is unable to bear children because of an undeveloped ovary; the second is Meg, a 27-year-old pop singer in a miniskirt who (like Wilson's pop singer, Gwen Landis, in *The Fifth of July*) outrages the community with her sexual affairs, profane language, and advanced life-style; and the third is Babe, a 24-year-old housewife (Miss Henley's creation entirely) who has just shot her husband in the stomach, reputedly because she didn't like his looks. Actually, Babe has been sleeping with a young black boy (she was lonely and he was "so good") and when her husband found out, decided it was more sensible to kill him than herself.

Babe's behavior after this murder attempt is typically flakey, but it is also typical of the way the author provides amusement at the cost of credibility. She mixes a pitcher of lemonade, then offers it to her husband bleeding on the floor. "He was looking up at me and trying to speak words. I said, 'What?' I said, 'Would you like a coke instead?'" When her husband recovers enough to speak he tries to institutionalize her—not surprisingly, though this is taken as further evidence of his miserable character. In the same mood of morbid hilarity, Babe attempts suicide twice; once by hanging (the rope breaks) and once by sticking her head inside the gas stove (she pulls it out to answer the phone). This proves to be a positive experience because it helps her to discover why her mother hanged herself along with a cat ("because she was afraid of dying all alone").

Babe will be saved from scandal and the insane asylum by a young lawyer who has discovered graft and forgery in her husband's past, and who also adores her; the more pressing charges against her may have been conveniently forgotten. As for her two sisters, they achieve equally happy resolutions to their dilemmas. Meg spends the night in a car with an old beau, thus reaffirming her faith in her capacity for love; and Lenny discovers that Charley, the man she abandoned because she couldn't give him offspring, doesn't want children anyway, thus allowing her to resume their old affair (Wilson created a similar sexual symmetry for Matt Friedman and Sally Talley). The play ends with the three sisters gathered around a birthday cake, gossiping and laughing together, having discovered that, whetever their difficulties, they are, like Mama, "not all alone." The author produces no Tchebutykin to disrupt this happy scene with any pessimistic mutterings.

Miss Henley manages a whimsical, goofy tone throughout her work which is quite ingratiating. She has a gift for outrageous reactions; she knows how to create picturesque characters. But she usually achieves her effects by damaging reality, and jamming events inside the plot like filling in a sausage casing. Within the two short days that comprise the action, Babe has not only shot her husband and made two attempts on her life but has found an admirer and developed a successful defense; Lenny's favorite horse has been struck by lightning; Meg has gone through three circles of despair and come out on the side of affirmation; and the girls' grandfather has suffered a near-fatal stroke and fallen into a coma. The grandfather's coma, however, evokes a response that suggests how effective Miss Henley's method can be when it operates in a convincing context: the girls react with a fit of giggling. "Gonna live?" "They don't [sadly] think so [breaking into laughter]"; "Oh, God, now I feel so bad [howling with laughter]." This is not different in style from the insouciance with which the sisters consistently greet awful news; but it is different in kind because it comes out of the event, not out of the author's desire to entertain.

Melvin Bernhardt's production meets the play entirely on its own terms, which is to say, it makes no effort to resolve any stylistic incongruities. Like the play, the direction is textured, witty, well-modeled, suggestive of depths without actually revealing them. Bernhardt's character work with the actors is particularly strong. Aside from a tendency (not shared by Mary Beth Hurt, attractively knife-edged, though vaguely Western as Meg) to break into shrill Southern shrieks at levels that could shatter all the glassware in the kitchen, the women in the cast are uniformly appealing, giving performances that are rich and fruity and packed with nuance. Mia Dillon brings a ripe, winsome simple-mindedness to the part of Babe; Lizbeth MacKay displays repressed hysteria as Lenny, as she speeds across the linoleum, sticking birthday candles into chocolate chip cookies; Peter MacNicol is boyishly charming as Babe's smitten lawyer; and Sharon Ullrich and Raymond Porter play other friends and family with economy and strength.

In short, *Crimes of the Heart* is an entirely harmless evening at a decent level of professionalism. It is not cheap; it is not pretentious; it is generally amusing. The play, however, is unlikely to survive as anything more than a stock company favorite, Pulitzer Prize or not, because like most romantic literature, it raises issues it is unwilling to face. William Gibson once complained that Broadway was a place to be likable, not serious. *Crimes of the Heart* is eminently likable, but it is not really serious. A healthy commercial theater would be offering two or three such plays a month; it would also be generating plays that were not just cuddly and ingratiating but penetrating and profound.

CRITICAL COMMENTARY

William W. Demastes (essay date 1988)

SOURCE: "New Voices Using New Realism: Fuller, Henley, and Norman," in *Beyond Naturalism: A New Realism in American Theatre,* Greenwood Press, 1988, pp. 125-54.

[*In the excerpt below, Demastes explores the manner in which Henley "has taken domestic comedy and infused it with an absurdist perspective" in* Crimes of the Heart.]

Winning the 1981 Pulitzer Prize for *Crimes of the Heart* at age 29, Beth Henley was the first woman to win the award in twenty-three years. As a successful female dramatist, her voice is a valuable addition to an under-represented element in the field. Her works do focus on women and even on their struggle for independence from a male-dominated hierarchy, but perhaps the unique contribution Henley makes to American theatre has its roots in her Southern heritage; through her, Southern drama returns to mainstream theatre. Concerning her Southern background, Brendan Gill [in *The New Yorker,* 16 November 1981] offers the following generalization: "Northern writers have inherited a Puritan disinclination to tell whoppers; Southern writers do little else." In Henley's case, being raised in Mississippi has certainly cultivated in her a penchant for "whoppers." But more important is her keen Southern sense of the grotesque and absurd experienced in daily existence, a sense that has often triggered loose comparisons between her and other Southern writers like Eudora Welty and Flannery O'Connor. The reason for the comparison, as one critic notes, is that "she writes with wit and compassion about good country people gone wrong or whacko" [Scot Haller, *Saturday Review,* November 1981].

The comparisons are valid if for no other reason than the fact that Henley has mastered the art of the grotesquely comic by co-mingling serious, life-threatening concerns with mundane daily activities. In her work what seem to be serious issues are reduced to trivialities, and the mundane is raised to seemingly unwarranted but nonetheless believable levels of importance. The result is she overturns whatever system of moralizing an audience may have, and then refuses to return us to any sense of order. The extreme subjectivity illustrated in the various characters' value systems leaves us in a state of uncertainty, but this uncertainty doesn't lead to despair; it is simply a state of being to be accepted. We shouldn't struggle to objectify the events, attributing to them some god-given meaning, nor should we fully expect to understand the events even under our own systems of order.

Edith Oliver [in *The New Yorker,* 12 January 1981] summarizes *Crimes of the Heart* as being "a comedy of private disasters among three sisters in Hazlehurst, Mississippi." She explains:

> The sisters . . . are Lenny . . , the oldest of them, whose thirtieth birthday is being insufficiently celebrated on the day the action takes place, and who is fading into spinsterhood; Meg . . , the middle one, who has been away from home unsuccessfully pursuing a career as a popular singer (she has spent the past year as a clerk in a dog-food store); and Babe . . , who has just shot her husband, Zachary, the best lawyer in town, because, she explains, she didn't like the way he looked, although she later reveals to Meg that she has been having delightful sexual episodes with a young black boy of fifteen, whom she is shielding.

In addition, it is variously revealed that Lenny's old horse had recently been struck and killed by lightning, that the mother had committed suicide several years earlier, hanging herself and her cat, that Lenny is sterile and that their guardian/grandfather is currently in the hospital following a stroke. And as a sort of climax, we witness a comically failed suicide attempt on stage by Babe.

This unlikely string of events, though, "marches," as Gill notes, "at a pace that keeps us from ever questioning the degree of clever manipulation that we are being made subject to." The separate incidents are added to the list in such an un-self-conscious way that they are looked at and weighted separately, given individual credibility and acceptance almost before we consider the "absurdity" of the entire menagerie. The success of this on-stage diffuseness establishes a singularly important element of realistic credibility—the play slips into the realm of realistic possibility—and because we don't pause to reflect, her "whopper" is allowed to stand. We simply turn to laughing at the "succession of misfortunes inflicted upon people who lack

the capacity to avoid them." The yarn is spun, we accept it, and can move on to the business of the play.

But as is typical with such Southern tales, *Crimes of the Heart* is not just an entertaining situation or laughing comedy. Her play goes well beyond such empty conventionality, as Haller observes:

> Although *Crimes of the Heart* is structured as a six-character, three-act, one-set comedy, Henley's accomplishment is not the resurrection of the traditional well-made play, but rather the ransacking of it. She has chosen the family drama as her framework—the play takes place entirely in the MaGrath kitchen—but she has populated the household with bizarre characters. In effect, she has mated the conventions of the naturalistic play with the unconventional protagonists of absurdist comedy.

Despite its wealth of comic material, it is a palatable presentation of material previously reserved for more esoteric forms of theatre—theatre of the absurd—and that is Henley's triumph, the triumph in fact that is a product of her Southern heritage. Henley's play presents, as Kauffmann argues, "the tension between the fierce lurking lunacy underlying the small-town life she knows so well and the sunny surface that tries to accommodate it" [Stanley Kauffmann, in *Saturday Review,* January 1982]. As such, her work escapes the intellectual detachment of the French absurdists and existentialists, and because it takes the horrors of life out of the lecture halls and puts them in a kitchen, it argues that the absurd has an immediacy and relevance to daily existence that other works can't claim to argue. "In short," says Kauffmann, "what begins as more wistfulness under the wisteria eventually becomes a compound of giggle and decay on the edge of an abyss." Henley has taken domestic comedy and infused it with an absurdist perspective.

The fusion of these two components is primarily effected by Henley's use of a disconnected, fragmented style of dialogue, a style comically reminiscent of another playwright, David Mamet, who works in another dialect from another region of the country but whose approach to that dialect is similar. Because her play focuses on dialogue, she has also met with criticism similar to that which Mamet received. For example, Kauffmann notes, "Too much of the action occurs offstage and is reported." But the actions, finally, aren't what bring on the humor; it's the *recounting* of the actions. The opening lines set the pattern. The sisters' first cousin, Chick, introduces Babe's crime to the play with the following: "It's just too awful! It's just way too awful! How I'm gonna continue holding my head up high in this community, I do not know. Did you remember to pick up those pantyhose for me?" The incident of the shooting shifts to egocentric concerns of Chick's own reputation and finally to concern about a pantyhose purchase. The psychological consistency is evident—we learn of Chick's character very efficiently in this passage—but the weighting of events does not coincide with any logical consistency other than Chick's own extremely subjective logic.

Within the first minutes of the play, confusion completely asserts itself. The news of the shooting is replaced by concern for the death of an old horse—apparently "struck by lightning"—followed by news that "Old Granddaddy's gotten worse," and concluded with anxiety over a child's "first time at the dentist." Additionally, the important decision of determining who should defend Babe is settled by hiring a son of a friend (Annie) because they would "be doing Annie a favor by hiring him up."

Discrepancies between feelings and expression of those feelings add to the confusion. Babe reports that she shot Zachary because she "just didn't like his stinking looks." Other disclosures inform against this claim, but nothing actually reported and confirmed justifies the attempted murder, at least from an objective/rational point of view. Babe also recounts making lemonade and offering some to Zachary, lying wounded on the floor. Dramatizing the event as Kauffmann seems to wish (and as the movie version did), would draw out the horror of the event, but the choice of simply having Babe describe the events comically reveals the discrepancy between Babe's feelings and a perhaps more "proper," though unfelt, expression of feelings. Added to the unfolding of central events is a string of similar interchanges. And though overall events in the play are perhaps painful to the sisters, the reports they give are far from despairing and often make for pure comedy. Lenny, for example, reminds Meg of an unanswered letter explaining Granddaddy's stroke: "I wrote you about all those blood vessels popping in his brain?" And Meg mumbles about the shooting: "So, Babe shot Zachary Bottrell . . . slap in the gut."

In many ways, the dialogue is a refreshing break from the coldly clinical analyses often given of such events. But the dialogue goes a step further and suggests a certain solipsism among the characters, the result of an inevitable self-interest and resulting miscommunication. The above line of Meg's is followed by a typical example of miscommunication. Meg continues, saying, "It's hard to believe," to which Lenny replies, "It certainly is. Little Babe—shooting off a gun," Whether or not Meg is thinking in the same way as Lenny, one point is likely: the audience has been led to assume that it is "hard to believe" that Babe shooting her husband would happen. Lenny—and perhaps Meg—is thinking of the unlikelihood of "little" Babe shooting a gun under any circumstances; she isn't even thinking of a circumstance where Babe's husband would be in front of it. Lenny has lost focus on Zach's involvement altogether, shifting her thoughts to how Babe has grown up, a musing having started by first considering current events. In fact, the play continues with Lenny: "She was always the prettiest and most perfect of the three of us." As with the opening scene with Chick, no one can seem to keep on the subject at hand, continually shifting from subject matter of seemingly vastly varying significance. The varied layers produce a completely interwoven product that confuses any rational, ordered, "objective" hierarchy that an audience may have come to expect in more conventional works of art.

The method Henley uses is a simple one of inserting horrifyingly significant events into a world of the mundane. The result is two-fold. First, the facts of death, suicide, and assault take on a certain intimacy. They are no longer only distantly experienced, and neither are they either abstractly or exotically/sensationally experienced as in much literature, drama, and the media in general. The potential for Henley is that such presentation of events, set in a household that could be our neighbor's, could lead to the terrifying surmise that assault and death lurk at every corner, even in the most normal of neighborhoods. Forwarding this thesis alone, however, is not the play's purpose. If it were, it would be a work, like many others, striving to alert its audience to painful visions of apocalyptic doom, and its effect would be to have its audience look at the world with some fearfully heightened sense of tragic potentialities.

But not only does Henley succeed in giving these threatening facts of life a certain intimacy, she also moves to a level where this fusion of the significant with the mundane succeeds in convincing us that death, suicide, and assault are realities that we face every day to some extent. And the comic touch suggests that we do not need any heightened, redirected awareness about such things because such responses are little more than misguided over-reactions. People are currently equipped to handle tragedy and handle it successfully, especially when they are aware that such events are not the result of some mystical curse handed down only to those chosen to suffer, but rather are random, inexplicable events that we are all subject to but that we can overcome, or at least endure. In a way, the Southern "superstition" of Christian mystery has been updated to embrace a modernist posture of the absurd.

Doc Porter is an example of a character in the play who has endured without bitterness, a man whose life was ruined by a crippling accident caused by Hurricane Camille several years earlier. Though he never fulfills his (and the community's) dream of becoming a doctor, he does settle down and raise a family. He even confronts the ghost of his past catastrophe, in the person of Meg. Meg is partially responsible for Doc's accident, and though the two presumably were in love, she abandons him shortly after the storm. New hopes seem to rekindle when Meg returns home during the action of the play, but rather than running away with Meg and beginning a new life, Doc seemingly accepts his "fate" and opts for the life he has already made. Meg reports their meeting together:

> I was out there thinking, What will I say when he begs me to run away with him? . . . But . . . he didn't ask me. He didn't even want to ask me. I could tell by this certain look in his eyes that he didn't even want to ask me.

For Doc, the confrontation has demystified the past and the despair (if there was any) over lost opportunity. The events weren't the result of some curse handed down by a conscious god who required confrontation and defiance, but were random accidents requiring acceptance. So Doc's acceptance of his current life is less an expression of defeat than an acknowledgment of his having accepted the "mystery."

The confrontation defuses some sense of loss for Meg, too. She asks herself: "Will I have pity on his wife and those two half-Yankee children? I mean, can I sacrifice their happiness for mine? Yes! Oh, yes! Yes, I can!" He never asks her, of course, and her response is, "Why aren't I miserable! Why aren't I morbid! . . . I don't know. But for now it was . . . just such fun. I'm happy." The hoped-for escape doesn't come, the easy, romanticized solution isn't offered, but a sobering relief from the depression of an unfulfilled existence is the result.

Relief of another sort is found by the sisters as a group, in the form of an attack of hysterical laughter when it is announced that "Old Granddaddy" is about to die. Tension, at the very least, is released. And when the mystery of their mother's suicide is "solved," another burden is lifted. Babe discovers through her own suicide attempt why their mother hung the cat with her in the suicide: "She needed him with her because she felt so alone." The discovery leads to the conclusion that the family's string of bad luck is not the result of some curse of insanity. It's not a curse of any sort. It has been the result of a series of "bad days," as it is simply but finally and authoritatively put. Says Babe of her day of shooting her husband, of having her affair with a black youth revealed, of being threatened with blackmail and commitment to an asylum: "I'm having a bad day. It's been a real bad day."

The general answer that Henley offers is that survival requires a concerted effort of love and community support. Babe, we feel, will survive. She says, "I'm not like Mama. I'm not so all alone." And Meg learns the same lesson. After her night with Doc, she says, "I realized I could care about someone. I could want someone." Lenny's revelation is similar, only her problems are given instant relief through the traditional and somewhat overworked entrance of a lost suitor. For the two other central characters, Meg and Babe, the lesson is learned but less euphorically resolved. Their lessons in the play lead to the fair conclusion that "we've just got to learn to get through these real bad days," and that one cannot do so alone. No "prince charming" is offered; rather, the learning process has taken on the realistic dimension of just beginning for them, and the play ends without resolution, only a set determination to face the next, inevitable crisis together and endure it as well.

In a way, Henley's argument is similar to Mamet's. Her characters have demonstrated an at times extreme sense of solipsistic subjectivity that logic and language can't fully overcome and in fact seem to encourage. As such, "community" seems impossible. But if they move beyond the efforts to rationally objectify life and find an alternative unifying bond, then survival is tolerable. In the play, this alternative is found. Very simply put, in the face of other failed answers, love in general and the comforts of family in particular are what Henley offers as "solutions."

The answer Henley offers is by no means profound. It is a common-sense abstraction that is far from a set, soundly articulated philosophy. But solid answers aren't what the play is designed to offer. As Kauffmann says:

> *Crimes* moves to no real resolution, but this is part of its power. It presents a condition that, in minuscule, implies much about the state of the world . . . and about human chaos; it says, "Resolution is not my business. Ludicrously horrifying honesty is."

Exactly how these characters resolve their current dilemmas is irrelevant, finally. Even the events themselves are irrelevant. Henley's play is one that presents a common condition of isolation, posits a general means to handle the isolation, but promises no particular prescriptive solutions to the dilemma. As with Mamet, Henley senses first a need to re-establish the basic bonds of human existence before more artificial social bonds can be sufficiently established.

And it is up to humanity itself to exact the necessary changes because there is, finally, no perceivable grand design giving meaning to events and actions in our lives. Henley's technique of binding the significant and the mundane into a confusion that clouds the relative importance of each event fairly illustrates that point. Our efforts to see an importance in various events assume that the events have "meaning." We must realize, however, that such meaning is purely subjective and finally arbitrary. It is this revelation that uncovers Henley's vision of the essentially absurd nature of the human condition. And that condition infiltrates what could very well be our own homes.

That her work has been taken perhaps too lightly by critics and audiences is possibly the result of the fact that it is a laughing comedy, which downplays the seriousness of its design, and the fact that its simplistic—incidental—"solution" bears too much of the critical weight of the play: critics, looking for results, see little and so look less deeply at the rest of the play. But closer scrutiny reveals a serious design behind that laughter and prior to the resolution. Henley has taken the conventional realistic format and has infused it with the esoteric reflections of absurdist thinkers and writers.

Martin Esslin, in *Theatre of the Absurd,* points out that the end of absurdist drama is to challenge "the possibility of knowing the laws of conduct and ultimate values, as deducible from a firm foundation of revealed certainty about the purpose of man in the universe." Absurdist theatre strives "to re-establish an awareness of man's situation when confronted with the ultimate reality of his condition." It is these tenets that are seen in Henley, but they are presented in a context—a middle-class kitchen—familiar to its audience rather than being presented in an abstracted setting of intentionally unfamiliar conditions. The material has become accessible to a broader audience as a result. For Henley, Southern Christian mysticism has been replaced by and updated with a perhaps equally mystifying absurdist perception of existence, but updated nonetheless.

Though Henley has dispensed with the classical Southern outlook on existence, she has transferred to that new perception a key ingredient of the old: a sense of inevitable triumph over despair (though sufficiently guarded from easy, romanticized answers), something the absurdists themselves, arguably, never ventured to do, or at best, only ambiguously hinted at.

FURTHER READING

AUTHOR COMMENTARY

Betsko, Kathleen and Koenig, Rachel. "Beth Henley." In *Interviews with Contemporary Women Playwrights,* pp. 211-22. New York: Beech Tree Books, 1987.

> Conversation in which Henley discusses the creative process, winning the Pulitzer Prize, politics, and feminist issues.

OVERVIEWS AND GENERAL STUDIES

Gagen, Jean. "'Most Resembling Unlikeness, and Most Unlike Resemblance': Beth Henley's *Crimes of the Heart* and Chekhov's *Three Sisters.*" *Studies in American Drama* 4 (1989): 119-28.

> Examines some parallels and differences between Henley's and Chekhov's plays, including structure, theme, and vision in the two works.

Guerra, Jonnie. "Beth Henley: Female Quest and the Family-Play Tradition." In *Making a Spectacle: Feminist Essays on Contemporary Women's Theatre,* edited by Lynda Hart, pp. 118-30. Ann Arbor: University of Michigan Press, 1989.

> Examines the female characters' journeys to autonomy in Henley's plays.

Hargrove, Nancy D. "The Tragicomic Vision of Beth Henley's Drama." *The Southern Quarterly* XXII, No. 4 (Summer 1984): 54-70.

> Takes aim at the overemphasis on the comic elements of Henley's plays and their neglect of serious concerns.

McDonnell, Lisa J. "Diverse Similitude: Beth Henley and Marsha Norman." *The Southern Quarterly* XXV, No. 3 (Spring 1987): 95-104.

> Focuses on "the distinguishing characteristics" of the two playwrights and "emphasizes their striking originality as they work within common literary and dramatic traditions."

Shepard, Alan Clarke. "Aborted Rage in Beth Henley's Women." *Modern Drama* XXXVI, No. 1 (March 1993): 97-108.

> Analyzes the "murderous and suicidal fantasies" of Henley's female characters.

CRIMES OF THE HEART

Gill, Brendan. Review of *Crimes of the Heart. The New Yorker* LVII, No. 39 (16 November 1981): 182-83.

> Praises *Crimes of the Heart* for its "daffy complexity of plot" and its "pace that keeps us from ever questioning the degree of clever manipulation that we are being made subject to."

Kauffmann, Stanley. "Two Cheers for Two Plays." *Saturday Review* 9, No. 1 (January 1982): 54-5.

> Mixed assessment of *Crimes* that hold that Henley "has struck a rich, if not inexhaustible, dramatic lode: the tension between the fierce lurking lunacy underlying the small-town life she knows so well and the sunny surface that tries to accommodate it."

Rich, Frank. Review of *Crimes of the Heart. The New York Times* (22 December 1980): C 16.

> Admiring review that observes: "Miss Henley is a beguiling writer. She meets her characters on their own terms and then embraces them; in her compassionate view, every conceivable crime of the heart is pardonable."

———. Review of *Crimes of the Heart. The New York Times* (5 November 1981): C 21.

> Argues that in *Crimes* Henley "builds from a foundation of wacky but consistent logic until she's constructed a funhouse of perfect-pitch language and ever-accelerating misfortune."

THE MISS FIRECRACKER CONTEST

Nightingale, Benedict. "A Landscape that Is Unmistakably by Henley." *The New York Times* (3 June 1984): H 3, H 7.

> Admires *The Miss Firecracker Contest* as a "thoroughly beguiling addition to the Henley archives" but finds the production too frenetic in tone and mood.

Oliver, Edith. Review of *The Miss Firecracker Contest. The New Yorker* LX, No. 17 (11 June 1984): 112-13.

> Favorable evaluation of *Miss Firecracker* that asserts that "where it shines is in the imagination of the playwright, in the characters she has created, in the strangeness and depth and validity of their emotions, in the lines she has written for them to speak, and in her own astonishing, humorous vision."

Rich, Frank. Review of *The Miss Firecracker Contest. The New York Times* (28 May 1984): 11.

> Highly favorable notice that asserts: "For all the play's hyperbolic comic shenanigans, Miss Henley never loses sight of the sad, real people within."

Simon, John. "Repeaters." *New York* Magazine 17, No. 23 (4 June 1984): 79-80.

> Negative review of *The Miss Firecracker Contest* that contends that "much of the writing and all the characters

writing is, so to speak, born affiliated with yourself. Anybody can teach the craft of playwriting, just as I can teach myself how to make a blueprint and construct a house, on paper. But what cannot be taught, and what I was fortunate in discovering, was simply being myself, with my own problems and my own relationships to life.

Without the Group Theatre I doubt that I would have become a playwright. I might have become some other kind of writer, but the Group Theatre and the so-called "method" forced you to face yourself and really function out of the kind of person you are, not as you thought the person had to function, or as another kind of person, but simply using your own materials. The whole "method" acting technique is based on that. Well, after attempting to write for eight or ten years, I finally started a short story that made me really understand what writing was about in the sense of personal affiliation to the material.

I was holed up in a cheap hotel, in a kind of fit of depression, and I wrote about a young kid violinist who didn't have his violin because the hotel owner had appropriated it for unpaid bills. He looked back and remembered his mother and his hard-working sister, and although I was not that kid and didn't have that kind of mother or sister, I did fill the skin and the outline with my own personal feeling, and for the first time I realized what creative writing was.

A playwright who writes about things that he is not connected with, or to, is not a creative writer. He may be a very skilled writer, and it may be on a very high level of craft, but he's not going to be what I call an artist, a poet. We nowadays use the term creative arts, or a creative person, very loosely. A movie writer thinks of himself as a creative person who writes films or TV shows. Well, in the sense that I'm using the word, he's just a craftsman, like a carpenter. He has so many hammers, so many nails, so much dimension to fill, and he can do it with enormous skill. But the creative writer always starts with a state of being. He doesn't start with something outside of himself. He starts with something inside himself, with a sense of unease, depression, or elation, and only gradually finds some kind of form for what I'm calling that "state of being." He doesn't just pick a form and a subject and a theme and say this will be a hell of a show.

The form, then, is always dictated by the material; there can be nothing ready-made about it. It will use certain dramatic laws because, after all, you have to relate this material to an audience, and a form is the quickest way to get your content to an audience. That's all form is. Form is viability.

I was twenty-six years old when I started *Awake and Sing!*, my first play. I wrote the first two acts, and six months later, in the spring of 1933, I went home to my folks' house in Philadelphia and finished the last act there. That summer the Group Theatre went to a place called Green Mansions Camp [in the Adirondacks], where we sang for our supper by being the social staff. After he read *Awake and Sing!* Harold Clurman announced one night at a meeting of the entire company that the Group Theatre idea—that we would develop from our ranks not only our own actors, but our own directors and perhaps our own playwrights—was really working out in practice. "Lo and behold!" he said, "sitting right here in this room is the most talented new young playwright in the United States." And everybody, including me, turned around to see who was in the room and then with a horrible rush of a blush I realized he was talking about me.

But the Group Theatre didn't want to do the play. Although Harold Clurman, who was kind of the ideological head, liked it, he didn't have the strength to push it through to production against the wishes of the other two directors, Lee Strasberg and Cheryl Crawford. Lee Strasberg particularly didn't like the play. He kept saying, "It's a mere genre study." Strasberg and I were always on the outs. . . .

This was now August or September of 1934, and the Group Theatre was determined in the purity of its heart, that it would have to go away and do a new play when it might very well have continued the run of the very successful, and by this time Pulitzer Prize, *Men in White*. But purity prevailed and we went up to Ellenville, New York, to a big, rambling, broken-down hotel—don't forget, with its office and managerial staff the Group Theatre consisted of maybe thirty-six men and women and their children—and we had to find quite a large place to live in. We arrived practically when autumn was setting in at this old Saratoga-type wooden hotel, with all the bedding piled up, and we lived in an itchy and uncomfortable way there for about five or six weeks while we put into rehearsal a play by Melvin Levy, called *Gold Eagle Guy*. I had, perhaps unfairly, only scorn and contempt for the play because I thought *Awake and Sing!* was far superior as a piece of writing. Indeed, we all felt that *Gold Eagle Guy* was a stillborn script, and Luther Adler summed it up for us one morning at rehearsal when he said, kind of *sotto voce*, "Boys, I think we're working on a stiff." That morning we were almost improvising certain scenes, which we would later scale down to the playwright's words. Levy would get alarmed because the actors were not quite saying his words, and not using his punctuation. To this day there are playwrights who don't know their punctuation isn't very important in the recreation of the character they've written, or that, as we used to say in the Group Theatre, their script is only a series of stenographic notes.

In any case, I had been given my own room at this old hotel, which gave me a certain lift. It's surprising how very important a small satisfaction can be in the life of one who is moving away from what I can only call illness to some kind of health or strength. (You must remember the background to all of this was that before I was twenty-five I had tried to commit suicide three times; once I stopped it myself and twice my life was saved by perfect strangers.) Before this I had always been quartered with one or two and sometimes three other actors, but when they gave me my own room, with clean, white-washed walls, I began to feel they had some sense that I had some kind of distinction, and I was very happy.

I had by now started *Paradise Lost,* about a man, Leo, who was trying to be a good man in the world and meets raw, evil, and confused conditions where his goodness means nothing. Almost all of that play came out of my experiences as a boy in the Bronx. I saw people evicted, I saw block parties, I knew a girl who stayed at the piano all day, a boy who drowned, boys who went bad and got in trouble with the police. As a matter of fact, two of the boys I graduated with ended up in the electric chair and another boy became a labor racketeer. Not too much of that play was invented; it was felt, remembered, celebrated.

One night I had the idea for the scene in the play which I call the Fire Bug Scene. It just impelled itself to be written, and since I had no paper I wrote the whole scene as fast as I could on the white wall. The words just gushed out; my hand couldn't stop writing. Then later, I copied it down on the typewriter, but to this day the scene may still be on the wall of that old hotel. . . .

Well, now we move up to Boston in the late fall of 1934 to open *Gold Eagle Guy,* and that's when I wrote **"Waiting for Lefty."** I now had behind me the practically completed *Awake and Sing!* and about half of *Paradise Lost,* but somehow **"Waiting for Lefty"** just kind of slipped itself in there. Its form and its feeling are different from the other two plays, and I actually wrote it in three nights in the hotel room in Boston after returning home from the theater about midnight. It just seemed to gush out, and it took its form necessarily from what we then called the agit-prop form, which, of course, stands for agitational propaganda.

I really saw the play as a kind of collective venture—something we would do for a Sunday night benefit in New York for the *New Theatre Magazine,* a Left magazine that was always in need of money. My demands were so modest that I tried to get two other actors in the Group Theatre who I thought had writing talent to assist me. One of them, Art Smith, came up with me one night to my hotel room and we talked around and around this thing, but he seemed rather listless about working with me, so I went ahead by myself.

As a matter of fact, the form of **"Waiting for Lefty"** is very rooted in American life, because what I semi-consciously had in mind was actually the form of the minstrel show. I had put on two or three minstrel shows in camp and had seen three or four other ones. It's a very American, indigenous form—you know, an interlocutor, end men, people doing their specialities, everyone sitting on the stage, and some of the actors sitting in the audience. There were a number of plays then, usually cheap and shoddy plays, that had actors in the audience. I had played in one called, I think, *The Spider,* in Camden, New Jersey, when I was in stock. I guess all these things conglomerated in my mind, but what's important for **"Waiting for Lefty"** is how it matched my conversion from a fellow who stood on the side and watched and then finally, with a rush, agreed—in this drastic social crisis in the early 'thirties—that the only way out seemed to be a kind of socialism, or the Communist party, or something. And the play represents that kind of ardor and that kind of conviction.

About ten days after the tryout in Boston we opened *Gold Eagle Guy* at the Morosco Theater in New York, and the play got very bad notices. In all New York theaters you automatically lose the theater when the play receipts fall below a certain figure, so we moved over to the Belasco. It happened that three or four or even five of my plays were done at that theater, which people thought was very glamorous, but I always thought it a rather crummy old joint, shabby, with uncomfortable seats. Anyway, to keep the play going the actors and the playwright took cuts in salary, but in a few weeks it closed and we were forced out into the cold winter. We had no new play to put into rehearsal and there was a sadness around the place.

In the meantime I'd gotten some of the actors together and had started to rehearse **"Waiting for Lefty."** I gave Sandy Meisner, an actor friend of mine, some of the scenes to direct, and I directed the bulk of the play. Strasberg, who was quite resentful of it, told Harold Clurman, "Let 'em fall and break their necks." One of the main things about Strasberg was that he always hated to go out on a limb. He must save his face at all times. Almost Oriental. I suspect that the thing about Strasberg was that whenever the Group Theatre name was used or represented, it was as though his honor was at stake. He didn't like me, he didn't like what I had written, and he felt it would in some way be a reflection on him, on the entire Group Theatre. This man who could be so generous, sometimes could be so niggardly and begrudging. It was with great trepidation that I had proposed putting on this play at all, and when I asked him a few questions about handling a group, an ensemble, he'd answer me very curtly, and I thought to myself, "Oh, the hell with him. I'll just go ahead and do this myself."

And then; the night of the benefit, I had an enormous fight down at the old Civic Repertory Theatre on 14th Street to get my play put on last. They used to put on eight or nine vaudeville acts there for the Sunday night benefits and they wanted some dance group to close the show, but finally, because I threatened to pull it, they agreed to put **"Waiting for Lefty"** on last.

It was very lucky they did because there would have been no show after that. The audience stopped the show after each scene; they got up, they began to cheer and weep. There have been many great opening nights in the American theater but not where the opening and the performing of the play were a cultural fact. You saw a cultural unit functioning. From stage to theater and back and forth the identity was so complete, there was such an at-oneness with audience and actors, that the actors didn't know whether they were acting and the audience didn't know whether they were sitting and watching it, or had changed position. I was sitting in the audience with my friend, Elia Kazan, sitting next to me (I wouldn't have dared take on one of the good parts myself) and after the Luther Adler scene, the young doctor scene, the audience got up and shouted, "Bravo! Bravo!" I was thinking, "Shh, let the play continue," but I found myself up on my feet shouting, "Bravo, Luther! Bravo, Luther!" In fact, I was part of the audience. I forgot I wrote the play, I forgot I was in the play, and many of the actors forgot. The proscenium arch disappeared. That's the key phrase. Before and since, in the American theater people have tried to do that by theater-in-the-round, theater this way, that way, but here, psychologically and emotionally, the proscenium arch dissolved away. When that happens, not by technical innovation, but emotionally and humanly, then you will have great theater—theater at its most primitive and grandest.

Of course, the nature of the times had a good deal to do with this kind of reaction. I don't think a rousing play today could have this kind of effect because there are no positive, ascending values to which a play can attach itself.

OVERVIEWS AND GENERAL STUDIES

Michael J. Mendelsohn (essay date 1963)

SOURCE: "Clifford Odets: The Artist's Commitment," in *Literature and Society*, edited by Bernice Slote, University of Nebraska Press, 1964, pp. 142-52.

[*The following was originally presented as a conference paper in 1963. Mendelsohn views Odets' social and personal beliefs in the context of his early plays.*]

Early in Clifford Odets' 1949 melodrama, *The Big Knife,* the central character recalls something significant about his youth:

> My uncle's books—for that neighborhood—I'll bet he had a thousand! He had a nose for the rebels—London, Upton Sinclair—all the way back to Ibsen and Hugo. Hugo's the one who helped me nibble my way through billions of polly seeds. Sounds grandiose, but Hugo said to me: "Be a good boy, Charlie. Love people, do good, help the lost and fallen, make the world happy, if you can!" [I]

These words spoken by Charlie Castle have clear autobiographical overtones for anyone familiar with Odets' early life. More important, they provide one clue to our understanding of the mixture of proletarianism, humanitarianism, and intellectualism that is Clifford Odets.

But books are of secondary importance in Odets' career compared with the anxieties and ferment of the early depression years. The claim that Odets' work was a product of the 1930's is an oversimplification. Yet there is at least partial truth in the comment frequently made in various forms that Odets is characteristically *the* playwright of the Thirties. Odets was nurtured in the highly charged emotional atmosphere that has been admirably chronicled in Harold Clurman's history of the Group Theatre, *The Fervent Years* [1945]. In our era of more staid theatre manners, it is sometimes difficult to find credible the excitement which surrounded the Federal Theatre Project, various workers' theatre groups, the Mercury Theatre's production of *The*

Cradle Will Rock, the Garment Workers' *Pins and Needles,* or Odets' own **"Waiting for Lefty."**

One incident in Odets' early career, duly reported by the New York *Times* [24 July 1935], perhaps best illustrates the reputation already attached to him at the time. With John Howard Lawson and three other writers, Odets called on Luigi Pirandello, who was visiting New York in 1935. Pirandello apparently wanted to talk about literature, but his visitors were more interested in politics. The Italian playwright claimed that "politics and social questions 'are of the moment' but that 'an artistic moment lives forever.' He insisted that Mr. Odets' plays were good plays 'not because they are social, but because they are artistic.'" The *Times* reporter, apparently somewhat overwhelmed by the whole exchange, added, "the conference broke up with some rancor."

Thus, the turbulent Thirties demanded of any artist involvement with society, and Odets would hardly be accused of being an ivory-tower writer. Social consciousness was a way of life for this angry generation, replacing the Bohemianism of the preceding generation. Odets and the other angry writers were too deeply committed to people and their problems to create art for art's sake. "I have never been able to finish a Henry James novel," said Odets when he spoke with me. He went on:

> This may be some defect in me . . . but I don't think so; I cannot think so. The cult of Henry James with [a] certain kind of stable values. I think it's the stable values that interest people. You know, the fixed world, a closed world, a world that's not changing. We live in a time where you say something in one decade, and a decade later you're old-fashioned.

Such a statement itself tells much about the concepts of the playwright. The world revealed in the plays of Odets is a dynamic, fluid, lived-in world. In this essay I intend to examine that world, with particular attention to **"Waiting for Lefty"** and *Golden Boy,* in order to demonstrate Odets' clear and continuing commitment to the lost and fallen in American society.

It is clear from a great number of statements in his plays that Odets believes that each of us has a firm responsibility to work for the general improvement of society. Often this belief is put in very vague terms, as it is in Leo Gordon's vision of the future, at the end of *Paradise Lost.* In this early play, Odets tries to show an entire sterile society floundering aimlessly in a futile effort to prevent its own erosion; *Paradise Lost* is Odets' *Cherry Orchard.* But the drama is a weak one, mainly because of its central character. Odets' brave attempt to raise Leo Gordon to tragic stature in the final speech fails badly. The acquisition of wisdom through suffering brings a fitting end to the reign of Oedipus; it is not sufficiently plausible for Leo Gordon.

In certain other plays, Odets phrases his beliefs in slightly more specific terms, as in the detective's injunction to the young hero and heroine of *Night Music* to "conquer disease and poverty, dirt and ignorance" (III, ii). But this is as close as Odets comes to spelling out a program. The most specific action taken is the call to strike in **"Waiting for Lefty,"** and even this, of course, is not an end in itself, but only an initial step toward achieving the brave new world. No Odets character is shown joining any kind of Peace Corps; no Faust is present to undertake an irrigation project. The idealistic endings of Odets' plays are not endings at all, but, as the playwright has said, are only beginnings:

> Frequently, the simplicity of some of my endings comes from the fact that I did not say at the same time, "This is a beginning; this will give you the right to begin in a clean and simple way." But these things are not ends in themselves. A strike and a better wage is not an end in itself. . . . It will give you the chance, in a democracy, to find your place, to assume your place and be responsible for your growth and happiness in that place.

Ralph Berger in *Awake and Sing* starts to learn when his grandfather admonishes him to "look on the world, not on yourself so much" (I). And the beginning comes for Ralph when he follows that advice, gives up his self-centered complaining about skates, and obeys his grandfather's command to "go out and fight so life shouldn't be printed on dollar bills" (I). The beginning comes for Dr. Ben Stark in *Rocket to the Moon* when he takes a close look at his relationship with his wife. The beginning comes for Leo Gordon when he recognizes a bond uniting his middle class and the unemployed worker.

More often than not, Odets speaks through his plays as a kind of middle-class conscience. The middle class must, as in *Paradise Lost,* abandon its self-delusion, or, as in *Awake and Sing,* educate itself to tell the difference between dollar bills and life. Odets' characters are constantly enjoined to use whatever resources they possess—violin or printing press—to work for the Utopian paradise which Jacob describes to Ralph in *Awake and Sing*: "From 'L'Africana' . . . a big explorer comes on a new land—'O Paradiso.' From act four this piece. Caruso stands on the ship and looks on a Utopia. You hear? 'Oh paradise! Oh paradise on earth!'" This striving for a better world is an underlying theme of virtually every Odets play. Even in *The Big Knife* there is an unmistakable feeling that America must be freed of the Marcus Hoffs if the middle-class conscience is to be placated.

The evident correlate of a need to improve society is the premise that society is susceptible of betterment. In this concept is the basis of Odets' optimism, and in this optimism is the basis of Odets' first success, **"Waiting for Lefty."** This play of labor union strife is so often pointed to as the typical leftist drama of the Thirties that the comment is as trite as it is oversimplified. The drama is militant, propagandistic, and strident, but, unlike so many of the angry plays of the period, it is also frequently human and touching. Part of the importance of **"Lefty"** certainly lies in the acclaim it received; since subtlety is not one of the play's strong points, the fact that audiences were able to lose themselves in such a direct assault is in itself a

good indication of the mood in that turbulent depression year, 1935. Harold Clurman has termed the play "the birth cry of the thirties" and it is quite natural that the drama has assumed for him a large, almost mystic halo. Others less emotionally involved with the play find that in retrospect it is hard to become so excited as this. Great drama is indestructible; **"Waiting for Lefty,"** for all its merits, often seems as dead as last year's newspaper.

There are many fine qualities about **"Waiting for Lefty,"** not the least of them being that the author approached his work with imagination and technique that far surpass what might be expected from a first play. As a result, **"Waiting for Lefty"** displays an artistry generally absent from previous labor plays of the period. In a series of vignettes, sharply telescoped in time, the drama takes up the story of several characters associated in different ways with the proposed taxi drivers' strike. As Odets envisioned the structure, it was related to that of a minstrel show, with various characters emerging from the darkened stage into the spotlight to tell their stories. Although seemingly episodic in structure, **"Waiting for Lefty"** has a basic unity imposed upon it, first by the theatrical framework of the strike meeting and second by the gradually developed thesis that everyone involved is a part of Lefty.

There is a double framework involved in **"Waiting for Lefty,"** and Odets handles it cleverly, never allowing his audience to forget the significance of his dramatic point. Time and again as the play builds its intensity, he wrenches the audience away from a scene with a violent reminder that there is a strike to be considered, action to be taken. The interplay between personal lives and collective action is masterfully handled: Joe and Edna need food for their children; a strike will provide it. The "young hack" can't afford to marry at all: a strike will enable him to do so. Dr. Benjamin is fired by an anti-Semitic hospital board; the clenched fist offers the solution. Each character is a fragment of Lefty, and the wait that is taking place is a wait for the submerging of the individual in the group.

Every scene adds to the intensity that is necessary for this play's success. The earliest is the least militant, as a wife tries through quiet persuasion to push her lethargic husband toward action. The second ends with direct personal action as the laboratory assistant strikes his employer in the mouth. The following scene moderates the pace somewhat with a tender consideration of a love problem under the financial stress of the depression. But immediately after scene three, the tempo quickens and the undertone of violent action becomes overwhelming. An unemployed actor is handed a copy of the *Communist Manifesto* and told that it contains the real answers. [The scene with the unemployed actor is omitted in the Random House *Six Plays of Clifford Odets* (1939) but may be found in several texts including Willard H. Durham and John W. Dodds, *British and American Plays, 1830-1945*, 1947. Odets has stated (Interview) that the reason for the omission was his decision that the problem was not sufficiently universal, that it had special meaning only for actors—Mendelsohn's note.] Dr. Benjamin, an intellectual, learns the necessity of collective action to erase inequities in American society. Dismissing the idea of going to Russia, "the wonderful opportunity to do good work in their socialized medicine," he proclaims that his work is in America and stands, at the end of the final vignette, with clenched fist raised high.

By this time the pace is unrelenting, and all that remains is the achievement of a new leader's birth in Lefty's death. A crucial part of the message of labor solidarity is that many spring up where one dies. And so Lefty is not dead. Instead he arrives in the body and voice of Agate Keller. The wait is not in vain. And the tocsin rings clearly—if somewhat shrilly—in Keller's emotionally charged call to arms, the famous "stormbirds of the workingclass" speech. Keller shouts of dying for the cause, but he also talks of the new world that will emerge, of the fruit trees that will grow from the ashes. Such is the optimistic premise in which **"Waiting for Lefty"** is solidly rooted.

Although the playwright has disavowed the label "optimist," on the grounds that he has depicted a great deal of sordidness in his plays, everything in the plays is tinged with an idealistic belief that mankind is capable of improving its own position. The paradise on earth seen by Caruso the explorer can be achieved—if man is willing to work for it. Fay, the young heroine of *Night Music,* best expresses this indomitable spirit:

> The last cricket, the very last. . . . Crickets are my favorite animals in all the world. They're never down in the mouth. All night they make their music. . . . Night music. . . . If they can sing, I can sing. I'm more than them. We're more than them. . . . We can sing through any night! [II, iv]

Closely connected with his idealistic pronouncements on American society are Odets' opinions of the artist's place in that society. In both *Golden Boy* and *The Big Knife* the playwright employed a familiar metaphor, gold and the soul, to express an idea obviously close to his heart. On the immediate story level Odets was able to make *Golden Boy* a salable commodity which provided excitement and entertainment for large numbers of playgoers. At the same time he was able to satisfy his own propensity for dealing with significant themes. For *Golden Boy* was not a prize fight story to Odets; it was an allegory, or, better, a parable, in which the playwright examines both an individual's relationship to society and his duty to himself. Joe Bonaparte's first sin stems from his betrayal of the individual's debt to the group. "My boy usta coulda be great for all man," says his father. Instead, with no grandfather Jacob to lecture him, Joe squanders his life in the sin of self-centeredness. Of course that sin is also shared by the country as a whole. American society, suggests the playwright, has glorified material possessions (Joe's Deusenberg car) and the champion (who may destroy others in order to reach the top) at the expense of the artistic and the creative. For the success worshippers of America, there is no place for the second best, a theme Arthur Miller was to stress even more emphatically in *Death of a Salesman.* Those critics who wished to carp at Odets grasped at the thought that it is incredible to imagine a good violinist becoming a good fighter. But for purposes of sharp dra-

matic contrast to underscore his theme, Odets is perfectly justified in his choice of symbols. The extremes are exactly what he needs. There may be slightly more plausibility in the story of a successful doctor who gives up his society practice and retreats to the New England woods to do theoretical research, or a stockbroker who disappears in the South Pacific to paint murals on the walls of his native hut. But if there is more plausibility, there is also less contemporary social applicability in these situations.

Joe's other sin is in suppressing his own better nature. Within him, Odets' hero has some small gifts that should be developed. When he neglects the development of his artistic gifts in favor of his muscular ones, he is indulging in a self-punishment, a destruction of the human side of his nature. The realization that he has completely destroyed the better side of himself, coupled with the loathing of what he has become, drives the golden boy to suicide. The morality-play aspect of all this is evident: Everyman-Bonaparte forsakes his duty to do good works for God, sells himself to the Devil in return for some large status symbols, repents too late for salvation. There is no turning back for Joe. Odets would like the reader to identify closely with Joe, for the success of *Golden Boy* on its allegorical level depends on just such an identification. The choice confronting Joe is everyone's choice.

Odets' later plays, those beginning with *Night Music* (1940), are free of the excesses and overwrought curtain speeches which mark the earlier plays. His early work exposed him to valid charges of excessive emotionalism. But Odets, while retaining his characteristic richness and strength of dialogue, abandoned this kind of writing along with the doctrinaire speeches. What he did not abandon, however, was his social awareness. His recent comment about the social protest plays of the Thirties underlines once more the persistence of his views:

> The plays undoubtedly came out of ascending values, out of positive values, out of the search of millions of American citizens for some way out of a horrifying dilemma—a dilemma which, by the way, I don't think is over. And the writer, or the playwright like myself, simply had to be alive and aware and partaking of this extraordinary ferment around him. The playwright then, as he always is, became the articulate voice of the aspiration of millions of people. . . . When you have a community of values in the theatre (which is, of course, what we *don't* have), when you have that profound community of values in the theatre, the proscenium arch disappears. The audience is not watching a play, and the actors are not playing to an audience which is seated passively somewhere in that dark pit or that dark hole which is the auditorium. Theatre in its profoundest sense—*all* literature in its profoundest sense—has come out of writers, has come in periods when the plight or problem expressed by the actors was completely at one with the plight and problems and values or even moralities of the audience. This is why literature the size of Homer and the Greek drama and the Bible, or, in music, of the early Reformation writers, composers like Bach, has such size. It's because the artist . . . is not someone apart and inimical to his audience, not a man in opposition to the values he is

expressing, but one who is completely at one, who shares organically the very values of the audience for whom he is writing.

It would seem, then, that while he submerged certain other traits, Odets was still vitally concerned with human dignity and with the place of the individual in modern society.

In his later plays and film scripts, Odets moved somewhat away from socio-political subject matter and closer toward problems of individual human needs, with no consequent lessening of what I would call his intellectual-proletarian attitude. The more mature Odets emphasized right and wrong in individual relationships rather than economic exploitation or class struggle. And the ironic result is that Odets more often achieved his dramatic goal using less obviously didactic or emotionally tinted materials.

It is evident that Odets still loves People, in that vague, abstract, idealistic way which makes the Thirties writers of the Left admirable and, at the same time, difficult to understand for the more cynical and more individualistic succeeding generation. Undoubtedly Odets' contributions to American dramatic literature are, at least in part, the product of that love and of the sensitivity or social consciousness which compelled him to give up an acting career in the first place. There is little reason to believe that he would have written anything had he not been motivated by the inequities of American society that he observed. As a young playwright Odets once asserted in an article, "I see it every day all over the city, girls and boys were not getting a chance. . . . No special pleading is necessary in a play which says that people should have fuller and richer lives" [cited by Joseph Mersand, *The American Drama, 1930-1940,* 1941]. And he continued to say the same thing. His characters are obliged to burst the bonds that restrict them in their middle-class milieu, to avoid being tied down by family and tradition, to seek their own place in the sun. This concept was repeated often in Odets' works, but with ever-diminishing stridency. Early in his career Odets believed that he had a mission, and, like so many mission-inspired men, he occasionally allowed the cause to obscure the logic of his work.

To me it is a sign of artistic maturity that Odets gradually learned to stress his themes in a quieter, less didactic manner. In his last produced play, *The Flowering Peach,* some loss of missionary zeal is apparent in the words of a fatigued Noah: "Evil is a stone wall. I hurt my head a lotta times." Militant activists may see Noah's compromises as a "sellout" of the playwright's own beliefs, but this view is unrealistic. The change—if there is one at all—is only a matter of degree. The successful wedding of theme and structure which characterizes *The Flowering Peach* can only be considered an artistic advancement over the too insistent pounding of message in **"Waiting for Lefty."** And running through all of Odets' work is his concern for the dignity of the common man. There was, then, no dimming of Odets' basic optimistic belief in the goodness of people or of his hopes for a better society. If there is one dominant attitude to be found in all of Odets' dramas, it is the one which Charlie Castle says he learned

from reading Victor Hugo: "'Love people, do good, help the lost and fallen, make the world happy, if you can!'"

Gerald Rabkin (essay date 1964)

SOURCE: "The Road from Marxist Commitment: Clifford Odets," in *Drama and Commitment: Politics in the American Theatre of the Thirties,* Indiana University Press, 1964, pp. 169-212.

[*In the excerpt below, Rabkin examines Odets' incorporation of elements of agitprop into his writings of the 1930s.*]

Clifford Odets scrawled his name across the page marked 1935 in American dramatic history. In the course of that year he had five plays produced, four of them on Broadway: **"Waiting for Lefty," "Till the Day I Die,"** *Awake and Sing!,* and *Paradise Lost.* His short monologue, **"I Can't Sleep,"** was produced at a union benefit, and the aforementioned **"Lefty"** began a theatrical career that was to carry it, not only from one end of the United States to the other, but all over the world. The name of Odets became the number one topic of literary conversation, and the hitherto unknown and struggling young actor became one of the foremost celebrities of the day. The *Literary Digest* [6 April 1935] described his emergence:

> In less than ninety days, toiling with the unrest of his times as a central theme, a young actor in the New York theatre . . . has become the most exciting spokesman the world of workers yet has produced, and he has become perhaps the most articulate dramatist available in the theatre.

For once the Broadway and Marxist critics were unanimous in their praise. Richard Watts wrote in the *Herald Tribune* [31 March 1935], "It is pretty clear by now that Mr. Odets' talent for dramatic writing is the most exciting thing to appear in the American drama since the flaming emergence of O'Neill. . . . " And the Marxist critics, despite specific reservations, found much to cheer about in the fact that the new young dramatist had emerged from their own ranks, for Odets' initial discovery was indeed the result of his radical affiliations. **"Lefty"** had been written in response to a contest by the left-wing New Theatre League which was looking for one-act plays on a revolutionary theme which might be easily produced. The play was written at fever heat in three days and nights, won the contest, and was produced at one of the New Theatre League's Sunday night benefit performances by members of the Group Theatre (to which Odets belonged). The performance on January 5, 1935, was one of the electrifying moments in American theatre. Harold Clurman [in *The Fervent Years,* 1945] relates its initial impact:

> The first scene of **"Lefty"** had not played two minutes when a shock of delighted recognition struck the audience like a tidal wave. Deep laughter, hot assent, a kind of joyous fervor seemed to sweep the audience

toward the stage. The actors no longer performed; they were being carried along as if by an exultancy of communication such as I had never witnessed in the theatre before. Audience and actors had become one. . . . When the audience at the end of the play responded to the militant question from the stage: "Well, what's the answer?" with a spontaneous roar of "Strike! Strike!" it was something more than a tribute to the play's effectiveness, more even than a testimony of the audience's hunger for constructive social action. It was the birth cry of the '30s. Our youth had found its voice.

Odets had succeeded where other revolutionary dramatists before him had failed. He had written a militant "agit-prop" drama which succeeded in appealing to unaffiliated liberals as well as to convinced Marxists, and he had done so by humanizing a form of drama whose avowed purpose, as we have observed, was to present political doctrine directly to the audience by means of broadly theatrical play-lets. The following titles indicate the thematic simplicity of the agitprop: *Work or Wages, Unemployment, The Miners are Striking, Vote Communist.* To achieve overtly didactic ends, a variety of dramaturgical devices were employed, many of them stemming from the theatrical experimentation of the twenties: choral recitation, episodic structure, satiric caricature, theatrical stylization. . . .

It is apparent that **"Waiting for Lefty"** is essentially in the agit-prop tradition. Its purpose is overtly didactic in its affirmation of communist doctrine; it is episodic in structure, cartoon-like in its character delineation, directly presentational in technique, and replete with slogans and political comment. Yet while its conclusion is strikingly similar to that of [Art Smith and Elia Kazan's] *Dimitroff* in its merging of actor and audience, in its militant cry to action, we may observe that Odets' plea to strike is essentially a device. The answer and response of actor and audience is not designed to achieve an immediate goal as in the case of Kazan and Smith's play, but is rather a symbolic call to arms, a demonstration of unity and achieved class consciousness. **"Lefty's"** success lay in the fact that it appealed to the unconverted as well as to the committed; it swept all of a liberal persuasion into militant participation, at least in the theatre, by virtue of the precision with which Odets enunciated the Depression malaise. Odets' achievement lay in his ability to humanize the agit-prop without forgoing its theatricality and didacticism. He succeeded not only in presenting the conversion to militancy of a series of taxi-cab workers, but in forcing the audience to see in the plight of these characters a reflection of their own social predicament. Several Marxist critics, among them John Howard Lawson, objected to the designation of **"Lefty"** as a proletarian play because "the militant strike committee [is] made up largely of declassed members of the middle class. One cannot reasonably call these people 'stormbirds of the working class.'" But **"Lefty's"** strength as a conversion drama lay precisely in the fact that Odets' appeal was directed essentially to the class to which he belonged. Of the principal characters only two, Joe and Sid, are proletarians; the others represent various members of the declassed bourgeoisie: a lab assistant who refuses to become an informer, an actor who can't find work on the Broadway market, an interne who is fired because of the anti-Semitism of his superiors. All are forced into activism by social circumstances. "Don't call me red," shouts Joe. "You know what we are? The black and blue boys! We been kicked around so long we're black and blue from head to toes!" But Joe had not always been as adamant as he is now. He had been goaded to militancy by his wife's threat to leave him unless he organized and fought for his rights: "Get those hack boys together! . . . Stand up like men and fight for the crying kids and wives. Goddamnit! I'm tired of slavery and sleepless nights."

Joe's social awakening is but one in the series of conversions that constitute **"Waiting for Lefty."** Each episode presents the road to commitment of each of the several characters against the backdrop of various capitalist evils: labor spying, informing, anti-Semitism, economic aggression, etc. One by one the dramas of conversion are enacted: the interne finds that Jewish and Gentile capitalists are cut from the same cloth; the lab assistant recognizes that the logic of capitalism demands war; the workers, Sid and Joe, realize that the cards are stacked against the proletariat; and the young actor, turned down by a producer who cares more for his pet dog than for human beings, is taken in hand by a radical stenographer who undertakes his ideological enlightenment:

> One dollar buys ten loaves of bread, Mister. Or one dollar buys nine loaves of bread and one copy of the Communist Manifesto. Learn while you eat. . . . Read while you run. . . . From Genesis to Revelation . . . the meek shall not inherit the earth! The MILITANT! Come out in the light, Comrade!

All roads lead to Agate's final peroration, his cry for alliance with the proletariat: "It's war! Working class, unite and fight! Tear down the slaughter house of our old lives!" The basic metaphor of the play is, of course, the futility of waiting for something that will never come, the hope that somehow conditions may be alleviated by other than direct action. Fatt, the personification of the capitalist system, had counseled the workers to put their faith in "the man in the White House" in his attempt to dissuade them from striking; but half-way measures are doomed to failure. Salvation must be earned; Lefty never comes because he has been murdered—the ritual martyrdom of proletarian literature—and the act of waiting must be replaced by militancy.

> Hello America! Hello! We're Stormbirds of the Working Class. Workers of the world . . . our bones and blood! And when we die they'll know what we did to make a new world! Christ, cut us up to little pieces. We'll die for what is right! Put fruit trees where our ashes are!

The impact of **"Waiting for Lefty"** is irrevocably dependent upon its contemporaneity. In the thirties the play was a formidable weapon. Within weeks after its initial production it became the public property of the left, and groups were organized all over the country to perform it. Odets later doubted if he had earned a thousand dollars out of the play: "People just did it. . . . It has been done all over the world . . . and I have not received five cents of royalties. . . . It was at one time a kind of light machine gun that you wheeled in to use whenever there was any kind of strike trouble." A storm of censorship accompanied its production in many different cities. In Boston, the actors were arrested for language that was "extremely blasphemous"; in Philadelphia, the theatre in which the play was to be produced was suddenly called "unsafe," and the performance was canceled. Will Geer produced the play in Hollywood despite threats and was severely beaten by hoodlums; and in general, the stridency of conservative criticism revealed that Odets' "machine gun" was not far off target.

The instantaneous success of **"Lefty"** at the New Theatre League Sunday performances caused the Group Theatre to present the play as one of its scheduled productions. In moving to Broadway, however, a new companion piece was needed to fill out the bill, since *Dimitroff* would hardly have succeeded uptown, and Odets wrote a play based upon contemporary life in Nazi Germany called **"Till the Day I Die."** Based upon a letter in the *New Masses,* the plot concerns Ernst Taussig, a German communist captured by the Nazis in a raid and subjected by them to torture in an effort to force him to inform upon his associates. Although he is never completely broken, Taussig is made to appear a traitor to his comrades. Blacklisted by his former friends, fearful of compromising the revolutionary cause, Ernst commits suicide.

Odets' achievement lay in his ability to humanize the agit-prop without forgoing its theatricality and didacticism.

—*Gerald Rabkin*

Lawson objected that "the sustained conflict, the conscious will of man pitted against terrible odds is omitted. We see [Taussig] . . . only *before* and *after*. The crucial stage, in which his will is tested and broken, occurs between scenes five and seven." The significant fact is that the audience is never really sure whether or not Taussig *was* broken by the Nazis or whether or not he retained his integrity to the end. At the beginning of the play he is a convinced revolutionary fervently viewing the classless future. Has he indeed changed when he is released from his initial Nazi captivity? It does not seem so. To Tilly's query as to whether or not he was afraid Ernst answered, "A man who knows that the world contains millions of brothers and sisters can't be afraid. . . . In the cell there—I know I stayed alive because I knew my comrades were with me in the same pain and chaos."

All the evidence of the play supports Ernst's contention that he kept the revolutionary faith, that he had been forced to accompany storm troopers on their round-ups of radicals, that he was forcibly brought into court at political trials, that, in short, it was planned to make him appear to be an informer. Nowhere is it implied that Taussig was actually broken. The important fact is that the issue of his innocence or guilt is not the crucial dramatic question which the play posits. It is rather involved with the problem of political loyalty; the play affirms the revolutionary contention that the individual is less important than the cause to which he is dedicated. In the best scene in the play—best because it smacks of the authentic logic of political debate—the local cell excommunicates Taussig because his comrades cannot afford to take the chance that he may be guilty; he cannot be trusted, whether he is innocent or not. Love and fraternal affection must bow before the iron exigencies of the revolutionary situation, since in a warring world "it is brother against brother." Just as the labor spy in **"Waiting for Lefty"** is exposed by his brother, Ernst Taussig is disavowed by his brother Carl:

> Many a comrade has found with deep realization that he has no home, no brother—even no mothers or fathers! What must we do here? . . . We must expose this one brother wherever he is met. Whosoever looks in his face is to point the finger. Children will jeer at him in the darkest streets of his life! Yes, the brother, the erstwhile comade cast out! There is no brother, no family, no deeper mother than the working class.

Ernst recognizes that there is but one action left him, and he asks his brother to administer the *coup de grâce*. He knows that he must be cast away, that the individual is unimportant in the greater struggle, that his realization will come through the work of his comrades: "the day is coming, and I'll be in the final result." Unlike the traditional martyrs of Marxist literature, whose deaths serve as the catalysts for the awakening of others, Ernst believes that he is the phoenix that will arise from the ashes of his necessary death. Thus the play ends, not with the conversion of the previously uncommitted, but with the affirmation by the committed that their existence is contained in the collective of which they are a part.

When he was writing **"Waiting for Lefty"** and **"Till the Day I Die,"** Odets expressed himself in typically Marxist tones, maintaining that the function of art was primarily propagandistic. "It may be said that anything which one writes on 'the side' of the large majority of people is propaganda. But today the truth followed to its logical conclusion is inevitably revolutionary." It is not surprising, then, that the author of such a statement should be, in fact, a member of the Communist party, having been recruited by the small core of communists within the Group Theatre. Years later, in the familiar purgative drama of the fifties, Odets related to the House Un-American Activities Committee the circumstances of his enrollment:

> In a time of great social unrest many people found themselves reaching out for new ideas, new ways of solving depressions or making a better living, fighting for one's rights. . . . These were . . . horrendous days . . . there was a great deal of talk about amelioration of conditions, about how should one live. . . . One read literature; there were a lot of . . . pamphlets . . . I read

them along with a lot of other people, and finally joined the Communist party in the belief, in the honest and real belief, that this was some way out of the dilemma in which we found ourselves.

Odets testified that he remained in the party "from toward the end of 1934 to the middle of '35, covering maybe anywhere from six to eight months." It is not our purpose here to scrutinize the motivations which resulted in Odets' disavowal. We are concerned primarily with the dramatist, not the individual; we may observe, however, that Odets' act of disaffiliation in 1935 is in no way clearly obvious from either his public statements or his dramatic work. As the counsel for the Un-American Activities Committee embarrassingly pointed out, Odets continued to affiliate with leftwing groups throughout the Depression and war years. Perhaps the answer lies in the intellectual climate of the mid-thirties, the era of the Popular Front. Unless one was, as an intellectual, directly involved with the vagaries and variations of social doctrine (e.g., Edmund Wilson, Sidney Hook), it was quite possible to drift away from overt commitment without the painful process of making a clean break.

Thus Odets' Marxist commitment was very different from that of John Howard Lawson. The latter came to his political beliefs, as we have seen, after a long period of conflict and indecision; once he made his commitment, Lawson became a political man, his role as artist receding behind the ideological facade. Odets, however, did not arrive at his radicalism after a long period of intellectual debate. He was, in a sense, born to it; radicalism was in the air his generation breathed. Since his commitment was never primarily intellectual, he never formally rejected it in the manner of the intellectuals who, having made themselves political men, one day awake with horror to a sense of betrayal and find it necessary to destroy their radical roots.

We cannot, therefore, discover any crucial moment of commitment or disaffiliation in the life and work of Clifford Odets. For whatever reasons he left the party, there can be no denying the pervasive influence of Marxism upon the great bulk of his work. Surely Odets' temperament, particularly after his sudden access to fame and his defection to Hollywood, was unsuited to political obligation. He was too concerned with his own problems ever to assent fully to the role of party member. But since his commitment to Marxism was essentially more emotional than intellectual, he retained, throughout the Depression, an umbilical connection with the radical movement. It is interesting that despite Odets' statement to the Un-American Activities Committee that he left the Party in 1935 because "it came to the point of where I thought . . . I can't respect these people on a so-called cultural basis" Odets was still talking in terms of the social "usefulness" of art in the preface to his *Six Plays* (1939). He stated his esthetic aim as follows: "Much of my concern during the past years has been with fashioning a play immediately and dynamically useful and yet as psychologically profound as my present years and experience will permit." This is the artist's great problem "since we are living in a time when new art works should shoot bullets. . . . "

Odets' aggressive Marxism of the mid-decade is reflected in a short monologue, **"I Can't Sleep,"** written for performance at a benefit for the Marine Workers Industrial Union in 1935. It, too, is a party play in that it overtly considers the greatest of revolutionary sins, heresy. It is reminiscent of the Grand Inquisitor sequence in [Fyodor Dostoevsky's] *The Brothers Karamazov,* in which the silence of Christ forces the Inquisitor into self-revelation. Odets' hero—played originally by Morris Carnovsky—rejects a beggar's appeal for charity, and finds himself imprisoned in a cell of guilt constructed by the disavowed radicalism of his youth. He initially answers the beggar's unpitying stare with belligerence—"Listen, don't be so smart. When a man offers you money, take it!"—but soon he turns from aggressive self-justification to personal revelation. He tells of his inability to communicate with his wife, of the gulf of misunderstanding which separates him from his children, of all the bitter frustrations which afflict him, symbolized by the ever-present fact of his insomnia. Consumed by loneliness, he yearns to cry "Brother" to his fellow man but is constrained by the fear of appearing a fool.

And slowly the last layer of artifice is pulled away and the true cause of the man's depression is revealed: "I spoke last week to a red in the shop. Why should I mix in with politics? With all my other troubles I need yet a broken head? I can't make up my mind—what should I do? . . . Join up, join up. But for what? For trouble?" This question reaches the heart of the man's dilemma, and in a torrent of words he reveals the source of his guilt, the renunciation of his working-class roots, his acceptance, against his better nature, of the capitalist ethic. . . .

The source of much of Odets' strength as a "proletarian" playwright lay precisely in the fact that he did not force himself to write about the proletariat. Unlike other middle-class writers of Marxist persuasion, he had the esthetic sense to write about areas of his direct experience. In his early days in the Group he started several plays, one in particular on the subject of his much-beloved Beethoven. A diary entry of the time reveals his dissatisfaction with these early attempts: "Now I see again in myself flight, always flight. Here I am writing the Beethoven play, which when it is finished may not be about Beethoven. Why not write something about the Greenberg family, something I know better, something that is closer to me?"

The resultant play, initially entitled *I Got the Blues,* was started in a cold-water flat on West 57th Street, New York City, and finished at Warrensburg, New York, during the rehearsals of *Men in White*. It was finally produced by the Group, after the success of the subsequently written **"Lefty,"** under the title of *Awake and Sing!* In it the Greenberg family emerged as the Berger family of the Bronx, and Odets revealed himself not only as a young writer of intense revolutionary fervor, but as a skillful recorder of the pungent detail of Jewish lower middle-class life.

The basic image of *Awake and Sing!* is resurrection, the emergence of life from death. For the life of the Berger family in Depression-age America is spiritual death, dehumanized by a thousand irritants, frustrated by the exigencies of economic breakdown. Yet precisely because the sources of the Bergers' difficulties are primarily social, *Awake and Sing!* is an essentially optimistic play; dangers are without, not within, and they may be combatted. The fundamental activity of the Bergers—"a struggle for life amidst petty conditions"—is a noble one; nor is it meaningless. Significantly Odets changed the title of the play from *I Got the Blues*—a statement of the Depression malaise—to *Awake and Sing!*—and the imperative commanded by the exclamation point is no accident. "Awake and sing, ye that dwell in the dust," he is crying, the American blues can be eliminated. But the play is not a direct call to militancy; its strength rests in the depiction of the social dislocation of the middle class and the skill with which this dislocation is personalized in the several characters. . . .

Awake and Sing! is not merely a catalogue of frustration. In the portrayal of old Jacob, the radical of the family, Odets provides the play with its explicit social commentary without violating the demands of character. Throughout the early action Jacob serves as a kind of chorus, drawing the Marxist moral from the statements and activities of the other characters. When his somber social analyses are laughed at by his family, particularly by his business-man son, Morty, he responds: "Laugh, laugh . . . tomorrow not." It is in the hope of achieving this tomorrow in the person of Ralph, the young son of the Berger household, that Jacob commits the sacrifice of leaping to his death so that Ralph might have his insurance money as a means to escape the strangle hold of the family and society. When Ralph learns of the old man's sacrifice he vows that it will not have been in vain. Jacob's legacy is not money, which Ralph in fact rejects, but social awareness. To his mother's justification of life in America, he retorts, "It don't make sense. If life made you this way, then it's wrong." Bessie answers, "So go out and change the world if you don't like it," and Ralph affirms, "I will! And why? 'Cause life's different in my head. Gimme the earth in two hands. I'm strong." Jacob's books, his ideas, are Ralph's real inheritance, and he has become infused with the old man's revolutionary fervor:

> Get teams together all over. Spit on your hands and get to work. And with enough teams together maybe we'll get steam in the warehouse so our fingers don't freeze off. Maybe we'll fix it so life won't be printed on dollar bills.

And the play ends on the note of resurrection. "The night he died," states Ralph about Jacob, "I saw it like a thunder-bolt! I saw he was dead and I was born! I swear to God, I'm one week old! I want the whole city to hear it—fresh blood, arms. We got 'em. We're glad we're living."

Thus, despite the effectiveness of realistic detail, it is apparent that *Awake and Sing!* still retains strong agit-prop roots. But instead of appealing directly for revolutionary action, it attempts to demonstrate the thesis of revolutionary awareness in the relationship between Jacob and Ralph against the family background of middle-class decay. Its success is dependent upon this conjunction of

thesis and detail. Odets never was a genre painter; his strokes are broad, his dialogue heightened. What he succeeded in delineating were the specific images of social dislocation. The importance of the Marxist premise from a dramatic point of view does not lie in its specific truth or falsity; it serves rather as a dramatic metaphor which orders the disparate elements of the play, which relates the images of frustration and dislocation to a guiding thematic concept. The spine of the play is the conviction that the world of the Bergers must be changed if human potentiality is to be realized. For Odets at that time this faith was affirmed by Marxism; far from marring the play, the Marxist metaphor gathers the various dramatic strands and relates them to the basic theme of social resurrection.

Odets, then, was never primarily a realist. *Awake and Sing!* and his next play, *Paradise Lost,* are essentially allegories of middle-class decay. It was the inability to recognize this fact which was primarily responsible for the critical furor which attended the production of the latter play. The Broadway critics, who had greeted *Awake and Sing!* in uniformly commendatory tones ("a triumph for the Group and . . . Mr. Odets," "Something of an event, not to say a miracle," "a stirring play") now turned their guns upon Odets' new play, most finding it marred by "frowzy characterization, random form and . . . inchoate material." Nor did Odets receive any consolation from the radical press. For the most part, Marxist critics rejected the play on the grounds of unsound social analysis. Stanley Burnshaw, for example, questioned the validity of Odets' portrait of the American middle class. He maintained that the American bourgeoisie "is *not* a homogenous group withering into oblivion. . . . Overwhelming numbers of middle-class people . . . are part and parcel of the advancing social group. . . . Can their life be truthfully conveyed by such symbols as sexual impotence, heart disease . . . barrenness and arson, larcency, racketeering, cuckoldry, feeblemindedness and sex neuroses?"

The Marxist attacks were predicted on a literal interpretation of the dissolution of the Gordon family as a result of economic pressures. Under such an interpretation it is obvious that physical disease cannot fairly be credited to capitalism. But as Clurman, the play's director, noted, neither in direction, acting nor set design was *Paradise Lost* naturalistic: "The 'reading' I have given the script gives the play a definite *line* or what certain reviewers would call a propagandistic slant." And, despite the fact that the play displeased the left, the "line" was clearly Marxist: "The middle-class carries out the orders of the ruling class with the illusion of complete freedom."

At the beginning of Act III of *Paradise Lost,* Clara Gordon relates to her dying son, Julie, the parable of the golden idol:

> Well, Moses stayed in the mountain forty days and forty nights. They got frightened at the bottom. . . . What did those fools do? They put all the gold pieces together, all the jewelry, and melted them, and made a baby cow of gold. . . . Moses ran down the hill so fast. . . . He took the cow and broke it into a thousand

pieces. Some people agreed, but the ones who didn't? Finished. God blotted them out of the book. Here today, gone tomorrow!

Paradise Lost is itself Odets' parable of the decadence of contemporary capitalism, and his idolators are as surely condemned as those who worshipped the golden calf. The characters in the play are all condemned—some by disease, some by economics—but they are all presented as denizens of a world made unreal by false hope and futile illusion. The image is starker than that of *Awake and Sing!* because the seeds of redemption, although present in the play, are not allowed to flower. Ralph, Moe, Hennie escape to attempt to create a better world; despite his realization that he must do the same, Leo's final affirmation has come too late. He, too, is condemned. Thus, redemption must come from without, in the creation of a world unmarred by the abortiveness and sickness which dominate the world of *Paradise Lost.*

Such a vision is unquestionably grim, and *Paradise Lost* is a grim play, relieved but briefly by the humor that characterized much of *Awake and Sing!* The several characters, despite particularization, are more overtly allegorical; all represent to a greater or lesser degree the smothering of the individual by capitalist society. . . .

The image which pervades *Paradise Lost* is the "sweet smell of decay." The world of the Gordons is a microcosm of the "profound dislocation" of the middle class in capitalist society. Leo Gordon, a man of fundamentally noble instincts, comes finally to recognize that he is the representative of a dying class. Throughout the play he is appalled by the misery which he sees around him and is determined not to build his happiness on the exploitation of others. But his fortune and his family are crushed by personal tragedy and his refusal to recoup the loss of his business by approving an arranged insurance fire. "So in the end," he laments, "nothing is real. Nothing is left but our memory of life." But, despite his condemnation, he is allowed one glimpse of the new future that will replace the false paradise:

> No! There is more to life than this! . . . There is a future. Now we know, we dare to understand. . . . I tell you the whole world is for men to possess. Heartbreak and terror are not the heritage of mankind! No fruit tree wears a lock and key. . . . The world is in its morning . . . and *no man fights alone!*

Despite dramaturgic preparation, there can be no denying that this peroration is inconsistent with the basic metaphor of *Paradise Lost*. Perhaps Odets feared that if he did not explicitly state what was generally implied in the play, it might have been open to the criticism of "negativism." And yet, even without the obviousness of Leo's final awareness, it is apparent that the very frustration which dominates the play implies a social protest. As John Gassner has pointed out, "Airing one's discontents is a patent form of rebellion, dramatization of frustration is already a form of acting out, exposing a situation is criticism and often a challenge to action."

The unreality which critics of the play objected to is a reflection of the dream world constructed by the middle class in its futile attempt to escape the economic realities of capitalism. The Marxist metaphor lies at the heart of *Paradise Lost*; it is basic to its very conception. The very title implies that there is a paradise to be regained. The play also represents the end of Odets' period of overt political commitment, the last expression of the bitter years of anonymity which preceded his emergence. Downcast by the bad critical reaction to the play, which long remained his favorite, he wrote a short biographical piece in which he lamented the vagaries of sudden success:

> The young writer comes out of obscurity with a play or two. Suppose he won't accept the generous movie offers. Why, that means he's holding out for more. Suppose he accepts—he's an ingrate, rat, renegade. . . .

> If he's written two plays about the same kind of people everyone knows that's all he can write about. . . . If the reviewers praise him Tuesday, it's only because they're gentle, quixotic fellows. But watch them tear him apart on Wednesday! . . . The young writer is now ready for a world cruise!

And as Clurman pointed out, "for a New York playwright this means almost inevitably Hollywood."

The problem of artistic integrity is necessarily difficult to define; it invariably mires the critic in the quicksands of the intentional fallacy. But biographical concerns are not necessarily extrinsic to an evaluation of literature. In the case of Odets, for example, it is crucial to an understanding of much of his later work—in particular *Golden Boy* and *The Big Knife*—to recognize the ambivalent attitudes which he displayed toward the symbol of American success, Hollywood. Indeed, we are faced here with a not unfamiliar problem: if the roots of an artist lie in the fact of his knowledge of an environment which is economically deprived, how is he to prevent the withering of these roots by the fact of his newfound success? Is the artist, by virtue of his status as celebrity, now cut off by this very status from the sources of his previous vitality? These questions have relevance not only to Odets but to many others of his generation. Hollywood's siren song dashed the talents of many young radical writers on the rocks of hack screenwriting.

In the case of Odets, Hollywood meant not only separation from the roots of New York radicalism, but separation as well from his theatre, the Group. Odets' debt to the Group was manifest: it produced all of the plays that he wrote in the thirties. Odets is one of the few playwrights of our time to have a theatre which enabled him to speak in a consistent voice. In the direction of Clurman and the acting talent of the Adlers, Carnovsky, Bromberg, Garfield, Cobb, *et al.,* he was fortunate in having a well-trained ensemble which offered the perfect medium for the expression of his dramatic vision.

Perhaps for several reasons—the failure of *Paradise Lost,* the lure of the fantastic salary ($2,500 a week), the desire to explore that most powerful of mass media—Odets, to the dismay of the Group, went to Hollywood in 1936 to "look around"; as he himself stated to Clurman, he had a need "to sin." Thus began a tortured love affair between Odets and the film capital which lasted until his death there in 1963. Ironically enough, his last work of any significance was his screenplay for the cynical *The Sweet Smell of Success* (1957). Alternately praising and reviling Hollywood, Odets was never able either fully to accept or reject its values. He viewed the cinema alternately as a medium particularly suited to the dramatist because of its directness, fluidity, and universality, and as a medium which, because of its subjugation to commercial exigencies, vitiates and destroys artistic integrity.

On the one hand, Odets offered the justification that Hollywood, by virtue of its fantastic salaries, might serve as the new patron which would free the writer for his more creative work; while, on the other, he continually recognized that isolation from the source of his material was the artist's real danger. Ironically, less than a year before he went to Hollywood for the first time, Odets wrote: "Shortly I'm getting to the coal fields and the textile centers. Let New York see the rest of the country. Hollywood too. Play material enough to keep six dozen writers going. . . ." [New York *World Telegram,* 19 March 1935].

Odets' major, and only, dramatic effort for the year 1936 consisted of the film, *The General Died at Dawn*; it was eagerly awaited by radical circles in the hope that the fair-haired boy of leftist drama had succeeded in striking a few blows for the revolutionary cause. Sidney Kaufman reported upon the film's progress in the *New Masses*: "This melodramatic yarn rings like a coin from the nickelodeon mint," he admitted, "but, godalmighty, what a different face it wears." This different face was, for Kaufman, reflected in several speeches of implied social consciousness. An examination of the script, however, reveals them as hardly inflammatory. Judy (played by Madeleine Carroll) has decoyed O'Hara (Gary Cooper) into a train compartment.

> *Judy:* Why do they make these attempts on your life?
>
> *O'Hara:* Politics. A certain honorable tootsie roll named Yang thinks he has a right to control the lives of tens of thousands of poor Chinese.
>
> *Judy:* How?
>
> *O'Hara:* Military dictatorship! Taxes! You put, he takes! You protest, he shoots! A head-breaker, a heart-breaker, a strike-breaker! Altogether a four-star rat!

The General Died at Dawn found few champions in either the radical or nonradical camps, and the artist in Odets soon recognized that the media of the film and the stage were not equally hospitable to seriousness, that the powers that controlled the film industry were not interested in fully utilizing the talent in their employ. The stage, and the Group, beckoned, and Odets returned to New York with *Golden Boy*. But while he was anxious to be free of the encumbrances of the film colony, Odets was excited by the possibility of applying film technique and subject matter to the medium of the stage. The cinema was indeed "the authentic folk theatre of America," but producers were not interested in presenting their material significantly; on the contrary, "their chief problem is the one of keeping the level of human experience in their pictures as low as possible." But the film has opened up the possibility of a true portrayal of American life by virtue of the range and color of its subject matter and technique. Inasmuch as Hollywood will not permit the serious use of this authentic material, it remains the task of the playwright to do so within the freer confines of the stage: "It is about time that the talented American playwright began to take the gallery of American types, the assortment of fine vital themes away from the movies."

This is precisely what Odets attempted to achieve in *Golden Boy*. "Where is there a more interesting theme in this country than a little Italian boy who wants to be rich? Provided, of course, you place him in his true social background and . . . present the genuine pain, meaning and dignity of life within your characters." In short, Odets took as his self-appointed task the infusion of a typical Hollywood theme with a sense of reality, "to tell the truth where the film told a lie. . . ." The difficulty with such an approach is that the triteness of the traditional subject matter may negate the seriousness of theme. *Golden Boy* treads the uncertain line between cliché and seriousness. But, on the whole, one must, in the case of this play, acknowledge Odets' success in achieving his avowed purpose. Although the story of Joe Bonaparte's rise and fall is indeed sheer Hollywood—it is the stuff of a hundred fight films—Odets has succeeded in covering the bones of melodrama with sterner stuff. He has done so by reverting to his role of allegorist.

Golden Boy is not primarily concerned with the decay of a class, it is concerned with the decadence of an ideal, success. The very nature of Odets' personal situation in Hollywood offered him his theme; for Joe Bonaparte in gaining the world loses his soul, and he loses it because he relinquishes his artistic integrity for immediate success in the world of the quick buck. It is not my intention to draw any invidious biographical parallels, but it is apparent that Joe's dilemma to a great extent parallels Odets'. The worlds of the prize ring and the motion-picture studios betray uncomfortable similarities. Both exploit talent for specifically commercial ends; both deal in forms of mass entertainment. But in the case of Joe Bonaparte the choice is not ambiguous; the pugilistic talent which he must employ to achieve success is clearly demarcated from his ability to play the violin. The Hollywood screenwriter could bask in the illusion that he was pursuing the dramatic craft.

Whether or not the world of the prize ring is intended to represent the world of Hollywood, it is apparent that the values of both are those which Odets had previously attacked in his early plays. The theme of *Golden Boy* is made meaningful in terms of a specific condemnation of the values of a society in which false values are able to pervert man's better instincts.

Joe Bonaparte's decision to fight, to show the world, is given credence by a society in which "five hundred fiddlers stand on Broadway and 48th Street, on the corner, every day, rain or shine, hot or cold." In such a world the artistic gesture appears futile, and if success must be gained at the expense of art, then art must be sacrificed. But Joe's success, based upon false values, is doomed to prove insubstantial. Slowly he is turned into that which runs against his better nature, a killer; ultimately no longer faced with an alternative, he must fight because that is the only thing he can do. Joe has become a killer in spirit: "When a bullet sings through the air it has no past—only a future—like me! Nobody, nothing stands in my way!" It is not long before he becomes a killer in fact, the fit companion for the homosexual racketeer, Fuseli; in the course of a fight he knocks out his opponent and finds that the blow has killed him. Remorse has come too late; Joe recognizes that in the act of violence he has killed as well the man he might have become. Too late he realizes that it is not the kings and dictators who conquer the world, but "the boy who might have said, 'I have myself; I am what I want to be!'"

Joe's death in an auto crash is not gratuitous; it is the fitting conclusion to a life which he chose to lead according to the laws of the jungle. The final verdict is delivered by Joe's union-organizer brother, Frank: "What waste!" The creative energy which might have produced beautiful music has been destroyed in a false crusade. Joe's killer instinct had been bred in a world in which such talent is highly prized. If Joe was destroyed by his false image of success he was not entirely culpable; this image was created by a society in which man's basest instincts are glorified.

Such are the implications of Odets' parable. It is apparent that beneath the surface melodrama lies the familiar Marxist metaphor, albeit somewhat diluted by personal considerations. Odets' involvement in the problem of success, however, reveals more than merely personal concerns; it reflects his awareness of its mythic role in our society. It is significant that Joe was presented with an alternative. Although he rejected it because of the pressure of false values, the alternative nonetheless exists: to refuse to acquiesce in these values, to build a society in which art has a place. This conclusion is not directly affirmed, but it is strongly implied, particularly in the person of Frank, who serves as a foil to Joe's destructive energy. It is noteworthy that Odets should turn Hollywood subject matter and technique (the short, cinematic scenes, the use of fade-outs) against itself, in order to combat the mythic Hollywood success story (and Hollywood, in retaliation, reversed Odets' logic by putting a "happy ending" upon the screen version of *Golden Boy*). The moral of Odets' allegory might not be overtly revolutionary, but it is nonetheless rooted in severe social criticism.

Odets was not, however, through with Hollywood. Over the course of the next decade he was alternately to make his peace with the film colony and then reject it anew. (A 1944 interview [*New York Times,* 27 August] was entitled "Going Their Way Now? Clifford Odets Has Given Up Tilting at the Hollywood Windmill, or So He Says.") In 1948, for example, he returned to Broadway after a seven-

year absence, and castigated the movie colony in the harshest terms possible. He deeply resented the accusations of "sell out" which had plagued him ever since he initially left for Hollywood, and offered several explanations for his long defection: he wanted to recoup the "small fortune" he had invested in the Group in its dying years, to forget "the distress of several misplaced personal allegiances"; he was looking for a period of "creative repose: money, rest, and simple clarity." But Hollywood, he averred, offered few consolations beyond the monetary; since his talents were still ignored, he came to detest the lethargy into which he had fallen; he consoled himself with the plays he was going to write, "took my filthy salary every week and rolled an inner eye around an inner landscape." Apparently Odets never quite escaped the sense of guilt born of accepting Hollywood gold, and was performing an act of purgation in returning to the New York theatre, "where personal affiliation with one's writing (the first premise of truth) does not constitute lese majesty."

Odets' specific act of contrition was represented by his play *The Big Knife* (1949), in which he attempted to expose the mendacity of Hollywood and the corrosive effect of its guiding ethic. "The big knife," he stated, "is that force in modern life which is against people and their aspirations, which seeks to cut people off in their best flower," but, we must ask, in what precisely does this force reside? For the difficulty with the play is that we are never exactly sure what the playwright is railing against. In *Golden Boy,* Odets used some of the conventions of melodrama in order to construct an allegory which depicted the pernicious effect of a destructive ethic; in *The Big Knife* he attempts much the same thing, but fails to demonstrate the play's thesis through dramatic action. Joe Bonaparte is destroyed because society has made him a killer; why does Charlie Castle destroy himself? Hank, the New York writer who symbolizes the man of integrity, presents Charlie's eulogy: "He killed himself . . . because that was the only way he could live." Charlie's suicide was "a final act of faith." Faith, however, in what? Castle's predicament, as revealed in the play, seems magnified beyond all dramatic credibility precisely because it is forcibly wedded to melodramatic circumstance instead of arising inexorably from a genuine moral dilemma. The real issue involved is simple: should the artist, luxuriating in material splendor at the expense of his artistic integrity, chuck it all to return to a meaningful existence? Stated in these terms, the issue seems hardly one to induce suicide. But Odets obviously felt that the problem was not dramatically sufficient, and therefore felt constrained to project this dilemma in terms of a plot which deals with intrigue and suggested murder. The difficulty with this scheme from a dramatic viewpoint is that the real issue—the acceptance or rejection of Hollywood values—is in no way related to the machinery of the plot. If Charlie Castle is blackmailed into signing his contract, what happens to the element of choice which is crucial to the larger, more serious, dramatic issue?

Thus the prevalent tone of *The Big Knife* is hysteria. Odets attacks many evils of the Hollywood scene—the malicious gossip-monger, the amoral aide-de-camp, the hypocritical, vicious producer—but he fails to achieve what he succeeded in accomplishing in *Golden Boy,* to relate these specific evils, and the drama's basic structure, to a guiding metaphor which clarifies the main lines of the intended allegory. The boxing world becomes, in *Golden Boy,* a microcosm of the larger society of which it is a part; Hollywood, in *The Big Knife,* fails not only as a microcosm, but as a realistic portrayal of the film capital. God knows there are sufficient grounds for criticism without implying that producers and agents are would-be murderers.

The crucial fact is that *Golden Boy* presents a social alternative; *The Big Knife* does not. "Does the man in your book get out of here?" cries Charlie to Hank. "Where does he go? What, pray tell, does he do? (*bitterly*) Become a union organizer?" This alternative, objectified in the person of Frank in *Golden Boy,* has become unthinkable. Charlie's anguish springs from the recognition that he is a part of the world which he wants to reject. The problem with the play resides in this very ambivalence. Odets—in the character of Castle—alternately vilifies and accepts Hollywood captivity. Charlie wants to reject the malicious world of which he is a part, but feels unable to substitute another. Although he recognizes that "everyone needs a cause to touch greatness," he has lost his capacity to believe in causes. He has, as hank points out, sold out, and is consequently tormented by guilt: "Look at me! Could you ever know that all my life I yearned for a world and people to call out the best in me?" In short, although Odets *has* a theme, he is unwilling to face its direct implications. For the real question, left unanswered in *The Big Knife,* is in what or in whom does the responsibility lie for the destruction of Charlie Castle? In society? In his own weakness? Perhaps Odets was too personally involved in Charlie's dilemma to objectify it truthfully. As Clurman noted, the play "is neither the true story of Odets nor the clear account of a freely conceived Charlie Castle. Its subjectivity is muddled by its pretense of objectivity; its objectivity is compromised by the author's inability to distinguish between his creature and himself."

The importance of Odets' political commitment from a dramatic point of view resided in its affording him an intellectual substructure upon which to construct his several dramas. Since Odets' virtues were never primarily intellectual, his social orientation enabled him to relate his characters and themes to a coherent world-view. Either explicit or implicit in all his dramas of the thirties lies the metaphor born of his Marxist commitment. At first overtly stated, it later becomes the philosophical undercurrent which relates his several portraits of frustration to a gesture of protest. The Marxist eschatology provided the dramatist with a structural referent, for implicit in the dialectical struggle is an essential drama, the vanquishing of the old class by the new. It is this dialectic which informs Odets' Depression dramas; either explicitly in **"Waiting for Lefty"** or implicitly in *Rocket to the Moon,* they all offer the hope of the future against the frustration of the present. The structural failure of *The Big Knife* lies in Odets' inability, after the loss of political commitment, to substitute a suitable unifying dramatic metaphor. With the absence of the substructure of social protest, the drama flounders in a sea of hysteria. I am not implying the *necessity* of a social metaphor in drama, but merely pointing out the crucial role it played in Odets' career as dramatist. Odets has lost his status as major dramatist because, unlike Tennessee Williams, for example, he failed to suggest in his later dramas that he was presenting us with a vision of reality which transcended his several plays.

The consequences of the loss of metaphor may be observed in a comparison of two domestic dramas written in the thirties and the fifties respectively. *Rocket to the Moon* (1938) is not an overtly political play. In fact, the Marxist critics complained that "Odets has stopped listening to the people he knows so well." It is concerned with the frustrations of a middle-class dentist and his futile love affair with his young secretary. But despite Odets' essentially personal concerns, despite his emphasis upon psychological rather than social factors, there can be no denying that beneath the play resides the basic social metaphor.

The very positing of the metaphor of the rocket to the moon—the illusion of escape—has meaning because it is an illusion, because there is an alternative. Cleo, the young secretary, rejects both Stark and Prince, the denizens of a dying world, to seek fulfillment elsewhere:

> Don't you think there's a world of joyful men and women? Must all men live afraid to laugh and sing? Can't we sing at work and love our work? It's getting too late to play at life; I want to *live* it.

Thus *Rocket to the Moon,* despite its psychological emphasis, is still structured by the redemption motif which characterizes Odets' earlier plays. And the redemption resides both in an affirmation and a rejection, since the one predicates the other. The play succeeds, therefore, in relating the confusion and frustration of its major characters to the larger world of which they are a part; Stark, Prince, Belle, and Cleo speak in the authentic voice of the Depression generation, reaching, grasping for a way out. But personal problems are grounded in a larger social context; Ben Stark cannot really love because his bourgeois world is rooted in futility and illusion. Odets draws the social moral—the moral Clurman chose as the "spine" of his production of the play:

> Who's got time and place for "love and the grace to use it?" [asks Stark] Is it something apart, love? . . . An entertainment? Christ, no! It's a synthesis of good and bad, economics, work, play, all contacts. . . . Love is no solution of life! . . . The opposite. You have to bring a whole balanced normal life to love if you want it to go!

It is revealing to compare *Rocket to the Moon* with Odets' later domestic drama, *The Country Girl* (1951). Although in the latter play Odets again treats the themes of frustration and redemption, he does so this time within a self-contained personal world removed from social causation. Odets formally acknowledged his restriction of emphasis in an interview in the New York *Times* [5 November 1950]. In omitting "social significance," he admitted that he may have taken "a step backward" as a playwright. However, by insulating his characters from the raging complexities of the world beyond their own private heartbreak, he believed that he was able to write more proficiently than ever before. He deliberately undertook to limit himself to but one aspect of life, the search for personal values. He acknowledged the self-imposed limitation, but mused, "It may be that limitation is the beginning of wisdom."

The Country Girl is endowed with virtues hitherto unassociated with Odets; it is neat, well-ordered, and theatrically sound—a *pièce bien faite*. "I wanted to take simple elements and make something sharp and theatrical about them. I stated a fact, the story of these two people, rather than speculated about the fact." But in restricting his scope, Odets robbed the play of his salient virtue, the necessary connection between the characters on the stage and the world of which they are a part. Frank Elgin's redemption is portrayed but it is never related to any specific cause. The key questions, left unanswered, are why did he go to pieces and why was he saved? The esthetic difficulties in *The Big Knife* resulted from Odets' inability to realize Charlie Castle's real anguish in effective dramatic terms; the esthetic difficulty with *The Country Girl* is that one is never fully convinced of Elgin's anguish. Since he remains the skeleton of a character rather than its flesh and bones, his redemption by his faithful wife seems, in the context of the play, almost gratuitous. He might well have gone on another bender and failed to achieve his theatrical triumph. At the end of the play Georgie, the country girl of the title, herself admits that "neither of us has really changed," but none the less discerns some "new element of hope," although she is not sure what. Neither are we as audience or reader convinced of this new possibility of hope because we are never presented with any dramatic alternative except that of the conventional backstage drama: will Frank Elgin succeed in making a comeback or not?

Insofar as there is a theme, it involves the fact of human responsibility, the necessity of looking forward not back. Georgie attempts to make Frank look life in the eye, to emerge from behind the myriad of evasions with which he has buttressed his life. But this theme is itself evaded because the roots of Frank's irresponsibility—symbolized in his alcoholism—are never explained. Responsibility implies a correlative: responsibility to what, and evasion of what? Frank's theatrical triumph does not arise out of the fact of his coming to terms with himself; it is merely presented. The last scene of the play might well have demonstrated his inability to cope with the responsibilities of opening on Broadway without marring the essential logic of the play.

In *Rocket to the Moon* the outside world continually intrudes, but in *The Country Girl* the social metaphor has been eschewed, exposing the bare bones of theatrical contrivance. It is as if Odets were saying to Broadway: "You want me to meet you on your terms? Very well, I'll show you that I'm able to do so." But in accepting Broadway's terms—an acceptance rewarded by commercial success—he surrendered the very real virtue which distinguished his earlier work, the adamant refusal to be con-

fined by the structure of the conventional Broadway play, the fervent desire to change the theatre, and ultimately the world outside it.

Odets, in losing his political commitment, enacted the drama of his generation. It is not inappropriate that disenchantment with Marxist principles should have specific esthetic results, for Marxism had indeed attempted to create a specific esthetic. We have observed that although Odets never adhered rigidly to the strict logic of the doctrine of proletarian literature, none the less his Depression dramas are rooted in the *metaphor* of the Marxist dialectic. Thus the theme of redemption or resurrection is wedded to the concept of the necessary vanquishing of the old class by the new. Odets' problem as a dramatist, although never explicitly viewed as such, was to find a substitute metaphor to order the various elements of his artistic experience. Once the Marxist metaphor had lost its validity, once the substructure of the Marxist dialectic no longer sufficed, Odets was deprived of the structural framework upon which he had consciously or unconsciously built.

The consequences of the absence of this framework may be observed in an examination of Odets' last play with the Group, *Night Music* (1940). Although certain persistent Odetsian themes appear in the play, in particular the redemption of the young by the old, they are no longer related to a guiding, thematic concept; instead Odets attempts to substitute an esthetic metaphor, musical structure, for thematic structure, and the resultant play is characterized by a general diffuseness and uncertainty which robs its social implications of any vitality. In attempting to portray contemporary homelessness and uncertainty, Odets committed the esthetic mistake of being himself uncertain and erratic.

Odets possessed an aural rather than a visual imagination; his plays have always been characterized by the specific quality of their dialogue, the authentic sound of colloquial, urban speech. In commenting on New York City, he once noted that "I don't see it visually—though it's beautiful enough—so much as I hear it and feel it." And in the story of Steve Takis' erratic weekend on the town, Odets attempts, in *Night Music,* to record the sounds and music of twentieth-century New York and, by extension, America. But the myriad variations of the play serve to muddy rather than to clarify the theme. Hearing the sound of crickets, Fay, the young heroine, remarks, "Night Music . . . if they can sing, I can sing. . . . We can sing through any night!" This faith in the ability of the human being to transcend his difficulties is, at best, most generally stated. True, the play raises some specific social issues. Steve's predicament, for example, is given an economic base, since his aggression is motivated by the fact of his deprivation. The "big international question" for him is still "when do we eat?" But a sense of man's inability to confront reality and change the world vitiates the social implications of *Night Music*. If there is one essential theme it is that of homelessness, the individual's inability to find someone or something to belong to. Although Steve Takis is indeed a proletarian, despite occasional outbursts of indignation, he displays no real sense of class. He is a boy without credentials, the "All-American bum," striking back at friend and foe alike with a defensive hospitality, which is merely a mask for his sense of homelessness. The theme of *Night Music* is, thus, not the determination of the economically deprived to gain their deserved rights, but rather a despairing acknowledgment of the futility of gestures of protest. Not merely Steve and Fay, but *all* the characters in the play, regardless of class, are characterized by this similar sense of dislocation. Where previously dislocation had served Odets as a class image, it now informs *all* strata of society.

Odets seems to acquiesce in the mood of futility which pervades the play. His attempt to dispel it, in the person of the Guardian Angel, the detective Rosenberger, is so generalized in its optimism as to be fundamentally unconvincing. For Odets' answer seems to be nothing so much as to affirm a blind faith in man's possibilities. Rosenberger's role in the play serves merely to demonstrate the gratuitousness of his solutions; whenever the young couple finds itself in difficult straits, he appears to set the situation right, and to present them with his optimistic gospel: "Where there is life there is hope, in my humble opinion. Only the living can cry out against life."

It is precisely this sense of false solution—of conquering life by merely living it—which provides the play with the Saroyanesque note that many of the critics noted ("Now that Odets writes like Saroyan," wrote Atkinson, "doomsday is near"). Rosenberger's relationship to Steve is not unlike that of Jacob to Ralph, but whereas the latter's redemption was predicated on the acceptance of a specific road out of the frustrations of the present, Steve's redemption is based upon his acceptance of the vaguest kind of social philosophy: "In the time of your life, live." Although Saroyan's particular talent was able to inform this false optimism with a kind of wistfulness and nostalgia which made it work theatrically, Odets' talent did not lend itself to such manipulation. Ultimately, despite his attempt at wistfulness, his world is a real one, and demands real solutions. *Night Music* is one of those works which catches a specific moment in history; the spirit of the thirties had disappeared, employment was up, and the European war hovered ominously on the horizon. The major social issue was soon to become the simple act of survival. In such a world, in which catastrophe appeared imminent, it is not strange that the playwright should turn to themes of uncertainty, despair, and a desperate optimism. But Odets' dramatic dilemma was to find a means of structuring these various themes. He failed, despite the musical metaphor, because the implications of the various elements in the play continually led him in different directions. Thus the play is alternately wistful, nostalgic, bitter, farcical, optimistic, and despairing. The theme of redemption seems gratuitous because it does not seem warranted; if there is any moral in Steve's redemption, it lies in the cliché, love conquers all. Yet the seriousness of much of the play makes us unwilling to accept the conventional romantic ending. Rosenberger advises Steve to "make a Party-To-Marry-My-Girl." Even as a comic statement, it is significant that Odets' specific political solution to Steve's problems should be marriage.

In *Clash By Night* (1941) the vision of uncertainty and homelessness which found whimsical reflection in *Night Music* had turned stark and grim. The war clouds which had appeared on the horizon in the earlier play now seemed poised to drench the American landscape, and, in fact, less than one month after the play was produced in November, 1941, the Depression era found its violent interment in the cataclysm of world war.

The mood of the play may be gathered from Odets' diary notes pertaining to its genesis:

> July 27: The climate of the . . . play will be exactly that of the weather here. Muggy, foreboding, the never bursting open sky Why? I feel it must be that way. It is weather in which anything can happen. All courses of conduct are possible, men and women may suddenly weep, reverse their entire lives under this leaden sky; relaxed amiabilities, hatreds, exquisite tenderness . . . sudden murderous wrath, all may happen. . . . Out of a long chain of seeming dull trivia is born a shattering explosion that is the line of the new play.

> . . . . .

> August 8: The theme is taking shape in my mind, intensely personal but generally significant feeling behind it. The theme . . . has to do with the need of a new morality, with a return to voluntarily imposed morals, to voluntarily assumed forms in a world . . . where there are no forms but plenty of appetite and irresponsibility.

> . . . . .

> October 21: Part of the theme of this play is about how men irresponsibly wait for the voice and strong arm of Authority to bring them to life. . . . Nothing stands for Authority and we wait for its voice! . . . The children are looking for the father to arrange their lives for them!

Clash By Night represents Odets' final testament to the themes which informed his earlier dramas. The vision which had celebrated human possibility has turned sour, and the image of redemption is overshadowed by that of death. Like Odets' early characters, the people whose struggles are recorded in *Clash By Night* are frustrated by circumstance. Mae, like Hennie, is trapped in a loveless marriage; Earl's bluster, like that of Moe and Steve, masks a basic insecurity; the good-hearted Jerry wants nothing so much as to feel that he is needed. The dream of love, the desire to escape a life which is devoid of joy—"a life lived on the installment plan"—these pathetic gropings set the stage for the enactment of the love triangle which constitutes the plot of the play. But whereas Hennie, Moe, and Ralph were able to escape, Jerry, Mae, and Earl are condemned. There is no escape afforded them; Jerry, goaded by the fascistic Kress, is overwhelmed by jealousy and kills Earl rather than lose his wife.

Odets attempts to use the redemption theme by posing, in opposition to the tragedy of his major characters, the healthy relationship of a young couple, Joe and Peggy.

Unlike Earl or Jerry, Joe "knows his address," he is not torn away from the roots of life. He states what, we may assume, Odets intended as the moral of the play:

> We're all afraid! Earl, Jerry, Mae, millions like them, clinging to a goofy dream—expecting life to be a picnic. Who taught them that? Radio, Songs, the Movies . . . paradise is just around the corner. . . . But . . . we know the facts, the anti-picnic facts. We know that Paradise begins in responsibility. . . . Yes, it's a time to learn, a time to begin—it's time to love and face the future!

We must ask in what manner this theme is realized in *Clash By Night*. Despite this statement, and Mae's final advice to the young couple—"You're young and strong, you got a future"—it is apparent that Odets is merely going through the motions. He had become so acclimated to the structural support of the Marxist-redemption metaphor that he used it in this play as a dramatic device even though it is never validated. The drama of Earl, Jerry, and Mae is in no way logically connected to the drama of Joe and Peggy. Indeed, the latter might well have been eliminated without impairing the play one iota. Nowhere in the play is it implied that the dilemma of the principal characters is motivated by the false ideals which they have learned from society. Nowhere is the corrosive influence of radio, songs, and the movies manifest. Mae, Jerry and Earl are trapped by circumstances, by the inexorable fact that in a love triangle someone's fingers must be burned. Is the desire to escape from the frustration of the present necessarily a false ideal? Nowhere does Odets imply this. The metaphor of social redemption which served as a dramatic aid as long as Odets accepted the implications of Marxism, serves, in the case of *Clash By Night,* to falsify the play; for all elements of the play enforce the conviction that there is no escape. The world is seen, in Arnold's image as "a darkling plain . . . where ignorant armies clash by night." All the characters in the play confirm this pessimistic view, even the untormented Peggy, who states, "It's a nervous world, a shocking world. I don't understand it, I just don't understand it."

The ritual of violence which Odets enacted in *Clash By Night* was soon enacted in the world at large, and the world war which inaugurated the forties fittingly ended both the decade and the Great Depression itself. We have already traced much of Odets' subsequent career. Like many of his generation he was unable to replace the faith which had made him one of the most representative dramatists of the Depression era; and what is more significant for his art, he was unable to find a new dramatic metaphor to replace the one born of his political commitment. The failure of *The Big Knife* brought forth the compromise of *The Country Girl,* in which the rebel in Odets deferred to the Broadway craftsman. And yet his dissatisfaction with the compromise is attested by his last play, *The Flowering Peach* (1954), in which we find the playwright groping towards a new metaphor he never succeeded in finding.

Once again, Odets is concerned with an allegory of redemption; but redemption in this case is not born of a specific act of faith, but rather the attempt to replace the loss of faith. For in *The Flowering Peach* Odets attempts to define the dilemma both of his generation and of his own art. It represents that moment in an artist's career when reassessment seems to be demanded, when the artist must stop and take stock of his personal and esthetic resources. "I'm not a kid anymore," Odet acknowledged to a *Times* interviewer [26 December] 1954, "I'm 47. And at this age I began to ask myself, what happened? Do you want to begin all over again? Who are you and where are you?"

The significance of the play lies in the fact that Odets finally attempted to come to terms with the esthetic consequences of the loss of his political commitment. It was an acknowledgment long overdue, for, as we have observed, the attempt to exploit the structural advantages of the Marxist metaphor after rejecting its meaning vitiated Odets' post-Depression plays. The essence of *The Flowering Peach* is the acceptance of the loss of political faith. If there is one key line in the play it is perhaps Rachel's cry to the idealistic Japheth: "There is idealism now in just survival." Odets affirmed this conviction in the *Times*:

> When you start out you have to champion something. Every artist begins as if he were the first one painting, every composer as if there were no Beethoven. But if you still feel that way after ten or fifteen years, you're nuts. . . . I couldn't have written *The Flowering Peach* twenty years ago. As you grow older, you mature. The danger is that in broadening, as you mature, you dilute your art. A growing writer always walks that tight rope.

Odets' utilization of the Noah myth is not subject to a one-to-one allegorical interpretation. There can be no doubt, however, that the play represents an intensely personal statement. Odets is basically concerned with man's reaction to cosmic injustice, his attempt to construct a means whereby he can *accept* this injustice. It is this concept of acceptance which dominates *The Flowering Peach*. Despite everything, Noah accepts the will of God, the fact of human destruction. The rebel, Japheth, prefers to remain off the ark rather than accept the divine edict, but Noah knocks him unconscious and carries him aboard; thus man, Odets, implies, must accept the inequities of life; the gesture of protest must not be carried to extremes. And yet the rebellious gesture is not futile. It is Japheth's insistence that the ship have a rudder, his skill in fixing leaks, which saves the ship from foundering. Man must not merely accept, he must act. He cannot assume that God will necessarily prevent catastrophe; he must have faith in himself, for he can never be sure what God wants. Noah, however, *does* know what God wants. He wants to prevent the extinction of life, to provide the basis for the construction of a new world. The necessity of this preservation—and the acceptance of the capriciousness of divine law—transcends the meaning of Japheth's gesture of protest. Ultimately, he too must accept the way of the world. The rebel may attempt to guide his destiny, but he cannot change it. Significantly, the world which is renewed at the end of the play, it is implied, will not be very different from the world which was destroyed. Shem, who symbolizes man's acquisitive nature, has not been changed by the catastrophe. At the beginning of the play he was loath to accept Noah's demand to aid in the construction of the Ark because it meant the sacrifice of his worldly possessions; during the voyage he had planned for the future by saving the manure of the animals in anticipation of the time when fuel would be needed and he could sell dried manure briquettes. But Noah, who had previously berated Shem's avariciousness, finally, and significantly, comes to live with it. Previously Noah had attacked Shem's desire to live again by the principle of exploitation, but after his initial anger at his son's attempt to "begin a new world . . . with manure," at the risk of endangering the safety of the ark, Noah finally comes to accept his wife's logic: "Shem made a useful thing from nothing. . . . Why kill the man with brains? No, make him use it for the *family*!" Ultimately it is *not* the rebel, Japheth, that Noah goes to live with in the new world; it is Shem. "Why? It's more comfortable."

Thus, the rebel in Odets came to accept the futility of the radical gesture; there is sufficient idealism in the fact of survival. "You say to the eagle, fly!" cries Noah to God at the moment of his designation, "Even to a little bitty of an eagle like me, fly, fly, higher and higher! You have shrinked away his wings and he couldn't do it! Why did You pick me?" But every man is chosen, and every man must face the contradiction between his aspirations and his achievements. The fire of youth is gone, the desire to change the world is gone; but the world endures. And what has Noah learned from his journey through catastrophe? "To walk in humility, I learned. And listen, even to *myself* . . . and to speak softly, with the voices of consolation."

Thus redemption is ultimately born of acceptance, not protest; Agate Keller had cried in **"Waiting For Lefty"** that "when we die they'll know what we did to make a new world! Christ, cut us up to little pieces . . . put fruit trees where our ashes are!" But Noah accepts a small branch of the flowering peach as a "precious gift . . . from the new earth." Regeneration indeed, but this time without the ashes of man's effort.

C. W. E. Bigsby (essay date 1982)

SOURCE: "The Group Theatre and Clifford Odets," in *A Critical Introduction to Twentieth-Century American Drama, Volume 1: 1900-1940,* Cambridge University Press, 1982, pp. 159-88.

[*In the excerpt below, Bigsby surveys Odets' work with the Group Theatre, paying particular attention to* Awake and Sing!]

Odets's Berger family [of *Awake and Sing!*] is trapped, in a mental no less than a physical world. The limits are partly those imposed by an urban setting which itself has been shaped by a history of speculation and exploitation, and partly by a mental geography which they regard as implacable as a physical terrain. Most of the family accept

as unyielding what is mutable, constructing their own prisons out of economic fiats to which they give metaphysical authority. The primary space which they surrender is the crucial territory within which the self defines its own possibilities. Dreams are mistaken for visions and vice versa. The harsh realities of economic life are allowed to deform the moral imagination. The falsehoods of public mythology become the falsehoods of private life. The social lie, which proposes the inevitability of success and which accounts for failure by locating it in the weakness of the individual or the incorrigible wilfulness of a particular group, becomes the private lie, which demeans by forcing the individual to respect externalities, to allow a dangerous gap to open up between appearance and reality. The Berger family are on the verge of the middle class and as such are especially vulnerable. To deny the reality of the American dream is ostensibly to condemn themselves to permanent deprivation. The constant image is one of flight, escape. They look to escape the reality of their situation through marriage, through luck, through a desperate commitment to political or social myths, through a sardonic humour, through self-deceit, or even, most desperately, through suicide, albeit a suicide which, like that which was to send Willy Loman to his death in *Death of a Salesman,* is designed to liberate the next generation.

All the material is there for a social play which indicts a brutal and brutalising system. Certainly it is possible to make money. Bessie Berger's brother does so by dint of caring nothing for anyone, remaining blandly unaware of others' suffering and evidencing the crudest intolerance. Otherwise, it is really only the gambler and the cynic who can survive, and they do so by taking society on its own terms. But Odets is less interested in offering an indictment of capitalism than he is with asserting the need for a morally improved world, for the individual to wake up to a failure which is as much private as public. Odets was now a Communist Party member, but the mood of *Awake and Sing* is much closer to Roosevelt than to Marx. The awakening with which the play climaxes is very much that moral regeneration for which Roosevelt had called and which he was to continue to call for in his Second Inaugural, where he was to assert that:

> Old Truths have been relearned; untruths have been unlearned . . . We are beginning to wipe out the line that divides the practical from the ideal; and in so doing we are fashioning an instrument of unimagined power for the establishment of a morally better world. This new understanding undermines the old admiration of worldly success as such. We are beginning to abandon our tolerance of the abuse of power by those who betray for profit the elementary decencies of life . . . Shall we pause now and turn our back upon the road that lies ahead? Shall we call this the promised land? Or, shall we continue on our way? For 'each age is a dream that is dying, or one that is coming to birth'.

Awake and Sing recounts the personal growth to a kind of maturity of Ralph Berger and, ostensibly, of his sister Hennie. Condemned to play their required roles in the social drama which their mother has formulated from shreds of American pietism and capitalist propaganda, wedded to the lower middle-class insecurities of immigrant life, they are caught between her pretensions and the constraining power of their far from genteel poverty. Having failed to win her own place in the sun, she relies on her children to justify her and is implacable in the zeal with which she seeks to mould them. By the end of the play they have apparently learnt the need to break free, though the suicide of their grandfather offers an exemplary warning of the futility of a commitment and a vision not rooted in practical action.

Odets's is a world in which language is warped by circumstance. The language of familiarity cloaks a fundamental estrangement. The pressure of the city erodes the word, insinuates a space between language and meaning.

—C. W. E. Bigsby

Clifford Odets is an urban writer. The pressure which his characters feel is that of the city. The collapse of personal space, the closing off of social possibilities, the erosion of familial cohesion, the betrayal of moral values, the loss of transcendent vision, are the product of a world which is seen as essentially urban. The Bergers live in a tenement building. Their dog is exercised on the roof; their son sleeps in the living room; the different generations are crowded together, making the ironies of lost lives inescapable. Lost opportunities, denied hopes, frustrated plans, are ruthlessly exposed. Nothing can be concealed. The loss of space is the loss, too, of privacy, the exposure of failure and weakness. The transformation of this circumstance by simple ideological shift is not credible nor presented as such by Odets. Jacob's communism is a fantasy, rooted neither in knowledge nor action, while Ralph's personal liberation is drained of ideological content. Indeed that lack of ideological content emphasises the individual nature of that transformation, and its slender foundation. The ambiguity of this conversion is an indication of some of the play's more disabling contradictions. Odets delineates with care the pressures which destroy personal relations, individual conscience and communal values; he is less capable of identifying the source of regeneration which survives in language but not in action. Hennie's pursuit of personal fulfilment at the expense of her child, whom she abandons at the end of the play, is ostensibly endorsed by Ralph, suggesting a concern for self at the heart of his own bid for freedom which stains it with an egotism at odds with his language, and with the logic of the play which suggests a movement towards a self-realisation linked to national recovery.

Odets's is a world in which language is warped by circumstance. The language of familiarity cloaks a funda-

mental estrangement. The pressure of the city erodes the word, insinuates a space between language and meaning. Jacob's romantic radicalism is born out of a desire to bring word and referent into some kind of dialectical relationship, to close the space opened up by time and the loss of an environment in which such a relationship would be possible. The pathos of Jacob is clear. He dies without closing that space and, worse than that, he dies with a kind of betrayal. In plunging to the sidewalk from the rooftop he offers his life to buy his grandson a future by leaving him $3000. It is a gesture which denies the life that he has constructed in his mind. It is a bribe offered to the world he thinks he holds in contempt. It is a gift which will taint the young man; which, if accepted, will pull him down into the material world, which will locate him with the forces he affects to despise. Like Willy Loman, in *Death of a Salesman,* he offers a dubious inheritance. The proof of Ralph's maturity lies, like Biff's, in his realisation that it is an inheritance which has to be refused. But where Willy Loman prides himself, no matter how self-deceivingly, on his success, desperately trying to relate to the public myths of America, Jacob consoles himself for his failure by condemning that society. In doing so, he inevitably defuses Odets's own indictment of the system. In both cases the weakness lies as much in the individual, wilfully self-blinding, vacillating, visionary without cogent perception, as it does in society. It is a weakness which blunts the social critique.

By the same token Ralph's decision to hand the money over to his mother and stay in the tenement leaves him in a social world unreconstructed except by his new version of a world which he now believes, without any evidence, to be susceptible to his transforming imagination. But that imagination is too insubstantially rooted to carry conviction. The density of the city, the accumulated evidence of loss, betrayal and surrender, is too great for his new perception to sustain the weight which Odets would place on it. What is presented as a triumph, as perception transmuted into action, is invaded by an irony generated less by his own weaknesses, though these are plain, than by the subversive power of a social world whose force lies more in its demeaning materialism than in the capitalist injustice. The play's action implies a determinism scarcely neutralised by a quixotic gesture, a commitment to transformation pushed not simply into the future and hence untested in action, but into a spiritual world which is perhaps indistinguishable from the fantasy which had animated his grandfather.

In the context of *Awake and Sing,* in which disillusionment, the blunting of aspirations and the slow depletion of energy are demonstrable facts of personal and public life, there is a terrible symmetry in Ralph's decision. The naive enthusiasm which he feels in the closing moments of the play is indistinguishable from that with which Moe Axelrod had gone off to war, Bessie had married her now dispirited husband and Jacob had responded to the images of human solidarity which had filled him with sufficient energy to purchase, but not read, a library of radical texts. There is a logic established which cannot be neutralised by simple rhetoric. He exchanges one dream for another;

the vaguely-felt social commitment which now engages him. As he puts down the telephone, following the ending of a brief, but apparently passionately-felt affair, he announces, 'No girl means anything to me until . . . Till I can take care of her. Till we don't look out on an air shaft. Till we can take the world in two hands and polish off the dirt.' The extent of the rationalisation seems clear, though it threatens the integrity of his new commitment. Indeed his failure to sustain that personal relationship in the face of opposition, the collapse of will which leads him to sacrifice her to her vindictive relatives, is of a kind with his sister's willing sacrifice of her child, abandoned so that she can seek happiness unencumbered. It cannot be viewed unambiguously and it must be presumed to have implications for his new faith, which is expressed with precisely that enthusiasm which he had previously reserved for his private world.

And the risk clearly exists that for Ralph the future will become a kind of crystalline myth, as the past does for his father. Teddy Roosevelt and Valentino define the parameters of his fantasy world, as Marx and Lenin do those of Jacob. The present is evacuated. It contains the threat of uncontrolled emotion; it demands a human response. It is Jacob who is described by Odets as being 'a sentimental idealist with no power to turn ideal into action' but it is not clear why this should not also prove an adequate description of Ralph.

For Odets, the change in the lives of Ralph and Hennie, at least, though minor in origin and in immediate effect, was to be a public act. To newspaper interviewers he asserted that 'The play represents an adjustment in the lives of the characters, not an adjustment of environment . . . just a minor family turmoil, an awakening to life of the characters, a change in attitude . . . But today the truth followed to its logical conclusions is inevitably revolutionary. No special pleading is necessary in a play which says that people should have full and richer lives' [Gerald Weales, *Clifford Odets,* 1971]. When Jacob is particularly depressed or harassed he plays a recording of Caruso singing 'O Paradiso' and explains that 'a big explorer comes on a new land—"O Paradiso". . . You hear? Oh paradise! Oh paradise on earth!' This, presumably, is the America, now destroyed by greed, which must be redeemed.

The family, central to American mythology, becomes, if not the source of corruption, then its most obvious evidence. Jacob's comment, 'Marx said it—abolish such families', is a genuine reference to the Communist manifesto, which does indeed assert that the bourgeoisie have made the family relationship into a financial relationship. This is exemplified here not merely by Bessie's willing sacrifice of moral value to financial security but also by the legacy left by Jacob. It is a temptation which has to be resisted. And yet the family is not to be abandoned, or, as in Hennie's case, not to be abandoned without moving into a dubious moral world. It is to be transformed by changing the nature of the society in which it is located. But this merely serves to underline the inadequacy of Ralph to the task which he wishes to take on. 'Get teams togeth-

er all over. Spit on your hands and get to work,' he insists, 'And with enough teams together maybe we'll get steam in the warehouse so our fingers don't freeze off. Maybe we'll fix it so life won't be printed on dollar bills.' But the agency for this transformation, the process whereby he will move from perception to action, is unclear.

The play's final speech signals his private rebirth in his own mind, but the link between that and a public act of reconstruction is dubious while the tone of the speech is scarcely different from that in which he had earlier announced his love-affair. At the beginning of the play he had explained that 'I'm telling you I could sing . . . We just walked along like that, see, without a word, see. I never was so happy in all my life . . . She looked at me . . . right in the eyes . . ." I love you," she says, "Ralph." I took her home . . . I wanted to cry. That's how I felt.' At the end of the play it is an abstract cause rather than a girl, but the tone and indeed the language are the same: 'My days won't be for nothing . . . I'm twenty-two and kickin'! I'll get along. Did Jake die for us to fight about nickels? No. "Awake and sing," he said . . . The night he died, I saw it like a thunderbolt! I saw he was dead and I was born! I swear to God, I'm one week old! I want the whole city to hear it—fresh blood, arms. We got 'em. We're glad we're living.' For Odets, his was an affirmative voice, just as below what he acknowledged to be the 'dirty lie' implicit in Hennie and Moe's escape to Cuba he could bring himself to assert that 'I do believe that, as the daughter in the family does, she can make a break with the groundling lies of her life, and try to find happiness by walking off with a man not her husband' [Weales]. The flouting of convention is offered as itself adequate evidence of rebellion, but it is difficult to sustain this interpretation given Hennie's weakness and her casual abandonment of her child, and given Moe's strategy of neutralising the crude immorality of society with his own homeopathic corruption. Marx did not propose adultery as a solution to capitalism, nor the exchange of one failed capitalist paradise for another. But the confusion does not only operate in Odets's mind; it is endemic in the play. A drama of praxis requires both the possibility of change and characters capable of imagining and sustaining that change. Neither Hennie nor Moe has this imagination. They gamble on the future, on a radical change in Moe's personality for which there is no evidence; on the existence and desirability of a static world of romantic delight which will make no demands on their sensibilities or their consciences. Odets is caught between a social play of public revolt and a private drama of personal rebellion. The two are never successfully welded together except at the level of language.

There is perhaps an explanation of sorts in the fact that *Awake and Sing* had originally been deeply pessimistic. Indeed Clurman had called it 'almost masochistically pessimistic'. In an early version Moe is arrested before his proposition to Hennie; Bessie is a cruder figure, drained of what sympathy attaches itself to her in the final version. The changes may explain something of the obvious tensions in a play whose realism of dialogue and character was not matched by a coherent dramatic or social vision.

AWAKE AND SING!

PRODUCTION REVIEWS

Stark Young (review date 13 March 1935)

SOURCE: "Awake and Whistle at Least," in *The New Republic,* Vol. LXXXII, No. 1058, 13 March 1935, p. 134.

[*In the following, Young offers a mixed review of* Awake and Sing!, *judging it a "workaday drama."*]

There are a number of pertinent things to be said of the Group Theatre's last production. It is, in the first place, a piece written by a member of the Group itself; and that is a notable point. The direction was under Mr. Harold Clurman, one of the heads of the Group, and it was good directing in general, intelligent, full of a stage sense, and thoroughly foreseen. I thought it needed only greater variations in pitch. The company in general shows growth; technically, the whole performance of the play is more even and distributed among the individual players than has often been the case in the past. The play itself deserves genuine attention critically.

Awake and Sing shows great promise, especially in the field of melodrama. It begins, moves along and develops with real skill. The attention it exacts is definite and constant. The only boredom I felt was with the recurring ugliness, sometimes so prolonged that I was led to wonder why I should bother with such people as these characters seemed to be.

This effect of stridency and ugliness, however, diminished after the first act. The growing intensity of the play replaced that yapping quality which, if spread throughout the household of characters, passes endurance. It is practically impossible to feel either the tragedy or the comedy of such rowing, jawing, prideless and uninspired human beings. This sort of judgment of that type of Jewish life seems to me necessary and right; how otherwise are we to measure and evaluate the nobler and more beautiful forms of Jewish life that are to be found? Any general front rigidly preserved, merely means that the lower Jewish forms of life gain, the higher lose.

Awake and Sing tells the story of a family, the Bergers, in the Bronx, whose daughter has slipped into perilous ways, and is beginning a baby. There is, also, a son, well written, whose mind is revolutionary but somewhat frightened: the maternal control these many years has been too strong. He has a girl, Blanche, an orphan without money, whom the mother fights. The Berger daughter is married off to a suitor who is all confusion, a wretched little sample of bourgeois goodness—which, plainly, is to be despised in this family that has always kicked about its chances. There is the old grandfather, full of Marx—however

diluted with Caruso records (it is not easy to believe that Caruso's notions of Marxian principles would have accorded with this old man's). And there is a sort of bootlegger or free person of discolor, Moe Axelrod, who has been the first in the daughter's life, who comes to board, and who in the end carries the girl off, away from her husband, away from her baby. The grandfather assists in the son's future by making out his $3,000 insurance policy to him and then jumping off the roof; though, as a matter of fact, the son, well warned of his family's plans to cheat him, resolves to let them all have the paltry sum. Deserted by his girl, thrilled with the old grandfather's spirit, inheriting his handful of books, the young man determines to fight for the revolution, for good heat in the factory, the right to et cetera, et cetera. Meanwhile we hear uttered the sentence about all the bourgeois: "house filled with hate!" Such houses crowd the length and breadth of the country; the revolution will change all that by giving such families as the Bergers a right to lie in the sun, to bring their children up as—it is not clear what. As to the hate-filled houses, I know so many that are not so that I remain a poor judge of the idea promulgated. I know a great many families where hate does not rule, some of them very close to me. I am reminded, also, that hate as a dramatic motif has small purpose unless it be conceived and portrayed either in most intense or tragic terms, not all mere commonness or envy.

As a workaday drama *Awake and Sing* seems to me far above the average. The author of it has talent, a sense of character drawing and a clear sense of emotional contrasts. The scene of the grandfather cutting the rich son's hair is genuine drama and is moving. What the play lacks is a deep basis in the dramatist's own conception. What life, beneath the incidental, has he in mind? What, for instance, does he think of their constant patter about getting on, in money, in advantages, when all the time there lie within his Jews' grasp their own marvelous inheritance? Are we to weep because this family that might have possessed one of the great racial traditions of the world, its poetry and prayer, are sour because they cannot have Packards? Where, for Mr. Odets, is the race's dream and shadow of divinity? From the dramatist's point of view we have a right to ask a more fundamental conception on his own part. On what, in his opinion, does this life that he portrays rest? The actual conveyance technically of the bases on which a play rests is a part of the dramatist's technical problem.

One comment remains on the playwright's achievement in *Awake and Sing,* which is that it lacks tonality. The use of English at its best may be denied these aliens or these dwellers in the Bronx, whose agitations can so stridently take the charm out of life. But there is in Mr. Odets' play far too much of a certain vulgar animation of phrase, of forcing of the comparison and epithet, gutterism, as it were, that seeks after vivacity. Why not more either of the English language or of plain speech stumbling? For example, at the end, when the girl and her lover are going away, upsetting meanwhile a whole social system, why should not someone speak simply, in key, leaving vivacious vulgarity to those whose character it dramatically expresses?

Theatre liveliness is one thing, but we do not sell out for it. If we do, we merely show that we passed through an important human scene like a spoon through soup, without perceiving the savor. You cannot have everything; if you wish to jazz, do please jazz; if you wish to stand by the wailing wall, then wail. But you must not be afraid that your matter will fail in liveliness for the vulgar, unless, that is, you think the enlivening element is its vulgarity. Watching the last scene of *Awake and Sing,* I was unable to tell whether or not he thought of value the reactions to life of people who asked of life so little that is valuable or profound; or whether, with his young man's final curtain, the dramatist is thinking of revolution as one more stage cliché or as a pathetic canvas of possibility on which passionate or starved youth can begin to draw the pattern of the life it desires for itself.

Grenville Vernon (review date 15 March 1935)

SOURCE: A review of *Awake and Sing!,* in *The Commonweal,* Vol. XXI, No. 20, 15 March 1935, p. 570.

[*Vernon provides a glowing assessment of* Awake and Sing!, *declaring it "one of the truest, most vital productions of the year."*]

The Group Theatre got off none too happily in its first production of the season, *Gold Eagle Guy,* but in *Awake and Sing* it has hit its stride. In Clifford Odets's play of a Jewish family in the Bronx, not only do the Group actors find themselves peculiarly at home, but Mr. Odets's play proves to be one of the truest, most vital productions of the year, a play which deserves a place in the front rank of American drama. The story of *Awake and Sing* is simple enough. It is the tale of the love of Hennie Berger for Moe Axelrod. Hennie after an unfortunate love affair has married a rather moronic young Jew, Sam Feinschreiber, or rather has been married to him by her mother, Bessie Berger, who knows she is to have a child and wants to save the reputation of the family. This is done against the protest of the girl's grandfather, Jacob. In the end Hennie goes off with the man she really loves, Moe Axelrod. The play cannot be defended on moral grounds, but it is none the less a story which bears only too clearly the marks of truth in a civilization in which moral standards are fast disintegrating. But it isn't the story itself that makes the play important; it is the dramatist's masterly evocation of Jewish character and his splendid sense of dialogue. In his depiction of the matriarch, Bessie, with her insistence on the age-old ideas of the Jewish race, its courage, its belief in the family as a unit, Mr. Odets has proved himself a master. Yet he is none the less sure in his etching of the older liberal Jew, Jacob, with his ideas of personal dignity and love for humanity; of the erring daughter, Hennie, torn between her family's tradition and her love, which until the end seems almost hate, of Moe; and of Moe Axelrod himself, brutal yet honest, a masterly portrait of the young Jew who has lost belief in everything except himself. Splendidly done, too, are the figures of Uncle Morty, the cynical Jew of business; of Myron Berger,

Bessie's futile husband; and of Sam, the half moron husband. They are not pretty pictures, any of them, except old Jacob, but they have the ring of truth and life. *Awake and Sing* is a study of the old against the new, and though the dramatist's sympathy is evidently with the latter, he never preaches, and the triumph of the new cannot hide the fact that the faith which upheld the old has found nothing substantial to take its place.

The acting was flawless. Perhaps first honors go to Luther Adler for his splendid portrayal of Moe; to Morris Carnovsky for his idealistic but futile Jacob; to Stella Adler for her indomitable matriarch. Yet almost equally fine are Phoebe Brand's Bessie, J. E. Bromberg's Uncle Morty, and Sanford Meisner's Sam Feinschreiber. No one but Jewish actors could have given these characters as they are given, actors who know not only the flavor and ideas of the characters themselves, but who are able to speak their lines veritably. *Awake and Sing* is a true folk-drama, but it is more than that. It is a document truly appalling in its truth. It shows the old ideals of Jewry crumbling under the pressure of an alien civilization and a racial emancipation. That Jewry will be willing to remain long so utterly hopeless and disillusioned would be too painful to believe. The spirit which animates the idealistic Jacob, twisted though it is, will some day emerge and assert its rights.

CRITICAL COMMENTARY

Richard H. Goldstone (essay date 1964)

SOURCE: "The Making of Americans: Clifford Odets's Implicit Theme," in *Proceedings of the IVth Congress of the International Comparative Literature Association,* edited by François Jost, Mouton & Co., 1966, pp. 654-60.

[*In the excerpt below from a conference paper presented in 1964, Goldstone asserts that* Awake and Sing! *is Odets' most profound play and explores the significance of money to the characters.*]

Awake and Sing is a turning away from naturalism, the mode which Zola, Gorki, Elmer Rice and Eugene O'Neill had exploited in their dramatic writings about the poor. Odets chose realism over naturalism, sensing that the time had come when an American dramatist could write realistically about the emerging lower middle class—in this instance, immigrant Eastern European Jews. Realistic drama had previously focused upon the middle and upper middle classes, social groups with whom the theater-going public could identify; only [Sean] O'Casey had successfully used the lower middle class as the subject for realistic drama and Odets sensed that what O'Casey had done for the tenement dwellers of Dublin, an American playwright could do for the Jewish denizens of the Bronx. . . .

A scene from a production of Awake and Sing!

Odets had two objectives. More explicitly than O'Casey he wished to make the theater the expression of his social conscience, of his awareness of the need for social reform. At the same time, Odets wished to lay bare the truth, as he saw it, about the lives of his own people, to reveal and interpret their confusions, their fears, their aspirations and their failures.

We encounter, then, in **Awake and Sing** a family of Jews, East European in origin. Of the nine persons of the play, five were born in Europe and the others are children of immigrants. No one in the play is very far from the memory of the squalor of their origins—the squalor both of the European ghettoes and lower East Side slums. Jacob, the grandfather, says to his grandson, Ralph: "Go out and fight so life shouldn't be printed on dollar bills." But life for these people *was* printed on dollar bills, on dimes, nickels and pennies. Their life was the struggle to survive. In ghettoes and slums the energies of people were devoted to getting and clutching the coins and bills on which life depended.

This is a play *about* money, or more particularly, about money and Jews. As such, it is a harsh, ugly, and—in certain respects—an unfair play. Yet it makes something clear about Jews and money which even today after pogroms and genocide, the world does not now, nor did not in 1935, really understand. Odets, in coming to terms with Jews and money (or to be more accurate, *some* Jews and

money), composed a remarkable play, but one susceptible to misunderstanding and misinterpretation.

Money clearly dominates the play—the accumulating, the hoarding, the utter absorption with it. Money is the play's central image, its all encompassing symbol.

In any complex society, money is important and the less there is of it the more important it becomes. For the poor Europeans, money meant clothing, food, staples, horses or draft animals. In short, money provided the necessaries of life, which were hard to come by. For the European Jew, the Eastern European Jew, in particular, money had an additional function. It not only provided the necessaries, it was the means of buying life itself; for Jews, the accumulation of money was the only possible guaranty of life and breath.

The nineteenth and early twentieth century Jew of Russia, Poland, Galicia, Hungary and the Balkans was not generally permitted to own land, follow a profession or attend secular schools. Traditionally and by necessity the Jew was a money-lender, a barterer of cheap merchandise, a repairer of pots and pans, a clothing mender, or a fiddler. Because the professions, farming and government service were closed to him, the Jew's only avenues of escape from a life of hopeless drudgery were the amassing of small capital or expatriation.

Life in the ghettoes had, besides crippling poverty, worse hazards. Money was a necessity to protect one's life and family against the depredations of the police, petty officials, mounted soldiers and a bigoted peasantry, any of whom could, capriciously and with impunity, pillage and murder Jews. Immunity from such attacks might be bought; the only defense was money.

Expatriation also required the accumulation of more than travel expenses. Beyond railroad and ship passage, money was needed to bribe border officials and sentries, in lieu of passports not available to most of the Jewish population.

In America, the memory of what money *was* haunts the Berger family of *Awake and Sing*. Money was Bessie Berger's passion, for Bessie was the real head of the family, the one on whose shoulders lay ultimate responsibilities. Bessie's obsession with money explains her intransigent denial of Blanche, the penniless orphan; it explains no roller skates for the child, Ralph, and Bessie's willingness to defraud the grown Ralph of his inheritance. But Bessie was no miser; money to her was something to be spent, provided it was spent to secure life. No roller skates for little Ralph, but twenty-five dollars for a specialist when the child was ill. (Twenty-five dollars was a month's rent.) Bessie believed that money bought life; that you were dead without it.

Odets's point is that Bessie is wrong. Morty, her rich brother, is the proof. Here is a man who *has* money—all he needs—but his life is sterile and his soul is dead. If only the Jew in America could liberate himself from the idea that money, rather than spiritual freedom, is the key to life. Most of the characters in the play never learn this; Jake knew but he was too old and broken to act upon it. (He hadn't even cut the pages of the books he had bought to liberate his mind.) Ralph is the only one who makes the full transition from the ghetto to a free land. Myron, Jake, Bessie, Sam are victims caught between two worlds: the crippling, stifling memory of a Europe which in a few years was to become a crematorium for Jews, and America where a Jew could breathe, and walk erect so long as he used his heart and mind and body with courage and purpose and decency. The play's theme is expressed in the title: Awake and sing (ye that dwell in the dust).

But Odets qualifies this idea of American freedom. Hennie's elopement with Moe represents her impulse to escape the constrictions of her environment, just as her brother Ralph needs to escape his. But Hennie is not admirable and her actions serve as a counterpoint to the main theme of the play.

After Hennie's seduction and abandonment by Moe Axelrod (before the play begins), she becomes promiscuous and reckless. When she can no longer conceal her pregnancy, she reluctantly agrees to her mother's scheme to deceive Sam Feinschreiber. But her reluctance is not at all like her grandfather Jacob's moral repugnance to taking advantage of a simple and ingenuous greenhorn; on the contrary, Hennie is appalled at having to marry an immigrant, "a poor foreigner", she calls him, who "can't even speak an English word."

What we see here operating in Hennie, Odets observes, is the impulse of the first generation American to turn his back on his roots and in doing so begin to develop the characteristic American xenophobia which was particularly virulent in the decades preceding the Second World War. Hennie marries and mistreats the luckless Sam; finally she abandons him and her child whom she foists upon her parents without a second thought because, presumably, Moe—as he himself reminds her over and over again—is more exciting in bed than Sam.

Hennie might be described as the kind of Jew, who having liberated herself from the strict regimen of Mosaic law, plunges into a world of moral anarchy because—like Moe—she has found nothing to replace the stern faith of her ancestors. Whatever Marxist ideas infiltrate the play, in Hennie's instance they are irrelevant. One cannot see how Hennie's moral disintegration and her final act of defiance have any economic basis; she is a girl with a strong sexual libido and no moral values or intellectual resources to hold it in check.

The situation of Hennie and Moe—two Jews who have liberated themselves from their past, from their religion and culture, from American concepts of respectability—is stated but not developed in the play. Yet we have a clear sense that the kind of specious freedom that this couple has won for themselves is taking them down an ugly blind alley with no exit. For what future is there for two bitter and spiritually crippled individuals whose basic tie extends no further than the double bed of adultery and self-absorption?

The Hennie-Moe-Sam Feinschreiber triangle set off against the central drama involving Bessie-Jacob-Ralph has a clear thematic function suggesting as it does that self-realization is no more to be obtained through moral anarchy and self-indulgence than it is through the accumulation of money and its spurious security. Ralph's drive toward freedom from his family's values is to be made possible by Jacob's suicide, a suicide undertaken so that Ralph will be the beneficiary of the old man's insurance. But Ralph's rebirth begins at the moment that he rejects the legacy.

Ralph cannot put behind his oppressive ghetto origins and take his place as an American unless he divests himself of the symbol of those origins—the hoard of gold and silver. At the moment that Ralph rejects the symbolic hoard and spiritually disassociates himself from the household which has remained a symbolic ghetto, he becomes an American and a free man.

In the middle thirties when the play was first produced, audiences assumed that Ralph was going to join the Communist movement. The text, however, does not justify such an assumption; Ralph's only explicit objective is to help organize the workers in his warehouse so as to improve working conditions.

No matter. Ralph has made a basic transition. He has crossed the line which separates those concerned only with family and self from those who seek or accept responsibility for those outside family and self. It is at the moment of crossing that line that Ralph is, as he says, "reborn." Ralph's rebirth coincides with Hennie's decision to abandon her responsibilities. Her decision—the choice of a loveless elopement—contrasts ironically with Ralph's. Hennie, already defeated by life, has met her final defeat: the loss of her role as wife and mother.

Whatever Marxist impulses the play may have once transmitted to its audiences are no longer felt in the reading of the text. Essentially what Odets portrayed—objectively, but with compassion—is a family group whose likeness could be found wherever large clusters of immigrant Jews betook themselves. What makes the play both arresting and important is that from unpromising basic materials—the Bergers are, after all, a commonplace group—Odets has created characters who join the line of older American families: the Laphams, the Babbitts, the Compsons, the Gants, and the Joads. In illuminating the lives of those in the process of becoming Americans, Odets somehow enables us to know what it is to be an American. Most of those who left the Old World behind were people whose dissatisfactions were sufficiently intense that they were willing to uproot themselves from what was safe, or at least familiar; Americans, as Thornton Wilder once observed, are a people without roots whose strength lies in the circumstance that they don't really want them.

"WAITING FOR LEFTY"

PRODUCTION REVIEWS

The Literary Digest (review date 6 April 1935)

SOURCE: "An Exciting Dramatist Rises in the Theater," in *The Literary Digest,* 6 April 1935, p. 18.

[*In the following, the anonymous critic gives the dual bill of "Till the Day I Die" and "Waiting for Lefty" a favorable reception.*]

In less than ninety days, toiling with the unrest of his times as a central theme, a young actor in the New York theater, a young actor who was competent, but never performance-material to make the heavens sing in praise of him, has become the most exciting spokesman the world of workers yet has produced, and, as something more than mere lagnappe to that feat, he has become perhaps the most articulate dramatist available in the theater.

Clifford Odets, almost a boy, lean, nervous, aflame with indignation at what he sees around him, is the author of three plays which have made his name a new force in drama, and his work a new power for the restoration of drama.

A few weeks ago the theater was slipping naturally and quietly into the sleep of spring. When everything else in nature awakens, it is the custom of the drama to close its eyes for the long snooze.

This season was no different, until, one night, not long ago, the Group Theater presented *Awake and Sing!* Superficially, this was a play about middle-class Jewish family-life in the Bronx. Beneath it, however, beat a new rhythm, a new voice was being heard, and it spoke eloquently, persuasively, and with passion, against the confusion of these times.

There have been dozens of plays with the same theme, some comedies, some tragedies, most of them clumsy and self-conscious. This one was none of these, and, next morning, Mr. Odets was hailed by every critic in New York.

He had written a short play about the 1934 taxicab-drivers' strike in New York. A bitter arraignment of the forces which herded the deluded drivers and exploited them, the Group gave it special Sunday night performances in a downtown theater.

In a few weeks the public clamor for the work of Odets had risen to that point where this producing organization had to bring it up into Broadway for regular showing. To it was added another short Odets play: **"Till the Day I Die,"** an anti-Nazi preachment based on the information smuggled out of Germany in a letter.

This play and **"Waiting for Lefty,"** the taxicab-strikers' play, have been made into a single evening's program. It is an evening of, candidly, propaganda. His Nazi play is the first one to take note of the plight of Communists in Germany.

Until now, three previous Nazi plays have concerned themselves only with the persecution of the Jews. Odets ignores this point completely, and centers his violent protest on the Hitler-Brownshirt activities against Communists. He details the subterfuges to which they are driven, he recites the tortures, he makes a ringing, courageous appeal for consolidation of the united front in Germany.

He works with the simples of the problem, deriving his power from showing the actual impact of the situation on humans as recognizable as a next-door neighbor. There is a place for propaganda in the theater; indeed, it is its natural pulpit. Odets appears to have recognized that, and rationalized it.

"Waiting for Lefty" is Mr. Odets at the sum of his best. His play roves the entire theater. It is played simultaneously on stage, in the orchestra section, and from the gallery. The audience is, in effect, a meeting of desperate taxicab-drivers.

Audiences at the three Odets plays have been mixed, mixed, that is, from a political point of view. Liberals, Communists, middle-class men and women with good jobs, and

Elia Kazan, with arms raised, as Clancy in the Group Theatre production of "Waiting for Lefty."

men in the ranks which still represent capitalism, mingle together, and watch these plays. The roar and surge of the propaganda in them inflames the Communistic patrons, but not once has it, also, failed to impress and give pause to those who, at heart, and in their minds, are opposed to what the plays represent.

And in that lies the strange, exciting magic which Clifford Odets has brought to the theater in this short, short time. The humanity of his plays is irresistible to all.

Joseph Wood Krutch (review date 10 April 1935)

SOURCE: "Mr. Odets Speaks His Mind," in *The Nation*, New York, Vol. 140, No. 3640, 10 April 1935, pp. 427-28.

[*In the following review of "Till the Day I Die" and "Waiting for Lefty," Krutch states that with these plays "Mr. Odets has invented a form which turns out to be a very effective dramatic equivalent of soap-box oratory."*]

A new production by the Group Theater supplies the answer to a question I asked in this column three weeks ago. Mr. Clifford Odets, the talented author of *Awake and Sing,* has come out for the revolution and thrown in his artistic lot with those who use the theater for direct propaganda. The earlier play, it seems, was written some three years ago before his convictions had crystallized, and it owes to that fact a certain contemplative and brooding quality. The new ones—there are two on a double bill at the Longacre—waste no time on what the author now doubtless regards as side issues, and they hammer away with an unrelenting insistency upon a single theme: Workers of the World Unite!

"Waiting for Lefty," a brief sketch suggested by the recent strike of taxi drivers, is incomparably the better of the two, and whatever else one may say of it, there is no denying its effectiveness as a tour de force. It begins *in media res* on the platform at a strikers' meeting, and "plants" interrupting from the audience create the illusion that the meeting is actually taking place at the very moment of representation. Brief flashbacks reveal crucial moments in the lives of the drivers, but the scene really remains in the hall itself, and the piece ends when the strike is voted. The pace is swift, the characterization is for the most part crisp, and the points are made, one after another, with bold simplicity. What Mr. Odets is trying to do could hardly be done more economically or more effectively.

Cold analysis, to be sure, clearly reveals the fact that such simplicity must be paid for at a certain price. The villains are mere caricatures and even the very human heroes occasionally freeze into stained-glass attitudes, as, for example, a certain lady secretary in one of the flashbacks does when she suddenly stops in her tracks to pay a glowing tribute to "The Communist Manifesto" and to urge its perusal upon all and sundry. No one, however, expects subtleties from a soap-box, and the interesting fact is that Mr. Odets has invented a form which turns out to be a very effective dramatic equivalent of soap-box oratory.

Innumerable other "proletarian" dramatists have tried to do the same thing with far less success. Some of them have got bogged in futuristic symbolism which could not conceivably do more than bewilder "the worker"; others have stuck close to the usual form of the drama without realizing that this form was developed for other uses and that their attempt to employ it for directly hortatory purposes can only end in what appears to be more than exceedingly crude dramaturgy. Mr. Odets, on the other hand, has made a clean sweep of the conventional form along with the conventional intentions. He boldly accepts as his scene the very platform he intends to use, and from it permits his characters to deliver speeches which are far more convincing there than they would be if elaborately worked into a conventional dramatic story. Like many of his fellows he has evidently decided that art is a weapon, but unlike many who proclaim the doctrine, he has the full courage of his conviction. To others he leaves the somewhat nervous determination to prove that direct exhortation can somehow be made compatible with "art" and that "revolutionary" plays can be two things at once. The result of his downrightness is to succeed where most of the others have failed. He does not ask to be judged by any standards except those which one would apply to the agitator, but by those standards his success is very nearly complete.

"Waiting for Lefty" is played upon what is practically a bare stage. It could be acted in any union hall by amateur actors, and the fact accords well with the intention of a play which would be wholly in place as part of the campaign laid out by any strike committee. Indeed, it is somewhat out of place anywhere else for the simple reason that its appeal to action is too direct not to seem almost absurd when addressed to an audience most of whose members are not, after all, actually faced with the problem which is put up to them in so completely concrete a form. The play might, on the other hand, actually turn the tide at a strikers' meeting, and that is more than can be said of most plays whose avowed intention is to promote the class war.

As for the other piece, **"Till the Day I Die,"** there is much less to be said in its favor. The hero is a young German whose loyalty to the Communist Party survives the tortures applied by fiendish storm troopers, but a note

on the program suggests the reason why the play lacks the air of reality. It was "suggested by a letter from Germany printed in the *New Masses,*" and obviously the author had too little to go on. However much **"Waiting for Lefty"** may owe to a Marxian formula, both the characters and the situation come within the range of the author's experience and there is a basis of concrete reality. **"Till the Day I Die"** is founded upon nothing except the printed word, and the characters are mere men of wax. In so far as we believe it at all, we do so only because we have been told that such things do happen. There is little in the play itself to carry conviction, and neither its hero nor its villains seem very much more real than those of the simplest and most old-fashioned melodramas. The acting in the two pieces is as different as they are themselves. Mr. Odets's Germans strike attitudes and declaim. His strikers are so real—perhaps so actual would be better—that when the play is over one expects to find their cabs outside.

Grenville Vernon **(review date 12 April 1935)**

SOURCE: "Two Communist Plays," in *The Commonweal,* Vol. XXI, No. 24, 12 April 1935, p. 682.

[*Vernon finds "Waiting for Lefty" energetically performed but expresses reservations about its political message.*]

In *Awake and Sing,* the play of Jewish life in the Bronx, the Group Theatre recently revealed to the New York public a new dramatist of real ability—Clifford Odets. In that play Mr. Odets showed a keen sense of dramatic values and for a young playwright an unusual mastery of theatrical technique; but far more important than these, the ability to visualize and project living men and women by means of significant action, and vivid, realistic, pungent dialogue. The characters of *Awake and Sing* were entirely Jewish, and Mr. Odets was evidently working in a milieu and in a spirit which he thoroughly understood. That Mr. Odets is a radical, even perhaps a Communist, might have been gathered from the play, not so much by what was definitely spoken, but what was implicit. Neither his sense of character nor his telling of the story were hobbled by the intrusion of the author speaking in his own person. And this was good art. In the two one-act plays which the Group Theatre has now presented, Mr. Odets is unfortunately no longer the artist, but frankly the propagandist, and the result is far less satisfying. Moreover in these plays the characters are primarily non-Jewish, and Mr. Odets gives to them no such sense of verity either in action or dialogue as he displayed in *Awake and Sing.* Indignation and intensity may be admirable things in the drama, but only when they are held in check; if they are left to run wild they destroy verity of character and of theme, leaving the figures of the play mere puppets, devoid of their own life, and existing only in the heated fancy of the author. This was what happened in **"Till the Day I Die"** and to a large extent in **"Waiting for Lefty."** **"Till the Day I Die"** is laid in Germany under the rule of the Nazis. The story is of a young Communist who is forced by the Nazis to become an informer, or rather he pretends to become an informer to save his life and reason. He does not really betray his comrades, but his comrades, including his own brother and the girl he loves, think he has betrayed them, and in the end he shoots himself as the only way to prove that he has remained faithful to his ideal. In the course of the play are introduced a number of stock characters; the Nazis all either hysterical, degenerate, brutal or stupid; the Communists, idealistic heroes. The result is that without exception the characters are as unreal in action and speech as the figures of old-time bourgeois melodrama. Moreover, the author is forever present, striking dramatic attitudes, spouting communistic sentiments in communistic jargon. Not for a moment is there the sense of reality, and what effects are obtained are obtained through the most obvious melodramatic means. In short, Mr. Odets neither feels nor understands the people he is trying to depict. That the actors are most of them excellent helps little. Such artists as Alexander Kirkland, Margaret Barker, Bob Lewis, Lewis Lev-erett and Roman Bohnen are thrown away.

"Waiting for Lefty" is a much better play. Here at least Mr. Odets is dealing with a scene and with characters he has seen and known, at least superficially. When he condescends to have them speak in their own persons, they speak the language of the New York streets, the language of taxi-drivers, labor leaders, *agents provocateurs*. The main action, and by far the most interesting and vital portion of the play, takes place in the scenes representing a meeting of taxi-drivers, with the officers of the union trying to prevent a strike, and the radicals insisting on one. Speeches are made from the stage, and actors are interspersed in the audience to heckle the speakers. These scenes are exciting, and despite the overdose of communistic propaganda are on the whole true to life. But the scenes between, depicting the evils of capitalistic civilization, of what happens in the homes of the workers, in the hospitals, in theatrical offices, are stereotyped bits of communistic hokum, and not particularly good hokum. Mr. Odets hasn't taken the trouble to saturate himself with the spirit which might have informed his figures; he has simply taken age-old puppets and situations, given them a revolutionary twist, and let them go at that. That this isn't enough for a serious dramatist goes without saying; it isn't enough even for effective propaganda. As in its companion piece, the acting in **"Waiting for Lefty"** is better than the play. Especially good are Russell Collins, Lewis Lev-erett, Bob Lewis, Roman Bohnen, George Heller and Mr. Odets himself.

Yet the production of these plays by radical writers and the interest they have aroused ought to be pondered by the established dramatists, as well as by the playwrights of the future. Such plays as Mr. Odets's and Mr. Maltz's *Black Pit* have, it is true, little to do with the great mass of the American people. They are distinctly foreign in emphasis and appeal primarily to a small coterie. They are not American or for the average American. But one thing they have—earnestness. Perhaps hate and envy rather than love are their basic passions, but at least they are not trivial. They are coarse in language and crude in action, but they

are alive. Too many of our established playwrights have lately been turning out mere confections, plays which are amusing but little more. It is time the playwrights who believe Communism to be destructive of all our civilization has built up through the centuries show some of the earnestness displayed by these communistic writers. In Emmet Lavery we have one such new dramatist. It is only through such dramatists that the theatre will reach the heights, for Communism is essentially materialistic, and materialism is barren of the things of the imagination. The spirit alone can fructify.

GOLDEN BOY

PRODUCTION REVIEWS

Joseph Wood Krutch (review date 13 November 1937)

SOURCE: A Review of *Golden Boy,* in *The Nation,* New York, Vol. 145, No. 20, 13 November 1937, p. 540.

[*In the following review, Krutch states: "There are moments when* Golden Boy *seems near to greatness; there are others when it trembles on the edge of merely strident melodrama."*]

In *Golden Boy* Clifford Odets has written what is certainly his best play since *Awake and Sing*. To say this is to say that the piece exhibits unmistakable power and genuine originality, even though it is not, unfortunately, to deny that there is still in his work something which suggests imperfect mastery of a form he will probably have to invent for himself if he is ever to become completely articulate. There are moments when *Golden Boy* seems near to greatness; there are others when it trembles on the edge of merely strident melodrama.

Ostensibly the play deals with the career of a young Italian boy who abandons the fiddle for the prize ring because "you can't pay people back with music," and because he wants the money which will make him forget an embittered youth. Actually the theme is the same as the theme of *Awake and Sing,* and the power which Odets exhibits is again the power to suggest the lonely agony of souls imprisoned in their own private hells of frustrated desire and inarticulate hate. No one that I know can more powerfully suggest the essential loneliness of men and women, their inability to explain the varied forms assumed by the symbols of their desire, and the powerlessness of any one of them to help the other. His dialogue is often brilliantly suggestive, especially when he puts it into the mouths of ignorant or uncultivated people; even the vulgarest of his villains rises to the dignity of the tortured; and he involves the spectator in the agonies of his characters until the palms sweat and one goes out of the theater tense with an emotion which the author has been unwilling or unable to resolve.

I suppose that the interpretation which Mr. Odets puts upon his own play is obvious enough. It is, I assume, that suffering like this "is inevitable under capitalism," and that the fiddler turned prize fighter is the type of those in whom rebellion assumes a merely symbolic instead of an effective form. But this time, at least, Mr. Odets keeps his political theories in the background where they belong and writes a play which does not depend for its appeal upon a concern with his economic opinions. The agonies of his characters are real and affecting whatever one may think of the reasons for their existence.

Stark Young (review date 17 November 1937)

SOURCE: A review of *Golden Boy,* in *The New Republic,* Vol. LXXXXIII, No. 1198, 17 November 1937, pp. 44-5.

[*In this assessment of* Golden Boy, *Young praises Odets' handling of dialogue, adding: "In this respect Mr. Odets is the most promising writer our theatre can show."*]

It seems to me the first thing about Mr. Odets' new play that we should mention is a certain quality in the dialogue. He has a sense of character drawing that exhibits the courage of outline. An unusual number of the characters in *Golden Boy* are set beside one another with the right bold theatre instinct, a perception of the fact, unknown to most playwrights nowadays, that character in fiction and character on the stage are two very different matters—see the fuzzy nonsense in most British plays that come to Broadway. He has an intuition of emotional impacts that make real theatre instead of mere description. The story in *Golden Boy* wanders for a few moments at the start but goes straight on after that. The number of motifs in personality, reactions, inheritance, hurts, secrecies, hopes, happiness, fate, bodily conditions, and so forth may seem crowded in at times, to lack a steady, or mature, distribution and proportion; but the direction is a good one nevertheless, it makes for abundance, it interweaves elements that promise a living fabric. His conception of the scenes, where to emphasize, where bring down the curtain, has grown neater and sharper. And the insistence, more or less adolescent, that once threw things in our faces is warmed now into both better persuasion and better taste.

The point I wanted to stress as where his theatre gift most appears is in the dialogue's avoidance of the explicit. The explicit, always to be found in poor writers trying for the serious, is the surest sign of lack of talent. To write in terms of what is not said, of combinations elusive and in detail, perhaps, insignificant, of a hidden stream of sequences, and a resulting air of spontaneity and true pressure—that is quite another matter. In this respect Mr. Odets is the most promising writer our theatre can show. The effect very often, and always the promise, of such a manner of dialogue is glowing, impressive and worthy of the response and applause that the audience gives it.

The performance of the play—under Mr. Harold Clurman's direction—is here and there tense at present but can soon be eased; it is on the whole varied, truly theatric and admirable. The Group Theatre seems to have contrived a genuine renewal. Mr. Carnovsky as the old Italian father, Mr. Adler as the golden boy, Mr. Kazan as the killer boss, etc., give capital performances, better than can be shown in a few words here. Miss Frances Farmer, following other starry leads eastward from Hollywood, played well. She needs only more fluency in order to vary the rhythm of her performance; and she might wisely ask of the author or the director some change from a perpetual coming in at the door, entrance after entrance. Much of the other playing was good.

Brooks Atkinson (review date 21 November 1937)

SOURCE: "*Golden Boy:* Clifford Odets Rewards the Group Theatre with One of His Best Plays," in *The New York Times,* 21 November 1937, Section II, p. 1.

[*Atkinson compares the construction of the themes and dialogue in* Golden Boy *to a symphony.*]

After doing a long stretch in Hollywood, Clifford Odets has returned to the theatre with one of his best plays. In *Golden Boy* he has dissected the success story of a prize fighter. For the most part it is a pithy and thoroughly absorbing drama that restores to the theatre a pungent theatrical talent. It is not so devastatingly simple in form as **"Waiting for Lefty,"** which was the inspiration of a lifetime, nor so complete an expression of life as *Awake and Sing!* but it stands head and shoulders above the self-conscious *Paradise Lost.* When Mr. Odets first came into the theatre with an actor's talent for dramatic writing there was much throwing about of brains in all the neighborhood drama columns. Although his talent is not yet mature, his instinct for storytelling on the stage is sound enough in *Golden Boy* to confirm the early enthusiasm for his writings and to raise again the hope that he will see the job of playwrighting through to a workmanlike conclusion.

First of all, he is a concrete writer, as an actor is likely to be. He does not discuss the idea in *Golden Boy* so much as he shows it—symbolizing the prize fighter's choice of career in the violin he might have played with artistic glory if he had not broken his hands in the ring. The violin he loves: the broken hands he sadistically gloats over—those are the conflicting concrete facts that give a practical structure to the craftsmanship of *Golden Boy.* In the second place, Mr. Odets has the virtuoso's instinct for form. He is a lover of symphonic music. Perhaps he has learned from the composition of symphonies how to keep more than one theme running through his work, how to play one off against the other for emphasis and contrast and how to draw them all together for smashing conclusion. Apart from the main theme of the prize fighter who is pursuing his career in cold malevolence, *Golden Boy* develops the subordinate themes of the manager and his pathetic love affair, the compassionate father who knows good

*Luther Adler, Morris Carnovsky, and Frances Farmer in a scene
from* Golden Boy.

from bad and cannot be stampeded into cynicism, the giggling sister and her exuberant husband, the melancholy
neighborhood intellectual, the laconical brother who finds
spiritual peace in the warfare of trade unionism. Although
"contrapuntal" is a big word, it roughly describes the style
Mr. Odets is mastering to give his dramas some fullness of
body and to relate his story to the life of his times.

His dialogue is the best and the worst of his talent. It is
the best instrument in his expression because it is vigorous, crisp and salty and because it gets at the truth of
characters by indirection. For his chief character, Joe
Bonaparte, is a queer tangle of hostile impulses. He wants
to succeed sensationally; he wants to be in the newspapers; he wants the cheers and the awe of the multitudes,
and he wants to make a fortune fast. Under his rancorous
callousness, however, he is too sensitive to believe in the
validity of any of these things, and he is constantly under
the necessity of hiding his scruples and perhaps destroying them by heedless action. Although he looks hard on
the surface, he is tender under the skin—lonely, unhappy,
thwarted, confused. His fierce success in the prize ring is
a manifestation of the authentic inferiority complex; it puts
a bold front on a timid disposition. Sometimes Mr. Odets
says so plainly, but he has conjured most of the truth out
of his prize fighter's character by elliptical phrases that
ricochet off the mind in startling directions. This has come
to be known as the Chekhovian style, for Chekhov, a doctor
by training, first brought into the drama the art of packing

truth between the lines. Although Mr. Odets's use of it in
Paradise Lost sounded and was imitative, he has made it
very much his own in *Golden Boy* and plucked the heart
out of his chief character's mystery.

But Mr. Odets's taste is unsettled. In fact, his dialogue is
by turns so genuine and so counterfeit that he can almost
be said to have no taste at all. Especially in the first act
of *Golden Boy*, when he is still feeling around for the best
way to get started, he writes with a braggart's want of
discrimination—joining cheap cleverness and Broadway
flippancies to genuine improvisations. In his eagerness to
avoid a dull statement of a situation Mr. Odets sounds like
a medley of popular songs; he echoes all the brassy bits
of argot he has ever heard. Perhaps he is suffering a little
from his prize fighter's neurosis. Perhaps he is not so sure
of himself in the prize fighter's ring as he would have us
believe. At any rate, it is significant that when he gets his
play well started toward a logical conclusion he writes
with a rugged sureness of accent. The bite of phrase and
the truth of character are superbly blended. The big scene
in the last act, when the prize fighter discovers that he has
accidentally killed his opponent, is written with the austere economy of a playwright who knows that a superfluous word distorts a crucial episode. Although the last scene
of drunken carousal is not written with that much accuracy of ear and imagination it is nevertheless a stunning
piece of theatre. Mr. Odets's instinct for dialogue is frequently treacherous, but his instinct for the design of a
scene seldom fails him.

This is his first play on a theme that is not rooted in the
class struggle. He has been congratulated for abandoning
his politico-economic point of view toward life. Whether
that is a strength or a weakness in a playwright's career
depends entirely upon his personal convictions as he acquires more experience in the world. A writer needs the
subjects that give his talent the freest scope. In *Golden
Boy* Mr. Odets has trenchantly illustrated the pernicious-
ness of choices that are false to a man's private character.
Among other things, he has illustrated the false choices
that our economic system frequently imposes upon original people. But the main thing is that at the present time
it has released Mr. Odets's talent and proved that, despite
certain flaws in his sense of taste, he can write with gusto
and versatility.

CRITICAL COMMENTARY

Harold Clurman (essay date 1939)

SOURCE: An introduction to *Golden Boy,* in *Six Plays of
Clifford Odets,* The Modern Library, 1939, pp. 429-33.

[*In the essay below, Clurman explores the allegorical
nature of* Golden Boy.]

Golden Boy has already been praised as a good show,
common-sense entertainment, and effective melodrama. It

has also been blamed for betraying Hollywood influence in its use of terse, typical situations, story motifs which resemble that of either popular fiction or movies, and possibly too in its use of an environment (the prize-fight world) that somehow seems unworthy of the serious purpose professed by its author. There has been, in addition, almost universal admiration for many separate scenes and long passages of brilliant dialogue.

What has not been discussed very fully, however, is the total significance of these divers elements, the meaning that their configuration within one framework might have. And it is this meaning, both in relation to the American scene and to Clifford Odets' work and progress within it, that might be most valuable to examine.

An early draft of **Golden Boy** bore the designation "a modern allegory." An allegory, I take it, is an extremely simple but boldly outlined tale in which a series of images is used to suggest a meaning of a more general, and usually a moral, nature. The good allegory will hold one's interest by the sheer directness or vividness of its story, the suggested meaning of which may occur to us only in retrospect, or which may be so organically imbedded in the structure of the story that in absorbing the story details we are almost automatically and spontaneously aware of their meaning. The allegory, in other words, deals in symbols that are so pointed and unmistakable that they transform themselves easily into the truth that their author hopes to express.

Whether or not Clifford Odets has chosen the happiest symbols in **Golden Boy,** it is a fact that his intention was to convey such a truth, and to convey it in terms that would not only avoid preachment, but entertain us by the mere raciness of its presentation.

The story of this play is not so much the story of a prize-fighter as the picture of a great fight—a fight in which we are all involved, whatever our profession or craft. What the golden boy of this allegory is fighting for is a place in the world as an individual; what he wants is to free his ego from the scorn that attaches to "nobodies" in a society in which every activity is viewed in the light of a competition. He wants success not simply for the soft life—automobiles, etc.—which he talks about, but because the acclaim that goes with it promises him acceptance by the world, peace with it, safety from becoming the victim that it makes of the poor, the alien, the unnoticed minorities. To achieve this success, he must exploit an accidental attribute of his make-up, a mere skill, and abandon the development of his real self.

It so happens that Odets thought of embodying this fight for achievement in terms of the *fight business.* For it is obvious on reflection that though the use of the prize-fight world is central to the play's plot, in the playwright's larger intention it may be considered almost incidental. . . . Further than that, to dramatize the conflict between what a man might be and what he becomes, the author has conceived a youth who is essentially an artist in a modest, unspectacular way. The hero is a violinist; and the fiddle

in this allegory is employed as the symbolic antithesis of the fighting game.

The play tells the story then of an artist, or even more generally of a sensitive human being, growing up in a world where personal achievement is measured in terms of that kind of sensational success that our newspapers, our mania for publicity slogans, indeed our whole large-scale production psychology make into almost the only kind of success we can recognize. To tell this story two worlds are mirrored in the swiftest, barest terms: the artists' world with its humble pleasures, its small but basic contentments, and the business world with its fundamental uncertainty, hysteria, indifference to and impatience with human problems as such, its inevitable ruthlessness, its ultimate killer tendencies.

The home scenes with their funny lines, their petty "philosophical" disputes between the two old cronies, their healthy naïveté and even their vulgarity are not haphazardly designed to show off the author's faculty for salty speech or clever characterization. They are part of a pattern to illustrate both the sweet human earthiness that the hero leaves for the hard world where success is made, and the slight shabbiness which makes the hero look upon his background as an almost shameful world—futile, unglamorous, lamentably unaware of the advantages it is missing.

What happens to the boy when he makes the compromise with his true nature? Odets' allegory proceeds to show that the boy becomes a commodity, something that can be bought and sold, maneuvered, that he who begins by trying to beat the competitive world by playing its game becomes himself a thing possessed. Odets' hero is literally taken over by a whole ring of exploiters: agents, managers, merchants and middlemen of every description, including the criminal racketeer. And it is most characteristic of the situation that while the hero tries to use these people for his own ends he despises them, while they who are to a large extent dependent on him resent the intrusion of any of his personal problems into their business considerations.

Beyond this, the activity involved in performing his new task—fighting his way to "fame and fortune"—finally incapacitates him from ever doing his true work or going back to his old and real self. In realistic terms, he breaks his hands in a fight so that he no longer can hope to play the violin which once meant so much to him. And when he has become a fighter a certain coarseness develops in him, a certain despair. He is denatured to the point of becoming a killer, figuratively and, thanks to a ring accident, literally. In the interim, he has fallen in love, hoping, by a romantic attachment to a woman equally lost in the hurly-burly of the success world, to solve his inner dilemma. But he is a defeated man. He has nothing to live by now. Both worlds are closed to him, and he must die.

It is necessary to repeat the bare features of the story to show the particular scheme, at once ideological and narrative, that gives the play its basic form. If we analyze it even further we shall find that the choice and placement of almost every character fit into this scheme. Take, for example, the momentary presence of the older brother Frank, the C.I.O. organizer. What is his significance here? His wounded head, his quiet retort "I fight," his sureness, are all minute indications that there is nothing abhorrent to the author in the thought of physical struggle as such, but that for people like his hero to have a world in which they might ultimately feel at home in being what they are and to have honor in such a world as well, it is necessary for the Franks to exist and fight. Our hero fights as a lone ego; Frank fights, as he says, together with and for millions of others. Frank is a free man; our hero is destroyed.

If there is any Hollywood influence in this play beyond the mere quick action and stock figures employed, it must be in the fact that in an important sense Hollywood and what it represents have provided the play with its inner theme, its true subject matter. So many artists today stand in relation to Hollywood as our hero in relation to his double career. From this point of view *Golden Boy* might be regarded as Clifford Odets' most subjective play.

Yet with this deeply and subtly subjective material, Odets has attempted to write his most objective play—a play that would stand on its own feet, so to speak, as a good show, a fast-moving story, a popular money-making piece. He has tried, in short, to bridge the gap between his own inner problems and the need he feels, like his hero and all of us in the audience, to make "fame and fortune." In his own work, he has tried to reconcile the fiddle and the fist; he has tried to yield himself a positive result out of a contradiction that kills his hero. He has done this by making the whole thing into a morality which would instruct and read us all a lesson (himself and his audience) even while it amused.

The strength and weakness of the play lie in this fusion of elements, admirable in intention, more varied in effect than in any of his former plays, but still imperfect as a whole. The strength of the present play is shown by its definite audience impact in the theatre; its imperfection comes from a certain lack of concreteness in details of plot and character—an objective flaw due to his mere nodding acquaintance with most of the play's locale, and from an insistence on certain character touches that mislead rather than clarify, such as the reference to the hero's eyes—a subjective flaw due to a reliance on a personal interpretation where a social one is required.

It must be pointed out in conclusion that the technical problem for a playwright—the problem of making himself completely articulate as well as sound—increases with the depth and richness of his material. The content of Clifford Odets' talent is greater than that of any young playwright in America today, and the line of his development must necessarily be arduous and complex. In certain instances, pat advice is more flattering to the critic than helpful to the writer. With Clifford Odets, we should simply be grateful for each of the endeavors that mark his progress. *Golden Boy* is a step ahead in the career of one of the few American playwrights who can be discussed as an artist.

FURTHER READING

BIBLIOGRAPHY

Demastes, William W. *Clifford Odets: A Research and Production Sourcebook.* New York: Greenwood Press, 1991, 209 p.

> Offers exhaustive lists of works by and about Odets as well as thorough descriptions of each play, including characters, plot summary, and critical overview for each.

BIOGRAPHIES

Brenman-Gibson, Margaret. *Clifford Odets: American Playwright: The Years from 1906 to 1940.* New York: Atheneum, 1981, 749 p.

> Focuses on Odets' psychological characteristics, providing insight into the person behind the plays.

Mendelsohn, Michael J. *Clifford Odets: Humane Dramatist.* Deland, Fla.: Everett/Edwards, 1969, 138 p.

> Standard biographical material supplemented by personal interviews and correspondence with Odets.

Shuman, R. Baird. *Clifford Odets.* New York: Twayne Publishers, 1962, 160 p.

> Argues that Odets' later plays are as important as his earlier work and explores allegorical significance in all his writings.

Weales, Gerald. *Odets the Playwright.* New York: Methuen, 1985, 205 p.

> Studies all of Odets' writings, from stage plays to screen plays, and includes newspaper interviews, reviews, and memoirs.

AUTHOR COMMENTARY

Odets, Clifford. "Genesis of a Play." *The New York Times* (1 February 1942): IX, 3.

> Offers extracts from his journal regarding the composition of *Clash by Night* in order to "demonstrate how certain remote thoughts and feelings collect themselves around a theatrical spine and become a play."

———. "Two Approaches to the Writing of a Play." *The New York Times* (22 April 1951): II, 1-2.

> Discusses the difference between creating a play to express "a personal state of being" and merely "fabricating" one.

———. *The Time is Ripe: The 1940 Journal of Clifford Odets.* New York: Grove Press, 1988, 369 p.

> An in-depth look at one year in the playwright's life, in which he surveys the creative process, his mind-set, and his career to date.

OVERVIEWS AND GENERAL STUDIES

Atkinson, Brooks. "Clifford Odets Revealed as the Most Promising New American Dramatist." *The New York Times* (10 March 1935): VIII, 1.

Considers Odets "a new dramatist of exciting potentialities" and praises "Waiting for Lefty" and *Awake and Sing!*

Cantor, Harold. *Clifford Odets: Playwright-Poet.* Metuchen, N.J.: The Scarecrow Press, 1978, 235 p.

Attempts to correct the "mistaken and simplistic view" that Odets is a playwright whose works no longer have relevance or validity.

Miller, Gabriel. *Clifford Odets.* New York: Continuum, 1989, 253 p.

Seeks to "present Odets as a playwright who experimented with dramatic form while giving significant thematic and social concerns that evolved over the course of his career."

Murray, Edward. *Clifford Odets: The Thirties and After.* New York: Frederick Ungar Publishing Co., 1968, 229 p.

Maintains that "Clifford Odets is the only American dramatist, with the possible exception of Edward Albee, worthy to be considered in the same class with Eugene O'Neill, Arthur Miller, and Tennessee Williams."

Pells, Richard H. "The Radical Stage and the Hollywood Film in the 1930s." In his *Radical Visions and American Dreams: Culture and Social Thought in the Depression Years,* pp. 252-91. Middletown, Conn.: Wesleyan University Press, 1984.

Considers how Odets' plays were intimately related to the political and social conditions of the 1930s.

Styan, J. L. "Realism in America: Early Variations." In his *Modern Drama in Theory and Practice, Volume 1: Realism and Naturalism,* pp. 122-36. Cambridge: Cambridge University Press, 1981.

Examines Odets' use of realism in staging his agitprop plays.

Vernon, Grenville. "Clifford Odets." *The Commonweal* XXIX, No. 8 (16 December 1938): 215.

Contends that, regardless of their stated ethnic background, Odets' characters are "always Jewish in mode of thought, in emotion, and in expression."

Warshow, Robert. "Poet of the Jewish Middle Class." *Commentary* 1, No. 7 (May 1946): 17-22.

Explores aspects of Jewish culture and experience in Odets' works.

Weales, Gerald. "Clifford's Children: It's a Wise Playwright Who Knows His Own Father." *Studies in American Drama, 1945-Present* 2 (1987): 3-18.

Analyzes the settings, language, and ideology of Odets' plays.

Willett, Ralph. "Clifford Odets and Popular Culture." *The South Atlantic Quarterly* LXIX, No. 1 (Winter 1970): 68-78.

Argues that Odets' stage plays are as immersed in popular culture as his film scripts.

"WAITING FOR LEFTY" and "TILL THE DAY I DIE"

Atkinson, Brooks. Review of "Waiting for Lefty" and "Till the Day I Die." *The New York Times* (27 March 1935): 24.

Laudatory assessment that declares "Mr. Odets continues to be our most promising new dramatist."

Isaacs, Edith J. R. "Going Left with Fortune." *Theatre Arts Monthly* XIX, No. 5 (May 1935).

States "Waiting for Lefty" has "no clear outline or point of view except a general one of sympathy with the poor and the oppressed." Isaacs also contends that "Till the Day I Die" "takes too much for granted in its minor roles and situations; acts too quickly . . . ; and is too brutal."

MacLeish, Archibald. "Theatre Against War and Fascism." *New Theatre* 11, No. 8 (August 1935): 3.

Favorable review of a performance of "Waiting for Lefty." MacLeish observes that "Clifford Odets and the Group and a crowded sweltering audience created among them something moving and actual and alive."

Young, Stark. "Lefty and Nazi." *The New Republic* LXXXII, No. 1062 (10 April 1935): 247.

Positive evaluation of "Waiting for Lefty" and "Till the Day I Die" that focuses on the controversial nature of their content.

AWAKE AND SING!

Atkinson, Brooks. Review of *Awake and Sing! The New York Times* (20 February 1935): 23.

Admiring assessment that nevertheless notes that Odets "does not quite finish what he has started in this elaborately constructed piece. Although he is very much awake, he does not sing with the ease and clarity of a man who has mastered his score."

Dozier, Richard J. "The Making of *Awake and Sing! The Markham Review* 6 (Summer 1977): 61-5.

Compares the play in its original form and the shape it finally took with its controversial "affirmative" ending.

Isaacs, Edith J. R. Review of *Awake and Sing!" Theatre Arts Monthly* XIX, No. 4 (April 1935): 254-56.

Argues that while the play "is full of promise," it is "thin and weak in important spots and not always clear in the action."

GOLDEN BOY

Atkinson, Brooks. Review of *Golden Boy. The New York Times* (5 November 1937): 18.

>   Asserts that *Golden Boy* "confirms the original convictions that Mr. Odets is an instinctive writer for the stage. He can compose dialogue with a fugue-like tossing around of themes; he can create vigorous characters; he can exploit scenes and enclose his narrative within the fullness of [a] wholly written play."

Choudhuri, A. D. "*Golden Boy*: Public Face of Illusion." In *The Face of Illusion in American Drama,* pp. 59-73. Atlantic Highlands, N.J.: Humanities Press, 1979.

>   Examines Odets' play from the perspective of the "manipulation of the concept of illusion and its conflict with reality."

Review of *Golden Boy. Time* XXX, No. 20 (15 November 1937): 25-6.

>   Admires the "swift mounting of scenes [and] the extravagance of dramatic energy" in *Golden Boy.*

Additional coverage of Odets' life and career is contained in the following sources published by Gale Research: *Contemporary Authors,* **Vols. 85-88;** *Contemporary Literary Criticism,* **Vols. 2, 28;** *Dictionary of Literary Biography,* **Vols. 7, 26;** *Major Twentieth-Century Writers.*

Plautus
c. 254 B.C.-184 B. C.

(Full name Titus Maccius Plautus.)

INTRODUCTION

Plautus was one of ancient Rome's most popular play-wrights. Of the roughly one hundred and thirty comedies attributed to him in antiquity, twenty-one survive, one of which is a fragment. Plautus derived the plots for his plays from Greek originals by such playwrights as Menander, Diphilus, Philemon, and Alexis, adapting them to the tastes and interests of his Roman audience. Plautus' plays, like their models, are characterized as New Comedy, which is generally concerned with exploring the personal relationships of ordinary men and women, their fears, loves, and financial preoccupations.

BIOGRAPHICAL INFORMATION

Very little is known of Plautus's life. He was born into a poor family—some scholars suggest they were slaves—in the village of Sarsina in Umbria. As a youth he traveled to Rome, finding employment as a craftsman in the theater. Tradition holds that during his youth Plautus endured the hardships of poverty and suffered a variety of setbacks, such as the loss of money in a business enterprise. He was therefore compelled to work in a mill to earn a living. Sometime in the middle of his life Plautus turned to adapting Greek plays and eventually became the most successful Roman playwright of his time.

MAJOR WORKS

The New Comedy of Plautus is generally characterized by complex plot structures—typically involving love affairs or intrigues—elaborately delineated characters, and scenes filled with topical allusions, ingenious trickery, and reversals of expectations. Furthermore, the comedies of Plautus are suffused with jokes, puns, surprises of all sorts, elaborate songs and vibrant action. Of Plautus's twenty-one comedies, several have been particularly influential. *Menaechmi* (*Twin Menaechmi*), about the twin sons of a Syracusan merchant, one of whom was abducted, became the source of Shakespeare's *The Comedy of Errors*. *Amphitruo* (*Amphitryon*), which is concerned with mistaken identities, later formed the basis of comedies by Molière, John Dryden, and Jean Giradoux. The title character of *Miles Gloriosus* (*Braggart Warrior*) became an important stock figure in Elizabethan comedy, especially in plays by Ben Jonson. Other notable plays by Plautus include *Aulularia* (*Pot of Gold*), which concerns a miserly old man

Engraving of a likeness of Plautus.

obsessed with a buried pot of gold; and *Mostellaria* (*Haunted House*), which deals with the imaginative trickery of a slave, Tranio, in the service of his master.

CRITICAL RECEPTION

In his lifetime Plautus achieved great acclaim and renown. An astute and shrewd observer of his times, he tailored his comedies to a theater and an audience which he understood intimately. Scholars note that these conditions permitted the numerous changes Plautus introduced into his adaptations of Greek originals. Among the Plautine innovations critics have identified are characters who directly address the audience, the prominence of the Cunning Slave as a central figure, an emphasis on bawdy or cynical jokes, and a marked increase in the amount of song and musical accompaniment. Critics have also pointed to the energetic farce, rapid pace, and lively dialogue as factors in the immense popularity of Plautus' plays. After his death, the comedies of Plautus became classics. His most popular works were revived throughout antiquity and into modern times. They have frequently been translated and have served as models and inspirations for countless comedies throughout the world.

*PRINCIPAL WORKS

PLAYS

Amphitruo [*Amphitryon*] c. 186 B. C.
Asinaria [*Comedy of Asses*]
Aulularia [*Pot of Gold*]
Bacchides [*Two Bacchides*]
Captivi [*Captives*]
Casina
Cistellaria [*Casket*]
Curculio
Epidicus
Menaechmi [*Twin Menaechmi*]
Mercator [*Merchant*]
Miles Gloriosus [*Braggart Warrior*] c. 211 B. C.
Mostellaria [*Haunted House*]
Persa [*Persian*]
Poenulus [*Carthaginian*]
Pseudolus 191 B. C.
Rudens [*Rope*]
Stichus 200 B. C.
Trinummus [*Three Bob Day*]
Truculentus
†*Vidularia*

* As the dates of many of Plautus' plays are unknown, the works in this list are presented in alphabetical order. Dates are provided when they are known or conjectured.

† This work survives only in a fragment of about 100 lines.

OVERVIEWS AND GENERAL STUDIES

Philip Whaley Harsh (essay date 1944)

SOURCE: "Plautus," in *A Handbook of Classical Drama*, Stanford University Press, 1944, pp. 333-74.

[*In the following excerpt, Harsh provides a survey of Plautus's major plays.*]

The twenty extant plays of Plautus constitute an astonishingly varied collection of good, bad, and indifferent comedies. Even the worst, however, usually have one or more effective scenes, and most of the indifferent ones doubtless were successful in his theater. For modern dramatists, good and bad alike have served as a continually plundered storehouse of interesting comic characters and amusing situations. The structure of the *Amphitryon,* for instance, is not well proportioned, to say the least; but the play's situation is so infallibly amusing that it has attracted innumerable adapters. Nor have imitators been frightened away from the *Twin Menaechmi* merely because its basic situation is fantastically improbable. The *Braggart Warrior* is very poorly constructed, but its title character remains eternally popular. The widely adapted *Pot of Gold,* how-

ever, calls for no apology on any score, for it is a masterpiece. These four plays, the most influential ones, well illustrate the variety of Plautus' work.

It is obviously difficult to determine the personal contributions of a dramatist all of whose plays are adaptations of Greek plays now lost. Still this can be done for Terence with comparative clarity, for his literary prologues and the ancient commentaries give much detailed information. Besides, his plays themselves are remarkably consistent in subject matter, structure, and various other features of dramatic technique, some of which are known not to have been characteristic of Greek comedy. But for Plautus the situation is quite different. He has no literary prologues, and no commentaries have been preserved. We are thrown back, therefore, upon the plays themselves; and, except in style, these show great variation.

In meter the variation is great but consistent and significant: Plautus began his career using little or no lyric measure and gradually increased its use as time went on. The *Braggart Warrior,* for instance, is dated by its reference to the imprisonment of Naevius (lines 209-12) about 205 B.C. It has no elaborate lyric and, except for a single passage in anapests, it is confined to iambic and trochaic lines of six or seven and one-half feet. This is the simplest metrical structure of any Plautine play. The *Stichus,* produced in 200 B.C., opens with an elaborate lyric, has two passages in anapests, and one passage in lyric iambic measure of eight feet, as well as a few lyric lines at the end of the play. The *Pseudolus,* dated 191 B.C., is literally filled with lyric and anapestic measures. These are the only plays which can be dated with certainty, and with these three as a framework modern scholars have arranged the other plays in the order of their metrical elaborateness and have assumed that this was more or less the order of their composition. This assumption must not be pressed too closely, however, for presumably a serious comedy of character like the *Pot of Gold* admits fewer true lyrics and requires more restrained dialogue than an extravagent farce like the *Casina*. It is hardly necessary to add that in Plautine comedy, as in Greek tragedy and Aristophanes, the meters are skillfully adapted to the subject matter. Changes in meter emphasize changes in tone and are especially effective in a melodramatic play like the *Rope*.

In subject matter, Plautus seems to run the gamut of New Comedy and perhaps to reach into that of Middle Comedy; nor has any clear and significant development in this regard been observed. The mythological travesty of the *Amphitryon* is certainly the oldest material, but the elaborate meter of this play places it in the period of Plautus' maturity. The *Captives,* usually assigned to this same period, is an extraordinary play concerning the exchange of prisoners of war. The majority of Plautus' plays, however, like most of those of New Comedy, concern the gay life of the gilded youth of Athens, their eternal need of money with which to purchase sweethearts, and the frequent recognition of these sweethearts as Attic citizens.

The dramatist's attitude toward his material shows equal variety. Thus the *Pot of Gold* is a serious comedy of character, the **Haunted House** a farce, and the **Two Bacchides** a comedy of character and intrigue. These are all from the mature or late periods, and Plautus seems to have undergone no development in this regard, although comedies of intrigue are the most frequent from the beginning of his career to the end. Thus the **Comedy of Asses** presumably comes near the beginning and the **Pseudolus** near the end; the intrigue of the one is very similar to that of the other, although the **Pseudolus** is in every way vastly superior.

In dramatic structure, also, the plays vary tremendously. The **Braggart Warrior,** the **Comedy of Asses,** and the **Merchant,** all having simple metrical structure, are usually classed together as the earliest plays. But of these three, the **Merchant** is constructed excellently, the other two miserably. The **Stichus,** slightly later, has practically no plot at all—not, of course, necessarily a fault. Among the later plays, however, it is not so easy to point to such indisputable contrasts, and it may be that Plautus improved somewhat in this regard. Still, certain of the late plays, such as the **Persian,** are surely not distinguished in structure or in their general technique.

Another item of remarkable variation is found in the total length of the different comedies. The longest are the early **Braggart Warrior** (1,437 lines), the **Carthaginian** (1,422), and the middle or late **Rope** (1,423) and **Pseudolus** (1,334). The shortest are the **Curculio** (729), the **Epidicus** (733), the **Stichus** (775), and the **Persian** (858). These plays are from the early, middle, and late periods.

This astonishing variation of the plays, in the opinion of the present writer, seems to indicate that Plautus took his plays without much critical discrimination from a wide variety of authors and that these authors are responsible for the main features of the plays. It is conceivable, of course, that the actual manuscripts available to Plautus at Rome may have been limited. If he used any criterion consistently, it was that of theatrical effectiveness. Horace was not wholly unjustified in saying that Plautus rushed over the stage in loose "socks" and cared only for popular success. Many modern critics, however, assume that Plautus so mauled the original Greek comedies that he himself is responsible for most of the faults of his plays. Perhaps these critics would have a higher opinion of Plautus' intellect if they set their hands to translating the delightfully delicate ironies and the brilliant wit of the **Amphitryon.** Certainly all but the very keenest modern translators have fallen far short of Plautus' attainment.

That Plautus had no slavish respect for the Greek originals is obvious from the plays themselves. As he changes the meters to suit himself, so he introduces various Roman allusions. References to Greek places or customs or events that would be obscure to a Roman audience are usually eliminated. Greek gods are changed to Roman. This, of course, is mere expert translation, and even Terence regularly followed this practice. But Plautus has the habit of mixing Greek and Roman in a way offensive to the modern reader, though it doubtless seemed natural enough to his original audience. It is now disconcerting, for instance,

to have the Greek atmosphere broken by a reference to the Praetor. Even more disconcerting is a reference to a particular place in the city of Rome or—for comic effect—to the country town Praeneste or Plautus' own Sarsina. Terence was careful to avoid all such confusion.

Plautus sometimes combined two Greek plays into one Roman or omitted a scene from the original, and in general he adapted with considerable freedom. So says Terence in defense of his own practice. Modern scholars have expended a huge amount of energy in attempting to analyze the comedies and determine the innovations of Plautus; but most of these studies have been made without sufficient literary background and consist, as someone has said, of a comparison of the known with the unknown. To assume that the very prolific Greek writers of New Comedy made no blunders or allowed no inconsistencies to creep in is obviously fallacious. In short, a detailed reconstruction of the original plays from the plays of Plautus is quite impossible.

In matters of style, the personality of Plautus, greatly influenced by the conventions of his day, is observable throughout his works. His dialogue is vigorous and rapid and filled with delightful humor. In general, however, his style, like that of his contemporaries, is far more exuberant than the chaste elegance of Greek New Comedy. Plautus' Latin abounds in alliteration, redundancy, puns, and word play. This exuberance is seen in its most extreme manifestation in his anapestic and lyric passages, an English prose translation of which often sounds utterly ridiculous. Such passages should, of course, be translated into the idiom of modern popular songs. Ancient critics such as Cicero give Plautus credit for an admirable mastery of colloquial Latin. He is very bold in his word coinages, which are often made for comic effect, such as in the awkward "loan translation" of a Greek compound, *turpilucricupidus* ("filthy-lucre-grabber"). Occasionally a bit of Greek or local dialect is admitted for the same effect. But very few cases of merely bad translation are found.

In certain respects Plautus distantly resembles Aristophanes. Certainly his sense of humor is robust and all-inclusive. He is fond of comedy based on physical effects, such as the pouring of slops on Amphitryon near the end of that play, the vomiting of Labrax in the **Rope,** and the drunken belching of Pseudolus. He likes indecent jests; but these usually seem a little prim in comparison with those of Aristophanes or those of Naevius. His language and his meters are similarly exuberant. His use of interminable lists, as in the **Pot of Gold** (508-19), and his employment of a dinning repetition line after line, as in the **Rope** (1212-24), also strike Aristophanic notes. He is similarly informal. So the property manager in the **Curculio** interrupts the play to give a discourse on the various quarters of Rome. More frequently, the dramatic illusion is broken by direct address to the audience or by directly insulting the audience. So Euclio in the **Pot of Gold** (718) declares that many of those in the audience, as he well knows, are thieves. We need not assume that any of these characteristics of Old Comedy had wholly died out in the Greek tradition, but possibly they are somewhat more frequent in Plautus than in his originals. The contrast with the dignified and formal Terence, at least, is again most striking. Nor need we assume that Plautus is consciously following the Aristophanic tradition—it is merely that he has a strain of the immortal comic spirit.

Amphitryon

Though constructed with something of the careless nonchalance of Old Comedy, the *Amphitryon* is so filled with delightful irony and irrepressible low comedy and tells such an immortal story that it is one of the most interesting plays of Plautus.

About three hundred verses, it is usually assumed, are missing from the text after line 1034.

LEGEND.—The legend concerning the twin birth of Heracles and Iphicles, like that of the triple birth of Helen, Castor, and Pollux, finds its eventual origin in the old popular superstition which attributed multiple births to supernatural causes. Thus the strong twin, Heracles, was thought to be the son of a divinity and only the weaker Iphicles the true son of the mortal Amphitryon.

The most striking features of the legend of Heracles' birth were the disguise of Jupiter, the long night which was necessary for the conception of this mighty child, the divine manifestations at his birth, and the miracles wrought by him in infancy. Obviously there should be at least seven months between the long night and the birth, and some months more between the birth and the miracles. But if Aristophanes in the *Acharnians* could have Amphitheus go to Sparta, arrange truces there, and return to Athens all within the space of fifty lines, his contemporaries, if they so chose, could doubtless combine the long night—transformed, as in Plautus' play, perhaps from the night of generation to a night of incidental dalliance—the birth, and the miracles all into one comedy.

SOURCE.—No subject material has held the boards so long and successfully as the story of Alcmena and Amphitryon. Only the story of Oedipus and possibly that of Medea and a few others were more frequently dramatized by the Greek poets. Aeschylus wrote an *Alcmene*. So did Euripides and each of at least three minor poets of the fifth and fourth centuries. Other plays entitled *Amphitryon,* which may have dealt with entirely different phases of the story, were written by Sophocles, an Alexandrine poet, and the Roman Accius.

This subject would seem naturally to lend itself readily to parody; and the comic writers, as usual, doubtless centered their attention on the version of Euripides. A reference at the opening of Plautus' *Rope* (86) amusingly recalls the realistic stage effects which were employed at the climax of Euripides' play. Two contemporaries of Aristophanes essayed the subject—one, Archippus, calling his play the *Amphitryon;* the other, Plato "Comicus," calling his the *Long Night (Nux Makra)*. Philemon also wrote a *Night,* and Rhinthon, a Greek of southern Italy writing burlesque, was the author of an *Amphitryon.* Almost nothing is known of these plays.

It is usually assumed that the immediate original of the Latin play was a comedy of the Middle or New period. This may be correct. But the *Amphitryon,* though in some ways typical of New Comedy, exhibits more technical characteristics of early comedy than any other play of Plautus. One can hardly doubt that such writers as Archippus and Plato "Comicus," perhaps Rhinthon also, have left their marks upon the play. Informality is its most striking feature. The scene at one time seems to be laid before the house of Amphitryon, at another somewhere near the harbor. Such variation was not unnatural on the long Roman stage, however, and less striking examples are found in other plays. The very fact that Thebes is placed near the sea is a bold distortion, like the coast of Bohemia in Shakespeare. The utter contempt for the dramatic illusion, also, is reminiscent of Old Comedy. So are the various effects of low comedy: the beating of Sosia and Mercury's pouring ashes and slops down on Amphitryon. Time is boldly telescoped. There is something too of the inimitable spirit and verve of Old Comedy.

INFLUENCE.—There are vast numbers of modern adaptations of Plautus' *Amphitryon*. One of the most famous of these is Molière's *Amphitryon* (1668), which has been translated into many languages and frequently reproduced. Especially noteworthy in his version is the introduction of Sosia's wife. Sosia's "girl friend" is given only a brief reference in the play of Plautus (659). Well known also are the version of Rotrou (*Les Sosies,* 1638), which had considerable influence on Molière, that of John Dryden (1690), and that of von Kleist (1807). In the *Comedy of Errors* Shakespeare adopted certain motives from the *Amphitryon*.

Most interesting of all, however, is the brilliant contemporary production of Jean Giraudoux, *Amphitryon 38*. This is an astonishingly original reworking of material so often dramatized before, and it has very little in common with the play of Plautus. Indeed the story has been made into delightfully high comedy. In a bedroom scene filled with subtle irony Jupiter praises the night just past in the most effusive terms, but for his every adjective Alcmène insists upon recalling a night (with Amphitryon, of course) that was much superior. Thus the comedy is mainly at the expense not of Amphitryon but of the god himself! Alcmène also pays her generous share, for she mistakes the real Amphitryon for the god and, thinking that she is playing a clever deception upon him, sends him in to the bed of Jupiter's former play-fellow, Leda. The comedy closes with a gift of forgetfulness—a faint reminiscence perhaps of Molière's ending. An English adaptation of this play was produced in America with great success.

DISCUSSION.—Except for the *Plutus* of Aristophanes, the *Amphitryon* is the only example of mythological travesty that has been preserved. This genre, though occasionally written at Athens during the fifth century, came into great popularity during the first half of the fourth century and to some extent prepared the way for the development of intimate social comedy.

The basic plot of the *Amphitryon,* a wife's adultery and the duping of a husband, was one which convention usually forbade comedy. The cruel irony of the situation, difficult for any husband to enjoy wholly without misgivings, is well exploited, however, even in the *Iliad* (3. 369-454), where Menelaus still toils on the field of battle while Paris, rescued from him by Aphrodite, has taken Helen to bed. The situation is softened in the comedy of Plautus because a well-known myth is being parodied and because Alcmena is morally innocent. Here the duping of the husband is played up into a comedy of errors and, to make confusion worse confounded, Mercury is introduced in the disguise of Sosia.

The opening of the *Amphitryon* is remarkably recitational and farcical. Here is the best example of the proverbially long-winded god of the prologue. Almost a hundred lines of clever foolery have gone by before Mercury finally begins with the argument of the play. Another fifty lines are used for explaining the situation. Since this is a comedy of errors, the poet is careful here and throughout the play to instruct the audience with painful explicitness before every new development. Incidentally Mercury reminds us that some Roman actors, being slaves, might be whipped for a poor performance, and he makes interesting revelations concerning *claqueurs* in the ancient theater.

The entrance of Sosia does not begin the action but leads to another prologue! Now we hear in detail the story of Amphitryon's campaign, and the mortal is no more concise—and no less clever—than the immortal has been. Practically nothing in this long monody, occasionally punctuated by a remark of Mercury, has any structural significance except the reference to the gold cup of Pterela (260). No normal dramatic conversation develops until almost three hundred fifty verses have been spoken in these two prologues. Still, this opening, though static, is far from dull.

After the amusing low comedy between Sosia and Mercury, the slave departs, and the god speaks another prologue! We are now told the complications that are about to take place, and even precisely how everything will be made right in the end.

The two scenes between Jupiter and Alcmena are among the best of the play and prove that, after all, ancient dramatists could write scenes of sentimental dalliance. The exchanges here, of course, are pervaded by a delicate irony. Alcmena can well say, "Gracious me! I am discovering how much regard you have for your wife (508)." And Mercury can be quite sure that he is telling the truth when he says to Alcmena: ". . . . I don't believe there's a mortal man alive loves his own wife (*glancing slyly at Jupiter*) so madly as the mad way he dotes on you." Incidentally in this scene Jupiter gives Alcmena the gold cup which, as we have heard before (260, 419-21), Amphitryon has received as his special reward, and which is to play such an important role in the subsequent action.

The comedy of errors now continues with the introduction of Amphitryon; and the structural function of the earlier mystification of the slave, it now appears, is to furnish the first step in the gradual mystification and maddening of the master. The second step quickly follows with the strangely cold reception which Amphitryon receives from Alcmena. Her production of the gold cup adds a third. Meanwhile the irony continues, but it is not always as delicate as it is in the very proper oath of Alcmena (831-34): "By the realm of our Ruler above and by Juno, mother and wife, whom I should most reverence and fear, I swear that no mortal man save you alone has touched my body with his to take my shame away."

When Amphitryon, convinced of his wife's infidelity, has rushed off to find her kinsman, Jupiter returns for another session of dalliance and to set the stage for the supreme humiliation of Amphitryon. He also foretells the coming action and solution, repeating in part what Mercury has said previously. Later Mercury reappears as the "running slave," and carefully explains how he will mock Amphitryon.

Failure to locate the kinsman of Alcmena aggravates Amphitryon's ill humor, and when he returns to find the house closed to him his frustration knows no bounds. But this is only the beginning of his grief. He must be taunted unmercifully by the divine lackey and finally have ashes dumped upon him and slops poured over him—a scene which doubtless brought down the house, be it Greek or Roman. All this time Jupiter is taking his pleasure of Alcmena inside. Finally Jupiter himself comes forth and tows the conquering hero Amphitryon about the stage by the nape of his neck. There is not a scene even in Aristophanes that carries low comedy quite so far as this.

When Amphitryon finally regains his feet, now stark mad, he resolves to rush into the house and slay everyone whom he meets. But at this crucial moment come thunder and lightning, and he is struck down before his house. There can be no vacant stage here, and doubtless Bromia quickly enters, though her subsequent account reveals that a great deal of time is supposed to have elapsed. Amphitryon, recognizing the unmistakable signs of divinity, is thoroughly placated. He considers it an honor to have had his wife adulterated by Jupiter. Nevertheless, the play must end in true tragic fashion with an appearance of Jupiter as the god from the machine. The last line of all, reminiscent of the humor of Mercury in the prologue, is perhaps the best of the play (Nixon's translation): "Now, spectators, for the sake of Jove almighty, give us some loud applause."

. . . . .

Pot of Gold (Aulularia)

The *Pot of Gold* is a delightful comedy of character with an abundance of dramatic action. Unfortunately the final scene has been lost, but fragments and the arguments of the play indicate the main features of the solution.

It is thought that Menander was the author of the original—a very attractive but unproved assumption. The miser was a favorite type with Menander, as may be seen in his *Arbitration*, where also a cook is used for a scene of low comedy.

SIGNIFICANT NAMES.—The name Staphyla ("bunch of grapes") suggests that this character, like so many of the old women of comedy, is addicted to winebibbing, and certain of her lines confirm this (354-55). The cooks, too, are picturesquely named Congrio (*gongros,* "eel") and Anthrax ("a coal"). From the point of view of American slang, however, the most aptly named character is that of the young man who has violated Euclio's daughter—Lyconides ("wolfling").

INFLUENCE.—The *Pot of Gold* has been a very influential play. Ben Jonson's *The Case Is Altered* is an adaptation of this and of the *Captives.* But by far the most famous adaptation is Molière's *L'Avare* (1668), which itself inspired various imitations, including comedies entitled *The Miser* by Shadwell (1672) and by Fielding (1732).

A comparison of the play of Molière with that of Plautus is a profitable study; but only a few points can here be noted. Molière, like Plautus, employs significant names. Among these Harpagon ("grappling hook," "snatcher") is a Greek-Latin formation and was doubtless suggested by the cognate verb which occurs in the *Pot of Gold* (201), or by the name Harpax in the *Pseudolus* (esp. 654). Moliere has enriched the plot by adding a son and his love affair, in which Harpagon himself is involved. Several passages closely follow Plautus. Harpagon rages at the loss of his gold much as Euclio does and even descends to making similar remarks directly to the audience (IV, vii). The scene where Valère confesses to Harpagon also follows Plautus very closely in its elaborate irony. The Menandrean humanity of Euclio, however, has been wholly lost in the grossly exaggerated Harpagon.

DISCUSSION.—The main plot of the *Pot of Gold* is an unusual one. A miser, Euclio, through excess of caution, is made to lose his recently discovered treasure. By the good offices of a young man who has violated his daughter, however, he recovers the treasure. Meanwhile he has learned a lesson; and so he apparently gives the money to his daughter as a dowry and is happy to be relieved of the task of guarding it. Thus this comedy, like the *Brothers* of Terence, has a serious theme. The minor plot concerning the daughter and her violation is trite, but skill is shown in combining it very closely with the main plot. Indeed it is employed almost wholly to bring out the character of Euclio and facilitate the main action.

The play opens with an omniscient prologue by the patron divinity of the household. Noteworthy here is the explanation that the proposal of the old man, Megadorus, is merely a device of the divinity for uniting the girl to the father of her child. Surely a modern playwright would have preferred to dispense with the prologue altogether and to reserve Megadorus' proposal for an exciting complication. But the ancient dramatist has some justification for rejecting this method. He is anxious in no way to detract from the emphasis on Euclio's character. Even in the pro-

logue, the primary concern is to show that the miserliness of Euclio has been inherited for generations. Indeed the proposal of Megadorus itself is primarily designed to bring out the point, essential to the plot, that the present Euclio will not even give a dowry to his daughter though she must inevitably lose social status if she marries a wealthy man without one. So the very liberal character of Megadorus is designed by contrast to display the niggardliness of Euclio.

The scenes between Euclio and Staphyla, also, serve to illustrate the character of the miser. Incidentally, preparation for his subsequent distrust of the very bland Megadorus is contained in his complaint that all his fellow citizens, seeming to know that he has found a treasure, now greet him more cordially.

Eunomia and Megadorus are introduced with an elaborate duet in which it is brought out that an old brother is being forced to do his duty to society by an old sister who has already done hers. Since Eunomia must have a role later in the play, the dramatist has done well to introduce her here, and she is very nicely drawn. Her slightly archaic Latin perhaps suggests that she belongs to that class of staid matrons whom attention to the home has caused to lose contact with the latest developments of a changing world—a type of old-fashioned womanhood well known and admired by Cicero.

The cooks furnish low comic relief in this very serious play but are also necessary in the machinery of the plot. Significantly emphatic are the repeated references to the notorious thievery of cooks, especially the slave's monologue devoted exclusively to this subject immediately before the re-entrance of Euclio (363-70). The distinctly lower atmosphere of these menials is subtly suggested also by a few indecent jests.

So Euclio is brought to the fatal mistake of removing his hoarded gold and burying it elsewhere. Megadorus' genial threat to make him drunk merely adds to his uneasiness, though he has been pleased with Megadorus' disgust of rich wives and their extravagance.

The action which leads the slave of Lyconides to steal Euclio's treasure is well motivated; but the technique of eavesdropping is awkward in the extreme, for misers, however old or fond of talking to themselves, are careful not to talk of their treasures aloud. To present their thoughts in soliloquies may be permissible, but to have another discover the secret by overhearing such a soliloquy violates all probability.

The best scene of the play, perhaps, is that in which Lyconides confesses one sin but Euclio thinks that he is confessing another. The ambiguity here is more easily maintained in Latin or French than in English. Highly amusing, too, is the later effort of Lyconides' slave to withdraw his confession of having stolen the treasure.

Doubtless little of importance has been lost at the end except Euclio's final speech of reformation.

Two Bacchides (Bacchides)

... The *Two Bacchides,* somewhat like the *Self-Tormentor* of Terence, opens as a splendid Menandrean comedy of character but soon hastens off into the usual stereotyped play of intrigue. Noteworthy is the rapid shift in the fortunes of the various individuals. Mnesilochus now has an abundance of money, now none, and soon an abundance again. The fortunes of his father change even more rapidly and, of course, end at a humiliatingly low level.

An undetermined number of verses have been lost from the opening, but the play is essentially intact.

SOURCE.—The source of Plautus' play is revealed by verses 816-17, which translate one of Menander's most famous lines, "Whom the gods love dies young." Menander's play was called the *Double Deceiver (Dis Exapaton).* From the title it is obvious that Menander's play also centered about the intrigue to secure money. Some modern scholars, however, have insisted that Plautus has added one deception—the second letter. Chrysalus does cite three deceptions (953-78). That later Nicobulus (1090) and one of the sisters (1128) count only two has been taken to indicate that Plautus here reverts to the original text of Menander. But it is ridiculous for modern scholars to assume that Plautus could become confused on such a simple score. The inconsistency is only apparent. Indeed, Bacchis clearly says that Nicobulus has been "trimmed" twice; and this certainly, as presumably the earlier phrase of Nicobulus and the Greek title, can only refer to actual financial losses. In short, there is no evidence that Plautus has changed the plot, though we can feel certain that he has greatly elaborated the simple meters of the original.

INFLUENCE.—More important than the few adaptations in modern times has been the influence of certain of the play's many types of characters, especially the strait-laced pedagogue and the deceiving servant. Chrysalus' wild tale of the sloop (279-305) eventually, perhaps, turns up in Molière's *Les Fourberies de Scapin* (1671; II, xi) after appearing in various intermediary plays, including Cyrano de Bergerac's *Le Pédant Joué* (possibly 1654).

DISCUSSION.—The *Two Bacchides* exhibits an embryonic double plot, for it contains two young men and their difficulties in love. The best of the play is doubtless found in the opening scenes between the naïvely innocent Pistoclerus and the more than competent Bacchis. Both are delightfully characterized, and Bacchis shows great skill in ensnaring him as she and her sister are later to ensnare the fathers of both young men. Very amusing is the reaction of Pistoclerus' pedagogue, Lydus, who cannot realize that his ward is no longer a child and whose moral code, in comparison with that of his masters, is ridiculously high.

From the first, Pistoclerus has been acting as the agent of Mnesilochus, and with the return of this second young man, the need of money to save his love from the soldier becomes the chief concern of the action. Pistoclerus practically disappears after he has caused the minor complication of Mnesilochus' returning all the money brought from Ephesus to his father. Part of this money must now be recovered through the usual type of intrigue engineered by the usual clever slave. The victim is forewarned repeatedly, as in the *Pseudolus,* and yet repeatedly deceived. As in the *Pseudolus,* also, return of part of the money is promised to the victim at the end of the play. The intrigue itself and especially the elaborate comparison which Chrysalus draws between himself and Ulysses are clever and amusing, though of course the whole depends upon the mechanically pat entrance of the soldier. As a comic character, however, Chrysalus falls far below the level of the colorful Pseudolus.

In general the portrayal of characters is masterly. But contrast of characters, except for the indirect contrast between the strait-laced Lydus and the unscrupulous Chrysalus, is not here employed as effectively as in the *Brothers* of Terence and in other Menandrean plays. This shortcoming is all the more striking because the cast includes two young men, two old men, and two courtesans.

The final scene wherein the sister courtesans take in the old men has often been criticized on moral grounds. Though amusing, it is undeniably crude. Satire is often so. There is not the slightest ground, however, for thinking that either crudity or satire is not Menandrean. The Greeks saw life whole and honestly recorded what they saw.

Captives

The *Captives* is a quiet comedy of delightful humor and somewhat melodramatic pathos. Lessing considered it the finest comedy ever produced because, in his opinion, it best fulfills the purpose of comedy and because it is richly endowed with other good qualities. The opinion of Lessing, however, was attacked in his own day, and the merit of the *Captives* is still a matter of debate and violent disagreement. This arises in part from differences of opinion concerning the purpose of comedy and from attempts to compare incomparables. Various types of comedy naturally have various appeals, and the *Captives* is admittedly lacking in the robust gaiety and occasional frank indecencies of the *Pseudolus* as it is lacking also in the verve and activity and romance of the *Rope*. It is nevertheless a very successful play.

Nothing is known concerning the Greek original.

INFLUENCE.—Among comedies indebted to the *Captives* may be mentioned the following: Ariosto's *I Suppositi* (about 1502, adapted into English by George Gascoigne [1566]), Ben Jonson's *The Case Is Altered* (about 1598, combining the *Captives* and the *Pot of Gold*), and Rotrou's *Les Captifs* (1638).

SIGNIFICANT NAMES.—The significance of the name Ergasilus ("working for a living," but here, as elsewhere, with the connotation of "courtesan") is explained by the parasite himself in his opening lines. The name Hegio ("leading citizen") obviously suggests a gentleman. The names Philocrates ("lover of mastery"), Aristophontes ("best-slayer"), and Philopolemus ("lover of war") all suggest mighty warriors, and there is more than a shade of irony in the fact that all these men have been captured in war. Stalagmus ("drop") is a derisive name applied to a slave of diminutive stature. The name Tyndarus is apparently taken from the legendary Tyndareos, father of Helen, and is obviously a slave's name.

STRUCTURE.—The *Captives,* like most of the plays of Plautus, was probably presented without intermission or interlude; but the traditional "acts," which date from the Renaissance, here divide the play into well-defined chapters of action. It is not unlikely, therefore, that these divisions are the same as those of the original Greek play, which probably had five sections marked off by four choral interludes.

The first section (126 lines) is designed to put the audience into a pleasant mood, characterize Hegio, and repeat the essential facts of the exposition (for the play is a unit practically independent of the prologue). The second section (266 lines) again explains the confusion of identity and successfully launches the intrigue by which Hegio is made to send away the gentleman, Philocrates, rather than the servant, Tyndarus. The third section (307 lines) presents Hegio's discovery of the ruse and the downfall of Tyndarus. The fourth (154 lines) announces the return of Hegio's captive son and is mainly concerned with the foolery of the parasite Ergasilus. The fifth (107 lines) contains the actual arrival of Philocrates, Philopolemus, and the wicked slave Stalagmus. Most important of all, Tyndarus is here recognized as the long-lost son of Hegio.

DISCUSSION.—An intrigue by which two enslaved captives cheat their purchaser furnishes subject matter refreshingly different from that of most later Greek comedies. But the *Captives* still has many conventional features. The parasite is the usual stereotyped character, and to eliminate him would be to sacrifice the most amusing character of the play. Stock incidents, too, are found in the confusion of identities and in the use of intrigue and recognition. The appearance of Stalagmus, also, is too happy a coincidence for serious drama. No proper explanation is given for his return, although some preparation for this and for the recognition is made by Hegio's account of his earlier loss of a son (760). Nor is it true, as the speaker of the prologue alleges, that the play contains no indecent lines, although moral purity has contributed more than its share to the popularity of this play in modern times. In order to be fair to the poet, however, we must admit that even the conventional features are handled with unusual skill and freshness. The indecent jests are few and are employed almost exclusively to emphasize Ergasilus' irrepressible exuberance when he is bringing the good news to Hegio (867, 888). The confusion of identities is here entirely credible—although this has been disputed—and bears no resemblance to the implausibly maintained confusion in the *Twin Menaechmi.* The actors may well commend this play, therefore, for its effort to break away from the stereotyped characters and the stock incidents of New Comedy.

Unique in New Comedy is the appearance of two actors along with the speaker of the prologue in order that the audience may understand the true identity of Philocrates and Tyndarus beyond all doubt. The prologue also reveals that Tyndarus is the son of Hegio, although Tyndarus and Philocrates do not know this during the subsequent scenes. This inconsistency should hardly be considered a fault, for it is here assumed that the play has not yet begun.

Although most of the information given in the prologue is as usual repeated in the following scenes, a prologue was absolutely essential in this play, for without the knowledge that Tyndarus is Hegio's son the audience would fail to appreciate much of the dramatic irony which pervades the whole action and constitutes perhaps the chief virtue of the play.

Dramatic irony and suspense tend to be mutually exclusive, since the one often depends upon the superior knowledge of the audience and the other upon its ignorance; yet the *Captives* combines both to a remarkable extent and with unusual subtlety. The suspense concerns the return of Philocrates, of course, and it is built up primarily by means of the irony of Philocrates' lines and the earnest anxiety of Tyndarus in their scene of farewell.

The dramatic irony of the play begins when Hegio first addresses his two captives. Philocrates plays the role of the confidential slave with consummate skill especially in his assured self-reliance and in his impudent boldness, whereas Tyndarus assumes the modest restraint of a gentleman. Many of these speeches obviously have one meaning for Hegio but another, truer, meaning for the captives and the audience. This humorous irony is very materially aided in Latin by the usual omission of articles and pronouns. Thus when Tyndarus, posing as the gentleman, speaks of sending the "slave" Philocrates *ad patrem,* the reference is amusingly ambiguous.

The dramatic irony reaches its greatest height, however, in the scene of farewell. When the supposed master recites at great length the virtues of the slave, he is really praising himself; and when the supposed slave recites the virtues of the master, he, too, is really praising himself. But the poor naïve Hegio is so taken in by the deception that he is greatly impressed with what he thinks to be the sincere mutual praise of master and slave (418-21). The effect here is primarily comic; but there is real pathos in the true Tyndarus' fear of being abandoned, a fear which Hegio cannot understand but which the audience fully appreciates. The high point of this aspect of the dramatic irony comes when the "slave" who is being sent home gives an oath to Hegio and to his former "master" that he will never be false to Philocrates. Such an oath reassures Hegio, but it can only disquiet the true Tyndarus.

The most serious and pathetic irony in these scenes, however, is contained in those speeches in which the truth can be appreciated only by the audience. The true Tyndarus in his first conversation with Hegio, for instance, says that he was formerly just as much a free man as Hegio's own son and that his father misses him just as much as Hegio misses his own son. Whereas Tyndarus here intends to lie and Hegio thinks that Tyndarus is Philocrates and is telling the truth, the audience know that Tyndarus is really saying what is true because he is the son of Hegio.

Another scene of pathetic irony is that in which Hegio undertakes to punish Tyndarus, really his own son. When Tyndarus boldly insists that his action has been commendable and proper, Hegio himself is forced to admit that he would have been very grateful indeed if a slave had performed such an action for a son of his. This is precisely what Tyndarus has done, for by securing the release of Philocrates he has really made possible the return of his own brother, the captured son of Hegio.

Indirectly, of course, Tyndarus has also made his own recognition possible. Yet Hegio thinks that this action of Tyndarus has made him lose his second and last son. Although this scene is not without its touches of humor, the tone is on the whole very serious, and the solemn simplicity of the iambic meter here, as Lindsay points out, is reminiscent of tragedy and offers a very strong contrast with the bustling comedy of the preceding scene.

Hegio is not the stupid old man characteristic of comedy, although his figure has its amusing aspects; nor is he the stereotyped kindly old gentleman. He is thoroughly an individual. Before his entrance he is described briefly by Ergasilus as a man of the old school whose present business of trading in captives is most alien to his character. Thus we are prepared for Hegio's being taken in by the clever ruse of the captives. Undeniably amusing is his meticulous but naïve and wholly ineffectual caution in handling the captives. This caution is brought out both in his directions to the Guard and in his first conversation with the "slave" Philocrates. Amusing also is the manner in which Tyndarus and Philocrates talk to each other in their scene of farewell with an irony which wholly deceives the old man.

Sudden changes in the emotional tone of the play are emphasized by the figure of Ergasilus. Besides enlivening this unusually serious play with the usual low comedy, Ergasilus serves as an emotional foil for Hegio. At the beginning of the play both Hegio and Ergasilus are worried and not too optimistic. But as the play progresses and arrangements are made for sending the "slave" to Elis, Hegio becomes elated at the prospect of securing the return of his captured son. Just at this point, Ergasilus appears and, in strong contrast to Hegio's elation, pours forth his woeful tale of hopeless failure to discover a patron in the forum or even to raise a laugh. He would gladly dig the eyes out of this day that has made him so hateful to everyone. Immediately after this depressing monologue and the exit of Ergasilus, Hegio reappears in a state of elation greater than before, relating how he has been congratulated by everyone for successfully arranging the return of his son. The irony of his situation again presents the old man in a somewhat humorous light.

After the deception of the captives has been discovered, Hegio himself falls into a dreadfully depressed state and presents a figure of almost tragic pathos. But Ergasilus now appears in a state of ecstatic elation over the good news which he has for Hegio. The day which before was so hateful to him he now recognizes as his greatest benefactor. Ergasilus has time for only a few lines, however, before Hegio reappears. In a brief song, very different in tone from his earlier song of self-congratulation, Hegio now bitterly complains of his disappointment and chagrin, anticipating the scorn of everyone when they learn of the way in which he has been taken in. Here the irony of Hegio's depressed state fuses the pathos and the humor of his figure to make him the most appealing character of the play. A final brief song by Hegio, in the same meter, opens the last section of the play and expresses Hegio's solemn gratitude for the return of his captive son.

Tyndarus and Philocrates, like Hegio, are entirely admirable characters, and their virtues are fittingly rewarded as we should expect in a comedy. Still, they do not become saccharine in their goodness. Tyndarus is more than willing, for instance, to see Stalagmus punished. Sentimentality, which might have run rampant in the final scene, has been avoided by maintaining the usual classic restraint and honesty.

Casina

Like much of Aristophanes, this spirited musical farce is grossly indecent and irresistibly amusing. Its popularity is well-attested in the prologue, part of which, at least, was written for a reproduction some time after Plautus' death. The text in the broad scenes near the end of the play is only partially preserved. The play as a whole is the most lyric of Plautus' comedies, and many a delightfully extravagant line of the original falls very flat in translation.

The *Casina* has had some unimportant modern adaptations, but the resemblance of its plot to the *Mariage de Figaro* of Beaumarchais is thought to be fortuitous.

The original Greek version of this play, like that of the *Rope,* was written by Diphilus, who called his comedy the *Lot-Drawers (Kleroumenoi).* Modern scholars often assume that Plautus has revamped the whole play and introduced much of its grossness. Diphilus, however, was distinguished among the poets of New Comedy for his frankness, and it is not easy to imagine how this material could be handled very differently from the way in which Plautus has handled it. It is obvious from Diphilus' title that his play too centered about a contest, and it is likely that this contest was the rivalry of two slaves, reflecting, as in Plautus, the rivalry of father and son. Certainly if the father was involved, the subject was a scandalous one and fitted only for broad farce.

If Plautus is responsible for the suppression of the nauseatingly frequent motive of recognition, he is to be heartily congratulated; but there is no trustworthy evidence on this point. Certainly the play is skillfully constructed, and the tone is consistent throughout. Quite in keeping with this tone is the burlesque of tragedy when Pardalisca first comes rushing upon the stage in pretended mortal terror (621). Similar is Palaestra's song of more genuine terror in the *Rope* (664). But to discuss at length a play which makes its simple point—uproarious laughter—so obviously and so adequately would be mere pedantry.

. . . . .

Epidicus

The *Epidicus* is another play of intrigue and recognition. Though not as gay and spirited as the *Pseudolus,* it is interesting from several points of view. The intrigue is extraordinarily complicated, although the action as a whole, lacking any elaboration of the love affair or of the involved past of Periphanes, is too slight. This play and the *Curculio* are the shortest ancient comedies.

The crafty slave Epidicus, who dominates the action from the beginning to the end, has played an important role in the formation of modern counterparts such as Scapin, Scaramouche, and Figaro.

The plot begins as the usual one of a young man in love and desperately needing money to secure his sweetheart. The situation here, however, is somewhat complicated; for Epidicus has previously secured a slave girl, Acropolistis, of whom the young Stratippocles has until recently been enamored. This girl is already within the house at the opening of the play, and the father is convinced that she is his natural daughter. But now Stratippocles returns from the wars with his newer sweetheart, who is hardly his own until he pays the banker her purchase price. The stress placed upon the virtue of this second girl foreshadows her recognition, but we may well be astounded when by this recognition the girl turns out to be Stratippocles' half-sister. Nowhere in New Comedy, perhaps, is there a more startling surprise. This has been made possible by the absence of an omniscient prologue and—even more strikingly—by the failure to elaborate the story of Periphanes' illegitimate daughter, references to whom are enigmatically brief, though the matter is subtly maintained before the minds of the audience by Periphanes' references to his past indiscretions (382-92, 431-32).

Many scholars think that Plautus is responsible for the omission of a prologue. If so, it would seem that he is deliberately striving for suspense and surprise and is thus anticipating the regular practice of Terence. Similar to Terentian technique also is the excellent scene of dramatic exposition and the employment of a protatic character to facilitate it. But the original existence of a prologue is at least doubtful. Though it is customary to inform the audience in plays where recognition occurs, the *Epidicus* gives no opportunity for effective dramatic irony on this score. It should be noted also that the whole emphasis of the piece is upon the machinations of Epidicus and not upon the love of Stratippocles. Indeed it is obvious that this infatuation is only a few days old. Its frustration in the end, therefore, is a matter of little consequence, especially since his former sweetheart, as Epidicus himself points out (653), has already been secured for him.

The play has been criticized, also, for the nature of its ending, which leaves various incidental matters unsettled.

But perhaps the playwright is superior to his critics here again; for Epidicus must remain the center of attention, and his affairs certainly are beautifully concluded in the amusing final scene. He is saved by a highly improbable coincidence—Stratippocles' buying his own sister—but this, of course, is typical of New Comedy.

The comic ironies are noteworthy. Epidicus feigns great modesty before the old men, and they praise the cleverness of his scheme. With less truth but with equal comic effectiveness Epidicus praises the shrewdness of Apoecides. Epidicus convinces the old men that he has bought the flute player, who is actually only hired; he also convinces them that the girl herself has been deceived into thinking she is only hired. Thus, when the ruse is discovered, the girl proves to be hired as she has claimed to be from the start. This phase of the humor reaches its high point when Apoecides says that he too pretended that the girl was only hired and assumed an expression of dullness and stupidity. Then he proceeds to illustrate this expression for Periphanes and the audience; in production, we can be sure, his actor did not make the slightest change in his expression to illustrate dullness and stupidity on the face of Apoecides (420).

Twin Menaechmi (Menaechmi)

This skillfully constructed farce is very spirited and amusing. It has fared unusually well at the hands of English translators, furthermore, and it is said to be the Latin comedy most frequently reproduced in American schools and colleges.

Nothing is known of the Greek original, although Athenaeus, an ancient scholar who had read more than eight hundred plays of Middle Comedy alone and whose interest was centered in cooks and foods, says that slave cooks can be found only in the plays of Poseidippus. Cylindrus in this play, of course, is a household slave. Except for the elaboration of monologues into cantica, the Latin version presumably follows the Greek original.

SIGNIFICANT NAMES.—Especially noteworthy among the names used in the play is that of the parasite, whose Latin name, Peniculus, means "Sponge," perhaps the most apt name for a parasite that occurs in Plautus. Erotium, "Lovey," is an effective but not uncommon name for a courtesan, and her cook is well-named Cylindrus, "Roller."

INFLUENCE.—Along with the *Amphitryon,* the *Pot of Gold,* and the *Braggart Warrior,* the *Twin Menaechmi* has been one of the most influential plays of Plautus. Various adaptations have appeared, including those of Trissino (1547, *Simillimi*), Rotrou (1636), Regnard (1705), and Goldoni (*I Due Gemelli Veneziani*). But Shakespeare's adaptation (1594 or earlier), of course, is by far the most famous.

The Comedy of Errors takes certain motives from the *Amphitryon,* especially the twin slaves and the exclusion of Antipholus from his own house while his twin is inside; but it is primarily an elaboration of the *Twin Menaechmi.* Here we may observe Shakespeare at work and may analyze that fusion of the classical and romantic traditions which characterized Elizabethan drama. From the romantic come its abundance of incident and its utter disregard of plausibility, its plethora of youthful emotional appeal, its insistence upon a romantic love affair, its melodramatic suspense, its vacillation between the comic and the tragic—both sentimentalized—and its grand finale where almost everyone shares in the general happiness. From the classic tradition come its elaborate plot, its observation of the essential unities, and its fundamentally realistic dramatic outlook.

DISCUSSION.—Basically the plot of the *Twin Menaechmi* is one of recognition. A great deal of complication, however, is built up about the somewhat involved personal relations of the Epidamnian Menaechmus. The similarity of the appearance of the twins naturally leads to a comedy of errors. This was a favorite motive, and no less than eight Greek comedies are known to have been given the title or subtitle "Twins." Indeed this motive plays an important role in several other comedies of Plautus himself, including the *Amphitryon,* the *Two Bacchides,* and the *Braggart Warrior*.

In a comedy of errors, the ancient playwright thinks it essential to explain the real situation very carefully beforehand to the audience, and the *Twin Menaechmi* opens with a long omniscient prologue. This is followed by another long monologue when Sponge enters. Two such speeches make for a slow opening. But with the amusing song of the Epidamnian Menaechmus the play assumes that rapid pace which is necessary for successful farce.

The scene between this sporty gentleman and Erotium finishes in the details of the setting and with the theft of the wife's mantle initiates the dramatic action. As gentleman, parasite, and courtesan withdraw, the Syracusan Menaechmus, accompanied by his slave Messenio, steps into the situation which has been nicely elaborated for them.

The weary Messenio warns his master that here in Epidamnus the world finds its greatest voluptuaries and drinkers; it is full of sycophants and flattering parasites; the courtesans are the most seductive on earth, and the city is so named because almost no one stops here without his purse's suffering damnation. The amusing reaction of his master is to demand the purse in order to avoid at least one risk in Epidamnus! The cook Cylindrus immediately appears and seems to prove the accuracy of Messenio's description beyond all question. Indeed, Messenio is taken in by his own cleverness, as we should expect in a comedy of errors; and, instead of realizing at once that his master is being mistaken for his lost twin brother, Messenio feels certain that they are being attacked by the pirate courtesans of this Barbary coast. His worst fears seem quite justified when the seductive Erotium appears. Thus the dramatist creates a very amusing situation while he is furnishing some plausibility for the long continuation of the comedy of errors.

There now follows a series of scenes wherein one person after another mistakes the Syracusan for the Epidamnian.

After Cylindrus and Erotium comes Sponge, and then a servant of Erotium. In these episodes the twins are shown to resemble each other as closely in their dishonesty as in their appearance. The Syracusan is also mistaken by the wife of the Epidamnian Menaechmus and finally by the father-in-law as well. All the complications which these errors involve are skillfully manipulated. Especially noteworthy is the way in which the parasite, usually an unessential figure, is worked into the mechanism of the plot to become the link between the double lives which the Epidamnian Menaechmus is living.

The best of the episodes of error, however, is that with the physician. Of all the galaxy of comic characters none perhaps surpasses the medical quack in age. He is listed in accounts of early Greek improvisations. Though this passage is the only one in Roman comedy where he has survived, he must have been a stock figure. His most striking characteristics in any age are here well brought out—his technical jargon, his endless number of impertinent questions, his extravagant claims, and of course his utterly incorrect diagnosis. Characteristic too of quack or expert in all ages is his prescription of the most expensive treatment possible.

Only near the end of the play does Messenio meet the Epidamnian Menaechmus and mistake him for his master. This error quickly leads to the climax, where no one except the slave, apparently, has enough sense to bring about the solution. If the gentlemen had been given more, the play could not have continued so long!

Very different is the ending of Plautus from that of Shakespeare. Far from arranging a reconciliation between the Epidamnian Menaechmus and his wife—to say nothing of Sponge—the cold cynicism of the author remains to the last lines, where along with the other chattel to be offered at auction is included the wife—if anyone is so foolish as to wish to buy her.

. . . . .

Braggart Warrior (*Miles Gloriosus*)

The *Braggart Warrior,* usually assumed to be one of the earliest extant plays of Plautus, is interesting for several reasons. Of all ancient comedies it presents the most complete portrait of the immortal braggart soldier, and it has therefore been very influential. The two plots of the play, also, are immortal. Its characters are vividly drawn, and the final scenes are uproariously funny. But the whole play is very crude farce, and the deception of Sceledrus in the opening sections has little to do with the later entrapment of the soldier.

SIGNIFICANT NAMES.—Pyrgopolinices is an elaborate Greek compound meaning "victor of fortresses and cities." The name Artotrogus signifies "bread-chewer," Acroteleutium "tip-top," Philocomasium "fond of drinking bouts," Sceledrus "dirt," and Palaestrio "wrestler," or "trickster."

SOURCE.—The title of the Greek play is given in the internal prologue, the *Braggart (Alazon)*; but nothing is known of the Greek author. Most scholars assume that two plays have here been combined by Plautus; and this may well be so, but any Greek dramatist who would stoop to the crudity of such farce might also fail to appreciate the niceties of plot construction.

The literary motive of the secret passageway is very old. In an age when lack of transportation and the need of protection necessitated extreme conservation of space within cities, common walls between houses were the rule, and secret passageways must not have been such very rare exceptions.

The second plot also is a very ancient one. A man, usually husband or lover, is persuaded to send away a girl with another man and even to give them gifts or the means of escape. The deception is threatened by various complications in its final stages; but all comes out well, and pursuit or revenge is prevented by some device. This plot is used by Euripides in the *Iphigenia in Tauris* and especially in the *Helen*. The scene of departure in the *Helen* is notably similar to that in the *Braggart Warrior;* comic irony plays a major role in both. Palaestrio's grief in this comedy, furthermore, shows more than a tinge of Oriental deception, resembling the grief of an Egyptian prince taking leave of Caesar during his Alexandrine campaign.

The motive of the secret passageway is found combined with this second plot of deception not only in Plautus. In a fascinating Albanian tale, a priest is duped into marrying his own pretty wife to a merchant next door. At the ensuing wedding banquet, the priest is made drunk, his beard is shaved off, and he is disguised as a robber and left by the side of the road. When he awakes in the morning he actually joins a band of robbers. But here, although the secret passageway is used precisely as in Plautus, the person deceived by it is the main character, and the two plots are closely and effectively joined.

INFLUENCE.—The professional soldier of fortune was a very common figure on the streets of Athens during the period of New Comedy, and nowhere was he more popular than on the comic stage. This is evidenced by many plays of New Comedy, including Menander's *Shearing of Glycera (Perikeiromene)*, Terence's *Eunuch,* and various other plays of Plautus, especially the *Two Bacchides,* the *Carthaginian,* and the *Truculentus*. This type is exploited in innumerable modern plays and finally results in such masterpieces as Falstaff. Indeed, Pyrgopolinices' boast that his children live for a thousand years (1079), as has been pointed out, is a gross understatement.

Many comedies have been directly influenced by the *Braggart Warrior*. Among the most notable may be mentioned Nicholas Udall's *Ralph Roister Doister* (before 1553; indebted also to the *Eumuch* of Terence), Dolce's *Il Capitano* (published 1560), Baïf's *Le Brave* (1567), Mareschal's *Le Capitan Fanfaron* (published 1640), and Holberg's *Jacob von Tyboe.*

DISCUSSION.—The *Braggart Warrior* is very clumsily constructed, for only a feeble effort has been made to connect its two actions. The soldier, the main character of the second action, is well characterized and his propensity for the fairer sex is given significant emphasis at the opening of the play. Thus the minor plot, which follows immediately, is suspended within the major. Several incidental references are made to the twin sister, an important element of the first action, during the latter part of the play. Sceledrus, too, is there mentioned and may reappear at the very end. Both actions, furthermore, are engineered by Palaestrio, and both are crude and farcical. But the first makes no real contribution to the second. The long episode with the genial old Periplectomenus has little to do with either. Incidentally annoying are the innumerable asides used to elaborate obvious jests. At times Palaestrio's handling of the soldier, however, shows real cleverness.

Haunted House (*Mostellaria*)

Like the *Three Bob Day* (*Trinummus*), the *Haunted House* begins with a series of excellent scenes presenting situation and characters but soon hastens off into the most obvious farce. Here, however, the farce is as good as farce can be.

The Greek original seems to have been entitled the *Ghost (Phasma)*. Records of three such comedies have been preserved, and it is usually assumed that the original of this play was the one written by Philemon. This assumption, even though no sound evidence for it exists, is attractive because of the play's structural similarity to the *Three Bob Day,* which was certainly written by Philemon. The tendency of high comedy to degenerate into farce, however, is observable in other plays such as the *Two Bacchides*.

The *Haunted House* has been very influential. Among adaptations may be mentioned Thomas Heywood's *The English Traveller* (printed 1633), Regnard's *Le Retour Imprévu* (1700) and its adaptation by Fielding, *The Intriguing Chambermaid* (1733), and Holberg's *Huus-Spögelse* or *Abracadabra*. The names Tranio and Grumio, furthermore, are used for servants in *The Taming of the Shrew,* in which perhaps certain motives also are taken from Plautus.

The *Haunted House* has very little plot. A young Athenian gentleman, Philolaches, has been living a gay life in the absence of his father. Upon the father's unexpected return, Philolaches is surprised in a very embarrassing daytime carousal. The clever slave Tranio, therefore, undertakes to prevent the father from entering the house until the members of the party have sobered and dispersed. Constantly threatened with exposure, Tranio constantly becomes involved in more and more elaborate deceptions. Finally, after his ruses are all discovered, he is rescued by the boon companion of Philolaches, who smoothes things over with the ease of a *deus ex machina*. All the activity of Tranio, of course, has really been much ado about nothing, for at best he could hope to deceive the old man for only a few hours. The initial pretext, however, is not implausible at first glance, and the rapidity of the action allows us no time for cogitation.

Although the whole play is amusing, the opening scenes are by far the best. Their primary function, of course, is to create the atmosphere of gay living. Various characters also are brilliantly presented here. But both creation of atmosphere and portrayal of character are carried far beyond the length justified by their importance in the main action. Obviously the dramatist intends these scenes to be enjoyed for their intrinsic charm.

In all New Comedy, no better scene of exposition is found than that of Grumio and Tranio. Not only is the situation most vividly presented but an effective warning of a day of reckoning is sounded, and the brazen Tranio is thoroughly individualized by contrast with the honest Grumio. The one fault of the scene is that Grumio, who is characterized even more interestingly than Tranio, does not reappear in the play.

The scenes presenting Philolaches and his companions also are delightful. The humor of Philolaches' remarks as he watches his love Philematium ("Little Kiss") complete her toilet and the masterly portrait of this delightfully naïve girl more than justify the theatrical awkwardness of the staging. The carousal too is skillfully presented. The drunken man, of course, is almost infallible low comedy; but Callidamates, with all the seriousness and moral callousness of inebriation, plays the role so entertainingly that we forget the triteness of the motive. Indeed this whole group of characters is so interesting that we, somewhat like Philolaches, may well regret the return of father Theopropides; for he is merely the stereotyped old man of comedy, conservative to—and beyond—the point of stupidity, so cautious where there is no need of caution and elsewhere so rash. He forms the perfect dupe for the wily Tranio, and these two monopolize the stage for the remainder of the play.

Persian (Persa)

The **Persian** is a thin but amusing little farce of "high life below stairs." It is unique, however, in certain respects. The original Greek play is thought by some scholars to have been written before the conquests of Alexander (line 506, very doubtful evidence) and therefore to have belonged to Middle Comedy. A free girl who is a virgin takes an active role in the play; and the whole seems more closely to approach comic opera than any other play of Plautus.

The simple plot concerns the intrigue of a slave, Toxilus, who in the absence of his master is living the life of a king (31), which of course includes being in love with a strumpet and keeping a parasite. Toxilus, like any young gentleman, wishes to free his sweetheart. With the aid of a friend and of the parasite's daughter he succeeds in doing so and in thoroughly humiliating the slave dealer. Perhaps it is unfortunate that this material has not been more effectively employed as a burlesque of the life of Athenian gilded youth.

The comic opera elements are many, of which lyricism is the first and most important. External formalism also is noteworthy. The first lines between Toxilus and Sagaristio constitute the only certain case of metrical responsion in Plautus. Balanced speeches are the rule throughout this first scene and frequently occur elsewhere in the play, especially in the scene of pert repartee between Sophoclidisca and Paegnium. The very admission of such a scene is suggestive of comic opera, for it is obviously inserted merely for its quaint buffoonery. Below the ordinary level of New Comedy, furthermore, is much of the stage action, especially the "planting" of the girl and Sagaristio to come in just at the right moment, and later the similar "planting" of Saturio. The extravagant implausibility of the intrigue, the use of disguises, and the way in which the intrigue is made a mere joke in the final scene—these, too, are proper to comic opera or burlesque. The saucy Paegnium ("play-thing"), though far from the harmless innocent of the modern stage, belongs to this same sphere. Perhaps the daughter of the parasite might here be included. The reversal of nature by which daughter lectures father on honesty and reputation is ridiculously incongruous with the girl's lowly position in life, as with her unenviable role in the intrigue—incongruous, indeed, with the whole atmosphere of this comedy of low life. Last of all may be mentioned the exotic costumes and the carefully identified dances in the very gay final scene. While some of these features may well be due to Plautine originality, they would not be unnatural developments of the lyricism and extravagance of Old Comedy. Certainly the Persian's four-line name (702-5) and the drunken revel (*komos*) of the final scene are reminiscent of Aristophanes.

. . . . .

Rope (Rudens)

The **Rope** more nearly approaches the spirit of romantic comedy than any other ancient play. It contains more important characters and more dramatic action than almost any other, and it is among the longest (1,423 lines). It is noteworthy not only for its romantic atmosphere but also for its unsurpassed vivacity, its irrepressible and sometimes sardonic humor, its dramatic irony, and its melodramatic pulsation of emotions.

SOURCE AND INFLUENCE.—The god of the prologue intimates that the author of the Greek original was Diphilus, but the name of that play is not given. It has been argued that Plautus made many important alterations in the play, but these arguments seem unconvincing.

Among adaptations, which have not been numerous, may be mentioned Thomas Heywood's *The Captives* (1624).

DISCUSSION.—The **Rope** is primarily a play of discovery in which, somewhat as in Menander's *Arbitration,* a father unwittingly adjudicates the fate of his own lost daughter. Various exciting complications are furnished by the daughter's shipwreck, the quarrel between her lover and the slave dealer who is attempting to recover her, and the contest of the two slaves over the trunk. That honesty is the best policy is the obvious moral to be drawn from the action.

The locale of this comedy is as picturesque and striking as it is unusual: the desolate seashore near the North African city of Cyrene, an ancient Brighton or Deauville.

Since the play is to contain concealed identities and a recognition, the author has considered an omniscient prologue essential in order that the irony of the action may be fully appreciated. Perhaps such a prologue is also the simplest method of revealing the complicated exposition of the play—the soundest justification for the Euripidean prologue, which seems to have been used regularly by Diphilus. Not much of the coming action, however, is here foreshadowed in the prologue.

Very unusual is the scene in which Sceparnio pretends to look off and sight the shipwrecked men and the two girls in a lifeboat. Action that could not be presented "on stage" frequently occurs in tragedy, where it is usually described in a messenger's speech. In comedy, such action is rare, and the method of describing it here employed, though informal, is very effective.

As soon as the stage is cleared—the exit of Daemones is dramatically necessary but surely somewhat forced and implausible—Palaestra, like a tragic heroine, appears singing her monody of complaint against Heaven and her cruel fate. The pathos of this is more significant for the audience, since they know that she is actually standing very close to the house of her long-lost parents. After Ampelisca has entered with a few plaintive lines we have a charming duet with the tragic cretic meter beautifully adapted to the scene (esp. lines 235-37). Indeed, this whole episode is one of the most charming in Plautus. As poetry, however, it is hardly superior to the "chorus" of fishermen who appear soon afterward. Here we have a passage of real beauty such as is common in Aristophanes but rare in New Comedy and apparently unknown in Menander. This chorus is usually considered a vestige of the old comic chorus, and their introduction here is certainly very felicitous. With their reed poles and, doubtless, fishermen's hats, they add a delightful bit of local color—obviously an artistic addition rather than an interruption like the ordinary interlude chorus. Their quaint humor forms a winsomely comic relief for the tragic tone of the two girls in distress.

Lovers' dalliance on stage is rare in ancient comedy, but slaves are allowed more liberty of action in certain situations than ladies and gentlemen, and we find an amusing if somewhat risqué example of love-making in the scene between the slaves, Ampelisca and Sceparnio. We may assume that Ampelisca starts this flirtation by ogling Sceparnio and caressing her words in a manner most likely to win over a stranger from whom she wishes to ask a favor. Sceparnio, however, is won over even more effectively than she wished, and it is all the girl can do to keep the situation in hand. With the aid of feminine tact and deceit, however, she succeeds in gaining her request by mere promises. While Sceparnio is gone to fetch the water, she is put to flight by the approach of the slave dealer. When Sceparnio returns with his high hopes of an easy conquest, he presents a figure whose ridiculousness can hardly be appreciated without actually seeing him as he carries the

jug and searches eagerly about the stage for the vanished girl. His fear now of being caught as a thief and, finally, his utter disgust at having done some real work for nothing form a very amusing contrast with his high spirits at the opening of the scene.

Various scenes of low comedy occur throughout the play which set off and relieve the more serious episodes. Amusing is the scene wherein the slave dealer Labrax and his friend Charmides first emerge from their shipwreck. They come on stage with their garments drenched, shivering and, as the meter apparently indicates, chattering from cold. They curse their fortune and each other. They run the gamut of low comedy from miserable puns to vomiting.

The influence of melodramatic tragedy is evident in many scenes of the *Rope,* but most of all in the scene where the girls flee from the temple of Venus to the altar. Palaestra's monody here is remarkably similar to a fragmentary monody from a tragedy of Plautus' contemporary, Ennius, wherein a woman, Andromache, is seeking refuge. Both songs are in part written in cretic meter, characterized by elaborate alliteration and assonance, the use of synonyms and various artificialities of high style. The grouping about the altar, furthermore, is remarkably similar to that of a scene from an unknown tragedy represented on a Greek vase. The whole scene here, then, may be a parody of a definite tragedy.

The amusing Sceparnio does not appear in the second half of the play; but a counterpart for him is found in the fisherman, Gripus, the slave of Daemones, who is not mentioned in the prologue and of whom we hear nothing until Daemones comes on stage to deliver a short monologue and then returns into the house (892-905). Obviously this somewhat awkward speech is designed solely to introduce Gripus, who enters immediately after Daemones makes his exit. The emotions of Gripus, like those of Sceparnio, shift very rapidly: he enters in the greatest elation over his discovery of the wicker trunk, and in an amusing monody he daydreams aloud on becoming a millionaire, a tycoon in the world of trade, and on founding a city to commemorate his fame. The humorous irony of these lines may easily be overlooked in reading the play; but it could not be lost in the theater, for we may be sure that during his monody, as he walks slowly toward the center of the stage, his spying adversary, Trachalio, is already on stage behind him.

One of the most delightful scenes of the play is the ensuing one between Gripus and Trachalio with their mock juristic arguments. It is easy to understand why Plautus chose to name the play after this scene and the tug of war of the two slaves over the trunk. Especially delightful is the naïve way in which the slaves, when their casuistry runs short, resort to barefaced lies and elaborate threats of violence which reveal that each is actually very much afraid of the other.

The scene in which both slaves appeal to Daemones is a continuation of this argument, in which Gripus is at least more consistent than Trachalio, who at one time renounces all personal claims (1077) and at another demands half of the booty (1123). The zeal of Gripus increases as the apparent justice of his case fades away, and he does not fail to anticipate every possible device of his opponents.

Comedies usually come to a close very shortly after the solution of the plot, but the **Rope** continues for some time after the main complication has been solved with Palaestra's restoration to her parents. Still, there are minor threads of the plot that must be neatly finished off. The play does not, therefore, appear to be unduly extended, especially since the final scenes are so gay and amusing; throughout this comedy, gaiety and amusement are more important than the progression of the plot.

The romantic pulsation of emotions, already noted in the earlier parts of the play, continues to the very end and is nicely emphasized by appropriate metrical variation. Trachalio and Daemones are in high spirits, Trachalio and Plesidippus in even higher spirits—especially Plesidippus, who is ecstatic over the good fortune of Palaestra and their coming marriage. These scenes, of course, are in the gay trochaic meter which was probably accompanied by music. But between these scenes with Trachalio, wherein the author runs riot in word play in a manner more characteristic of Aristophanes or Rabelais than of New Comedy, the ill-humored Gripus in prosaic iambics continues his haggling argument with his master over the ownership of the trunk. This ill-humor is even more amusing, of course, than the gaiety of the other characters.

The ironic humor, also, with an occasional thrust of real satire, is maintained to the last line, where the audience, if they will applaud loudly, are invited to a drinking party—all, that is, under sixteen years of age. Sixteen was the usual age for the assumption of a man's dress and status at Rome, and from this passage it has been concluded that minors were not allowed in the Roman theater.

. . . . .

Three Bob Day (Trinummus)

Lessing considered this play second only to the **Captives** among Plautus' comedies, but such a high rating seems hardly justified. There are certainly some excellent scenes of high comedy, especially in the first part of the play; but the climax falls off disappointingly into obvious farce.

The Greek original, as we are plainly told, was the *Treasure* of Philemon (*Thesauros*). Probably some monologues of the original have been elaborated into monodies, but otherwise perhaps few if any changes have been made.

No female role is found in the **Three Bob Day**. This feature, so entirely natural in a play like the **Captives,** is here somewhat unfortunate from the modern point of view, in that this unusual plot seems ideally suited for intimate romantic comedy. Such development, however, was left for a Frenchman, Néricault Destouches, whose adaptation, *Le Trésor Caché,* brought to life the two girls that are to be married to the young men at the end of Plautus' play.

Another adaptation, Lessing's *Der Schatz* (1750), is well-known.

DISCUSSION.—Precisely to define the plot of the **Three Bob Day** is difficult, and this very fact marks the play out as extraordinary in New Comedy, where the plots are usually all too stereotyped. The main problem, however, concerns the honor of Lesbonicus, a young man who in the absence of his father has so dissipated his property that he finds himself greatly embarrassed over the prospect of his sister's being forced to marry without a dowry. The modern reader may easily underestimate the seriousness of this situation. According to the Athenian moral code, this young man's first duty in life was to look to the honor and decent marriage of his sister. For her to marry without a dowry and thus to sacrifice all social prestige naturally meant utter disgrace for him. A minor problem of the play is centered about the honor of Callicles, an old friend whom the father of Lesbonicus has charged with something of the family interests during his absence. Both these problems are excellent dramatic material.

After a quaint prelude which well strikes the moral tone of the play and also serves as a literary prologue, the play opens with a very delightful scene between Callicles and a friend, Megaronides, who has come to castigate him for his apparent breach of faith. Both are nicely characterized as old men by their jests on wives and marriage, their use of proverbs, and their complaints of the moral degeneration of the times. Their main function, of course, is to give the exposition; and this they succeed in doing in a most natural fashion. Megaronides is not, as we might expect, a protatic character but has been skillfully worked into the subsequent action. One fault, however, may be found with this scene: no immediate dramatic action or complication is suggested. The mention of Lesbonicus' sister has been too brief, and nothing has been said that might suggest her marrying in the near future.

When this episode is ended, Lysiteles, a young man of whom we have heard nothing, appears with a charming monody, the length of which, if nothing else, indicates the importance of the speaker. His problem is a serious one: to be or not to be—in love. Seeing only too clearly that love is a waster of property and a corrupter of good morals, this strange young man decides that he will not be. He wishes, as we later discover, to marry instead!

When Lysiteles has reached this very virtuous decision, his father, Philto, opportunely comes on, and the ensuing scene is even more delightful high comedy than that between Callicles and Megaronides. Philto lectures his son in a moral fashion that qualifies him to rank as an ancestor of Polonius. But Lysiteles is somewhat cleverer than Laertes. He actually encourages his father; indeed he anticipates Philto in reaching the extreme limit of virtue and suggests a definite virtuous action—marrying a girl without a dowry. Any translation of virtuous words into action would doubtless have been disconcerting enough for Philto; and this particular action carries virtue far beyond the limits which he had envisaged even in his most abstract cogitations. But the receptiveness and docility of Lysiteles have been so great that the father is now embarrassed to refuse. Never in New Comedy is a father thrown for a neater and less-expected fall than this. The whole scene is a masterpiece.

Philto agrees to his son's marrying the sister of Lesbonicus without a dowry. This initiates the dramatic action at last, and it also sets the stage for the entrance of Lesbonicus, whose efforts to trace down the rapid flight of his funds are very amusing. Philto, as if he had not learned his lesson, continues with philosophizing, and his subsequent interview with Lesbonicus nicely points up the dilemma of this young man. Indeed, Lesbonicus becomes so desperate that he actually longs for the return of his father! Stasimus, his impudent slave, furnishes the low comedy of the scene. This reduces the level of the play's humor somewhat, although, in his not very successful efforts to deceive Philto, Stasimus is made the butt rather than the author of the humor.

Lesbonicus has been unable to settle the problem of the dowry with Philto, and so goes off to find Lysiteles. Meanwhile Callicles reappears and makes known his intention of somehow providing for the dowry. Lesbonicus knows nothing of this, however, and he is still desperate when he returns with Lysiteles and they debate the matter at great length. This scene might be called the climax of the play, for here the complication reaches its point of highest tension.

The play now degenerates rapidly. Megaronides' plan to provide the dowry from the secret treasure of Charmides is too much the usual comic intrigue. With the timely arrival of Charmides, furthermore, the working out of this plan becomes obvious farce. The stage technique, also, especially the continual use of asides, is somewhat awkward.

The farce in these later sections of the play can hardly be said to strike an inharmonious note, for the tone of the play has been charmingly light throughout. But it seems unfortunate that the serious moral dilemma of the young men is not exploited in a more satisfactory manner. The solution adopted, of course, is purely external. Another fault of the play is its failure at an early point to focus upon a single character and to maintain him as the center of interest. Unfortunate also is the continual h.rping on the moral degeneration of the times. This theme, a commonplace in New Comedy, is put to real service where Philto is concerned, and possibly the play as a whole would have been more effective if it had been reserved for him alone.

Truculentus

The *Truculentus* is a remarkable but not an amusing play. Like the novel *Sapho* of Alphonse Daudet, it is written for the enlightenment of a young man on youth's eternal problem. Vice would flourish less, says Diniarchus in his "prologue" (57-63), if the experience of one generation could be passed on to the next. The play, then, is very serious. We might be tempted to call its outcome tragic. Certainly few tragedies are so depressing. But Aristotle (*Poetics*)

says that the spectacle of the evil prospering is the most untragic of all. Phronesium is certainly evil, and she certainly prospers. An amazing detachment is maintained by the dramatist throughout, and he coldly refuses to display the slightest sympathy with his characters. Indeed, this play is one of the most remarkable pieces of stark realism in classical drama. Its ending is similar to that of the *Two Bacchides* and the *Eunuchus;* but those plays seem very light and gay compared to this.

The *Truculentus* has been somewhat neglected by modern scholars because the text tradition is deplorably bad— the worst of all the plays of Plautus, though there are no lengthy lacunae.

The author of the Greek original is unknown.

DISCUSSION.—The play has almost no plot. It is merely the spectacle of a very real Circe turning men into swine. Four men are chosen for purposes of illustration. They are all typical, and properly so, for the author wishes to include all mankind; but they are treated in a far from typical manner. The various episodes dealing with these four are adeptly interwoven, though there is no artificial complexity about the play. The young Athenian gentleman, Diniarchus, is the first to be taken up and the only one whose case history is given in some detail. He has long since been a lover of courtesan and of courtesan's maid alike and, now bankrupt, he still is their lover. After he has been introduced and retires into Phronesium's house, the truculent slave comes on. He is the most picturesque character of the play. From his first line he is most aptly characterized as a bumpkin. His metaphors are rustic, and he swears by the hoe. Such referential swearing, though common in Aristophanes, is not frequent in Roman comedy. He is also characterized by his quaint perversity in the use of language, something like Antipho's use of riddles in the *Stichus*. Though this slave shows some signs of human frailty to the courtesan's maid, we naturally expect him to remain truculent throughout the play; and when he leaves the stage with the declaration that he will inform his old master of the young master's goings on, we anticipate the appearance of the old man. Such action would recall that of Lydus in the *Two Bacchides*.

Diniarchus now returns to the stage, and after the splendid fanfare of the early scenes, Phronesium makes her entrance and works her magic spell upon him. Much of this scene is concerned incidentally with the story of the soldier and the suppositious child, thus anticipating the appearance of the next victim and preparing for the discovery of the child's true identity. When Diniarchus has gone off to scrape up gifts, the stage is carefully set and the preparations perhaps include a seductive negligee. As the soldier enters he informs the audience by direct address not to expect the usual foolery of the braggart soldier from him; and indeed this soldier does not strut in the ordinary comic fashion, though a few mild jokes are admitted. The theme of Diniarchus is now fused with that of the soldier upon the entrance of the young gentleman's slaves bearing his gifts to Phronesium under the very eyes of the soldier. Nothing could better portray the soldier's enslavement; and after this scene has passed, we put little faith in his wrathful decision to remain aloof for a few days in order to bring Phronesium to her knees. At this point Strabax, the rustic young master of the truculent slave, comes on with money which he has purloined from his father for the woman whom he loves more than his mother (662). He is taken in with little ado, and immediately his slave reappears, no longer truculent and not with his old master, as we expected, but actually with his savings and a determination to take a fling at the type of life which is so attractive to his betters. Thus free and servile, weak and strong, all are here enslaved.

Diniarchus returns in the greatest elation over Phronesium's reception of his gifts and her invitation to rejoin her. The unexpected appearance of Strabax with far more money, however, has already changed Phronesium's situation and given her an actor for the role of the soldier's rival. So the maid keeps Diniarchus outside the house and regales him with a description of Strabax' enjoying the provisions which Diniarchus himself has lately furnished. Diniarchus is bitterly disillusioned. His futile protests before the house are interrupted by the episode with Callicles. No hint of Diniarchus' violation of Callicles' daughter has been given previously. But the dramatist here, as in the sudden change of the truculent slave, is not striving for surprise; he merely wishes to repress the minor phases of the play and maintain an effective unity. This incident with Callicles is designed merely to illustrate the utter ruin of Diniarchus. After he learns that his lack of restraint has cost him so dearly, he is still unable to master his passions and to demand the child—discovered to be that of Callicles' daughter and himself—from Phronesium, who now comes

on mildly intoxicated but still having far more self-mastery than her lovers, drunk or sober. With a view to securing her favors after his marriage, Diniarchus weakly allows her temporarily to retain the child in order to swindle the soldier. After this moral nihilism, the baseness of the soldier and Strabax in their final agreement to share Phronesium seems almost an anticlimax.

Erich Segal (essay date 1972)

SOURCE: "The Business of Roman Comedy," in *Perspectives of Roman Poetry: A Classics Symposium*, edited by G. Karl Galinsky, University of Texas Press, 1974, pp. 93-103.

[*In this essay from a 1972 symposium, Segal examines the concern with financial and business affairs displayed in Plautus's works.*]

Comedy is, in one sense, the perfect crime. It effects a magic larceny that temporarily diverts the moral bill collector. Normal checks and balances cease to operate; perpetrators of outrageous acts are not called into account. Comic heroes get away with behavior that would normally require them to pay a debt to society.

The preponderance of financial imagery in the preceding paragraph is hardly coincidental. Similar language often describes moral and monetary attitudes. Debt and guilt are really two sides of the same coin that buys comedy its laughter. It is all a funny business wherein business contributes richly to the fun—especially in ancient Rome. But before turning to a specific appraisal of Roman comedy, let us examine further the ambiguous association between money and morality.

Nietzsche [in *Zur Genealogie der Moral,* 1887] went so far as to assert that the cardinal notion of guilt originates from the very material notion of debt. In an important essay on comedy ["On the Psychology of Comedy," 1926], Ludwig Jekels remarked that "the substitution of the idea of money debt for that of moral guilt is hardly surprising to the psycho-analyst, who frequently observes this substitutive relation in the dreams and resistances of his patients." Moreover, this linkage finds philological substantiation in the many languages that employ the same word to denote both debt and guilt. Shakespeare's *Henry IV Part I* best dramatizes this Janus-like concept, offering a clear paradigm of the comic process. With the reader's indulgence, a digression to Elizabeth's England will enable us to return with greater perspective to Plautus's Rome. *Sauter,* as it were, *pour mieux reculer.*

Shakespeare's Prince Hal lives in a magnetic field between dalliance and duty, which is to say between palace and pub. In the first, solemn statecraft is the business, and a common psychological attitude becomes a literal fact: the hero's father is a king. At the opposite pole is Eastcheap, where Hal plays the truant from duty, sporting under the aegis of that devilish surrogate father, Falstaff. Fat Jack is the unchallenged champion in the art of avoiding every kind of responsibility. Which is, of course, what makes him the king of comic heroes. Whatever the debt, he never pays.

At every level, *Henry IV* is replete with monetary imagery. At the play's outset, after much lighthearted banter with Falstaff, Hal reveals that his delinquency is itself an involvement calculated to enhance his worth upon "redemption":

> So, when this loose behavior I throw off
> And pay the debt I never promisèd,
> By how much better than my word I am,
> By so much shall I falsify men's hopes;
> And, like bright metal on a sullen ground,
> My reformation, glitt'ring o'er my fault,
> Shall show more goodly and attract more eyes
> Than that which hath no foil to set it off.
> I'll so offend to make offense a skill,
>   Redeeming time when men least think I will.
>   (I.ii.197-205)

Even the overplot deals with debt and payment, whether it be the king's guilt feelings for the death of Richard II or his refusal to ransom captured Mortimer:

>   Shall our coffers, then,
> Be emptied to redeem a traitor home?
> Shall we buy treason? and indent with fears
>   When they have lost and forfeited themselves?
>   (I.iii.85-88)

Heroic Hotspur is no less concerned with the balance sheet, as when he cries for reparation against King Henry:

> To answer all the debt he owes to you
>   Even with the bloody payment of your deaths.
>   (I.iii.185-186)

Financial preoccupations are ubiquitous, whether they be Falstaff's scheme to rob cash en route to the king's exchequer or his rich excuses when he is subsequently outthieved. Later Hal also discovers in Falstaff's pocket a gigantic unpaid bill for pleasures past (II.iv.505). But Falstaff pays only in puns:

> *Prince.* Sirrah, do I owe you a thousand pound?
> *Falstaff.* A thousand pound, Hal? A million! Thy
>   love is worth a million; thou owest me thy love.
>   (III.iii.129-131)

Likewise, the only "reckonings" Fat Jack acknowledges are sexual (cf. I.ii.44-64). Falstaff would even evade man's ultimate debt:

> *Prince.* Why, thou owest God a death.
> *Falstaff.* 'Tis not due yet: I would be loath to pay
>   him before his day.
>   (V.i.126-128)

In direct and deliberate contrast, Prince Hal eventually accepts all his responsibilities. When he arrives at the palace he informs the king that he regards Hotspur as nothing more than his bill collector and that he intends to "tear the reckoning from his heart" (II.ii.147-152). In leaving the Boar's Head, Hal is forsaking the world of what he has called "playing holidays" (I.ii.192). In as many words, the world of Comedy.

Shakespeare's palace–pub dynamic may be readily translated into Roman terms. To Plautus the antinomies were *forum* and *festivus locus*. The first was, of course, the financial center of ancient Rome; the second, the playwright's own concept of the Roman theater. And we must bear in mind that, when Plautus composed, the stage was constructed especially for the play, then immediately dismantled on the morrow. The theatrical occasion was unique, officially a holiday. The celebrants gathered in a place as unusual as it was ephemeral:

> nunc qua adsedistis caussa in festivo loco,
> comoediai quam nos acturi sumus
> et argumentum et nomen vobis eloquar.
>   (*Miles Gloriosus* 83-85)

> [I'll tell you why you've gathered in this festive
>   spot,
> The comedy we will enact, its name and plot.]

This prologue to one of Plautus's earliest plays indicates that both artist and audience were aware of the holiday nature of the theatrical event. And while the citizenry packed the *festivus locus,* the business district was completely deserted. As Plautus remarks in another prologue, *tranquillum est, Alcedonia sunt circum forum* (*Casina* 26) [All's calm, a halcyon quiet floats about the forum]. This is a most atypical state of affairs; the forum normally bustled with business activity as the Romans frantically pursued profit. Horace testifies to the acquisitive, avaricious character of the Romans:

> "O cives, cives, quaerenda pecunia primum est;
> virtus post nummos." haec Ianus summus ab imo
> prodocet, haec recinunt iuvenes dictata senesque.
> (*Epist.* I.1.53-55)

> ["O citizens, citizens, get money, first of all get
>   money.
> Be worth a lot—then afterward be worthy." These
>   words
> great Janus, banking deity, proclaims across the
>   forum,
> and these same dictates are echoed by the young
>   and by the old.]

What makes the business of Plautine comedy so extraordinary is the obsessive emphasis on business in ordinary Roman life. Since other accounts echo Horace's description, the contrast in Roman comedy becomes all the more significant. Take the passage from the *Casina* prologue that we have already quoted in brief:

Eicite ex animo curam atque alienum aes,
ne quis formidet flagitatorem suom:
ludi sunt, ludus datus est argentariis;
tranquillum est, Alcedonia sunt circum forum.

(lines 23-26)

[Just kick out all your cares, and as for debts,
   ignore'em.
Let no one fear fierce creditors will sue.
It's holiday for everyone—for bankers, too.
All's calm, a halcyon quiet floats around the
   forum.]

Every line contains a specific financial or business reference to debts, creditors, bankers, and finally to the banking center itself. Most significant for this essay is the collocation in line 23 of anxiety and debt, *cura* and *alienum aes.* Once again moral and monetary obligations merge into nonspecific "worries." But specifically worrisome to the people of Rome.

The Romans were obsessed with payment in both senses of the word. Theirs was a patriarchal society where one owed one's father the debt of absolute obedience. The country's leaders were *patres;* treason was *parricidium.* Indeed, Sallust calls Catiline's co-conspirators *parricidae rei publicae* (*Cat.* 51.25). Moreover, finance was a filial duty, profit a moral obligation, waste a cardinal sin. In fact, the association between moral and material debt may find its strongest expression in the Roman mind. Which is why its frequent flouting in Roman comedy makes the genre both comic and Roman.

Plautus's **Menaechmi** dramatizes the contrast between everyday Roman *industria* and holiday *voluptas.* Here the house of Menaechmus is, broadly speaking, like King Henry's palace, the locus of duty, restraint, obligations—and even economy. The house of Erotium likewise corresponds to the Boar's Head Tavern as the center of indulgence, prodigality, and pleasure enhanced by payment evaded. And yet the **Menaechmi** is in many ways atypical of Plautus, a comedy of errors and not guile. Other plays more Plautine (and hence more Roman) easily illustrate the argument of this essay. Let us pay some attention to the **Mostellaria**. This "little ghost story" contains all the elements that combined to make Plautus the most successful comic author in history. No playwright better understood, or catered to, his public's preoccupations.

The **Mostellaria** begins with a lively agon between clever slave Tranio and loyal (ergo unclever) slave Grumio. In their master's absence Tranio has led astray the old man's once paragonal son. The puritanical Grumio is outraged:

nam ego illum corruptum duco quom his factis
   studet;
quo nemo adaeque iuuentute ex omni Attica
antehac est habitus parcus nec magi' continens,
is nunc in aliam partem palmam possidet.
uirtute id factum tua et magisterio tuo. (lines 28-32)

[That boy, who out of all the boys in Attica
Was once so chaste, so frugal, once so well-
   behaved,
Now takes the prizes in completely different sports
Thanks to all your tutoring and all your talent.]

The translation does not really do justice to the special Roman connotations of *virtus* in the final line. For Grumio's terminology implies that Tranio has subverted every good Roman virtue in the lad and become—like Falstaff to Hal—a devilish corrupter of youth.

Indeed, Grumio's words resemble those of King Henry when he laments that all the good qualities of Hotspur are lacking in his heir. The king envies:

A son who is the theme of honor's tongue,
Amongst a grove the very straightest plant;
Who is sweet fortune's minion and her pride;
Whilst I, by looking on the praise of him,
See riot and dishonor stain the brow
Of my young Harry.

(I.i.81-86)

In the **Mostellaria,** riot and dishonor likewise stain the brow of young Philolaches. And the imagery of his delinquency is also expressed in financial terms. While his father was abroad he has "invested" in pleasure. He has purchased a slave girl and freed her. When the old man unexpectedly returns, clever Tranio must put him off the track by pretending that the cash has gone to buy a new house. As any good (Roman) father would, Theopropides rejoices at the news:

patrissat: iam homo in mercatura vortitur.

(line 639)

[He is his father's son, he's going into business!]

Of course his son has actually been neither filial nor frugal. In fact, his true behavior is alliteratively described:

Et, postquam eius hinc pater
sit profectus peregre, perpotasse adsiduo.

(lines 975-976)

[And following his father's faring forth
For foreign parts, the fellow fell to full-time frolic.]

The real situation is not *patrissare* but *perdidit patrem* (line 983). Not taking after father but merely taking him. And early in the play we have seen the lad utter parricidal thoughts. When he first spies his mistress he exclaims:

utinam meus nunc mortuos pater ad me nuntietur,
ut ego exheredem me meis bonis faciam atque haec
   sit heres.

(lines 233-234)

[Oh, someone bring the news right now—the news
   my father's dead!]

I'd disinherit myself and make her heir to all my goods!]

The puritanical, parsimonious Roman would virtually equate prodigality with parricide. Yet Plautus's young hero thinks of both deeds and joyfully merges the two.

As Philolaches eavesdrops, his sweetheart's cynical maid warns her that the young lad will soon bankrupt himself since he shows no *parsimonia*. Eventually, *"iam ista quidem apsumpta res erit"* (line 235) [all his current wealth will soon be in a state of ruin]. The Roman spectator would not fail to appreciate the ironic echo in Tranio's subsequent exclamation. When he learns that his elder master has inopportunely returned, he cries, *"apsumpti sumus"* (line 366).

The irony persists. Just what is a good investment? To Philolaches it is pleasure, the purchase of Philematium's freedom:

> *Philolaches.* nec quicquam argenti locaui iam diu
>   usquam aeque bene.
> *Philematium.* certe ego, quod te amo, operam
>   nusquam melius potui ponere.
> *Philolaches.* bene igitur ratio accepti atque expensi
>   inter nos conuenit.
>
> (lines 302-304)

[*Philolaches.* You're the best investment deal I've
  ever made in my whole life.
Philematium. Nor could I have better placed my
  whole concern than in your love.
Philolaches. Look at our account: income and outgo
  balance perfectly.]

On the other hand, Philolaches' father prefers more lucrative affairs. To him investment evokes thoughts solider and stolider. Real estate, for example. Thus, when he is informed by Tranio that his money has been used to purchase the house next door, Theopropides tours the place and then enthuses: "bene res nostra conlocata est istoc mercimonio" (line 915) [Our cash is well invested in this merchandise]. The contrasting life styles between father and son center on the *locatio* or investment of *res nostra*.

And there is always the presence of debt. In an early scene we witness the enactment of what will later metamorphose into metaphor. When the neighbor complains that his house has no shady areas, he laments that the sun never leaves, but rather "quasi flagitator astat usque ad ostium" (line 768) [It hangs around my door as if it were a debt collector].

The image is anything but coincidental. Indeed, the basic conflict and essential comic joy of the *Mostellaria* are vividly enacted in the scene with an actual *flagitator,* a debt collector. Just as clever Tranio has appeased old Theopropides with his real estate acquisition fable, who should enter but the very man who lent him the now-squandered cash? This moneylender is obsessed with profit. In fact, he has just come from the forum where he has been trying desperately to make more investments (the

verb is again *locare,* line 535). Spying Tranio, his debtor, he wastes no words:

> *Tranio.* Salvere iubeo te, Misargyrides, bene.
> *Misargyrides.* Salve et tu. quid de argentost?
>
> (lines 568-569)

[*Tranio.* Hello, Misargyrides, hope you're feeling
  well.
Misargyrides. Hello to you. *Now what about my
  money?*]

A squabble ensues in which Tranio deftly evades the banker's demands for his interest. Meanwhile, the slave's master stands ingenuously by. Should old Theopropides ever catch on to what the matter is, there will also be hell to pay. The scene rises to comic crescendo with the debt collector shrieking:

> *Misargyrides.* cedo faenus, redde faenus, faenus
>   reddite.
> daturin estis faenus actutum mihi?
> datur faenus mi?
> *Tranio.*   faenus illic, faenus hic!
> nescit quidem nisi faenus fabularier.
>
> (lines 603-606)

[*Misargyrides.* My interest now, my interest,
  interest; pay
me interest! Will you please pay my interest
to me right away? I want my interest!
Tranio.   "Interest" here and "interest"
there. The only interest this man has in life is
  "interest"!]

But Misargyrides never does collect, for this is comedy and the pun is the only coin of the realm. The bilking of a bill collector is a favorite theme of Roman comedy—especially since the creditor is most often trying to collect the price of pleasure, that is, a girl. In this very special world there is not even a moral price to pay. A prime example is the finale of the *Mostellaria*. Here Tranio's rogueries are at last exposed—and he glories in them:

> fateor peccauisse, amicam liberasse apsente te,
> faenori argentum sumpsisse; id esse apsumptum
>   praedico.
>
> (lines 1139-1140)

[Yes I will confess: he sinned while you were gone.
  He freed his girl,
Drew a lot of cash on interest, threw the lot of cash
  away.]

But his master Theopropides is determined to punish him. In real life, Roman masters could actually put disobedient slaves to death, a fact that would not have been lost on the audience. Yet note how Tranio finally escapes:

> *Tranio.* quid gravaris? quasi non cras iam
>   commeream aliam noxiam:
> ibi utrumque, et hoc et illud, poteris ulcisci probe . . .

Theopropides. . . . abi inpune . . .
(lines 1178-1180)

[*Tranio*. Why be annoyed? You know tomorrow I'll
commit some fresh new crime.
Then you'll collect revenge for both—for what I've
done and what I'll do . . .
Theopropides. . . . all right, no punishment . . .]

The key word is *cras,* tomorrow. Tomorrow there will be
business as usual; tomorrow payments will be made. This
very same word had earlier convinced the moneylender to
relent: *petito cras* (line 64), collect tomorrow. And so the
money-mad Misargyrides quits the stage, thinking, "sat
habeo si cras fero" (line 654) [I'm satisfied if I collect
tomorrow].

Tomorrow is also the excuse offered by the **Casina** prologue to make the audience forget *cura, alienum aes*—
and even fear of a *flagitator* (lines 23-24). The bankers
are on holiday—at least for today. But:

ratione utuntur, ludis poscunt neminem,
secundum ludos reddunt autem nemini.
(lines 27-28)

[While the games are on, they wisely never try to
dun,
But after, when the games are through, they pay off
none!]

Employing their *ratio,* their mental balance sheet, the
bankers realize that they can always make their shrewd-
thinking profit *secundum ludos,* after the festival. This
peripheral awareness that business will resume tomorrow
permits the insouciance of Roman holiday humor. The
occasion is extraordinary and so is the place where they
have gathered. In this *festivus locus,* all Roman thoughts
are banished be they of *cura, alienum aes,* or, as would be
more likely, both combined. Pseudolus's remark epitomizes the spectator's own experience: "in loco festiuo
sumus festiue accepti" (line 1254) [we have had festive
entertainment in a festive spot]. And tomorrow everyone
would be back in the forum. The *festivus locus* would
literally have disappeared.

Thus, there is a simple if paradoxical explanation for the
abundance of financial imagery in Plautus: it was intended
precisely to distract the audience from financial thoughts.
To make the Roman spectator forget his business was, in
fact, the very business of Roman comedy.

F. H. Sandbach (essay date 1977)

SOURCE: "Plautus," in *The Comic Theatre of Greece and
Rome,* W. W. Norton & Company, 1977, pp. 118-34.

[*In the excerpt below, Sandbach analyzes Plautus's use
of language, observing: "Words were a source of delight" for the playwright.*]

Plautus, the most original and vigorous writer of Roman
comedy, came from Sarsina in Umbria, half-way between
modern Florence and Rimini. It was an Italian town subjected to the Romans a dozen years before his birth.
Whether Plautus was his real name or one humorously
adopted for professional purposes [the name means "flat-
footed"], and whether he had been an actor before he was
a writer are questions which admit of fascinating discussion but no certain answer; fortunately they are of no
importance to the historian of drama. Nothing shows that
he acted in or produced his own plays, but he gives a
strong impression that he understood the theatre for which
he wrote. He would have an inexperienced audience, not
very quick on the uptake, and so it was necessary to proceed more slowly than a Greek dramatist would, to say
things twice, to introduce reminders about essential elements in the plot, and above all not to allow the spectators
to become bored. They did not require complete coherence nor expect that characterisation should be consistent;
these are merits demanded by a theatre-goer who can take
a wide view; what was important for Plautus was the
immediate effect.

All his twenty-one surviving plays are adaptations of Greek
comedies. Three and probably a fourth are from Menander,
two from Diphilus, two from Philemon, one apparently
from Alexis, all authors of the great period of New Comedy. Of the other twelve one is from an otherwise unknown Demophilus, but all the rest have anonymous originals. There is nothing to show that any of them came
from the Greek dramatists who were his contemporaries
or belonged to the immediately preceding generation. On
the contrary some of their original authors certainly lived
about a hundred years earlier than he, and may even have
been members of the great trio of that time.

Unfortunately it is impossible to say how Plautus got hold
of these Greek plays. They may have formed part of the
repertory of the Artists of Dionysus, but it is no more than
a plausible guess that these visited the theatres of Greek
cities in southern Italy, and there is no evidence that Plautus had any contact with them or with southern Italy at all.
Perhaps the players for whom he wrote in some way obtained texts with which they provided him. It would be
rash to suppose that he always admired the plays he adapted
or thought them particularly suitable for his purposes; he
may have had to use what he could get.

However that may be, the Greek authors provided him
with stories of ingenious construction and scenes of dramatic tension. When these were embroidered and diversified, when their jests were multiplied and their comic
possibilities exploited by a writer who possessed an un-
failing vigour of expression and a rich abundance of language there resulted a new kind of popular drama which
could entertain a wide range of tastes.

Variety is the obvious device to hold the attention of any
audience. Metrical variety had become less and less used
by the Greeks, and it is possible that in Menander's later
plays it was entirely abandoned, in order to maintain a
homogeneous medium; but the choral intermezzi were still

---

there, to provide a change of metre and the charms of music. Deprived of a chorus, Plautus re-introduced these elements into the body of his plays. Whether the first to do it or not, he increased the number of scenes written in the long trochaic or iambic lines, and on the Roman stage, whatever may have been done in Greece, these were delivered to an accompaniment by the piper. This makes likely a manner of speech not quite like that adopted by the actors for the unaccompanied iambic senarii (lines of six feet). Certainly differences can be detected in the language employed; often the vocabulary has a more elevated tone, the sentences use a greater wealth of words, and opportunities are seized for sound-effects; in particular the Roman delight in alliteration was catered for.

But this was not Plautus' only metrical means to variety. Far more striking and far more individual to him were scenes in various other metres, mainly cretics, bacchiacs and anapaests, which had in Greece been associated with song. They became more and more common as time went on, and in the late *Casina,* if the prologue is excluded from the count, nearer a half than a third of the play proper is of this kind. Sometimes several metres are used in conjunction; there may even be change from line to line, as occurs in the lyrics of Greek tragedy.

It is customary today to call these scenes *cantica.* The word was used by Cicero, but the late grammarians' attempts to define its meaning are confused and unhelpful. There is no certainty that it had the same denotation for him as for us; it may have covered everything apart from the iambic senarii. It is derived from the verb *canere,* which we translate 'sing', but there are many different ways of interpreting the word 'sing'; we even talk of a 'sing-song' voice. Perhaps the minimum sense of *canere* is 'to speak with attention to pitch and rhythm'. It is possible that there was no fundamental difference in delivery between the long iambic and trochaic lines and what we call *cantica.*

Certainly the latter were not sung in the style of arias in grand opera; the words were important and often indeed essential to the progress of the play; the vocalist must have concentrated more on getting the meaning across than on the musical qualities of his 'song'. There are even lines which an accumulation of consonants make it almost impossible to sing, in the usual modern sense of the word. Here at least emphasis must have been more on rhythm than on notes. Nevertheless there are passages in ancient authors which suggest that these 'lyrics' made greater demands on the voice, and it may be that, particularly in the monologues, which are numerous, the actor was required to produce sounds that we should unhesitatingly call song.

Here may be mentioned an odd story in Livy; he says that Livius Andronicus, who acted in his own plays, found his voice giving way as a result of repeated encores and therefore obtained leave to employ a slave to sing the words while he put his unhampered energy into silent miming. This, Livy asserts, was the origin of the custom by which someone sang in time with the actors' gestures, the latter's voice being required for the spoken scenes only. Even if he had no opportunities himself to see literary dramas performed, he must have known men old enough to have seen them. Yet if he believed it to have been the normal custom for one person to sing while another mimed, he must have been mistaken, since Cicero speaks of the singing of the famous actor Roscius.

There has been much argument about possible precedents for Plautus' use of *cantica.* At first sight an origin may be sought in imitation of the sung lyrics, mostly monodies, which became increasingly common in the tragedies of Euripides. Plautus often used the form for passages of elevated tone, whether meant to be pathetic or ridiculous, in which a character laments his or her situation, and the language is often singularly like that of serious laments to be found in the fragments of Ennius, the leading tragedian of the early second century. Both writers use much alliteration and assonance. But Plautus was the older of the two; chronology forbids any assumption that the initiative came from Ennius.

But whatever the origin of the *cantica,* they lend a peculiar flavour to Plautus' plays. They could be enjoyed not only by the mass of the audience, whom we can imagine to have been readier to listen to a 'musical' than to a straight play, but also by the more cultured hearer, who could appreciate the way in which changes of rhythm coincided with changes of feeling or subject.

By variety of metre and the use of musical numbers Plautus introduced into his Latin versions of plays that had belonged to Greek New Comedy elements that had formed part of the attraction of Old Comedy for its diversified audience. There were also other ways of responding to the simpler tastes of his spectators which recall features to be seen in Aristophanes. Nothing shows that he knew that writer's work, but he may have come across isolated precedents in the authors of New Comedy; on the other hand he may have acted independently, knowing what would please in the theatre; certainly, if he found any hints in his originals, he developed them vastly.

First, there is the spicing of scenes with indecencies, mostly sexual, often homosexual, and largely depending on ambiguous words. These passages seem to occur more at random than they do in Aristophanes; they may be completely absent from long stretches of text. Some few of them suit their speakers, but for the most part they stand out as inappropriate interruptions to the course of events; the actor momentarily becomes an entertainer with a line of dirty jokes.

Another kind of entertainment was provided by playing upon words, a device even more prominent in Plautus than in Old Comedy. This can be done with wit; it can be suitable to the speaker; it can be pregnant with meaning. Nothing could be more effective than Hamlet's

> A little more than kin and less than kind.

But whereas it is credible enough that an excluded lover should make a bitter play on words as he upbraids the *pessuli pessumi* (most wicked bolts) which keep him out, or that a parasite should repeat syllables as he gloats over his expected dinner, *quanta sumini apsumedo, quanta callo calamitas* (What consumption there'll be of cow's udder, what damage I'll do to the flesh!), yet often Plautus aims at nothing more than creating a sound-effect by capping one word with another that is similar. This is just a game irrelevant to plot or character. But there are also puns and sometimes the similarity of words is made the basis for repartee, as when one character says *nihil sentio,* and the other replies *non enim es in senticeto; eo non sentis.* That might be represented by

> (A) I'm not aware of anything. (B) No, you're not in a warehouse; that's why you're not aware.

Jokes of this sort can be heard in popular entertainments today.

Words were a source of delight for Plautus. Not only did he use a rich vocabulary drawn from colloquial speech, but he loved to invent comical new compounds and derivatives. His inventiveness and fancy did not desert him in his treatment of personal proper names. Greek New Comedy, as we have seen, used many over and over again for different characters. Since Plautus' audiences were not familiar with the conventions that attached each name to a particular type of person, he adopted the natural practice, usual in the modern theatre, of providing each character with his own individual name. In all his twenty-one plays there are only three instances of duplication: two young slaves called Pinacium, or 'Little Picture', two young men called Charinus, and two old men called Callicles. These names may have been taken over from the Greek originals, a procedure he sometimes followed, as for example in **The Bacchis Sisters** the slave Lydus kept his name from Menander's *A Double Deceit.* But the other slave in that play became Chrysalus instead of Syros, while the young men Sostratos and Moschos exchanged those

names for the less trite Mnesilochus and Pistoclerus. The former was common in real life, Pistoclerus is not recorded, although a quite possible compound. This illustrates Plautus' normal practice: many of his names are genuine; many may be his own inventions, but they are made on correct principles by analogy with forms he knew. Some of the latter kind are intended to have some point: Pistoclerus is a loyal (*pistos*) friend. A soldier, who is probably a parvenu, is called Therapontigonus, 'Son of a Servant', a theoretically possible but improbable and ridiculous name. A few are openly comic, although correct, formations: a parasite Artotrogus, 'Nibbleloaf', and a moneylender Misargyrides, 'Money Haterson'. A few others, Pyrgopolinices, 'Forte Grandstrife', and Polymachaeroplagides, 'Mickledagger McStrike', which improperly combine three elements, have parallels in Aristophanes' Tisamenophainippos and Panourgipparchides and conceivably had precedents in New Comedy, but are probably the products of his own fertile invention, like the magnificent double-barrelled Bumbomachides Clutumistaridisarchides.

These names, which have more point for those who know Greek, are only a particular case of a problem presented by the occurrence in Plautus' text of fairly numerous words of Greek origin, which are sometimes given Latin terminations or even compounded with a Latin element, e.g. *thermopotasti,* 'you've had a hot drink'. Are these words which had been adopted in the popular language of Rome? Or were they introduced to mark the fact that the characters were Greeks? Would they be understood by the majority of the audience or only by a select few? One is tempted to compare modern plays in which a foreigner speaks a line or two in his own tongue, which only a part of the audience will understand, but then considerately uses English, even to his compatriots, with occasional lapses into supposed vernacular expletives like *'Donnerwetter'.* But there are only a few places where one of Plautus' characters utters a phrase in Greek with apparently no reason but that he is a Greek. On the other hand there are many passages where Greek words are used with the apparent expectation that they will be understood by many in the theatre. A spectator will not resent elements that are above his head, provided that they are not excessive and that his own tastes are adequately catered for. A dramatist does not have to write down to the lowest level in his audience. Many French words have today a meaning for Englishmen who could not follow a French sentence, and similarly English is invading French. It may be guessed that Greeks, both slaves and free men looking for employment or trade, were already common enough in Rome to have made a considerable contribution to vocabulary.

Consistently with this Plautus seems to have relied on an elementary knowledge of Greek mythology among many of his audience. That his references to it were automatically translated from the original Greek, without any care whether they would be understood, was a theory once propounded by scholars unable to imagine how a successful dramatist works. It is quite untenable because these references occur not only in passages which may have a Greek origin but also in some which clearly are of his own composition. One need not suppose that every spectator had heard, for example, of Argus, but it was sufficient if many had done; and for those whose memories were hazy Plautus added a reminder: 'If Argus were their watcher, *he who was all eyes, whom Juno once attached as warder to Io,* he would never succeed in watching them.' Familiarity with Greek mythology will have come not only through contact with Greeks in person but also through its representation on works of art, which must have been explained and at least partially understood. Greek art and mythology had long been accepted by the Etruscans, the Romans' neighbours on the other side of the Tiber, from whom they received much cultural influence.

Another appeal to popular taste was provided by scenes in which characters exchange insults or threats. This seems to have been a standard form of entertainment in Italy. Horace recounts in the fifth satire of his first book how his travelling party, which included Maecenas and Virgil, were amused one night by the personalities exchanged by two 'parasites', a freed man and an Oscan (perhaps one should think of the Oscan plays from Atella) and the emperor Marcus Aurelius remembers another supper at which the company was diverted by the backchat between country-folk. Roman taste was also met by passages in which slaves are threatened with horrific and sometimes impossibly exaggerated physical maltreatment. The slaves themselves also anticipate or remember these punishments, frequently using comic language to refer to them.

Common to all this Plautine material is the characteristic of being designed for an immediate effect, to raise a laugh, without any regard for the progress of the action or appropriateness to the situation or to the character of the speaker, except in so far as scurrilities and foolish jokes are delivered mainly by slaves and men of low social standing. A standard motif developed for its own sake is the 'running slave', who often comes on in haste to deliver some piece of news, pretending to push aside invisible persons who crowd the street. Once Plautus doubles the absurdity by making such a slave, who carries information it is essential his master should have without delay, withhold it when he finds him until he has indulged in a long passage of backchat (*Mercator* 111-75).

As Plautus introduces jokes for their own sake, the actors lose connection with the character they are portraying; they cease to represent Greeks in Athens, and become entertainers on the Roman stage. 'Don't you know, woman, why the Greeks called Hecuba a bitch?' A slave, boasting of his success in cheating his master, which he represents by military metaphors such as were dear to Plautus, concludes 'I am not having a triumph; that has become such a common thing these days'; he is referring to the frequency of triumphs celebrated by Roman generals in the early second century, perhaps to the year 189, which saw no fewer than four (*Bacchides* 1072).

Unconcerned though Plautus is to maintain dramatic illusion and ready to forget the plot temporarily, he was by no means indifferent to the story, but carried it on clearly, making the progress of the intrigue plain. For its main lines he was indebted to the Greek original and, particularly in early plays, he took pains to see that the spectators followed it. Thus in *Poenulus* the trick to deceive the slave-dealer is explained three times (170-87, 547-65, 591-603). The interruptions to the plot by the miscellaneous jokes may even be seen as testimony to its importance. Close attention was necessary to follow Menander's dramas and his rivals probably wrote in the same manner. Plautus, with an audience on which such demands could not be made, caused the play to proceed by shorter steps than the integrated acts of his models. Then, after a passage of light relief, he would often return to the thread of the plot by repeating a phrase which had immediately preceded the insertion.

Important though the plot was, Plautus was sometimes ready to truncate it. To take an example, in Diphilus' *Klerumenoi* (*Drawers of Lots*) a girl of free birth had been exposed, rescued, and brought up in a household where both father and son fell in love with her. The father hoped to obtain her by marrying her to a complaisant slave; his wife, taking the part of the son, who had been sent abroad, wished the bridegroom to be another slave, who would be ready to make way for him on his return. All analogy shows that the girl's free birth would be established and she be united with the young man in legal marriage. But, says the prologue to *Casina,* Plautus' adaptation,

> The youth will not come back to town today in this comedy. Don't except it. Plautus was against it; he broke down a bridge on the young man's route.

The Latin poet was satisfied to concentrate on the earlier parts of the play, the manoeuvres of the husband and the wife, and the substitution, if that can be assigned to Diphilus, of a man for the girl in the bed where the father expected to find her.

Another way in which he altered the proportions of his originals appears in those plays where, as has been securely established, he greatly expanded and elaborated the role of a slave, making him much more prominent than he had been in the Greek. Three of these have as their title the name of a slave whose part was probably taken by the leading actor, as that of Chrysalus must have been in ***The Bacchis Sisters***.

Plautine slaves are of two main types, the ingenious trickster and the loyal servant. The former not only carries out the intrigue invented by the Greek author but is given to boasting elaborately of his cleverness; the supreme example is Chrysalus, who in a long *canticum* compares himself to Ulysses and the other characters to various figures who had parts, on either side, in the Trojan War. These slaves are sometimes incredibly insolent to their masters, in a manner which Plautus found it amusing to ascribe to servants of Greeks, who had strange ideals about freedom of speech. The honest retainers, on the other hand, often moralise at length about duty to their masters, uttering sentiments that would be highly approved by the slave-owners in the audience. Plautus may have found hints in his originals for what he so developed, but the prominence he gave it was his own.

In 1968 publication of a papyrus containing parts of a section of Menander's *Dis Exapaton* which correspond to *Bacchides* 494-562 threw new light on the subject of Plautus' independence; it was found that he had made quite unsuspected changes. To explain the situation it will suffice to say that Mnesilochus had, while abroad in Ephesus to collect some money belonging to his father, fallen in love with a hetaira who was about to be taken to Athens. He wrote to his friend Pistoclerus there, asking him to find the girl, with whom he hoped to resume relations on his return. Pistoclerus succeeded, but fell under the spell of her twin sister, who used the same name, Bacchis. Mnesilochus, coming home, and hearing of this, is not unnaturally led to believe that the girl he loves has become the mistress of his friend. Before this he had intended to buy her release from a contract to a soldier, entered into before he had met her. His slave Chrysalus had made this possible for him by telling his father a false story explaining that they had been obliged to leave the money in Ephesus.

Plautus has changed the names of these three characters; in Menander Mnesilochus was Sostratos, Pistoclerus was Moschos, and Chrysalus was Syros. Sostratos, left alone after hearing of what he supposes to be his friend's disloyalty, reflects as follows:

> He's gone then . . . She'll keep her hold on him. You made Sostratos your prey first.—She'll deny it, no doubt about that; she's brazen enough; every god in heaven will be brought into it. A curse on that wicked woman! (*Makes for the door of the house in which she is*). Back, Sostratos! She may talk you over. I've been her slave (?) . . . but let her use her persuasion on me when my pockets are empty and I've got nothing. I'll give my father all the money. She'll stop making herself attractive when she finds herself telling her tale to a dead man, as the proverb has it. I must go to him at once.

At this moment the father returns from the market and Sostratos tells him that there was no truth in the story spun by Syrus: 'forget it, and come with me to get the money.' The pair go off into the town, where it must have been left, and the act ends.

How did Plautus deal with this?

> Whether I should now believe my friend and companion or Bacchis to be my greater enemy, is a big problem. Did she prefer him? Let her have him! Excellent! I'll say she's done herself no good by that. Let no one ever take me for a prophet if I don't absolutely and completely—love her! I'll see to it that she can't say she got hold of a man she could laugh at; I'll go home— and steal something from my father to give her! I'll be revenged on her one way or another and make a beggar or—my father! But am I really in my right mind when I talk like this about what is still in the future? I love her, I think, if there's anything I can be sure of, but I'd rather outbeggar any beggar than let her get a feather-weight of gold from my money. My God, she shan't have the laugh of me! I've decided to hand over all the gold to my father. So then she'll coax me when my

pockets are empty and I've no resources, when it will mean as little to me as if she were telling tales to a dead man at his grave. It's quite decided that I give the gold back to my father.

Adding that he will prevail on his father not to be angry with Chrysalus, he goes in. Menander's scene between father and son has disappeared. Plautus had to make some cuts to compensate for his expansions, and this he thought he could dispense with. He must have observed that Nicobulus, as the father is called in his play, had earlier gone to the forum and had not yet come back, but perhaps he hoped that the spectators would not notice.

Menander allowed it to be understood from Sostratos' words that he still felt the girl's attraction—'she may talk you over'. Plautus makes it explicit in a sentence striking for its unexpected termination: 'if I don't absolutely and completely—' the context suggests 'ruin her', but surprisingly the conclusion is 'love her'. Pleased with this device, he repeats it twice, to produce jests that do not suit Mnesilochus' character but drive home the point that he is still prepared to put the girl before his father. His infatuation is then confirmed, for the slowest hearer, 'I love her'. That is an avowal that Sostratos did not make; anger was uppermost in his mind. After declaring his love Mnesilochus expresses a determination not to let Bacchis get her hands on any of his money; this resolve is inadequately explained.

Plautus also modifies the purpose of the young man's action over the money. Sostratos thought of the effect on the girl: she would have no use for a poor man. Mnesilochus, whose whole speech is self-centred, thinks of himself; if he has nothing, he will be unable to respond to her wiles. Almost all that Sostratos said was concerned with how *she* would behave. The same preoccupation with her and her thoughts coloured a second soliloquy, which he delivered in the next act. He came back with his father, who left once again; then he broke out:

> Yes, I believe I should enjoy seeing this perfect lady, this love of mine now that my pockets are empty, making herself attractive and expecting—'rightaway' she says to herself—all the money I'm bringing her. 'O, yes, he's bringing it all right, generously by heaven—could anyone be more generous?—and don't I deserve it?' She has turned out well enough to be exactly what I once thought her—one can be thankful for that—and I pity that fool Moschos. In one way I'm angry, but on the other hand I don't reckon he's responsible for the wrong I've been done, but that woman, who's the most brazen-faced of the lot of them.

With that Moschos came impatiently out of the house where the two sisters were.

> *Moschos.* Then if he's heard I'm here, where on earth is he?—Oh, welcome, Sostratos.
>
> *Sostratos.* (*sulkily*) Welcome.
>
> *Moschos.* Why so downcast and gloomy? And the hint

of a tear in your look? You've not found some unexpected trouble here?

Sostratos. Yes.

Moschos. Then aren't you going to tell me?

Sostratos. It's in the house, Moschos, you know.

Moschos. What do you mean?

Sostratos. [*A sentence is lost.*] That's the first wrong you've done me.

Moschos. I? Wronged you? Heaven forbid, Sostratos.

Sostratos. I didn't expect it, either.

Moschos. What are you talking about?

Here the papyrus ends, but it seems probable that the misunderstanding was rapidly cleared up.

Plautus, who had no chorus to cover a lapse of time, could not plausibly make Mnesilochus return instantly after going off to give his father the gold and to explain away the slave's story. Instead he advanced the entry of Pistoclerus. No sooner has Mnesilochus gone in than his friend comes out from the other house, into which he directs his opening words:

> Your instructions, Bacchis, shall take first place ahead of all else; I'm to look out for Mnesilochus and bring him back here to you in my company. Indeed, if my message has reached him, it's a puzzle what can be delaying him. I'll go and call here, in case he's at home.

Moschos did not babble like this nor did he need instructions from Bacchis; his single entrance line expresses his own eagerness to meet his long-absent old friend. Pistoclerus' laboured explanations provide, even if it be inadequately, for a passage of time during which Mnesilochus may be supposed to have dealt with his father. So he can now emerge, and Plautus continues, summarising events since the end of Menander's act.

> *Mnesilochus.* I've returned my father all the gold. I'd like her to meet me now, now that my pockets are empty, she who despises me. But how reluctantly my father pardoned Chrysalus when I asked! But I did finally prevail on him not to harbour any anger.

> *Pistoclerus.* Is this my friend?

> *Mnesilochus.* Is this my enemy I see?

> *Pistoclerus.* It is, to be sure.

> *Mnesilochus.* It is he. I will go up and meet him face to face.

> *Pistoclerus.* Welcome to you, Mnesilochus.

Mnesilochus. And to you.

Pistoclerus. Let us have a dinner to celebrate your safe return from foreign parts.

Mnesilochus. I've no liking for a dinner that will make me sick!

Pistoclerus. You don't say that you have been faced with something to upset you on your return?

Mnesilochus. Yes, and a very violent upset.

Pistoclerus. What caused it?

Mnesilochus. A man I previously thought my friend.

Pistoclerus. There are many men alive today who act in that manner and that fashion. When you count them as friends, they are found to be false in their falsity, busy with their tongues, but sluggish in service and light in loyalty. There is not a soul whose success they do not envy; but their inactivity makes it sure enough that no one envies them.

Mnesilochus. I'll swear that you've studied their ways well and have a good grip on them. But there is one thing more: their bad character brings them bad luck; they have no friends and make enemies all round. And in their folly they reckon they are cheating others, when they are really cheating themselves. That is how it is with the man I thought as good a friend to me as I am to myself. He took all the pains in his power to do me any harm he could and to get everything that belonged to me into his own hands.

Pistoclerus. He must be a wicked man.

Mnesilochus. I think so.

Pistoclerus. Speak out, I beg you, tell me who he is.

Mnesilochus. One who wishes you well. Otherwise I would pray you to do him any harm you could.

Pistoclerus. Just say who the man is. If I don't hurt him somehow, call me the worst of slackers.

Mnesilochus. The man's a rogue, but he's a friend of yours.

Pistoclerus. The more reason for telling me who he is. I don't care much for the friendship of a rogue.

Mnesilochus. I see that I can't do anything but tell you his name. Pistoclerus, you have utterly ruined me, your friend.

Menander made Moschos see at once that something was wrong, just as an intimate friend would, and Sostratos was quickly brought to explain his resentment. For Plautus this was missing an opportunity; he could use a motif that he were essential to the progress of the plot, making the new version do all that was necessary to carry the play forward, but substituting his own characterisation.

The result of this new evidence must be to show that greater difficulty than some have imagined must attend any effort to work back from Plautus to the Greek play he adapted. On the other hand since the failure to account for the movements of the father is proved to be due to him and not to Menander, there is support for those who think such imperfections reliable clues to Plautine workmanship. But although he is here convicted of carelessness, there is new proof of his independence; it seems he is to be credited with responsibility for a greater part of his plays than some scholars have supposed.

Wolfgang Riehle (essay date 1990)

SOURCE: "The Structure of Plautine Comedy and Its Impact on Shakespeare," in *Shakespeare, Plautus, and the Humanist Tradition,* D. S. Brewer, 1990, pp. 77-110.

[*In this essay, Riehle examines the structural and comedic devices Shakespeare derived from Plautus and employed in* The Comedy of Errors *and other works.*]

may well have met in some other play. If Mnesilochus were to denounce the man he supposed to have injured him, but without giving his name, Pistoclerus with nothing on his conscience could be made to speak unwittingly in his own condemnation, and Mnesilochus could be made to lead him on. (More accurately, Pistoclerus condemns not himself, but the man whom his friend supposes him to be.) Plautus' scene is somewhat contrived, but it might be effective on the stage, as the audience enjoyed Pistoclerus' repeated failures to understand. One should not condemn it for not being Menander's; its explicit vigour will have made it more attractive to the Roman audience than his would have been. But it must be realised that Menander conceived the young men quite differently. His Moschos is sensitive and direct, immediately perceives the other's distress, and would not meet it with four pompous lines of generalisation about false friends; Sostratos, although not unresentful, does not see an enemy in Moschos, but puts the blame on the girl, not on his old companion. Plautus worked with stock motifs, Menander with lifelike figures of his own invention.

Now that it is possible to compare a passage of Menander with Plautus' version, there is proof that in his later works at least the Latin dramatist dealt very freely with his original. It was not just a matter of inserting extraneous jokes into a more or less faithfully translated text. Scholars had realised that there must have been changes when a *canticum* replaced a spoken scene, but not that a scene could remain spoken yet be given a new form. We now know that he could refashion both monologue and dialogue which

1. SOME BASIC ELEMENTS OF SCENIC DRAMATURGY

In turning to questions of plot and the dramaturgic organization of the action, we shall not be concerned with a detailed structural comparison between [Shakespeare's *Comedy of Errors*] and *Menaechmi,* since several critics have already examined the process by which Shakespeare transforms the plot of Plautine comedy. Nor shall we consider the question of the Elizabethan attitude towards the classical unities which has also been previously discussed. We shall, instead, choose to concentrate on a number of essential structural aspects of New Comedy, and shall investigate the ways in which Shakespeare makes use of them. The first area we shall look at is that of scenic dramaturgy.

It is well known that in New Comedy there are no changes of locality, whereas in tragedy as well as in Old Comedy such changes are common. The acting area in New Comedy is always a street or the space in front of a house. Indoor scenes, when they become necessary, are also sometimes played in front of the house, and the dramatist is unconcerned about dramatic verisimilitude. This kind of scenic dramaturgy has important implications. As the action unfolds in one place, there is no need for the characters on stage to clear it so as to create the illusion that the next scene will take place in a different setting. In New Comedy, therefore, one scene is distinguished from the next by a change in character grouping, brought about either by the arrival of a further character or (much less frequently) by a character's exit.

In his *Errors,* Shakespeare has not only preserved the unity of time, for the most part he has also remained remarkably faithful to the dramaturgy of space in New Comedy. For example, Menander's *Dyskolos* is opened by the Prologue spoken by Pan who invites the audience to 'Imagine that the scene's in Attica' and the Prologue to **Menaechmi** concludes with the remark that today the stage 'is' Epidamnus and tomorrow it may 'be' any other place, depending upon the plot of the next play (72-76). Shakespeare's attitude towards the creation of dramatic space through the imagination of the audience is very similar; we need only think of the Prologue to *Troilus and Cressida,* which begins by informing us: 'In Troy there lies the scene . . . ', then the bare stage is given a particular individuality in a manner corresponding to the transformation of the Menandrian or Plautine stage. The similarities between the Plautine and the Elizabethan dramaturgy of space are very close indeed. And there is surely no *decisive* qualitative difference between the so-called Terentian screen stage, for which *Errors* was most probably written, and the Elizabethan popular stage. The neutral space where the action develops becomes an individual place only through the action. That this dramaturgy in *Errors* is not simply concerned about 'realism', can be seen, for example, in the interesting situation in IV, i. When Antipholus E is hard pressed by Angelo and the Second Merchant, who want his money, he orders Dromio to fetch it. Dromio, however, does not do what would be the most obvious thing from a realistic point of view, namely cross the stage and enter the house of Antipholus E; instead, he exits hurriedly and returns only after some time, sweating. The audience are not disturbed by this anti-illusionist dramaturgy, since they have no time to become aware of it, for Shakespeare uses Dromio's absence as an opportunity for Adriana's and Luciana's reappearance, so that Dromio's hasty and exhausted return and his encounter with the two ladies produce another very effective confusion.

In a discussion of the dramaturgy of space, the use of offstage localities cannot be ignored. Plautus is one of the very first dramatists to make offstage scenery into an important part of the total dramatic design. There is an effective contrast between the everyday business world of the Forum and the offstage holiday area of the harbour, with the pleasures of Erotium lying in wait. Menaechmus E oscillates between the two worlds, whereas Menaechmus S belongs entirely to the latter. He is a born traveller and uses the search for his brother almost as a pretext for travelling. For a few moments, his narration of his long journeys creates an imaginary world which forms a contrast to the action of the play itself. Again, in the brilliant scene V, ii, he succeeds in imaginatively extending the actual space when he plays the madman and suggests that he is performing a chariot race on the orders of Apollo.

In *Errors,* offstage locality becomes even more important; it can be seen as an extension and transformation of the Plautine dramaturgy of space. Whereas Menaechmus E is saved from being carried off to the clinic, Antipholus E is actually sent to prison, which Dromio metaphorically associates with Hell, and is then thrown into a 'dark and dankish vault' (V, i, 248). This dark vault, which marks the nadir of Antipholus's fortunes, is the exact counterpart of the Priory in which his brother is detained. In the one place, identity is about to be destroyed, while by the other its final attainment is made possible.

Scene III, i of *Errors* deserves our special attention. Here, the acting space is again extended beyond the visible part of the stage. It is often claimed that, for the scene to make its proper impact, both pairs of twins should be clearly visible to the audience. I am rather inclined to believe that the overall effect of this magnificent scene is greater if the acting space is divided into a visible and an invisible half. Staged in this way, the scene is extremely funny. In my own production, both Dromios were visible to the audience only for the short moment when Dromio E succeeded in pulling open the door, whereupon Dromio S at once pulled it to again.

In our discussion of the characters in **Menaechmi** we have seen that two contrasting backstage locations—the Forum and the harbour—are essential for a proper understanding of the play's movements because the one represents the everyday world of business and constraint, whereas the other symbolizes the spirit of holiday and sexual liberty, and the comedy moves between these two worlds. It is, I think, very likely that there are direct links between this kind of spatial opposition and the contrasting of localities in some of Shakespeare's comedies. Again Shakespeare may have taken up a suggestion which he developed into a dramaturgic device of great originality. In fact, as early as the 'classical' *Errors,* we find that Shakespeare employs two contrasting *kinds* of space. In the very first scene, which is exceptional in that it takes place within the Duke's palace, Shakespeare widens the narrow confines of the play by evoking an *imaginary* space in the minds of the audience. Egeon mentions his misfortunes on the boundless ocean, and from then on, as R. Berry has remarked [in *Shakespeare and the Awareness of the Audience,* 1985], 'always at the back of the action is the sea'. This boundlessness of the imaginary space is reinforced by Luciana in II, i, when she describes the cosmic order and refers to the creatures 'in earth, in sea, in sky', 'The beasts, the fishes, and the winged fowls', and then goes on to call Man 'Lord of the wide world and wild wat'ry seas' (18ff.). Thus Shakespeare achieves an effective contrast with the real acting space, the city of Ephesus, which gives the impression of a continually narrowing acting area: whereas, as the play progresses, the major characters increasingly experience a feeling of claustrophobia, the references to the sea provide the audience with a momentary relief by offering a view outside the narrowing confines of the play world. Shakespeare further elaborates this same technique in his later plays, for example in *A Midsummer Night's Dream,* where we find a comparable narrowing of space in the woods of Athens, while the poetical and mythological descriptions, such as the picture of Oberon sitting on a 'promontory', hearing 'a mermaid on a dolphin's back' (II, i, 148ff.), briefly open up a liberating vista into the world outside the woods, as Young has shown [D. P. Young, *Something of Great Constancy. The Art of 'A Midsummer Night's Dream',* 1966].

The city of Ephesus is a common locality in New Comedy. However, Shakespeare is not content merely to distance the action of his play by transferring it to a far-off place; he is concerned to evoke in the audience the opposing reactions of 'engagement and detachment'. Not only in the second scene but on some later occasions, too, there are references to familiar English locations, particularly when Dromio S gives his description of Nell, the buxom kitchen wench. Berry was the first to conclude that these associations give the audience the 'reassurance that all will be well'.

In this context a further interesting aspect of the dramaturgic affinity between Shakespeare and Plautus becomes evident. As is well known, Plautus takes over the Greek settings of his sources; on the other hand, however, he occasionally includes in his plays some references to Roman place names as well as official and legal terms. One effect of the combination of Greek and Roman elements is certainly to create an imaginary world of play set at some removes from everyday experience; at the same time these Roman references reassure the audience of the eventual resolution in a way quite comparable to Shakespeare's homely allusions in *Errors*. This is particularly striking since, in contrast to Plautus, we do not find any references to contemporary Rome in the plays of Terence.

We must now pay special attention to the way in which in Plautine Comedy and in Elizabethan drama space is used for the meeting and parting of the *dramatis personae*. As both classical and many Elizabethan comedies are 'plays of meeting', to use a term coined by Clifford Leech [in 'The Function of Locality in the Plays of Shakespeare and his Contemporaries', in D. Galloway, ed., *The Elizabethan Theatre*, 1969], we find a great many variations on the act of meeting. In both traditions we have frequent scenes in which the action develops simultaneously on different parts of the stage, as envisaged by [D. Bain, in *Actors and Audience*, 1977]:

> That X can be on stage concurrently with Y and unaware of Y's presence or that they can be mutually unaware of each other's presence is an established convention of the Greek stage. When an actor enters an already occupied stage, he is in comedy usually represented as at first unaware of the presence of the other people on stage. On some occasions they are represented as unaware of him and the two actors or groups of actors proceed in mutual unawareness for some time.

Bain rightly points out that this dramaturgic convention, which is related to the multiple setting familiar to us from the medieval tradition, does not put great strain on the audience's belief because 'the [. . .] characters are [. . .] too occupied in their own thoughts to notice each other.' The very length of the Plautine stage too adds credibility to this convention. It is nevertheless clear that these scenic situations, with the exception of the 'classical' eavesdropping convention, are far less dramatic than situations beginning with a dialogue. In Plautus and in New Comedy proper, we find many examples of these scenic types. Yet

Plautus also knows how to make good dramatic use of an 'open' dialogue, where characters appear to be continuing on stage a discussion which they had already begun beforehand.

In Shakespeare's plays, we admire the 'infinite variety' of the ways in which his characters meet. In our present context, it is particularly interesting to note that he shows an increasing reserve in the use of less 'dramatic' scene openings involving soliloquies or the soliloquy of a new character which is overheard and commented on by another; when this latter situation is necessary, Shakespeare, as a rule, sees to it that after a short while a dialogue between the characters is established. On the other hand, his art of beginning a scene in the middle of a dialogue can already be studied in *Errors*, where this technique adds a strong touch of 'realism' to the play's overall impact. The beginning of the so-called wooing scene, III, ii, is especially noteworthy because . . . the pattern of an ordinary wooing is, as it were, undercut by the fact that we meet Luciana and Antipholus *after* they have already exchanged a dialogue behind the stage, and the new scene opens with Luciana taking the initiative and giving Antipholus some strikingly odd advice for what she interprets as an amorous adventure.

In New Comedy, there are frequent scenes in which a newcomer on stage does not notice that his arrival has been observed by a character or a group of characters hiding behind a suitable object; these eavesdropping scenes always provide opportunities for effective stage comedy. The great variety of eavesdropping scenes in the comedies of Plautus served Shakespeare as a kind of skeletal basis around which he built his own brilliant scenes of overhearing. Two of the best scenes of this kind appear in plays well known during the Renaissance, namely in *Miles Gloriosus* (IV, iv) and *Amphitruo* (I, i). In *Amphitruo*, the way in which Mercury and Sosia observe each other and comment on one another from a distance is masterfully contrived. *Menaechmi* also contains an interesting example: at first, Peniculus thinks his Patron, who has just returned from the Forum, has come from the dinner and cheated him, whereupon he plans his revengeful intrigue in his cynical asides. Plautus adds complexity to the situation through the fact that, just as Menaechmus is unaware of Peniculus's thoughts of revenge, so Peniculus fails to realize that he is being deceived about Menaechmus's real identity. In *Errors* Shakespeare disposed of the eavesdropping convention because, unlike his Latin sources, he had no real need for it. Since *deliberate* deception is the prerequisite of an intrigue, it would be wrong to call *Errors* a comedy of intrigue. The Courtesan, it is true, plans to avenge herself on Antipholous, but she is prevented from putting her plans into practice; nothing else in the play can properly be called an intrigue. Nevertheless, we have, of course, in *Errors* a great deal of *passive* self-deception. It would exceed the limits of this book to examine Shakespeare's reception of the dramaturgic elements of intrigue and disguise, particularly Roman elements occurring in Plautus, not least in the splendid *Amphitruo*; instead we must refer the reader to existing studies on these points.

Vase painting of a scene used by Plautus in Amphitruo:
Zeus visits Alcmene.

Shakespeare's transformation of the eavesdropping convention in his later comedies is stunning, especially in *Troilus and Cressida* and in the famous gulling of Benedick and Beatrice in *Much Ado About Nothing*. Benedick begins scene II, iii with a soliloquy and then, as so often happens in New Comedy, the soliloquizer notices other people coming on stage and decides to overhear them. At this point, the pattern of the scene becomes more and more complicated because, when Benedick starts reflecting about Claudio's having become a 'fool of love', he does not realize that at this very moment that is precisely what he himself is about to become too. The complexity of the situation is then further increased by a doubling of eavesdropping: just as Benedick reacts in asides to what he has heard, so the intriguers secretly comment on the progress of their scheme. Benedick's aside: 'I should think this a gull, but that the white-bearded fellow speaks it. Knavery cannot sure hide himself in such reverence' (II, iii, 118-120) is overheard by them and interpreted as signalling their success: 'He hath ta'en th'infection' (121). In the gulling of Beatrice, the situation is then paralleled, most skilfully varied and even contrasted, because, although the intrigue takes on a parallel form, the method which Hero, Margaret and Ursula employ is different: whereas the men had cajoled Benedick into believing that Beatrice was deeply in love with him, the women point out to the eavesdropping Beatrice her own proud and disdainful attitude towards Benedick.

The great length of the Plautine stage and the vast size of the Elizabethan platform were certainly favourable to the frequent employment not only of eavesdropping, but also of the aside, which occurs above all in the superb overhearing scenes in both Plautus and Shakespeare and which has an interesting and even contrasting variety of forms in Roman comedy. Plautus often has a character secretly address the audience and is not concerned about illusion, when a character produces a whole chain of asides, yet he also knows how to add credibility to this convention when he wants to. We find this especially in his eavesdropping scenes, where a character's aside is often a *spontaneous* but brief emotional reaction; and spontaneous asides, not simply directed at the audience, occur in ordinary dialogue as well. The speaker may even secretly address his partner, so that the aside retains a dialogic element. Although Plautus ultimately 'derived' this convention from Greek New Comedy, it has been shown that he sometimes transforms it into something new and original and even *increases* the dramatic plausibility of the aside by additional devices. This happens when an aside is noticed or 'discovered' by the dialogue partner(s); either the character's silence is commented on, or the aside has been heard indistinctly, and therefore the speaker of the aside is asked to repeat his comment; formulae such as the following are used: 'Quid tu solus *tecum* loquere?' (*Auluaria* 190); 'quid tute *tecum*?' (*Mostellaria* 551). The aside may be noticed as an inarticulate murmur (*Aulularia*), or one character may make a secret remark while another is engaged with an occupation of some kind, so that he does not notice that an aside is being made.

Plautus developed a further type, namely the aside accompanied by the actor's turning or even moving away from his partner. Thus, in **Truculentus,** for example, a character addresses the following question to another *dramatis persona*: 'Quo te avortisti?' (357); this implies no less than a '*post eventum* stage direction for the delivery of the aside' [Bain], because here the speaker, besides talking secretly, has also changed his position. This device too is clearly meant to add verisimilitude to the convention, and the size of the platform stage provides the opportunity for this kind of delivery. According to Bain, the aside which is observed but not understood by the partner can even be traced back to Euripidean tragedy.

In the plays of Shakespeare, the aside holds a very important dramaturgic position, and there are some interesting connections between Plautus and Shakespeare in the use of this technique. If Plautus employs both the anti-illusionist secret address to the audience and the more 'realistic' forms of the aside, so does Shakespeare. It would be wrong to claim that Shakespeare gradually replaced the direct address to the audience by types fully compatible with the dramatic illusion. Yet we may say that there is a gradual increase of the latter types until the final plays, where a new 'Plautine' unconcern about more primitive dramaturgic elements makes itself felt. We find a similar 'Plautine' disregard of realism in the aside in the very early trilogy *Henry VI* and the early *Richard III*. Like Plautus, Shakespeare here inserts whole 'chains' of asides which awkwardly interrupt the regular flow of the dialogue. In the first part of *Henry VI,* Suffolk ponders in frequent asides whether he should woo Margaret (V, iii, 60-99), and in *Richard III,* Margaret, having entered the stage from a back door, showers Gloucester with curses in a series of asides (I, iii, 109-156).

On the other hand, *Richard III* also contains Gloucester's famous and 'realistic' aside-comment on a remark made by young Prince Edward. Since the young Prince has indistinctly heard, but not understood, Gloucester's aside: 'So wise so young, they say do never live long', Gloucester turns the original meaning of his comment into its very opposite and then, in a second aside, he compares his own verbal ingenuity, by which he manages to produce deceptive ambiguity, with that of the Vice of the Moralities.

> I say, without characters fame lives long.
> [Aside] Thus, like the formal Vice, Iniquity,
> I moralize two meanings in one word.
>
> III, i, 79-83

Like a Vice character, Gloucester deceives his victim with a double meaning so that young Edward is bound to mistake his words. Not only does Gloucester deceive Edward, but in two asides he even makes the audience aware of his deceptive verbal ambiguity. The fact that his first aside has been half perceived by his victim, and has to be reformulated in order to provide it with an opposite meaning, reminds us of an aside-type in Plautus. The very content of Gloucester's first remark, too, is connected with the New Comedy tradition because it closely resembles the famous tag: 'Whom the gods love die young', found in Menander. Furthermore, it is no mere coincidence that Shakespeare's *Errors,* too, contains this Plautine technique of a person 'discovering', but not fully understanding, an aside. In the first encounter of Antipholus S and Dromio with Adriana and Luciana, Dromio, imitating his master, tries in an aside to account for the incredible situation he finds himself in: 'O for my beads; I cross me for a sinner. / This is the fairy land . . . ' (187-192). Again, this aside, spoken in an 'incredible' situation, is given dramatic verisimilitude by the fact that Luciana has noticed Dromio talking aside: 'Why prat'st thou to thyself and answer'st not?'. With regard to its form, this aside corresponds to the Plautine type of 'Quid tute tecum?'. Elsewhere in Shakespeare, we find a variety of responses from characters who observe another character talking aside. For example, in *Cymbeline,* Belarius notices that Arviragus, who has just spoken aside, 'wrings at some distress' (III, vi, 78), and in *The Tempest,* Ferdinand remarks to Miranda that her father, speaking aside, must be 'in some passion' (V, i, 143). There are, then, a number of dramatic situations in Shakespeare in which the content of an aside remains hidden from both the audience and certain of the characters on stage because the aside is merely whispered.

The turning or even moving away of the character who speaks the aside was taken over in Elizabethan and Shakespearean drama as an effective means of adding plausibility to the convention. In the anonymous play *A Pleasant Comedie of Faire Em The Miller's Daughter,* a stage direction suggests that the character Blanche is to make her aside-comment 'secretly at one end of the stage'. Another stage direction in *The Famous Victories of Henry V* shows that Lady Katheren, who wants to make an aside, thinks it best to withdraw for a while from the dialogue situation and to conceal her words by moving away: 'She goes aside, and speakes as followeth'. In Tourneur's *Revenger's Tragedy,* Lussurioso asks his partner, who has spoken an aside, 'Why dost walk aside?'. Likewise, the 'turning away' of a character in order to make an aside is found in Elizabethan drama, as in *The Taming of a Shrew.* All these examples clearly continue the Plautine tradition. Shakespeare does not find the need to insert stage directions suggesting the moving away of a character speaking aside; instead, he prefers to use situations for an aside in which a character is already standing outside the ordinary dramatic situation or in which two separate groups have been formed. These types of the aside are, however, surpassed in effectiveness by those which, in form and content, are spontaneous reactions of a speaker to a certain dramatic situation. Effective instances of these can already be found in *Errors.* The way in which Adriana in II, ii addresses Antipholus as her husband evokes an emotional response from him which is released in his talking to himself . . . :

> To me she speaks, she moves me for her theme;
> What, was I married to her in my dream?
> Or sleep I now, and think I hear all this?
> What error drives our eyes and ears amiss?
>
> 181-184

His secret attempt to cope with the confused situation culminates in his resolution: 'Until I know this sure uncertainty, / I'll entertain the offer'd fallacy.' Some moments later, he again tries to explain to himself the unexplainable: 'Am I in earth, in heaven, or in hell?', and again he makes up his mind to act according to what the people of Ephesus expect of him: 'I'll say as they say, and persever so, / And in this mist at all adventures go' (212-216). It would be quite wrong to assume that these asides were designed to be directly addressed to the audience in order to inform them beforehand of Antipholus's intentions; on the contrary, judged from the point of view of providing information, they are superfluous because the plot will soon develop in quite a different direction from that which Antipholus has anticipated, and therefore he fails to carry out his intention of *deliberately playing* the madman; all he can do is to *react* to situations which become increasingly threatening. A comparison with **Menaechmi** makes the point abundantly clear. In V, ii Menaechmus S notices that Senex and Matrona are beginning to take him for a madman. Then the idea occurs to him on the spur of the moment that *playing* the madman may be the only way to escape from them. In an aside directly addressed to the audience Menaechmus informs them of his intentions. Here the aside is necessary because the audience have to know in advance that his ensuing mad behaviour is to be taken as deliberate role-playing.

In *Errors,* soliloquies as well as asides are used very economically; they are always brief and do not get in the way of the dramatic opening of a scene, as they often do in the comedies of Plautus. Shakespeare seems already to have become aware of the dangers inherent in this convention. It would be beyond the scope of this book to give a survey of the variety of the asides in Shakespeare; suffice it to say that Shakespeare enormously extended the ways in which a speaker may express his emotional condition and articulate his innermost thoughts and feelings. It is, therefore, not surprising that the greatest examples occur in Shakespeare's tragedies, rather than in his comedies. In no other play is the convention of the aside transformed with such originality and perfection as in *Macbeth*. Here the dramatic situation created by the Weird Sisters with their prophecies releases in Macbeth an inner process during which he becomes conscious of his secret desires and expresses them in a series of asides. He thus becomes increasingly isolated from his companions (I, iii, 116ff.). They notice his change of behaviour and observe how he is 'rapt'. At the end of this process Macbeth is absorbed in his evil thoughts to the point of forgetting that he is not alone, and so his asides give way to mere soliloquizing, whereupon he leaves the stage in order to put his evil plans into practice.

The structure of a play is essentially determined by the interaction of the characters' entrances and exits. It is therefore worth asking the question how and with what kind of motivation the playwright causes his characters to meet and to separate; yet, strangely enough, this aspect is too often neglected in scholarly research. Menander's dramaturgy of entrances and exits produces a natural effect. Plautus is sometimes not concerned with motivating the appearance of his characters; thus he has them enter 'on cue', just as they are expected or mentioned by the persons present on stage. This *lupus in fabula* effect may seem clumsy or artificial, and indeed, on one occasion Plautus makes fun of himself, as it were, when a character comments on the sudden arrival of another as an appearance similar to the 'lupum in sermone' (*Stichus,* V, 577). But in the theatre, rules other than 'realistic' ones are valid. Nor, indeed, is this convention so completely unrealistic; we all know from everyday experience that the 'speak of the devil' effect occurs in real life as well. Like Plautus, Shakespeare makes quite frequent use of this technique. Yet he very often adds credibility to the convention. We find a very good example in *Richard III,* where much is made of the contrast between reality and dramatic illusion. Richard, who is an excellent actor as well as a director, suggests that the action on stage is 'real' by the very fact that he occasionally compares it with a stage play; and Buckingham likens Richard's appearance in III, iv at the right moment to the entrance of an actor on his cue (26).

How, then, do *Errors* and its Plautine sources compare in their motivation of the characters' entrances and exits? It has recently been suggested that Plautus motivates both entrances and exits carefully, but this is not entirely borne out by *Menaechmi* and *Amphitruo*. Exits are sometimes not provided with credible motivation and are not always conducive to the further development of the plot. For example, after she has convicted her husband of his theft, the Matrona exits in IV, ii with the remark: 'never shall you enter the house unless you bring the mantle with you.' ('nam domum numquam introibis, nisi feres pallam simul.'

662). She does not suggest that she intends to take any further action against him; it appears that she is waiting at home for his return. In V, i she re-enters unexpectedly because she wants to see why her husband has been away for so long: 'I'll go out and see if my husband won't soon be back home.' ('Provisam quam mox vir meus redeat domum.' 704). This re-entry, which lacks any connection with her earlier exit, is necessary at this point because Menaechmus S must have a chance to meet her. Peniculus and Erotium leave the stage for good while the action is still in full flow, and the Matrona, having fled in panic from her 'mad husband', does not return either. As these loose ends show, we have in **Menaechmi** some comparatively slack links between scenes.

There are a good many examples where the entrance of a character lacks motivation. When Menaechmus S enters from Erotium's house, he appears with no particular intention—he is still relishing in his mind the pleasures he has just experienced. The other Menaechmus, too, enters on several occasions without having a real motive. For example, in IV, iii he leaves the stage with the intention of asking his friends what he should do next after Erotium has turned her back on him. This is a somewhat clumsy trick the author is forced to use in order to keep him offstage for some time. When he returns in V, i, he still does not know what to do, and is complaining even more bitterly: 'Well! By Jove, I certainly do lead a miserable life!' ('eu edepol! ne ego homo vivo miser.' 908). His reappearance is, however, necessary from a dramaturgic point of view because the Senex and the Medicus have to mistake him for his 'mad' twin brother.

In *Amphitruo,* most entrances and exits are much better motivated, but even here some of them serve merely to provide opportunities for new mistakings of identity. Thus Alcumena on one occasion enters from her house for the sole purpose of delivering a reflective soliloquy, whereupon she meets her real husband (II, ii, 633-653). Later on, the real Amphitruo leaves the stage with the intention of fetching Naucrates from the boat; again, it is necessary for Amphitruo to be temporarily absent so as to provide an opportunity for another mistaking of identity. Yet, he returns without Naucrates, because the introduction of a new character at this point would have been superfluous. However, this should not be condemned as lack of motivation, for, as Marti has shown, there is a dramatic purpose behind Amphitruo's failure to fetch Naucrates: it is a further disappointment for him, and thus his isolation increases dangerously [H. Marti, *Untersuchungen zur dramatischen Technik bei Plautus und Terenz,* 1959]. Moreover, inconsistencies of motivation are not noticed during a performance; indeed, they are perfectly in tune with the 'logic' of theatrical game-playing.

Our comparison with Plautus helps us to realize that Shakespeare, by contrast, pays much closer attention to both the entrances and the exits of his characters. There is practically no exit in *Errors* which is not clearly motivated in the sense that it is the immediate cause of the character's re-entry. Thus, in contrast to the convention of New Comedy, the scenes in Shakespeare are on the one hand frequently distinguished from one another by the 'clear stage' convention, while on the other hand they are closely linked together by the interdependence of exits and entrances. Shakespeare's principal device here is the series of orders which the Dromios are given and which they attempt to carry out. Whereas in *Menaechmi* there is only one occasion on which the slave Messenio exits with a particular order, in *Errors* most of the confusions occur precisely because one of the Dromios is carrying out the order of his own Antipholus, when he happens to meet the other one. The knot of the action is thus bound much more tightly than in Plautus. This produces a certain 'cogency' completely lacking in **Menaechmi**.

2. THE PROBLEM OF ACT DIVISION

It is impossible to examine Shakespeare's reception of the comedies of Plautus without discussing the vexed question of Act division. The view shared by most Shakespeare critics has been discussed at length by H.C. Snuggs, who tries to show that Shakespeare did not care much about the convention of the five-Act structure, but rather composed his plays in terms of scenes [*Shakespeare and Five Acts,* 1960]. There is, however, far too much evidence which speaks against this conclusion. The soundest view appears to be that of Emrys Jones and G.K. Hunter, who take a middle position: Shakespeare did not abandon the five-Act convention altogether, but neither did he adhere to it strictly and consistently. Nevertheless, 'many of Shakespeare's plays observe the five-Act arrangement' [Jones, *Scenic Form in Shakespeare,* 1971; Hunter, 'Were there Act-Pauses on Shakespeare's Stage?' in *English Renaissance Drama. Essays in Honor of Madeleine Doran & Mark Eccles,* ed. S. Henning, R. Kimbrough, R. Knowles, 1976].

This whole question is far from being of secondary importance because it would be interesting to know whether Shakespeare wrote in terms of five rhythmically alternating movements; if he did, then they must in some way or other have been conveyed to the audience during a performance. In his fine article G.K. Hunter also argued in favour of short Act pauses because 'it often seems that a pause, of the appropriate length, can cause tension to increase rather than elapse'. And these pauses must have been filled by brief music performed by the musicians of the public theatres. In any case, Hunter has collected enough evidence for the existence of the five Act convention even on the popular stages. Our own considerations will confirm Hunter's findings from a different perspective.

The confusions that arise in this matter can mainly be traced back to T.W. Baldwin's lengthy study, which, like his book on the compositional genetics of *Errors,* distorts the facts. Baldwin calls his book *Shakspere's Five-Act Structure,* but in fact only about a quarter of the work is concerned with Shakespeare. He starts with the assumption that 'Terence was at the basis of the grammar-school system. Along with him, Plautus was frequently used as a supplement'. Because of his strong bias against Plautus his argument falters and even becomes contradictory, and

it is most strange that practically all critics have nevertheless accepted his 'conclusions'. He tries to persuade us into believing that Lambinus's edition of Plautus of 1576 was the 'standard annotated edition'—he has to base his argument on an edition like this one which does not always use Act divisions. However, even Baldwin has to concede two facts which completely undermine his argument: a) Lambinus was 'exceptional in that he regarded these act-divisions as unwarranted innovations'. b) As the overwhelming majority of Plautus editions had these divisions, Shakespeare 'may [. . .] also still have had his old grammar school edition of Plautus in addition to that of Lambinus.' This old edition might have proved handy on act-divisions. There is, then, no reason to doubt that Shakespeare worked with a text of Plautine comedies containing these divisions, and indeed, as we shall see, the evidence for this is overwhelming. Many English dramatists looked to Plautus rather than Terence for their classical model for comic drama. The plain facts are that no Terentian play served Shakespeare as a source for any of his comedies, whereas he made extensive use of the Plautine **Menaechmi** and **Amphitruo**. I shall argue, therefore, that Shakespeare quite 'naturally' became familiar with the convention of Act division through the plays of Plautus and that it is absurd to assume with Baldwin that he 'reconstructs [**Menaechmi** and **Amphitruo**] into the *Andria* formula of Terentian structure'. Yet first of all it is necessary to consider briefly the use of the Act convention in the tradition of New Comedy.

In the comedies of Menander and those of his contemporaries whose names have been preserved, the action was divided into Acts by the appearance from time to time of a Chorus. Plautus and Terence disposed of this Chorus completely and this, together with the fact that the Plautine and Terentian manuscripts do not contain Act divisions, has led scholars to assume that Acts lost their importance in Roman comedy, despite the fact that both Horace and Varro define a play as being divided into five Acts. Along with other classicists, Duckworth argues that, since the plays of New Comedy have an *actio continua,* a 'continuous action', the question of whether there were acts becomes immaterial. However, it seems to me that such a view does not do full justice to the practical concerns of the theatre. It is helpful to the audience if they are made to realize that the action is unfolding in several units and movements, and these may be pointed out by the rhythmic recurrence of brief pauses, filled, perhaps, by a few 'flourishes' of music or other pointers which do not really interrupt the continuous flow of the action, but which help to make the structural organization more lucid. The written text of Plautine and Terentian comedy as we have it does not, of course, indicate these non-verbal elements of the original performance; yet we can be fairly certain that such devices were used, and may indeed have contributed considerably to the overall effect, because there is an interesting exception: in the Plautine **Pseudolus** a character leaves the stage telling the audience: 'I'll soon be back, though, and won't keep you waiting. Meantime you'll be entertained by the fluteplayer here.' ('sed mox exibo, non ero vobis morae; tibicen vos interibi hic delectaverit', 573a), and then Act II starts afresh.

The Act divisions of modern editions of Plautus go back to manuscripts of the 15th century, and in the 16th century the humanist J.B. Pio inserted them into all editions. The same had first been done with the comedies of Terence. The humanists took it for granted that comedies had to be divided into Acts, not least because Donatus discussed the plays of Terence in terms of Acts. How, then, did Pio decide where an Act division had to be? He followed the *scaena vacua* or 'clear stage' criterion that somehow seems to reflect the Act division of the Greek models of the Roman comedies. However, since the Roman transformations are often considerable, and since in a play there are sometimes more and sometimes fewer than the four required *scaena vacua* situations, his decision must necessarily have been difficult or even haphazard. Nevertheless, many of his divisions make very good sense, and those Renaissance humanist editions of Terence which have Act divisions generally accepted his decisions.

Since Baldwin has a marked and even 'irrational' preference for Terence and a much lower opinion of Plautus, he presents the factual evidence uncritically: For instance, while he has a chapter on 'Terence Texts in England', he fails to give us a corresponding account of the spread of Plautine texts in England. What makes his whole line of argument so wrong is that he does not see that Shakespeare's own dramatic temperament is far more akin to Plautus than to Terence. Since most Plautus editions, too, were divided into Acts, we have the best of reasons for assuming that the edition Shakespeare used will also have contained these divisions. Yet the really important question has still to be asked: in what way are Act divisions that were inserted by the humanists structurally motivated and plausible? If there is a positive answer to this question, we are fully justified in examining the effect they had on Shakespeare.

Before beginning our closer inspection, two misunderstandings must be cleared up which have so far hindered critics from taking an unbiased view of the problem. Just as classicists have argued that the *actio continua* in New Comedy makes the question of Act division irrelevant, so Shakespeare critics have adduced the 'continuous action' of Shakespeare's plays as proof that he composed his plays without paying any attention to dividing them into Acts. Thus W.W. Greg [in *The Shakespeare First Folio*, 1955] pointed out that, shortly after the beginning of Act V, Antipholus and his Dromio reappear, although they left the stage only a short while before, at the end of the preceding Act. From this Greg concluded that Act division in the Folio was inserted by the editors in the process of printing. Given the correspondence of the *actio continua* and the 'continuous action', Greg's argument appears to be really without force. He failed to realize, for example, that at the end of Act IV in the **Amphitruo** comedy Amphitruo falls to the ground and continues to lie there until the beginning of Act V. Similar occasions can be found in French classical drama, and in the division between Acts III and IV of *A Midsummer Night's Dream* the Folio has the famous stage direction that the lovers should 'sleepe all the Act'. We must therefore conclude that continuous action and Act division need not be mutually exclusive, as long as the interval between the Acts remains short.

The second misunderstanding is the notion that the exposition of a drama is complete only after *all* the characters have been introduced to the audience. Snuggs, who takes this view, thinks that in **Menaechmi** the exposition ends *after* the first appearance of the traveller twin in II, i, so that he considers the Act division before the end of the first scene of Act II unjustified. Snuggs and others do not seem to have read carefully enough the Evanthian definition of *protasis,* according to which, as we shall see, part of the action is withheld from the audience in order to create suspense. Besides, the very Prologue to a play like **Menaechmi** mentions the arrival of the traveller Menaechmus so that there is no need to regard the exposition as extending to II, 1.

As far as **Menaechmi** and **Amphitruo** are concerned, the Act divisions do on the whole make good sense in that they coincide with the various stages of the plot development and agree with the Evanthian and Donatian definitions of the structure of comedy. . . . The first Act of both **Menaechmi** and **Amphitruo** contains the exposition, although not all the characters have been introduced yet. The action of **Menaechmi,** which consists mainly of confusions of identity, starts with the beginning of Act II, when the other twin arrives only to be taken for Menaechmus E by the Cook and Erotium. The third Act forms a unit of its own, since the Parasite, having returned from the Forum in disappointment, mistakes the identity of Menaechmus S and therefore begins to plan his revenge on his Patron. It is very interesting that the beginning of each new Act appears to be emphasized by the entry of a *new* character. If Acts II and III started with an emphatic beginning in the first appearance of Menaechmus S and the return of the Parasite, the fourth Act is again set off as a separate entity by the very first entry of the Matrona, who immediately joins in the revenge of the Parasite. This revenge, carried out as an intrigue, then forms the dramatic focus of Act IV. Act V of **Menaechmi** is exceptional in so far as here the confusions continue right into the *anagnorisis*. In any case, this final Act presents a new phase of the play's dramatic development, especially in the appearance of the Senex as an entirely new character. In **Menaechmi,** the dramatist succeeds in maintaining dramatic suspense right until the end, not least by means of the appearance of a new character in each Act (even if in Act III the new character is only the maid of the Courtesan).

In a perceptive article ['Zur Komposition von Plautus' "Menaechmi",' *RhM* 114, 1971] W. Steidle has shown that scene III, i should be regarded as the pivotal centre of the whole play. This scene consists of Peniculus's soliloquy, which he delivers returning from the Forum in disappointment about his missed lunch. Here it can be seen that Plautus is a master of symmetrical structure. The soliloquy is symmetrically flanked on each side by two scenes of mistaken identity—the two scenes preceding III, i, (in II, ii Menaechmus S is mistaken by the Cook and in II, iii by Erotium) and the two scenes following it (in these he is taken for his brother by Peniculus and Erotium's maid). Steidle also points out that the two scenes next to the pivot, namely II, iii and III, ii, are the more important ones.

The Act structure of **Amphitruo** presents a surprisingly comparable picture. The exposition in Act I is followed by the beginning of the complications in Act II with the return of the real Amphitruo, and the Act then focuses on Alcumena's despair. Scene III, i is again the pivot of the play: Jupiter enters as the 'stage director' of his own play and informs the audience of what he intends to do in order to make sure that the play ends like a proper comedy. This soliloquy is then flanked by two scenes resembling each other, since they are both dominated by Alcumena. All these Acts are marked by an emphatic beginning with the appearance of an important character: Act IV, for example, begins with the return of the real Amphitruo, who finds himself locked out of his own house. Jupiter, who has come from the house in order to face Amphitruo, at the end of the same Act exits into the house with thunder and lightning, whereupon Amphitruo falls to the ground. After Jupiter's theophany, Act V starts by bringing the truth gradually to light. The answer to the question of what the individual Acts contribute to the development of the action is simply: dramatic intensification.

Some interesting connections between Plautus's technique of paralleling and contrasting and Shakespeare's use of the same devices have been pointed out above all by H.F. Brooks [in 'Themes and Structures in "The Comedy of Errors",' in *Early Shakespeare,* Stratford-upon-Avon Studies 3, 1961], and it is unnecessary to repeat his findings. Instead, we shall concentrate here on the fact that Shakespeare's use of symmetry and Act division should be seen in close relation to the Plautine **Menaechmi** and **Amphitruo**. Just as Plautus makes scene III, i the centre of his comedies, so does Shakespeare. In III, i of *Errors,* the real husband Antipholus E is locked out of his own house, and this produces a splendid major climax in the long series of confusions beginning as early as Act I. Whereas in **Menaechmi** Peniculus in a soliloquy complains about having been tricked out of a meal he had been promised, in Shakespeare the real husband returns home to have his meal, only to be locked out by his own wife. The soliloquy is replaced by a brilliant dramatic scene, which ironically anticipates the final 'gossips' feast'. Yet the symmetrical structure bears an astonishing resemblance to that of **Menaechmi**. Just as the central scene in the latter play is flanked by scenes which have important features in common, so in *Errors* the scenes next to the pivotal centre III, i are related to each other by a thematic similarity, although at first sight this is perhaps less clearly noticeable than in **Menaechmi**. If in III, ii Antipholus S voices feelings of possessive love towards Luciana, then this was in a way 'triggered off' in II, ii by Adriana, when she articulated her possessive desire for him as her supposed husband. Furthermore, at the end of Act III Antipholus S comes very close to meeting his twin brother; he, as it were, just fails to find him by the 14 lines which are exchanged between Angelo, the Second Merchant and the Officer. Interestingly enough, at the end of Act III of **Menaechmi**, too, the twins likewise miss each other by a

few moments—the 12 lines by which Menaechmus E comes too late.

Although surprisingly close links between the structural symmetry in Plautus and Shakespeare have emerged, we have to bear in mind Brooks's sound warning which he expressed when he discussed the balanced groupings of characters, namely 'that one and the same feature commonly has antecedents in more than one tradition', and especially in the Moralities and Interludes. This is quite true, although the authors of these plays were 'humanists' themselves and may owe to classical drama more than is usually recognized. We remember that . . . , for example, the comic subplot of *Cambises* reflects quite clearly the atmosphere of Plautine comedy.

There can be no doubt that the structural correspondences between *Errors* and **Menaechmi** are anything but accidental. Over and above these, however, there is the dramaturgic similarity of Act division. Shakespeare employs the same technique of marking the beginning of a new Act by the appearance of a new character. After the exposition has been presented in Act I, a new tone is set by the first appearance of the two sisters Adriana and Luciana. At the beginning of III, i the denizen Antipholus makes his first, delayed entrance. At the opening of Act IV, we encounter the second merchant as a new character, and the Act reaches its climax in the only situation in which Dr Pinch is seen on stage. Act V opens with characters we already know, but before long a final new character, Aemilia, makes her entrance as the important *dea ex machina*.

Shakespeare not only emphasizes the beginning of most Acts in *Errors* by a new character, he also concludes Acts II to IV by means of deliberately parallel situations, a fact which was remarked by Baldwin. He shows that at the end of each of these Acts Antipholus soliloquizes about the effects of witchcraft, to which he attributes his predicament, and declares that he wishes to leave the city as soon as possible. The effect of this concluding situation is reinforced by a final couplet. (Only the two concluding lines of Antipholus S in Act IV are exceptional in that they do not form a rhyming couplet.) These parallel endings make a strong impact of their own in a performance; with them, Shakespeare achieves a rhythm which makes the audience aware of the great movements of the plot, each of which marks an intensification of the confusions of the major characters.

It is now clear that in *Errors* Shakespeare adopted the structural convention of Act division, and evidence from elsewhere in his dramatic work points in the same direction. Apart from the four appearances of the Chorus in *Henry V* and *Pericles,* this evidence is very strong in *The Tempest,* where the Act divisions are generally believed to derive from Shakespeare's own hand. Here he begins Act V with the same characters who have just left the stage. There can, then, be no serious doubt that, when Shakespeare studied the Plautine **Menaechmi** and **Amphitruo**, he became directly acquainted with the five-Act convention. Since most editions of Plautus, too, had Act divisions, there is no need whatsoever to follow Baldwin's curious view that, in order to study this convention, Shakespeare had to turn to Terence. . . . [In] a good number of his later plays he employed the convention and . . . he adopted it in some of his tragedies as well. G.K. Hunter is, I think, right in claiming that in this respect New Comedy was more influential than Senecan tragedy. However, Hunter concludes that the ultimate authority behind Elizabethan Act division was Terence because he, rather than Seneca, was the major author studied in the Grammar Schools ['Seneca and the Elizabethans: a case-study in "influence",' in *Dramatic Identities and the Cultural Tradition. Critical Essays by G.K. Hunter,* 1978]. Although this is true, it must be objected that what really counts is not what the immature schoolboy studied at school but what the adult dramatist took as his model; in England, as we have seen, the dramatists in most cases preferred to follow Plautus in the art of play-writing. However, Hunter's attempt to argue in favour of Act pauses on the Elizabethan stage is convincing and confirms our own results. In any case, the view [expressed by M. Mincoff in 'Shakespeare's Comedies and the Five-Act Structure', *Bulletin de la Faculté des Lettres de Strasbourg* 63, 1965] that the 'theory of the five-act structure is largely a red herring' should at last be discarded.

ASINARIA

David Konstan   (essay date 1978)

SOURCE: "Plot and Theme in Plautus' *Asinaria,*" in *The Classical Journal,* Vol. 73, No. 3, February-March, 1978, pp. 215-21.

[*Here, Konstan examines the theme of materialism and its corrosive effect on morality in the* Asinaria.]

Four-fifths the way through the play, the plot of Plautus' *Asinaria* takes a sudden and surprising turn. Briefly, what happens is this. Argyrippus, the young lover in the comedy, is madly infatuated with a *meretrix,* a harlot, whose name is Philaenium. Unfortunately, there is also a rival called Diabolus, who plans to hire the girl exclusively for himself for an entire year. To forestall him, Argyrippus has to produce the sum of twenty minae before Diabolus can, and thereby preempt the contract. He himself is destitute. At the beginning of the drama we discover that his father, Demaenetus, has learned all about the affair and the role of Libanus, a household slave, in abetting it. Libanus is in a state of great anxiety, since he expects to be sent to the mills, but Demaenetus is at pains to calm him down. "Listen to me," he says. "Why should I want to do a thing like that? Why should I threaten you just because you kept me in ignorance? And really, why should I get angry with my son, the way other fathers do?" (46-50). Demaenetus has, of course, answered his own question.

Roman fathers typically disapproved of such liaisons, which could prove both costly and embarrassing. At all events, this was certainly the comic stereotype, and Demaenetus is a character in a comedy. When Libanus replies, "Now this is something new, isn't it?" (quid istuc novi est? 50) he would seem to be bearing a message from Plautus to notice a novel departure from the familiar pattern. Demaenetus soon expounds his philosophy: "All parents, Libanus, if they will hear me out, will indulge their children, and will treat their sons with sympathy and friendship. This is what I try to do, I want to be loved by mine. I want to be like my father, who dressed up like a merchant for my sake and managed to steal the woman I was in love with from her pimp. And he wasn't ashamed in spite of his age to play tricks like that and buy me, his own son, with his kindness. I've decided to follow in the ways of my father. Just today my boy Argyrippus begged me for the money he needed for this romance, and I want passionately to help him out. I want to be loved for helping him, I want him to love his father" (65 77). For all his good intentions, however, Demaenetus is not in a position to grant his son the money, for it is his well-endowed wife—this expression is meant, for once, in the literal sense—who controls the purse-strings. As Demaenetus himself puts it, "I took the money, and for a dowry I sold my authority" (argentum accepi, dote imperium vendidi, 87). She, moreover, keeps her son neatly under control, he observes, "as fathers normally do" (79). Therefore he enlists Libanus and Leonida, another slave, to find a way to defraud his wife, Artemona, of the twenty minae so that Argyrippus may have his girl.

This basic information is presented in the first scene, which takes up a little over a hundred lines. Most of what follows simply exhibits the situation of Argyrippus and the rival Diabolus, and dramatizes the intrigue by which Demaenetus and the slaves obtain the money. Then, suddenly, at line 735, without warning, without so much as a hint to prepare the audience, comes the startling development which I mentioned at the beginning of this paper: Libanus and Leonida, on the point of granting the silver to Argyrippus, mention a stipulation which Demaenetus has imposed, that he have the privilege of a night, that very night with Philaenium. Argyrippus suffers agonies of jealousy, but at last Artemona is summoned on stage by the enraged Diabolus to witness her husband's debauchery, whereupon she unceremoniously drives the old lecher home, leaving Argyrippus in sole possession of his paramour. Two questions immediately suggest themselves. The first is, how did Plautus motivate so extraordinary a transition from Demaenetus' sympathetic support for his son's affair to the sordid competition with which the play concludes? The second question is, why?

I believe that the first step toward understanding the transition is to recognize that the change in the character of Demaenetus, which appears as the critical discontinuity in the play, is in fact a secondary phenomenon, a function of an alteration in the plot. In the first scene of the *Asinaria,* Plautus planted certain expectations for how the story would unfold. The expectations are based on the audience's familiarity with the standard paradigms of plot forms in ancient comedy. Toward the end of the play, he switched from one paradigm to another. This entailed some adjustments in characterization, and also left visible seams at the critical juncture. I shall indicate the chief anomalies presently, but first I should like to describe or classify the basic story patterns which Plautus made use of in the *Asinaria,* in order to show what the sequence is.

The most common paradigm in classical comedy is based on a simple triangle involving a father, a son, and a girl. The son is torn between passion for the girl who is, at least to all appearances, ineligible as a partner in marriage, and fear of his father, a stern *paterfamilias* of the old school. It is a familiar story: Plautus used it in several comedies, the **Cistellaria,** for instance, and it informs practically all of Terence's plays. Frequently, the dilemma is resolved by means of a recognition scene, in which the girl is revealed to be a legitimate citizen, whom the son may marry with the blessing of his father. Stories of this type, in general, are predicated upon the supposition of a fundamental tension between the personal desires, on one side, and, on the other, the social restraints or conventions by which the community is defined and preserved. The social rule is: citizens may marry only citizens. Love, however, pays no regard to such prohibitions. Because this moral tension between youthful passion and social responsibility, as represented by the father, is the basis of the type I am discussing, I have called it the ethical paradigm. The *Asinaria,* as we have seen, opens with an evocation of this type: the confrontation between the deceived and irate *senex* and the clever and intriguing slave belongs to the denouement of such plays, like the **Mostellaria** and the **Epidicus,** for example. However, no sooner does Plautus suggest the ethical paradigm than he dismisses it, as Libanus shrewdly observes, for a different pattern. I shall now attempt to analyze this new form.

Plautus' most successful story type is based on the competition between two rival lovers for a single girl. This type, familiar from the **Miles Gloriosus** and the **Pseudolus,** is built essentially on the struggle between two contending factions or parties. On one side are the supporters of young lover, on the other the satellites, parasites, cooks and other hangers-on of the rival. The rival himself is generally a stranger, a foreign soldier, for example. He is full of bombast but not powerless: either he already owns the girl or he is in a position to purchase her, in which case the procurer is his natural ally. Against such an enemy the lover requires guile, and the cooperation of loyal friends and advisers. No moral inhibitions operate here: the problem is essentially one of strategy. In plays of this sort the *senex* may have the role of an indulgent, humane and even libertarian figure who encourages the intrigues of the lover, rather than that of the severe and conservative father in the ethical paradigm. The urbane Periplectomenus in the **Miles Gloriosus,** Callipho in the **Pseudolus,** and Micio in Terence's *Adelphoe* are representatives of this figure, which, I believe, deserves a general name: I call it the avuncular role. Not that the relationship is necessarily that of uncle, of course; in the **Pseudolus,** Callipho is merely a friend of the family. In the *Asinaria,* Demaenetus appears to have doffed the usual patriarchal

persona for the part of the sympathetic elder of this second paradigm, to assist Argyrippus against the superior resources of his rival, Diabolus. Yet it is extraordinary, even unique, that a *paterfamilias* should assume this role.

There is yet another crucial difference between the situation in the *Asinaria* and the usual type of the rival play. The deception by which the *meretrix* will be won has for its victim not the rival himself or the procurer, but Artemona, Demaenetus' own wife. This brings the dimension of ethical conflict right back into the play, albeit in a distorted form. As we have seen, Artemona, by virtue of the large dowry she controls, has actually been playing the role of the *paterfamilias,* while Demaenetus has been reduced to a status of dependency. Demaenetus' position is essentially like that of the young lover in the first paradigm I described, who struggles against the restrictions of traditional authority, although there is this difference, that Demaenetus' passion is so far vicarious. This circumstance necessarily casts some suspicion on the character of Demaenetus' sympathy for his son. He is not simply a hip old gentleman lending a helping hand to a passionate adolescent. His desire for the boy's affection in place of respect is tarnished, because he does not have the title to respect: he sold it, as he confesses. This situation really presents two problems, not just one. The first is that Argyrippus must win his girl; the second is that Demaenetus must be put in his place, which means not only that his deception of Artemona must be exposed—this would merely leave Demaenetus where he was to begin with—but that he must somehow reassume his proper position in the household. The surprising conclusion to the *Asinaria* is designed precisely to accomplish both these objectives simultaneously.

At the risk of trying the reader's patience, I must now describe still a third plot paradigm, one which Plautus employs in the **Mercator** and **Casina.** This one is essentially a blend of the first two, the ethical and rival types, for in it the father is cast as the rival to the son. It may be useful to consider it this way. In the first plot type, the father is the obstacle to the son's affair, while in the second type, the obstacle, or "blocking character," in the language of Northrop Frye, is the rival. In the third or hybrid form, the father as rival is the obstacle to the son. But the passionate *paterfamilias* has an obstacle of his own in the person of his wife, from whom he must conceal the intrigue. Thus the wife becomes a natural ally of the son. The exposure, or threatened exposure, of the old man's infatuation simultaneously restores him to his family and leaves the field of love to the boy. Despite a certain indelicacy inherent in this plot form, it actually achieves a splendid reconciliation of passion and duty. The success of the son's affair is contingent upon restoring the moral integrity of the father.

It will now have been perceived that the sudden turn toward the end of the *Asinaria* may be described as a shift into the third paradigm. In many ways, it is an excellent move. The tension between husband and wife, which is a basic feature of this type, had been built into the initial conditions of the play, because of Demaenetus' resentment of Artemona. Best of all, it solves at one stroke the problem of Argyrippus, who triumphs over Diabolus and then in turn over his father, and also the matter of Demaenetus' abdication of his paternal responsibilities: he must now, according to the conventions of this story, mend his ways and take up his proper position in his house. To be sure, Artemona still has her dowry, if we wish to be sticklers on the point. But Demaenetus' weakness was in any case really a moral fault. His humiliation is intended to bring him to his senses, and make him play the role, at least, of a Roman head of household.

Nevertheless, so abrupt a switch in the story form was bound to leave its mark on the text. We can see the signs of strain in the way the intrigue develops. Saurea, the chief steward of Artemona, has sold some asses to a dealer (from whom the play apparently derives its name) at a price of twenty minae, and the dealer has sent a young man to render payment. Leonida meets the man in a barber shop, catches wind of his purpose, and pretends at once to be Saurea. Leonida then rushes home, enjoins Libanus to fall in with the ruse, and the two together put on elaborate act to induce the merchant boy to deposit the money with them. This action takes up a shade less than a third of the entire play. Nevertheless, it comes utterly to naught. The boy will surrender the silver to no one but Demaenetus, who is the only member of the household he knows by sight. The slaves pursue him from the stage. Then, after a brief interlude, Libanus and Leonida return. They engage for a while in comic banter, which Libanus at last cuts short with the remark, "Enough of this, answer what I ask you." "What would you like to know?" replies Leonida. Libanus gets right to the point: "Do you have the twenty minae?" "You're a prophet," answers Leonida. "As a matter of fact, old Demaenetus was as tricky as could be. It was hilarious the way he went along with the game that I was Saurea. I could hardly keep from laughing, when he hollered at the poor foreigner because he wouldn't trust me in his absence. He never once forgot to call me Saurea the steward" (578-584). It is easy to see the awkwardness here. If the merchant will pay the money only to Demaenetus, why do the two slaves go to such trouble to impersonate Saurea? Why not just take him straightway to Demaenetus and be done with it? As it is, a great portion of the drama is sacrificed to a useless action, while the twenty minae are acquired in an offstage transaction, effortlessly and without deceit. Finally, there is no point whatsoever to Demaenetus' connivance in his slave's imposture. He has only to receive the money in his own name; Artemona's steward has nothing to do with it. Clearly, there is patchwork here, and the seams are showing. I do not wish to speculate about Plautus' methods of composition, whether he freely invented certain episodes in the *Asinaria,* or welded together two Greek originals, or found the contamination of the plot already present in his model. I have no doubt, however, that at some time a joint was made. The reason for it, moreover, is obvious. Throughout most of the play—so long as it conforms to the simple rival paradigm—all that is required is that Libanus and Leonida obtain the money intended for Saurea, who was responsible for the sale of the asses, and then make it over to Argyrippus so that he may anticipate Diabolus and hire

the harlot. But to effect the transition to the concluding paradigm, in which the father appears as the rival, Demaenetus has to be the actual possessor of the silver. Only thus is he in the position to attach the cruel stipulation to his gift to Argyrippus. Accordingly, he was made the direct recipient of the twenty minae, despite the dramatic and perhaps also ethical improprieties that this entailed.

Up to now I have been examining how the transformation in the plot of the *Asinaria* works. I should like to conclude by suggesting briefly what it means. To be sure, it may be there for its own sake, as an ingenious new combination of the standard forms, although at the cost of a serious dislocation in the plot. But the sequence of paradigms which I have described is not without significance. Demaenetus is presented to us at first as a man who has voluntarily given up his claim on the filial piety of his son—and that was a powerful obligation in Rome—and in its place established the ideal of a bond of pure affection. But, as we have seen, there is also something sham about Demaenetus' philosophy. He sold his authority in the home. The avuncular role is only a disguise. The truth is, a *paterfamilias* has abandoned or been driven from his position as guardian and representative of the Roman moral tradition, and is now guided wholly by sentiment. But there is nothing to prevent his uninhibited feelings from fastening on the paramour of his son. This is in the nature of passion: it is indifferent to social customs and constraints. And when this happens, the sentimental bond with his son dissolves. All that remains is selfish desire. In a pathetic and rather touching scene between Demaenetus and Argyrippus in the presence of the girl Philaenium, the father insists upon his privilege. Argyrippus professes to be moved by *pietas* (831). This is a stroke of Plautine irony: it is not the duty of a son to promote his father's debaucheries. Demaenetus then appeals to Argyrippus' affections: "I don't want to be feared," he whines, "I want to be loved" (835). Nevertheless, Argyrippus is unable to conceal his anguish. At last, Demaenetus bares his teeth: "Put up with this one day," he orders; "I gave you the power to have her for a year, it was I provided the lover with his money." Argyrippus' answer is revealing: "Yes, that's what you bound me to you with" (em istoc me facto tibi devinxti, 849). The father who sold his right to respect now relies on the naked power of cash to bend his son to his will. Thematically, then, this scene recapitulates the movement of the drama as a whole.

There is a scene earlier in the play between Philaenium and her mother—also her procuress—Cleareta, by name, which is analogous to the confrontation between Argyrippus and Demaenetus. Cleareta accuses the girl of defying her mother's authority (imperium, 505, 509) by yielding to her love for Argyrippus rather than respecting her mother's orders as filial piety requires. The dialogue here is plainly a parody of the commonplace comic situation in which the tension between youthful infatuation and parental authority is exhibited. It is unusual, however, in two respects. First, the lover is not a young man but a woman, and a prostitute at that. Second, and more important, Cleareta's appeal to her daughter's sense of duty has nothing to do with the communal norms of behavior; she objects to the irregular liaison only when it brings no profit. The ethical content of the *pietas* (509) or filial duty which she demands is wholly perverted. Philaenium is for her mother no more than an instrument of her avarice. To cloak this exploitation in the guise of filial virtue is an ironic travesty of the moral basis of relations in the family. The entire scene is a comic exposé of the materialistic abuse of conventional values, from Cleareta's opening demand for reverence to Philaenium's closing words: "Mother, you have raised an obedient daughter" (544).

Cleareta has made no secret of her materialism. A long scene between her and Diabolus is devoted to the expression of her acquisitiveness, which she defends as a matter of principle against Diabolus' appeal for gratitude and fairness (Act 1, Scene 3). The image of corrupt and selfish authority is represented also in two other scenes in the *Asinaria,* and in both the source of power is money. When Leonida masquerades as Saurea, in his attempt to inveigle the merchant's boy out of the twenty minae, he affects a blustering rage, in order to display his high position in the household and thus impose upon the boy to render up the money, if for no other reason than out of pity for the cringing and whining Libanus (371 ff.). The humor of Leonida's despotic posturing perhaps derives in part from parody or inversion of the strict and repressive discipline of the Roman family. But his arbitrary and violent imperiousness is wholly different from the moral ideal of *patria potestas*. Saurea's status in the household is, we may recall, a reflection of that of his mistress, and thus rests ultimately upon the power of her dowry. We may perhaps, then, understand the caricature of Saurea as another example of the corrosive effect of money on the natural order of the household, as the Romans perceived it.

After Libanus and Leonida have obtained the twenty minae, through the intervention of Demaenetus himself, as I have mentioned above, there follows a saucy burlesque in which the two slaves subject Argyrippus and Philaenium to outrageous indignities. They force embraces from the girl, piggy-back rides from her lover, and demand to be beseeched by both as the very gods of Providence and Salvation, before they consent to surrender the silver (Act 3, Scene 3). There is perhaps no better example in Roman comedy of sheer Saturnalian perversity, the elevation of the slave and humiliation of the master. Again, the only motive for this grovelling is cash.

The theme of materialism pervades the play. Where money is the basis of authority, customary moral restraints are swept away. This effect is exhibited in the first instance in Demaenetus' sentimental or vicarious attachment to his son's love affair. We, the audience, may have been seduced for a while into sympathizing with the decadence of Demaenetus, because his liberal attitude seemed to offer a reprieve from the oppressiveness of patriarchal authority. Argyrippus would have an ally in his father. But we are compelled by the development of the plot, by the switch to the final paradigm, to acknowledge the necessity of

traditional ethical restraints. Without them, the family becomes a shambles, and the son, free of his father's moral control, must now face him as a rival governed solely by naked self-interest. Sentimentality is revealed as a cloak for materialism. At the heart of the problem is the moral disorder introduced into the household by the abuses of the dowry system, about which Plautus expressed his concern also in the *Aulularia*. The *Asinaria* is thus more than a clever variation on comic paradigms; it is also a defense of the ethical structure of the ancient patriarchal family against the corruption of money and passion, and reflects the profound moral conservatism of its author.

AULULARIA

David Konstan   (essay date 1983)

SOURCE: "*Aulularia*: City-State and Individual," in *Roman Comedy,* Cornell, 1983, pp. 33-46.

[*In the essay below, Konstan discusses "the theme of avarice and the romantic theme" in the* Aulularia.]

In the characteristic story-type of new comedy, a young man's passionate infatuation with a girl who is ineligible for marriage is fulfilled in a respectable way through a turn in the plot—a recognition scene, for example—which reveals the maiden's citizen status. It is discovered, then, that the wayward passion had all along aspired to a permissible object, and the original tension turns out to be illusory. In plays of this type, the prohibited passion drives outward beyond the limits of the community. Love fastens in its willful way upon a stranger, and thereby threatens to violate the exclusiveness by which the community is defined. But a special class of stories, relatively rare in new comedy, looks not so much to urges that push across the boundary as to figures who withdraw into isolation from their fellow citizens. These are the tales of the misanthrope and the misogynist, the miser and the prude. Their challenge to the community manifests itself as a secession, rather than as the pursuit of a forbidden relationship. Characters of this sort bear a certain affinity to the stern fathers who are typically the obstacle to love. By his withdrawal from society the misanthrope or miser may for example block a romantic alliance involving his daughter. Nevertheless, the differences between the two types are essential. In the amatory plays the "blocking characters" prevent or oppose the romantic union, but they do so as representatives of the claims of marriage, that is, of legitimate social communion. The recognition scene is an essential part of a plot of this kind because it permits the fulfillment both of the erotic impulse and of the social requirement of marriage among citizens, which had seemed to be opposed in their demands. The misanthrope and the miser, on the contrary, have themselves severed their ties with society. It is they who will not marry or allow their

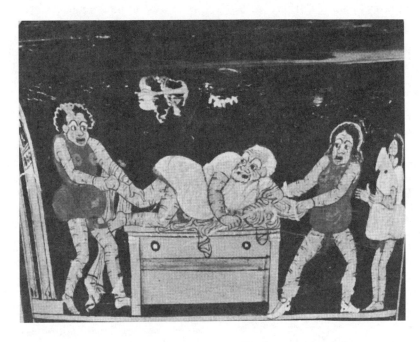

Vase painting of a scene used by Plautus in Aulularia:
thieves pull a miser off his money chest.

daughters to marry, they who will not engage in commerce with their fellows which is the right use of wealth. Consumed as they are by a private passion, they are more akin to the lover than they are to the conventional morality of the blocking character. Where the lover threatens to defy the boundaries of the community, the miser and the misanthrope dissolve its inner bonds and encyst themselves within society as internal exiles. They cannot be brought back into society by a dramatic coincidence or revelation. They must rather be made to realize the insufficiency of their isolation, so that they turn back of their own will to the community of men. Hence such plays depend essentially upon a change in character. The recusant foregoes his specious autarky, recognizes his insufficiency and the insufficiency of the ideal or symbol which he had made the sole object of his desire, whether it is the miser's gold or the misanthrope's virtue and sincerity. In a word, he gives up his fetish, which, from the point of view of community, consists in the worship of an abstract value at the expense of the social relationship that its function is to mediate. This paradigm defines the general form of Plautus's comedy, the *Aulularia*.

E. J. Thomas begins the introduction to his commentary on this play: "The *Aulularia* stands alone among the comedies of Plautus as a character piece." He continues: "The character of the miser is developed in connexion with a simple plot dealing with middle-class life, but it is the picture of the avaricious Euclio that gives unity to the whole" [E. J. Thomas, ed., *T. Macci Plauti Aulularia,* 1913]. I shall begin my analysis of the *Aulularia* by undoing its apparent unity to reveal the separate strands, woven together to compose a plot that in fact is double or complex. The initial conditions of the drama are these. Euclio has discovered buried in his hearth a pot of gold, which his grandfather had concealed, and with it his native stinginess grows into a grand passion. The Lar—the household deity who speaks the prologue and gives the mise-en-scène, explains that he has revealed the treasure so that Euclio may arrange a proper marriage for his daughter Phaedria, whose generosity and devotion have touched the god. The Lar also relates that the unfortunate Phaedria has been raped. The offender is Lyconides, the nephew of Euclio's wealthy neighbor Megadorus. Finally, the Lar declares that, to induce Lyconides to marry Phaedria, he will inspire Megadorus to propose to the girl himself. The prologue thus introduces two distinct components of the story, which for convenience I call the theme of avarice and the romantic theme. The discovery of the gold and the violation of the miser's daughter are not logically related events. Only the intention of the Lar that the gold be used as a dowry for Phaedria (27) brings the themes together at this point.

In the first act, Plautus exhibits the character of the miser and the significance of his obsession as a withdrawal from social life. The action neatly lays bare the difference between the miser's passion for his gold and ordinary acquisitiveness or parsimony, which the Romans regarded as a virtue. Despite a paranoid anxiety for his gold, Euclio is obliged to leave it unguarded while he goes to the forum to receive a handout which the head of his *curia* or political unit has advertised. Now, Euclio does not want the dole, inasmuch as his trip to the forum puts his treasure in jeopardy, but he fears that if he did not go out to get it, the danger would be worse, since others would suspect him of harboring some hidden wealth. Because his hoard is secret, Euclio is caught in a double bind: If he stays home with his pot of gold, he may arouse the curiosity of his neighbors, so he must, however reluctantly, engage in public life in order to keep up appearances. All of the miser's social activity is a sham—even commerce or, as here, a petition for a free bequest. The miser wishes not to make money but to have it, and to keep it out of social circulation. The irony in Euclio's behavior is that, in his obsession with his gold, he would reject, if he dared, even the minimal public commitment involved in receiving a donation.

Before he sets out, Euclio torments his old servant, Staphyla, with suspiciousness and orders her to extinguish the fire in his hearth, lest anyone enter his house with the purpose of borrowing a light (91-92). Perhaps he is particularly worried about the fire because the pot of gold, as we have noted, was buried in the fireplace. Nevertheless, the quenching of the hearth fire in Greece and Rome, as in all communities before the invention of matches, was a serious matter. More than this, Euclio also orders Staphyla to deny that she has any water. Now, the symbol of banishment in Rome was the *aquae et ignis interdictio,* the prohibition on the lending of water and fire. Fixated on his private treasure, Euclio has in effect estranged his society from himself. The scene abounds in farcical humor, and Euclio extends his interdiction to knives, hatches, mortars and pestles, and jugs of any kind. But the elements of parody or exaggeration do not conceal Euclio's attempt, in abolishing the commerce in fire and water which define symbolically the mutual ties of community, to exile the whole community from himself.

The romantic theme is brought to the foreground in the second act, in which Megadorus bids and wins consent for the hand of Phaedria from her father Euclio. In anticipation of the wedding, Megadorus arranges for a troupe of slaves and retainers to prepare the festivities. Congrio, a cook, is dispatched to Euclio's house, because the old miser is too niggardly to provide for his daughter's marriage celebration. Euclio himself, who has been out shopping but has found everything too expensive except some incense and flowers, returns to find his house wide open and Congrio hollering for a larger pot (end of Act II).

"Pot" is all the miser hears, and he rushes in to drive the poor cook from his house under a storm of blows. Suspicious of Megadorus and everyone else, he decides at last to remove the pot of gold from the house and conceal it in the temple of Fides, good faith (end of Act III). While Euclio is in the temple, a slave of Lyconides marches on stage. He has been sent to reconnoiter the wedding preparations on behalf of his master, who, he tells us, is in love with Phaedria (603). Plautus does not explain Lyconides' sudden feeling for the girl he raped nine months before. Presumably he is anxious lest, thus violated, she should become his uncle's wife, and Megadorus's interest in her may also have awakened a slumbering passion of his own. The Greek original, if it at all resembled Plautus's play at this point, may have accounted more clearly for Lyconides' change of heart. However this may be, Lyconides' slave is on hand to overhear Euclio's injunction to Fides to preserve his gold. With a vow of his own to Fides, the slave enters the temple to search out the gold, but is violently driven out by Euclio, whom the cry of a crow had sent scurrying back to check on his treasure. Euclio thoroughly frisks and abuses the slave, who in fact is empty-handed. He then reenters the temple, repossesses his pot of gold and, charging that Fides has not kept faith and that it took a crow to save him, announces that he will hide it outside the city walls in a thick and lonely grove of Silvanus, the woodland god, whom he trusts more than Faith herself (674-76). Lyconides' slave, quite angry now and determined to cheat the miser of his gold, has been eavesdropping. He beats Euclio to the grove, conceals himself in a tree where he can watch the old man bury the gold, digs it up himself, and steals home with it. The next words we hear are Euclio's after he discovers his loss: "I'm dead, finished and done for" (713).

As to the plot alone, the concealment of the gold twice, first in the temple of Fides and then in the grove of Silvanus, is plainly a doublet, a redundant repetition of a single act. Lyconides' slave could as well have found the gold in his first attempt. But to the theme of the play, the pairing of the actions is crucial. It is in the character of the miser, we have said, to exempt himself from the bonds of community. For the Romans, the spirit of these bonds was represented above all in the concept of *fides,* which variously meant good faith, trustworthiness, and, most concretely, the warranty on a pledge. *Fides* was the basis of all contracts, the soul of all honest exchange. From this spirit of collective good faith, Euclio withdraws his confidence. We must observe that, despite Euclio's ingratitude, his gold had been kept safe in the temple of Fides. The miser's trust did not betray him; he thought more of a crow's cackle than the personified force of social ties and rejected the good faith of his community. Instead he went beyond the city walls, which for the Romans especially represented the sacred boundary of the civilized community where law and honor reigned, and trusted his gold to the uncultivated precinct of a god of the wilderness. Euclio has deliberately and explicitly abandoned the city and committed himself to the chance concern of nature. And there, outside the city, he is treated like the outcast he has made himself. Beyond the rule of Fides, his gold is appropriated by cunning and theft. There is no injustice here: Having withdrawn from society, the miser endures the fate of the stranger.

Thematically, then, the theft of the miser's gold is a function of secession from society. At the same time, it exposes his lack of self-sufficiency and establishes the conditions under which he may elect to be reintegrated into the community, and thus to satisfy the dramatic demands of comedy. To return to the romantic component of the plot, the rape of Phaedria represents exactly the same kind of assault on Euclio as the stealing of his treasure. The twin principle upon which citizenship was constituted in ancient Rome was the *ius connubii et commercii,* the right of marriage and of commerce. These two rights have in common that both are based upon the sanctity of the contract and therefore rest upon the communal principle of good faith. Outside the citizen community, the rule of violence, of *vis et violentia,* holds sway, except where special agreements may be mutually recognized. Where the *ius commercii,* the right of commerce, is abrogated, there robbery, a relationship of force alone, prevails. Similarly, rape is the mode of sexual appropriation where the right of marriage, the *ius connubii,* ceases to prevail. Because of his withdrawal, the miser is no longer sheltered under the laws of the community. Despite the absence of a causal connection between Euclio's obsession with his pot of gold and the rape of Phaedria, thematically the two facts are intimately related: The rape is the expression in the sphere of sex of the miser's isolation, just as the theft is its expression in the sphere of property. The rape and the theft are all the closer, in that women were not in Roman society so far removed from other forms of property. Phaedria's dishonor is thus her father's loss.

The love story is advanced through the proposal of Megadorus which, for reasons that Plautus's version does not make very clear, kindles or rekindles in Lyconides the desire for Phaedria. After his change of heart, Lyconides tells his mother, Eunomia, of the rape, and begs her to intercede with her brother Megadorus, who apparently retracts his offer of marriage: He is not seen again in our text. In this brief scene of nineteen lines (682-700), Phaedria is heard offstage to cry out in the agony of her labor pangs, and Lyconides wonders out loud where his slave might be, possibly a reminder of the connection between the theft and the rape. In the following scene, the slave appears with the stolen pot of gold, and in the next, Euclio bursts in with the vehement lament over his loss. Lyconides hears the howling, recognizes Euclio, and concludes that he has found out about the birth of Phaedria's baby (729). After a moment's hesitation, he decides to confess outright to the crime. An extraordinary exchange for some twenty-five lines follows, in which Euclio mistakenly believes that Lyconides has admitted to the theft of his gold. Without giving details of the misunderstanding, which accommodates even Lyconides' plea that love (*amor,* 745) was the cause of his offense, we note that the scene demonstrates the essential equivalence, from Euclio's point of view, of the rape and the robbery. Both are violations of his proprietary rights.

When Euclio at last dispels the ambiguity with an explicit mention of his pot of gold (763), Lyconides vigorously disclaims any part or knowledge of the theft. Then, just when he has persuaded Euclio of his innocence he discloses the rape. Finally, he mollifies the old miser, who by now is utterly overwhelmed, by reaffirming his wish to marry the girl, which the laws require (793), and he assures Euclio that thanks to him the old man can attend the wedding as a grandfather.

From this point on, the play moves into the phase of reintegration. Lyconides learns what has happened to the gold from his slave, who expects a liberal reward but instead is ordered to return it to Euclio. Thus, the recovery of the treasure too is predicated upon Lyconides' change of heart, which was poorly motivated if we look only to the plot. Thematically, however, it is exactly right, and probably Plautus's dramatic instinct assured him it would work. For having refused the mutual exchange which is the basis of the communal bond, the miser has been humbled. He has been dealt with as an outsider, plundered and stripped without regard to the laws of fair dealing which he himself had set aside by hoarding, which only those who give and take may invoke. He has learned the lesson of his insufficiency, the same way Menander's misanthrope discovers his need of others when he falls down a well. In accord with the comic convention, he can now rejoin society, renew the rites of exchange that define the group. In a stroke, the violation of Phaedria and the plunder of the gold are undone. Made wiser by his losses, Euclio is once more granted the chance of giving his daughter in marriage, and of using the gold as was intended, for a dowry. In the dowry, in fact, are symbolized and joined both terms of the *ius connubii et commercii.* In the relations of the community, the dowry is the exemplary use of wealth, for it represents the exchange of kin and property on which the solidarity of the several clans, of the society as a whole, is based. The giving of the dowry, Euclio's ultimate assent to the mutuality of the communal bond, must have been the culminating action of the *Aulularia.* Unfortunately, the conclusion to the final act has not survived. Nevertheless, we may be quite certain about the disposition of the treasure. We know the Lar's intention in the prologue; the last line of an acrostic argument prefixed to the play reports the transfer of the gold; and finally, a fragment of our play preserved by the grammarian Nonius and undoubtedly to be attributed to Euclio reads: "Night or day I was never at rest. Now I shall sleep." The miser's hoard is at last restored to use, its abstract value is reembodied in the practical relations of social life.

I turn now to the discussion of Megadorus; no treatment of the *Aulularia* can be complete without an analysis of his role, which brings out some of the most complex and challenging aspects of its theme. Back in the second act, after Euclio's initial scenes with his servant, Lyconides' mother, Eunomia, appeals to her brother Megadorus to take a wife. Nothing in particular motivates her intervention, but we sense the influence of the Lar. When Megadorus learns what she wants, he replies: "Aii! I'm dead!" (150). Megadorus may at once be recognized as a type:

the inveterate bachelor, rich and contented with his lot, and loath to undertake either the responsibilities or the expense of a wife and family, like Micio in Terence's *Adelphoe.* Megadorus thus stands aloof from one of the bonds of community and neglects the obligation to continue his line (cf. 147-48). He does confess, however, to a special passion for Phaedria, despite her poverty, and declares his intention to ask Euclio for her hand. Because Megadorus was already infatuated with Phaedria before Eunomia's intervention, her advice to her brother serves no function in the plot, but again is a significant contribution to the theme. The dialogue between Eunomia and Megadorus underscores that Megadorus's interest is not in marriage as such, but has its source solely in desire. In terms of popular Roman psychology, he is motivated by irrational passion rather than by customary duty which, as Eunomia makes clear, would enjoin him to contract an advantageous alliance. Megadorus's desire thus resembles that of the young lover in the amatory plots—so characteristic of ancient comedy—to which we referred earlier. In those stories the erotic impulse usually attaches itself to an object outside the limits of the community. The same is true of Megadorus's passion, for Phaedria, because she has been raped, is according to the conventional taboo in ancient comedy ineligible to marry anyone but the man who assaulted her, and so she is removed beyond that circle of potential kin which defines the boundary of society. As we know, when Megadorus learns of the rape he will repudiate her. On the most general level, the stigma on Phaedria may be regarded as a sign of Euclio's voluntary withdrawal from social relations which is implicit in the fetish of his secret hoard. Of course, Megadorus is in complete ignorance of both the rape and the pot of gold. But his motive, which is erotic rather than connubial, and the relationship he is prepared to establish not between members of a common group but as a personal tie beyond communal sanctions, are reflected in the circumstances that Euclio and Phaedria are of an inferior social order, and that Megadorus, whose name literally means "Great-Gift," is willing to remit the dowry.

When Megadorus approaches Euclio, the old miser immediately suspects him of being after his gold. He distractedly mumbles threats to his servant; when Megadorus asks him what he is grumbling about, he claims it is his poverty that prevents him for want of a dowry from marrying off his daughter (190-92). The connection here is overt between the hoarding of wealth and the denial of conjugality, the double abrogation of the *ius connubii et commercii* which isolates the miser. After a further display of Euclio's paranoid antics, Megadorus makes his proposal. Euclio, who has all along been leery of this untoward regard of a rich man for a poor one, at first accuses Megadorus of mocking him. Assured of his neighbor's earnestness, he laboriously expounds his concern that for a poor man to join himself to a rich is like an ass consorting with bulls: His own order will reject him, and Megadorus's will never accept him, the asses will tear him with their teeth while the bulls will attack him with their horns (226-35). Euclio's analogy between the different orders and different biological species points to the extreme separation of social classes in Plautus's Rome, whether or not

the language goes back to the Greek original of the *Aulularia.* The wealthy and the poor constitute distinct communities within the society, not to be crossed by ties of marriage. Euclio then stipulates that there will be no dowry, lest Megadorus imagine that he has found some hidden treasure, as he says (240), and at last the nuptial agreement is struck, even though Euclio's fears are not altogether allayed.

If we look to the theme of the *Aulularia,* clearly Megadorus's proposal cannot possibly resolve the tensions of the play. If the miser is to be reintegrated into society, his treasure must be revealed and put to use in an exchange that confirms the communal bonds among families. Thus the dowry is crucial, and for Megadorus to waive it is to block the redemption of Euclio and leave him estranged by his obsession. That marriage to Megadorus is no solution is made all the clearer by Phaedria's pregnancy, which Staphyla proceeds to lament. To put it another way, marrying off Phaedria without a dowry is no better than giving her away to a total stranger. This point is developed at considerable length in acts II and III of the *Trinummus,* where the young, impoverished Lesbonicus expresses his anxiety to his friend Lysiteles that "they will spread the report that I have given my sister to you in concubinage, rather than in marriage, if I give her without a dowry" (689-91). The dowry is the sign of the communal sanction. Without it, marriage is not a bond but an appropriation. We have seen that Megadorus's offer is prompted by an erotic impulse rather than by a sense of civic obligation, and that his class is socially discrete from hers. In the plot as a whole, Megadorus's involvement is not so much the cause of Lyconides' reversal as a foil to it. Where Lyconides is in a position to convert the rape of Phaedria to marriage and the stolen gold to a dowry, Megadorus can do neither. He reaches out but cannot mend the breach created by Euclio's self-imposed exile. The class distinction between Megadorus and Euclio only mimics the separation between the miser and his fellows and may thus be regarded thematically as a metaphor for Euclio's isolation. Structurally, Megadorus's appeal across the barrier of class is only another manifestation of Euclio's being beyond the pale, as the erotic nature of Megadorus's attraction also suggests, and thus at bottom his proposal but reiterates the theme, albeit in a more gentle way, of the rape and the theft. Megadorus's proposal, then, is not the answer; it is rather another aspect of the problem of the play.

In the context of the play's dominant theme, the difference in order between Megadorus and Euclio may be interpreted as a representation of Euclio's estrangement from society. Once it has been introduced, however, Plautus takes up the theme of class distinctions and develops it for its own value. We have already noticed indications of its seriousness in the first interview between Megadorus and Euclio. After Euclio drives Congrio the cook from his house, a scene occurs with Megadorus and the miser in which many critics have seen the hand of Plautus himself at work. Sandwiched between Euclio's hostile complaints against his neighbor's suspected machinations (462, 551ff.), Megadorus delivers a soliloquy, overheard and heartily endorsed by Euclio, on the faults of the dowry system and the manners of contemporary women. Megadorus makes the following points: Dowries are the cause of discord between and among the social orders (481); they contribute also to the prodigality of women, who regard the money they bring into a marriage as their own to spend on luxuries as they choose (498-502); and finally, as a corollary of the preceding, women are becoming, thanks to the dowry, freer of the authority of their husbands (534). Scholars have in fact arrived at an approximate date for Plautus's *Aulularia* by interpreting this speech of Megadorus as a protest against the repeal of the *lex Oppia* in 195 B.C., which regulated the sumptuary expenses of women. The most important feature of Megadorus's soliloquy, however, is that this intrusive condemnation of dowries and above all of their corrosive effect on the solidarity and harmony of the community runs exactly counter to the role of the dowry in the entire play. We have to do here with an independent set piece, in which the divisive social forces are represented not as the withdrawal of the individual householder from a community of equals, but as a general disintegration of social ties consequent upon the corruption of the dowry system by the qualitative but unequal increment in the wealth of the citizen body. The contrast may be put more pointedly: The extravagance of the aristocracy is precisely the opposite of the miser's retentiveness. To be sure, these contrary causes have a like effect, the weakening of the conjugal bond. But in the one case, this enfeeblement is due, as Plautus sees it, to the growing independence of moneyed matrons, whose subservience may be restored by the abolition of the dowry, while in the case of the miser the dowry is the substantial symbol of the communal relationship. What Plautus has added to the *Aulularia,* if indeed the scene is his own invention, is a piece of social criticism which violates the thematic coherence of the drama.

Yet on the deepest level Plautus's inclusion of Megadorus's complaint may not be misguided. After all, the archetypal story of the miser is, like all archetypes, abstracted from the realities of social life. The miser's gold is not real wealth, it is a pure symbol. Euclio's grandfather never bought a thing with it, but buried it, as he thought, for all time in the earth from which it had come. No more is the miser's withdrawal from society an expression of true autarky or power. In his helpless isolation, he is easily brought low and as easily regenerated. His is a docile defiance, perfectly suited to a moral tale exalting the ideology of community. No such character ever seriously threatened the solidarity of society. But what, then, is the real danger which the miser represents, and which is imaginatively overcome in the reconciliation with which the comedy must end? At the heart of the miser's nature is the priority he assigns to money over the actual human relationships with other members of his community. In the creation of the mythic imagination, this character worships the inert form of gold, as may in real life occur with the pathological personality. But the truly destructive manifestation of this spirit is not miserliness but materialism, which dissolves the ties of traditional obligation and restraint and leaves in their place the naked aspiration to wealth and power. The ostentatious spending of the aris-

tocracy and the weakening of the marriage relationship are early symptoms of this spirit. The dowry was its victim: It ceased to be the material token of the communal identity of the clans, and became mere money. In this aspect, the dowry was a sign not of social integration but of fragmentation, both within the aristocracy and between the orders. In attacking it, Plautus did what the comic temper and the ultimate theme of the *Aulularia* itself demanded. He disdained the consistency of the formal idea of the dowry and reaffirmed the claims of community against the real centrifugal tendencies of his day.

MOSTELLARIA

Dana F. Sutton (essay date 1993)

SOURCE: "Plautus and the Nature of Roman Comedy," in *Ancient Comedy: The War of the Generations,* Twayne Publishers, 1993, pp. 55-108.

[*In the excerpt below, Sutton offers two differing interpretive approaches to the* Mostellaria: *psychological and social.*]

Mostellaria (*The Haunted House*) is based on the play *Phasma* (*The Ghost*) by the New Comedy poet Philemon. It begins with an acrimonious scene between two slaves, Grumio and Tranio, belonging to a master named Theopropides. Grumio is a slave from his rural estates, while Tranio works in his city home. Grumio is highly indignant because in the master's absence Tranio has been squandering his goods. Worse yet, he has been corrupting their master's son Philolaches, egging him on in his career of riotous living: drunk all the time, feasting, supporting parasites, buying slave girls their freedom, in general carrying on with his cronies like so many Greeks (22 and 64). He predicts dire consequences for Tranio, enumerating some of the punishments that await him, such as being dragged off to the country and placed on a labor gang, or even crucifixion. Tranio responds to this grumpy onslaught with *sang-froid*. All this drinking, loving, and whoring is his own affair. He is risking his own neck, not Grumio's. Come to think of it, Grumio, you reek of garlic, you stinking clodhopper. Aren't there some cows that need tending back on the farm? He sweeps off, leaving Grumio expostulating. Theopropides has been gone three years, and he hopes the master will return before all his estate is sent to rack and ruin.

The comic introduction consisting of a dialogue between slaves is a traditional device, found as early as such Aristophanic plays as *The Knights* and *The Wasps*. This one accomplishes more than informing the audience about the narrative's background and introducing the important character Tranio. It also limns the basic polarity that organizes the whole play. It plays off hedonism against the work ethic and the fun-loving against the dour, and if Grumio can scarcely be said to be an authority figure, he certainly is free in invoking authority's machinery of punishment in support of his values. Plautus firmly locates the former values and kinds of people in the city and the latter in the countryside.

Tranio exits and Philolaches enters, immediately launching into a remarkable extended address to the audience (84ff.). He's been thinking things over and has come to the conclusion that a man is very like a building. Even if its builder constructs it carefully, when its occupants neglect its upkeep it will deteriorate and finally collapse. Same with himself. He received a careful upbringing, but fell into profligate ways. Now his money, his credit, reputation, virtue, and prestige are shot to hell. "I don't seem to be able to repair my house before the whole thing falls down in total ruin, foundation and all, and nobody can help me. I'm heartsick when I see what I am now and what I used to be" (147-9). His conclusion: "I'm good for nothing, and I see I've been made this way by my own inner nature" (156). The boy is well aware that he is doing wrong, but admits that he is helpless to resist because he is bound to obey the imperatives of his innate nature or character (*ingenium*).

This soliloquy, however, leads nowhere. Philolaches may be aware of his shortcomings but, perhaps because he is using his final conclusion as an excuse, he is really unrepentant and has no intention of reforming. And even by the end of the play there is no indication that he will change his profligate ways.

Next follows a long scene in which Philolaches' girl friend Philematum converses with her maidservant Scapha with Philolaches overhearing and offering a running commentary. Scapha is urging Philematum to take a cynical attitude and spread her favors around, but Philolaches has purchased Philematum's freedom and so she feels she must show her gratitude by remaining loyal to the boy. Philolaches, overhearing, is thrilled. A couple of his remarks deserve to be singled out. When Philematum and Scapha are discussing the need for her financial support, Philolaches exclaims that he will sell his father into slavery before he will see her impoverished (229f.). When the girl expresses her gratitude to him, he goes even further (233f.): "would that my father's death would be reported to me right now, so that I might disinherit myself and make her his heir!" Here we have the same son's hope touched upon (in characteristically inverted form) by Philocleon near the end of *The Wasps,* that the father's death will leave the son with sufficient money to lavish on his love affairs.

After this scene is over, a boon blade named Callidamates comes reeling drunkenly up to Philolaches' house, accompanied by his own mistress. After a little byplay he unabashedly collapses on a handy couch and passes out. Thus ends Act I.

Act II begins on a very much more agitated note. Tranio bursts in and, in horror, announces some catastrophic news to the audience: he has just seen old man Theopropides down at the harbor. All is lost! He himself is bound for

ruin. Anybody in the audience want to be paid to be crucified in his place? Guess not. Philolaches appears, hears the news, and is reduced to a helpless state of shock. Callidamates had better be woken up and removed. When he has been shaken awake, he sits up and cheerfully offers to murder the old man (384). The offer is refused and he is hustled into the house.

Faced with Philolaches' panicky despair, Tranio takes charge. He has a plan, whereby Theopropides will not only refuse to enter the house but will also flee far away. The only thing Philolaches and his friends have to do is shut themselves up inside and not make a sound. They should all place their trust in him: a tricky business like this needs the management of an experienced man, a man who can make everything turn out right without landing himself in the soup (408ff.).

The preparations are quickly made and Theopropides soon appears. His first words are a prayer of gratitude to Neptune for sparing his life during his voyage. Tranio, overhearing, offers his own running commentary: "By god, Neptune, you've made a huge mistake, missing such a grand opportunity" (438f.). Theopropides imagines his homecoming will be welcome. Again, Tranio: "By heaven, the man who came to announce your death would be a great deal more welcome!" (442f.). Then the two men confront each other. The old man wants to go in the house, but Tranio reacts with horror. He spins a complicated and fantastic story about how in Theopropides' absence it was discovered that the house is haunted because of a murder once having been committed in it. Therefore the house has been boarded up. This fiction manages to play on Theopropides' superstitious side, and he is quickly infected by Tranio's spurious sense of dread, much to the slave's secret delight.

So far, so good, but when comic deceptions of this sort are woven, unforeseen complications are bound to arise that all but ruin the deceiver's scheme. In the present instance, an indignant moneylender named Misargyrides unexpectedly turns up demanding repayment for all the money he has lent Philolaches. Theopropides is puzzled by this, especially when he learns of the enormous debt that his son has run up. When Tranio urges him to settle the debt, he asks the inevitable embarrassing question: for what purpose was the money borrowed? On the spur of the moment, Tranio comes up with the answer that Philolaches borrowed it to raise the down payment on a new house. After all, since the old one proved to be haunted, a new one was necessary. Theopropides is pleased by this sensible purchase, but asks another inevitable and equally awkward question: precisely where is this house? For he would very much like to inspect it.

Tranio is once more thrown back on his inventive resources. In desperation he points to the house of their next-door neighbor. Theopropides naturally wants to go inside, provoking yet another crisis. Fortunately Tranio is able to stall Theopropides by saying that the women within must have the chance to get ready for the entry, and so the old man is hustled off the stage long enough for Tranio to collect his wits.

By a stroke of good luck, at this point the owner of the house next door appears. This is Simo, another old man but cut from entirely different cloth than Theopropides. We first meet him sneaking out of his house. His wife has given him a wonderful lunch and now wants him to go to bed. So he is going off to the Forum. From the insistence with which this issue of his going to bed is mentioned throughout his monologue and his extreme repugnance at the idea, it is evident that he is really avoiding her sexual advances: "the old hag wanted to drag me off to the bedroom!" (696). Tranio overhears and commiserates. But then he has a bright idea and engages Simo in conversation. The old man asks if the usual goings-on are still happening in the house, and he adds that he thoroughly approves: "indulge yourself—think how short life is" (724f.).

Tranio reveals the terrible news of Theopropides' return, and Simo sympathizes. He immediately recognizes the danger facing Tranio. First he will receive a whipping. Then irons await him, and finally the cross (743f.). The slave pretends to be terror-stricken, falling at Simo's knees and begging for help. Then he launches into another of his lies. Theopropides has decided to add women's quarters to his house, looking forward to the time his son marries. His architect greatly admires Simo's house and has proposed it as a model. Would it be possible for Theopropides to inspect the building? Simo genially agrees.

So Tranio goes to fetch Theopropides. As he crosses the stage from the one house to the other, he delivers himself of a crowing monologue in which he brags about his control over these two old men. "Muleteers have their pack-mules, but I have pack-men, and they're really laden down—they'll carry whatever you load 'em with" (780-2). As he escorts Theopropides back across the stage he carefully prepares him. That old gentleman you see is the individual who sold the house to Philolaches. Now he deeply regrets having done so. This bit of misinformation allows Tranio to glide over some rough spots. For example, when Simo cheerfully invites Theopropides to look the house over "as if it were your own," Theopropides naturally asks Tranio what this "as if" is about, and Tranio is able to explain that away in terms of Simo's alleged regret over its sale.

In the course of the house inspection, Tranio solemnly points out a picture in the portico. The two old men cannot see it, so the slave is so good as to describe it (832ff.): a crow stands between two vultures and is pecking at the both of them in turns. Since they still can't see it, he is even more specific: "look in my direction, then you'll see the crow—and if you can't make it out, then look in your own direction and perhaps you'll see the vultures" (835ff.).

Act IV begins with a monologue, by Callidamates' philosophical slave Phaniscus (858ff.). He reflects on a slave's lot. Some slaves grow to fear nothing. Then they fall into bad ways and earn nothing but whippings. His own plan is to build his life on the principle of not getting whipped, and therefore he sticks to the good old straight and narrow. After all, a master's only what his slaves make him. If they're good, so is he. If they are rascals, he becomes one himself. In the present instance, all of Callidamates' other slaves were too lazy to go fetch their master, so he is undertaking the task by himself—won't they be in for a scourging when Master returns!

Theopropides and Tranio emerge from Simo's house. Theopropides is overjoyed about the supposed purchase and is eager to pay off the moneylender. No problem, says Tranio; just give me the money and I'll make sure he gets it. When Theopropides gets a bit suspicious, he blandly asks "would I dare play a trick on you in word or deed? . . . Since I came into your service have I ever deceived you?" (924, 926).

Phaniscus and another slave of Callidamates reappear in order to retrieve their master. When they start knocking on the door Theopropides is puzzled and enters into conversation with Phaniscus. They are unaware of Theopropides' identity and so innocently reveal the truth to the old man, informing him of all the loose living that has gone on in the house during his absence and supplying some lurid details of his son's dissipation. And he also reveals that one slave in particular has distinguished himself by his misdeeds, a man named Tranio. Won't Philolaches' father be aghast when he comes home and finds out about all this roistering!

Theopropides indeed is aghast, and matters grow even worse because as soon as Phaniscus disappears Simo arrives and, after some humorous dialogue as they talk at cross-purposes, the two old men compare notes and figure out how they have been swindled by Tranio. At the end of Act IV Theopropides howls that he has been ruined. All he can think of is revenge, so he asks Simo if he can borrow some whips. Genial as ever, Simo agrees.

Act V has to do with the impending punishment of Tranio. When he sees Theopropides standing in front of the house waiting for him, Tranio realizes that the jig is up. Nevertheless he has sufficient confidence in his cleverness that he is not unduly perturbed. He knows that Theopropides has decided to feign ignorance and so he plays along. When the old man innocently informs him that Simo has denied receiving any money for his house, he pretends surprise. Theopropides claims that Simo has agreed to let him have all his slaves in order to be put to the question about the missing money (1086)—yet another reference to the torture of slaves, because this is the only way in which slave testimoney could be taken under Roman law—and so Tranio proposes to help him wait. But as they continue their conversation he sits on a handy altar in mock-innocence. Theopropides, with equally fake innocence, tries to cajole him off the altar, but he politely refuses. Thus, when pretenses are dropped, he is in a place of sanctuary and beyond his master's reach. So when Theopropides begins ranting at him, he can jeer back from a position of security. Theopropides promises condign punishments, but Tranio continues to mock him for the fool he is.

The impasse is broken by the entrance of Callidamates. Newly sober, he has come as a representative of Philolaches and his pals. In the most urbane way he tries to calm Theopropides. At first to no avail: master and slave continue their mutual threats and jeers until Callidamates reveals that Philolaches' friends have managed to scrape together enough money to make a full restitution. This news produces the desired change of attitude. At first Theopropides is reluctant to let Tranio off the hook, but the slave says he is sorry and points out that if his master forgives the crimes he has committed today, then he can doubly punish him for those he will undoubtedly commit tomorrow. Theopropides relents and the play comes to an abrupt end.

It would be possible to imagine a cheerful and straightforward play in which a series of practical jokes are played on a father so that a son might enjoy his ladylove. But *Mostellaria* is not quite that play. Two elements serve to darken and complicate its tone. During the course of the play Theopropides' death is repeatedly hoped for, and this wish is placed in the mouths of no less than three characters. And repeated allusions to crucifixion and the similar horrors that await a disobedient slave serve to raise the stakes by reminding the audience of the very genuine perils involved in Tranio's self-imposed tightrope act. The presence of both of these elements entitle the reader to wonder what precisely is going on.

Mostellaria seems susceptible to two readings, each by itself inadequate, but neither excluding the possibility or diminishing the value of the other. First, one can apply a psychological interpretation. We shall see a distinctly Oedipal undercurrent in *Asinaria* and *Casina,* where sons and fathers are competing for the same woman. In the case of *Mostellaria* and plays with similar plots, it would seem possible to carry the argument a step farther. In *Mostellaria* father and son are scarcely in competition for an erotic object, but one can argue that in any play where a father stands between a son and the fulfillment of his erotic ambitions, and where the father is therefore cast in the role of an obstacle that must be circumvented or defeated, we are really confronted with a plot in which the Oedipal situation is disguised by displacement but is nonetheless hovering in the background.

The usefulness of this suggestion lies in its explanatory power. Such a reading renders fully understandable Philolaches' openly expressed wish for the death of his father, and similar hopes placed in the mouths of Callidamates and Tranio are then seen as the son's wish displaced onto other characters. Furthermore, this suggestion perhaps makes Tranio's motivation more comprehensible.

For one must wonder exactly why Tranio is willing to launch on the complicated and risky business of trying to fool his master, and why he goes about the job with such relish. A partial reason is of course supplied by the speech he makes when he first learns of Theopropides' return (348ff.): in his master's absence he has been playing the rascal and so he has every reason to fear imminent retribution. But when Tranio and Philolaches collide shortly thereafter and he agrees to help the boy (388ff.), this motivation goes unmentioned, and we never hear of it again except when Tranio alludes to it as a device for playing on Simo's sympathies. Certainly, Tranio is not

Zero Mostel, and in view of the popularity of *A Funny Thing Happened on the Way to the Forum* it is worth bearing in mind that the ambition of the clever Plautine slave of the Tranio-Pseudolus type is not usually to gain his manumission. Rather, it appears that Tranio's major motivation is clever deception for the pure joy of it. He seems to act out of the uncomplicated pleasure of demonstrating his intelligence and general superiority and taking advantage of his master's foolish gullibility. Certainly his self-satisfied asides and monologues and his phoney "painting" of the highly symbolic crow and vultures show the fun he has in manipulating and outthinking his supposed betters. Everything he does is calculated to show that he is the better man.

But a psychological reading points to a deeper understanding of such slaves' motivations. In a recent article, Holt Parker has suggested:

> The Plautine *adulescens* is naïve in his monomaniac pursuit of the girl. He has no inhibitions at all, and we in the audience can enjoy vicariously his evil wishes against his father and his ultimate triumph, while protected from guilt by our own sense of superiority. Likewise, the Plautine *servus* is monomaniac in his pursuit of trickery as an end in itself. He too has no inhibitions, and we vicariously enjoy his evil deeds against the father. . . . However, it is the impudent slave who allows the youth to be naïve, by removing the intentionality. It is the slave who acts, plans, intends, does, and so takes on (and takes away) all the guilt that would have fallen on the son.

So, according to a Freudian reduction of the dramatic situation to the level of Oedipal psychodrama, important components of the Oedipal son's personality are displaced onto Tranio. Because of his ridiculous and slavelike nature he is able to translate into action the son's inmost wishes. For a Freudian interpreter, at any rate, a sort of "proof" that such a projection is occurring lies in the fact that Tranio too gives voice to Philolaches' wish that Theopropides might die. Such a psychological understanding that the son's expected intentionality and guilt are not really absent, but are merely displaced, serves to explain the extreme passivity and strange helplessness of Philolaches and similar comic sons.

A notorious characteristic of "clever slave" plays is that this type of slave dominates, and that the upper-class youths on whose behalf they intervene are eternally passive and feckless. This slave is the cleverest, most adventurous, and most dynamic character in the repertoire of New Comedy characters, and his scheming serves to drive the plot. The psychological interpretation proposed here provides a theoretical explanation both of the slaves' dynamism and of the young men's passivity. The element of displacement also makes the play less censorable and more acceptable to the audience.

By the same token, part of the Oedipal son's personality is also displaced onto Callidamates. Like Tranio, he can speak and act in ways that Philolaches cannot. While Philolaches can only wistfully hope for Theopropides' death, Callidamates proposes to translate this desire into bold action. If Tranio embodies the Oedipal son's dynamism, Callidamates represents his aggressive side. This too has the effect of shifting the burden of guilt away from the son. And again, if the audience is protected from feelings of guilt vis-à-vis the slave Tranio out of a sense of superiority, Callidamates' extreme drunkenness serves to engender a similar sense in the spectator.

This interpretation of Tranio's function renders explicable one of the play's most striking peculiarities, the complete disappearance of Philolaches before the play is even half over. Tranio volunteers to help Philolaches even though the boy does not ask for his assistance, and Philolaches places himself completely in the slave's hands. His exit line in this scene (407) consists of the significant words "I place myself and my hopes in your custody, Tranio." Then he vanishes.

In accordance with comic convention, the play must end with a reconciliation. Since *Mostellaria* is about a boy's rebellion against his father, one would predict that Philolaches would appear again at play's end, and that the essential reconciliation to be effected would be that of Philolaches and Theopropides. Rather remarkably, therefore, the reconciliation achieved in Act V is between Tranio, Callidamates, and Theopropides. Philolaches, to be sure, is mentioned, but he does not appear, and the final resolution of the play consists of Theopropides' at least temporary forgiveness of Tranio. If we are to think that on a deep psychological level Tranio and Callidamates embody the Oedipal son's dynamic and aggressive side, then the inner logic of the play's reconciliation becomes comprehensible. Indeed, according to this logic, a reconciliation that merely occurred between father and son would not be fully satisfactory since this would not embrace a reconciliation between the father and the son's more aggressive aspects, personified by other characters.

One might expect that the conclusion of the play would feature some sort of change of heart in Philolaches that would resolve the issue of his awareness of his malfeasances expressed in the monologue delivered as we first meet him. This long speech contains at least the germ of a repentant attitude, which Plautus could have built upon later in the play. As it stands, the monologue is really only a kind of red herring: it is a sign pointing nowhere, and it raises expectations that are left unfulfilled. As the play stands this speech (perhaps inherited from Plautus' Greek original) is its main weakness. It seems intrusive, and Plautus might have been well advised if he had eliminated it.

The same kind of psychologizing interpretation also helps one understand another of the play's most salient features. The audience is constantly reminded that Theopropides has at his disposal whips, crosses, and all the machinery for meting out authoritarian punishment. Although he never gets to use this machinery (by the rules of comedy, it would be unthinkable for him to do so), this steady barrage of allusions has the effect of adding an element of tension and menace to the situation and of reminding the audience of serious and consequential issues lurking in the background. Such allusions raise two questions. Why is the issue belabored in such a programmatic way? Also, these threats serve to remind us of the armory of punishment and repressive violence available to a truly authoritarian father. And yet at the same time they establish a problematic contrast between the figure of such a terrifying father and the weak simpleton who actually embodies fatherhood in the play. Why did Plautus adopt this strategy?

The answers to these questions cannot be fully answered until we turn to a second way of reading *Mostellaria,* which employs social rather than psychological insights. Nevertheless, according to a psychological reading we can understand at least one component of Plautus' intentions in loading this play with so many allusions to the condign punishment of slaves. If Tranio is a kind of son-surrogate embodying the Oedipal son's dynamism and aggression, then surely such threatened violence equally represents the Oedipal son's guilt-induced dread of paternal retribution. Having these punishments hang over Tranio has the effect of shifting the anxiety as well as the guilt away from the son-figure in the play: it is notable that Theopropides, who has every reason in the world to be irate at Philolaches, never issues any especially dire threats against him. The audience is invited to laugh at these threats in their transmuted and comical guise: comical because the audience knows full well that they will not be put into effect, and because they hang over a character toward whom the spectator is invited to adopt an attitude of superiority.

Theopropides is not characterized as especially austere or as pathologically authoritarian, and so is not a figure of great menace. Rather, his salient qualities are stupidity, gullibility, silly superstition, and weakness, and throughout the play he is humiliated and reduced to a figure of fun as his powerlessness is revealed to the spectator. The object here is obviously to deflate the prestige of fatherhood. It may not be entirely amiss to suggest that, just as the more dynamic aspects of the Oedipal son's personality are shifted onto Tranio, so some of the Oedipal father's grim and austere characteristics are transferred to the slave Grumio. What is left is a silly, impotent old man.

Seen from one point of view, Simo is another of those young-at-heart old men who remain fun-loving and in touch with the values of Dionysus. But viewed from another angle he is a kind of surrogate figure onto whom have been shifted the attractive features that a father like Theopropides should but does not have. He is an elder man who is tolerant, nonthreatening, and who poses no obstacles to the son and therefore elicits no feelings of guilt. Like Micio in Terence's *Adelphoe,* he therefore stands as a kind of son's fantasy figure of what an ideal father might be like and how he could be perceived, if only the whole burden of the Oedipal situation and its attendant feelings of hostility and guilt could be dispensed with.

The analysis of comedy, no less than any other kind of literature, requires some sort of theoretical underpinning. It also requires some sort of agreed-upon discourse. If Aristotle did write a Book II of the *Poetics,* he evidently made catharsis the centerpiece of his discussion of comedy as well as of tragedy. It is easy to see the attraction of this strategy; it is in fact easier than in the case of tragedy insofar as comic psychic catharsis can be correlated with a distinctly cathartic physiological event, laughter. Over the past couple of decades in particular, the idea of the cathartic value of comedy has begun to resurface in critical discussions of ancient comedy, as modern students become increasingly aware of the necessity of some theoretical foundation for their discussions (although one must admit that there exists a wide spectrum of opinions as to what comic catharsis actually is and how it may work).

The idea that the primary function of ancient comedy was to purge the spectator of Oedipal tensions and feelings of guilt, which might be suggested by some of Sigmund Freud's observations on the subject of humor, would be intolerably and absurdly reductionist. But it seems both possible and attractive to argue that such was one kind of catharsis that ancient comedy could provide on occasion. In plays such as *Mostellaria* the Oedipal situation is invoked in more or less disguised, but nevertheless penetrable, forms and its associated hostilities are ventilated. The situation is presented as seen through the son's eyes, so that the son and his allies are represented favorably and the father and his supporters are not. The father is bamboozled, defeated, subjected to various outrages, if not by his son, then at least by the son's allies and surrogates. And so the father (although he is not killed, as some characters have wished) is ultimately shown to be impotent. Divestiture and demystification of paternal power and prestige amount to a kind of symbolic castration. In result, the son achieves his erotic aims. Nonetheless, despite the dark elements provided by the potential violence of paternal authority and the symbolic fulfillment of the wish for the father's death, part and parcel of the plot is a final reconciliation that serves to defuse the situation and eliminate the feelings of guilt and anxiety it has evoked. For, by the invariable rules of the game, the world of comedy is a safe one. This is both because its characters are people to whom the audience is invited to feel superior, and because all of the dangers, threats, and menaces in comedy's world are understood to be spurious and unthreatening.

The insight that both Tranio and Callidamates embody displaced fragments of the Oedipal son's personality serves to render the absence of the son at the play's conclusion comprehensible. The reconciliation between Tranio, Callidamates, and Theopropides, rather than between father and son, has already been discussed. Then too, Plautus helps along the psychological effect of the reconciliation scene by supplying an extra anxiety-reducing detail. At 1149ff. Tranio jeers at Theopropides: "If you are a friend of Diphilus or Philemon, tell them how your slave played a practical joke on you. You would provide them with an excellent example of a baffled man for their comedies." This metadramatic touch, which occurs at an emotionally critical moment, serves to remind the spectator that what he is witnessing is, after all, just a play that need not be taken overseriously.

So, on the psychological level, plays like *Mostellaria* work by evoking Oedipal feelings in the spectator and then purging him of them. But it is doubtful that Freudian analysis by itself tells the whole story, or that *Mostellaria* could be adequately understood by interpreting it as displaced projections of a psychic melodrama. The trouble is that if you adhere rigidly to the Freudian program and place an exclusively Oedipal interpretation on father-son confrontations in Roman comedy, this reading has the effect of pushing off such conflicts into the abstract realm of "the eternal human condition" and thereby depriving them of any sense of immediacy.

For generational conflict is part of the fabric of life. The young envy the power, prestige, and efficacy possessed by their elders, nurturing hopes and dreams of inheriting all of this themselves (presumably not unmixed with complex feelings of aggression and guilt). For them to achieve their personal, economic, social, and professional ambitions, sooner or later their elders must be thrust aside. Or at the very least a "place in the sun" must eventually be negotiated for a younger generation, which involves an element of compromise and yielding on the part of society's seniors. In any male-dominated society, this amounts to a formula for competition and conflict between young men and old men. Within the family context, this means competition and conflict between sons and fathers. The would-be parricide in *The Birds* may be taken as emblematic of this fact. There is nothing visibly Oedipal about him. His stated ambition is purely and simply to inherit his father's property, and there is no reason for doubting his word. With prizes such as prestige, power, and property at stake, the competition for the mother begins to look not so much like an all-powerful, all-determining inner psychic melodrama, but rather (as I have already suggested) like a metaphor for a concrete social reality.

Despite its fictive Greek setting, the actual Romanness of the situation in *Mostellaria* is shown by a number of touches introduced by the author. Thus, for instance, we are thrice told that characters in the play "live like a bunch of Greeks" (22, 64, 960). Tranio speaks of convening a senate in his heart, and also of convening a senate of slaves (688, 1049f.). Simo announces his intention of going to the Forum to dodge his wife (708f.). But the most significant such detail has to do with the punishments threatened to be applied to Tranio. In the absence of any evidence about the Greek prototype of this play, we cannot be sure whether this whole element of slave punishment was at least partially present in Philemon's *Phasma* or whether it has been entirely contributed by Plautus. But we can be sure that, if this element was at all present in his Greek model, Plautus significantly changed and Romanized it. Throughout the play crucifixion is pressed into service as a symbol of the punitive authority of the *paterfamilias,* and crucifixion is of course a distinctively Roman means of punishment. Taken in combination, these considerations suggest a specifically Roman reading of the play. Even though *Mostellaria* has a putatively Greek setting, they are Plautus' means of inviting us to view the play's events as if they were occurring in a Roman social context.

If we are to read the play in this manner, its events acquire a specific and somewhat different meaning. Viewed in this light, *Mostellaria* tells the story of a rebellion within the *familia*. Philolaches may be a free son and Tranio a slave but, each in his own way, both are supposed to be bound by *familia* discipline and to display upward-directed obedience and loyalty toward the *paterfamilias*. Besides ignoring his duty of *pietas*, Philolaches is guilty of a second serious infraction of *familia* discipline. He squanders family property for his own dubious purposes, thereby placing his own interests ahead of the collective welfare of the *familia*. On the other hand, he does not commit a second possible breach of *pietas*. Roman sons were supposed to submit to arranged marriages contracted for the advancement of the *familia*, and inappropriate self-chosen love matches were out of the question. In *Mostellaria* it is never said that Philolaches' ambition is to marry his girlfriend. But in other plays similarly disloyal sons indeed are guilty of this form of disloyalty, although a frequent part of inevitable final reconciliations is that such girlfriends are ultimately discovered to be not as inappropriate choices as they first seem.

Ostensibly Philolaches, always egged on by Tranio, is rebelling against the constraints of *pietas* out of sheer hedonism, and from this limited standpoint Mommsen's harsh judgement of comic values is not entirely unjustified. But on a deeper level, Philolaches' real malfeasance is that he is flying the Jolly Roger of individualism. He has placed his own values and interests ahead of the welfare of the *familia*, and in this sense it scarcely matters exactly what these values and interests are.

According to a Roman interpretation, the comic handling of Theopropides also acquires a different significance. A large part of the play's purpose is to lampoon a *paterfamilias*. Various tactics are adopted to achieve this. When Theopropides is shown to be stupid, gullible, superstitious, and wholly ineffectual, his essential weakness is revealed. Even a lowly slave can outthink him and is a more dynamic and creative human being than himself. There is thus a striking contrast between what a *paterfamilias* is supposed to be and what this father actually is. Furthermore, the steady barrage of references to the machinery of torture, whipping, and crucifixion at the disposal of the *paterfamilias* for the purpose of enforcing *familia* discipline can now be seen to play a significant function. They serve as a sort of baseline whereby we can measure the disparity between the powers theoretically vested in Theopropides and his actual weakness, making the latter appear all the more thoroughgoing.

This is especially so because, on this level, the play does not conclude on any real note of reconciliation. To be sure, *Mostellaria* has a plot resolution sufficient to satisfy the needs of comedy and a reconciliation that is adequate for an emotionally satisfying conclusion. But from the present viewpoint it is striking and significant that the play features a reconciliation between Theopropides, Tranio, and Callidamates, but nothing of the kind between Theopropides and Philolaches. There are no grounds for thinking that a repentant son will mend his ways, abandon his expensive habits, and resume the proper discipline of *pietas* toward his father. And we are given plenty of reason for suspecting that Tranio will continue on his roguish career. And so the play does not end with any kind of recuperation of Theopropides' paternal authority or restoration of *familia* discipline. Rather, the concluding impression is that the erstwhile wholeness of the *familia* has been ruptured permanently—and that this is no bad—or fatal—thing. In this sense, the only genuine reconciliation at the play's conclusion is that Theopropides is obliged to reconcile himself to a changed state of affairs within his household. The success of the rebellion is acknowledged. We [can] see similar endings in the other Plautine comedies . . . , which conclude with a gesture of paternal surrender.

Mostellaria is another play in which the characters fall into two distinct and readily identifiable camps. On one side are the fun-lovers (Philolaches, which is what the name means in Greek, Tranio, Callidamates, with Simo as an ally) and on the other the *paterfamilias* Theopropides and his gloomily harsh slave Grumio, to whom can probably be added the badgering moneylender Misargyrides, since he is a representative of the workaday world and its responsibilities. True to the logic of comedy, the members of the former camp are portrayed as attractive human beings, while those on the agelastic side are represented unsympathetically. This of course helps orient the spectator's feelings: everything about the play invites the audience to sympathize with and cheer for the rebels against *pietas* and to hope for the defeat of the characters ranged against them.

In view of all that has been said, it is obvious that one of *Mostellaria*'s major functions is to exert some sort of cathartic function vis-à-vis the figure of the *paterfamilias*, over and above any kind of cathartic value it may have in connection with the spectator's Oedipal guilts and anxieties. The idea of the play is not just to expose Theopropides as a weak and ineffectual father, but in so doing to mount an attack on the very idea of authoritarian fatherhood.

As intimated earlier, a major function of comic catharsis is a debunking one. The comic poet takes a look at some individual or institution that has the power to intimidate the spectator in real life. More precisely, he establishes a stage-surrogate for that person or institution. Then, by a series of techniques he strips this surrogate of its aura of prestige. Such techniques include exposing the surrogate's actual weakness and consequent hypocrisy and portraying it in a grotesque and unflattering light. The surrogate is thus held up to public humiliation. The spectator is invited to laugh at this surrogate, and the laughter has the value of purging him of some of the awe and intimidation that the surrogate's real-life equivalent inspires, and also invites him to adopt an attitude of superiority to and dislike for the surrogate. The ultimate idea is that something of these attitudes will rub off on the spectator toward the person or thing represented by the surrogate, and that person or thing's prestige and capacity to intimidate will be impaired. Thus comedy has the power to instruct the spectator's feelings toward people and things in the real world.

This kind of comic mechanism can be seen at work in any editorial-page cartoon, and this is the psychological mechanism at work in his plays when Aristophanes lampoons pretentious people and institutions and particularly when he lambastes his enemies. So by invoking the cathartic-deflative machinery of comic ridicule, Plautus is trying to instruct the feelings of the spectator no less than did Aristophanes.

This is why the suggestion deserves to be made that *Mostellaria* be read as a contemporary Roman sociopolitical document. *Mostellaria* does two things that are highly subversive of the *mosmaiorum*. It mounts a comic attack on the figure of the *paterfamilias* and at the same time it suggests an alternative to *pietas,* insinuating that junior members of the *familia* have lives of their own, have their own ambitions to fulfill, and deserve the freedom to pursue them. It also suggests that slaves are interesting and worthwhile human beings in their own right (in some of his other plays Plautus makes the same point about women).

Mostellaria is scarcely an isolated example. A number of other Plautine comedies also seem calculated to undermine the austere and forbidding image of the *paterfamilias*. . . . Some of these more or less resemble *Mostellaria* in that practical jokes are played on a father so that a son may enjoy a ladylove. In several of these, the trickery is achieved by a clever slave of the Tranio type. Such plays are **Bacchides, Epidicus, Pseudolus,** and **Trinummus**. Three Plautine comedies (**Asinaria, Casina,** and **Mercator**) are variants of a different type of father-son conflict, in which father and son are competing for the same sexual object.

FURTHER READING

OVERVIEWS AND GENERAL STUDIES

Anderson, William S. *Barbarian Play: Plautus' Roman Comedy.* Toronto: University of Toronto Press, 1993, 184 p.
  Investigates "the special genius of Plautus," which, Anderson claims, rivalled that of his Greek predecessors.

Arnott, W. Geoffrey. "Plautus and Terence." In his *Menander, Plautus, Terence,* pp. 28-62. Oxford: Clarendon Press, 1975.
  Provides a bibliography of Plautus' works in Latin and in English translation; a survey of Plautus' career; and a consideration of his adaptation of Greek plays.

Bruster, Douglas. "Comedy and Control: Shakespeare and the Plautine *Poeta.*" *Comparative Drama* 24, No. 3 (Fall 1990): 217-31.
  Contends that the "controlling playwright figure," a character common to many of Shakespeare's works, is ultimately derived from Plautus' cunning slave, or *poeta.*

Dorey, T. A., and Dudley, Donald R. *Roman Drama.* New York: Basic Books, 1965, 229 p.
  Contains three essays relating to Plautus: "Plautus and His Audience," by Walter R. Chambers; "The Glorious Military," by John Arthur Hanson; and "The Amphitryo Theme," by C. D. N. Costa.

Hall, F. W. "Repetitions and Obsessions in Plautus." *Classical Quarterly* XX (January 1926): 20-6.
  Explores the significance of Plautus' "constantly repeating himself, often verbatim" within and among various plays.

Handley, E. W. *Menander and Plautus: A Study in Comparison.* London: H. K. Lewis & Co., 1968, 23 p.
  Assesses Plautus' debt to his Greek predecessor.

Kent, Roland G. "Variety and Monotony in Plautine Plots." *Philological Quarterly* II, No. 3 (July 1923): 164-72.
  Compares the plots of plays by Plautus to ones by Menander and Terence, finding those of Plautus to be the most varied.

Ryder, K. C. "The *Senex Amator* in Plautus." *Greece and Rome* XXXI, No. 2 (October 1984): 181-89.
  Examines the figure of the *senex amator*—the passionate old man—in several of Plautus' comedies.

Slater, Niall W. *Plautus in Performance: The Theatre of the Mind.* Princeton, N.J.; Princeton University Press, 1985, 190 p.
  Attempts to reconstruct both the initial performances of, and original audiences for, Plautus's plays.

Zagagi, Netta. "Tradition and Originality in Plautus: Studies of the Amatory Motifs in Plautine Comedy." *Hypomnemata* 62 (1980): 1-159.
  Assesses the extent to which Plautus is indebted to his Greek models for the depiction of love in his works.

AMPHITRUO

Forehand, Walter E. "Irony in Plautus' *Amphitruo.*" *American Journal of Philology* XCII, No. 4368 (October 1971): 633-51.
  Examines the play "with respect to the matrix of ironies found within its language and plot" and notes "the implications of these ironies for our view of the play as a whole."

ASINARIA

Lowe, J. C. B. "Aspects of Plautus' Originality in the *Asinaria.*" *Classical Quarterly* 42, No. 1 (1992): 152-75.
  Analyzes key scenes from the play in an effort to evaluate Plautus' handling of his Greek models.

BACCHIDES

Goldberg, Sander M. "Act to Action in Plautus' *Bacchides*." *Classical Philology* 85, No. 3 (July 1990): 191-201.

Compares *Bacchides* to its source play, Menander's *Dis Exapaton,* which survives only in fragments. What, according to Goldberg, this comparison shows "is ultimately a matter not so much of different techniques, or even of aesthetic gains and losses, as of fundamental changes in the idea of comic theater."

Owens, William M. "The Third Deception in *Bacchides*: Fides and Plautus' Originality." *American Journal of Philology* 115 (Fall 1994): 381-407.

Argues that *Bacchides* "is about trust and deception, a thematic antithesis which Plautus has characterized in ethnic terms: on the one hand, trust is romanized as *fides*; on the other, deception is characterized as Greek."

CAPTIVI

Lowe, J. C. B. "Prisoners, Guards, and Chains in Plautus, *Captivi*." *American Journal of Philology* 112, No. 1 (Spring 1991): 29-44.

Finds contradictory evidence in the play regarding how Plautus meant the play to be staged.

CASINA

O'Bryhim, Shawn. "The Originality of Plautus' *Casina*."

American Journal of Philology 110, No. 1 (Spring 1989): 81-103.

Demonstrates that "in the *Casina,* Plautus carefully selected portions of two comedies, made major changes in them, blended his own material, and molded the results into a coherent, tightly constructed plot."

MENAECHMI

Levin, Harry. "Two Comedies of Errors." In his *Refractions: Essays in Comparative Literature,* pp. 128-50. New York: Oxford University Press, 1966.

Illustrates the ways in which the comedic techniques Plautus employs in the *Menaechmi* influenced Shakespeare and other playwrights.

MILES GLORIOSUS

Cleary, Vincent J. "*Se Sectari Simiam*: Monkey Business in the *Miles Gloriosus*." *The Classical Journal* 67, No. 1 (October-November 1971): 299-305.

Asserts that the "monkey scene" of Act 2, scene 2, provides a unifying image for the entire comedy.

PERSA

Lowe, J. C. B. "The *Virgo Callida* of Plautus, *Persa*." *Classical Quarterly* 39, No. 2 (1989): 390-99.

Examines the theme of trickery and deception in the play.

Tom Stoppard
1937-

(Born Tomas Straussler.)

INTRODUCTION

Since the mid-1960s Stoppard has been recognized as a leading playwright in contemporary theater. Like George Bernard Shaw and Oscar Wilde, with whom he is often compared, Stoppard examines serious issues within the context of comedy, using such devices as word games and slapstick to address complex questions regarding authority, morality, the existence of God, the nature of art and reality, the supposed progress of science, and other issues. This mixture of the comic and the serious in Stoppard's work has led some to characterize his plays as "philosophical farce." Although some critics argue that Stoppard's theatrical devices mask their lack of real profundity, most praise him for his wit and technical virtuosity.

BIOGRAPHICAL INFORMATION

Stoppard was born in Zlin, in the former Czechoslovakia, the second son of Eugene and Martha Straussler. His father was a doctor employed by the shoe manufacturer Bata, which moved the family to Singapore in 1939. Soon thereafter, just prior to the Japanese invasion of Singapore, Stoppard, his mother, and his brother were evacuated to Darjeeling, India. Dr. Straussler remained behind and was killed in 1941. Five years later Stoppard's mother married Major Kenneth Stoppard, a British army officer stationed in India, and after the war the family moved to England. Stoppard left school at the age of seventeen to become a journalist with the Bristol newspaper the *Western Daily Press.* Two years later he became a freelance journalist and began writing plays. His first work, *A Walk on the Water,* was written in 1960. In the early 1960s, while continuing to work as a journalist—including a stint as drama critic for the short-lived magazine *Scene* in 1963—Stoppard composed radio and televisions plays, the novel *Lord Malquist and Mr. Moon,* and several short stories. He also wrote *Tango*—an adaptation of a play by Slawomir Mrozek—and "The Gamblers." In 1964 Stoppard spent five months in Berlin participating in a colloquium of young playwrights. While there he wrote the one-act verse drama "Rosencrantz and Guildenstern meet King Lear," based on a question his agent had posed whether Lear was king of England during the time period in which Shakespeare's *Hamlet* is set. During the next three years, the work evolved into Stoppard's first major success, *Rosencrantz and Guildenstern Are Dead.* The play opened to near-universal acclaim and Stoppard received several prizes, including the *Evening Standard* Drama Award for most promising playwright and a Tony Award. Stoppard

has continued to write for radio, stage, and screen, winning a *Evening Standard* Drama Award for *Jumpers,* a New York Drama Critics Circle Award for *The Real Thing,* a Tony Award for *Travesties,* and an Olivier Award for *Arcadia.*

MAJOR WORKS

Rosencrantz and Guildenstern Are Dead explores such themes as identity, chance, freedom, and death. It centers on two minor characters from *Hamlet* who, while waiting to act their roles in Shakespeare's tragedy, pass the time by telling jokes and pondering the nature of reality. These two "bit players" in a drama not of their making are bewildered by their predicament and face death as they search for the meaning of their existence. *Rosencrantz and Guildenstern Are Dead* has often been compared with Samuel Beckett's *Waiting for Godot* for its mixture of humor and philosophic speculation on the absurdity of existence. *Jumpers* reinforced Stoppard's reputation as a playwright who flamboyantly examines important questions. In this play, which parodies both modern philosophy and the "thriller" genre, George Moore—a philosopher attempting to prove the existence of God and of moral absolutes—and his wife Dotty—a nightclub singer who believes in the sentimental songs she sings—are stripped of their moral ideals and romantic notions. *Travesties* marked a new development in Stoppard's career: the presentation of detailed political and ethical analysis. This play fictionally depicts Vladimir Ilych Lenin, James Joyce, and Tristan Tzara residing in Zurich during World War I. By juxtaposing the theories of the three men—Lenin's Marxism, Joyce's Modernism, and Tzara's Dadaism—Stoppard offers observations on the purpose and significance of art. Stoppard's next four major works are commonly referred to as his "dissident comedies." *Every Boy Deserves Favour, Professional Foul, Night and Day,* and the two interlocking plays *Dogg's Hamlet, Cahoot's Macbeth* blend themes of art, illusion and reality, marital infidelity, the freedom and responsibility of the press, and the moral implications of political issues. *The Real Thing* examines art, metaphysical concerns, and political commitment, while marking Stoppard's most significant treatment of the theme of love. As with the dissident comedies, *The Real Thing* continues Stoppard's movement toward conventional comedy, de-emphasizing farcical action while increasingly concentrating on witty dialogue and exploring human relationships. *Hapgood* is a comic espionage thriller that employs theories regarding the behavior of subatomic particles to explore uncertainty and the subjective nature of truth. Stoppard's two most recent works, *Arcadia* and *Indian Ink,* both possess structures that divide the action between the historical past and the present. As the scenes set in the present uncover and comment on the scenes set in the past, Stoppard explores the elusiveness of certainty, be it in human relationships, historical events, or knowledge of the universe.

CRITICAL RECEPTION

Many critics rank Stoppard, together with Harold Pinter, at the forefront of contemporary British theater. The 1966 production of *Rosencrantz and Guildenstern Are Dead* was an immediate critical and popular success; when the play premiered in London, Harold Hobson declared it "the most important event in British professional theatre of the last nine years." *Jumpers* and *Travesties* solidified Stoppard's reputation as a major dramatist, as reviewers praised the moral and philosophical complexities presented in these plays, as well as their verbal and visual wit. While generally less well received, Stoppard's dissident comedies nevertheless have been admired for their broadening of the scope of Stoppard's art to include political themes. In *Hapgood* critics have detected a new note of optimism and a movement away from the absurdism of Stoppard's earlier work. Further growth has been observed in the highly acclaimed *The Real Thing,* which has been hailed as the playwright's most personal and autobiographical work and praised for its examination of the power of love. *Arcadia* has been judged a theatrical *tour de force* for its fusion of science, philosophy, and human emotion. Vincent Canby has pronounced it Stoppard's "richest, most ravishing comedy to date." Since 1966, Stoppard's theater has evolved from depicting the absurd view of existence

to presenting artistic and philosophical attacks on absurdity. The political positions of his plays have moved from detachment to a commitment to personal and artistic freedom, while Stoppard's dominant theatrical mode has varied from farce to romantic comedy. Throughout these changes in Stoppard's career, critics have consistently extolled his wit and brilliant use of language, as well as his technical skill.

PRINCIPAL WORKS

STAGE PLAYS

*A Walk on the Water 1960
"The Gamblers" 1960 [performed 1965]
Rosencrantz and Guildenstern Are Dead 1966
Tango [adaptor; from a play by Slawomir Mrozek] 1966
Enter a Free Man 1968
"The Real Inspector Hound" 1968
"Albert's Bridge" 1969
"If You're Glad I'll Be Frank" 1969
"After Magritte" 1970
"Dogg's Our Pet" 1971
Jumpers 1972
The House of Bernarda Alba [adaptor; from play by Federico Garcia Lorca] 1973
Travesties 1974
Dirty Linen 1976
Every Good Boy Deserves Favour 1977
Night and Day 1978
Dogg's Hamlet, Cahoot's Macbeth 1979
Undiscovered Country [adaptor; from a play by Arthur Schnitzler] 1979
On the Razzle [adaptor; from a play by Johann Nestroy] 1981
The Real Thing 1982
The Love for Three Oranges [adaptor; from an opera by Sergei Prokofiev] 1983
Rough Crossing [adaptor; from a play by Ferenc Molnár] 1984
Dalliance [adaptor; from a play by Schnitzler] 1986
Largo Desolato [adaptor; from a play by Václav Havel] 1986
Hapgood 1988
Arcadia 1993
†*Indian Ink* 1995

RADIO PLAYS

"The Dissolution of Dominic Boot" 1964
"M Is for Moon among Other Things" 1964
A Walk on the Water 1965
"If You're Glad I'll Be Frank" 1966
"Albert's Bridge" 1967
"Where Are They Now?" 1970
Artist Descending a Staircase 1972
The Dog It Was that Died 1982
In the Native State 1991

ment. There we all were, busting a gut with great mono-logues and pyrotechnics, and this extraordinary genius just put this play together with enormous refinement, and then with two completely unprecedented and uncategorizable bursts of architecture in the middle—terrible metaphor—and there it was, theatre! So that was liberating.

It's only too obvious that there's a sort of Godotesque element in *Rosencrantz.* I'm an enormous admirer of Beckett, but if I have to look at my own stuff objectively, I'd say that the Beckett novels show as much as the plays, because there's a Beckett joke which is the funniest joke in the world to me. It appears in various forms but it consists of confident statement followed by immediate refutation by the same voice. It's a constant process of elaborate structure and sudden—and total—dismantlement. In *Travesties,* when John Wood is saying Joyce was this without being that, each sentence radically qualifies the statement before it until he ends up with 'a complex per-sonality'. That sort of Beckettian influence is much more important to me than a mere verbal echo of a line or a parallelism at the end of *Jumpers.* That, if you like, is an open, shy bit of tribute-making, whereas the debt is rather larger than that.

There's an element of coincidence in what's usually called influence. One's appetites and predilections are obviously not unique. They overlap with those of countless other people, one of whom—praise be God—is Samuel Beck-ett. And it's not surprising if there are fifty writers in England who share in some way a predilection for a cer-tain kind of intellectual or verbal humour or conceit which perhaps in some different but recognizable way is one which Beckett likes and uses.

From play to play Beckett's stage directions progressive-ly give less freedom to the director and actors. How do you feel about that?

I think, truth be told, that were there a language one could do it in, like musical notation, I'd like to notate my plays so that there's only one way of doing everything in them. That's not to say that that would produce the best result. I know from past experience that I've been quite wrong about the way things ought to look and how lines ought to be spoken. One ought to be there for the first production and chance the rest. The first production in France of *Rosencrantz* was a nonsense and I haven't been done in France since.

What about T. S. Eliot and Prufrock?

There are certain things written in English which make me feel as a diabetic must feel when the insulin goes in. Pruf-rock and Beckett are the twin syringes of my diet, my arterial system.

How much did you change the text of **Rosencrantz** *after the Edinburgh production?*

I added a scene. Laurence Olivier pointed out that the section in which they're asked by Claudius to go and find

Hamlet after he's killed Polonius ought to be in the play. So I went off and wrote that. Otherwise it's the same. There was one speech that was cut at the National which went back in later, but on the whole the Edinburgh text was shorter.

Is there ever a conflict between literary and theatrical pressures?

I realized quite a long time ago that I was in it because of the theatre rather than because of the literature. I like theatre, I like showbiz, and that's what I'm true to. I really think of the theatre as valuable and I just hope very much that it'll remain like that as an institution. I think it's vital that the theatre is run by people who like showbiz. 'If a thing doesn't work, why is it there in that form?' is rough-ly the philosophy, and I've benefited greatly from Peter Wood's down-to-earth way of telling me, 'Right, I'm sit-ting in J 16, and I don't understand what you're trying to tell me. It's not clear.' There's none of this stuff about 'When Faber and Faber bring it out, I'll be able to read it six times and work it out for myself.' Too late.

What happens in practice is that after a certain number of weeks elapse I can't see the play any more. I've lost my view of it, and I'm at the mercy of anybody who nudges me. That can work to my disadvantage because it can make the play unnecessarily broad, when I should have kept faith with the delicacy of it. At the same time, it's meant that Peter has actually saved the play. The speech in which Joyce justifies his art wasn't in the text of *Trav-esties* that I gave to Peter. It was he who said it was necessary, and I now think it's the most important speech in the play. It's showbiz, but the speech is there because of its place in the argument.

What about Cecily's lecture at the beginning of Act Two? Surely you're not expecting the audience to digest so much information so quickly?

There are several levels going here, and one of them is that what I personally like is the theatre of audacity. I thought, 'Right. We'll have a rollicking first act, and they'll all come back from their gin-and-tonics thinking "Isn't it fun? What a lot of lovely jokes!" And they'll sit down, and this pretty girl will start talking about the theory of Marxism and the theory of capitalism and the theory of value. And the smiles, because they're not prepared for it, will atrophy.' And that to me was like a joke in itself. But the important thing was that I'd ended the first act with what at that stage was a lengthy exposition of Dada. I wanted to begin the second with a corresponding exposi-tion of how Lenin got to Zurich, not in geographical but political terms. I chose to do that from square one by starting from *Das Kapital,* Marxian theory of profit, the-ory of labour, theory of value, and then to slide into the populist movement, the terrorism, Ulyanov's brother and so on. If I could have brought that off, I'd have been prouder of that than anything else I'd ever written. There wasn't a joke in it but I felt I could get away with it because it was going to be a new set—to start with, we weren't going to begin in the library—a new character and a new scene after the interval. I overplayed that hand very badly, and at the first preview I realized that the speech had to be about Lenin only. The second act is Lenin's act really, and I just blue-pencilled everything up to the mention of Lenin. So now it was one page instead of five.

In my original draft I took the Lenin section out of the play far more radically than in the version you saw. I actually stopped the play and had actors coming down to read that entire passage from clipboards or lecterns, because I felt very strongly—and now I believe I was right—that one thing I could not do was to integrate the Lenins into the *Importance* scheme. Irving Wardle said he'd have liked to see Lenin as Miss Prism, but that would have killed the play because of the trivialization. It would have been disastrous to Prismize and Chasublize the Lenins, and I believe that that section saves *Travesties* because I think one's just about *had* that particular Wilde joke at that point. I wanted the play to stop—to give the audience documentary illustration of what Lenin felt about art and so on, and then carry on with the play. Peter Wood's objection was unarguable: the whole thing is within the framework of Carr's memory except this bit. How do you get back people's belief if you interrupt it?

What I was trying was this. What I'm always trying to say is 'Firstly, A. Secondly, minus A.' What was supposed to be happening was that we have this rather frivolous nonsense going on, and then the Lenin section comes in and says, 'Life is too important. We can't afford the luxury of this artificial frivolity, this nonsense going on in the arts.' Then he says, 'Right. That's what I've got to say,' and he sits down. Then the play stands up and says, 'You thought *that* was frivolous? You ain't seen nothin' yet.' And you go into the Gallagher and Shean routine. That was the architectural thing I was after.

What's altered is the sympathy level you have with Lenin. When you read the words on the page there's a sense in which Lenin keeps convicting himself out of his own mouth. It's absurd. It's full of incredible syllogisms. All the publishing and libraries and bookshops and newspapers must be controlled by the Party. The press will be free. Anybody can write anything they like but anybody who uses the Party press to speak against the Party naturally won't be allowed to do it. And then you go back to the first proposition that everything's controlled by the Party, and you're going round in circles. It's sheer nonsense. And at the end he says, 'I can't listen to music. It makes you want to pat people's heads when you really have to HATE them without MERCY. Though ideally we're against doing violence to people.'

In the text one's trying to demonstrate that he was in an impossible position. The ethics of necessity syndrome was operating. But in theatrical terms Frank Windsor and Barbara Leigh Hunt are 98.4 degrees from top to bottom. They're just blood heat, they're so human. When they walk on the stage you don't really think that man has contradicted himself throughout and condemned himself out of his own mouth. You think he really had a burden to carry, and Ashkenazy is doing his bit in the loudspeaker, playing the Apassionata. The equation is different, and even I am seduced by it.

Generally speaking, are long speeches dangerous?

I always think that they're the safe parts of the play, and they've proved to be so. With *Jumpers* a certain amount of boggling went on when they saw the script. Michael Hordern was worried; Peter was worried. In practice the monologues played themselves, and all the conventionally easy bits—the dialogue—were very difficult indeed to get right. In *Travesties* John Wood, who has the grave disadvantage of being about four times as intelligent as it's good for an actor to be, came in when we were talking about the monologue and he simply said, 'I've looked at it at home. There are no problems in it.' And we didn't rehearse it—just went through it a few times when we were doing the run-throughs and I think I spent two hours with him one day talking about little details of inflection.

What about this question of increasing architectural complexity? It must have the effect of multiplying the unpredictables and the variables and the points where balance will change from one performance to the next.

Yes, I really have a deep desire not to get involved in that kind of play for a long time. It's wonderful that Peter brought *Travesties* off in theatrical terms, but it's like an egg-and-spoon race. As he says. It could have dropped off in previews at any moment. One's energy as a writer is going into *theatricality,* and that's okay, but one doesn't want to do that each time, and ideally what I'd like to write now is something that takes place in a whitewashed room with no music and no jumping about, but which is a literary piece—so that the energy can go into the literary side of what I do. I'd like to write a quiet play.

Jumpers and *Travesties* are very similar plays. No one's said that, but they're so similar that were I to do it a third time it would be a bore. You start with a prologue which is slightly strange. Then you have an interminable monologue which is rather funny. Then you have scenes. Then you end up with another monologue. And you have unexpected bits of music and dance, and at the same time people are playing ping-pong with various intellectual arguments.

I can see they have that in common, but the relationship between the abstract ideas and the concrete characters seems different.

Yes, and there are senses in which *Travesties* is a great advance on *Jumpers,* but it's the same kind of pig's breakfast, and I'd really like to abandon that particular paintbox and do a piece of literature for three voices and a dog. One is playing a double game with a play like *Jumpers* and *Travesties:* one is judged as a writer on the strength of what one manages to bring off theatrically, and I'm afraid, with respect to those critics whom I feel to be perceptive, that the chances of a play being judged in isolation from what is done to that play are not great. I was the beneficiary of that happening once, in the case of

Ronald Bryden's review of **Rosencrantz.** The play was done in a church hall on a flat floor so that people couldn't actually see it. There was no scenery, student actors. The director didn't show up. Someone else filled in. I turned up for thirty-six hours and tried to put a few things right. It went on in some kind of state or other, and Ronald Bryden, writing for the *Observer,* just saw straight through to the text. But if Peter had got **Travesties** wrong, he would have been said to have failed as a director and I would have been said to have failed as a writer, with the same text with which Peter succeeded. It's a nonsense. There's an equation to be got right and there are a number of variables in it. It's not a question of something being right or wrong, it's a question of the variables adding up to the right answer. Things are so interrelated.

OVERVIEWS AND GENERAL STUDIES

Philip Roberts (essay date 1978)

SOURCE: "Tom Stoppard: Serious Artist or Siren?" in *Critical Quarterly,* Vol. 20, No. 3, Autumn, 1978, pp. 84-92.

[*Attempting to assess Stoppard's view of drama, Roberts notes the playwright's ambiguous pronouncements about his own work.*]

Tom Stoppard's writing career is a remarkable one. Since 1963, when his play **A Walk on the Water** was transmitted on television a few days after the assassination of President Kennedy 'as a substitute for a play deemed inappropriate in the circumstances', he has had performed some eleven stage plays (including two adaptations), seven television plays, six radio plays and one music piece ('Every good boy deserves favour'). There have also been some short stories and a single novel. He is said by his agent to have 'grossed well over £300,000' from **Rosencrantz and Guildenstern are Dead** alone. He is the most consistently eulogised dramatist of our time. Only Beckett and Pinter, significantly, are able to match his glowing reviews, which is possibly why, in the midst of wittily decrying critics in general, he has a good word for reviewers: 'I hope it is obvious that generally I am not referring to theatre-reviewers, who are performing a useful public service [the *Times Literary Supplement,* 13 October 1972]. He has been praised, albeit with a few reservations by Bigsby, deified pedantically by Hayman, championed aggressively by James and mythologised unctuously by Tynan. His critical cup runneth over, and although what is said about his plays is not his fault, what he says about his plays should make one wonder why the accolades are so fulsome, and why his particular brand of theatre should have drawn quite so much attention over the last fifteen years.

Stoppard is never less than articulate about his position. In 1968, he stated that he had 'very few social preoccu-

pations . . . Some writers write because they burn with a cause which they further by writing about it. I burn with no causes. I cannot say that I write with any social objective. One writes because one loves writing [*Sunday Times,* 25 February 1968]. The statement is one of many in which the terms of the antithesis set up are disguised as mutually exclusive. The inference is that those whose medium is the theatre who are judged to have something to say are lesser writers who merely employ the theatre. Any other medium would do as well. Again, those with social preoccupations are defined as writers who 'burn with a cause'. In order to take the position that a love of writing is the only reason for so doing, it becomes necessary to denigrate those who apparently work differently. Elsewhere, Stoppard confesses himself

> deeply embarrassed by the statements and postures of 'committed' theatre. There is no such thing as 'pure' art—art is a commentary on something else in life—it might be adultery in the suburbs or the Vietnamese war. I think that art ought to involve itself in contemporary social and political history as much as anything else, but I find it deeply embarrassing when large claims are made for such an involvement: when, because art takes notice of something important, it's claimed that the art is important. It's not [quoted by C. W. E. Bigsby, in *Tom Stoppard: Writers and Their Work,* 1976].

What is being said here amounts to a refusal to believe in the efficacy, in any sense, of theatre to affect anything, including an audience. It is perfectly reasonable to feel embarrassed about 'committed' theatre but to equate it with 'pure' art and then to feel embarrassed when 'large claims are made' for it is to attribute non-Stoppardian theatre with an arrogance which might make even the hardest of hard-line 'political' groups wince. In another context, Stoppard goes so far as to pronounce the theatre 'valuable, and I just hope very much that it'll remain like that as an institution. I think it's vital that the theatre is run by people who like showbiz' [interview with Stoppard in *Tom Stoppard* by Ronald Hayman, 1977]. He does not, however, define in what sense the theatre is valuable. There is a consistent jokiness to Stoppard's sayings about the theatre and himself. In a second interview with Hayman, he confessed that 'I never quite know whether I want to be a serious artist or a siren'. It is the case that watching the plays at least reflects a comparable unease, especially if one's doubts are reinforced by (they may be deliberately provocative) such airy notions as 'I'm not actually hooked on form. I'm not even hooked on content if one means message. I'm hooked on style' and 'For me the particular use of a particular word in the right place, or a group of words in the right order, to create a particular effect is important; it gives me more pleasure than to make a point which I might consider to be profound . . . ' [interview with Stoppard in *Behind the Seenes: Theatre and Film Interviews from the Transatlantic Review,* ed. J. F. McCrindle, 1971]. What is peculiar about this is the supposition that writing is about one thing *or* the other.

What Stoppard has resisted steadily both in his plays and in his opinions expressed in interviews is any idea of the theatre as an agent of change, as a form of art which is in any sense expressive of and contributory to the nature of the society of which it is a part. In order to do this, he uses a definition of the term 'political' which excludes what he does, and thereby begs the question as to the status of his own work. Stoppard comfortably acquiesces in the *status quo:* 'I lose less sleep if a policeman in Britian beats somebody up than if it happens in a totalitarian country, because I know it's an exceptional case. It's a sheer perversion of speech to describe the society I live in as one that inflicts violence on the underprivileged [quoted by Kenneth Tynan in the *Sunday Times,* 15 February 1978]. It might be thought that the perversion of speech resides more in Stoppard's deliberate restriction of the word 'violence' to physical beating so as to enable him to assert smugly that the underprivileged in Britain are not done *any* violence. Consequently, he becomes exasperated at those who dissent and whose writing reflects such dissent. In an interview in 1974, Stoppard attempted to stretch the term 'political' into meaninglessness:

> there are political plays which are about specific situations, and there are political plays which are about a general political situation, and there are plays which are *political acts* in themselves, insofar as it can be said that attacking or insulting or shocking an audience is a political act . . . The Term 'political play' is a loose one if one is thinking of *Roots* as well as *Lear*— I mean Bond's—as well as *Lay By.* So much so that I don't think it is meaningful or useful to make that distinction between them and *Jumpers*—still less so in the case of *Travesties* . . . *Jumpers* obviously isn't a political act, nor is it a play about politics, nor is it a play about ideology . . . On the other hand the play reflects my belief that all political acts have a moral basis to them and are meaningless without them [*Theatre Quarterly* 14, May-June 1974].

In other words, there are just plays and no label works for all of them. Or, perhaps, could it be that all plays are political? The stance is that of the liberal humanist with a corresponding belief that mankind will sort itself out eventually, without anyone prodding it in any particular direction. Stoppard recently put this very plainly: 'I believe in the perfectibility of society, and the concomitant of that belief is a recognition of its imperfections. That's why I am not a revolutionary person. I don't believe that the painful progress towards the perfect society happens in revolutionary spasms. I think it is a gradualist thing of growing enlightenment. I believe in the contagious values [interview with Stoppard by Marina Warner in *Vogue,* January 1978].

It is curious that someone whose approach is gradualist should continue to demonstrate the chaos in the world via, initially, a series of characters out of Prufrock, Beckett (the novels), Flann O'Brien, *Ulysses* and Sterne, and that, as far as he is concerned, the great liberator theatrically was *Waiting for Godot.* His initial heroes, as Bigsby has well annotated, are all trapped within a hostile mechanistic world which is at odds with individual aspiration. The telephonist who is the speaking clock in **"If You're Glad I'll Be Frank"** (radio 1966; stage 1969) cannot prevail. Albert in **"Albert's Bridge"** (radio 1967; stage 1969) finds

order in the structure of the bridge which is not available on the ground. George in ***Enter a Free Man*** (television 1963 as ***A Walk on the Water***; stage 1968) defends his eccentricity as a means of surviving in the face of an illogical world. ***Rosencrantz and Guildenstern are Dead*** (1966) shows two figures entirely outdistanced by the few facts of their situation and forced into the Beckettian situation of playing theatre games. If the world is the true Beckettian one as delineated by Stoppard, then there seems little sense even in a gradulist optimism. There is to date nothing written about the play that made Stoppard famous which shows how it is essentially different from its equally famous parent. All that appears to have happened is that Vladimir and Estragon have been moved up-market. The two plays which followed were **"The Real Inspector Hound"** and **"After Magritte"** (1968 and 1970), both of which Stoppard accurately describes as 'an attempt to bring off a sort of comic coup in pure mechanistic terms. They were *conceived* as short plays' [*Theatre Quarterly*]. In both, what appears to be central is the opportunity for wit, parody and metaphysical dalliance to do with the nature of perception. The plays reel away from seriousness as from a contagious disease.

Only in the two most recently available full-length plays does Stoppard confess himself entangled with more disturbing matters, and again the questions are severely diffused by the shifting insistence upon farce which both feather-beds and suffocates them. Out of the fashionable Beckettian context of the early sixties emerged Stoppard's preoccupation with 'the points of view play' so that he could assert in 1974 that 'there is very often *no* single, clear statement in my plays. What there is, is a series of conflicting statements made by conflicting characters, and they tend to play a sort of infinite leap-frog. You know, an argument, a refutation, then a rebuttal of the refutation, then a counter-rebuttal, so that there is never any point in this intellectual leap-frog at which I feel *that* is the speech to stop it on, *that* is the last word [*Theatre Quarterly*]. The structure and way of proceeding given here are accurate descriptions of both ***Jumpers*** (1972) and ***Travesties*** (1974). George, a professor of Moral Philosphy, attempts to establish the validity of God and morality via a lecture which he is composing throughout ***Jumpers***. He does so in the face of a world and society which is busily engaged in doing precisely the opposite. As before in Stoppard's plays, there is the little man or the eccentric *contra mundum.* He is the lonely figure holding out against overwhelming pressure, whether from his retired show-business wife, his all-purpose Vice-Chancellor, or the irresistible march to power of the radical liberal party (a deliberate contradiction in terms?). The play is pessimistic despite its acutely clever portrayal of certain aspects of the academic life, for George never engages with the real world, and can struggle with metaphysics only on the luxurious level of a private study. While he wanders in abstractions, the world gets on with its business. George is Stoppard's hero, someone who despite the odds, the self-contradictions, even the topical fallacies, and especially despite the realities of the situation, insists upon the existence and survival of values other than the ones which rule. The fact that George is shown to be hopelessly adrift is what makes him so attractive to Stoppard, for in his confusions he is said to represent essential man. Conceptually, George's rational means advance him no further than Watt [in Beckett's *Watt*] confronted with the problem of Mr Knott's leftovers who, having found 'the solution that seemed to have prevailed', furnishes the household with hordes of famished dogs, each in their turn to eat Mr Knott's food and numbers of families to supply the dogs and 'For reasons that remain obscure Watt was, for a time, greatly interested, and even fascinated, by this matter of the dog . . . and he attached to this matter an importance, and even a significance, that seems hardly warranted. For otherwise would he have gone into the matter at such length.'

It is true that Stoppard remarks that he believes 'all political acts must be judged in moral terms, in terms of their consequences. Otherwise, they are simply attempts to put the boot on some other foot' [*Theatre Quarterly*]. What is equally true is that any sense that George provides moral judgements has to be mediated both through the bones of a murder enquiry and through the technique of argument and counter argument which is Stoppard's main structural device. He heads unerringly for the joke, the parodic moment, the visually witty contrast to a degree which makes one doubt whether anything of what George struggles with, albeit in a vacuum, is able to locate itself solidly in such a texture. The confusions engendered lead to bizarre criticism. Thus Lucina P. Gabbard argues [in *Modern Drama* XX, No. 1, March, 1977] that Stoppard 'daringly weaves a serious philosophical dialectic in and out of this Absurdist drama', as if the debate in George's lecture is a complex one. She concludes that 'Absurdism, usually so depressing to audiences, emerges in a new configuration with entertainment', which suggests she has only read and not seen Beckett, Ionesco *et al*. The same writer is sufficiently entranced to instance the use of a screen and a slide projector as examples of 'Brechtian technique'.

Stoppard himself has pointed out the similarity between *Jumpers* and *Travesties*. They are 'very similar plays. No-one's said that . . . You start with a prologue which is slightly strange. Then you have an interminable monologue which is rather funny. Then you have scenes. Then you end up with another monologue. And you have unexpected bits of music and dance, and at the same time people are playing ping-pong with various intellectual arguments [interview with Hayman]. His sense of the two plays is that 'A lot of things in *Jumpers* and *Travesties* seem to me to be the terminus of the particular kind of writing which I can do'. Once again, what Stoppard may have to say is, perhaps defensively, insulated via the recollections of Henry Carr and by the other clever weaving of Carr's memories with *The Importance of Being Earnest*. Carr's origins, once again, are Beckettian: 'My memoirs, is it, then? Life and times, friend of the famous . . . Joyce . . . a liar and a hypocrite, a tight-fisted, sponging, fornicating drunk not worth the paper, that's that bit done . . . (*He makes an effort*) . . . (*He gives up again*).' What he does is to summon up the occasion when Joyce, Tzara and Lenin were all in Zurich in 1918. They are all three engaged in revolution in one form or another. Other than that and the historical fact that Carr was involved with

Joyce in a production of Wilde, there seems no good reason why connections should be apparent between them. Except that Stoppard appears to want to endorse the farce and the frivolity at the expense of Lenin, because of the implications of the ideology represented by Lenin. The play is broken backed and oscillates between farce figures jumping through comic hoops and Lenin's ostensibly dour reality. Characters pirouette around a situation which they do not advance, and of which they are not the product. They *observe* the situation as wittily as possible. Most of the speeches are not dialogue but elegant reflections upon a general theme. Each of the central characters makes pronouncements upon himself and the others, scores points, and is in turn rebuffed by another character. When at a loss, they move into pages of limericks or adaptations of music-hall songs. They as characters hardly exist. What is paramount is the shape of the remark, the delicacy of the wit. The play concentrates upon its own hermetic premise. Tzara and Joyce are created as mad and eccentric, exaggerated so as to provide a focal point for the sparks which can be struck. Carr is equally concerned only with his own cleverness and disdain. And then there's Lenin.

Stoppard has said that *Travesties* 'puts the question in a more extreme form. It asks whether an artist has to justify himself in political terms *at all*', 'whether the words "revolutionary" and "artist" are capable of being synonymous or whether they are mutually exclusive, or something in between'. His three main figures represent aspects of this curious question, on the one hand Joyce, on the other Lenin and in between Tzara. The question is never seriously debated, however. It is stated dogmatically in three forms, and the fact that Joyce and Tzara are joined with Carr means that they all perform a manic dance, mouthing belief but not substantiating it. Joyce in fact is absent from the play for long stretches at a time. Where the scheme falters is with the introduction of Lenin himself and Stoppard, as ever, is sensitive to the problem. He had ended Act One with an exposition of Dada and

> I wanted to begin the second with a corresponding exposition of how Lenin got to Zurich, not in geographical but political terms. I chose to do that from square one by starting with *Das Kapital* . . . I overplayed that hand very badly, and at the first preveiw I realised that the speech had to be about Lenin only. The second act is Lenin's act really, and I just bluepencilled everything up to the mention of Lenin. So now it was one page instead of five [interview with Hayman].

The unease shows in the text at the beginning of Act Two where it is stated that 'The performance of the whole of this lecture is not a requirement, but is an option. After "To resume" it could pick up at any point, e.g. "Lenin was convinced . . ." or "Karl Marx had taken it as an axiom", but no later than that'. The opening series of Act Two may thus begin with the statement that the beginning of the war caught Lenin and his wife in Galicia and that they came eventually to Zurich: 'Here could be seen James Joyce . . . and here, too the Dadaists were performing nightly . . . '. Now there is nothing objectionable in worrying away at those speeches of Lenin which are self-contradictory and in turn pondering the situation of the artist. Yet when the form and procedure of the play is such as in *Travesties,* it is the case that Lenin's massive historical presence in the play creates a boomerang effect with regard to Joyce and to Tzara. If the only seriousness in the play is of the self-regarding kind, then Lenin's pronouncements must inevitably carry weight, since the others are busily absorbed in playing Wildean antics. Consequently, the targets are easy to aim at. Cecily's passionate defence of Lenin is ridiculed suavely by Carr who insists on viewing her as a sexual object. The sequence closes with Cecily in Carr's mind's eye dancing on a table to the tune of 'The stripper' and Carr's roaring *'Get 'em off!'*. It is true that this is Carr and not Stoppard. It is also true that her passion is ridiculed and that she is made to love Carr because she wants to reform him. The centre of the play is not a debate about the artist and revolution. It is contained more obviously in Carr's remark to Tzara: 'You're an artist. And multi-coloured micturition is no trick to those boys, they'll have you pissing blood.' Lenin, in spite of the author in the end stands as a critical comment on the rest of the characters.

At the moment, Stoppard's work is beloved by those for whom theatre is an end and not a means, diversionary and not central, a ramification and not a modifier of the *status quo,* a soother of worried minds and not an irritant. He is the wittiest of our West End playwrights and his plays assure the reactionary that theatre was and is what they always trusted it was, anodyne and anaesthetising. It is difficult to know whether Stoppard at present takes himself too seriously enough. The novelist Derek Marlowe suggests that 'He's startled by the smallest minutiae of life. But the grand events, the highs and lows of human behaviour, he sees with a sort of aloof, omniscient amusement. The world doesn't impinge on his work, and you'd think after reading his plays that no emotional experience had ever impinged on his world' to which Stoppard characteristically and ambiguously replied, 'That criticism is always being presented to me as if it were a membrane that I must somehow break through in order to grow up . . .' [Tynan]. It remains to be seen whether the serious writer or the siren triumphs.

Andrew K. Kennedy (essay date 1982)

SOURCE: "Tom Stoppard's Dissident Comedies," in *Modern Drama,* Vol. XXV, No. 4, December, 1982, pp. 469-76.

[*In the following essay, Kennedy discusses Stoppard's moral and political satire in* Jumpers, Every Good Boy Deserves Favour, *and* Professional Foul.]

> To thy own self be true
> One and one is always two.

How many readers and theatre-goers would find the hallmarks of Tom Stoppard's verbal wit in those Peer Gyntian lines from *Every Good Boy Deserves Favour*? The lines are spoken rapidly by Alexander, the political prisoner detained in a "hospital," to his absent son; every word is *meant,* without ambiguity or irony either in the phrasing or in the situation; and the verse is a mnemonic, in case the prisoner is not allowed writing material "on medical grounds." This is only a local example of the remarkable change in Stoppard's comedy from a relativistic and parodic universe of wit to a new kind of comedy that combines moral and political commitment with a newly stable satire of real/absurd worlds, recognizably located in Russia and Czechoslovakia. It is an interesting transformation of comic vision, strategy and language.

Stoppard's comedy has, until this new direction, been most notable for the creation of a "pan-parodic" theatre. We were right to stress the vertiginous interplay of two kinds of theatre (Renaissance and Modernist) in the tragical-comical-farcical-melodramatic *Rosencrantz and Guildenstern are Dead,* and the cross-weaving of style parodies from Dada and Joyce, caught in the threads of Wilde's famous farce, in turn misperformed by the British Consul's decaying memory, in *Travesties*. In that kind of comedy—with its rapidly shifting perspectives, surrealistic quasi-encounters, and self-breeding verbal games—a "centre of gravity" was not to be looked for too gravely. That comedy did release vision, but no stable point of view. When a committed spokesman does appear amid the whirling worlds and words—George meditating on the meaning of God and morality in *Jumpers,* and Lenin's speeches on art and revolution in *Travesties*—critics complain that the comedy is all but undone: "his footing slips in his play-long parody of philosophy . . . polysyllables are dull weapons with which to cut at logical positivism" [Ruby Cohn in *Contemporary English Drama,* ed. C. W. E. Bigsby, 1981] and the "authentic speeches" of Lenin dislocate the "baroque farce" in the play [C. W. E. Bigsby, in *Tom Stoppard,* 1976]. Cecily's lecture on the origins of the Russian Revolution at the opening of act two of *Travesties* was judged to be so anti-comic by a French director that he procured, if that is the word, an actress who was willing to deliver the tedium-risking speech in the nude, slowly getting dressed as she went on speaking the unwitty lines (Stoppard's anecdote). In sum, the universal parody, the instability of focus, and the sometimes indulgent but nearly always theatrically well-timed verbal wit *have* created a comedy-farce in which the importance of being serious was a risky ingredient.

Every Good Boy Deserves Favour and *Professional Foul* are relatively modest in scope; they also differ in genre and style, preserving only a family resemblance with the universal parody of the earlier plays. It may well be that we have been given a wholly new *kind* of political comedy, still to be defined. Placing these two short Stoppard comedies on the generic map may be provisional; but before we turn to the plays themselves, it is worth recalling that there has been a certain poverty of political comedy in contemporary (English) drama. Some of the most interesting plays by roughly "New Left" dramatists (plays like Howard Brenton's *Weapons of Happiness* and David Hare's *Fanshen*) border on the ponderously solemn. A generation of dramatists has found it difficult to combine

didactic purpose—including a feeling for ideological subtleties and contradictions—with anything resembling full-
blooded comic vision. Traces of the robust Shavian and
Brechtian political comedy—with its fusion of theatricality and ideology, comedy and ideas, the direct use of platform, stage, arena and circus, from *Major Barbara* to
Arturo Ui—are now rare, or rarefied. When a bolder kind
of political comedy is attempted, it often leads to a catastrophe of pity and terror, deliberately and didactically
contrived, as in Trevor Griffiths's fine *Comedians* and
Edward Bond's recent *Restoration* (in which the triumphant pastiche comedy suggested by the title is pushed
towards a melodramatic execution through aristocratic
villainy).

Stoppard's combination of "lightness of touch" in comedy and a new political purpose is in itself noteworthy;
and if we decide that he is successful in keeping the
balance between intermirroring theatre worlds and recognizable real worlds, then he has achieved something
rare in our time. Shaw tried something comparable in
one line of development from *Androcles and the Lion* to
The Apple Cart—a pantomime comedy of belief and
political extravaganza. But Stoppard's scale is smaller,
and his control arguably greater, more concentrated. There
may be another point of affinity between the two dramatists. In the plays under discussion, Stoppard (who once
created university wits who had dined on Beckett) seems
to be governed by a non-absurd vision of absurdity. By
this I mean the relatively stable exposure of the lunacies
and brutalities of a political system; the multiple irrationality is seen rationally enough to let the audience watch
from a stable standpoint. The worlds which persecute a
Bukovsky and a Havel are shown to be grotesquely dis-
located in their pursuit of absolute "rationality" and
power, and the audience is made to perceive the madness; yet the foundations of the theatre and its language
are not shaken in this kind of committed comedy.

Every Good Boy Deserves Favour (1977) is serio-comic
from the opening scene on. The confusion of roles and
planes of action—between Ivanov's insane musical hallucinations and Alexander's state-fabricated "hallucinations"—
is situational wit developed with great economy. The scene
serves as a prelude and shorthand exposition to the whole
play. Ivanov's manic mime, as he conducts his imaginary
orchestra, involves the audience in "listening" to the un-
heard music first, and then to the audible orchestra, seemingly dominated by the mad Ivanov's wonder-working
triangle. Since Ivanov assumes that his fellow-prisoner is
a fellow-musician, he proceeds to cross-examine his musical credentials in a way that is at once comic and menacing:

> IVANOV . . . Let me put it like this: if I smashed this
> instrument of yours over your head, would you need a
> carpenter, a welder, or a brain surgeon?

> ALEXANDER I do not play an instrument. If I played an
> instrument I'd tell you what it was. But I do not play
> one. I have never played one. I do not know how to
> play one. I am not a musician.

> IVANOV What the hell are you doing here?

> ALEXANDER I was put here.

> IVANOV What for?

> ALEXANDER For slander.

> IVANOV Slander? What a fool! *Never speak ill of a
> musician!*—those bastards won't rest. They're animals,
> to a man.

> ALEXANDER This was political.

> IVANOV Let me give you some advice. Number one—
> never mix music with politics. Number two—never
> confide in your psychiatrist. Number three—*practise!*

> ALEXANDER Thank you.

The dark overtones of this comic opening provide the key
to the mode and the mood of this dark comedy. Apart
from the delightful yet sinister mixing of music and politics, we get an early inkling of the orchestra being used
as a central play-metaphor, going well beyond "musical
accompaniment" or "melo-drama" in the old sense. For
the fantasy of conducting a kind of cosmic orchestra, letting a triangle dictate its perfect concord, is itself a totalitarian fantasy which mirrors the ideologue's dream of
universal order. No discord in the music, no dissent in the
state. Beating in measure is all. Meanwhile, the miserable
plight and the incongruous collisions of Ivanov and Alexander mock the human desire for perfect order and hege-
mony, from the start.

In the play's design, the two cell-mates do not, however,
interact to any great extent. It is possible to see this as
an underexplored possibility, probably due to the limited
scope of the play. Furthermore, Stoppard must have
wanted to avoid the relatively mechanical pattern of a
comedy of errors. Instead, he modulates into his darkest
key by scene two: Alexander delivers a long speech to
the passive Ivanov, expounding the crazy ABC of justice
in the police state. In a later cell-scene (scene five),
Alexander is given a solo speech addressed to his absent
young son Sacha, in which he describes the horrifying
effects of being on hunger-strike, when the flesh starts to
smell of acetone, nail varnish. All this sounds and is
authentic (some of it taken directly from an eyewitness
account by Victor Fainberg in *Index on Censorship*). And
since such speeches form the centre of the play's political protest against the abuses of psychiatry for political
ends, they are an integral element of Stoppard's strategy.
But they are directly didactic—not parable, not comic;
they resemble the Lenin speeches in ***Travesties*** in tilting
the play away from its comic-satirical moorings. It is
possible that an Ionesco—or Mrozek or Havel, who had
been directly submerged in the Kafka world of East
European totalitarianism—would have handled even such
scenes on the level of absurdist gallows humour, still within
the frame of a comic political parable.

The comic potential of the play is developed in lateral scenes, away from the cell, in the other two acting areas: the school where Sacha is being taught *and* indoctrinated, and the hospital office where bizarre interviews take place. Much of the comedy of confused levels hinges on the triangle, now both a musical instrument and a geometrical figure calling out for absolute definition. Thus is a pun transmuted into a multilevel comedy of ideas. One particularly effective scene shows the boy Sacha parroting the axioms of Euclid (which he has to copy ten times, as his father has to copy political slogans a million times). The teacher then matches each axiom with some doctrine considered axiomatic in the Soviet state:

SACHA 'A point has position but no dimension.'

TEACHER The asylum is for malcontents who don't know what they're doing.

SACHA 'A line has length but no breadth.'

TEACHER They know what they are doing but they don't know it's anti-social.

SACHA 'A straight line is the shortest distance between two points.'

TEACHER They know it's anti-social but they're fanatics.

SACHA 'A circle is the path of a point moving equidistant to a given point.'

TEACHER They're sick.

SACHA 'A polygon is a plane area bounded by straight lines.'

TEACHER And it's not a prison, it's a hospital.

(*Pause.*)

This Orwellian scene is intensified into further satire in the second schoolroom scene, when Sacha twists the absolutes of geometry into strange home-made formulations like "A triangle is the shortest distance between three points" and "A circle is the longest distance to the same point." Stoppard, a master of verbal distortion, is here letting a dissident geometry make its point against pseudo-Euclidean politics.

Later in the hospital office, as in distorting mirrors, the axiom-drill of the schoolroom is twisted into still more grotesque shapes. Ivanov, the madman, happens to be in the office when Sacha arrives, and the boy is at once subjected to a manic and intimidating music lesson:

SACHA I can't play anything, really.

IVANOV Everyone is equal to the triangle. That is the first axiom of Euclid, the Greek musician.

SACHA Yes, Sir.

IVANOV The second axiom! It is easier for a sick man to play the triangle than for a camel to play the triangle.

All these episodes are threaded on a plot of sorts, which is itself broadly comic, involving as it does a doctor who plays the violin (in the "real" orchestra) and the Colonel in charge of the psychiatric hospital who is said to be an expert in semantics. The final scene modulates into a formal "happy ending" as the Colonel descends theatrically, *deus ex machina* of our time, to sort out the bitter confusions of mere mortals. The Colonel confuses Alexander and Ivanov (or, rather, confuses Alexander Ivanov with Alexander Ivanov), and in his genius discovers that Ivanov does *not* believe sane people are put in mental hospitals while Alexander does not hear music of any kind. Evil is averted—as in the finale of a tragicomedy like *Measure for Measure*—the patients/prisoners are released. Comic release follows.

Professional Foul is lighter in texture than ***Every Good Boy,*** with a fine balance between comedy, ideas, and the personal drama of a dissident and his family. That balance brings this small-scale play near to Stoppard's "perfect marriage between the play of ideas and farce or even high comedy" [Stoppard, in *Theatre Quarterly* 4, May-July 1974]. It is, however, very much a television play, to be judged partly for its success in using the medium: the rapid succession of scenes, the comedy of close-ups (e.g., the philosopher caught by the camera reading a girlie magazine in the aeroplane), and, above all, the ingenious variations played on stock character and situation. Ordinary muddles and misunderstandings gradually crystallize into the cruel farce of the Prague secret police chasing and bugging a gentle and philosophical dissident. Popular topics, like football and an absent-minded professor, are woven into an ongoing argument over the rights of the individual in the state. The criss-crossing of three fields— philosophy, football, and politics—is as amusing as any of Stoppard's galleries of interreflecting mirrors.

Like ***Jumpers,*** the play is structured around a central character, at first a caricature: the liberal, vague, and seemingly gutless Oxford philosopher, Professor Anderson, whose hidden motive for travelling to a colloquium on ethics in Prague is to watch football there. The surface comedy begins with the opening scene, set in the aeroplane, where Anderson in his vagueness unintentionally creates the impression of being condescending to a junior academic from a provincial university, and also casts some doubt on the nature of the "extra-curricular activities" he has in mind for the Prague conference—politics, football, or an amorous adventure could all be meant. It is essential to Stoppard's purpose to establish this elegantly world-weary Oxbridge don "type" early in the play. For the gentlemanly manner and the well-meaning detachment bordering on inanity ("A cleaner? What is that?", he asks Hollar, the Czech philosophy student now compelled to do menial work) exhibit the weaknesses of liberal/non-committal/Anglo-Saxon attitudes. Anderson appears to have reduced ethics to good manners and so casts himself for the role of the innocent abroad in a comedy of manners.

Asked by Hollar to take back with him to England the only copy of his doctoral thesis on correct behaviour—a dangerous topic in Prague—Anderson responds first with inbred evasion:

> ANDERSON . . . Oh, Hollar . . . now, you know, really, I'm a guest of the government here.
>
> HOLLAR They would not search you.
>
> ANDERSON That's not the point. I'm sorry . . . I mean it would be bad manners, wouldn't it?
>
> HOLLAR Bad manners?
>
> ANDERSON I know it sounds rather lame. But ethics and manners are interestingly related. The history of human calumny is largely a series of breaches of good manners.

Anderson's hypercorrect attitude is gradually, and serio-comically, transformed into cunning. He becomes a political fox who can perform a minor breach of "manners"— a breach of the law in a police state—by first rousing himself to make an impermissible speech in favour of individual rights at the conference, and then deciding after all to hide Hollar's thesis (in a colleague's brief-case). "It's not quite playing the game is it?", growls the pseudo-committed colleague as they fly out of Prague, with the undetected thesis, in the final scene.

It is a comedy of conversion—let us call it the liberal's progress from fatuousness to commitment—worked out in scenes of personal confrontation, flanked by scenes of hilariously overlapping *fields*. In the dark core-scenes of the dissident's drama (scenes six and seven), Anderson is accidentally made to participate in a police raid on Hollar's flat, witnessing the slick brutality of the procedures, the panic of wife, son and other residents. He is indignantly protesting because he has to miss England playing (though allowed to listen to a radio report, in Czech, by courtesy of the secret police). The ordinary confusion of who is doing what for what purpose is dovetailed into the larger confusion of a police state apparatus that is efficient in function but "absurd" in purpose. And Anderson, the disconnected philosopher, is learning to connect things. In the second personal scene, Hollar's son (called Sacha again, as if to underline the link with *Every Good Boy*) movingly acts as the interpreter, in halting English, between Mrs. Hollar and the increasingly moved Anderson. Even this scene has a comic point of entry, as Anderson's suspicious colleague thinks he has his hypothesis concerning certain "extra-curricular activities" confirmed when he spots an attractive woman waving to Anderson in the hotel dining-room—it is Mrs. Hollar come to ask for help ("Bloody hell, it *was* a woman. Crafty old beggar").

The overlapping fields accommodate Stoppard's characteristic picnic of speech-styles. The title itself is taken from a footballer's intentional foul to stop a goal; and, clearly, Anderson is about to commit "a professional foul,"

in the light of his own professional etiquette. Then there are the local puns, for instance, the confusion of "left wing" in its political and footballing contexts. The most successful verbal comedy is the barrage of football reports being telephoned by assorted British journalists who all seem to have a flair for parodying their particular style ("Only Crisp looked as if he had a future outside Madame Tussaud's—a.u.d.s.—stop"). The parody of linguistic philosophy (scene eight) is more laboured and more superficial than the parody of Anderson's earlier liberal-humanist wishy-washiness. (The parody of linguistic philosophy has, of course, a bearing on Stoppard's general post-Wittgenstein openness to situational "language games"—but that is another point.) Nor is the political centre-piece, Anderson's committed speech in defence of freedom and individual rights at the conference, quite as effective as it is probably intended to be. Here television may be a handicap, for a fragmented Western television audience (I am speaking from experience and observation) cannot quite re-create for itself the force of hearing such a speech in an East European assembly. Further, it is not at all easy to integrate a "straight" and resounding defence of values into the structure of a comedy, as even Chaplin found when he marred the ending of his superbly controlled Hitler satire in *The Great Dictator* by shouting the truths of the gospel at the audience in the final episode of the film. However, having said that, I may add that Stoppard himself is not always at ease in handling a tirade of ideas—he is no Shaw in this respect (witness sections of **Jumpers**).

The play of ideas is much more successfully handled in shorter spurts, where an idea is aired and then left to float back into the main body of the play at a later stage. Such an idea is the "audacious application" by McKendrick of the "catastrophe theory" to ethics—roughly the view that "'Morality'" and "'Immorality'" represent not opposite planes, but rather two lines running along the same plane until at a certain point—the catastrophe or breaking-point— "your progress along one line of behaviour jumps you into the opposite line; the principle reverses itself . . .". McKendrick is carried away by waves of enthusiasm, uses a knife and a hand for emphasis, and then directly (*argumentum ad hominem*) accuses Anderson of wanting to treat values he knows to be fictions as if they were "God-given absolutes": "So you end up using a moral principle as your excuse for acting against a moral interest. It's a sort of funk—."

The over-ingenious argument gathers strength and point when we see Anderson, as it were, having learnt the lesson of a reversed principle—though he is really acting under the direct impact of the emotional scene with Mrs. Hollar and Sacha—in promising to "do everything I can" to help the persecuted dissident. And Anderson has the last word too, when he defends his act of having placed Hollar's suppressed thesis in McKendrick's brief-case, with a practical application of the same catastrophe theory: "I'm afraid I reversed a principle." Committed action has grown out of non-absolutist ethics for Anderson. And committed comedy has grown out of political catastrophe, through Stoppard.

Joseph J. Feeney (essay date 1982)

SOURCE: "Fantasy in Structure: Layered Metaphor in Stoppard," in *Forms of the Fantastic: Selected Essays from the Third International Conference on the Fantastic in Literature and Film,* edited by Jan Hokenson and Howard Pearce, Greenwood Press, 1986, pp. 233-39.

[*The following was first presented at a 1982 conference. Feeney contends that the seeming spontaneity of Stoppard's imagination obscures the careful craftsmanship of his plays, which, he claims, are structured around set of "parallel metaphors."*]

Tom Stoppard has an imagination that feeds on analogies. "Things are so interrelated," he once commented in an interview [in Ronald Hayman's *Tom Stoppard,* 1979]; and in writing his plays Stoppard frequently finds himself discovering (often to his own surprise) various "convergences of different threads," "structural pivots," and points of "cross reference." In these plays, the themes, characters, plots, language, and setting somehow become curiously linked and, through multiple metaphors, end up standing parallel to each other. In *Jumpers,* for example, philosophy resembles gymnastics, which is like casual sex, which resembles academic politics, which . . . And so the metaphor-making sparkles along in the Stoppard imagination. These metaphors, furthermore—often bizarre and fantastic ones—then get built into the very structure of a Stoppard play.

For the casual theatergoer, the Stoppard imagination seems only a near-bottomless source of fantastic puns, incongruities, plot twists, and verbal surprises. Critics, too, often concentrate on Stoppard's absurdity and celebration of irrationality. But underneath the surface of Stoppard's plays—and of his imagination—is an intelligence and a dramatic craft that are carefully ordering those diverse elements that only *seem* to be so spontaneous, arbitrary, and chaotic. The real Stoppard, however, is a supreme organizer, a craftsman who knows that his plays "hinge around incredibly carefully thought-out structural pivots which I arrive at as thankfully and as unexpectedly as an explorer parting the pampas grass which is head-high and seeing a valley full of sunlight and maidens."

This "structural pivot" is very frequently a set of parallel metaphors whose points of similarity Stoppard works out as carefully as a seventeenth-century metaphysical poet. Through metaphor after metaphor Stoppard links together bizarrely diverse elements, and this metaphor—or, more accurately, series of metaphors or layers of metaphor—provides structure, form, and shape for the play. These layers of metaphor continue for the full length of the play, and each layer of the comparison illuminates and is illuminated by the others. Thus, Stoppard's dreamiest flights of fantasy are reined in, through metaphor, by his mind and his imagination. He sees similarities, works out continuing points of comparison, and builds these metaphors into his plays in such a way that the parallels are fantastic yet consistently coherent. Fantasy becomes structured through metaphor. And this rare combination of wild fantasy and clear structure becomes a Stoppard trademark that forms a potentially centrifugal play into a coherent unit. A number of his plays demonstrate this characteristic of Stoppard's imagination; here I consider three of them: *Jumpers, Every Good Boy Deserves Favor,* and *Professional Foul.*

A preliminary clarification may help on the question of structure. Each of these plays, to be sure, has a traditional plot structure; the traditional urge of suspense drives each play forward: Who murdered the gymnast, and what will happen to George Moore? What will be Alexander's fate for speaking the truth about Russia's political freedom? Will Hollar's philosophical essay be successfully smuggled out of Czechoslovakia? These questions, and the plots they spawn, propel each play forward and provide its basic structure. But Stoppard adds his layers of metaphor as an alternate structure. This layered metaphor, with its multiple levels of similarities, adds its own form, unity, and structure to each play. These fantastic metaphors also provide much of each play's brilliance, its *tour-de-force* quality; the metaphors—together with Stoppard's verbal pyrotechnics—also give the play its sense of fun.

Jumpers (1972) is a play whose major conflict is a dispute between philosophies, and all the other conflicts in the play—about sex, gymnastics, academic appointments, murder, even the astronauts on the moon—are merely metaphoric parallels for the central philosophical dispute. On one side is George Moore, a philosopher, who generally follows the philosophical positions of the English philosopher G. E. Moore (1873—1958) (whose name, of course, is also George Moore). The philosophical hero (like Stoppard I will call him "George") is, at the beginning of the play, preparing a lecture for a university symposium that very evening. Opposing recent developments in English philosophy and ethics, he comments that he "hoped [that evening] to set British moral philosophy back forty years, which is roughly when it went off the rails." Following what he, and historians of philosophy, call the "intuitionist philosopher" G. E. Moore, George holds that there is an absolute metaphysical base for affirming what is *good* and what is *bad;* goodness, he maintains, is a *fact* that, by intuition, is recognized when it is seen. Moreover (and unlike G. E. Moore), George, arguing as a philosopher, actually affirms that there is a God. Standing in the long tradition of Aristotle, Aquinas, and the Judeo-Christian philosophical heritage, he affirms a God of Creation and a God of Goodness "to account for existence and . . . to account for moral values".

On the other side of the philosophical dispute stand the more recent English philosophers—the current "orthodox mainstream" according to George—who are represented in the play by Sir Archibald Jumper ("Archie," says Stoppard) and his followers, including the recently murdered Professor McFee. These contemporary philosophers are, at one point, catalogued and lumped together as "logical positivists, mainly, with a linguistic analyst or two, a couple of Benthamite Utilitarians . . . lapsed Kantians and empiricists generally . . . and of course the usual Behaviourists." This group holds, according to George, that "things and actions . . . can have any number of real and verifiable properties. But good and bad, better and worse . . . are not real properties of things . . . just expressions of our feelings about them." The play's question, then, becomes this: Can goodness and badness be objectively grounded (at least by intuition), or are they only subjective feelings without any objective philosophical foundation? This is the play's philosophical conflict and the crux of its plot.

In *Jumpers,* however, this cerebral dramatic conflict, itself enfleshed in George and Archie, is further expressed in a series of bizarre metaphors; Stoppard finds parallels of this philosophical disagreement in the realms of gymnastics, sex, academic power, national politics, murder, astronauts on the moon, and human feeling. And while these metaphors at first seem fantastic and strange, on examination they make full sense and provide a complex structural network for the play. Archie (Sir Archibald Jumper, the philosopher without metaphysical foundation) is himself a gymnast—physically and philosophically— and also the manager of a group of gymnasts whom he hires out to perform at parties; these jumpers are young and "relevant," physically skilled, technically brilliant at somersaults, but have no solid foundation. In contrast, George is physically dull, boringly stable, but grounded on the firm, solid earth. Furthermore, Archie—the jumper—also leaps from bed to bed and has seduced George's own wife; George, his marriage shaky, is troubled—both morally and sexually—by Archie's actions, but is himself moral enough to refrain from such sexual acrobatics. Archie, further, is a man of academic power, vice-chancellor of George's university and the professor in charge of academic appointments; George, seeker of truth and man of moral integrity, is totally powerless and holds the lowly reputed chair of moral philosophy. In politics (to go the next metaphor), the jumpers are Radical-Liberals; George holds a more traditional position. In life, the jumpers, since they hold no moral position as absolute, are willing to resort even to murder; George, recognizing moral limits, could not imagine himself murdering anyone. The characters' habits, too, differ: During the play the jumpers are enjoying a free-flying party in George's living room and bedroom while George is in his study preparing his lecture in isolation from others. Even the lunar astronauts take part in *Jumpers'* multilayered metaphor. On television the American astronauts are seen walking on and violating the moon, and when they take off for the return to earth, one astronaut chooses self-preservation at the cost of the other's life; George and even his wife prefer altruistic courage and also mourn the loss of the old romantic, stable view of a distant and lovely moon. The jumpers, finally, see their bodies as only brilliant machines, are always coolly in control of a situation, but care little about love; George, though he cannot express his love to his wife, still cares about her, and even about his tortoise, Pat, and his hare, Thumper. Yet George, isolated but still holding to objective morality, even at play's end, remains a victim of slapstick and a philosopher in a pratfall.

On this set of incongruous metaphors, then, is the play built: philosophy = gymnastics = sex = academic chairs =

national politics = murder = parties = astronauts = love = slapstick = George and Archie. Stoppard has chosen such fantastic linkings to dramatize his worries about order, reason, morality, and responsibility in the modern world. The play *Jumpers,* then, while funny and sparkling, is also very serious and—most to the point—very carefully structured.

Every Good Boy Deserves Favour (1977) and *Professional Foul* (1977) are equally funny and equally serious; they are both also structured with great care. Dealing with political repression and with freedom of expression, *Every Good Boy Deserves Favour* shows a political prisoner kept in a Russian mental hospital, and *Professional Foul* is a television play about free expression in Czechoslovakia. Both plays, like *Jumpers,* are built on parallel layers of metaphor carefully linked together.

The title of *Every Good Boy Deserves Favour* puns on the musical notation E, G, B, D, F (the play's title is the British version of our "Every Good Boy Does Fine"), and the work is described [by Stoppard in the Hayman interview] as "a piece for actors and orchestra." André Previn wrote the music, and both actors and orchestra share the stage. On the stage two men are confined in a Russian mental hospital; Alexander, a political prisoner because he criticized the repression of dissent, and Ivanov, a certified madman who believes he has an orchestra in his head (he thinks the cellos are rubbish!). At issue in the play is the difference between clinical madness and the human sanity-political madness of dissent in a repressive society. The play, as it progresses, jokes about Ivanov's imaginary orchestra, shows Alexander's determination to be honest and to speak the truth frankly, and dramatizes his young son's desire to free him. The plot—such as it is—is resolved crazily when a colonel enters and unwittingly confuses the two men; he asks Alexander whether he hears an orchestra in his head ("No," he says) and Ivanov whether the Soviet government puts sane men in lunatic asylums ("I shouldn't think so," he says). Both men are sent home and the play ends happily.

Despite the ghastly political and human situation, the play is funny. Many of the lines and situations are zanily comic; Ivanov is a humorous character; even the musical score is a parody of modern Russian music. Stoppard adds to the humor and incongruity with layers of incongruous metaphors. In Russia any statement about government repression—statements that are morally right and as obvious as geometry and logic ("To thine own self be true. / One and one is always two.")—somehow means political dissent. Such dissent is treated as madness and as a refusal to play one's part in the orchestra of the State (here, ironically, existing only in the mind of a madman). These political themes and conflicts appear in the lines of the characters, in the logic or illogic of their utterances, in the mental-hospital setting, and in the orchestra's music. On one side stands the sane, dissenting Alexander: frank in politics, morally truthful, logically and mathematically accurate (one and one *do* make two), quite sane, possessing no imaginary orchestra, forthright in word, honest to his opinions; on the other side, the madman and good Communist Ivanov: amoral in his madness, inventing an unreal world of relations and even a new orchestra in his mind, crazy in word, with opinions unconnected with reality. Like Russian Communism he lives within a crazy, closed system. And even the State-as-orchestra is not very competent and plays music that is a parody. Thus, Stoppard builds up the incongruous but clear metaphors on which the play's structure stands: Alexander and Ivanov = politics = morality = logical mathematics = sanity = madness = music = verbal style = character = society. The play's richness as well as its humor and irony are all based on these layers of metaphor.

Even a play as seemingly—and actually—realistic as *Professional Foul* is based on similar fantastic parallels structured through metaphor. The play, one of Stoppard's rare pieces for television, dramatizes a lesson in applied ethics as learned by Professor Anderson, a Cambridge ethicist and rabid soccer fan. This ninety-minute drama begins as several British philosophers are flying to Prague to deliver papers at an international philosophical congress. Anderson, who has always carefully kept his philosophy separate from his life and politics, has prepared a lecture on "Ethical Fictions as Ethical Foundations." (The treatment of ethics as a fiction, incidentally, recapitulates Archie Jumper's position.) But if truth were to be told, Professor Anderson is *really* going to Prague to catch the World Cup qualifier soccer match between England and Czechoslovakia, which will be played in the Czech capital at the time of the congress. But when Anderson reaches his Prague hotel, he is unexpectedly visited by his former Czech student, Pavel Hollar, who asks Anderson to carry his thesis—on human rights—to England for publication. Anderson, unwilling to offend his Czech hosts by such smuggling and "bad manners," refuses. But the next day, on his way to the soccer match, Anderson finds that Hollar has been arrested; angered, he then presents to the international congress not his own paper on "ethical fictions" but Hollar's strong views on human rights and on their real, objective foundation. Anderson, then, chooses to speak out in place of the imprisoned Hollar and even decides to smuggle Hollar's thesis to the English printers. The play ends as Anderson smuggles the thesis out of Czechoslovakia in the briefcase of an unsuspecting British philosopher—a relativist in moral theory—who unreasonably complains that a "principle" has been violated. Anderson counters that since for the relativist philosophy is merely a "game" anyway, how could an alleged non-real "principle" be violated? (Hollar, a traditional objectivist in moral theory, with philosophical consistency was willing to be imprisoned for his opinions and principles.) In any case, says Anderson, the smuggling was merely a "professional foul" or "necessary foul"—an action similar to England's tackle in the soccer game as the Czech player was driving to the goal. And why should an English relativist complain in such a case?

In *Professional Foul,* then, Stoppard once again creates a very odd, layered metaphor: in this case soccer = politics = philosophy = academic life = Anderson and the other characters. The soccer foul is necessary for England to prevent a Czech goal; similarly, it is necessary to hide the thesis to protect (from the Czech police) Hollar's statement on political freedom and individual rights. Hiding the thesis in a relativist's briefcase (unknown to the relativist) is furthermore just part of the philosophical game for a man who holds to no objective principles. Whether such a concealment is "foul," then—much less immoral—is seen to depend on one's ethical theories and principles. Thus, at the drama's end, the relativist's complaint—"It's not quite playing the game is it?"—sets Anderson up for the play's brilliant final lines: "Ethics is a very complicated business. That's why they have these congresses." All five levels of the play—soccer/politics/philosophy/acdemics/characters—come to-gether beautifully and ironically in the play's closing words. The comparisons generated in Stoppard's imagination have been organized and controlled through the play's structure of metaphor. Through the ironies of the metaphor, the reader comes to see that philosophy, politics, and the commitment involved in both cannot be called games in any sense at all.

Tom Stoppard has frequently shown himself willing to discuss the creative process behind his plays, and in many interviews he offers glimpses of how his imagination works. A few of his comments, when read together, clarify the metaphor-making typical of his imagination. In 1979 he said, for example, that he "enjoys writing dialogue but has a terrible time writing plays" [Mel Gussow, "Stoppard's Intellectual Cartwheels Now with Music," *New York Times,* 29 July 1979]. It is at this "terrible time," one might speculate, that Stoppard surprises himself by discovering the "convergences of different threads," the "cross references," and "structural pivots" that characterize his plays [Hayman interview]. At such moments, it seems, Stoppard sees new similarities and proceeds to construct the complex interlinkings that constitute his plays. He characteristically catches those interrelations he talked of through a series of metaphors.

Stoppard himself once described the joining of these interrelations in a play as "carpet-making" with its "different threads" [Hayman interview]. But this particular metaphor of crosshatching, though offered by the playwright himself, does not fully catch the great clarity and parallelism of Stoppard's metaphor-making. Rather, Stoppard seems to express his clearly perceived parallels by clearly designed metaphors that overlie and enrich each other like the layers of a French petit-four, a Viennese torte, or even, perhaps, an English trifle. Or again, in less gustatory terms, Stoppard's imagination is as rich, as analytically clear, and as enticing as the imagination of a Donne, of a Herbert, or of some medieval exegete or allegorist.

Joan F. Dean (essay date 1988)

SOURCE: "Unlikely Bedfellows: Politics and Aesthetics in Tom Stoppard's Recent Work," in *Tom Stoppard: A Casebook,* edited by John Harty, III, Garland Publishing, Inc., 1988, pp. 243-59.

[Dean explores the interrelation of politics and playwriting throughout much of Stoppard's work.]

Throughout Stoppard's plays questions concerning the artist, his responsibilities, and his work frequently surface. His characters are often painters, writers (including poets, journalists, and dramatists), musicians, or actors. Some are based on historical personages; some cut from whole cloth; one or two even suggest a close connection with Stoppard himself. Many of these characters are directly concerned with the creative, artistic process. Others, notably the many actors who populate his plays—Dorothy Moore in *Jumpers* (1972) and the players in *Rosencrantz* (1967)—are not primarily imaginative, but interpretive artists. Still others, like the journalists in *Night and Day* (1978), are marginally connected with art itself: first, because like other writers, they work in the medium of language and, second, because they share similar responsibilities with imaginative artists who deal with political questions.

Stoppard's own recent works also address political issues. Especially since *Jumpers,* his characters inhabit well-defined social and historical contexts—hyperbolic and futuristic as they may be—rather than timeless, abstract, or universal realms. *Travesties* (1974), like *Artist* (1972), is set in Zurich during World War I just before the Russian Revolution. *Night and Day* deals with a political situation in Africa in a specific phase of post-colonial development. *Professional Foul* (1977), *Every Good Boy Deserves Favour* (1977), *Cahoot's Macbeth* (1979), and *Squaring the Circle* (1984) all examine the plight of those trying to work under the oppression of totalitarian governments in the late twentieth century. These four all rely heavily upon specific situations in Czechoslovakia, the Soviet Union, or Poland in the very recent past. Among Stoppard's works, these are his most explicitly political. *The Real Thing* (1982) is set in present-day England against a backdrop of anti-nuclear, anti-Establishment agitation. In each case, the social and political backdrop is essential to the thematic concerns—specifically those regarding the nature of playwrighting—in a way that is not at all characteristic of the plays before *Jumpers*.

Over the past decade, these two recurrent themes, politics and playwrighting, have become curiously interrelated. Stoppard's efforts to sway what Henry in *The Real Thing* calls "that axis of behaviour where we locate politics or justice" focuses on communist repression in no fewer than five works: *Professional Foul, Every Good Boy Deserves Favour, Cahoot's Macbeth, Squaring the Circle,* and, to a lesser extent, *Travesties*. The immediate concern with the affairs and responsibilities of the artist appear in *Artist, Travesties,* and *The Real Thing*; *Night and Day* deals with journalists rather than artists.

Despite critical charges that his early characters were subordinate to the ideas they represented, Stoppard's more recent characters often face the same challenges as the playwright himself. They take up questions that Stoppard as a journalist, a playwright, an individual has addressed in interviews, non-fictional articles, and lectures. A dramatist, to be sure, has many more options open to him than a journalist, but the dramatist has the additional responsibility of creating art. Insofar as the playwright concerns himself with political matters, he can, as Stoppard often does, disseminate information and shape opinion. Moreover, in *Night and Day, Every Good Boy Deserves Favour, Cahoot's Macbeth,* and *Squaring the Circle,* freedom of artistic expression and freedom of the press are portrayed as dual manifestations of the same basic liberty. Those freedoms of expression are critical for Stoppard. Speaking before the National Press Club 1979, Stoppard asserted: "A reasonable litmus test for any society in my view [is] is it a society where you can publish within the law?" Ultimately, in Stoppard's works the responsibilities of the political playwright are not unlike those of the political reporter.

In his recent works, on the one hand, Stoppard's characters persistently encounter problems related to the nature of drama—specifically, those pertaining to the relationship between dramatic representation and reality, between life and art. On the other hand, artists and others (journalists, the narrator in *Squaring the Circle,* et al.) are often forced to account for or to justify themselves and their work. While these two questions are distinct, they are hardly unrelated. This is especially true for those works that deal directly with specific political situations. The possibilities for oversimplifying or misrepresenting a political situation are strong; the consequences of such distortions are potentially disastrous.

The pitfalls of the intentional fallacy are particularly troublesome in evaluating Stoppard's characters. There are no straw men in his plays and few characters, like Brodie in *The Real Thing,* who elicit an immediate dislike. The creation of villainous or even unsympathetic characters would undermine one of the foundations of Stoppard's dramatic technique: what he himself has referred to [in *Theatre Quarterly* 4, May-July 1976] as a "kind of infinite leapfrog." Characters with diametrically opposed views are pitted against one another, but both sides of the argument are given strong voices. *Jumpers* provides the best example in the contrast between the dapper though unctuous Sir Archibald Jumper and the sincere but hapless George Moore. Whereas Archie is powerful, successful, and thoroughly cynical ("At the graveside, the undertaker doffs his hat and impregnates the prettiest mourner. Wham, Bam, thank you Sam"), George succeeds neither in marriage nor in academe. Yet, as Kenneth Tynan observes [in *Show People,* 1979], George's ineffable faith in man's spirit and the existence of a moral order approximates Stoppard's own convictions:

> In that great debate there is no question where Stoppard stands. He votes for the spirit—although he did not state his position in the first person until June of this year [1977], when in the course of a book review, he defined himself as a supporter of "Western liberal democracy, favouring an intellectual elite and a progressive middle class and based on a moral order derived from Christian absolutes."

Yet though it may be helpful to link Moore and Stoppard on this point alone, to identify Stoppard and Moore is patently foolhardy.

Moreover, the fact that Stoppard writes comedy rather than tragedy presents another obstacle to examining the playwright's aesthetic and political position. Aristophanes and all who followed him not withstanding, comedy, especially in post-WWII British drama, is too often seen as escapist entertainment rather than politic commentary. As Catherine Itzin amply demonstrates in her study *Stages in the Revolution*: *Political Theatre in Britain Since 1968* [1980], the British stage has frequently and forcefully been used as a political platform for issues ranging from gay rights to government funding of the arts, from anti-war and anti-nuclear views to the I.R.A. But the vast majority of these political plays are overtly polemical and decidedly mirthless—two characteristics that immediately distinguish them from Stoppard's works. Their single-mindedness and dreariness are implicitly mocked in *The Real Thing* by Brodie's dogmatic television script.

In *Artist*, a radio play, and its full-length theatrical descendent, *Travesties,* Stoppard focuses on questions concerning the artist and his relationship to society that he had only touched upon in earlier works. While none of the characters in *Artist* reappear in *Travesties,* the former is clearly a preamble to the latter in its themes, setting, and comments about the artist in society. Both plays deal with characters who as artists find that global conflict ranging about them and who, to varying degrees, attempt to ignore it by seeking refuge in Switzerland. In *Artist* the aural images of the war are all too obvious: the discussions concerning art are punctuated by "a convoy of rattletrap lorries," explosions, the thundering hooves of the German cavalry. In *Travesties* the reminders of war appear in Carr's personal experience in the trenches, Lenin's exile in Zurich, and Joyce's insistence that "[a]s an artist, naturally I attach no importance to the swings and roundabout of political history."

Whereas *Artist* is principally focused on a story of unrequited love and the difficulty of expressing that love in art, *Travesties* more pointedly confronts the relationship between art and politics and the artist's responsibility to his society. As I have shown elsewhere [in *Tom Stoppard: Comedy as a Moral Matrix,* 1981], *Travesties* pits the proponents of socialist realism (Lenin), Dadaism (Tzara), art for art's sake (Joyce), and conventional bourgeois art (Carr). Among these views, Lenin's view of art is the one most discredited in *Travesties* because it is contradicted by Lenin's own response to art. The appropriate, doctrinaire response on art is learned rather than felt by Lenin. He initially prefers the bourgeois Pushkin to the revolutionary Mayakovsky; Beethoven's "Appassionata" "makes [him] want to say nice stupid things and pat the heads of those people who while living in this vile hell can create such beauty."

Yet the most substantial hinge between *Artist* and *Travesties* lies in the repetition of two statements concerning art and the artists. [In *Artist*] Donner, the artist in love with Sophie who ultimately commits himself to realistic painting, and Henry Carr [in *Travesties*] both offer definitions of the artist: "An artist is someone who is gifted in some way that [which] enables him to do something more or less well which can only be done badly or not at all by someone who is not thus gifted." That definition anticipates Henry's comparison of those who craft cricket bats and those who write plays in *The Real Thing*. Donner, an artist capable of realistic painting, Carr, and Henry agree that the prerequisite of the artist is the mastery of his medium; what is often simply called talent.

Travesties also shares with *Artist* nearly identical statements appearing in very different contexts concerning the artist's standing in and responsibility to society. As Carr says in *Travesties*: "What is an artist? For every thousand people there's nine hundred doing the work, ninety doing well, nine doing good, and one lucky bastard who's the artist." Carr is suspicious of, if not hostile to, art. He distrusts art because he fears that he may not understand it, that it may be a ruse perpetrated by artists. Stoppard's *Squaring the Circle* and *The Real Thing* also present characters who distrust art, often for political reasons.

Squaring the Circle follows the pattern of *Professional Foul* (both television plays), *Cahoot's Macbeth,* and *Every Good Boy Deserves Favour* in focusing expressly on a specific political situation. Unlike *Jumpers* and *Night and Day, Squaring the Circle* does not distance the work in an imaginary setting, but directly addresses a political reality as well as the problems involved in presenting that situation. In the course of *Squaring the Circle* Stoppard communicates an enormous amount of purely factual information: the history of Poland since 1720, the reason Poland is less likely to receive loans from Western governments than other equally economically imperiled countries, why moral leadership in Poland has been in the hands of the Church, the fact that 70 per cent of Polish agriculture is privately owned. This is no mean feat. At a time when most of the media coverage, at least in America, depicted the conflict between the Polish unions and the country's communist government in highly charged emotional terms, *Squaring the Circle* approaches its subject with an even-handedness. The play's approach to its subject seems predicated on the conviction that before the audience can undertake political action, it must factually and objectively understand the situation. As much as the image that General Jaruzelski presents to the Western world may fit the caricature of a Communist puppet dictator, complete with sinister tinted glasses, overbearing demeanor, and Fearless Leader uniform, and Lech Walesa may appear as his perfect foil—with his work clothes, unkept mustache, and insistent family—these are not the basis on which Stoppard draws their characters. Both are far more complex because they are presented not just as symbols, but as individuals. Audience expectations are continually reversed, for *Squaring the Circle* does not focus on the charismatic personality of Walesa, but rather on the complexities and ambiguities of the situation in Poland. Here, perhaps more convincingly than in any other play, Stoppard demonstrates how thoroughly he has researched his subject.

In some ways *Squaring the Circle* contains Stoppard's most "Brechtian" dramaturgy. (Ironically, its politics are decidedly anti-Brechtian or at least anti-communist.) The dramatic progress of the work expediently guided by the direct address of the Narrator. But that progress is repeatedly thwarted, qualified, or interrupted by the voice of the Witness who objects to or criticizes the dramatization of a particular situation. Despite its didacticism, *Squaring the Circle,* like all of Stoppard's political plays, does not intend to galvanize the audience to action.

The difficulty of accurately reporting or recreating a political situation becomes a thematic concern, just as it had in *Night and Day*. Stoppard's attention is expressly focused on the problem of presenting the words and deeds of actual people with honesty. His preface to *Squaring the Circle* confirms his sensitivity to this inherent dilemma:

> Documentary fiction, by definition, is always in danger of seeming to claim to know more than a film maker *can* know. Accurate detail mingles with arty detail, without distinguishing marks, and history mingles with good and bad guesses. . . . It was the fear of just such imponderables and just such confusion between large speculation and small truths . . . that led me to the idea of having a narrator with acknowledged fallibility.

Technically, this is not an innovative device in Stoppard's dramaturgy. The most obvious precedent is Henry Carr, the "narrator" as well as a character in *Travesties*. Carr's memory, the stage directions record, "occasionally jumps the rails and has to be restarted at the point where it goes wild." Stoppard's own work employs other analogous dramatic devices, many of which evoke Pirandello's manipulations of dramatic reality. For Stoppard, as for Pirandello, multiple perspectives or renditions are not only stylistic devices, but because of their very nature and tacit commentary on drama itself, they become an important thematic component of these works.

As early as *Rosencrantz,* characters concerned themselves, often in an alarmingly disinterested way, with various explanations or interpretations of events. Rosencrantz, for instance, offers a "list of possible explanations" for his run of incredibly bad luck at coin-tossing. In **"After Magritte"** (1970) various characters, all eyewitnesses, provide radically different descriptions of the identical event. But in the works since *Jumpers,* those that are more directly concerned with political or aesthetic issues, Stoppard moves through different planes of dramatic reality to indicate how restricted any single perspective on a political situation must be.

Stoppard's solution to the dilemma of this limited perspective in *Squaring the Circle* was the creation of the Witness who periodically interrupts the narrator to challenge his authority. The very presence of the witnesses raises the question of "the qualified reality" which is all any account, whether it aspires to the status of art or claims to be wholly documentary, can achieve. Any perspective is necessarily limited—be it by camera position (in the case of a film documentary), by editing, or by inherent if inadvertent bias—and the best, the most objective and fair-minded solution for Stoppard is to acknowledge that fact.

Consequently, in *Squaring the Circle* the exchanges between the narrator and the Witness make explicit the problem Stoppard as a playwright and commentator confronted.

The Narrator is closer to Stoppard than virtually any of his earlier characters. Like the playwright, the Narrator operates from a position of presumed authority. Throughout most of the history of drama, until very recently in fact, one of the conventions governing the use of direct address (soliloquies, asides, choric statements, etc.) was that the character speak the truth, or at least what he perceived to be the truth at that moment. But Stoppard, through the Narrator, not only acknowledges but also exploits that assumption.

Much of the humor in *Squaring the Circle* lies in the conscious manipulation of the dramatic conventions governing veracity in direct address and awareness of the clichés of television journalism or its "docu-dramas." The Narrator often explains or tries to justify the interjection of literary images, such as a chess game or a game of cards, as a matter of artistic license. When the party bosses appear dressed as gangsters, the Witness objects:

WITNESS: What's all this gangster stuff?

NARRATOR: It's a metaphor.

WITNESS: Wrong. You people—

NARRATOR: All right.

The Witness is not about to allow the imposition of simplistic or clichéd images, no matter how convenient, on his reality. He resists all attempts of the Narrator (and author) to reduce the political circumstances to an easily accessible, tidy scenario. During the confrontation of General Jaruzelski, Walesa, and Cardinal Glemp, which is portrayed as a card game, the Narrator admits: "Everything is true except the words and the pictures."

Stoppard meticulously develops the ironies inherent in the political situation in *Squaring the Circle*. The play opens, for example, with the striking contrast between the official, public language that Leonid Brezhnev might have addressed to Edward Gierek ("Comrade! As your friends and allies in the progress towards the inevitable triumph of Marxist-Leninism, we are concerned, deeply concerned, by recent departures from Leninist norms by Polish workers manipulated by a revisionist element of the Polish Intelligentsia!") and what is closer in tone to, but certainly not exactly, the actual words uttered by Brezhnev: "What the hell is going on with you guys? Who's running the country? You or the engine drivers? Your work force has got you by the short hairs because you're up to your neck in hock to the German bankers, American bankers, Swiss bankers—you're in hock to us to the tune of . . . is it millions or billions . . . ?"

In *Every Good Boy Deserves Favour,* the incompetence of the authorities and their desperate attempts to conceal that incompetence, forces the play's action to the borders of farce. Bureaucrats posing as doctors struggle to disguise their bungling just as Feydeau's philanderers fought to safeguard their illicit liaisons. Only the stupidity and hypocrisy of the authorities assure the nominal, momentary (and hollow) happy ending of *Every Good Boy Deserves Favour*. Similarly, the ending of *Professional Foul,* recalling the recovery of Miss Prism's long-lost handbag and, in its self-conscious artificiality, obliquely suggests that such contrived happy endings are not about to resolve the oppression depicted. But in *Squaring the Circle* there is not only a more sustained, methodical delineation of the political issues, there is far less of the frenetic action of farce, very little of the intricate wordplay and wit so often identified with Stoppard, and none of the sleight-of-hand happy endings found in *Professional Foul* or *Every Good Boy Deserves Favour. Squaring the Circle* ends when the political situation reaches an impasse, not a resolution.

Thematically, *Squaring the Circle* deals with the political reality in Poland as well as the difficulty of writing about that situation. Stoppard's *The Real Thing* considers the difficulty of writing not only about politics, but also about love.

The Real Thing moves between the illusive and the real, the impersonal and the personal, the false and the true. Its opening scene initially lures the audience into mistaking *House of Cards* for the real thing, or *The Real Thing*. Conflating Henry's play and Stoppard's play is as natural and as dangerous as conflating Henry and Stoppard, the character and his creator. This is not the only opportunity the audience has to conflate art and life. In *The Real Thing* Stoppard again interpolates scenes from other works as a play-within-a-play much as *Hamlet* is used in *Rosencrantz* or *Earnest* in *Travesties*. The intimate conversations of Stoppard's characters flow into the rhetorical formality of Ford's *'Tis Pity She's a Whore* or Strindberg's *Miss Julie*.

Life, of course, does imitate art. When in *The Real Thing* Annie and Billy drift into the dialogue taken from Ford's *'Tis Pity She's a Whore,* Billy, at least, is sincere in borrowing from a character to express his own feelings. In the next scene in *The Real Thing,* Henry's first wife, Charlotte, reminds Henry that she lost her virginity to the actor playing Giovanni to her Annabella, fuelling Henry's suspicions about Annie's infidelity.

Moreover, *House of Cards* establishes the image of a suspicious husband searching through his wife's possessions for evidence of adultery that is twice replayed in the course of *The Real Thing*. First, Charlotte, Henry's ex-wife, reports that her affair with an architect (a profession shared with the jealous husband in *House of Cards*) ended when he was unable to find her diaphragm in their home while she was away. Later, Henry himself ransacks Annie's belongings, presumably with the same goal in mind, while she is in Glasgow playing Annabella to Billy's Giovanni. The crucial difference is that in a highly emotional state, the razor-sharp wit of the characters in *House of*

Cards yields to the untidy and unliterary anger of characters who present themselves as more real, or at least more human. As Hersh Zeifman observes, "the reaction of the 'real' husband to his wife's betrayal is, in both cases, utterly opposite to the graceful wit under pressure displayed by the theatrical husband in *House of Cards*" [*Modern Drama* XXV, No. 2, June, 1983].

The ambivalence of the play's title, referring both to true love and true art, is indicative of not only the play's structure, but its subject as well. Those subjects—love and art—are approached with a reverence anomalous in Stoppard's canon. Rarely does Stoppard treat his subject with such vulnerable sincerity and without the detachment of witty barbs.

The Real Thing contains some of Stoppard's most direct statements concerning love as well as the nature of the artist and his creation. In Henry, Stoppard has created a character who suggests not just tangential but direct comparison with his author. Among all Stoppard's characters, Henry offers the most tempting invitation to identify a character as the spokesman of his creator. Beside age, profession, and an interest in cricket, Henry and Stoppard share similar if not identical notions of playwriting. Outside of his interviews, the most forthright statements from Stoppard concerning playwrighting come from Henry. None of Henry's ideas on art in general or playwrighting contradict or are at variance with what Stoppard has said about playwrighting in interviews. Moreover, Henry's comments on drama are unrefuted, even unqualified by any other character in *The Real Thing*. The only possible opposition to Henry's ideas on playwrighting lies with Brodie, a singularly dislikable character, who ends with dip rather than pie on his face.

Yet Henry is hardly a self-serving idealization of the playwright. Unlike what Tynan has said of Stoppard's meticulous preparation, Henry "doesn't like research." Certainly, the little of what we know of *House of Cards* suggests Stoppard's characteristic wit and wordplay, but its subject, self-knowledge through pain, is hardly typical of his work. Although Henry respects language to the point of twice correcting his friend's grammar, he is not above writing a hack screenplay to earn the money to pay his alimony. He does, in fact, eventually doctor Brodie's play for television production. But he never manages to write the play he has promised Annie, largely because, as he says, "Loving and being loved is unliterary. It's happiness expressed in banality and lust." As tempting as it is, identifying Stoppard and Henry is as misguided as mistaking *House of Cards* for *The Real Thing*.

For Henry the real thing is as illusive and rare in love as it is in art. Just as he doesn't "believe in debonair relationships," he objects to the single-mindedness of Brodie's dramatic effort. Henry, in fact, despises Brodie as "a lout with language," and Brodie's play as invective drivel. In regard to "politics, justice, patriotism," Henry believes:

> There's nothing real there separate from our perception
> of them. So if you try to change them as though there

were something there to change, you'll get frustrated, and frustration will finally make you violent. If you know this and proceed with humility, you may perhaps alter people's perceptions so that they behave a little differently at that axis of behaviour where we locate politics or justice; but if you don't know this, then you're acting on a mistake. Prejudice is the expression of this mistake.

What Henry here suggests is precisely what Stoppard's political works, especially and most successfully *Squaring the Circle,* attempt to do. Polemical works are likely only to polarize already divided groups. But if properly used, words "can build bridges across incomprehension and chaos". For both Henry and Stoppard political action is wedded not to a particular ideology or cause, but to moral intelligence and sensibility. Without that fusion, political statement can easily become, as it does for Brodie, violence.

Moreover, if political statement is to be expressed artistically, both Henry and Stoppard would argue that precision with language and talent are necessary. Henry's already famous comparison of writing and crafting a cricket bat recall what Donner in *Artist* and Carr in *Travesties* say about the artist's talent:

This thing here, which looks like a wooden club, is actually several pieces of particular wood cunningly put together in a certain way so that the whole thing is sprung, like a dance floor. . . . What we're trying to do is to write cricket bats, so that when we throw up an idea and give it a little knock, it might . . . travel. . . .

In the ability to make an idea "travel" lies the possibility of quickening the moral and political sensibilities of the artist's audiences. And therein lies the power as well as the genius of Stoppard as a dramatist.

The dramatic device most characteristic of Stoppard's approach to both political and aesthetic problems is to establish a dramatic reality on one plane and then to qualify, deny, or undercut it by introducing a higher plane which announces itself as closer to the Truth. The structure of his recent works, especially those which address political or aesthetic questions, reflects the games of leap-frog played by characters who offer "an argument, a refutation, then a rebuttal of the refutation, then a counter-rebuttal. . ." [*Theatre Quarterly*].

Established, fixed texts—the official party line in the case of *Squaring the Circle,* Shakespeare's *Hamlet,* Wilde's *Earnest*—only partially illuminate a given situation. Yet another perspective is provided by the vastly more personal, intimate and individualized portraits of Stoppard's characters.

The introduction of multiple perspectives on a single situation is hardly a recent development in Stoppard's work; "After Magritte" provides a much earlier example as various characters attempt to report what they saw. But in

Squaring the Circle and *The Real Thing* this device effectively interpolates alternative versions of reality specifically to indicate the ambiguities and complexities of human situations that variously deal with art, love, or politics. In earlier works, this same device was used but to vastly different ends: the text of Shakespeare's *Hamlet* was interpolated into *Rosencrantz* and fragments of Wilde's *Earnest* appeared in *Travesties*. In *Squaring the Circle* and *The Real Thing* Stoppard's deft manipulation of dramatic realities and interpolated scenes has realized a new maturity in suggesting the limits of art and the complex relationship between art and life.

In 1975, Stoppard told Charles Marowitz:

I'm not impressed by art *because* it's political. I believe in art being good art or bad art, not relevant or irrelevant art. The plain truth is that if you are angered or disgusted by a particular injustice or immorality, and you want to do something about it, *now,* at *once,* then you can hardly do worse than write a play about it. That's what art is bad at [*New York Times,* 19 October 1975].

Despite the political content in the works since *Jumpers,* there is nothing in any of Stoppard's works that contradicts this statement. His sights have always been on the "axis of behaviour where we locate politics or justice"; his concern for the integrity of art has always preceded his political statements. Political commitments are matter left for the audience to discover in their own moral sensibility.

Mary A. Doll (essay date 1993)

SOURCE: "Stoppard's Theatre of Unknowing," in *British and Irish Drama since 1960,* edited by James Acheson, The Macmillan Press Ltd., 1993, pp. 117-29.

[*In the essay below, Doll provides an overview of Stoppard's drama, noting the use of paradox, ambiguity, and humor, which characterize his work as "post-Absurdist."*]

It should come as no surprise, given his background, that Tom Stoppard should be a playwright of paradox. His personal as well as professional life speak of a penchant for double, not stable, coding. Born in Zlin, Czechoslovakia, 3 July 1937, Tom Straussler became a child without a country, fleeing the effects of World War II by living with his family in Singapore, then in India, and finally in England—all before the age of nine. When his mother remarried after his father was killed, his name changed to Stoppard and his life changed from that of an immigrant—he called himself a 'bounced Czech'—to that of a privileged student in English preparatory schools. Stoppard began his career as a journalist and theatre reviewer, although his real interest was in creating, not critiquing, plays. When at the age of twenty-nine he achieved world fame with his first play, *Rosencrantz and Guildenstern are Dead,* he became known as a university wit—without yet having attended university.

Such contradictions in Stoppard's personal life helped shape his multifaceted career. Unlike most of his artistic contemporaries, Stoppard has produced work in all media and in all genres, including critical articles in journals and newspapers; short stories; one novel; radio, television, and film scripts; and, of course, stage plays (twenty-four: sixteen original, eight adaptations) for which he is best known. True to his sensibility Stoppard demonstrates that any attempt to name, point, place, picture or record any event as fact is completely ironic—irony being his chosen mode since it puts the point beside the point. Stoppard presents serious issues—like war, death, love, art, deceit, and treachery—with a light touch. His intention is to divest us of certainty, which he sees as an arrogant attitude inherited from the postures of logical positivism and classical science.

The nearest attempt to categorise Stoppard has been made by Martin Esslin, who places the playwright beyond the Absurd in what he calls the post-Absurdist tradition [The Theatre of the Absurd, 1961]. Post-Absurdists go even farther than Absurdists in dispensing with unities of plot, character, and action, together with the illusion of certainty such unities assume. Esslin's word replacing 'unity' is 'mystery' or 'mystification'—the latter a word Stoppard uses. Another word for Absurdism, 'paradox', Stoppard also employs to suggest the doubling quality inside his drama. 'Paradox and tautology', he once said. 'They don't have to mean anything, lead anywhere, be part of anything else. I just like them' [quoted by Stephen Shiff, Vanity Fair, May, 1989]. In a Stoppard play doubling is a recognisable feature, including motifs of doubletiming, coincidence, and doublecrossing. There are—and this is a Stoppard hallmark—plays-within-plays; characters who are twins; characters who are different characters with the same names; and characters who are at the same time spies and counter-spies.

A second post-Absurdist trait of Stoppard's work is ambiguity. 'My plays', he has said, 'are a lot to do with the fact that I JUST DON'T KNOW'; such not-knowing he calls the "definite maybe"' [Author 78, Spring, 1967]. He often features a detective, a philosopher, a sleuth or a spy who, in the spirit of Isaac Newton or Sherlock Holmes, applies cause-and-effect logic to any problem at hand. Newton's postulate—from same beginnings will follow same ends—is ludicrously explored by Stoppard s detectives. Instead of a Newtonian universe, where problems can be solved, Stoppard ascribes to what post-modern science calls 'chaos theory'. Gaps, punctures and breaks in sequence sabotage every logical attempt to formulate a hypothesis. Indeed, Stoppard's greatest contribution to theatre may be his concept of the indeterminacies of what it is 'to know' as a hired professional, a spectator, or even as an ordinary human being.

A third quality of Absurdist drama is its plumbing of comedy for the presentation of serious themes. Where Stoppard clearly departs from the Absurdist tradition is in tone. Stoppard's tone is paradoxically both lighter—'English high comedy' as Esslin puts it—and weightier. Important issues are presented elegantly, often in the guise of gaming, including everything from bridge and billiards to ping pong, charades and cricket. But these games are really stylised rituals, meant to be seen as the games people play against two parts of themselves, against others, or against some higher ethical code.

Stoppard's first play, **Rosencrantz and Guildenstern are Dead** (1967) earned him deserved world-wide recognition. A comic-tragedy, it proposes a theme that runs through all his work—that what we witness is unrelated to reality or truth—and sets forth his post-Absurdist use of doubling, ambiguity, and elegant play. Doublecoded here, of course, is Shakespeare's Hamlet, which, like Stoppard's later **Dogg's Hamlet, Cahoot's Macbeth** (1979), places traditional theatre with its expectations of top-down authority and elevated blank verse alongside post-Absurdist theatre with its confusion in rank ordering and idiomatic speech. Stoppard thus deconstructs Shakespeare. 'Ros' and 'Guil'—mere functionaries in Shakespeare's world—enter Stoppard's world centre stage. It is they, not Hamlet, who ponder the serious issues of death, probability, relationship. It is they, not Hamlet, who emphasise the metaphor of theatre as a place where one can 'come to know'—but only in play time; for while Ros and Guil play-act their Shakespeare lines, we watch them watch the king watch the Players play the role of Hamlet's father ghosting the play. No one 'comes to know' with an assured Aristotelian sense.

Stoppard's second play, **Enter a Free Man** (1968), takes the existential themes of being and the impossibility of knowing into a new situation. The essence of being, Stoppard suggests, consists in playing ourselves as different people when we enter different situations. We are never 'free' since within our seemingly stable orders lie strange attractors luring us into other trajectories. The play concerns the underhanded schemes of George (he would like to escape his average home life) and daughter Linda (she would like to marry her motorcycle boyfriend), both of whom seek adventure outside the realm of the wife-mother Persephone (whose real home, we know from myth, is in the underworld, the realm of the hidden other self). To have an identity that stays the same in all situations is to engage in myth; but myth, Stoppard suggests, is a reality of sorts.

In **"The Real Inspector Hound"** (1968) Stoppard again takes up the issue of reality, this time inside the context of the whodunnit. What better character type to illustrate the indeterminacies of problem solving than an inspector and a spectator? The play is ostensibly about two drama critics reviewing a production, but the play-within-a-play motif provides a frame for Stoppard's borrowings from chaos theory. Indeed, as the philosopher of science Steven Toulmin comments, Stoppard has put to death the whole notion of what it is to be a spectator, since would-be spectators are transformed into agents, making us all agents in what we observe [Steven Toulmin, The Return of Cosmology: Postmodern Science and the Theology of Nature, 1982]. Stoppard plays with the idea of 'the death of the spectator' on two levels, both in terms of plot (one of the drama critic spectators, drawn into the living room whodunnit, gets murdered) and in terms of the spectator's role.

The play is not about drama critics but about perception. If classical theatre, like classical science, depended on a stable order, then the study of chaos, like a Stoppard play, depends on dynamic orders. Perception shifts, disequilibrium ensues, and the part-whole relationship of observer to thing-observed—once considered fixed—erupts. Chaos theorists call the eruption of these new patterns 'fractals' or structures which are self-similar at different levels. Fractal patterns arise spontaneously and engage in activity that doubles, echoes, and mirrors—producing thereby an irregular order that does not depend on individual components. Stoppard spectators similarly must relinquish their role, classically defined as objective observers.

Part of the erupting order in this play is Stoppard's parodies of criticisms levelled at his work. The two critics, Moon and Birdboot, comment on the play they are viewing, which concerns a drawing room murder at Muldoon Manor. The play, they say, is a trifle; the characters are ciphers; the second act fails to fulfil the promise of the first act; there is hardly a whiff of social realism. More to Stoppard's point, however, is his fascination with the possibilities afforded art by non-linear dynamics. At issue is a storm, a house party, an intruder, a murder. A cosy order is disrupted by a murdered body. The statement about killing Simon Gascoyne seems to be a clue to the murder but is attributed to every suspect, making conclusion impossible. This particle of information loops and repeats, embedding layers of complexity. Like the manor house set apart in the storm with no roads leading to it, the observed problem cannot be 'gotten at' by traditional channels of thinking. We spectators are in the midst of a chaotic situation, adrift from tradition.

"After Magritte" (1971) contains a similar comment on methods of logical deduction leading to smug conclusions—falsely, of course. Matters which appear to the senses defy eye witness accounts and 'private eye' ratiocinations. Not only is Stoppard critiquing again the spectator theory of knowledge—where what one sees is what one knows—but he is also presenting issues concerning non-mimetic art, which in *Travesties* (1975) and *Artist Descending a Staircase* (1973, 1989) become central foci.

René Magritte (1898-1967) is a natural model for Stoppard since, like Stoppard's, Magritte's work multiplies ambiguities. In what Michel Foucault [in *This is Not a Pipe,* 1982] describes as a 'calligram', Magritte's painting 'aspires playfully to efface the oldest oppositions of our alphabetical civilisation: to show and to name; to shape and to say; to reproduce and to articulate; to imitate and to signify; to look and to read'. Art's role is *not* to name, signify, shape, or show; it is to be insouciant, to celebrate difference. Magritte names his paintings wrongly in order to focus attention upon the very act of naming. But, as Foucault observes, 'in this split and drifting space, strange bonds are knit'. Just as Foucault's writing about Magritte is a cornucopia of wisecracks meant to draw attention to absurdities, so too are Stoppard's plays.

Overlaps with Stoppard and Magritte are instructive. In **"After Magritte"** the stereotype detective Foot (flat-foot-ed, literal) and police constable Holmes (after Sherlock) formulate a false hypothesis based on simple sensory data and mere shreds of evidence. Stoppard employs the metaphor of a light bulb—there are numerous references to Thomas Edison, inventor of electricity—to indicate ironically that with such reliance on ratiocination there can be no light, no sudden inspiration, and certainly no real seeing. 'Eye' witness accounts all prove wrong, and details which 'speak volumes to an experienced detective' speak the wrong volumes loudly. The situation in this play is of witnessing a bizarre spectacle—Mother lying on her back on an ironing board—presuming she is dead; witnessing the strange behaviour of Harris and Thelma—Harris dressed in thigh-length waders, Thelma dressed for ballroom dancing—and presuming there has been a crime. The absurdity of the situation might seem merely derivative of Magritte were it not for the fact that a similar incident actually occurred in the United States, when a museum guard observed through a museum window a grey-haired woman seated in a chair, not breathing; he called the fire department, which rushed to the rescue—of an art exhibit of a woman in a chair.

Ambiguities of naming and knowing are centrally shown in *Jumpers* (1972), which features a professor/philosopher, George Moore, named after George Edward Moore (1873-1958). The real George Moore's preoccupation, expressed in *Principia Ethica* (1903), had to do with questions of ethical theory (the meaning of 'good', 'right', and 'duty'), the theory of knowledge, and the nature of philosophical analysis. Of Stoppardian interest is Moore's obsession with the verb 'to know': how the act of 'knowing' relates to observation, to perception, and to expression. In the tradition of logical positivism, Moore attempted to define 'to know', endowing knowledge with qualities of certainty above and beyond what can be discovered through the five senses or articulated through imprecise language. George Edward Moore's leaps of logic become the ironic metaphor of *Jumpers,* where eight amateur acrobats form the backdrop against the speechifying character George Moore.

George is attempting to pinpoint the existence of God by examining data, looking for logical inferences, putting two and two together, and coming up with God. His mental gymnastics—spoofed by the somersaultings of gymnasts—only prove that 'the point' will not stand its ground. The positions of the acrobats shift—we learn they are trying to hide a corpse. So too does the position of George shift as he tries to hide his logic behind such philosophical corpses as those of Plato, Newton, and Russell. His jargon recalls the speech of Lucky, a slave to a tyrannical master in Samuel Beckett's *Waiting for Godot,* where phrases like 'established beyond all doubt' are positioned against phrases like 'for reasons unknown'. Dorothy, George's wife, is 'dotty': she sings stereotypical moon songs and needs therapy because her fantasies about the moon, thus about love, have been invaded either by technological moon landings or by her husband's excessive rationalism. While Stoppard's satire is clever, if overworked, a more serious theme runs through the play: the yearning for carnal knowing and for another kind of mind-knowing.

Stoppard continues to raise issues inside high comedy with *Travesties* (1975). The play takes its energy from a little-known event in literary history—a travesty of seriousness—and Oscar Wilde's *The Importance of Being Earnest*—a travesty of earnestness, the first event intersecting with the second. Amused by the anti-art Dada movement, Stoppard cheerfully seeks to dislocate his audience. Henry Carr, for instance, is the improbable fringe catalyst of chaos who remembers his time in war chiefly through recollecting what he wore (war/wore)—twill jodhpurs, silk cravats—war a metaphor for fashion. The first act introduces historical and fictional characters, who play with issues of art (Tristan Tzara, the Dadaist, is a character), history (Karl Marx is a character), and literature (James Joyce is a character). The first act, however, is parodied by the second act when a pretty girl delivers heavy speeches on Marxism and the theory of value—undercutting, thereby, the clever speeches of the fashionable first-act men.

Travesties shares many of the same concerns as the radio play *Artist Descending a Staircase* (1973), later turned into a stage play (1989). In both, art—not history or philosophy—conveys insight (to those who are not blindsighted), since the necessary 'fall' artists must make from the literal staircase of rationalism opens up the province of imagination. Tristan Tzara becomes perhaps the first Stoppard mouthpiece to articulate a clear position on the seriousness of play. Not only does he insist on the right of the artist to delude audience expectation but he insists on the ethical function of such denunciation, noting that wars are really fought for words like 'oil' and 'coal', not for words like 'freedom' and 'patriotism'. Dada art, like post-Absurdism, is thus committed to the serious enterprise of exposing the sophistry within every rational argument.

Stoppard has been criticised for trivialising serious issues or for being too neutral in the exposition of political ideas. Such indeterminacy, the critics argue, reduces the author's intent. Rather than answering his critics, Stoppard utilises their thinking to his own post-Absurdist effect. Switzerland, a neutral ground with its reassuring air of permanence, becomes in *Travesties* the centre of flux; a little-known event becomes the raw material from which the story draws its energy; uncertainty and confusion are like the cuckoos of Swiss clocks. It is not that chaos is chaotic, but that order has a false sense of security dressed in fancy clothes (tra-vesties).

Dirty Linen and New-Found-Land (1976), a 'knickers farce', were reviewed negatively as 'undergraduate satire' or as 'altogether intolerable' [see Thomar R. Whitaker, *Tom Stoppard*, 1983]. While Stoppard's post-Absurdism here leans toward panache, it nevertheless reflects a serious Orwellian point about politics and the English language that the critics seemed to have missed. Spoofed in *Dirty Linen* is Parliamentary procedure, instituted to safeguard government from corruption, but in fact safeguarding government from the people's right to know. Similar to other social rituals, government committee proceedings

provide gaming situations where politicians can 'score' with Maddie Gotobed (an unsubtle name), and journalists covering committee deliberations can 'win' readers. 'Public trust', which must 'air its dirty linen', becomes just a meaningless phrase like *che sara sara, c'est la vie,* or *quel dommage.* Stoppard suggests that the devaluing of democratic principles is as universally accepted as the degeneration of plain talk. This concern about democracy and language is mirrored in the second play, where America, the supposed new-found-land, is exposed as merely a trite idea propped up by stereotypes. The character Arthur takes us on a Whitmanesque celebration of 'America' coast to coast. But poetry dies inside bombast, as does meaning inside politics. Doublespeak leads to adultery in the private sphere and disinformation in the public sphere, and what mediates the lie in each is the noble-sounding word.

Every Good Boy Deserves Favour: A Piece for Actors and Orchestra (1977)—André Previn conducting—places Stoppard's comedy squarely inside a post-Absurdist framework, where the really serious issues of our time can no longer be discussed seriously (we have lost the capacity to hear) and so a new strategy must be found. One of Stoppard's new strategies is music, which speaks to the soul, not the mind. The setting, a mental institution inside a Soviet totalitarian regime, offers Stoppard yet another occasion to critique the logics that uphold institutions, be these 'democratic' or 'communist', and to show these logics as false. But with music as a background to the grim themes of torture, political prisoners, repressive regimes and mental illness, Stoppard softens his attack; and by exposing interrogation methods as bizarre, he shows the craziness of logic.

Recognisably Stoppardian is the situation of two men with the same name, Alexander Ivanov, one 'sane', the other 'insane'. Both characters rebel against the norm, but for different reasons. The case of the 'insane' Alexander reveals the validity of Greek culture, which saw a harmony between music and math. Deluded by the notion that his body contains an orchestra, Ivanov the lunatic brings back the wisdom of the Greeks, which in Euclidean geometry proclaimed two fascinating axioms: first, everyone is equal to the triangle; second, a point has position but no dimension. The first axiom warns against dichotomous, either/or rigidities. Accordingly, the lunatic plays a triangle, an instrument he uses to sabotage rigid regimes; he 'plays' against two-sided oppositional thinking with the triangle. His delusion, therefore, is ludic, a gaming protection against absolutes. The second axiom applies to the other Ivanov, the political prisoner, whose protest against totalitarianism has given him his public 'point' but has denied him his private 'dimension' with his son, Sacha. This character is thus a prisoner inside a belief system that excludes the middle: life lived among and between other people, like sons. That he is imprisoned by a totalitarian regime is symbolic of a frozen relationship with his son, a touching sub-theme.

In ***Night and Day*** (1978) the focus is again on language and politics and the war between the two. Set in a fictional black African country, Kambawe, the play concerns a nation faced with an internal revolution caused by conflicting economic and political systems. But of greater interest than the revolution is the attitude of the two journalists covering the war, their at-war viewpoints about reporting and factuality. Milne and Wagner are like night and day: the former a cynic, a self-seeking capitalist and a scab; the latter an idealist who believes that his profession is the Fourth Estate, capable of correcting the lies of politicians.

The play is also about colonisation: how not just countries or journalists but ordinary people like Ruth Carson can be occupied by foreign forces. Ruth engages inner speech, delivered outwardly, to suggest her contrast to the double-talk of politicians; hers is the speaking back and forth from one 'country' of the self to another, in clear recognition that she has been colonised. In a particularly dramatic moment Ruth rails against the cant for which people die. Speaking between her two selves, she comes to see that winning wars is not for the liberation of Kambawe but for the ownership of Kambawe's resources: *King Solomon's Mines* played for 'reel'.

Stoppard continues language considerations in ***Dogg's Hamlet, Cahoot's Macbeth*** (1979), where in the preface he suggests that the play is an answer to Ludwig Wittgenstein's philosophical investigation proposing that different words describe different shapes and sizes. Ever fascinated with systems of thought, Stoppard exposes the assumption within the assumption, playfully and hilariously. In ***Dogg's Hamlet*** the language system to be learned is Dogg talk. Professor Dogg, to whom the play is dedicated, has his own set of words which Abel, Baker, and Charlie, in fine military fashion, understand. These three schoolboys are erecting a stage for a performance, but to put all the planks in place they need to know the lingo. The audience watches as they place planks on cue by a single command, much as dogs perform for masters. Spectators, not understanding the language, must themselves become doglike, trying to master tricks. The first thirty pages of playtext are, subsequently, Dogg talk, followed by the last fourteen pages, which derive from Shakespeare's *Hamlet,* including Hamlet's loaded line, 'Words, words, words', and Polonius' response, 'Though this be madness, yet there is method in it'.

Doublecoded within this situation is another situation, that of another Shakespeare play, *Macbeth,* dedicated to the Czechoslovakian playwright Pavel Kohout. Stoppard has instructed his audience sufficiently in the first part of his production so that when Easy enters, speaking only Dogg language, he becomes easily understood. The point of the nonsense seems to be this: plays within plays illustrate political situations; the Czech revolution, with its accompanying censorship of artists like Pavel Kohout, 'ghost' every attempt by Tom Stoppard, born in Czechoslovakia, to write in the free world. Both Macbeth and Hamlet have at their dramatic centres a ghost; so does Stoppard have at his centre a ghost—his own dead father and the censored artist from his fatherland. While British audiences are well schooled in understanding such rituals as parlor games

and tea, these same audiences have no way of dealing with the black holes of totalitarianism. Stoppard brings forth spectres of his 'checkered' past (re-presented through Shakespeare) so that British ears may acquire new hearing, British eyes deeper seeing.

With ***The Real Thing*** (1982) Stoppard further engages serious themes. Like his first play, it won a Tony Award, deservedly so; it is a gem of a play, raising all of Stoppard's issues of the sixties and seventies with a new eighties elegance. The problem of language, the question of art's role in politics, the question of reality: these comprise the concerns which have almost become Stoppard hallmarks. Less familiar is Stoppard's treatment of 'knowing' as a carnal, not just an intellectual concern. *Knowing*—the yearning *to be known* without the mask—becomes a powerful theme because an impossible reality.

Two members of the writing profession, Brodie and Henry, are professional antagonists with different ideas of their trade. Brodie, committed to politics, believes that art should make a point about public policy; his language is unequivocal but trite. Henry believes that art is not 'about' anything: it is the thing itself. His play *House of Cards* is a metaphor for his theory of aesthetics as a house decked to fall. The spectator must acquire the skill to see that false claims or noble words are flimsy frames for truth. With its emphasis on the title word 'real', this play addresses the impossibility of knowing—in relationships, particularly—when truth is obscured by language.

Of central interest is Henry's desire to find for himself the undealt card of carnal knowledge. Knowing the flesh *in extremis* is stripping off the public mask, becoming finally naked to one's lover, one's self. But carnal knowing offers no guarantee of fidelity. In this play everyone carnally loves everyone else's spouse. Stoppard once again double codes Shakespeare—this time *Othello*—to show the tragic ends to which logical proofs can lead. A mere handkerchief 'stands' for more than it can define—betrayal—a reality which can never be defined to satisfy the condition of pain.

The Real Thing is central to Stoppard's aesthetic intention. Through a mix of doubling, ambiguity, and playfully elegant wit, Stoppard makes his post-Absurdist point. Not only is it impossible to equate the thing 'named' or shown to the thing 'experienced', it is wrong, ethically and morally, so to do. In an impassioned speech for the function of paradox in language, Henry (speaking for Stoppard), says this:

> Words don't deserve . . . malarkey. They're innocent, neutral, precise, standing for this, describing that, meaning the other, so if you look after them you can build bridges across incomprehension and chaos. But when they get their corners knocked off, they're no good any more. . . .

Words have corners, just as truth does: shades of meaning, opposite definitions, different parts of speech. The terrible irony is that words standing for 'this' while describing 'that' invite lying, publicly as well as privately. The solution is not to make ever more precise the terms of our knowing; the solution is to open up our ability to see the dead ends to which big words can lead when their corners get knocked off.

Hapgood (1988) is the most recent of Stoppard's work to advance the post-Absurdist motifs of mystification, ambiguity, and playfulness—this time with overt reference to spectator notions borrowed from scientific chaos theory. According to David Bohm, no continuous motion such as that presupposed by Newtonian cause-and-effect logic actually exists in nature. Instead, an examination of the dual role of both matter and energy reveals that things can be connected any distance away without any apparent force to carry that connection [See *The Reenactment of Science*, ed. David Ray Griffin, 1988]. Rather than parts organising wholes—deduction's code of reasoning—it seems that parts *are* wholes. It seems, too, that discrete individual units (called 'the quantum' in science, 'the spectator' in theatre) are constantly attracted by turbulence and self-contradiction. How we know is a mystery based on an overall interrelatedness of things—a statement which chaos theorists readily accept. An interesting irony here is that Stoppard may ultimately appeal more to scientists schooled in chaos theory than to literary critics schooled in Aristotle.

Hapgood is a play about a character who is unable to pinpoint the truth she is seeking, either in her professional life as chief intelligence officer (called Mother) or in her private life as a single parent (also called Mother). No matter how Elizabeth Hapgood figures it, her seeing always eludes reality. The pivotal character is a Russian physicist, Joseph Kerner, who, like Barley Blair of the Stoppard-scripted movie, *The Russia House* (1990), has defected to the West to continue his research but who feeds back to the Soviet Union information that will mislead the Soviet scientists. That Kerner, Hapgood's lover, has a twin complicates the problem Hapgood has in trying to 'see' who he is (she, however, also plays at twinning). This doubled situation demonstrates the scientific property of electrons, which in quantum mechanics can be in two places at the same time.

While something subversive pervades Stoppard's post-Absurdist perspective, it is also curiously liberating. Stoppard shows us that every ordered system has rituals, which he delights in stylising so that we can see their mannered form. To consider any code as single-layered is totally to misrepresent reality. Reality seen through a Stoppard lens is always ambiguous; but its pain, though real, is not tragic. Stoppard's sharp wit cuts through the nonsense, giving us the grace to accept unknowing when confronted with such axioms as these: I am not who you think I am; the games we play are more serious than we think they are; the wars we fight are not for the causes they tell us they are.

ROSENCRANTZ AND GUILDENSTERN ARE DEAD

R. H. Lee   (essay date 1969)

SOURCE: "The Circle and its Tangent," in *Theoria*, Pietermaritzburg, Vol. XXXIII, October, 1969, pp. 37-43.

[*In the essay below, Lee employs the image of a circle and a line tangential to it—representing the world in Stoppard's play in which Rosencrantz and Guildenstern are "people" and its intersection with the world of* Hamlet, *in which they are "characters"—to elucidate the structure of Stoppard's drama and its relation to Shakespeare's tragedy.*]

Almost every critic or reviewer who has written on Tom Stoppard's *Rosencrantz and Guildenstern are Dead* has paid tribute to the dramatist's "brilliant idea" in linking his play about two supporting actors with the play in which they act their parts. But once they have shown that they understand that a "brilliant" and even audacious idea is involved, they stop without doing justice either to the full brilliance of the idea, or to the detail in which it is worked out. In this article I want, first, to explain what I think the idea is, and how the structure and intention of the play should be seen; and, secondly, to analyse some parts of the play to show that the dramatist embodies this idea in the substance as well as the structure of the play.

When Rosencrantz and Guildenstern first meet the Player on the way to Elsinore, this exchange takes place:

Rosencrantz: What is your line?

Player: Tragedy, sir. Deaths and disclosures, universal and particular, denouements both unexpected and inexorable, transvestite melodrama on all levels including the suggestive. We transport you into a world of intrigue and illusion . . . clowns, if you like, murderers—we can do you ghosts and battles, on the skirmish level, heroes, villains, tormented lovers—set pieces in the poetic vein; we can do you rapiers or rape or both, by all means, faithless wives and ravished virgins—flagrante delicto at a price, but that comes under realism for which there are special terms. Getting warm, am I?

It has already been established that one of the primary verbal modes of the play is punning, and so we are not surprised to find that "line" can mean "special interest or concern" or "the long narrow mark linking two or more points". The Player thus performs tragedies as his special interest or concern, and his specialisation as a form of drama is also described as a line. Tragedy as a literary form *is* predominantly linear, and this fact suggests to me that a helpful way of looking at the structure of the play is to see it as a circle with a tangent to it. The circle is the world of Rosencrantz and Guildenstern as people, and the tangent is the world of *Hamlet*, and Hamlet, play and character. The tangent touches the circle in the lives of

Rosencrantz and Guildenstern, at the very point where we see them as *people* (expressed, in dramatic terms, by their being characters in **Rosencrantz and Guildenstern are Dead**) and at the same time as characters in *Hamlet*. Their confusion arises from the intermittent and, to them, inexplicable movements from one kind of world to another.

The diagram of the circle and its tangent is helpful also in suggesting the nature of the two worlds touching each other. We have already discussed the pun on the 'line' of tragedy linking *Hamlet* with the tangent. In the action and image of spinning coins, and in the plain allusions to *Waiting for Godot,* we see the nature of the other world—the circular, repetitive experience of Beckettian comedy. In his play, Stoppard provides us with the point of contact of seventeenth and twentieth century views of the world, as these are crystallised in the drama of each century. Let us look at each separately.

The understanding of and response to tragedy as a literary form depends upon the acceptance of the idea of causality: that certain events will have certain consequences which, in turn, become the causes of certain events which have their own consequences. One could go further and say that belief in tragedy also involves acceptance of the belief that the whole linked chain of events has a purpose, and is therefore theoretically explicable by someone in possession of all the necessary information. The two central elements of tragedy are indicated in the terms "inevitability" and "understanding"; or to quote Northrop Frye [in his *Anatomy of Criticism*]:

> . . . tragedy shows itself to be primarily a vision of the supremacy of the event or 'mythos'. The response to tragedy is 'this must be', or, perhaps more accurately, 'this *does* happen': the event is primary, the explanation of it, secondary and variable.

In our own lives, the possibility of seeing clearly the full course of the linked chain of events, and understanding its inevitable end, is limited. It is limited by our individual participation in the event which colours our view of them, and by physical death, which cuts off our participation in the sequence at the moment it reaches its conclusion, and the moment *before* we can understand it. The fact and prospect of death also complicates and confuses our necessary emotional acceptance that this *is* where the whole tragic sequence is leading. We are thus in our own lives partially unable and partially unwilling to contemplate the straight line of tragedy to death.

And therein lies the great satisfaction and arguable moral value of dramatic tragedy. The tragic play compels us to see a tragic sequence, and, because we are not involved in it, and because the dramatist can give us all the information for understanding, we cannot flinch from the inevitable end—death. This is what Aristotle means in his theory of the cathartic value of tragedy—it enables us to contemplate through art a vision of life too horrifying to contemplate at first hand. In fact, artistic death is the only death most of us *can* contemplate—as the Player argues to Rosencrantz and Guildenstern, when they object that stage deaths are unbelievable:

> *Guildenstern:* Actors! The mechanics of cheap melodrama! That isn't *death!* You scream and choke and sink to your knees, but it doesn't bring death home to anyone—it doesn't catch them unawares and start the whisper in their skulls that says—" One day you are going to die". You die so many times; how can you expect them to believe in your death!

> *Player:* On the contrary, it's the only kind they do believe. They're conditioned to it. I had an actor once who was condemned to hang for stealing a sheep—or a lamb, I forget which—so I got permission to have him hanged in the middle of a play—had to change the plot a bit but I thought it would be effective, you know—and you wouldn't believe it, he just *wasn't* convincing! It was impossible to suspend one's disbelief—and what with the audience jeering and throwing peanuts, the whole thing was a *disaster!*—he did nothing but cry all the time—right out of character—just stood there and cried . . . Never again . . . Audiences know what to expect, and that is all that they are prepared to believe in.

A tragic drama, then, focusses our attention on and, as Aristotle's theory suggests, helps us to come to terms with what is assumed by the dramatist to be the situation in real life. Whether this theory actually describes the effect, desired and actual, of tragedy is hotly disputed, and modern critics tend not to accept these wide claims. Frye, for instance, narrows them considerably, but still indicates belief in the "line" of tragedy when he writes:

> The machinery of fate (in tragedy) is administered by a set of remote invisible gods, whose freedom and pleasure are ironic because they exclude man, and who intervene in human affairs chiefly to safeguard their own prerogatives. They demand sacrifices, punish presumption, and enforce obedience to natural and moral law as an end in itself. Here we are not trying to describe, for instance, the gods in Greek tragedy: we are trying to isolate the sense of human remoteness and futility in relation to the divine order which is only one element among others in most tragic visions of life, though an essential one in all.

Stoppard's "brilliant idea" consists essentially in using the actual tragic play *Hamlet* (to which we already attach feelings of "human remoteness and futility") as an image of "the machinery of fate" in the lives of Rosencrantz and Guildenstern themselves. A tragedy becomes the vehicle for a sense of tragedy in another play. Rosencrantz and Guildenstern are caught up in it "without possibility of reprieve or hope of explanation".

The Player and the tragedians (we notice that though they are usually called the Players, Stoppard chooses to focus upon their playing of tragedy alone) are given many opportunities of describing this view of life. The central example, perhaps, is this:

> *Player:* There's a design at work in all art—surely you know that? Events must play themselves out to aesthetic, moral and logical conclusion.

Guildenstern: And what's that, in this case?

Player: It never varies—we aim at the point where everyone who is marked for death dies.

Guildenstern: Marked?

Player: Between "just deserts" and "tragic irony" we are given quite a lot of scope for our particular talent. Generally speaking, things have gone about as far as they can possibly go when things have got about as bad as they reasonably get. (*He switches on a smile.*)

Guildenstern: Who decides?

Player (switching off his smile): Decides? It is *written*. (*He turns away.* GUIL. *grabs him and spins him back violently.*) (*Unflustered*) Now if you're going to be subtle, we'll miss each other in the dark. I'm referring to oral tradition. So to speak.

(GUIL. *releases him.*)

We're tragedians, you see. We follow directions—there is no *choice* involved. The bad end unhappily, the good unluckily. That is what tragedy means.

(*Calling.*)

Positions!

(*The* TRAGEDIANS *have taken up positions for the continuation of the mime: which in this case means a love scene, sexual and passionate, between the* QUEEN *and the* POISONER/KING.)

Player: Go!

Death is the goal of the design of all tragic art, and the actor can manoeuvre only in the determining of the kind of death, and the moral attitude to death. Once we have established those, we can begin. Wittily, as he explains this theory, the tragedians take their places *and begin*. This is the world into which Rosencrantz and Guildenstern are dragged initially by the messenger, uncomprehending of its causes or consequences, barely understanding the minute parts they have to play, and thus carried along to their deaths. There is a small growth of self-awareness, expressed in their attitude to being on the boat in Act III. Though they disbelieve in their destination, they do realise that they are being carried somewhere:

Guildenstern: Where we went wrong was getting on a boat. We can move, of course, change direction, rattle about, but our movement is contained within a larger one that carries us along as inexorably as the wind and current . . .

Rosencrantz: They had it in for us, didn't they? Right from the beginning. Who'd have thought that we were so important?

Guildenstern: But why? Was it all for this? Who are we that so much should converge on our little deaths? (*In anguish to the* PLAYERS.) Who are *we*?

They do develop slightly, moving away from the world they begin in, into the Hamlet world. Their original world is caught at once for us, in the play, in the action and image of spinning coins, and especially in the remarkable run of heads with which the play has opened. Around this phenomenon, which the simpler and more satisfied Rosencrantz finds simply "luck", Guildenstern nervously erects certain pertinent philosophical dilemmas. For our purpose, the most important is that it suggests a world in which all causality is absent, and presents us with the notion that the sequence of eighty-five heads is both amazing and expected:

Guildenstern: It must be indicative of something, besides the redistribution of wealth. (*He muses.*) List of possible explanations. One: I'm willing it. Inside where nothing shows, I am the essence of a man spinning double-headed coins, and betting against himself in private atonement for an unremembered past. (*He spins a coin at* ROS.)

Rosencrantz: Heads.

Guildenstern: Two: time has stopped dead, and the single experience of one coin being spun once has been repeated ninety times . . . (*He flips a coin, looks at it, tosses it to* ROS.) On the whole, doubtful. Three: divine intervention that is to say, a good turn from above concerning him, cf. children of Israel, or retribution from above concerning me, cf. Lot's wife. Four: a spectacular vindication of the principle that each individual coin spun individually (*he spins one*) is as likely to come down heads as tails and therefore should cause no surprise each individual time it does.

The final explanation is statistically accurate, and presents us with a world of total unreliability—an amazing combination of phenomena simply cannot be made to yield either a sequence or a precedent. The eighty-sixth spin is totally undetermined by the previous eighty-five. Facts remain isolated, refuse to form chains, and explanations remain forever "possible", the nature of circumstances determining the run being beyond our comprehension.

Guildenstern himself specifically draws the comparison between the two kinds of world:

Guildenstern: The equanimity of your average tosser of coins depends upon a low, or rather a tendency, or let us say a probability, or at any rate a mathematically calculable chance, which ensures that he will not upset himself by losing too much nor upset his opponent by winning too often. This made for a kind of harmony and a kind of confidence. It related the fortuitous and the ordained into a reassuring union which we recognized as nature. The sun came up about as often as it went down, in the long run, and a coin showed heads about as often as it showed tails. Then a messenger arrived. We had been sent for. Nothing else happened. Ninety-two coins spun consecutively have come down ninety-two consecutive times . . . and for the last three minutes on the wind of a windless day I have heard the sound of drums and flute . . .

The messenger summons them from the endless cycle of fortuitous, repetitive facts, to a world which proceeds in an ordained linear, sequential manner to a pre-determined goal. The use of *Waiting for Godot* is balanced by the use of *Hamlet,* and in the play the seventeenth century world view (focussed in its drama) touches the absurd universe (focussed in *its* drama). The Rosencrantz and Guildenstern exits from *Hamlet* become "entrances somewhere else", "which is a kind of integrity"; but I think Stoppard goes beyond this, to suggest that there is no end to the futile round of the absurd universe, unless we seize again on tragedy. Guildenstern says in the play: "We need Hamlet for our release", and we feel that Stoppard is obliquely telling us that modern drama needs some infusion of the attitudes behind *Hamlet* for its release from being forever waiting for Godot.

Normand Berlin (essay date 1973)

SOURCE: "*Rosencrantz and Guildenstern Are Dead*: Theater of Criticism," in *Modern Drama,* Vol. XVI, Nos. 3-4, December, 1973, pp. 269-77.

[*Berlin argues that, rather than encouraging active involvement in the play's events,* Rosencrantz and Guildenstern Are Dead *promotes a distanced, critical response. Stoppard, he asserts, "forces us to be conscious observers of a play frozen before us in order that it may be examined critically."*]

Tom Stoppard's *Rosencrantz and Guildenstern Are Dead* entered the theater world of 1966-67 with much fanfare, and in the ensuing years it has acquired a surprisingly high reputation as a modern classic. It is an important play, but its importance is of a very special kind up to now not acknowledged. The play has fed the modern critics' and audiences' hunger for "philosophical" significances, and as absurdist drama it has been compared favorably and often misleadingly with Beckett's *Waiting for Godot.* However, its peculiar value as theater of criticism has received no attention. To help recognize this value I offer the following discussion.

Rosencrantz and Guildenstern Are Dead is a derivative play, correctly characterized by Robert Brustein [in the *New Republic,* November 1967] as a "theatrical parasite." It feeds on *Hamlet,* on *Six Characters in Search of an Author,* and on *Waiting for Godot.* Stoppard goes to Shakespeare for his characters, for the background to his play's action, and for some direct quotations, to Pirandello for the idea of giving extra-dramatic life to established characters, to Beckett for the tone, the philosophical thrust, and for some comic routines. The play takes Shakespeare's Rosencrantz and Guildenstern—time-servers, who appear rather cool and calculating in Shakespeare, and whose names indicate the courtly decadence they may represent—

and transforms them into garrulous, sometimes simple, often rather likable chaps. Baffled, imprisoned in a play they did not write, Rosencrantz and Guildenstern must act out their pre-arranged dramatic destinies. Like Beckett's Vladimir and Estragon, they carry on vaudeville routines, engage in verbal battles and games, and discourse on the issues of life and death. However, whereas Beckett's play, like Shakespeare's, defies easy categories and explanations, and remains elusive in the best sense of the word, suggesting the mystery of life, Stoppard's play welcomes categories, prods for a clarity of explanation, and seems more interested in substance than shadow.

Stoppard's play is conspicuously intellectual; it "thinks" a great deal, and consequently it lacks the "feeling" or union of thought and emotion that we associate with *Waiting for Godot* and *Hamlet.* This must be considered a shortcoming in Stoppard's art, but a shortcoming that Stoppard shares with other dramatists and one that could be explained away if only his intellectual insights were less derivative, seemed less canned. To be sure, plays breed plays, and it would be unfair to find fault with Stoppard for going to other plays for inspiration and specific trappings. In fact, at times he uses Shakespeare and Beckett ingeniously and must be applauded for his execution. But when the ideas of an essentially intellectual play seem too easy, then the playwright must be criticized. Whenever Stoppard—his presence always felt although his characters do the talking—meditates on large philosophical issues, his play seems thin, shallow. His idiom is not rich enough to sustain a direct intellectual confrontation with Life and Death. Consider, for example, Guildenstern's question: "The only beginning is birth and the only end is death—if you can't count on that, what can you count on?" Put in this pedestrian way, the idea behind the question loses its force. Or take Guildenstern's remarks on Death: "Dying is not romantic, and death is not a game which will soon be over . . . Death is not anything . . . death is not . . . It's the absence of presence, nothing more . . . the endless time of never coming back . . . a gap you can't see, and when the wind blows through it, it makes no sound. . . ." Examples of this kind of direct philosophical probing can be found throughout the play. We hear a man talking but do not feel the pressure of death behind the words. The passage seems false because the language does not possess the elusiveness and the economy that are essential if a writer wishes to confront large issues directly.

But there are indirect ways to deal with life and death, and here Stoppard is highly successful. And here we arrive at the heart of the discussion of Stoppard's art. According to Stoppard himself [in an article by Tom Prideaux in *Life,* February, 1968], his play was "not written as a response to anything about alienation in our times. . . . It would be fatal to set out to write primarily on an intellectual level. Instead, one writes about human beings under stress—whether it is about losing one's trousers or being nailed to the cross." Stoppard's words run counter to our experience of the play and indicate once again that writers are not the best judges of their own writing. Like all writers of drama, Stoppard wishes to present human beings under stress, but he does so in the most intellectual way. In fact, there is only one level to the play, one kind of stance, and that level is intellectual. The audience witnesses no forceful sequence of narrative, since the story is known and therefore already solidified in the audience's mind. One could say that the audience is given not sequence but status-quo, and status-quo points to a "critical stance"—a way of looking at the events of the play as a critic would, that is, experiencing the play as structure, complete, unmoving, unsequential.

In the act of seeing a stage play, which moves in time, we are in a pre-critical state, fully and actively engaged in the play's events. When the play is over, then we become critics, seeing the play as a structural unity and, in fact, able to function as critics only because the play has stopped moving. In the act of seeing *Rosencrantz and Guildenstern Are Dead,* however, our critical faculty is not subdued. We are always *observing* the characters and are not ourselves participating. We know the results of the action because we know *Hamlet,* so that all our references are backward. Not witnessing a movement in time, we are forced to contemplate the frozen state, the status-quo, of the characters who carry their Shakespearean fates with them. It is *during* Stoppard's play that we function as critics, just as Stoppard, through his characters, functions as critic within the play. It is precisely this critical stance of Stoppard, of his characters, and of his audience that allows me to attach the label "theater of criticism" to the play, thereby specifying what I believe to be Stoppard's distinctiveness as a modern dramatist.

We recognize and wonder at those points in Shakespeare's plays where he uses the "theater" image to allow us to see, critically, the play before us from a different angle, where, for example, we hear of the future re-creations of Caesar's murder at the very point in the play where it is re-created, or where we hear Cleopatra talk about her greatness presented on stage "i' th' posture of a whore" at the moment when it is presented in that posture. At these moments Shakespeare engages us on a cerebral level, forcing us to think, stopping the action to cause us to consider the relationship between theater and life. These Shakespearean moments are expanded to occupy much of Stoppard's play, just as Shakespeare's minor characters are expanded to become Stoppard's titular non-heroes.

I have indicated Stoppard's shortcomings when he wishes to express truths about Life and Death. However, as critic discussing *Hamlet* and Elizabethan drama, he is astute, sometimes brilliant, and his language is effective because it need not confront head-on the large issues that only poetry, it seems, is successful in confronting directly. In a *New Yorker* interview [4 November 1967] with actors Brian Murray and John Woods, who played Rosencrantz and Guildenstern in the New York production of Stoppard's play, Murray says: "I have been an actor most of my life, and I've played all kinds of parts with the Royal Shakespeare Company, but I never realized how remarkable Shakespeare is until I saw what Tom Stoppard could do with a couple of minor characters from *Hamlet*." This fleeting statement in a rather frivolous interview pinpoints what Stoppard does best: what he can "do with" Shake-

speare's minor characters to help us realize "how remarkable Shakespeare is." That is, Stoppard helps us to see more clearly not "human beings under stress" but Shakespeare. The actor Murray is applauding a critical function, and as we thread our way through the play Stoppard must be praised for precisely that function. . . .

Stoppard, a drama critic before turning playwright and in this play a playwright as drama critic, crisply pinpoints the characteristics of Greek and Elizabethan tragedy and, enlarging the range of his criticism, uses these tragic characteristics to indicate what "we"—players and audience—do.

I am arguing that Stoppard is most successful when he functions as a critic of drama and when he allows his insights on the theater to lead him to observations on life. He is weakest, most empty, when he attempts to confront life directly. Stoppard is at his artistic best when he follows the advice of Polonius: "By indirections find directions out." This is as it should be, I think, because Stoppard's philosophical stance depends so heavily on the "play" idea, the mask, the game, the show. Not only is the entire *Rosencrantz and Guildenstern Are Dead* a play within a play that Shakespeare has written, but throughout Stoppard uses the idea of play. Rosencrantz and Guildenstern, and of course the Player, are conscious of themselves as players, acting out their lives, and baffled, even anguished, by the possibility that no one is watching the performance. All the world is a stage for Stoppard, as for Shakespeare, but Shakespeare's art fuses world and stage, causing the barrier between what is real and what is acted to break down, while Stoppard's art separates the two, makes us observers and critics of the stage, and allows us to see the world through the stage, ever conscious that we are doing just that. The last is my crucial point: Stoppard forces us to be conscious observers of a play frozen before us in order that it may be examined critically. Consequently, what the play offers us, despite its seeming complexity and the virtuosity of Stoppard's technique, is clarity, intellectual substance, rather than the shadows and mystery that we find in *Hamlet* or the pressure of life's absurdity that we find in *Waiting for Godot.* Of course, we miss these important aspects of great drama, and some critics and reviewers have correctly alluded to the play's deficiencies in these respects, but we should not allow what is lacking to erase what is there—bright, witty, intellectual criticism and high theatricality.

I present one final example, taken from the end of the play, to demonstrate Stoppard's fine ability to make criticism and theater serve as a commentary on man. In this incident—"Incidents! All we get is incidents! Dear God, is it too much to expect a little sustained action?!"—Guildenstern, who all along has shown contempt for the players and for their cheap melodrama in presenting scenes of death, becomes so filled with vengeance and scorn that he snatches the dagger from the Player's belt and threatens the Player:

> I'm talking about death—and you've never experienced *that.* And you cannot *act* it. You die a thousand casual deaths—with none of that intensity which squeezes

out life . . . and no blood runs cold any where. Because even as you die you know that you will come back in a different hat. But no one gets up after *death*—there is no applause—there is only silence and some second-hand clothes, and that's—*death*—

He then stabs the Player, who "with huge, terrible eyes, clutches at the wound as the blade withdraws: he makes small weeping sounds and falls to his knees, and then right down." Hysterically, Guildenstern shouts: "If we have a destiny, then so had he—and if this is ours, then that was his—and if there are no explanations for us, then let there be none for him—" At which point the other players on stage applaud the Player, who stands up, modestly accepts the admiration of his fellow tragedians, and proceeds to show Guildenstern how the blade of the play dagger is pushed into the handle.

Here we seem to witness, for the only time in the play, an *act* being performed, a *choice* being made, not dictated by the events of Shakespeare's play—only to discover that we have witnessed playing, theater. Guildenstern and Rosencrantz are taken in by the performance of a false death, bearing out the Player's belief, stated earlier in the play, that audiences believe *only* false deaths, that when he once had an actor, condemned for stealing, really die on stage the death was botched and unbelievable. What we have in Guildenstern's "killing" of the Player, therefore, is a theatrical re-enforcement of the earlier observations on audiences by the Player as critic. As we spectators watch the event—Rosencrantz had remarked earlier that he feels "like a spectator"—we intellectually grasp the fact that we had no real action, that no choice was made, Stoppard thereby making his philosophical point indirectly and with fine effect. In Stoppard a condition of life is most clearly understood, it seems, only when reflected in a critical, theatrical mirror.

In *Rosencrantz and Guildenstern Are Dead* we do not have the kind of theater characterized by such phrases as direct involvement, emotional, pre-critical, theater of the heart, but rather a theater of criticism, intellectual, distanced, of the mind. In a very real sense, Stoppard is an artist-critic writing drama for audience-critics, a dramatist least effective when he points his finger directly at the existential dilemma—"What does it all add up to?"—and most effective when he confronts the play *Hamlet* and Elizabethan drama and theatrical art, thereby going roundabout to get to the important issues. Stoppard's play, because it feeds on both an Elizabethan tragedy and a modern tragicomedy, gives us the opportunity to consider the larger context of modern drama, especially Joseph Wood Krutch's well-known and ominous observations [in *The Modern Temper*, 1957] on the death of tragedy and his prediction of the devolution of tragedy from Religion to Art to Document. Krutch finds an interesting answer, I believe, in *Rosencrantz and Guildenstern Are Dead*. Using Krutch's words, but not in the way he uses them, we can say that *Rosencrantz and Guildenstern Are Dead* is art that studies art, and therefore serving as a document, dramatic criticism as play presenting ideas on *Hamlet,* on Elizabethan drama, on theatrical art, and by so doing

commenting on the life that art reveals. That is, Stoppard's play is holding the mirror of art up to the art that holds the mirror up to nature.

This double image causes the modern audience to take the kind of stance often associated with satire. And yet, Stoppard's play cannot be called satirical, for it makes no attempt to encourage the audience into any kind of action, as do Brecht's plays, or to cause the audience to change the way things are. The play examines the way things are, or, more precisely stated, it intellectually confronts and theatricalizes the condition of man the player and the world as theater. By the pressure of its *critical* energy, the play awakens in the audience a recognition of man's condition, not in order to change that condition, but to see it clearly. In short, by presenting a theatrical, artistic document, Stoppard makes us think—the words "document" and "think" pointing to the modernity, the impoverishment, and the particular value of *Rosencrantz and Guildenstern Are Dead*. The play presents not revelation but criticism, not passionate art—Hamlet in the graveyard—but cool, critical, intellectual art—Hamlet playing with the recorders. *Rosencrantz and Guildenstern Are Dead,* in its successful moments, brilliantly displays the virtues of theater of criticism, and perhaps shows the direction in which some modern drama will be going—"times being what they are."

William E. Gruber (essay date 1981-82)

SOURCE: "'Wheels within Wheels, etcetera': Artistic Design in *Rosencrantz and Guildenstern Are Dead,*" in *Comparative Drama,* Vol. 15, No. 4, Winter, 1981-82, pp. 291-310.

[*In the following essay, Gruber maintains that* Rosencrantz and Guildenstern Are Dead *is not merely a pastiche of elements of* Hamlet; *rather it is a technically innovative play that mirrors classical tragedy.*]

Tom Stoppard's *Rosencrantz and Guildenstern Are Dead* ought to cause us to acknowledge some inadequacies in the vocabulary we currently use to discuss plays, and the nature of our shortcoming can be demonstrated, I think, with some representative summaries of Stoppard's art. Ruby Cohn, for example, suggests that Stoppard proved "extremely skillful in dovetailing the *Hamlet* scenes into the *Godot* situation" [*Modern Shakespeare Offshoots,* 1976]; Ronald Hayman writes that "Stoppard appeared at the right moment with his beautifully engineered device for propelling two attendant lords into the foreground" [*Tom Stoppard,* 1977]; Charles Marowitz comments that "Stoppard displays a remarkable skill in juggling the donnees of existential philosophy" ["Confessions of a Conterfeit Critic"]; and Thomas Whitaker argues that "the *raisonneur* of this clever pastiche is of course The Player . . . [who] knowingly plays himself" [*Fields of Play in Modern Drama,* 1977].

Such language—"skillful in dovetailing," "beautifully engineered," "clever pastiche"—condemns while it praises, subtly labeling Stoppard's play as a derivative piece of workmanship. We tend to mistrust anything which is not obviously new, not wholly original; yet surely our modern bias here obscures crucial differences between Stoppard's play and, say, the *Hamlet*-collages of Marowitz and Joseph Papp. These latter works may be summarized accurately as examples of skillful joinery. But Stoppard's drama does not simply "fit" together different pieces of theater. His play has no clear theatrical precedent, and a workshop vocabulary proves unable to explain what occurs when the script of *Hamlet* mingles with the script of *Rosencrantz and Guildenstern Are Dead*.

Part of the reason this subject has not been clarified is that it is impossible to assess accurately the extent to which the audience will recognize allusions to *Hamlet*. Even one of Stoppard's stage directions poses insoluble problems: *"Hamlet enters upstage, and pauses, weighing up the pros and cons of making his quietus."* Is this a reference which only readers who are familiar with Hamlet's soliloquy can pick up? Or can the actor who mimes Hamlet's actions somehow call the audience's attention to a specific portion of an unspoken soliloquy? Or, to cite a related problem, what is the audience to make of references to *Hamlet* which occur out of immediate literary context? For example, Guildenstern, on board the ship for England, suddenly speaks portions of Hamlet's "pipe-playing" speech, a speech he had heard (yet can we really assume this?) during an earlier scene from Shakespeare's play which Stoppard does not reproduce. Is it possible that Stoppard here intends to show that Guildenstern ironically is locked into the text of *Hamlet*? But if this is Stoppard's intent, how many viewers, in passing, could make the necessary connections between the two plays? Because of these and other similar instances, it is clear that different kinds of audiences are going to experience significantly different responses to the various allusions to *Hamlet*. Those who read *Rosencrantz and Guildenstern Are Dead* are more acutely aware of the numerous subtle references to *Hamlet*; and, of course, those readers and viewers who are thoroughly familiar with Shakespeare's drama will recognize many more interactions between the two plays than those members of the audience who know *Hamlet* only as a famous old tragedy.

The key to Stoppard's design, however, cannot be found by wrestling with ambiguities such as these, and there is no point in laboring to answer what percentage or what audience catches which *Hamlet* allusion. Instead, it will be more profitable to speculate regarding the general expectations of one who comes to see or to read the play. It would be a mistake to underestimate the pervasive influence of Shakespeare's most famous tragedy, even among those whose interest in the theater is minimal. Our belief that *Hamlet* is *the* central drama of our culture has been growing since late in the eighteenth century, so that the language of the play shapes our idiom, governs the way we think on certain critical matters. Indeed, the play's status is mythic. Stoppard can assume of every member of his audience an almost religious attitude toward *Hamlet*, a belief that this play comes closer than any other to capturing the mystery of human destiny. The audience does not

expect *Hamlet* itself, and this is an important distinction. Stoppard's audience is not prepared for any specific response to the *Hamlet* material; and the great secret of his method is that he offers us a wonderfully suggestive way of seeing human action performed simultaneously in several modes.

If one assumes that Stoppard is using *Hamlet* as ancient playwrights used myth—and not for irony or for plot line or for laughs—one sees his play in ways which are wholly invisible to those who mistakenly treat it as a "worm's eye" view of tragedy, or as a witty experiment in Absurdist drama, or as a clever Shakespearean pastiche. From this perspective, I plan to review three noteworthy features of *Rosencrantz and Guildenstern Are Dead*. My aim is to correct a number of misconceptions regarding the play, misconceptions which have persisted for so long that they are in danger of becoming accepted as facts.

The first thing that impresses one about the play is its peculiar "literariness." So marked, in fact, is this quality that no one seems able to avoid mentioning it. Though there has been no agreement as to its effect, it is generally taken to be more-or-less undesirable. Robert Brustein, for example, once called the play a "theatrical parasite" [*New Republic*, November 1967]; Normand Berlin has dissected the play into specific borrowings from Shakespeare, Beckett, and Pirandello, concluding that the play exists exclusively on an intellectual level rather than an emotional one [*Modern Drama* 16, 1973]; Andrew Kennedy believes that "the real pressure in the play comes from thought about the theater rather than from personal experience" [*Modern Drama* 11, 1969]; and almost every other commentary on review of *Rosencrantz and Guildenstern Are Dead* stresses Stoppard's indebtedness to Absurdist dramatists, Beckett in particular. Clearly, *Rosencrantz and Guildenstern Are Dead* is so consciously a distillation of literature and literary method that, to paraphrase Maynard Mack's point about *Hamlet*'s mysteriousness, the play's literariness seems to be part of its point. We feel this literariness in numberless ways. We feel it in the particular use of the Shakespearean materials: in the characters, certainly, and in the numerous scenes or part-scenes from *Hamlet*, in the broad sweep of the action, and in the incessant probing of familiar questions as to Hamlet's madness, his motives, his ambitions, fears, loves. And we feel it in a less specific sense, too: partly because of The Player, of course, who points the thought of the play with his frequent discussions of tragedy, of melodrama, and of the significance of playing and acting; but partly, too, because of the general bookish consciousness which seems to be diffused evenly throughout the play, manifest in a score or more of literary or linguistic biases: syllogisms, puns, rhetoricians' games, pointed repetitions, along with a host of allusions to literature and literary topics that at times threaten to make the play into an exclusively literary epistemology, shifting our attention from pictorial to verbal theater.

In this respect, in fact, the play is remarkably exploratory. "Like a Metaphysical poet," Hayman writes, "or a dog with a bone, Stoppard plays untiringly with his central conceit, never putting it down except to pick it up again, his teeth gripping it even more firmly." One feels here enormous pressures of language operating through the characters, pressures which, say, in the work of Ionesco or Beckett, are distinguished only in a negative sense, as they are in the broken discourse of Lucky in *Godot* or in the ludicrous absurdities of *The Bald Soprano*. Here, however, language is not an imperfect instrument, a thing to be scorned. There is so much conscious experimentation with language, it is as if Stoppard were permitting his characters the freedom to strive for the linguistic combination, so to speak, that will unlock their mystery. Ros and Guil often exchange banalities, to be sure; but sometimes, too, their words frame truths, as when they analyze the history of Hamlet's condition (end of Act I), or when they discover (on board ship in Act III) the purpose of their voyage to England.

For these reasons, the dramatic power of *Rosencrantz and Guildenstern Are Dead* involves more than skillful juggling or witty commentary, and Stoppard has done more than to dovetail his story with an older one in the manner, for example, that Eugene O'Neill created *Mourning Becomes Electra*. The staged events of *Rosencrantz and Guildenstern Are Dead* in fact have little in common with the events of *Hamlet;* they are not the same play, but different plays, jostling for the same space. And the outcome of the duel, so to speak, between the respective plots of *Rosencrantz and Guildenstern Are Dead* and *Hamlet* is hardly a foregone conclusion. Stoppard's play is not an "interpretation" of *Hamlet,* if by "interpretation" one refers merely to a modern rendering of a fixed text. The real technical innovation of *Rosencrantz and Guildenstern Are Dead* can be understood only when we see that, for Stoppard, the text of *Hamlet* is potentially invalid, or at least incomplete—something to be tested, explored, rather than accepted without proof, just as a myth may generate endless versions of itself, some contradictory. Hence Stoppard is not using *Hamlet* as a script; rather, the script of *Hamlet* forms part of the material for a discursive experiment, a literary exercise, as it were. In this most superficial sense, Stoppard's play may be considered simply an honest effort to clarify some matters of Hamlet's story that Shakespeare for unknown reasons ignored. Thus Brian Murray [quoted by Cohn] commented of the play: "This strikes a blow for everyone who was ever puzzled by a minor Shakespeare part."

In a more profound sense, however, the play does not clarify mysteries, only multiplies them. Yet this does not mean that Stoppard equivocates, teases his audience with a methodical changing of signs. Like its famous Elizabethan predecessor, *Rosencrantz and Guildenstern Are Dead* attempts to close with the fact of meaninglessness, to enfold it with words. Here we touch the core, I think, of the play's literariness, perceive the motive behind its experimentation with a variety of scripts. What, this play asks again and again, is valid dramatic language, and what is its relationship to the modes of human action? Is that relationship heroic? or is it comic, a poignant statement of our own insignificance? Two possible and variant texts, one willed and one predicted, here compete for the same

stage in a contest which is mediated by the figure of The Player, who moves easily between the heroics of Hamlet's court and the anterior world of Ros and Guil. It is important when experiencing Stoppard's play to be alive to its rich variety of contrasts. We must wince at the jolt, so to speak, whenever the play shifts from one mode to another, from one cast and its story to its alternate, and back again. Iambics and prose, vigor and lassitude, seriousness and silliness, skill and ineptitude, all coexist, alternately and repeatedly testing the efficacy and theatrical appeal of each. We must not hold up one mode at the expense of the other, but must be sensitive to each of the two as an element in an ongoing dialectic. Moreover, we ought not to see these incompatible elements as an experiment in Absurdist drama, either in philosophy or in form. For the play does not advance a simplistic philosophy by means of its constantly shifting perspectives, but develops a debate: Do we wish our drama in meter, or in prose? Do we prefer silly gaming, or coherent action? Do we, like Ros, want a "good story, with a beginning, middle and end"? Or do we, like Guil, prefer "art to mirror life"? And finally, are these ancient classical directives of any relevance nowadays, times being what they are?

Thus the literariness of Stoppard's play is pervasive, total. Its significance cannot be grasped simply by documenting the numerous specific echoes of earlier plays and playwrights, "intellectualizing" the play and its author, assigning them the appropriate thematic and technical camp, or postcamp. Not a failure of words, which proves the playwright's lack of originality or demonstrates his place in the Absurdist ranks, but a bold assertion of language's worth: for all the theatrical and literary elements, it turns out, are not ends in themselves, but help clearly to frame deeply personal considerations of human action, its motives and limitations and values. From its earliest moments, Stoppard's play reopens a number of very old questions related to the meaning of the simple *event,* questions which *Waiting for Godot* had effectively closed. The play begins by posing such questions: a coin falls "heads" almost ninety times in succession. It must, as Guil says, be "indicative of something besides the redistribution of wealth. List of possible explanations. One: I'm willing it. . . . Two: time has stopped dead. . . . Three: divine intervention. . . . Four: a spectacular vindication of the principle that each individual coin spun individually is as likely to come down heads as tails and therefore should cause no surprise each individual time it does."

Since the operations of their world lie generally beyond their comprehension, it is not surprising that critics, used to modern theater, have found in Ros and Guil's plight yet one more image of humans' bafflement as to their proper roles. Ros and Guil have usually been seen (in Thomas Whitaker's words) as "two characters in search of an *explication de texte,* two muddled players in reluctant pursuit of the roles they already play." It is in this respect, of course, that the play seems most closely to resemble Beckett's *Godot*. For we hear echoes of Vladimir and Estragon in the repetitious emptiness of Ros and Guil's conversations as they, like Beckett's clowns, wait to play their parts: "Where's it going to end?" "That's the question."

"It's *all* questions." "Do you think it matters?" "Doesn't it matter to you?" "Why should it matter?" "What does it matter why?" "Doesn't it *matter* why it matters?" "What's the *matter* with you?" "It doesn't matter." "What's the game?" "What are the rules?" Whether or not Ros and Guil's bewilderment suggests the play's essential kinship with the work of Beckett is a matter I would like to take up later. One final point concerning the two courtiers: it is clear that their essence—hence their character—is conceived in terms of emptiness: "*Two Elizabethans* [establishes the opening stage direction] *passing the time in a place without any visible character.*"

Concomitant with this emptiness of act and motive, of course, is a second important feature of **Rosencrantz and Guildenstern Are Dead,** an emphasis on play and playing. Like *Hamlet,* **Rosencrantz and Guildenstern Are Dead** examines human acts and acting within a variety of contexts ranging from practical to the metaphysical to the theological. Central to Stoppard's play are the figures of Rosencrantz and Guildenstern, two of literature's most unimportant people, mere concessions to the expediencies of plot. Shakespeare jokes about the courtiers' lack of individuality by playing on their metric interchangeability. And Stoppard, as did Shakespeare, first conceives his creations as broadly comic. That there should exist two persons with a corporate identity, as it were, mocks some of the fundamentals of human order both on stage and off. The world may well be a stage; if so, however, the metaphor requires identities to be unique: each must play his part. Hence the concept of identical twins—two actors playing one role—is inherently chaotic, traditionally comic. In fact, we may trace the dramatic lineage of Ros and Guil back much further than Beckett and the music hall, back at least to Roman Comedy, and even further to the primitive notion that there is something downright foolish in two people who compete for a single identity.

But if the actions of Ros and Guil seem foolish and aimless, it is equally true that divine secrets seem to govern their madness. There is no doubt that the various collisions of identity and motive that occur in **Rosencrantz and Guildenstern Are Dead**—taken singly—are humorous. Yet here, as is true of the comic elements that are characteristic of mature Shakespearean tragedy, what is funny and what is serious seem interchangeable—or, rather, seem independent analogues of a grim reality. We realize very soon, for example, that the Fool's witticisms in *Lear* are "no play." Something similar conditions our appreciation of Stoppard's drama: grappling with the concept of death as a state of negative existence, for example, Guildenstern concludes that, "You can't not-be on a boat," a statement which is mocked immediately by Ros's foolish misinterpretation, "I've frequently not been on boats." Yet the courtiers' inept mishandling of language does not long remain a comic malapropism, but bends, to use Robert Frost's image, with a crookedness that is straight. Both twisted syntax and twisted logic are appallingly true: wherever they are—on boats, on the road, within a court—it is the fate of Ros and Guil never to be.

The play returns us, then, to thoroughly familiar territory, to a consideration of some of the fundamental perplexities that gave shape and lasting meaning to *Hamlet.* We of this century do not know with any greater clarity what it might require for a man "to be." Nor are we any closer to the secret which resolves the separate meanings of "play," whereby we fill empty time with arbitrary activity, and "play," that art which defines for us human time endowed with maximum meaning, maximum consequence. Here it has seemed to many that Stoppard's answer lies with The Player: always in character, always in costume, The Player's essence is his abiding changeability. The simple fact of his endurance argues for his wisdom. At the play's end, corpses litter the stage. Yet The Player, like Brecht's Mother Courage, seems infinitely adaptable, infinitely resourceful. Although his numerous "deaths" are impressive and even credible, he inevitably returns to life for his next performance. In a world in which everyone is marked for death, The Player's survival capabilities seem especially significant.

Because of the apparent emphasis Stoppard places on "play," it has been frequently suggested that Stoppard wants us to believe that *mimesis* fosters understanding. In Act I, for example, Ros and Guil deepen their awareness of Hamlet's transformation through an act of role-playing, whereby Ros questions Guil, who pretends to be Hamlet:

> *Ros* (lugubriously): His body was still warm.
>
> *Guil:* So was hers.
>
> *Ros:* Extraordinary.
>
> *Guil:* Indecent.
>
> *Ros:* Hasty.
>
> *Guil:* Suspicious.
>
> *Ros:* It makes you think.
>
> *Guil:* Don't think I haven't thought of it.

Even more important is their playing in Act III, in which they act out a possible script for their arrival in England. Here Ros, who is taking the part of the King of England, becomes so convinced of the reality of his situation that he tears open their letter of instructions and discovers the order for Hamlet's execution. Suddenly, unexpectedly, Ros and Guil are illuminated by moral crisis; "Their playing," Robert Egan writes [in *Theatre Journal* 31, March, 1979], "has made available to them the opportunity to define significant versions of self through a concrete moral decision and a subsequent action, even if a useless action."

It is inevitable, perhaps, in this shadow world made of parts of old plays that one of the largest roles should be that of the Player. And it is also inevitable that in such a shifting and ofttimes morally weightless world the advice of The Player should carry the negative equivalent of weight. Regarding the question of how to act in their situation, for example, he advises Guildenstern to "Relax. Respond. That's what people do. You can't go through life questioning your situation at every turn." Or, later, his professional comments seem universally applicable: "We follow directions—there is no *choice* involved. The bad end unhappily, the good unluckily. That is what tragedy means." And, finally, it is The Player who convinces Guil (and us) of the impressive efficacy of mimetic understanding. Indeed, for a time it seems as if *mimesis* represents the only valid mode of knowing: the play's closing scenes forcefully demonstrate that what we considered a "real" stabbing and a "real" death was merely competent acting, merely the fulfillment of the bargain between actor and audience. "You see," The Player explains to the dumbfounded Guildenstern, "it *is* the kind they do believe in—it's what is expected." And the truth of this seems to be reinforced a few lines later, when we truly witness "real" deaths as merely an actor's casual exit. Ros simply disappears, disappears so quietly that his friend does not notice his passing. And Guil makes death into a game of hide-and-seek: "Now you see me, now you—."

There is a series evident here, of course: Hamlet is to Ros and Guil as Ros and Guil are to Alfred. And naturally this projects an engulfing form, an engulfing dramatist for *Hamlet,* and so for Stoppard's audience. Yet we ought not to presume to have uncovered the message of the play within this problematical series of regessions. The mind wearies of such esoteric speculations; and Stoppard's aim here may well be to cause us eventually to reject any fancies regarding our own wispy theatricality. Indeed, the line of argumentation which makes play the only reality can be pursued too far, resulting at best in empty theatricality, at worst in excessively sophisticated dogma. It is, in Horatio's words, "to consider too curiously." This is not to deny the concept of playing an important place in Stoppard's work. Nevertheless, to make The Player exclusively into a source of affirmation betrays the meaning of the remainder of the characters, ultimately of the entire drama. "Do you know what happens to old actors?" inquires The Player, setting the context for still one more joke about occupations. Ros, here playing the comic-hall straight man, obediently asks "What?" "Nothing," replies The Player, "They're still acting." Here, in a single word, is focussed the whole of the play's chilling analysis of human freedom and providential design. Actors are *nothing*. As The Player admits elsewhere, actors are the opposite of people. It is not a matter of how we take the sense of "nothing"; for in a play whose deepest levels of meaning concern the minimum essentials for human action and human identity, "nothing" can refer only to a waste of being, the squandering of human potential through cowardice. Perhaps the play's literariness may help clarify this crucial point: to be "nothing," in literary terms, has been considered the most terrible fate of all. Recall, for example, the horde of lost souls whirling endlessly outside Dante's Hell, desperately pursuing all banners, any banner that might ultimately give them human shape, human meaning.

As is true of so much of the superficial horseplay in *Rosencrantz and Guildenstern Are Dead,* then, words here

turn on their user, twisting themselves into enigmatic truth. The Player, because his role is eternally to be someone else, is thus no one in particular. Free of every human limitation, he exists wholly within the sphere of play. Thus nothing happens to the actor because nothing can: he is wholly amorphous, wholly uncertain, without identity, feeling or meaning apart from that conferred on him by his audience, without—and this is most important—responsibility for who he is. What The Player espouses is that a person should "act natural." That is, he argues that one should merely respond to circumstances, secure in the belief that in the end all one can do is to follow one's script. This is of course an acceptable concept to propose to explain human activity, but let us acknowledge it for what it is: fatalism. And there is little evidence in this play—less in later plays—that Stoppard holds such a view. The point is this: in this play, as in most of the important tragic statements of Western theater, there is no single perspective that hits the mark.

We are left, then, with a third problem, possibly the most intriguing: what sort of play is ***Rosencrantz and Guildenstern Are Dead***? To call the play a burlesque or a parody betrays one's insensitivity to its rich and manifold significances; and "tragicomedy" is a term grown so vague as to be almost without meaning. Clearly, Stoppard has surrealist longings in him (**"After Magritte"**; *Travesties*; *Artist Descending a Staircase*), but ***Rosencrantz and Guildenstern Are Dead,*** despite its veneer of gimmickry, proves instead the lasting power of straightforward theater. There is a small measure of truth in Brustein's term for the play—"theatrical parasite"—for it is obvious that Stoppard needs *Hamlet* if his play is to exist at all. Stoppard's play seems to vibrate because of the older classic, as a second tuning fork resonates by means of one already in motion.

Nevertheless, the tone of the modern play is distinct. Properly speaking, Stoppard has not composed a "play within a play," nor has he written a lesser action which mirrors a larger. The old text and the new text are not simply "joined"; they exist as a colloidal suspension, as it were, rather than as a permanent chemical solution. Or, to change metaphors to illustrate an important point more clearly, the texts of Hamlet's play and Ros and Guil's play form two separate spheres of human activity which, like two heavenly bodies, impinge upon each other because of their respective gravitational fields. The history of Rosencrantz and Guildenstern swings into line the scattered chunks of *Hamlet;* and the courtiers' story in turn is warped by the immense pull of Hamlet's world. Even though we cannot see much of that world, we may deduce its fulness. Though it exists largely offstage, or on another stage, we nevertheless sense that world's glitter, its nobility, and its grandeur, and we feel its awesome power.

This is not to imply that the sum of the two texts results in determinism, or that we leave the theater pitying Ros and Guil for being victimized. To the contrary: Helene Keysson-Franke [in *Educational Theatre Journal* 27, No. 1, March, 1975] speculates that the juxtaposition of *Hamlet* scenes and invented scenes "creates a sense of the possibility of freedom and the tension of the improbability of escape." Such is Stoppard's economy of technique that he chills us with Fate's whisper without a single line of exposition, without an elaborate setting of mood or of theme. Immediately the play begins our attention is mesmerized, as the two courtiers spin their recordbreaking succession of coins. The atmosphere is charged with dramatic potential, tense with impending crisis. The coin which falls "heads" scores of times in succession defines what has been called a "boundary situation"; the technique is notably Shakespearean, reminding one of the tense, foreboding beginnings invoked by the witches of *Macbeth,* or, of course, by the ghost of *Hamlet.* Ros and Guil's playing is not the aimless play of Beckett's tramps, with which it has been compared, but a play obviously freighted with imminent peril. We are impressed not by the absurdity of their situation, but by its terrible sense; one senses the chilling presence of *Hamlet,* waiting menacingly in the wings.

But *Hamlet,* as is true of all myths, is what is predicted, not what is ordained. The two courtiers are not sniveling, powerless victims of time and circumstance, and their story does not illustrate the baffling absurdity or the blind fatality that has sometimes been said to arrange their lives. This is the conclusion which many who comment upon the play have reached, guided, in part, by the anguish of Guil: "No—it is not enough. To be told so little—to such an end—and still, finally, to be denied an explanation—." We are wrong here to view events wholly through the eyes of the characters, and our pity for them must be conditioned with a little judgment. It is necessary to recognize that the Ros and Guil whom we see in the final scene are in no important way different from the Ros and Guil of the opening scene, and that such implied insensitivity to their world—puny though that world may be—bespeaks a deeper, mortal insensitivity to humanity and to themselves. Facing death, speaking his final lines of the play, the burden incumbent upon him to touch the shape of his life and so give it meaning, Ros one last time chooses to evade responsibility: "I don't care. I've had enough. To tell you the truth, I'm relieved." Nor is the more speculative Guil alive to his context: "Our names shouted in a certain dawn," he ponders; ". . . a message . . . a summons. . . . There must have been a moment, at the beginning, where we could have said—no. But somehow we missed it."

The context of men's action remains forever a mystery. It was a mystery for Hamlet, it is a mystery for Ros and Guil, it is a mystery for us. Yet between the two plays there exists an important difference in the quality of the characters' responses to what must remain forever hidden from their sight. We do not here—as we did in the closing scenes of *Hamlet*—discover new men. Hamlet, it is true, submits to his world with weary resignation. But Hamlet acknowledges human limitations without lapsing wholly into despair. The difference is between Hamlet, who accepts an ambiguous world while yet believing in the need for human exertion at critical junctures in time, and Ros and Guil, who quail before their world's haunting mysteries, wishing never to have played the game at all. Guil despairs, groping for his freedom "at the beginning," when

he might—so he reasons—have refused to participate. He wishes—there is no other way to put it—to avoid human responsibility. Thus his undeniably moving cry must be understood in the light of our clearer knowledge that his real opportunity came not at the beginning, but near the end of the play, when he accidentally discovered that his mission was to betray Hamlet. He misunderstands, in other words, the nature of his freedom, misunderstands as well the meaning of his choice. Too, we must not overlook the fact that Guil's misreading of his life provokes one final confusion of names: unaware that Ros has silently departed—died—Guil asks, "Rosen—? Guil?" In a play in which the floating identities of the two central characters has steadily deepened in seriousness, this final misunderstanding is especially important. Guil's fate is never to know who he is. Ultimately, as Robert Egan has pointed out, "Guildenstern does die the death he has opted for."

To insist on Ros and Guil's freedom, and therefore on their responsibility, may seem wrongheaded, particularly because one is reluctant to condemn them for being confused by a script which they have not read. The courtiers are baffled by offstage events; hence it is not surprising that critics and playgoers have been tempted to draw parallels between this play and *Waiting for Godot.* Yet in truth the dramaturgy of Stoppard does not simply grow out of the theater of Beckett. True, Stoppard employs elements of that theater; but the effect of this is to call the validity of Absurdist theater into question. Stoppard uses Absurdist techniques, as he uses the *Hamlet* material, to frame questions concerning the efficacy and significance of these diverse ways of understanding human action.

Evidence for this may be found by examining Stoppard's handling of the *Hamlet* material, and by noting how this handling varies over the course of the three-act structure of ***Rosencrantz and Guildenstern Are Dead.*** Act I first poses the dilemma, defining, as it were, the conflict of the play as a struggle between two plots, between the story an individual (here, two individuals) wills for himself and the story the myth tells about him. Here the two texts seem most at odds, for *Hamlet* intervenes in two large chunks, each time unexpectedly, almost forcing its way on stage. In the second Act, however, the compositional pattern shifts: here Shakespeare's text intrudes more frequently, and in shorter bits, as if the completed play were being broken down and assimilated by—or accommodated to—the play in the making. In this second Act we feel the maximum presence of *Hamlet,* the increased pull of the myth. Structure here may be clarified by reference to classical terminology: in this Act we witness the *epitasis,* the complication, or the tying of the knot. Between the growing design of *Hamlet* and the intertextual freedom of Ros and Guil's discussions there develops maximum tension, maximum interplay between what Keysson-Franke calls "the possibility of freedom and the improbability of escape." Then, in the final Act, the process whereby *Hamlet* is accommodated to ***Rosencrantz and Guildenstern Are Dead*** seems completed. Here is staged the famous sea voyage of Hamlet, for which no dramatic precedent exists. No lines from Shakespeare's play can here intrude, for none is available. In *Hamlet,* we

John Stride and Edward Petherbridge as the title characters in the 1967 National Theatre production of Rosencrantz and Guildenstern Are Dead *at the Old Vic Theatre in London.*

learn of the events of the voyage only in retrospect, during a subsequent conversation between Horatio and Hamlet. So, even though those of us who know the play remember what happened at sea, we know nothing of the causes of that action. Even knowledgeable playgoers, then, assume that the events at sea had resulted from chance, or, as Hamlet later suggests, from heaven's ordinance. This is an important point: most of Act III of *Rosencrantz and Guildenstern Are Dead* exists between the lines, as it were, of *Hamlet,* in what has always represented an undefined, unwritten zone. Stoppard here invites his characters to invent their history according to their will. He offers them alternatives, if not absolute choice. This is confirmed by the courtiers' imaginings concerning their arrival in England. Ros mourns:

> I have no image. I try to picture us arriving, a little harbour perhaps . . . roads . . . inhabitants to point the way . . . horses on the road . . . riding for a day or a fortnight and then a palace and the English king. . . . That would be the logical kind of thing. . . . But my mind remains a blank. No we're slipping off the map.

The passage chills us, and invites us to recall that for Rosencrantz and Guildenstern there will be no future. Yet does it not invite us equally to reflect upon the courtiers' imaginative shortcomings, their own sinful—not too strong a word—despair? Indeed, soon afterwards they are graced with the opportunity to devise their own script, but they fail to do so because they cannot transcend their own banality, cannot for one moment rise out of their slough. Upon reading the letter which discloses the King's intent to have Hamlet executed, Guil lapses into an empiricism so bland, so callous as to lack utterly moral context:

> Assume, if you like, that they're going to kill him. Well, he is a man, he is mortal, death comes to us all, etcetera, and consequently he would have died anyway, sooner or later. Or to look at it from the social point of view—he's just one man among many, the loss would be well within reason and convenience. And then again, what is so terrible about death? As Socrates so philosophically put it, since we don't know what death is, it is illogical to fear it. It might be . . . very nice. Certainly it is a release from the burden of life, and, for the godly, a haven and a reward. Or to look at it another way—we are little men, we don't know the ins and outs of the matter, there are wheels within

wheels, etcetera—it would be presumptuous of us to interfere with the designs of fate or even of kings. All in all, I think we'd be well advised to leave well alone. Tie up the letter—there—neatly—like that.—They won't notice the broken seal, assuming you were in character.

Only by considering Guil's comments in full can we appreciate their slowly deepening repulsiveness. They are spoken, recall, while our hearts are yet moved by Ros' intuitive reaction to the letter ordering Hamlet's death: "We're his *friends*." As Guil speaks, the stage grows quiet, empty: we feel the crisis, feel the awful pressure of a thing about to be done, feel that (in Brutus' words) "between the acting of a dreadful thing and the first motion, all the interim is like a hideous dream." Given the opportunity for meaningful action, Guil (and thus, by way of tacit compliance, Ros) refuses to act. Given suddenly—one is tempted to say beneficently—ample room and time to define their selves, the courtiers cannot swell to fit their new roles. For a moment, *Hamlet* is swept away, suspended powerless; for a brief interim we sense that the fate of the prince and his play rests in Ros and Guil's hands. That interim is theirs alone; it does not belong to *Hamlet*. And they refuse to act. To choose not to choose, of course, is a manner of choosing. Ros and Guil fill their moment of time, their *season,* with emptiness—until the text of Shakespeare's *Hamlet* rushes back to fill the vacuum. Scarcely has Ros concluded, "We're on top of it now," than Shakespeare's text looms to meet them.

In this light, then, Guil's desperate attempt to slay The Player who brings the courtiers the news of their deaths seems triply ironic. Guil is wrong about death, in that it *can* be counterfeited by a successful actor. And he is wrong about the shape of his life, too, and about the meaning of human action. No one—not Fate, not Shakespeare, and not Tom Stoppard—"had it in for them." Where Guil and Ros erred was not in getting on a boat; they failed when they chose freely to be cowards, chose freely, that is, to be themselves. Stoppard stresses their cowardice, not their ignorance, and his irony here flatly contradicts those who see Ros and Guil as powerless victims. And Guil is wrong, finally, in his desperate attempt to murder The Player. Guil seems here to hope to win dramatic stature by an act of violence, to gain identity from a conventionally heroic act of will. In fact, Stoppard seems to be saying, such conventional heroism is not necessary; all that was required of Guil was the destruction of a single letter.

Thus it is inevitable that the stage lights dim on Ros and Guil's play and shine in the end on *Hamlet:* "immediately," Stoppard directs, "the whole stage is lit up, revealing, upstage, arranged in the approximate positions last held by the dead tragedians, the tableau of court and corpses which is the last scene of *Hamlet*." The text of Shakespeare's play suddenly appears to overwhelm its modern analogue, as the old play and the new play here converge in a genuine *coup de théâtre*. Yet the point here is more than mere theatrics, more, too, than weary fatalism or anguish at the absurdity of human life. The sudden sweeping reduction of Ros and Guil completes Stoppard's play at the same time it affirms unconditionally the morality of

Shakespeare's. On this crucial point, Stoppard is unequivocal: in rehearsals, and in all published editions of the play after the first, Stoppard excised a bit of action which brought his drama full circle, so that it ended with someone banging on a shutter, shouting two names. Stoppard's alteration moves his play away from the cultivated theatricality and ambiguity one finds often in Absurdist drama; and we are left with the clear knowledge that Ros and Guil, despite their being given an entire play of their own, have not advanced beyond the interchangeable, nondescript pair who took the boards more than three hundred years ago. Just as he disappears from view, Guil quips, "Well, we'll know better next time." But the evidence from *two* plays, now, suggests that they won't. Oddly, Stoppard is here not following Shakespeare's script so much as he is redefining and reasserting its tragic validity: *Rosencrantz and Guildenstern Are Dead* proves that Shakespeare had it right after all. For this reason, Ros and Guil are not permitted to "die" on stage; they merely disappear from view. Is this not one final demonstration of Stoppard's consistent dramatic technique?—for he merely whisks the courtiers off the stage, lest their corpses—visible proof that they had lived—convince an audience of their dramatic substance.

Wheels within wheels: *Rosencrantz and Guildenstern Are Dead* is deeply ironic, yet the irony is not at all the mocking, ambivalent irony we have come to expect of the modern theater. To be sure, to rank the orders of reality in this haunting play is to invert *mimesis,* for here the admitted fiction—the world of *Hamlet*—possesses most substance. It turns out, in fact, that even The Player is more real, that is, of more worth, than Ros and Guil. But this does not mean that The Player—whose essence is his artifice—forms the play's thematic center. Like *Hamlet, Rosencrantz and Guildenstern Are Dead* brings into conjunction a number of states of being, examines from a variety of perspectives some modes of human action. What the play *means,* it means largely by virtue of these numerous contrasts and resulting tensions. No one perspective is so broad as to embrace the whole; each, by itself, is faulty, both intellectually and morally. Nevertheless, together they assert a view of human activity that stresses men's ultimate responsibility—whether prince or actor or lackey—for what they do, and so for who they are.

It is simply incorrect, for this reason, to call *Rosencrantz and Guildenstern Are Dead* an example of Absurdist drama, even to call it "post-Absurdist" drama (in all but the literal sense). In the first place, we do not find here a "sense of metaphysical anguish at the absurdity of the human condition," a theme which Martin Esslin long ago defined as central to Absurdist playwrights [*The Theatre of the Absurd,* 1961]. Certainly, Ros and Guil die without knowing what their lives were all about. But the whole point of the *Hamlet* material is to define for the audience—if not for Ros and Guil—a knowable logic that shapes men's fortunes, even as it permits them a part in the process. We must distinguish here the difference between two varieties of offstage material, such as one finds, say, in *Waiting for Godot* or in *The Birthday Party,* on the one hand, and in *Oedipus Rex* and in *Rosencrantz and*

Guildenstern Are Dead, on the other. In the former plays, the offstage material functions exclusively to deepen the audience's awareness of human ignorance; it is mockingly obscure, purposely baffling to characters and to spectators. But in the latter plays, the offstage material functions both as mystery *and* as myth, the myth with its powerful implications of logic, design, even—in the right circumstances—knowability.

In other ways, too, *Rosencrantz and Guildenstern Are Dead* rejects much of the Absurdist canon. It is not "antiliterary"; it does not "abandon rational devices and discursive thought," but instead depends upon them; and finally, it does not lament the loss of opportunities for meaning, even for heroism, because Ros and Guil enjoy, albeit briefly, such potential. This play, as has been said of Stoppard's **"The Real Inspector Hound,"** is "comfortingly classical" [Kennedy]. It testifies to the informing aesthetic power even today of a tragic dramatic form far older than the Elizabethan play which inspired it. *Rosencrantz and Guildenstern Are Dead* offers its audience the vision of two characters caught in the agony of moral choice. At a moment when they least expect it, and in a place they had never forseen, they must decide the shape of their lives. To be sure, the information upon which they must base their decision comes to them in the form of riddles, half-truths, things only partly-known; but when has it ever been otherwise? Like other tragic protagonists before them, Ros and Guil must choose, and they choose in error. Leading up to and away from this moral crisis which forms the dramatic center of his play, Stoppard constructs a linear plot, set in time, and moved by a group (or, if you will, two groups) of characters who are consistent in both motive and response. Behind the play stands an ancient way of ordering experience, a way which is both mythic and ritualistic. And for his theme, Stoppard (with the aid of *Hamlet*) offers a version of justice: all the characters get what they deserve. So simple, so moving, so regrettable, but, finally, so consoling: what, in the end, could be more like classical tragedy than that?

JUMPERS

Lucina P. Gabbard (essay date 1977)

SOURCE: "Stoppard's *Jumpers:* A Mystery Play," in *Modern Drama,* Vol. 20, No. 1, March, 1977, pp. 87-95.

[*In this essay, Gabbard categorizes* Jumpers *as a metaphysical detective story.*]

Tom Stoppard's *Jumpers* is a many-splendored mystery play—so many-splendored that it is, metaphorically, a kaleidoscope. Bright fragments of many forms and many themes make new configurations with each twist of the dial. The most obvious ingredients are rollicking comedy

and metaphysics. This combination recalls the mystery plays of medieval times which mixed morality and Bible stories with humorous and grotesque details. Stopping there, however, would misrepresent and over-simplify the generic classification of *Jumpers* for the kaleidoscope contains bits of many genres assembled in the overall design of a "whodunit."

Applied to form, the mystery is not "whodunit?" but "whatisit?" Some critics call the play a farce, and it does employ many farcical techniques. It makes beautiful mischief with mistaken identity. George assumes that Dotty's casserole is made from his missing rabbit, Thumper. So he tells Crouch, the porter: "Do you realize she's in there now, eating him?" Crouch, thinking George refers to the murdered Professor McFee, replies: "You mean—raw?" Compounding Crouch's horror, George answers crossly: "No, of course not!—*cooked*—with gravy and mashed potatoes." The play is alive with broad comic action. McFee's corpse swings in and out of sight on the back of the bedroom door. Nobody drops his pants, but Dotty drops her robe, revealing a lovely body naked from the thighs up. Traditionally, however, farce is devoid of profundity, whereas *Jumpers* is not. Stoppard's slapstick takes place in the midst of cosmic tragedy and metaphysical inquiry. Astronaut Oates has been abandoned on the moon, and George addresses himself to the question, "Is God?" More-over, the play ridicules man's institutions—education, justice, morality—thereby taking on the weight of a satire.

Intermingled with these ancient forms are all the cultural features of twentieth century drama. The two astronauts on the moon represent Space Age technology; their fight for the single berth on the crippled space capsule depicts the Darwinian commonplace of survival of the fittest. The image of Astronaut Oates "waving forlornly from the featureless wastes of the lunar landscape" objectifies man facing the existential void. Dotty's analyst is a Freudian. The Jumpers, flipflopping between political and philosophical roles while Archie calls the tune, suggest the Marxian masses controlled by society. The amorality of Archie and his acrobats is typical of the Absurdist's world which Richard Corrigan describes well: "There are no value judgments or distinctions in values in the world of the Absurd. In Admov's *Ping Pong*, the aesthetic, economic, and philosophic implications of pinball machines are discussed with religious fervor. In Ionesco's *Jack or the Submission* the whole action is to convince Jack to accept the family's chief value: 'I love potatoes with bacon'" [Richard Corrigan, *The Theatre in Search of a Fix,* 1973]. Another example in Corrigan's elaboration might well have been George's analogy between McFee's beliefs about *good* and *bad* and "the rules of tennis without which Wimbledon Fortnight would be a complete shambles."

Brechtian technique also contributes to this kaleidoscope. In his description of the set, Stoppard calls for a screen forming a backdrop for film and slide projections. But the farce, the satire, the contemporary milieu—even the Brechtian screen—are all elements of Absurdism; and to this accumulation, Stoppard adds his and the Absurdists' principal method—the use of concrete images to convey meaning. In *Endgame*, Beckett places Nagg and Nell in giant garbage cans to represent the discarding of old and useless parents. Stoppard makes a pyramid of acrobats out of the university's Philosophy Department, bodying forth the intellectual's mental gymnastics. The Coda, a full-fledged dream, adds still another Absurd ingredient.

Other nondramatic literary forms also claim mention in *Jumpers*. Titles of novels and songs constitute the charades which are the basis of Dotty's relationship with George. Overt allusions to classic poets—Milton, Keats—mingle with covert references to modern masters like Eliot and Beckett. The tortoise and the hare recall an oft-told fable—as do Dotty's cries of "Wolf!" A large portion of the play, however, is devoted to George's preparations for the symposium. Thus, Stoppard daringly weaves a serious philosophical dialectic in and out of this Absurdist drama; the whole is thinly wrapped in the Londoner's favorite genre—the detective story. Inspector Bones and the characters of *Jumpers* are confronted with three obvious mysteries: who killed McFee? where is Thumper? does God exist? Analysis of the play soon reveals, however, that these three questions are only starters. The kaleidoscope is as full of posers as of forms.

Thus, the emphasis of this "whodunit" shifts from "whatisit?" to "whatsitsay?" To investigate this mystery requires examination of the play's inseparable mixture of images and characters. Like the fragments in the kaleidoscope, the images, when juxtaposed, create meaningful designs; they all deal with man's problems—with himself, his beliefs, and his institutions. The people within these images have dual roles. On the one hand, they reveal the personal problems and relationship of the characters in the murder mystery; and on the other hand, they represent differing facets of the troubled Space Age.

At the center of the design are George and Dorothy Moore and Sir Archibald Jumpers. George Moore is a professor of Moral Philosophy, but his identity is diminished by his namesake, the famed author of *Principa Ethica*. George is totally absorbed in preparing a paper to be presented at the university's symposium on "Man—good, bad, or indifferent?"; his paper poses the question—"Is God?" George's eccentricity is captured in the image he presents opening the door to Inspector Bones. Brandishing a bow and arrow in one hand, holding a tortoise in the other, George appears with his face covered in shaving foam. The effect is appropriate to his later self-description: ". . . I cut a ludicrous figure in the academic world . . . largely due to my aptitude for traducing a complex and logical thesis to a mysticism of staggering banality." George is also central to the "whodunit," even though for a long time he seems unaware of the tragedy. Nevertheless, the murder occurred at a party at George's house; George summoned the police by an anonymous complaint about the noise; the victim, Professor McFee, was George's philosophical adversary; and finally, the discovery of George's absent-minded murder of Thumper presents the possibility that he may also have unwittingly killed McFee.

George is married to Dotty, "a prematurely-retired musical-comedy actress of some renown." Dotty is dotty: "unreliable and neurotic," she calls herself. She can no longer distinguish one moon song from another. Nevertheless, her fans enthusiastically await her comeback. At the party, scene of the murder, they applaud despite her inability to remember her song. She has withdrawn into the darkness before the shot is fired; afterwards she steps into the light only to have the dying man pull himself up against her legs. The others quickly depart, and Dotty is left, whimpering under the weight of the corpse. Her frock stained with his blood, she is the image of the prime suspect. She calls out to George for help, and he, unaware of the murder, responds indifferently. To gain his attention she makes an offer which reveals the emptiness of their marriage: "Georgie!—I'll let you." He replies: "I don't want to be 'let.' Can't you see that it's an insult?" Their only communication seems to be through charades. Finding Dotty nude and despondent on the bed, George responds quickly—*"The Naked and the Dead!"* On the contrary, Archie comforts Dotty by removing the corpse and visiting her every day—in her bedroom. He claims to be her doctor-psychiatrist, but evidence indicates a love affair. The nature of Archie's relationship with Dotty is another of the mysteries with which George wrestles.

Sir Archibald Jumpers is a man of many talents? roles?—all of them authoritative. Near the opening of the play, he stands in a white spot as his voice barks out: "And now!—ladies and gentlemen!—the INCREDIBLE—RADICAL!—LIBERAL!!—JUMPERS!! As the music swells and eight Jumpers come somersaulting in, Archie is the image of the ringmaster of this whole circus. And indeed he is! He is Vice-Chancellor of the university, thereby George's boss. He is organizer of the Jumpers—"a mixture of the more philosophical members of the university gymnastics team and the more gymnastic members of the Philosophy School." As chief Jumper, he is also head of the Radical Liberal Party which is celebrating its victory at the polls. When he signs the report on the cause of McFee's death, he insists he is coroner. He is not only Dotty's psychiatrist but also her legal adviser. He explains: "I'm a doctor of medicine, philosophy, literature and law, with diplomas in psychological medicine and P.T. including gym." Archie is totally amoral and pragmatical. He solves his problems by lies, bribery, blackmail, or whatever is necessary. In short, he is George's opposite—in temperament and belief. Archie is very much involved with the murder. The victim, Professor McFee, was one of the Jumpers—holder of the Chair of Logic. Archie disposes of the body and attempts to defend Dotty. He also makes himself a suspect by admitting that McFee, his faithful protégé, was threatening to become "St. Paul to Moore's Messiah."

Also involved in the murder mystery are three other characters: Inspector Bones, Crouch, and a nameless secretary. Inspector Bones, like all the others, displays Cognomen Syndrome; he is a detective, a rattler of skeletons in closets. (He also has a brother who was an osteopath!) Bones has been summoned to the scene by two anonymous telephone calls, but he comes, flowers in hand, as one of Dotty's ardent fans. He hopes for her autograph, perhaps even "the lingering touch of a kiss brushed against an admirer's cheek. . . ." Nevertheless, if he discovers the allegations to be true, he will let her feel "the full majesty of the law." Upon seeing Dotty, however, he is struck dumb by infatuation and desires only to protect her. He suggests an eminent psychiatric witness might get her off. Although incorruptible by Archie's attempted bribery, he is easy prey to a blackmail scheme. While he is alone in the bedroom with Dotty, she cries "Rape!" Archie enters to find Bones—a frozen image pleading with a smile: "It's not what you think." Archie moves in quickly to "tsk tsk" at the "tragic end" of "an incorruptible career." To George, it is all another mystery: "How the hell does one know what to believe?" In any event, the investigation is ended, and the "whodunit" is unsolved.

Crouch is the porter. As his name suggests, he maintains a servile posture. He carries out the rubbish and serves drinks at the party. In this latter capacity, he was at the scene of the crime. In fact, he made the second anonymous report to the police. His involvement is deepened by his friendship with the deceased. He used to converse with McFee when the learned professor called for his girl—George's secretary. As a result of these conversations and "a bit of reading," Crouch has become something of a philosopher himself. He demonstrates his knowledge by pointing to a flaw in George's treatise. But when George rebuts his point, Crouch, true to his name, withdraws humbly: "I expect you're right, sir. I mean, it's only a hobby with me."

The secretary is nameless and wordless. At the party she strips while swinging from a trapeze. Through the rest of the play she sits silent and grim, taking George's dictation. Only at the close of Act II is her involvement revealed: she was secretly betrothed to McFee, who was already married. Just before his death, McFee had "to make a clean breast and tell her it was all off" because he was going into the monastery. Thus, the failures of modern marriage are reaffirmed, and the secretary joins the list of suspects with a motive for murdering McFee. This last message is transmitted vividly by the image of the secretary turning to reveal blood on her back.

Two other characters, appearing only on Dotty's giant television screen, are too crucial to be omitted—the astronauts Scott and Oates. Their images are seen stalking the surface of the moon, and the announcer reports their private drama. Only one man could return in the crippled space capsule. While the world of viewers watched, the astronauts—the twentieth century's heroes—struggled until Oates was knocked to the ground by Scott, the commanding officer. Dotty's word image speaks the rest: "Poor moon man, falling home like Lucifer." Later she adds: "it certainly spoiled that Juney old moon." It also caused Dotty's breakdown and, according to Crouch, McFee's reversal. So the moon men are indirectly responsible for the course of events.

A twist of the kaleidoscope and all these private characters assume an almost allegorical significance. Each becomes a symbol of some segment of society; each becomes a fragment in a new configuration showing the topsy-turvy world of the Space Age and the mind-defying mystery of life. Through all time man has sought to right the world and solve the mystery of his presence on this planet. All of his systems and institutions have been devised to approach one or the other of these problems.

For centuries man's solution was belief in God and the morality of man. George is the defender of these beliefs, but his progressive deterioration represents their precarious position. From the outset George explains: "There is presumably a calender date—a *moment*—when the onus of proof passed from the aetheist to the believer, when, quite suddenly, secretly, the noes had it." This tenuous state is magnified when George, elevated to the symbolic level, becomes the universal representative of theology and ethics. This ineffectual, pedantic little man stands alone against the swollen tide of Jumpers—"Logical positivists, mainly, with a linguistic analyst or two, a couple of Benthamite Utilitarians . . . lapsed Kantians and empiricists generally . . . and of course the usual Behaviourists. . . ." George himself admits his bottom rank: "I was lucky to get the Chair of Moral Philosophy. . . . Only the Chair of Divinity lies further below the salt, and *that's* been vacant for six months. . . ." Furthermore, even with this lone defender, God's position is eroding, for George has turned Him into "a philosopher's God, logically inferred from self-evident premises." Consequently, God has fallen victim to the tricks of language—another failure among man's inventions. George confesses that "words betray the thoughts they are supposed to express." By George's own semantic twists, God becomes "a theological soubriquet" for the "first Cause"; or, as "the first term of the series," George explains, "God, so to speak, is nought." At the height of his frustration, George cries out: "How does one know what it is one believes when it's so difficult to know what it is one knows. I don't claim to *know* that God exists, I only claim that he does without my knowing it, and while I claim as much I do not claim to know as much; indeed I cannot know and God knows I cannot." However despondent, George's words ring with atrophying heroism when juxtaposed with Dotty's admission: "And yet, Professor, one can't help wondering at the persistence of the reflex, the universal constant unthinking appeal to the non-existent God who is presumed dead."

Morality suffers from the same confusion. How can the world of *Jumpers* right its wrongs when no one can agree on what is wrong? George is the solitary spokesman for moral absolutes; he summarizes the culture's dilemma while stating his agreement with his namesake: ". . . by insisting that goodness was a fact, and on his right to recognize it when he saw it, Moore avoided the moral limbo devised by his successors, who are in the unhappy position of having to admit that one man's idea of good is no more meaningful than another man's. . . ." A principal cause of this moral confusion is again—language. George says that every year the symposium's subject is the same, "Man—good, bad, or indifferent?" but "there is enough disagreement about its meaning to ensure a regular change of topic." Unfortunately, George's egocentric and unfeeling reactions to Dotty and the others indicate that his own morality is smothered by pedantry.

At the end of Act II, theology and ethics seem bereft of their last defender. George discovers that he, not Dotty, has killed Thumper—with the arrow shot to prove God's existence. In the shock of realizing himself a killer, George steps backward, and "*CRRRRRRRRUNCH*!!" he kills his tortoise, Pat. His sobs are amplified and blend into the Coda, where the prostrate George is gripped by a bizarre dream. Has George suffered a total collapse? Or has he merely found escape?

Even in George's dream, Archie is in charge. Symbolically, Archie is leadership—the repository of man's hopes and abdicated responsibilities. And Archie has led all segments of society down the path of expediency and amorality. Archie's intellectuals—education—are corrupt and ineffective, jumping from one pose to another at Archie's convenience and command. According to George, they are all as mad as McFee, who thinks lying and murder are merely antisocial, not inherently wrong. The general acceptance of such beliefs is witnessed by their philosophical classification—"Orthodox mainstream." The ineptitude of all these thinkers is exposed when Archie reveals the basis of their selection. For the new chairman of the Philosophy Department, he wants "someone of good standing; he won't have to know much philosophy."

As leader of the Radical Liberals, winners of the recent election, Archie also represents politics—the foundation of man's self-government. But like morality, "Democracy is all in the head," Archie has told Dotty. In fact, Dotty explains, the election was actually a *coup d'état*. When George protests that he voted, she retorts: "It's not the voting that's democracy, it's the counting." Language plays its tricks again. As a result of this "election," the Church Commissioners were dispossessed, the Newspaper proprietors found themselves in a police car, Clegthorpe—agricultural spokesman and agnostic—has been appointed Archbishop of Canterbury, and early next week "the Police Force will be thinned out to a ceremonial front for the peacekeeping activities of the Army." The image of the failure of politics is intensified by recalling that the Rad-Libs are "a mixed bunch," more than just party workers and academics. Moreover, in the first scene the whole pyramid of Rad-Lib Jumpers has been seen to collapse under the removal of logic—the death of McFee. In the Coda the pyramid is rebuilt with Archbishop Clegthorpe, "The highpoint of scientism," as its pinnacle. But once more a gunshot—violence—intervenes. Clegthorpe is toppled, and the pyramid disintegrates. Are Archie's Jumpers like a pile of dominoes, doomed to fall each time Someone somewhere gives a nudge?

Dotty, of course, stands for escapism. She is sex, show business, and romance—rolled into one. Her songs about Juney moons, her millions of undaunted admirers, her flirtations and infidelities speak of man's wishes—his fantasies of beautiful bodies and perpetual love-making under a spangled moon. But this symbol too has collapsed. Dotty faltered in the middle of her act and addressed herself to the mystery of another absolute: ". . . why must the damned show go on anyway?"

Summoned by fearful anonymity is Bones—symbol of law, order, and justice. He is supposed to be evenhanded and incorruptible, able to detect the evil-doers and empowered to right their wrongs by punishment. Alas! Bones, the implacable law, is also human. Victimized by Dotty's charms, Bones instructs Archie to temper justice with romantic illusion, dirty tricks, and prejudice: "Put her in the box and you're half-way there. The other half is, get something on Mad Jock McFee, and if you don't get a Scottish judge it'll be three years probation and the sympathy of the court." Finally, made vulnerable by his fantasies, Bones—the full majesty of the law—is frightened into retreat by Dotty's blackmail. But the mystery remains: who killed McFee? And the criminal is still at large. Is there no protection under the law?

The secretary and Crouch, of course, represent the mute, lowly ones who only watch and serve. That American Jumper, Richard Nixon, might have called them the silent majority. But they are victims too. Stripping on the flying trapeze, the secretary symbolizes man swinging between the darknesses of ignorance and false hopes, from the innocence of the womb to the reality of the tomb. The moments of light in between represent those flashes of insight which strip him, little by little, of his beliefs and illusions. Crouch, representing the servile ones, is so blinded by his workaday world that he doubts neither his own inferiority nor the Jumpers' expertise. Unseeing, he "*backs into the path of the swing and is knocked arse over tip by a naked lady.*" He never knows what has hit him until he is blacked out and broken in the crash. But in the Coda, Crouch has become Chairman of the Symposium. Do the meek inherit the earth?

Catalysts to it all are the moon men—science and technology raised to the ultimate power. The scientific method was intended to provide the objectivity that would unlock the secrets of the universe. Instead it unloosed an invasion by machines—television cameras exploring the surface of the moon and the skin of Dotty's body. Can external coverings reveal the soul—of Dotty or the moon? It unloosed astronauts in goldfish bowls violating God's heaven, landing their amorality on the moon. In the Coda, Archie puts rationalizations into Captain Scott's mouth. He orders Scott to explain his "instinctive considerations" with "special reference" to his "seniority" over Oates, their "respective usefulness to society," and his responsibility to himself. Captain Scott has only to answer, "That's it." The spectacle of these astronauts fighting on the moon caused McFee to doubt himself. Before his murder, he confided to Crouch: "I am giving philosophical respectability to a new pragmatism in public life, of which there have been many disturbing examples both here and on the moon." Perhaps the most far-reaching effect was on Dotty: the moon was no longer fantasy land, no longer Juney or spooney or crooney. For Dotty it was all over once man set foot on the moon and could see us "whole, all in one go, little—local" with all our absolutes looking like "the local customs of another place." Dotty's final declaration paraphrases into an awesome interrogative: What is going to happen when the people on the bottom discover that the truths they have taken on trust now have edges?

Dotty's concern adds to the principal accumulated questions: Is God? Is man good, bad or indifferent? What do *good* and *bad* mean? And, of course, who shot McFee? Stoppard lets Archie give the answer: "Unlike mystery novels, life does not guarantee a denouement; and if it came, how would one know whether to believe it?" Thus, the play states that life is a mystery no one can solve. Stoppard's advice seems to be—dream! look on the better side!—because the Coda ends on an optimistic note. Dotty sings again, perched on "a spangled crescent moon." George exclaims that even disbelievers agree that "life is better than death, that love is better than hate." And Archie revives an extended version of the old paradox that the half empty cup is also half full. He sanctions: "Do not despair—many are happy much of the time. . . ." Or does the Coda merely suggest that life, like this play, is one bizarre dream after another?

One thing is clear: Stoppard's Absurd "Whodunit" about the multiple mysteries of life is an almost perfect blend of form and content. Moreover, in production the fast pace and overlapping images of *Jumpers* create a three-ring circus effect. The swinging trapeze, the songs, the jokes, and the nudity mix bits of vaudeville, musical comedy, and burlesque into this legitimate stage play. The result is that Absurdism, usually so depressing to audiences, emerges in a new configuration with entertainment.

TRAVESTIES

Carol Billman (essay date 1980)

SOURCE: "The Art of History in Tom Stoppard's *Travesties*," in *Kansas Quarterly,* Vol. 12, No. 4, Fall, 1980, pp. 47-52.

[*In the essay below, Billman explores the connection between art and history in* Travesties: *"Through his characterization of Carr, Stoppard yokes the roles of artist and historian . . . , affirming through Carr the importance of history and the individual 'making' it."*]

In his profile of Tom Stoppard for the *New Yorker* [December 19, 1977] Kenneth Tynan, pursuing a biblical distinction, divides contemporary British dramatists into two camps:

> On one side were the hairy men—heated, embattled, socially committed playwrights, like John Osborne, John Arden, and Arnold Wesker, who had come out fighting in the late fifties. On the other side were the smooth men—cool, apolitical stylists, like Harold Pinter, the late Joe Orton, Christopher Hampton . . . , Alan Ayckbourn . . . , Simon Gray . . . , and Stoppard.

Stoppard himself said in 1974, "I think that in future I

must stop compromising my plays with this whiff of social application [found in *Jumpers*]. They must be entirely untouched by any suspicion of usefulness. I should have the courage of my lack of convictions." This is not to say that Stoppard's stylistically dazzling plays are devoid of substance or lack themes. Indeed, one of his favorite issues in *Travesties* as well as a number of his preceding works is the definition of art and of an artist's social obligations. But *Travesties* is also a history play, a fact that may seem surprising given the playwright's avowedly asocial, therefore ahistorical, perspective. As historical drama the play is not unlike such other contemporary works as Weiss's *Marat/Sade,* Camus' *Caligula,* or Kopit's *Indians*—each represents history as a random and mysterious course of events rather than as a logical, easily understood narrative. Nor is *Travesties* out of line with Stoppard's earlier plays, for it extends the discussion of art and the artist's social responsibilities to include history, first defining the subject and ultimately determining the historian's function.

The absence of absolutes has been another longstanding concern for Stoppard. In the plays before *Travesties* the relativity of everything from word meaning to political stances and philosophical arguments is illustrated dramatically. The way one looks at things is always a question of point of view, an idea expressed first by Stoppard in the 1967 radio play **"Albert's Bridge,"** in which the character Fraser suddenly finds life tolerable when he joins the painter Albert atop the Clufton Bridge:

> . . . So I climb up again and prepare to cast myself off, without faith in angels to catch me—or desire that they should—and lo! I look down at it all and find that the proportions have been re-established. My confidence is restored, by perspective.

Stoppard relates this theme to the subject of art and its legitimacy. For him the products of his profession, literary works, are not inviolable, as he shows when he rewrites *Hamlet* from the perspective of two minor characters in **Rosencrantz and Guildenstern Are Dead** and when he parodies the convolutions of British detective stories in **"The Real Inspector Hound."** In *Travesties,* too, Stoppard works in the tradition of literary imitation. Beyond echoing great modern dramatists from Ionesco and Beckett to Brecht, the obvious source for imitation is Oscar Wilde's *The Importance of Being Earnest.* *Travesties* contains a play within a play in that four of Stoppard's characters act out (without knowing it) the roles of the confused quartet in Wilde's comedy: Henry Carr is Algernon; Tristan Tzara, Jack Worthing; Cecily and Gwendolen, their namesakes.

The dialogue in the play includes, moreover, travestied limericks and Shakespearean sonnets. And Stoppard parodies less poetic but nonetheless well-known word groups: Carr repeatedly turns clichés on end—e.g., "my art belongs to dada" and "post hock, propter hock." As this last snippet of rewritten Latin illustrates, the playwright does not stop with parodies of English. By choosing more than one way of saying something—"Pardon! . . . Entschuldigung! . . . Scusi! . . . Excuse me!"—Stoppard makes Ionesco's point about the arbitrary relationship of word form and meaning. What is more, Stoppard dramatizes the fact that word meaning is relative; even when speaker and listener use the same language, the meanings they assign a word vary, a point demonstrated by Carr and Tzara's argument over the meaning of the word *artist*. Responding to Tzara's loose construction of the term, Carr counters:

> If there is any point in using language at all it is that a word is taken to stand for a particular fact or idea and not for other facts or ideas. . . . Don't you see my dear Tristan you are simply asking me to accept that the word Art means whatever you wish it to mean; but I do not accept it.

Carr's diehard absolutism notwithstanding, he cannot convince others to abide by his (belief in) precise denotation; they have their own points of view.

It should come as no surprise that works of literature and their medium, language, are presented as malleable in a play that has Dadaism as one of its central concerns, since the absence of absolute or rational explanation is what Dada is all about: "*Dada!* down with reason, logic, causality, coherence, tradition, proportion, sense and consequence." What is more extraordinary is the application of the tenets of this artistic and literary movement to historical events. Tzara acts out the Dadaist credo when he creates a poem by arbitrarily pulling lines out of a hat. Significantly, he extends the theory of random choice: "To a Dadaist history comes out of a hat too."

A sign of Stoppard's own attention in *Travesties* to larger historical patterns is the long monologue delivered by Cecily at the beginning of Act II. "Cecily's Lecture," as it is termed in the text, is a Brechtian newsreel of the historical events providing the backdrop against which the action of the play takes place. This indication of conventional historical narrative aside, events are reviewed in a piecemeal fashion that disorients audiences used to thinking of history along such orderly lines as chronology or progression. The play provides no linear design allowing for easy assimilation of historical fact. It moves forward by fits and starts and often circles back to one event time and again—e.g., the repeated allusions to Carr and Joyce's dispute over the cost of the trousers the former wore in Joyce's Zurich production of *The Importance of Being Earnest*. *Travesties* does provide, however, if not a readily understandable presentation of historical fact, a lesson about the recapitulation of history. Stoppard's point, of course, is that the unorthodox, convoluted structure of his play is more mimetic than the tidily sequential and causally related chain of events in which historical records are frequently served up.

But the playwright's point of departure—a questionable occurrence, the meeting of Joyce, Lenin, and Tzara while they were in Zurich concurrently—makes it clear that he, too, is *shaping* an historical account. Again, it is a subjective question of point of view. Speaking of his own dra-

matic piecing together of Shakespeare's personal history, Stoppard's contemporary, British playwright Edward Bond, writes [in his introduction to *Bingo,* 1974]:

> Of course, I can't insist that my description of Shakespeare's death is true. I'm like a man who looks down from a bridge at the place where an accident has happened. The road is wet, there's a skid mark, the car's wrecked, and a dead man lies by the road in a pool of blood. I can only put the various things together and say what probably happened.

Likewise, Stoppard's history play dramatizes a view from the bridge, as his earlier **"Albert's Bridge"** did literally. Somebody stands back and plays the role of investigator or detective, whose job it is to reconstruct the events. History, then, does have a pattern, not one rising naturally from events under scrutiny but one imposed inevitably by the person recounting what happened.

A minor character in most accounts, including Joyce's *Ulysses,* in which he is found in a footnote, Henry Carr becomes in *Travesties* the reconstructer through whom the stories of three great men are channeled. Drama does not require an onstage narrator of events, but Stoppard has provided one and in so doing has found a visual means of underscoring the creativity of the history-teller. Beyond being a conspicuous raconteur, Carr is a conspicuously eccentric source of information. His recollections of the way things were in Zurich include not only remembrances of public events and great men but also those of a distinctly personal nature, and he makes no attempt to integrate the two. For example,

> You forget that I was there, in the mud and blood of a foreign field, unmatched by anything in the whole history of human carnage. Ruined several pairs of trousers. Nobody who has not been in the trenches can have the faintest conception of the horror of it. I had hardly set foot in France before I sank in up to the knees in a pair of twill jodhpurs with pigskin straps handstitched by Ramidge and Hawkes. And so it went on—the sixteen ounce serge, the heavy worsteds, the silk flannel mixture—until I was invalided out with a bullet through the calf of an irreplaceable lambs-wool dyed khaki in the yarn to my own specification. I tell you, there is nothing in Switzerland to compare with it.

The reader of *Travesties* is told directly that Carr's account is idiosyncratic: Stoppard explains in a stage direction at the outset of the play that "the story (like a toy train perhaps) occasionally jumps the rails and has to be restarted at the point where it goes wild." He then gives these railments a name, "time slips," and makes suggestions for their staging. The viewer of the play also knows that Carr's perception of the past is not always lucid or concise. By the character's own admission in the dialogue: ". . . I digress. No apologies required, constant digression being the saving grace of senile reminiscence."

Moreover, Stoppard structures his work so that it is obviously a memory play, even though he resorts to no such apparent device as the tape recorder used by Beckett in

Krapp's Last Tape. Aside from the parody of Wilde's play, *Travesties* contains in a second sense a play within a play, the inner performance equaling the psychodrama of Carr's retrospection. Carr, in fact, splits into two on-stage characters, Old and Young Carr. At the conclusion Stoppard moves forward to the present time of the play as Old Carr and Old Cecily argue about how things went:

> *Old Cecily:* And I never helped him write *Imperialism, the Highest Stage of Capitalism.* That was the year before, too. 1916.
>
> *Carr:* Oh, Cecily, I wish I'd known then that you'd turn out to be a pedant! (*getting angry*) Wasn't this—Didn't do that—1916—1917—*What of it*? I was here. They were here. They went on. I went on. We all went on.

This exchange nicely points up how stories are influenced not just by personal interests but by less conscious factors as well, such as forgetfulness and the inability to sort out what is important.

Carr's manner of speaking further emphasizes the fact that a person is in control of the history he tells. First, the pace of Carr's story is noticeably uneven. Sometimes he so deletes or compresses information that the audience is left behind; sometimes he is circumlocutory to the point that the narrative virtually comes to a halt. His language, too, draws attention to itself as in this passage:

> 'Twas in the bustling metropolis of swiftly gliding trams and greystone banking houses, of cosmopolitan restaurants on the great stone banks of the swiftly-gliding snot-green (mucus mutandis) Limmat River, of jewelled escapements and refugees of all kinds, e.g. Lenin, there's a point . . . Lenin As I Knew Him. . . . To be in his presence was to be aware of a complex personality, enigmatic, magnetic, but not, I think, astigmatic, his piercing brown (if memory serves) eyes giving no hint of it.

Here he relies on the stock formulas of the oral storyteller ("'Twas in the . . .") as well as his own uniquely additive syntactic patterns and ability to turn a phrase ("mucus mutandis").

Despite his own acknowledgment that he digresses, Carr believes that his "memory serves." As his debate over semantics with Tzara illustrates, Carr believes, most fundamentally, in objectivity and absolutes. And he believes in order; throughout his reminiscences, for example, he resorts to labels as a device to give structure to his discourse: "Memories of James Joyce," "The Ups and Downs of Consular life in Zurich During the Great War: A Sketch," "Lenin As I Knew Him." Of course, all that he does and says belies his principles—he is a living reminder of the erratic subjectivity of the history-teller and the relativity of his product.

Accordingly, audiences cannot take all that Carr recounts and preaches seriously. But Stoppard means for the man himself to be taken seriously, and he is. Carr's idiosyncra-

sies and ways of putting things are arresting, and even his sartorial obsession is, after all, a humanizing vanity. Finally, he—not Tzara, Lenin, or Joyce—is the focal character of the play. His arguments negating Tzara's nihilism are more persuasive than the pontifications of the Dadaist, and he can effectively counter the Marxist rhetoric and Joycean banter when in the situation to do so. In short, Stoppard leads audiences to support Carr and his story; Old Cecily's nitpicking attention to correcting details at the end of the play *is* silly. Since history comes "out of a hat," Carr might as well be doing the pulling. His account is as good as any . . . and better than many, for as we have seen, it implicitly but strongly points up the fact that creation is involved in marshaling historical facts into narrative.

Old Carr sums up his documented legal battle with Joyce over Carr's theatrical costume and concludes:

> I dreamed about him, dreamed I had him in the witness box, a masterly cross-examination, case practically won, admitted it all, the whole thing, the trousers, everything, and I *flung* at him—"And what did you do in the Great War?" "I wrote *Ulysses,*" he said. "What did you do?"

In this passage Joyce, sounding like Stoppard demanding the courage of his lack of convictions, cooly asserts *art pour l'art,* a position Carr would condone despite personal squabbles with the writer. But elsewhere, in a speech whose importance Stoppard now dwells on, Joyce defends the artist against Tzara's attacks on the grounds that he is the recorder and shaper of history:

> An artist is the magician put among men to gratify—capriciously—their urge for immortality. The temples are built and brought down around him, continuously and contiguously, from Troy to the fields of Flanders. If there is any meaning in any of it, it is what survives as art, yes even in the celebration of tyrants, yes even in the celebration of nonentities. What now of the Trojan War if it had been passed over by the artist's touch? Dust. A forgotten expedition prompted by Greek merchants looking for new markets. A minor redistribution of broken pots.

Even though Carr would not be quick to second this opinion, Joyce's comment in effect sums up what the bit player dramatizes in *Travesties,* for Carr performs the function Joyce assigns to the artist. Through his characterization of Carr, Stoppard yokes the roles of artist and historian: he goes beyond the travesty of existing histories, affirming through Carr the importance of history and of the individual "making" it.

In much of his subsequent work Stoppard shows that he learned the lesson his history play teaches. The plays that immediately follow *Travesties*—*Dirty Linen* and *New-Found-Land*—are social comedies in that they both depict the practices of bumbling British politicians, in the House of Commons and a local Home Office respectively. But his more recent works—the television drama *Foul Play, Every Good Boy Deserves Favor,* and *Night and Day*—are plays that truly represent social engagements on Stoppard's part: these plays face squarely such issues as governmental restriction of individual freedom. In characteristic fashion Carr lists at the conclusion of *Travesties* the things he learned in Zurich:

> I learned three things in Zurich during the war. I wrote them down. Firstly, you're either a revolutionary or you're not, and if you're not you might as well be an artist as anything else. Secondly, if you can't be an artist, you might as well be a revolutionary . . .
>
> I forget the third thing.

What he has forgotten but Stoppard has learned is that the two categories are not necessarily mutually exclusive, and thus the playwright has gone on to show he has the courage to state his social convictions on stage.

THE REAL THING

Paul Delaney (essay date 1985)

SOURCE: "Cricket Bats and Commitment: The Real Thing in Art and Life," in *Critical Quarterly*, Vol. 27, No. 1, Spring, 1985, pp. 45-60.

[*In the essay below, Delaney explores the intersection of life and art, genuine and ersatz love, in* The Real Thing.]

That Tom Stoppard's plays are neither imprecise nor obscurantist, that his ambiguities are intended neither to dazzle nor confuse but 'to be precise over a greater range of events', was perhaps the most signal contribution of Clive James's [November] 1975 *Encounter* article: 'It is the plurality of contexts that concerns Stoppard: ambiguities are just places where contexts join'. And in *The Real Thing* (1982) the interstices come between art and life. Stoppard's attempt, a breathtakingly ambitious one, is to deal at once with what is real in life, what is real in art, and what the real differences are between art and life. *The Real Thing* endeavours to indicate what constitutes a more real life as opposed to the glib, the trendy, the ersatz; what endures as a living reality in an age that demands disposable relationships, pragmatic alliances. In art, *The Real Thing* endeavours to distinguish the authentic from propagandistic imitations, the liveliness of the right words in the right order from the ham-fisted butchery of language, what endures as the marbled reality in an age that demands the polystyrene, what endures as alabaster when the age demands plaster. But if the real thing exists in life and the real thing exists in art, the differences between life and art remain no less real. Indeed the very form of *The Real Thing*, opening as it does with a play within a play serves to dramatise the differences between reality and imaginative reality.

The contrast between the real and the imaginative accounts for the genesis not only of the play's form but for the emergence of a playwright as its protagonist. 'I've just finished a play', Stoppard told an American audience [at a lecture] in March 1982, 'which is about a playwright—not for reasons of autobiographical megalomania'. Rather, Stoppard continued, 'I wanted to write a play in which the first scene turns out to have been written by one of the characters in the second scene and consequently he had to be a playwright of course.'

As the curtain rises on that first scene, *The Real Thing* seems the direct opposite of Stoppard's earlier plays. Whereas *Jumpers* and *Travesties* begin with a 'pig's breakfast' of incongruous, seemingly random images, *The Real Thing* opens on a seemingly straightforward domestic scene. At second glance, the plays appear to be mirror images of each other. In *Jumpers* and *Travesties* we gradually learn that the seemingly unreal opening scene is in fact real; in *The Real Thing* we gradually learn that the seemingly real is in fact imaginative, is a play within a play. But eventually we should come to see—whether we begin with the seemingly unreal and then learn that it is the real thing or whether we begin with the seemingly real and then subsequently encounter the real thing—that Tom Stoppard has been writing about real things for quite some time now.

Even *Rosencrantz and Guildenstern are Dead* (1967) springs, as James told us, from "the perception—surely a compassionate one—that the fact of their deaths mattering so little to Hamlet was something which ought to have mattered to Shakespeare." If such art is unarguably self-referential, what it is arguing for is for a greater sympathy, and that in the sublimest of works, for ordinary ramshackle humanity. At the heart of the extraordinary *Rosencrantz and Guildenstern* we find a celebration of the merely ordinary. Just so, the bounding wit of *Jumpers* (1972), endlessly cartwheeling us from George's study to Dottie's bedroom, finally leads us to see—as an urbane sophisticated world does not—the validity of the insights of the ploddingly pedestrian George who affirms the inherently moral nature of experience in the real world; and to see—as George does not—the loneliness and anguish of the pathetically real Dottie. In the intricately erudite *Travesties* (1974) we find the ordinary decent consul Henry Carr at the centre not only of the play's structure but of the play's sympathy. If Joyce is celebrated, as he is, it is because his art deals with the likes of Henry Carr, his art emerges from, even immortalises, the real. Even more clearly, the more recent plays deal with ordinary humanity in all their creatureliness: husbands and wives, fathers and—again and again—sons. Just as George in *Jumpers* may offer moral affirmations which are valid in theory but which need to be demonstrated in practice, the tensions in *Professional Foul* (1977) involve the disjunction between the realms of Professor Anderson's abstract philosophising and the real world of Pavel Hollar's wife and son. Stoppard has described the play as an education by experience. Although Anderson may have 'a perfectly respectable philosophical thesis', Stoppard says, 'what happens is something extremely simple . . . he just brushes up against the specific reality of the mother and the child, especially the child' [interview in *Gambit* 10, No. 37,

1981]. But in the disjunction between precept and practice, between moral abstractions and moral applications,
there is not the absurdist assertion of a chaotic universe,
nor the aesthete's withdrawal into sublimely stylish siren
song, nor the obscurantist's perverse or inadvertent confusion. From the first, Stoppard's plays have depicted real
people in real time and space rather than offering a surrealistic or absurdist vision of unreality.

The Real Thing's primary connection with the earlier plays
is not just its verbal felicity (which many reviewers have
noted) nor the naturalistic form which the play shares with
Night and Day (1978). *The Real Thing*—as remarkable
for its emotional richness as for its wit—extends, deepens,
and refines the concerns with which Stoppard has been
dealing at least since *Jumpers*. Like *Jumpers, The Real
Thing* depicts human experience as inherently, fundamentally moral. With equal clarity, Stoppard's most recent
play affirms that the real thing exists in the realm of art
and thus continues *Travesties*' concern with the difference
between genuine and bogus art. Further, *The Real Thing*
extends and deepens the concern in *Travesties* and *Dogg's
Hamlet, Cahoot's Macbeth* (1979) over the connection
between art and politics. If such plays as *Every Good Boy
Deserves Favour* (1977) and *Professional Foul* narrowed
the focus of the universal moral values adumbrated in
Jumpers to an examination of the body politic and affirmed that 'the ethics of the State must be judged against
the fundamental ethic of the individual'—that is, 'one
man's dealings with another man'—*The Real Thing* narrows the focus still further precisely to the arena of one
person's dealings with another person. Thus, the affirmation in *Jumpers* of moral absolutes; the apologia com-
menced in *Travesties* and continued in *Dogg's Hamlet,
Cahoot's Macbeth* for art as a moral matrix; the application in *Every Good Boy Deserves Favour* and *Professional Foul* of moral judgement to the political arena; the
assertion in *Night and Day* that corruption in language is
connected with corruption in moral vision; all coalesce in
The Real Thing with a deepened concern for the inherently moral commitment made between a man and a woman
who know and are known by each other in the most intimate and most real of human relationships. Perhaps what
The Real Thing most fundamentally shares with Stoppard's earlier plays is its assumption that reality exists,
that life is meaningful, that the universe is not random or
chaotic, that the difference between the real and the unreal, between the genuine and the artificial is knowable
and that the real thing can be recognised.

Thus, if the opening causes the audience to experience
disorientation, it also allows the audience to experience
the shock of recognition. Hersh Zeifman's observation that
the form of the play involves the audience viscerally in
the questions being dealt with is undoubtedly correct
[*Modern Drama* 26, 1983]. We are taken in by that first
scene. Indeed, it is not until some way into the second
scene that we recognise the opening as having been a play
within a play. But the point, surely, is that we can recognise the real thing when it comes along. If the play shows
that appearances can be deceiving, that we may momentarily mistake the imaginative construct for actual reality,

it also shows that we can recognise appearances for what
they are—appearances. If it is sometimes difficult to tell
the real from the ersatz, if the artificial can sometimes
deceive us into believing it to be real, that in no way
suggests that the real thing does not exist and cannot,
upon discovery, be recognised.

The form of the play does not mystify, baffle, or confuse;
it does not—as it is possible for a different sort of play to
do—leave us up in the air as to which is the imaginative
realm and which is actual experience, which is waking
reality and which is the dream. Actually, in performance
the play is surprisingly straightforward and easy to follow.
Even the least sophisticated member of the audience would
not emerge from Stoppard's play wondering if the opening scene about an architect were 'real' and the remaining
two and a quarter hours constituted an elaborate play within
a play. Perhaps, however, it must be ruefully noted that
more sophisticated viewers may be taken in either by the
play's form or by the sophistries which the play refutes.
One of the things which complicates argument at the
moment, as Stoppard has remarked elsewhere, 'is that
people are so clever that, paradoxically, they can be persuaded of almost anything' [interview in the *Wall Street
Journal,* 1 February 1980]. Given the general level of
academic twaddle about Stoppard as an 'absurdist', 'post-
absurdist', or 'pan-parodist', we may yet encounter sophisticated academic nonsense about this play. Nevertheless, to emerge from *The Real Thing* with a sense that it
is impossible to tell what is real and what is unreal within
the play, one must be clever indeed.

Although disclaiming any autobiographical impulse behind the selection of a playwright as the protagonist for
his play, Stoppard nevertheless reports [in the 1982 lec-
ture] that 'in the course of writing it, I found this man
expressing some of the notions I have about writing',
notions, he continued, 'which I probably will not disown
in the near future.' Indeed, less than a week after finishing
the play, Stoppard offered Henry's statements on writing
to an American audience with the explanation that he would
be 'reading them out as though they are mine.' *The Real
Thing*'s affirmation of art is rooted in a celebration of
language, a celebration which extends Stoppard's previous concern that language not be subjected to the abuse of
pedestrian cliché, political cant, or totalitarian obfuscation. Henry's role as guardian of the language at times
takes the form of mere grammatical finickiness, the 'professional fastidiousness' of a playwright who corrects his
guests' use of the gerund. However, when Henry objects
to describing a conviction for arson as being 'hammered'
by an emotional 'backlash', he is not merely being pedantic. He is objecting to jargon which misrepresents real
events, as well as objecting to the misuse of words in a
mixed metaphor.

Such a concern for language extends the denunciation in
Night and Day of both journalistic and political jargon,
both the 'Lego-set language' of the London tabloids and
the political cant of the labour unions. '"Betrayal" . . .
"Confrontation" . . . "Management" . . . My God, you'd
need a more supple language than that to describe an ar-

gument between two amoebas', says Jacob Milne as he mimics the debased language which evicts 'ordinary English' when the 'house Trots' speak of a strike. More sweepingly, when the arsonist Brodie attempts to take up writing, Henry exposes the vacuity of his revolutionary rhetoric in what Roger Scruton rightly calls a 'masterly and devastating criticism of the radical butchery of language' [*Encounter,* February 1983]: 'I can't help somebody who thinks, or thinks he thinks, that editing a newspaper is censorship, or that throwing bricks is a demonstration while building tower blocks in social violence, or that unpalatable statement is provocation while disrupting the speaker is the exercise of free speech . . . Words don't deserve that kind of malarkey'. Eventually, however, Henry's celebration of words as 'innocent, neutral, precise, standing for this, describing that, meaning the other' not only affirms a connectedness between the word and the thing named but emerges as a sacramental view of language: 'I don't think writers are sacred, but words are.'

Just as *Travesties* celebrates the 'immortality' of art 'that will dance for some time yet', *The Real Thing* celebrates the sacredness of words which can grant a form of immortality: 'If you get the right ones in the right order, you can . . . make a poem which children will speak for you when you're dead.' Indeed, like *Travesties, The Real Thing* celebrates a non-propagandistic art, praises art which 'works' aesthetically whether or not it 'works' in terms of social utility, by, for example, securing the immediate release of prisoners. The two conceptions of art collide in the play's last scene in which Brodie sees a videotape of his own play in a version completely revised by Henry. When Annie, who had requested her husband Henry to rewrite Brodie's fumbling dialogue, says of the television play, 'It did work', Brodie—with no conception of how a play could 'work' aesthetically—asks uncomprehendingly, 'You mean getting me sprung?' 'No', Annie replies, 'I didn't mean that.' The difference between writing well and writing rubbish, between art which 'works' and plays 'which go "clunk" every time someone opens his mouth', springs not from the social or political importance of the subject ('something to write about, something real') or from the immediate social or political effect ('getting me sprung'), but from the liveliness or loutishness in the use of language, the carelessness or precision in putting words together.

The writer can 'get it right' or can fail to get it right. And the difference between the two is, in one of the memorable images of the play, as great as the difference between a cricket bat and a cudgel. 'This thing here', Henry says of the real thing, 'which looks like a wooden club, is actually several pieces of particular wood cunningly put together in a certain way so that the whole thing is sprung, like a dance floor.' Both Henry's explanation of the intricate composition of the cricket bat (metaphorically 'well chosen words nicely put together') and his association of it with the dance recall Joyce's apologia in *Travesties* for art. By contrast, the turgid prose of Brodie's dialogue is a cudgel, 'a lump of wood of roughly the same shape trying to be a cricket bat, and if you hit a ball with it, the ball will travel about ten feet and you will drop the bat and dance about shouting "Ouch!" with your hands stuck

into your armpits'. To demonstrate that the difference between the two (metaphorically the difference between 'good writing' and writing that is 'no good') is not just a matter of opinion, Henry points to Brodie's script and suggests that Annie try for herself: 'You don't believe me, so I suggest you go out to bat with this and see how you get on. "You're a strange boy, Billy, how old are you?" "Twenty, but I've lived more than you'll ever live." Ooh, ouch!' What Henry is suggesting, basically, is an education by experience. What he affirms, he argues, is not contingent on his skill in arguing, but is verifiable by experience, is—quite simply—true: 'This isn't better because someone says it's better. . . . It's better because it's better.'

Although *The Real Thing* continues to celebrate language, continues to associate complexity in composition and liveliness in writing with the dance, nevertheless implicit in the image of the cricket bat is a significant departure from some of Stoppard's previous descriptions of the genesis and purpose of art. If a cricket bat is 'for hitting cricket balls with', what, we may ask, is art 'for'? 'What we're trying to do', Henry explains, 'is to write cricket bats, so that when we throw up an idea and give it a little knock, it might . . . travel.' Art, as Henry explains it, is for launching ideas. Such a conception of art differs substantially from the much-quoted epigram Stoppard coined some years ago that 'plays are not the end-products of ideas, ideas are the end-products of plays'. More recently, however, when the quote came bouncing back to him from yet another interviewer, Stoppard tossed it aside as having 'the overstatement of most epigrams'. Indeed, that quip, Stoppard continued, 'of course . . . stopped being applicable round about the time I started writing *Jumpers*. There the play was the end-product of an idea as much as the converse' (*Gambit*). Just so, as Henry explains it, the idea seems to be preexistent, to be already rolled up into, well, a ball, which the artist—if he wields his art lightly, forcefully, and well; if he avoids ham-fisted bludgeoning—can send soaring.

If Henry's explanation of the lofting of ideas demonstrates development in Stoppard's perspective on the genesis of art, Henry's reflections on the effect of art more profoundly clarify Stoppard's position from his treatment in previous plays of the connection between art and politics. Just as Tzara, in *Travesties,* could not change art into something it was not simply by abusing the word 'art', so in *The Real Thing* an artist cannot change 'politics, justice, patriotism' by trying to stick labels on them. However, Henry continues in clarification of what the artist can change, 'if you know this and proceed with humility, you may perhaps alter people's perceptions so that they behave a little differently at that axis of behaviour where we locate politics or justice.' Art, that is, can in some way effect social change toward justice. However, art is not useful in some kind of immediate way that gets Brodie free from prison next month. Rather, art is a civilising force, a humanising force, a 'moral matrix' as Stoppard told an interviewer in [*Theatre Quarterly* IV, No. 4, May–July 1974], 'from which we make our judgements about the world'.

If Joyce in *Travesties* affirmed art for art's sake, art completely removed from any kind of social or political obli-

Michael Hordern as George in the 1972 National Theatre production of Jumpers *at the Old Vic Theatre in London.*

gations, art which exists in a separate realm where it 'will dance for some time yet and *leave the world precisely as it finds it*', Henry in *The Real Thing* affirms art which can both teach and delight, art which exists both in the realm of time and the timeless, the power of words with which an artist 'can nudge the world a little or make a poem which children will speak for you when you're dead'. Henry's climactic statement on art continues *Travesties'* affirmation that art need not be social, continues to see art as gratifying 'a hunger that is common to princes and peasants' or, even, children. However, the acknowledgement that art can 'nudge' the world, significantly, if modestly, extends Stoppard's claims for art. Social impact may not be art's major purpose; and art may not accomplish social change with immediate effect. Nevertheless, art need not leave the world precisely as it finds it; art can move the world, at least fractionally; and that movement can be in the direction of justice. Henry's climactic statements on art thus conflate a number of themes from the play. The world that is there to be nudged is real; a world in which people need to act with justice is inherently moral; and art, by faithfully reflecting the real world, can enable people to see the real world and their own actions with greater precision, to act with greater comprehension and clarity.

Thus, however distinct the plane of imaginative reality may be from reality, there are, finally, interconnections between them. There are points at which the aesthetic intersects the epistemological and even the ethical. Distortions in one plane can lead to distortions in the other planes. Abuse of words in writing can lead to a warped vision of the real world, a bent toward seeing justice as fraud, property as theft, patriotism as propaganda, religion as a con trick. And such skewed perception of the real world can lead to the acting out of prejudice, to behaviour in the ethical plane which is likewise skewed. Thus clarity of artistic vision is not, finally, divorced from accuracy of epistemological perception or even from rightness of ethical action. Writing aright can lead, or can help lead, or—to put it as modestly as possible—can 'nudge' human beings 'a little' toward acting aright in the real world.

Stoppard's vision of the intersecting planes of the aesthetic, the epistemological, and the ethical may be intricate—and intricacy may characterise the art which bodies forth such complexity—but what it is not is chaotic. To abandon precision in epistemological perception of the real world is to make a 'mistake'; to abandon precision in moral vision is to manifest 'prejudice'; and to abandon precision in writing is to create works which do not square with the real world, works which do not even square with themselves, architectural follies which should be 'bridges across incomprehension and chaos' but which are in fact 'jerry-built', 'rubbish', incapable of supporting even their own clumsy weight.

If Stoppard's plays grow, or apparently grow, from the demand that Art should be its own subject, they inevitably break through this new and alien and artificial turf and sink their roots into the timeless truth that the evanescent beauty of art can only blossom from the ordinary mundane soil of real life. Stoppard eschews the example of committed playwrights who 'grapple' with 'weighty' issues, argues James, 'not because he can't do what they can do, but because he can do what they can do so easily' (*Encounter,* November 1975). Having demonstrated his mastery of the form, Stoppard finally leaves behind the inherently circular world of art which is merely self-referential for much the same reason.

Stoppard's is a paradoxical art. He writes cavortingly clever plays which wittily expose as effete the merely clever. He writes exuberantly risqué plays which ruefully reflect on human experience as ineluctably moral. He writes disarmingly stylish plays which expose the danger of mere style. He writes extraordinary plays which celebrate ordinary mundane human beings. He writes seemingly surreal plays that affirm the existence and the value of the real. In a farrago of words he affirms that the essential truths are simple and monolithic and precede language. And in one of the surpassing ironies of his paradoxical plays, Stoppard creates a self-referential art which celebrates only that art which is not merely self-referential, celebrates that art which is mimetically rooted in its representation of ordinary human experience, art which eschews the surreal for the real.

Having established the contrast between real life and art in the juxtaposition of scene one with scene two, having celebrated the existence of the real thing in art in Henry's memorable contrast of cricket bats with cudgels in the middle of the second act, what remains as the ultimate concern of the play is the contrast between the ersatz—however alluring or deceptive or temporarily misleading—and the real thing in human relationships. 'Does the world "love" mean anything at all?' a character asks in Harold Pinter's most recent play ['Family Voices']. Stoppard's play asks a much harder question. *The Real Thing* asks if commitment, fidelity, trust have meaning even in an age which insists that relationships are negotiable commodities, even in a hedonistic environment which is as surfeited with sensuality as 'this poncy business' of the theatre, even—indeed—in a relationship which has its very inception in an adulterous affair. *The Real Thing* asks if there can be affirmation of commitment, fidelity, trust between lovers who were themselves brought together by infidelity, the breaking of commitments, the betrayal of trust.

Just as the play opens with two quite different scenes both of which—initially—appear to be real; just as we are presented with two characters who embody different views of writing; just so *The Real Thing* presents us with characters who embody several different views of love and different views of the nature of human relationships. Charlotte, Henry's first wife, discounts the significance of love—romantic, marital, or even parental—from her first appearance. Although she is primarily trying to insult Henry's plays as unreal, there is also undisguised condescension toward the whole notion of fidelity in Charlotte's assertion that if Henry were to catch her with a lover his 'sentence structure would go to pot, closely followed by his sphincter'. Indeed, in some of the coarsest language of the play, Charlotte describes fidelity in a wife as merely a matter of having 'a stiff upper lip, and two semi-stiff lower ones'. She even jeers at Henry's love for his daughter and describes parental love as abnormal, saying that 'normal is the other way round'—normal, that is, is the response of one who 'just can't stand the little buggers'. Ultimately Charlotte's view of relationships is articulated in mercantile metaphors. 'There are', she asserts, 'no commitments, only bargains'. If Charlotte dismisses relationships as 'bargains', Debbie puts a different price on relationships in her advocacy of 'free love'. Like her mother, Debbie contemptuously dismisses the necessity or significance of fidelity. Infidelity is 'a crisis only if you want to make it' one, Debbie reasons, arguing that her boiler room trysts had shown her that sex is not 'secret and ecstatic and wicked and a sacrament' but, merely, 'turned out to be biology after all'.

Whereas Charlotte and Debbie demonstrate a pragmatic devaluing of relationships, Annie—who marries Henry after both have divorced their first spouses—values commitment but sees it as negotiable. Certainly she is more willing than Henry to jettison a first marriage. However, she is intense in her affection, her love, for Henry and she sees their subsequent marriage as something more than a bargain, as a relationship involving a measure of commitment. But she does not equate love or commitment, necessarily, with fidelity. Having embarked on an adulterous affair with the actor Billy, Annie endeavours nevertheless to assert her continuing love for Henry. She says she has learned not to care about the affairs she had suspected Henry of having, and that while her affair with Billy may continue, it is quite separate from her relationship with Henry: 'You weren't replaced, or even replaceable.'

As opposed to such denials of the possibility of love, or of the need for love to be accompanied by marriage, or of the need for marriage to be accompanied by fidelity, Henry from the first affirms the insularity of passion, the significance of commitment, the value of fidelity. While Henry the playwright confesses that he does not 'know how to write love' because 'loving and being loved is unliterary', Henry the man can turn to Annie at the peak of an argument and say, however unliterarily, 'I love you so.' In performance the chemistry between Roger Rees and Felicity Kendal, the unselfconscious physical affection they share, may provide compelling emphasis to Annie's response, 'I love you so, Hen.'

At least in part, however, the resonance of such an exchange is established precisely by the dialogue's unpolished simplicity. Scruton's description of Stoppard's dialogue as 'an exchange not of feelings, but of epigrams' (*Encounter,* February 1983), might well apply to the play within the play, the scene from 'House of Cards' written by Henry. But applied to *The Real Thing* Scruton's charge simply leaves out more than it includes. To fail to distinguish the verbal veneer of that first scene from the emotional richness of much of the rest of the play is to call attention only to the discussion of art and miss the immediate personal experience of love and betrayal, the offering of commitment and the discovery of infidelity which undergirds the fabric of the play, One of the most moving speeches of the play, Henry's anguished cry, restrained until after Annie has already departed for another adulterous rendezvous, 'Oh, please, please, please, please *don't*' is scarcely aphoristic. Indeed, precisely what we do not get at the play's most emotional moments is what Henry and Charlotte identify as 'badinage', 'smart talk', sitting around 'being witty about place mats'. Even Henry's first act curtain speech, 'I love love', although—perhaps—impassioned, can scarcely be described as eloquent: 'I love having a lover and being one. The insularity of passion. I love it. I love the way it blurs the distinction between everyone who isn't one's lover. Only two kinds of presence in the world. There's you and there's them.' Indeed, by having the climactic speech of act one couched in sentence fragments, Stoppard is deliberately undercutting the rhetorical possibilities of the moment.

While it may be true, as [Zeifman] has observed, that in Stoppard's play 'love speaks in many different tongues, with many different accents', it does not necessarily follow that it is impossible to tell 'which of them, finally, is "the real thing". Such a view offers the sophisticated interpretation that while a stoppard play might engage in elaborate theatre games, might recount the process of trying to define the real thing, it surely would not do anything quite so simplistic as to define the real thing, well at least—dear me—not in terms of the morality of sexual relationships.

Despite such critical reluctance to recognise anything but relativity, Stoppard asserts that when his characters speak on various sides of a question, one may be voicing a position which is not just more persuasive or more eloquent or more generally accepted, but is, quite simply, true. Of *Night and Day* Stoppard asserts, 'Ruth has got a gift for sarcastic abuse, but what Milne says is true'. 'I mean', Stoppard continues somewhat insistently, 'it is true . . . I believe it to be a true statement. Milne has my prejudice if you like. Somehow unconsciously, I wanted him to be known to be speaking the truth' (*Gambit*). And such truths just might be surprisingly simple. A moment later Stoppard offers a blunt assessment of *Professional Foul*: 'it's to do with the morality between individuals.' 'Something which has preoccupied me for a long time', he continues, 'is the desire to simplify questions and take the sophistication out. A fairly simple question about morality, if debated by highly sophisticated people, can lead to almost any conclusion.' When Stoppard takes the sophistication out, when he cuts through the sophistries and gets down to the real thing, what he finds is a question of 'the morality between individuals'.

Similarly, when *The Real Thing* cuts through the sophisticated badinage that 'little touches' can 'lift adultery out of the moral arena and make it a matter of style' the play leads us to a question about morality between individuals, a question about one person's dealings with another person in the most intimate of human relationships, a question that remains squarely in 'the moral arena'. But this matter of morality, the sophisticated observer may ask, it is still a question, n'est-ce pas? It is, how you say, an 'intellectual leap-frog' [Zeifman]. Skewering those who continue to find leap-frogging in his plays, Stoppard declares 'I can say that in the last few years I haven't been writing about questions whose answers I believe to be ambivalent. In *Every Good Boy* and *Professional Foul,* the author's position isn't ambiguous' (*Gambit*). Nor is it in *The Real Thing*.

Whatever Charlotte's gift for sarcastic abuse, whatever Debbie's gift for verbal sophistry, whatever Annie's gift for persuasive nonsense, we should eventually recognise the difference between the real thing and the bogus imitation as being as great as, well, the difference between a cricket bat and a cudgel. Indeed, like Brodie's attempt at playwriting, Charlotte's pronouncements on fidelity are undercut by their own 'crudity'. We discover, subsequently, that while married to Henry, Charlotte had embarked on an adulterous tour of the Home Counties with no fewer than nine different 'chaps'. 'I thought we'd made a commitment', Henry says in surprise, evoking Charlotte's disparaging comment that there are no commitments, 'only bargains'. Indeed, after Henry's marriage to Annie, we discover Charlotte is 'shacked up' with a real-life architect, has other affairs alongside that affair, and gives the architect the elbow when he objects. Charlotte may be an entrepreneur; but she's no bargain.

More persuasive, perhaps, is Debbie's advocacy of free love. If sex is mere biology, relationships need make no pretense of even aspiring to fidelity: 'That's what free love is free of—propaganda.' Brodie's prose may be hamfisted, whereas Debbie's phrase-making is 'flawless', 'neat'. But Henry faults both of them for using language to falsify reality: 'You can do that with words, bless 'em.' What Debbie does with words is create 'sophistry in a phrase so neat you can't see the loose end that would unravel it. It's flawless but wrong. A perfect dud.' Henry demonstrates the ease of spinning out such phrases with a neat epigram of his own: 'What free love is free of is love.' Later in the conversation Debbie unpops another pithy pronouncement: 'Exclusive rights isn't love, it's colonisation.' Though he dismisses such a cleverty as 'another *ersatz* masterpiece', Henry's affection for his daughter is clear—as is his disapproval of her misuse of her gift for language—in saying she is 'like Michelangelo working in polystyrene'. The scene does not, however, merely offer a battle of wits, a mock-epic exchange of epigrams. 'Don't write it, Fa', Debbie interrupts, 'Just say it.'

So Henry just says it. His daughter's glib devaluing of commitment prompts Henry's climactic statement on the nature of relationships—a statement which lacks eloquence or gloss or polish, but which for all that carries far greater weight than Debbie's 'polystyrene' philosophising: 'It's to do with knowing and being known. I remember how it stopped seeming odd that in biblical Greek knowing was used for making love. Whosit knew so-and-so. Carnal knowledge. It's what lovers trust each other with. Knowledge of each other, not of the flesh but through the flesh, knowledge of self, the real him, the real her, *in extremis,* the mask slipped from the face.' Against such a standard Debbie's burblings about free love and non-exclusive rights seem sophomoric, as, indeed, they are. Her glib sophistries are finally faulted, much as Charlotte's sardonic crudities, not merely as glib or wrong-headed or reductivist—though they are all of those—but because they are unreal. They lack reality.

Affirming a knowledge 'not of the flesh but through the flesh' Henry asserts that there is more to sex than just biology, more to a human being than meets the microscope, more to human actions than amoral glandular functions. Henry, that is, affirms human interaction, intimacy between 'the real him' and 'the real her' as inherently, ineluctably, moral. Writing in 1977 on the ubiquitous attacks of relativists on objective truth and absolute morality, Stoppard declared his own belief in 'a moral order derived from Christian absolutes' [*Times Literary Supplement*, 3 June 1977]. Just so, more than Henry's language is derived from biblical Greek. Henry's view of relationships is derived from a biblical view of relationships: 'in pairs we insist that we give ourselves to each other. What selves? What's left? . . . A sort of knowledge. Personal, final, uncompromised. Knowing, being known. I revere that.' From a sacramental view of language to a reverential view of relationships, *The Real Thing* continues to depict both life and the language which faithfully represents life as meaningful.

In contrast both to Charlotte's sardonic pragmatism and the trendy promiscuity that Debbie so glibly espouses, Annie demonstrates some degree of commitment. Even amid her affair with Billy, Annie maintains that she loves Henry, and tries to assure him that Billy is not a threat. However, her expectations that Henry should manifest 'dignity', should learn 'not to care', should 'find a part of yourself where I'm not important' are shown to be unrealistic. Just as *Professional Foul* shows a professor 'being educated by experience beyond the education he's received from thinking' (*Gambit,*), *The Real Thing* shows a playwright's education by experience when, after having written about infidelity in his plays, he has to experience the real thing in his own life. Just as reality can cut through the seemingly seamless tissue that philosophers or professors are able to spin, so reality can cut through the fanciful figures that playwrights can weave. As a playwright, Henry has written about the discovery of infidelity and shown the cuckolded husband continuing to run on a witty line of banter. But when Henry the man discovers the infidelity of his own wife, he disclaims privacy, dignity and stagey sophistication: 'I don't believe in debonair relationships. "How's your lover today, Amanda?" "In the pink, Charles. How's yours?" I believe in mess, tears, pain, self-abasement, loss of self-respect, nakedness. Not

caring doesn't seem much different from not loving.' Rejecting the brittle stage banter of Noel Coward sophisticates, Henry also explodes Debbie's dicta on free love as simply sophisticated masks for indifference. What free love is free of is love because not to care is not to love.

Henry can swallow his pride; he can resist being 'pathetic' or 'tedious' or 'intrusive', but he cannot learn to 'not care'. The reviewer who came away with the impression that Henry 'comes to realise that exclusive rights to a person is not love' got it, rather spectacularly, wrong [John Barber, *The Daily Telegraph*, 17 November 1982]. Henry quotes his daughter's epigram but does so with bitter irony. 'We have got beyond hypocrisy, you and I', Henry says, wryly hypocritical: 'Exclusive rights isn't love, it's colonisation.' 'Stop it—please stop it', Annie interrupts, unable to endure the irony in Henry's voice. 'The trouble is', Henry continues more straightforwardly, 'I can't *find* a part of myself where you're not important. I write in order to be worth your while and to finance the way I want to live with you. Not the way *you* want to live. The way *I* want to live with *you*.' However eloquent Henry may be in defence of art, he is quick to deny that his commitment to his art in any way supercedes or is even separable from the commitments he makes to relationships in real life. He is even willing to 'tart up Brodie's unspeakable drivel into speakable drivel' if Annie wants him to. We see in what sense this is a 'committed' playwright. Henry's is a commitment not to causes or ideologies but to a person. Although his memorable image of the cricket bat may be the springboard for an articulate apologia for the real thing in art, what finally matters to Henry more than art or even articulacy is love—the genuine article, the real thing, however haltingly expressed—in real life.

Despite Scruton's charge that Stoppard 'does not portray characters, who develop in relation to each other', the play finally hinges precisely on the transformation, the development, the growth we see in Annie. Even if Annie's espousal of commitment without concomitant fidelity seems a more formidable position than either Charlotte's or Debbie's, the play does not leave such a view as just another option alongside Henry's conception of love. In a series of crucial revelations in the play's final scene Annie abandons such a position along with a number of other falsehoods. We learn, first of all, that Brodie's ostensibly revolutionary offense had been wholly apolitical in motivation, had been performed, Annie says, with 'not an idea in his head except to impress me'.

Thus, for at least the second time in his career, Stoppard has written a play in which a shadowy Scot proves of pivotal significance. Just as *Jumpers* springs from George's attempts to compose a response to the philosophically radical McFee, so the putative political radical Brodie prompts Henry's response from the first scene. In both plays the off-stage Scot serves as the catalyst for an entire line of argument by the protagonist throughout the play, and then, at the penultimate moment of the play is discovered to be radically unlike what we had thought him to be. Further, such a radical alteration in our perception of him has the effect not of undercutting what the protagonist has been saying throughout the evening but of supporting, underscoring, reinforcing it. The posthumous revelation that McFee had rejected moral relativism, abandoned a materialist view of humankind, experienced a religious conversion, broken off an affair, and made plans to enter a monastery, does not go much further to support the theist affirmations of the moral absolutist George than Henry's position is supported by the revelation of Brodie, in the last scene, as a hooligan whose 'political' act of setting a fire on the Cenotaph had been prompted by a wholly apolitical desire, using the only means such an inarticulate lout had at hand, to impress a girl.

If the penultimate revelaton of Brodie reaffirms all that Henry—as playwright—has said about writing, the ultimate revelation of a transformation in Annie reaffirms what Henry—as a lover—has said about love. The two long arcs of the play—the concern with writing and the concern with loving—thus meet and are resolved in the play's final scene. However much weight Henry's impassioned plea for commitment may have carried during the preceding scenes the play's affirmations are not, finally, based on Henry's words alone. In the closing scene, Annie, sick of the freedom—the licence—of her extramarital experimentation, rejects her adulterous involvement, recoiling from the prospect of another contact with Billy with a vehement 'No'. Moments later she turns to her husband and speaks six words. If Henry and Annie's reconciliation is almost 'wordless', as Scruton pejoratively describes it, we should recall, as Anderson says in *Professional Foul,* that 'the important truths are simple and monolithic. The essentials of a given situation speak for themselves, and language is as capable of obscuring the truth as of revealing it.' The simple and monolithic truth here is that the relationship of a husband and wife, a relationship bent to the breaking point, has been restored. The words are, merely:

Annie: I've had it. Look after me.

Henry: Don't worry. I'm your chap.

But what has been exchanged is a world of feeling. And if the utter simplicity of Annie's words, if the expressiveness of her embrace, if the significance of her smile as she turns out the lights, if all this is not compelling, would it have been more compelling if they had discussed it? As the curtain descends on that luminous bedroom portal, the play ends not—as in Shakespearean comedy—with marriage as restoration, but—having attained the more mature vision of Shakespearean romance—with a restoration within marriage.

Just as we can tell the difference between a cricket bat and a cudgel, just as we can tell the difference between conscious artistry and the political hack-writing of Brodie, so we can tell the difference between ersatz pronouncements on love and the real thing, the difference between the real thing and bogus imitations in life. The real thing is real life as opposed to imaginative reality, actual experience rather than art. The real thing is love rather than, just, sex. The real thing is the word rather than the sophistry, the faithful use of language rather than the corrupt abuse of language into jargon. The real thing is art rather than its propagandistic imitation, writing that grows out of authentic human experience rather than doctrinaire posturing, the right words in the right order rather than hamfisted rubbish. The real thing is the clear-sighted perception of politics, justice, patriotism rather than the obfuscation of prejudice. The real thing is the recognition of a relationship as a commitment rather than a mere bargain, the willingness to accept commitment in relationship rather than casualness in affairs, the fulfilment—and sometimes pain—of promise rather than the mere pleasure of promiscuity; costly love rather than free. And in facing the fact of infidelity, the real thing is the pain and nakedness of caring rather than the debonair front of witty repartee or the indifference of not caring.

The measure of Stoppard's achievement is not that he is able to depict the ecstatic passion of love, or the sweet pangs of unrequited love, or the attractiveness of illicit love, or—finally—even the agonies of betrayed love, though *The Real Thing* does all that. The measure of Stoppard's achievement is that he is able to depict and vivify and make compelling the enduring happiness—deeper than ecstasy if less spectacular, more satisfying than illicit love if sometimes less attractive, more profoundly moving than free love if more painful—of loving and being loved, knowing and being known, the giving and receiving of commitment, fidelity. If *Jumpers,* as Kenneth Tynan aptly observed, is unique in the theatre as 'a farce whose main purpose is to affirm the existence of God' [*The New Yorker,* 19 December 1977], *The Real Thing* has its own uniqueness as a West End comedy of adulterous alliances—a play about 'infidelity among the architect class. Again'—whose main purpose is to affirm the vital importance of fidelity, yes even the vital importance, in the commitment which love entails, of being earnest. And if it seems even less likely in our time than in Wilde's that a playwright could affirm the importance of being earnest and be in earnest about it, could affirm fidelity and not be ironic or cynical or, merely, flippant about it, that too is a measure of Stoppard's achievement. Stoppard has the unmitigated audacity, the perfectly scandalous nerve—simply washing one's clean linen in public—to dedicate the text of his adulterous comedy to his wife; and while that sort of thing may not be enormously on the increase in London, Stoppard sends his audience streaming out into the West End night—the lyrics 'I'm a Believer' ringing in their ears—convinced that such dedication, 'For Miriam', just might, after all, be the real thing.

HAPGOOD

Hersh Zeifman (essay date 1990)

SOURCE: "A Trick of the Light: Tom Stoppard's *Hapgood* and Postabsurdist Theater," in *Around the Absurd: Essays on Modern and Postmodern Drama,* edited by

John Wood as Henry Carr in the 1974 Royal Shakespeare Company production of Travesties *at the Aldwych Theatre in London.*

Enoch Brater and Ruby Cohn, The University of Michigan Press, 1990, pp. 175-201.

[*In this essay, Zeifman focuses on* Hapgood *to uncover a note of optimism which distinguishes Stoppard's plays from works by Samuel Beckett and other writers of absurdist drama.*]

In a 1974 interview with the editors of *Theatre Quarterly,* Tom Stoppard was questioned about the genesis of his playwriting career [*Theatre Quarterly* IV, No. 4, May-July 1974]. *A Walk on the Water,* written in 1960 (but not staged in England until 1968, as *Enter a Free Man*), was considered "an unusual kind of first play" by the interviewers, containing little that was "autobiographical or seminal." Stoppard responded:

> I don't think a first play tends to be that—it tends to be the sum of all the plays you have seen of a type you can emulate technically and have admired. So *A Walk on the Water* was in fact *Flowering Death of a Salesman*. . . . *I don't think it's a very true play, in the sense that I feel no intimacy with the people I was writing about. It works pretty well as a play, but it's actually phoney because it's play written about other people's characters.*

The "other people's characters" Stoppard was referring to were abducted, as he himself pointed out, from Robert

Bolt's *Flowering Cherry* and Arthur Miller's *Death of a Salesman:* a strange theatrical amalgam that perhaps explains the play's uncertain tone. For his second play Stoppard turned to an entirely different source: "The next play I wrote, **"The Gamblers,"** was over-influenced by Beckett, set in a condemned cell with only two people in it" [quoted by Charles Marowitz, in the *New York Times,* 19 October 1975]. While this imitation of Beckett was originally likewise "a kind of feint," it has proved to be of more lasting significance: Samuel Beckett has remained an important influence on Stoppard's drama.

Stoppard has expressed his intense admiration of Beckett on numerous occasions. "There's just no telling," he has written [in the *Sunday Times,* 25 February 1968], "what sort of effect [*Waiting for Godot*] had on our society, who wrote because of it, or wrote in a different way because of it. . . . Of course it would be absurd to deny my enormous debt to it, and love for it. Precisely what Stoppard loved in Beckett was, first of all, the structure of Beckett's humor: "There's Beckett joke which is the funniest joke in the world to me. It appears in various forms but it consists of confident statement followed by immediate refutation by the same voice. It's constant process of elaborate structure and sudden—and total—dismantlement" [quoted by Ronald Hayman in his *Tom Stoppard,* 1977]. Stoppard was also heavily influenced by the poetic cadences of Beckett's language, especially the stichomythia characteristic of much of Gego's and Didi's dialogue. But his greatest "debt" was to Beckett's absurdist vision (hence his ironic description of **"The Gamblers"** as "Waiting Godot in the Condemned Cell"). As he [in the *Theatre Quarterly* interview] wrote while still a theater critic in a review of Jack MacGowran's Beckett compilation *End of Day*: "[Beckett's] characters vacillate in a wasteland between blind hope and dumb despair. . . . Everything is canceled out; Beckett (see Martin Esslin's *The Theatre of the Absurd*) is much impressed by St. Augustine's words, 'Do not despair—one of the thieves was saved. Do not presume—one of the thieves was damned" [*Scene 7,* 25 October 1962].

The characters of Stoppard's next stage play similarity "vacillate in a wasteland between blind hope and dumb despair." ***Rosencrantz and Guildenstern Are Dead,*** the work that established Stoppard's fame (and fortune), is a deeply Beckettian play—as almost every critic who has analyzed it has acknowledged. (That acknowledgement has not always been a positive one. Robert Brustein, for example, labeled the play "a theatrical parasite" and dismissed its author as a mere "university wit," offering audiences "a form of Beckett without tears" [*New Republic,* 4 November 1967]. But whether positive or negative, Beckett's influence on the play is clearly evident.) Mirroring "the Beckett joke," the structure of ***Rosencrantz and Guildenstern Are Dead*** is a series of comic "statements" constantly refuting themselves, playing in effect "a sort of infinite leap-frog" [Stoppard, *Theatre Quarterly*]. ("I write plays," Stoppard has noted, "because dialogue is the most respectable way of contradicting myself" [quoted by Jon Bradshaw in *New York* Magazine, 10 January 1977]. Further, the stichomythic exchanges of the title characters eerily echo the language of *Godot's* tramps; what Stoppard wrote in a 1963 review of James Saunders's *Next Time I'll Sing To You*—"Some of his dialogue is so Beckettian as to be pastiche" [*Scene* 18, 9 February 1963]—proved to be prophetically applicable to Stoppard's own play, not yet written. And the play's central conceit—two shadowy courtiers on the fringes of *Hamlet,* trapped in the margins of a "text" about which they know nothing, adrift in a world that makes no sense—embodies the heart of a Beckettian endgame, the quintessence of Camus's definition of the absurd [in *The Myth of Sisyphus*]:

> A world that can be explained even with bad reasons is a familiar world. But, on the other hand, in a universe suddenly divested of illusions and lights, man feels an alien, a stranger. His exile is without remedy since he is deprived of the memory of a lost home or the hope of a promised land. This divorce between man and his life, the actor and his setting, is properly the feeling of absurdity.

Beckett's absurdist influence is equally strong in *Jumpers,* Stoppard's next full-length work for the theater. The argument of the play has been neatly summarized by the philosopher A. J. Ayer [in the *Sunday Times,* 9 April 1972]: it is "between those who believe in absolute values, for which they seek a religious sanction, and those, more frequently to be found among contemporary philosophers, who are subjectivists or relativists in morals, utilitarians in politics, and atheists or at least agnostics." (It was mischievous of the *Sunday Times* to commission this review from Ayer, the preeminent logical positivist [i.e., relativist] of his generation, whose first initials just "happen" to be reflected in the name of the play's "arch-villain," Archibald Jumper.) Although many of the play's characters "seek," however, they do not find: nothing in *Jumpers* appears certain, least of all absolute values. As I have argued elsewhere [*Yearbook of English Studies* 9, 1979], *Jumpers* is a parodic mystery play, in both senses of the term. There are in fact two linked mysteries at the core of the play: (*a*) Who killed Duncan McFee? and (*b*) Does God exist? The play's central character, a professor of ethics named George Moore, thinks he knows the answers, but in neither instance can he prove his case: the physical mystery and the metaphysical mystery remain equally unsolved (and unsolvable). (As the prisoner wryly informs the jailer in **"The Gamblers"**: "I think you may have stumbled across the definition of divine will—an obsession with mystery.") The world of *Jumpers* is thus maddeningly, absurdly ambiguous, with both the earth and the heavens refusing to divulge their secrets.

The metaphysical absurdism of *Jumpers* is dramatized not simply in the play's theme but in its structure as well: if the world is "divested of illusions and lights," if it no longer makes sense, why then should plays that attempt to reflect that world? In absurdist theater, as Martin Esslin proclaimed in his seminal study [*Theatre of the Absurd*], form mirrors content: "The Theatre of the Absurd has renounced arguing *about* the absurdity of the human condition; it merely *presents* it in being—that is, in terms of

concrete stage images." One of the first stage images we encounter in the play's bizarre prologue sets the tone for everything that follows: a (progressively) naked lady is seen swinging from a chandelier. "*Like a pendulum between darkness and darkness, the* Secretary *swings into the spotlight, and out . . . , in sight for a second, out of sight for a second, in sight for a second, out of sight for a second. . . .*" Now you see it, now you don't; the audience is in effect "ambushed" from the play's opening moments. Reflecting the play's theme in a maze of mirrors, the structure of *Jumpers* is rife with ambiguity, a conjuror's trick that has the audience echoing George's baffled "How the hell does one know what to believe?" Just when we think we "know" where we are, just when the picture finally seems to come into focus, the angle suddenly shifts and we are left once more with a blur.

Take, for example, the first postprologue encounter between George and his "dotty" wife Dotty. From the darkened space of her bedroom, Dotty has been uttering piteous, and increasingly urgent, cries for help: "Murder—Rape—Wolves!" George, feverishly attempting to "invent" God in his study, is convinced she is merely "crying wolf" ("Dorothy, I will not have my work interrupted by these gratuitous acts of lupine delinquency!"), but he finally breaks down and decides to look in on her. As he enters the bedroom, the lights come up to display Dotty's nude body "*sprawled face down, and apparently lifeless on the bed.*" Dotty *appears* to be dead, and the audience is allowed a brief interval to register the shock of that fact. But even as we are jumping to that conclusion, George's reaction to the scene puzzles us: "George *takes in the room at a glance, ignores* Dotty, *and still calling for* Thumper *goes to look in the bathroom.*" Is this professor so absent-minded that he fails to notice the nude corpse of his wife? Is he so indifferent that he doesn't care? While we are pondering, George returns from the bathroom and suddenly addresses the "corpse":

> *George:* Are you a proverb?
>
> *Dotty:* No, I'm a book.
>
> *George: The Naked and the Dead.*

An audience invariably laughs at this point, partly in relief that Dotty is alive and partly in embarrassment at having been so easily misled: Dotty was simply "acting out" a charade, as she will continue to do throughout the play. Now you see it, now you don't: the whole play is, structurally, a series of "charades" that constantly challenges our perceptions of "truth."

And yet, though the truth in *Jumpers* proves to be elusive, though the world appears meaningless and absurd, there is a significant counterthread of optimism running defiantly through the fabric of the play. On the surface, the absurdist vision originally "inherited" from Beckett is brilliantly sustained, but *under* the surface that vision is continually being eroded and sabotaged. The source of the play's optimism is George's heartfelt belief that, whether he "knows" it or not, God *does* exist, that moral absolutes are valid. Camus would have argued that George is suffering from what he termed "the fatal evasion" of hope: "Hope of another life one must 'deserve' or trickery of those who live not for life itself but for some great idea that will transcend it, refine it, give it meaning, and betray it." It is an evasion practiced by almost all of Beckett's characters as well, desperately attempting to wrest meaning out of the very heart of meaninglessness. ("How one hoped above, on and off," comments the speaker of one of Beckett's "Texts for Nothing" from beyond the grave. "With what diversity.") The crucial difference is that everything in a Beckett play conspires to invalidate that hope: in a circular text reflecting the unattainability of desire, Godot will never come. Unlike his characters, Beckett has no illusions; the absurdity of his dramatic world continually denies man's "pernicious and incurable optimism." Stoppard, on the other hand, *shares* George's faith: "Our view of good behaviour *must* not be relativist. . . . I wanted to write a theist play, to combat the arrogant view that anyone who believes in God is some kind of cripple, using God as a crutch" [quoted by Oleg Kerensky in *The New British Drama: Fourteen Playwrights since Osborne and Pinter,* 1977].

The faith expressed by George (and Stoppard), however, is never allowed to wrench the play completely out of its absurdist framework. Stoppard is careful not to sentimentalize George, to "vindicate" him: despite his faith, George is frequently buffoonish and ineffectual, and his values by no means triumph. George's belief in moral absolutes, for example, cannot save Thumper and Pat from their spectacularly absurd deaths, deaths that George himself, however unwittingly, causes. Thus the play comes full circle, ending as it began with the anguished cries of "Help! Murder!" ringing in our ears. Nor—in spite of Stoppard's attempts to "soften" George's inertia in his latest revision of the play's coda—is George's belief translated into the kind of action that might prevent (or, at the very least, *try* to prevent) the murder of Clegthorpe. And finally, although George's closing argument in the coda is emotionally moving, it is Archie who not only scores points (literally) for his intellectual "bounce," but, in the debate between relativism and absolutes, is given the last word:

> Do not despair—many are happy much of the time; more eat than starve, more are healthy than sick, more curable than dying, not so many dying as dead; and one of the thieves was saved. Hell's bells and all's well—half the world is at peace with itself, and so is the other half; vast areas are unpolluted; millions of children grow up without suffering deprivation, and millions, while deprived, grow up without suffering cruelties, and millions, while deprived and cruelly treated, none the less grow up. No laughter is sad and many tears are joyful. At the graveside the undertaker doffs his top hat and impregnates the prettiest mourner. Wham, bam, thank you Sam.

As many critics have noted, there is something deeply cynical and offensive about Archie's Beckettian/Augustinian parody, especially as it immediately follows the shooting of Clegthorpe. Previously Archie employed the phrase "do not despair" as a prelude to bribery; now it serves as a cover under which to dismiss murder. If the "Wham, bam, thank you Sam" refers to *Sam* Clegthorpe, the saying is hideously apt, for Clegthorpe has indeed been screwed—royally (note the coda's ironic allusions to the murders commissioned by Richard III and Henry II) and briskly.

But there is also a strange sense in which Archie's closing words are meant to be taken "straight," as a kind of consolation. *Jumpers* clearly dramatizes metaphysical anguish, the anguish underlying Beckett's absurdist view of the world; at the same time, however, it suggests that, despite that absurdity, there are genuine grounds for optimism, for not giving in to despair. If Beckett sums up existence in haunting images of death [in *Waiting for Godot*] (Pozzo's mournful "They give birth astride of a grave, the light gleams an instant, then it's night once more," later expanded by Vladimir: "Astride of a grave and a difficult birth. Down in the hole, lingeringly, the grave-digger puts on the forceps"), Stoppard focuses instead on life: "At the graveside the undertaker doffs his top hat and impregnates the prettiest mourner." Archie's "Wham, bam, thank you Sam" is directed, then, more at Sam Beckett than at Sam Clegthorpe, but the acknowledgment is double-edged. While the "thank you" is obviously sincere—Stoppard has much to thank Beckett for—it also denotes a leave-taking: Stoppard's salute to Beckett is both a hail and a farewell. *Jumpers* thus marks a demarcation point in Stoppard's drama, his reluctant parting of the ways from the all-encompassing absurdism of Beckett's vision. The metaphysical optimism felt so insistently as an undercurrent in the play, pulsing faintly but tenaciously beneath its absurdist surface, produces a powerful tension. And it is out of this tension—a manifestly absurd "text" just as manifestly subverted by its own subtext—that Stoppard has created what is in effect a distinctively postabsurdist theater.

Hapgood, . . . which opened in London in the spring of 1988, brilliantly exemplifies his unique brand of postabsurdist theater. On the surface, the play is filled with all manner of dazzling absurdist trappings, but the tension produced by the play's subtext continually undermines that surface. Like its radio predecessor *The Dog It Was That Died, Hapgood* is, on the most obvious level, a play about espionage. (Stoppard frequently uses short media plays as "trial runs" for his longer and more complex stage plays: thus *Jumpers* derives from the earlier television play *Another Moon Called Earth,* while much of *Travesties* was anticipated in the radio play *Artist Descending a Staircase.*) In *The Dog It Was That Died,* the absurdities of the espionage world are instantly evoked by the play's title, an allusion to Goldsmith's "An Elegy on the Death of a Mad Dog":

> The dog, to gain some private ends.
> Went mad, and bit the man.
>
> . . . .
>
> The man recovered of the bite—
> The dog it was that died.

As the radio play opens, a dog indeed has died—an unfortunate mutt that just happened to be lying on a barge that just happened to be passing under Chelsea Bridge at the precise moment Purvis, a double agent who no longer knew which side he was spying for, decided to jump off it in a suicide attempt. Purvis recovered; that dog it was that died. Like the comic reversal of Goldsmith's elegy, there is thus something immediately topsy-turvy about the play and the world it is dramatizing, a world so absurd that the whole concept of espionage ultimately becomes meaningless.

Hapgood opens in a similar absurdist vein: what Stoppard once said of *Jumpers* and *Travesties*—"You start with a prologue which is slightly strange" [quoted by Hayman in *Tom Stoppard*]—is true of all his full-length stage plays. Set in the men's changing room of an old-fashioned municipal swimming-bath, the opening scene of the play resembles a Feydeau farce peopled by the characters of a John LeCarré novel on speed. In a totally confusing "ballet" impossible to make sense of (and choreographed, in Peter Wood's production, to the limpid strains of Bach's *Brandenburg Concerto*), spy chases counterspy chases countercounterspy in and out of slamming cubicle doors and all around the Burberry bush (for the still center of this storm is the raincoat-clad Elizabeth Hapgood, code-named "Mother," waiting patiently in the men's shower under a pink umbrella). Adding to the bewilderment are identical briefcases, identical towels, and—crucial to the plot but impossible to detect at this point—identical twins. The confusion of this opening scene is deliberate; there is no way an audience can possibly follow all those comings and going, and Stoppard knows that. We are thus immediately made to experience, structurally, what the play's characters are suffering from thematically: an inability to figure out what's going on, to determine precisely who is the traitor in their midst.

For it turns out that the mayhem of the opening scene is the result of a complicated espionage operation designed to trap that traitor, a "mole" who is passing sensitive scientific data to the Russians. The "prime" suspect (a word we shall return to later) is the defector Joseph Kerner, a physicist and double agent: a Soviet "sleeper" apparently spying for the KGB, he is in fact, unbeknownst to the Russians, a British "joe" who has been "turned" by Hapgood and is working for British Intelligence. Or is he? Could he be, unbeknownst to the British, a *triple* agent? Hapgood is convinced he is loyal—*"Kerner is my joe!"*—but Blair, a senior colleague, and the American Wates, representing the CIA, have their doubts. As the action of the play progresses, a second major suspect emerges in the figure of Ridley, another member of the intelligence unit. Ultimately, however, everyone in the unit becomes suspect. "How are you at telling lies?" Wates asks Hapgood at one point; "I make a living," she replies. When lying is a part of the job description, how does one know whom to believe? And what if the problem is not about lying per se (which implies that there is a specific truth deliberately being obscured), but rather about the very nature of "truth" itself?

This difficulty in determining the truth is emphasized in the play through an analogy with physics (specifically, quantum mechanics)—an analogy continually pointed out by Kerner, who, as both spy and physicist, is uniquely qualified to make the connection. During an early "interrogation" scene set at the zoo, Blair confronts Kerner directly about his suspect allegiances, expecting the Russian to provide him with an unequivocal answer. Despite his professed ignorance of physics, Blair has, paradoxically, a "scientific" perspective on life: obviously Kerner must be working for one side or the other.

> *Blair:* One likes to know what's what.
>
> *Kerner:* Oh yes! Objective reality.
>
> *Blair:* I thought you chaps believed in that.
>
> *Kerner:* "You chaps?" Oh, *scientists.* (*Laughs*) "You chaps!" Paul, objective reality is for zoologists. "Ah, yes, definitely a giraffe." But a double agent is not like a giraffe. A double agent is more like a trick of the light.

In the London production, Kerner's point was cleverly underlined by Carl Tom's witty set design: this conversation at the zoo occurred directly in front of an enormous giraffe—or, rather, a pair of giraffes, positioned in such a way that we seemed to be seeing a two-headed giraffe emanating from a single body. "Ah, yes, definitely a giraffe"—but *nothing* is definite in this play when even a giraffe appears to be a "double agent."

Kerner then proceeds to clarify what he meant by the phrase "a trick of the light," launching into a minilecture on whether light is wave or particle. Confused by this apparent digression, Blair tries to return to the ostensible subject, "Joseph—I want to know if you're ours or theirs, that's all," only to have Kerner reply, "I'm telling you but you're not listening." Kerner *is* answering Blair's question, but by analogy:

> [We scientists] watch the bullets of light to see which way they go. . . . Every time we don't look we get wave pattern. Every time we look to see how we get wave pattern, we get particle pattern. The act of observing determines the reality. . . . Somehow light is particle and wave. The experimenter makes the choice. You get what you interrogate for. And you want to know if I'm a wave or a particle.

There is a conundrum here: light appears to have the mutually exclusive properties of *both* wave *and* particle. As the physicist Richard Feynman has written, in a passage Stoppard selected as the epigraph to the play, "We choose to examine a phenomenon which is impossible, *absolutely* impossible, to explain in any classical way, and which has in it the heart of quantum mechanics. In reality it contains the *only* mystery. . . ." If light is both wave and particle (depending on who's looking, or not looking), then can a double agent be both "sleeper" and "joe"? The "mystery" within the espionage plot is as baffling as the "mystery" in physics: both are explicitly referred to as a "puzzle," and both seem impossible to solve.

The analogy in the play between espionage and physics depends—and becomes even more disturbing—as Kerner goes on to describe the strange behavior of electrons ("Electrons," Feynman notes [in *The Feynman Lectures on Physics: Quantum Mechanics,* 1966], "behave just like light"):

> The particle world is the dream world of the intelligence officer. . . . An electron . . . is like a moth, which was there a moment ago, it gains or loses a quantum of energy and it jumps, and at the moment of the quantum jump it is like two moths, one to be here and one to stop being there; an electron is like twins, each one unique, a unique twin.

A true double agent, then, like an electron, defeats surveillance because he's a "twin," seemingly in two places at the same time: now you see it, now you don't. Kerner, for example, appears to be both "sleeper" and "joe"; but which is the "mask" and which the "face"? Or, to phrase the question in slightly different terms that are more familiar to students of Stoppard's drama, which is "the real thing"? Does "the real thing" even exist? And can we ever hope to plumb the depths of so complex a mystery?

Although Stoppard has great fun immersing himself (and us) in the unsettling world of quantum mechanics, the analogy between particle physics and espionage in *Hapgood* extends far beyond espionage specifically to embrace a much more general concept: the "puzzle" of human identity itself. Confronted once more with Blair's accusations near the end of the play, Kerner responds, "So now I am a prime suspect":

> A prime is a number which cannot be divided except by itself. . . . But really suspects are like squares, the product of twin roots. . . . You . . . think everybody has no secret or one big secret, they are what they seem or the opposite. You look at me and think: *Which is he?* Plus or minus? If only you could figure it out like looking into me to find my root. And then you still wouldn't know. We're all doubles. . . . The one who puts on the clothes in the morning is the working majority, but at night—perhaps in the moment before unconsciousness—we meet our sleeper—the priest is visited by the doubter, the marxist sees the civilizing force of the bourgeoisie, the captain of industry admits the justice of common ownership.

Like electrons, like espionage agents, all human beings are "doubles": "squares," not primes; "the product of twin roots," each of us embodying our own "sleeper." And of no one is this more true than the enigmatic eponymous heroine of *Hapgood*. Kerner recalls, significantly, that he never saw Hapgood sleeping: "Interrogation hours, you know. She said, 'I want to *sleep* with you.' But she never did. And when I learned to read English books I realized that she never said it, either." Yet Hapgood, too, is a "sleeper," a "double agent"—not in terms of the espionage plot but in the ontological sense for which espionage (and physics) acts as a controlling metaphor in the play.

Who and what is Hapgood (that all our swains commend her)? In the "technical," macho world of espionage, she is Mother: a crack shot with both a gun and a quip, a coolly intelligent and efficient executive who plays chess without a board and is fiercely protective of her "joes." But at the same time she is also a mother with a conflicting set of "Joes": her eleven-year-old son Joe, and *Joseph* Kerner. (Kerner is not only Hapgood's agent, he is also the father of her son; not only, then, one of her "joes" but also, as he explicitly reminds her, "one of your Joes.") Hapgood's "schizophrenic" existence is neatly dramatized structurally in our first glimpses of her. In scene 1 she is Mother anxiously watching her espionage joe (Kerner) deliver a possibly incriminating briefcase to his Russian contact; in scene 3, the next time we see her, she is mother anxiously watching her son Joe play a rugby game at his school. This "personal" Hapgood is both deeply attached to her son ("He's the handsome one with the nicest knees") and deeply guilty that her demanding work consigns Joe to a boarding school, alienating her from the day-to-day activities of his life.

The two "worlds" of Hapgood—mother and Mother—wage a constant battle throughout the play: in order to accommodate the former, she must repeatedly jeopardize the latter, thereby blurring the boundaries and breaking all the rules. But this collision course between the split sides of her character is only one sense in which Stoppard dramatizes the enigma of her identity. For Hapgood is many different things to many different people, a multiple personality reflected in the various names by which other characters address her; if one's name is the "key" to one's identity, then Elizabeth Hapgood is truly protean. To agents Ridley and Merryweather, she is "Mother"; Blair refers to her as "Elizabeth"; Joe calls her "Mum" or "Mummy"; her secretary Maggs says "Mrs Hapgood"; Wates calls her "ma'am"; her "sister" Celia speaks of "Betty"; and Kerner uses the Russian form of her first name, "Yelizaveta," along with various endearments derived from it: "Lilya," "Lilitchka."

The question of Hapgood's identity becomes even more complex with the appearance of Celia Newton, the "twin sister" she fabricates in order to expose Ridley as the unit's traitor. Hapgood's impersonation of Celia links her with all the other "reflectors" in the play, scientific and human—decoys designed to deceive. Having been informed by Kerner that the only logical solution to the apparent contradictions of the opening scene is to posit twin Ridleys, Hapgood sets out to trap him (them?) with the aid of her own "twin." She thus makes a quantum jump, "impossibly" present in two places at the same time: as Ridley will discover to his peril, "she's here and she's not here." In terms of personality and behavior, Celia and Hapgood are as different as (to allude to yet another Stoppard play title) night and day. To cite just one example: prim and proper Hapgood never swears, as Blair for one points out both directly—"Do you never use bad language, never ever?"—and indirectly, in his constant teasing: "Oh, f-f-fiddle!"; pot-smoking, "bohemian" Celia, on the other hand, swears a blue streak (indeed, the first word out of her mouth is scatological).

Faced with a physically identical Hapgood who is nothing like Hapgood, Ridley is dumbfounded. On one level, this non-Hapgood in Hapgood's body excites him. Earlier in the play, having been rebuffed by Hapgood's "You're not my type," he exploded: "You come on like you're running your joes from the senior common room and butter wouldn't melt in your pants but . . . if you could have got your bodice up past your brain you would have screwed me and liked it." Now his fantasy seems to have been made flesh; the battle between bodice and brain is, for Celia, not much of a contest. On another level, however, the transformation terrifies him. *"Who the hell are you?"* he cries out in anguish. "I'm your dreamgirl, Ernie—," Celia replies, "Hapgood without the brains or the taste." *"Who the hell are you?"* is, of course, the key question in the play. Celia is not only *Ridley's* "dreamgirl" but *Elizabeth's:* her "sleeper," her "double." The complicated trap Hapgood has sprung for Ridley hinges on his being totally convinced that Celia is *not* Hapgood, and it works: despite his espionage training, despite his street smarts, despite his suspicions, Ridley is taken in. (He calls her "Auntie," Mother's sister.) But in order to "become" Celia so convincingly, there must be something of Celia locked deep within Hapgood. Ironically, Celia *is* Hapgood's "twin"; Kerner may have never seen her "sleeping," but *we* have. Who, then, is the "real" Elizabeth Hapgood? Is it possible to answer? Ridley is fooled the way all of us are ultimately fooled, expecting people to be "what they seem or . . . the opposite," to be either "particle" or "wave."

As always in Stoppard's plays, the elusiveness of the truth proves to be a matter of form as well as of content: just as the characters are constantly being "ambushed" in **Hapgood,** so too is the audience. Thus, when the lights come up on the second scene of act 2 and "Celia" suddenly comes flying out the kitchen door to answer Ridley's ring, we are in the same shocked position as he is: who *is* this creature who looks exactly like Hapgood but who dresses, speaks, and behaves so differently? When she identifies herself as Hapgood's twin, there is no real reason to doubt her—especially since we have not been told the exact details of Hapgood's plan to trap Ridley. As far as we know, Hapgood's having a twin may be part of the plan. After Celia exits briefly, allowing Ridley to contact Hapgood on his two-way radio and thus enabling us to hear Hapgood's voice, we are even more convinced that Celia is legitimate: can one person, after all, be in two different places at the same time? (There is an obvious answer to this apparent impossibility, but the pace of the theater production is such that we don't have the time to work it out.) Celia seems so different from Hapgood that, despite ourselves, we get taken in.

This adds immeasurably, of course, to the humor of the later scene in which Celia, now dressed like Hapgood and occupying her office, finds herself having to impersonate Hapgood when Maggs unexpectedly enters the office with important classified documents from Australia:

> *Maggs:* I was in the pub. . . . I got the desk to bleep me if you came in—just the top one, really, it's green-routed and Sydney's been on twice this morning.

> *Hapgood:* Has he?

We laugh because Celia is way out of her depth and trying desperately to disguise that fact. When Ridley attempts to help her out by reaching for one of the documents, Maggs cautions her, "It's yo-yo, Mrs Hapgood." "Is it, is it really?" Celia replies. "Yes, indeed. It's yo-yo, Ridley, you know what yo-yo is." Luckily, Ridley does, since Celia, treading cautiously through the minefield of this foreign language, clearly doesn't have a clue. Nor can she respond when Maggs passes on the cryptic message "Bishop to queen two"—a move in one of Hapgood's ongoing boardless chess games with McPherson in Canada, played via the security link with Ottawa. At the very end of the scene, however, Ridley departs before her, leaving her alone on stage for a moment; as she prepares to follow him, Maggs enters once more wondering if everything is all right:

> *Hapgood:* Yes, Maggs—everything's fine. (*She heads through the open door.*) Queen to king one.

Like pawns rooked by a grand master, we have suddenly been checkmated: Hapgood's "Celia" turns out to be the queen of disguises.

This structural dislocation of the audience's perspective is by now a Stoppardian signature: an absurdist world, after all, defies comprehension. The scene transitions in **Hapgood** exemplify this conundrum brilliantly. At the end of scene 1, for example, Blair, in the municipal baths, speaks into his two-way radio: "I want Kerner in Regent's Park, twelve o'clock sharp. (*He puts the radio away and looks at his wrist-watch. The next time he moves, it is twelve o'clock and he is at the zoo*)." Blair has made, in effect, a quantum jump; like an electron or a "twin" moth, he is one moment at the baths and then "instantly" at the zoo. Blair's "elusiveness" sets the pattern for the majority of the play's scene changes, the most stunning of which involves Ridley in act 2. At the end of his first encounter with Celia, "Ridley *stays where he is. The next time he moves, he's somebody else. So we lose the last set without losing* Ridley. *When the set has gone,* Ridley *is in some other place . . . , a man arriving somewhere. He carries a suitcase. He is a different* Ridley. *It's like a quantum jump.*" What we are seeing, in effect, is Ridley's literal twin materializing out of "nowhere." But as we have seen, all the play's characters are "twins," literally or metaphorically: the audience's difficulty in determining who is who on the physical plane simply mirrors its confusion on the ontological plane. Thus, in the play's climactic scene, set once again full-circle in the municipal baths, we see, "impossibly," two Ridleys at the same time. The illusion is created, significantly, through lighting: the flashlight Ridley is carrying at the beginning of the scene (allowing much of the stage to be in darkness) and the strobe light at the end (distorting our perception). But then, as **Hapgood** has dramatized so convincingly, all human identity is finally "a trick of the light."

The unmasking of the Ridley twins as the play's traitors seems to solve one of the major mysteries posed by **Hap-**

good, at least on the surface level of its espionage plot; unlike *Jumpers,* say, this mystery play *does* offer a "dénouement" in which the guilty party is identified. But Stoppard's surfaces are deceptive, and his surprises never stop. For Ridley, as his name suggests, is, like all the play's central characters, a riddle: both "wave" and "particle." On the one hand, he is indeed a traitor who has been spying for the Russians, and he can certainly be extremely ruthless. On the other hand, the motives behind his "selling out" to the Russians are complex: feeling betrayed by the English class system ("We're in a racket which identifies national interest with the interests of the officer class"), he has come to distrust all ideology, viewing espionage as a round dance of futility, a "game" that nobody ever wins. When he falls into Hapgood's trap, then, and agrees to help her hand over secret scientific data to the Russians, he acts not so much for ideological reasons as for "personal" ones: his genuine concern both for Hapgood's son, who he believes has been kidnapped by the KGB, and, more important, for Hapgood herself. In Ridley's view, the information they are meant to be passing on to the Russians is worthless ("It's a joke"), especially when weighed against the safety of Joe. Given the absurdist nature of espionage dramatized in the play, it is hard not to sympathize with Ridley's point of view—especially with his feelings for Joe. Hapgood's son is the latest in a long line of "wise children" in Stoppard's drama; a template of ethical behavior, he serves, like young Alastair in *Night and Day,* "as a catalyst for revealing the moral propensities of others" [Richard Corballis, in *Tom Stoppard: A Casebook,* ed. John Harty, 1988]. And Ridley's feelings for Hapgood are likewise a mitigating factor. When he precedes her into the darkened baths with flashlight in hand, thus initiating the events that will expose him as a traitor, the torch he is carrying exists on more than one level: Ridley's "treason" here stems primarily from his love for Hapgood.

This ambiguity surrounding Ridley's identification as the play's traitor is mirrored in Stoppard's treatment of the other "prime" suspects in the unit, Kerner and Blair. Although the exposure of Ridley as a double agent would appear to let them both off the hook, Stoppard's surprises are not yet over. For we ultimately discover that Kerner too has been spying for the Russians. The story he told about being blackmailed into betraying the British (the KGB figured out Joe's paternity and were threatening to harm the boy)—a story we initially viewed as a fabrication, a web in the strand of Hapgood's trap for Ridley—turns out to be genuine; as Hapgood paradoxically observes, "You made up the truth." The ground keeps shifting beneath our feet: Kerner's sardonic comment to Hapgood earlier in the play—"You think you have seen to the bottom of things, but there is no bottom"—is meant equally as a warning to the audience. Kerner is thus as much a riddle as Ridley. "When things get very small," Kerner once noted when discussing the atom, "they get truly crazy"; the enigma of Kerner's identity, like Ridley's, is embodied in his very name (German *Kern:* the nucleus of an atom). And yet, can treason resulting from blackmail—motivated, even more than Ridley's, by love for Hapgood and their son—really be considered transon? Technically,

perhaps, but then the "technical," as opposed to the "personal," is one of Stoppard's central concerns in the play. Thus Blair, while "technically" the only one of the three men to emerge "clean" from the espionage betrayal plot, proves to be, in yet another surprise, the most significant "traitor" of all. As an accomplished Intelligence agent, Blair is a master of "Newspeak," the lies that posed as truth in Orwell's *Nineteen Eighty-four.* (Orwell, we recall, was born Eric *Blair.*) Blair's doublespeak, however, extends to friends as well as enemies, to the "personal" as well as the "technical." But then for Blair it's *all* technical, as Kerner had sensed from the beginning. Proclaiming his concern for Hapgood's safety, Blair at one point threatened Kerner: "I've got one of my people working on the inside lane on false papers and if she's been set up I'll feed you to the crocodiles. . . ." But Blair's language gives himself away. "One of your *people*?" Kerner replies. "Oh, Paul. *You* would betray her before I would. My mamushka." Kerner's prediction turns out to be correct: perfectly willing to deceive Hapgood and jeopardize Joe's safety for the "larger," fictive safety of British security, Blair is technically loyal but personally traitorous. Kerner's "mamushka" is, for Blair, only Mother.

As Hapgood (and the audience) discovers, then, the quest to determine the play's "real" traitor is a deeply enigmatic one: everybody is a "double agent" one way or another—even, as we have seen, Hapgood. Especially Hapgood. In the struggle between the "personal" and the "technical," between heart and brains, between mother and Mother, Hapgood has consistently sacrificed the former—has sacrificed, in effect, her Joes for her joes. Joseph Kerner was finally more valuable to her as a spy than as a father for Joe; as Ridley taunts her: "We aren't in the daddy business, we're in the mole business." And while she clearly loves her son, he too gets subsumed in "the mole business": when Hapgood phones Joe to check that he is safe and closes the conversation, ominously, with "Yes, Joe, I'm here to be told"—the precise words she has addressed throughout the play to her operatives—a shudder passes through the audience. Who is speaking here: mother or Mother? And if Hapgood no longer knows the difference, is it any wonder that—even without her direct knowledge—Joe gets sucked in as "bait" in the espionage trap she is setting? What, finally, is Hapgood accomplishing that is so worthwhile that it could justify the sacrifice of Joe? In a quantum world that is random, quixotic and indeterminate, espionage is merely another "trick of the light." As Ridley informs Celia:

> Telling lies is Betty's job, sweetheart— . . . so Betty can know something which the opposition thinks she doesn't know, most of which doesn't matter a fuck, and that's just the half they didn't *plant* on her—so she's lucky if she comes better than even, that's the edge she's in it for, and if she's thinking now it wasn't worth one sleepless night for her little prep-school boy, good for her, she had it coming.

"Maybe she did," Celia agrees, and then proceeds to deride the madness of the espionage world: "Everybody's lying to everybody. You're all at it. Liars. Nutters' corner. You deserve each other. . . . You're out on a limb for a boy she put there, while she was making the world safe for him to talk properly in and play the game . . .".

But this is Celia talking, not Hapgood: the "sleeper," not "the working majority." In the play's penultimate scene, Ridley gives Hapgood one last chance to awaken that "sleeper":

> Listen, be yourself. These people are not for you, in the end they get it all wrong, the dustbins are gaping for them. Him [Blair] most. He's had enough out of you and you're getting nothing back, he's dry and you're the juice. We can walk out of here, Auntie.

Ridley persists in addressing her as "Auntie," as Celia, even though at this point he has discovered the ruse. But "Celia" won't, or can't, respond; feeling betrayed, Ridley reaches for his gun and Hapgood shoots him. "Oh, you *mother*" Wates spits at her in a particularly well-chosen epithet; by betraying her Joes, Ridley, and "Celia"—by choosing Mother over mother—Hapgood has become an obscenity. The sight of Ridley's dead body, coupled with her anger at Blair for placing Joe at risk, finally shocks Hapgood to her senses. Responding to Blair's attempt to justify his actions—"It's them or it's us, isn't it?"—Hapgood's scorn is withering, an acknowledgment of her "personal" treason: "Who? Us and the KGB? The opposition! We're just keeping each other in business, we should send each other Christmas cards—oh, f-f-fuck it, Paul!" That final phrase is, of course, Celia's, not Hapgood's; the "sleeper" has at last awakened, with an outraged howl of despair.

What Hapgood awakens to is, paradoxically, an absurdist nightmare, a world "suddenly divested of illusions and lights." The play's analogy between espionage and quantum mechanics, then, seen on one level as a metaphor for the elusiveness of human identity, is, on the deepest level, a metaphor for the structure of the universe itself, for the elusiveness of cosmic identity: the mystery of physics mirrors the mystery of metaphysics. As Kerner explains to Hapgood:

> It upset Einstein very much, you know, all that damned quantum jumping, it spoiled his idea of God. . . . He believed in the same God as Newton, causality, nothing without a reason, but now one thing led to another until causality was dead. Quantum mechanics made everything finally random, things can go this way or that way, the mathematics deny certainty, they reveal only probability and chance, and Einstein couldn't believe in a God who threw dice. . . . There is a straight ladder from the atom to the grain of sand, and the only real mystery in physics is the missing rung. Below it, particle physics; above it, classical physics; but in between, metaphysics. All the mystery in life turns out to be the same mystery. . . .

"If it's all random, then what's the point?" cried Bone, the forerunner of George in Stoppard's television play *Another Moon Called Earth* (the "original" of *Jumpers*). And George later echoes his lament: "Copernicus cracked our

confidence, and Einstein smashed it: for if one can no longer believe that a twelve-inch ruler is always a foot long, how can one be sure of relatively less certain propositions, such as that God made the Heaven and the Earth . . ."

In the quantum world of *Hapgood,* a world where light is both wave and particle, a twelve-inch ruler may not always be a foot long. This is indeed a terrifying concept, for the pragmatist Blair, such conclusions are not acceptable. When Kerner mocks his belief in objective reality, Blair replies: "What other kind is there? You're this or you're that, and you know which. Physics is a detail I can't afford . . .". Orwell's Winston Smith [in *Nineteen Eighty-four*] sought psychic security in certain immutable scientific laws: "The solid world exists, its laws do not change. . . . *Freedom is the freedom to say that two plus two make four,*" a claim reiterated (though "halved") by Alexander, the hero of Stoppard's *Every Good Boy Deserves Favour*: "One and one is always two." But Winston and Alexander were struggling against repressive totalitarian regimes that cynically distort truths for their own power-driven ends; the characters in *Hapgood,* on the other hand, are struggling against an absurdist universe in which the very essence of such "truths" has been exploded. Despite George's impassioned belief in the original coda of *Jumpers* that "it remains an independent metaphysical truth that two and two make four," the most one seems able to say in a post-Newtonian world is Dotty's "two and two make *roughly* four" (my emphasis).

The sweet security of Newtonian physics has thus been forever shattered, destroying in its wake such complementary consolations as *"God's in his heaven—/ All's right with the world!"*—in an absurdist universe, Pippa has passed on. The resulting randomness is ironically acknowledged in Hapgood's choice of an alias when impersonating her "twin sister": portraying a "decoy," a "trick of the light," she slyly names herself *Celia* [Latin *caelum:* heaven] *Newton*. The joke, however, is ultimately on Hapgood, for "Celia Newton" turns out to be an illusion in more ways than one: the certainties that name once embodied no longer apply, replaced by a God rolling dice. "What's the game?" queried a bewildered Rosencrantz, a *"voice in the wilderness";* "What are the rules?" added Guildenstern. The characters of *Hapgood* appear equally forlorn. Invited by Celia to play a deckless game of cards while waiting for Joe's "ransom" call, Ridley responds, "Well, what are we playing?" Celia's silence forces Ridley to guess, to plunge into the void. Unfortunately, Ridley guesses wrong: "*Snap*!! Bad luck . . .". When the "game" of life proves to be so inscrutable, so arbitrary, what are the chances of winning? Certainly the dice never roll in Ridley's favor; in the program of the London production of *Hapgood,* Stoppard casually informs us that the fateful day on which Ridley plays and loses the game of "Snap"—and, later, his life—is a Friday the thirteenth: "bad luck" indeed. The question twice posed in *Hapgood* about a particular espionage scheme, "Who's in charge and is he sane?", might thus well be asked of the universe; the mocking laughter that serves as an answer—the sound of rolling dice—echoes repeatedly through the play.

And yet, for all its absurdist trappings, Stoppard's drama refuses to succumb to despair. In Beckett's ironically titled *Happy Days,* Winnie's desperate mask of cheerfulness keeps slipping, exposing the face of pain underneath; as Winnie notes, "sorrow keeps breaking in." In *Hapgood,* by contrast, it is happiness that keeps breaking in: the optimistic note sounded continually as the play's counterthread beats a muted but persistent refrain. Kerner, for example, while acknowledging his "estrangement" in a seemingly absurd and pointless universe, nevertheless continues to make value judgments, continues to believe in *something.* Against the theorems of quantum mechanics suggesting randomness, Kerner places an opposed set of "theorems":

> The West is morally superior, in my opinion. It is in different degrees unjust and corrupt like the East. Its moral superiority lies in the fact that the system contains the possibility of its own reversal—I am enthralled by the voting, to me it has power of an equation in nature, the masses converted to energy. Highly theoretical, of course. . . .

"The masses converted to energy" implicitly evokes Einstein's celebrated equation $e = mc^2$, Kerner's equation transposes it into the social and political sphere and discovers consolation. Similarly consoling is Kerner's transformation of Einstein's metaphysical angst, his shattered faith in God. Einstein's inability to believe in a God who threw dice is, for Kerner, "the only idea of Einstein's I never understood. . . . He should have come to me, I would have told him, 'Listen, Albert, He threw *you*—look around, He never stops'." The world may be random, uncertain, but hopelessness and despair are certainly not the inevitable response.

The subtext of optimism running through *Hapgood* is at its clearest—and, because of the structural position, its strongest—in the play's brief final scene. On the surface, we seem to have reached the nadir of despair. All of Hapgood's illusions have been totally shattered: her espionage work has been exposed as a farce; Ridley is dead, killed by her own hand; Blair has "betrayed" her; Kerner is about to return to Russia ("[Blair] thinks I was a triple, but I was definitely not, I was past that, quadruple at least, maybe quintuple.") Having repudiated espionage and resigned her job, Hapgood is now simply a mother: the final scene is set once more at Joe's school as Hapgood watches her son play rugby. When Kerner, who has come to say farewell before departing for Russia—to Hapgood and, not so incidentally, to his son, whom he is seeing for the first time—turns to leave, Hapgood cries out: "How can you go? *How can you?*"

(She turns away. The game starts. Referee's whistle, the kick. After a few moments Hapgood *collects herself and takes notice of the rugby.*

When the game starts Kerner's *interest is snagged. He stops and looks at the game.)*

Hapgood: Come on St Christopher's!—We can win this one! Get those tackles in!

(She turns round and finds that Kerner *is still there. She turns back to the game and comes alive.)*

Hapgood: Shove!—heel!—well heeled!—well out—move it!—*move it, Hapgood*—that's good—that's *better!*

Like everything else in the play, the ending is enigmatic but charged with hope: Kerner does *not* leave; Hapgood, registering his hesitation, *"comes alive."* Kerner's interest has been snagged specifically by the "game." The "game" of espionage may be elusive and futile, but *this* game—*Joe's* "game"—is worth playing. As Hapgood herself has discovered in her "liberating" impersonation of Celia, there *are* values worth believing in, the values noted by Michael Billington in his astute review of the play: "that democracy is better than dictatorship, that love is a possibility and that—a persistent Stoppard theme—children anchor one in the real world" [*The Guardian,* 9 March 1988]. The universe may be random and subject to chance; the metaphysical "game" may be purely arbitrary, played by a God capricious as a child ("Snap") or made giddy by the sound of rolling dice; but not every Friday, luckily, is the thirteenth. Chance may be positive as well as negative, a belief embodied in the very name of Stoppard's title character: Hap (defined by the OED as "Chance or fortune . . . ; luck, lot") is specifically linked to *good.* The clouds of absurdism are dispersed in the play by Stoppard's postabsurdist search for silver linings; "the need to make things better," Stoppard noted in a 1981 interview [in *Gambit* 10, No. 37], "is constant and important. Otherwise you're into a sort of nihilism." Temperamentally opposed to nihilism, Stoppard has chosen to write plays in which a "crazy" world is, crazily but persistently, imbued with hope. And so *Hapgood* closes with both Elizabeth and Kerner facing front, facing the audience, as they recommence their journey of faith, rooting for St. Christopher's (the patron saint of travelers, the bearer of divinity) and cheering on *Hap-good.* The last word we hear when all is said and done, echoing in our ears as the curtain falls, is, significantly in this postabsurdist play, *"better!"*

In the addendum to Beckett's early novel *Watt,* we find the following little poem:

> who may tell the tale
> of the old man?
> weigh absence in a scale?
> mete want with a span?
> the sum assess
> of the world's woes?
> nothingness
> in words enclose?

This is the daunting task absurdist writers like Beckett have set for themselves: the dramatization of "negatives" (age, absence, want, woes, nothingness). Beckett's plays—frequently, like the *Watt* poem, couched in the interrogative—are thus a series of paradoxes; it is enormously difficult to make absence present on stage, to concretize a void, to create something out of nothing, to "eff" the "ineffable." In doing so they explore, in Esslin's words, "the ultimate realities of the human condition . . . Like ancient Greek tragedy and the medieval mystery plays and baroque allegories, the Theatre of the Absurd is intent on making its audience aware of man's precarious and mysterious position in the universe."

Tom Stoppard is similarly concerned in his drama with the metaphysically "precarious" and "mysterious"—thus his attraction to the Theater of the Absurd. But while frequently exhibiting an absurdist outer shell, Stoppard's plays contain at their core a subversive "sweetness" that ultimately bursts forth and cracks that shell; this unique blend of shell and core produces the distinctive postabsurdist tone of much of Stoppard's theater. The measure of Stoppard's departure from true absurdism can be gauged partly by comparing the humor of his plays with that of Beckett. Beckett's is almost literally graveyard humor, the rueful laughter of skeletons littering the road to Calvary (as Nell observes in a quintessentially Beckettian line in *Endgame*: "Nothing is funnier than unhappiness, I grant you that"). At the close of Shakespeare's *Love's Labour's Lost*, a sudden shadow blots the merriment of that last act in the figure of Marcade, an emissary of death. Infected by the darkness of his presence, Rosaline delays for a year the expected comic resolution by imposing a "service" on her lover Berowne:

> *Rosaline:* You shall this twelve month term from
> day to day,
> Visit the speechless sick, and still converse
> With groaning wretches; and your task shall be,
> With all the fierce endeavour of your wit
> To enforce the pained impotent to smile.
> *Berowne:* To move wild laughter in the throat of
> death?
> It cannot be; it is impossible:
> Mirth cannot move a soul in agony.

"Wild laughter in the throat of death" precisely sums up the humor of Beckett's plays. Stoppard's humor, by contrast, is "tomfoolery," marked by its buoyancy, its exultation in life—a torrent of unstoppable puns and hilarious jokes, full-throated and irrepressible.

This disparity in the tone of their humor leads us to the heart of Stoppard's divergence from Beckett and genuine absurdism. Although I disagree with much of Brustein's criticism of *Rosencrantz and Guildenstern Are Dead,* his assessment of the "derivative" nature of Stoppard's despair in that play strikes me as accurate: "[Stoppard's insights] all seem to come to him, prefabricated, from other plays—with the result that his air of pessimism seems affected, and his philosophical meditations, while witty and urbane, never obtain the thickness of *felt* knowledge." As admiring as Stoppard is of the art of Beckett's absurdism, that art is, finally, not Stoppard's. In the "arguments with himself" that constitute his drama, part of him clearly acknowledges the absurdism of man's existence in a world "divested of illusions and lights," but another part of him—

a major part—consistently subverts that acknowledgment. In the last analysis, Stoppard's eschatology is ameliorist; the rich vein of optimism running through the subtext of his plays thus converts what could easily be a threnody into an aubade. There is light at the end of the tunnel of Stoppard's drama—elusive, inscrutable, perhaps even deceptive, but still light. Whereas Beckett's absurdist theater fearlessly explores the darkness, the "black hole" of nothingness ("The fable of one with you in the dark. The fable of one fabling of one with you in the dark. And how better in the end labour lost and silence" [*Company*]), the postabsurdist plays of Tom Stoppard hopefully explore this "trick of the light."

FURTHER READING

AUTHOR COMMENTARY

Delaney, Paul, ed. *Tom Stoppard in Conversation.* Ann Arbor: University of Michigan Press, 1994, 300 p.
> Collection of interviews dating from 1967 to 1993, containing comprehensive coverage of Stoppard's plays.

Gordon, Giles. Interview with Tom Stoppard. *The Transatlantic Review,* No. 29 (Summer 1968): 17-25.
> Conversation in which Stoppard discusses the conception and composition of *Rosencrantz and Guildenstern Are Dead.*

Gussow, Mel. *Conversations with Stoppard.* London: Nick Hern Books, 1995, 146 p.
> Series of interviews, spanning the years 1974 to 1995, in which Stoppard talks about his works from "The Real Inspector Hound" to *Indian Ink.*

OVERVIEWS AND GENERAL STUDIES

Bareham, T., ed. *Tom Stoppard:* Rosencrantz and Guildenstern Are Dead, Jumpers, Travesties: *A Casebook.* Houndsmills, Basingstoke, Hampshire: Macmillan, 1990, 220 p.
> Contains critical studies and early reviews of the three plays as well as interviews with Stoppard, surveys of his work, and a bibliography.

Bloom, Harold, ed. *Tom Stoppard: Modern Critical Views.* New York: Chelsea House, 1986, 191 p.
> Collection of thirteen essays on various facets of Stoppard's art and career. In his introduction, Bloom assesses Stoppard's achievements and notes his affinity to his precursors, particularly Samuel Beckett and Oscar Wilde.

Brassell, Tim. *Tom Stoppard: An Assessment.* New York: St. Martin's Press, 1985, 299 p.

Book-length critical study of Stoppard's major and minor works.

Chetta, Peter N. "Multiplicities of Illusion in Tom Stoppard's Plays." In *Staging the Impossible: The Fantastic Mode in Modern Drama,* edited by Patrick D. Murphy, pp. 127-36. Westport, Conn.: Greenwood Press, 1992.
Examines elements of fantasy in Stoppard's works.

Corballis, Richard. *Stoppard: The Mystery and the Clockwork.* Oxford: Amber Lane Press, 1984. 204 p.
Examines Stoppard's stage plays, arguing that each presents a clash between two worlds: the real world, which is marked by uncertainty and mystery, and the dream world of artifice and abstraction.

Delaney, Paul. *Tom Stoppard: The Moral Vision of the Major Plays.* New York: St. Martin's Press, 1990, 202 p.
Traces the "paths by which Stoppard's theater develops from moral affirmation to moral application, from the assertion of moral principles to the enactment of moral practice."

Gitzen, Julian. "Tom Stoppard: Chaos in Perspective." *Southern Humanities Review* 10, No. 2 (Spring 1976): 143-52.
Maintains that even in his farcical plays Stoppard conveys a serious premise: "that our society is in imminent danger of going out of control."

Hayman, Ronald. *Tom Stoppard.* Contemporary Playwrights Series. London: Heinemann, 1977, 143 p.
Includes two interviews with Stoppard, discussions of more than twenty plays, biographical and bibliographical materials, and a list of performances.

Hu, Stephen. *Tom Stoppard's Stagecraft.* New York: Peter Lang, 1989, 274 p.
Studies the lighting, scenery, costumes, action, dramatic structure, and other elements of Stoppard's major works.

James, Clive. "Count Zero Splits the Infinite." *Encounter* XLV, No. 5 (November 1975): 68-76.
Appreciative survey of Stoppard's works that defends their complexity and intellectual depth.

Jenkins, Anthony. *The Theatre of Tom Stoppard.* Cambridge: Cambridge University Press, 1987, 189 p.
Critical study of the plays that pays particular attention to the interconnection of Stoppard's texts.

Kelly, Katherine E. "Tom Stoppard Radioactive: A Sounding of the Radio Plays." *Modern Drama* XXXII, No. 3 (September 1989): 440-52.
Delineates the ways the medium of radio helped Stoppard master his craft.

———. *Tom Stoppard and the Craft of Comedy: Medium and Genre at Play.* Ann Arbor: University of Michigan Press, 1991, 179 p.
Traces thematic and formal elements in Stoppard's major plays.

Mackenzie, Ian. "Tom Stoppard: The Monological Imagination." *Modern Drama* XXXII, No. 4 (December 1989): 574-86.
Draws on Mikhail Bakhtin's theories regarding dialogue—that texts may "speak" with multiple "voices" simultaneously—to argue that Stoppard's political plays are monologic, that is, speak with Stoppard's own voice, despite the playwright's insistence that they do not.

Page, Malcolm, ed. *File on Stoppard.* London: Methuen, 1986, 96 p.
Features extracts of reviews and criticism, a bibliography, a chronology, and other materials.

Robinson, Gabrielle Scott. "Plays without Plot: The Theatre of Tom Stoppard." *Educational Theatre Journal* 29, No. 1 (March 1977): 37-48.
Illustrates how Stoppard unites farce and philosophy in his plays.

Rusinko, Susan. *Tom Stoppard.* Boston: Twayne Publishers, 1986, 164 p.
Examines Stoppard's use of language, manipulation of ideas, and "creative plagiarizing of other writers."

Sammells, Neil. *Tom Stoppard: The Artist as Critic.* Houndsmills, Basingstoke, Hampshire: Macmillan Press, 1988, 162 p.
Analyzes elements of aesthetic and political commentary and criticism in Stoppard's plays.

Tynan, Kenneth. "Withdrawing with Style from the Chaos." *The New Yorker* LIII, No. 43 (12 December 1977): 41-111.
Broad-ranging survey of Stoppard's life and professional career.

Whitaker, Thomas. *Tom Stoppard.* Grove Press Modern Dramatist Series. New York: Grove Press, 1983, 177 p.
Includes a brief biography and analysis of the major plays.

Zeitman, Hersh. "Tomfoolery: Stoppard's Theatrical Puns." *The Yearbook of English Studies* 9 (1979): 204-20.
Contends that "Stoppard uses puns, carefully and deliberately, as structural devices in his plays, as an integral part of a play's basic 'meaning'."

ROSENCRANTZ AND GUILDENSTERN ARE DEAD

Callen, Anthony. "Stoppard's Godot: Some French Influences on Post-war English Drama." *New Theatre Magazine* X, No. 1 (Winter 1969): 22-30.
Details the influence of Samuel Beckett's *Waiting for Godot* on *Rosencrantz and Guildenstern Are Dead.*

Gianakaris, C. J. "Absurdism Altered: *Rosencrantz and Guildenstern Are Dead.*" *Drama Survey* 7, Nos. 1-2 (Winter 1968-69): 52-8.
Proposes that Stoppard joins absurdism with social activist theater in *Rosencrantz and Guildenstern Are Dead.*

Hobson, Harold. Review of *Rosencrantz and Guildenstern Are Dead. The Times,* London (17 April 1967).

> Favorable evaluation in which Hobson asserts that *Rosencrantz and Guildenstern Are Dead* is "the most important event in British professional theatre of the last nine years."

Keyssar-Franke, Helene. "The Strategy of *Rosencrantz and Guildenstern Are Dead." Educational Theatre Journal* 27, No. 1 (March 1975): 85-97.

> Argues that, despite being a derivative work, *Rosencrantz and Guildenstern Are Dead* is theatrically effective because it "has a potent and appropriate dramatic strategy, a lucid and meaningful grasp on the relationship of every moment of the play to the audience."

Perlette, John M. "Theatre at the Limit: *Rosencrantz and Guildenstern Are Dead." Modern Drama* XXVIII, No. 4 (December 1985): 659-69.

> Explores the play's concern with our inability to perceive "the reality of death."

JUMPERS

Crump, G. B. "The Universe as Murder Mystery: Tom Stoppard's *Jumpers." Contemporary Literature* 20, No. 3 (Summer 1979): 354-68.

> Analyzes the use of philosophical material in *Jumpers* to refute the charge that Stoppard is a "superficial dilettante."

Kreps, Barbara. "How Do We Know That We Know What We Know in Tom Stoppard's *Jumpers?" Twentieth Century Literature* 32, No. 2 (Summer 1986): 187-208.

> Argues that *Jumpers* "poses serious questions about both the basis and the limits of human knowledge, human values, and human behavior."

Thomson, Leslie. "'The Curve Itself' in *Jumpers." Modern Drama* XXXIII, No. 4 (December 1990): 470-85.

> Examines the thematic significance of the central image pattern or arcs, arches, and circles in *Jumpers,* noting how the visual images echo the verbal "curves"—allusions, cross-references, and word play.

TRAVESTIES

Corballis, Richard. "Wilde . . . Joyce . . . O'Brien . . . Stoppard: Modernism and Postmodernism in *Travesties.*" In *Joycean Occasions: Essays from the Milwaukee James Joyce Conference,* edited by Janet E. Dunleavy, Melvin J. Friedman, and Michael Patrick Gillespie, pp. 157-70. Newark: University of Delaware Press, 1991.

> Investigates the treatment in *Travesties* of the postmodernist concern with power and of the modernist preoccupation with the relationship between art and politics. Corballis finds the two approaches in harmony rather than at odds in the play.

Sammells, Neil. "Earning Liberties: *Travesties* and *The Importance of Being Earnest." Modern Drama* XXIX, No. 3 (September 1986): 376-87.

> Explores how Stoppard's play "critically engages" Wilde's *The Importance of Being Earnest,* interpreting and transforming the central theme and form.

PROFESSIONAL FOUL

Cobley, Evelyn. "Catastrophe Theory in Tom Stoppard's *Professional Foul." Contemporary Literature* XXV, No. 1 (Spring 1984): 53-65.

> Maintains that the world presented in *Professional Foul* offers no absolutes but rather "a complex network of interrelationships where any statement or action is a 'both-and' issue."

Eldridge, Michael. "Drama as Philosophy: *Professional Foul* Breaks the Rules." In *Drama and Philosophy,* edited by James Redmond, pp. 199-208. Cambridge: Cambridge University Press, 1990.

> Considers *Professional Foul* a mystery play "that is both philosophically interesting and dramatically effective."

THE REAL THING

Rusinko, Susan. "The Last Romantic: Henry Boot, Alias Tom Stoppard." *World Literature Today* 59, No. 1 (Winter 1985): 17-21.

> Proposes that Henry Boot, the main character of *The Real Thing,* "embodies Stoppard's view of the artist and his function in society."

Thomson, Leslie. "The Subtext of *The Real Thing*: It's 'all right'." *Modern Drama* XXX, No. 4 (December 1987): 535-48.

> Explores the significance of the recurring phrase "all right" in *The Real Thing,* arguing that it is a kind of subtext which "becomes a means of furthering our evaluation and understanding, or confirming our subjective perceptions of the characters and their relationships."

Zeifman, Hersh. "Comedy of Ambush: Tom Stoppard's *The Real Thing." Modern Drama* XXVI, No. 2 (June 1983): 139-49.

> Discusses Stoppard's device of the "comic ambush," which continually alters the audience's perception of events and thus underscores the thematic concern with what is real and what is not.

ARCADIA

Canby, Vincent. "Stoppard's Comedy of 1809 and Now." *The New York Times* (31 March 1995).

> Highly favorable review of *Arcadia* in which Canby declares: "There's no doubt about it. *Arcadia* is Tom Stoppard's most ravishing comedy to date, a play of wit, intellect, language, brio and, new for him, emotion."

Lahr, John. "Blowing Hot and Cold." *The New Yorker* (22 April 1995).

> Laudatory review of *Arcadia* that considers it Stoppard's "best play so far." Lahr particularly admires "Stoppard's labyrinthine plot, whose ingenious twists and turns involve greed, rapacity, vainglory, skullduggery, cruelty, delusion, confusion, and genius."

Nightingale, Benedict. Review of *Arcadia. The Times,* London (14 April 1993).

> Favorable assessment that finds *Arcadia* brilliantly structured. Nightingale describes the play as "Stoppard's tribute to the complexity, unpredictability and inscrutability of the world."

Additional coverage of Stoppard's life and career is contained in the following sources published by Gale Research: *Concise Dictionary of British Literary Biography,* Vol. 8; *Contemporary Authors,* Vols. 81-84; *Contemporary Authors New Revision Series,* Vol. 39; *Contemporary Literary Criticism,* Vols. 1, 3, 4, 5, 8, 15, 29, 34, 63; *Dictionary of Literary Biography,* Vol. 13; *Dictionary of Literary Biography Yearbook 1985; DISCovering Authors; Major Twentieth-Century Writers; World Literature Criticism.*

CUMULATIVE INDEXES

How to Use This Index

The main references

Calvino, Italo
1923-1985.....CLC 5, 8, 11, 22, 33, 39,
73; SSC 3

list all author entries in the following Gale Literary Criticism series:

BLC = Black Literature Criticism
CLC = Contemporary Literary Criticism
CLR = Children's Literature Review
CMLC = Classical and Medieval Literature Criticism
DA = DISCovering Authors
DAB = DISCovering Authors: British
DAC = DISCovering Authors: Canadian
DC = Drama Criticism
HLC = Hispanic Literature Criticism
LC = Literature Criticism from 1400 to 1800
NCLC = Nineteenth-Century Literature Criticism
PC = Poetry Criticism
SSC = Short Story Criticism
TCLC = Twentieth-Century Literary Criticism
WLC = World Literature Criticism, 1500 to the Present

The cross-references

See also CANR 23; CA 85-88;
obituary CA 116

list all author entries in the following Gale biographical and literary sources:

AAYA = Authors & Artists for Young Adults
AITN = Authors in the News
BEST = Bestsellers
BW = Black Writers
CA = Contemporary Authors
CAAS = Contemporary Authors Autobiography Series
CABS = Contemporary Authors Bibliographical Series
CANR = Contemporary Authors New Revision Series
CAP = Contemporary Authors Permanent Series
CDALB = Concise Dictionary of American Literary Biography
CDBLB = Concise Dictionary of British Literary Biography
DAM = DISCovering Authors: Modules
    DRAM: *Dramatists Module;* **MST:** *Most-Studied Authors Module;*
    MULT: *Multicultural Authors Module;* **NOV:** *Novelists Module;*
    POET: *Poets Module;* **POP:** *Popular Fiction and Genre Authors Module*
DLB = Dictionary of Literary Biography
DLBD = Dictionary of Literary Biography Documentary Series
DLBY = Dictionary of Literary Biography Yearbook
HW = Hispanic Writers
JRDA = Junior DISCovering Authors
MAICYA = Major Authors and Illustrators for Children and Young Adults
MTCW = Major 20th-Century Writers
NNAL = Native North American Literature
SAAS = Something about the Author Autobiography Series
SATA = Something about the Author
YABC = Yesterday's Authors of Books for Children

Literary Criticism Series
Cumulative Author Index

A. E. . . . . TCLC 3, 10
See also Russell, George William

Abasiyanik, Sait Faik 1906-1954
See Sait Faik
See also CA 123

Abbey, Edward 1927-1989 . . . . . . CLC 36, 59
See also CA 45-48; 128; CANR 2, 41

Abbott, Lee K(ittredge) 1947- . . . . . . CLC 48
See also CA 124; CANR 51; DLB 130

Abe, Kobo 1924-1993 . . . . . CLC 8, 22, 53, 81
See also CA 65-68; 140; CANR 24;
DAM NOV; MTCW

Abelard, Peter c. 1079-c. 1142 . . . CMLC 11
See also DLB 115

Abell, Kjeld 1901-1961 . . . . CLC 15
See also CA 111

Abish, Walter 1931- . . . . CLC 22
See also CA 101; CANR 37; DLB 130

Abrahams, Peter (Henry) 1919- . . . . . CLC 4
See also BW 1; CA 57-60; CANR 26;
DLB 117; MTCW

Abrams, M(eyer) H(oward) 1912- . . . CLC 24
See also CA 57-60; CANR 13, 33; DLB 67

Abse, Dannie 1923- . . . . CLC 7, 29; DAB
See also CA 53-56; CAAS 1; CANR 4, 46;
DAM POET; DLB 27

Achebe, (Albert) Chinua(lumogu)
1930- . . . . . CLC 1, 3, 5, 7, 11, 26, 51, 75;
BLC; DA; DAB; DAC; WLC
See also AAYA 15; BW 2; CA 1-4R;
CANR 6, 26, 47; CLR 20; DAM MST,
MULT, NOV; DLB 117; MAICYA;
MTCW; SATA 40; SATA-Brief 38

Acker, Kathy 1948- . . . . CLC 45
See also CA 117; 122

Ackroyd, Peter 1949- . . . . CLC 34, 52
See also CA 123; 127; CANR 51; DLB 155;
INT 127

Acorn, Milton 1923- . . . . CLC 15; DAC
See also CA 103; DLB 53; INT 103

Adamov, Arthur 1908-1970 . . . . . . CLC 4, 25
See also CA 17-18; 25-28R; CAP 2;
DAM DRAM; MTCW

Adams, Alice (Boyd) 1926- . . . CLC 6, 13, 46
See also CA 81-84; CANR 26; DLBY 86;
INT CANR-26; MTCW

Adams, Andy 1859-1935 . . . . TCLC 56
See also YABC 1

Adams, Douglas (Noel) 1952- . . . CLC 27, 60
See also AAYA 4; BEST 89:3; CA 106;
CANR 34; DAM POP; DLBY 83; JRDA

Adams, Francis 1862-1893 . . . . NCLC 33

Adams, Henry (Brooks)
1838-1918 . . . . . . TCLC 4, 52; DA; DAB;
DAC
See also CA 104; 133; DAM MST; DLB 12,
47

Adams, Richard (George)
1920- . . . . CLC 4, 5, 18
See also AAYA 16; AITN 1, 2; CA 49-52;
CANR 3, 35; CLR 20; DAM NOV;
JRDA; MAICYA; MTCW; SATA 7, 69

Adamson, Joy(-Friederike Victoria)
1910-1980 . . . . CLC 17
See also CA 69-72; 93-96; CANR 22;
MTCW; SATA 11; SATA-Obit 22

Adcock, Fleur 1934- . . . . CLC 41
See also CA 25-28R; CAAS 23; CANR 11,
34; DLB 40

Addams, Charles (Samuel)
1912-1988 . . . . CLC 30
See also CA 61-64; 126; CANR 12

Addison, Joseph 1672-1719 . . . . LC 18
See also CDBLB 1660-1789; DLB 101

Adler, Alfred (F.) 1870-1937 . . . . . . TCLC 61
See also CA 119

Adler, C(arole) S(chwerdtfeger)
1932- . . . . CLC 35
See also AAYA 4; CA 89-92; CANR 19,
40; JRDA; MAICYA; SAAS 15;
SATA 26, 63

Adler, Renata 1938- . . . . CLC 8, 31
See also CA 49-52; CANR 5, 22; MTCW

Ady, Endre 1877-1919 . . . . TCLC 11
See also CA 107

Aeschylus
525B.C.-456B.C. . . . . CMLC 11; DA;
DAB; DAC
See also DAM DRAM, MST

Afton, Effie
See Harper, Frances Ellen Watkins

Agapida, Fray Antonio
See Irving, Washington

Agee, James (Rufus)
1909-1955 . . . . TCLC 1, 19
See also AITN 1; CA 108; 148;
CDALB 1941-1968; DAM NOV; DLB 2,
26, 152

Aghill, Gordon
See Silverberg, Robert

Agnon, S(hmuel) Y(osef Halevi)
1888-1970 . . . . CLC 4, 8, 14
See also CA 17-18; 25-28R; CAP 2; MTCW

Agrippa von Nettesheim, Henry Cornelius
1486-1535 . . . . LC 27

Aherne, Owen
See Cassill, R(onald) V(erlin)

Ai 1947- . . . . CLC 4, 14, 69
See also CA 85-88; CAAS 13; DLB 120

Aickman, Robert (Fordyce)
1914-1981 . . . . CLC 57
See also CA 5-8R; CANR 3

Aiken, Conrad (Potter)
1889-1973 . . . CLC 1, 3, 5, 10, 52; SSC 9
See also CA 5-8R; 45-48; CANR 4;
CDALB 1929-1941; DAM NOV, POET;
DLB 9, 45, 102; MTCW; SATA 3, 30

Aiken, Joan (Delano) 1924- . . . . CLC 35
See also AAYA 1; CA 9-12R; CANR 4, 23,
34; CLR 1, 19; DLB 161; JRDA;
MAICYA; MTCW; SAAS 1; SATA 2,
30, 73

Ainsworth, William Harrison
1805-1882 . . . . NCLC 13
See also DLB 21; SATA 24

Aitmatov, Chingiz (Torekulovich)
1928- . . . . CLC 71
See also CA 103; CANR 38; MTCW;
SATA 56

Akers, Floyd
See Baum, L(yman) Frank

Akhmadulina, Bella Akhatovna
1937- . . . . CLC 53
See also CA 65-68; DAM POET

Akhmatova, Anna
1888-1966 . . . . CLC 11, 25, 64; PC 2
See also CA 19-20; 25-28R; CANR 35;
CAP 1; DAM POET; MTCW

Aksakov, Sergei Timofeyvich
1791-1859 . . . . NCLC 2

Aksenov, Vassily
See Aksyonov, Vassily (Pavlovich)

Aksyonov, Vassily (Pavlovich)
1932- . . . . CLC 22, 37
See also CA 53-56; CANR 12, 48

Akutagawa Ryunosuke
1892-1927 . . . . TCLC 16
See also CA 117

Alain 1868-1951 . . . . TCLC 41

Alain-Fournier . . . . TCLC 6
See also Fournier, Henri Alban
See also DLB 65

Alarcon, Pedro Antonio de
1833-1891 . . . . NCLC 1

Alas (y Urena), Leopoldo (Enrique Garcia)
1852-1901 . . . . TCLC 29
See also CA 113; 131; HW

Albee, Edward (Franklin III)
1928- . . . . . . CLC 1, 2, 3, 5, 9, 11, 13, 25,
53, 86; DA; DAB; DAC; WLC
See also AITN 1; CA 5-8R; CABS 3;
CANR 8; CDALB 1941-1968;
DAM DRAM, MST; DLB 7;
INT CANR-8; MTCW

Alberti, Rafael 1902- . . . . CLC 7
See also CA 85-88; DLB 108

Albert the Great 1200(?)-1280 . . . . CMLC 16
See also DLB 115

Alcala-Galiano, Juan Valera y
See Valera y Alcala-Galiano, Juan

Andrews, Elton V.
See Pohl, Frederik

Andreyev, Leonid (Nikolaevich)
1871-1919 . . . . TCLC 3
See also CA 104

Andric, Ivo 1892-1975 . . . . CLC 8
See also CA 81-84; 57-60; CANR 43;
DLB 147; MTCW

Angelique, Pierre
See Bataille, Georges

Angell, Roger 1920- . . . . CLC 26
See also CA 57-60; CANR 13, 44

Angelou, Maya
1928- . . . . CLC 12, 35, 64, 77; BLC; DA;
DAB; DAC
See also AAYA 7; BW 2; CA 65-68;
CANR 19, 42; DAM MST, MULT,
POET, POP; DLB 38; MTCW; SATA 49

Annensky, Innokenty Fyodorovich
1856-1909 . . . . TCLC 14
See also CA 110

Anon, Charles Robert
See Pessoa, Fernando (Antonio Nogueira)

Anouilh, Jean (Marie Lucien Pierre)
1910-1987 . . . . . . CLC 1, 3, 8, 13, 40, 50
See also CA 17-20R; 123; CANR 32;
DAM DRAM; MTCW

Anthony, Florence
See Ai

Anthony, John
See Ciardi, John (Anthony)

Anthony, Peter
See Shaffer, Anthony (Joshua); Shaffer,
Peter (Levin)

Anthony, Piers 1934- . . . . CLC 35
See also AAYA 11; CA 21-24R; CANR 28;
DAM POP; DLB 8; MTCW; SAAS 22;
SATA 84

Antoine, Marc
See Proust, (Valentin-Louis-George-Eugene-)
Marcel

Antoninus, Brother
See Everson, William (Oliver)

Antonioni, Michelangelo 1912- . . . . . CLC 20
See also CA 73-76; CANR 45

Antschel, Paul 1920-1970
See Celan, Paul
See also CA 85-88; CANR 33; MTCW

Anwar, Chairil 1922-1949 . . . . TCLC 22
See also CA 121

Apollinaire, Guillaume . . TCLC 3, 8, 51; PC 7
See also Kostrowitzki, Wilhelm Apollinaris
de
See also DAM POET

Appelfeld, Aharon 1932- . . . . CLC 23, 47
See also CA 112; 133

Apple, Max (Isaac) 1941- . . . . CLC 9, 33
See also CA 81-84; CANR 19; DLB 130

Appleman, Philip (Dean) 1926- . . . . . CLC 51
See also CA 13-16R; CAAS 18; CANR 6,
29

Appleton, Lawrence
See Lovecraft, H(oward) P(hillips)

Apteryx
See Eliot, T(homas) S(tearns)

Apuleius, (Lucius Madaurensis)
125(?)-175(?) . . . . CMLC 1

Aquin, Hubert 1929-1977 . . . . CLC 15
See also CA 105; DLB 53

Aragon, Louis 1897-1982 . . . . CLC 3, 22
See also CA 69-72; 108; CANR 28;
DAM NOV, POET; DLB 72; MTCW

Arany, Janos 1817-1882 . . . . NCLC 34

Arbuthnot, John 1667-1735 . . . . LC 1
See also DLB 101

Archer, Herbert Winslow
See Mencken, H(enry) L(ouis)

Archer, Jeffrey (Howard) 1940- . . . . CLC 28
See also AAYA 16; BEST 89:3; CA 77-80;
CANR 22; DAM POP; INT CANR-22

Archer, Jules 1915- . . . . CLC 12
See also CA 9-12R; CANR 6; SAAS 5;
SATA 4, 85

Archer, Lee
See Ellison, Harlan (Jay)

Arden, John 1930- . . . . CLC 6, 13, 15
See also CA 13-16R; CAAS 4; CANR 31;
DAM DRAM; DLB 13; MTCW

Arenas, Reinaldo
1943-1990 . . . . CLC 41; HLC
See also CA 124; 128; 133; DAM MULT;
DLB 145; HW

Arendt, Hannah 1906-1975 . . . . CLC 66
See also CA 17-20R; 61-64; CANR 26;
MTCW

Aretino, Pietro 1492-1556 . . . . LC 12

Arghezi, Tudor . . . . CLC 80
See also Theodorescu, Ion N.

Arguedas, Jose Maria
1911-1969 . . . . CLC 10, 18
See also CA 89-92; DLB 113; HW

Argueta, Manlio 1936- . . . . CLC 31
See also CA 131; DLB 145; HW

Ariosto, Ludovico 1474-1533 . . . . LC 6

Aristides
See Epstein, Joseph

Aristophanes
450B.C.-385B.C. . . . . CMLC 4; DA;
DAB; DAC; DC 2
See also DAM DRAM, MST

Arlt, Roberto (Godofredo Christophersen)
1900-1942 . . . . TCLC 29; HLC
See also CA 123; 131; DAM MULT; HW

Armah, Ayi Kwei 1939- . . . . CLC 5, 33; BLC
See also BW 1; CA 61-64; CANR 21;
DAM MULT, POET; DLB 117; MTCW

Armatrading, Joan 1950- . . . . CLC 17
See also CA 114

Arnette, Robert
See Silverberg, Robert

**Arnim, Achim von (Ludwig Joachim von
Arnim)** 1781-1831 . . . . NCLC 5
See also DLB 90

Arnim, Bettina von 1785-1859 . . . . NCLC 38
See also DLB 90

Arnold, Matthew
1822-1888 . . . . . NCLC 6, 29; DA; DAB;
DAC; PC 5; WLC
See also CDBLB 1832-1890; DAM MST,
POET; DLB 32, 57

Arnold, Thomas 1795-1842 . . . . . . NCLC 18
See also DLB 55

Arnow, Harriette (Louisa) Simpson
1908-1986 . . . . CLC 2, 7, 18
See also CA 9-12R; 118; CANR 14; DLB 6;
MTCW; SATA 42; SATA-Obit 47

Arp, Hans
See Arp, Jean

Arp, Jean 1887-1966 . . . . CLC 5
See also CA 81-84; 25-28R; CANR 42

Arrabal
See Arrabal, Fernando

Arrabal, Fernando 1932- . . . CLC 2, 9, 18, 58
See also CA 9-12R; CANR 15

Arrick, Fran . . . . CLC 30
See also Gaberman, Judie Angell

Artaud, Antonin (Marie Joseph)
1896-1948 . . . . TCLC 3, 36
See also CA 104; 149; DAM DRAM

Arthur, Ruth M(abel) 1905-1979 . . . . CLC 12
See also CA 9-12R; 85-88; CANR 4;
SATA 7, 26

Artsybashev, Mikhail (Petrovich)
1878-1927 . . . . TCLC 31

Arundel, Honor (Morfydd)
1919-1973 . . . . CLC 17
See also CA 21-22; 41-44R; CAP 2;
CLR 35; SATA 4; SATA-Obit 24

Asch, Sholem 1880-1957 . . . . TCLC 3
See also CA 105

Ash, Shalom
See Asch, Sholem

Ashbery, John (Lawrence)
1927- . . . . . . CLC 2, 3, 4, 6, 9, 13, 15, 25,
41, 77
See also CA 5-8R; CANR 9, 37;
DAM POET; DLB 5; DLBY 81;
INT CANR-9; MTCW

Ashdown, Clifford
See Freeman, R(ichard) Austin

Ashe, Gordon
See Creasey, John

Ashton-Warner, Sylvia (Constance)
1908-1984 . . . . CLC 19
See also CA 69-72; 112; CANR 29; MTCW

Asimov, Isaac
1920-1992 . . . CLC 1, 3, 9, 19, 26, 76, 92
See also AAYA 13; BEST 90:2; CA 1-4R;
137; CANR 2, 19, 36; CLR 12;
DAM POP; DLB 8; DLBY 92;
INT CANR-19; JRDA; MAICYA;
MTCW; SATA 1, 26, 74

Astley, Thea (Beatrice May)
1925- . . . . CLC 41
See also CA 65-68; CANR 11, 43

Aston, James
See White, T(erence) H(anbury)

Balzac, Honore de
1799-1850 . . . . **NCLC 5, 35, 53; DA;
DAB; DAC; SSC 5; WLC**
See also DAM MST, NOV; DLB 119

Bambara, Toni Cade
1939-1995 . . . . . . **CLC 19, 88; BLC; DA;
DAC**
See also AAYA 5; BW 2; CA 29-32R; 150;
CANR 24, 49; DAM MST, MULT;
DLB 38; MTCW

Bamdad, A.
See Shamlu, Ahmad

Banat, D. R.
See Bradbury, Ray (Douglas)

Bancroft, Laura
See Baum, L(yman) Frank

Banim, John 1798-1842 . . . . **NCLC 13**
See also DLB 116, 158, 159

Banim, Michael 1796-1874 . . . . . . **NCLC 13**
See also DLB 158, 159

Banks, Iain
See Banks, Iain M(enzies)

Banks, Iain M(enzies) 1954- . . . . **CLC 34**
See also CA 123; 128; INT 128

Banks, Lynne Reid . . . . **CLC 23**
See also Reid Banks, Lynne
See also AAYA 6

Banks, Russell 1940- . . . . **CLC 37, 72**
See also CA 65-68; CAAS 15; CANR 19;
DLB 130

Banville, John 1945- . . . . **CLC 46**
See also CA 117; 128; DLB 14; INT 128

Banville, Theodore (Faullain) de
1832-1891 . . . . **NCLC 9**

Baraka, Amiri
1934- . . . . **CLC 1, 2, 3, 5, 10, 14, 33;
BLC; DA; DAC; DC 6; PC 4**
See also Jones, LeRoi
See also BW 2; CA 21-24R; CABS 3;
CANR 27, 38; CDALB 1941-1968;
DAM MST, MULT, POET, POP;
DLB 5, 7, 16, 38; DLBD 8; MTCW

Barbauld, Anna Laetitia
1743-1825 . . . . **NCLC 50**
See also DLB 107, 109, 142, 158

Barbellion, W. N. P. . . . . **TCLC 24**
See also Cummings, Bruce F(rederick)

Barbera, Jack (Vincent) 1945- . . . . . . **CLC 44**
See also CA 110; CANR 45

Barbey d'Aurevilly, Jules Amedee
1808-1889 . . . . **NCLC 1; SSC 17**
See also DLB 119

Barbusse, Henri 1873-1935 . . . . **TCLC 5**
See also CA 105; DLB 65

Barclay, Bill
See Moorcock, Michael (John)

Barclay, William Ewert
See Moorcock, Michael (John)

Barea, Arturo 1897-1957 . . . . **TCLC 14**
See also CA 111

Barfoot, Joan 1946- . . . . **CLC 18**
See also CA 105

Baring, Maurice 1874-1945 . . . . **TCLC 8**
See also CA 105; DLB 34

Barker, Clive 1952- . . . . **CLC 52**
See also AAYA 10; BEST 90:3; CA 121;
129; DAM POP; INT 129; MTCW

Barker, George Granville
1913-1991 . . . . **CLC 8, 48**
See also CA 9-12R; 135; CANR 7, 38;
DAM POET; DLB 20; MTCW

Barker, Harley Granville
See Granville-Barker, Harley
See also DLB 10

Barker, Howard 1946- . . . . **CLC 37**
See also CA 102; DLB 13

Barker, Pat(ricia) 1943- . . . . **CLC 32, 91**
See also CA 117; 122; CANR 50; INT 122

Barlow, Joel 1754-1812 . . . . **NCLC 23**
See also DLB 37

Barnard, Mary (Ethel) 1909- . . . . **CLC 48**
See also CA 21-22; CAP 2

Barnes, Djuna
1892-1982 . . . **CLC 3, 4, 8, 11, 29; SSC 3**
See also CA 9-12R; 107; CANR 16; DLB 4,
9, 45; MTCW

Barnes, Julian 1946- . . . . **CLC 42; DAB**
See also CA 102; CANR 19; DLBY 93

Barnes, Peter 1931- . . . . **CLC 5, 56**
See also CA 65-68; CAAS 12; CANR 33,
34; DLB 13; MTCW

Baroja (y Nessi), Pio
1872-1956 . . . . **TCLC 8; HLC**
See also CA 104

Baron, David
See Pinter, Harold

Baron Corvo
See Rolfe, Frederick (William Serafino
Austin Lewis Mary)

Barondess, Sue K(aufman)
1926-1977 . . . . **CLC 8**
See also Kaufman, Sue
See also CA 1-4R; 69-72; CANR 1

Baron de Teive
See Pessoa, Fernando (Antonio Nogueira)

Barres, Maurice 1862-1923 . . . . **TCLC 47**
See also DLB 123

Barreto, Afonso Henrique de Lima
See Lima Barreto, Afonso Henrique de

Barrett, (Roger) Syd 1946- . . . . **CLC 35**

Barrett, William (Christopher)
1913-1992 . . . . **CLC 27**
See also CA 13-16R; 139; CANR 11;
INT CANR-11

Barrie, J(ames) M(atthew)
1860-1937 . . . . **TCLC 2; DAB**
See also CA 104; 136; CDBLB 1890-1914;
CLR 16; DAM DRAM; DLB 10, 141,
156; MAICYA; YABC 1

Barrington, Michael
See Moorcock, Michael (John)

Barrol, Grady
See Bograd, Larry

Barry, Mike
See Malzberg, Barry N(athaniel)

Barry, Philip 1896-1949 . . . . **TCLC 11**
See also CA 109; DLB 7

Bart, Andre Schwarz
See Schwarz-Bart, Andre

Barth, John (Simmons)
1930- . . . . . . **CLC 1, 2, 3, 5, 7, 9, 10, 14,
27, 51, 89; SSC 10**
See also AITN 1, 2; CA 1-4R; CABS 1;
CANR 5, 23, 49; DAM NOV; DLB 2;
MTCW

Barthelme, Donald
1931-1989 . . . . . . **CLC 1, 2, 3, 5, 6, 8, 13,
23, 46, 59; SSC 2**
See also CA 21-24R; 129; CANR 20;
DAM NOV; DLB 2; DLBY 80, 89;
MTCW; SATA 7; SATA-Obit 62

Barthelme, Frederick 1943- . . . . **CLC 36**
See also CA 114; 122; DLBY 85; INT 122

Barthes, Roland (Gerard)
1915-1980 . . . . **CLC 24, 83**
See also CA 130; 97-100; MTCW

Barzun, Jacques (Martin) 1907- . . . . **CLC 51**
See also CA 61-64; CANR 22

Bashevis, Isaac
See Singer, Isaac Bashevis

Bashkirtseff, Marie 1859-1884 . . . **NCLC 27**

Basho
See Matsuo Basho

Bass, Kingsley B., Jr.
See Bullins, Ed

Bass, Rick 1958- . . . . **CLC 79**
See also CA 126

Bassani, Giorgio 1916- . . . . **CLC 9**
See also CA 65-68; CANR 33; DLB 128;
MTCW

Bastos, Augusto (Antonio) Roa
See Roa Bastos, Augusto (Antonio)

Bataille, Georges 1897-1962 . . . . **CLC 29**
See also CA 101; 89-92

Bates, H(erbert) E(rnest)
1905-1974 . . . . . . **CLC 46; DAB; SSC 10**
See also CA 93-96; 45-48; CANR 34;
DAM POP; DLB 162; MTCW

Bauchart
See Camus, Albert

Baudelaire, Charles
1821-1867 . . . . . **NCLC 6, 29; DA; DAB;
DAC; PC 1; SSC 18; WLC**
See also DAM MST, POET

Baudrillard, Jean 1929- . . . . **CLC 60**

Baum, L(yman) Frank 1856-1919 . . . **TCLC 7**
See also CA 108; 133; CLR 15; DLB 22;
JRDA; MAICYA; MTCW; SATA 18

Baum, Louis F.
See Baum, L(yman) Frank

Baumbach, Jonathan 1933- . . . . . . **CLC 6, 23**
See also CA 13-16R; CAAS 5; CANR 12;
DLBY 80; INT CANR-12; MTCW

Bausch, Richard (Carl) 1945- . . . . . . **CLC 51**
See also CA 101; CAAS 14; CANR 43;
DLB 130

Baxter, Charles 1947- . . . . **CLC 45, 78**
See also CA 57-60; CANR 40; DAM POP;
DLB 130

Baxter, George Owen
See Faust, Frederick (Schiller)

Baxter, James K(eir) 1926-1972 .... **CLC 14**
See also CA 77-80

Baxter, John
See Hunt, E(verette) Howard, (Jr.)

Bayer, Sylvia
See Glassco, John

Baynton, Barbara 1857-1929..... **TCLC 57**

Beagle, Peter S(oyer) 1939-......... **CLC 7**
See also CA 9-12R; CANR 4, 51;
DLBY 80; INT CANR-4; SATA 60

Bean, Normal
See Burroughs, Edgar Rice

Beard, Charles A(ustin)
1874-1948 .... **TCLC 15**
See also CA 115; DLB 17; SATA 18

Beardsley, Aubrey 1872-1898 ..... **NCLC 6**

Beattie, Ann
1947- .... **CLC 8, 13, 18, 40, 63; SSC 11**
See also BEST 90:2; CA 81-84; DAM NOV,
POP; DLBY 82; MTCW

Beattie, James 1735-1803 .... **NCLC 25**
See also DLB 109

Beauchamp, Kathleen Mansfield 1888-1923
See Mansfield, Katherine
See also CA 104; 134; DA; DAC;
DAM MST

Beaumarchais, Pierre-Augustin Caron de
1732-1799 .... **DC 4**
See also DAM DRAM

Beaumont, Francis 1584(?)-1616...... **DC 6**
See also CDBLB Before 1660; DLB 58, 121

**Beauvoir, Simone (Lucie Ernestine Marie
Bertrand) de**
1908-1986 .... **CLC 1, 2, 4, 8, 14, 31, 44,
50, 71; DA; DAB; DAC; WLC**
See also CA 9-12R; 118; CANR 28;
DAM MST, NOV; DLB 72; DLBY 86;
MTCW

Becker, Jurek 1937-............ **CLC 7, 19**
See also CA 85-88; DLB 75

Becker, Walter 1950-............. **CLC 26**

Beckett, Samuel (Barclay)
1906-1989 ...... **CLC 1, 2, 3, 4, 6, 9, 10,
11, 14, 18, 29, 57, 59, 83; DA; DAB;
DAC; SSC 16; WLC**
See also CA 5-8R; 130; CANR 33;
CDBLB 1945-1960; DAM DRAM, MST,
NOV; DLB 13, 15; DLBY 90; MTCW

Beckford, William 1760-1844 .... **NCLC 16**
See also DLB 39

Beckman, Gunnel 1910-.......... **CLC 26**
See also CA 33-36R; CANR 15; CLR 25;
MAICYA; SAAS 9; SATA 6

Becque, Henri 1837-1899........ **NCLC 3**

Beddoes, Thomas Lovell
1803-1849 .... **NCLC 3**
See also DLB 96

Bedford, Donald F.
See Fearing, Kenneth (Flexner)

Beecher, Catharine Esther
1800-1878 .... **NCLC 30**
See also DLB 1

Beecher, John 1904-1980.......... **CLC 6**
See also AITN 1; CA 5-8R; 105; CANR 8

Beer, Johann 1655-1700............. **LC 5**

Beer, Patricia 1924-.............. **CLC 58**
See also CA 61-64; CANR 13, 46; DLB 40

Beerbohm, Henry Maximilian
1872-1956 .... **TCLC 1, 24**
See also CA 104; DLB 34, 100

Beerbohm, Max
See Beerbohm, Henry Maximilian

Beer-Hofmann, Richard
1866-1945 .... **TCLC 60**
See also DLB 81

Begiebing, Robert J(ohn) 1946-..... **CLC 70**
See also CA 122; CANR 40

Behan, Brendan
1923-1964 .... **CLC 1, 8, 11, 15, 79**
See also CA 73-76; CANR 33;
CDBLB 1945-1960; DAM DRAM;
DLB 13; MTCW

Behn, Aphra
1640(?)-1689 ...... **LC 1, 30; DA; DAB;
DAC; DC 4; PC 13; WLC**
See also DAM DRAM, MST, NOV, POET;
DLB 39, 80, 131

Behrman, S(amuel) N(athaniel)
1893-1973 .... **CLC 40**
See also CA 13-16; 45-48; CAP 1; DLB 7,
44

Belasco, David 1853-1931 .... **TCLC 3**
See also CA 104; DLB 7

Belcheva, Elisaveta 1893- .... **CLC 10**
See also Bagryana, Elisaveta

Beldone, Phil "Cheech"
See Ellison, Harlan (Jay)

Beleno
See Azuela, Mariano

Belinski, Vissarion Grigoryevich
1811-1848 .... **NCLC 5**

Belitt, Ben 1911-................. **CLC 22**
See also CA 13-16R; CAAS 4; CANR 7;
DLB 5

Bell, James Madison
1826-1902 .... **TCLC 43; BLC**
See also BW 1; CA 122; 124; DAM MULT;
DLB 50

Bell, Madison (Smartt) 1957- ...... **CLC 41**
See also CA 111; CANR 28

Bell, Marvin (Hartley) 1937-..... **CLC 8, 31**
See also CA 21-24R; CAAS 14;
DAM POET; DLB 5; MTCW

Bell, W. L. D.
See Mencken, H(enry) L(ouis)

Bellamy, Atwood C.
See Mencken, H(enry) L(ouis)

Bellamy, Edward 1850-1898 ...... **NCLC 4**
See also DLB 12

Bellin, Edward J.
See Kuttner, Henry

Belloc, (Joseph) Hilaire (Pierre)
1870-1953 .... **TCLC 7, 18**
See also CA 106; DAM POET; DLB 19,
100, 141; YABC 1

Belloc, Joseph Peter Rene Hilaire
See Belloc, (Joseph) Hilaire (Pierre)

Belloc, Joseph Pierre Hilaire
See Belloc, (Joseph) Hilaire (Pierre)

Belloc, M. A.
See Lowndes, Marie Adelaide (Belloc)

Bellow, Saul
1915- ...... **CLC 1, 2, 3, 6, 8, 10, 13, 15,
25, 33, 34, 63, 79; DA; DAB; DAC;
SSC 14; WLC**
See also AITN 2; BEST 89:3; CA 5-8R;
CABS 1; CANR 29; CDALB 1941-1968;
DAM MST, NOV, POP; DLB 2, 28;
DLBD 3; DLBY 82; MTCW

Belser, Reimond Karel Maria de
See Ruyslinck, Ward

Bely, Andrey .... **TCLC 7; PC 11**
See also Bugayev, Boris Nikolayevich

Benary, Margot
See Benary-Isbert, Margot

Benary-Isbert, Margot 1889-1979... **CLC 12**
See also CA 5-8R; 89-92; CANR 4;
CLR 12; MAICYA; SATA 2;
SATA-Obit 21

Benavente (y Martinez), Jacinto
1866-1954 .... **TCLC 3**
See also CA 106; 131; DAM DRAM,
MULT; HW; MTCW

Benchley, Peter (Bradford)
1940-...................... **CLC 4, 8**
See also AAYA 14; AITN 2; CA 17-20R;
CANR 12, 35; DAM NOV, POP;
MTCW; SATA 3

Benchley, Robert (Charles)
1889-1945 .... **TCLC 1, 55**
See also CA 105; DLB 11

Benda, Julien 1867-1956 .... **TCLC 60**
See also CA 120

Benedict, Ruth 1887-1948 .... **TCLC 60**

Benedikt, Michael 1935- .... **CLC 4, 14**
See also CA 13-16R; CANR 7; DLB 5

Benet, Juan 1927-................ **CLC 28**
See also CA 143

Benet, Stephen Vincent
1898-1943 .... **TCLC 7; SSC 10**
See also CA 104; DAM POET; DLB 4, 48,
102; YABC 1

Benet, William Rose 1886-1950 ... **TCLC 28**
See also CA 118; DAM POET; DLB 45

Benford, Gregory (Albert) 1941-.... **CLC 52**
See also CA 69-72; CANR 12, 24, 49;
DLBY 82

Bengtsson, Frans (Gunnar)
1894-1954 .... **TCLC 48**

Benjamin, David
See Slavitt, David R(ytman)

Benjamin, Lois
See Gould, Lois

Benjamin, Walter 1892-1940..... **TCLC 39**

Benn, Gottfried 1886-1956........ **TCLC 3**
See also CA 106; DLB 56

Bennett, Alan 1934- ..... **CLC 45, 77; DAB**
See also CA 103; CANR 35; DAM MST;
MTCW

Bennett, (Enoch) Arnold
1867-1931 . . . . TCLC 5, 20
See also CA 106; CDBLB 1890-1914;
DLB 10, 34, 98, 135

Bennett, Elizabeth
See Mitchell, Margaret (Munnerlyn)

Bennett, George Harold 1930-
See Bennett, Hal
See also BW 1; CA 97-100

Bennett, Hal . . . . CLC 5
See also Bennett, George Harold
See also DLB 33

Bennett, Jay 1912- . . . . CLC 35
See also AAYA 10; CA 69-72; CANR 11,
42; JRDA; SAAS 4; SATA 41;
SATA-Brief 27

Bennett, Louise (Simone)
1919- . . . . CLC 28; BLC
See also BW 2; DAM MULT; DLB 117

Benson, E(dward) F(rederic)
1867-1940 . . . . TCLC 27
See also CA 114; DLB 135, 153

Benson, Jackson J. 1930- . . . . CLC 34
See also CA 25-28R; DLB 111

Benson, Sally 1900-1972 . . . . CLC 17
See also CA 19-20; 37-40R; CAP 1;
SATA 1, 35; SATA-Obit 27

Benson, Stella 1892-1933 . . . . TCLC 17
See also CA 117; DLB 36, 162

Bentham, Jeremy 1748-1832 . . . . . NCLC 38
See also DLB 107, 158

Bentley, E(dmund) C(lerihew)
1875-1956 . . . . TCLC 12
See also CA 108; DLB 70

Bentley, Eric (Russell) 1916- . . . . CLC 24
See also CA 5-8R; CANR 6; INT CANR-6

Beranger, Pierre Jean de
1780-1857 . . . . NCLC 34

Berendt, John (Lawrence) 1939- . . . . CLC 86
See also CA 146

Berger, Colonel
See Malraux, (Georges-)Andre

Berger, John (Peter) 1926- . . . . . . CLC 2, 19
See also CA 81-84; CANR 51; DLB 14

Berger, Melvin H. 1927- . . . . CLC 12
See also CA 5-8R; CANR 4; CLR 32;
SAAS 2; SATA 5

Berger, Thomas (Louis)
1924- . . . . CLC 3, 5, 8, 11, 18, 38
See also CA 1-4R; CANR 5, 28, 51;
DAM NOV; DLB 2; DLBY 80;
INT CANR-28; MTCW

Bergman, (Ernst) Ingmar
1918- . . . . CLC 16, 72
See also CA 81-84; CANR 33

Bergson, Henri 1859-1941 . . . . TCLC 32

Bergstein, Eleanor 1938- . . . . CLC 4
See also CA 53-56; CANR 5

Berkoff, Steven 1937- . . . . CLC 56
See also CA 104

Bermant, Chaim (Icyk) 1929- . . . . . . CLC 40
See also CA 57-60; CANR 6, 31

Bern, Victoria
See Fisher, M(ary) F(rances) K(ennedy)

Bernanos, (Paul Louis) Georges
1888-1948 . . . . TCLC 3
See also CA 104; 130; DLB 72

Bernard, April 1956- . . . . CLC 59
See also CA 131

Berne, Victoria
See Fisher, M(ary) F(rances) K(ennedy)

Bernhard, Thomas
1931-1989 . . . . CLC 3, 32, 61
See also CA 85-88; 127; CANR 32;
DLB 85, 124; MTCW

Berriault, Gina 1926- . . . . CLC 54
See also CA 116; 129; DLB 130

Berrigan, Daniel 1921- . . . . CLC 4
See also CA 33-36R; CAAS 1; CANR 11,
43; DLB 5

Berrigan, Edmund Joseph Michael, Jr.
1934-1983
See Berrigan, Ted
See also CA 61-64; 110; CANR 14

Berrigan, Ted . . . . CLC 37
See also Berrigan, Edmund Joseph Michael,
Jr.
See also DLB 5

Berry, Charles Edward Anderson 1931-
See Berry, Chuck
See also CA 115

Berry, Chuck . . . . CLC 17
See also Berry, Charles Edward Anderson

Berry, Jonas
See Ashbery, John (Lawrence)

Berry, Wendell (Erdman)
1934- . . . . CLC 4, 6, 8, 27, 46
See also AITN 1; CA 73-76; CANR 50;
DAM POET; DLB 5, 6

Berryman, John
1914-1972 . . . . . . CLC 1, 2, 3, 4, 6, 8, 10,
13, 25, 62
See also CA 13-16; 33-36R; CABS 2;
CANR 35; CAP 1; CDALB 1941-1968;
DAM POET; DLB 48; MTCW

Bertolucci, Bernardo 1940- . . . . CLC 16
See also CA 106

Bertrand, Aloysius 1807-1841 . . . . NCLC 31

Bertran de Born c. 1140-1215 . . . . . CMLC 5

Besant, Annie (Wood) 1847-1933 . . . TCLC 9
See also CA 105

Bessie, Alvah 1904-1985 . . . . CLC 23
See also CA 5-8R; 116; CANR 2; DLB 26

Bethlen, T. D.
See Silverberg, Robert

Beti, Mongo . . . . CLC 27; BLC
See also Biyidi, Alexandre
See also DAM MULT

Betjeman, John
1906-1984 . . . CLC 2, 6, 10, 34, 43; DAB
See also CA 9-12R; 112; CANR 33;
CDBLB 1945-1960; DAM MST, POET;
DLB 20; DLBY 84; MTCW

Bettelheim, Bruno 1903-1990 . . . . . . CLC 79
See also CA 81-84; 131; CANR 23; MTCW

Betti, Ugo 1892-1953 . . . . TCLC 5
See also CA 104

Betts, Doris (Waugh) 1932- . . . . CLC 3, 6, 28
See also CA 13-16R; CANR 9; DLBY 82;
INT CANR-9

Bevan, Alistair
See Roberts, Keith (John Kingston)

Bialik, Chaim Nachman
1873-1934 . . . . TCLC 25

Bickerstaff, Isaac
See Swift, Jonathan

Bidart, Frank 1939- . . . . CLC 33
See also CA 140

Bienek, Horst 1930- . . . . CLC 7, 11
See also CA 73-76; DLB 75

Bierce, Ambrose (Gwinett)
1842-1914(?) . . . . TCLC 1, 7, 44; DA;
DAC; SSC 9; WLC
See also CA 104; 139; CDALB 1865-1917;
DAM MST; DLB 11, 12, 23, 71, 74

Billings, Josh
See Shaw, Henry Wheeler

Billington, (Lady) Rachel (Mary)
1942- . . . . CLC 43
See also AITN 2; CA 33-36R; CANR 44

Binyon, T(imothy) J(ohn) 1936- . . . . CLC 34
See also CA 111; CANR 28

Bioy Casares, Adolfo
1914- . . . CLC 4, 8, 13, 88; HLC; SSC 17
See also CA 29-32R; CANR 19, 43;
DAM MULT; DLB 113; HW; MTCW

Bird, Cordwainer
See Ellison, Harlan (Jay)

Bird, Robert Montgomery
1806-1854 . . . . NCLC 1

Birney, (Alfred) Earle
1904- . . . . CLC 1, 4, 6, 11; DAC
See also CA 1-4R; CANR 5, 20;
DAM MST, POET; DLB 88; MTCW

Bishop, Elizabeth
1911-1979 . . . . . . CLC 1, 4, 9, 13, 15, 32;
DA; DAC; PC 3
See also CA 5-8R; 89-92; CABS 2;
CANR 26; CDALB 1968-1988;
DAM MST, POET; DLB 5; MTCW;
SATA-Obit 24

Bishop, John 1935- . . . . CLC 10
See also CA 105

Bissett, Bill 1939- . . . . CLC 18; PC 14
See also CA 69-72; CAAS 19; CANR 15;
DLB 53; MTCW

Bitov, Andrei (Georgievich) 1937- . . . CLC 57
See also CA 142

Biyidi, Alexandre 1932-
See Beti, Mongo
See also BW 1; CA 114; 124; MTCW

Bjarme, Brynjolf
See Ibsen, Henrik (Johan)

Bjornson, Bjornstjerne (Martinius)
1832-1910 . . . . TCLC 7, 37
See also CA 104

Black, Robert
See Holdstock, Robert P.

Blackburn, Paul 1926-1971 . . . . . . CLC 9, 43
See also CA 81-84; 33-36R; CANR 34;
DLB 16; DLBY 81

Black Elk 1863-1950 . . . . **TCLC 33**
See also CA 144; DAM MULT; NNAL

Black Hobart
See Sanders, (James) Ed(ward)

Blacklin, Malcolm
See Chambers, Aidan

Blackmore, R(ichard) D(oddridge)
1825-1900 . . . . **TCLC 27**
See also CA 120; DLB 18

Blackmur, R(ichard) P(almer)
1904-1965 . . . . **CLC 2, 24**
See also CA 11-12; 25-28R; CAP 1; DLB 63

Black Tarantula, The
See Acker, Kathy

Blackwood, Algernon (Henry)
1869-1951 . . . . **TCLC 5**
See also CA 105; 150; DLB 153, 156

Blackwood, Caroline 1931- . . . . **CLC 6, 9**
See also CA 85-88; CANR 32; DLB 14;
MTCW

Blade, Alexander
See Hamilton, Edmond; Silverberg, Robert

Blaga, Lucian 1895-1961 . . . . **CLC 75**

Blair, Eric (Arthur) 1903-1950
See Orwell, George
See also CA 104; 132; DA; DAB; DAC;
DAM MST, NOV; MTCW; SATA 29

Blais, Marie-Claire
1939- . . . . **CLC 2, 4, 6, 13, 22; DAC**
See also CA 21-24R; CAAS 4; CANR 38;
DAM MST; DLB 53; MTCW

Blaise, Clark 1940- . . . . **CLC 29**
See also AITN 2; CA 53-56; CAAS 3;
CANR 5; DLB 53

Blake, Nicholas
See Day Lewis, C(ecil)
See also DLB 77

Blake, William
1757-1827 . . . . **NCLC 13, 37; DA; DAB;
DAC; PC 12; WLC**
See also CDBLB 1789-1832; DAM MST,
POET; DLB 93; MAICYA; SATA 30

Blake, William J(ames) 1894-1969 . . . **PC 12**
See also CA 5-8R; 25-28R

Blasco Ibanez, Vicente
1867-1928 . . . . **TCLC 12**
See also CA 110; 131; DAM NOV; HW;
MTCW

Blatty, William Peter 1928- . . . . **CLC 2**
See also CA 5-8R; CANR 9; DAM POP

Bleeck, Oliver
See Thomas, Ross (Elmore)

Blessing, Lee 1949- . . . . **CLC 54**

Blish, James (Benjamin)
1921-1975 . . . . **CLC 14**
See also CA 1-4R; 57-60; CANR 3; DLB 8;
MTCW; SATA 66

Bliss, Reginald
See Wells, H(erbert) G(eorge)

Blixen, Karen (Christentze Dinesen)
1885-1962
See Dinesen, Isak
See also CA 25-28; CANR 22, 50; CAP 2;
MTCW; SATA 44

Bloch, Robert (Albert) 1917-1994 . . . **CLC 33**
See also CA 5-8R; 146; CAAS 20; CANR 5;
DLB 44; INT CANR-5; SATA 12;
SATA-Obit 82

Blok, Alexander (Alexandrovich)
1880-1921 . . . . **TCLC 5**
See also CA 104

Blom, Jan
See Breytenbach, Breyten

Bloom, Harold 1930- . . . . **CLC 24**
See also CA 13-16R; CANR 39; DLB 67

Bloomfield, Aurelius
See Bourne, Randolph S(illiman)

Blount, Roy (Alton), Jr. 1941- . . . . . **CLC 38**
See also CA 53-56; CANR 10, 28;
INT CANR-28; MTCW

Bloy, Leon 1846-1917. . . . . **TCLC 22**
See also CA 121; DLB 123

Blume, Judy (Sussman) 1938- . . . **CLC 12, 30**
See also AAYA 3; CA 29-32R; CANR 13,
37; CLR 2, 15; DAM NOV, POP;
DLB 52; JRDA; MAICYA; MTCW;
SATA 2, 31, 79

Blunden, Edmund (Charles)
1896-1974 . . . . **CLC 2, 56**
See also CA 17-18; 45-48; CAP 2; DLB 20,
100, 155; MTCW

Bly, Robert (Elwood)
1926- . . . . **CLC 1, 2, 5, 10, 15, 38**
See also CA 5-8R; CANR 41; DAM POET;
DLB 5; MTCW

Boas, Franz 1858-1942. . . . . **TCLC 56**
See also CA 115

Bobette
See Simenon, Georges (Jacques Christian)

Boccaccio, Giovanni
1313-1375 . . . . **CMLC 13; SSC 10**

Bochco, Steven 1943- . . . . **CLC 35**
See also AAYA 11; CA 124; 138

Bodenheim, Maxwell 1892-1954 . . . **TCLC 44**
See also CA 110; DLB 9, 45

Bodker, Cecil 1927- . . . . **CLC 21**
See also CA 73-76; CANR 13, 44; CLR 23;
MAICYA; SATA 14

Boell, Heinrich (Theodor)
1917-1985 . . . . **CLC 2, 3, 6, 9, 11, 15, 27,
32, 72; DA; DAB; DAC; WLC**
See also CA 21-24R; 116; CANR 24;
DAM MST, NOV; DLB 69; DLBY 85;
MTCW

Boerne, Alfred
See Doeblin, Alfred

Boethius 480(?)-524(?) . . . . **CMLC 15**
See also DLB 115

Bogan, Louise
1897-1970 . . . . **CLC 4, 39, 46; PC 12**
See also CA 73-76; 25-28R; CANR 33;
DAM POET; DLB 45; MTCW

Bogarde, Dirk . . . . **CLC 19**
See also Van Den Bogarde, Derek Jules
Gaspard Ulric Niven
See also DLB 14

Bogosian, Eric 1953- . . . . **CLC 45**
See also CA 138

Bograd, Larry 1953- . . . . **CLC 35**
See also CA 93-96; SAAS 21; SATA 33

Boiardo, Matteo Maria 1441-1494 . . . . **LC 6**

Boileau-Despreaux, Nicolas
1636-1711 . . . . **LC 3**

Boland, Eavan (Aisling) 1944- . . . **CLC 40, 67**
See also CA 143; DAM POET; DLB 40

Bolt, Lee
See Faust, Frederick (Schiller)

Bolt, Robert (Oxton) 1924-1995 . . . . **CLC 14**
See also CA 17-20R; 147; CANR 35;
DAM DRAM; DLB 13; MTCW

Bombet, Louis-Alexandre-Cesar
See Stendhal

Bomkauf
See Kaufman, Bob (Garnell)

Bonaventura. . . . . **NCLC 35**
See also DLB 90

Bond, Edward 1934- . . . . **CLC 4, 6, 13, 23**
See also CA 25-28R; CANR 38;
DAM DRAM; DLB 13; MTCW

Bonham, Frank 1914-1989. . . . . **CLC 12**
See also AAYA 1; CA 9-12R; CANR 4, 36;
JRDA; MAICYA; SAAS 3; SATA 1, 49;
SATA-Obit 62

Bonnefoy, Yves 1923- . . . . **CLC 9, 15, 58**
See also CA 85-88; CANR 33; DAM MST,
POET; MTCW

Bontemps, Arna(ud Wendell)
1902-1973 . . . . **CLC 1, 18; BLC**
See also BW 1; CA 1-4R; 41-44R; CANR 4,
35; CLR 6; DAM MULT, NOV, POET;
DLB 48, 51; JRDA; MAICYA; MTCW;
SATA 2, 44; SATA-Obit 24

Booth, Martin 1944- . . . . **CLC 13**
See also CA 93-96; CAAS 2

Booth, Philip 1925- . . . . **CLC 23**
See also CA 5-8R; CANR 5; DLBY 82

Booth, Wayne C(layson) 1921- . . . . . **CLC 24**
See also CA 1-4R; CAAS 5; CANR 3, 43;
DLB 67

Borchert, Wolfgang 1921-1947 . . . . . **TCLC 5**
See also CA 104; DLB 69, 124

Borel, Petrus 1809-1859. . . . . **NCLC 41**

Borges, Jorge Luis
1899-1986 . . . **CLC 1, 2, 3, 4, 6, 8, 9, 10,
13, 19, 44, 48, 83; DA; DAB; DAC;
HLC; SSC 4; WLC**
See also CA 21-24R; CANR 19, 33;
DAM MST, MULT; DLB 113; DLBY 86;
HW; MTCW

Borowski, Tadeusz 1922-1951 . . . . . . **TCLC 9**
See also CA 106

Borrow, George (Henry)
1803-1881 . . . . **NCLC 9**
See also DLB 21, 55

Bosman, Herman Charles
1905-1951 . . . . **TCLC 49**

Bosschere, Jean de 1878(?)-1953 . . . **TCLC 19**
See also CA 115

Boswell, James
1740-1795 . . . . . . **LC 4; DA; DAB; DAC;
WLC**
See also CDBLB 1660-1789; DAM MST;
DLB 104, 142

Bottoms, David 1949- . . . . **CLC 53**
See also CA 105; CANR 22; DLB 120;
DLBY 83

Boucicault, Dion 1820-1890 . . . . . . **NCLC 41**

Boucolon, Maryse 1937-
See Conde, Maryse
See also CA 110; CANR 30

Bourget, Paul (Charles Joseph)
1852-1935 . . . . **TCLC 12**
See also CA 107; DLB 123

Bourjaily, Vance (Nye) 1922- . . . . **CLC 8, 62**
See also CA 1-4R; CAAS 1; CANR 2;
DLB 2, 143

Bourne, Randolph S(illiman)
1886-1918 . . . . **TCLC 16**
See also CA 117; DLB 63

Bova, Ben(jamin William) 1932- . . . . **CLC 45**
See also AAYA 16; CA 5-8R; CAAS 18;
CANR 11; CLR 3; DLBY 81;
INT CANR-11; MAICYA; MTCW;
SATA 6, 68

Bowen, Elizabeth (Dorothea Cole)
1899-1973 . . . . . . **CLC 1, 3, 6, 11, 15, 22;
SSC 3**
See also CA 17-18; 41-44R; CANR 35;
CAP 2; CDBLB 1945-1960; DAM NOV;
DLB 15, 162; MTCW

Bowering, George 1935- . . . . **CLC 15, 47**
See also CA 21-24R; CAAS 16; CANR 10;
DLB 53

Bowering, Marilyn R(uthe) 1949- . . . **CLC 32**
See also CA 101; CANR 49

Bowers, Edgar 1924- . . . . **CLC 9**
See also CA 5-8R; CANR 24; DLB 5

Bowie, David . . . . **CLC 17**
See also Jones, David Robert

Bowles, Jane (Sydney)
1917-1973 . . . . **CLC 3, 68**
See also CA 19-20; 41-44R; CAP 2

Bowles, Paul (Frederick)
1910- . . . . **CLC 1, 2, 19, 53; SSC 3**
See also CA 1-4R; CAAS 1; CANR 1, 19,
50; DLB 5, 6; MTCW

Box, Edgar
See Vidal, Gore

Boyd, Nancy
See Millay, Edna St. Vincent

Boyd, William 1952- . . . . **CLC 28, 53, 70**
See also CA 114; 120; CANR 51

Boyle, Kay
1902-1992 . . . . . **CLC 1, 5, 19, 58; SSC 5**
See also CA 13-16R; 140; CAAS 1;
CANR 29; DLB 4, 9, 48, 86; DLBY 93;
MTCW

Boyle, Mark
See Kienzle, William X(avier)

Boyle, Patrick 1905-1982 . . . . **CLC 19**
See also CA 127

Boyle, T. C. 1948-
See Boyle, T(homas) Coraghessan

Boyle, T(homas) Coraghessan
1948- . . . . **CLC 36, 55, 90; SSC 16**
See also BEST 90:4; CA 120; CANR 44;
DAM POP; DLBY 86

Boz
See Dickens, Charles (John Huffam)

Brackenridge, Hugh Henry
1748-1816 . . . . **NCLC 7**
See also DLB 11, 37

Bradbury, Edward P.
See Moorcock, Michael (John)

Bradbury, Malcolm (Stanley)
1932- . . . . **CLC 32, 61**
See also CA 1-4R; CANR 1, 33;
DAM NOV; DLB 14; MTCW

Bradbury, Ray (Douglas)
1920- . . . . **CLC 1, 3, 10, 15, 42; DA;
DAB; DAC; WLC**
See also AAYA 15; AITN 1, 2; CA 1-4R;
CANR 2, 30; CDALB 1968-1988;
DAM MST, NOV, POP; DLB 2, 8;
INT CANR-30; MTCW; SATA 11, 64

Bradford, Gamaliel 1863-1932 . . . . . **TCLC 36**
See also DLB 17

Bradley, David (Henry, Jr.)
1950- . . . . **CLC 23; BLC**
See also BW 1; CA 104; CANR 26;
DAM MULT; DLB 33

Bradley, John Ed(mund, Jr.)
1958- . . . . **CLC 55**
See also CA 139

Bradley, Marion Zimmer 1930- . . . . . **CLC 30**
See also AAYA 9; CA 57-60; CAAS 10;
CANR 7, 31, 51; DAM POP; DLB 8;
MTCW

Bradstreet, Anne
1612(?)-1672 . . . . . . **LC 4, 30; DA; DAC;
PC 10**
See also CDALB 1640-1865; DAM MST,
POET; DLB 24

Brady, Joan 1939- . . . . **CLC 86**
See also CA 141

Bragg, Melvyn 1939- . . . . **CLC 10**
See also BEST 89:3; CA 57-60; CANR 10,
48; DLB 14

Braine, John (Gerard)
1922-1986 . . . . **CLC 1, 3, 41**
See also CA 1-4R; 120; CANR 1, 33;
CDBLB 1945-1960; DLB 15; DLBY 86;
MTCW

Brammer, William 1930(?)-1978 . . . . **CLC 31**
See also CA 77-80

Brancati, Vitaliano 1907-1954 . . . . . **TCLC 12**
See also CA 109

Brancato, Robin F(idler) 1936- . . . . . **CLC 35**
See also AAYA 9; CA 69-72; CANR 11,
45; CLR 32; JRDA; SAAS 9; SATA 23

Brand, Max
See Faust, Frederick (Schiller)

Brand, Millen 1906-1980 . . . . **CLC 7**
See also CA 21-24R; 97-100

Branden, Barbara . . . . **CLC 44**
See also CA 148

Brandes, Georg (Morris Cohen)
1842-1927 . . . . **TCLC 10**
See also CA 105

Brandys, Kazimierz 1916- . . . . **CLC 62**

Branley, Franklyn M(ansfield)
1915- . . . . **CLC 21**
See also CA 33-36R; CANR 14, 39;
CLR 13; MAICYA; SAAS 16; SATA 4,
68

Brathwaite, Edward Kamau 1930- . . . **CLC 11**
See also BW 2; CA 25-28R; CANR 11, 26,
47; DAM POET; DLB 125

Brautigan, Richard (Gary)
1935-1984 . . . . **CLC 1, 3, 5, 9, 12, 34, 42**
See also CA 53-56; 113; CANR 34;
DAM NOV; DLB 2, 5; DLBY 80, 84;
MTCW; SATA 56

Braverman, Kate 1950- . . . . **CLC 67**
See also CA 89-92

Brecht, Bertolt
1898-1956 . . . . . . **TCLC 1, 6, 13, 35; DA;
DAB; DAC; DC 3; WLC**
See also CA 104; 133; DAM DRAM, MST;
DLB 56, 124; MTCW

Brecht, Eugen Berthold Friedrich
See Brecht, Bertolt

Bremer, Fredrika 1801-1865 . . . . . **NCLC 11**

Brennan, Christopher John
1870-1932 . . . . **TCLC 17**
See also CA 117

Brennan, Maeve 1917- . . . . **CLC 5**
See also CA 81-84

Brentano, Clemens (Maria)
1778-1842 . . . . **NCLC 1**
See also DLB 90

Brent of Bin Bin
See Franklin, (Stella Maraia Sarah) Miles

Brenton, Howard 1942- . . . . **CLC 31**
See also CA 69-72; CANR 33; DLB 13;
MTCW

Breslin, James 1930-
See Breslin, Jimmy
See also CA 73-76; CANR 31; DAM NOV;
MTCW

Breslin, Jimmy . . . . **CLC 4, 43**
See also Breslin, James
See also AITN 1

Bresson, Robert 1901- . . . . **CLC 16**
See also CA 110; CANR 49

Breton, Andre
1896-1966 . . . . . **CLC 2, 9, 15, 54; PC 15**
See also CA 19-20; 25-28R; CANR 40;
CAP 2; DLB 65; MTCW

Breytenbach, Breyten 1939(?)- . . **CLC 23, 37**
See also CA 113; 129; DAM POET

Bridgers, Sue Ellen 1942- . . . . **CLC 26**
See also AAYA 8; CA 65-68; CANR 11,
36; CLR 18; DLB 52; JRDA; MAICYA;
SAAS 1; SATA 22

Bridges, Robert (Seymour)
1844-1930 . . . . **TCLC 1**
See also CA 104; CDBLB 1890-1914;
DAM POET; DLB 19, 98

Bridie, James . . . . **TCLC 3**
See also Mavor, Osborne Henry
See also DLB 10

Brin, David 1950- . . . . **CLC 34**
See also CA 102; CANR 24;
INT CANR-24; SATA 65

Buchner, (Karl) Georg
1813-1837 . . . . NCLC 26

Buchwald, Art(hur) 1925- . . . . CLC 33
See also AITN 1; CA 5-8R; CANR 21;
MTCW; SATA 10

Buck, Pearl S(ydenstricker)
1892-1973 . . . . CLC 7, 11, 18; DA; DAB;
DAC
See also AITN 1; CA 1-4R; 41-44R;
CANR 1, 34; DAM MST, NOV; DLB 9,
102; MTCW; SATA 1, 25

Buckler, Ernest 1908-1984. . . . CLC 13; DAC
See also CA 11-12; 114; CAP 1;
DAM MST; DLB 68; SATA 47

Buckley, Vincent (Thomas)
1925-1988 . . . . CLC 57
See also CA 101

Buckley, William F(rank), Jr.
1925- . . . . CLC 7, 18, 37
See also AITN 1; CA 1-4R; CANR 1, 24;
DAM POP; DLB 137; DLBY 80;
INT CANR-24; MTCW

Buechner, (Carl) Frederick
1926- . . . . CLC 2, 4, 6, 9
See also CA 13-16R; CANR 11, 39;
DAM NOV; DLBY 80; INT CANR-11;
MTCW

Buell, John (Edward) 1927- . . . . CLC 10
See also CA 1-4R; DLB 53

Buero Vallejo, Antonio 1916- . . . CLC 15, 46
See also CA 106; CANR 24, 49; HW;
MTCW

Bufalino, Gesualdo 1920(?)- . . . . CLC 74

Bugayev, Boris Nikolayevich 1880-1934
See Bely, Andrey
See also CA 104

Bukowski, Charles
1920-1994 . . . . CLC 2, 5, 9, 41, 82
See also CA 17-20R; 144; CANR 40;
DAM NOV, POET; DLB 5, 130; MTCW

Bulgakov, Mikhail (Afanas'evich)
1891-1940 . . . . TCLC 2, 16; SSC 18
See also CA 105; DAM DRAM, NOV

Bulgya, Alexander Alexandrovich
1901-1956 . . . . TCLC 53
See also Fadeyev, Alexander
See also CA 117

Bullins, Ed 1935- . . CLC 1, 5, 7; BLC; DC 6
See also BW 2; CA 49-52; CAAS 16;
CANR 24, 46; DAM DRAM, MULT;
DLB 7, 38; MTCW

Bulwer-Lytton, Edward (George Earle Lytton)
1803-1873 . . . . NCLC 1, 45
See also DLB 21

Bunin, Ivan Alexeyevich
1870-1953 . . . . TCLC 6; SSC 5
See also CA 104

Bunting, Basil 1900-1985. . . . CLC 10, 39, 47
See also CA 53-56; 115; CANR 7;
DAM POET; DLB 20

Bunuel, Luis 1900-1983 . . CLC 16, 80; HLC
See also CA 101; 110; CANR 32;
DAM MULT; HW

Bunyan, John
1628-1688 . . . . . . LC 4; DA; DAB; DAC;
WLC
See also CDBLB 1660-1789; DAM MST;
DLB 39

Burckhardt, Jacob (Christoph)
1818-1897 . . . . NCLC 49

Burford, Eleanor
See Hibbert, Eleanor Alice Burford

Burgess, Anthony
. CLC 1, 2, 4, 5, 8, 10, 13, 15, 22, 40, 62,
81; DAB
See also Wilson, John (Anthony) Burgess
See also AITN 1; CDBLB 1960 to Present;
DLB 14

Burke, Edmund
1729(?)-1797 . . . . LC 7; DA; DAB; DAC;
WLC
See also DAM MST; DLB 104

Burke, Kenneth (Duva)
1897-1993 . . . . CLC 2, 24
See also CA 5-8R; 143; CANR 39; DLD 45,
63; MTCW

Burke, Leda
See Garnett, David

Burke, Ralph
See Silverberg, Robert

Burney, Fanny 1752-1840 . . . . NCLC 12, 54
See also DLB 39

Burns, Robert 1759-1796. . . . . PC 6
See also CDBLB 1789-1832; DA; DAB;
DAC; DAM MST, POET; DLB 109;
WLC

Burns, Tex
See L'Amour, Louis (Dearborn)

Burnshaw, Stanley 1906- . . . . . CLC 3, 13, 44
See also CA 9-12R; DLB 48

Burr, Anne 1937- . . . . CLC 6
See also CA 25-28R

Burroughs, Edgar Rice
1875-1950 . . . . TCLC 2, 32
See also AAYA 11; CA 104; 132;
DAM NOV; DLB 8; MTCW; SATA 41

Burroughs, William S(eward)
1914- . . . . CLC 1, 2, 5, 15, 22, 42, 75;
DA; DAB; DAC; WLC
See also AITN 2; CA 9-12R; CANR 20;
DAM MST, NOV, POP; DLB 2, 8, 16,
152; DLBY 81; MTCW

Burton, Richard F. 1821-1890. . . . NCLC 42
See also DLB 55

Busch, Frederick 1941- . . . CLC 7, 10, 18, 47
See also CA 33-36R; CAAS 1; CANR 45;
DLB 6

Bush, Ronald 1946- . . . . CLC 34
See also CA 136

Bustos, F(rancisco)
See Borges, Jorge Luis

Bustos Domecq, H(onorio)
See Bioy Casares, Adolfo; Borges, Jorge
Luis

Butler, Octavia E(stelle) 1947- . . . . . CLC 38
See also BW 2; CA 73-76; CANR 12, 24,
38; DAM MULT, POP; DLB 33;
MTCW; SATA 84

Butler, Robert Olen (Jr.) 1945- . . . . . CLC 81
See also CA 112; DAM POP; INT 112

Butler, Samuel 1612-1680 . . . . LC 16
See also DLB 101, 126

Butler, Samuel
1835-1902 . . . . . . TCLC 1, 33; DA; DAB;
DAC; WLC
See also CA 143; CDBLB 1890-1914;
DAM MST, NOV; DLB 18, 57

Butler, Walter C.
See Faust, Frederick (Schiller)

Butor, Michel (Marie Francois)
1926- . . . . CLC 1, 3, 8, 11, 15
See also CA 9-12R; CANR 33; DLB 83;
MTCW

Buzo, Alexander (John) 1944- . . . . . . CLC 61
See also CA 97-100; CANR 17, 39

Buzzati, Dino 1906-1972 . . . . CLC 36
See also CA 33-36R

Byars, Betsy (Cromer) 1928- . . . . CLC 35
See also CA 33-36R; CANR 18, 36; CLR 1,
16; DLB 52; INT CANR-18; JRDA;
MAICYA; MTCW; SAAS 1; SATA 4,
46, 80

Byatt, A(ntonia) S(usan Drabble)
1936- . . . . CLC 19, 65
See also CA 13-16R; CANR 13, 33, 50;
DAM NOV, POP; DLB 14; MTCW

Byrne, David 1952- . . . . CLC 26
See also CA 127

Byrne, John Keyes 1926-
See Leonard, Hugh
See also CA 102; INT 102

Byron, George Gordon (Noel)
1788-1824 . . . . . NCLC 2, 12; DA; DAB;
DAC; WLC
See also CDBLB 1789-1832; DAM MST,
POET; DLB 96, 110

C. 3. 3.
See Wilde, Oscar (Fingal O'Flahertie Wills)

Caballero, Fernan 1796-1877 . . . . . NCLC 10

Cabell, James Branch 1879-1958 . . . TCLC 6
See also CA 105; DLB 9, 78

Cable, George Washington
1844-1925 . . . . TCLC 4; SSC 4
See also CA 104; DLB 12, 74; DLBD 13

Cabral de Melo Neto, Joao 1920- . . . CLC 76
See also DAM MULT

Cabrera Infante, G(uillermo)
1929- . . . . CLC 5, 25, 45; HLC
See also CA 85-88; CANR 29;
DAM MULT; DLB 113; HW; MTCW

Cade, Toni
See Bambara, Toni Cade

Cadmus and Harmonia
See Buchan, John

Caedmon fl. 658-680 . . . . CMLC 7
See also DLB 146

Caeiro, Alberto
See Pessoa, Fernando (Antonio Nogueira)

Cage, John (Milton, Jr.) 1912- . . . . . CLC 41
See also CA 13-16R; CANR 9;
INT CANR-9

Cain, G.
See Cabrera Infante, G(uillermo)

Cary, (Arthur) Joyce (Lunel)
1888-1957 .... TCLC 1, 29
See also CA 104; CDBLB 1914-1945;
DLB 15, 100

Casanova de Seingalt, Giovanni Jacopo
1725-1798 .... LC 13

Casares, Adolfo Bioy
See Bioy Casares, Adolfo

Casely-Hayford, J(oseph) E(phraim)
1866-1930 .... TCLC 24; BLC
See also BW 2; CA 123; DAM MULT

Casey, John (Dudley) 1939-....... CLC 59
See also BEST 90:2; CA 69-72; CANR 23

Casey, Michael 1947-............. CLC 2
See also CA 65-68; DLB 5

Casey, Patrick
See Thurman, Wallace (Henry)

Casey, Warren (Peter) 1935-1988 ... CLC 12
See also CA 101; 127; INT 101

Casona, Alejandro................. CLC 49
See also Alvarez, Alejandro Rodriguez

Cassavetes, John 1929-1989........ CLC 20
See also CA 85-88; 127

Cassill, R(onald) V(erlin) 1919-... CLC 4, 23
See also CA 9-12R; CAAS 1; CANR 7, 45;
DLB 6

Cassirer, Ernst 1874-1945 .... TCLC 61

Cassity, (Allen) Turner 1929- ... CLC 6, 42
See also CA 17-20R; CAAS 8; CANR 11;
DLB 105

Castaneda, Carlos 1931(?)-........ CLC 12
See also CA 25-28R; CANR 32; HW;
MTCW

Castedo, Elena 1937- .... CLC 65
See also CA 132

Castedo-Ellerman, Elena
See Castedo, Elena

Castellanos, Rosario
1925-1974 .... CLC 66; HLC
See also CA 131; 53-56; DAM MULT;
DLB 113; IIW

Castelvetro, Lodovico 1505-1571..... LC 12

Castiglione, Baldassare 1478-1529 ... LC 12

Castle, Robert
See Hamilton, Edmond

Castro, Guillen de 1569-1631........ LC 19

Castro, Rosalia de 1837-1885 ..... NCLC 3
See also DAM MULT

Cather, Willa
See Cather, Willa Sibert

Cather, Willa Sibert
1873-1947 .... TCLC 1, 11, 31; DA;
DAB; DAC; SSC 2; WLC
See also CA 104; 128; CDALB 1865-1917;
DAM MST, NOV; DLB 9, 54, 78;
DLBD 1; MTCW; SATA 30

Catton, (Charles) Bruce
1899-1978 .... CLC 35
See also AITN 1; CA 5-8R; 81-84;
CANR 7; DLB 17; SATA 2;
SATA-Obit 24

Cauldwell, Frank
See King, Francis (Henry)

Caunitz, William J. 1933- .... CLC 34
See also BEST 89:3; CA 125; 130; INT 130

Causley, Charles (Stanley) 1917-..... CLC 7
See also CA 9-12R; CANR 5, 35; CLR 30;
DLB 27; MTCW; SATA 3, 66

Caute, David 1936-.............. CLC 29
See also CA 1-4R; CAAS 4; CANR 1, 33;
DAM NOV; DLB 14

Cavafy, C(onstantine) P(eter)
1863-1933 .... TCLC 2, 7
See also Kavafis, Konstantinos Petrou
See also CA 148; DAM POET

Cavallo, Evelyn
See Spark, Muriel (Sarah)

Cavanna, Betty .... CLC 12
See also Harrison, Elizabeth Cavanna
See also JRDA; MAICYA; SAAS 4;
SATA 1, 30

Cavendish, Margaret Lucas
1623-1673 .... LC 30
See also DLB 131

Caxton, William 1421(?)-1491(?)..... LC 17

Cayrol, Jean 1911 .... CLC 11
See also CA 89-92; DLB 83

Cela, Camilo Jose
1916- .... CLC 4, 13, 59; HLC
See also BEST 90:2; CA 21-24R; CAAS 10;
CANR 21, 32; DAM MULT; DLBY 89;
HW; MTCW

Celan, Paul ...... CLC 10, 19, 53, 82; PC 10
See also Antschel, Paul
See also DLB 69

Celine, Louis-Ferdinand
.... CLC 1, 3, 4, 7, 9, 15, 47
See also Destouches, Louis-Ferdinand
See also DLB 72

Cellini, Benvenuto 1500-1571 .... LC 7

Cendrars, Blaise .... CLC 18
See also Sauser-Hall, Frederic

Cernuda (y Bidon), Luis
1902-1963 .... CLC 54
See also CA 131; 89-92; DAM POET;
DLB 134; HW

Cervantes (Saavedra), Miguel de
1547-1616 .... LC 6, 23; DA; DAB;
DAC; SSC 12; WLC
See also DAM MST, NOV

Cesaire, Aime (Fernand)
1913- .... CLC 19, 32; BLC
See also BW 2; CA 65-68; CANR 24, 43;
DAM MULT, POET; MTCW

Chabon, Michael 1965(?)- .... CLC 55
See also CA 139

Chabrol, Claude 1930- .... CLC 16
See also CA 110

Challans, Mary 1905-1983
See Renault, Mary
See also CA 81-84; 111; SATA 23;
SATA-Obit 36

Challis, George
See Faust, Frederick (Schiller)

Chambers, Aidan 1934- .... CLC 35
See also CA 25-28R; CANR 12, 31; JRDA;
MAICYA; SAAS 12; SATA 1, 69

Chambers, James 1948-
See Cliff, Jimmy
See also CA 124

Chambers, Jessie
See Lawrence, D(avid) H(erbert Richards)

Chambers, Robert W. 1865-1933... TCLC 41

Chandler, Raymond (Thornton)
1888-1959 .... TCLC 1, 7
See also CA 104; 129; CDALB 1929-1941;
DLBD 6; MTCW

Chang, Jung 1952-................ CLC 71
See also CA 142

Channing, William Ellery
1780-1842 .... NCLC 17
See also DLB 1, 59

Chaplin, Charles Spencer
1889-1977 .... CLC 16
See also Chaplin, Charlie
See also CA 81-84; 73-76

Chaplin, Charlie
See Chaplin, Charles Spencer
See also DLB 44

Chapman, George 1559(?)-1634...... LC 22
See also DAM DRAM; DLB 62, 121

Chapman, Graham 1941-1989 ...... CLC 21
See also Monty Python
See also CA 116; 129; CANR 35

Chapman, John Jay 1862-1933 ..... TCLC 7
See also CA 104

Chapman, Walker
See Silverberg, Robert

Chappell, Fred (Davis) 1936-.... CLC 40, 78
See also CA 5-8R; CAAS 4; CANR 8, 33;
DLB 6, 105

Char, Rene(-Emile)
1907-1988 .... CLC 9, 11, 14, 55
See also CA 13-16R; 124; CANR 32;
DAM POET; MTCW

Charby, Jay
See Ellison, Harlan (Jay)

Chardin, Pierre Teilhard de
See Teilhard de Chardin, (Marie Joseph)
Pierre

Charles I 1600-1649 .... LC 13

Charyn, Jerome 1937- .... CLC 5, 8, 18
See also CA 5-8R; CAAS 1; CANR 7;
DLBY 83; MTCW

Chase, Mary (Coyle) 1907-1981 ...... DC 1
See also CA 77-80; 105; SATA 17;
SATA-Obit 29

Chase, Mary Ellen 1887-1973....... CLC 2
See also CA 13-16; 41-44R; CAP 1;
SATA 10

Chase, Nicholas
See Hyde, Anthony

Chateaubriand, Francois Rene de
1768-1848 .... NCLC 3
See also DLB 119

Chatterje, Sarat Chandra 1876-1936(?)
See Chatterji, Saratchandra
See also CA 109

Chatterji, Bankim Chandra
1838-1894 .... NCLC 19

Chatterji, Saratchandra .... TCLC 13
See also Chatterje, Sarat Chandra

Chatterton, Thomas 1752-1770 .... LC 3
See also DAM POET; DLB 109

Chatwin, (Charles) Bruce
1940-1989 .... CLC 28, 57, 59
See also AAYA 4; BEST 90:1; CA 85-88;
127; DAM POP

Chaucer, Daniel
See Ford, Ford Madox

Chaucer, Geoffrey
1340(?)-1400 ... LC 17; DA; DAB; DAC
See also CDBLB Before 1660; DAM MST,
POET; DLB 146

Chaviaras, Strates 1935-
See Haviaras, Stratis
See also CA 105

Chayefsky, Paddy .... CLC 23
See also Chayefsky, Sidney
See also DLB 7, 44; DLBY 81

Chayefsky, Sidney 1923-1981
See Chayefsky, Paddy
See also CA 9-12R; 104; CANR 18;
DAM DRAM

Chedid, Andree 1920- .... CLC 47
See also CA 145

Cheever, John
1912-1982 ...... CLC 3, 7, 8, 11, 15, 25,
64; DA; DAB; DAC; SSC 1; WLC
See also CA 5-8R; 106; CABS 1; CANR 5,
27; CDALB 1941-1968; DAM MST,
NOV, POP; DLB 2, 102; DLBY 80, 82;
INT CANR-5; MTCW

Cheever, Susan 1943- .... CLC 18, 48
See also CA 103; CANR 27, 51; DLBY 82;
INT CANR-27

Chekhonte, Antosha
See Chekhov, Anton (Pavlovich)

Chekhov, Anton (Pavlovich)
1860-1904 ..... TCLC 3, 10, 31, 55; DA;
DAB; DAC; SSC 2; WLC
See also CA 104; 124; DAM DRAM, MST

Chernyshevsky, Nikolay Gavrilovich
1828-1889 .... NCLC 1

Cherry, Carolyn Janice 1942-
See Cherryh, C. J.
See also CA 65-68; CANR 10

Cherryh, C. J. .... CLC 35
See also Cherry, Carolyn Janice
See also DLBY 80

Chesnutt, Charles W(addell)
1858-1932 .... TCLC 5, 39; BLC; SSC 7
See also BW 1; CA 106; 125; DAM MULT;
DLB 12, 50, 78; MTCW

Chester, Alfred 1929(?)-1971 .... CLC 49
See also CA 33-36R; DLB 130

Chesterton, G(ilbert) K(eith)
1874-1936 .... TCLC 1, 6; SSC 1
See also CA 104; 132; CDBLB 1914-1945;
DAM NOV, POET; DLB 10, 19, 34, 70,
98, 149; MTCW; SATA 27

Chiang Pin-chin 1904-1986
See Ding Ling
See also CA 118

Ch'ien Chung-shu 1910- .... CLC 22
See also CA 130; MTCW

Child, L. Maria
See Child, Lydia Maria

Child, Lydia Maria 1802-1880 .... NCLC 6
See also DLB 1, 74; SATA 67

Child, Mrs.
See Child, Lydia Maria

Child, Philip 1898-1978 .... CLC 19, 68
See also CA 13-14; CAP 1; SATA 47

Childress, Alice
1920-1994 .. CLC 12, 15, 86; BLC; DC 4
See also AAYA 8; BW 2; CA 45-48; 146;
CANR 3, 27, 50; CLR 14; DAM DRAM,
MULT, NOV; DLB 7, 38; JRDA;
MAICYA; MTCW; SATA 7, 48, 81

Chislett, (Margaret) Anne 1943- .... CLC 34

Chitty, Thomas Willes 1926- .... CLC 11
See also Hinde, Thomas
See also CA 5-8R

Chivers, Thomas Holley
1809-1858 .... NCLC 49
See also DLB 3

Chomette, Rene Lucien 1898-1981
See Clair, Rene
See also CA 103

Chopin, Kate
.... TCLC 5, 14; DA; DAB; SSC 8
See also Chopin, Katherine
See also CDALB 1865-1917; DLB 12, 78

Chopin, Katherine 1851-1904
See Chopin, Kate
See also CA 104; 122; DAC; DAM MST,
NOV

Chretien de Troyes
c. 12th cent. - .... CMLC 10

Christie
See Ichikawa, Kon

Christie, Agatha (Mary Clarissa)
1890-1976 ...... CLC 1, 6, 8, 12, 39, 48;
DAB; DAC
See also AAYA 9; AITN 1, 2; CA 17-20R;
61-64; CANR 10, 37; CDBLB 1914-1945;
DAM NOV; DLB 13, 77; MTCW;
SATA 36

Christie, (Ann) Philippa
See Pearce, Philippa
See also CA 5-8R; CANR 4

Christine de Pizan 1365(?)-1431(?) .... LC 9

Chubb, Elmer
See Masters, Edgar Lee

Chulkov, Mikhail Dmitrievich
1743-1792 .... LC 2
See also DLB 150

Churchill, Caryl 1938- ... CLC 31, 55; DC 5
See also CA 102; CANR 22, 46; DLB 13;
MTCW

Churchill, Charles 1731-1764 .... LC 3
See also DLB 109

Chute, Carolyn 1947- .... CLC 39
See also CA 123

Ciardi, John (Anthony)
1916-1986 .... CLC 10, 40, 44
See also CA 5-8R; 118; CAAS 2; CANR 5,
33; CLR 19; DAM POET; DLB 5;
DLBY 86; INT CANR-5; MAICYA;
MTCW; SATA 1, 65; SATA-Obit 46

Cicero, Marcus Tullius
106B.C.-43B.C. .... CMLC 3

Cimino, Michael 1943- .... CLC 16
See also CA 105

Cioran, E(mil) M. 1911-1995 ...... CLC 64
See also CA 25-28R; 149

Cisneros, Sandra 1954- ...... CLC 69; HLC
See also AAYA 9; CA 131; DAM MULT;
DLB 122, 152; HW

Cixous, Helene 1937- .... CLC 92
See also CA 126; DLB 83; MTCW

Clair, Rene .... CLC 20
See also Chomette, Rene Lucien

Clampitt, Amy 1920-1994 .... CLC 32
See also CA 110; 146; CANR 29; DLB 105

Clancy, Thomas L., Jr. 1947-
See Clancy, Tom
See also CA 125; 131; INT 131; MTCW

Clancy, Tom .... CLC 45
See also Clancy, Thomas L., Jr.
See also AAYA 9; BEST 89:1, 90:1;
DAM NOV, POP

Clare, John 1793-1864 ...... NCLC 9; DAB
See also DAM POET; DLB 55, 96

Clarin
See Alas (y Urena), Leopoldo (Enrique
Garcia)

Clark, Al C.
See Goines, Donald

Clark, (Robert) Brian 1932- .... CLC 29
See also CA 41-44R

Clark, Curt
See Westlake, Donald E(dwin)

Clark, Eleanor 1913- .... CLC 5, 19
See also CA 9-12R; CANR 41; DLB 6

Clark, J. P.
See Clark, John Pepper
See also DLB 117

Clark, John Pepper
1935- .... CLC 38; BLC; DC 5
See also Clark, J. P.
See also BW 1; CA 65-68; CANR 16;
DAM DRAM, MULT

Clark, M. R.
See Clark, Mavis Thorpe

Clark, Mavis Thorpe 1909- .... CLC 12
See also CA 57-60; CANR 8, 37; CLR 30;
MAICYA; SAAS 5; SATA 8, 74

Clark, Walter Van Tilburg
1909-1971 .... CLC 28
See also CA 9-12R; 33-36R; DLB 9;
SATA 8

Clarke, Arthur C(harles)
1917- ...... CLC 1, 4, 13, 18, 35; SSC 3
See also AAYA 4; CA 1-4R; CANR 2, 28;
DAM POP; JRDA; MAICYA; MTCW;
SATA 13, 70

Clarke, Austin 1896-1974 .... CLC 6, 9
See also CA 29-32; 49-52; CAP 2;
DAM POET; DLB 10, 20

Clarke, Austin C(hesterfield)
1934- .... CLC 8, 53; BLC; DAC
See also BW 1; CA 25-28R; CAAS 16;
CANR 14, 32; DAM MULT; DLB 53,
125

Clarke, Gillian   1937- . . . .   CLC 61
See also CA 106; DLB 40

Clarke, Marcus (Andrew Hislop)
1846-1881   . . . .   NCLC 19

Clarke, Shirley   1925- . . . .   CLC 16

Clash, The
See Headon, (Nicky) Topper; Jones, Mick;
Simonon, Paul; Strummer, Joe

Claudel, Paul (Louis Charles Marie)
1868-1955   . . . .   TCLC 2, 10
See also CA 104

Clavell, James (duMaresq)
1925-1994   . . . .   CLC 6, 25, 87
See also CA 25-28R; 146; CANR 26, 48;
DAM NOV, POP; MTCW

Cleaver, (Leroy) Eldridge
1935- . . . .   CLC 30; BLC
See also BW 1; CA 21-24R; CANR 16;
DAM MULT

Cleese, John (Marwood)   1939- . . . . .   CLC 21
See also Monty Python
See also CA 112; 116; CANR 35; MTCW

Cleishbotham, Jebediah
See Scott, Walter

Cleland, John   1710-1789   . . . .   LC 2
See also DLB 39

Clemens, Samuel Langhorne   1835-1910
See Twain, Mark
See also CA 104; 135; CDALB 1865-1917;
DA; DAB; DAC; DAM MST, NOV;
DLB 11, 12, 23, 64, 74; JRDA;
MAICYA; YABC 2

Cleophil
See Congreve, William

Clerihew, E.
See Bentley, E(dmund) C(lerihew)

Clerk, N. W.
See Lewis, C(live) S(taples)

Cliff, Jimmy . . . .   CLC 21
See also Chambers, James

Clifton, (Thelma) Lucille
1936- . . . .   CLC 19, 66; BLC
See also BW 2; CA 49-52; CANR 2, 24, 42;
CLR 5; DAM MULT, POET; DLB 5, 41;
MAICYA; MTCW; SATA 20, 69

Clinton, Dirk
See Silverberg, Robert

Clough, Arthur Hugh   1819-1861 . .   NCLC 27
See also DLB 32

Clutha, Janet Paterson Frame   1924-
See Frame, Janet
See also CA 1-4R; CANR 2, 36; MTCW

Clyne, Terence
See Blatty, William Peter

Cobalt, Martin
See Mayne, William (James Carter)

Cobbett, William   1763-1835   . . . . .   NCLC 49
See also DLB 43, 107, 158

Coburn, D(onald) L(ee)   1938- . . . . . .   CLC 10
See also CA 89-92

Cocteau, Jean (Maurice Eugene Clement)
1889-1963 . . . .   CLC 1, 8, 15, 16, 43; DA;
DAB; DAC; WLC
See also CA 25-28; CANR 40; CAP 2;
DAM DRAM, MST, NOV; DLB 65;
MTCW

Codrescu, Andrei   1946- . . . .   CLC 46
See also CA 33-36R; CAAS 19; CANR 13,
34; DAM POET

Coe, Max
See Bourne, Randolph S(illiman)

Coe, Tucker
See Westlake, Donald E(dwin)

Coetzee, J(ohn) M(ichael)
1940- . . . .   CLC 23, 33, 66
See also CA 77-80; CANR 41; DAM NOV;
MTCW

Coffey, Brian
See Koontz, Dean R(ay)

Cohan, George M.   1878-1942 . . . . .   TCLC 60

Cohen, Arthur A(llen)
1928-1986   . . . .   CLC 7, 31
See also CA 1-4R; 120; CANR 1, 17, 42;
DLB 28

Cohen, Leonard (Norman)
1934- . . . .   CLC 3, 38; DAC
See also CA 21-24R; CANR 14;
DAM MST; DLB 53; MTCW

Cohen, Matt   1942- . . . .   CLC 19; DAC
See also CA 61-64; CAAS 18; CANR 40;
DLB 53

Cohen-Solal, Annie   19(?)- . . . .   CLC 50

Colegate, Isabel   1931- . . . .   CLC 36
See also CA 17-20R; CANR 8, 22; DLB 14;
INT CANR-22; MTCW

Coleman, Emmett
See Reed, Ishmael

Coleridge, Samuel Taylor
1772-1834 . . . . .   NCLC 9, 54; DA; DAB;
DAC; PC 11; WLC
See also CDBLB 1789-1832; DAM MST,
POET; DLB 93, 107

Coleridge, Sara   1802-1852 . . . .   NCLC 31

Coles, Don   1928- . . . .   CLC 46
See also CA 115; CANR 38

Colette, (Sidonie-Gabrielle)
1873-1954 . . . . . .   TCLC 1, 5, 16; SSC 10
See also CA 104; 131; DAM NOV; DLB 65;
MTCW

Collett, (Jacobine) Camilla (Wergeland)
1813-1895   . . . .   NCLC 22

Collier, Christopher   1930- . . . .   CLC 30
See also AAYA 13; CA 33-36R; CANR 13,
33; JRDA; MAICYA; SATA 16, 70

Collier, James L(incoln)   1928- . . . . .   CLC 30
See also AAYA 13; CA 9-12R; CANR 4,
33; CLR 3; DAM POP; JRDA;
MAICYA; SAAS 21; SATA 8, 70

Collier, Jeremy   1650-1726 . . . .   LC 6

Collier, John   1901-1980 . . . .   SSC 19
See also CA 65-68; 97-100; CANR 10;
DLB 77

Collins, Hunt
See Hunter, Evan

Collins, Linda   1931- . . . .   CLC 44
See also CA 125

Collins, (William) Wilkie
1824-1889   . . . .   NCLC 1, 18
See also CDBLB 1832-1890; DLB 18, 70,
159

Collins, William   1721-1759 . . . .   LC 4
See also DAM POET; DLB 109

Collodi, Carlo   1826-1890 . . . .   NCLC 54
See also Lorenzini, Carlo
See also CLR 5

Colman, George
See Glassco, John

Colt, Winchester Remington
See Hubbard, L(afayette) Ron(ald)

Colter, Cyrus   1910- . . . .   CLC 58
See also BW 1; CA 65-68; CANR 10;
DLB 33

Colton, James
See Hansen, Joseph

Colum, Padraic   1881-1972 . . . .   CLC 28
See also CA 73-76; 33-36R; CANR 35;
CLR 36; MAICYA; MTCW; SATA 15

Colvin, James
See Moorcock, Michael (John)

Colwin, Laurie (E.)
1944-1992 . . . .   CLC 5, 13, 23, 84
See also CA 89-92; 139; CANR 20, 46;
DLBY 80; MTCW

Comfort, Alex(ander)   1920- . . . .   CLC 7
See also CA 1-4R; CANR 1, 45; DAM POP

Comfort, Montgomery
See Campbell, (John) Ramsey

Compton-Burnett, I(vy)
1884(?)-1969 . . . . . .   CLC 1, 3, 10, 15, 34
See also CA 1-4R; 25-28R; CANR 4;
DAM NOV; DLB 36; MTCW

Comstock, Anthony   1844-1915 . . . .   TCLC 13
See also CA 110

Comte, Auguste   1798-1857 . . . .   NCLC 54

Conan Doyle, Arthur
See Doyle, Arthur Conan

Conde, Maryse   1937- . . . .   CLC 52, 92
See also Boucolon, Maryse
See also BW 2; DAM MULT

Condillac, Etienne Bonnot de
1714-1780   . . . .   LC 26

Condon, Richard (Thomas)
1915- . . . .   CLC 4, 6, 8, 10, 45
See also BEST 90:3; CA 1-4R; CAAS 1;
CANR 2, 23; DAM NOV;
INT CANR-23; MTCW

Congreve, William
1670-1729 . . . .   LC 5, 21; DA; DAB;
DAC; DC 2; WLC
See also CDBLB 1660-1789; DAM DRAM,
MST, POET; DLB 39, 84

Connell, Evan S(helby), Jr.
1924- . . . .   CLC 4, 6, 45
See also AAYA 7; CA 1-4R; CAAS 2;
CANR 2, 39; DAM NOV; DLB 2;
DLBY 81; MTCW

Crawford, Isabella Valancy
1850-1887 . . . . NCLC 12
See also DLB 92

Crayon, Geoffrey
See Irving, Washington

Creasey, John 1908-1973 . . . . CLC 11
See also CA 5-8R; 41-44R; CANR 8;
DLB 77; MTCW

Crebillon, Claude Prosper Jolyot de (fils)
1707-1777 . . . . LC 28

Credo
See Creasey, John

Creeley, Robert (White)
1926- . . . . . CLC 1, 2, 4, 8, 11, 15, 36, 78
See also CA 1-4R; CAAS 10; CANR 23, 43;
DAM POET; DLB 5, 16; MTCW

Crews, Harry (Eugene)
1935- . . . . CLC 6, 23, 49
See also AITN 1; CA 25-28R; CANR 20;
DLB 6, 143; MTCW

Crichton, (John) Michael
1942- . . . . CLC 2, 6, 54, 90
See also AAYA 10; AITN 2; CA 25-28R;
CANR 13, 40; DAM NOV, POP;
DLBY 81; INT CANR-13; JRDA;
MTCW; SATA 9

Crispin, Edmund . . . . CLC 22
See also Montgomery, (Robert) Bruce
See also DLB 87

Cristofer, Michael 1945(?)- . . . . CLC 28
See also CA 110; DAM DRAM; DLB 7

Croce, Benedetto 1866-1952 . . . . . . TCLC 37
See also CA 120

Crockett, David 1786-1836 . . . . NCLC 8
See also DLB 3, 11

Crockett, Davy
See Crockett, David

Crofts, Freeman Wills
1879-1957 . . . . TCLC 55
See also CA 115; DLB 77

Croker, John Wilson 1780-1857 . . NCLC 10
See also DLB 110

Crommelynck, Fernand 1885-1970 . . CLC 75
See also CA 89-92

Cronin, A(rchibald) J(oseph)
1896-1981 . . . . CLC 32
See also CA 1-4R; 102; CANR 5; SATA 47;
SATA-Obit 25

Cross, Amanda
See Heilbrun, Carolyn G(old)

Crothers, Rachel 1878(?)-1958 . . . . . TCLC 19
See also CA 113; DLB 7

Croves, Hal
See Traven, B.

Crowfield, Christopher
See Stowe, Harriet (Elizabeth) Beecher

Crowley, Aleister . . . . TCLC 7
See also Crowley, Edward Alexander

Crowley, Edward Alexander 1875-1947
See Crowley, Aleister
See also CA 104

Crowley, John 1942- . . . . CLC 57
See also CA 61-64; CANR 43; DLBY 82;
SATA 65

Crud
See Crumb, R(obert)

Crumarums
See Crumb, R(obert)

Crumb, R(obert) 1943- . . . . CLC 17
See also CA 106

Crumbum
See Crumb, R(obert)

Crumski
See Crumb, R(obert)

Crum the Bum
See Crumb, R(obert)

Crunk
See Crumb, R(obert)

Crustt
See Crumb, R(obert)

Cryer, Gretchen (Kiger) 1935- . . . . . . CLC 21
See also CA 114; 123

Csath, Geza 1887-1919 . . . . TCLC 13
See also CA 111

Cudlip, David 1933- . . . . CLC 34

Cullen, Countee
1903-1946 . . . . . . TCLC 4, 37; BLC; DA;
DAC
See also BW 1; CA 108; 124;
CDALB 1917-1929; DAM MST, MULT,
POET; DLB 4, 48, 51; MTCW; SATA 18

Cum, R.
See Crumb, R(obert)

Cummings, Bruce F(rederick) 1889-1919
See Barbellion, W. N. P.
See also CA 123

Cummings, E(dward) E(stlin)
1894-1962 . . . . . . CLC 1, 3, 8, 12, 15, 68;
DA; DAB; DAC; PC 5; WLC 2
See also CA 73-76; CANR 31;
CDALB 1929-1941; DAM MST, POET;
DLB 4, 48; MTCW

Cunha, Euclides (Rodrigues Pimenta) da
1866-1909 . . . . TCLC 24
See also CA 123

Cunningham, E. V.
See Fast, Howard (Melvin)

Cunningham, J(ames) V(incent)
1911-1985 . . . . CLC 3, 31
See also CA 1-4R; 115; CANR 1; DLB 5

Cunningham, Julia (Woolfolk)
1916- . . . . CLC 12
See also CA 9-12R; CANR 4, 19, 36;
JRDA; MAICYA; SAAS 2; SATA 1, 26

Cunningham, Michael 1952- . . . . CLC 34
See also CA 136

Cunninghame Graham, R(obert) B(ontine)
1852-1936 . . . . TCLC 19
See also Graham, R(obert) B(ontine)
Cunninghame
See also CA 119; DLB 98

Currie, Ellen 19(?)- . . . . CLC 44

Curtin, Philip
See Lowndes, Marie Adelaide (Belloc)

Curtis, Price
See Ellison, Harlan (Jay)

Cutrate, Joe
See Spiegelman, Art

Czaczkes, Shmuel Yosef
See Agnon, S(hmuel) Y(osef Halevi)

Dabrowska, Maria (Szumska)
1889-1965 . . . . CLC 15
See also CA 106

Dabydeen, David 1955- . . . . CLC 34
See also BW 1; CA 125

Dacey, Philip 1939- . . . . CLC 51
See also CA 37-40R; CAAS 17; CANR 14,
32; DLB 105

Dagerman, Stig (Halvard)
1923-1954 . . . . TCLC 17
See also CA 117

Dahl, Roald
1916-1990 . . . . . . CLC 1, 6, 18, 79; DAB;
DAC
See also AAYA 15; CA 1-4R; 133;
CANR 6, 32, 37; CLR 1, 7; DAM MST,
NOV, POP; DLB 139; JRDA; MAICYA;
MTCW; SATA 1, 26, 73; SATA-Obit 65

Dahlberg, Edward 1900-1977 . . . CLC 1, 7, 14
See also CA 9-12R; 69-72; CANR 31;
DLB 48; MTCW

Dale, Colin . . . . TCLC 18
See also Lawrence, T(homas) E(dward)

Dale, George E.
See Asimov, Isaac

Daly, Elizabeth 1878-1967 . . . . CLC 52
See also CA 23-24; 25-28R; CAP 2

Daly, Maureen 1921- . . . . CLC 17
See also AAYA 5; CANR 37; JRDA;
MAICYA; SAAS 1; SATA 2

Damas, Leon-Gontran 1912-1978 . . . CLC 84
See also BW 1; CA 125; 73-76

Dana, Richard Henry Sr.
1787-1879 . . . . NCLC 53

Daniel, Samuel 1562(?)-1619 . . . . LC 24
See also DLB 62

Daniels, Brett
See Adler, Renata

Dannay, Frederic 1905-1982 . . . . CLC 11
See also Queen, Ellery
See also CA 1-4R; 107; CANR 1, 39;
DAM POP; DLB 137; MTCW

D'Annunzio, Gabriele
1863-1938 . . . . TCLC 6, 40
See also CA 104

Danois, N. le
See Gourmont, Remy (-Marie-Charles) de

d'Antibes, Germain
See Simenon, Georges (Jacques Christian)

Danticat, Edwidge 1969- . . . . CLC 91

Danvers, Dennis 1947- . . . . CLC 70

Danziger, Paula 1944- . . . . CLC 21
See also AAYA 4; CA 112; 115; CANR 37;
CLR 20; JRDA; MAICYA; SATA 36,
63; SATA-Brief 30

Da Ponte, Lorenzo 1749-1838 . . . . NCLC 50

Dario, Ruben
1867-1916 . . . . TCLC 4; HLC; PC 15
See also CA 131; DAM MULT; HW;
MTCW

Darley, George 1795-1846 . . . . NCLC 2
See also DLB 96

de Man, Paul (Adolph Michel)
    1919-1983 . . . . **CLC 55**
    See also CA 128; 111; DLB 67; MTCW

De Marinis, Rick 1934- . . . . **CLC 54**
    See also CA 57-60; CANR 9, 25, 50

Demby, William 1922- . . . . . . **CLC 53; BLC**
    See also BW 1; CA 81-84; DAM MULT;
    DLB 33

Demijohn, Thom
    See Disch, Thomas M(ichael)

de Montherlant, Henry (Milon)
    See Montherlant, Henry (Milon) de

Demosthenes 384B.C.-322B.C. . . . **CMLC 13**

de Natale, Francine
    See Malzberg, Barry N(athaniel)

Denby, Edwin (Orr) 1903-1983 . . . . . **CLC 48**
    See also CA 138; 110

Denis, Julio
    See Cortazar, Julio

Denmark, Harrison
    See Zelazny, Roger (Joseph)

Dennis, John 1658-1734 . . . . **LC 11**
    See also DLB 101

Dennis, Nigel (Forbes) 1912-1989 . . . . **CLC 8**
    See also CA 25-28R; 129; DLB 13, 15;
    MTCW

De Palma, Brian (Russell) 1940- . . . . **CLC 20**
    See also CA 109

De Quincey, Thomas 1785-1859 . . . **NCLC 4**
    See also CDBLB 1789-1832; DLB 110; 144

Deren, Eleanora 1908(?)-1961
    See Deren, Maya
    See also CA 111

Deren, Maya . . . . **CLC 16**
    See also Deren, Eleanora

Derleth, August (William)
    1909-1971 . . . . **CLC 31**
    See also CA 1-4R; 29-32R; CANR 4;
    DLB 9; SATA 5

Der Nister 1884-1950 . . . . **TCLC 56**

de Routisie, Albert
    See Aragon, Louis

Derrida, Jacques 1930- . . . . **CLC 24, 87**
    See also CA 124; 127

Derry Down Derry
    See Lear, Edward

Dersonnes, Jacques
    See Simenon, Georges (Jacques Christian)

Desai, Anita 1937- . . . . . . **CLC 19, 37; DAB**
    See also CA 81-84; CANR 33; DAM NOV;
    MTCW; SATA 63

de Saint-Luc, Jean
    See Glassco, John

de Saint Roman, Arnaud
    See Aragon, Louis

Descartes, Rene 1596-1650 . . . . **LC 20**

De Sica, Vittorio 1901(?)-1974 . . . . . **CLC 20**
    See also CA 117

Desnos, Robert 1900-1945 . . . . **TCLC 22**
    See also CA 121

Destouches, Louis-Ferdinand
    1894-1961 . . . . **CLC 9, 15**
    See also Celine, Louis-Ferdinand
    See also CA 85-88; CANR 28; MTCW

Deutsch, Babette 1895-1982 . . . . **CLC 18**
    See also CA 1-4R; 108; CANR 4; DLB 45;
    SATA 1; SATA-Obit 33

Devenant, William 1606-1649 . . . . **LC 13**

Devkota, Laxmiprasad
    1909-1959 . . . . **TCLC 23**
    See also CA 123

De Voto, Bernard (Augustine)
    1897-1955 . . . . **TCLC 29**
    See also CA 113; DLB 9

De Vries, Peter
    1910-1993 . . . . **CLC 1, 2, 3, 7, 10, 28, 46**
    See also CA 17-20R; 142; CANR 41;
    DAM NOV; DLB 6; DLBY 82; MTCW

Dexter, Martin
    See Faust, Frederick (Schiller)

Dexter, Pete 1943- . . . . **CLC 34, 55**
    See also BEST 89:2; CA 127; 131;
    DAM POP; INT 131; MTCW

Diamano, Silmang
    See Senghor, Leopold Sedar

Diamond, Neil 1941- . . . . **CLC 30**
    See also CA 108

Diaz del Castillo, Bernal 1496-1584 . . **LC 31**

di Bassetto, Corno
    See Shaw, George Bernard

Dick, Philip K(indred)
    1928-1982 . . . . **CLC 10, 30, 72**
    See also CA 49-52; 106; CANR 2, 16;
    DAM NOV, POP; DLB 8; MTCW

Dickens, Charles (John Huffam)
    1812-1870 . . . . . . **NCLC 3, 8, 18, 26, 37,**
       50; DA; DAB; DAC; SSC 17; WLC
    See also CDBLB 1832-1890; DAM MST,
    NOV; DLB 21, 55, 70, 159; JRDA;
    MAICYA; SATA 15

Dickey, James (Lafayette)
    1923- . . . . **CLC 1, 2, 4, 7, 10, 15, 47**
    See also AITN 1, 2; CA 9-12R; CABS 2;
    CANR 10, 48; CDALB 1968-1988;
    DAM NOV, POET, POP; DLB 5;
    DLBD 7; DLBY 82, 93; INT CANR-10;
    MTCW

Dickey, William 1928-1994 . . . . . . **CLC 3, 28**
    See also CA 9-12R; 145; CANR 24; DLB 5

Dickinson, Charles 1951- . . . . **CLC 49**
    See also CA 128

Dickinson, Emily (Elizabeth)
    1830-1886 . . . . **NCLC 21; DA; DAB;**
       DAC; PC 1; WLC
    See also CDALB 1865-1917; DAM MST,
    POET; DLB 1; SATA 29

Dickinson, Peter (Malcolm)
    1927- . . . . **CLC 12, 35**
    See also AAYA 9; CA 41-44R; CANR 31;
    CLR 29; DLB 87, 161; JRDA; MAICYA;
    SATA 5, 62

Dickson, Carr
    See Carr, John Dickson

Dickson, Carter
    See Carr, John Dickson

Diderot, Denis 1713-1784 . . . . **LC 26**

Didion, Joan 1934- . . . . . **CLC 1, 3, 8, 14, 32**
    See also AITN 1; CA 5-8R; CANR 14;
    CDALB 1968-1988; DAM NOV; DLB 2;
    DLBY 81, 86; MTCW

Dietrich, Robert
    See Hunt, E(verette) Howard, (Jr.)

Dillard, Annie 1945- . . . . **CLC 9, 60**
    See also AAYA 6; CA 49-52; CANR 3, 43;
    DAM NOV; DLBY 80; MTCW;
    SATA 10

Dillard, R(ichard) H(enry) W(ilde)
    1937- . . . . **CLC 5**
    See also CA 21-24R; CAAS 7; CANR 10;
    DLB 5

Dillon, Eilis 1920-1994 . . . . **CLC 17**
    See also CA 9-12R; 147; CAAS 3; CANR 4,
    38; CLR 26; MAICYA; SATA 2, 74;
    SATA-Obit 83

Dimont, Penelope
    See Mortimer, Penelope (Ruth)

Dinesen, Isak . . . . **CLC 10, 29; SSC 7**
    See also Blixen, Karen (Christentze
    Dinesen)

Ding Ling . . . . **CLC 68**
    See also Chiang Pin-chin

Disch, Thomas M(ichael) 1940- . . . **CLC 7, 36**
    See also AAYA 17; CA 21-24R; CAAS 4;
    CANR 17, 36; CLR 18; DLB 8;
    MAICYA; MTCW; SAAS 15; SATA 54

Disch, Tom
    See Disch, Thomas M(ichael)

d'Isly, Georges
    See Simenon, Georges (Jacques Christian)

Disraeli, Benjamin 1804-1881 . . **NCLC 2, 39**
    See also DLB 21, 55

Ditcum, Steve
    See Crumb, R(obert)

Dixon, Paige
    See Corcoran, Barbara

Dixon, Stephen 1936- . . . . . . **CLC 52; SSC 16**
    See also CA 89-92; CANR 17, 40; DLB 130

Dobell, Sydney Thompson
    1824-1874 . . . . **NCLC 43**
    See also DLB 32

Doblin, Alfred . . . . **TCLC 13**
    See also Doeblin, Alfred

Dobrolyubov, Nikolai Alexandrovich
    1836-1861 . . . . **NCLC 5**

Dobyns, Stephen 1941- . . . . **CLC 37**
    See also CA 45-48; CANR 2, 18

Doctorow, E(dgar) L(aurence)
    1931- . . . . . **CLC 6, 11, 15, 18, 37, 44, 65**
    See also AITN 2; BEST 89:3; CA 45-48;
    CANR 2, 33, 51; CDALB 1968-1988;
    DAM NOV, POP; DLB 2, 28; DLBY 80;
    MTCW

Dodgson, Charles Lutwidge 1832-1898
    See Carroll, Lewis
    See also CLR 2; DA; DAB; DAC;
    DAM MST, NOV, POET; MAICYA;
    YABC 2

Dodson, Owen (Vincent)
1914-1983 .... **CLC 79; BLC**
See also BW 1; CA 65-68; 110; CANR 24;
DAM MULT; DLB 76

Doeblin, Alfred 1878-1957 .... **TCLC 13**
See also Doblin, Alfred
See also CA 110; 141; DLB 66

Doerr, Harriet 1910- .... **CLC 34**
See also CA 117; 122; CANR 47; INT 122

Domecq, H(onorio) Bustos
See Bioy Casares, Adolfo; Borges, Jorge
Luis

Domini, Rey
See Lorde, Audre (Geraldine)

Dominique
See Proust, (Valentin-Louis-George-Eugene-)
Marcel

Don, A
See Stephen, Leslie

Donaldson, Stephen R. 1947- .... **CLC 46**
See also CA 89-92; CANR 13; DAM POP;
INT CANR-13

Donleavy, J(ames) P(atrick)
1926- .... **CLC 1, 4, 6, 10, 45**
See also AITN 2; CA 9-12R; CANR 24, 49;
DLB 6; INT CANR-24; MTCW

Donne, John
1572-1631 .... **LC 10, 24; DA; DAB;**
DAC; PC 1
See also CDBLB Before 1660; DAM MST,
POET; DLB 121, 151

Donnell, David 1939(?)- .... **CLC 34**

Donoghue, P. S.
See Hunt, E(verette) Howard, (Jr.)

Donoso (Yanez), Jose
1924- .... **CLC 4, 8, 11, 32; HLC**
See also CA 81-84; CANR 32;
DAM MULT; DLD 113; HW; MTCW

Donovan, John 1928-1992 .... **CLC 35**
See also CA 97-100; 137; CLR 3;
MAICYA; SATA 72; SATA-Brief 29

Don Roberto
See Cunninghame Graham, R(obert)
B(ontine)

Doolittle, Hilda
1886-1961 ..... **CLC 3, 8, 14, 31, 34, 73;**
DA; DAC; PC 5; WLC
See also H. D.
See also CA 97-100; CANR 35; DAM MST,
POET; DLB 4, 45; MTCW

Dorfman, Ariel 1942- .... **CLC 48, 77; HLC**
See also CA 124; 130; DAM MULT; HW;
INT 130

Dorn, Edward (Merton) 1929- ... **CLC 10, 18**
See also CA 93-96; CANR 42; DLB 5;
INT 93-96

Dorsan, Luc
See Simenon, Georges (Jacques Christian)

Dorsange, Jean
See Simenon, Georges (Jacques Christian)

Dos Passos, John (Roderigo)
1896-1970 ...... **CLC 1, 4, 8, 11, 15, 25,**
34, 82; DA; DAB; DAC; WLC
See also CA 1-4R; 29-32R; CANR 3;
CDALB 1929-1941; DAM MST, NOV;
DLB 4, 9; DLBD 1; MTCW

Dossage, Jean
See Simenon, Georges (Jacques Christian)

Dostoevsky, Fedor Mikhailovich
1821-1881 ..... **NCLC 2, 7, 21, 33, 43;**
DA; DAB; DAC; SSC 2; WLC
See also DAM MST, NOV

Doughty, Charles M(ontagu)
1843-1926 .... **TCLC 27**
See also CA 115; DLB 19, 57

Douglas, Ellen .... **CLC 73**
See also Haxton, Josephine Ayres;
Williamson, Ellen Douglas

Douglas, Gavin 1475(?)-1522 .... **LC 20**

Douglas, Keith 1920-1944 .... **TCLC 40**
See also DLB 27

Douglas, Leonard
See Bradbury, Ray (Douglas)

Douglas, Michael
See Crichton, (John) Michael

Douglass, Frederick
1817(?)-1895 .... **NCLC 7; BLC; DA;**
DAC; WLC
See also CDALB 1640-1865; DAM MST,
MULT; DLB 1, 43, 50, 79; SATA 29

Dourado, (Waldomiro Freitas) Autran
1926- .... **CLC 23, 60**
See also CA 25-28R; CANR 34

Dourado, Waldomiro Autran
See Dourado, (Waldomiro Freitas) Autran

Dove, Rita (Frances)
1952- .... **CLC 50, 81; PC 6**
See also BW 2; CA 109; CAAS 19;
CANR 27, 42; DAM MULT, POET;
DLB 120

Dowell, Coleman 1925-1985 .... **CLC 60**
See also CA 25-28R; 117; CANR 10;
DLB 130

Dowson, Ernest (Christopher)
1867-1900 .... **TCLC 4**
See also CA 105; 150; DLB 19, 135

Doyle, A. Conan
See Doyle, Arthur Conan

Doyle, Arthur Conan
1859-1930 .... **TCLC 7; DA; DAB;**
DAC; SSC 12; WLC
See also AAYA 14; CA 104; 122;
CDBLB 1890-1914; DAM MST, NOV;
DLB 18, 70, 156; MTCW; SATA 24

Doyle, Conan
See Doyle, Arthur Conan

Doyle, John
See Graves, Robert (von Ranke)

Doyle, Roddy 1958(?)- .... **CLC 81**
See also AAYA 14; CA 143

Doyle, Sir A. Conan
See Doyle, Arthur Conan

Doyle, Sir Arthur Conan
See Doyle, Arthur Conan

Dr. A
See Asimov, Isaac; Silverstein, Alvin

Drabble, Margaret
1939- .... **CLC 2, 3, 5, 8, 10, 22, 53;**
DAB; DAC
See also CA 13-16R; CANR 18, 35;
CDBLB 1960 to Present; DAM MST,
NOV, POP; DLB 14, 155; MTCW;
SATA 48

Drapier, M. B.
See Swift, Jonathan

Drayham, James
See Mencken, H(enry) L(ouis)

Drayton, Michael 1563-1631 .... **LC 8**

Dreadstone, Carl
See Campbell, (John) Ramsey

Dreiser, Theodore (Herman Albert)
1871-1945 .... **TCLC 10, 18, 35; DA;**
DAC; WLC
See also CA 106; 132; CDALB 1865-1917;
DAM MST, NOV; DLB 9, 12, 102, 137;
DLBD 1; MTCW

Drexler, Rosalyn 1926- .... **CLC 2, 6**
See also CA 81-84

Dreyer, Carl Theodor 1889-1968 .... **CLC 16**
See also CA 116

Drieu la Rochelle, Pierre(-Eugene)
1893-1945 .... **TCLC 21**
See also CA 117; DLB 72

Drinkwater, John 1882-1937 ...... **TCLC 57**
See also CA 109; 149; DLB 10, 19, 149

Drop Shot
See Cable, George Washington

Droste-Hulshoff, Annette Freiin von
1797-1848 .... **NCLC 3**
See also DLB 133

Drummond, Walter
See Silverberg, Robert

Drummond, William Henry
1854-1907 .... **TCLC 25**
See also DLB 92

Drummond de Andrade, Carlos
1902-1987 .... **CLC 18**
See also Andrade, Carlos Drummond de
See also CA 132; 123

Drury, Allen (Stuart) 1918- .... **CLC 37**
See also CA 57-60; CANR 18;
INT CANR-18

Dryden, John
1631-1700 .... **LC 3, 21; DA; DAB;**
DAC; DC 3; WLC
See also CDBLB 1660-1789; DAM DRAM,
MST, POET; DLB 80, 101, 131

Duberman, Martin 1930- .... **CLC 8**
See also CA 1-4R; CANR 2

Dubie, Norman (Evans) 1945- ...... **CLC 36**
See also CA 69-72; CANR 12; DLB 120

Du Bois, W(illiam) E(dward) B(urghardt)
1868-1963 ...... **CLC 1, 2, 13, 64; BLC;**
DA; DAC; WLC
See also BW 1; CA 85-88; CANR 34;
CDALB 1865-1917; DAM MST, MULT,
NOV; DLB 47, 50, 91; MTCW; SATA 42

Dubus, Andre 1936- ... **CLC 13, 36; SSC 15**
See also CA 21-24R; CANR 17; DLB 130;
INT CANR-17

Duca Minimo
See D'Annunzio, Gabriele

Ducharme, Rejean 1941- .... **CLC 74**
See also DLB 60

Duclos, Charles Pinot 1704-1772 ..... **LC 1**

Dudek, Louis 1918- .... **CLC 11, 19**
See also CA 45-48; CAAS 14; CANR 1;
DLB 88

Duerrenmatt, Friedrich
1921-1990 ...... **CLC 1, 4, 8, 11, 15, 43**
See also CA 17-20R; CANR 33;
DAM DRAM; DLB 69, 124; MTCW

Duffy, Bruce (?)- .... **CLC 50**

Duffy, Maureen 1933- .... **CLC 37**
See also CA 25-28R; CANR 33; DLB 14;
MTCW

Dugan, Alan 1923- .... **CLC 2, 6**
See also CA 81-84; DLB 5

du Gard, Roger Martin
See Martin du Gard, Roger

Duhamel, Georges 1884-1966 .... **CLC 8**
See also CA 81-84; 25-28R; CANR 35;
DLB 65; MTCW

Dujardin, Edouard (Emile Louis)
1861-1949 .... **TCLC 13**
See also CA 109; DLB 123

Dumas, Alexandre (Davy de la Pailleterie)
1802-1870 .... **NCLC 11; DA; DAB;**
DAC; WLC
See also DAM MST, NOV; DLB 119;
SATA 18

Dumas, Alexandre
1824-1895 .... **NCLC 9; DC 1**

Dumas, Claudine
See Malzberg, Barry N(athaniel)

Dumas, Henry L. 1934-1968 ..... **CLC 6, 62**
See also BW 1; CA 85-88; DLB 41

du Maurier, Daphne
1907-1989 .... **CLC 6, 11, 59; DAB;**
DAC; SSC 18
See also CA 5-8R; 128; CANR 6;
DAM MST, POP; MTCW; SATA 27;
SATA-Obit 60

Dunbar, Paul Laurence
1872-1906 ...... **TCLC 2, 12; BLC; DA;**
DAC; PC 5; SSC 8; WLC
See also BW 1; CA 104; 124;
CDALB 1865-1917; DAM MST, MULT,
POET; DLB 50, 54, 78; SATA 34

Dunbar, William 1460(?)-1530(?) .... **LC 20**
See also DLB 132, 146

Duncan, Lois 1934- .... **CLC 26**
See also AAYA 4; CA 1-4R; CANR 2, 23,
36; CLR 29; JRDA; MAICYA; SAAS 2;
SATA 1, 36, 75

Duncan, Robert (Edward)
1919-1988 .... **CLC 1, 2, 4, 7, 15, 41, 55;**
PC 2
See also CA 9-12R; 124; CANR 28;
DAM POET; DLB 5, 16; MTCW

Duncan, Sara Jeannette
1861-1922 .... **TCLC 60**
See also DLB 92

Dunlap, William 1766-1839 .... **NCLC 2**
See also DLB 30, 37, 59

Dunn, Douglas (Eaglesham)
1942- .... **CLC 6, 40**
See also CA 45-48; CANR 2, 33; DLB 40;
MTCW

Dunn, Katherine (Karen) 1945- ..... **CLC 71**
See also CA 33-36R

Dunn, Stephen 1939- .... **CLC 36**
See also CA 33-36R; CANR 12, 48;
DLB 105

Dunne, Finley Peter 1867-1936.... **TCLC 28**
See also CA 108; DLB 11, 23

Dunne, John Gregory 1932- .... **CLC 28**
See also CA 25-28R; CANR 14, 50;
DLBY 80

Dunsany, Edward John Moreton Drax
Plunkett 1878-1957
See Dunsany, Lord
See also CA 104; 148; DLB 10

Dunsany, Lord .... **TCLC 2, 59**
See also Dunsany, Edward John Moreton
Drax Plunkett
See also DLB 77, 153, 156

du Perry, Jean
See Simenon, Georges (Jacques Christian)

Durang, Christopher (Ferdinand)
1949- .... **CLC 27, 38**
See also CA 105; CANR 50

Duras, Marguerite
1914- ...... **CLC 3, 6, 11, 20, 34, 40, 68**
See also CA 25-28R; CANR 50; DLB 83;
MTCW

Durban, (Rosa) Pam 1947- .... **CLC 39**
See also CA 123

Durcan, Paul 1944- .... **CLC 43, 70**
See also CA 134; DAM POET

Durkheim, Emile 1858-1917 ...... **TCLC 55**

Durrell, Lawrence (George)
1912-1990 .... **CLC 1, 4, 6, 8, 13, 27, 41**
See also CA 9-12R; 132; CANR 40;
CDBLB 1945-1960; DAM NOV; DLB 15,
27; DLBY 90; MTCW

Durrenmatt, Friedrich
See Duerrenmatt, Friedrich

Dutt, Toru 1856-1877........... **NCLC 29**

Dwight, Timothy 1752-1817...... **NCLC 13**
See also DLB 37

Dworkin, Andrea 1946- .... **CLC 43**
See also CA 77-80; CAAS 21; CANR 16,
39; INT CANR-16; MTCW

Dwyer, Deanna
See Koontz, Dean R(ay)

Dwyer, K. R.
See Koontz, Dean R(ay)

Dylan, Bob 1941- ...... **CLC 3, 4, 6, 12, 77**
See also CA 41-44R; DLB 16

Eagleton, Terence (Francis) 1943-
See Eagleton, Terry
See also CA 57-60; CANR 7, 23; MTCW

Eagleton, Terry .... **CLC 63**
See also Eagleton, Terence (Francis)

Early, Jack
See Scoppettone, Sandra

East, Michael
See West, Morris L(anglo)

Eastaway, Edward
See Thomas, (Philip) Edward

Eastlake, William (Derry) 1917- ..... **CLC 8**
See also CA 5-8R; CAAS 1; CANR 5;
DLB 6; INT CANR-5

Eastman, Charles A(lexander)
1858-1939 .... **TCLC 55**
See also DAM MULT; NNAL; YABC 1

Eberhart, Richard (Ghormley)
1904- .... **CLC 3, 11, 19, 56**
See also CA 1-4R; CANR 2;
CDALB 1941-1968; DAM POET;
DLB 48; MTCW

Eberstadt, Fernanda 1960- .... **CLC 39**
See also CA 136

Echegaray (y Eizaguirre), Jose (Maria Waldo)
1832-1916 .... **TCLC 4**
See also CA 104; CANR 32; HW; MTCW

Echeverria, (Jose) Esteban (Antonino)
1805-1851 .... **NCLC 18**

Echo
See Proust, (Valentin-Louis-George-Eugene-)
Marcel

Eckert, Allan W. 1931- .... **CLC 17**
See also CA 13-16R; CANR 14, 45;
INT CANR-14; SAAS 21; SATA 29;
SATA-Brief 27

Eckhart, Meister 1260(?)-1328(?) .. **CMLC 9**
See also DLB 115

Eckmar, F. R.
See de Hartog, Jan

Eco, Umberto 1932- .... **CLC 28, 60**
See also BEST 90:1; CA 77-80; CANR 12,
33; DAM NOV, POP; MTCW

Eddison, E(ric) R(ucker)
1882-1945 .... **TCLC 15**
See also CA 109

Edel, (Joseph) Leon 1907- ...... **CLC 29, 34**
See also CA 1-4R; CANR 1, 22; DLB 103;
INT CANR-22

Eden, Emily 1797-1869 .... **NCLC 10**

Edgar, David 1948- .... **CLC 42**
See also CA 57-60; CANR 12;
DAM DRAM; DLB 13; MTCW

Edgerton, Clyde (Carlyle) 1944- ..... **CLC 39**
See also AAYA 17; CA 118; 134; INT 134

Edgeworth, Maria 1768-1849... **NCLC 1, 51**
See also DLB 116, 159; SATA 21

Edmonds, Paul
See Kuttner, Henry

Edmonds, Walter D(umaux) 1903- .. **CLC 35**
See also CA 5-8R; CANR 2; DLB 9;
MAICYA; SAAS 4; SATA 1, 27

Edmondson, Wallace
See Ellison, Harlan (Jay)

Edson, Russell .... **CLC 13**
See also CA 33-36R

Edwards, Bronwen Elizabeth
See Rose, Wendy

Edwards, G(erald) B(asil)
1899-1976 .... **CLC 25**
See also CA 110

Edwards, Gus 1939- .... **CLC 43**
See also CA 108; INT 108

Edwards, Jonathan
1703-1758 . . . . **LC 7; DA; DAC**
See also DAM MST; DLB 24

Efron, Marina Ivanovna Tsvetaeva
See Tsvetaeva (Efron), Marina (Ivanovna)

Ehle, John (Marsden, Jr.) 1925- . . . . **CLC 27**
See also CA 9-12R

Ehrenbourg, Ilya (Grigoryevich)
See Ehrenburg, Ilya (Grigoryevich)

Ehrenburg, Ilya (Grigoryevich)
1891-1967 . . . . **CLC 18, 34, 62**
See also CA 102; 25-28R

Ehrenburg, Ilyo (Grigoryevich)
See Ehrenburg, Ilya (Grigoryevich)

Eich, Guenter 1907-1972 . . . . **CLC 15**
See also CA 111; 93-96; DLB 69, 124

Eichendorff, Joseph Freiherr von
1788-1857 . . . . **NCLC 8**
See also DLB 90

Eigner, Larry . . . . **CLC 9**
See also Eigner, Laurence (Joel)
See also CAAS 23; DLB 5

Eigner, Laurence (Joel) 1927-1996
See Eigner, Larry
See also CA 9-12R; CANR 6

Eiseley, Loren Corey 1907-1977 . . . . . **CLC 7**
See also AAYA 5; CA 1-4R; 73-76;
CANR 6

Eisenstadt, Jill 1963- . . . . **CLC 50**
See also CA 140

Eisenstein, Sergei (Mikhailovich)
1898-1948 . . . . **TCLC 57**
See also CA 114; 149

Eisner, Simon
See Kornbluth, C(yril) M.

Ekeloef, (Bengt) Gunnar
1907-1968 . . . . **CLC 27**
See also CA 123; 25-28R; DAM POET

Ekelof, (Bengt) Gunnar
See Ekeloef, (Bengt) Gunnar

Ekwensi, C. O. D.
See Ekwensi, Cyprian (Odiatu Duaka)

Ekwensi, Cyprian (Odiatu Duaka)
1921- . . . . **CLC 4; BLC**
See also BW 2; CA 29-32R; CANR 18, 42;
DAM MULT; DLB 117; MTCW;
SATA 66

Elaine . . . . **TCLC 18**
See also Leverson, Ada

El Crummo
See Crumb, R(obert)

Elia
See Lamb, Charles

Eliade, Mircea 1907-1986 . . . . **CLC 19**
See also CA 65-68; 119; CANR 30; MTCW

Eliot, A. D.
See Jewett, (Theodora) Sarah Orne

Eliot, Alice
See Jewett, (Theodora) Sarah Orne

Eliot, Dan
See Silverberg, Robert

Eliot, George
1819-1880 . . . . . **NCLC 4, 13, 23, 41, 49;**
DA; DAB; DAC; WLC
See also CDBLB 1832-1890; DAM MST,
NOV; DLB 21, 35, 55

Eliot, John 1604-1690 . . . . **LC 5**
See also DLB 24

Eliot, T(homas) S(tearns)
1888-1965 . . . . . **CLC 1, 2, 3, 6, 9, 10, 13,**
15, 24, 34, 41, 55, 57; DA; DAB; DAC;
PC 5; WLC 2
See also CA 5-8R; 25-28R; CANR 41;
CDALB 1929-1941; DAM DRAM, MST,
POET; DLB 7, 10, 45, 63; DLBY 88;
MTCW

Elizabeth 1866-1941 . . . . **TCLC 41**

Elkin, Stanley L(awrence)
1930-1995 . . . . . . **CLC 4, 6, 9, 14, 27, 51,**
91; SSC 12
See also CA 9-12R; 148; CANR 8, 46;
DAM NOV, POP; DLB 2, 28; DLBY 80;
INT CANR-8; MTCW

Elledge, Scott . . . . **CLC 34**

Elliott, Don
See Silverberg, Robert

Elliott, George P(aul) 1918-1980 . . . . . **CLC 2**
See also CA 1-4R; 97-100; CANR 2

Elliott, Janice 1931- . . . . **CLC 47**
See also CA 13-16R; CANR 8, 29; DLB 14

Elliott, Sumner Locke 1917-1991 . . . **CLC 38**
See also CA 5-8R; 134; CANR 2, 21

Elliott, William
See Bradbury, Ray (Douglas)

Ellis, A. E. . . . . **CLC 7**

Ellis, Alice Thomas . . . . **CLC 40**
See also Haycraft, Anna

Ellis, Bret Easton 1964- . . . . **CLC 39, 71**
See also AAYA 2; CA 118; 123; CANR 51;
DAM POP; INT 123

Ellis, (Henry) Havelock
1859-1939 . . . . **TCLC 14**
See also CA 109

Ellis, Landon
See Ellison, Harlan (Jay)

Ellis, Trey 1962- . . . . **CLC 55**
See also CA 146

Ellison, Harlan (Jay)
1934- . . . . **CLC 1, 13, 42; SSC 14**
See also CA 5-8R; CANR 5, 46;
DAM POP; DLB 8; INT CANR-5;
MTCW

Ellison, Ralph (Waldo)
1914-1994 . . . . **CLC 1, 3, 11, 54, 86;**
BLC; DA; DAB; DAC; WLC
See also BW 1; CA 9-12R; 145; CANR 24;
CDALB 1941-1968; DAM MST, MULT,
NOV; DLB 2, 76; DLBY 94; MTCW

Ellmann, Lucy (Elizabeth) 1956- . . . . **CLC 61**
See also CA 128

Ellmann, Richard (David)
1918-1987 . . . . **CLC 50**
See also BEST 89:2; CA 1-4R; 122;
CANR 2, 28; DLB 103; DLBY 87;
MTCW

Elman, Richard 1934- . . . . **CLC 19**
See also CA 17-20R; CAAS 3; CANR 47

Elron
See Hubbard, L(afayette) Ron(ald)

Eluard, Paul . . . . **TCLC 7, 41**
See also Grindel, Eugene

Elyot, Sir Thomas 1490(?)-1546 . . . . . **LC 11**

Elytis, Odysseus 1911- . . . . **CLC 15, 49**
See also CA 102; DAM POET; MTCW

Emecheta, (Florence Onye) Buchi
1944- . . . . **CLC 14, 48; BLC**
See also BW 2; CA 81-84; CANR 27;
DAM MULT; DLB 117; MTCW;
SATA 66

Emerson, Ralph Waldo
1803-1882 . . . . . **NCLC 1, 38; DA; DAB;**
DAC; WLC
See also CDALB 1640-1865; DAM MST,
POET; DLB 1, 59, 73

Eminescu, Mihail 1850-1889 . . . . . **NCLC 33**

Empson, William
1906-1984 . . . . **CLC 3, 8, 19, 33, 34**
See also CA 17-20R; 112; CANR 31;
DLB 20; MTCW

Enchi Fumiko (Ueda) 1905-1986 . . . . **CLC 31**
See also CA 129; 121

Ende, Michael (Andreas Helmuth)
1929-1995 . . . . **CLC 31**
See also CA 118; 124; 149; CANR 36;
CLR 14; DLB 75; MAICYA; SATA 61;
SATA-Brief 42; SATA-Obit 86

Endo, Shusaku 1923- . . . . . **CLC 7, 14, 19, 54**
See also CA 29-32R; CANR 21;
DAM NOV; MTCW

Engel, Marian 1933-1985 . . . . **CLC 36**
See also CA 25-28R; CANR 12; DLB 53;
INT CANR-12

Engelhardt, Frederick
See Hubbard, L(afayette) Ron(ald)

Enright, D(ennis) J(oseph)
1920- . . . . **CLC 4, 8, 31**
See also CA 1-4R; CANR 1, 42; DLB 27;
SATA 25

Enzensberger, Hans Magnus
1929- . . . . **CLC 43**
See also CA 116; 119

Ephron, Nora 1941- . . . . **CLC 17, 31**
See also AITN 2; CA 65-68; CANR 12, 39

Epsilon
See Betjeman, John

Epstein, Daniel Mark 1948- . . . . **CLC 7**
See also CA 49-52; CANR 2

Epstein, Jacob 1956- . . . . **CLC 19**
See also CA 114

Epstein, Joseph 1937- . . . . **CLC 39**
See also CA 112; 119; CANR 50

Epstein, Leslie 1938- . . . . **CLC 27**
See also CA 73-76; CAAS 12; CANR 23

Equiano, Olaudah
1745(?)-1797 . . . . **LC 16; BLC**
See also DAM MULT; DLB 37, 50

Erasmus, Desiderius 1469(?)-1536 . . . . **LC 16**

Erdman, Paul E(mil) 1932- . . . . **CLC 25**
See also AITN 1; CA 61-64; CANR 13, 43

Author Index

Feinberg, David B. 1956-1994 . . . . . . **CLC 59**
See also CA 135; 147

Feinstein, Elaine 1930- . . . . **CLC 36**
See also CA 69-72; CAAS 1; CANR 31;
DLB 14, 40; MTCW

Feldman, Irving (Mordecai) 1928- . . . . **CLC 7**
See also CA 1-4R; CANR 1

Fellini, Federico 1920-1993 . . . . . **CLC 16, 85**
See also CA 65-68; 143; CANR 33

Felsen, Henry Gregor 1916- . . . . **CLC 17**
See also CA 1-4R; CANR 1; SAAS 2;
SATA 1

Fenton, James Martin 1949- . . . . **CLC 32**
See also CA 102; DLB 40

Ferber, Edna 1887-1968 . . . . **CLC 18**
See also AITN 1; CA 5-8R; 25-28R; DLB 9,
28, 86; MTCW; SATA 7

Ferguson, Helen
See Kavan, Anna

Ferguson, Samuel 1810-1886 . . . . . **NCLC 33**
See also DLB 32

Fergusson, Robert 1750-1774 . . . . **LC 29**
See also DLB 109

Ferling, Lawrence
See Ferlinghetti, Lawrence (Monsanto)

Ferlinghetti, Lawrence (Monsanto)
1919(?)- . . . . **CLC 2, 6, 10, 27; PC 1**
See also CA 5-8R; CANR 3, 41;
CDALB 1941-1968; DAM POET; DLB 5,
16; MTCW

Fernandez, Vicente Garcia Huidobro
See Huidobro Fernandez, Vicente Garcia

Ferrer, Gabriel (Francisco Victor) Miro
See Miro (Ferrer), Gabriel (Francisco
Victor)

Ferrier, Susan (Edmonstone)
1782-1854 . . . . **NCLC 8**
See also DLB 116

Ferrigno, Robert 1948(?)- . . . . **CLC 65**
See also CA 140

Feuchtwanger, Lion 1884-1958 . . . . . **TCLC 3**
See also CA 104; DLB 66

Feuillet, Octave 1821-1890 . . . . . . **NCLC 45**

Feydeau, Georges (Leon Jules Marie)
1862-1921 . . . . **TCLC 22**
See also CA 113; DAM DRAM

Ficino, Marsilio 1433-1499 . . . . **LC 12**

Fiedeler, Hans
See Doeblin, Alfred

Fiedler, Leslie A(aron)
1917- . . . . **CLC 4, 13, 24**
See also CA 9-12R; CANR 7; DLB 28, 67;
MTCW

Field, Andrew 1938- . . . . **CLC 44**
See also CA 97-100; CANR 25

Field, Eugene 1850-1895 . . . . **NCLC 3**
See also DLB 23, 42, 140; DLBD 13;
MAICYA; SATA 16

Field, Gans T.
See Wellman, Manly Wade

Field, Michael . . . . **TCLC 43**

Field, Peter
See Hobson, Laura Z(ametkin)

Fielding, Henry
1707-1754 . . . . . . **LC 1; DA; DAB; DAC;**
WLC
See also CDBLB 1660-1789; DAM DRAM,
MST, NOV; DLB 39, 84, 101

Fielding, Sarah 1710-1768 . . . . **LC 1**
See also DLB 39

Fierstein, Harvey (Forbes) 1954- . . . **CLC 33**
See also CA 123; 129; DAM DRAM, POP

Figes, Eva 1932- . . . . **CLC 31**
See also CA 53-56; CANR 4, 44; DLB 14

Finch, Robert (Duer Claydon)
1900- . . . . **CLC 18**
See also CA 57-60; CANR 9, 24, 49;
DLB 88

Findley, Timothy 1930- . . . . . . **CLC 27; DAC**
See also CA 25-28R; CANR 12, 42;
DAM MST; DLB 53

Fink, William
See Mencken, H(enry) L(ouis)

Firbank, Louis 1942-
See Reed, Lou
See also CA 117

Firbank, (Arthur Annesley) Ronald
1886-1926 . . . . **TCLC 1**
See also CA 104; DLB 36

Fisher, M(ary) F(rances) K(ennedy)
1908-1992 . . . . **CLC 76, 87**
See also CA 77-80; 138; CANR 44

Fisher, Roy 1930- . . . . **CLC 25**
See also CA 81-84; CAAS 10; CANR 16;
DLB 40

Fisher, Rudolph
1897-1934 . . . . **TCLC 11; BLC**
See also BW 1; CA 107; 124; DAM MULT;
DLB 51, 102

Fisher, Vardis (Alvero) 1895-1968 . . . . **CLC 7**
See also CA 5-8R; 25-28R; DLB 9

Fiske, Tarleton
See Bloch, Robert (Albert)

Fitch, Clarke
See Sinclair, Upton (Beall)

Fitch, John IV
See Cormier, Robert (Edmund)

Fitzgerald, Captain Hugh
See Baum, L(yman) Frank

FitzGerald, Edward 1809-1883 . . . . **NCLC 9**
See also DLB 32

Fitzgerald, F(rancis) Scott (Key)
1896-1940 . . . . **TCLC 1, 6, 14, 28, 55;**
DA; DAB; DAC; SSC 6; WLC
See also AITN 1; CA 110; 123;
CDALB 1917-1929; DAM MST, NOV;
DLB 4, 9, 86; DLBD 1; DLBY 81;
MTCW

Fitzgerald, Penelope 1916- . . . **CLC 19, 51, 61**
See also CA 85-88; CAAS 10; DLB 14

Fitzgerald, Robert (Stuart)
1910-1985 . . . . **CLC 39**
See also CA 1-4R; 114; CANR 1; DLBY 80

FitzGerald, Robert D(avid)
1902-1987 . . . . **CLC 19**
See also CA 17-20R

Fitzgerald, Zelda (Sayre)
1900-1948 . . . . **TCLC 52**
See also CA 117; 126; DLBY 84

Flanagan, Thomas (James Bonner)
1923- . . . . **CLC 25, 52**
See also CA 108; DLBY 80; INT 108;
MTCW

Flaubert, Gustave
1821-1880 . . . . **NCLC 2, 10, 19; DA;**
DAB; DAC; SSC 11; WLC
See also DAM MST, NOV; DLB 119

Flecker, Herman Elroy
See Flecker, (Herman) James Elroy

Flecker, (Herman) James Elroy
1884-1915 . . . . **TCLC 43**
See also CA 109; 150; DLB 10, 19

Fleming, Ian (Lancaster)
1908-1964 . . . . **CLC 3, 30**
See also CA 5-8R; CDBLB 1945-1960;
DAM POP; DLB 87; MTCW; SATA 9

Fleming, Thomas (James) 1927- . . . . **CLC 37**
See also CA 5-8R; CANR 10;
INT CANR-10; SATA 8

Fletcher, John 1579-1625 . . . . **DC 6**
See also CDBLB Before 1660; DLB 58

Fletcher, John Gould 1886-1950 . . . **TCLC 35**
See also CA 107; DLB 4, 45

Fleur, Paul
See Pohl, Frederik

Flooglebuckle, Al
See Spiegelman, Art

Flying Officer X
See Bates, H(erbert) E(rnest)

Fo, Dario 1926- . . . . **CLC 32**
See also CA 116; 128; DAM DRAM;
MTCW

Fogarty, Jonathan Titulescu Esq.
See Farrell, James T(homas)

Folke, Will
See Bloch, Robert (Albert)

Follett, Ken(neth Martin) 1949- . . . . **CLC 18**
See also AAYA 6; BEST 89:4; CA 81-84;
CANR 13, 33; DAM NOV, POP;
DLB 87; DLBY 81; INT CANR-33;
MTCW

Fontane, Theodor 1819-1898 . . . . . **NCLC 26**
See also DLB 129

Foote, Horton 1916- . . . . **CLC 51, 91**
See also CA 73-76; CANR 34, 51;
DAM DRAM; DLB 26; INT CANR-34

Foote, Shelby 1916- . . . . **CLC 75**
See also CA 5-8R; CANR 3, 45;
DAM NOV, POP; DLB 2, 17

Forbes, Esther 1891-1967 . . . . **CLC 12**
See also AAYA 17; CA 13-14; 25-28R;
CAP 1; CLR 27; DLB 22; JRDA;
MAICYA; SATA 2

Forche, Carolyn (Louise)
1950- . . . . **CLC 25, 83, 86; PC 10**
See also CA 109; 117; CANR 50;
DAM POET; DLB 5; INT 117

Ford, Elbur
See Hibbert, Eleanor Alice Burford

Ford, Ford Madox
1873-1939 . . . . **TCLC 1, 15, 39, 57**
See also CA 104; 132; CDBLB 1914-1945;
DAM NOV; DLB 162; MTCW

Ford, John 1895-1973. . . . . **CLC 16**
See also CA 45-48

Ford, Richard 1944- . . . . **CLC 46**
See also CA 69-72; CANR 11, 47

Ford, Webster
See Masters, Edgar Lee

Foreman, Richard 1937-. . . . . **CLC 50**
See also CA 65-68; CANR 32

Forester, C(ecil) S(cott)
1899-1966 . . . . **CLC 35**
See also CA 73-76; 25-28R; SATA 13

Forez
See Mauriac, Francois (Charles)

Forman, James Douglas 1932-. . . . . . **CLC 21**
See also AAYA 17; CA 9-12R; CANR 4,
19, 42; JRDA; MAICYA; SATA 8, 70

Fornes, Maria Irene 1930-. . . . . . **CLC 39, 61**
See also CA 25-28R; CANR 28; DLB 7;
HW; INT CANR-28; MTCW

Forrest, Leon 1937- . . . . **CLC 4**
See also BW 2; CA 89-92; CAAS 7;
CANR 25; DLB 33

Forster, E(dward) M(organ)
1879-1970 . . . . . **CLC 1, 2, 3, 4, 9, 10, 13,
15, 22, 45, 77; DA; DAB; DAC; WLC**
See also AAYA 2; CA 13-14; 25-28R;
CANR 45; CAP 1; CDBLB 1914-1945;
DAM MST, NOV; DLB 34, 98, 162;
DLBD 10; MTCW; SATA 57

Forster, John 1812-1876 . . . . **NCLC 11**
See also DLB 144

Forsyth, Frederick 1938-. . . . . . **CLC 2, 5, 36**
See also BEST 89:4; CA 85-88; CANR 38;
DAM NOV, POP; DLB 87; MTCW

Forten, Charlotte L. . . . . **TCLC 16; BLC**
See also Grimke, Charlotte L(ottie) Forten
See also DLB 50

Foscolo, Ugo 1778-1827. . . . . **NCLC 8**

Fosse, Bob . . . . **CLC 20**
See also Fosse, Robert Louis

Fosse, Robert Louis 1927-1987
See Fosse, Bob
See also CA 110; 123

Foster, Stephen Collins
1826-1864 . . . . **NCLC 26**

Foucault, Michel
1926-1984 . . . . **CLC 31, 34, 69**
See also CA 105; 113; CANR 34; MTCW

Fouque, Friedrich (Heinrich Karl) de la Motte
1777-1843 . . . . **NCLC 2**
See also DLB 90

Fourier, Charles 1772-1837 . . . . . . **NCLC 51**

Fournier, Henri Alban 1886-1914
See Alain-Fournier
See also CA 104

Fournier, Pierre 1916-. . . . . **CLC 11**
See also Gascar, Pierre
See also CA 89-92; CANR 16, 40

Fowles, John
1926- . . . . . . **CLC 1, 2, 3, 4, 6, 9, 10, 15,
33, 87; DAB; DAC**
See also CA 5-8R; CANR 25; CDBLB 1960
to Present; DAM MST; DLB 14, 139;
MTCW; SATA 22

Fox, Paula 1923-. . . . . **CLC 2, 8**
See also AAYA 3; CA 73-76; CANR 20,
36; CLR 1; DLB 52; JRDA; MAICYA;
MTCW; SATA 17, 60

Fox, William Price (Jr.) 1926- . . . . . **CLC 22**
See also CA 17-20R; CAAS 19; CANR 11;
DLB 2; DLBY 81

Foxe, John 1516(?)-1587 . . . . **LC 14**

Frame, Janet . . . . **CLC 2, 3, 6, 22, 66**
See also Clutha, Janet Paterson Frame

France, Anatole. . . . . **TCLC 9**
See also Thibault, Jacques Anatole Francois
See also DLB 123

Francis, Claude 19(?)- . . . . **CLC 50**

Francis, Dick 1920- . . . . **CLC 2, 22, 42**
See also AAYA 5; BEST 89:3; CA 5-8R;
CANR 9, 42; CDBLB 1960 to Present;
DAM POP; DLB 87; INT CANR-9;
MTCW

Francis, Robert (Churchill)
1901-1987 . . . . **CLC 15**
See also CA 1-4R; 123; CANR 1

Frank, Anne(lies Marie)
1929-1945 . . . . **TCLC 17; DA; DAB;
DAC; WLC**
See also AAYA 12; CA 113; 133;
DAM MST; MTCW; SATA-Brief 42

Frank, Elizabeth 1945-. . . . . **CLC 39**
See also CA 121; 126; INT 126

Franklin, Benjamin
See Hasek, Jaroslav (Matej Frantisek)

Franklin, Benjamin
1706-1790 . . . . . **LC 25; DA; DAB; DAC**
See also CDALB 1640-1865; DAM MST;
DLB 24, 43, 73

Franklin, (Stella Maraia Sarah) Miles
1879-1954 . . . . **TCLC 7**
See also CA 104

Fraser, (Lady) Antonia (Pakenham)
1932- . . . . **CLC 32**
See also CA 85-88; CANR 44; MTCW;
SATA-Brief 32

Fraser, George MacDonald 1925-. . . . **CLC 7**
See also CA 45-48; CANR 2, 48

Fraser, Sylvia 1935-. . . . . **CLC 64**
See also CA 45-48; CANR 1, 16

Frayn, Michael 1933-. . . . . . . **CLC 3, 7, 31, 47**
See also CA 5-8R; CANR 30;
DAM DRAM, NOV; DLB 13, 14;
MTCW

Fraze, Candida (Merrill) 1945-. . . . . **CLC 50**
See also CA 126

Frazer, J(ames) G(eorge)
1854-1941 . . . . **TCLC 32**
See also CA 118

Frazer, Robert Caine
See Creasey, John

Frazer, Sir James George
See Frazer, J(ames) G(eorge)

Frazier, Ian 1951-. . . . . **CLC 46**
See also CA 130

Frederic, Harold 1856-1898. . . . . . **NCLC 10**
See also DLB 12, 23; DLBD 13

Frederick, John
See Faust, Frederick (Schiller)

Frederick the Great 1712-1786 . . . . . . **LC 14**

Fredro, Aleksander 1793-1876. . . . . **NCLC 8**

Freeling, Nicolas 1927- . . . . **CLC 38**
See also CA 49-52; CAAS 12; CANR 1, 17,
50; DLB 87

Freeman, Douglas Southall
1886-1953 . . . . **TCLC 11**
See also CA 109; DLB 17

Freeman, Judith 1946-. . . . . **CLC 55**
See also CA 148

Freeman, Mary Eleanor Wilkins
1852-1930 . . . . **TCLC 9; SSC 1**
See also CA 106; DLB 12, 78

Freeman, R(ichard) Austin
1862-1943 . . . . **TCLC 21**
See also CA 113; DLB 70

French, Albert 1943- . . . . **CLC 86**

French, Marilyn 1929-. . . . . . **CLC 10, 18, 60**
See also CA 69-72; CANR 3, 31;
DAM DRAM, NOV, POP;
INT CANR-31; MTCW

French, Paul
See Asimov, Isaac

Freneau, Philip Morin 1752-1832. . **NCLC 1**
See also DLB 37, 43

Freud, Sigmund 1856-1939 . . . . **TCLC 52**
See also CA 115; 133; MTCW

Friedan, Betty (Naomi) 1921-. . . . . . **CLC 74**
See also CA 65-68; CANR 18, 45; MTCW

Friedlaender, Saul 1932- . . . . **CLC 90**
See also CA 117; 130

Friedman, B(ernard) H(arper)
1926- . . . . **CLC 7**
See also CA 1-4R; CANR 3, 48

Friedman, Bruce Jay 1930-. . . . **CLC 3, 5, 56**
See also CA 9-12R; CANR 25; DLB 2, 28;
INT CANR-25

Friel, Brian 1929-. . . . . **CLC 5, 42, 59**
See also CA 21-24R; CANR 33; DLB 13;
MTCW

Friis-Baastad, Babbis Ellinor
1921-1970 . . . . **CLC 12**
See also CA 17-20R; 134; SATA 7

Frisch, Max (Rudolf)
1911-1991 . . . . . **CLC 3, 9, 14, 18, 32, 44**
See also CA 85-88; 134; CANR 32;
DAM DRAM, NOV; DLB 69, 124;
MTCW

Fromentin, Eugene (Samuel Auguste)
1820-1876 . . . . **NCLC 10**
See also DLB 123

Frost, Frederick
See Faust, Frederick (Schiller)

Graduate of Oxford, A
See Ruskin, John

Graham, John
See Phillips, David Graham

Graham, Jorie 1951-.............. **CLC 48**
See also CA 111; DLB 120

Graham, R(obert) B(ontine) Cunninghame
See Cunninghame Graham, R(obert) B(ontine)
See also DLB 98, 135

Graham, Robert
See Haldeman, Joe (William)

Graham, Tom
See Lewis, (Harry) Sinclair

Graham, W(illiam) S(ydney)
1918-1986 .... **CLC 29**
See also CA 73-76; 118; DLB 20

Graham, Winston (Mawdsley)
1910- .... **CLC 23**
See also CA 49-52; CANR 2, 22, 45;
DLB 77

Grant, Skeeter
See Spiegelman, Art

Granville-Barker, Harley
1877-1946 .... **TCLC 2**
See also Barker, Harley Granville
See also CA 104; DAM DRAM

Grass, Guenter (Wilhelm)
1927-..... **CLC 1, 2, 4, 6, 11, 15, 22, 32,
49, 88; DA; DAB; DAC; WLC**
See also CA 13-16R; CANR 20;
DAM MST, NOV; DLB 75, 124; MTCW

Gratton, Thomas
See Hulme, T(homas) E(rnest)

Grau, Shirley Ann
1929- .... **CLC 4, 9; SSC 15**
See also CA 89-92; CANR 22; DLB 2;
INT CANR-22; MTCW

Gravel, Fern
See Hall, James Norman

Graver, Elizabeth 1964-........... **CLC 70**
See also CA 135

Graves, Richard Perceval 1945- .... **CLC 44**
See also CA 65-68; CANR 9, 26, 51

Graves, Robert (von Ranke)
1895-1985 ...... **CLC 1, 2, 6, 11, 39, 44,
45; DAB; DAC; PC 6**
See also CA 5-8R; 117; CANR 5, 36;
CDBLB 1914-1945; DAM MST, POET;
DLB 20, 100; DLBY 85; MTCW;
SATA 45

Gray, Alasdair (James) 1934- ...... **CLC 41**
See also CA 126; CANR 47; INT 126;
MTCW

Gray, Amlin 1946- .... **CLC 29**
See also CA 138

Gray, Francine du Plessix 1930-.... **CLC 22**
See also BEST 90:3; CA 61-64; CAAS 2;
CANR 11, 33; DAM NOV;
INT CANR-11; MTCW

Gray, John (Henry) 1866-1934 .... **TCLC 19**
See also CA 119

Gray, Simon (James Holliday)
1936- .... **CLC 9, 14, 36**
See also AITN 1; CA 21-24R; CAAS 3;
CANR 32; DLB 13; MTCW

Gray, Spalding 1941- .... **CLC 49**
See also CA 128; DAM POP

Gray, Thomas
1716-1771 ...... **LC 4; DA; DAB; DAC;
PC 2; WLC**
See also CDBLB 1660-1789; DAM MST;
DLB 109

Grayson, David
See Baker, Ray Stannard

Grayson, Richard (A.) 1951-........ **CLC 38**
See also CA 85-88; CANR 14, 31

Greeley, Andrew M(oran) 1928-.... **CLC 28**
See also CA 5-8R; CAAS 7; CANR 7, 43;
DAM POP; MTCW

Green, Brian
See Card, Orson Scott

Green, Hannah
See Greenberg, Joanne (Goldenberg)

Green, Hannah .... **CLC 3**
See also CA 73-76

Green, Henry................... **CLC 2, 13**
See also Yorke, Henry Vincent
See also DLB 15

Green, Julian (Hartridge) 1900-
See Green, Julien
See also CA 21-24R; CANR 33; DLB 4, 72;
MTCW

Green, Julien................ **CLC 3, 11, 77**
See also Green, Julian (Hartridge)

Green, Paul (Eliot) 1894-1981...... **CLC 25**
See also AITN 1; CA 5-8R; 103; CANR 3;
DAM DRAM; DLB 7, 9; DLBY 81

Greenberg, Ivan 1908-1973
See Rahv, Philip
See also CA 85-88

Greenberg, Joanne (Goldenberg)
1932- .... **CLC 7, 30**
See also AAYA 12; CA 5-8R, CANR 14,
32; SATA 25

Greenberg, Richard 1959(?)-....... **CLC 57**
See also CA 138

Greene, Bette 1934- .... **CLC 30**
See also AAYA 7; CA 53-56; CANR 4;
CLR 2; JRDA; MAICYA; SAAS 16;
SATA 8

Greene, Gael .... **CLC 8**
See also CA 13-16R; CANR 10

Greene, Graham
1904-1991 .... **CLC 1, 3, 6, 9, 14, 18, 27,
37, 70, 72; DA; DAB; DAC; WLC**
See also AITN 2; CA 13-16R; 133;
CANR 35; CDBLB 1945-1960;
DAM MST, NOV; DLB 13, 15, 77, 100,
162; DLBY 91; MTCW; SATA 20

Greer, Richard
See Silverberg, Robert

Gregor, Arthur 1923-.............. **CLC 9**
See also CA 25-28R; CAAS 10; CANR 11;
SATA 36

Gregor, Lee
See Pohl, Frederik

Gregory, Isabella Augusta (Persse)
1852-1932 .... **TCLC 1**
See also CA 104; DLB 10

Gregory, J. Dennis
See Williams, John A(lfred)

Grendon, Stephen
See Derleth, August (William)

Grenville, Kate 1950-............. **CLC 61**
See also CA 118

Grenville, Pelham
See Wodehouse, P(elham) G(renville)

Greve, Felix Paul (Berthold Friedrich)
1879-1948
See Grove, Frederick Philip
See also CA 104; 141; DAC; DAM MST

Grey, Zane 1872-1939 .... **TCLC 6**
See also CA 104; 132; DAM POP; DLB 9;
MTCW

Grieg, (Johan) Nordahl (Brun)
1902-1943 .... **TCLC 10**
See also CA 107

Grieve, C(hristopher) M(urray)
1892-1978 .... **CLC 11, 19**
See also MacDiarmid, Hugh; Pteleon
See also CA 5-8R; 85-88; CANR 33;
DAM POET; MTCW

Griffin, Gerald 1803-1840 .... **NCLC 7**
See also DLB 159

Griffin, John Howard 1920-1980.... **CLC 68**
See also AITN 1; CA 1-4R; 101; CANR 2

Griffin, Peter 1942- .... **CLC 39**
See also CA 136

Griffiths, Trevor 1935-......... **CLC 13, 52**
See also CA 97-100; CANR 45; DLB 13

Grigson, Geoffrey (Edward Harvey)
1905-1985 .... **CLC 7, 39**
See also CA 25-28R; 118; CANR 20, 33;
DLB 27; MTCW

Grillparzer, Franz 1791-1872...... **NCLC 1**
See also DLB 133

Grimble, Reverend Charles James
See Eliot, T(homas) S(tearns)

Grimke, Charlotte L(ottie) Forten
1837(?)-1914
See Forten, Charlotte L.
See also BW 1; CA 117; 124; DAM MULT,
POET

Grimm, Jacob Ludwig Karl
1785-1863 .... **NCLC 3**
See also DLB 90; MAICYA; SATA 22

Grimm, Wilhelm Karl 1786-1859 .. **NCLC 3**
See also DLB 90; MAICYA; SATA 22

**Grimmelshausen, Johann Jakob Christoffel
von** 1621-1676 .... **LC 6**

Grindel, Eugene 1895-1952
See Eluard, Paul
See also CA 104

Grisham, John 1955- .... **CLC 84**
See also AAYA 14; CA 138; CANR 47;
DAM POP

Grossman, David 1954- .... **CLC 67**
See also CA 138

Grossman, Vasily (Semenovich)
1905-1964 .... **CLC 41**
See also CA 124; 130; MTCW

Grove, Frederick Philip . . . . **TCLC 4**
See also Greve, Felix Paul (Berthold Friedrich)
See also DLB 92

Grubb
See Crumb, R(obert)

Grumbach, Doris (Isaac)
1918- . . . . **CLC 13, 22, 64**
See also CA 5-8R; CAAS 2; CANR 9, 42;
INT CANR-9

Grundtvig, Nicolai Frederik Severin
1783-1872 . . . . **NCLC 1**

Grunge
See Crumb, R(obert)

Grunwald, Lisa 1959- . . . . **CLC 44**
See also CA 120

Guare, John 1938- . . . . **CLC 8, 14, 29, 67**
See also CA 73-76; CANR 21;
DAM DRAM; DLB 7; MTCW

Gudjonsson, Halldor Kiljan 1902-
See Laxness, Halldor
See also CA 103

Guenter, Erich
See Eich, Guenter

Guest, Barbara 1920- . . . . **CLC 34**
See also CA 25-28R; CANR 11, 44; DLB 5

Guest, Judith (Ann) 1936- . . . . **CLC 8, 30**
See also AAYA 7; CA 77-80; CANR 15;
DAM NOV, POP; INT CANR-15;
MTCW

Guevara, Che . . . . **CLC 87; HLC**
See also Guevara (Serna), Ernesto

Guevara (Serna), Ernesto 1928-1967
See Guevara, Che
See also CA 127; 111; DAM MULT; HW

Guild, Nicholas M. 1944- . . . . **CLC 33**
See also CA 93-96

Guillemin, Jacques
See Sartre, Jean-Paul

Guillen, Jorge 1893-1984 . . . . **CLC 11**
See also CA 89-92; 112; DAM MULT,
POET; DLB 108; HW

Guillen (y Batista), Nicolas (Cristobal)
1902-1989 . . . . . **CLC 48, 79; BLC; HLC**
See also BW 2; CA 116; 125; 129;
DAM MST, MULT, POET; HW

Guillevic, (Eugene) 1907- . . . . **CLC 33**
See also CA 93-96

Guillois
See Desnos, Robert

Guiney, Louise Imogen
1861-1920 . . . . **TCLC 41**
See also DLB 54

Guiraldes, Ricardo (Guillermo)
1886-1927 . . . . **TCLC 39**
See also CA 131; HW; MTCW

Gumilev, Nikolai Stephanovich
1886-1921 . . . . **TCLC 60**

Gunesekera, Romesh . . . . **CLC 91**

Gunn, Bill . . . . **CLC 5**
See also Gunn, William Harrison
See also DLB 38

Gunn, Thom(son William)
1929- . . . . **CLC 3, 6, 18, 32, 81**
See also CA 17-20R; CANR 9, 33;
CDBLB 1960 to Present; DAM POET;
DLB 27; INT CANR-33; MTCW

Gunn, William Harrison 1934(?)-1989
See Gunn, Bill
See also AITN 1; BW 1; CA 13-16R; 128;
CANR 12, 25

Gunnars, Kristjana 1948- . . . . **CLC 69**
See also CA 113; DLB 60

Gurganus, Allan 1947- . . . . **CLC 70**
See also BEST 90:1; CA 135; DAM POP

Gurney, A(lbert) R(amsdell), Jr.
1930- . . . . **CLC 32, 50, 54**
See also CA 77-80; CANR 32;
DAM DRAM

Gurney, Ivor (Bertie) 1890-1937 . . . **TCLC 33**

Gurney, Peter
See Gurney, A(lbert) R(amsdell), Jr.

Guro, Elena 1877-1913 . . . . **TCLC 56**

Gustafson, Ralph (Barker) 1909- . . . . **CLC 36**
See also CA 21-24R; CANR 8, 45; DLB 88

Gut, Gom
See Simenon, Georges (Jacques Christian)

Guterson, David 1956- . . . . **CLC 91**
See also CA 132

Guthrie, A(lfred) B(ertram), Jr.
1901-1991 . . . . **CLC 23**
See also CA 57-60; 134; CANR 24; DLB 6;
SATA 62; SATA-Obit 67

Guthrie, Isobel
See Grieve, C(hristopher) M(urray)

Guthrie, Woodrow Wilson 1912-1967
See Guthrie, Woody
See also CA 113; 93-96

Guthrie, Woody . . . . **CLC 35**
See also Guthrie, Woodrow Wilson

Guy, Rosa (Cuthbert) 1928- . . . . **CLC 26**
See also AAYA 4; BW 2; CA 17-20R;
CANR 14, 34; CLR 13; DLB 33; JRDA;
MAICYA; SATA 14, 62

Gwendolyn
See Bennett, (Enoch) Arnold

H. D. . . . . **CLC 3, 8, 14, 31, 34, 73; PC 5**
See also Doolittle, Hilda

H. de V.
See Buchan, John

Haavikko, Paavo Juhani
1931- . . . . **CLC 18, 34**
See also CA 106

Habbema, Koos
See Heijermans, Herman

Hacker, Marilyn
1942- . . . . **CLC 5, 9, 23, 72, 91**
See also CA 77-80; DAM POET; DLB 120

Haggard, H(enry) Rider
1856-1925 . . . . **TCLC 11**
See also CA 108; 148; DLB 70, 156;
SATA 16

Hagiwara Sakutaro 1886-1942 . . . . **TCLC 60**

Haig, Fenil
See Ford, Ford Madox

Haig-Brown, Roderick (Langmere)
1908-1976 . . . . **CLC 21**
See also CA 5-8R; 69-72; CANR 4, 38;
CLR 31; DLB 88; MAICYA; SATA 12

Hailey, Arthur 1920- . . . . **CLC 5**
See also AITN 2; BEST 90:3; CA 1-4R;
CANR 2, 36; DAM NOV, POP; DLB 88;
DLBY 82; MTCW

Hailey, Elizabeth Forsythe 1938- . . . **CLC 40**
See also CA 93-96; CAAS 1; CANR 15, 48;
INT CANR-15

Haines, John (Meade) 1924- . . . . **CLC 58**
See also CA 17-20R; CANR 13, 34; DLB 5

Hakluyt, Richard 1552-1616 . . . . **LC 31**

Haldeman, Joe (William) 1943- . . . . . **CLC 61**
See also CA 53-56; CANR 6; DLB 8;
INT CANR-6

Haley, Alex(ander Murray Palmer)
1921-1992 . . . . **CLC 8, 12, 76; BLC; DA;
DAB; DAC**
See also BW 2; CA 77-80; 136; DAM MST,
MULT, POP; DLB 38; MTCW

Haliburton, Thomas Chandler
1796-1865 . . . . **NCLC 15**
See also DLB 11, 99

Hall, Donald (Andrew, Jr.)
1928- . . . . **CLC 1, 13, 37, 59**
See also CA 5-8R; CAAS 7; CANR 2, 44;
DAM POET; DLB 5; SATA 23

Hall, Frederic Sauser
See Sauser-Hall, Frederic

Hall, James
See Kuttner, Henry

Hall, James Norman 1887-1951 . . . **TCLC 23**
See also CA 123; SATA 21

Hall, (Marguerite) Radclyffe
1886-1943 . . . . **TCLC 12**
See also CA 110; 150

Hall, Rodney 1935- . . . . **CLC 51**
See also CA 109

Halleck, Fitz-Greene 1790-1867 . . **NCLC 47**
See also DLB 3

Halliday, Michael
See Creasey, John

Halpern, Daniel 1945- . . . . **CLC 14**
See also CA 33-36R

Hamburger, Michael (Peter Leopold)
1924- . . . . **CLC 5, 14**
See also CA 5-8R; CAAS 4; CANR 2, 47;
DLB 27

Hamill, Pete 1935- . . . . **CLC 10**
See also CA 25-28R; CANR 18

Hamilton, Alexander
1755(?)-1804 . . . . **NCLC 49**
See also DLB 37

Hamilton, Clive
See Lewis, C(live) S(taples)

Hamilton, Edmond 1904-1977 . . . . **CLC 1**
See also CA 1-4R; CANR 3; DLB 8

Hamilton, Eugene (Jacob) Lee
See Lee-Hamilton, Eugene (Jacob)

Hamilton, Franklin
See Silverberg, Robert

Howes, Barbara 1914- . . . . **CLC 15**
See also CA 9-12R; CAAS 3; SATA 5

Hrabal, Bohumil 1914- . . . . **CLC 13, 67**
See also CA 106; CAAS 12

Hsun, Lu
See Lu Hsun

Hubbard, L(afayette) Ron(ald)
1911-1986 . . . . **CLC 43**
See also CA 77-80; 118; CANR 22;
DAM POP

Huch, Ricarda (Octavia)
1864-1947 . . . . **TCLC 13**
See also CA 111; DLB 66

Huddle, David 1942- . . . . **CLC 49**
See also CA 57-60; CAAS 20; DLB 130

Hudson, Jeffrey
See Crichton, (John) Michael

Hudson, W(illiam) H(enry)
1841-1922 . . . . **TCLC 29**
See also CA 115; DLB 98, 153; SATA 35

Hueffer, Ford Madox
See Ford, Ford Madox

Hughart, Barry 1934- . . . . **CLC 39**
See also CA 137

Hughes, Colin
See Creasey, John

Hughes, David (John) 1930- . . . . **CLC 48**
See also CA 116; 129; DLB 14

Hughes, Edward James
See Hughes, Ted
See also DAM MST, POET

Hughes, (James) Langston
1902-1967 . . . . . **CLC 1, 5, 10, 15, 35, 44;**
BLC; DA; DAB; DAC; DC 3; PC 1;
SSC 6; WLC
See also AAYA 12; BW 1; CA 1-4R;
25-28R; CANR 1, 34; CDALB 1929-1941;
CLR 17; DAM DRAM, MST, MULT,
POET; DLB 4, 7, 48, 51, 86; JRDA;
MAICYA; MTCW; SATA 4, 33

Hughes, Richard (Arthur Warren)
1900-1976 . . . . **CLC 1, 11**
See also CA 5-8R; 65-68; CANR 4;
DAM NOV; DLB 15, 161; MTCW;
SATA 8; SATA-Obit 25

Hughes, Ted
1930- . . . . **CLC 2, 4, 9, 14, 37; DAB;**
DAC; PC 7
See also Hughes, Edward James
See also CA 1-4R; CANR 1, 33; CLR 3;
DLB 40, 161; MAICYA; MTCW;
SATA 49; SATA-Brief 27

Hugo, Richard F(ranklin)
1923-1982 . . . . **CLC 6, 18, 32**
See also CA 49-52; 108; CANR 3;
DAM POET; DLB 5

Hugo, Victor (Marie)
1802-1885 . . . . **NCLC 3, 10, 21; DA;**
DAB; DAC; WLC
See also DAM DRAM, MST, NOV, POET;
DLB 119; SATA 47

Huidobro, Vicente
See Huidobro Fernandez, Vicente Garcia

Huidobro Fernandez, Vicente Garcia
1893-1948 . . . . **TCLC 31**
See also CA 131; HW

Hulme, Keri 1947- . . . . **CLC 39**
See also CA 125; INT 125

Hulme, T(homas) E(rnest)
1883-1917 . . . . **TCLC 21**
See also CA 117; DLB 19

Hume, David 1711-1776 . . . . **LC 7**
See also DLB 104

Humphrey, William 1924- . . . . **CLC 45**
See also CA 77-80; DLB 6

Humphreys, Emyr Owen 1919- . . . . . **CLC 47**
See also CA 5-8R; CANR 3, 24; DLB 15

Humphreys, Josephine 1945- . . . . **CLC 34, 57**
See also CA 121; 127; INT 127

Hungerford, Pixie
See Brinsmead, H(esba) F(ay)

Hunt, E(verette) Howard, (Jr.)
1918- . . . . **CLC 3**
See also AITN 1; CA 45-48; CANR 2, 47

Hunt, Kyle
See Creasey, John

Hunt, (James Henry) Leigh
1784-1859 . . . . **NCLC 1**
See also DAM POET

Hunt, Marsha 1946- . . . . **CLC 70**
See also BW 2; CA 143

Hunt, Violet 1866-1942 . . . . **TCLC 53**
See also DLB 162

Hunter, E. Waldo
See Sturgeon, Theodore (Hamilton)

Hunter, Evan 1926- . . . . **CLC 11, 31**
See also CA 5-8R; CANR 5, 38;
DAM POP; DLBY 82; INT CANR-5;
MTCW; SATA 25

Hunter, Kristin (Eggleston) 1931- . . . **CLC 35**
See also AITN 1; BW 1; CA 13-16R;
CANR 13; CLR 3; DLB 33;
INT CANR-13; MAICYA; SAAS 10;
SATA 12

Hunter, Mollie 1922- . . . . **CLC 21**
See also McIlwraith, Maureen Mollie
Hunter
See also AAYA 13; CANR 37; CLR 25;
DLB 161; JRDA; MAICYA; SAAS 7;
SATA 54

Hunter, Robert (?)-1734 . . . . **LC 7**

Hurston, Zora Neale
1903-1960 . . . . **CLC 7, 30, 61; BLC; DA;**
DAC; SSC 4
See also AAYA 15; BW 1; CA 85-88;
DAM MST, MULT, NOV; DLB 51, 86;
MTCW

Huston, John (Marcellus)
1906-1987 . . . . **CLC 20**
See also CA 73-76; 123; CANR 34; DLB 26

Hustvedt, Siri 1955- . . . . **CLC 76**
See also CA 137

Hutten, Ulrich von 1488-1523 . . . . **LC 16**

Huxley, Aldous (Leonard)
1894-1963 . . . . . **CLC 1, 3, 4, 5, 8, 11, 18,**
35, 79; DA; DAB; DAC; WLC
See also AAYA 11; CA 85-88; CANR 44;
CDBLB 1914-1945; DAM MST, NOV;
DLB 36, 100, 162; MTCW; SATA 63

Huysmans, Charles Marie Georges
1848-1907
See Huysmans, Joris-Karl
See also CA 104

Huysmans, Joris-Karl . . . . **TCLC 7**
See also Huysmans, Charles Marie Georges
See also DLB 123

Hwang, David Henry
1957- . . . . **CLC 55; DC 4**
See also CA 127; 132; DAM DRAM;
INT 132

Hyde, Anthony 1946- . . . . **CLC 42**
See also CA 136

Hyde, Margaret O(ldroyd) 1917- . . . **CLC 21**
See also CA 1-4R; CANR 1, 36; CLR 23;
JRDA; MAICYA; SAAS 8; SATA 1, 42,
76

Hynes, James 1956(?)- . . . . **CLC 65**

Ian, Janis 1951- . . . . **CLC 21**
See also CA 105

Ibanez, Vicente Blasco
See Blasco Ibanez, Vicente

Ibarguengoitia, Jorge 1928-1983 . . . . **CLC 37**
See also CA 124; 113; HW

Ibsen, Henrik (Johan)
1828-1906 . . . . **TCLC 2, 8, 16, 37, 52;**
DA; DAB; DAC; DC 2; WLC
See also CA 104; 141; DAM DRAM, MST

Ibuse Masuji 1898-1993 . . . . **CLC 22**
See also CA 127; 141

Ichikawa, Kon 1915- . . . . **CLC 20**
See also CA 121

Idle, Eric 1943- . . . . **CLC 21**
See also Monty Python
See also CA 116; CANR 35

Ignatow, David 1914- . . . . . . **CLC 4, 7, 14, 40**
See also CA 9-12R; CAAS 3; CANR 31;
DLB 5

Ihimaera, Witi 1944- . . . . **CLC 46**
See also CA 77-80

Ilf, Ilya . . . . **TCLC 21**
See also Fainzilberg, Ilya Arnoldovich

Immermann, Karl (Lebrecht)
1796-1840 . . . . **NCLC 4, 49**
See also DLB 133

Inclan, Ramon (Maria) del Valle
See Valle-Inclan, Ramon (Maria) del

Infante, G(uillermo) Cabrera
See Cabrera Infante, G(uillermo)

Ingalls, Rachel (Holmes) 1940- . . . . . **CLC 42**
See also CA 123; 127

Ingamells, Rex 1913-1955 . . . . **TCLC 35**

Inge, William Motter
1913-1973 . . . . **CLC 1, 8, 19**
See also CA 9-12R; CDALB 1941-1968;
DAM DRAM; DLB 7; MTCW

Ingelow, Jean 1820-1897 . . . . **NCLC 39**
See also DLB 35; SATA 33

Ingram, Willis J.
See Harris, Mark

Innaurato, Albert (F.) 1948(?)- . . **CLC 21, 60**
See also CA 115; 122; INT 122

Innes, Michael
See Stewart, J(ohn) I(nnes) M(ackintosh)

Jewsbury, Geraldine (Endsor)
1812-1880 . . . . **NCLC 22**
See also DLB 21

Jhabvala, Ruth Prawer
1927- . . . . **CLC 4, 8, 29, 92; DAB**
See also CA 1-4R; CANR 2, 29, 51;
DAM NOV; DLB 139; INT CANR-29;
MTCW

Jibran, Kahlil
See Gibran, Kahlil

Jibran, Khalil
See Gibran, Kahlil

Jiles, Paulette 1943- . . . . **CLC 13, 58**
See also CA 101

Jimenez (Mantecon), Juan Ramon
1881-1958 . . . . **TCLC 4; HLC; PC 7**
See also CA 104; 131; DAM MULT,
POET; DLB 134; HW; MTCW

Jimenez, Ramon
See Jimenez (Mantecon), Juan Ramon

Jimenez Mantecon, Juan
See Jimenez (Mantecon), Juan Ramon

Joel, Billy . . . . **CLC 26**
See also Joel, William Martin

Joel, William Martin 1949-
See Joel, Billy
See also CA 108

John of the Cross, St. 1542-1591 . . . . **LC 18**

Johnson, B(ryan) S(tanley William)
1933-1973 . . . . **CLC 6, 9**
See also CA 9-12R; 53-56; CANR 9;
DLB 14, 40

Johnson, Benj. F. of Boo
See Riley, James Whitcomb

Johnson, Benjamin F. of Boo
See Riley, James Whitcomb

Johnson, Charles (Richard)
1948- . . . . **CLC 7, 51, 65; BLC**
See also BW 2; CA 116; CAAS 18;
CANR 42; DAM MULT; DLB 33

Johnson, Denis 1949- . . . . **CLC 52**
See also CA 117; 121; DLB 120

Johnson, Diane 1934- . . . . **CLC 5, 13, 48**
See also CA 41-44R; CANR 17, 40;
DLBY 80; INT CANR-17; MTCW

Johnson, Eyvind (Olof Verner)
1900-1976 . . . . **CLC 14**
See also CA 73-76; 69-72; CANR 34

Johnson, J. R.
See James, C(yril) L(ionel) R(obert)

Johnson, James Weldon
1871-1938 . . . . **TCLC 3, 19; BLC**
See also BW 1; CA 104; 125;
CDALB 1917-1929; CLR 32;
DAM MULT, POET; DLB 51; MTCW;
SATA 31

Johnson, Joyce 1935- . . . . **CLC 58**
See also CA 125; 129

Johnson, Lionel (Pigot)
1867-1902 . . . . **TCLC 19**
See also CA 117; DLB 19

Johnson, Mel
See Malzberg, Barry N(athaniel)

Johnson, Pamela Hansford
1912-1981 . . . . **CLC 1, 7, 27**
See also CA 1-4R; 104; CANR 2, 28;
DLB 15; MTCW

Johnson, Samuel
1709-1784 . . . . . **LC 15; DA; DAB; DAC;
WLC**
See also CDBLB 1660-1789; DAM MST;
DLB 39, 95, 104, 142

Johnson, Uwe
1934-1984 . . . . **CLC 5, 10, 15, 40**
See also CA 1-4R; 112; CANR 1, 39;
DLB 75; MTCW

Johnston, George (Benson) 1913- . . . **CLC 51**
See also CA 1-4R; CANR 5, 20; DLB 88

Johnston, Jennifer 1930- . . . . **CLC 7**
See also CA 85-88; DLB 14

Jolley, (Monica) Elizabeth
1923- . . . . **CLC 46; SSC 19**
See also CA 127; CAAS 13

Jones, Arthur Llewellyn 1863-1947
See Machen, Arthur
See also CA 104

Jones, D(ouglas) G(ordon) 1929- . . . . **CLC 10**
See also CA 29-32R; CANR 13; DLB 53

Jones, David (Michael)
1895-1974 . . . . **CLC 2, 4, 7, 13, 42**
See also CA 9-12R; 53-56; CANR 28;
CDBLB 1945-1960; DLB 20, 100; MTCW

Jones, David Robert 1947-
See Bowie, David
See also CA 103

Jones, Diana Wynne 1934- . . . . **CLC 26**
See also AAYA 12; CA 49-52; CANR 4,
26; CLR 23; DLB 161; JRDA; MAICYA;
SAAS 7; SATA 9, 70

Jones, Edward P. 1950- . . . . **CLC 76**
See also BW 2; CA 142

Jones, Gayl 1949- . . . . **CLC 6, 9; BLC**
See also BW 2; CA 77-80; CANR 27;
DAM MULT; DLB 33; MTCW

Jones, James 1921-1977 . . . . **CLC 1, 3, 10, 39**
See also AITN 1, 2; CA 1-4R; 69-72;
CANR 6; DLB 2, 143; MTCW

Jones, John J.
See Lovecraft, H(oward) P(hillips)

Jones, LeRoi . . . . **CLC 1, 2, 3, 5, 10, 14**
See also Baraka, Amiri

Jones, Louis B. . . . . **CLC 65**
See also CA 141

Jones, Madison (Percy, Jr.) 1925- . . . **CLC 4**
See also CA 13-16R; CAAS 11; CANR 7;
DLB 152

Jones, Mervyn 1922- . . . . **CLC 10, 52**
See also CA 45-48; CAAS 5; CANR 1;
MTCW

Jones, Mick 1956(?)- . . . . **CLC 30**

Jones, Nettie (Pearl) 1941- . . . . **CLC 34**
See also BW 2; CA 137; CAAS 20

Jones, Preston 1936-1979 . . . . **CLC 10**
See also CA 73-76; 89-92; DLB 7

Jones, Robert F(rancis) 1934- . . . . **CLC 7**
See also CA 49-52; CANR 2

Jones, Rod 1953- . . . . **CLC 50**
See also CA 128

Jones, Terence Graham Parry
1942- . . . . **CLC 21**
See also Jones, Terry; Monty Python
See also CA 112; 116; CANR 35; INT 116

Jones, Terry
See Jones, Terence Graham Parry
See also SATA 67; SATA-Brief 51

Jones, Thom 1945(?)- . . . . **CLC 81**

Jong, Erica 1942- . . . . . . **CLC 4, 6, 8, 18, 83**
See also AITN 1; BEST 90:2; CA 73-76;
CANR 26; DAM NOV, POP; DLB 2, 5,
28, 152; INT CANR-26; MTCW

Jonson, Ben(jamin)
1572(?)-1637 . . . . **LC 6; DA; DAB; DAC;
DC 4; WLC**
See also CDBLB Before 1660;
DAM DRAM, MST, POET; DLB 62,
121

Jordan, June 1936- . . . . **CLC 5, 11, 23**
See also AAYA 2; BW 2; CA 33-36R;
CANR 25; CLR 10; DAM MULT,
POET; DLB 38; MAICYA; MTCW;
SATA 4

Jordan, Pat(rick M.) 1941- . . . . **CLC 37**
See also CA 33-36R

Jorgensen, Ivar
See Ellison, Harlan (Jay)

Jorgenson, Ivar
See Silverberg, Robert

Josephus, Flavius c. 37-100 . . . . . . **CMLC 13**

Josipovici, Gabriel 1940- . . . . **CLC 6, 43**
See also CA 37-40R; CAAS 8; CANR 47;
DLB 14

Joubert, Joseph 1754-1824 . . . . **NCLC 9**

Jouve, Pierre Jean 1887-1976 . . . . . . **CLC 47**
See also CA 65-68

Joyce, James (Augustine Aloysius)
1882-1941 . . . . **TCLC 3, 8, 16, 35, 52;
DA; DAB; DAC; SSC 3; WLC**
See also CA 104; 126; CDBLB 1914-1945;
DAM MST, NOV, POET; DLB 10, 19,
36, 162; MTCW

Jozsef, Attila 1905-1937 . . . . **TCLC 22**
See also CA 116

Juana Ines de la Cruz 1651(?)-1695 . . . **LC 5**

Judd, Cyril
See Kornbluth, C(yril) M.; Pohl, Frederik

Julian of Norwich 1342(?)-1416(?) . . . . **LC 6**
See also DLB 146

Juniper, Alex
See Hospital, Janette Turner

Just, Ward (Swift) 1935- . . . . **CLC 4, 27**
See also CA 25-28R; CANR 32;
INT CANR-32

Justice, Donald (Rodney) 1925- . . **CLC 6, 19**
See also CA 5-8R; CANR 26; DAM POET;
DLBY 83; INT CANR-26

Juvenal c. 55-c. 127 . . . . **CMLC 8**

Juvenis
See Bourne, Randolph S(illiman)

Kacew, Romain 1914-1980
See Gary, Romain
See also CA 108; 102

Kadare, Ismail 1936- . . . . **CLC 52**

Kadohata, Cynthia . . . . **CLC 59**
See also CA 140

Kafka, Franz
1883-1924 . . . . **TCLC 2, 6, 13, 29, 47, 53;**
DA; DAB; DAC; SSC 5; WLC
See also CA 105; 126; DAM MST, NOV;
DLB 81; MTCW

Kahanovitsch, Pinkhes
See Der Nister

Kahn, Roger 1927- . . . . **CLC 30**
See also CA 25-28R; CANR 44; SATA 37

Kain, Saul
See Sassoon, Siegfried (Lorraine)

Kaiser, Georg 1878-1945 . . . . **TCLC 9**
See also CA 106; DLB 124

Kaletski, Alexander 1946- . . . . **CLC 39**
See also CA 118; 143

Kalidasa fl. c. 400- . . . . **CMLC 9**

Kallman, Chester (Simon)
1921-1975 . . . . **CLC 2**
See also CA 45-48; 53-56; CANR 3

Kaminsky, Melvin 1926-
See Brooks, Mel
See also CA 65-68; CANR 16

Kaminsky, Stuart M(elvin) 1934- . . . **CLC 59**
See also CA 73-76; CANR 29

Kane, Paul
See Simon, Paul

Kane, Wilson
See Bloch, Robert (Albert)

Kanin, Garson 1912- . . . . **CLC 22**
See also AITN 1; CA 5-8R; CANR 7;
DLB 7

Kaniuk, Yoram 1930- . . . . **CLC 19**
See also CA 134

Kant, Immanuel 1724-1804 . . . . . . **NCLC 27**
See also DLB 94

Kantor, MacKinlay 1904-1977 . . . . . . **CLC 7**
See also CA 61-64; 73-76; DLB 9, 102

Kaplan, David Michael 1946- . . . . . . **CLC 50**

Kaplan, James 1951- . . . . **CLC 59**
See also CA 135

Karageorge, Michael
See Anderson, Poul (William)

Karamzin, Nikolai Mikhailovich
1766-1826 . . . . **NCLC 3**
See also DLB 150

Karapanou, Margarita 1946- . . . . **CLC 13**
See also CA 101

Karinthy, Frigyes 1887-1938 . . . . . **TCLC 47**

Karl, Frederick R(obert) 1927- . . . . . **CLC 34**
See also CA 5-8R; CANR 3, 44

Kastel, Warren
See Silverberg, Robert

Kataev, Evgeny Petrovich 1903-1942
See Petrov, Evgeny
See also CA 120

Kataphusin
See Ruskin, John

Katz, Steve 1935- . . . . **CLC 47**
See also CA 25-28R; CAAS 14; CANR 12;
DLBY 83

Kauffman, Janet 1945- . . . . **CLC 42**
See also CA 117; CANR 43; DLBY 86

Kaufman, Bob (Garnell)
1925-1986 . . . . **CLC 49**
See also BW 1; CA 41-44R; 118; CANR 22;
DLB 16, 41

Kaufman, George S. 1889-1961 . . . . . **CLC 38**
See also CA 108; 93-96; DAM DRAM;
DLB 7; INT 108

Kaufman, Sue . . . . **CLC 3, 8**
See also Barondess, Sue K(aufman)

Kavafis, Konstantinos Petrou 1863-1933
See Cavafy, C(onstantine) P(eter)
See also CA 104

Kavan, Anna 1901-1968 . . . . . . **CLC 5, 13, 82**
See also CA 5-8R; CANR 6; MTCW

Kavanagh, Dan
See Barnes, Julian

Kavanagh, Patrick (Joseph)
1904-1967 . . . . **CLC 22**
See also CA 123; 25-28R; DLB 15, 20;
MTCW

Kawabata, Yasunari
1899-1972 . . . . . **CLC 2, 5, 9, 18; SSC 17**
See also CA 93-96; 33-36R; DAM MULT

Kaye, M(ary) M(argaret) 1909- . . . . . **CLC 28**
See also CA 89-92; CANR 24; MTCW;
SATA 62

Kaye, Mollie
See Kaye, M(ary) M(argaret)

Kaye-Smith, Sheila 1887-1956 . . . . . **TCLC 20**
See also CA 118; DLB 36

Kaymor, Patrice Maguilene
See Senghor, Leopold Sedar

Kazan, Elia 1909- . . . . **CLC 6, 16, 63**
See also CA 21-24R; CANR 32

Kazantzakis, Nikos
1883(?)-1957 . . . . **TCLC 2, 5, 33**
See also CA 105; 132; MTCW

Kazin, Alfred 1915- . . . . **CLC 34, 38**
See also CA 1-4R; CAAS 7; CANR 1, 45;
DLB 67

Keane, Mary Nesta (Skrine) 1904-
See Keane, Molly
See also CA 108; 114

Keane, Molly . . . . **CLC 31**
See also Keane, Mary Nesta (Skrine)
See also INT 114

Keates, Jonathan 19(?)- . . . . **CLC 34**

Keaton, Buster 1895-1966 . . . . **CLC 20**

Keats, John
1795-1821 . . . . **NCLC 8; DA; DAB;**
DAC; PC 1; WLC
See also CDBLB 1789-1832; DAM MST,
POET; DLB 96, 110

Keene, Donald 1922- . . . . **CLC 34**
See also CA 1-4R; CANR 5

Keillor, Garrison . . . . **CLC 40**
See also Keillor, Gary (Edward)
See also AAYA 2; BEST 89:3; DLBY 87;
SATA 58

Keillor, Gary (Edward) 1942-
See Keillor, Garrison
See also CA 111; 117; CANR 36;
DAM POP; MTCW

Keith, Michael
See Hubbard, L(afayette) Ron(ald)

Keller, Gottfried 1819-1890 . . . . **NCLC 2**
See also DLB 129

Kellerman, Jonathan 1949- . . . . **CLC 44**
See also BEST 90:1; CA 106; CANR 29, 51;
DAM POP; INT CANR-29

Kelley, William Melvin 1937- . . . . . . **CLC 22**
See also BW 1; CA 77-80; CANR 27;
DLB 33

Kellogg, Marjorie 1922- . . . . **CLC 2**
See also CA 81-84

Kellow, Kathleen
See Hibbert, Eleanor Alice Burford

Kelly, M(ilton) T(erry) 1947- . . . . **CLC 55**
See also CA 97-100; CAAS 22; CANR 19,
43

Kelman, James 1946- . . . . **CLC 58, 86**
See also CA 148

Kemal, Yashar 1923- . . . . **CLC 14, 29**
See also CA 89-92; CANR 44

Kemble, Fanny 1809-1893 . . . . **NCLC 18**
See also DLB 32

Kemelman, Harry 1908- . . . . **CLC 2**
See also AITN 1; CA 9-12R; CANR 6;
DLB 28

Kempe, Margery 1373(?)-1440(?) . . . . . **LC 6**
See also DLB 146

Kempis, Thomas a 1380-1471 . . . . **LC 11**

Kendall, Henry 1839-1882 . . . . **NCLC 12**

Keneally, Thomas (Michael)
1935- . . . . . . **CLC 5, 8, 10, 14, 19, 27, 43**
See also CA 85-88; CANR 10, 50;
DAM NOV; MTCW

Kennedy, Adrienne (Lita)
1931- . . . . **CLC 66; BLC; DC 5**
See also BW 2; CA 103; CAAS 20; CABS 3;
CANR 26; DAM MULT; DLB 38

Kennedy, John Pendleton
1795-1870 . . . . **NCLC 2**
See also DLB 3

Kennedy, Joseph Charles 1929-
See Kennedy, X. J.
See also CA 1-4R; CANR 4, 30, 40;
SATA 14, 86

Kennedy, William 1928- . . . **CLC 6, 28, 34, 53**
See also AAYA 1; CA 85-88; CANR 14,
31; DAM NOV; DLB 143; DLBY 85;
INT CANR-31; MTCW; SATA 57

Kennedy, X. J. . . . . **CLC 8, 42**
See also Kennedy, Joseph Charles
See also CAAS 9; CLR 27; DLB 5;
SAAS 22

Kenny, Maurice (Francis) 1929- . . . . **CLC 87**
See also CA 144; CAAS 22; DAM MULT;
NNAL

Kent, Kelvin
See Kuttner, Henry

Kenton, Maxwell
See Southern, Terry

Kenyon, Robert O.
See Kuttner, Henry

Kerouac, Jack . . . . . CLC 1, 2, 3, 5, 14, 29, 61
See also Kerouac, Jean-Louis Lebris de
See also CDALB 1941-1968; DLB 2, 16;
DLBD 3

Kerouac, Jean-Louis Lebris de 1922-1969
See Kerouac, Jack
See also AITN 1; CA 5-8R; 25-28R;
CANR 26; DA; DAB; DAC; DAM MST,
NOV, POET, POP; MTCW; WLC

Kerr, Jean 1923- . . . . CLC 22
See also CA 5-8R; CANR 7; INT CANR-7

Kerr, M. E. . . . . CLC 12, 35
See also Meaker, Marijane (Agnes)
See also AAYA 2; CLR 29; SAAS 1

Kerr, Robert . . . . CLC 55

Kerrigan, (Thomas) Anthony
1918- . . . . CLC 4, 6
See also CA 49-52; CAAS 11; CANR 4

Kerry, Lois
See Duncan, Lois

Kesey, Ken (Elton)
1935- . . . . . . CLC 1, 3, 6, 11, 46, 64; DA;
DAB; DAC; WLC
See also CA 1-4R; CANR 22, 38;
CDALB 1968-1988; DAM MST, NOV,
POP; DLB 2, 16; MTCW; SATA 66

Kesselring, Joseph (Otto)
1902-1967 . . . . CLC 45
See also CA 150; DAM DRAM, MST

Kessler, Jascha (Frederick) 1929- . . . . CLC 4
See also CA 17-20R; CANR 8, 48

Kettelkamp, Larry (Dale) 1933- . . . . CLC 12
See also CA 29-32R; CANR 16; SAAS 3;
SATA 2

Keyber, Conny
See Fielding, Henry

Keyes, Daniel 1927- . . . . CLC 80; DA; DAC
See also CA 17-20R; CANR 10, 26;
DAM MST, NOV; SATA 37

Khanshendel, Chiron
See Rose, Wendy

Khayyam, Omar
1048-1131 . . . . CMLC 11; PC 8
See also DAM POET

Kherdian, David 1931- . . . . CLC 6, 9
See also CA 21-24R; CAAS 2; CANR 39;
CLR 24; JRDA; MAICYA; SATA 16, 74

Khlebnikov, Velimir . . . . TCLC 20
See also Khlebnikov, Viktor Vladimirovich

Khlebnikov, Viktor Vladimirovich 1885-1922
See Khlebnikov, Velimir
See also CA 117

Khodasevich, Vladislav (Felitsianovich)
1886-1939 . . . . TCLC 15
See also CA 115

Kielland, Alexander Lange
1849-1906 . . . . TCLC 5
See also CA 104

Kiely, Benedict 1919- . . . . CLC 23, 43
See also CA 1-4R; CANR 2; DLB 15

Kienzle, William X(avier) 1928- . . . . CLC 25
See also CA 93-96; CAAS 1; CANR 9, 31;
DAM POP; INT CANR-31; MTCW

Kierkegaard, Soren 1813-1855. . . . NCLC 34

Killens, John Oliver 1916-1987. . . . . CLC 10
See also BW 2; CA 77-80; 123; CAAS 2;
CANR 26; DLB 33

Killigrew, Anne 1660-1685. . . . . LC 4
See also DLB 131

Kim
See Simenon, Georges (Jacques Christian)

Kincaid, Jamaica 1949- . . . CLC 43, 68; BLC
See also AAYA 13; BW 2; CA 125;
CANR 47; DAM MULT, NOV;
DLB 157

King, Francis (Henry) 1923- . . . . . CLC 8, 53
See also CA 1-4R; CANR 1, 33;
DAM NOV; DLB 15, 139; MTCW

King, Martin Luther, Jr.
1929-1968 . . . . CLC 83; BLC; DA; DAB;
DAC
See also BW 2; CA 25-28; CANR 27, 44;
CAP 2; DAM MST, MULT; MTCW;
SATA 14

King, Stephen (Edwin)
1947- . . . . . . CLC 12, 26, 37, 61; SSC 17
See also AAYA 1, 17; BEST 90:1;
CA 61-64; CANR 1, 30; DAM NOV,
POP; DLB 143; DLBY 80; JRDA;
MTCW; SATA 9, 55

King, Steve
See King, Stephen (Edwin)

King, Thomas 1943- . . . . CLC 89; DAC
See also CA 144; DAM MULT; NNAL

Kingman, Lee. . . . . CLC 17
See also Natti, (Mary) Lee
See also SAAS 3; SATA 1, 67

Kingsley, Charles 1819-1875 . . . . . NCLC 35
See also DLB 21, 32; YABC 2

Kingsley, Sidney 1906-1995. . . . . . . CLC 44
See also CA 85-88; 147; DLB 7

Kingsolver, Barbara 1955- . . . . . . CLC 55, 81
See also AAYA 15; CA 129; 134;
DAM POP; INT 134

Kingston, Maxine (Ting Ting) Hong
1940- . . . . CLC 12, 19, 58
See also AAYA 8; CA 69-72; CANR 13,
38; DAM MULT, NOV; DLBY 80;
INT CANR-13; MTCW; SATA 53

Kinnell, Galway
1927- . . . . CLC 1, 2, 3, 5, 13, 29
See also CA 9-12R; CANR 10, 34; DLB 5;
DLBY 87; INT CANR-34; MTCW

Kinsella, Thomas 1928- . . . . CLC 4, 19
See also CA 17-20R; CANR 15; DLB 27;
MTCW

Kinsella, W(illiam) P(atrick)
1935- . . . . CLC 27, 43; DAC
See also AAYA 7; CA 97-100; CAAS 7;
CANR 21, 35; DAM NOV, POP;
INT CANR-21; MTCW

Kipling, (Joseph) Rudyard
1865-1936 . . . . . . TCLC 8, 17; DA; DAB;
DAC; PC 3; SSC 5; WLC
See also CA 105; 120; CANR 33;
CDBLB 1890-1914; CLR 39; DAM MST,
POET; DLB 19, 34, 141, 156; MAICYA;
MTCW; YABC 2

Kirkup, James 1918- . . . . CLC 1
See also CA 1-4R; CAAS 4; CANR 2;
DLB 27; SATA 12

Kirkwood, James 1930(?)-1989 . . . . . . CLC 9
See also AITN 2; CA 1-4R; 128; CANR 6,
40

Kirshner, Sidney
See Kingsley, Sidney

Kis, Danilo 1935-1989 . . . . CLC 57
See also CA 109; 118; 129; MTCW

Kivi, Aleksis 1834-1872. . . . . NCLC 30

Kizer, Carolyn (Ashley)
1925- . . . . CLC 15, 39, 80
See also CA 65-68; CAAS 5; CANR 24;
DAM POET; DLB 5

Klabund 1890-1928. . . . . TCLC 44
See also DLB 66

Klappert, Peter 1942- . . . . CLC 57
See also CA 33-36R; DLB 5

Klein, A(braham) M(oses)
1909-1972 . . . . CLC 19; DAB; DAC
See also CA 101; 37-40R; DAM MST;
DLB 68

Klein, Norma 1938-1989 . . . . CLC 30
See also AAYA 2; CA 41-44R; 128;
CANR 15, 37; CLR 2, 19;
INT CANR-15; JRDA; MAICYA;
SAAS 1; SATA 7, 57

Klein, T(heodore) E(ibon) D(onald)
1947- . . . . CLC 34
See also CA 119; CANR 44

Kleist, Heinrich von
1777-1811 . . . . NCLC 2, 37
See also DAM DRAM; DLB 90

Klima, Ivan 1931- . . . . CLC 56
See also CA 25-28R; CANR 17, 50;
DAM NOV

Klimentov, Andrei Platonovich 1899-1951
See Platonov, Andrei
See also CA 108

Klinger, Friedrich Maximilian von
1752-1831 . . . . NCLC 1
See also DLB 94

Klopstock, Friedrich Gottlieb
1724-1803 . . . . NCLC 11
See also DLB 97

Knebel, Fletcher 1911-1993. . . . . CLC 14
See also AITN 1; CA 1-4R; 140; CAAS 3;
CANR 1, 36; SATA 36; SATA-Obit 75

Knickerbocker, Diedrich
See Irving, Washington

Knight, Etheridge
1931-1991 . . . . CLC 40; BLC; PC 14
See also BW 1; CA 21-24R; 133; CANR 23;
DAM POET; DLB 41

Knight, Sarah Kemble 1666-1727 . . . . . LC 7
See also DLB 24

Knister, Raymond 1899-1932. . . . . . TCLC 56
See also DLB 68

Knowles, John
1926- . . . . . . CLC 1, 4, 10, 26; DA; DAC
See also AAYA 10; CA 17-20R; CANR 40;
CDALB 1968-1988; DAM MST, NOV;
DLB 6; MTCW; SATA 8

L'Ymagier
   See Gourmont, Remy (-Marie-Charles) de

Lynch, B. Suarez
   See Bioy Casares, Adolfo; Borges, Jorge
   Luis

Lynch, David (K.) 1946-.......... **CLC 66**
   See also CA 124; 129

Lynch, James
   See Andreyev, Leonid (Nikolaevich)

Lynch Davis, B.
   See Bioy Casares, Adolfo; Borges, Jorge
   Luis

Lyndsay, Sir David 1490-1555 ...... **LC 20**

Lynn, Kenneth S(chuyler) 1923-.... **CLC 50**
   See also CA 1-4R; CANR 3, 27

Lynx
   See West, Rebecca

Lyons, Marcus
   See Blish, James (Benjamin)

Lyre, Pinchbeck
   See Sassoon, Siegfried (Lorraine)

Lytle, Andrew (Nelson) 1902-1995 .. **CLC 22**
   See also CA 9-12R; 150; DLB 6

Lyttelton, George 1709-1773........ **LC 10**

Maas, Peter 1929- .... **CLC 29**
   See also CA 93-96; INT 93-96

Macaulay, Rose 1881-1958 ..... **TCLC 7, 44**
   See also CA 104; DLB 36

Macaulay, Thomas Babington
   1800-1859 .... **NCLC 42**
   See also CDBLB 1832-1890; DLB 32, 55

MacBeth, George (Mann)
   1932-1992 .... **CLC 2, 5, 9**
   See also CA 25-28R; 136; DLB 40; MTCW;
   SATA 4; SATA-Obit 70

MacCaig, Norman (Alexander)
   1910- .... **CLC 36; DAB**
   See also CA 9-12R; CANR 3, 34;
   DAM POET; DLB 27

MacCarthy, (Sir Charles Otto) Desmond
   1877-1952 .... **TCLC 36**

MacDiarmid, Hugh
   .... **CLC 2, 4, 11, 19, 63; PC 9**
   See also Grieve, C(hristopher) M(urray)
   See also CDBLB 1945-1960; DLB 20

MacDonald, Anson
   See Heinlein, Robert A(nson)

Macdonald, Cynthia 1928-...... **CLC 13, 19**
   See also CA 49-52; CANR 4, 44; DLB 105

MacDonald, George 1824-1905..... **TCLC 9**
   See also CA 106; 137; DLB 18; MAICYA;
   SATA 33

Macdonald, John
   See Millar, Kenneth

MacDonald, John D(ann)
   1916-1986 .... **CLC 3, 27, 44**
   See also CA 1-4R; 121; CANR 1, 19;
   DAM NOV, POP; DLB 8; DLBY 86;
   MTCW

Macdonald, John Ross
   See Millar, Kenneth

Macdonald, Ross..... **CLC 1, 2, 3, 14, 34, 41**
   See also Millar, Kenneth
   See also DLBD 6

MacDougal, John
   See Blish, James (Benjamin)

MacEwen, Gwendolyn (Margaret)
   1941-1987 .... **CLC 13, 55**
   See also CA 9-12R; 124; CANR 7, 22;
   DLB 53; SATA 50; SATA-Obit 55

Macha, Karel Hynek 1810-1846 .. **NCLC 46**

Machado (y Ruiz), Antonio
   1875-1939 .... **TCLC 3**
   See also CA 104; DLB 108

Machado de Assis, Joaquim Maria
   1839-1908 .... **TCLC 10; BLC**
   See also CA 107

Machen, Arthur........... **TCLC 4; SSC 20**
   See also Jones, Arthur Llewellyn
   See also DLB 36, 156

Machiavelli, Niccolo
   1469-1527 ...... **LC 8; DA; DAB; DAC**
   See also DAM MST

MacInnes, Colin 1914-1976...... **CLC 4, 23**
   See also CA 69-72; 65-68; CANR 21;
   DLB 14; MTCW

MacInnes, Helen (Clark)
   1907-1985 .... **CLC 27, 39**
   See also CA 1-4R; 117; CANR 1, 28;
   DAM POP; DLB 87; MTCW; SATA 22;
   SATA-Obit 44

Mackay, Mary 1855-1924
   See Corelli, Marie
   See also CA 118

Mackenzie, Compton (Edward Montague)
   1883-1972 .... **CLC 18**
   See also CA 21-22; 37-40R; CAP 2;
   DLB 34, 100

Mackenzie, Henry 1745-1831 .... **NCLC 41**
   See also DLB 39

Mackintosh, Elizabeth 1896(?)-1952
   See Tey, Josephine
   See also CA 110

MacLaren, James
   See Grieve, C(hristopher) M(urray)

Mac Laverty, Bernard 1942-....... **CLC 31**
   See also CA 116; 118; CANR 43; INT 118

MacLean, Alistair (Stuart)
   1922-1987 .... **CLC 3, 13, 50, 63**
   See also CA 57-60; 121; CANR 28;
   DAM POP; MTCW; SATA 23;
   SATA-Obit 50

Maclean, Norman (Fitzroy)
   1902-1990 .... **CLC 78; SSC 13**
   See also CA 102; 132; CANR 49;
   DAM POP

MacLeish, Archibald
   1892-1982 .... **CLC 3, 8, 14, 68**
   See also CA 9-12R; 106; CANR 33;
   DAM POET; DLB 4, 7, 45; DLBY 82;
   MTCW

MacLennan, (John) Hugh
   1907-1990 .... **CLC 2, 14, 92; DAC**
   See also CA 5-8R; 142; CANR 33;
   DAM MST; DLB 68; MTCW

MacLeod, Alistair 1936- ..... **CLC 56; DAC**
   See also CA 123; DAM MST; DLB 60

MacNeice, (Frederick) Louis
   1907-1963 ...... **CLC 1, 4, 10, 53; DAB**
   See also CA 85-88; DAM POET; DLB 10,
   20; MTCW

MacNeill, Dand
   See Fraser, George MacDonald

Macpherson, James 1736-1796 ...... **LC 29**
   See also DLB 109

Macpherson, (Jean) Jay 1931-...... **CLC 14**
   See also CA 5-8R; DLB 53

MacShane, Frank 1927-........... **CLC 39**
   See also CA 9-12R; CANR 3, 33; DLB 111

Macumber, Mari
   See Sandoz, Mari(e Susette)

Madach, Imre 1823-1864........ **NCLC 19**

Madden, (Jerry) David 1933- .... **CLC 5, 15**
   See also CA 1-4R; CAAS 3; CANR 4, 45;
   DLB 6; MTCW

Maddern, Al(an)
   See Ellison, Harlan (Jay)

Madhubuti, Haki R.
   1942- .... **CLC 6, 73; BLC; PC 5**
   See also Lee, Don L.
   See also BW 2; CA 73-76; CANR 24, 51;
   DAM MULT, POET; DLB 5, 41;
   DLBD 8

Maepenn, Hugh
   See Kuttner, Henry

Maepenn, K. H.
   See Kuttner, Henry

Maeterlinck, Maurice 1862-1949 ... **TCLC 3**
   See also CA 104; 136; DAM DRAM;
   SATA 66

Maginn, William 1794-1842....... **NCLC 8**
   See also DLB 110, 159

Mahapatra, Jayanta 1928-......... **CLC 33**
   See also CA 73-76; CAAS 9; CANR 15, 33;
   DAM MULT

Mahfouz, Naguib (Abdel Aziz Al-Sabilgi)
   1911(?)-
   See Mahfuz, Najib
   See also BEST 89:2; CA 128; DAM NOV;
   MTCW

Mahfuz, Najib................. **CLC 52, 55**
   See also Mahfouz, Naguib (Abdel Aziz
   Al-Sabilgi)
   See also DLBY 88

Mahon, Derek 1941-.............. **CLC 27**
   See also CA 113; 128; DLB 40

Mailer, Norman
   1923- ...... **CLC 1, 2, 3, 4, 5, 8, 11, 14,**
            28, 39, 74; DA; DAB; DAC
   See also AITN 2; CA 9-12R; CABS 1;
   CANR 28; CDALB 1968-1988;
   DAM MST, NOV, POP; DLB 2, 16, 28;
   DLBD 3; DLBY 80, 83; MTCW

Maillet, Antonine 1929-...... **CLC 54; DAC**
   See also CA 115; 120; CANR 46; DLB 60;
   INT 120

Mais, Roger 1905-1955 .... **TCLC 8**
   See also BW 1; CA 105; 124; DLB 125;
   MTCW

Maistre, Joseph de 1753-1821 .... **NCLC 37**

Maitland, Sara (Louise) 1950-...... **CLC 49**
   See also CA 69-72; CANR 13

Major, Clarence
1936- . . . . CLC 3, 19, 48; BLC
See also BW 2; CA 21-24R; CAAS 6;
CANR 13, 25; DAM MULT; DLB 33

Major, Kevin (Gerald)
1949- . . . . CLC 26; DAC
See also AAYA 16; CA 97-100; CANR 21,
38; CLR 11; DLB 60; INT CANR-21;
JRDA; MAICYA; SATA 32, 82

Maki, James
See Ozu, Yasujiro

Malabaila, Damiano
See Levi, Primo

Malamud, Bernard
1914-1986 . . . . . . CLC 1, 2, 3, 5, 8, 9, 11,
18, 27, 44, 78, 85; DA; DAB; DAC;
SSC 15; WLC
See also AAYA 16; CA 5-8R; 118; CABS 1;
CANR 28; CDALB 1941-1968;
DAM MST, NOV; DLB 2, 28, 152;
DLBY 80, 86; MTCW

Malaparte, Curzio 1898-1957 . . . . . TCLC 52

Malcolm, Dan
See Silverberg, Robert

Malcolm X . . . . CLC 82; BLC
See also Little, Malcolm

Malherbe, Francois de 1555-1628 . . . . . LC 5

Mallarme, Stephane
1842-1898 . . . . NCLC 4, 41; PC 4
See also DAM POET

Mallet-Joris, Francoise 1930- . . . . . . CLC 11
See also CA 65-68; CANR 17; DLB 83

Malley, Ern
See McAuley, James Phillip

Mallowan, Agatha Christie
See Christie, Agatha (Mary Clarissa)

Maloff, Saul 1922- . . . . CLC 5
See also CA 33-36R

Malone, Louis
See MacNeice, (Frederick) Louis

Malone, Michael (Christopher)
1942- . . . . CLC 43
See also CA 77-80; CANR 14, 32

Malory, (Sir) Thomas
1410(?)-1471(?) . . . . . . LC 11; DA; DAB;
DAC
See also CDBLB Before 1660; DAM MST;
DLB 146; SATA 59; SATA-Brief 33

Malouf, (George Joseph) David
1934- . . . . CLC 28, 86
See also CA 124; CANR 50

Malraux, (Georges-)Andre
1901-1976 . . . . . . CLC 1, 4, 9, 13, 15, 57
See also CA 21-22; 69-72; CANR 34;
CAP 2; DAM NOV; DLB 72; MTCW

Malzberg, Barry N(athaniel) 1939- . . . CLC 7
See also CA 61-64; CAAS 4; CANR 16;
DLB 8

Mamet, David (Alan)
1947- . . . . . . CLC 9, 15, 34, 46, 91; DC 4
See also AAYA 3; CA 81-84; CABS 3;
CANR 15, 41; DAM DRAM; DLB 7;
MTCW

Mamoulian, Rouben (Zachary)
1897-1987 . . . . CLC 16
See also CA 25-28R; 124

Mandelstam, Osip (Emilievich)
1891(?)-1938(?) . . . . . TCLC 2, 6; PC 14
See also CA 104; 150

Mander, (Mary) Jane 1877-1949. . . TCLC 31

Mandiargues, Andre Pieyre de . . . . . . CLC 41
See also Pieyre de Mandiargues, Andre
See also DLB 83

Mandrake, Ethel Belle
See Thurman, Wallace (Henry)

Mangan, James Clarence
1803-1849 . . . . NCLC 27

Maniere, J.-E.
See Giraudoux, (Hippolyte) Jean

Manley, (Mary) Delariviere
1672(?)-1724 . . . . LC 1
See also DLB 39, 80

Mann, Abel
See Creasey, John

Mann, (Luiz) Heinrich 1871-1950. . . TCLC 9
See also CA 106; DLB 66

Mann, (Paul) Thomas
1875-1955 . . . . TCLC 2, 8, 14, 21, 35, 44,
60; DA; DAB; DAC; SSC 5; WLC
See also CA 104; 128; DAM MST, NOV;
DLB 66; MTCW

Manning, David
See Faust, Frederick (Schiller)

Manning, Frederic 1887(?)-1935 . . . TCLC 25
See also CA 124

Manning, Olivia 1915-1980 . . . . . . CLC 5, 19
See also CA 5-8R; 101; CANR 29; MTCW

Mano, D. Keith 1942- . . . . CLC 2, 10
See also CA 25-28R; CAAS 6; CANR 26;
DLB 6

Mansfield, Katherine
. . . . . TCLC 2, 8, 39; DAB; SSC 9; WLC
See also Beauchamp, Kathleen Mansfield
See also DLB 162

Manso, Peter 1940- . . . . CLC 39
See also CA 29-32R; CANR 44

Mantecon, Juan Jimenez
See Jimenez (Mantecon), Juan Ramon

Manton, Peter
See Creasey, John

Man Without a Spleen, A
See Chekhov, Anton (Pavlovich)

Manzoni, Alessandro 1785-1873 . . NCLC 29

Mapu, Abraham (ben Jekutiel)
1808-1867 . . . . NCLC 18

Mara, Sally
See Queneau, Raymond

Marat, Jean Paul 1743-1793 . . . . LC 10

Marcel, Gabriel Honore
1889-1973 . . . . CLC 15
See also CA 102; 45-48; MTCW

Marchbanks, Samuel
See Davies, (William) Robertson

Marchi, Giacomo
See Bassani, Giorgio

Margulies, Donald . . . . CLC 76

Marie de France c. 12th cent. -. . . . CMLC 8

Marie de l'Incarnation 1599-1672. . . . LC 10

Mariner, Scott
See Pohl, Frederik

Marinetti, Filippo Tommaso
1876-1944 . . . . TCLC 10
See also CA 107; DLB 114

Marivaux, Pierre Carlet de Chamblain de
1688-1763 . . . . LC 4

Markandaya, Kamala . . . . CLC 8, 38
See also Taylor, Kamala (Purnaiya)

Markfield, Wallace 1926-. . . . . CLC 8
See also CA 69-72; CAAS 3; DLB 2, 28

Markham, Edwin 1852-1940 . . . . . . TCLC 47
See also DLB 54

Markham, Robert
See Amis, Kingsley (William)

Marks, J
See Highwater, Jamake (Mamake)

Marks-Highwater, J
See Highwater, Jamake (Mamake)

Markson, David M(errill) 1927- . . . . CLC 67
See also CA 49-52; CANR 1

Marley, Bob . . . . CLC 17
See also Marley, Robert Nesta

Marley, Robert Nesta 1945-1981
See Marley, Bob
See also CA 107; 103

Marlowe, Christopher
1564-1593 . . . . . LC 22; DA; DAB; DAC;
DC 1; WLC
See also CDBLB Before 1660;
DAM DRAM, MST; DLB 62

Marmontel, Jean-Francois
1723-1799 . . . . LC 2

Marquand, John P(hillips)
1893-1960 . . . . CLC 2, 10
See also CA 85-88; DLB 9, 102

Marquez, Gabriel (Jose) Garcia
See Garcia Marquez, Gabriel (Jose)

Marquis, Don(ald Robert Perry)
1878-1937 . . . . TCLC 7
See also CA 104; DLB 11, 25

Marric, J. J.
See Creasey, John

Marrow, Bernard
See Moore, Brian

Marryat, Frederick 1792-1848 . . . . NCLC 3
See also DLB 21

Marsden, James
See Creasey, John

Marsh, (Edith) Ngaio
1899-1982 . . . . CLC 7, 53
See also CA 9-12R; CANR 6; DAM POP;
DLB 77; MTCW

Marshall, Garry 1934-. . . . . CLC 17
See also AAYA 3; CA 111; SATA 60

Marshall, Paule
1929- . . . . CLC 27, 72; BLC; SSC 3
See also BW 2; CA 77-80; CANR 25;
DAM MULT; DLB 157; MTCW

Marsten, Richard
See Hunter, Evan

Martha, Henry
See Harris, Mark

Martial c. 40-c. 104 .... **PC 10**

Martin, Ken
See Hubbard, L(afayette) Ron(ald)

Martin, Richard
See Creasey, John

Martin, Steve 1945- .... **CLC 30**
See also CA 97-100; CANR 30; MTCW

Martin, Valerie 1948- .... **CLC 89**
See also BEST 90:2; CA 85-88; CANR 49

Martin, Violet Florence
1862-1915 .... **TCLC 51**

Martin, Webber
See Silverberg, Robert

Martindale, Patrick Victor
See White, Patrick (Victor Martindale)

Martin du Gard, Roger
1881-1958 .... **TCLC 24**
See also CA 118; DLB 65

Martineau, Harriet 1802-1876.... **NCLC 26**
See also DLB 21, 55, 159; YABC 2

Martines, Julia
See O'Faolain, Julia

Martinez, Jacinto Benavente y
See Benavente (y Martinez), Jacinto

Martinez Ruiz, Jose 1873-1967
See Azorin; Ruiz, Jose Martinez
See also CA 93-96; HW

Martinez Sierra, Gregorio
1881-1947 .... **TCLC 6**
See also CA 115

Martinez Sierra, Maria (de la O'LeJarraga)
1874-1974 .... **TCLC 6**
See also CA 115

Martinsen, Martin
See Follett, Ken(neth Martin)

Martinson, Harry (Edmund)
1904-1978 .... **CLC 14**
See also CA 77-80; CANR 34

Marut, Ret
See Traven, B.

Marut, Robert
See Traven, B.

Marvell, Andrew
1621-1678 ...... **LC 4; DA; DAB; DAC;**
PC 10; WLC
See also CDBLB 1660-1789; DAM MST,
POET; DLB 131

Marx, Karl (Heinrich)
1818-1883 .... **NCLC 17**
See also DLB 129

Masaoka Shiki .... **TCLC 18**
See also Masaoka Tsunenori

Masaoka Tsunenori 1867-1902
See Masaoka Shiki
See also CA 117

Masefield, John (Edward)
1878-1967 .... **CLC 11, 47**
See also CA 19-20; 25-28R; CANR 33;
CAP 2; CDBLB 1890-1914; DAM POET;
DLB 10, 19, 153, 160; MTCW; SATA 19

Maso, Carole 19(?)- .... **CLC 44**

Mason, Bobbie Ann
1940- .... **CLC 28, 43, 82; SSC 4**
See also AAYA 5; CA 53-56; CANR 11,
31; DLBY 87; INT CANR-31; MTCW

Mason, Ernst
See Pohl, Frederik

Mason, Lee W.
See Malzberg, Barry N(athaniel)

Mason, Nick 1945- .... **CLC 35**

Mason, Tally
See Derleth, August (William)

Mass, William
See Gibson, William

Masters, Edgar Lee
1868-1950 ...... **TCLC 2, 25; DA; DAC;**
PC 1
See also CA 104; 133; CDALB 1865-1917;
DAM MST, POET; DLB 54; MTCW

Masters, Hilary 1928- .... **CLC 48**
See also CA 25-28R; CANR 13, 47

Mastrosimone, William 19(?)- ...... **CLC 36**

Mathe, Albert
See Camus, Albert

Matheson, Richard Burton 1926- ... **CLC 37**
See also CA 97-100; DLB 8, 44; INT 97-100

Mathews, Harry 1930- .... **CLC 6, 52**
See also CA 21-24R; CAAS 6; CANR 18,
40

Mathews, John Joseph 1894-1979... **CLC 84**
See also CA 19-20; 142; CANR 45; CAP 2;
DAM MULT; NNAL

Mathias, Roland (Glyn) 1915- ..... **CLC 45**
See also CA 97-100; CANR 19, 41; DLB 27

Matsuo Basho 1644-1694 .... **PC 3**
See also DAM POET

Mattheson, Rodney
See Creasey, John

Matthews, Greg 1949- .... **CLC 45**
See also CA 135

Matthews, William 1942- .... **CLC 40**
See also CA 29-32R; CAAS 18; CANR 12;
DLB 5

Matthias, John (Edward) 1941- ...... **CLC 9**
See also CA 33-36R

Matthiessen, Peter
1927- .... **CLC 5, 7, 11, 32, 64**
See also AAYA 6; BEST 90:4; CA 9-12R;
CANR 21, 50; DAM NOV; DLB 6;
MTCW; SATA 27

Maturin, Charles Robert
1780(?)-1824 .... **NCLC 6**

Matute (Ausejo), Ana Maria
1925- .... **CLC 11**
See also CA 89-92; MTCW

Maugham, W. S.
See Maugham, W(illiam) Somerset

Maugham, W(illiam) Somerset
1874-1965 ...... **CLC 1, 11, 15, 67; DA;**
DAB; DAC; SSC 8; WLC
See also CA 5-8R; 25-28R; CANR 40;
CDBLB 1914-1945; DAM DRAM, MST,
NOV; DLB 10, 36, 77, 100, 162; MTCW;
SATA 54

Maugham, William Somerset
See Maugham, W(illiam) Somerset

Maupassant, (Henri Rene Albert) Guy de
1850-1893 ..... **NCLC 1, 42; DA; DAB;**
DAC; SSC 1; WLC
See also DAM MST; DLB 123

Maurhut, Richard
See Traven, B.

Mauriac, Claude 1914- .... **CLC 9**
See also CA 89-92; DLB 83

Mauriac, Francois (Charles)
1885-1970 .... **CLC 4, 9, 56**
See also CA 25-28; CAP 2; DLB 65;
MTCW

Mavor, Osborne Henry 1888-1951
See Bridie, James
See also CA 104

Maxwell, William (Keepers, Jr.)
1908- .... **CLC 19**
See also CA 93-96; DLBY 80; INT 93-96

May, Elaine 1932- .... **CLC 16**
See also CA 124; 142; DLB 44

Mayakovski, Vladimir (Vladimirovich)
1893-1930 .... **TCLC 4, 18**
See also CA 104

Mayhew, Henry 1812-1887 ...... **NCLC 31**
See also DLB 18, 55

Mayle, Peter 1939(?)- .... **CLC 89**
See also CA 139

Maynard, Joyce 1953- .... **CLC 23**
See also CA 111; 129

Mayne, William (James Carter)
1928- .... **CLC 12**
See also CA 9-12R; CANR 37; CLR 25;
JRDA; MAICYA; SAAS 11; SATA 6, 68

Mayo, Jim
See L'Amour, Louis (Dearborn)

Maysles, Albert 1926- .... **CLC 16**
See also CA 29-32R

Maysles, David 1932- .... **CLC 16**

Mazer, Norma Fox 1931- .... **CLC 26**
See also AAYA 5; CA 69-72; CANR 12,
32; CLR 23; JRDA; MAICYA; SAAS 1;
SATA 24, 67

Mazzini, Guiseppe 1805-1872 .... **NCLC 34**

McAuley, James Phillip
1917-1976 .... **CLC 45**
See also CA 97-100

McBain, Ed
See Hunter, Evan

McBrien, William Augustine
1930- .... **CLC 44**
See also CA 107

McCaffrey, Anne (Inez) 1926- ...... **CLC 17**
See also AAYA 6; AITN 2; BEST 89:2;
CA 25-28R; CANR 15, 35; DAM NOV,
POP; DLB 8; JRDA; MAICYA; MTCW;
SAAS 11; SATA 8, 70

McCall, Nathan 1955(?)- .... **CLC 86**
See also CA 146

McCann, Arthur
See Campbell, John W(ood, Jr.)

McCann, Edson
See Pohl, Frederik

Meredith, William (Morris)
1919- .... **CLC 4, 13, 22, 55**
See also CA 9-12R; CAAS 14; CANR 6, 40;
DAM POET; DLB 5

Merezhkovsky, Dmitry Sergeyevich
1865-1941 .... **TCLC 29**

Merimee, Prosper
1803-1870 .... **NCLC 6; SSC 7**
See also DLB 119

Merkin, Daphne 1954-............. **CLC 44**
See also CA 123

Merlin, Arthur
See Blish, James (Benjamin)

Merrill, James (Ingram)
1926-1995 .... **CLC 2, 3, 6, 8, 13, 18, 34,**
                                          91
See also CA 13-16R; 147; CANR 10, 49;
DAM POET; DLB 5; DLBY 85;
INT CANR-10, MTCW

Merriman, Alex
See Silverberg, Robert

Merritt, E. B.
See Waddington, Miriam

Merton, Thomas
1915-1968 .. **CLC 1, 3, 11, 34, 83; PC 10**
See also CA 5-8R; 25-28R; CANR 22;
DLB 48; DLBY 81; MTCW

Merwin, W(illiam) S(tanley)
1927- ... **CLC 1, 2, 3, 5, 8, 13, 18, 45, 88**
See also CA 13-16R; CANR 15, 51;
DAM POET; DLB 5; INT CANR-15;
MTCW

Metcalf, John 1938-.............. **CLC 37**
See also CA 113; DLB 60

Metcalf, Suzanne
See Baum, L(yman) Frank

Mew, Charlotte (Mary)
1870-1928 .... **TCLC 8**
See also CA 105; DLB 19, 135

Mewshaw, Michael 1943-........... **CLC 9**
See also CA 53-56; CANR 7, 47; DLBY 80

Meyer, June
See Jordan, June

Meyer, Lynn
See Slavitt, David R(ytman)

Meyer-Meyrink, Gustav 1868-1932
See Meyrink, Gustav
See also CA 117

Meyers, Jeffrey 1939- .... **CLC 39**
See also CA 73-76; DLB 111

Meynell, Alice (Christina Gertrude Thompson)
1847-1922 .... **TCLC 6**
See also CA 104; DLB 19, 98

Meyrink, Gustav .... **TCLC 21**
See also Meyer-Meyrink, Gustav
See also DLB 81

Michaels, Leonard
1933- .... **CLC 6, 25; SSC 16**
See also CA 61-64; CANR 21; DLB 130;
MTCW

Michaux, Henri 1899-1984 ...... **CLC 8, 19**
See also CA 85-88; 114

Michelangelo 1475-1564............ **LC 12**

Michelet, Jules 1798-1874 ...... **NCLC 31**

Michener, James A(lbert)
1907(?)- .... **CLC 1, 5, 11, 29, 60**
See also AITN 1; BEST 90:1; CA 5-8R;
CANR 21, 45; DAM NOV, POP; DLB 6;
MTCW

Mickiewicz, Adam 1798-1855 ..... **NCLC 3**

Middleton, Christopher 1926-...... **CLC 13**
See also CA 13-16R; CANR 29; DLB 40

Middleton, Richard (Barham)
1882-1911 .... **TCLC 56**
See also DLB 156

Middleton, Stanley 1919-........ **CLC 7, 38**
See also CA 25-28R; CAAS 23; CANR 21,
46; DLB 14

Middleton, Thomas 1580-1627........ **DC 5**
See also DAM DRAM, MST; DLB 58

Migueis, Jose Rodrigues 1901-..... **CLC 10**

Mikszath, Kalman 1847-1910 ..... **TCLC 31**

Miles, Josephine
1911-1985 .... **CLC 1, 2, 14, 34, 39**
See also CA 1-4R; 116; CANR 2;
DAM POET; DLB 48

Militant
See Sandburg, Carl (August)

Mill, John Stuart 1806-1873..... **NCLC 11**
See also CDBLB 1832-1890; DLB 55

Millar, Kenneth 1915-1983 .... **CLC 14**
See also Macdonald, Ross
See also CA 9-12R; 110; CANR 16;
DAM POP; DLB 2; DLBD 6; DLBY 83;
MTCW

Millay, E. Vincent
See Millay, Edna St. Vincent

Millay, Edna St. Vincent
1892-1950 ...... **TCLC 4, 49; DA; DAB;**
                                DAC; PC 6
See also CA 104; 130; CDALB 1917-1929;
DAM MST, POET; DLB 45; MTCW

Miller, Arthur
1915- .... **CLC 1, 2, 6, 10, 15, 26, 47, 78;**
                       DA; DAB; DAC; DC 1; WLC
See also AAYA 15; AITN 1; CA 1-4R;
CABS 3; CANR 2, 30;
CDALB 1941-1968; DAM DRAM, MST;
DLB 7; MTCW

Miller, Henry (Valentine)
1891-1980 .... **CLC 1, 2, 4, 9, 14, 43, 84;**
                              DA; DAB; DAC; WLC
See also CA 9-12R; 97-100; CANR 33;
CDALB 1929-1941; DAM MST, NOV;
DLB 4, 9; DLBY 80; MTCW

Miller, Jason 1939(?)- .... **CLC 2**
See also AITN 1; CA 73-76; DLB 7

Miller, Sue 1943- .... **CLC 44**
See also BEST 90:3; CA 139; DAM POP;
DLB 143

Miller, Walter M(ichael, Jr.)
1923- .... **CLC 4, 30**
See also CA 85-88; DLB 8

Millett, Kate 1934-............... **CLC 67**
See also AITN 1; CA 73-76; CANR 32;
MTCW

Millhauser, Steven 1943-....... **CLC 21, 54**
See also CA 110; 111; DLB 2; INT 111

Millin, Sarah Gertrude 1889-1968 .. **CLC 49**
See also CA 102; 93-96

Milne, A(lan) A(lexander)
1882-1956 .... **TCLC 6; DAB; DAC**
See also CA 104; 133; CLR 1, 26;
DAM MST; DLB 10, 77, 100, 160;
MAICYA; MTCW; YABC 1

Milner, Ron(ald) 1938-....... **CLC 56; BLC**
See also AITN 1; BW 1; CA 73-76;
CANR 24; DAM MULT; DLB 38;
MTCW

Milosz, Czeslaw
1911- ... **CLC 5, 11, 22, 31, 56, 82; PC 8**
See also CA 81-84; CANR 23, 51;
DAM MST, POET; MTCW

Milton, John
1608-1674 ...... **LC 9; DA; DAB; DAC;**
                                                    WLC
See also CDBLB 1660-1789; DAM MST,
POET; DLB 131, 151

Min, Anchee 1957-............... **CLC 86**
See also CA 146

Minehaha, Cornelius
See Wedekind, (Benjamin) Frank(lin)

Miner, Valerie 1947- .... **CLC 40**
See also CA 97-100

Minimo, Duca
See D'Annunzio, Gabriele

Minot, Susan 1956- .... **CLC 44**
See also CA 134

Minus, Ed 1938-................. **CLC 39**

Miranda, Javier
See Bioy Casares, Adolfo

Mirbeau, Octave 1848-1917....... **TCLC 55**
See also DLB 123

Miro (Ferrer), Gabriel (Francisco Victor)
1879-1930 .... **TCLC 5**
See also CA 104

Mishima, Yukio
.... **CLC 2, 4, 6, 9, 27; DC 1; SSC 4**
See also Hiraoka, Kimitake

Mistral, Frederic 1830-1914 ...... **TCLC 51**
See also CA 122

Mistral, Gabriela............ **TCLC 2; HLC**
See also Godoy Alcayaga, Lucila

Mistry, Rohinton 1952-....... **CLC 71; DAC**
See also CA 141

Mitchell, Clyde
See Ellison, Harlan (Jay); Silverberg, Robert

Mitchell, James Leslie 1901-1935
See Gibbon, Lewis Grassic
See also CA 104; DLB 15

Mitchell, Joni 1943-.............. **CLC 12**
See also CA 112

Mitchell, Margaret (Munnerlyn)
1900-1949 .... **TCLC 11**
See also CA 109; 125; DAM NOV, POP;
DLB 9; MTCW

Mitchell, Peggy
See Mitchell, Margaret (Munnerlyn)

Mitchell, S(ilas) Weir 1829-1914 .. **TCLC 36**

Naipaul, V(idiadhar) S(urajprasad)
    1932- .... **CLC 4, 7, 9, 13, 18, 37; DAB;
                                        DAC**
    See also CA 1-4R; CANR 1, 33, 51;
        CDBLB 1960 to Present; DAM MST,
        NOV; DLB 125; DLBY 85; MTCW

Nakos, Lilika 1899(?)- .... **CLC 29**

Narayan, R(asipuram) K(rishnaswami)
    1906- .... **CLC 7, 28, 47**
    See also CA 81-84; CANR 33; DAM NOV;
        MTCW; SATA 62

Nash, (Frediric) Ogden 1902-1971 .. **CLC 23**
    See also CA 13-14; 29-32R; CANR 34;
        CAP 1; DAM POET; DLB 11;
        MAICYA; MTCW; SATA 2, 46

Nathan, Daniel
    See Dannay, Frederic

Nathan, George Jean 1882-1958 ... **TCLC 18**
    See also Hatteras, Owen
    See also CA 114; DLB 137

Natsume, Kinnosuke 1867-1916
    See Natsume, Soseki
    See also CA 104

Natsume, Soseki .... **TCLC 2, 10**
    See also Natsume, Kinnosuke

Natti, (Mary) Lee 1919-
    See Kingman, Lee
    See also CA 5-8R; CANR 2

Naylor, Gloria
    1950- ..... **CLC 28, 52; BLC; DA; DAC**
    See also AAYA 6; BW 2; CA 107;
        CANR 27, 51; DAM MST, MULT,
        NOV, POP; MTCW

Neihardt, John Gneisenau
    1881-1973 .... **CLC 32**
    See also CA 13-14; CAP 1; DLB 9, 54

Nekrasov, Nikolai Alekseevich
    1821-1878 .... **NCLC 11**

Nelligan, Emile 1879-1941 .... **TCLC 14**
    See also CA 114; DLB 92

Nelson, Willie 1933- .... **CLC 17**
    See also CA 107

Nemerov, Howard (Stanley)
    1920-1991 .... **CLC 2, 6, 9, 36**
    See also CA 1-4R; 134; CABS 2; CANR 1,
        27; DAM POET; DLB 5, 6; DLBY 83;
        INT CANR-27; MTCW

Neruda, Pablo
    1904-1973 ..... **CLC 1, 2, 5, 7, 9, 28, 62;
                DA; DAB; DAC; HLC; PC 4; WLC**
    See also CA 19-20; 45-48; CAP 2;
        DAM MST, MULT, POET; HW; MTCW

Nerval, Gerard de
    1808-1855 ..... **NCLC 1; PC 13; SSC 18**

Nervo, (Jose) Amado (Ruiz de)
    1870-1919 .... **TCLC 11**
    See also CA 109; 131; HW

Nessi, Pio Baroja y
    See Baroja (y Nessi), Pio

Nestroy, Johann 1801-1862 ...... **NCLC 42**
    See also DLB 133

Neufeld, John (Arthur) 1938- ...... **CLC 17**
    See also AAYA 11; CA 25-28R; CANR 11,
        37; MAICYA; SAAS 3; SATA 6, 81

Neville, Emily Cheney 1919- .... **CLC 12**
    See also CA 5-8R; CANR 3, 37; JRDA;
        MAICYA; SAAS 2; SATA 1

Newbound, Bernard Slade 1930-
    See Slade, Bernard
    See also CA 81-84; CANR 49;
        DAM DRAM

Newby, P(ercy) H(oward)
    1918- .... **CLC 2, 13**
    See also CA 5-8R; CANR 32; DAM NOV;
        DLB 15; MTCW

Newlove, Donald 1928- .... **CLC 6**
    See also CA 29-32R; CANR 25

Newlove, John (Herbert) 1938- ..... **CLC 14**
    See also CA 21-24R; CANR 9, 25

Newman, Charles 1938- .... **CLC 2, 8**
    See also CA 21-24R

Newman, Edwin (Harold) 1919- .... **CLC 14**
    See also AITN 1; CA 69-72; CANR 5

Newman, John Henry
    1801-1890 .... **NCLC 38**
    See also DLB 18, 32, 55

Newton, Suzanne 1936- .... **CLC 35**
    See also CA 41-44R; CANR 14; JRDA;
        SATA 5, 77

Nexo, Martin Andersen
    1869-1954 .... **TCLC 43**

Nezval, Vitezslav 1900-1958 ...... **TCLC 44**
    See also CA 123

Ng, Fae Myenne 1957(?)- .... **CLC 81**
    See also CA 146

Ngema, Mbongeni 1955- .... **CLC 57**
    See also BW 2; CA 143

Ngugi, James T(hiong'o) .... **CLC 3, 7, 13**
    See also Ngugi wa Thiong'o

Ngugi wa Thiong'o 1938- ..... **CLC 36; BLC**
    See also Ngugi, James T(hiong'o)
    See also BW 2; CA 81-84; CANR 27;
        DAM MULT, NOV; DLB 125; MTCW

Nichol, B(arrie) P(hillip)
    1944-1988 .... **CLC 18**
    See also CA 53-56; DLB 53; SATA 66

Nichols, John (Treadwell) 1940- .... **CLC 38**
    See also CA 9-12R; CAAS 2; CANR 6;
        DLBY 82

Nichols, Leigh
    See Koontz, Dean R(ay)

Nichols, Peter (Richard)
    1927- .... **CLC 5, 36, 65**
    See also CA 104; CANR 33; DLB 13;
        MTCW

Nicolas, F. R. E.
    See Freeling, Nicolas

Niedecker, Lorine 1903-1970.... **CLC 10, 42**
    See also CA 25-28; CAP 2; DAM POET;
        DLB 48

Nietzsche, Friedrich (Wilhelm)
    1844-1900 .... **TCLC 10, 18, 55**
    See also CA 107; 121; DLB 129

Nievo, Ippolito 1831-1861 .... **NCLC 22**

Nightingale, Anne Redmon 1943-
    See Redmon, Anne
    See also CA 103

Nik. T. O.
    See Annensky, Innokenty Fyodorovich

Nin, Anais
    1903-1977 ...... **CLC 1, 4, 8, 11, 14, 60;
                                        SSC 10**
    See also AITN 2; CA 13-16R; 69-72;
        CANR 22; DAM NOV, POP; DLB 2, 4,
        152; MTCW

Nishiwaki, Junzaburo 1894-1982 .... **PC 15**
    See also CA 107

Nissenson, Hugh 1933-........... **CLC 4, 9**
    See also CA 17-20R; CANR 27; DLB 28

Niven, Larry .... **CLC 8**
    See also Niven, Laurence Van Cott
    See also DLB 8

Niven, Laurence Van Cott 1938-
    See Niven, Larry
    See also CA 21-24R; CAAS 12; CANR 14,
        44; DAM POP; MTCW

Nixon, Agnes Eckhardt 1927-...... **CLC 21**
    See also CA 110

Nizan, Paul 1905-1940........... **TCLC 40**
    See also DLB 72

Nkosi, Lewis 1936-.......... **CLC 45; BLC**
    See also BW 1; CA 65-68; CANR 27;
        DAM MULT; DLB 157

Nodier, (Jean) Charles (Emmanuel)
    1780-1844 .... **NCLC 19**
    See also DLB 119

Nolan, Christopher 1965-.......... **CLC 58**
    See also CA 111

Noon, Jeff 1957-................. **CLC 91**
    See also CA 148

Norden, Charles
    See Durrell, Lawrence (George)

Nordhoff, Charles (Bernard)
    1887-1947 .... **TCLC 23**
    See also CA 108; DLB 9; SATA 23

Norfolk, Lawrence 1963-.......... **CLC 76**
    See also CA 144

Norman, Marsha 1947- .... **CLC 28**
    See also CA 105; CABS 3; CANR 41;
        DAM DRAM; DLBY 84

Norris, Benjamin Franklin, Jr.
    1870-1902 .... **TCLC 24**
    See also Norris, Frank
    See also CA 110

Norris, Frank
    See Norris, Benjamin Franklin, Jr.
    See also CDALB 1865-1917; DLB 12, 71

Norris, Leslie 1921- .... **CLC 14**
    See also CA 11-12; CANR 14; CAP 1;
        DLB 27

North, Andrew
    See Norton, Andre

North, Anthony
    See Koontz, Dean R(ay)

North, Captain George
    See Stevenson, Robert Louis (Balfour)

North, Milou
    See Erdrich, Louise

Northrup, B. A.
    See Hubbard, L(afayette) Ron(ald)

North Staffs
See Hulme, T(homas) E(rnest)

Norton, Alice Mary
See Norton, Andre
See also MAICYA; SATA 1, 43

Norton, Andre 1912- .... **CLC 12**
See also Norton, Alice Mary
See also AAYA 14; CA 1-4R; CANR 2, 31;
DLB 8, 52; JRDA; MTCW

Norton, Caroline 1808-1877...... **NCLC 47**
See also DLB 21, 159

Norway, Nevil Shute 1899-1960
See Shute, Nevil
See also CA 102; 93-96

Norwid, Cyprian Kamil
1821-1883 .... **NCLC 17**

Nosille, Nabrah
See Ellison, Harlan (Jay)

Nossack, Hans Erich 1901-1978..... **CLC 6**
See also CA 93-96; 85-88; DLB 69

Nostradamus 1503-1566........... **LC 27**

Nosu, Chuji
See Ozu, Yasujiro

Notenburg, Eleanora (Genrikhovna) von
See Guro, Elena

Nova, Craig 1945-.............. **CLC 7, 31**
See also CA 45-48; CANR 2

Novak, Joseph
See Kosinski, Jerzy (Nikodem)

Novalis 1772-1801 .... **NCLC 13**
See also DLB 90

Nowlan, Alden (Albert)
1933-1983 .... **CLC 15; DAC**
See also CA 9-12R; CANR 5; DAM MST;
DLB 53

Noyes, Alfred 1880-1958.......... **TCLC 7**
See also CA 104; DLB 20

Nunn, Kem 19(?)-................ **CLC 34**

Nye, Robert 1939- .... **CLC 13, 42**
See also CA 33-36R; CANR 29;
DAM NOV; DLB 14; MTCW; SATA 6

Nyro, Laura 1947- .... **CLC 17**

Oates, Joyce Carol
1938-......CLC 1, 2, 3, 6, 9, 11, 15, 19,
33, 52; DA; DAB; DAC; SSC 6; WLC
See also AAYA 15; AITN 1; BEST 89:2;
CA 5-8R; CANR 25, 45;
CDALB 1968-1988; DAM MST, NOV,
POP; DLB 2, 5, 130; DLBY 81;
INT CANR-25; MTCW

O'Brien, Darcy 1939-............. **CLC 11**
See also CA 21-24R; CANR 8

O'Brien, E. G.
See Clarke, Arthur C(harles)

O'Brien, Edna
1936- ... CLC 3, 5, 8, 13, 36, 65; SSC 10
See also CA 1-4R; CANR 6, 41;
CDBLB 1960 to Present; DAM NOV;
DLB 14; MTCW

O'Brien, Fitz-James 1828-1862... **NCLC 21**
See also DLB 74

O'Brien, Flann........ **CLC 1, 4, 5, 7, 10, 47**
See also O Nuallain, Brian

O'Brien, Richard 1942- .... **CLC 17**
See also CA 124

O'Brien, Tim 1946-......... **CLC 7, 19, 40**
See also AAYA 16; CA 85-88; CANR 40;
DAM POP; DLB 152; DLBD 9;
DLBY 80

Obstfelder, Sigbjoern 1866-1900... **TCLC 23**
See also CA 123

O'Casey, Sean
1880-1964 ...... CLC 1, 5, 9, 11, 15, 88;
DAB; DAC
See also CA 89-92; CDBLB 1914-1945;
DAM DRAM, MST; DLB 10; MTCW

O'Cathasaigh, Sean
See O'Casey, Sean

Ochs, Phil 1940-1976............. **CLC 17**
See also CA 65-68

O'Connor, Edwin (Greene)
1918-1968 .... **CLC 14**
See also CA 93-96; 25-28R

O'Connor, (Mary) Flannery
1925-1964 .... CLC 1, 2, 3, 6, 10, 13, 15,
21, 66; DA; DAB; DAC; SSC 1; WLC
See also AAYA 7; CA 1-4R; CANR 3, 41;
CDALB 1941-1968; DAM MST, NOV;
DLB 2, 152; DLBD 12; DLBY 80;
MTCW

O'Connor, Frank........... **CLC 23; SSC 5**
See also O'Donovan, Michael John
See also DLB 162

O'Dell, Scott 1898-1989........... **CLC 30**
See also AAYA 3; CA 61-64; 129;
CANR 12, 30; CLR 1, 16; DLB 52;
JRDA; MAICYA; SATA 12, 60

Odets, Clifford
1906-1963 .... **CLC 2, 28; DC 6**
See also CA 85-88; DAM DRAM; DLB 7,
26; MTCW

O'Doherty, Brian 1934-........... **CLC 76**
See also CA 105

O'Donnell, K. M.
See Malzberg, Barry N(athaniel)

O'Donnell, Lawrence
See Kuttner, Henry

O'Donovan, Michael John
1903-1966 .... **CLC 14**
See also O'Connor, Frank
See also CA 93-96

Oe, Kenzaburo
1935-......... **CLC 10, 36, 86; SSC 20**
See also CA 97-100; CANR 36, 50;
DAM NOV; DLBY 94; MTCW

O'Faolain, Julia 1932-....... **CLC 6, 19, 47**
See also CA 81-84; CAAS 2; CANR 12;
DLB 14; MTCW

O'Faolain, Sean
1900-1991 .... CLC 1, 7, 14, 32, 70;
SSC 13
See also CA 61-64; 134; CANR 12;
DLB 15, 162; MTCW

O'Flaherty, Liam
1896-1984 .... **CLC 5, 34; SSC 6**
See also CA 101; 113; CANR 35; DLB 36,
162; DLBY 84; MTCW

Ogilvy, Gavin
See Barrie, J(ames) M(atthew)

O'Grady, Standish James
1846-1928 .... **TCLC 5**
See also CA 104

O'Grady, Timothy 1951- .... **CLC 59**
See also CA 138

O'Hara, Frank
1926-1966 .... **CLC 2, 5, 13, 78**
See also CA 9-12R; 25-28R; CANR 33;
DAM POET; DLB 5, 16; MTCW

O'Hara, John (Henry)
1905-1970 .... CLC 1, 2, 3, 6, 11, 42;
SSC 15
See also CA 5-8R; 25-28R; CANR 31;
CDALB 1929-1941; DAM NOV; DLB 9,
86; DLBD 2; MTCW

O Hehir, Diana 1922- .... **CLC 41**
See also CA 93-96

Okigbo, Christopher (Ifenayichukwu)
1932-1967 ..... **CLC 25, 84; BLC; PC 7**
See also BW 1; CA 77-80; DAM MULT,
POET; DLB 125; MTCW

Okri, Ben 1959- .... **CLC 87**
See also BW 2; CA 130; 138; DLB 157;
INT 138

Olds, Sharon 1942-......... **CLC 32, 39, 85**
See also CA 101; CANR 18, 41;
DAM POET; DLB 120

Oldstyle, Jonathan
See Irving, Washington

Olesha, Yuri (Karlovich)
1899-1960 .... **CLC 8**
See also CA 85-88

Oliphant, Laurence
1829(?)-1888 .... **NCLC 47**
See also DLB 18

Oliphant, Margaret (Oliphant Wilson)
1828-1897 .... **NCLC 11**
See also DLB 18, 159

Oliver, Mary 1935-............. **CLC 19, 34**
See also CA 21-24R; CANR 9, 43; DLB 5

Olivier, Laurence (Kerr)
1907-1989 .... **CLC 20**
See also CA 111; 150; 129

Olsen, Tillie
1913- ..... CLC 4, 13; DA; DAB; DAC;
SSC 11
See also CA 1-4R; CANR 1, 43;
DAM MST; DLB 28; DLBY 80; MTCW

Olson, Charles (John)
1910-1970 ..... CLC 1, 2, 5, 6, 9, 11, 29
See also CA 13-16; 25-28R; CABS 2;
CANR 35; CAP 1; DAM POET; DLB 5,
16; MTCW

Olson, Toby 1937- .... **CLC 28**
See also CA 65-68; CANR 9, 31

Olyesha, Yuri
See Olesha, Yuri (Karlovich)

Ondaatje, (Philip) Michael
1943- ... CLC 14, 29, 51, 76; DAB; DAC
See also CA 77-80; CANR 42; DAM MST;
DLB 60

Oneal, Elizabeth 1934-
See Oneal, Zibby
See also CA 106; CANR 28; MAICYA;
SATA 30, 82

Oneal, Zibby .... CLC 30
See also Oneal, Elizabeth
See also AAYA 5; CLR 13; JRDA

O'Neill, Eugene (Gladstone)
1888-1953 ...... TCLC 1, 6, 27, 49; DA;
DAB; DAC; WLC
See also AITN 1; CA 110; 132;
CDALB 1929-1941; DAM DRAM, MST;
DLB 7; MTCW

Onetti, Juan Carlos 1909-1994 ... CLC 7, 10
See also CA 85-88; 145; CANR 32;
DAM MULT, NOV; DLB 113; HW;
MTCW

O Nuallain, Brian 1911-1966
See O'Brien, Flann
See also CA 21-22; 25-28R; CAP 2

Oppen, George 1908-1984 .... CLC 7, 13, 34
See also CA 13-16R; 113; CANR 8; DLB 5

Oppenheim, E(dward) Phillips
1866-1946 .... TCLC 45
See also CA 111; DLB 70

Orlovitz, Gil 1918-1973 .... CLC 22
See also CA 77-80; 45-48; DLB 2, 5

Orris
See Ingelow, Jean

Ortega y Gasset, Jose
1883-1955 .... TCLC 9; HLC
See also CA 106; 130; DAM MULT; HW;
MTCW

Ortese, Anna Maria 1914-........ CLC 89

Ortiz, Simon J(oseph) 1941- .... CLC 45
See also CA 134; DAM MULT, POET;
DLB 120; NNAL

Orton, Joe .... CLC 4, 13, 43; DC 3
See also Orton, John Kingsley
See also CDBLB 1960 to Present; DLB 13

Orton, John Kingsley 1933-1967
See Orton, Joe
See also CA 85-88; CANR 35;
DAM DRAM; MTCW

Orwell, George
..... TCLC 2, 6, 15, 31, 51; DAB; WLC
See also Blair, Eric (Arthur)
See also CDBLB 1945-1960; DLB 15, 98

Osborne, David
See Silverberg, Robert

Osborne, George
See Silverberg, Robert

Osborne, John (James)
1929-1994 ..... CLC 1, 2, 5, 11, 45; DA;
DAB; DAC; WLC
See also CA 13-16R; 147; CANR 21;
CDBLB 1945-1960; DAM DRAM, MST;
DLB 13; MTCW

Osborne, Lawrence 1958- .... CLC 50

Oshima, Nagisa 1932- .... CLC 20
See also CA 116; 121

Oskison, John Milton
1874-1947 .... TCLC 35
See also CA 144; DAM MULT; NNAL

Ossoli, Sarah Margaret (Fuller marchesa d')
1810-1850
See Fuller, Margaret
See also SATA 25

Ostrovsky, Alexander
1823-1886 .... NCLC 30

Otero, Blas de 1916-1979......... CLC 11
See also CA 89-92; DLB 134

Otto, Whitney 1955-.............. CLC 70
See also CA 140

Ouida .... TCLC 43
See also De La Ramee, (Marie) Louise
See also DLB 18, 156

Ousmane, Sembene 1923- .... CLC 66; BLC
See also BW 1; CA 117; 125; MTCW

Ovid 43B.C.-18(?).......... CMLC 7; PC 2
See also DAM POET

Owen, Hugh
See Faust, Frederick (Schiller)

Owen, Wilfred (Edward Salter)
1893-1918 ...... TCLC 5, 27; DA; DAB;
DAC; WLC
See also CA 104; 141; CDBLB 1914-1945;
DAM MST, POET; DLB 20

Owens, Rochelle 1936-............ CLC 8
See also CA 17-20R; CAAS 2; CANR 39

Oz, Amos 1939- ... CLC 5, 8, 11, 27, 33, 54
See also CA 53-56; CANR 27, 47;
DAM NOV; MTCW

Ozick, Cynthia
1928- .... CLC 3, 7, 28, 62; SSC 15
See also BEST 90:1; CA 17-20R; CANR 23;
DAM NOV, POP; DLB 28, 152;
DLBY 82; INT CANR-23; MTCW

Ozu, Yasujiro 1903-1963.......... CLC 16
See also CA 112

Pacheco, C.
See Pessoa, Fernando (Antonio Nogueira)

Pa Chin .... CLC 18
See also Li Fei-kan

Pack, Robert 1929-.............. CLC 13
See also CA 1-4R; CANR 3, 44; DLB 5

Padgett, Lewis
See Kuttner, Henry

Padilla (Lorenzo), Heberto 1932-... CLC 38
See also AITN 1; CA 123; 131; HW

Page, Jimmy 1944-.............. CLC 12

Page, Louise 1955-.............. CLC 40
See also CA 140

Page, P(atricia) K(athleen)
1916- .... CLC 7, 18; DAC; PC 12
See also CA 53-56; CANR 4, 22;
DAM MST; DLB 68; MTCW

Paget, Violet 1856-1935
See Lee, Vernon
See also CA 104

Paget-Lowe, Henry
See Lovecraft, H(oward) P(hillips)

Paglia, Camille (Anna) 1947-....... CLC 68
See also CA 140

Paige, Richard
See Koontz, Dean R(ay)

Pakenham, Antonia
See Fraser, (Lady) Antonia (Pakenham)

Palamas, Kostes 1859-1943 .... TCLC 5
See also CA 105

Palazzeschi, Aldo 1885-1974 .... CLC 11
See also CA 89-92; 53-56; DLB 114

Paley, Grace 1922-.... CLC 4, 6, 37; SSC 8
See also CA 25-28R; CANR 13, 46;
DAM POP; DLB 28; INT CANR-13;
MTCW

Palin, Michael (Edward) 1943-..... CLC 21
See also Monty Python
See also CA 107; CANR 35; SATA 67

Palliser, Charles 1947-............ CLC 65
See also CA 136

Palma, Ricardo 1833-1919........ TCLC 29

Pancake, Breece Dexter 1952-1979
See Pancake, Breece D'J
See also CA 123; 109

Pancake, Breece D'J.............. CLC 29
See also Pancake, Breece Dexter
See also DLB 130

Panko, Rudy
See Gogol, Nikolai (Vasilyevich)

Papadiamantis, Alexandros
1851-1911 .... TCLC 29

Papadiamantopoulos, Johannes 1856-1910
See Moreas, Jean
See also CA 117

Papini, Giovanni 1881-1956....... TCLC 22
See also CA 121

Paracelsus 1493-1541.............. LC 14

Parasol, Peter
See Stevens, Wallace

Parfenie, Maria
See Codrescu, Andrei

Parini, Jay (Lee) 1948- .... CLC 54
See also CA 97-100; CAAS 16; CANR 32

Park, Jordan
See Kornbluth, C(yril) M.; Pohl, Frederik

Parker, Bert
See Ellison, Harlan (Jay)

Parker, Dorothy (Rothschild)
1893-1967 .... CLC 15, 68; SSC 2
See also CA 19-20; 25-28R; CAP 2;
DAM POET; DLB 11, 45, 86; MTCW

Parker, Robert B(rown) 1932-...... CLC 27
See also BEST 89:4; CA 49-52; CANR 1,
26; DAM NOV, POP; INT CANR-26;
MTCW

Parkin, Frank 1940-.............. CLC 43
See also CA 147

Parkman, Francis, Jr.
1823-1893 .... NCLC 12
See also DLB 1, 30

Parks, Gordon (Alexander Buchanan)
1912- .... CLC 1, 16; BLC
See also AITN 2; BW 2; CA 41-44R;
CANR 26; DAM MULT; DLB 33;
SATA 8

Parnell, Thomas 1679-1718 .... LC 3
See also DLB 94

Parra, Nicanor 1914-........ CLC 2; HLC
See also CA 85-88; CANR 32;
DAM MULT; HW; MTCW

Parrish, Mary Frances
See Fisher, M(ary) F(rances) K(ennedy)

Parson
See Coleridge, Samuel Taylor

Parson Lot
See Kingsley, Charles

Partridge, Anthony
See Oppenheim, E(dward) Phillips

Pascoli, Giovanni 1855-1912 ..... **TCLC 45**

Pasolini, Pier Paolo
1922-1975 .... **CLC 20, 37**
See also CA 93-96; 61-64; DLB 128;
MTCW

Pasquini
See Silone, Ignazio

Pastan, Linda (Olenik) 1932- ...... **CLC 27**
See also CA 61-64; CANR 18, 40;
DAM POET; DLB 5

Pasternak, Boris (Leonidovich)
1890-1960 ...... **CLC 7, 10, 18, 63; DA;
DAB; DAC; PC 6; WLC**
See also CA 127; 116; DAM MST, NOV,
POET; MTCW

Patchen, Kenneth 1911-1972 ... **CLC 1, 2, 18**
See also CA 1-4R; 33-36R; CANR 3, 35;
DAM POET; DLB 16, 48; MTCW

Pater, Walter (Horatio)
1839-1894 .... **NCLC 7**
See also CDBLB 1832-1890; DLB 57, 156

Paterson, A(ndrew) B(arton)
1864-1941 .... **TCLC 32**

Paterson, Katherine (Womeldorf)
1932- .... **CLC 12, 30**
See also AAYA 1; CA 21-24R; CANR 28;
CLR 7; DLB 52; JRDA; MAICYA;
MTCW; SATA 13, 53

Patmore, Coventry Kersey Dighton
1823-1896 .... **NCLC 9**
See also DLB 35, 98

Paton, Alan (Stewart)
1903-1988 ...... **CLC 4, 10, 25, 55; DA;
DAB; DAC; WLC**
See also CA 13-16; 125; CANR 22; CAP 1;
DAM MST, NOV; MTCW; SATA 11;
SATA-Obit 56

Paton Walsh, Gillian 1937-
See Walsh, Jill Paton
See also CANR 38; JRDA; MAICYA;
SAAS 3; SATA 4, 72

Paulding, James Kirke 1778-1860.. **NCLC 2**
See also DLB 3, 59, 74

Paulin, Thomas Neilson 1949-
See Paulin, Tom
See also CA 123; 128

Paulin, Tom .... **CLC 37**
See also Paulin, Thomas Neilson
See also DLB 40

Paustovsky, Konstantin (Georgievich)
1892-1968 .... **CLC 40**
See also CA 93-96; 25-28R

Pavese, Cesare
1908-1950 ..... **TCLC 3; PC 13; SSC 19**
See also CA 104; DLB 128

Pavic, Milorad 1929- .... **CLC 60**
See also CA 136

Payne, Alan
See Jakes, John (William)

Paz, Gil
See Lugones, Leopoldo

Paz, Octavio
1914- .... **CLC 3, 4, 6, 10, 19, 51, 65;
DA; DAB; DAC; HLC; PC 1; WLC**
See also CA 73-76; CANR 32; DAM MST,
MULT, POET; DLBY 90; HW; MTCW

Peacock, Molly 1947-............. **CLC 60**
See also CA 103; CAAS 21; DLB 120

Peacock, Thomas Love
1785-1866 .... **NCLC 22**
See also DLB 96, 116

Peake, Mervyn 1911-1968 .... **CLC 7, 54**
See also CA 5-8R; 25-28R; CANR 3;
DLB 15, 160; MTCW; SATA 23

Pearce, Philippa .... **CLC 21**
See also Christie, (Ann) Philippa
See also CLR 9; DLB 161; MAICYA;
SATA 1, 67

Pearl, Eric
See Elman, Richard

Pearson, T(homas) R(eid) 1956- .... **CLC 39**
See also CA 120; 130; INT 130

Peck, Dale 1967- .... **CLC 81**
See also CA 146

Peck, John 1941- .... **CLC 3**
See also CA 49-52; CANR 3

Peck, Richard (Wayne) 1934- ...... **CLC 21**
See also AAYA 1; CA 85-88; CANR 19,
38; CLR 15; INT CANR-19; JRDA;
MAICYA; SAAS 2; SATA 18, 55

Peck, Robert Newton
1928- .... **CLC 17; DA; DAC**
See also AAYA 3; CA 81-84; CANR 31;
DAM MST; JRDA; MAICYA; SAAS 1;
SATA 21, 62

Peckinpah, (David) Sam(uel)
1925-1984 .... **CLC 20**
See also CA 109; 114

Pedersen, Knut 1859-1952
See Hamsun, Knut
See also CA 104; 119; MTCW

Peeslake, Gaffer
See Durrell, Lawrence (George)

Peguy, Charles Pierre
1873-1914 .... **TCLC 10**
See also CA 107

Pena, Ramon del Valle y
See Valle-Inclan, Ramon (Maria) del

Pendennis, Arthur Esquir
See Thackeray, William Makepeace

Penn, William 1644-1718 .... **LC 25**
See also DLB 24

Pepys, Samuel
1633-1703 ..... **LC 11; DA; DAB; DAC;
WLC**
See also CDBLB 1660-1789; DAM MST;
DLB 101

Percy, Walker
1916-1990 .... **CLC 2, 3, 6, 8, 14, 18, 47,
65**
See also CA 1-4R; 131; CANR 1, 23;
DAM NOV, POP; DLB 2; DLBY 80, 90;
MTCW

Perec, Georges 1936-1982 .... **CLC 56**
See also CA 141; DLB 83

Pereda (y Sanchez de Porrua), Jose Maria de
1833-1906 .... **TCLC 16**
See also CA 117

Pereda y Porrua, Jose Maria de
See Pereda (y Sanchez de Porrua), Jose
Maria de

Peregoy, George Weems
See Mencken, H(enry) L(ouis)

Perelman, S(idney) J(oseph)
1904-1979 ... **CLC 3, 5, 9, 15, 23, 44, 49**
See also AITN 1, 2; CA 73-76; 89-92;
CANR 18; DAM DRAM; DLB 11, 44;
MTCW

Peret, Benjamin 1899-1959 .... **TCLC 20**
See also CA 117

Peretz, Isaac Loeb 1851(?)-1915... **TCLC 16**
See also CA 109

Peretz, Yitzkhok Leibush
See Peretz, Isaac Loeb

Perez Galdos, Benito 1843-1920... **TCLC 27**
See also CA 125; HW

Perrault, Charles 1628-1703 .... **LC 2**
See also MAICYA; SATA 25

Perry, Brighton
See Sherwood, Robert E(mmet)

Perse, St.-John .... **CLC 4, 11, 46**
See also Leger, (Marie-Rene Auguste) Alexis
Saint-Leger

Perutz, Leo 1882-1957 .... **TCLC 60**
See also DLB 81

Peseenz, Tulio F.
See Lopez y Fuentes, Gregorio

Pesetsky, Bette 1932-............. **CLC 28**
See also CA 133; DLB 130

Peshkov, Alexei Maximovich 1868-1936
See Gorky, Maxim
See also CA 105; 141; DA; DAC;
DAM DRAM, MST, NOV

Pessoa, Fernando (Antonio Nogueira)
1888-1935 .... **TCLC 27; HLC**
See also CA 125

Peterkin, Julia Mood 1880-1961 .... **CLC 31**
See also CA 102; DLB 9

Peters, Joan K. 1945-............. **CLC 39**

Peters, Robert L(ouis) 1924-........ **CLC 7**
See also CA 13-16R; CAAS 8; DLB 105

Petofi, Sandor 1823-1849........ **NCLC 21**

Petrakis, Harry Mark 1923-........ **CLC 3**
See also CA 9-12R; CANR 4, 30

Petrarch 1304-1374................. **PC 8**
See also DAM POET

Petrov, Evgeny .... **TCLC 21**
See also Kataev, Evgeny Petrovich

Petry, Ann (Lane) 1908- ...... **CLC 1, 7, 18**
See also BW 1; CA 5-8R; CAAS 6;
CANR 4, 46; CLR 12; DLB 76; JRDA;
MAICYA; MTCW; SATA 5

Petursson, Halligrimur 1614-1674 .... **LC 8**

Philips, Katherine 1632-1664........ **LC 30**
See also DLB 131

Philipson, Morris H. 1926- .... **CLC 53**
See also CA 1-4R; CANR 4

Phillips, David Graham
1867-1911 .... **TCLC 44**
See also CA 108; DLB 9, 12

Phillips, Jack
See Sandburg, Carl (August)

Phillips, Jayne Anne
1952- .... **CLC 15, 33; SSC 16**
See also CA 101; CANR 24, 50; DLBY 80;
INT CANR-24; MTCW

Phillips, Richard
See Dick, Philip K(indred)

Phillips, Robert (Schaeffer) 1938-... **CLC 28**
See also CA 17-20R; CAAS 13; CANR 8;
DLB 105

Phillips, Ward
See Lovecraft, H(oward) P(hillips)

Piccolo, Lucio 1901-1969......... **CLC 13**
See also CA 97-100; DLB 114

Pickthall, Marjorie L(owry) C(hristie)
1883-1922 .... **TCLC 21**
See also CA 107; DLB 92

Pico della Mirandola, Giovanni
1463-1494 .... **LC 15**

Piercy, Marge
1936- .... **CLC 3, 6, 14, 18, 27, 62**
See also CA 21-24R; CAAS 1; CANR 13,
43; DLB 120; MTCW

Piers, Robert
See Anthony, Piers

Pieyre de Mandiargues, Andre 1909-1991
See Mandiargues, Andre Pieyre de
See also CA 103; 136; CANR 22

Pilnyak, Boris .... **TCLC 23**
See also Vogau, Boris Andreyevich

Pincherle, Alberto 1907-1990 ... **CLC 11, 18**
See also Moravia, Alberto
See also CA 25-28R; 132; CANR 33;
DAM NOV; MTCW

Pinckney, Darryl 1953- .... **CLC 76**
See also BW 2; CA 143

Pindar 518B.C.-446B.C......... **CMLC 12**

Pineda, Cecile 1942- .... **CLC 39**
See also CA 118

Pinero, Arthur Wing 1855-1934 ... **TCLC 32**
See also CA 110; DAM DRAM; DLB 10

Pinero, Miguel (Antonio Gomez)
1946-1988 .... **CLC 4, 55**
See also CA 61-64; 125; CANR 29; HW

Pinget, Robert 1919- .... **CLC 7, 13, 37**
See also CA 85-88; DLB 83

Pink Floyd
See Barrett, (Roger) Syd; Gilmour, David;
Mason, Nick; Waters, Roger; Wright,
Rick

Pinkney, Edward 1802-1828 ..... **NCLC 31**

Pinkwater, Daniel Manus 1941-.... **CLC 35**
See also Pinkwater, Manus
See also AAYA 1; CA 29-32R; CANR 12,
38; CLR 4; JRDA; MAICYA; SAAS 3;
SATA 46, 76

Pinkwater, Manus
See Pinkwater, Daniel Manus
See also SATA 8

Pinsky, Robert 1940-..... **CLC 9, 19, 38, 91**
See also CA 29-32R; CAAS 4;
DAM POET; DLBY 82

Pinta, Harold
See Pinter, Harold

Pinter, Harold
1930- ..... **CLC 1, 3, 6, 9, 11, 15, 27, 58,
73; DA; DAB; DAC; WLC**
See also CA 5-8R; CANR 33; CDBLB 1960
to Present; DAM DRAM, MST; DLB 13;
MTCW

Pirandello, Luigi
1867-1936 ...... **TCLC 4, 29; DA; DAB;
DAC; DC 5; WLC**
See also CA 104; DAM DRAM, MST

Pirsig, Robert M(aynard)
1928- .... **CLC 4, 6, 73**
See also CA 53-56; CANR 42; DAM POP;
MTCW; SATA 39

Pisarev, Dmitry Ivanovich
1840-1868 .... **NCLC 25**

Pix, Mary (Griffith) 1666-1709 ...... **LC 8**
See also DLB 80

Pixerecourt, Guilbert de
1773-1844 .... **NCLC 39**

Plaidy, Jean
See Hibbert, Eleanor Alice Burford

Planche, James Robinson
1796-1880 .... **NCLC 42**

Plant, Robert 1948- .... **CLC 12**

Plante, David (Robert)
1940- .... **CLC 7, 23, 38**
See also CA 37-40R; CANR 12, 36;
DAM NOV; DLBY 83; INT CANR-12;
MTCW

Plath, Sylvia
1932-1963 ..... **CLC 1, 2, 3, 5, 9, 11, 14,
17, 50, 51, 62; DA; DAB; DAC; PC 1;
WLC**
See also AAYA 13; CA 19-20; CANR 34;
CAP 2; CDALB 1941-1968; DAM MST,
POET; DLB 5, 6, 152; MTCW

Plato
428(?)B.C.-348(?)B.C..... **CMLC 8; DA;
DAB; DAC**
See also DAM MST

Platonov, Andrei .... **TCLC 14**
See also Klimentov, Andrei Platonovich

Platt, Kin 1911- .... **CLC 26**
See also AAYA 11; CA 17-20R; CANR 11;
JRDA; SAAS 17; SATA 21, 86

Plautus c. 251B.C.-184B.C.......... **DC 6**

Plick et Plock
See Simenon, Georges (Jacques Christian)

Plimpton, George (Ames) 1927-..... **CLC 36**
See also AITN 1; CA 21-24R; CANR 32;
MTCW; SATA 10

Plomer, William Charles Franklin
1903-1973 .... **CLC 4, 8**
See also CA 21-22; CANR 34; CAP 2;
DLB 20, 162; MTCW; SATA 24

Plowman, Piers
See Kavanagh, Patrick (Joseph)

Plum, J.
See Wodehouse, P(elham) G(renville)

Plumly, Stanley (Ross) 1939- ...... **CLC 33**
See also CA 108; 110; DLB 5; INT 110

Plumpe, Friedrich Wilhelm
1888-1931 .... **TCLC 53**
See also CA 112

Poe, Edgar Allan
1809-1849 ..... **NCLC 1, 16; DA; DAB;
DAC; PC 1; SSC 1; WLC**
See also AAYA 14; CDALB 1640-1865;
DAM MST, POET; DLB 3, 59, 73, 74;
SATA 23

Poet of Titchfield Street, The
See Pound, Ezra (Weston Loomis)

Pohl, Frederik 1919- .... **CLC 18**
See also CA 61-64; CAAS 1; CANR 11, 37;
DLB 8; INT CANR-11; MTCW;
SATA 24

Poirier, Louis 1910-
See Gracq, Julien
See also CA 122; 126

Poitier, Sidney 1927- .... **CLC 26**
See also BW 1; CA 117

Polanski, Roman 1933- .... **CLC 16**
See also CA 77-80

Poliakoff, Stephen 1952- .... **CLC 38**
See also CA 106; DLB 13

Police, The
See Copeland, Stewart (Armstrong);
Summers, Andrew James; Sumner,
Gordon Matthew

Polidori, John William
1795-1821 .... **NCLC 51**
See also DLB 116

Pollitt, Katha 1949- .... **CLC 28**
See also CA 120; 122; MTCW

Pollock, (Mary) Sharon
1936- .... **CLC 50; DAC**
See also CA 141; DAM DRAM, MST;
DLB 60

Polo, Marco 1254-1324 .... **CMLC 15**

Polonsky, Abraham (Lincoln)
1910- .... **CLC 92**
See also CA 104; DLB 26; INT 104

Polybius c. 200B.C.-c. 118B.C.... **CMLC 17**

Pomerance, Bernard 1940-......... **CLC 13**
See also CA 101; CANR 49; DAM DRAM

Ponge, Francis (Jean Gaston Alfred)
1899-1988 .... **CLC 6, 18**
See also CA 85-88; 126; CANR 40;
DAM POET

Pontoppidan, Henrik 1857-1943 ... **TCLC 29**

Poole, Josephine .... **CLC 17**
See also Helyar, Jane Penelope Josephine
See also SAAS 2; SATA 5

Popa, Vasko 1922-1991 .... **CLC 19**
See also CA 112; 148

Pope, Alexander
1688-1744 ...... **LC 3; DA; DAB; DAC;
WLC**
See also CDBLB 1660-1789; DAM MST,
POET; DLB 95, 101

Porter, Connie (Rose) 1959(?)- ..... **CLC 70**
See also BW 2; CA 142; SATA 81

Reid, Desmond
See Moorcock, Michael (John)

Reid Banks, Lynne 1929-
See Banks, Lynne Reid
See also CA 1-4R; CANR 6, 22, 38;
CLR 24; JRDA; MAICYA; SATA 22, 75

Reilly, William K.
See Creasey, John

Reiner, Max
See Caldwell, (Janet Miriam) Taylor (Holland)

Reis, Ricardo
See Pessoa, Fernando (Antonio Nogueira)

Remarque, Erich Maria
1898-1970 .... CLC 21; DA; DAB; DAC
See also CA 77-80; 29-32R; DAM MST, NOV; DLB 56; MTCW

Remizov, A.
See Remizov, Aleksei (Mikhailovich)

Remizov, A. M.
See Remizov, Aleksei (Mikhailovich)

Remizov, Aleksei (Mikhailovich)
1877-1957 .... TCLC 27
See also CA 125; 133

Renan, Joseph Ernest
1823-1892 .... NCLC 26

Renard, Jules 1864-1910 .... TCLC 17
See also CA 117

Renault, Mary .... CLC 3, 11, 17
See also Challans, Mary
See also DLBY 83

Rendell, Ruth (Barbara) 1930- .. CLC 28, 48
See also Vine, Barbara
See also CA 109; CANR 32; DAM POP; DLB 87; INT CANR-32; MTCW

Renoir, Jean 1894-1979 .... CLC 20
See also CA 129; 85-88

Resnais, Alain 1922- .... CLC 16

Reverdy, Pierre 1889-1960 .... CLC 53
See also CA 97-100; 89-92

Rexroth, Kenneth
1905-1982 ...... CLC 1, 2, 6, 11, 22, 49
See also CA 5-8R; 107; CANR 14, 34;
CDALB 1941-1968; DAM POET;
DLB 16, 48; DLBY 82; INT CANR-14; MTCW

Reyes, Alfonso 1889-1959 .... TCLC 33
See also CA 131; HW

Reyes y Basoalto, Ricardo Eliecer Neftali
See Neruda, Pablo

Reymont, Wladyslaw (Stanislaw)
1868(?)-1925 .... TCLC 5
See also CA 104

Reynolds, Jonathan 1942- .... CLC 6, 38
See also CA 65-68; CANR 28

Reynolds, Joshua 1723-1792 .... LC 15
See also DLB 104

Reynolds, Michael Shane 1937- .... CLC 44
See also CA 65-68; CANR 9

Reznikoff, Charles 1894-1976 .... CLC 9
See also CA 33-36; 61-64; CAP 2; DLB 28, 45

Rezzori (d'Arezzo), Gregor von
1914- .... CLC 25
See also CA 122; 136

Rhine, Richard
See Silverstein, Alvin

Rhodes, Eugene Manlove
1869-1934 .... TCLC 53

R'hoone
See Balzac, Honore de

Rhys, Jean
1890(?)-1979 .... CLC 2, 4, 6, 14, 19, 51;
SSC 21
See also CA 25-28R; 85-88; CANR 35;
CDBLB 1945-1960; DAM NOV; DLB 36, 117, 162; MTCW

Ribeiro, Darcy 1922- .... CLC 34
See also CA 33-36R

Ribeiro, Joao Ubaldo (Osorio Pimentel)
1941- .... CLC 10, 67
See also CA 81 84

Ribman, Ronald (Burt) 1932- .... CLC 7
See also CA 21-24R; CANR 46

Ricci, Nino 1959- .... CLC 70
See also CA 137

Rice, Anne 1941- .... CLC 41
See also AAYA 9; BEST 89:2; CA 65-68;
CANR 12, 36; DAM POP

Rice, Elmer (Leopold)
1892-1967 .... CLC 7, 49
See also CA 21-22; 25-28R; CAP 2;
DAM DRAM; DLB 4, 7; MTCW

Rice, Tim(othy Miles Bindon)
1944- .... CLC 21
See also CA 103; CANR 46

Rich, Adrienne (Cecile)
1929- .... CLC 3, 6, 7, 11, 18, 36, 73, 76;
PC 5
See also CA 9-12R; CANR 20;
DAM POET; DLB 5, 67; MTCW

Rich, Barbara
See Graves, Robert (von Ranke)

Rich, Robert
See Trumbo, Dalton

Richard, Keith .... CLC 17
See also Richards, Keith

Richards, David Adams
1950- .... CLC 59; DAC
See also CA 93-96; DLB 53

Richards, I(vor) A(rmstrong)
1893-1979 .... CLC 14, 24
See also CA 41-44R; 89-92; CANR 34;
DLB 27

Richards, Keith 1943-
See Richard, Keith
See also CA 107

Richardson, Anne
See Roiphe, Anne (Richardson)

Richardson, Dorothy Miller
1873-1957 .... TCLC 3
See also CA 104; DLB 36

Richardson, Ethel Florence (Lindesay)
1870-1946
See Richardson, Henry Handel
See also CA 105

Richardson, Henry Handel .... TCLC 4
See also Richardson, Ethel Florence (Lindesay)

Richardson, Samuel
1689-1761 ...... LC 1; DA; DAB; DAC;
WLC
See also CDBLB 1660-1789; DAM MST, NOV; DLB 39

Richler, Mordecai
1931- .... CLC 3, 5, 9, 13, 18, 46, 70;
DAC
See also AITN 1; CA 65-68; CANR 31;
CLR 17; DAM MST, NOV; DLB 53;
MAICYA; MTCW; SATA 44;
SATA-Brief 27

Richter, Conrad (Michael)
1890-1968 .... CLC 30
See also CA 5-8R; 25-28R; CANR 23;
DLB 9; MTCW; SATA 3

Ricostranza, Tom
See Ellis, Trey

Riddell, J. H. 1832-1906 .... TCLC 40

Riding, Laura .... CLC 3, 7
See also Jackson, Laura (Riding)

Riefenstahl, Berta Helene Amalia 1902-
See Riefenstahl, Leni
See also CA 108

Riefenstahl, Leni .... CLC 16
See also Riefenstahl, Berta Helene Amalia

Riffe, Ernest
See Bergman, (Ernst) Ingmar

Riggs, (Rolla) Lynn 1899-1954 .... TCLC 56
See also CA 144; DAM MULT; NNAL

Riley, James Whitcomb
1849-1916 .... TCLC 51
See also CA 118; 137; DAM POET;
MAICYA; SATA 17

Riley, Tex
See Creasey, John

Rilke, Rainer Maria
1875-1926 .... TCLC 1, 6, 19; PC 2
See also CA 104; 132; DAM POET;
DLB 81; MTCW

Rimbaud, (Jean Nicolas) Arthur
1854-1891 ...... NCLC 4, 35; DA; DAB;
DAC; PC 3; WLC
See also DAM MST, POET

Rinehart, Mary Roberts
1876-1958 .... TCLC 52
See also CA 108

Ringmaster, The
See Mencken, H(enry) L(ouis)

Ringwood, Gwen(dolyn Margaret) Pharis
1910-1984 .... CLC 48
See also CA 148; 112; DLB 88

Rio, Michel 19(?)- .... CLC 43

Ritsos, Giannes
See Ritsos, Yannis

Ritsos, Yannis 1909-1990..... CLC 6, 13, 31
See also CA 77-80; 133; CANR 39; MTCW

Ritter, Erika 1948(?)- .... CLC 52

Rivera, Jose Eustasio 1889-1928... TCLC 35
See also HW

Rivers, Conrad Kent 1933-1968...... CLC 1
See also BW 1; CA 85-88; DLB 41

Rivers, Elfrida
See Bradley, Marion Zimmer

Riverside, John
See Heinlein, Robert A(nson)

Rizal, Jose 1861-1896. . . . . NCLC 27

Roa Bastos, Augusto (Antonio)
1917- . . . . CLC 45; HLC
See also CA 131; DAM MULT; DLB 113;
HW

Robbe-Grillet, Alain
1922- . . . . . . CLC 1, 2, 4, 6, 8, 10, 14, 43
See also CA 9-12R; CANR 33; DLB 83;
MTCW

Robbins, Harold 1916- . . . . CLC 5
See also CA 73-76; CANR 26; DAM NOV;
MTCW

Robbins, Thomas Eugene 1936-
See Robbins, Tom
See also CA 81-84; CANR 29; DAM NOV,
POP; MTCW

Robbins, Tom. . . . . CLC 9, 32, 64
See also Robbins, Thomas Eugene
See also BEST 90:3; DLBY 80

Robbins, Trina 1938- . . . . CLC 21
See also CA 128

Roberts, Charles G(eorge) D(ouglas)
1860-1943 . . . . TCLC 8
See also CA 105; CLR 33; DLB 92;
SATA-Brief 29

Roberts, Kate 1891-1985 . . . . CLC 15
See also CA 107; 116

Roberts, Keith (John Kingston)
1935- . . . . CLC 14
See also CA 25-28R; CANR 46

Roberts, Kenneth (Lewis)
1885-1957 . . . . TCLC 23
See also CA 109; DLB 9

Roberts, Michele (B.) 1949- . . . . CLC 48
See also CA 115

Robertson, Ellis
See Ellison, Harlan (Jay); Silverberg, Robert

Robertson, Thomas William
1829-1871 . . . . NCLC 35
See also DAM DRAM

Robinson, Edwin Arlington
1869-1935 . . . . TCLC 5; DA; DAC; PC 1
See also CA 104; 133; CDALB 1865-1917;
DAM MST, POET; DLB 54; MTCW

Robinson, Henry Crabb
1775-1867 . . . . NCLC 15
See also DLB 107

Robinson, Jill 1936- . . . . CLC 10
See also CA 102; INT 102

Robinson, Kim Stanley 1952- . . . . . . CLC 34
See also CA 126

Robinson, Lloyd
See Silverberg, Robert

Robinson, Marilynne 1944- . . . . CLC 25
See also CA 116

Robinson, Smokey. . . . . CLC 21
See also Robinson, William, Jr.

Robinson, William, Jr. 1940-
See Robinson, Smokey
See also CA 116

Robison, Mary 1949- . . . . CLC 42
See also CA 113; 116; DLB 130; INT 116

Rod, Edouard 1857-1910 . . . . TCLC 52

Roddenberry, Eugene Wesley 1921-1991
See Roddenberry, Gene
See also CA 110; 135; CANR 37; SATA 45;
SATA-Obit 69

Roddenberry, Gene . . . . CLC 17
See also Roddenberry, Eugene Wesley
See also AAYA 5; SATA-Obit 69

Rodgers, Mary 1931- . . . . CLC 12
See also CA 49-52; CANR 8; CLR 20;
INT CANR-8; JRDA; MAICYA;
SATA 8

Rodgers, W(illiam) R(obert)
1909-1969 . . . . CLC 7
See also CA 85-88; DLB 20

Rodman, Eric
See Silverberg, Robert

Rodman, Howard 1920(?)-1985 . . . . . CLC 65
See also CA 118

Rodman, Maia
See Wojciechowska, Maia (Teresa)

Rodriguez, Claudio 1934- . . . . CLC 10
See also DLB 134

Roelvaag, O(le) E(dvart)
1876-1931 . . . . TCLC 17
See also CA 117; DLB 9

Roethke, Theodore (Huebner)
1908-1963 . . . . . . CLC 1, 3, 8, 11, 19, 46;
PC 15
See also CA 81-84; CABS 2;
CDALB 1941-1968; DAM POET; DLB 5;
MTCW

Rogers, Thomas Hunton 1927- . . . . . CLC 57
See also CA 89-92; INT 89-92

Rogers, Will(iam Penn Adair)
1879-1935 . . . . TCLC 8
See also CA 105; 144; DAM MULT;
DLB 11; NNAL

Rogin, Gilbert 1929- . . . . CLC 18
See also CA 65-68; CANR 15

Rohan, Koda . . . . TCLC 22
See also Koda Shigeyuki

Rohmer, Eric. CLC 16
See also Scherer, Jean-Marie Maurice

Rohmer, Sax . . . . TCLC 28
See also Ward, Arthur Henry Sarsfield
See also DLB 70

Roiphe, Anne (Richardson)
1935- . . . . CLC 3, 9
See also CA 89-92; CANR 45; DLBY 80;
INT 89-92

Rojas, Fernando de 1465-1541 . . . . . . LC 23

**Rolfe, Frederick (William Serafino Austin
Lewis Mary)** 1860-1913 . . . . . . TCLC 12
See also CA 107; DLB 34, 156

Rolland, Romain 1866-1944 . . . . TCLC 23
See also CA 118; DLB 65

Rolvaag, O(le) E(dvart)
See Roelvaag, O(le) E(dvart)

Romain Arnaud, Saint
See Aragon, Louis

Romains, Jules 1885-1972 . . . . CLC 7
See also CA 85-88; CANR 34; DLB 65;
MTCW

Romero, Jose Ruben 1890-1952 . . . TCLC 14
See also CA 114; 131; HW

Ronsard, Pierre de
1524-1585 . . . . LC 6; PC 11

Rooke, Leon 1934- . . . . CLC 25, 34
See also CA 25-28R; CANR 23; DAM POP

Roper, William 1498-1578 . . . . LC 10

Roquelaure, A. N.
See Rice, Anne

Rosa, Joao Guimaraes 1908-1967 . . . CLC 23
See also CA 89-92; DLB 113

Rose, Wendy 1948- . . . . CLC 85; PC 13
See also CA 53-56; CANR 5, 51;
DAM MULT; NNAL; SATA 12

Rosen, Richard (Dean) 1949- . . . . CLC 39
See also CA 77-80; INT CANR-30

Rosenberg, Isaac 1890-1918 . . . . . . TCLC 12
See also CA 107; DLB 20

Rosenblatt, Joe . . . . CLC 15
See also Rosenblatt, Joseph

Rosenblatt, Joseph 1933-
See Rosenblatt, Joe
See also CA 89-92; INT 89-92

Rosenfeld, Samuel 1896-1963
See Tzara, Tristan
See also CA 89-92

Rosenthal, M(acha) L(ouis) 1917- . . . CLC 28
See also CA 1-4R; CAAS 6; CANR 4, 51;
DLB 5; SATA 59

Ross, Barnaby
See Dannay, Frederic

Ross, Bernard L.
See Follett, Ken(neth Martin)

Ross, J. H.
See Lawrence, T(homas) E(dward)

Ross, Martin
See Martin, Violet Florence
See also DLB 135

Ross, (James) Sinclair
1908- . . . . CLC 13; DAC
See also CA 73-76; DAM MST; DLB 88

Rossetti, Christina (Georgina)
1830-1894 . . . . . NCLC 2, 50; DA; DAB;
DAC; PC 7; WLC
See also DAM MST, POET; DLB 35;
MAICYA; SATA 20

Rossetti, Dante Gabriel
1828-1882 . . . . NCLC 4; DA; DAB;
DAC; WLC
See also CDBLB 1832-1890; DAM MST,
POET; DLB 35

Rossner, Judith (Perelman)
1935- . . . . CLC 6, 9, 29
See also AITN 2; BEST 90:3; CA 17-20R;
CANR 18, 51; DLB 6; INT CANR-18;
MTCW

Rostand, Edmond (Eugene Alexis)
1868-1918 . . . . . . TCLC 6, 37; DA; DAB;
DAC
See also CA 104; 126; DAM DRAM, MST;
MTCW

Roth, Henry   1906-1995 . . . . . . **CLC 2, 6, 11**
See also CA 11-12; 149; CANR 38; CAP 1;
DLB 28; MTCW

Roth, Joseph   1894-1939 . . . . **TCLC 33**
See also DLB 85

Roth, Philip (Milton)
1933- . . . . . . **CLC 1, 2, 3, 4, 6, 9, 15, 22,
31, 47, 66, 86; DA; DAB; DAC; WLC**
See also BEST 90:3; CA 1-4R; CANR 1, 22,
36; CDALB 1968-1988; DAM MST,
NOV, POP; DLB 2, 28; DLBY 82;
MTCW

Rothenberg, Jerome   1931- . . . . **CLC 6, 57**
See also CA 45-48; CANR 1; DLB 5

Roumain, Jacques (Jean Baptiste)
1907-1944 . . . . **TCLC 19; BLC**
See also BW 1; CA 117; 125; DAM MULT

Rourke, Constance (Mayfield)
1885-1941 . . . . **TCLC 12**
See also CA 107; YABC 1

Rousseau, Jean-Baptiste   1671-1741 . . . **LC 9**

Rousseau, Jean-Jacques
1712-1778 . . . . . **LC 14; DA; DAB; DAC;
WLC**
See also DAM MST

Roussel, Raymond   1877-1933 . . . . . **TCLC 20**
See also CA 117

Rovit, Earl (Herbert)   1927- . . . . **CLC 7**
See also CA 5-8R; CANR 12

Rowe, Nicholas   1674-1718 . . . . **LC 8**
See also DLB 84

Rowley, Ames Dorrance
See Lovecraft, H(oward) P(hillips)

Rowson, Susanna Haswell
1762(?)-1824 . . . . **NCLC 5**
See also DLB 37

Roy, Gabrielle
1909-1983 . . . . . **CLC 10, 14; DAB; DAC**
See also CA 53-56; 110; CANR 5;
DAM MST; DLB 68; MTCW

Rozewicz, Tadeusz   1921- . . . . **CLC 9, 23**
See also CA 108; CANR 36; DAM POET;
MTCW

Ruark, Gibbons   1941- . . . . **CLC 3**
See also CA 33-36R; CAAS 23; CANR 14,
31; DLB 120

Rubens, Bernice (Ruth)   1923- . . . **CLC 19, 31**
See also CA 25-28R; CANR 33; DLB 14;
MTCW

Rudkin, (James) David   1936- . . . . . . **CLC 14**
See also CA 89-92; DLB 13

Rudnik, Raphael   1933- . . . . **CLC 7**
See also CA 29-32R

Ruffian, M.
See Hasek, Jaroslav (Matej Frantisek)

Ruiz, Jose Martinez . . . . **CLC 11**
See also Martinez Ruiz, Jose

Rukeyser, Muriel
1913-1980 . . . . **CLC 6, 10, 15, 27; PC 12**
See also CA 5-8R; 93-96; CANR 26;
DAM POET; DLB 48; MTCW;
SATA-Obit 22

Rule, Jane (Vance)   1931- . . . . **CLC 27**
See also CA 25-28R; CAAS 18; CANR 12;
DLB 60

Rulfo, Juan   1918-1986 . . . . **CLC 8, 80; HLC**
See also CA 85-88; 118; CANR 26;
DAM MULT; DLB 113; HW; MTCW

Runeberg, Johan   1804-1877 . . . . . . **NCLC 41**

Runyon, (Alfred) Damon
1884(?)-1946 . . . . **TCLC 10**
See also CA 107; DLB 11, 86

Rush, Norman   1933- . . . . **CLC 44**
See also CA 121; 126; INT 126

Rushdie, (Ahmed) Salman
1947- . . . . . . **CLC 23, 31, 55; DAB; DAC**
See also BEST 89:3; CA 108; 111;
CANR 33; DAM MST, NOV, POP;
INT 111; MTCW

Rushforth, Peter (Scott)   1945- . . . . . **CLC 19**
See also CA 101

Ruskin, John   1819-1900 . . . . **TCLC 20**
See also CA 114; 129; CDBLB 1832-1890;
DLB 55; SATA 24

Russ, Joanna   1937- . . . . **CLC 15**
See also CA 25-28R; CANR 11, 31; DLB 8;
MTCW

Russell, George William   1867-1935
See A. E.
See also CA 104; CDBLB 1890-1914;
DAM POET

Russell, (Henry) Ken(neth Alfred)
1927- . . . . **CLC 16**
See also CA 105

Russell, Willy   1947- . . . . **CLC 60**

Rutherford, Mark . . . . **TCLC 25**
See also White, William Hale
See also DLB 18

Ruyslinck, Ward   1929- . . . . **CLC 14**
See also Belser, Reimond Karel Maria de

Ryan, Cornelius (John)   1920-1974 . . . **CLC 7**
See also CA 69-72; 53-56; CANR 38

Ryan, Michael   1946- . . . . **CLC 65**
See also CA 49-52; DLBY 82

Rybakov, Anatoli (Naumovich)
1911- . . . . **CLC 23, 53**
See also CA 126; 135; SATA 79

Ryder, Jonathan
See Ludlum, Robert

Ryga, George   1932-1987 . . . . . **CLC 14; DAC**
See also CA 101; 124; CANR 43;
DAM MST; DLB 60

S. S.
See Sassoon, Siegfried (Lorraine)

Saba, Umberto   1883-1957 . . . . **TCLC 33**
See also CA 144; DLB 114

Sabatini, Rafael   1875-1950 . . . . **TCLC 47**

Sabato, Ernesto (R.)
1911- . . . . **CLC 10, 23; HLC**
See also CA 97-100; CANR 32;
DAM MULT; DLB 145; HW; MTCW

Sacastru, Martin
See Bioy Casares, Adolfo

Sacher-Masoch, Leopold von
1836(?)-1895 . . . . **NCLC 31**

Sachs, Marilyn (Stickle)   1927- . . . . . **CLC 35**
See also AAYA 2; CA 17-20R; CANR 13,
47; CLR 2; JRDA; MAICYA; SAAS 2;
SATA 3, 68

Sachs, Nelly   1891-1970 . . . . **CLC 14**
See also CA 17-18; 25-28R; CAP 2

Sackler, Howard (Oliver)
1929-1982 . . . . **CLC 14**
See also CA 61-64; 108; CANR 30; DLB 7

Sacks, Oliver (Wolf)   1933- . . . . **CLC 67**
See also CA 53-56; CANR 28, 50;
INT CANR-28; MTCW

Sade, Donatien Alphonse Francois Comte
1740-1814 . . . . **NCLC 47**

Sadoff, Ira   1945- . . . . **CLC 9**
See also CA 53-56; CANR 5, 21; DLB 120

Saetone
See Camus, Albert

Safire, William   1929- . . . . **CLC 10**
See also CA 17-20R; CANR 31

Sagan, Carl (Edward)   1934- . . . . **CLC 30**
See also AAYA 2; CA 25-28R; CANR 11,
36; MTCW; SATA 58

Sagan, Francoise . . . . **CLC 3, 6, 9, 17, 36**
See also Quoirez, Francoise
See also DLB 83

Sahgal, Nayantara (Pandit)   1927- . . . **CLC 41**
See also CA 9-12R; CANR 11

Saint, H(arry) F.   1941- . . . . **CLC 50**
See also CA 127

St. Aubin de Teran, Lisa   1953-
See Teran, Lisa St. Aubin de
See also CA 118; 126; INT 126

Sainte-Beuve, Charles Augustin
1804-1869 . . . . **NCLC 5**

**Saint-Exupery, Antoine (Jean Baptiste Marie
Roger) de**
1900-1944 . . . . **TCLC 2, 56; WLC**
See also CA 108; 132; CLR 10; DAM NOV;
DLB 72; MAICYA; MTCW; SATA 20

St. John, David
See Hunt, E(verette) Howard, (Jr.)

Saint-John Perse
See Leger, (Marie-Rene Auguste) Alexis
Saint-Leger

Saintsbury, George (Edward Bateman)
1845-1933 . . . . **TCLC 31**
See also DLB 57, 149

Sait Faik . . . . **TCLC 23**
See also Abasiyanik, Sait Faik

Saki . . . . **TCLC 3; SSC 12**
See also Munro, H(ector) H(ugh)

Sala, George Augustus . . . . **NCLC 46**

Salama, Hannu   1936- . . . . **CLC 18**

Salamanca, J(ack) R(ichard)
1922- . . . . **CLC 4, 15**
See also CA 25-28R

Sale, J. Kirkpatrick
See Sale, Kirkpatrick

Sale, Kirkpatrick   1937- . . . . **CLC 68**
See also CA 13-16R; CANR 10

Salinas, Luis Omar   1937- . . . **CLC 90; HLC**
See also CA 131; DAM MULT; DLB 82;
HW

Salinas (y Serrano), Pedro
1891(?)-1951 . . . . **TCLC 17**
See also CA 117; DLB 134

Schnitzler, Arthur
1862-1931 . . . . **TCLC 4; SSC 15**
See also CA 104; DLB 81, 118

Schopenhauer, Arthur
1788-1860 . . . . **NCLC 51**
See also DLB 90

Schor, Sandra (M.) 1932(?)-1990 . . . **CLC 65**
See also CA 132

Schorer, Mark 1908-1977 . . . . **CLC 9**
See also CA 5-8R; 73-76; CANR 7;
DLB 103

Schrader, Paul (Joseph) 1946- . . . . . . **CLC 26**
See also CA 37-40R; CANR 41; DLB 44

Schreiner, Olive (Emilie Albertina)
1855-1920 . . . . **TCLC 9**
See also CA 105; DLB 18, 156

Schulberg, Budd (Wilson)
1914- . . . . **CLC 7, 48**
See also CA 25-28R; CANR 19; DLB 6, 26,
28; DLBY 81

Schulz, Bruno
1892-1942 . . . . **TCLC 5, 51; SSC 13**
See also CA 115; 123

Schulz, Charles M(onroe) 1922- . . . . **CLC 12**
See also CA 9-12R; CANR 6;
INT CANR-6; SATA 10

Schumacher, E(rnst) F(riedrich)
1911-1977 . . . . **CLC 80**
See also CA 81-84; 73-76; CANR 34

Schuyler, James Marcus
1923-1991 . . . . **CLC 5, 23**
See also CA 101; 134; DAM POET; DLB 5;
INT 101

Schwartz, Delmore (David)
1913-1966 . . . **CLC 2, 4, 10, 45, 87; PC 8**
See also CA 17-18; 25-28R; CANR 35;
CAP 2; DLB 28, 48; MTCW

Schwartz, Ernst
See Ozu, Yasujiro

Schwartz, John Burnham 1965- . . . . **CLC 59**
See also CA 132

Schwartz, Lynne Sharon 1939- . . . . . **CLC 31**
See also CA 103; CANR 44

Schwartz, Muriel A.
See Eliot, T(homas) S(tearns)

Schwarz-Bart, Andre 1928- . . . . **CLC 2, 4**
See also CA 89-92

Schwarz-Bart, Simone 1938- . . . . **CLC 7**
See also BW 2; CA 97-100

Schwob, (Mayer Andre) Marcel
1867-1905 . . . . **TCLC 20**
See also CA 117; DLB 123

Sciascia, Leonardo
1921-1989 . . . . **CLC 8, 9, 41**
See also CA 85-88; 130; CANR 35; MTCW

Scoppettone, Sandra 1936- . . . . **CLC 26**
See also AAYA 11; CA 5-8R; CANR 41;
SATA 9

Scorsese, Martin 1942- . . . . **CLC 20, 89**
See also CA 110; 114; CANR 46

Scotland, Jay
See Jakes, John (William)

Scott, Duncan Campbell
1862-1947 . . . . **TCLC 6; DAC**
See also CA 104; DLB 92

Scott, Evelyn 1893-1963 . . . . **CLC 43**
See also CA 104; 112; DLB 9, 48

Scott, F(rancis) R(eginald)
1899-1985 . . . . **CLC 22**
See also CA 101; 114; DLB 88; INT 101

Scott, Frank
See Scott, F(rancis) R(eginald)

Scott, Joanna 1960- . . . . **CLC 50**
See also CA 126

Scott, Paul (Mark) 1920-1978 . . . . **CLC 9, 60**
See also CA 81-84; 77-80; CANR 33;
DLB 14; MTCW

Scott, Walter
1771-1832 . . . . **NCLC 15; DA; DAB;
DAC; PC 13; WLC**
See also CDBLB 1789-1832; DAM MST,
NOV, POET; DLB 93, 107, 116, 144, 159;
YABC 2

Scribe, (Augustin) Eugene
1791-1861 . . . . **NCLC 16; DC 5**
See also DAM DRAM

Scrum, R.
See Crumb, R(obert)

Scudery, Madeleine de 1607-1701 . . . . . **LC 2**

Scum
See Crumb, R(obert)

Scumbag, Little Bobby
See Crumb, R(obert)

Seabrook, John
See Hubbard, L(afayette) Ron(ald)

Sealy, I. Allan 1951- . . . . **CLC 55**

Search, Alexander
See Pessoa, Fernando (Antonio Nogueira)

Sebastian, Lee
See Silverberg, Robert

Sebastian Owl
See Thompson, Hunter S(tockton)

Sebestyen, Ouida 1924- . . . . **CLC 30**
See also AAYA 8; CA 107; CANR 40;
CLR 17; JRDA; MAICYA; SAAS 10;
SATA 39

Secundus, H. Scriblerus
See Fielding, Henry

Sedges, John
See Buck, Pearl S(ydenstricker)

Sedgwick, Catharine Maria
1789-1867 . . . . **NCLC 19**
See also DLB 1, 74

Seelye, John 1931- . . . . **CLC 7**

Seferiades, Giorgos Stylianou 1900-1971
See Seferis, George
See also CA 5-8R; 33-36R; CANR 5, 36;
MTCW

Seferis, George . . . . **CLC 5, 11**
See also Seferiades, Giorgos Stylianou

Segal, Erich (Wolf) 1937- . . . . **CLC 3, 10**
See also BEST 89:1; CA 25-28R; CANR 20,
36; DAM POP; DLBY 86;
INT CANR-20; MTCW

Seger, Bob 1945- . . . . **CLC 35**

Seghers, Anna . . . . **CLC 7**
See also Radvanyi, Netty
See also DLB 69

Seidel, Frederick (Lewis) 1936- . . . . . **CLC 18**
See also CA 13-16R; CANR 8; DLBY 84

Seifert, Jaroslav 1901-1986 . . . . . **CLC 34, 44**
See also CA 127; MTCW

Sei Shonagon c. 966-1017(?) . . . . . . **CMLC 6**

Selby, Hubert, Jr.
1928- . . . . **CLC 1, 2, 4, 8; SSC 20**
See also CA 13-16R; CANR 33; DLB 2

Selzer, Richard 1928- . . . . **CLC 74**
See also CA 65-68; CANR 14

Sembene, Ousmane
See Ousmane, Sembene

Senancour, Etienne Pivert de
1770-1846 . . . . **NCLC 16**
See also DLB 119

Sender, Ramon (Jose)
1902-1982 . . . . **CLC 8; HLC**
See also CA 5-8R; 105; CANR 8;
DAM MULT; HW; MTCW

Seneca, Lucius Annaeus
4B.C.-65 . . . . **CMLC 6; DC 5**
See also DAM DRAM

Senghor, Leopold Sedar
1906- . . . . **CLC 54; BLC**
See also BW 2; CA 116; 125; CANR 47;
DAM MULT, POET; MTCW

Serling, (Edward) Rod(man)
1924-1975 . . . . **CLC 30**
See also AAYA 14; AITN 1; CA 65-68;
57-60; DLB 26

Serna, Ramon Gomez de la
See Gomez de la Serna, Ramon

Serpieres
See Guillevic, (Eugene)

Service, Robert
See Service, Robert W(illiam)
See also DAB; DLB 92

Service, Robert W(illiam)
1874(?)-1958 . . . . . . **TCLC 15; DA; DAC;
WLC**
See also Service, Robert
See also CA 115; 140; DAM MST, POET;
SATA 20

Seth, Vikram 1952- . . . . **CLC 43, 90**
See also CA 121; 127; CANR 50;
DAM MULT; DLB 120; INT 127

Seton, Cynthia Propper
1926-1982 . . . . **CLC 27**
See also CA 5-8R; 108; CANR 7

Seton, Ernest (Evan) Thompson
1860-1946 . . . . **TCLC 31**
See also CA 109; DLB 92; DLBD 13;
JRDA; SATA 18

Seton-Thompson, Ernest
See Seton, Ernest (Evan) Thompson

Settle, Mary Lee 1918- . . . . **CLC 19, 61**
See also CA 89-92; CAAS 1; CANR 44;
DLB 6; INT 89-92

Seuphor, Michel
See Arp, Jean

**Sevigne, Marie (de Rabutin-Chantal) Marquise
de** 1626-1696 . . . . **LC 11**

Sexton, Anne (Harvey)
    1928-1974 .... CLC 2, 4, 6, 8, 10, 15, 53;
                    DA; DAB; DAC; PC 2; WLC
    See also CA 1-4R; 53-56; CABS 2;
    CANR 3, 36; CDALB 1941-1968;
    DAM MST, POET; DLB 5; MTCW;
    SATA 10

Shaara, Michael (Joseph, Jr.)
    1929-1988 .... CLC 15
    See also AITN 1; CA 102; 125; DAM POP;
    DLBY 83

Shackleton, C. C.
    See Aldiss, Brian W(ilson)

Shacochis, Bob .... CLC 39
    See also Shacochis, Robert G.

Shacochis, Robert G.   1951-
    See Shacochis, Bob
    See also CA 119; 124; INT 124

Shaffer, Anthony (Joshua)   1926-.... CLC 19
    See also CA 110; 116; DAM DRAM;
    DLB 13

Shaffer, Peter (Levin)
    1926- ...... CLC 5, 14, 18, 37, 60; DAB
    See also CA 25-28R; CANR 25, 47;
    CDBLB 1960 to Present; DAM DRAM,
    MST; DLB 13; MTCW

Shakey, Bernard
    See Young, Neil

Shalamov, Varlam (Tikhonovich)
    1907(?)-1982 .... CLC 18
    See also CA 129; 105

Shamlu, Ahmad   1925- .... CLC 10

Shammas, Anton   1951-............ CLC 55

Shange, Ntozake
    1948- .... CLC 8, 25, 38, 74; BLC; DC 3
    See also AAYA 9; BW 2; CA 85-88;
    CABS 3; CANR 27, 48; DAM DRAM,
    MULT; DLB 38; MTCW

Shanley, John Patrick   1950-....... CLC 75
    See also CA 128; 133

Shapcott, Thomas W(illiam)   1935- .. CLC 38
    See also CA 69-72; CANR 49

Shapiro, Jane...................... CLC 76

Shapiro, Karl (Jay)   1913- .. CLC 4, 8, 15, 53
    See also CA 1-4R; CAAS 6; CANR 1, 36;
    DLB 48; MTCW

Sharp, William   1855-1905 .... TCLC 39
    See also DLB 156

Sharpe, Thomas Ridley   1928-
    See Sharpe, Tom
    See also CA 114; 122; INT 122

Sharpe, Tom...................... CLC 36
    See also Sharpe, Thomas Ridley
    See also DLB 14

Shaw, Bernard................... TCLC 45
    See also Shaw, George Bernard
    See also BW 1

Shaw, G. Bernard
    See Shaw, George Bernard

Shaw, George Bernard
    1856-1950 ... TCLC 3, 9, 21; DA; DAB;
                    DAC; WLC
    See also Shaw, Bernard
    See also CA 104; 128; CDBLB 1914-1945;
    DAM DRAM, MST; DLB 10, 57;
    MTCW

Shaw, Henry Wheeler
    1818-1885 .... NCLC 15
    See also DLB 11

Shaw, Irwin   1913-1984....... CLC 7, 23, 34
    See also AITN 1; CA 13-16R; 112;
    CANR 21; CDALB 1941-1968;
    DAM DRAM, POP; DLB 6, 102;
    DLBY 84; MTCW

Shaw, Robert   1927-1978 .... CLC 5
    See also AITN 1; CA 1-4R; 81-84;
    CANR 4; DLB 13, 14

Shaw, T. E.
    See Lawrence, T(homas) E(dward)

Shawn, Wallace   1943- .... CLC 41
    See also CA 112

Shea, Lisa   1953-................. CLC 86
    See also CA 147

Sheed, Wilfrid (John Joseph)
    1930- .... CLC 2, 4, 10, 53
    See also CA 65-68; CANR 30; DLB 6;
    MTCW

Sheldon, Alice Hastings Bradley
    1915(?)-1987
    See Tiptree, James, Jr.
    See also CA 108; 122; CANR 34; INT 108;
    MTCW

Sheldon, John
    See Bloch, Robert (Albert)

Shelley, Mary Wollstonecraft (Godwin)
    1797-1851 .... NCLC 14; DA; DAB;
                    DAC; WLC
    See also CDBLB 1789-1832; DAM MST,
    NOV; DLB 110, 116, 159; SATA 29

Shelley, Percy Bysshe
    1792-1822 .... NCLC 18; DA; DAB;
                    DAC; PC 14; WLC
    See also CDBLB 1789-1832; DAM MST,
    POET; DLB 96, 110, 158

Shepard, Jim   1956-.............. CLC 36
    See also CA 137

Shepard, Lucius   1947- .... CLC 34
    See also CA 128; 141

Shepard, Sam
    1943- .... CLC 4, 6, 17, 34, 41, 44; DC 5
    See also AAYA 1; CA 69-72; CABS 3;
    CANR 22; DAM DRAM; DLB 7;
    MTCW

Shepherd, Michael
    See Ludlum, Robert

Sherburne, Zoa (Morin)   1912-...... CLC 30
    See also AAYA 13; CA 1-4R; CANR 3, 37;
    MAICYA; SAAS 18; SATA 3

Sheridan, Frances   1724-1766......... LC 7
    See also DLB 39, 84

Sheridan, Richard Brinsley
    1751-1816 .... NCLC 5; DA; DAB;
                    DAC; DC 1; WLC
    See also CDBLB 1660-1789; DAM DRAM,
    MST; DLB 89

Sherman, Jonathan Marc........... CLC 55

Sherman, Martin   1941(?)-......... CLC 19
    See also CA 116; 123

Sherwin, Judith Johnson   1936-... CLC 7, 15
    See also CA 25-28R; CANR 34

Sherwood, Frances   1940-.......... CLC 81
    See also CA 146

Sherwood, Robert E(mmet)
    1896-1955 .... TCLC 3
    See also CA 104; DAM DRAM; DLB 7, 26

Shestov, Lev   1866-1938.......... TCLC 56

Shevchenko, Taras   1814-1861.... NCLC 54

Shiel, M(atthew) P(hipps)
    1865-1947 .... TCLC 8
    See also CA 106; DLB 153

Shields, Carol   1935-......... CLC 91; DAC
    See also CA 81-84; CANR 51

Shiga, Naoya   1883-1971........... CLC 33
    See also CA 101; 33-36R

Shilts, Randy   1951-1994 .... CLC 85
    See also CA 115; 127; 144; CANR 45;
    INT 127

Shimazaki Haruki   1872-1943
    See Shimazaki Toson
    See also CA 105; 134

Shimazaki Toson................. TCLC 5
    See also Shimazaki Haruki

Sholokhov, Mikhail (Aleksandrovich)
    1905-1984 .... CLC 7, 15
    See also CA 101; 112; MTCW;
    SATA-Obit 36

Shone, Patric
    See Hanley, James

Shreve, Susan Richards   1939-...... CLC 23
    See also CA 49-52; CAAS 5; CANR 5, 38;
    MAICYA; SATA 46; SATA-Brief 41

Shue, Larry   1946-1985............. CLC 52
    See also CA 145; 117; DAM DRAM

Shu-Jen, Chou   1881-1936
    See Lu Hsun
    See also CA 104

Shulman, Alix Kates   1932- ...... CLC 2, 10
    See also CA 29-32R; CANR 43; SATA 7

Shuster, Joe   1914- .... CLC 21

Shute, Nevil...................... CLC 30
    See also Norway, Nevil Shute

Shuttle, Penelope (Diane)   1947- ..... CLC 7
    See also CA 93-96; CANR 39; DLB 14, 40

Sidney, Mary   1561-1621 .... LC 19

Sidney, Sir Philip
    1554-1586 ..... LC 19; DA; DAB; DAC
    See also CDBLB Before 1660; DAM MST,
    POET

Siegel, Jerome   1914- .... CLC 21
    See also CA 116

Siegel, Jerry
    See Siegel, Jerome

Sienkiewicz, Henryk (Adam Alexander Pius)
    1846-1916 .... TCLC 3
    See also CA 104; 134

Sierra, Gregorio Martinez
    See Martinez Sierra, Gregorio

Sierra, Maria (de la O'LeJarraga) Martinez
    See Martinez Sierra, Maria (de la
    O'LeJarraga)

Sigal, Clancy   1926- . . . . CLC 7
    See also CA 1-4R

Sigourney, Lydia Howard (Huntley)
    1791-1865 . . . . NCLC 21
    See also DLB 1, 42, 73

Siguenza y Gongora, Carlos de
    1645-1700 . . . . LC 8

Sigurjonsson, Johann   1880-1919 . . . TCLC 27

Sikelianos, Angelos   1884-1951 . . . . TCLC 39

Silkin, Jon   1930- . . . . CLC 2, 6, 43
    See also CA 5-8R; CAAS 5; DLB 27

Silko, Leslie (Marmon)
    1948- . . . . CLC 23, 74; DA; DAC
    See also AAYA 14; CA 115; 122;
    CANR 45; DAM MST, MULT, POP;
    DLB 143; NNAL

Sillanpaa, Frans Eemil   1888-1964 . . . CLC 19
    See also CA 129; 93-96; MTCW

Sillitoe, Alan
    1928- . . . . CLC 1, 3, 6, 10, 19, 57
    See also AITN 1; CA 9-12R; CAAS 2;
    CANR 8, 26; CDBLB 1960 to Present;
    DLB 14, 139; MTCW; SATA 61

Silone, Ignazio   1900-1978 . . . . CLC 4
    See also CA 25-28; 81-84; CANR 34;
    CAP 2; MTCW

Silver, Joan Micklin   1935- . . . . CLC 20
    See also CA 114; 121; INT 121

Silver, Nicholas
    See Faust, Frederick (Schiller)

Silverberg, Robert   1935- . . . . CLC 7
    See also CA 1-4R; CAAS 3; CANR 1, 20,
    36; DAM POP; DLB 8; INT CANR-20;
    MAICYA; MTCW; SATA 13

Silverstein, Alvin   1933- . . . . CLC 17
    See also CA 49-52; CANR 2; CLR 25;
    JRDA; MAICYA; SATA 8, 69

Silverstein, Virginia B(arbara Opshelor)
    1937- . . . . CLC 17
    See also CA 49-52; CANR 2; CLR 25;
    JRDA; MAICYA; SATA 8, 69

Sim, Georges
    See Simenon, Georges (Jacques Christian)

Simak, Clifford D(onald)
    1904-1988 . . . . CLC 1, 55
    See also CA 1-4R; 125; CANR 1, 35;
    DLB 8; MTCW; SATA-Obit 56

Simenon, Georges (Jacques Christian)
    1903-1989 . . . . CLC 1, 2, 3, 8, 18, 47
    See also CA 85-88; 129; CANR 35;
    DAM POP; DLB 72; DLBY 89; MTCW

Simic, Charles   1938- . . . CLC 6, 9, 22, 49, 68
    See also CA 29-32R; CAAS 4; CANR 12,
    33; DAM POET; DLB 105

Simmons, Charles (Paul)   1924- . . . . . CLC 57
    See also CA 89-92; INT 89-92

Simmons, Dan   1948- . . . . CLC 44
    See also AAYA 16; CA 138; DAM POP

Simmons, James (Stewart Alexander)
    1933- . . . . CLC 43
    See also CA 105; CAAS 21; DLB 40

Simms, William Gilmore
    1806-1870 . . . . NCLC 3
    See also DLB 3, 30, 59, 73

Simon, Carly   1945- . . . . CLC 26
    See also CA 105

Simon, Claude   1913- . . . . CLC 4, 9, 15, 39
    See also CA 89-92; CANR 33; DAM NOV;
    DLB 83; MTCW

Simon, (Marvin) Neil
    1927- . . . . CLC 6, 11, 31, 39, 70
    See also AITN 1; CA 21-24R; CANR 26;
    DAM DRAM; DLB 7; MTCW

Simon, Paul   1942(?)- . . . . CLC 17
    See also CA 116

Simonon, Paul   1956(?)- . . . . CLC 30

Simpson, Harriette
    See Arnow, Harriette (Louisa) Simpson

Simpson, Louis (Aston Marantz)
    1923- . . . . CLC 4, 7, 9, 32
    See also CA 1-4R; CAAS 4; CANR 1,
    DAM POET; DLB 5; MTCW

Simpson, Mona (Elizabeth)   1957- . . . CLC 44
    See also CA 122; 135

Simpson, N(orman) F(rederick)
    1919- . . . . CLC 29
    See also CA 13-16R; DLB 13

Sinclair, Andrew (Annandale)
    1935- . . . . CLC 2, 14
    See also CA 9-12R; CAAS 5; CANR 14, 38;
    DLB 14; MTCW

Sinclair, Emil
    See Hesse, Hermann

Sinclair, Iain   1943- . . . . CLC 76
    See also CA 132

Sinclair, Iain MacGregor
    See Sinclair, Iain

Sinclair, Mary Amelia St. Clair   1865(?)-1946
    See Sinclair, May
    See also CA 104

Sinclair, May . . . . TCLC 3, 11
    See also Sinclair, Mary Amelia St. Clair
    See also DLB 36, 135

Sinclair, Upton (Beall)
    1878-1968 . . . . . . CLC 1, 11, 15, 63; DA;
                                    DAB; DAC; WLC
    See also CA 5-8R; 25-28R; CANR 7;
    CDALB 1929-1941; DAM MST, NOV;
    DLB 9; INT CANR-7; MTCW; SATA 9

Singer, Isaac
    See Singer, Isaac Bashevis

Singer, Isaac Bashevis
    1904-1991 . . . . CLC 1, 3, 6, 9, 11, 15, 23,
                38, 69; DA; DAB; DAC; SSC 3; WLC
    See also AITN 1, 2; CA 1-4R; 134;
    CANR 1, 39; CDALB 1941-1968; CLR 1;
    DAM MST, NOV; DLB 6, 28, 52;
    DLBY 91; JRDA; MAICYA; MTCW;
    SATA 3, 27; SATA-Obit 68

Singer, Israel Joshua   1893-1944 . . . TCLC 33

Singh, Khushwant   1915- . . . . CLC 11
    See also CA 9-12R; CAAS 9; CANR 6

Sinjohn, John
    See Galsworthy, John

Sinyavsky, Andrei (Donatevich)
    1925- . . . . CLC 8
    See also CA 85-88

Sirin, V.
    See Nabokov, Vladimir (Vladimirovich)

Sissman, L(ouis) E(dward)
    1928-1976 . . . . CLC 9, 18
    See also CA 21-24R; 65-68; CANR 13;
    DLB 5

Sisson, C(harles) H(ubert)   1914- . . . . . CLC 8
    See also CA 1-4R; CAAS 3; CANR 3, 48;
    DLB 27

Sitwell, Dame Edith
    1887-1964 . . . . CLC 2, 9, 67; PC 3
    See also CA 9-12R; CANR 35;
    CDBLB 1945-1960; DAM POET;
    DLB 20; MTCW

Sjoewall, Maj   1935- . . . . CLC 7
    See also CA 65-68

Sjowall, Maj
    See Sjoewall, Maj

Skelton, Robin   1925- . . . . CLC 13
    See also AITN 2; CA 5-8R; CAAS 5;
    CANR 28; DLB 27, 53

Skolimowski, Jerzy   1938- . . . . CLC 20
    See also CA 128

Skram, Amalie (Bertha)
    1847-1905 . . . . TCLC 25

Skvorecky, Josef (Vaclav)
    1924- . . . . CLC 15, 39, 69; DAC
    See also CA 61-64; CAAS 1; CANR 10, 34;
    DAM NOV; MTCW

Slade, Bernard . . . . CLC 11, 46
    See also Newbound, Bernard Slade
    See also CAAS 9; DLB 53

Slaughter, Carolyn   1946- . . . . CLC 56
    See also CA 85-88

Slaughter, Frank G(ill)   1908- . . . . . . CLC 29
    See also AITN 2; CA 5-8R; CANR 5;
    INT CANR-5

Slavitt, David R(ytman)   1935- . . . . CLC 5, 14
    See also CA 21-24R; CAAS 3; CANR 41;
    DLB 5, 6

Slesinger, Tess   1905-1945 . . . . TCLC 10
    See also CA 107; DLB 102

Slessor, Kenneth   1901-1971 . . . . CLC 14
    See also CA 102; 89-92

Slowacki, Juliusz   1809-1849 . . . . . NCLC 15

Smart, Christopher
    1722-1771 . . . . LC 3; PC 13
    See also DAM POET; DLB 109

Smart, Elizabeth   1913-1986 . . . . CLC 54
    See also CA 81-84; 118; DLB 88

Smiley, Jane (Graves)   1949- . . . . CLC 53, 76
    See also CA 104; CANR 30, 50;
    DAM POP; INT CANR-30

Smith, A(rthur) J(ames) M(arshall)
    1902-1980 . . . . CLC 15; DAC
    See also CA 1-4R; 102; CANR 4; DLB 88

Smith, Anna Deavere   1950- . . . . CLC 86
    See also CA 133

Smith, Betty (Wehner)   1896-1972 . . . CLC 19
    See also CA 5-8R; 33-36R; DLBY 82;
    SATA 6

Spenser, Edmund
1552(?)-1599 .... **LC 5; DA; DAB; DAC;
PC 8; WLC**
See also CDBLB Before 1660; DAM MST,
POET

Spicer, Jack 1925-1965 ...... **CLC 8, 18, 72**
See also CA 85-88; DAM POET; DLB 5, 16

Spiegelman, Art 1948- .... **CLC 76**
See also AAYA 10; CA 125; CANR 41

Spielberg, Peter 1929- .... **CLC 6**
See also CA 5-8R; CANR 4, 48; DLBY 81

Spielberg, Steven 1947- .... **CLC 20**
See also AAYA 8; CA 77-80; CANR 32;
SATA 32

Spillane, Frank Morrison 1918-
See Spillane, Mickey
See also CA 25-28R; CANR 28; MTCW;
SATA 66

Spillane, Mickey .... **CLC 3, 13**
See also Spillane, Frank Morrison

Spinoza, Benedictus de 1632-1677 .... **LC 9**

Spinrad, Norman (Richard) 1940-... **CLC 46**
See also CA 37-40R; CAAS 19; CANR 20;
DLB 8; INT CANR-20

Spitteler, Carl (Friedrich Georg)
1845-1924 .... **TCLC 12**
See also CA 109; DLB 129

Spivack, Kathleen (Romola Drucker)
1938- .... **CLC 6**
See also CA 49-52

Spoto, Donald 1941-.............. **CLC 39**
See also CA 65-68; CANR 11

Springsteen, Bruce (F.) 1949- ...... **CLC 17**
See also CA 111

Spurling, Hilary 1940-............ **CLC 34**
See also CA 104; CANR 25

Spyker, John Howland
See Elman, Richard

Squires, (James) Radcliffe
1917-1993 .... **CLC 51**
See also CA 1-4R; 140; CANR 6, 21

Srivastava, Dhanpat Rai 1880(?)-1936
See Premchand
See also CA 118

Stacy, Donald
See Pohl, Frederik

Stael, Germaine de
See Stael-Holstein, Anne Louise Germaine
Necker Baronn
See also DLB 119

**Stael-Holstein, Anne Louise Germaine Necker
Baronn** 1766-1817 .... **NCLC 3**
See also Stael, Germaine de

Stafford, Jean 1915-1979 ... **CLC 4, 7, 19, 68**
See also CA 1-4R; 85-88; CANR 3; DLB 2;
MTCW; SATA-Obit 22

Stafford, William (Edgar)
1914-1993 .... **CLC 4, 7, 29**
See also CA 5-8R; 142; CAAS 3; CANR 5,
22; DAM POET; DLB 5; INT CANR-22

Staines, Trevor
See Brunner, John (Kilian Houston)

Stairs, Gordon
See Austin, Mary (Hunter)

Stannard, Martin 1947-.......... **CLC 44**
See also CA 142; DLB 155

Stanton, Maura 1946- .... **CLC 9**
See also CA 89-92; CANR 15; DLB 120

Stanton, Schuyler
See Baum, L(yman) Frank

Stapledon, (William) Olaf
1886-1950 .... **TCLC 22**
See also CA 111; DLB 15

Starbuck, George (Edwin) 1931-.... **CLC 53**
See also CA 21-24R; CANR 23;
DAM POET

Stark, Richard
See Westlake, Donald E(dwin)

Staunton, Schuyler
See Baum, L(yman) Frank

Stead, Christina (Ellen)
1902-1983 .... **CLC 2, 5, 8, 32, 80**
See also CA 13-16R; 109; CANR 33, 40;
MTCW

Stead, William Thomas
1849-1912 .... **TCLC 48**

Steele, Richard 1672-1729 .... **LC 18**
See also CDBLB 1660-1789; DLB 84, 101

Steele, Timothy (Reid) 1948-....... **CLC 45**
See also CA 93-96; CANR 16, 50; DLB 120

Steffens, (Joseph) Lincoln
1866-1936 .... **TCLC 20**
See also CA 117

Stegner, Wallace (Earle)
1909-1993 .... **CLC 9, 49, 81**
See also AITN 1; BEST 90:3; CA 1-4R;
141; CAAS 9; CANR 1, 21, 46;
DAM NOV; DLB 9; DLBY 93; MTCW

Stein, Gertrude
1874-1946 ...... **TCLC 1, 6, 28, 48; DA;
DAB; DAC; WLC**
See also CA 104; 132; CDALB 1917-1929;
DAM MST, NOV, POET; DLB 4, 54, 86;
MTCW

Steinbeck, John (Ernst)
1902-1968 ...... **CLC 1, 5, 9, 13, 21, 34,
45, 75; DA; DAB; DAC; SSC 11; WLC**
See also AAYA 12; CA 1-4R; 25-28R;
CANR 1, 35; CDALB 1929-1941;
DAM DRAM, MST, NOV; DLB 7, 9;
DLBD 2; MTCW; SATA 9

Steinem, Gloria 1934-............. **CLC 63**
See also CA 53-56; CANR 28, 51; MTCW

Steiner, George 1929-............. **CLC 24**
See also CA 73-76; CANR 31; DAM NOV;
DLB 67; MTCW; SATA 62

Steiner, K. Leslie
See Delany, Samuel R(ay, Jr.)

Steiner, Rudolf 1861-1925 .... **TCLC 13**
See also CA 107

Stendhal
1783-1842 .... **NCLC 23, 46; DA; DAB;
DAC; WLC**
See also DAM MST, NOV; DLB 119

Stephen, Leslie 1832-1904 .... **TCLC 23**
See also CA 123; DLB 57, 144

Stephen, Sir Leslie
See Stephen, Leslie

Stephen, Virginia
See Woolf, (Adeline) Virginia

Stephens, James 1882(?)-1950...... **TCLC 4**
See also CA 104; DLB 19, 153, 162

Stephens, Reed
See Donaldson, Stephen R.

Steptoe, Lydia
See Barnes, Djuna

Sterchi, Beat 1949-.............. **CLC 65**

Sterling, Brett
See Bradbury, Ray (Douglas); Hamilton,
Edmond

Sterling, Bruce 1954-.............. **CLC 72**
See also CA 119; CANR 44

Sterling, George 1869-1926....... **TCLC 20**
See also CA 117; DLB 54

Stern, Gerald 1925- .... **CLC 40**
See also CA 81-84; CANR 28; DLB 105

Stern, Richard (Gustave) 1928-... **CLC 4, 39**
See also CA 1-4R; CANR 1, 25; DLBY 87;
INT CANR-25

Sternberg, Josef von 1894-1969..... **CLC 20**
See also CA 81-84

Sterne, Laurence
1713-1768 ...... **LC 2; DA; DAB; DAC;
WLC**
See also CDBLB 1660-1789; DAM MST,
NOV; DLB 39

Sternheim, (William Adolf) Carl
1878-1942 .... **TCLC 8**
See also CA 105; DLB 56, 118

Stevens, Mark 1951- .... **CLC 34**
See also CA 122

Stevens, Wallace
1879-1955 .... **TCLC 3, 12, 45; DA;
DAB; DAC; PC 6; WLC**
See also CA 104; 124; CDALB 1929-1941;
DAM MST, POET; DLB 54; MTCW

Stevenson, Anne (Katharine)
1933- .... **CLC 7, 33**
See also CA 17-20R; CAAS 9; CANR 9, 33;
DLB 40; MTCW

Stevenson, Robert Louis (Balfour)
1850-1894 ..... **NCLC 5, 14; DA; DAB;
DAC; SSC 11; WLC**
See also CDBLB 1890-1914; CLR 10, 11;
DAM MST, NOV; DLB 18, 57, 141, 156;
DLBD 13; JRDA; MAICYA; YABC 2

Stewart, J(ohn) I(nnes) M(ackintosh)
1906-1994 .... **CLC 7, 14, 32**
See also CA 85-88; 147; CAAS 3;
CANR 47; MTCW

Stewart, Mary (Florence Elinor)
1916- .... **CLC 7, 35; DAB**
See also CA 1-4R; CANR 1; SATA 12

Stewart, Mary Rainbow
See Stewart, Mary (Florence Elinor)

Stifle, June
See Campbell, Maria

Stifter, Adalbert 1805-1868 ...... **NCLC 41**
See also DLB 133

Still, James 1906-................ **CLC 49**
See also CA 65-68; CAAS 17; CANR 10,
26; DLB 9; SATA 29

Sting
See Sumner, Gordon Matthew

Stirling, Arthur
See Sinclair, Upton (Beall)

Stitt, Milan 1941- .... **CLC 29**
See also CA 69-72

Stockton, Francis Richard 1834-1902
See Stockton, Frank R.
See also CA 108; 137; MAICYA; SATA 44

Stockton, Frank R. .... **TCLC 47**
See also Stockton, Francis Richard
See also DLB 42, 74; DLBD 13;
SATA-Brief 32

Stoddard, Charles
See Kuttner, Henry

Stoker, Abraham 1847-1912
See Stoker, Bram
See also CA 105; DA; DAC; DAM MST,
NOV; SATA 29

Stoker, Bram
1847-1912 .... **TCLC 8; DAB; WLC**
See also Stoker, Abraham
See also CA 150; CDBLB 1890-1914;
DLB 36, 70

Stolz, Mary (Slattery) 1920- .... **CLC 12**
See also AAYA 8; AITN 1; CA 5-8R;
CANR 13, 41; JRDA; MAICYA;
SAAS 3; SATA 10, 71

Stone, Irving 1903-1989 .... **CLC 7**
See also AITN 1; CA 1-4R; 129; CAAS 3;
CANR 1, 23; DAM POP;
INT CANR-23; MTCW; SATA 3;
SATA-Obit 64

Stone, Oliver 1946- .... **CLC 73**
See also AAYA 15; CA 110

Stone, Robert (Anthony)
1937- .... **CLC 5, 23, 42**
See also CA 85-88; CANR 23; DLB 152;
INT CANR-23; MTCW

Stone, Zachary
See Follett, Ken(neth Martin)

Stoppard, Tom
1937- ...... **CLC 1, 3, 4, 5, 8, 15, 29, 34,
63, 91; DA; DAB; DAC; DC 6; WLC**
See also CA 81-84; CANR 39;
CDBLB 1960 to Present; DAM DRAM,
MST; DLB 13; DLBY 85; MTCW

Storey, David (Malcolm)
1933- .... **CLC 2, 4, 5, 8**
See also CA 81-84; CANR 36;
DAM DRAM; DLB 13, 14; MTCW

Storm, Hyemeyohsts 1935- .... **CLC 3**
See also CA 81-84; CANR 45;
DAM MULT; NNAL

Storm, (Hans) Theodor (Woldsen)
1817-1888 .... **NCLC 1**

Storni, Alfonsina
1892-1938 .... **TCLC 5; HLC**
See also CA 104; 131; DAM MULT; HW

Stout, Rex (Todhunter) 1886-1975 ... **CLC 3**
See also AITN 2; CA 61-64

Stow, (Julian) Randolph 1935- .. **CLC 23, 48**
See also CA 13-16R; CANR 33; MTCW

Stowe, Harriet (Elizabeth) Beecher
1811-1896 ..... **NCLC 3, 50; DA; DAB;
DAC; WLC**
See also CDALB 1865-1917; DAM MST,
NOV; DLB 1, 12, 42, 74; JRDA;
MAICYA; YABC 1

Strachey, (Giles) Lytton
1880-1932 .... **TCLC 12**
See also CA 110; DLB 149; DLBD 10

Strand, Mark 1934- ...... **CLC 6, 18, 41, 71**
See also CA 21-24R; CANR 40;
DAM POET; DLB 5; SATA 41

Straub, Peter (Francis) 1943- ...... **CLC 28**
See also BEST 89:1; CA 85-88; CANR 28;
DAM POP; DLBY 84; MTCW

Strauss, Botho 1944- .... **CLC 22**
See also DLB 124

Streatfeild, (Mary) Noel
1895(?)-1986 .... **CLC 21**
See also CA 81-84; 120; CANR 31;
CLR 17; DLB 160; MAICYA; SATA 20;
SATA-Obit 48

Stribling, T(homas) S(igismund)
1881-1965 .... **CLC 23**
See also CA 107; DLB 9

Strindberg, (Johan) August
1849-1912 ...... **TCLC 1, 8, 21, 47; DA;
DAB; DAC; WLC**
See also CA 104; 135; DAM DRAM, MST

Stringer, Arthur 1874-1950 .... **TCLC 37**
See also DLB 92

Stringer, David
See Roberts, Keith (John Kingston)

Strugatskii, Arkadii (Natanovich)
1925-1991 .... **CLC 27**
See also CA 106; 135

Strugatskii, Boris (Natanovich)
1933- .... **CLC 27**
See also CA 106

Strummer, Joe 1953(?)- .... **CLC 30**

Stuart, Don A.
See Campbell, John W(ood, Jr.)

Stuart, Ian
See MacLean, Alistair (Stuart)

Stuart, Jesse (Hilton)
1906-1984 .... **CLC 1, 8, 11, 14, 34**
See also CA 5-8R; 112; CANR 31; DLB 9,
48, 102; DLBY 84; SATA 2;
SATA-Obit 36

Sturgeon, Theodore (Hamilton)
1918-1985 .... **CLC 22, 39**
See also Queen, Ellery
See also CA 81-84; 116; CANR 32; DLB 8;
DLBY 85; MTCW

Sturges, Preston 1898-1959 .... **TCLC 48**
See also CA 114; 149; DLB 26

Styron, William
1925- .... **CLC 1, 3, 5, 11, 15, 60**
See also BEST 90:4; CA 5-8R; CANR 6, 33;
CDALB 1968-1988; DAM NOV, POP;
DLB 2, 143; DLBY 80; INT CANR-6;
MTCW

Suarez Lynch, B.
See Bioy Casares, Adolfo; Borges, Jorge
Luis

Su Chien 1884-1918
See Su Man-shu
See also CA 123

Suckow, Ruth 1892-1960 .... **SSC 18**
See also CA 113; DLB 9, 102

Sudermann, Hermann 1857-1928 .. **TCLC 15**
See also CA 107; DLB 118

Sue, Eugene 1804-1857 .... **NCLC 1**
See also DLB 119

Sueskind, Patrick 1949- .... **CLC 44**
See also Suskind, Patrick

Sukenick, Ronald 1932- ..... **CLC 3, 4, 6, 48**
See also CA 25-28R; CAAS 8; CANR 32;
DLBY 81

Suknaski, Andrew 1942- .... **CLC 19**
See also CA 101; DLB 53

Sullivan, Vernon
See Vian, Boris

Sully Prudhomme 1839-1907 ...... **TCLC 31**

Su Man-shu .... **TCLC 24**
See also Su Chien

Summerforest, Ivy B.
See Kirkup, James

Summers, Andrew James 1942- ..... **CLC 26**

Summers, Andy
See Summers, Andrew James

Summers, Hollis (Spurgeon, Jr.)
1916- .... **CLC 10**
See also CA 5-8R; CANR 3; DLB 6

**Summers, (Alphonsus Joseph-Mary Augustus)
Montague** 1880-1948 .... **TCLC 16**
See also CA 118

Sumner, Gordon Matthew 1951-.... **CLC 26**

Surtees, Robert Smith
1803-1864 .... **NCLC 14**
See also DLB 21

Susann, Jacqueline 1921-1974....... **CLC 3**
See also AITN 1; CA 65-68; 53-56; MTCW

Su Shih 1036-1101 .... **CMLC 15**

Suskind, Patrick
See Sueskind, Patrick
See also CA 145

Sutcliff, Rosemary
1920-1992 .... **CLC 26; DAB; DAC**
See also AAYA 10; CA 5-8R; 139;
CANR 37; CLR 1, 37; DAM MST, POP;
JRDA; MAICYA; SATA 6, 44, 78;
SATA-Obit 73

Sutro, Alfred 1863-1933........... **TCLC 6**
See also CA 105; DLB 10

Sutton, Henry
See Slavitt, David R(ytman)

Svevo, Italo .... **TCLC 2, 35**
See also Schmitz, Aron Hector

Swados, Elizabeth (A.) 1951-....... **CLC 12**
See also CA 97-100; CANR 49; INT 97-100

Swados, Harvey 1920-1972 .... **CLC 5**
See also CA 5-8R; 37-40R; CANR 6;
DLB 2

Swan, Gladys 1934- .... **CLC 69**
See also CA 101; CANR 17, 39

Thakura, Ravindranatha
See Tagore, Rabindranath

Tharoor, Shashi 1956- .... **CLC 70**
See also CA 141

Thelwell, Michael Miles 1939- ..... **CLC 22**
See also BW 2; CA 101

Theobald, Lewis, Jr.
See Lovecraft, H(oward) P(hillips)

Theodorescu, Ion N. 1880-1967
See Arghezi, Tudor
See also CA 116

Theriault, Yves 1915-1983.... **CLC 79; DAC**
See also CA 102; DAM MST; DLB 88

Theroux, Alexander (Louis)
1939- .... **CLC 2, 25**
See also CA 85-88; CANR 20

Theroux, Paul (Edward)
1941- .... **CLC 5, 8, 11, 15, 28, 46**
See also BEST 89:4; CA 33-36R; CANR 20,
45; DAM POP; DLB 2; MTCW;
SATA 44

Thesen, Sharon 1946- .... **CLC 56**

Thevenin, Denis
See Duhamel, Georges

Thibault, Jacques Anatole Francois
1844-1924
See France, Anatole
See also CA 106; 127; DAM NOV; MTCW

Thiele, Colin (Milton) 1920- .... **CLC 17**
See also CA 29-32R; CANR 12, 28;
CLR 27; MAICYA; SAAS 2; SATA 14,
72

Thomas, Audrey (Callahan)
1935- .... **CLC 7, 13, 37; SSC 20**
See also AITN 2; CA 21-24R; CAAS 19;
CANR 36; DLB 60; MTCW

Thomas, D(onald) M(ichael)
1935- .... **CLC 13, 22, 31**
See also CA 61-64; CAAS 11; CANR 17,
45; CDBLB 1960 to Present; DLB 40;
INT CANR-17; MTCW

Thomas, Dylan (Marlais)
1914-1953 ... **TCLC 1, 8, 45; DA; DAB;**
DAC; PC 2; SSC 3; WLC
See also CA 104; 120; CDBLB 1945-1960;
DAM DRAM, MST, POET; DLB 13, 20,
139; MTCW; SATA 60

Thomas, (Philip) Edward
1878-1917 .... **TCLC 10**
See also CA 106; DAM POET; DLB 19

Thomas, Joyce Carol 1938- .... **CLC 35**
See also AAYA 12; BW 2; CA 113; 116;
CANR 48; CLR 19; DLB 33; INT 116;
JRDA; MAICYA; MTCW; SAAS 7;
SATA 40, 78

Thomas, Lewis 1913-1993 .... **CLC 35**
See also CA 85-88; 143; CANR 38; MTCW

Thomas, Paul
See Mann, (Paul) Thomas

Thomas, Piri 1928- .... **CLC 17**
See also CA 73-76; HW

Thomas, R(onald) S(tuart)
1913- .... **CLC 6, 13, 48; DAB**
See also CA 89-92; CAAS 4; CANR 30;
CDBLB 1960 to Present; DAM POET;
DLB 27; MTCW

Thomas, Ross (Elmore) 1926-1995 .. **CLC 39**
See also CA 33-36R; 150; CANR 22

Thompson, Francis Clegg
See Mencken, H(enry) L(ouis)

Thompson, Francis Joseph
1859-1907 .... **TCLC 4**
See also CA 104; CDBLB 1890-1914;
DLB 19

Thompson, Hunter S(tockton)
1939- .... **CLC 9, 17, 40**
See also BEST 89:1; CA 17-20R; CANR 23,
46; DAM POP; MTCW

Thompson, James Myers
See Thompson, Jim (Myers)

Thompson, Jim (Myers)
1906-1977(?) .... **CLC 69**
See also CA 140

Thompson, Judith .... **CLC 39**

Thomson, James 1700-1748...... **LC 16, 29**
See also DAM POET; DLB 95

Thomson, James 1834-1882...... **NCLC 18**
See also DAM POET; DLB 35

Thoreau, Henry David
1817-1862 ..... **NCLC 7, 21; DA; DAB;**
DAC; WLC
See also CDALB 1640-1865; DAM MST;
DLB 1

Thornton, Hall
See Silverberg, Robert

Thucydides c. 455B.C.-399B.C.... **CMLC 17**

Thurber, James (Grover)
1894-1961 .... **CLC 5, 11, 25; DA; DAB;**
DAC; SSC 1
See also CA 73-76; CANR 17, 39;
CDALB 1929-1941; DAM DRAM, MST,
NOV; DLB 4, 11, 22, 102; MAICYA;
MTCW; SATA 13

Thurman, Wallace (Henry)
1902-1934 .... **TCLC 6; BLC**
See also BW 1; CA 104; 124; DAM MULT;
DLB 51

Ticheburn, Cheviot
See Ainsworth, William Harrison

Tieck, (Johann) Ludwig
1773-1853 .... **NCLC 5, 46**
See also DLB 90

Tiger, Derry
See Ellison, Harlan (Jay)

Tilghman, Christopher 1948(?)- ..... **CLC 65**

Tillinghast, Richard (Williford)
1940- .... **CLC 29**
See also CA 29-32R; CAAS 23; CANR 26,
51

Timrod, Henry 1828-1867 .... **NCLC 25**
See also DLB 3

Tindall, Gillian 1938- .... **CLC 7**
See also CA 21-24R; CANR 11

Tiptree, James, Jr. .... **CLC 48, 50**
See also Sheldon, Alice Hastings Bradley
See also DLB 8

Titmarsh, Michael Angelo
See Thackeray, William Makepeace

Tocqueville, Alexis (Charles Henri Maurice
Clerel Comte) 1805-1859..... **NCLC 7**

Tolkien, J(ohn) R(onald) R(euel)
1892-1973 ...... **CLC 1, 2, 3, 8, 12, 38;**
DA; DAB; DAC; WLC
See also AAYA 10; AITN 1; CA 17-18;
45-48; CANR 36; CAP 2;
CDBLB 1914-1945; DAM MST, NOV,
POP; DLB 15, 160; JRDA; MAICYA;
MTCW; SATA 2, 32; SATA-Obit 24

Toller, Ernst 1893-1939 .... **TCLC 10**
See also CA 107; DLB 124

Tolson, M. B.
See Tolson, Melvin B(eaunorus)

Tolson, Melvin B(eaunorus)
1898(?)-1966 .... **CLC 36; BLC**
See also BW 1; CA 124; 89-92;
DAM MULT, POET; DLB 48, 76

Tolstoi, Aleksei Nikolaevich
See Tolstoy, Alexey Nikolaevich

Tolstoy, Alexey Nikolaevich
1882-1945 .... **TCLC 18**
See also CA 107

Tolstoy, Count Leo
See Tolstoy, Leo (Nikolaevich)

Tolstoy, Leo (Nikolaevich)
1828-1910 ...... **TCLC 4, 11, 17, 28, 44;**
DA; DAB; DAC; SSC 9; WLC
See also CA 104; 123; DAM MST, NOV;
SATA 26

Tomasi di Lampedusa, Giuseppe 1896-1957
See Lampedusa, Giuseppe (Tomasi) di
See also CA 111

Tomlin, Lily..................... **CLC 17**
See also Tomlin, Mary Jean

Tomlin, Mary Jean 1939(?)-
See Tomlin, Lily
See also CA 117

Tomlinson, (Alfred) Charles
1927- .... **CLC 2, 4, 6, 13, 45**
See also CA 5-8R; CANR 33; DAM POET;
DLB 40

Tonson, Jacob
See Bennett, (Enoch) Arnold

Toole, John Kennedy
1937-1969 .... **CLC 19, 64**
See also CA 104; DLBY 81

Toomer, Jean
1894-1967 ...... **CLC 1, 4, 13, 22; BLC;**
PC 7; SSC 1
See also BW 1; CA 85-88;
CDALB 1917-1929; DAM MULT;
DLB 45, 51; MTCW

Torley, Luke
See Blish, James (Benjamin)

Tornimparte, Alessandra
See Ginzburg, Natalia

Torre, Raoul della
See Mencken, H(enry) L(ouis)

Torrey, E(dwin) Fuller 1937-....... **CLC 34**
See also CA 119

Torsvan, Ben Traven
See Traven, B.

Torsvan, Benno Traven
See Traven, B.

Torsvan, Berick Traven
See Traven, B.

Torsvan, Berwick Traven
See Traven, B.

Torsvan, Bruno Traven
See Traven, B.

Torsvan, Traven
See Traven, B.

Tournier, Michel (Edouard)
1924- . . . . CLC 6, 23, 36
See also CA 49-52; CANR 3, 36; DLB 83;
MTCW; SATA 23

Tournimparte, Alessandra
See Ginzburg, Natalia

Towers, Ivar
See Kornbluth, C(yril) M.

Towne, Robert (Burton) 1936(?)- . . . . CLC 87
See also CA 108; DLB 44

Townsend, Sue 1946- . . CLC 61; DAB; DAC
See also CA 119; 127; INT 127; MTCW;
SATA 55; SATA-Brief 48

Townshend, Peter (Dennis Blandford)
1945- . . . . CLC 17, 42
See also CA 107

Tozzi, Federigo 1883-1920 . . . . TCLC 31

Traill, Catharine Parr
1802-1899 . . . . NCLC 31
See also DLB 99

Trakl, Georg 1887-1914 . . . . TCLC 5
See also CA 104

Transtroemer, Tomas (Goesta)
1931- . . . . CLC 52, 65
See also CA 117; 129; CAAS 17;
DAM POET

Transtromer, Tomas Gosta
See Transtroemer, Tomas (Goesta)

Traven, B. (?)-1969 . . . . CLC 8, 11
See also CA 19-20; 25-28R; CAP 2; DLB 9,
56; MTCW

Treitel, Jonathan 1959- . . . . CLC 70

Tremain, Rose 1943- . . . . CLC 42
See also CA 97-100; CANR 44, DLB 14

Tremblay, Michel 1942- . . . . . . CLC 29; DAC
See also CA 116; 128; DAM MST; DLB 60;
MTCW

Trevanian . . . . CLC 29
See also Whitaker, Rod(ney)

Trevor, Glen
See Hilton, James

Trevor, William
1928- . . . . . CLC 7, 9, 14, 25, 71; SSC 21
See also Cox, William Trevor
See also DLB 14, 139

Trifonov, Yuri (Valentinovich)
1925-1981 . . . . CLC 45
See also CA 126; 103; MTCW

Trilling, Lionel 1905-1975 . . . . CLC 9, 11, 24
See also CA 9-12R; 61-64; CANR 10;
DLB 28, 63; INT CANR-10; MTCW

Trimball, W. H.
See Mencken, H(enry) L(ouis)

Tristan
See Gomez de la Serna, Ramon

Tristram
See Housman, A(lfred) E(dward)

Trogdon, William (Lewis) 1939-
See Heat-Moon, William Least
See also CA 115; 119; CANR 47; INT 119

Trollope, Anthony
1815-1882 . . . . . NCLC 6, 33; DA; DAB;
DAC; WLC
See also CDBLB 1832-1890; DAM MST,
NOV; DLB 21, 57, 159; SATA 22

Trollope, Frances 1779-1863 . . . . . NCLC 30
See also DLB 21

Trotsky, Leon 1879-1940 . . . . TCLC 22
See also CA 118

Trotter (Cockburn), Catharine
1679-1749 . . . . LC 8
See also DLB 84

Trout, Kilgore
See Farmer, Philip Jose

Trow, George W. S. 1943- . . . . CLC 52
See also CA 126

Troyat, Henri 1911- . . . . CLC 23
See also CA 45-48; CANR 2, 33; MTCW

Trudeau, G(arretson) B(eekman) 1948-
See Trudeau, Garry B.
See also CA 81-84; CANR 31; SATA 35

Trudeau, Garry B. . . . . CLC 12
See also Trudeau, G(arretson) B(eekman)
See also AAYA 10; AITN 2

Truffaut, Francois 1932-1984 . . . . . . CLC 20
See also CA 81-84; 113; CANR 34

Trumbo, Dalton 1905-1976 . . . . CLC 19
See also CA 21-24R; 69-72; CANR 10;
DLB 26

Trumbull, John 1750-1831 . . . . . . NCLC 30
See also DLB 31

Trundlett, Helen B.
See Eliot, T(homas) S(tearns)

Tryon, Thomas 1926-1991 . . . . CLC 3, 11
See also AITN 1; CA 29-32R; 135;
CANR 32; DAM POP; MTCW

Tryon, Tom
See Tryon, Thomas

Ts'ao Hsueh-ch'in 1715(?)-1763 . . . . . . LC 1

Tsushima, Shuji 1909-1948
See Dazai, Osamu
See also CA 107

Tsvetaeva (Efron), Marina (Ivanovna)
1892-1941 . . . . TCLC 7, 35; PC 14
See also CA 104; 128; MTCW

Tuck, Lily 1938- . . . . CLC 70
See also CA 139

Tu Fu 712-770 . . . . PC 9
See also DAM MULT

Tunis, John R(oberts) 1889-1975 . . . CLC 12
See also CA 61-64; DLB 22; JRDA;
MAICYA; SATA 37; SATA-Brief 30

Tuohy, Frank . . . . CLC 37
See also Tuohy, John Francis
See also DLB 14, 139

Tuohy, John Francis 1925-
See Tuohy, Frank
See also CA 5-8R; CANR 3, 47

Turco, Lewis (Putnam) 1934- . . . CLC 11, 63
See also CA 13-16R; CAAS 22; CANR 24,
51; DLBY 84

Turgenev, Ivan
1818-1883 . . . . NCLC 21; DA; DAB;
DAC; SSC 7; WLC
See also DAM MST, NOV

Turgot, Anne-Robert-Jacques
1727-1781 . . . . LC 26

Turner, Frederick 1943- . . . . CLC 48
See also CA 73-76; CAAS 10; CANR 12,
30; DLB 40

Tutu, Desmond M(pilo)
1931- . . . . CLC 80; BLC
See also BW 1; CA 125; DAM MULT

Tutuola, Amos 1920- . . . CLC 5, 14, 29; BLC
See also BW 2; CA 9-12R; CANR 27;
DAM MULT; DLB 125; MTCW

Twain, Mark
. . . . . TCLC 6, 12, 19, 36, 48, 59; SSC 6;
WLC
See also Clemens, Samuel Langhorne
See also DLB 11, 12, 23, 64, 74

Tyler, Anne
1941- . . . . CLC 7, 11, 18, 28, 44, 59
See also BEST 89:1; CA 9-12R; CANR 11,
33; DAM NOV, POP; DLB 6, 143;
DLBY 82; MTCW; SATA 7

Tyler, Royall 1757-1826 . . . . NCLC 3
See also DLB 37

Tynan, Katharine 1861-1931 . . . . TCLC 3
See also CA 104; DLB 153

Tyutchev, Fyodor 1803-1873 . . . . . NCLC 34

Tzara, Tristan . . . . CLC 47
See also Rosenfeld, Samuel
See also DAM POET

Uhry, Alfred 1936- . . . . CLC 55
See also CA 127; 133; DAM DRAM, POP;
INT 133

Ulf, Haerved
See Strindberg, (Johan) August

Ulf, Harved
See Strindberg, (Johan) August

Ulibarri, Sabine R(eyes) 1919- . . . . . CLC 83
See also CA 131; DAM MULT; DLB 82;
HW

Unamuno (y Jugo), Miguel de
1864-1936 . . . . TCLC 2, 9; HLC; SSC 11
See also CA 104; 131; DAM MULT, NOV;
DLB 108; HW; MTCW

Undercliffe, Errol
See Campbell, (John) Ramsey

Underwood, Miles
See Glassco, John

Undset, Sigrid
1882-1949 . . . . TCLC 3; DA; DAB;
DAC; WLC
See also CA 104; 129; DAM MST, NOV;
MTCW

Ungaretti, Giuseppe
1888-1970 . . . . CLC 7, 11, 15
See also CA 19-20; 25-28R; CAP 2;
DLB 114

Unger, Douglas 1952- . . . . CLC 34
See also CA 130

Unsworth, Barry (Forster) 1930- . . . . CLC 76
See also CA 25-28R; CANR 30

Updike, John (Hoyer)
1932- . . . . . . CLC 1, 2, 3, 5, 7, 9, 13, 15,
23, 34, 43, 70; DA; DAB; DAC; SSC 13;
WLC
See also CA 1-4R; CABS 1; CANR 4, 33,
51; CDALB 1968-1988; DAM MST,
NOV, POET, POP; DLB 2, 5, 143;
DLBD 3; DLBY 80, 82; MTCW

Upshaw, Margaret Mitchell
See Mitchell, Margaret (Munnerlyn)

Upton, Mark
See Sanders, Lawrence

Urdang, Constance (Henriette)
1922- . . . . CLC 47
See also CA 21-24R; CANR 9, 24

Uriel, Henry
See Faust, Frederick (Schiller)

Uris, Leon (Marcus) 1924- . . . . . . CLC 7, 32
See also AITN 1, 2; BEST 89:2; CA 1-4R;
CANR 1, 40; DAM NOV, POP; MTCW;
SATA 49

Urmuz
See Codrescu, Andrei

Urquhart, Jane 1949- . . . . CLC 90; DAC
See also CA 113; CANR 32

Ustinov, Peter (Alexander) 1921- . . . . CLC 1
See also AITN 1; CA 13-16R; CANR 25,
51; DLB 13

Vaculik, Ludvik 1926- . . . . CLC 7
See also CA 53-56

Valdez, Luis (Miguel)
1940- . . . . CLC 84; HLC
See also CA 101; CANR 32; DAM MULT;
DLB 122; HW

Valenzuela, Luisa 1938- . . . CLC 31; SSC 14
See also CA 101; CANR 32; DAM MULT;
DLB 113; HW

Valera y Alcala-Galiano, Juan
1824-1905 . . . . TCLC 10
See also CA 106

Valery, (Ambroise) Paul (Toussaint Jules)
1871-1945 . . . . TCLC 4, 15; PC 9
See also CA 104; 122; DAM POET; MTCW

Valle-Inclan, Ramon (Maria) del
1866-1936 . . . . TCLC 5; HLC
See also CA 106; DAM MULT; DLB 134

Vallejo, Antonio Buero
See Buero Vallejo, Antonio

Vallejo, Cesar (Abraham)
1892-1938 . . . . TCLC 3, 56; HLC
See also CA 105; DAM MULT; HW

Valle Y Pena, Ramon del
See Valle-Inclan, Ramon (Maria) del

Van Ash, Cay 1918- . . . . CLC 34

Vanbrugh, Sir John 1664-1726 . . . . . . LC 21
See also DAM DRAM; DLB 80

Van Campen, Karl
See Campbell, John W(ood, Jr.)

Vance, Gerald
See Silverberg, Robert

Vance, Jack . . . . CLC 35
See also Vance, John Holbrook
See also DLB 8

Vance, John Holbrook 1916-
See Queen, Ellery; Vance, Jack
See also CA 29-32R; CANR 17; MTCW

Van Den Bogarde, Derek Jules Gaspard Ulric
Niven 1921-
See Bogarde, Dirk
See also CA 77-80

Vandenburgh, Jane . . . . CLC 59

Vanderhaeghe, Guy 1951- . . . . CLC 41
See also CA 113

van der Post, Laurens (Jan) 1906- . . . CLC 5
See also CA 5-8R; CANR 35

van de Wetering, Janwillem 1931- . . CLC 47
See also CA 49-52; CANR 4

Van Dine, S. S. . . . . TCLC 23
See also Wright, Willard Huntington

Van Doren, Carl (Clinton)
1885-1950 . . . . TCLC 18
See also CA 111

Van Doren, Mark 1894-1972 . . . . . CLC 6, 10
See also CA 1-4R; 37-40R; CANR 3;
DLB 45; MTCW

Van Druten, John (William)
1901-1957 . . . . TCLC 2
See also CA 104; DLB 10

Van Duyn, Mona (Jane)
1921- . . . . CLC 3, 7, 63
See also CA 9-12R; CANR 7, 38;
DAM POET; DLB 5

Van Dyne, Edith
See Baum, L(yman) Frank

van Itallie, Jean-Claude 1936- . . . . CLC 3
See also CA 45-48; CAAS 2; CANR 1, 48;
DLB 7

van Ostaijen, Paul 1896-1928 . . . . . TCLC 33

Van Peebles, Melvin 1932- . . . . . . CLC 2, 20
See also BW 2; CA 85-88; CANR 27;
DAM MULT

Vansittart, Peter 1920- . . . . CLC 42
See also CA 1-4R; CANR 3, 49

Van Vechten, Carl 1880-1964 . . . . . . CLC 33
See also CA 89-92; DLB 4, 9, 51

Van Vogt, A(lfred) E(lton) 1912- . . . . . CLC 1
See also CA 21-24R; CANR 28; DLB 8;
SATA 14

Varda, Agnes 1928- . . . . CLC 16
See also CA 116; 122

Vargas Llosa, (Jorge) Mario (Pedro)
1936- . . . . CLC 3, 6, 9, 10, 15, 31, 42, 85;
DA; DAB; DAC; HLC
See also CA 73-76; CANR 18, 32, 42;
DAM MST, MULT, NOV; DLB 145;
HW; MTCW

Vasiliu, Gheorghe 1881-1957
See Bacovia, George
See also CA 123

Vassa, Gustavus
See Equiano, Olaudah

Vassilikos, Vassilis 1933- . . . . CLC 4, 8
See also CA 81-84

Vaughan, Henry 1621-1695 . . . . LC 27
See also DLB 131

Vaughn, Stephanie . . . . CLC 62

Vazov, Ivan (Minchov)
1850-1921 . . . . TCLC 25
See also CA 121; DLB 147

Veblen, Thorstein (Bunde)
1857-1929 . . . . TCLC 31
See also CA 115

Vega, Lope de 1562-1635 . . . . LC 23

Venison, Alfred
See Pound, Ezra (Weston Loomis)

Verdi, Marie de
See Mencken, H(enry) L(ouis)

Verdu, Matilde
See Cela, Camilo Jose

Verga, Giovanni (Carmelo)
1840-1922 . . . . TCLC 3; SSC 21
See also CA 104; 123

Vergil
70B.C.-19B.C. . . . . . CMLC 9; DA; DAB;
DAC; PC 12
See also DAM MST, POET

Verhaeren, Emile (Adolphe Gustave)
1855-1916 . . . . TCLC 12
See also CA 109

Verlaine, Paul (Marie)
1844-1896 . . . . NCLC 2, 51; PC 2
See also DAM POET

Verne, Jules (Gabriel)
1828-1905 . . . . TCLC 6, 52
See also AAYA 16; CA 110; 131; DLB 123;
JRDA; MAICYA; SATA 21

Very, Jones 1813-1880 . . . . NCLC 9
See also DLB 1

Vesaas, Tarjei 1897-1970 . . . . CLC 48
See also CA 29-32R

Vialis, Gaston
See Simenon, Georges (Jacques Christian)

Vian, Boris 1920-1959 . . . . TCLC 9
See also CA 106; DLB 72

Viaud, (Louis Marie) Julien 1850-1923
See Loti, Pierre
See also CA 107

Vicar, Henry
See Felsen, Henry Gregor

Vicker, Angus
See Felsen, Henry Gregor

Vidal, Gore
1925- . . . . . CLC 2, 4, 6, 8, 10, 22, 33, 72
See also AITN 1; BEST 90:2; CA 5-8R;
CANR 13, 45; DAM NOV, POP; DLB 6,
152; INT CANR-13; MTCW

Viereck, Peter (Robert Edwin)
1916- . . . . CLC 4
See also CA 1-4R; CANR 1, 47; DLB 5

Vigny, Alfred (Victor) de
1797-1863 . . . . NCLC 7
See also DAM POET; DLB 119

Vilakazi, Benedict Wallet
1906-1947 . . . . TCLC 37

Villiers de l'Isle Adam, Jean Marie Mathias
Philippe Auguste Comte
1838-1889 . . . . NCLC 3; SSC 14
See also DLB 123

Villon, Francois 1431-1463(?) . . . . PC 13

Vinci, Leonardo da 1452-1519 . . . . LC 12

Vine, Barbara .... **CLC 50**
See also Rendell, Ruth (Barbara)
See also BEST 90:4

Vinge, Joan D(ennison) 1948- ...... **CLC 30**
See also CA 93-96; SATA 36

Violis, G.
See Simenon, Georges (Jacques Christian)

Visconti, Luchino 1906-1976 .... **CLC 16**
See also CA 81-84; 65-68; CANR 39

Vittorini, Elio 1908-1966 ..... **CLC 6, 9, 14**
See also CA 133; 25-28R

Vizinczey, Stephen 1933- .... **CLC 40**
See also CA 128; INT 128

Vliet, R(ussell) G(ordon)
1929-1984 .... **CLC 22**
See also CA 37-40R; 112; CANR 18

Vogau, Boris Andreyevich 1894-1937(?)
See Pilnyak, Boris
See also CA 123

Vogel, Paula A(nne) 1951- .... **CLC 76**
See also CA 108

Voight, Ellen Bryant 1943- .... **CLC 54**
See also CA 69-72; CANR 11, 29; DLB 120

Voigt, Cynthia 1942- .... **CLC 30**
See also AAYA 3; CA 106; CANR 18, 37,
40; CLR 13; INT CANR-18; JRDA;
MAICYA; SATA 48, 79; SATA-Brief 33

Voinovich, Vladimir (Nikolaevich)
1932- .... **CLC 10, 49**
See also CA 81-84; CAAS 12; CANR 33;
MTCW

Vollmann, William T. 1959- .... **CLC 89**
See also CA 134; DAM NOV, POP

Voloshinov, V. N.
See Bakhtin, Mikhail Mikhailovich

Voltaire
1694-1778 ..... **LC 14; DA; DAB; DAC;**
SSC 12; WLC
See also DAM DRAM, MST

von Daeniken, Erich 1935- .... **CLC 30**
See also AITN 1; CA 37-40R; CANR 17,
44

von Daniken, Erich
See von Daeniken, Erich

von Heidenstam, (Carl Gustaf) Verner
See Heidenstam, (Carl Gustaf) Verner von

von Heyse, Paul (Johann Ludwig)
See Heyse, Paul (Johann Ludwig von)

von Hofmannsthal, Hugo
See Hofmannsthal, Hugo von

von Horvath, Odon
See Horvath, Oedoen von

von Horvath, Oedoen
See Horvath, Oedoen von

von Liliencron, (Friedrich Adolf Axel) Detlev
See Liliencron, (Friedrich Adolf Axel)
Detlev von

Vonnegut, Kurt, Jr.
1922- ...... **CLC 1, 2, 3, 4, 5, 8, 12, 22,**
40, 60; DA; DAB; DAC; SSC 8; WLC
See also AAYA 6; AITN 1; BEST 90:4;
CA 1-4R; CANR 1, 25, 49;
CDALB 1968-1988; DAM MST, NOV,
POP; DLB 2, 8, 152; DLBD 3; DLBY 80;
MTCW

Von Rachen, Kurt
See Hubbard, L(afayette) Ron(ald)

von Rezzori (d'Arezzo), Gregor
See Rezzori (d'Arezzo), Gregor von

von Sternberg, Josef
See Sternberg, Josef von

Vorster, Gordon 1924- .... **CLC 34**
See also CA 133

Vosce, Trudie
See Ozick, Cynthia

Voznesensky, Andrei (Andreievich)
1933- .... **CLC 1, 15, 57**
See also CA 89-92; CANR 37;
DAM POET; MTCW

Waddington, Miriam 1917- .... **CLC 28**
See also CA 21-24R; CANR 12, 30;
DLB 68

Wagman, Fredrica 1937- .... **CLC 7**
See also CA 97-100; INT 97-100

Wagner, Richard 1813-1883 .... **NCLC 9**
See also DLB 129

Wagner-Martin, Linda 1936- ...... **CLC 50**

Wagoner, David (Russell)
1926- .... **CLC 3, 5, 15**
See also CA 1-4R; CAAS 3; CANR 2;
DLB 5; SATA 14

Wah, Fred(erick James) 1939- ...... **CLC 44**
See also CA 107; 141; DLB 60

Wahloo, Per 1926-1975 .... **CLC 7**
See also CA 61-64

Wahloo, Peter
See Wahloo, Per

Wain, John (Barrington)
1925-1994 .... **CLC 2, 11, 15, 46**
See also CA 5-8R; 145; CAAS 4; CANR 23;
CDBLB 1960 to Present; DLB 15, 27,
139, 155; MTCW

Wajda, Andrzej 1926- .... **CLC 16**
See also CA 102

Wakefield, Dan 1932- .... **CLC 7**
See also CA 21-24R; CAAS 7

Wakoski, Diane
1937- ..... **CLC 2, 4, 7, 9, 11, 40; PC 15**
See also CA 13-16R; CAAS 1; CANR 9;
DAM POET; DLB 5; INT CANR-9

Wakoski-Sherbell, Diane
See Wakoski, Diane

Walcott, Derek (Alton)
1930- .... **CLC 2, 4, 9, 14, 25, 42, 67, 76;**
BLC; DAB; DAC
See also BW 2; CA 89-92; CANR 26, 47;
DAM MST, MULT, POET; DLB 117;
DLBY 81; MTCW

Waldman, Anne 1945- .... **CLC 7**
See also CA 37-40R; CAAS 17; CANR 34;
DLB 16

Waldo, E. Hunter
See Sturgeon, Theodore (Hamilton)

Waldo, Edward Hamilton
See Sturgeon, Theodore (Hamilton)

Walker, Alice (Malsenior)
1944- .... **CLC 5, 6, 9, 19, 27, 46, 58;**
BLC; DA; DAB; DAC; SSC 5
See also AAYA 3; BEST 89:4; BW 2;
CA 37-40R; CANR 9, 27, 49;
CDALB 1968-1988; DAM MST, MULT,
NOV, POET, POP; DLB 6, 33, 143;
INT CANR-27; MTCW; SATA 31

Walker, David Harry 1911-1992 .... **CLC 14**
See also CA 1-4R; 137; CANR 1; SATA 8;
SATA-Obit 71

Walker, Edward Joseph 1934-
See Walker, Ted
See also CA 21-24R; CANR 12, 28

Walker, George F.
1947- .... **CLC 44, 61; DAB; DAC**
See also CA 103; CANR 21, 43;
DAM MST; DLB 60

Walker, Joseph A. 1935- .... **CLC 19**
See also BW 1; CA 89-92; CANR 26;
DAM DRAM, MST; DLB 38

Walker, Margaret (Abigail)
1915- .... **CLC 1, 6; BLC**
See also BW 2; CA 73-76; CANR 26;
DAM MULT; DLB 76, 152; MTCW

Walker, Ted .... **CLC 13**
See also Walker, Edward Joseph
See also DLB 40

Wallace, David Foster 1962- .... **CLC 50**
See also CA 132

Wallace, Dexter
See Masters, Edgar Lee

Wallace, (Richard Horatio) Edgar
1875-1932 .... **TCLC 57**
See also CA 115; DLB 70

Wallace, Irving 1916-1990 ...... **CLC 7, 13**
See also AITN 1; CA 1-4R; 132; CAAS 1;
CANR 1, 27; DAM NOV, POP;
INT CANR-27; MTCW

Wallant, Edward Lewis
1926-1962 .... **CLC 5, 10**
See also CA 1-4R; CANR 22; DLB 2, 28,
143; MTCW

Walley, Byron
See Card, Orson Scott

Walpole, Horace 1717-1797 .... **LC 2**
See also DLB 39, 104

Walpole, Hugh (Seymour)
1884-1941 .... **TCLC 5**
See also CA 104; DLB 34

Walser, Martin 1927- .... **CLC 27**
See also CA 57-60; CANR 8, 46; DLB 75,
124

Walser, Robert
1878-1956 .... **TCLC 18; SSC 20**
See also CA 118; DLB 66

Walsh, Jill Paton .... **CLC 35**
See also Paton Walsh, Gillian
See also AAYA 11; CLR 2; DLB 161;
SAAS 3

Walter, Villiam Christian
See Andersen, Hans Christian

Wambaugh, Joseph (Aloysius, Jr.)
1937- . . . . CLC 3, 18
See also AITN 1; BEST 89:3; CA 33-36R;
CANR 42; DAM NOV, POP; DLB 6;
DLBY 83; MTCW

Ward, Arthur Henry Sarsfield 1883-1959
See Rohmer, Sax
See also CA 108

Ward, Douglas Turner 1930- . . . . CLC 19
See also BW 1; CA 81-84; CANR 27;
DLB 7, 38

Ward, Mary Augusta
See Ward, Mrs. Humphry

Ward, Mrs. Humphry
1851-1920 . . . . TCLC 55
See also DLB 18

Ward, Peter
See Faust, Frederick (Schiller)

Warhol, Andy 1928(?)-1987 . . . . CLC 20
See also AAYA 12; BEST 89:4; CA 89-92;
121; CANR 34

Warner, Francis (Robert le Plastrier)
1937- . . . . CLC 14
See also CA 53-56; CANR 11

Warner, Marina 1946- . . . . CLC 59
See also CA 65-68; CANR 21

Warner, Rex (Ernest) 1905-1986 . . . . CLC 45
See also CA 89-92; 119; DLB 15

Warner, Susan (Bogert)
1819-1885 . . . . NCLC 31
See also DLB 3, 42

Warner, Sylvia (Constance) Ashton
See Ashton-Warner, Sylvia (Constance)

Warner, Sylvia Townsend
1893-1978 . . . . CLC 7, 19
See also CA 61-64; 77-80; CANR 16;
DLB 34, 139; MTCW

Warren, Mercy Otis 1728-1814 . . . NCLC 13
See also DLB 31

Warren, Robert Penn
1905-1989 . . . . CLC 1, 4, 6, 8, 10, 13, 18,
39, 53, 59; DA; DAB; DAC; SSC 4; WLC
See also AITN 1; CA 13-16R; 129;
CANR 10, 47; CDALB 1968-1988;
DAM MST, NOV, POET; DLB 2, 48,
152; DLBY 80, 89; INT CANR-10;
MTCW; SATA 46; SATA-Obit 63

Warshofsky, Isaac
See Singer, Isaac Bashevis

Warton, Thomas 1728-1790 . . . . LC 15
See also DAM POET; DLB 104, 109

Waruk, Kona
See Harris, (Theodore) Wilson

Warung, Price 1855-1911 . . . . TCLC 45

Warwick, Jarvis
See Garner, Hugh

Washington, Alex
See Harris, Mark

Washington, Booker T(aliaferro)
1856-1915 . . . . TCLC 10; BLC
See also BW 1; CA 114; 125; DAM MULT;
SATA 28

Washington, George 1732-1799 . . . . . . LC 25
See also DLB 31

Wassermann, (Karl) Jakob
1873-1934 . . . . TCLC 6
See also CA 104; DLB 66

Wasserstein, Wendy
1950- . . . . CLC 32, 59, 90; DC 4
See also CA 121; 129; CABS 3;
DAM DRAM; INT 129

Waterhouse, Keith (Spencer)
1929- . . . . CLC 47
See also CA 5-8R; CANR 38; DLB 13, 15;
MTCW

Waters, Frank (Joseph)
1902-1995 . . . . CLC 88
See also CA 5-8R; 149; CAAS 13; CANR 3,
18; DLBY 86

Waters, Roger 1944- . . . . CLC 35

Watkins, Frances Ellen
See Harper, Frances Ellen Watkins

Watkins, Gerrold
See Malzberg, Barry N(athaniel)

Watkins, Paul 1964- . . . . CLC 55
See also CA 132

Watkins, Vernon Phillips
1906-1967 . . . . CLC 43
See also CA 9-10; 25-28R; CAP 1; DLB 20

Watson, Irving S.
See Mencken, H(enry) L(ouis)

Watson, John H.
See Farmer, Philip Jose

Watson, Richard F.
See Silverberg, Robert

Waugh, Auberon (Alexander) 1939- . . CLC 7
See also CA 45-48; CANR 6, 22; DLB 14

Waugh, Evelyn (Arthur St. John)
1903-1966 . . . . . . CLC 1, 3, 8, 13, 19, 27,
44; DA; DAB; DAC; WLC
See also CA 85-88; 25-28R; CANR 22;
CDBLB 1914-1945; DAM MST, NOV,
POP; DLB 15, 162; MTCW

Waugh, Harriet 1944- . . . . CLC 6
See also CA 85-88; CANR 22

Ways, C. R.
See Blount, Roy (Alton), Jr.

Waystaff, Simon
See Swift, Jonathan

Webb, (Martha) Beatrice (Potter)
1858-1943 . . . . TCLC 22
See also Potter, Beatrice
See also CA 117

Webb, Charles (Richard) 1939- . . . . . . CLC 7
See also CA 25-28R

Webb, James H(enry), Jr. 1946- . . . . CLC 22
See also CA 81-84

Webb, Mary (Gladys Meredith)
1881-1927 . . . . TCLC 24
See also CA 123; DLB 34

Webb, Mrs. Sidney
See Webb, (Martha) Beatrice (Potter)

Webb, Phyllis 1927- . . . . CLC 18
See also CA 104; CANR 23; DLB 53

Webb, Sidney (James)
1859-1947 . . . . TCLC 22
See also CA 117

Webber, Andrew Lloyd . . . . CLC 21
See also Lloyd Webber, Andrew

Weber, Lenora Mattingly
1895-1971 . . . . CLC 12
See also CA 19-20; 29-32R; CAP 1;
SATA 2; SATA-Obit 26

Webster, John 1579(?)-1634(?) . . . . DC 2
See also CDBLB Before 1660; DA; DAB;
DAC; DAM DRAM, MST; DLB 58;
WLC

Webster, Noah 1758-1843 . . . . NCLC 30

Wedekind, (Benjamin) Frank(lin)
1864-1918 . . . . TCLC 7
See also CA 104; DAM DRAM; DLB 118

Weidman, Jerome 1913- . . . . CLC 7
See also AITN 2; CA 1-4R; CANR 1;
DLB 28

Weil, Simone (Adolphine)
1909-1943 . . . . TCLC 23
See also CA 117

Weinstein, Nathan
See West, Nathanael

Weinstein, Nathan von Wallenstein
See West, Nathanael

Weir, Peter (Lindsay) 1944- . . . . CLC 20
See also CA 113; 123

Weiss, Peter (Ulrich)
1916-1982 . . . . CLC 3, 15, 51
See also CA 45-48; 106; CANR 3;
DAM DRAM; DLB 69, 124

Weiss, Theodore (Russell)
1916- . . . . CLC 3, 8, 14
See also CA 9-12R; CAAS 2; CANR 46;
DLB 5

Welch, (Maurice) Denton
1915-1948 . . . . TCLC 22
See also CA 121; 148

Welch, James 1940- . . . . CLC 6, 14, 52
See also CA 85-88; CANR 42;
DAM MULT, POP; NNAL

Weldon, Fay
1933- . . . . CLC 6, 9, 11, 19, 36, 59
See also CA 21-24R; CANR 16, 46;
CDBLB 1960 to Present; DAM POP;
DLB 14; INT CANR-16; MTCW

Wellek, Rene 1903-1995 . . . . CLC 28
See also CA 5-8R; 150; CAAS 7; CANR 8;
DLB 63; INT CANR-8

Weller, Michael 1942- . . . . CLC 10, 53
See also CA 85-88

Weller, Paul 1958- . . . . CLC 26

Wellershoff, Dieter 1925- . . . . CLC 46
See also CA 89-92; CANR 16, 37

Welles, (George) Orson
1915-1985 . . . . CLC 20, 80
See also CA 93-96; 117

Wellman, Mac 1945- . . . . CLC 65

Wellman, Manly Wade 1903-1986 . . CLC 49
See also CA 1-4R; 118; CANR 6, 16, 44;
SATA 6; SATA-Obit 47

Wells, Carolyn 1869(?)-1942 . . . . . . TCLC 35
See also CA 113; DLB 11

Wells, H(erbert) G(eorge)
1866-1946 .... **TCLC 6, 12, 19; DA;**
DAB; DAC; SSC 6; WLC
See also CA 110; 121; CDBLB 1914-1945;
DAM MST, NOV; DLB 34, 70, 156;
MTCW; SATA 20

Wells, Rosemary 1943-............ **CLC 12**
See also AAYA 13; CA 85-88; CANR 48;
CLR 16; MAICYA; SAAS 1; SATA 18,
69

Welty, Eudora
1909- ...... **CLC 1, 2, 5, 14, 22, 33; DA;**
DAB; DAC; SSC 1; WLC
See also CA 9-12R; CABS 1; CANR 32;
CDALB 1941-1968; DAM MST, NOV;
DLB 2, 102, 143; DLBD 12; DLBY 87;
MTCW

Wen I-to 1899-1946 .... **TCLC 28**

Wentworth, Robert
See Hamilton, Edmond

Werfel, Franz (V.) 1890-1945 ..... **TCLC 8**
See also CA 104; DLB 81, 124

Wergeland, Henrik Arnold
1808-1845 .... **NCLC 5**

Wersba, Barbara 1932-............ **CLC 30**
See also AAYA 2; CA 29-32R; CANR 16,
38; CLR 3; DLB 52; JRDA; MAICYA;
SAAS 2; SATA 1, 58

Wertmueller, Lina 1928- .... **CLC 16**
See also CA 97-100; CANR 39

Wescott, Glenway 1901-1987....... **CLC 13**
See also CA 13-16R; 121; CANR 23;
DLB 4, 9, 102

Wesker, Arnold 1932- .. **CLC 3, 5, 42; DAB**
See also CA 1-4R; CAAS 7; CANR 1, 33;
CDBLB 1960 to Present; DAM DRAM;
DLB 13; MTCW

Wesley, Richard (Errol) 1945-....... **CLC 7**
See also BW 1; CA 57-60; CANR 27;
DLB 38

Wessel, Johan Herman 1742-1785 .... **LC 7**

West, Anthony (Panther)
1914-1987 .... **CLC 50**
See also CA 45-48; 124; CANR 3, 19;
DLB 15

West, C. P.
See Wodehouse, P(elham) G(renville)

West, (Mary) Jessamyn
1902-1984 .... **CLC 7, 17**
See also CA 9-12R; 112; CANR 27; DLB 6;
DLBY 84; MTCW; SATA-Obit 37

West, Morris L(anglo) 1916-..... **CLC 6, 33**
See also CA 5-8R; CANR 24, 49; MTCW

West, Nathanael
1903-1940 ..... **TCLC 1, 14, 44; SSC 16**
See also CA 104; 125; CDALB 1929-1941;
DLB 4, 9, 28; MTCW

West, Owen
See Koontz, Dean R(ay)

West, Paul 1930- .... **CLC 7, 14**
See also CA 13-16R; CAAS 7; CANR 22;
DLB 14; INT CANR-22

West, Rebecca 1892-1983 .. **CLC 7, 9, 31, 50**
See also CA 5-8R; 109; CANR 19; DLB 36;
DLBY 83; MTCW

Westall, Robert (Atkinson)
1929-1993 .... **CLC 17**
See also AAYA 12; CA 69-72; 141;
CANR 18; CLR 13; JRDA; MAICYA;
SAAS 2; SATA 23, 69; SATA-Obit 75

Westlake, Donald E(dwin)
1933-..................... **CLC 7, 33**
See also CA 17-20R; CAAS 13; CANR 16,
44; DAM POP; INT CANR-16

Westmacott, Mary
See Christie, Agatha (Mary Clarissa)

Weston, Allen
See Norton, Andre

Wetcheek, J. L.
See Feuchtwanger, Lion

Wetering, Janwillem van de
See van de Wetering, Janwillem

Wetherell, Elizabeth
See Warner, Susan (Bogert)

Whalen, Philip 1923- .... **CLC 6, 29**
See also CA 9-12R; CANR 5, 39; DLB 16

Wharton, Edith (Newbold Jones)
1862-1937 ...... **TCLC 3, 9, 27, 53; DA;**
DAB; DAC; SSC 6; WLC
See also CA 104; 132; CDALB 1865-1917;
DAM MST, NOV; DLB 4, 9, 12, 78;
DLBD 13; MTCW

Wharton, James
See Mencken, H(enry) L(ouis)

Wharton, William (a pseudonym)
.... **CLC 18, 37**
See also CA 93-96; DLBY 80; INT 93-96

Wheatley (Peters), Phillis
1754(?)-1784 .... **LC 3; BLC; DA; DAC;**
PC 3; WLC
See also CDALB 1640-1865; DAM MST,
MULT, POET; DLB 31, 50

Wheelock, John Hall 1886-1978.... **CLC 14**
See also CA 13-16R; 77-80; CANR 14;
DLB 45

White, E(lwyn) B(rooks)
1899-1985 .... **CLC 10, 34, 39**
See also AITN 2; CA 13-16R; 116;
CANR 16, 37; CLR 1, 21; DAM POP;
DLB 11, 22; MAICYA; MTCW;
SATA 2, 29; SATA-Obit 44

White, Edmund (Valentine III)
1940- .... **CLC 27**
See also AAYA 7; CA 45-48; CANR 3, 19,
36; DAM POP; MTCW

White, Patrick (Victor Martindale)
1912-1990 .. **CLC 3, 4, 5, 7, 9, 18, 65, 69**
See also CA 81-84; 132; CANR 43; MTCW

White, Phyllis Dorothy James 1920-
See James, P. D.
See also CA 21-24R; CANR 17, 43;
DAM POP; MTCW

White, T(erence) H(anbury)
1906-1964 .... **CLC 30**
See also CA 73-76; CANR 37; DLB 160;
JRDA; MAICYA; SATA 12

White, Terence de Vere
1912-1994 .... **CLC 49**
See also CA 49-52; 145; CANR 3

White, Walter F(rancis)
1893-1955 .... **TCLC 15**
See also White, Walter
See also BW 1; CA 115; 124; DLB 51

White, William Hale 1831-1913
See Rutherford, Mark
See also CA 121

Whitehead, E(dward) A(nthony)
1933- .... **CLC 5**
See also CA 65-68

Whitemore, Hugh (John) 1936-..... **CLC 37**
See also CA 132; INT 132

Whitman, Sarah Helen (Power)
1803-1878 .... **NCLC 19**
See also DLB 1

Whitman, Walt(er)
1819-1892 ..... **NCLC 4, 31; DA; DAB;**
DAC; PC 3; WLC
See also CDALB 1640-1865; DAM MST,
POET; DLB 3, 64; SATA 20

Whitney, Phyllis A(yame) 1903-.... **CLC 42**
See also AITN 2; BEST 90:3; CA 1-4R;
CANR 3, 25, 38; DAM POP; JRDA;
MAICYA; SATA 1, 30

Whittemore, (Edward) Reed (Jr.)
1919- .... **CLC 4**
See also CA 9-12R; CAAS 8; CANR 4;
DLB 5

Whittier, John Greenleaf
1807-1892 .... **NCLC 8**
See also CDALB 1640-1865; DAM POET;
DLB 1

Whittlebot, Hernia
See Coward, Noel (Peirce)

Wicker, Thomas Grey 1926-
See Wicker, Tom
See also CA 65-68; CANR 21, 46

Wicker, Tom .... **CLC 7**
See also Wicker, Thomas Grey

Wideman, John Edgar
1941- .... **CLC 5, 34, 36, 67; BLC**
See also BW 2; CA 85-88; CANR 14, 42;
DAM MULT; DLB 33, 143

Wiehe, Rudy (Henry)
1934- .... **CLC 6, 11, 14; DAC**
See also CA 37-40R; CANR 42;
DAM MST; DLB 60

Wieland, Christoph Martin
1733-1813 .... **NCLC 17**
See also DLB 97

Wiene, Robert 1881-1938........ **TCLC 56**

Wieners, John 1934-............... **CLC 7**
See also CA 13-16R; DLB 16

Wiesel, Elie(zer)
1928- ...... **CLC 3, 5, 11, 37; DA; DAB;**
DAC
See also AAYA 7; AITN 1; CA 5-8R;
CAAS 4; CANR 8, 40; DAM MST,
NOV; DLB 83; DLBY 87; INT CANR-8;
MTCW; SATA 56

Wiggins, Marianne 1947-.......... **CLC 57**
See also BEST 89:3; CA 130

Wight, James Alfred 1916-
See Herriot, James
See also CA 77-80; SATA 55;
SATA-Brief 44

Wilbur, Richard (Purdy)
1921- ... CLC 3, 6, 9, 14, 53; DA; DAB;
DAC
See also CA 1-4R; CABS 2; CANR 2, 29;
DAM MST, POET; DLB 5;
INT CANR-29; MTCW; SATA 9

Wild, Peter 1940-................ CLC 14
See also CA 37-40R; DLB 5

Wilde, Oscar (Fingal O'Flahertie Wills)
1854(?)-1900 .... TCLC 1, 8, 23, 41; DA;
DAB; DAC; SSC 11; WLC
See also CA 104; 119; CDBLB 1890-1914;
DAM DRAM, MST, NOV; DLB 10, 19,
34, 57, 141, 156; SATA 24

Wilder, Billy .... CLC 20
See also Wilder, Samuel
See also DLB 26

Wilder, Samuel 1906-
See Wilder, Billy
See also CA 89-92

Wilder, Thornton (Niven)
1897-1975 ...... CLC 1, 5, 6, 10, 15, 35,
82; DA; DAB; DAC; DC 1; WLC
See also AITN 2; CA 13-16R; 61-64;
CANR 40; DAM DRAM, MST, NOV;
DLB 4, 7, 9; MTCW

Wilding, Michael 1942-........... CLC 73
See also CA 104; CANR 24, 49

Wiley, Richard 1944-............. CLC 44
See also CA 121; 129

Wilhelm, Kate .... CLC 7
See also Wilhelm, Katie Gertrude
See also CAAS 5; DLB 8; INT CANR-17

Wilhelm, Katie Gertrude 1928-
See Wilhelm, Kate
See also CA 37-40R; CANR 17, 36; MTCW

Wilkins, Mary
See Freeman, Mary Eleanor Wilkins

Willard, Nancy 1936-........... CLC 7, 37
See also CA 89-92; CANR 10, 39; CLR 5;
DLB 5, 52; MAICYA; MTCW;
SATA 37, 71; SATA-Brief 30

Williams, C(harles) K(enneth)
1936-................... CLC 33, 56
See also CA 37-40R; DAM POET; DLB 5

Williams, Charles
See Collier, James L(incoln)

Williams, Charles (Walter Stansby)
1886-1945 .... TCLC 1, 11
See also CA 104; DLB 100, 153

Williams, (George) Emlyn
1905-1987 .... CLC 15
See also CA 104; 123; CANR 36;
DAM DRAM; DLB 10, 77; MTCW

Williams, Hugo 1942-............. CLC 42
See also CA 17-20R; CANR 45; DLB 40

Williams, J. Walker
See Wodehouse, P(elham) G(renville)

Williams, John A(lfred)
1925-................ CLC 5, 13; BLC
See also BW 2; CA 53-56; CAAS 3;
CANR 6, 26, 51; DAM MULT; DLB 2,
33; INT CANR-6

Williams, Jonathan (Chamberlain)
1929-...................... CLC 13
See also CA 9-12R; CAAS 12; CANR 8;
DLB 5

Williams, Joy 1944-.............. CLC 31
See also CA 41-44R; CANR 22, 48

Williams, Norman 1952-.......... CLC 39
See also CA 118

Williams, Sherley Anne
1944-.................. CLC 89; BLC
See also BW 2; CA 73-76; CANR 25;
DAM MULT, POET; DLB 41;
INT CANR-25; SATA 78

Williams, Shirley
See Williams, Sherley Anne

Williams, Tennessee
1911-1983 ..... CLC 1, 2, 5, 7, 8, 11, 15,
19, 30, 39, 45, 71; DA; DAB; DAC;
DC 4; WLC
See also AITN 1, 2; CA 5-8R; 108;
CABS 3; CANR 31; CDALB 1941-1968;
DAM DRAM, MST; DLB 7; DLBD 4;
DLBY 83; MTCW

Williams, Thomas (Alonzo)
1926-1990 .... CLC 14
See also CA 1-4R; 132; CANR 2

Williams, William C.
See Williams, William Carlos

Williams, William Carlos
1883-1963 .... CLC 1, 2, 5, 9, 13, 22, 42,
67; DA; DAB; DAC; PC 7
See also CA 89-92; CANR 34;
CDALB 1917-1929; DAM MST, POET;
DLB 4, 16, 54, 86; MTCW

Williamson, David (Keith) 1942-.... CLC 56
See also CA 103; CANR 41

Williamson, Ellen Douglas 1905-1984
See Douglas, Ellen
See also CA 17-20R; 114; CANR 39

Williamson, Jack.................. CLC 29
See also Williamson, John Stewart
See also CAAS 8; DLB 8

Williamson, John Stewart 1908-
See Williamson, Jack
See also CA 17-20R; CANR 23

Willie, Frederick
See Lovecraft, H(oward) P(hillips)

Willingham, Calder (Baynard, Jr.)
1922-1995 .... CLC 5, 51
See also CA 5-8R; 147; CANR 3; DLB 2,
44; MTCW

Willis, Charles
See Clarke, Arthur C(harles)

Willy
See Colette, (Sidonie-Gabrielle)

Willy, Colette
See Colette, (Sidonie-Gabrielle)

Wilson, A(ndrew) N(orman) 1950- .. CLC 33
See also CA 112; 122; DLB 14, 155

Wilson, Angus (Frank Johnstone)
1913-1991 .. CLC 2, 3, 5, 25, 34; SSC 21
See also CA 5-8R; 134; CANR 21; DLB 15,
139, 155; MTCW

Wilson, August
1945-....... CLC 39, 50, 63; BLC; DA;
DAB; DAC; DC 2
See also AAYA 16; BW 2; CA 115; 122;
CANR 42; DAM DRAM, MST, MULT;
MTCW

Wilson, Brian 1942-.............. CLC 12

Wilson, Colin 1931-............ CLC 3, 14
See also CA 1-4R; CAAS 5; CANR 1, 22,
33; DLB 14; MTCW

Wilson, Dirk
See Pohl, Frederik

Wilson, Edmund
1895-1972 .... CLC 1, 2, 3, 8, 24
See also CA 1-4R; 37-40R; CANR 1, 46;
DLB 63; MTCW

Wilson, Ethel Davis (Bryant)
1888(?)-1980 .... CLC 13; DAC
See also CA 102; DAM POET; DLB 68;
MTCW

Wilson, John 1785-1854......... NCLC 5

Wilson, John (Anthony) Burgess 1917-1993
See Burgess, Anthony
See also CA 1-4R; 143; CANR 2, 46; DAC;
DAM NOV; MTCW

Wilson, Lanford 1937-....... CLC 7, 14, 36
See also CA 17-20R; CABS 3; CANR 45;
DAM DRAM; DLB 7

Wilson, Robert M. 1944-........ CLC 7, 9
See also CA 49-52; CANR 2, 41; MTCW

Wilson, Robert McLiam 1964- ..... CLC 59
See also CA 132

Wilson, Sloan 1920-.............. CLC 32
See also CA 1-4R; CANR 1, 44

Wilson, Snoo 1948-.............. CLC 33
See also CA 69-72

Wilson, William S(mith) 1932- ..... CLC 49
See also CA 81-84

Winchilsea, Anne (Kingsmill) Finch Counte
1661-1720 .... LC 3

Windham, Basil
See Wodehouse, P(elham) G(renville)

Wingrove, David (John) 1954-...... CLC 68
See also CA 133

Winters, Janet Lewis .... CLC 41
See also Lewis, Janet
See also DLBY 87

Winters, (Arthur) Yvor
1900-1968 .... CLC 4, 8, 32
See also CA 11-12; 25-28R; CAP 1;
DLB 48; MTCW

Winterson, Jeanette 1959-........ CLC 64
See also CA 136; DAM POP

Winthrop, John 1588-1649......... LC 31
See also DLB 24, 30

Wiseman, Frederick 1930-........ CLC 20

Wister, Owen 1860-1938 .... TCLC 21
See also CA 108; DLB 9, 78; SATA 62

Witkacy
See Witkiewicz, Stanislaw Ignacy

Witkiewicz, Stanislaw Ignacy
1885-1939 .... TCLC 8
See also CA 105

Yezierska, Anzia 1885(?)-1970 ..... **CLC 46**
See also CA 126; 89-92; DLB 28; MTCW

Yglesias, Helen 1915-.......... **CLC 7, 22**
See also CA 37-40R; CAAS 20; CANR 15;
INT CANR-15; MTCW

Yokomitsu Riichi 1898-1947 ...... **TCLC 47**

Yonge, Charlotte (Mary)
1823-1901 .... **TCLC 48**
See also CA 109; DLB 18; SATA 17

York, Jeremy
See Creasey, John

York, Simon
See Heinlein, Robert A(nson)

Yorke, Henry Vincent 1905-1974 ... **CLC 13**
See also Green, Henry
See also CA 85-88; 49-52

Yosano Akiko 1878-1942 .. **TCLC 59; PC 11**

Yoshimoto, Banana .... **CLC 84**
See also Yoshimoto, Mahoko

Yoshimoto, Mahoko 1964-
See Yoshimoto, Banana
See also CA 144

Young, Al(bert James)
1939- .... **CLC 19; BLC**
See also BW 2; CA 29-32R; CANR 26;
DAM MULT; DLB 33

Young, Andrew (John) 1885-1971 .... **CLC 5**
See also CA 5-8R; CANR 7, 29

Young, Collier
See Bloch, Robert (Albert)

Young, Edward 1683-1765 .... **LC 3**
See also DLB 95

Young, Marguerite (Vivian)
1909-1995 .... **CLC 82**
See also CA 13-16; 150; CAP 1

Young, Neil 1945-............... **CLC 17**
See also CA 110

Yourcenar, Marguerite
1903-1987 .... **CLC 19, 38, 50, 87**
See also CA 69-72; CANR 23; DAM NOV;
DLB 72; DLBY 88; MTCW

Yurick, Sol 1925-................. **CLC 6**
See also CA 13-16R; CANR 25

Zabolotskii, Nikolai Alekseevich
1903-1958 .... **TCLC 52**
See also CA 116

Zamiatin, Yevgenii
See Zamyatin, Evgeny Ivanovich

Zamora, Bernice (B. Ortiz)
1938- .... **CLC 89; HLC**
See also DAM MULT; DLB 82; HW

Zamyatin, Evgeny Ivanovich
1884-1937 .... **TCLC 8, 37**
See also CA 105

Zangwill, Israel 1864-1926........ **TCLC 16**
See also CA 109; DLB 10, 135

Zappa, Francis Vincent, Jr. 1940-1993
See Zappa, Frank
See also CA 108; 143

Zappa, Frank..................... **CLC 17**
See also Zappa, Francis Vincent, Jr.

Zaturenska, Marya 1902-1982.... **CLC 6, 11**
See also CA 13-16R; 105; CANR 22

Zelazny, Roger (Joseph)
1937-1995 .... **CLC 21**
See also AAYA 7; CA 21-24R; 148;
CANR 26; DLB 8; MTCW; SATA 57;
SATA-Brief 39

Zhdanov, Andrei A(lexandrovich)
1896-1948 .... **TCLC 18**
See also CA 117

Zhukovsky, Vasily 1783-1852 .... **NCLC 35**

Ziegenhagen, Eric .... **CLC 55**

Zimmer, Jill Schary
See Robinson, Jill

Zimmerman, Robert
See Dylan, Bob

Zindel, Paul
1936- ..... **CLC 6, 26; DA; DAB; DAC;**
DC 5
See also AAYA 2; CA 73-76; CANR 31;
CLR 3; DAM DRAM, MST, NOV;
DLB 7, 52; JRDA; MAICYA; MTCW;
SATA 16, 58

Zinov'Ev, A. A.
See Zinoviev, Alexander (Aleksandrovich)

Zinoviev, Alexander (Aleksandrovich)
1922- .... **CLC 19**
See also CA 116; 133; CAAS 10

Zoilus
See Lovecraft, H(oward) P(hillips)

Zola, Emile (Edouard Charles Antoine)
1840-1902 ...... **TCLC 1, 6, 21, 41; DA;**
DAB; DAC; WLC
See also CA 104; 138; DAM MST, NOV;
DLB 123

Zoline, Pamela 1941-............. **CLC 62**

Zorrilla y Moral, Jose 1817-1893.. **NCLC 6**

Zoshchenko, Mikhail (Mikhailovich)
1895-1958 .... **TCLC 15; SSC 15**
See also CA 115

Zuckmayer, Carl 1896-1977........ **CLC 18**
See also CA 69-72; DLB 56, 124

Zuk, Georges
See Skelton, Robin

Zukofsky, Louis
1904-1978 .... **CLC 1, 2, 4, 7, 11, 18;**
PC 11
See also CA 9-12R; 77-80; CANR 39;
DAM POET; DLB 5; MTCW

Zweig, Paul 1935-1984........ **CLC 34, 42**
See also CA 85-88; 113

Zweig, Stefan 1881-1942 .... **TCLC 17**
See also CA 112; DLB 81, 118

DC Cumulative Nationality Index

DC Cumulative Title Index

Title Index